W9-BUL-137

TRENTINO-ALTO ADIGE
Pages 160–169

THE VENETO AND FRIULI
Pages 132–159

VENICE
Pages 80–131

EMILIA-ROMAGNA
Pages 246–261

Ancona

Pescara

L'Aquila

ROMA

ROME AND LAZIO

Campobasso

Foggia

Bari

SOUTHERN ITALY

Napoli

Salerno

Potenza

Taranto

UMBRIA
Pages 338–353

LE MARCHE
Pages 354–363

ABRUZZO, MOLISE, AND PUGLIA
Pages 484–497

BASILICATA AND CALABRIA
Pages 498–505

Catanzaro

NAPLES AND CAMPANIA
Pages 466–483

Messina

Reggio di Calabria

Palermo

Catania

Agrigento

SICILY
Pages 506–527

EYEWITNESS *TRAVEL GUIDES*

ITALY

DK EYEWITNESS *TRAVEL GUIDES*

ITALY

DORLING KINDERSLEY PUBLISHING, INC.
LONDON • NEW YORK • SYDNEY • DELHI
PARIS • MUNICH • JOHANNESBURG
www.dk.com

Dorling Kindersley Publishing, Inc.

www.dk.com

PROJECT EDITOR Fiona Wild
ART EDITORS Vanessa Courtier, Annette Jacobs
EDITORS Francesca Machiavelli, Sophie Martin,
Helen Townsend, Nicky Tyrrell
US EDITORS Mary Sutherland, Michael T. Wise
DESIGNERS Jo Doran, Anthea Forlee,
Paul Jackson, Marisa Renzullo

MAIN CONTRIBUTORS
Ros Belford, Susie Boulton, Christopher Catling,
Sam Cole, Paul Duncan, Olivia Ercoli, Andrew Gumbel,
Tim Jepson, Ferdie McDonald, Jane Shaw

MAPS
Lovell Johns Ltd,
Dorling Kindersley Cartography

PHOTOGRAPHER
John Heseltine

ILLUSTRATORS
Stephen Conlin, Donati Giudici Associati srl, Stephen Gyapay,
Roger Hutchins, Maltings Partnership, Paul Weston, John Woodcock

Reproduced by Colourscan (Singapore)
Printed and bound by South China Printing Co. Ltd., China

First American Edition, 1996
6 8 10 9 7

First Published in the United States by
Dorling Kindersley, Inc.,
95 Madison Avenue, New York, New York 10016
Reprinted with revisions 1997 (twice), 1999, 2000, 2001

Copyright © 1996, 2001 Dorling Kindersley Limited, London

Library of Congress Cataloging-in-Publication Data
Italy.
    p.   cm. -- (Dorling Kindersley travel guides)
Includes index.
    ISBN 0-7894-0425-7
    1, Italy -- Guidebooks.   I. Dorling Kindersley Limited.
II. Series.
DG416.I8168 1996   95-4502
914.504' 929 -- dc20   CIP

THROUGHOUT THIS BOOK, FLOORS ARE REFERRED TO IN ACCORDANCE WITH EUROPEAN USAGE.
I.E, "FIRST FLOOR" IS ONE FLIGHT UP.

**The information in every
DK Eyewitness Travel Guide is checked annually.**
Every effort has been made to ensure that this book is as up-to-date as
possible at the time of going to press. Some details, however, such as
telephone numbers, opening hours, prices, gallery hanging arrangements
and travel information are liable to change. The publishers cannot accept
responsibility for any consequences arising from the use of this book.
We value the views of our readers very highly. Please write to: Senior
Managing Editor, DK Eyewitness Travel Guides, Dorling Kindersley,
9 Henrietta Street, London WC2E 8PS.

◁ **Fertile wine-growing region around Panzano in Chianti, Tuscany**

CONTENTS

David **by Bernini, Rome**

INTRODUCING ITALY

NORTHEAST ITALY

NORTHWEST ITALY

Gondolas weaving through the maze of canals in Venice

A traditional small shop in
Volterra, Tuscany

Basilica of San Francesco in Assisi, started in 1228

HOW TO USE THIS GUIDE

THIS GUIDE helps you get the most from your visit to Italy, providing expert recommendations as well as detailed practical information. *Introducing Italy* maps the whole country and sets it in its historical and cultural context. The 15 regional chapters, plus *Rome, Florence,* and *Venice,* describe important sights with the help of maps and images. Each section is introduced with features on regional architecture and food specialties. *Travelers' Needs* gives details on hotels and restaurants, and the *Survival Guide* contains practical information on everything from transportation to personal safety.

ROME

The center of Rome has been divided into five sightseeing areas. Each area has its own chapter that opens with a list of the sights described. All the sights are numbered and plotted on an *Area Map*. The detailed information for each sight is presented in numerical order, making it easy to locate within the chapter.

Sights at a Glance lists the chapter's sights by category: Churches, Museums and Galleries, Historic Buildings, Streets and Piazzas.

All pages relating to Rome have red thumb tabs.

A locator map shows where you are in relation to other areas of the city center.

1 Area Map
For easy reference, the sights are numbered and located on a map. The sights are also shown on the Street Finder *on pages 433–41.*

2 Street-by-Street Map
This gives a bird's-eye view of the heart of each sightseeing area.

A suggested route for a walk is shown in red.

Stars indicate the sights that no visitor should miss.

3 Detailed information
All the sights in Rome are described individually. Addresses and practical information are provided. The key to the symbols used in the information block is shown on the back flap.

1 Introduction
The landscape, history, and character of each region is described here, showing how the area has developed over the centuries and what it offers to the visitor today.

ITALY AREA BY AREA
Apart from Rome, Florence and Venice, Italy has been divided into 15 areas, each of which has a separate chapter. The most interesting towns and places to visit have been numbered on a *Pictorial Map*.

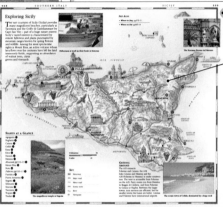

Each area of Italy can be identified quickly by its color coding, shown on the inside front cover.

2 Pictorial Map
This shows the main road network and gives an illustrated overview of the whole region. All entries are numbered, and there are also useful tips on getting around the region by car and train.

3 Detailed information
All the important towns and other places to visit are described individually. They are listed in order, following the numbering given on the Pictorial Map. Within each entry, information is given on the most important sights. The name of the provincial capital is given for smaller towns at the top of each entry.

Story boxes explore specific subjects further.

For all the top sights, a Visitors' Checklist provides the practical information you need to plan your visit.

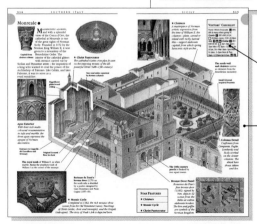

4 Italy's top sights
These are given two or more full pages. Historic buildings are dissected to reveal their interiors; museums and galleries have color-coded floor plans to help you locate the most interesting exhibits.

INTRODUCING
ITALY

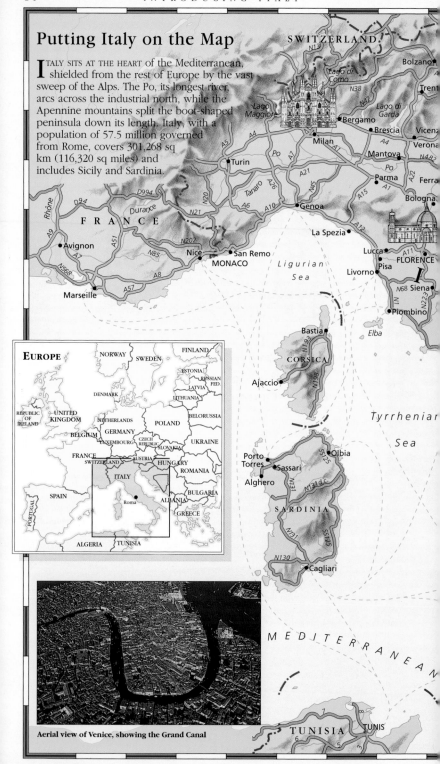

Putting Italy on the Map

ITALY SITS AT THE HEART of the Mediterranean, shielded from the rest of Europe by the vast sweep of the Alps. The Po, its longest river, arcs across the industrial north, while the Apennine mountains split the boot-shaped peninsula down its length. Italy, with a population of 57.5 million governed from Rome, covers 301,268 sq km (116,320 sq miles) and includes Sicily and Sardinia.

SWITZERLAND

Bolzano

Trent

Lago di Como

Lago Maggiore

Bergamo

Brescia

Vicenza

Verona

Milan

Mantova

Turin

Parma

Ferrara

Bologna

FRANCE

Rhône

Avignon

Marseille

Nice

San Remo

MONACO

Genoa

La Spezia

Lucca

Pisa

FLORENCE

Livorno

Siena

Piombino

Elba

Ligurian Sea

Bastia

CORSICA

Ajaccio

Tyrrhenian Sea

Porto Torres

Olbia

Sassari

Alghero

SARDINIA

Cagliari

EUROPE

NORWAY

SWEDEN

FINLAND

ESTONIA

LATVIA

RUSSIAN FED.

LITHUANIA

DENMARK

REPUBLIC OF IRELAND

UNITED KINGDOM

NETHERLANDS

BELGIUM

GERMANY

POLAND

BELORUSSIA

LUXEMBOURG

CZECH REPUBLIC

UKRAINE

FRANCE

SWITZERLAND

AUSTRIA

SLOVAKIA

HUNGARY

ROMANIA

ITALY

Roma

SPAIN

BULGARIA

ALBANIA

GREECE

PORTUGAL

ALGERIA

TUNISIA

MEDITERRANEAN

TUNISIA

TUNIS

Aerial view of Venice, showing the Grand Canal

◁ **View over Florence of the richly decorated 15th-century Duomo and Campanile**

Satellite photograph of southern Europe and the Mediterranean

KEY

———	Highway
———	Major road
- - -	Ferry service
–••–••–	International boundary

0 kilometers		200

0 miles		100

Northern Italy

Airline connections link the rest of Europe with the cities of Milan, Turin, Bologna, Pisa, Florence, Verona, and Venice. Major roads and railroads also provide excellent links to cities all over Europe. Transportation is very efficient, with highways and railroads along both coasts, and across the area's main east to west axis at the foot of the Alps. Milan, Verona, and Bologna are the key transportation hubs, while Florence forms the focus of links to the south.

Florence by Road

Good fast roads link Florence to Pisa to the west, Rome and Siena to the south, and Bologna to the north.

FLORENCE AND ENVIRONS

KEY

⛴ Ferry port

✈ Airport

FS Main train station

– – International boundary

– – Regional boundary

Highway

Main road

Railroad line

0 kilometers   4

0 miles   2

VENICE

Marco Polo

Mestre

FS

N14

N116

N11

Canale Osellino

Laguna Veneta

FS Santa Lucia

San Marco

Turkey·Egypt·
Greece·Ancona

0 kilometers   4

0 miles   2

Venice by Road
*Venice is joined to
the mainland by a
causeway. This pro-
vides easy access to
highway links with
Verona and Padua.*

AUSTRIA

Cortina d'Ampezzo

Tolmezzo

N52

Udine

N13

N56

A4

Cividale del Friuli

Pordenone

A28

Gorizia

Aquileia

eviso

A27

A57

Mestre

Grado   Trieste

VENICE

SLOVENIA

Greece·
Turkey·
Egypt·

Po
Delta

N309

di
cchio

Ravenna

A14

za

Rimini

A14

SAN MARINO

Pèsaro

Fano

San Leo

Urbino

N3

polcro

Urbania

rezzo

Cortona

Gubbio

Sibillini

Jesi

Grotte di
Frasassi

Ancona

Conero
Peninsula

Loreto

N76

Greece

Ionian Islands

Cyprus

Turkey

A26

Lago
Trasimeno

Perugia

Assisi

Spello

N3

Montefalco

Todi

Spoleto

Norcia

Ascoli Piceno

A14

Orvieto

rbo

N2

A1

Pescara

L'Aquila   SS17   A25

Lanciano

Sulmona

A24

A14

Scanno   SS17

San Severo

ROME

ATICAN CITY

A12

A1

N82

SS17

N4

Lucera

Foggia

N89

Troia

Brindisi

Sermoneta

Sperlonga

Terracina   Formia

Gaeta

Benevento

Caserta

0 kilometers   100

0 miles   50

Taranto

Reggio di
Calabria

NAPLES   Monte
Vesuvio

KEY TO COLOR-CODING

Northeast Italy

Venice

The Veneto and Friuli

Trentino-Alto Adige

Northwest Italy

Lombardy

Valle d'Aosta and Piedmont

Liguria

Central Italy

Emilia-Romagna

Florence

Tuscany

Umbria

Le Marche

Southern Italy

INTERNATIONAL AIRLINE services fly to Rome, Naples, and Palermo in southern Italy. Transportation links within the region are generally slower than in the north, particularly inland and on the islands of Sicily and Sardinia. Coastal road and rail links are good, however, especially those linking Rome and Naples, the region's main transportation hubs. Two trans-Apennine highways offer the quickest cross-country routes.

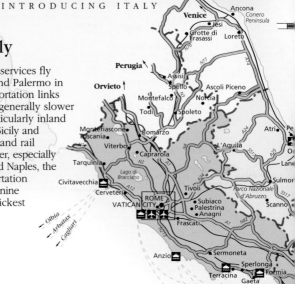

Sicily and Sardinia

Ferries operate to Sicily from Naples, Villa San Giovanni, and Reggio di Calabria. Further connections include boats to Malta and Tunisia. Ferries run to Sardinia from several mainland ports, notably from Genoa and Livorno.

KEY

⛴	Ferry port
✈	Airport
▬ ▬	International boundary
▬ ▬	Regional boundary
▬▬	Highway
▬▬	Main road
▬▬	Railroad line

ROME AND ENVIRONS

0 kilometers 10

0 miles 5

VATICAN CITY

FS

VIA FLAMINIA
VIA SALARIA
A1
VIA NOMENTANA
VIA CASSIA
VIA TIBURTINA
A24
VIA CASILINA
GRANDE RACCORDO ANULARE (GRA)
VIA AURELIA
VIA CRISTOFORO COLOMBO
VIA APPIA NUOVA
A12
A2

Leonardo da Vinci (Fiumicino)

Tevere (Tiber)

Ciampino

Rome by Road
Highway links approach Rome from Naples, Pescara, and Florence. All feed into the city's ring road, the Grande Raccordo Anulare.

Isole Tremiti

Vasto
Termoli
Rodi Garganico
Vieste
Gargano Peninsula
San Severo
Manfredonia
Lucera
Foggia
Troia
Trani
Bari
Albania →
Greece →
Egypt →
A14
Benevento
serta
Castel del Monte
Ruvo di Puglia
Melfi
Venosa
Alberobello
Greece →
Lagopesole
Brindisi
Monte Vesuvio
Matera
N379
N7
pei
Salerno
Amalfi
Taranto
Lecce
Greece →
Sorrento
Metaponto
ri
Paestum
Galatina
Otranto
Cilento
N9
Maratea
SS16
Rossano
Cosenza
N407
N106
Sant'Eufemia Lamezia
A290
Tropea
Stilo
Isole Eolie
Gerace
Naples
Messina
Milazzo
Villa San Giovanni
Tindari
Reggio di Calabria
A20
Taormina
Maltese
Naples
A18
na
A19
Catania
azza merina
Naples
Maltese
Pantalica
Siracusa
Noto

0 kilometers 100

0 miles 50

KEY TO COLOR-CODING

Rome and Lazio

Rome

Lazio

Southern Italy

Naples and Campania

Abruzzo, Molise, and Puglia

Basilicata and Calabria

Sicily

Sardinia

A PORTRAIT OF ITALY

ITALY HAS DRAWN PEOPLE *in search of culture and romance for many centuries. Few countries can compete with its Classical origins, its art, architecture, musical and literary traditions, its scenery or food and wine. The ambiguity of its modern image is also fascinating: since World War II Italy has climbed into the top ten world economies, yet at its heart it retains many of the customs, traditions, and regional allegiances of its agricultural heritage.*

Italy has no single cultural identity. From the northern snow-capped peaks of the Alps, to the long, rugged southern

Wedding Ferrari in typical Italian style

shores of Sicily, lies a plethora of distinctive regions and peoples. Politically, Italy is a young country; it did not exist as a unified nation state until 1861, and its 21 regions have maintained their cultural individuality. Visitors to Italy are often pleasantly surprised by the diversity of its dialects, cuisines, architecture, and craftsmanship. There is also a larger regional division. People speak of two distinct Italies: the rich industrial north and the poorer agricultural south, known as *Il Mezzogiorno* or Land of the Midday Sun. The frontier separating the two is indeterminate, lying somewhere between Rome and Naples.

The north is directly responsible for Italy's place among the world's top industrial nations. It has been the powerhouse behind the Italian economic miracle, its success achieved by internationally renowned names such as Fiat, Pirelli, Ferragamo, Olivetti, Zanussi, Alessi, and Armani. The south, in contrast, has high unemployment, earns less per capita

A secluded villa surrounded by cypress trees on a Tuscan hilltop

◁ **Three sundials covering the façade of Palazzo del Governatore, on Piazza Garibaldi, Parma**

than the north, is in the grip of organized crime, and has some areas that rank among the most depressed in Europe.

The historic divide between north and south is a powerful factor in contemporary politics. The newly formed federalist party, the Northern League, has based its popular campaign on this split. The party gained enough votes in recent elections to be included in the national government. Those in favor of separation complain that the south is a drain on resources: Milan is seen as efficient and rich, and Naples is viewed as chaotic, dirty and corrupt.

Conversation at Palazzo Farnese

History and geography have both contributed to the division. The north is closer in both location and spirit to Germany and France, while the south has suffered a succession of invasions from foreign powers: Carthaginians and Greeks in ancient times, Saracens and Normans in the Middle Ages, and until the middle of the last century, the Bourbons from Spain held sway.

TRADITION

Distinctive variations in Italy's regions have much to do with the mountainous landscape and inaccessible valleys. Tuscan and Ligurian hill towns, for instance, have quite different silhouettes; the farmhouses in Puglia are unlike those found in the landscape of Emilia-Romagna.

For many travelers, the Italian journey comes to an end in Campania, in southern Italy. Farther south the landscape, architecture, dialects, food, and even the appearance of the people, have closer affinities with the Eastern Mediterranean or North Africa than with Europe. In the far south, study of the local dialects has revealed traces of ancient Greek and old Albanian, preserved in tightly knit communities isolated by the rugged geography. Christianity and pagan ritual are closely linked; sometimes the Virgin is portrayed as a thinly disguised Demeter, the Earth goddess.

Throughout Italy, ancient techniques of husbandry endure, and many livelihoods are closely connected to the land and the seasons. Main crops include wheat, olives, and grapes; colorful Easter celebrations *(see p62)* pay tribute to the bounty of the soil. Although some of the north's post-war economic prosperity can be attributed to industry (especially car production in and around Turin), much of it has grown from the expansion of family-owned artisan businesses and the export of handmade goods abroad. This is recognized as a distinct sector of the economy. The internationally successful retail clothes chain,

Café-goers relaxing in Marina di Pisa, Tuscany

Medieval skyscrapers emerging from the Tuscan landscape of San Gimignano

Benetton, is a recent example. The "Made in Italy" label, found on goods such as clothes, shoes, and leather bags, guarantees a high standard.

CULTURE AND ARTS

Sophia Loren

The arts in Italy have had a long and glorious history, and Italians are very proud of this. Given the fact that Italy has more than 100,000 monuments (archaeological sites, cathedrals, churches, houses and statues), all of which have major historical significance, it is not surprising that there is a shortage of funds to keep them in good repair. Many museums in Italy, particularly those in the south, are closed, or partially closed. You may find churches in Venice hidden behind permanent scaffolding or those in Naples shut due to recent earthquake damage. However, with tourism now accounting for 3 percent of Italy's Gross Domestic Product, efforts are being made to put as many buildings and collections on show as possible.

The performing arts are also underfunded, yet there are some spectacular cultural festivals and other events. Opera is a forte, with almost every town of any size having its own opera house. Current stars include Luciano Pavarotti, and La Scala opera house in Milan shows world-class productions.

Film is another flourishing art form in Italy and has been so since its invention. The sets at Cinecittà, outside Rome, have been used by many famous directors such as Fellini,

Bernini's 17th-century Fontana del Tritone, Rome

Roadside stand near Positano, Campania

Pasolini, de Sica, Visconti, and many others. Italian films have always been an important export and continue to bring in money and acclaim from abroad. In Italy the arts belong to everyone: opera has traditionally been attended by people from all backgrounds, regardless of social status, as have movies and galleries.

SOCIAL CUSTOMS AND POLITICS

Italian society is still highly traditional, and Italians can be very formal. Between the generations degrees of familiarity exist: keep *ciao* (hello or goodbye) for friends your age or younger, and greet older people with *piacere* (pleased to meet you), *buon giorno* (good day) or *buona sera* (good evening), and on parting, say *arrivederci* (goodbye). Strangers are met with a handshake, but family and friends receive a kiss.

Italian chic, Armani style

Italian chic decrees that whatever clothes you wear should give the impression of wealth. If people wear similar outfits, it is because Italians are conformists in fashion as in many other aspects of daily life.

Italian politics, in contrast, are not so well regulated. Governments in the postwar era have consistently been short-lived coalitions dominated by the Christian Democrats. In 1993, however, Italy experienced a political crisis which blew its party system apart. Investigations in Milan into illegal party financing in 1992 revealed an organized network of bribery and corruption, which exposed a huge number of politicians and businessmen. Among the disgraced was Giulio Andreotti, Christian Democrat leader and six times prime minister. Silvio Berlusconi, leader of the Forza Italia party, became prime minister in 1994 but lasted only a short while as he, too, was accused of corruption. In 1998 Massimo D'Alema became Italy's first left wing Prime Minister. In 2000, the center-left coalition suffered heavy losses while Berlusconi's center-right coalition Polo gained in popularity.

MODERN LIFE

Food and soccer are the great constants; Italians live for both. Much time is spent on preparing food and eating.

Statue of Emperor Domitian in the Vatican Gardens

The solution to heavy traffic in Rome's Piazza Barberini: motorbikes and scooters

The Italian diet, particularly in the south, is among the healthiest in the world. Soccer is a national passion and inspires massive public interest and media attention, not least as a way of expressing regional loyalties.

As far as religion is concerned, the number of practicing Catholics has been in decline for some years. Although Rome lies at the center of world Catholicism, today many Italians are uninterested in religion, but still attend mass in number on saints' days or feast days.

The emphasis on conformity and a commitment to the institution of the family remain key factors in Italian society, despite the country's low, and falling, birth rate. Grandparents, children, and grandchildren, still live in family units, although this is becoming less common. All children are pampered but the most cherished ones are, usually

Strolling through one of Bologna's many porticoes

male. Women's liberation fought a powerful campaign in the 1970s and did much to change attitudes to women in the workplace, particularly in metropolitan areas. However, the idea that men should help with housework and the care of children is still a fairly foreign notion among the older generation.

With the miracle of its postwar economic recovery, where industry and technology were united with design, Italy has become a modern-day success story. Although the economy has been dented by the worldwide recession of the early 1990s, the exposure of corruption in all walks of public life and unprecedented political upheaval, Italy appears unchanged to foreign visitors. The ability of the country to keep its long-lasting regional identities and traditional values allows it to ride out any changes virtually unscathed.

Medieval and Early Renaissance Art

THE STORY OF early Italian art, from the 13th century until the late 15th century, illuminates one of the richest periods in European art history. For the first time since Classical antiquity, painters and sculptors created a convincing pictorial space in which figures, modeled "in the round," were given life. Ethereal buildings were replaced by those firmly rooted in the real world, reproducing what artists actually saw. This revolution in art included the reintroduction of the fresco technique, giving artists huge surfaces for telling pictorial stories.

c.1305 Giotto di Bondone, *The Meeting at the Golden Gate* (Cappella degli Scrovegni, Padua) Giotto broke away from the ornate Byzantine style to visualize naturalness and human emotions. His way of working would later be dubbed the Florentine style.

1235 Bonaventura Berlinghieri, *St. Francis Altarpiece* (San Francesco, Pescia)

1285 Duccio di Buoninsegna, *Rucellai Madonna*, panel (Uffizi, Florence). Duccio dominated the Sienese painting style that combined bold linear movements with a new human intimacy.

1339 Ambrogio Lorenzetti, *Good Government Enthroned* (Sala dei Nove, Palazzo Pubblico, Siena)

1220	1240	1260	1280	1300	1320

MIDDLE AGES　　　　　　　　　　　　　　　　　**FORERUNNERS TO RENAISSANCE**

1220	1240	1260	1280	1300	1320

c.1259 Nicola Pisano, Pulpit (Baptistry, Pisa cathedral)

c.1265 Coppo di Marcovaldo, *Madonna and Child* (Santa Monica dei Servi, Orvieto)

c.1280 Cimabue, *Madonna Enthroned with Angels and Prophets*, also known as *Santa Trinità Madonna* (Uffizi, Florence)

c.1291 Pietro Cavallini, *Last Judgment*, detail (Santa Cecilia, Trastevere, Rome)

c.1316–18 Simone Martini, *Vision of St. Martin* (Lower Church of San Francesco, Assisi)

c.1297 Giovanni Pisano, Pulpit (Sant'Andrea, Pistoia)

c.1336 Andrea Pisano, *Baptism of St. John the Baptist*, panel on the South Doors (Baptistry, Florence)

c.1425–52 Lorenzo Ghiberti, *Gates of Paradise*, panel on the East Doors. (Baptistry, Florence cathedral). These elaborate doors mark a transition from the Gothic style to the Early Renaissance style, in Florence.

c.1435 Donatello, *David* (Museo del Bargello, Florence)

1357 Andrea Orcagna, *Enthroned Christ with Madonna and Saints* (Strozzi Altarpiece, Santa Maria Novella, Florence)

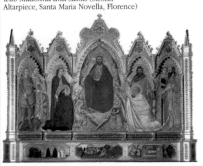

c.1452–65 Piero della Francesca, detail of *The Dream of Constantine* (San Francesco, Arezzo)

c.1456 Paolo Uccello, *Battle of San Romano* (Uffizi, Florence)

c.1410 Nanni di Banco, *Four Crowned Martyrs* (Orsanmichele, Florence)

| 1360 | 1380 | 1400 | 1420 | 1440 | 1460 | |

EARLY RENAISSANCE

| 1360 | 1380 | 1400 | 1420 | 1440 | 1460 | |

1423 Gentile da Fabriano, *Adoration of the Magi* (Uffizi, Florence)

c.1440 Fra Angelico, *Annunciation* (San Marco, Florence)

c.1350 Francesco Traini, *Triumph of Death* (Campo Santo, Pisa)

c.1463 Piero della Francesca, *Resurrection* (Pinacoteca, Sansepolcro)

c.1465 Fra Filippo Lippi, *Madonna with Child and Angels* (Uffizi, Florence)

c.1465–74 Andrea Mantegna, *Arrival of Cardinal Francesco Gonzaga* (Palazzo Ducale, Mantova)

c.1425–8 Masaccio, *The Tribute Money* (Cappella Brancacci, Florence)

c.1470 Andrea del Verrocchio, *David* (Bargello, Florence)

FRESCO TECHNIQUE

Fresco, meaning "fresh," refers to the technique of painting on-to a thin layer of damp, freshly laid plaster. Pigments are drawn into the plaster by surface tension, and the color becomes fixed as the plaster dries. The pigments react with the lime in the plaster to produce strong, rich colors, such as those in Masaccio's *The Tribute Money.*

The Tribute Money by Masaccio (Cappella Brancacci, Florence)

High Renaissance Art

THE HIGH RENAISSANCE in the late 15th century was marked by an increasing sense of realism in many religious works and the technical mastery of such renowned artists as Michelangelo, Leonardo da Vinci, and Raphael. The different schools of Renaissance painting, while drawing on Classical models, produced varying styles: Florentine painting was noted for its cool clarity, and sensuous color and warm light characterized many Venetian works. By the mid-16th century, however, these styles shifted to the fanciful, contorted imagery of Mannerism.

c.1480 Andrea Mantegna, *Dead Christ* (Brera, Milan)

1481–2 Sistine Chapel wall frescoes painted by various artists.

c.1481–2 Pietro Perugino, *Christ Delivering the Keys of the Kingdom to St. Peter*, wall fresco (Sistine Chapel, Rome)

c.1483–88 Andrea del Verrocchio, completed by Alessandro Leopardi, *Equestrian Monument of Bartolomeo Colleoni* (Campo dei Santi Giovanni e Paolo, Venice)

c.1487 Giovanni Bellini, *San Giobbe Altarpiece* (Accademia, Venice)

c.1495 Leonardo da Vinci, *Last Supper* (Santa Maria delle Grazie, Milan)

c.1503–1505 Leonardo da Vinci, *Mona Lisa* (Louvre, Paris)

1505 Raphael, *Madonna of the Goldfinch* (Uffizi, Florence)

1519–26 Titian, *Madonna of the Pesaro Family* (Santa Maria Gloriosa dei Frari, Venice)

1508–12 Michelangelo, *Sistine Chapel ceiling* (The Vatican, Rome). Over 200 preliminary drawings were made for this incredible vision of God's power and humanity's spiritual awakening.

| 1480 | 1500 | 15 |

HIGH RENAISSANCE

| 1480 | 1500 | 15 |

1485 Leonardo da Vinci, *Virgin of the Rocks* (Louvre, Paris)

c.1485 Sandro Botticelli, *Birth of Venus* (Uffizi, Florence)

c.1486 Leonardo da Vinci, *Uomo Vitruviano* (Accademia, Venice)

1499–1504 Luca Signorelli, *Damned Consigned to Hell* (Cappella Nuova, Orvieto cathedral)

1501–1504 Michelangelo, *David* (Galleria dell'Accademia, Florence)

1505 Giovanni Bellini, *Madonna and Child with Four Saints* (San Zaccaria altarpiece, Accademia, Venice)

c.1508 Giorgione, *Tempesta* (Accademia, Venice)

1509 Raphael, *School of Athens* (Stanza della Segnatura, The Vatican, Rome). The scale, magnificence, and harmony of this fresco represent the ideals of the High Renaissance. These ideals sought to express superhuman rather than human values.

1517 Sodom *Marriage of Alexander a Roxana* (Vill Farnesina, R

1516 Michela *Dying Slave* (Louvre, Paris)

1512–14 Raphael, *Ange Delivering St. Peter from Prison*, detail from the *Liberation of St. Peter from Prison* (Stanza di Eliodoro The Vatican, Rome)

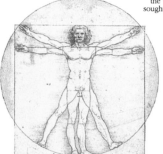

1523 Rosso Fiorentino, *Moses Defends the Daughters of Jethro* (Uffizi, Florence)

1530–32 Giulio Romano, *Ceiling and wall frescoes* (Sala dei Giganti, Palazzo del Tè, Mantova)

c.1532 Michelangelo, *"Blockhead" Captive* (Galleria dell' Accademia, Florence)

1534–5 Paris Bordone, *Fisherman Delivering the Ring* (Accademia, Venice)

c.1540–42 Titian, *David and Goliath* (Santa Maria della Salute, Venice)

c.1562–6 Jacopo Tintoretto, *Finding of the Body of St. Mark* (Brera, Milan)

c.1550 Moretto, *Ecce Homo with Angel* (Pinacoteca Tosio Martinengo, Brescia)

| 1540 | | 1560 |

MANNERISM

| 1540 | | 1560 |

1534–41 Michelangelo, *Last Judgment*, wall fresco (Sistine Chapel, Rome)

c.1546 Titian, *Portrait of Pope Paul III Farnese with his Nephews*, (Museo di Capodimonte, Naples)

c.1534–40 Parmigianino, *Madonna and Angels* or *Madonna with the Long Neck* (Uffizi, Florence). Attenuated proportions and contrasting colors make this a fine example of the Mannerist style.

1538 Titian, *Venus of Urbino* (Uffizi, Florence)

c.1540 Agnolo Bronzino, *Portrait of Lucrezia Panciatichi* (Uffizi, Florence). Elongated features, such as Lucrezia's fingers, are typical of the exaggerated Mannerist style.

1556 Veronese, *Triumph of Mordecai* (San Sebastiano, Venice)

c.1526–30 Correggio, *Assumption of the Virgin* (Dome of Parma cathedral). Neither a Mannerist nor a High Renaissance painter, Correggio was a master of illusion, skilled at making ascending figures float convincingly, as seen in the fresco above.

Italian Architecture

Corinthian capital

THE BUILDINGS OF ITALY span almost 3,000 years, drawing influences from a wide variety of sources. Etruscan and Roman buildings borrowed heavily from ancient Greece, and in later centuries Norman, Arabic, and Byzantine styles colored Italy's Romanesque and Gothic architecture. Classical ideals infused the country's Renaissance buildings, later giving way to the inspired innovations of the Baroque period.

Orvieto's duomo displays the ornate and intricate decoration, notably sculpture, common to many Gothic cathedrals. Building stretched from the 13th to the early 17th centuries.

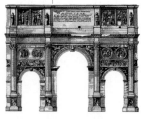

The Basilica di San Marco

The Basilica di San Marco (AD 832–1094) in Venice combines Classical, Romanesque, and Gothic architecture, but its key inspiration was Byzantine (see pp106–9).

200	400	600	800	1000
CLASSICAL		BYZANTINE		ROMANESQU
200	400	600	800	1000

Triumphal arches, such as Rome's Arch of Constantine (AD 313), were a uniquely Roman invention. Built to celebrate military victories, they were adorned with reliefs depicting episodes from successful campaigns (see p370).

The round-arched Romanesque style emerged from the Dark Ages in structures such as the duomo in Modena. The churches usually had simple interiors derived from Roman basilicas.

The building of domes over square or rectangular spaces was a major development of the Byzantine era.

ETRUSCAN ARCHITECTURE

Virtually the only architectural memorials to the Etruscans are their necropolises (c.6th century BC), found primarily in Tuscany, Lazio, and Umbria. Little else survives, probably because most day-to-day buildings were made from wood. The Etruscans' close cultural and trading ties with Greece, however, suggest their architecture would have borrowed heavily from Greek models. Rome, in turn, looked to Etruscan architecture for inspiration, and most early Roman public buildings were probably Etruscan in style.

Model of Etruscan temple with Classical Greek portico

The cathedral of Monreale in Sicily, built in the 12th century, contains Norman elements blended with exotic Arabic and Byzantine decoration (see pp514–15).

Bramante's Tempietto at San Pietro in Montorio, ne (built in 1502–10) was a Renaissance tribute to the recise, Classical temples of ancient Rome (see p370).

Baroque façades, such as this one added to Syracuse's duomo between 1728 and 1754, were often grafted onto older churches.

Industrial innovations in glass and metal were applied in new buildings, like Mengoni's imposing Galleria Vittorio Emanuele II (1865) in Milan (see p188).

The Classical ideals of Rome and ancient Greece were reintroduced into Italian architecture during the Renaissance.

Papal patronage and the vigor of the Counter-Reformation fueled the Baroque, a period of architectural splendor, invention, and exuberance.

The Mole Antonelliana (1863–89), in Turin, topped by a soaring granite spire, was for a time the tallest building in the world (p216).

Torre Velasca's 26-floor tower in Milan (1950s) pioneered the use of reinforced concrete.

1400	1600	1800	2000
RENAISSANCE	**BAROQUE**	**19th CENTURY**	**20th CENTURY**
1400	1600	1800	2000

Santa Maria Novella in Florence has a Renaissance façade (1456–70) by Alberti and a Gothic interior.

Gian Lorenzo Bernini (1598–1680), architect of St. Peter's Square, was a dominant figure in Roman Baroque.

Andrea Palladio (1508–80) built Neo-Classical villas and palazzi. His style was imitated in Europe for over two centuries (see p76).

lena's duomo 1136–1382), n imposing omanesque-Gothic cathedral, vent through 00 years of rchitectural ransformation see pp332–3).

Outer skin of dome, supported by 24 ribs

Lantern

Inner shell

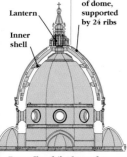

Brunelleschi's dome for the Duomo in Florence, completed in 1436, was a masterpiece of Renaissance design and ingenious engineering (see p245).

The Gesù in Rome was designed for the Jesuits by Vignola in 1568. With its powerful façade and lavish decoration it was the prototype for countless other Baroque churches (see p371).

The Pirelli building in Milan, designed by Ponti and Nervi (late 1950s), is a great example of modern Italian architecture (see p179).

Saints and Symbols in Italian Art

SAINTS AND SYMBOLS are especially important in Italian art. They form part of an established visual language used by artists to narrate stories of the Bible and the Catholic church to churchgoers. Paintings of the saints were the focus for prayer, and each offered assistance in a particular aspect of daily life. Patron saints protected specific cities or trades, and individuals who bore their name. Saints' days and religious festivals still play an important part in Italian life.

THE EVANGELISTS

The four evangelists, Matthew, Mark, Luke, and John are each represented by a winged creature, standing for a divine mission.

Eagle (St. John)

St. Dominic is usually portrayed wearing the habit of his order. The lily is another of his attributes.

St. Cosmas and St. Damian are always shown together, dressed in physicians' clothing.

St. Mark the Evangelist often holds his book of the Gospels.

St. John carries a book of the Gospel bearing his name.

St. Thomas Aquinas is usually shown with a star, barely visible in this painting on his Dominican habit.

St. Lawrence carries a palm leaf as well as the gridiron on which he was roasted.

Virgin Enthroned with the Child and Saints (c.1450) was painted on dry plaster by the Dominican friar, Fra Angelico. It is on display at the Museo di San Marco, Florence (see p268).

The Virgin, usually shown in blue robes, is depicted as Mater Amabilis – the "Mother Worthy of Love."

St. Peter Martyr, here with a palm leaf, is sometimes depicted with a head wound, carrying a sword.

SYMBOLS

In order to identify different saints or martyrs they were given "attributes" or symbols – particular objects to carry, or clothing to wear. These were items that played a particular role in their life story. Martyrs were known by their instruments of torture or death. Symbolism also appears in the sky, animals, flowers, colors, and numbers.

The lamb symbolizes Christ, the Lamb of God, or in early Christian art, the sinner.

The skull is a "memento mori" to remind us of death and impermanence.

**Winged man
(St. Matthew)**

**Winged lion
(St. Mark)**

**Winged ox
(St. Luke)**

Giovanni Bellini's painting of
*Madonna and Child with Four
Saints* (see p115)

St. Peter the Apostle, the
"rock" on which the Christian
church was founded, carries
the keys to heaven.

The Madonna, with the Christ
Child, is an emblem of perfect
motherly love.

St. Catherine of Alexandria
is shown here with a piece
of the wheel on which she
was martyred.

St. Jerome is always portrayed as an old man, often a
hermit, whose life was
devoted to scholarship.

Detail from **Madonna and Child with
Four Saints**, *by Giovanni Bellini. The
painting was produced for an altarpiece at San Zaccaria, Venice in 1505,
where it is still on display.*

The angel, a messenger
of God to man, is por-
trayed in this scene as a
musician of Heaven.

St. Lucy is depicted here
holding her own eyes in a dish.
She became the patron saint of
the blind and symbolizes light.

The lily, *flower of the Virgin,
is the symbol of purity, resurrection, peace, and chastity.*

The cockle shell *most often
represents pilgrimage. It is a
particular attribute of St. Roch.*

The palm *represents, in
Christian art, a martyr's
triumph over death.*

Writers, Poets, and Dramatists

ITALY HAS PRODUCED many writers (in Latin and Italian) who have won worldwide immortality. Each of them provides an illuminating insight into the country's turbulent past: the classical poets Virgil, Horace, and Ovid give vivid accounts of the concerns and values of ancient Rome; medieval Florence and Tuscany are brought to life in the poetry of Dante and Petrarch and the salacious tales of Boccaccio. In less than a century these three great writers created a new literary language to rank with any in Europe. Italy's modern literature still commands international attention – Umberto Eco has to his credit one of the most widely read books of this century.

Primo Levi *(1919–87) gave an astonishing account of his survival of the Jewish Holocaust and World War II's aftermath in* The Truce *and* If This Is A Man.

Trentino Alto Adige

Valle d'Aosta and Piedmont

Lombardy

Liguria

Emilia-Romagna

Tuscany

Dario Fo (born 1926) won the Nobel prize for Literature in 1997.

Umberto Eco *(born 1932), a professor at the University of Bologna, wrote the novel* The Name Of The Rose, *which explored his passion for the Middle Ages. The book was made into a film in 1986.*

Giovanni Boccaccio *(1313–75) is notable for providing a fascinating social record of his era.* The Decameron, *his captivating collection of 100 short stories, is set in the plague-stricken Florence of 1348.*

Pinocchio, *written by Carlo Collodi (1826–90) in 1911, is one of the world's best known children's stories. "Collodi" was Carlo Lorenzini's pseudonym, taken after his mother's birthplace in Tuscany.*

Dante's (1265–1321) Divine Comedy (c.1321), is a journey through Hell, Purgatory, and Paradise. It includes horrific accounts of the torments suffered by the damned.

Venetian author Carlo Goldoni (1707–93) reacted against the satirical tradition of La Commedia dell'Arte, *preferring to write more forgiving plays on contemporary Venice society.*

CLASSICAL ROMAN WRITERS

Texts in Latin by Classical Roman philosophers, poets, dramatists, and politicians are part of the bedrock of Western culture. Today the names Virgil *(The Aeneid)*, Ovid *(Metamorphoses)* and Pliny *(Historia Naturalis)* are literary legends. Fascinating histories such as Livy's *Early History of Rome*, Caesar's *Gallic Wars*, Tacitus's *Annals* and Suetonius's *The Twelve Caesars*, give us an invaluable window on the distant Roman past, as do the caustic *Satires* of Juvenal. Many Latin works owe their survival to the teams of medieval monks who diligently copied and illustrated them. In the Renaissance the stories of Ovid's *Metamorphoses* were plundered by many writers, and the works of Cicero had a profound influence on prose style; Seneca was seen as a master of tragedy, and Plautus's *Pot of Gold* served as a model for comedies.

Detail from medieval copy of Pliny's *Historia Naturalis*

Le Marche

ria

Petrarch (1304–74), one of the earliest and greatest lyric poets, produced works that showed the first indications of Humanism.

Lazio

Abruzzo, Molise, and Puglia

Campania

St. Francis of Assisi *(1182–1226) was the first author to write in Italian instead of formal Latin. As well as letters and sermons, he wrote poems and songs, including the popular Canticle of the Sun.*

Basilicata and Calabria

Roman writer Alberto Moravia (1907–90) is usually labeled a "Neo-Realist." His novels and short stories focus on the corrupt values of contemporary society. Among his best known works are *Gli Indifferenti* and *Agostino*.

Sicily

***The Sicilian** Nobel Prize-winner, Luigi Pirandello (1867–1936), was preoccupied with the theme of multiple personality.* Six Characters In Search Of An Author *is his most famous work.*

| 0 kilometers | 200 |
| 0 miles | 100 |

Veneto Friuli

Music and Opera in Italy

BEFORE ITALY'S UNIFICATION, particularly during the 17th and 18th centuries, each major city had its own traditions of music-making. Rome, as the papal city, had musical traditions less hedonistic than elsewhere, and avoided opera. Florence had its day at the turn of the 16th century, with its celebrated *camerata* (groups set on reviving the traditions of Ancient Greek spectacle). Venice fostered church music on a grand scale, and Naples, during the 18th century, was famous for comic opera. In the 19th century, Milan became the undisputed center of Italian opera, centered on La Scala.

Stradivarius violin

THE MEDIEVAL AND RENAISSANCE PERIODS

THROUGH BOCCACCIO *(see p30)*, among others, it is known that singing, dancing, and poetry often went hand in hand in medieval and Renaissance Italy. Italy concentrated on music as part of a spectacle rather than as a pure art form.

Important contributors to the music of these periods include Guido d'Arezzo (c.995–1050), a monk who developed musical notation, and Francesco Landini (1325–97), one of the first known composers whose songs displayed a distinct concern for lyricism. The next 150 years were to be characterized by the *Ars Perfecta* style, culminating with composer Giovanni Palestrina (1525–94). His vocal style subjected dissonance to strict control, and it was employed for most church music. Madrigals (vocal settings of poems by Petrarch and other poets) were also popular.

The early 17th century saw composers such as Carlo Gesualdo (c.1561–1613) and Claudio Monteverdi challenge these traditions by using more declamation and unexpected and unusual harmonies.

La Pietà, Venice, where Vivaldi performed

THE BAROQUE ERA

CLAUDIO MONTEVERDI'S music straddled the transition from the Renaissance period to 17th-century Baroque. The word "baroque" means highly ornamented, even bizarre, and embellishment was rife. Monteverdi's madrigals began as standard pieces for four voices but often ended up as mini-operas. This was due to the popularity of an individual instrumental style and the development of the *basso continuo* (a supporting organ, harpsichord, or lute that unleashed the possibility for solos and duets). At this point, the beginnings of the string orchestra were in place.

A new fashion for declamation meant that various emotional states were being represented with sighs and sobs rather than just description. Monteverdi's *Vespers* followed others' in exploiting the stereophonic possibilities of San Marco in Venice by contrasting different forces

MAJOR ITALIAN COMPOSERS THROUGH THE AGES

Claudio Monteverdi (1567–1643) was best known for his Vespers *of 1610. Both his madrigals and operas are considered major landmarks in the development of music.*

Antonio Vivaldi (1678–1741) wrote over 600 concertos, many of which are for the violin. The Four Seasons, *a set of concertos, is among the best-selling classical music of all time.*

Gioachino Rossini (1792–1868) was most famous for his comic operas, like The Barber of Seville. *The romantic, expressive side of his more serious works was often overlooked.*

Luciano Pavarotti performing in the most modern surroundings

in different parts of the building. In the 1680s, Arcangelo Corelli (1653–1713) turned to classicism. Corelli was famous for the *Concerto Grosso*, a style that contrasted the solo string group with the full ensemble. He was followed by Antonio Vivaldi (1678–1741), who concentrated his efforts on developing the solo form of the *Concerto Grosso*. He used wind and plucked instruments as well as violins.

THE EMERGENCE OF OPERA

OPERA FIRST emerged during the wedding celebrations of Italy's 16th-century wealthy families. Monteverdi was the first composer to establish

Giuseppe Verdi (1813–1901), whose first works were for La Scala, was the most important opera composer of the 19th century. His most celebrated works include Rigoletto *and* Aida.

his work firmly in the opera repertoire. During the 17th century, Alessandro Scarlatti (1660–1725) formulated a model that consisted of an orchestral overture followed by a sequence of narrative, set as *recitative*, and interrupted by *da capo* (three-part) arias. Themes for the weightier *opera seria* were largely drawn from mythology, while the lighter *opera buffa* had stock scenes that sometimes owed a large debt to the traditions of Commedia dell'Arte. Famous for his comic operas, such as *The Barber of Seville*, was the composer Gioachino Rossini. Among other contributors, Vincenzo Bellini (1801–35) and Gaetano Donizetti (1797–1848) developed *bel canto* singing, a style stressing fine tone and ornamentation.

The two most prominent opera composers of the latter half of the 19th century were Giuseppe Verdi and Giacomo Puccini (1858–1924). Verdi often turned to the works of Shakespeare as well as to more recent subjects in order to form a basis for his work, while many composers, like Puccini, turned to the new trend of *verismo* (slices of contemporary realism) – *La Bohème* is one of the most refined examples of this style.

Puccini's *Tosca*, first staged in 1900

THE 20TH CENTURY

IN THE EARLY 20th century, Puccini's *La Fanciulla del West* (The Girl of the Golden West) brought cowboys into opera, *Turandot* looked toward the Orient, and *Tosca* brought torture and murder. Some composers have attempted to emulate French and German music, and only a few Italian pieces, such as those by Ottorino Respighi (1879–1936), have been regularly performed. The most important name in Italian music today is Luciano Berio (born 1925), whose vocal and collage techniques have attracted numerous imitators. Berio also developed Music Theater, a relatively new art form lying somewhere between drama and opera. Recently, however, Berio has continued the tradition of Grand Opera with his elaborate production of *Un Re in Ascolto*. But it is perhaps Luciano Pavarotti who must be credited with renewing an international interest in opera. His (often televised) performances with "Three Tenors" stars José Carreras and Placido Domingo have secured a massive world audience for opera.

The illuminated interior of Rome's Teatro dell'Opera

Italian Design

ITALY HAS HAD PHENOMENAL success evolving stylish, desirable forms for everyday objects. Its 20th-century achievements can be credited to a handful of forward-thinking industrial giants, such as Olivetti, willing to entrust important product decisions to a group of inspired designers, like Ettore Sottsass. The design genius was to rethink the function of consumer objects, apply new technology, and then make the result look seductive.

The streamlined aesthetic of Italian design extends even to pasta; this Marille version was created by car designer Giorgio Giugiaro for Voiello in 1983.

Sleek, sculptural Alessi cutlery (1988), designed by Ettore Sottsass, combines maximum utility with elegance and aesthetic integrity.

The Alessi kettle (1985), designed by Michael Graves, achieved such popularity in its first year of production that over 100,000 were sold.

One of the best known coffeemakers is Bialetti's Moka Express. Although designed in 1930, it is still enormously popular today.

Combining elegance and function, the 1966 all-plastic Selene side chair was stackable and strong, and designed by Vico Magistretti for Artemide.

The folding Cumano table, designed by Achille Castiglione for Zanotta in 1979, is still revered as a "designer object."

The Patty Difusa chair, with unusual wooden arms that curve into legs, was designed by William Sawaya for Sawaya & Moroni in Milan.

Pininfarina's streamlined form for the Ferrari Testarossa (1986) pushes car design almost into the realms of sculpture.

Light in weight and compact in shape, Olivetti's Valentine typewriter revolutionized the role of the desk typewriter. Designed by Ettore Sottsass in 1969, its portability allowed the user to work anywhere.

B*abc*

Italian printer Giambattista Bodoni (1740–1813) designed the sophisticated typeface that bears his name and is still popular 200 years after its creation.

Milan's Giorgio Armani is best known for his updating of classic items such as the jacket, creating a flattering, smart, and comfortable "deconstructed" look.

The influential, Rome-based Valentino label has long excelled in sassy, well-tailored clothing, pitched at the very top end of the fashion market.

Florence has a long reputation as a producer of high quality crafts, particularly fashion accessories such as handbags, shoes, belts, jewelry, and briefcases.

Gucci's image has had a major revamp. Their classic items, including shoes, are once again a revered totem for the fashion-conscious.

The Artemide company is famous for combining metal and glass in many of their designs, especially lamps and lighting fixtures.

Piaggio's innovative Vespa scooter (1946), by Corradino d'Ascanio, provided cheap, fast, and reliable mobility at a time when few could afford the expense of a car. Hugely successful, the Vespa is still a common sight on Italy's streets.

The Fiat 500 (1957), like the Vespa, became a symbol of mobility and democratization, an expression of Italy's rapid postwar recovery.

Scientists, Inventors, and Explorers

ITALY HAS fostered a long tradition of important scientific thought and discovery, fueled in the Renaissance by such men as Galileo, who searched for a new understanding of the universe. Meanwhile, explorers such as Columbus had set off to find new worlds, a move heralded in the 13th century by Marco Polo. The spirit of scientific inquiry continued up to the 20th century, with the invention of radio and pioneering work in the field of nuclear physics.

Guglielmo Marconi *invented the first practical system for sending radio signals. In 1901, he succeeded in picking up a signal that had been sent to England from Newfoundland.*

Trent Alto A

Valle d'Aosta and Piedmont

Lombardy

The V and

After deducing *that an electric current made frogs' legs move, Alessandro Volta invented the electric battery, a "pile" of metal discs in contact with acid. He demonstrated it to Napoleon in 1801.*

Liguria

Tuscan

Genoese-born *Christopher Columbus sailed west from Spain in 1492. He reached the Indies in three months, navigating with such aids as an astrolabe.*

The explorer *Amerigo Vespucci established that the New World was a separate land mass. A pamphlet wrongly described him as its discoverer, and so, in 1507, America acquired its name.*

Leonardo da Vinci *was the ultimate Renaissance man, accomplished in both arts and sciences. He conceived his first design for a flying machine in c.1488, more than 400 years before the first airplane took off. This model is based on one of his technical drawings.*

The telescope *enabled astronomers to produce accurate lunar maps. Domenico Cassini, astronomy professor at Bologna University, refined the instrument. In 1665 he traced the meridian line in the church of San Petronio.*

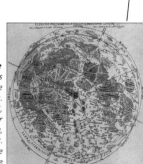

| 0 kilometers | 200 |
| 0 miles | 100 |

Padua University, founded in 1222, was a center of scientific learning in the Renaissance. Galileo, inventor of the telescope, taught physics here, and the lectern he used is still on display.

The Venetian Marco Polo set off for the east as a youth in 1271. He stayed at the court of the Mongol emperor, Kublai Khan, for nearly two decades before returning home. He is seen here arriving at Hormuz in the Persian Gulf from India.

Galileo Galilei proved that the earth revolved around the sun, overturning Church doctrine. He was convicted of heresy in 1633. Here he shows the rings of Saturn to Venetian senators.

Winner of the Nobel Prize for Physics in 1938, Enrico Fermi directed the first controlled nuclear chain reaction. He built the world's first nuclear reactor for producing power at the University of Chicago.

Pliny the Elder wrote his catalog of human knowledge, *Natural History*, in AD 77. He died when Vesuvius erupted two years later, but his book retained its authority for 1,500 years.

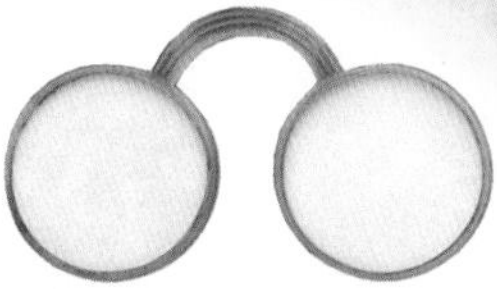

Le Marche

Umbria

ia-gna

Lazio

Abruzzo, Molise, and Puglia

Campania

Basilicata and Calabria

Eyeglasses were invented in Italy in the 13th century. They are first recorded in Venice, still an important center for glasswork today.

Sicily

The mathematician Archimedes was born in c.287 BC in Syracuse, Sicily, then a Greek colony. Legend has it that he discovered the principle of specific gravity while in the bath.

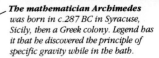

TEMPLA DOMVM EXPOSITIS·VICOS·FORA·MOENIA·PONTES·
VIRGINEAM TRIVII QVOD REPARARIS·AQVAM·
PRISCA LICET NAVTIS STATVAS DARE COMMODA PORTVS·
ET VATICANVM CINGERE SIXTE IVGVM·
PLVS TAMEN VRBS DEBET·NAM QVAE SQVALORE LATEBAT·
CERNITVR IN CELEBRI BIBLIOTHECA LOCO·

THE HISTORY OF ITALY

THE CONCEPT of Italy as a geographic entity goes back to the time of the Etruscans, but Italy's history is one of discord and division. Prior to the 19th century, the only time the peninsula was united was under the Romans, who, by the 2nd century BC, had subdued the other Italian tribes. Rome became the capital of a huge empire, introducing its language, laws, and calendar to most of Europe before succumbing to Germanic invaders in the 5th century AD.

Julius Caesar

Another important legacy of the Roman empire was Christianity and the position of the pope as head of the Catholic church. The medieval papacy summoned the Franks to drive out the Lombards and, in AD 800, crowned the Frankish king Charlemagne Holy Roman Emperor. Unfortunately, what seemed to be the dawn of a new age turned out to be anything but. For five centuries popes and emperors fought to decide which of them should be in charge of their nebulous empire.

Meanwhile, a succession of foreign invaders – Normans, Angevins, and Aragonese – took advantage of the situation to conquer Sicily and the south.

The north, in contrast, saw a growth of independent city states, the most powerful being Venice, fabulously wealthy through trade with the East. Other cities, such as Genoa, Florence, Milan, Pisa, and Siena, also had their days of glory. Northern Italy became the most prosperous and cultured region in western Europe, and it was the artists and scholars of 15th-century Florence who inspired the Renaissance. Small, fragmented states, however, could not compete with great powers. In the 16th century Italy's petty kingdoms fell prey to a foreign invader, this time to Spain, and the north subsequently came under the control of Austria.

One small kingdom that remained independent was Piedmont, but during a war between Austria and France it fell to Napoleon in 1796. In the 19th century, however, it was Piedmont that became the focus for a movement toward a united Italy, a goal that was achieved in 1870, thanks largely to the heroic military exploits of Garibaldi. In the 1920s, the Fascists seized power, and, in 1946, the monarchy was abandoned for today's republic.

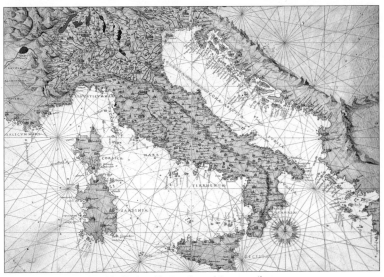

16th-century map of Italy, of the kind used by Venetian and Genoese sailors

◁ **Fresco by Melozzo da Forlì of the court of Sixtus IV (1471–84), a powerful and worldly Renaissance pope**

The Age of the Etruscans

THE ETRUSCANS were Italy's first major civilization. The frescoes, jewelry, and pottery found in their tombs are evidence of an artistic, cultured people. Their origin is a mystery, as is their language, but from the 9th century BC on they spread through central Italy, their chief rivals being the Greeks in the south. Etruria was never a unified state, just a loose confederation of cities. In the 6th century Etruscan kings ruled Rome, the city that would ultimately eclipse them.

ITALY IN 650 BC

☐	*Etruscan kingdoms*
☐	*Greek colonies*

The double flute was a specialty of the Etruscans. The instrument was played at festivals and funerals alike.

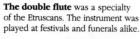

Terra-cotta Winged Horses
This beautiful relief of yoked horses (4th century BC) decorated the façade of the Ara della Regina temple at Tarquinia.

Bronze Sheep's Liver
The inscriptions served as a guide for telling the future from animals' entrails.

Terra-cotta Cremation Urn
The lid of the urn shows the deceased holding a writing tablet. The Etruscans intro-duced the alphabet to Italy.

TOMB OF THE LEOPARDS

Feasts and revelry are common themes in the frescoes that decorate Etruscan tombs. These musicians are from a tomb fresco (c.500 BC) at Tarquinia (*see p450*).

TIMELINE

9th century BC Pre-urban communities established along river valleys in Etruria	**753 BC** Legendary date of foundation of Rome by Romulus	**c.700 BC** Growth of cities in Etruria; earliest Etruscan inscriptions	**616 BC** Etruscan become rulers of Rome under Tarquino the Olde

900 BC	**800 BC**	**700 BC**

c.900 BC First traces of Iron Age in Italy; Villanovan period		
	c.800 BC Greeks settle in Sicily and south of Italy	**715–673 BC** Reign of the wise Numa Pompilius, second king of Rome

Etruscan gold earrings

A Boxing Match

Athletic competitions were held at funerals. This vase, which dates from about 500 BC, was made in Etruria, but imitates the Greek black-figure style of pottery.

The musicians and the dancer in the tomb painting are painted with a realism that indicates the influence of Greek art.

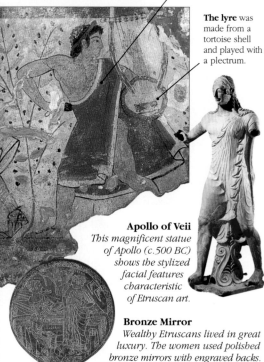

The lyre was made from a tortoise shell and played with a plectrum.

Apollo of Veii

This magnificent statue of Apollo (c.500 BC) shows the stylized facial features characteristic of Etruscan art.

Bronze Mirror

Wealthy Etruscans lived in great luxury. The women used polished bronze mirrors with engraved backs. This one shows Helen of Troy and the goddess Aphrodite.

WHERE TO SEE ETRUSCAN ITALY

Rock tombs *like these at Sovana (p336) are common in the volcanic tufa of central Italy.*

Tuscany, Lazio, and Umbria are rich in Etruscan remains, especially tombs. There are huge necropolises in Lazio at Cerveteri and Tarquinia (p450). The latter also has an important museum. Other museums with major collections of Etruscan art and artifacts include the Villa Giulia (p430) and the Vatican's Museo Gregoriano (p412) in Rome, the Museo Archeologico in Florence (p274), the Museo Civico in Chiusi (p322), and the Museo Guarnacci in Volterra (p336).

Temple of Neptune

This fine temple at Paestum (5th century BC) is a legacy of Greek colonization of the south.

---

509 BC Last Etruscan king, Tarquinius Superbus, expelled from Rome; establishment of Roman Republic

450 BC Roman law codified in the Twelve Tables

Mixing bowl, imported from Greece

390 BC Gauls sack Rome; Capitol saved thanks to alarm sounded by cackling geese

00 BC | **500 BC** | **400 BC**

499 BC Battle of Lake Regillus; Romans defeat alliance of Latins and Etruscans

474 BC Etruscan fleet defeated by Greeks off Cumae; blow to Etruscan naval power

c.400 BC Gauls start to settle along valley of the Po

396 BC Veii, a major Etruscan city in present-day Lazio, falls to Rome

Relief of Capitoline geese, found in the Roman Forum

From Republic to Empire

FROM THE SCORES of tribes inhabiting ancient Italy, one people, the Romans, emerged to conquer the peninsula and impose their language, customs, and laws on the rest.

Roman mask and helmet (1st century BC)

Rome's success was due to superb skill in military and civil organization. The state was a republic ruled by two consuls, elected each year, but as the extent of Rome's conquests grew, power passed to generals such as Julius Caesar. The Republic became unworkable and Caesar's heirs became the first Roman emperors.

Cisalpine Gaul
was annexed in 202–191 BC.

Etruria
was in Roman hands by 265 BC.

Julius Caesar
The great general, conqueror of Gaul, returned to Italy in 49 BC to defeat his rival Pompey. His rise to absolute power signaled the end of the Republic.

Oscan Inscription
The languages of the peoples conquered by Rome lived on for centuries before being replaced by Latin. The Oscans lived in what is now Campania.

War Elephant
In 218 BC the great Carthaginian general Hannibal brought 37 elephants across the Alps – to spread alarm in the Roman ranks.

Roman Aqueduct
The Romans' talent for engineering found its most spectacular expression in huge aqueducts. These could be up to 80 km (50 miles) long, though for most of that distance the water ran underground.

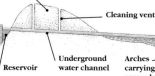

High ground

Cleaning vent

Reservoir

Underground water channel

Arches carrying water across low ground

AQUILEIA

VIA POSTUMIA

VERONA

Padus

PLACENTIA
Piacenza

VIA AEMILIA

BONONIA
Bologna

GENUA
Genoa

FLORENTIA
Florence

ARIMINUM
Rimini

FANUM FORTUNAE
Fano

PISAE
Pisa

Arnus

VIA CASSIA

ARRETIUM
Arezzo

POPULONIA

VIA AURELIA

CLUSIUM
Chiusi

Tiberis

VIA FLAMINIA

ALBA FUCENS

ROMA

TIBUR
Tivoli

PANORMUS
Palermo

TIMELINE

Via Appia

312 BC Building of Via Appia and Aqua Appia aqueduct

308 BC Etruscan city of Tarquinii falls to Rome

287–212 BC Life of Archimedes, the great Greek mathematician of Syracuse

275 BC Greek King Pyrrhus defeated by Romans at Beneventum

264–241 BC First Punic War (between Rome and Carthage)

265 BC Romans capture last Etruscan city

237 BC Romans occupy Corsica and Sardinia

Hannibal, Carthaginian leader in the Second Punic War

218 BC Second Punic War; Hannibal crosses the Alps

216 BC Roman defeat at Battle of Cannae

191 BC Gaulish territory south of the Alps falls to Rome

300 BC   250 BC   200 BC

THE HISTORY OF ITALY

Cicero Addresses the Senate
State business was debated in the Senate. The great orator Cicero (106 – 43 BC) argued for the Republic and against tyranny.

Roman Legionary
This bronze shows a legionnaire in standard kit of helmet, breastplate, leather kilt with iron plates, greaves on his shins, and sandals.

The Via Appia
was extended from Capua to Brindisi in 190 BC.

RFINIUM
LERIA

CAPUA
VIA APPIA
TARENTUM
Taranto
BRUNDISIUM
Brindisi

Sicily
became the first Roman province in 241 BC.

RHEGIUM
Reggio di Calabria

WHERE TO SEE ITALY FROM THE REPUBLICAN ERA

Republican structures are very rare, most having been rebuilt under the Empire. In Rome itself, two notable exceptions are the 2nd-century BC Temples of the Forum Boarium *(p423)*. However, the legacy of the age to modern Italy is not hard to appreciate. Countless roads, such as the Via Appia Antica *(p431)*, and towns were planned originally by Roman engineers. Two striking examples of towns with original Roman street plans are Lucca *(pp310–11)* and Como *(p185)*.

These huge basalt blocks *at Tharros in Sardinia* (p535) *were part of a Roman road.*

ROMAN ROADS

After conquering other tribes, the Romans imposed their authority by building roads along which legions could march rapidly to deal with any trouble. They also built towns. Many, such as Ariminum (Rimini), were "colonies," settlements for Roman citizens – often veteran legionnaires.

Aerial View of Bologna
Roman street plans are still visible in city centers today. The route of the old Via Aemilia cuts straight through the center of Bologna.

146 BC End of Third Punic War; Carthage destroyed

104 BC Slave revolt in Sicily

89 BC Social War: Rome's Italian allies granted citizenship

80 BC Building starts on the first Roman amphitheater, at Pompeii

31 BC Octavian defeats Mark Antony at Battle of Actium

30 BC Suicide of Mark Antony and Cleopatra in Egypt

| 150 BC | | 100 BC | | 50 BC | |

168 BC End of Third Macedonian War; Romans now masters of Greece

Milestone from the Via Aemilia

73 – 71 BC Slave revolt led by Spartacus

49 BC Caesar crosses the Rubicon and drives Pompey from Rome

44 BC Murder of Julius Caesar; end of Roman Republic

45 BC Introduction of 12-month Julian calendar

The Golden Age of Rome

FROM THE AGE of Augustus to the reign of Trajan, Rome's power grew until her empire stretched from Britain to the Red Sea. Despite the extravagance of emperors such as Nero, taxes and booty from military campaigns continually refilled the Imperial coffers. Under the wiser rule of Trajan, Hadrian, and Marcus Aurelius in the 2nd century AD, Roman citizens enjoyed wealth and comfort, with most of the work performed by slaves. Entertainment included visits to the baths, the theater, and the games. The town of Pompeii, buried when Vesuvius erupted in AD 79, preserves many fascinating details of everyday life.

ROMAN EMPIRE IN AD 117

☐ *Maximum extent of the Empire*

Mosaic of Gladiators
Bloodthirsty gladiatorial combats were very popular. The gladiators were mostly slaves captured in war.

Frescoes of festoons and medallions

Trajan's Column
The carvings record Trajan's successful campaigns in Dacia (present-day Romania) in the first decade of the 2nd century AD.

The triclinium
(main dining room) had a beautiful frieze of cupids.

Roman Shops
Buildings in towns were lined with small shops open to the street, like this pharmacy. The front was closed with wooden panels and locked at night.

HOUSE OF THE VETTII

This reconstruction shows one of Pompeii's finest houses *(see pp478–9)*. The Vettii were not aristocrats, but freedmen, former slaves, who had made a fortune through trade. The rooms were richly decorated with frescoes and sculptures.

TIMELINE

9 BC Dedication of Ara Pacis *(see p400)* in Rome to celebrate peace after wars in Gaul and Spain

AD 17 Tiberius fixes boundary of Empire along the Rhine and Danube

Bronze cooking pots from kitchen at Pompeii

AD 79 Eruption of Vesuvius destroys Pompeii and Herculaneu

50 BC	AD 1	AD 50

27 BC Augustus takes title Princeps, in effect becoming the first Roman emperor

AD 37–41 Reign of Caligula

AD 43 Roman conquest of Britain in reign of Claudius

AD 68 Deposition and suicide of Nero

AD 67 Traditional date for martyrdom of St. Peter and St. Paul in Rome

AD 80 Inaugural games in Colosseum

Augustus
The adopted son of Julius Caesar became the first emperor, reducing the Roman Senate to impotence and ruling by decree.

The atrium had a skylight in the roof with a pool that collected rainwater below.

Front entrance

WHERE TO SEE IMPERIAL ROME

The best places to discover how people lived are Pompeii *(pp478–9)* and Herculaneum. Artifacts and works of art from these sites are held at the Museo Archeologico in Naples *(pp474–5)*, and local museums all over Italy contain statues and other remains. Famous sights in Rome include the Pantheon *(p394)* and the Colosseum *(p383)*. Hadrian's Villa and Ostia *(p451)*, at Tivoli near Rome, are also fascinating to visit, but the whole country preserves traces of Rome's glory – from the Arch of Augustus in Aosta *(p207)* to Villa del Casale *(p521)* in Sicily.

The Forum (pp380–81), *with its temples and law courts, was the center of daily life in ancient Rome.*

Reception room

Mosaic of a Banquet
The Romans ate reclining on low couches. A popular accompaniment for many dishes was garum, a salty sauce made of dried fish.

Peristyle or colonnade

The internal garden was a feature borrowed by the Romans from the Greeks.

Household Shrine
Religious rites were practiced both in public and in private. This shrine from the House of the Vettii was dedicated to the lares, the household gods.

AD 97 Roman Empire reaches largest extent in reign of Trajan

AD 161–180 Reign of Marcus Aurelius

AD 193–211 Reign of Septimius Severus

AD 212 Roman citizenship extended to include people from all parts of the Empire

AD 100

AD 150

AD 200

Late 1st century AD Amphitheater of Verona built

AD 134 Hadrian's Villa at Tivoli completed

Emperor Septimius Severus

AD 216 Baths of Caracalla completed in Rome

AD 125 Pantheon rebuilt by Hadrian

The Splitting of the Empire

A DECISIVE TURNING POINT in the history of the Roman Empire came with Emperor Constantine's conversion to Christianity in AD 312 and his decision to build a new capital at Constantinople (Byzantium). By the 5th century the Empire was split in two. Rome and the Western Empire could not stem the tide of Germanic invaders migrating southward and Italy fell first to the Goths and later to the Lombards. The Eastern Empire retained nominal control over parts of Italy from its stronghold at Ravenna, which became the richest, most powerful city of the age, while the great palaces and arenas of Rome were reduced to ruins.

Glass flask with Christian symbol (4th century AD)

ITALY IN AD 600

◼ *Byzantine territories*
◻ *Lombard territories*

The Donation of Constantine
A medieval legend, encouraged by the papacy, tells how Constantine granted Pope Sylvester temporal power over Rome.

Belisarius
(500–565) was a general who won much of Italy back from the Goths.

Theodolinda of the Lombards
The 6th-century queen converted her people to orthodox Catholicism. Here, gold is melted for the church she built at Monza (see p178).

Justinian reigned from 527 to 565. He was a great lawgiver and one of the most powerful Byzantine emperors.

TIMELINE

303–5 Persecution of Christians throughout the Empire in the reign of Diocletian

404 Ravenna becomes seat of western emperor

312 Constantine defeats rival Maxentius at Battle of the Milvian Bridge

Gold coin of Theodoric

488 Italy invaded by the Theodoric the Ostrogoth

547 Church San Vita in Raven

| 300 | 400 | 500 |

270 Aurelian Wall built to protect Rome from Germanic invaders

313 Edict of Milan grants freedom of worship to Christians

324 Constantine becomes Rome's sole ruler

c.320 Building of first St. Peter's in Rome

410 Sack of Rome by Alaric the Visigoth

476 End of Western Empire

535 Belisarius lands in Sicily; reconquest of most of Italy by Byzantine Empire

564 Lombards invade Italy, establishing their capital at Pavia

Charlemagne
The King of the Franks was invited by the pope to crush the Lombards. In return, he was crowned Holy Roman Emperor in AD 800.

Saracens Besieging Messina *(843)*
In the 9th century Sicily was conquered by Muslims from Africa. Saracen raiders even reached Rome, where Pope Leo IV built a new wall to defend the Vatican.

The emperor holds a large gold paten, the dish on which the bread is placed for Mass.

Maximian, Archbishop of Ravenna

WHERE TO SEE EARLY CHRISTIAN AND BYZANTINE ITALY

Though the fall of the Roman Empire led to war, famine, and depopulation, the continuity of the Christian religion has preserved many monuments of the late Empire and Byzantine period. Rome has the catacombs *(p432)* and great basilicas, such as Santa Maria Maggiore *(p403)*. In Ravenna, the administrative capital of the Byzantine Empire, are the churches of San Vitale and Sant'Apollinare *(pp260–61)* with their magnificent mosaics. Sicily and the south also preserve many Byzantine churches, but the finest example of late Byzantine architecture is San Marco in Venice *(pp106–9)*.

Stilo *in Calabria has a beautiful Byzantine church, the Cattolica (p504), dating from the 10th century.*

Priests

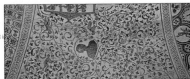

THE COURT OF JUSTINIAN
Byzantine churches were decorated with glorious mosaics of colored glass and gold leaf. This one from the apse of the church of San Vitale in Ravenna *(see p260)*, completed in 547, depicts members of the Imperial court.

Santa Costanza *in Rome (p431) was built in the 4th century as the mausoleum of Constantine's daughter. Late Roman mosaics decorate the vaults.*

	752 Lombard King Aistulf takes Byzantine stronghold of Ravenna	**774** Charlemagne conquers Italy and takes Lombard crown		**878** Saracens capture city of Syracuse from Byzantine Empire and gain control of Sicily
95 Lombards ...trol two ...ds of Italy		**800** Charlemagne crowned Holy Roman Emperor in St. Peter's		
600	**700**	**800**		**900**
Gregory the Great (reigned 590–604)	**754** Pope appeals to Franks for help; King Pepin invades Italy and defeats Lombards		*6th-century Lombard gold helmet in the Bargello museum, Florence (see p275)*	
99 Pope Gregory negotiates ...eace between the Lombards ...nd the Byzantine Empire				

The Rise of Venice

Enrico Dandolo, Doge of Venice (c.1120–1205)

Medieval Italy saw waves of foreign invaders joining in the struggle for power between popes and emperors. In the confusion, many northern cities asserted their independence from feudal overlords. The most powerful was Venice, governed by its doge and Great Council, which grew rich through trade with the East and by shipping Crusaders to fight the Saracens in the Holy Land. Its maritime rivals on the west coast were Genoa and Pisa.

MEDITERRANEAN IN 1250

— *Genoese trade routes*
— *Venetian trade routes*

Matilda of Tuscany

Matilda, Countess of Tuscany (1046–1115) supported the radical Pope Gregory VII against the Emperor Henry IV. When she died, she left her lands to the church.

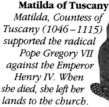

Canopy over the halfdeck

Sails – for added speed

Venetian Galley

The galleys used by Venice, both as warships and for carrying cargo, were similar to ancient Greek vessels.

The oars, pulled by slaves, were the principal means of propulsion.

The columns of San Marco and San Teodoro had been erected in the 12th century.

Basilica San Marco

Doge's Palace

MARCO POLO'S DEPARTURE FOR CHINA

Venice traded in Chinese silks and spices imported via the Middle East, but no Venetian had been to China before Marco Polo's father Nicolò. Marco Polo set off with his father in 1271, returning 25 years later with fantastic tales of his time at the court of Kublai Khan.

TIMELINE

1000 Doge of Venice, Pietro Orseolo II, defeats Dalmatian pirates in Adriatic

11th century School of Law at Bologna develops into Europe's first university

Medieval students

1139 Naples incorporated into Kingdom of Sicily

1000	1050	1100

1030 Norman knight Rainulf granted county of Aversa by Duke of Naples

1061 Normans Robert Guiscard and Roger de Hauteville capture Messina from the Arabs

1063 San Marco in Venice rebuilt

1084 Normans sack Rome

1076 Salerno, last Lombard city, falls to Normans

1073–85 Pope Gregory VII reforms church and papacy

1130 R[...] II crown[...] king of Sicily

1115 Death of Countess Matilda

St. Francis of Assisi
(1181–1226)
In The Dream of Pope Innocent III *by Giotto, painted around 1290–1295, St. Francis holds up the tottering edifice of the Roman church. The Franciscans' rule of poverty brought about a religious revival in reaction to the wealth of the church.*

WHERE TO SEE EARLY MEDIEVAL ITALY

Of the many churches built in this period, especially fine examples are Venice's San Marco *(p106)*, Sant'Antonio *(p152)* in Padua, and the duomo in Pisa *(p314)*. The Leaning Tower *(p316)* also dates back to the 12th century. Medieval castles include Frederick II's Castel del Monte in Puglia *(p493)* and Castello dell'Imperatore in Prato.

Castello dell' Imperatore, *Prato, was built about 1240.*

Monastery of Sant'Apollonia

Today's Riva degli Schiavoni

Nicolò Polo, his brother Maffeo, and son Marco prepare to embark. They sailed first to Acre in the Levant.

Fourth Crusade
Discord between the leaders of the crusade and Pope Innocent III culminated in the sacking of Constantinople in 1204.

Frederick II
(1194–1250)
The emperor kept a court of poets and scholars in Sicily. He won Jerusalem from the Arabs by diplomacy, but was constantly at war with the pope and the cities of Lombardy.

1155 Frederick Barbarossa crowned Holy Roman Emperor

1198 Frederick II becomes king of Sicily

1204 Sacking of Constantinople

1209 Franciscan Order founded

1216 Dominican Order founded

1250 Death of Frederick II

1260 Urban IV invites Charles of Anjou to rule Naples and Sicily

1265 Birth of Dante

1150   **1200**   **1250**

Frederick Barbarossa dressed as a Crusader

1220 Frederick II crowned Holy Roman Emperor

1228 Gregory IX excommunicates Frederick II; struggle between Guelphs (the papal party) and Ghibellines (supporters of the emperor)

1237 Lombard League defeat Frederick at Battle of Cortenuova

1271 Marco Polo sets off on journey to China

The Late Middle Ages

OLD FEUDS BETWEEN pope and emperor thrived throughout the 14th century, kept alive by two warring factions – the Guelphs, who backed the papacy, and the Ghibellines, who favored Imperial power. The cities of Lombardy and Tuscany used the political confusion to grow in strength. It was against this turbulent backdrop that a great new age in painting was inspired by artists such as Duccio and Giotto. Also at this time the Florentine poets Dante and Petrarch laid the foundations of Italian literature.

Sienese bishop's staff

ITALY IN 1350

- ☐ *Papal States*
- ☐ *Holy Roman Empire*
- ☐ *Angevin Kingdom of Naples*

MEDIEVAL TOWN SQUARE

Throughout central Italy, the town square was an expression of civic pride and independence. Towns such as Perugia *(see pp342–3)* tried to overshadow their rivals in the splendor of their town halls. The center of Perugia has changed little since the 14th century, when the town's main rival was Siena.

The campanile or bell tower

A griffin, symbol of Perugia

Condottieri
Cities paid condottieri, *leaders of bands of mercenaries, to fight their wars. Siena hired Guidoriccio da Fogliano, seen here in a fresco by Simone Martini (1330).*

The main chamber of the town hall, the Sala dei Notari, is decorated with the coats of arms of Perugia's mayors.

Dante's Inferno
One of the harshest punishments in Dante's vision of hell is reserved for corrupt popes, such as Boniface VIII (reigned 1294–1303), who are placed upside down in fiery pits.

The Fontana Maggiore was begun in 1275 and includes panels by Nicola Pisano. Prominently placed, it is an emblem of the town's wealth.

TIMELINE

1282 Sicilian Vespers; uprising against French rule in Palermo; 2,000 French soldiers killed

1298 Marco Polo returns from China to Venice

1296 Work begins on the Duomo in Florence

1309–43 Reign of Robert the Wise of Naples

1310 Work begins on Palazzo Ducale in Venice

1313 Birth of Boccaccio

1275	1300	1325

1282 Peter of Aragon lands at Trapani, conquers Sicily and is crowned king in Palermo

The poet and scholar Petrarch

1304 Birth of Petrarch

1309 Clement V moves papacy to Avignon

1321 Dante completes *La Divina Commedia* and dies the same year

1337 De[ath] of Gio[tto]

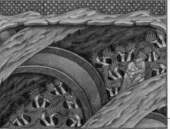

The Black Death
Bubonic plague reached Italy in 1347, carried on Genoese ships from the Black Sea. It killed over a third of the population, reducing those left to a state of superstitious terror.

WHERE TO SEE LATE MEDIEVAL ITALY

Many central Italian cities and towns have public buildings from the 13th and 14th centuries; among the most impressive are Palazzo Vecchio (*p283*) in Florence and Siena's Palazzo Pubblico (*p330*). Smaller towns that preserve much of their medieval character include Volterra (*p324*) and the walled Monteriggioni (*p324*) in Tuscany, Gubbio (*p342*) and Todi (*p349*) in Umbria, and Viterbo (*pp448–9*) in Lazio. The duomo in Orvieto (*pp348–9*) is a fine example of a late 13th-century Gothic cathedral.

Piazza dei Priori in Volterra (p324) *is one of the most beautiful medieval squares in Italy.*

The cathedral was started in 1350 and used to include an outside pulpit in the square.

Construction of Alessandria
Almost all towns were ringed with strong walls. This fresco (1407) by Spinello Aretino is a valuable record of medieval building techniques.

Return of Pope Gregory XI to Rome *(1378)*
For 70 years the popes had lived in Avignon, protected by the French kings, while nobles and republicans fought for control of Rome.

1339 Simon Boccanegra becomes first doge of Genoa; Giovanna I Queen of Naples

Medieval doctor

1378–1415 Period of Schism, with rival popes and antipopes in Rome and Avignon

1347–9 Black Death

1380 Genoese fleet surrenders to Venetians at Chioggia

| 1350 | 1375 | 1400 |

1354 Cola di Rienzo killed in Rome

1385 Gian Galeazzo Visconti becomes ruler of Milan

1406 Pisa annexed by Florence

1378 Gregory XI returns from Avignon to Rome

1347 Cola di Rienzo tries to reestablish Roman Republic

The Renaissance

Leonardo da Vinci (1452–1519)

FIFTEENTH-CENTURY ITALY saw a flowering of the arts and scholarship unmatched in Europe since the days of Greece and Rome. Architects turned from the Gothic to Classical models for inspiration, while painting, with its new understanding of perspective and anatomy, produced a generation of artists that included such giants as Leonardo da Vinci, Raphael, and Michelangelo. The patronage for this cultural "rebirth" came from the wealthy families that ruled the city states of the north, led by the Medici of Florence. In spite of intense rivalry, they oversaw a period of uneasy stability out of which the Renaissance grew.

ITALY IN 1492

▨	*Republic of Florence*
☐	*Papal States*
▨	*Aragonese possessions*

Handing over the Keys of St. Peter
Perugino's fresco in the Sistine Chapel (see p416) links the authority of the pope to the New Testament and, through the Classical buildings in the background, to ancient Rome.

Galeazzo Maria Sforza was the son of Milan's ruler.

Piero de' Medici, Lorenzo's father, was given the nickname "the Gouty."

Self-portrait of the artist

Execution of Savonarola *(1498)*
Having assumed the leadership of Florence in 1494, the fanatical monk was hanged, then burned for heresy in Piazza della Signoria.

TIMELINE

1420 Martin V re-establishes papacy in Rome	**1435** Publication of *On Painting* by Alberti, which contains the first system for the use of linear perspective	**1436** Brunelleschi completes dome of Florence cathedral		**1458–64** War between Houses of Aragon and Anjou over Kingdom of Naples	**1469** Lorenzo the Magnificent becomes ruler of Florence

1425   **1450**

Cosimo de' Medici

1434 Cosimo de' Medici comes to power in Florence	**1442** Naples captured by Alfonso of Aragon	**1452** Birth of Leonardo da Vinci
1444 Federico da Montefeltro becomes Duke of Urbino	**1453** Fall of Constantinople	*Filippo Brunelleschi*

The Battle of Pavia *(1525)*
The French King Francis I was captured at this battle against the army of the Hapsburg Emperor Charles V, who won control of Italy.

THE PROCESSION OF THE MAGI
Benozzo Gozzoli's fresco (1459) in the Palazzo Medici-Riccardi, Florence, depicts members of the Medici family and other contemporary notables. It contains many references to a great church council held in Florence in 1439.

Lorenzo de' Medici (the Magnificent) was depicted as one of the three kings traveling to Bethlehem.

WHERE TO SEE RENAISSANCE ITALY
Many cities were flourishing centers of the arts in the 15th century. None can rival Florence *(pp262–303)* with its great palazzi and the Uffizi gallery *(pp278–81)*, but Venice *(pp80–131)*, Urbino *(pp360–61)*, and Mantua *(p199)* all preserve great treasures. In Rome, do not miss the Vatican's Sistine Chapel and Raphael Rooms *(pp414–17)*.

The Spedale degli Innocenti *by Brunelleschi in Florence (p269) shows the Classical symmetry and restraint of Renaissance architecture.*

Humanism
Carpaccio's painting of St. Augustine is thought to show Cardinal Bessarion (c.1395–1472), one of the scholars who revived interest in Classical philosophy, especially Plato.

Pope Julius II
During his reign (1503–13), the worldly Julius made the papacy a major power in European politics. Raphael's portrait shows him as a shrewd old statesman.

1487 Birth of Titian
1483 Sixtus IV consecrates Sistine Chapel
1475 Birth of Michelangelo
1483 Birth of Raphael
Raphael
1494 Italy invaded by Charles VIII of France
1498 Savonarola executed; Machiavelli secretary to ruling Council in Florence
1500
1503 Giuliano della Rovere elected Pope Julius II; he proves the most powerful of the Renaissance popes
1512 Michelangelo completes Sistine Chapel ceiling
1513 Giovanni de' Medici crowned Pope Leo X
Niccolò Machiavelli
1527 Rome sacked by Imperial troops
1525 Francis I of France captured at Battle of Pavia
1532 Machiavelli's book *The Prince* is published, five years after his death
1475

The Counter-Reformation

Gian Lorenzo Bernini

AFTER THE SACK OF ROME in 1527, Italy was at the mercy of Charles V, Holy Roman Emperor and King of Spain. Pope Clement VII, who had opposed Charles, crowned him emperor in Bologna. In response to the growing threat from Protestantism, a series of reforms, known as the Counter-Reformation and backed by the Inquisition, imposed rigid orthodoxy. New religious orders, such as the Jesuits, were set up to take the battle for men's souls far overseas. The missionary spirit of the age inspired the dramatic forms of the Baroque.

ITALY IN 1550

- Spanish possessions
- States allied with Spain

Emperor Charles V and Pope Clement VII
The two former enemies settled their differences and the future destiny of Italy in the Treaty of Barcelona (1529).

The Virgin Mary intervenes on the side of the Christians.

BAROQUE STUCCO DECORATION
This stucco relief by Giacomo Serpotta (c.1690) in the Oratory of Santa Zita in Palermo is a magnificent example of Late Baroque exuberance. The subject is a favorite of the period, the Battle of Lepanto, a great naval triumph for the combined forces of Christendom against the Turks (1571).

The center of the ingenious creation is, in effect, a framed painting in perspective.

Baroque Architecture
Guarino Guarini's decoration of the dome of the Chapel of the Holy Shroud in Turin (see p213) *was completed in 1694.*

The young boy rests his hand on a helmet, symbol of the victorious Christians.

TIMELINE

1530–37 Alessandro de' Medici ruler of Florence

1542 Inquisition established in Rome

1545–63 Council of Trent sets out agenda of Counter-Reformation

Andrea Palladio

1580 Death of architect Palladio

1589 Palestrina publishes setting of the Latin Hymnal

1600 Philosopher Giordano Bruno burned for heresy in Rome

1550   1575

1540 Founding of Jesuit Order

1541 Michelangelo completes *Last Judgment* in Sistine Chapel

1529 Charles V crowned Holy Roman Emperor in San Petronio, Bologna

1571 Victory over Turkish fleet at Battle of Lepanto

1564 Birth of Galileo

1560 San Carlo Borromeo appointed Bishop of Milan

Giovanni Pierluigi da Palestrina

Trial of Galileo
The great astronomer was often in trouble with the Inquisition. He was summoned to Rome in 1633 and forced to deny that the Earth and planets moved around the sun.

Lepanto was the last major sea battle in which Venetian galleys played an important role.

Cherubs, a favorite motif in Baroque decoration

St. Ignatius Loyola
The Spanish saint was the founder of the Jesuits – sanctioned by the pope in Rome in 1540.

The turban, symbol of the defeated Turks

Revolt of Masaniello *(1647) High taxes made Spanish rule in Naples unpopular. A proposed tax on fruit sparked off this failed revolt.*

WHERE TO SEE BAROQUE ITALY

The Ecstasy of St. Teresa *by Bernini (p402) has the dynamic theatricality characteristic of the best Baroque sculpture.*

The Baroque is strongly associated with Rome and in particular with its great public spaces such as Piazza Navona *(pp388–9)* and the many churches by Borromini and Bernini. Other cities and towns with striking Baroque architecture include Lecce *(pp496–7)* in Puglia, Palermo *(pp510–13)*, Noto *(p527)* and Syracuse *(pp526–7)* in Sicily, and Turin *(pp212–17)*.

1625	1650	1675
1626 New St. Peter's consecrated in Rome	**1669** Venice loses island of Crete to the Turks	**1694** Andrea Pozzo completes ceiling fresco for the church of Sant'Ignazio in Rome
1631 Duchy of Urbino absorbed by Papal States		**1678** Birth of Vivaldi
1633 Galileo condemned by papal authorities	**1647** Revolt in Naples in response to tax on fruit	**1693** Eastern Sicily ruined by earthquake that kills 5 percent of the island's population
1642 *L'incoronazione di Poppea* by Monteverdi	**1669** Major eruption of Mount Etna	**1674** Revolt against Spanish rule in Messina

The Grand Tour

The Romantic poet Shelley, visitor to Italy

T HE TREATY of Aix-la-Chapelle in 1748 marked the start of 50 years of peace. It was about this time that Italy, with its great art treasures and Classical ruins, including the newly excavated Pompeii, became Europe's first great tourist destination. Young English "milords" visited Rome, Florence, and Venice as part of a new type of pilgrimage, the Grand Tour; while artists and poets sought inspiration in Rome's glorious past. In 1800, Napoleon, who conquered and briefly united Italy, threatened to destroy the old order, but in 1815 the status quo was restored.

Charles III's Fleet at Naples *(1753)*
Ruler of Naples from 1734 to 1759, when he became King of Spain, Charles attempted genuine political reforms.

Goethe in the Roman Campagna
Goethe toured Italy in the 1780s. Great poets who followed his example included the Romantics Keats, Shelley, and Byron.

Farnese Hercules
(see p475)

Venetian Carnival
The colorful folklore of Carnival attracted many tourists, but Venice's days of greatness were over. In 1797, the proud maritime republic was ceded to Austria by Napoleon.

The Dying Galatian
(see p376)

GALLERY OF VIEWS OF ANCIENT ROME BY PANNINI

Giovanni Pannini (1691–1765) painted views of Roman ruins for foreigners. This painting is a capriccio, an imaginary scene incorporating many well-known views and Classical statues

TIMELINE

1713 Treaty of Utrecht gives Naples and Sardinia to Austria and Sicily to Piedmont

Medici coat of arms

1725 *The Four Seasons* by Vivaldi

1735 Peace of Vienna confirms Charles III as King of the Two Sicilies (Naples and Sicily)

1748 First excavations at Pompeii

1700	1720	1740

1707 Birth of playwright Carlo Goldoni

1718 Piedmont and Sardinia united under House of Savoy; Sicily passes to Austria

1737 End of Medici dynasty in Florence; Grand Duchy of Tuscany passes to Austrian House of Lorraine

Antonio Vivaldi, great Venetian composer

View of the Roman Forum by Piranesi
The popular series of etchings Vedute di Roma *(Views of Rome) by Giovanni Battista Piranesi (1720–78) inspired a new interest in excavating the ruins of ancient Rome.*

WHERE TO SEE 18TH-CENTURY ITALY

The 18th century produced two of Rome's best-loved tourist attractions: the Spanish Steps *(p399)* and the Trevi Fountain *(p400)*. It was also the age of the first specially built museums, including the Vatican's Museo Pio-Clementino *(p411)*. The Neo-Classical sculpture of Antonio Canova (1757–1822) was immensely popular during this period. His tomb is in Santa Maria Gloriosa dei Frari in Venice *(pp94–5)*. Of Neo-Classical buildings, the most imposing is a vast monument to enlightened despotism: the Palazzo Reale at Caserta *(p480)*.

***Pauline Borghese**, Napoleon's sister, was the model for Antonio Canova's* Venus *(1805) in the Villa Borghese collection in Rome (p429).*

The Colosseum was as popular a subject in the 18th century as it is on today's picture postcards.

The Laocoön
(see p407)

View of the Pantheon
(see p394)

Napoleon
When Napoleon conquered Italy in 1800, he was seen by many as a liberator. The enchantment wore off as he took priceless works of art back to Paris.

Congress of Vienna *(1815)*
The conference decided that Austria should keep Lombardy and Venice, thereby sowing the seeds of the Italian unification movement.

La Scala Opera House, Milan (see p187)

1778 La Scala opened in Milan

1797 Venice given to Austria by Treaty of Campo Formio; France controls rest of northern Italy

1800–1801 Napoleon conquers Italy

1808 Murat becomes King of Naples

1809 Pope Pius VII exiled from Rome

1760	1780	1800

1773 Pope dissolves Jesuit Order

1780 Joseph II succeeds to Austrian throne; minor reforms in Lombardy

1806 Joseph Bonaparte becomes King of Naples

1768 Corsica sold by Genoa to France

1765–90 Reign of Leopold Grand Duke of Tuscany, who introduces enlightened reforms

1796–7 Napoleon's first campaign in northern Italy

1815 Congress of Vienna restores status quo in Italy, though Austria keeps Venice

The Risorgimento

THE WORD "RISORGIMENTO" (resurgence) describes the five decades of struggle for liberation from foreign rule, culminating in the unification of Italy in 1870. In 1848, patriots rose up against the Austrians in Milan and Venice, the Bourbons in Sicily, and the pope in Rome, where a republic was declared. Garibaldi valiantly defended the republic, but all the uprisings were too localized. By 1859, the movement was better organized with Vittorio Emanuele II at its head. Two years saw the conquest of all but Venice and Rome, both of which fell within a decade.

Vittorio Emanuele

ITALY IN 1861

⬜ *Kingdom of Italy*

The guns were rusty old converted flintlocks.

Giuseppe Mazzini
(1805–72)
An exile for much of his life, Mazzini fought alongside Garibaldi to unite Italy as a republic, rather than a kingdom.

The red shirt
was the badge of the Garibaldini.

Italian Railroads
The short railroad line from Naples to Portici was opened in 1839. Politically fragmented, Italy was slow to create an effective rail network.

Revolt of Messina
When, in 1848, Messina revolted, Ferdinand II subjected the town to a savage bombardment, earning himself the nickname King Bomba.

TIMELINE

1831 Insurrection in Romagna and Le Marche against papal rule

1840 First major railroad links established

1849 Accession of Vittorio Emanuele II as ruler of Piedmont

1820	1830	1840	1850

1820s Carbonari secret society active in Papal States

1831 Mazzini founds *Giovine Italia* (Young Italy) movement

1847 Economic crisis

1848 Revolutions throughout Italy

1852 Cavo becomes p minister of Piedmont

Daniele Manin, hero of the Venetian uprising of 1848

1849 Republic of Ror crushed by French tro

Battle of Solferino (1859)
With the help of a French army led by Napoleon III, the Piedmontese won Milan and Lombardy from the Austrians.

Two old paddle steamers brought the Thousand from Quarto near Genoa.

WHERE TO SEE RISORGIMENTO ITALY

Almost every town in Italy honors the heroes of the Risorgimento with a Via Garibaldi, a Via Cavour, a Piazza Vittorio, a Via Mazzini, and a Via XX Settembre (the date of the fall of Rome in 1870). Many cities also have Risorgimento museums. One of the best is in Turin *(p215).*

The Victor Emmanuel Monument (p374) *is a prominent, but largely unloved, Roman landmark.*

Count Camillo di Cavour (1810–61)
Cavour's diplomacy as prime minister of Piedmont ensured that the House of Savoy became rulers of the new Italy. He also coined the word "Risorgimento."

The skiffs were lent by other ships moored in Marsala harbor.

GARIBALDI AND THE THOUSAND
Giuseppe Garibaldi (1807–82) was a leader of courage and genius. In 1860, he landed at Marsala with 1,000 volunteers. The garrison at Palermo surrendered, Sicily fell, and he went on to conquer Naples, thus presenting Vittorio Emanuele with half a kingdom.

Giuseppe Verdi (1813–1901)
Composers such as Verdi, Donizetti, and Rossini made the 19th century the great era of Italian opera. Verdi's early operas inspired the Risorgimento.

1859 Battles of Magenta and Solferino; Piedmont acquires Lombardy from Austria and duchies of Parma, Modena, and Tuscany

1861 Kingdom of Italy proclaimed with capital at Turin

Pope Pius IX, who remained a virtual prisoner in the Vatican when Rome became capital of Italy

1882 Deaths of Garibaldi and Pope Pius IX

1893 Troops sent to suppress insurrection in Sicily

| 1860 | 1870 | 1880 | 1890 |

1866 Italy wins Venice from Austria

1860 Garibaldi and the Thousand capture Kingdom of the Two Sicilies

1870 Rome falls to royalist troops and is made capital of new kingdom; Vatican announces doctrine of papal infallibility

1878 Death of Vittorio Emanuele; accession of King Umberto I

1890 Italian colony of Eritrea established by royal decree

Twentieth-Century Italy

Fascism under Mussolini (1922–43) promised the Italians greatness, but delivered only humiliation. In spite of this, Italy has become one of Europe's leading economies with a standard of living undreamed of at the turn of the century. This has been achieved in the face of great obstacles. Since 1946, the Republic has passed through many crises: a series of unstable coalitions, the terrorist outrages in the 1970s and, recently, corruption scandals involving numerous government ministers and officials.

1936 Fiat produces first "Topolino" car

1922 Fascists march on Rome; Mussolini invited to form government

1918 Austrian advance halted at the river Piave, just north of Venice

1940 Italy enters World War II

1943 Allies land in Sicily; Italy signs armistice and new Badoglio government declares war on Germany

1900 Assassination of King Umberto I

1915 Italy enters World War I

1911–12 Italy conquers Libya

1900	1920	1940

1900	1920	1940

1908 Earthquake destroys many towns and villages in Calabria and eastern Sicily; Messina almost completely razed to the ground; over 150,000 die

1936 Italy conquers Abyssinia; pact with Germany, forming anti-Communist "Axis"

1920s Postwar years see continued emigration to the United States. Here, emigrants cheer as they reach New York aboard the *Giulio Cesare*

1943 Mussolini imprisoned, then freed by Germans

1946 Referendum in which Italy votes to become a republic; Christian Democrat party forms first of a long series of coalition governments

1917 Defeat at Caporetto on Italy's northeastern border; Italian troops, such as these Alpini, retreat to defensive positions

1909 In his *Futurist Manifesto*, Filippo Marinetti condemns all traditional art as too static. His idea of a new dynamic art is expressed in works such as Umberto Boccioni's bronze *Unique Forms of Continuity in Space*

1978 Prime Minister Aldo Moro kidnapped and assassinated by Red Brigades

1994 TV magnate Silvio Berlusconi becomes prime minister after forming new political party "Forza Italia". Alleged financial irregularities force him to resign later that year

1996 Fire destroys La Fenice theater in Venice

1996 Earthquake in Assisi seriously damages the Basilica di San Francesco, destroying Giotto's frescos

1960 *La Dolce Vita*, Federico Fellini's film satire on Rome's decadent café society, is released

1992 Judge Giovanni Falcone killed by Mafia in Sicily

1992 Scandals expose widespread corruption in the postwar political system

2000 Rome enters the 21st century with millions of pilgrims celebrating the Holy Year known as the Jubilee

1966 River Arno bursts its banks, flooding Florence and damaging many priceless works of art

1990 World Cup staged in Italy

1960	1980	2000

1960	1980	2000

1960 Olympic Games held in Rome

1978 Election of Pope John Paul II

1983 Bettino Craxi, Italy's first Socialist prime minister, forms government

1999 Roberto Benini wins 3 Oscars for his film *La Vita è Bella*, including best actor and best foreign language film

1969 Bomb outrage in Milan at Piazza Fontana; 13 killed and many injured

1982 Italian soccer team wins World Cup in Spain

1997 Dario Fo wins the Nobel prize for literature

1998 Italy joins the EU common currency

1957 Treaty of Rome; Italy one of the six founder members of the European Economic Community

ITALIAN FILM SINCE WORLD WAR II

The social problems of late 1940's Italy inspired a wave of film art known as Neo-Realism. Leading exponents included Roberto Rossellini, who made *Roma Città Aperta* (1945), Vittorio de Sica, the director of *Bicycle Thieves* (1948), Pierpaolo Pasolini and Luchino Visconti. Since that time, the major Italian directors have cultivated their own personal styles.

Visconti's later films, such as *Death in Venice* (1971), show formal beauty and decadence, while Federico Fellini's *La Dolce Vita* (1960) and *Roma* (1972) depict life as a grotesque carnival. Italy has also produced some successful commercial films. Sergio Leone's late 1960s westerns achieved worldwide acclaim, while Roberto Begnigni's *La Vita é Bella* won three Oscars in 1999.

Vittorio de Sica (1901–74)

ITALY THROUGH THE YEAR

THROUGHOUT ITALY, the variety of local character and color is astonishing. This is due mainly to the survival of regionalism, particularly in the southern parts of the country. Old traditions, customs, and lifestyles are still greatly respected and there is a deep attachment to the land, which is reflected in a healthy interest in the food and produce, as well as a perseverance of seasonal religious and secular events. Annual festivals, whether in rural or urban areas, range from wine-tasting and gastronomic celebrations to elaborate commemorations of every patron saint imaginable.

SPRING

THE ITALIAN SPRING begins early, particularly in the south. City streets and main sights are rarely overcrowded (except at Easter in Rome). The weather, however, can be unpredictable and wet in the central and northern parts of the country. Spring specialties, such as asparagus, spinach, and artichokes, begin to appear on restaurant menus. This is a season of great celebration; festivals and fairs abound, especially in Sicily, and the Easter papal address always draws massive crowds to St. Peter's.

Tuscan asparagus

MARCH

Mostra Vini Spumanti, *(mid-Mar)*, Madonna di Campiglio, Trentino-Alto Adige. Fair celebrating sparkling wine.
Sa Sartiglia, Oristano, Sardinia. Three-day carnival ending on Shrove Tuesday.

Procession of the Grieving Madonna on the isle of Procida

Su e zo per i ponti *(second Sun)*, Venice. Marathon-style race through the city's streets, up and down the bridges.

APRIL

Procession of the Grieving Madonna *(Good Friday)*, Procida, Campania. A colorful religious procession throughout the island.
Holy Week *(Easter Week)*. Numerous Easter celebrations from Palm Sunday to Easter Sunday, throughout the country.
Papal Address *(Easter Sunday)*, Rome. The pope makes his Easter address from the Vatican.
Dance of the Devils and Death *(Easter Sunday)*, Prizzi, Sicily. Dance recital symbolizing the attempts of evil to vanquish the forces of God.
Scoppio del Carro *(Easter Sunday)*, Florence. Fireworks display is lit by a mechanical dove in front of the Duomo.
Festa della Madonna che Scappa in Piazza *(Easter Sunday)*, Sulmona, Abruzzo. A meeting between the Virgin and the Risen Christ is enacted.
Festa degli Aquiloni *(first Sun after Easter)*, San Miniato, Tuscany. Kite lovers perform aerial acrobatics at this festival.
Festa di San Marco *(Apr 25)*, Venice. St. Mark, the patron saint of Venice, is commemorated by a gondola race across St. Mark's Basin.
Mostra Mercato Internazionale dell'Artigianato *(last week)*, Florence. An important European exhibition of arts and crafts.

Spring strawberries

Scoppio del Carro ("Explosion of the Carriage") in Florence

Sagra Musicale Lucchese *(Apr–Jul)*, Lucca, Tuscany. Extensive festival of sacred music, held in the city's many Romanesque churches.

MAY

Festa di Sant'Efisio *(May 1)*, Cagliari, Sardinia. Paraders in traditional Sardinian costume.
Festa dei Ceri *(May 5)*, Gubbio, Perugia. Festival, including a race with four teams carrying large candles.
Festa di San Domenico Abate *(May 6)*, Cocullo, Abruzzo. Includes a procession with a statue of St. Dominic covered with live snakes.
Festa della Mela *(late May)*, Ora (Auer), Trentino-Alto Adige. This annual "Festival of the Apple" takes place in a town known as the "gateway to the Dolomites."
Greek Drama in Theater *(May–Jun)*, Syracuse, Sicily. Festival of Greek drama.
Maggio Musicale *(May–Jun)*, Florence. This is the city's biggest arts festival, including music, drama, and dance.

Street carpeted with flowers for the Infiorata in Genzano

SUMMER

S UMMER brings the crowds to Italy, particularly the cities. Italians, however, flee and head for the coast, usually in August. The lines for tourist attractions can be long and hotels are often fully booked. Festivals vary; religious events are interspersed with those of the arts and local folklore.

JUNE

Festa della Fragola
(Jun 1), Borgo San Martino, Alessandria. Musical and folkloric performances in celebration of the strawberry.
Biennale *(Jun–Sep)*, Venice. The world's biggest exhibition of contemporary art, which takes place during odd-numbered years only.
Infiorata *(early Jun)*, Genzano, Castelli Romani. A procession through streets carpeted with flowers in this town just south of Rome.
Festa di San Giovanni *(mid-Jun – mid-Jul)*, Turin, Piedmont. Festival in honor of the city's patron saint, John, dating from the 14th century.
Calcio Storico Fiorentino *(Jun 24)*, Florence. Procession of people in 16th-century-style costumes; fireworks displays.

Festa di Sant'Andrea
(Jun 27), Amalfi, Campania. Fireworks and processions.
Festa dei Due Mondi *(late Jun–early Jul)*, Spoleto, Umbria. International festival of drama, music, and dance.
Gioco del Ponte *(last Sun)*, Pisa. "The Bridge Parade" of marchers in antique armor.
Tevere Expo *(end Jun)*, on the Tiber, Rome. Arts and crafts, food and wine stalls, folk music and fireworks.

JULY

Corsa del Palio *(Jul 2)*, Siena. Tuscany's most famous event *(see p331)* presents a medieval flag-waving exhibition and horse race.
Festa della Madonna della Bruna *(first Sun)*, Matera, Basilicata. A lively procession of clergymen and knights in costume.
Festa dei Noiantri *(last two weeks of Jul)*, Rome. A colorful race of the city's horse-drawn carriages.
Festa della Santa Maria del Carmine *(Jul 16)*, Naples. A sumptuous festival featuring the illumination of the city's *campanile* (bell tower).
International Film Festival *(Jul–Aug)*, Taormina, Sicily.

Musician from Florence's Calcio

The Sienese Palio in action

Opera Festival *(Jul–Aug)*, Verona, Veneto. Renowned opera festival *(see p137)* overlapping with the **Shakespeare Festival**, providing music, drama, opera, and dance.

AUGUST

Medieval Palio *(first week– end Aug)* Feltre, Veneto. Parades and archery competitions, medieval-style.
Festa del Mare *(Aug 15)*, Diano Marina, Liguria. This "Festival of the Sea" boasts a spectacular fireworks display.
Corsa del Palio *(Aug 16)*, Siena, Tuscany. See July entry.
Festa dei Candelieri *(Aug 16)*, Sassari, Sardinia. "Festival of the Candle," dating from the 16th century.
Venice Film Festival *(late Aug–early Sep)*. International festival on the Lido.
Rossini Festival *(Aug–Sep)*, Pèsaro, Le Marche. A celebration of the composer's work, in his birthplace.
Settimane Musicali di Stresa *(late Aug–end Sep)*, Stresa, Lombardy. Four weeks of concerts and recitals.

Sun, sand, and sea – essential ingredients of a Tuscan beach vacation

AUTUMN

Autumn is a slow, gentle season in Italy but that doesn't mean there are fewer festivals and fairs. In addition to the various religious events at this time of year, gastronomic festivals are especially popular, commemorating such delectables as chestnuts, local cheeses, sausages, and mushrooms. Autumn is the season of the *vendemmia*, the grape harvest, which is often used as an excuse for village festivities at which the latest local wines flow freely.

The climate *(see pp68–9)* in late autumn is often cold and wet in the north. The south, however, can be quite warm through October.

Advertisement for the September Palio in Asti, Piedmont

SEPTEMBER

Sagra dell'Uva *(early Sep)*, Rome. Harvest festival with grapes at bargain prices and lots of folk entertainment.
Neapolitan Song Contest *(Sep 7)*, Piazza di Piedigrotta, Naples. Usually entered by couples; the singer often plays a mandolin, while the partner plays the castanets.
Festa di San Sebastiano e Santa Lucia *(Sep 1–3)*, Sassari, Sardinia. Includes a contest where competitors improvise short poems.
Procession of the Macchina di Santa Rosa *(Sep 3)*, Viterbo, Lazio. Commemoration of the saint's body being transported to the Church of Santa Rosa in 1258.

The widely cultivated olive tree

Giostra del Saracino *(first Sun)*, Arezzo, Umbria. Joust of the Saracen and knights, dating from the 13th century.
Regata Storica *(first Sun)*, Venice. A procession of historic boats followed by a colorful gondola race.
Human chess game *(second week)*, Marostica, near Vicenza. A popular costumed game held in the main square every even year.
Rassegna del Chianti Classico *(second week)*, Chianti, Tuscany. Celebration of the local wines.
The Miracle of San Gennaro *(Sep 19)*, Naples. Re-enactment of the liquefaction of the saint's blood, in a lively mass at the duomo.
Palio *(third Sun)*, Asti, Piedmont. Includes a costumed medieval procession and bareback racing.

OCTOBER

Amici della Musica *(Oct–Apr)*, Florence, Tuscany. The "Friends of Music" concert season begins.
Fiera del Tartufo *(first Sun)*, Alba, Piedmont. A variety of events centered around the locally grown white truffle.
Festa di San Francesco *(Oct 4)*, Assisi, Umbria. Feast in honor of the saint.
Wine festivals *(first week)*, Castelli Romani, Lazio.
Sagra del Tordo *(last Sun)* Montalcino, Tuscany. Celebration of the thrush; costumed archery contests.
Festa dell'Uva *(dates vary)*, Bolzano, Trentino-Alto Adige. Grape festival with live music and a costumed procession featuring allegoric charts.

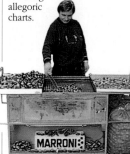

A roast chestnut stall in autumn

NOVEMBER

Festa dei Popoli *(Nov–Dec)*, Florence, Tuscany. Film festival showing films in their original languages with Italian subtitles.
Festa della Salute *(Nov 21)*, Venice. Loved by locals, this feast gives thanks to the Virgin Mary for deliverance from a 1630 plague.

The human chess game in the town square of Maròstica

WINTER

THERE ARE FAIRS, markets, and religious events up and down the country at this time of year. Neapolitan Christmas scenes are famous and nearly every church has one. The Christmas holiday itself is low key; more is made of other religious events such as the liquefaction of San Gennaro's blood in Naples and the Carnevale in Venice.

DECEMBER

Rome during one of its rare snowfalls

Festa di Sant'Ambrogio *(early Dec)*, Milan. The official opening of La Scala Opera season *(see p187)*.
Festa della Madonna di Loreto *(Dec 10)*, Loreto, Le Marche. Celebration of the Virgin's Holy House.
La Befana *(mid-Dec–mid-Jan)*, Rome. Well-known Christmas and children's fair held in Piazza Navona.
The Miracle of San Gennaro *(Dec 19)*, Naples. See September.
Christmas fair *(mid-Dec)*, Naples. Fair selling crèche figures and decorations.
Fiaccole di Natale *(Christmas Eve)*, Abbadia di San Salvatore, Tuscany. Features carols and processions in memory of the first shepherds.
Midnight Mass *(Dec 24)*, at churches all over the country.
Christmas Day *(Dec 25)*, St. Peter's Square, Rome. Public blessing by the pope.

La Befana at Piazza Navona, Rome

Carnevale, Viareggio

JANUARY

Capodanno *(Jan 1)*, all over the country. New Year's Day is celebrated with fireworks

and volleys from hunters firing into the air to scare off ghosts and spirits of the old year and welcome in the new.
La Befana *(mid-Dec–mid-Jan)*, Rome. The Christmas and children's fair continues.
Pitti Immagine Uomo, Pitti Immagine Donna, Pitti Immagine Bimbo, Fortezza da Basso, Florence. Month of international fashion shows for women, men, and children.
Festa di San Sebastiano *(Jan 20)*, Dolceacqua, Liguria. A tree covered with Hosts is carried through the town.
Festa d'o' Cippo di Sant'Antonio *(Jan 17)*, Naples. A procession for St. Anthony, protector of animals.
Carnevale *(Jan 22–Feb 7)*, Viareggio, Tuscany. A carnival famous for its lively floats, often inspired by topical themes.
Fair of St. Orsa *(Jan 30–31)*, Aosta, Valle d'Aosta. A popular exhibition of traditional arts and crafts.

FEBRUARY

Carnevale *(ten days before Lent, finishing Shrove Tuesday)*, Venice. The famous pre-Lent festival, meaning "farewell to meat." A variety of events is organized, but

PUBLIC HOLIDAYS

New Year's Day *(Jan 1)*
Epiphany *(Jan 6)*
Easter Sunday and Monday
Liberation Day *(Apr 25)*
Labor Day *(May 1)*
Ferragosto *(Aug 15)*
All Saints' Day *(Nov 1)*
Immaculate Conception *(Dec 8)*
Christmas Day *(Dec 25)*
Santo Stefano *(Dec 26)*

anyone can buy a mask and participate while watching an array of gorgeous costumes on show.
Sagra delle Mandorle in Fiore *(first or second week)*, Agrigento, Sicily. Annual almond blossom celebration.
Bacanal del Gnoco *(Feb 11)*, Verona. Traditional masked procession with both international and local allegorical floats. Masked balls are held in the town's squares.
Carnevale *(dates vary)*, Mamoiada, Sardinia. Processions include *mamuthones* wearing sinister black masks.

Carnevale revelers in Venice

The Year in Sports

SOCCER IS BY FAR the most important sport in Italy, uniting the country when the national team *(Azzurri)* plays. Other sports throughout the year also attract a large following, so fans are never at a loss for varied activities. For most big sports events, tickets can be obtained for cash at club outlets such as the arena itself. Agencies provide hard-to-get tickets often at higher prices. Beware of the inevitable scalpers at popular events since their expensive tickets may not be valid.

World Cup mania

Calcio Fiorentino, one of Italy's few indigenous sports, is said to be the medieval precursor of modern soccer.

Coppa Italia soccer final

Memorial d'Aloia rowing competition, held in Umbria

Italian Tennis Open, Rome

The professional water polo season takes place from March through July. The Canottieri Napoli team play consistently well through the championship.

Giro d'Italia is one of the world's most prestigious cycling races. Marco Pantani, left, won both the Giro and the Tour de France in 1998.

January	February	March	April	May	June

Indoor Athletics Championships

International Show jumping, Rome

Swimming is a popular competitive water sport and the Indoor Championships are held in February. Olympic medalist Luca Sacchi is one of Italy's top swimmers.

The Italian leg of the Circuito Mondiale in Mugello. Luca Cadalora was champion in 1991.

Although the San Marino Grand Prix is not technically an Italian motor race, it is held each May at Imola, near the home of Ferrari (see p252).

The Italian Outdoor Swimming Championships
*are held each year in July. Top swimmer Giorgio
Lamberti and his teammates, pictured above,
celebrate a relay team victory.*

Italy has some of the best *ski resorts in
Europe and hosts the middle stages of
the World Ski Cup each winter. Above is
Alberto Tomba, winner of the '94–'95 Cup.*

The Italian Grand Prix,
*held annually at Monza, is
Italy's round of the international Formula One
World Championship.
Giancarlo Fisichella is
one of Italy's best up-and-
coming young drivers.*

The San Remo Car Rally, *held
each year in October, was made
famous by driver Micky Biason
and the Lancia Delta Integrale.*

**Trofeo dei
Templi rowing
competition, Sicily**

August	September	October	November	December

**Roberto Baggio, below right, in
action at the 1994 World Cup**

**Siena Palio
(see p331),
held on
July 2 and
August 16**

The Italian soccer *season
runs from September through
June. It culminates with the Coppa
Italia final, which is equivalent to
the British FA Cup. Italy's soccer
obsession, however, reaches fever
pitch when the World Cup takes
place every four years.*

**The Outdoor Athletics
Championship** *has become very
popular in recent years, especially
the steeplechase, where Francesco
Panetta made his name.*

KEY TO SPORTING SEASONS

	Soccer
	Water polo
	Rugby
	Basketball
	Volleyball
	Skiing

The Climate of Italy

THE ITALIAN PENINSULA has a varied climate falling into three distinct geographical regions. Cold Alpine winters and warm, wet summers characterize the northern regions. In the extensive Po Valley, arid summers contrast with freezing, damp winters. The rest of Italy has a pleasant climate with long, hot summers and mild winters. Cooler weather along the backbone of the Apennines can bring snow during the winter months.

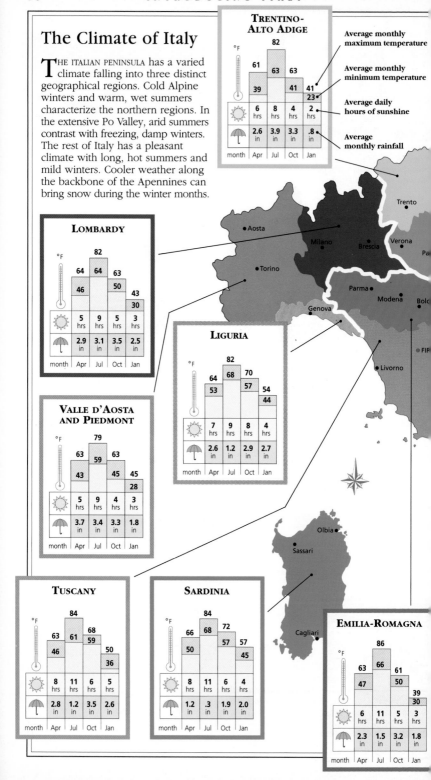

TRENTINO-ALTO ADIGE

°F			
82			
61	63	63	
39		41	41
			23

☀	6 hrs	8 hrs	4 hrs	2 hrs
☂	2.6 in	3.9 in	3.3 in	.8 in
month	Apr	Jul	Oct	Jan

Average monthly maximum temperature

Average monthly minimum temperature

Average daily hours of sunshine

Average monthly rainfall

Trento

Aosta
Milano
Brescia
Verona
Pa
Torino
Parma
Modena
Bolc
Genova
FIR
Livorno

LOMBARDY

°F			
	82		
64	64	63	
46		50	43
			30

☀	5 hrs	9 hrs	5 hrs	3 hrs
☂	2.9 in	3.1 in	3.5 in	2.5 in
month	Apr	Jul	Oct	Jan

LIGURIA

°F			
	82		
64	68	70	
53		57	54
			44

☀	7 hrs	9 hrs	8 hrs	4 hrs
☂	2.6 in	1.2 in	2.9 in	2.7 in
month	Apr	Jul	Oct	Jan

VALLE D'AOSTA AND PIEDMONT

°F			
	79		
63	59	63	
43		45	45
			28

☀	5 hrs	9 hrs	4 hrs	3 hrs
☂	3.7 in	3.4 in	3.3 in	1.8 in
month	Apr	Jul	Oct	Jan

Olbia
Sassari

TUSCANY

°F			
	84		
63	61	68	
46		59	50
			36

☀	8 hrs	11 hrs	6 hrs	5 hrs
☂	2.8 in	1.2 in	3.5 in	2.6 in
month	Apr	Jul	Oct	Jan

SARDINIA

°F			
	84		
66	68	72	
50		57	57
			45

☀	8 hrs	11 hrs	6 hrs	4 hrs
☂	1.2 in	.3 in	1.9 in	2.0 in
month	Apr	Jul	Oct	Jan

Cagliari

EMILIA-ROMAGNA

°F			
	86		
63	66	61	
47		50	
			39
			30

☀	6 hrs	11 hrs	5 hrs	3 hrs
☂	2.3 in	1.5 in	3.2 in	1.8 in
month	Apr	Jul	Oct	Jan

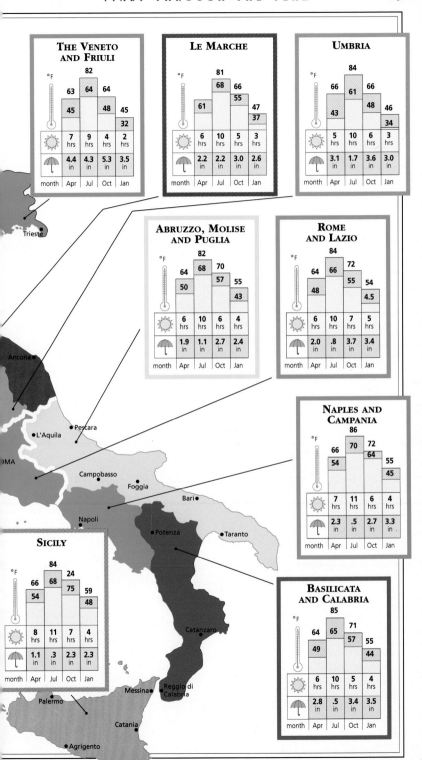

THE VENETO AND FRIULI

°F

month	Apr	Jul	Oct	Jan
	63	82	64	
	45	64	48	45
				32
☀	7 hrs	9 hrs	4 hrs	2 hrs
☂	4.4 in	4.3 in	5.3 in	3.5 in

LE MARCHE

°F

month	Apr	Jul	Oct	Jan
	61	81	66	
		68	55	47
				37
☀	6 hrs	10 hrs	5 hrs	3 hrs
☂	2.2 in	2.2 in	3.0 in	2.6 in

UMBRIA

°F

month	Apr	Jul	Oct	Jan
	66	84	66	
	43	61	48	46
				34
☀	5 hrs	10 hrs	6 hrs	3 hrs
☂	3.1 in	1.7 in	3.6 in	3.0 in

ABRUZZO, MOLISE AND PUGLIA

°F

month	Apr	Jul	Oct	Jan
	64	82	70	
	50	68	57	55
				43
☀	6 hrs	10 hrs	6 hrs	4 hrs
☂	1.9 in	1.1 in	2.7 in	2.4 in

ROME AND LAZIO

°F

month	Apr	Jul	Oct	Jan
	64	84	72	
	48	66	55	54
				4.5
☀	6 hrs	10 hrs	7 hrs	5 hrs
☂	2.0 in	.8 in	3.7 in	3.4 in

NAPLES AND CAMPANIA

°F

month	Apr	Jul	Oct	Jan
	66	86	72	
	54	70	64	55
				45
☀	7 hrs	11 hrs	6 hrs	4 hrs
☂	2.3 in	.5 in	2.7 in	3.3 in

SICILY

°F

month	Apr	Jul	Oct	Jan
	66	84	24	
	54	68	75	59
				48
☀	8 hrs	11 hrs	7 hrs	4 hrs
☂	1.1 in	.3 in	2.3 in	2.3 in

BASILICATA AND CALABRIA

°F

month	Apr	Jul	Oct	Jan
	64	85	71	
	49	65	57	55
				44
☀	6 hrs	10 hrs	5 hrs	4 hrs
☂	2.8 in	.5 in	3.4 in	3.5 in

Trieste
Ancona
L'Aquila · Pescara
OMA
Campobasso
Foggia
Bari
Napoli
Potenza · Taranto
Catanzaro
Palermo
Messina · Reggio di Calabria
Catania
Agrigento

NORTHEAST
ITALY

Northeast Italy at a Glance

THE SHEER VARIETY TO BE FOUND in northeast Italy makes it a fascinating area to explore. The majestic Dolomites dominate the north, straddling Trentino-Alto Adige and the Veneto, and are dotted with medieval castles and modern skiing resorts. On the plain, the cities of Verona, Vicenza, and Padua are all noted for outstanding architecture and museums, and the rural hinterland boasts beautiful villas. The incomparable and spectacular city of Venice, with its magnificent monuments, rises from the lagoon. Farther east, in Friuli, there are important Roman remains. This map pinpoints some of the highlights.

*Castel Tirolo,
Merano*

TRENTINO-ALTO ADIGE
(See pp160–69)

*Palazzo Pretorio,
Trento*

The Veneto

Alto Adige *is a dramatic region of snow-covered mountain valleys scattered with forbidding castles and onion-domed churches in the Tyrolean style (see pp164–5).*

The Dolomites (see pp78–9) *form the spectacular backdrop to many towns in northeast Italy, among them Trento, the region's capital (see pp168–9).*

*La Rotonda,
Vicenza*

*Ponte Scaligero,
Verona*

| 0 kilometers | 40 |
| 0 miles | 20 |

Verona *is one of the loveliest cities in the Veneto, boasting the Castelvecchio and a Roman arena now used for performances of opera (see pp136–41).*

Vicenza, *a model Renaissance city, is dominated by the buildings of Palladio, such as the Palazzo della Ragione and La Rotonda (see pp144–7).*

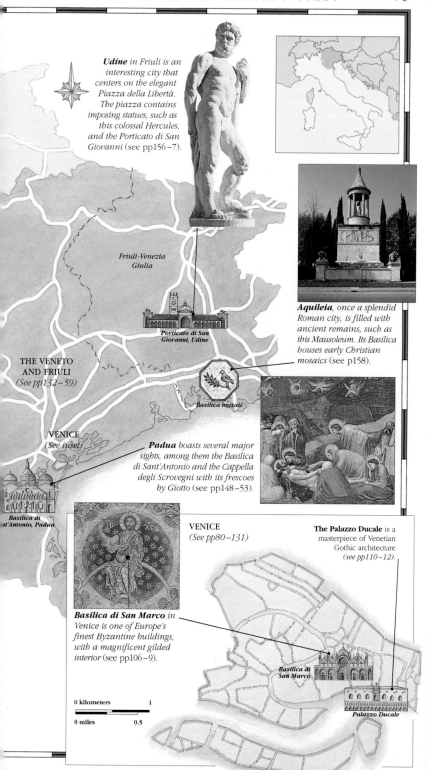

Udine in Friuli is an interesting city that centers on the elegant Piazza della Libertà. The piazza contains imposing statues, such as this colossal Hercules, and the Porticato di San Giovanni (see pp156–7).

Porticato di San Giovanni, Udine

Friuli-Venezia Giulia

Aquileia, once a splendid Roman city, is filled with ancient remains, such as this Mausoleum. Its Basilica houses early Christian mosaics (see p158).

THE VENETO AND FRIULI
(See pp132–59)

Basilica mosaic

VENICE
(See inset)

Padua boasts several major sights, among them the Basilica di Sant'Antonio and the Cappella degli Scrovegni with its frescoes by Giotto (see pp148–53).

Basilica di Sant'Antonio, Padua

VENICE
(See pp80–131)

Basilica di San Marco in Venice is one of Europe's finest Byzantine buildings, with a magnificent gilded interior (see pp106–9).

The Palazzo Ducale is a masterpiece of Venetian Gothic architecture (see pp110–12).

Basilica di San Marco

Palazzo Ducale

0 kilometers   1

0 miles   0.5

Regional Food: Northeast Italy

MANY TRADITIONAL SPECIALTIES of the Veneto are dominated, not surprisingly, by fresh fish and seafood from Lake Garda and the Adriatic. This is complemented by seasonal produce – peas, zucchini, asparagus from Bassano del Grappa, radicchio from Treviso – and meat and cheese from the mainland. Pasta is eaten throughout the

Gelati

northeast, but more typical is polenta, made from cornmeal, and also the many types of risotto. The influences from neighboring countries and trading partners may be tasted in the sweet and sour, spicy, or pickled dishes found throughout the region, from the mountains in the north to the beaches of the south.

Radicchio alla Griglia is a dish of slightly bitter red chicory leaves from Treviso that are grilled lightly over a hot fire.

Crab
Mussels
Bream
Squid
Shrimp
Scallops
Red mullet

Antipasto di Frutti di Mare *is a mixed seafood platter, dressed with a little olive oil and lemon juice. It is a particular favorite in Venice, where the seafood comes fresh from the Adriatic.*

Brodo di Pesce, *or fish soup, is typically Venetian and served all along the coast. It usually contains a mixture of fish, and is sometimes flavored with saffron from Friuli.*

Fiori di Zucchini, a seasonal delight, are zuccini flowers stuffed with delicate fish mousse then fried in a light batter.

Risotto alle Seppie *contains cuttlefish ink, which colors the rice a dramatic black in this traditional risotto.*

Risi e Bisi, *a soft and liquid risotto – almost a thick soup – is made of rice with fresh peas and small pieces of bacon.*

Carpaccio, *wafer-thin slices of raw beef sprinkled with oil, is here served with arugula leaves and slivers of Parmesan cheese.*

Zuppa di Cozze *is a classic way of cooking mussels, with a delicious sauce of white wine, garlic, and parsley.*

Spaghetti alle Vongole *often appears on coastal menus: it is spaghetti with fresh clams in a piquant, chili-pepper sauce.*

Polenta, *like pasta, is a filling staple of the Italian diet. Made from cornmeal it is often grilled and served with a tasty sauce.*

Sarde in Saor *is a traditional Venetian dish of fried fresh sardines marinated in a sweet and sour sauce.*

Anguille in Umido *are eels, gently stewed in an aromatic tomato sauce flavored with white wine and garlic.*

Fegato alla Veneziana *is a traditional Venetian specialty of tender calf's liver, lightly cooked on a bed of onions.*

Tiramisù, *Italy's most famous dessert, is a wonderfully rich blend of coffee-soaked sponge cake and mascarpone cheese.*

THE WINES OF THE NORTHEAST

The Veneto produces large quantities of everyday wines – red, white, and rosé *(chiaretto)*. When choosing an unknown white, you might select a Bianco di Custoza rather than an anonymous Soave. But don't rule out Soave; there are some fine examples, notably by Pieropan and Anselmi. The best whites from the northeast come from Friuli, where winemakers Puiatti, Schiopetto, Jermann, and Gravner excel in their craft. Trentino-Alto Adige, too, produces some crisp whites. Much light and fruity red wine is produced near Bardolino and Valpolicella, with some outstanding bottles coming from Allegrini and Masi. Recioto della Valpolicella is a rich, sweet dessert wine, and Recioto Amarone is less sweet, but stronger still.

Recioto Amarone *is a rich and full-bodied red wine, full of fruit, and very high in alcohol.*

Bianco di Custoza *is a dry white "super Soave" from the eastern shores of Lake Garda. Good white wine producers in the Veneto region include Pieropan, Anselmi, Maculan, Tedeschi, Allegrini and Cavalchina.*

Pieropan *produces some of Soave's finest quality wine. The single-vineyard wines from this famous estate are excellent.*

Prosecco *is the Veneto's own sparkling wine, and a delightful aperitivo. It may be secco (dry) or amabile (medium-sweet).*

Bianco di Custoza

Collio Pinot Bianco

Collio Pinot Bianco *is a superb, fragrant white wine made in the Collio hills next to the Slovenian border. Puiatti is a top producer.*

Understanding Architecture in Venice and the Veneto

TRADE CONTACT WITH THE EAST led medieval Venice to develop its own exotic style – known as Venetian Gothic – blending Byzantine domes and Islamic minarets with European Gothic pointed arches and quatrefoils. In the 16th century, Palladio introduced his interpretations of Classical architecture through a series of churches, public buildings, and rural villas in Venice and the Veneto. The 17th century brought the Baroque style, though its exuberance was tempered by Palladio-influenced restraint.

**Andrea Palladio
(1508 – 80)**

THE ARCHITECTURE OF VENICE: BYZANTINE TO BAROQUE

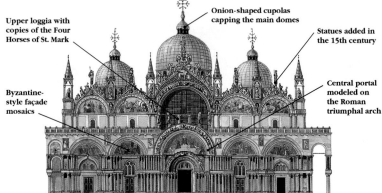

Upper loggia with copies of the Four Horses of St. Mark

Onion-shaped cupolas capping the main domes

Statues added in the 15th century

Byzantine-style façade mosaics

Central portal modeled on the Roman triumphal arch

The Basilica di San Marco, western Europe's finest Byzantine church (completed 11th century), was given lavish treatment to make it a dazzling shrine for the relics of St. Mark the Evangelist, and a fitting symbol of Venetian aspirations (see pp106–9).

THE GENIUS OF PALLADIO

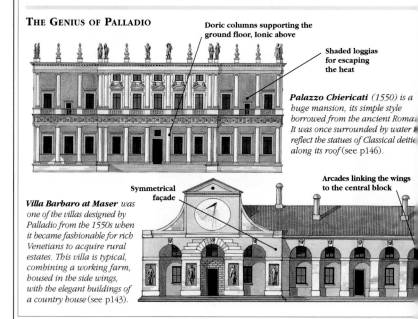

Doric columns supporting the ground floor, Ionic above

Shaded loggias for escaping the heat

Palazzo Chiericati (1550) is a huge mansion, its simple style borrowed from the ancient Roman. It was once surrounded by water t reflect the statues of Classical deitie along its roof (see p146).

Arcades linking the wings to the central block

Symmetrical façade

Villa Barbaro at Maser was one of the villas designed by Palladio from the 1550s when it became fashionable for rich Venetians to acquire rural estates. This villa is typical, combining a working farm, housed in the side wings, with the elegant buildings of a country house (see p143).

WHERE TO SEE THE ARCHITECTURE

A vaporetto trip along the Grand Canal in Venice *(see pp84–7)* is a splendid way of getting an over-view of Venetian architecture. Ca' d'Oro, Ca' Rezzonico, and Ca' Pesaro should be visited since they contain museums; a visit to the Basilica di San Marco

Typical Venetian Gothic window

and the Palazzo Ducale is a must. There are numerous examples of Palladio's architecture in the Veneto, but the star is the Villa Barbaro *(see p143)*. Several villas line the Brenta Canal (see p154), and the town of Vicenza *(see pp144–7)* is full of his buildings, including La Rotonda, his most famous villa.

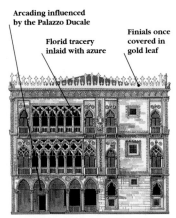

Arcading influenced by the Palazzo Ducale

Florid tracery inlaid with azure

Finials once covered in gold leaf

Ca d'Oro, the 15th-century "House of Gold," reveals Moorish influence in its roof finials and sinuous pointed arches (see p90).

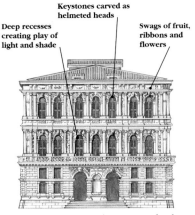

Keystones carved as helmeted heads

Deep recesses creating play of light and shade

Swags of fruit, ribbons and flowers

The 17th-century Ca' Pesaro typifies the Venetian Baroque style – Classical columns and rich but subtle ornamentation (see p85).

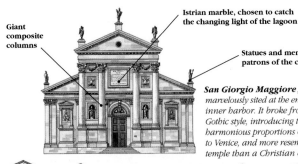

Giant composite columns

Istrian marble, chosen to catch the changing light of the lagoon

Statues and memorials to patrons of the church

San Giorgio Maggiore, built in 1559–80, is marvelously sited at the entrance to the Venetian inner harbor. It broke from the prevailing Gothic style, introducing the clean simplicity and harmonious proportions of Classical architecture to Venice, and more resembles an ancient Roman temple than a Christian church (see p116).

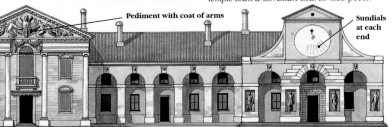

Pediment with coat of arms

Sundials at each end

The Dolomites

THE DOLOMITES ARE THE MOST DISTINCTIVE and beautiful mountains in Italy. They were formed of mineralized coral that was laid down beneath the sea during the Triassic era, and uplifted when the European and African continental plates dramatically collided 60 million years ago. Unlike the glacier-eroded saddles and ridges of the main body of the Alps, the pale rocks here have been carved by the corrosive effects of ice, sun, and rain, sculpting the cliffs, spires, and "organ pipes" that we see today. The eastern and western ranges of the Dolomites have slightly different characteristics; the eastern section is the more awe-inspiring, especially the Catinaccio (or Rosengarten) range which is particularly beautiful, turning rose pink in the dawn sunlight.

Onion dome, a common local feature

STRADA DELLE DOLOMITI

One of the most spectacular routes through the Dolomites links Bolzano *(see p166)* with Cortina d'Ampezzo *(see p155)*. The road twists and turns passing some of the greatest peaks, and the most majestic landscape.

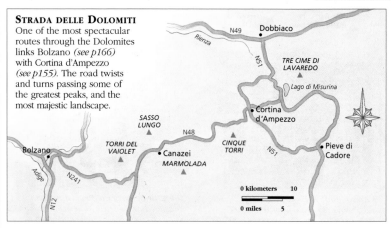

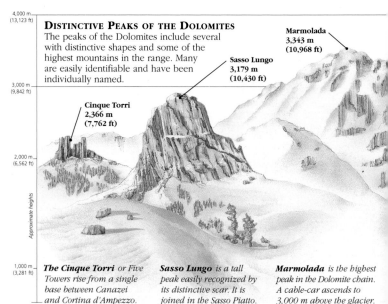

DISTINCTIVE PEAKS OF THE DOLOMITES

The peaks of the Dolomites include several with distinctive shapes and some of the highest mountains in the range. Many are easily identifiable and have been individually named.

Cinque Torri 2,366 m (7,762 ft)

Sasso Lungo 3,179 m (10,430 ft)

Marmolada 3,343 m (10,968 ft)

The Cinque Torri *or Five Towers rise from a single base between Canazei and Cortina d'Ampezzo.*

Sasso Lungo *is a tall peak easily recognized by its distinctive scar. It is joined in the Sasso Piatto.*

Marmolada *is the highest peak in the Dolomite chain. A cable-car ascends to 3,000 m above the glacier.*

Lago di Misurina is a large and beautiful lake lying beside the resort of Misurina. The crystal clear waters reflect the surrounding mountains, mirroring various peaks such as the distinctive and dramatic Sorapiss, in shimmering colors.

Outdoor activities in this area of dramatic landscapes include skiing in winter, biking the trails, and rambling along the paths to picnic sites in summer. Chairlifts from the main resorts provide easy access up into the mountains themselves, transporting you into some breathtaking scenery.

Torri del Vaiolet
2,243 m
(7,359 ft)

Tre Cime di Lavaredo
2,999 m
(9,839 ft)

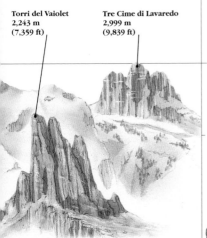

The Torri del Vaiolet is part of the beautiful Catinaccio range, known for its color.

Tre Cime di Lavaredo or Drei Zinnen dominate the valleys north of the Lago di Misurina.

NATURE IN THE DOLOMITES

Forests and meadows support a breathtaking richness of wildlife in the region. Alpine plants, which flower between June and September, have evolved their miniature form to survive the harsh winds.

The Flora

Gentian roots are used to make a bitter local liqueur.

The orange mountain lily thrives on sun-baked slopes.

The pretty burser's saxifrage grows in clusters on rocks.

Devil's claw has distinctive pink flower heads.

The Fauna

The ptarmigan changes its plumage from mottled brown in summer to snow white in winter for effective camouflage. It feeds on mountain berries and young plant shoots.

The chamois, a shy mountain antelope prized for its soft skin, is protected in the national parks, where hunting is forbidden.

Roe deer are common since their natural predators, wolves and lynx, have now died out. Their appetite for saplings causes problems for foresters.

VENICE

LYING IN THE *northeastern notch of Italy, Venice, gateway to the Orient, became an independent Byzantine province in the 10th century. Exclusive trading links with the East and victory in the Crusade of 1204 brought wealth and power, which were only gradually eroded by European and Turkish rivals. Today, Venice's ties are with the local Veneto region which stretches from the flat river plains to the Dolomites.*

Venice is one of the few cities in the world that can be truly described as unique. It survives against all the odds, built on a series of low mud banks amid the tidal waters of the Adriatic and regularly subject to floods. During the Middle Ages, under the leadership of successive doges, Venice expanded its power and influence throughout the Mediterranean to Constantinople (modern Istanbul). The immense wealth of the city was celebrated in art and architecture throughout the city.

The riches of St. Mark's alone bear witness to Venice's position as a world power from the 12th to 14th centuries. After slowly losing ground to the new states of Europe, however, it fell to Napoleon in 1797. Finally, Venice joined the Kingdom of Italy in 1866, so bringing unity to the country for the first time in its history. Today, Venice has found a new role. Her palazzi have become museums, shops, hotels, and apartments, and her convents have been turned into centers for art restoration. Yet little of the essential fabric of Venice has altered in 200 years. The city's sounds are still those of footsteps and the cries of boatmen. The only engines are those of barges delivering supplies or waterbuses ferrying passengers between stops. The same well-worn streets are still trod. More than 12 million visitors a year succumb to the magic of this improbable place whose "streets are full of water" and where the glories of the past are evident at every turn.

A busy street on the island of Burano, with its distinctive, brightly painted houses

◁ Gondola prows, with their characteristic *ferri*, and Santa Maria della Salute in the background

Exploring Venice

V ENICE IS DIVIDED into six ancient administrative districts or *sestieri*: Cannaregio, Castello, San Marco, Dorsoduro, San Polo, and Santa Croce. Visitors usually start at Piazza San Marco, heading for the magnificent basilica and the Palazzo Ducale, probably the busiest part of the city. You can walk to most places in Venice itself, and take a ride on a waterbus to any of the islands.

SIGHTS AT A GLANCE

Churches
Basilica di San Marco
  pp106–9 **18**
Madonna dell'Orto **1**
San Giacomo dell'Orio **6**
San Giorgio Maggiore **31**
San Giovanni
  Grisostomo **3**
San Giovanni in Bragora **29**
Santi Giovanni e Paolo **24**
Santa Maria Formosa **26**
Santa Maria Gloriosa
  dei Frari pp94–5 **8**
Santa Maria dei Miracoli **4**
Santa Maria della Salute **17**
San Nicolò dei
  Mendicoli **13**
San Pantalon **11**
San Polo **7**
San Rocco **10**
San Sebastiano **14**
Santo Stefano **23**
San Zaccaria **27**

Buildings and Monuments
Arsenale **30**
Campanile **21**

Palazzo Ducale
  pp110–12 **19**
Rialto **5**
Scuola di San Giorgio degli
  Schiavoni **28**
Statue of Colleoni **25**
Torre dell'Orologio **20**

Museums and Galleries
Accademia *pp102–3* **15**
Ca' d'Oro **2**
Ca' Rezzonico **12**
Guggenheim Collection **16**
Museo Correr **22**
Scuola Grande di
  San Rocco pp96–7 **9**

Lagoon
Burano **33**
Murano **32**
Torcello pp118–9 **34**

0 meters   500

0 yards   500

KEY

  Street-by-Street: San Polo
  pp92–3

  Street-by-Street: Dorsoduro
  pp98–9

  Street-by-Street: Piazza San
  Marco *pp104–5*

✈ International airport

FS Train station

⛴ Ferry boarding point

 Vaporetto boarding point

 Traghetto crossing *(see p636)*

 Gondola mooring

ℹ Tourist information

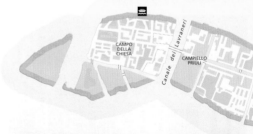

Santa Maria della Salute, at the mouth of the Grand Canal

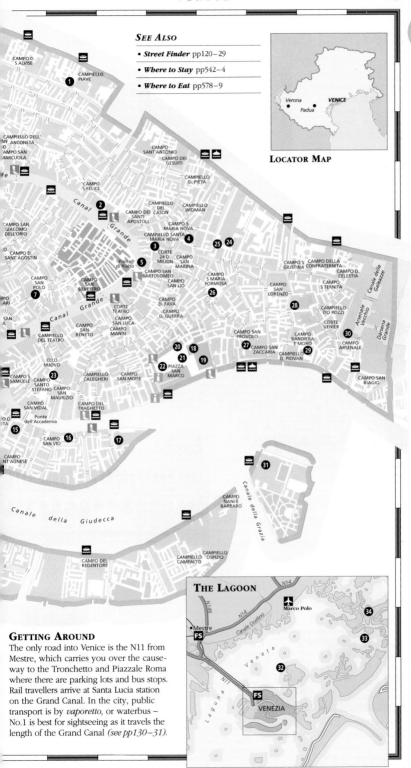

SEE ALSO

- *Street Finder* pp120–29
- *Where to Stay* pp542–4
- *Where to Eat* pp578–9

LOCATOR MAP

THE LAGOON

GETTING AROUND

The only road into Venice is the N11 from Mestre, which carries you over the causeway to the Tronchetto and Piazzale Roma where there are parking lots and bus stops. Rail travellers arrive at Santa Lucia station on the Grand Canal. In the city, public transport is by *vaporetto*, or waterbus – No.1 is best for sightseeing as it travels the length of the Grand Canal *(see pp130–31)*.

The Grand Canal: Santa Lucia to the Rialto

THE BEST WAY to view the Grand Canal as it winds through the heart of the city is from a *vaporetto*, or waterbus. Several lines travel the length of the canal *(see p636)*. The palaces lining the waterway were built over a span of five centuries and present a panoramic survey of the city's history, almost all bearing the name of some once-great Venetian family.

San Marcuola
The church was rebuilt in the 18th century, but the planned new façade overlooking the canal was never completed.

San Geremia houses the relics of St. Lucy, once kept in the church of Santa Lucia where the train station now stands.

Palazzo Labia
Between 1745–50, Giambattista Tiepolo decorated the ballroom with scenes from the life of Cleopatra.

Canale di Cannaregio

Palazzo Corner-Contarini

San Marcuo

Ferrovia

Ponte degli Scalzi

Fondaco dei Turchi
A warehouse for Turkish traders in the 17th–19th centuries, this is now the Natural History Museum.

San Simeone Piccolo
This 18th-century domed church is based on the Pantheon in Rome.

THE GONDOLAS OF VENICE

The gondola has been a part of Venice since the 11th century. With its slim hull and flat underside, the craft is perfectly adapted to negotiating narrow, shallow canals. There is a slight leftward curve to the prow, which counteracts the force of the oar, preventing the gondola from going around in circles.

In 1562 it was decreed that all gondolas should be black to stop people from making an ostentatious show of their wealth. For special occasions they are decorated with flowers. Today, gondola rides are expensive and usually taken by tourists *(see p637)*. However, *traghetti* (gondola ferries) are a cheap, convenient way of crossing the Grand Canal.

Gondolas tied up by steps

Ca' d'Oro
The delicate Gothic tracery of the façade makes this a striking landmark. Its art collection (see p90) includes Bernini's model for a fountain (c.1648).

Palazzo Vendramin Calergi
This is one of the finest early Renaissance palaces in Venice. The German composer Richard Wagner (left) died here in 1883.

The Pescheria has been the site of a busy fish market for six centuries.

Palazzo Sagredo
Graceful Veneto-Byzantine and Gothic arches are both featured on the waterfront façade.

Palazzo Michiel dalle Colonne takes its name from its distinctive colonnade.

The Rialto Bridge *(see p93)* spans the canal in the commercial heart of the city.

San Stae

Ca' d'Oro

San Stae
The façade of this Baroque church is richly adorned with statues. It is a popular concert venue.

Ca' Pesaro
The huge, stately Baroque palace today houses a gallery of modern art and the Oriental Museum.

Rialto

The Grand Canal: the Rialto to San Marco

Aᶠᵀᴱᴿ ᴾᴬˢˢᴵᴺᴳ the Rialto, the canal doubles back on itself along a stretch known as La Volta (the bend). It then widens out and the views become more spectacular approaching San Marco. Façades may have faded and foundations frayed with the tides, yet the canal remains, in the words of the French ambassador in 1495, "the most beautiful street in the world."

Palazzo Mocenigo
Lord Byron stayed in this huge 18th-century palace in 1818.

Sant' Angelo

San Tomà

Palazzo Garzoni
is a renovated Gothic palace, now part of the university.

Ca' Rezzonico
Now a museum of 18th-century Venice (see p99), the palace was the last home of the poet Robert Browning, seen here with his son Pen.

San Samuele

Ca' Rezzonico

Palazzo Grassi
The elegant palazzo dates from the 1730s. Bought by Fiat in 1984, it is now used for art exhibitions.

Ponte dell'Accademia

Accademia

Palazzo Capello Malipiero
The palace was rebuilt in 1622. Beside it stands the 12th-century campanile of San Samuele.

Accademia
The world's greatest collection of Venetian paintings is housed here in the former Scuola della Carità (see pp102–3), which has a Baroque façade by Giorgio Massari.

Palazzo Barbaro
Novelist Henry James wrote The Aspern Papers *here in 1888.*

LOCATOR MAP

☐ *See Venice Street Finder maps 6, 7*

The Riva del Vin is the dock where wine *(vin)* used to be unloaded. It is one of the few spots where you can sit and relax on the banks of the Grand Canal.

Palazzo Barzizza, rebuilt in the 17th century, preserves its early 13th-century façade.

Peggy Guggenheim Collection
A one-story palazzo houses Guggenheim's great modern art collection (see p100).

Santa Maria della Salute
The vast weight of this Baroque church is supported by over one million timber piles (see p101).

Palazzo Gritti-Pisani
The former home of the Gritti family is now the luxury Gritti Palace Hotel (see p544).

San Marco Vallaresso

Santa Maria del Giglio

Salute

Harry's Bar, founded in 1931 by Giuseppe Cipriani, is famous for its cocktails.

Palazzo Dario
Beautiful colored marbles give the 1487 palace a highly individual façade. Legend has it the building is cursed.

The Dogana di Mare (customs house), built in the 17th century, is crowned by two bronze Atlases supporting a golden globe topped by a weathervane.

Traveling slowly along the Grand Canal by gondola ▷

Madonna dell'Orto, with 15th-century façade statues of St. Christopher and the Apostles

Madonna dell'Orto ●

Campo Madonna dell'Orto. **Map** 2 F2.
[C] 041 275 04 62. ▧ *Madonna dell'Orto.* ○ *10am–5pm Mon–Sat; 1–5pm Sun.* ▨ ▨

THIS LOVELY Gothic church, founded in the mid-14th century, was dedicated to St. Christopher, patron saint of travelers, to protect the boatmen who ferried passengers to the islands in the northern lagoon. A 15th-century statue of the saint, recently restored by the Venice in Peril fund, still stands above the main portal. The dedication was changed and the church reconstructed in the early 15th century, following the strange discovery, in a nearby vegetable garden *(orto),* of a statue of the Virgin Mary said to have miraculous powers.

The interior, faced almost entirely in brick, is large, light, and uncluttered. Immediately on the right stands a magnificent painting by Cima da Conegliano, *St. John the Baptist and Other Saints* (c.1493). The vacant space in the chapel opposite belongs to Giovanni Bellini's *Madonna with Child* (c.1478), which was stolen for the third time in 1993.

The church's greatest remaining treasures are the works of art by Tintoretto, who was a parishioner of the church. His tomb, which is marked with a plaque, lies with that of his children, in the chapel to the

right of the chancel. The most dramatic of his works are the towering masterpieces that decorate the chancel (1562–4). On the right wall is *The Last Judgment,* whose turbulent content caused John Ruskin's wife, Effie, to flee the church in horror. In *The Adoration of the Golden Calf* on the left wall, the figure carrying the calf, fourth from the left, is believed to be a portrait of the artist. Inside the chapel of San Mauro, off the end of the right nave, stands a statue of the Madonna by Giovanni de' Santi. It was restored by the Venice in Peril fund, and inspired the rededication of the church.

Ca' d'Oro ●

Calle Ca' d'Oro. **Map** 3 A4.
[C] 041 523 87 90. ▧ *Ca' d'Oro.* ○ *9am–1.30pm daily.* ▨

IN 1420 Marino Contarini, a wealthy patrician, commissioned the construction of what he hoped would be the city's most magnificent palace *(see p77).* The building's intricate carving was entrusted to a team of Venetian and Lombard craftsmen, while the façade was beautifully adorned with the most elaborate and expensive decorative finishes of the day, including gold leaf, vermilion, and ultramarine.

Tullio Lombardo's Double Portrait

Over the years the palace was extensively remodeled and by the 18th century was in a state of semidereliction. In 1846 it was bought by the Russian Prince Troubetzkoy for the famous ballerina Maria Taglioni. Under her direction the palace suffered barbaric restoration, losing, among other things, its staircase and much of its original stonework. It was finally rescued by Baron Giorgio Franchetti, a wealthy patron of the arts, who bequeathed both the building and his private art collection to the state in 1915.

Pride of place on the first of the gallery's two floors goes to Andrea Mantegna's *St. Sebastian* (1506), the artist's last work, which occupies a special alcove of its own. Elsewhere, the floor's main exhibits are ranged around the *portego* (gallery). This is largely dominated by the vivid 15th-century *Double Portrait* (c.1493) by the sculptor Tullio Lombardo; Sansovino's lunette of the *Madonna and Child* (c.1530); and several bronze reliefs by the Paduan Andrea Briosco, "Il Riccio" (1470–1532). Rooms leading off the *portego* to the right contain numerous bronzes and medallions, with some examples by Pisanello and Gentile Bellini. Paintings here also include the famous *Madonna of the Beautiful Eyes,* attributed to Giovanni Bellini, a *Madonna and Child,* attributed to Alvise Vivarini (both late 15th century), and Carpaccio's *Annunciation* and *Death of the Virgin* (both c.1504). A room to the left of the *portego* contains non-Venetian paintings, notably a *Flagellation* by Luca Signorelli (c.1480). A lovely staircase leads to the second floor, which opens with a room hung with tapestries. It has bronzes by Alessandro Vittoria and paintings by

The magnificent Gothic façade of the Ca' d'Oro, or House of Gold

Titian and Van Dyck. The *portego* displays frescoes (c.1532) by Pordenone from the cloister of Santo Stefano, while an anteroom contains damaged frescoes by Titian and Giorgione taken from the Fondaco dei Tedeschi.

Giovanni Bellini's 1513 altarpiece in San Giovanni Grisostomo

San Giovanni Grisostomo ❸

Campo San Giovanni Grisostomo.
Map 3 B5. 🕻 *041 522 71 55.*
🚊 *Rialto.* ⏲ *4–5:30pm daily.*

THIS PRETTY little terracotta–colored church lies in a bustling quarter close to the Rialto. Built between 1479 and 1504, it is a lovely Renaissance design, the last work of Mauro Coducci.

The interior is built on a Greek-cross plan. The light meter illuminates Giovanni Bellini's *St. Jerome with Saints Christopher and Augustine* (1513) above the first altar on the right. This was most probably Bellini's last painting, executed when he was in his eighties.

Over the high altar hangs Sebastiano del Piombo's *St. John Chrysostom and Six Saints* (1509–11).

Santa Maria dei Miracoli ❹

Campo dei Miracoli. **Map** 3 B5.
🕻 *041 275 04 62.* 🚊 *Rialto.*
⏲ *10am–5pm Mon–Sat, 1–5pm Sun & public hols.* ✍ 🔔

AN EXQUISITE masterpiece of early Renaissance architecture, the Miracoli is the favorite church of many Venetians and the one where they like to get married. Tucked away in a maze of alleys and waterways in eastern Cannaregio, it is small and somewhat elusive.

Santa Maria dei Miracoli is decorated in various shades of marble, with some fine bas-reliefs and sculpture. It was built in 1481–9 by the architect Pietro Lombardo and his sons to enshrine *The Virgin and Child* (1408), a painting believed to have miraculous powers. The picture, by Nicolò di Pietro, can still be seen above the altar.

The interior of the church is embellished by pink, white, and gray marble, at its best when lit up by rays of pale

Decorative column from inside Santa Maria dei Miracoli

sunshine. It is crowned by a barrel-vaulted ceiling (1528), which has 50 portraits of saints and prophets. The balustrade, between the nave and the chancel, is decorated by Tullio Lombardo's carved figures of St. Francis, Archangel Gabriel, the Virgin, and St. Clare.

The screen around the high altar and the medallions of the Evangelists in the cupola spandrels are also Lombardo's work. Above the main door, the choir gallery was used by the nuns from the neighboring convent, who entered the church through an overhead gallery. The Miracoli has recently undergone a major restoration program, which was funded by the American Save Venice organization.

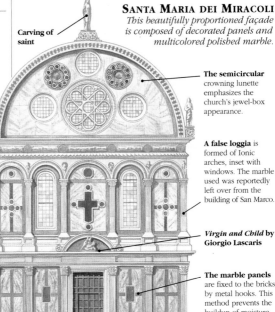

SANTA MARIA DEI MIRACOLI
This beautifully proportioned façade is composed of decorated panels and multicolored polished marble.

Carving of saint

The semicircular crowning lunette emphasizes the church's jewel-box appearance.

A false loggia is formed of Ionic arches, inset with windows. The marble used was reportedly left over from the building of San Marco.

***Virgin and Child* by Giorgio Lascaris**

The marble panels are fixed to the bricks by metal hooks. This method prevents the buildup of moisture and saltwater behind the panels and dates from the Renaissance.

Street-by-Street: San Polo

T HE RIALTO BRIDGE and markets make this
area a magnet for visitors. Traditionally
the city's commercial quarter, it was here that
bankers, brokers, and merchants conducted
their affairs. Streets are no longer lined with
stands selling spices and fine fabrics, but the
food markets and pasta shops are unmissable.
Away from the bridge, streets quickly become
less crowded, leading to tiny
piazzas and quiet churches.

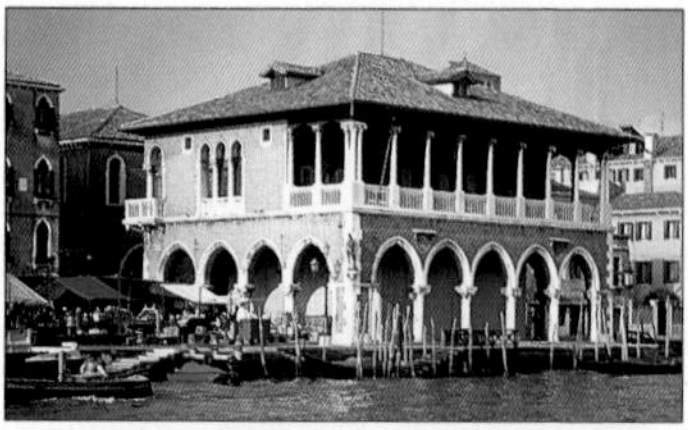

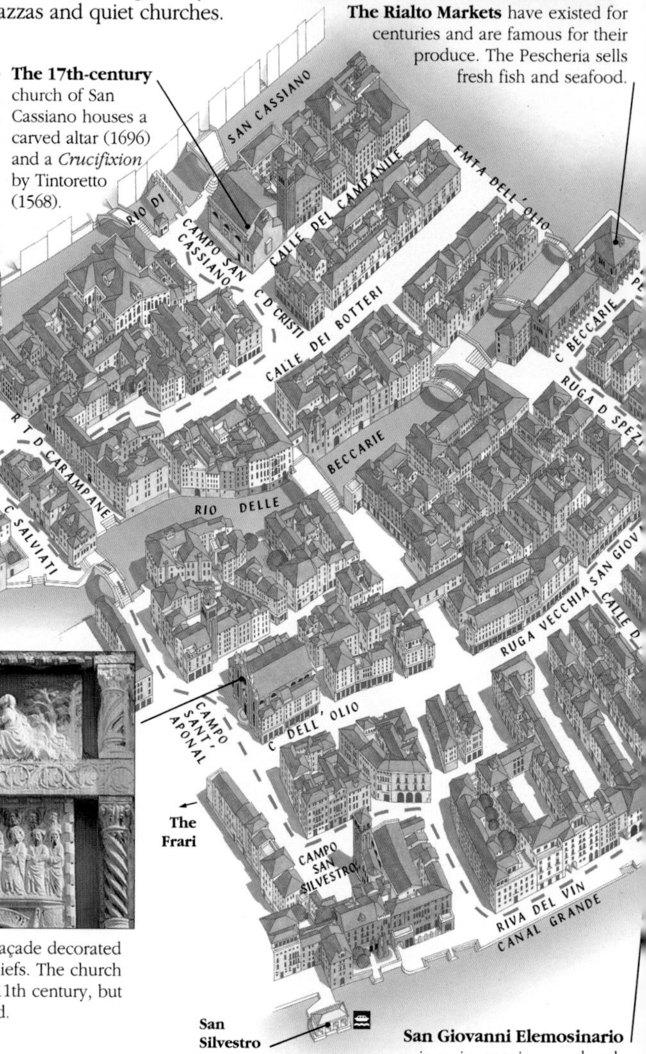

The Rialto Markets have existed for
centuries and are famous for their
produce. The Pescheria sells
fresh fish and seafood.

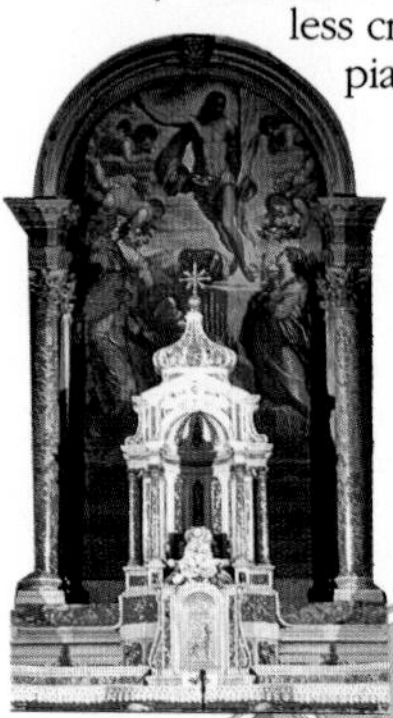

The 17th-century
church of San
Cassiano houses a
carved altar (1696)
and a *Crucifixion*
by Tintoretto
(1568).

The Frari

Sant'Aponal has a façade decorated
with worn Gothic reliefs. The church
was founded in the 11th century, but
is now deconsecrated.

**San
Silvestro**

San Giovanni Elemosinario
is an inconspicuous church
that was rebuilt in the early
16th century, although its
campanile dates from the
end of the 14th century.
Inside it are interesting
frescoes by Pordenone.

KEY

– – – Suggested route

0 meters   75

0 yards   75

STAR SIGHT

★ Rialto

LOCATOR MAP
*See Venice Street Finder
maps 2, 3, 6, 7*

The lively Erberia, selling fresh fruit and vegetables

Rialto ❺

Ponte di Rialto. **Map** 7 A1. 🚤 *Rialto.*

THE RIALTO takes its name from *rivo alto* (high bank) and was one of the first areas of Venice to be inhabited. A banking and then market district, it remains one of the city's busiest and most bustling areas. Locals and visitors alike jostle among the colorful stands of the Erberia (fruit and vegetable market) and Pescheria (fish market).

Stone bridges were built in Venice as early as the 12th century, but it was not until 1588, after the collapse, decay, or sabotage of earlier wooden structures, that a solid stone bridge was designed for the Rialto. Completed in 1591, the new bridge remained the only means of crossing the Grand Canal until 1854, when the Accademia bridge was built.

Few visitors leave Venice without crossing the famous bridge. It is a wonderful place to watch and photograph the constant activity of boats on the Grand Canal below.

San Giacomo dell'Orio ❻

Campo San Giacomo dell'Orio.
Map 2 E5. 📞 041 275 04 62.
🚤 *Riva di Biasio or San Stae.*
🕙 *10am–5pm Mon–Sat, 1–5pm Sun & public hols.* 🗲 🜨

THIS CHURCH is a focal point of a quiet quarter of Santa Croce. The name "dell'Orio" (locally dall'Orio) may derive from a laurel tree *(alloro)* that once stood near the church. San Giacomo was founded in the 9th century,

San Giacomo di Rialto's
clock face (1410), which has been a poor timekeeper over the years, adorns one of Venice's oldest churches.

DEGLI OREFICI

Market entrance

★ **Rialto**
One of Venice's most famous sights, the bridge offers fine views of the Grand Canal, and marks the heart of the city ❺

rebuilt in 1225, and thereafter repeatedly modified, resulting in a mixture of styles. The campanile, basilica ground plan, and Byzantine columns survive from the 13th century. The ship's keel roof and the columns are Gothic, while the apses are Renaissance.

In order to gain access to the Veronese ceiling and altar paintings in the new sacristy, apply to the custodian.

San Polo ❼

Campo San Polo. **Map** 6 F1.
📞 041 275 04 62. 🚤 *San Silvestro.*
🕙 *10am–5pm Mon–Sat, 1–5pm Sun & public hols.* 🗲 🜨

FOUNDED IN THE 9th century, rebuilt in the 15th, and revamped in the early 19th in Neo-Classical style, the church of San Polo is worth visiting for the lovely Gothic portal and the Romanesque lions at the foot of the 14th-century campanile – one holds a serpent between its paws, the other a human head.

Inside, follow the signs for the *Via Crucis del Tiepolo* – 14 pictures of the Stations of the Cross (1749) by the painter Giandomenico Tiepolo; many include vivid portraits of Venetian life. The church also has paintings by Veronese, Palma il Giovane (the Younger), and a dramatic *Last Supper* by Tintoretto.

A Romanesque lion at the base of San Polo's 14th-century campanile

Santa Maria Gloriosa dei Frari ⑧

MORE COMMONLY KNOWN as the Frari (a corruption of Frati, meaning brothers), this vast Gothic church dwarfs the eastern area of San Polo. The first church on the site was built by Franciscan friars in 1250–1338, but was replaced by a larger building completed in the mid-15th century. The airy interior is striking for its sheer size and for the quality of its works of art, including masterpieces by Titian and Giovanni Bellini, a statue by Donatello, and several grandiose tombs.

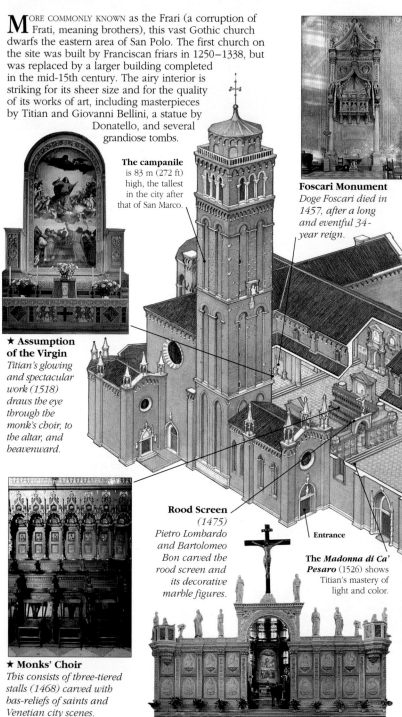

The campanile is 83 m (272 ft) high, the tallest in the city after that of San Marco.

Foscari Monument
Doge Foscari died in 1457, after a long and eventful 34-year reign.

★ **Assumption of the Virgin**
Titian's glowing and spectacular work (1518) draws the eye through the monk's choir, to the altar, and heavenward.

Rood Screen *(1475)*
Pietro Lombardo and Bartolomeo Bon carved the rood screen and its decorative marble figures.

Entrance

The ***Madonna di Ca' Pesaro*** (1526) shows Titian's mastery of light and color.

★ **Monks' Choir**
This consists of three-tiered stalls (1468) carved with bas-reliefs of saints and Venetian city scenes.

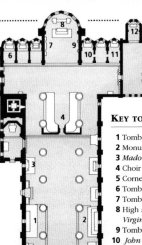

FLOORPLAN

The Frari's imposing cruciform interior, which is 90 m (295 ft) long, holds 12 sights that should not be missed.

KEY TO FLOORPLAN

1 Tomb of Canova
2 Monument to Titian
3 *Madonna di Ca' Pesaro* by Titian
4 Choir stalls
5 Corner Chapel
6 Tomb of Monteverdi
7 Tomb of Doge Nicolò Tron
8 High altar with *Assumption of the Virgin* (1518) by Titian
9 Tomb of Doge Francesco Foscari
10 *John the Baptist* (c.1450) by Donatello
11 B Vivarini's altar painting (1474), Bernardo Chapel
12 *Madonna and Child with Saints* (1488) by Bellini

VISITORS' CHECKLIST

Campo dei Frari. **Map** 6 D1.
041 275 04 62. *San Tomà*. 9am–6pm Mon–Sat, 1–6pm Sun & religious hols. except for those attending mass. frequent.

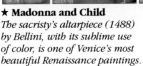

★ Madonna and Child
The sacristy's altarpiece (1488) by Bellini, with its sublime use of color, is one of Venice's most beautiful Renaissance paintings.

The former monastery, which houses the State Archives, has two cloisters: one in the style of Sansovino, another designed by Palladio.

Tomb of Canova
Canova designed, but never constructed, a Neo-Classical marble pyramid like this as a monument for Titian. After Canova's death in 1822, the sculptor's pupils used a similar design for their master's tomb.

STAR FEATURES

★ **Assumption of the Virgin by Titian**

★ **Madonna and Child by Bellini**

★ **Monks' Choir**

Scuola Grande di San Rocco 9

Restored main entrance to the Scuola di San Rocco

Founded in honor of San Rocco (St. Roch), a saint who dedicated his life to helping the sick, the Scuola started out as a charitable confraternity. Construction began in 1515 under Bartolomeo Bon and was continued by Scarpagnino until his death in 1549. The work was financed by donations from Venetians eager to invoke San Rocco's protection; the Scuola quickly became one of the wealthiest in Venice. In 1564 its members decided to commission Tintoretto to decorate its walls and ceilings. His earliest paintings, the first of over 50 works he eventually left in the Scuola, fill the small Sala dell'Albergo off the Upper Hall. His later paintings occupy the Ground Floor Hall, immediately inside the entrance.

Tintoretto's magnificent *Crucifixion*, painted in 1565 for the Sala dell'Albergo in the Scuola di San Rocco

GROUND FLOOR HALL

The GROUND FLOOR cycle was executed in 1583–7, when Tintoretto was in his sixties, and consists of eight paintings illustrating the life of Mary. The series starts with an *Annunciation* and ends with an *Assumption*, which was restored some years ago.

The tranquil scenes of *The Flight into Egypt*, *St. Mary Magdalene*, and *St. Mary of Egypt* are remarkable for their serenity. This is portrayed most

Detail from *The Flight into Egypt* (1582–7) by Tintoretto

lucidly by the Virgin's isolated spiritual contemplation in the *St. Mary of Egypt*. In all three paintings, the landscapes are rendered with rapid strokes and are an important part of the composition.

UPPER HALL AND SALA DELL'ALBERGO

Scarpagnino's great staircase (1544–6), with its upper flight decorated with two vast paintings commemorating the plague of 1630, leads to the Upper Hall. Here, biblical subjects decorate the ceiling and walls, painted by Tintoretto from 1575–81.

The ceiling paintings portray scenes from the Old Testament. The three large and dynamic square paintings in the center show episodes from the Book of Exodus: *Moses Strikes Water from the Rock*, *The Miracle of the Bronze Serpent*, and *The Fall of Manna in the Desert*. These all allude to the charitable

aims of the Scuola in alleviating thirst, sickness, and hunger respectively. All three paintings are crowded compositions displaying much violent movement.

The vast wall paintings in the hall feature episodes from the New Testament, linking with the ceiling paintings. Two of the most striking paintings are *The Temptation of Christ*, which shows a handsome young Satan offering Christ two loaves of bread, and *The Adoration of the Shepherds*. Like *The Temptation of Christ*, *The Adoration* is composed in two halves, with a female figure, shepherds, and ox below, and the Holy Family and onlookers above.

The beautiful carvings below the paintings were added in the 17th century by sculptor Francesco Pianta. The figures are allegorical and include (near the altar) a caricature of Tintoretto with his palette and brushes, representing Painting. Near the entrance to the Sala dell'

Detail from *The Temptation of Christ* (1578 – 81) by Tintoretto

Albergo, you can see the *Annunciation* by Titian. The Sala dell'Albergo itself is a room containing the most breathtaking of his master-pieces – the *Crucifixion* (1565). Henry James remarked of this painting: "no single picture contains more of human life; there is everything

in it, including the most exquisite beauty." Tintoretto began the cycle of paintings in this room in 1564, when he won the commission with the ceiling painting *San Rocco in Glory*. On the wall opposite the *Crucifixion* are paintings of episodes from the Passion: *Christ before Pilate, The Crowning with Thorns,* and *The Ascent to Calvary.*

The easel painting *Christ Carrying the Cross,* was once attributed to Giorgione, though many believe it to be by Titian.

San Rocco ⑩

Campo San Rocco. **Map** 6 D1. San Tomà. Apr–Oct: 8am–12:30pm, 3–5pm daily; Nov–Mar: 8am–12:30pm Mon–Sat, 2–4pm Sat, Sun, public hols.

Sharing the little square with the celebrated Scuola Grande di San Rocco is the church of the same name. Designed by Bartolomeo Bon in 1489 and largely rebuilt in 1725, the exterior suffers from a mixture of styles. The façade, similar in concept to the Scuola, was added in 1765–71.

Inside, the chancel is deco-rated with a series of paintings by Tintoretto depicting scenes from the life of San Rocco.

San Pantalon ⑪

Campo San Pantalon.
Map 6 D2. *041 523 58 934.*
San Tomà. 4–6pm Sun–Fri.

Fumiani's epic ceiling painting (1680–1740) in San Pantalon

The overwhelming feature of this late 17th-century church is its vast painted ceiling, dark, awe-inspiring, and remarkable for its illusionistic effect of height. The ceiling depicts a total of 40 scenes, and admirers claim that this is the world's largest work of art on canvas.

The scenes show the martyrdom and apotheosis of the physician St. Pantalon. The artist, Gian Antonio Fumiani, took 24 years (1680–1704) to achieve the masterpiece, before allegedly falling to his death from the scaffolding.

KEY TO PAINTINGS

GROUND FLOOR HALL 1 The Annunciation; **2** The Adoration of the Three Kings; **3** The Flight into Egypt; **4** The Massacre of the Innocents; **5** St. Mary Magdalene; **6** St. Mary of Egypt; **7** The Presentation in the Temple; **8** The Assumption.

UPPER HALL WALLS 9 San Rocco; **10** St. Sebastian; **11** The Adoration of the Shepherds; **12** The Baptism of Christ; **13** The Resurrection; **14** The Agony in the Garden; **15** The Last Supper; **16** The Vision of San Rocco; **17** The Miracle of the Loaves and Fishes; **18** The Resurrection of Lazarus; **19** The Ascension; **20** Christ Heals the Paralytic; **21** The Temptation of Christ.

UPPER HALL CEILING 22 Moses Saved from the Waters; **23** The Pillar of Fire; **24** Samuel and Saul; **25** Jacob's Ladder; **26** Elijah on a Chariot of Fire; **27** Elijah Fed by the Angels; **28** Daniel Saved by the Angels; **29** The Passover; **30** The Fall of Manna; **31** The Sacrifice of Isaac; **32** The Miracle of the Bronze Serpent; **33** Jonah Emerges from the Whale; **34** Moses Strikes Water from the Rock; **35** Adam and Eve; **36** Three Children in the Furnace; **37** God Appears to Moses; **38** Sampson Brings out Water from the Jawbone of an Ass; **39** The Vision of the Prophet Ezekiel; **40** The Vision of Jeremiah; **41** Elisha Distributes Bread; **42** Abraham and Melchizidek.

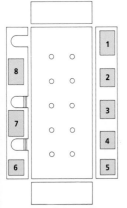

Ground Floor Hall

Upper Hall

Street-by-Street: Dorsoduro

THE SESTIERE OF DORSODURO was built up on a stratum of solid subsoil – the name means "hard backbone." It has as its focal point the lively Campo Santa Margherita, the largest open space in this part of Venice. The square bustles with activity, particularly in the morning when the market stalls are open, and in the evening when it is the haunt of students from nearby Ca' Foscari, now part of Venice University. The surrounding streets contain some architectural stunners, notably Ca' Rezzonico and the Scuola Grande dei Carmini, which has decorations by Tiepolo. Of the area's waterways, the delightful Rio San Barnaba is

Santa Margherita

best appreciated from the Ponte dei Pugni, near the barge selling fruit and vegetables – itself a time-honored Venetian sight. Alongside the Rio Terrà Canal there are some lively cafés and a fascinating shop selling masks for Carnevale.

Campo Santa Margherita is an ideal place for relaxing in a café.

Palazzo Zenobio, built at the end of the 17th century, has been an Armenian college since 1850. With permission, visitors can see the fine 18th-century ballroom.

Scuola Grande dei Carmini contains nine ceiling panels (1739–44) in the hall on the upper floor, painted by Tiepolo for the Carmelite confraternity.

Santa Maria dei Carmini has a Gothic side porch carved with Byzantine reliefs.

KEY

– – – Suggested route

| 0 meters | 50 |
| 0 yards | 50 |

Rio San Barnaba, flanked by Fondamenta Gherardini, is one of the prettiest canals in the *sestiere*.

LOCATOR MAP
*See Venice Street Finder
maps 5, 6*

Tiepolo's *New World* fresco, part
of a series in Ca' Rezzonico

Ca' Rezzonico ⑫

Fondamenta Rezzonico 3136.
Map 6 E3. [ ] *041 241 01 00.*
Ca' Rezzonico. ◯ *May–Oct:
10am–5pm daily; Nov–Apr: 10am–
4pm Sat–Thu.* ● *for restoration until
late 2000; Jan 1, May 1, Dec 25.*

THIS PALAZZO HOUSES the
museum of 18th-century
Venice, its rooms furnished
with frescoes, paintings, and
period pieces taken from other
palaces or museums. Building
began with Longhena (architect
of La Salute, *see p101*) in 1667,
but the funds of the Bon
family, who commissioned it,
ran out before the second
floor was started. In 1712 the
unfinished palace was bought
by the Rezzonico family of
Genoa. A large portion of
their fortune was spent on the
completion of the palace.

The Rezzonico family sold
it, in 1888, to the famous poet
Robert Browning and his son,
Pen. The outstanding
attraction in the palace today
is Giorgio Massari's ballroom,
which occupies the entire
width of the building. It
is adorned with gilded
chandeliers, carved
furniture by Andrea
Brustolon, and a ceiling
with *trompe l'oeil* frescoes.
Other rooms have frescoes
by Giambattista Tiepolo,
including his lively
Nuptial Allegory (1758),
and one by his son,
Giandomenico, originally
in his villa at Zianigo.

There are paintings by
Longhi, Guardi, and – rare in
Venice – Canaletto. On the top
floor is a reconstructed 18th-
century apothecary's shop
and a puppet theater.

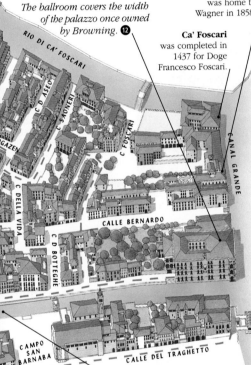

★ Ca' Rezzonico
*The ballroom covers the width
of the palazzo once owned
by Browning.* ⑫

Palazzo Giustinian
was home to
Wagner in 1858.

Ca' Foscari
was completed in
1437 for Doge
Francesco Foscari.

RIO DI CA' FOSCARI

CANAL GRANDE

C. D. ASEO

C. D. SAONERI

C. FOSCARI

MAGAZEN

C. DELLA VIDA

C. D. BOTTEGHE

CALLE BERNARDO

CAMPO
SAN
BARNABA

CALLE DEL TRAGHETTO

Ponte dei Pugni was
a traditional scene of
fist fights between rival
factions. They were
finally banned in 1705
for being too violent.

San Barnaba is a thriving
community, with its own
floating barge stall crammed
with fresh fruit and vegetables.
It is a focal point for tourists
and locals alike.

STAR SIGHT

★ Ca' Rezzonico

Nave of San Nicolò dei Mendicoli, one of the oldest churches in Venice

San Nicolò dei Mendicoli ⑬

Campo San Nicolò. **Map** 5 A3.
☎ 041 275 03 82. 🚤 San Basilio.
◯ 10am–noon, 4–6pm daily.

CONTRASTING WITH the remote and rundown area which surrounds it, this church still remains one of the most charming in Venice. Founded in the 7th century, it has been rebuilt extensively over the years. The little porch on the north flank is 15th century and once sheltered the beggars, or *mendicanti*, who gave the church its name.

Thanks to the Venice in Peril fund, in the 1970s the church underwent one of the most comprehensive restoration programs since the floods of 1966. Flooding had become such a problem that the priest often ferried himself around the church in a coracle (a small wicker boat). The floor, which was 30 cm (1 ft) below

the level of the canals, was rebuilt and raised slightly to prevent further flood damage. The roofs and lower walls were reconstructed, and paintings and statues restored.

The interior is delightfully embellished, particularly the nave with its 16th-century gilded wooden statues. These include the figure of San Nicolò himself. On the upper walls is a series of paintings of the life of Christ (c.1553) by Alvise dal Friso and other pupils of Veronese.

Outside, a small column supports a stone lion, in a humbler echo of the Column of San Marco in the Piazzetta.

San Sebastiano ⑭

Campo San Sebastiano. **Map** 5 C3.
☎ 041 275 04 62. 🚤 San Basilio.
◯ 10am–5pm Mon–Sat; 3–5pm Sun & public hols. 🅰 🎧

THIS CHURCH HAS one of the most homogeneous interiors in the whole of Venice. The splendor was created by Veronese, who, from 1555 to 1560 and again in the 1570s, was commissioned to deco-rate the sacristy ceiling, the nave ceiling, the frieze, the east end of the choir, the high altar, the doors of the organ panels, and the chancel.

The paintings, are typical of the artist, and feature radiant colors and rich costumes. Those on the sacristy ceiling depict the *Coronation of the Virgin* and the *Four Evangelists*.

Of the other paintings, the finest are the three which tell the story of Esther, Queen of Xerxes I of Persia, famous for securing the deliverance of the Jewish people.

Appropriately, the artist is buried in the church. His tomb is situated in front of the beautifully paved chapel to the left of the chancel.

Accademia ⑮

See pp102–3.

Peggy Guggenheim Collection ⑯

Palazzo Venier dei Leoni. **Map** 6 F4.
☎ 041 520 62 88. 🚤 Accademia.
◯ 10am–6pm Wed–Mon; 10am–10pm Sat. ◐ Dec 25. 🅰 🎧 🛇 📷 🗊

INTENDED AS A four-story palace, the 18th-century Palazzo Venier dei Leoni in fact never rose beyond the ground floor – hence its nickname, *Il*

The truncated palazzo housing the Peggy Guggenheim Collection

Palazzo Nonfinito (The Unfinished Palace). In 1949 the building was bought as a home by the American millionairess Peggy Guggenheim (1898–1979), a collector, dealer, and patron of the arts.

A perspicacious and high-spirited woman, she initially befriended, and then furthered the careers of, many innovative abstract and Surrealist artists. One was Max Ernst, who became her second husband. The collection consists of 200 fine paintings and sculptures, each representing the 20th century's most influential modern art movements. The dining room has notable Cubist works of art, including *The Poet* by Pablo Picasso, and an entire room is devoted to Jackson Pollock, who was "discovered" by Guggenheim. Other artists represented are Braque, Chagall, de Chirico, Dalí, Duchamp, Léger, Kandinsky, Klee, Mondrian, Miró, Malevich, Rothko, Bacon and Magritte, whose Surreal *Empire of Light* (1953–4) shows a night scene of a darkened house in a wooded setting with a bright day sky above. The sculpture collection, which includes Constantin Brancusi's elegant *Bird in Space* (c.1923), is laid out in the house and garden.

Bird in Space by Constantin Brancusi

Perhaps the most provocative piece is Marino Marini's *Angelo della Città* (Angel of the Citadel, 1948), located on the terrace overlooking the Grand Canal. This shows a prominently displayed man sitting on a horse, erect in all respects. Embarrassed onlookers avert their gaze to enjoy views of the Grand Canal.

The Guggenheim is one of the most visited sights of Venice, and the best place in the city to see modern art. Light-filled rooms and the large modern canvases provide a striking contrast to the Renaissance paintings that usually form the highlights in most Venetian churches and museums. A bonus for English speakers is the team of assistants, who are often visiting art graduates from Britain.

The garden has been paved and features an array of sculptures. Peggy Guggenheim's ashes are also preserved here, near the place where her pet dogs were buried. A shop and restaurant are housed in buildings off the garden. Call for information on temporary exhibits.

The Baroque church of Santa Maria della Salute, at the mouth of the Grand Canal

Santa Maria della Salute ⑰

Campo della Salute. **Map** 7 A4.
☎ 041 520 85 65. ⛴ Salute.
🕐 9am–noon, 3–6pm daily (6:30pm Jun–Sep). ⚏ to sacristy.

THE GREAT BAROQUE church of Santa Maria della Salute, standing at the entrance of the Grand Canal, is one of the most imposing architectural landmarks of Venice. Henry James likened it to "some great lady on the threshold of her salon."

Interior of the Salute with the octagonal space at its core

The church was built in thanksgiving for the city's deliverance from the plague epidemic of 1630, hence the name *Salute*, which means health and salvation.

Each November, in celebration, worshipers light candles and approach across a bridge of boats spanning the mouth of the Grand Canal for the occasion.

Baldassare Longhena started the church in 1630 at the age of 32 and worked on it for the rest of his life. It was not completed until 1687, five years after his death.

The interior is comparatively sober. It consists of a large octagonal space below the cupola and six chapels radiating from the ambulatory. The large domed chancel and grandiose high altar dominate the view from the main door.

The altar's sculptural group by Giusto Le Corte represents the Virgin and Child giving protection to Venice from the plague. The best of the paintings are in the sacristy to the left of the altar: Titian's early altarpiece of *St. Mark Enthroned with Saints Cosmas, Damian, Roch and Sebastian* (1511–12) and his dramatic ceiling paintings of *Cain and Abel*, *The Sacrifice of Abraham and Isaac*, and *David and Goliath* (1540–9). *The Wedding at Cana* (1551) on the wall opposite the entrance is a major work by Jacopo Tintoretto.

Accademia ⑮

SPANNING FIVE CENTURIES, the matchless collection of paintings in the Accademia provides a complete spectrum of the Venetian school, from the medieval Byzantine period through the Renaissance to the Baroque and later. The basis of the collection was the Accademia di Belle Arti, founded in 1750 by the painter Giovanni Battista Piazzetta. In 1807 Napoleon moved the collection to these premises and enriched it with works of art removed from churches and monasteries.

KEY TO FLOORPLAN

- ☐ Byzantine and International Gothic
- ☐ Renaissance
- ☐ Baroque, Genre, and Landscape
- ☐ Ceremonial Painting
- ☐ Temporary exhibitions
- ☐ Nonexhibition space

The former church of Santa Maria della Carità

The courtyard (1561) designed by Palladio

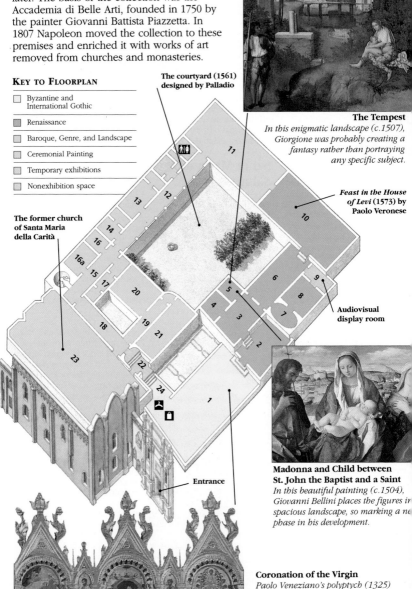

The Tempest
In this enigmatic landscape (c.1507), Giorgione was probably creating a fantasy rather than portraying any specific subject.

Feast in the House of Levi (1573) by Paolo Veronese

Audiovisual display room

Madonna and Child between St. John the Baptist and a Saint
In this beautiful painting (c.1504), Giovanni Bellini places the figures in spacious landscape, so marking a new phase in his development.

Entrance

Coronation of the Virgin
Paolo Veneziano's polyptych (1325) has a central image of the Virgin surrounded by a panoply of religious scenes. This detail shows episodes from the Life of St. Francis.

Healing of the Madman (c.1496) by Vittore Carpaccio

BYZANTINE AND INTERNATIONAL GOTHIC

Room 1 shows the influence of Byzantine art on the early Venetian painters. In Paolo Veneziano's glowing *Coronation of the Virgin* (1325), the linear rhythms are unmistakably Gothic, but the gold background and central panel are distinctly Byzantine.

In contrast, *The Coronation of the Virgin* (1448) by Michele Giambono reveals a delicate naturalism, typical of the International Gothic style.

RENAISSANCE

The renaissance came late to Venice, but by the second quarter of the 15th century it had transformed the city into a thriving art center rivaling Florence and Rome. Central to Venetian art in the 15th century was the *Sacra Conversazione*, in which the Madonna is portrayed with various saints in a harmonious composition. Giovanni Bellini's altarpiece for San Giobbe (c.1487) in Room 2 is one of the finest examples of this subject.

In contrast, the High Renaissance exuberance of Paolo Veronese is exemplified in the monumental *Feast in the House of Levi* (1573). The painting occupies a whole wall in Room 10. Tintoretto's huge masterpiece *The Miracle of St. Mark Freeing a Slave* (1548) is also on display here.

BAROQUE, GENRE AND LANDSCAPE

Venice lacked native Baroque painters, but a few non-Venetians kept the Venetian school alive in the 17th century. The most notable was the Genoese Bernardo Strozzi (1581–1644). The artist was a great admirer of the work of Veronese, as can be seen in his *Feast at the House of Simon* (1629) in

Room 11. Also represented in this room is Giambattista Tiepolo, the greatest Venetian painter of the 18th century.

The long corridor (12) and the rooms that lead from it are largely devoted to light-hearted landscape and genre paintings from the 18th century. Among them are pastoral scenes by Francesco Zuccarelli, works by Marco Ricci, scenes of Venetian society by Pietro Longhi, and a view of Venice by Canaletto (1763). This is a fine example of his sense of perspective.

CEREMONIAL PAINTING

Rooms 20 and 21 return to the Renaissance, featuring two great cycles of paintings from the late 16th century. The detail in these large-scale anecdotal canvases provides a fascinating glimpse of the life, customs, and appearance of Venice at the time.

Room 20 houses *The Stories of the Cross* by Venice's leading artists. In Room 21, minutely detailed *Scenes from the Legend of St. Ursula* (1490s) by Carpaccio mix reality and imagination by linking episodes from the life of the saint to the settings and costumes of 15th-century Venice.

Feast in the House of Levi (1573) by Paolo Veronese

Street-by-Street: Piazza San Marco

THROUGHOUT ITS LONG history Piazza San Marco has witnessed pageants, processions, political activities, and countless Carnival festivities. Visitors flock here in the thousands for two of the city's most important historic sights – the Basilica and the Palazzo Ducale. These magnificent buildings complement lesser sights, such as the Campanile, Museo Correr, and Torre dell'Orologio, not to mention the gardens of the Giardinetti Reali, open-air orchestras, elegant cafés – notably Quadri and Florian's – and numerous smart shops.

Lion of St. Mark

Torre dell'Orologio
The clock tower, with hidden clockwork figures, dates from the Renaissance **20**

Gondolas are moored in the Bacino Orseolo, named after Doge Pietro Orseolo who established a hospice for pilgrims here in 977.

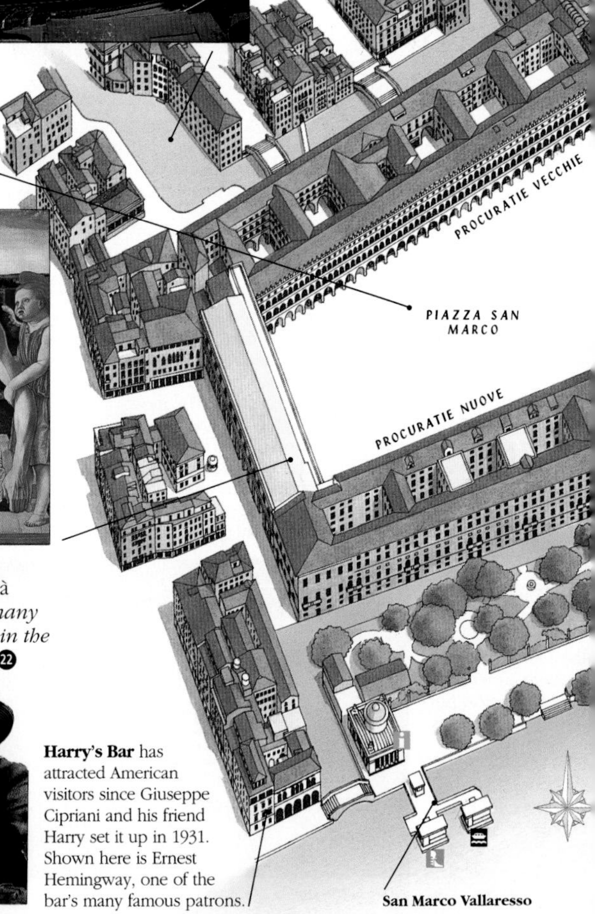

The Piazza was described by Napoleon as the "most elegant drawing room in Europe."

MERCERIE

PROCURATIE VECCHIE

PIAZZA SAN MARCO

PROCURATIE NUOVE

Museo Correr
Giovanni Bellini's Pietà
(1455–60) is one of many masterpieces hanging in the galleries of the Correr **22**

Harry's Bar has attracted American visitors since Giuseppe Cipriani and his friend Harry set it up in 1931. Shown here is Ernest Hemingway, one of the bar's many famous patrons.

San Marco Vallaresso

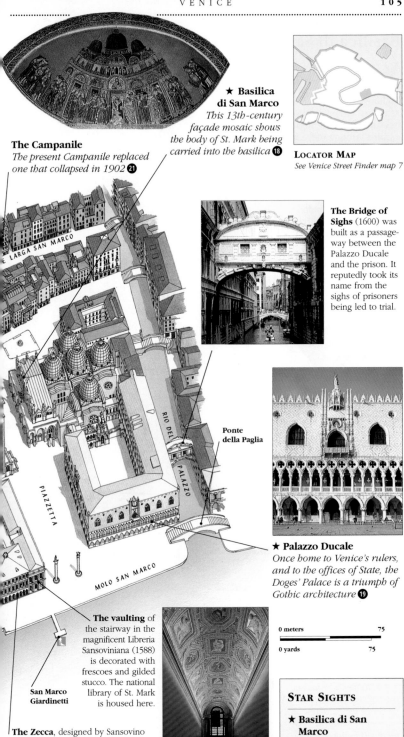

★ Basilica di San Marco
This 13th-century façade mosaic shows the body of St. Mark being carried into the basilica 🔞

LOCATOR MAP
See Venice Street Finder map 7

The Campanile
The present Campanile replaced one that collapsed in 1902 ㉑

E LARGA SAN MARCO

The Bridge of Sighs (1600) was built as a passageway between the Palazzo Ducale and the prison. It reputedly took its name from the sighs of prisoners being led to trial.

RIO DEL

PALAZZO

Ponte della Paglia

PIAZZETTA

★ Palazzo Ducale
Once home to Venice's rulers, and to the offices of State, the Doges' Palace is a triumph of Gothic architecture ⑲

MOLO SAN MARCO

0 meters	75
0 yards	75

The vaulting of the stairway in the magnificent Libreria Sansoviniana (1588) is decorated with frescoes and gilded stucco. The national library of St. Mark is housed here.

San Marco Giardinetti

The Zecca, designed by Sansovino and started in 1537, was the city mint until 1870, and gave its name to the *zecchino* or Venetian ducat.

STAR SIGHTS

★ **Basilica di San Marco**

★ **Palazzo Ducale**

Basilica di San Marco ⑱

Vᴇɴɪᴄᴇ'ꜱ ꜰᴀᴍᴏᴜꜱ ʙᴀꜱɪʟɪᴄᴀ blends the architectural and decorative styles of East and West to create one of the greatest buildings in Europe. The exterior owes its almost Oriental splendor to countless treasures from the Republic's overseas empire. Among these are copies of the famous bronze horses, brought from Constantinople in 1204, and a wealth of columns, bas reliefs, and colored marbles studded across the main façade. Mosaics from different epochs adorn the five doorways, while the main portal is framed by some of Italy's loveliest Romanesque carving (1240–65).

The Pentecost Dome, showing the Descent of the Holy Ghost as a dove, was probably the first dome to be decorated with mosaics.

St. Mark and Angels
The statues crowning the central arch are additions from the early 15th century.

The elegant arches echo those of the lower floor, forming a repeat pattern.

★ Horses of St. Mark
The four horses are replicas of the gilded bronze originals, now protected inside the Basilica's museum.

Sᴛᴀʀ Fᴇᴀᴛᴜʀᴇꜱ

★ **Façade Mosaics**

★ **Horses of St. Mark**

Romanesque carvings adorn the arches of the main portal.

Entrance

★ Façade Mosaics
A 17th-century mosaic shows the body of St. Mark being taken from Alexandria, reputedly smuggled past Muslim guards under slices of pork.

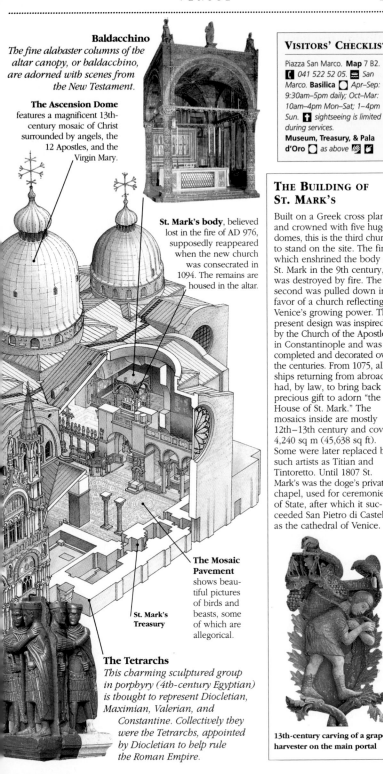

Baldacchino
The fine alabaster columns of the altar canopy, or baldacchino, are adorned with scenes from the New Testament.

The Ascension Dome
features a magnificent 13th-century mosaic of Christ surrounded by angels, the 12 Apostles, and the Virgin Mary.

St. Mark's body, believed lost in the fire of AD 976, supposedly reappeared when the new church was consecrated in 1094. The remains are housed in the altar.

The Mosaic Pavement shows beautiful pictures of birds and beasts, some of which are allegorical.

St. Mark's Treasury

The Tetrarchs
This charming sculptured group in porphyry (4th-century Egyptian) is thought to represent Diocletian, Maximian, Valerian, and Constantine. Collectively they were the Tetrarchs, appointed by Diocletian to help rule the Roman Empire.

VISITORS' CHECKLIST

Piazza San Marco. **Map** 7 B2.
📞 041 522 52 05. 🚉 *San Marco.* **Basilica** ⬤ *Apr–Sep: 9:30am–5pm daily; Oct–Mar: 10am–4pm Mon–Sat; 1–4pm Sun.* 🔲 *sightseeing is limited during services.*
Museum, Treasury, & Pala d'Oro ⬤ *as above* 🔲 🔲

THE BUILDING OF ST. MARK'S

Built on a Greek cross plan and crowned with five huge domes, this is the third church to stand on the site. The first, which enshrined the body of St. Mark in the 9th century, was destroyed by fire. The second was pulled down in favor of a church reflecting Venice's growing power. The present design was inspired by the Church of the Apostles in Constantinople and was completed and decorated over the centuries. From 1075, all ships returning from abroad had, by law, to bring back a precious gift to adorn "the House of St. Mark." The mosaics inside are mostly 12th–13th century and cover 4,240 sq m (45,638 sq ft). Some were later replaced by such artists as Titian and Tintoretto. Until 1807 St. Mark's was the doge's private chapel, used for ceremonies of State, after which it succeeded San Pietro di Castello as the cathedral of Venice.

13th-century carving of a grape harvester on the main portal

Exploring the Basilica

S⟨T. MARK'S⟩ MAGNIFICENT INTERIOR is clad with dazzling mosaics, which begin in the *narthex*, or atrium of the basilica, and culminate in the glittering panels of the Pentecost and Ascension domes. The Genesis Cupola in the atrium has a stunning Creation of the World described in concentric circles. The *pavimento* or floor is also patterned with mosaics in marble and glass. Steps from the atrium lead to the Museo Marciano, home to the basilica's famous horses. Other treasures include the jewel-encrusted Pala d'Oro, behind the high altar, the Nicopeia icon, and the precious hoards of silver, gold, and glassware in the Treasury.

Madonna di Nicopeia
This Byzantine icon, looted in 1204, is one of Venice's most revered images.

The Porta dei Fiori or Gate of Flowers is decorated with 13th-century reliefs.

Cappella dei Mascoli

North side aisle

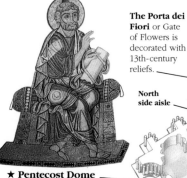

★ **Pentecost Dome**
Showing the Apostles touched by tongues of flame, the Pentecost Dome was lavishly decorated in the 12th century.

Atrium

Steps to Museo Marciano

Cappella Zen

Baptistry

★ **Ascension Dome**
A mosaic of Christ in Glory decorates the enormous central dome. This masterpiece was created by 13th-century Venetian craftsmen, who were strongly influenced by the art and architecture of Byzantium.

★ **Treasury**
A repository for precious artifacts from both Italy and Constantinople, the treasury houses objects such as this 11th-century silver-gilt coffer.

MOSAICS

Clothing the domes, walls, and floor of the basilica are over 4,000 sq m (43,000 sq ft) of gleaming golden mosaics. The earliest, dating from the 12th century, were the work of mosaicists from the East. Their delicate techniques were soon adopted by Venetian craftsmen, who gradually took over the basilica's decoration, combining Byzantine inspiration with Western influences. During the 16th century, many sketches by Tintoretto, Titian, Veronese, and other leading artists were reproduced in mosaic.

Among the most dazzling mosaics – many of which have been heavily restored – are those in the 13th-century central Ascension Dome and the 12th-century Pentecost Dome over the nave.

PALA D'ORO

Beyond the cappella di San Clemente lies the entrance to the most valuable treasure of San Marco: the Pala d'Oro. This jewel-spangled altarpiece, situated behind the high altar, consists of 250 enamel paintings on gold foil, enclosed within a gilded silver Gothic frame. Originally commissioned in Byzantium in AD 976, the altarpiece was further embellished over the

centuries. Napoleon stole some of the precious stones in 1797, but the screen still gleams with pearls, rubies, sapphires, and amethysts.

MUSEO MARCIANO

Steps from the atrium, signposted Loggia dei Cavalli, take you up to the church museum, where the gallery offers a splendid view into the basilica. The gilded bronze horses, housed in a room at the far end of the museum, were stolen from the top of the Hippodrome (ancient racecourse) in Constantinople (modern Istanbul) in 1204 but their origin, either Roman or Hellenistic, remains a mystery. Also displayed are mosaics, medieval manuscripts, and tapestries.

BAPTISTRY AND CHAPELS

The baptistry was added by Doge Andrea Dandolo (1343–54), who is buried here, with Sansovino, who designed the font. The adjoining Cappella Zen (currently closed to the public) became a funeral chapel for Cardinal Zen in 1504 in return for a bequest to the State. The left transept of the Cappella dei Mascoli is decorated with scenes from the life of the Virgin Mary, while the third chapel in the same transept houses the icon of the Madonna of Nicopeia. Looted in 1204, she was once carried into battle at the head of the Byzantine army.

★ **Pala d'Oro**
The altarpiece, created in the 10th century by medieval goldsmiths, is made up of 250 panels such as this one.

The sacristy door (often locked) has fine bronze panels by Sansovino, which include portraits of himself with Titian and Aretino.

The Altar of the Sacrament is decorated with mosaics of the parables and miracles of Christ dating from the late 12th or early 13th century.

The columns of the inner façade are thought to be fragments of the first basilica.

South side aisle

STAR FEATURES

★ Pala d'Oro

★ Treasury

★ Ascension and Pentecost Domes

Noah and the Flood, atrium mosaics from the 13th century

Palazzo Ducale ⑲

THE PALAZZO DUCALE (Doges' Palace) was the official residence of each Venetian ruler (doge) and was founded in the 9th century. The present palace owes its external appearance to the building work of the 14th and early 15th centuries. To create their airy Gothic masterpiece, the Venetians broke with tradition by perching the bulk of the palace (built in pink Veronese marble) on top of an apparent fretwork of loggias and arcades (built from white Istrian stone).

Mars by Sansovino

★ **Giants' Staircase**
This 15th-century staircase is crowned by Sansovino's statues of Mars and Neptune, symbols of Venice's power.

Sala del Senato

Sala del Collegio

Anticollegio

The Arco Foscari
has copies of Antonio Rizzo's 15th-century Adam and Eve.

Main entrance

★ **Porta della Carta**
This 15th-century Gothic gate is the principal entrance to the palace. From it, a vaulted passageway leads to the Arco Foscari and the internal courtyard.

Courtyard

★ **Sala del Maggior Consiglio**
This vast hall was used as a meeting place for members of Venice's Great Council. Tintoretto's huge Paradise *(1590) fills the end wall.*

Sala dello Scudo
The walls of this room, once part of the doge's private apartments, are covered with maps of the world. In the center of the room are two giant 18th-century globes.

VISITORS' CHECKLIST

Piazzetta. **Map** 7 C2. ☎ 041 522 49 51. 🚏 San Marco. ☼ Apr–Oct: 9am–7pm daily; Nov–Mar: 9am–5pm daily (last adm: 1 hr 30 mins before closing). ⬤ Jan 1, Dec 25. 🖳 🖒 🛗 ⬜

Sala delle
Quattro Porte

Sala del Consiglio
dei Dieci

Sala della
Bussola

Torture Chamber
Interrogations took place in the Torture Chamber. Suspects were hung by their wrists from a cord in the center of the room.

The Bridge
of Sighs

Drunkenness of Noah
This early 15th-century sculpture, symbolic of the frailty of man, is set on the corner of the palace.

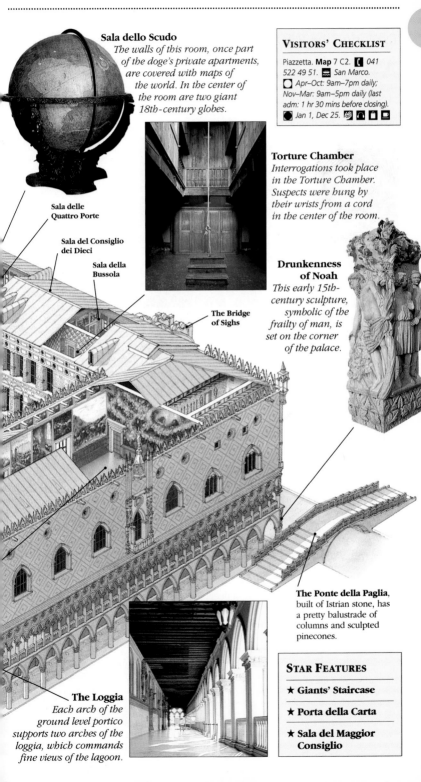

The Ponte della Paglia, built of Istrian stone, has a pretty balustrade of columns and sculpted pinecones.

The Loggia
Each arch of the ground level portico supports two arches of the loggia, which commands fine views of the lagoon.

STAR FEATURES

★ **Giants' Staircase**

★ **Porta della Carta**

★ **Sala del Maggior Consiglio**

Exploring the Palazzo Ducale

A TOUR OF THE PALAZZO DUCALE takes you through a succession of richly decorated chambers and halls, arranged over three floors, culminating with the Bridge of Sighs, which links the palace to the prisons. Casanova was once imprisoned here and made a daring escape from the Palazzo through a hole in the roof.

Jacopo and Domenico Tintoretto's *Paradise*, one of the world's largest paintings, in the Sala del Maggior Consiglio

SCALA D'ORO AND COURTYARD

A PASSAGE from the Porta del Frumento opens into the palace courtyard. The ticket office and palace entrance are to the left. At the top of Antonio Rizzo's 15th-century Giants' Staircase, the new doge would be crowned with the *zogia* or ducal cap. The Scala d'Oro (golden staircase), designed by Jacopo Sansovino, leads to the palace's upper floors. It takes its name, however, from the elaborate gilt stucco vault created by Alessandro Vittoria (1554–8).

SALA DELLE QUATTRO PORTE TO THE SALA DEL SENATO

T HE SECOND FLIGHT of the Scala d'Oro leads to the Sala delle Quattro Porte, with a ceiling designed by Palladio and frescoed by Tintoretto. The end walls of the next room, the Anticollegio, are decorated with mythological scenes by Tintoretto, and Veronese's masterly *Rape of Europa* (1580), opposite the window, is one of the palace's most dramatic works. The adjoining Sala del Collegio was where the doge and his counselors met to receive ambassadors and discuss matters of State. Embellishing the magnificent ceiling are 11 paintings by Veronese. In the next room, the Sala del Senato, the doge and some 200 senators discussed foreign affairs. The paintings are by Tintoretto and pupils.

A *bocca di leone* for denunciations

SALA DEL CONSIGLIO DEI DIECI TO THE ARMERIA

T HE Sala del Consiglio dei Dieci was the meeting room of the powerful Council of Ten, founded in 1310 to protect State security. Two fine works by Veronese adorn the ceiling: *Age and Youth* and *Juno Offering the Ducal Crown to Venice* (both

Dialectic (c.1577) by Veronese in the Palazzo Ducale's Sala del Collegio

1553–4). In the Sala della Bussola, offenders awaited their fate in front of the Council of Ten. The room's *bocca di leone* (lion's mouth), was used to post secret denunciations, and was just one of several in the palace. The wooden door here leads to the State Inquisitors' Room and thence to the torture chamber and prisons. The Armory – one of the finest such collections anywhere in Europe – occupies the following rooms.

SALA DEL MAGGIOR CONSIGLIO

T HE SCALA DEI CENSORI takes you to the second floor and past the Sala del Guariento and Antonio Rizzo's statues of Adam and Eve (1480s) to the magnificent Sala del Maggior Consiglio. A vast chamber, it was used as a meeting place for the Great Council and for grand state banquets. By the mid-16th century the Great Council had around 2,000 members. Any Venetian of high birth over 25 was entitled to a seat unless married to a commoner. Tintoretto's huge *Paradise* (1587–90) occupies the eastern wall. Measuring 7.45 by 24.65 m (25 by 81 ft), it is one of the largest paintings in the world. The itinerary then continues in more somber vein, crossing the Bridge of Sighs to enter the dank world of the prisons.

Torre dell'Orologio ⑳

Piazza San Marco. **Map** 7 B2. 🚌 San Marco. ⬤ for restoration.

Tᴴɪs ʀɪᴄʜʟʏ decorated clock tower on the north side of the piazza was built in the late 15th century. Mauro Coducci is thought to have worked on the design. With its display of the phases of the moon and the signs of the zodiac, the gilt and blue enamel clock face was designed with seafarers in mind. According to a gruesome local legend, once the clock was completed, the two inventors of the complex mechanism had their eyes gouged out to prevent them from ever creating a replica.

On the upper level, the winged lion of St. Mark stands against a star-spangled blue backdrop. At the very top the two huge bronze figures, known as the *Mori*, or Moors, because of their dark patina, strike the bell on the hour.

The clock face of the Torre dell'Orologio

Campanile ㉑

Piazza San Marco. **Map** 7 B2. 📞 041 522 40 64. 🚌 San Marco. ⬤ Jul–Sep: 9am–9pm; Oct–Dec, Feb–Jun: 9:30am–3:45pm daily. ⬤ Jan. 📷

Fʀᴏᴍ ᴛʜᴇ ᴛᴏᴘ of St. Mark's campanile, high above the piazza, visitors can enjoy views of the city, the lagoon and, visibility permitting, the peaks of the Alps. It was from this viewpoint that Galileo demonstrated his telescope to Doge Leonardo Donà in 1609. To do so he would have climbed the internal ramp. Access is achieved far less strenuously these days, by elevator.

The first tower, completed in 1173, was built as a lighthouse to assist navigators in the lagoon. It took on a less benevolent role in the Middle Ages, when offenders were imprisoned – and in some cases left to die – in a cage

hung near its summit. With the exception of several 16th-century renovations, the tower survived unharmed until July 14, 1902 when, with little warning, its foundations gave way and it suddenly collapsed. The only casualties were the Loggetta at the foot of the tower and the custodian's cat. Donations for reconstruction came flooding in, and the following year the foundation stone was laid for a campanile *"dov' era e com'era"* ("where it was and as it was"). The new tower was finally opened on April 25 (the Feast of St. Mark), 1912.

Museo Correr ㉒

Procuratie Nuove. Entrance in Ala Napoleonica. **Map** 7 B2. 📞 041 522 56 25. 🚌 San Marco. ⬤ Apr–Oct: 9am–7pm; Nov–Mar: 9am–5pm ⬤ Jan 1, Dec 25. 📷

Tᴇᴏᴅᴏʀᴏ ᴄᴏʀʀᴇʀ bequeathed his extensive collection of works of art to Venice in 1830, thus forming the core of the city's fine civic museum.

Its front rooms form a suitably Neo-Classical backdrop for early statues by Antonio Canova (1757–1822). The rest of the floor covers the history of the Venetian Republic, with maps, coins, armor, and a host of doge-related exhibits.

Young Man in a Red Hat (c.1490) by Carpaccio in the Museo Correr

The second floor contains the picture gallery, whose collection is comparable to that of the Accademia.

The paintings are hung chronologically, permitting you to trace the evolution of Venetian painting, and to see the influence that Ferrarese, Paduan, and Flemish artists had on the Venetian school.

The gallery's most famous works are by Carpaccio: *Portrait of a Young Man in a Red Hat* (c.1490), and *Two Venetian Ladies* (c.1507). The latter is traditionally, but probably incorrectly, known as *The Courtesans* because of the ladies' low-cut dresses. The Museo del Risorgimento on the same floor looks at the history of Venice until unification with Italy in 1866.

The ceiling of Santo Stefano, built in the form of a ship's keel

Santo Stefano ㉓

Campo Santo Stefano. **Map** 6 F2. 📞 041 275 04 62. 🚌 Accademia or Sant'Angelo. ⬤ 10am–5pm Mon–Sat, 1–5pm Sun.

Dᴇᴄᴏɴsᴇᴄʀᴀᴛᴇᴅ six times on account of the blood spilled within its walls, Santo Stefano – one of Venice's most beautiful churches – is now remarkably serene. Built in the 14th century, and altered in the 15th, the church has a carved portal by Bartolomeo Bon and a campanile with a typical Venetian tilt. The interior has a splendid ship's keel ceiling, carved tie-beams, and the sacristy crammed with valuable paintings.

Santi Giovanni e Paolo ㉔

KNOWN MORE COLLOQUIALLY as San Zanipolo, Santi Giovanni e Paolo vies with the Frari (see pp94–5) as the city's greatest Gothic church. Built by the Dominicans in the 14th century, it is striking for its vast scale and architectural austerity. Known as the Pantheon of Venice, it houses monuments to no fewer than 25 doges. Among these are several fine works of art, executed by the Lombardi family and other leading sculptors.

The bronze statue is a monument to Doge Sebastiano Venier, who was Commander of the Fleet at Lepanto.

The Nave
The cross-vaulted interior is tied by wooden beams and supported by stone columns.

★ Tomb of Nicolò Marcello
This magnificent Renaissance monument to Doge Nicolò Marcello (died 1474) was sculpted by Pietro Lombardo.

The doorway, which is decorated with Byzantine reliefs and carvings by Bartolomeo Bon, is one of Venice's earliest Renaissance architectural works.

Entrance

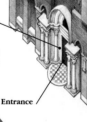

★ Tomb of Pietro Mocenigo
Pietro Lombardo's superb tomb (1481) commemorates the doge's military pursuits when he was Grand Captain of the Venetian forces.

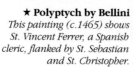

★ Polyptych by Bellini
This painting (c.1465) shows St. Vincent Ferrer, a Spanish cleric, flanked by St. Sebastian and St. Christopher.

**The Baroque high
altar,** begun in
1619, is attributed
to Baldassare
Longhena.

**16th-century
altar statues
by Vittoria**

**16th-century
frescoes
attributed to
Palma il Giovane**

★ **Tomb of Andrea
Vendramin**
*Lombardo's masterpiece
(1476–8) takes the form of
a Roman triumphal arch.*

STAR FEATURES

★ **Doges' Tombs**

★ **Polyptych by Bellini**

Statue of Colleoni 25

Campo Santi Giovanni e Paolo.
Map 3 C5. 🚌 *Ospedale Civile.*

Bartolomeo colleoni, the famous condottiere or commander of mercenaries, left his fortune to the Republic on condition that his statue was placed in front of San Marco. A prominent statue in the piazza would have broken with precedent, so the Senate cunningly had Colleoni raised before the Scuola di San Marco instead of the basilica. A touchstone of early Renaissance sculpture, the equestrian statue of the proud warrior (1481–8) is by the Florentine Andrea Verrocchio, but was cast in bronze after his death by Alessandro Leopardi. The statue has a strong sense of power and movement, which arguably ranks it alongside the works of Donatello.

Santa Maria Formosa 26

Campo Santa Maria Formosa.
Map 7 C1. 📞 *041 275 04 62.* 🚌
Rialto. ⭕ 10am–5pm Mon–Sat,
1–5pm Sun. 📷

Designed by Mauro Coducci in 1492, this church is most unusual in having two main façades – one which overlooks the campo, the other overlooks the canal. The bell tower or campanile, added in 1688, is noted for the grotesque face at its base. Two paintings stand out in the interior: a triptych (1473) by Bartolomeo Vivarini and Palma il Vecchio's *St. Barbara* (c.1510).

San Zaccaria 27

Campo San Zaccaria. **Map** 8 D2.
📞 *041 522 12 57.* 🚌 *San Zaccaria.*
⭕ 10am–noon, 4–6pm Mon–Sat,
11am–noon, 4–6pm Sun.

Set in a quiet square just a stone's throw from the Riva degli Schiavoni, the church of San Zaccaria is a successful blend of flamboyant Gothic

**Palma il Vecchio's *St. Barbara*
(c.1510) in Santa Maria Formosa**

and Classical Renaissance styles. Founded in the 9th century, its façade was later rebuilt by Antonio Gambello in Gothic style. When Gambello died in 1481, Mauro Coducci completed the upper section, adding many of its Renaissance panels.

The interior's artistic highlight is Giovanni Bellini's serene and sumptuously colored *Madonna and Child with Saints* (1505) in the north aisle. A door off the right nave leads to the Chapel of St. Athanasius, which in turn leads to the Chapel of San Tarasio. The chapel contains vault frescoes (1442) by the Florentine Andrea del Castagno, and polyptychs (1443–4) by Antonio Vivarini and Giovanni d'Alemagna.

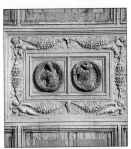

**A Renaissance panel by Coducci
on the façade of San Zaccaria**

Scuola di San Giorgio degli Schiavoni ㉘

Calle Furlani. **Map** 8 E1. **【** *041 522 88 28.* **🚤** *San Zaccaria.* **◯** *Apr–Oct: 9:30am–12:30pm, 3:30–6:30pm Tue–Sat (Sun am only); Nov–Mar: 10am–12:30pm, 3–6pm Tue–Sat (Sun am only).* **●** *Jan 1, May 1, Dec 25 and other religious hols.* 🖾

WITHIN THIS small gem are some of the finest paintings of Vittore Carpaccio. They were commissioned by the Schiavoni, or Dalmatian Slav community in Venice.

The Scuola was established in 1451 and rebuilt in 1551. It has changed very little since. The exquisite frieze, executed between 1502 and 1508, shows scenes from the lives of patron saints: St. George, St. Tryphone, and St. Jerome. Each episode of the narrative cycle is remarkable for its vivid coloring, minutely observed detail, and historic record of Venetian life. Outstanding among them are *St. George Slaying the Dragon* and *St. Jerome Leading the Tamed Lion to the Monastery*.

San Giovanni in Bragora ㉙

Campo Bandiera e Moro. **Map** 8 E2. **【** *041 520 59 06.* **🚤** *Arsenale.* **◯** *8:30am–7pm Mon–Fri, 8:30am–4pm Sat & Sun.*

THE EXISTING church is essentially Gothic (1475–9) and the interior contains major works of art that demonstrate the transition from Gothic to early Renaissance. Bartolomeo Vivarini's altarpiece *Madonna and Child with Saints* (1478) is unmistakably Gothic. Contrasting with this is Cima da Conegliano's large-scale *Baptism of Christ* (1492–5), which adorns the main altar.

Arsenale ㉚

Map 8 F1. **🚤** *Arsenale or Tana.* **Museo Storico Navale** Campo San Biagio. **Map** 8 F3. **【** *041 520 02 76.* **◯** *8:45am–1:30pm Mon–Fri; 8:45am–1pm Sat.* **●** *public hols.* 🖾

THE ARSENALE was founded in the 12th century and by the 16th had become the greatest naval shipyard in the world, capable of constructing a whole galley in 24 hours, using an assembly-line system. Surrounded by crenellated walls, it was like a city within a city. Today the site is largely unused. Its impressive 15th-century gateway, twin towers, and guardian lions can be viewed from the campo or bridge outside. The gateway was built by Antonio Gambello and is often cited as Venice's first Renaissance construction.

Around the corner, in Campo San Biagio, the **Museo Storico Navale** charts Venetian naval history from the heyday of the Arsenale to the present. Exhibits include friezes from famous galleys of the past and a replica of the *Bucintoro*, the Doge's ceremonial barge.

San Giorgio Maggiore ㉛

Map 8 D4. **【** *041 522 78 27.* **🚤** *San Giorgio.* **◯** *9:30am–12:30pm, 2:30–5pm daily (7pm May–Sep).* **Fondazione Cini** **【** *041 528 99 00* **◯** *Mon–Fri by appt.*

APPEARING LIKE a stage set across the water from the Piazzetta is the little island of

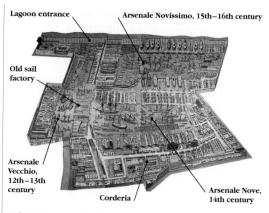

Lagoon entrance — **Arsenale Novissimo, 15th–16th century** — **Old sail factory** — **Arsenale Vecchio, 12th–13th century** — **Corderia** — **Arsenale Nove, 14th century**

18th-century engraving of the Arsenale

St. George Slaying the Dragon (1502–8) by Carpaccio, in the Scuola di San Giorgio degli Schiavoni

San Giorgio Maggiore. The church and monastery, constructed between 1559–80, are among Andrea Palladio's greatest architectural achievements. The church's temple front and the spacious interior with its perfect proportions and cool beauty are typically Palladian *(see pp76–7)*. These qualities are echoed by the church of Il Redentore on the nearby island of Giudecca, built by Palladio in 1577–92.

On the chancel walls of San Giorgio Maggiore, are two fine paintings by Tintoretto: *The Last Supper* and *Gathering of the Manna* (both 1594). In the Chapel of the Dead is his last work, *The Deposition* (1592–4), finished by his son Domenico.

The top of the campanile affords superb views of the city and lagoon. You can see the monastery cloisters below, now part of the **Fondazione Cini**, a cultural center that is used to host international exhibitions.

Palladio's San Giorgio Maggiore

Murano ㉜

🚤 *41, 42 from San Zaccaria; "navetta" from Fondamente Nuove.*

L IKE THE CITY of Venice, Murano consists of a cluster of small islands, connected by bridges. It has been the center of the glassmaking industry since 1291, when the furnaces and craftsmen were moved here from the city because of the risk of fire and the disagreeable effects of smoke. Some of the houses on the water date from this period.

The colonnaded exterior of Murano's Basilica dei Santi Maria e Donato

🏛 Museo Vetrario

Palazzo Giustinian, Fondamenta Giustinian. 🎧 *041 73 95 86.* ⬜ 10am–5pm (Nov–Mar: 4pm) Thu–Tue. ⬤ *Jan 1, May 1, Dec 25.* ▨

In the 15th and 16th centuries Murano was the principal glass-producing center in Europe and today most tourists visit for glass alone. The Museo Vetrario in the Palazzo Giustinian houses a fine collection of antique pieces. The prize exhibit is the dark blue Barovier wedding cup (1470–80), with enamel work by Angelo Barovier.

🔒 Basilica dei Santi Maria e Donato

Fondamenta Giustinian. 🎧 *041 73 90 56.* ⬜ daily.

The architectural highlight of the island is the Basilica dei Santi Maria e Donato, with its lovely colonnaded apse. Despite some heavy-handed restoration undertaken in the 19th century, this 12th-century church still retains much of its original beauty. Visitors should note the Gothic ship's keel roof, the apse with its mosaic Madonna, and the beautiful medieval mosaic floor, which dates from 1140.

Venetian glass goblet

Burano ㉝

🚤 *12 from Fondamente Nuove; 14 from San Zaccaria.*

B URANO IS THE MOST colorful of the lagoon islands and can be distinguished from a distance by the tilting tower of its church. In contrast with the haunting Torcello, the island is densely populated, its waterways fringed with brightly painted houses, such as the Casa Bepi.

The main thoroughfare is Via Baldassare Galuppi, named after the Burano-born composer. It features traditional lace and linen stalls and open-air trattorias serving fresh fish.

🏛 Scuola dei Merletti

Piazza Baldassare Galuppi. 🎧 *041 73 00 34.* ⬜ 10am–5pm (4pm Nov–Mar) Wed–Mon. ⬤ public hols. ▨

The people of Burano are fishermen and lacemakers by tradition. You can still see fishermen scraping their boats or mending nets, but today lacemakers are rare. In the 16th century, however, the local lace was the most sought after in Europe – it was so delicate it became known as *punto in aria* (point in the air). After a slump in the 18th century, the industry revived and a lace-making school, or Scuola dei Merletti, was set up in 1872. Although authentic Burano lace is hard to find today, you can watch it being made by Burano women at the school. There is also a museum attached that displays fine examples of antique lace.

The multicolored Casa Bepi on the island of Burano

Torcello 34

ESTABLISHED BETWEEN the 5th and 6th centuries, the island of Torcello boasts the oldest building in the lagoon – the cathedral of Santa Maria dell'Assunta. Founded in AD 639, it contains some splendid ancient mosaics. The adjoining church of Santa Fosca, of pure Byzantine design, is another mark of Torcello's former glory – before being eclipsed by Venice it had a population of 20,000.

★ **Apse Mosaic**
The 13th-century Madonna, set against a gold background, is one of the most beautiful mosaics in Venice.

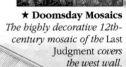

★ **Doomsday Mosaics**
The highly decorative 12th-century mosaic of the Last Judgment *covers the west wall.*

Pulpit
The present basilica dates from 1008, but includes earlier features. The pulpit contains 7th-century fragments.

The Roman sarcophagus below the altar is said to contain the relics of St. Heliodorus.

★ **Iconostasis**
The exquisite Byzantine marble panels of the rood screen are carved with peacocks, lions, and flowers.

Nave Columns
Two rows of slender marble columns, 18 in all, separate the three naves. Their finely carved capitals date from the 11th century.

VISITORS' CHECKLIST

🚊 No. 12 from Fondamente Nuove. **Santa Maria** 🅒 041 73 00 84. ☐ Apr–Sep: 10:30am–5:30pm; Oct–Mar: 10:30am–5pm daily. 🗺 **Campanile** 🅒 041 270 24 64. ☐ daily. 🗺 **Santa Fosca** 🅒 041 73 00 84. ☐ for masses. **Museo dell'Estuario** ☐ Apr–Sep: 10am–12:30pm, 2–5:30pm Tue–Sun; Oct–Mar: 10:30am–12:30pm, 2–4pm Tue–Sun. ⬤ public hols. 🗺

Torcello's Last Canals
Silted canals and malaria hastened Torcello's decline. One of the remaining waterways runs from the vaporetto *stop to the basilica.*

The altar
was rebuilt in 1939 and stands below a 15th-century wood relief of *Santa Fosca Sleeping.*

The central dome
and cross sections are supported by columns of Greek marble with Corinthian capitals.

Santa Fosca
Built in the 11th and 12th centuries on a Greek-cross plan, the church has a serene Byzantine interior with a central pentagonal apse.

The Portico of Santa Fosca, with its elegant stilted arches, is built on three sides of the church, and probably dates from the 12th century.

Vaporetto **boarding point** →

The Museo dell'Estuario houses many old church treasures.

STAR FEATURES

★ **Apse Mosaic**

★ **Doomsday Mosaics**

★ **Iconostasis**

Attila's Throne
It was said that the 5th-century king of the Huns used this marble seat as his throne.

VENICE STREET FINDER

ALL THE MAP REFERENCES given for sights, hotels, and restaurants in Venice refer to this section of the book. The key map below shows areas of the city that are covered by the Street Finder. The first figure of the map reference indicates which map to turn to, and the letter and number that follow are for the grid reference. Standard Italian spelling has been used on all the maps in this book, but when exploring Venice you will find that the names on many street signs are written in Venetian dialect. Mostly this means only a slight variation in spelling (as in the word Sotoportico/Sotoportego below), but some names look totally different. For example, the church of Santi Giovanni e Paolo *(see map 3)*, is frequently marked as "San Zanipolo." A further map showing the vaporetto routes follows the street maps.

RECOGNIZING STREET NAMES

The signs for street *(calle)*, canal *(rio)*, and square *(campo)* will soon become familiar, but the Venetians have a colorful vocabulary for the maze of alleys that makes up the city. When exploring, the following may help.

FONDAMENTA S.SEVERO

Fondamenta is a street that runs alongside a canal, often named after the canal it follows.

RIO TERRA GESUATI

Rio Terrà is a filled-in canal. Similar to a *rio terrà* is a *piscina*, which often forms a square.

SOTOPORTEGO E PONTE S.CRISTOFORO

Sotoportico or Sotoportego means a covered passageway.

SALIZADA PIO X

Salizzada is a main street (formerly a paved street).

RIVA DEI PARTIGIANI

Riva is a wide *fondamenta*, often facing the lagoon.

RUGAGIUFFA

Ruga is a street lined with shops.

CORTE DEI DO POZZI

Corte means a courtyard.

RIO MENUO O DE LA VERONA

Many streets and canals in Venice often have more than one name: *o* means "or."

1

5

Canal

Granc

0 meters ____ 500

0 yards ____ 500

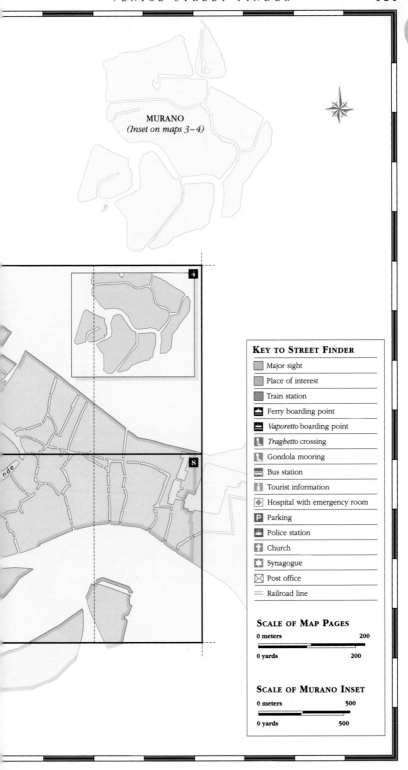

MURANO
(Inset on maps 3–4)

4

8

nde

KEY TO STREET FINDER

	Major sight
	Place of interest
	Train station
	Ferry boarding point
	Vaporetto boarding point
	Traghetto crossing
	Gondola mooring
	Bus station
	Tourist information
	Hospital with emergency room
P	Parking
	Police station
	Church
	Synagogue
	Post office
=	Railroad line

SCALE OF MAP PAGES

0 meters   200

0 yards   200

SCALE OF MURANO INSET

0 meters   500

0 yards   500

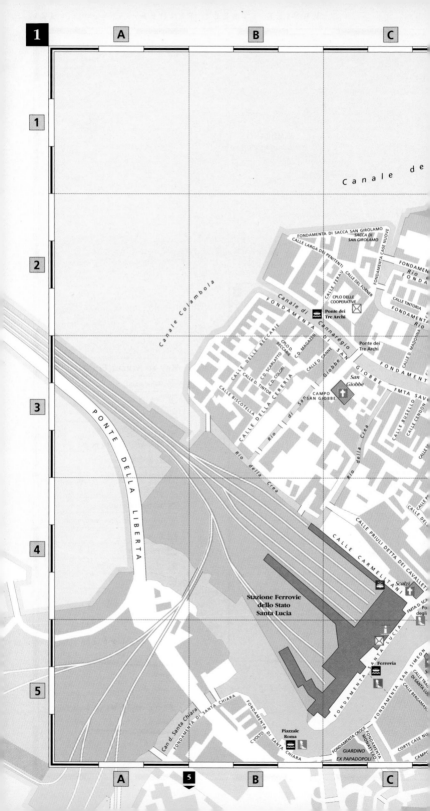

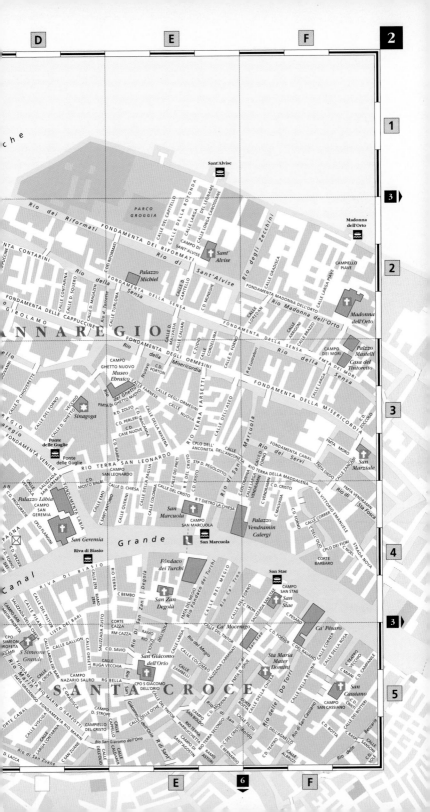

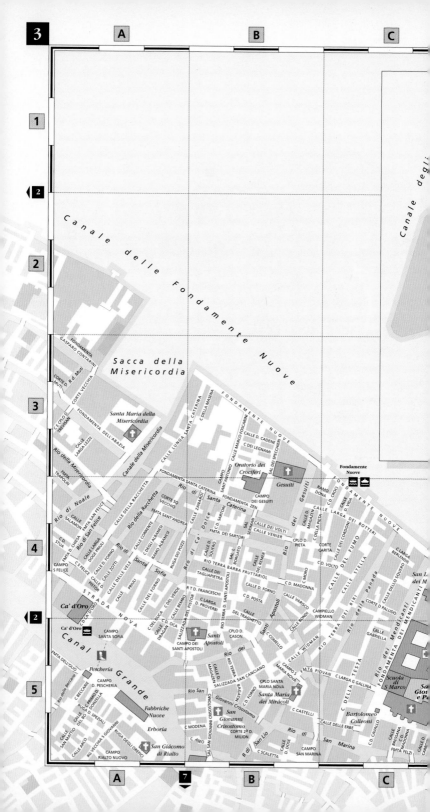

1

◄ **2**

2

Canale delle Fondamente Nuove

Canale degli

3

FONDAMENTA
GASPARO CONTARINI

Sacca della
Misericordia

CORTE VECCHIA

CORTE D.
MUTI

C. PO S.D.
TRENTON

FONDAMENTA DELL'ABAZIA

CALLE
LARGA LEZZE

Santa Maria della
Misericórdia

FONDAMENTA SANTA CATERINA

CALLE DELLA MASENA

FONDAMENTA NUOVE

CALLE MARCO FOSCARINI

CALLE D. CADENE

CALLE DEI LEGNAMI

CAMPO
SANT'ANTONIO

SAL. DELLO SPECCHIERI

Fondamente
Nuove

Rio della Misericordia

IMP.A
TRAPOLIN

Canale della Misericordia

CALLE LUNGA SANTA CATERINA

FONDAMENTA SANTA CATERINA

Oratorio dei
Crociferi

Gesuiti

RAMO
DONA

CO. CROCE

RAMO
D.DONA

Rio di Noale

CALLE
SALAMON

FMTA SAN FELICE

CORTE SO.
VECCHIO

FMTA SANT'ANDREA

CALLE DELLA RACCHETTA

Rio della Racchetta

CALLE ZANARDI

Rio di
Santa
Caterina

CD. SARTORI

CAMPO
DEI GESUITI

SERMAN

CALLE DEI VOLTI

CALLE VENIER

CPLO D.
PIETA

Gesuiti

CALLE
MAGAZEN

CALLE LARGA DEI BOTTERI

C. LARGA
BERLENDIS

CALLE D'OGA

CALLE MAGA

RIO TERRA SAN FELICE

RUGA DOI POZZI

FMTA DEI SARTORI

CALLE D.
SQUERO

SALI.
BORGATO

RIO DI
REMER

CORTE
CARITA

CO.
VOLTO

CD. VOLTO

CALLE DELLO SQUERO

CALLE DELLE CORDONI DELI

San L
dei M

CAMPO
S FELICE

C.S FELICE

CALLE D.
FORNO

DOGE PRIULI

RAMO ALBANESI

Rio di
Santa
Sofia

CALLE DEI
TAGLIAPIETRA

RIO TERRA BARBA FRUTTARIOL

CALLE DEI
FORNO

CD. MADONNA

CALLE DELLO SOVIRO

CORTE DEL PALUDO

CALLE DELLA STELLA

CALLE DEI BIRI

CALLE

CAMPO
S FELICE

CALLE ZOTTI

CALLE DEL FORNO

CALLE DELLE VELE

CALLE
PRIULI

RT. D. FRANCESCHI

CALLE LARGA
D. PROVERBI

CALLE VARICO

CALLE
DEL TRAGHETTO

CAMPIELLO
WIDMAN

CALLE
DEL FUMO

San L
dei M

STRADA

CALLE D.
PISTOR

CALLE DEL FORNO

CD. BUCA

CD. DRAGAN

SALIZADA DEL PISTOR

Santi
Apostoli

Rio dei

C. DELLA TESTA

CALLE
GABRIELLA

Scuola
di
S MARCO

Ca' d'Oro

NOVA

CD. CA' D'ORO

CD. ZAGA

CD. OCA

CPLO D.
CASON

CALLE WIDMAN

RIO TERRA

CAMPO S
MARIA NOVA

C. LARGA G GALLINA

Sa
Gio
e Pa

◄ **2**

Ca' d'Oro

CAMPO
SANTA SOFIA

CAMPO DEI
SANTI APOSTOLI

Santi
Apostoli

S. COMELLO

RIO DI
SANTA SOFIA

SALIZADA SAN CANCIANO

MARIA NOVA

MTA PIOVAN

RIO DEI MENDICANTI

FONDAMENTA DEI MENDICANTI

Canal

FMTA DELL'OLIO

Pescheria
Nuove

CAMPO
D. PESCHERIA

Rio San

RIO TERRA SAN
LEONARDO

SAN GIOVANNI CRISOSTOMO

CPLO SANTA
MARIA NOVA

Santa Maria
dei Mirácoli

C CASTELLI

CD. CAVALLO

Bartolomeo
Colleoni

Sa

CALLE
BRESSANA

CO.
MADONNA

Grande

CALLE delle Beccarie

C. BECCARIE

C. DO PRIMO

RUGA D. SPEZIALI

RUGA VECCHIA S GIOVANNI

Fabbriche
Nuove

Erboria

Rio San

Giovanni Crisostomo

San
Giovanni
Crisostomo

CORTE 2ª D.
MILION

C ASEO

C MODENA

Rio di

San Lio

CD.
DOSE

CD.
DOSE

San Marina

CAMPO
SAN MARINA

FMTA FELZI

CALLE
SAN MATTIO

CALLE D. DO SPEZIALI

CALLE ARCO

SAN GIOVANNI CRISOSTOMO

SALIZADA SAN GIOVANNI CRISOSTOMO

C. PO FONDO

C. SCALETTA

R. di

C. SCALETTA

San Giácomo
di Rialto

CAMPO
RIALTO NUOVO

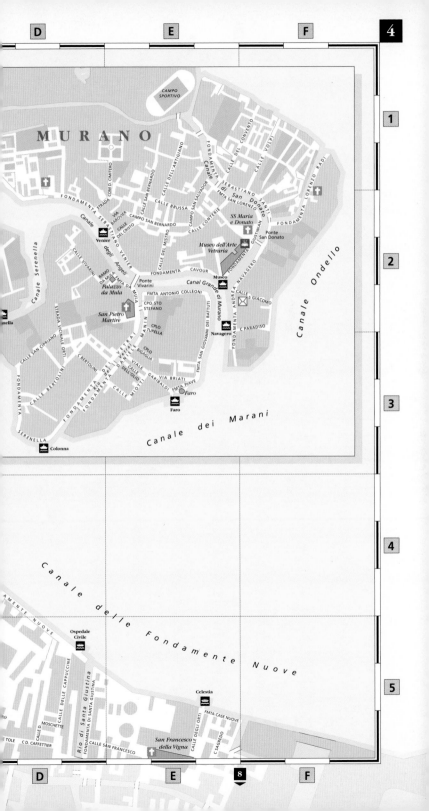

MURANO

CAMPO SPORTIVO

Canale Serenella

FONDAMENTA STRADA COM D. CIMITERO

Venier

Canale

FONDAMENTA SEBASTIANO VENIER

CALLE VIVARINI

CALLE SAN BERNARDO

CALLE DELL'ARTIGIANO

VIA BAROVIER

CALLE SAN SALVADOR

CAMPO SAN BERNARDO

CALLE DEL CRISTO

CALLE BRUSSA

CAMPO SAN STEFANO

CALLE COMTERIE

CALLE DEL MISTRO

FONDAMENTA SEBASTIANO SANTI

Canale di San Donato

FMTA SAN LORENZO

CALLE DEL CONVENTO

CALLE VOLPI

FONDAMENTA LORENZO RADI

SS Maria e Donato

Ponte San Donato

FONDAMENTA GIUSTINIAN

Museo dell'Arte Vetraria

FONDAMENTA CAVOUR

Canal Grande di Murano

Museo

FONDAMENTA ANDREA NAVAGERO

CALLE S GIACOMO

C PARADISO

Canale Ondello

RAMO DA MULA
CALLE DEGLI Angeli

Palazzo da Mula

Ponte Vivarini

FMTA ANTONIO COLLEONI

CPO STO STEFANO

San Pietro Martire

CALLE VIVARINI

STRADA VICINALE ORTI

CALLE SAN CIPRIANO

CALLE BERTOLINI

C BERTOLINI

FONDAMENTA SERENELLA

CALLE MANIN

CPLO TURELLA

CPLO BIGAGLIA

VETRAI

VIALE GARIBALDI

CALLE DEL'OLIO

FMTA SAN GIOVANNI DEI BATTUTI

Navagero

VIA BRIATI

FMTA PIAVE

Faro

Faro

Colonna

Canale dei Marani

Canale delle Fondamente Nuove

FONDAMENTE NUOVE

Ospedale Civile

CALLE DELLE CAPPUCCINE

Rio di Santa Giustina

FONDAMENTA DI SANTA GIUSTINA

CALLE SAN FRANCESCO

MOSCHETTE

C.D. CAFFETTIER

CALLE D.

TOLE

Celestia

FMTA CASE NUOVE

CALLE DEGLI ORTI

C SAGREDO

San Francesco della Vigna

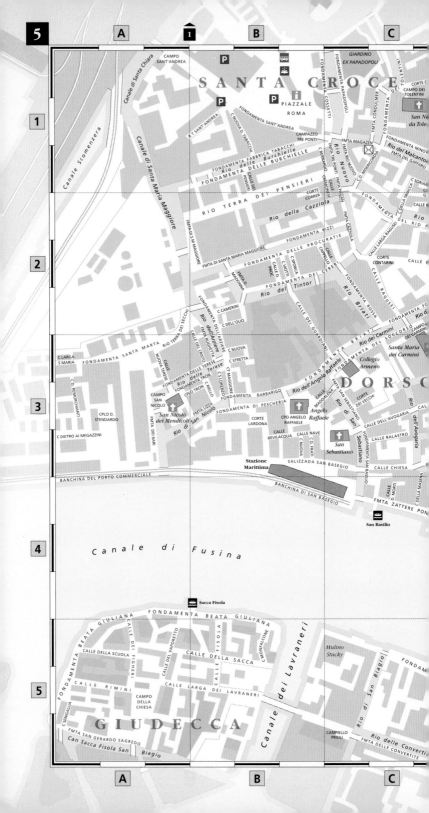

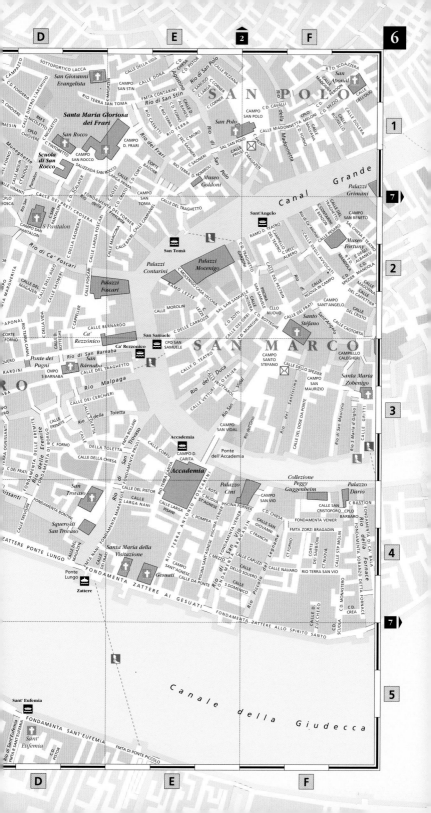

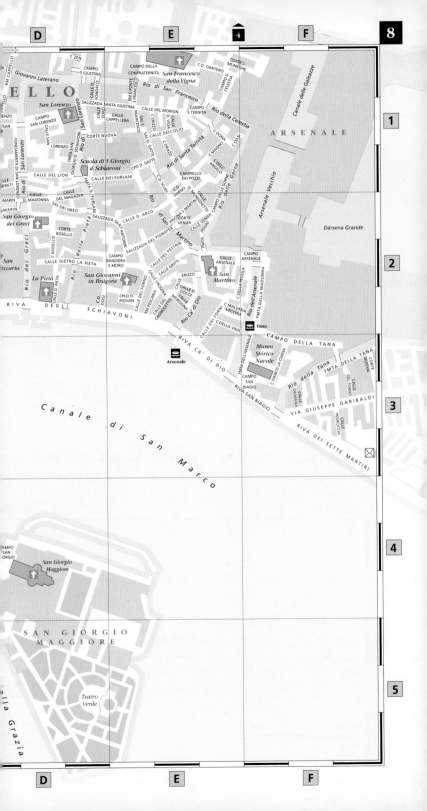

Venice Vaporetto Routes

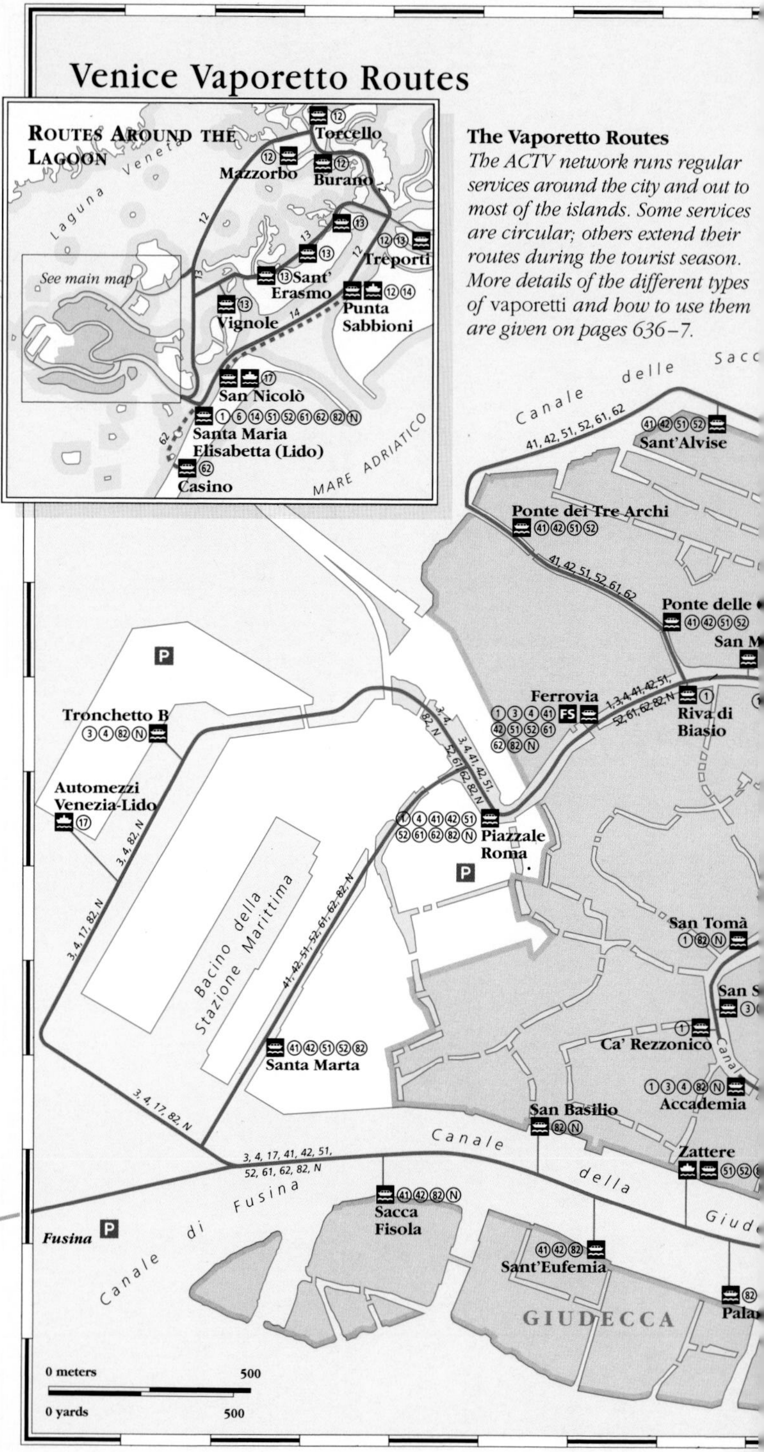

Torcello ⑫

Mazzorbo ⑫ ⑫ ⑫ Burano ⑫

Laguna Veneta

12

See main map

13

⑬ ⑫⑬ Treporti

⑬ Sant' Erasmo ⑫⑭ Punta Sabbioni

⑬ Vignole

14

⑰ San Nicolò

①⑥⑭51 61 62 82 N Santa Maria Elisabetta (Lido)

62 Casino

MARE ADRIATICO

The Vaporetto Routes

The ACTV network runs regular services around the city and out to most of the islands. Some services are circular; others extend their routes during the tourist season. More details of the different types of vaporetti and how to use them are given on pages 636–7.

Canale delle Sacc

41, 42, 51, 52, 61, 62

41 42 51 52 Sant'Alvise

Ponte dei Tre Archi
41 42 51 52

41, 42, 51, 52, 61, 62

Ponte delle
41 42 51 52
San M

Tronchetto B
③④82 N

P

Ferrovia 1, 3, 4, 41, 42, 51,
① ③ ④ 41 FS 52, 61, 62, 82, N ①
41 51 52 61
62 82 N Riva di Biasio

Automezzi Venezia-Lido
⑰

3, 4, 82, N

3, 4, 41, 42, 51, 52, 61, 62, 82, N

④ 41 42 51
52 61 62 82 N Piazzale Roma

P

San Tomà
① 82 N

Bacino della Stazione Marittima

San S
③

Ca' Rezzonico
①

①③④82 N Accademia

41, 42, 51, 52, 61, 62, 82, N

41 42 51 52 82 Santa Marta

Zattere
51 52

San Basilio
82 N

Canale della Giud

3, 4, 17, 41, 42, 51, 52, 61, 62, 82, N

3, 4, 17, 82, N

Fusina P

Canale di Fusina

41 42 82 N Sacca Fisola

41 42 82 Sant'Eufemia

82 Pala

GIUDECCA

0 meters 500

0 yards 500

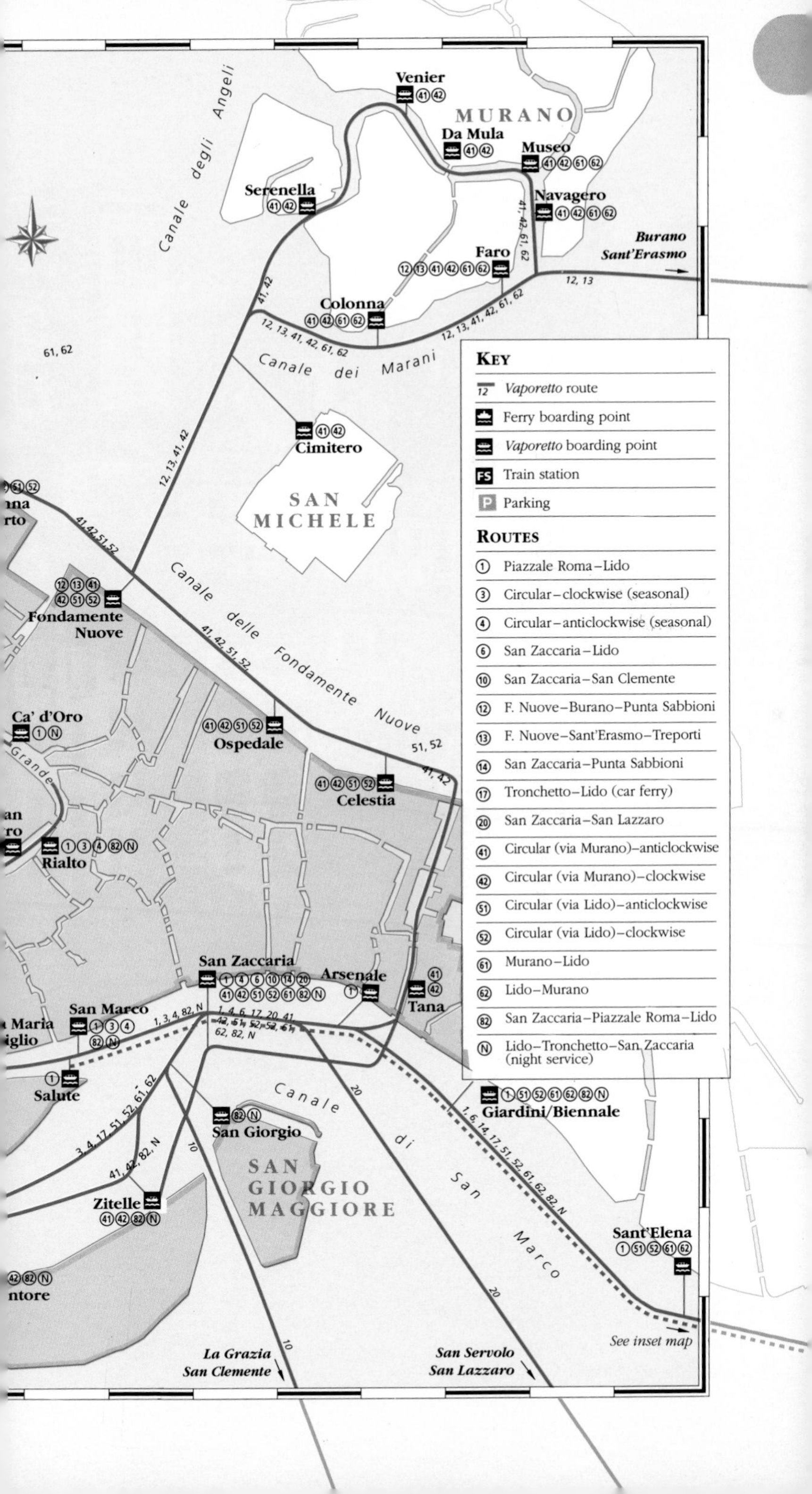

MURANO
Venier (41)(42)
Da Mula (41)(42)
Museo (41)(42)(61)(62)
Navagero (41)(42)(61)(62)
Serenella (41)(42)
Faro ⑫⑬(41)(42)(61)(62)
Colonna (41)(42)(61)(62)
Burano
Sant'Erasmo
12, 13
41, 42, 61, 62
41, 42
12, 13, 41, 42, 61, 62
12, 13, 41, 42, 61, 62
61, 62
Canale degli Angeli
Canale dei Marani
Cimitero (41)(42)
SAN MICHELE
12, 13, 41, 42
41,42,51,52
Fondamente Nuove ⑫⑬(41)(42)(51)(52)
Canale delle Fondamente Nuove
41, 42, 51, 52
Ca' d'Oro ①Ⓝ
Ospedale (41)(42)(51)(52)
51, 52
41, 42
Celestia (41)(42)(51)(52)
Grande
Rialto ①③④(82)Ⓝ
San Zaccaria ①④⑥⑩⑭⑳(41)(42)(51)(52)(61)(82)Ⓝ
Arsenale ①
Tana (41)(42)
San Marco ①③④(82)Ⓝ
Maria
iglio
1, 3, 4, 82, N
1, 4, 6, 17, 20, 41, 42, 51, 52, 53, 61, 62, 82, N
Salute ①
Canale di San Marco
Giardini/Biennale ①(51)(52)(61)(62)(82)Ⓝ
1, 6, 14, 17, 51, 52, 61, 62, 82, N
San Giorgio (82)Ⓝ
3, 4, 17, 51, 52, 61, 62
41, 42, 82, N
10
20
SAN GIORGIO MAGGIORE
Zitelle (41)(42)(82)Ⓝ
(42)(82)Ⓝ
ntore
Sant'Elena ①(51)(52)(61)(62)
See inset map
La Grazia
San Clemente
San Servolo
San Lazzaro
KEY
Vaporetto route
Ferry boarding point
Vaporetto boarding point
FS Train station
P Parking
ROUTES
① Piazzale Roma–Lido
③ Circular–clockwise (seasonal)
④ Circular–anticlockwise (seasonal)
⑥ San Zaccaria–Lido
⑩ San Zaccaria–San Clemente
⑫ F. Nuove–Burano–Punta Sabbioni
⑬ F. Nuove–Sant'Erasmo–Treporti
⑭ San Zaccaria–Punta Sabbioni
⑰ Tronchetto–Lido (car ferry)
⑳ San Zaccaria–San Lazzaro
(41) Circular (via Murano)–anticlockwise
(42) Circular (via Murano)–clockwise
(51) Circular (via Lido)–anticlockwise
(52) Circular (via Lido)–clockwise
(61) Murano–Lido
(62) Lido–Murano
(82) San Zaccaria–Piazzale Roma–Lido
Ⓝ Lido–Tronchetto–San Zaccaria (night service)

THE VENETO AND FRIULI

THE VENETO IS A REGION OF TREMENDOUS CONTRASTS, *encompassing the breathtaking natural beauty of the Dolomites, Lake Garda (Italy's largest lake) and the rolling Euganean Hills, and the man-made delights of magnificent ancient cities such as Verona, Vicenza, and Padua. Neighboring Friuli-Venezia Giulia lines the border with Slovenia to the east, taking in the Carnic Hills in the north, the Roman town of Aquileia and the bustling Adriatic port of Trieste.*

The Romans established their frontier posts here, on this fertile land of silt deposits, and these survive today as the cities of Vicenza, Padua, Verona, and Treviso. These were located on important trade routes such as the Serenissima, which connected the flourishing port cities of Venice and Genoa – and the Brenner Pass, which was used by commercial travelers crossing the Alps from northern Europe.

A strategic position at the hub of the empire's road network enabled the cities to prosper under Roman rule; this they continued to do under the benign rule of the Venetian empire more than 1,000 years later. Wealth from agriculture, commerce, and the spoils of war paid for the beautification of these cities through the building of Renaissance palaces and public buildings, many designed by the Veneto's great architect, Andrea Palladio. His palazzi and villas are telling symbols of the leisured existence once enjoyed by the area's aristocrats.

Today the Veneto is a thriving wine exporter, textile producer, and agricultural center, and Friuli is a focus for new technology, while remaining largely agricultural. Both regions are popular tourist destinations, despite lying a little in the shadow of Venice, and boast an abundant and enchanting variety of attractions.

A leisurely *passeggiata* in one of Verona's ancient streets

◁ **The Renaissance bridge by Palladio at Bassano del Grappa in the Veneto**

Exploring the Veneto and Friuli

THE FLAT LANDSCAPE of the Veneto plain is dramatically off-set by the spectacular Dolomite mountains that form the northwestern border to the Veneto. Friuli, Italy's most northeasterly region, lies tucked up against Austria to the north and Slovenia to the east. Both the Veneto and Friuli are bordered to the south by the Adriatic, with its beaches and ports, which provide a contrast with the area's gently rolling countryside, the vast stretch of Lake Garda, and the many attractive resorts and ancient towns.

View of Verona from the Teatro Romano

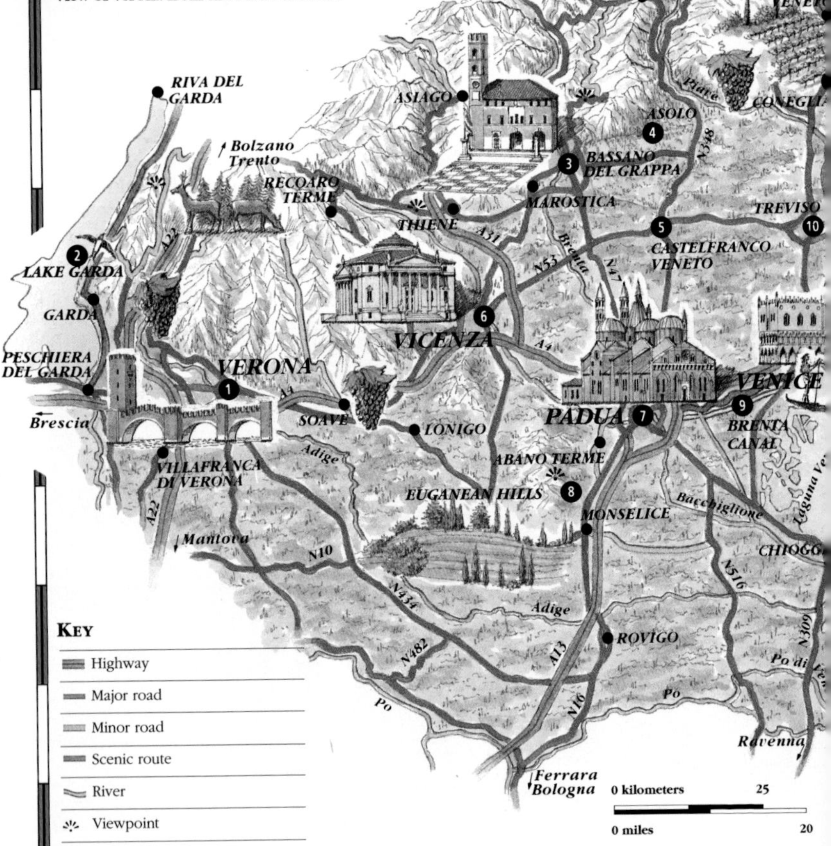

Innsbruck

CORTINA D'AMPEZZO

PIEVE CADOI

PARCO NAZIONALE DEI DOLOMITI BELLUNESI

BELLU

Trento   FELTRE

VITTORI VENETO

RIVA DEL GARDA

ASIAGO

ASOLO

CONEGL

Bolzano Trento

RECOARO TERME

BASSANO DEL GRAPPA

MAROSTICA

TREVISO

THIENE

CASTELFRANCO VENETO

LAKE GARDA

GARDA

VICENZA

PESCHIERA DEL GARDA

VERONA

VENICE

Brescia

SOAVE

LONIGO

BRENTA CANAL

PADUA

ABANO TERME

Adige

EUGANEAN HILLS

MONSELICE

Mantova

CHIOGG

Adige

ROVIGO

Po di

Po

Ferrara Bologna

Ravenna

KEY

━━━ Highway

━━ Major road

▬▬ Minor road

━━ Scenic route

〜 River

ᨏᨏ Viewpoint

0 kilometers   25

0 miles   20

GETTING AROUND

Extensive rail networks and good bus services make this region easy to explore by public transportation; only buses operate around Lake Garda. Highways and main roads provide good links between the main cities. The Venice Simplon-Orient-Express train, which operates from London to Venice, offers a novel approach to the area.

The bridge at Cividale del Friuli

A mountain chalet in Cortina d'Ampezzo

SIGHTS AT A GLANCE

Verona ①

Scaligeri statue in Castelvecchio

V ERONA IS A VIBRANT trading center, the second biggest city in the Veneto region (after Venice) and one of the most prosperous in northern Italy. Its ancient center boasts many magnificent Roman ruins, second only to those of Rome itself, and fine palazzi of *rosso di Verona*, the local pink-tinged limestone, built by the city's medieval rulers. Verona has two main focal points: the massive 1st-century AD Arena, which is still the setting for major events, and Piazza Erbe with its colorful market. One of the main attractions, however, is the church of San Zeno Maggiore (*see pp140–41*), which boasts unusual medieval bronze door panels, carved with extraordinary scenes, some biblical, others on the life of San Zeno.

View of Verona from the Museo Archeologico

Verona's Rulers

In 1263 the Scaligeri began their 127-year rule of Verona. They used ruthless tactics in their rise to power, but once established, the Scaligeri family brought peace to a city racked by civil strife and interfamily rivalry. They proved to be relatively just and cultured rulers – the poet Dante was welcomed to their court in 1301 and dedicated the final part of his epic *Divine Comedy* to the ruling Cangrande I. Today their legacy remains in their ornate tombs and in Castelvecchio.

In 1387 Verona fell to the Visconti of Milan, and a succession of outsiders – Venice, France, and Austria – then ruled the city until the Veneto was united with Italy in 1866.

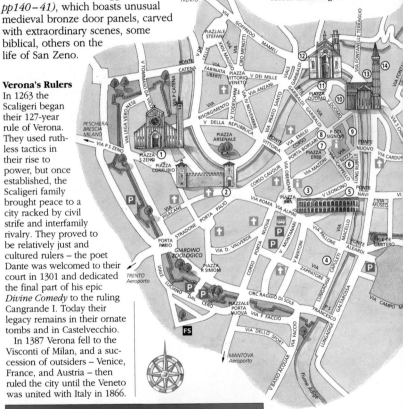

Verona's enormous Roman Arena seen from Piazza Brà

KEY

FS	Train station
🚌	Bus terminus
P	Parking
ℹ️	Tourist information
✝	Church

Ponte Scaligero, part of the old defense system of Castelvecchio

♣ Castelvecchio

Corso Castelvecchio 2. **C** 045 801 54 35. ☐ Tue–Sun.

This impressive castle, built by Cangrande II between 1355 and 1375, now houses one of the finest art galleries in the Veneto outside Venice. It is arranged to give striking views of the castle itself as well as the exhibits displayed within.

The first section contains a wealth of late Roman and early Christian material – silver plate, 5th-century brooches, glass painted with a portrait of Christ the Shepherd in gold, and the carved marble sarcophagus of Saints Sergius and Bacchus (1199).

The section on medieval and early Renaissance art vividly demonstrates the influence of northern art on local painters: the emphasis is on brutal realism as opposed to serene idealism. The late Renaissance works include a fine collection of 15th-century Madonnas.

Jewelry, suits of armor, swords and shield bosses, Veronese's *Deposition* (1565), and a portrait painting attributed to either Titian or to Lorenzo Lotto are on display in further sections.

Outside, a walkway offers views of the Adige River and the medieval **Ponte Scaligero** crossing it, and of the 14th-century equestrian statue of Cangrande I, which once graced his tomb *(see p138)*.

♠ Arena

Piazza Brà. **C** 045 800 32 04. ☐ Tue–Sun. ☐ Jan 1, Dec 25–26.

Verona's Roman amphitheater, completed in AD 30, is the third largest in the world, after Rome's Colosseum and the amphitheater at Santa Maria Capua Vetere, near Naples.

Visitors' Checklist

VISITORS' CHECKLIST

254,700. ✈ Villafranca 14 km (9 miles) SW. **FS** Porta Nuova, Piazza XXV Aprile. ☐ Piazza Citta-della. **i** Via degli Alpini II (045 806 86 80). ☐ daily. ☑ Tickets valid for churches. ☑ Apr: VinItaly wine fair; Jun– Aug: Estate Teatrale Veronese; Jul–Sep: Opera Festival.

The interior, still virtually intact, could hold almost the entire population of Roman Verona, and visitors came from across the Veneto to watch gladiatorial combats and mock battles. Since then, the Arena has seen executions, fairs, bullfights, and theater and opera productions.

♠ San Fermo Maggiore

Via San Fermo. **C** 045 59 28 13. ☐ Tue–Sat.

San Fermo Maggiore is not one but two churches: this is most clearly seen from the outside, where the apse has pointed Gothic elements rising above a sturdy Romanesque base. The lower church, begun in 1065 by Benedictine monks on the site of an earlier sanctuary, has frescoes on the simple arcades.

The more impressive upper church dates from 1313 and is covered with a splendid ship's keel roof. The interior also boasts much medieval fresco work, including a 14th-century section by Stefano da Zevio depicting Musician Angels. Nearby is the Brenzoni mauso-leum (c.1440) by Giovanni di Bartolo, and above it a 1426 fresco of the *Annunciation* by Pisanello (1377–1455).

BOSCO CHIESANUOVA

0 meters 500
0 yards 500

SIGHTS AT A GLANCE

The 11th-century apse of the lower church of San Fermo Maggiore

Exploring Verona

SINCE THE DAYS OF THE ROMAN EMPIRE, Piazza Erbe – built on the site of the ancient Roman forum – has been the center of Verona. Many of the city's fine palazzi, churches, and monuments are nearly as ancient, many dating from the medieval period.

The fountain, erected in the 14th century at the center of Piazza Erbe

⊞ Piazza Erbe
Piazza Erbe is named after the city's old herb market. Today's stands, shaded by umbrellas, sell everything from herb-flavored roast suckling pig in bread rolls to succulent fresh-picked fruit and delicious wild mushrooms.

At the northern end of Piazza Erbe stands the Baroque **Palazzo Maffei** (1668), surmounted by statues. In front of it rises a column supporting the **Venetian lion**, which marks Verona's absorption, in 1405, into the Venetian empire. On the west side is the **Casa dei Mercanti**, a largely 17th-century building that dates originally from 1301.

The **fountain** in the middle of the piazza is often overshadowed by the colorful market stands, though the statue at its center dates from Roman times. It serves as a reminder that this piazza has been used as a market place for 2,000 years.

⊞ Piazza dei Signori
Torre dei Lamberti 📞 045 803 27 26. 🔲 Tue–Sun. 🛈
In the center of the square stands an elegant 19th-century **statue of Dante**, whose gaze seems fixed on the forbidding **Palazzo del Capitano**, once the home of Verona's military commanders. Beside it is the equally intimidating **Palazzo della Ragione**, the Palace of Reason, or law court; both were built in the 14th century. The courtyard of the law court has a handsome external stone staircase, added in 1446–50. Stunning views of the Alps can be enjoyed by those prepared to climb the 84-m (275-ft) **Torre dei Lamberti**, which rises from the western side of the courtyard.

Behind the statue of Dante is the **Loggia del Consiglio** (1493), the council chamber topped by statues of Roman worthies born in Verona: they include Pliny the Elder, the natural historian, and Vitruvius, the architectural theorist.

The square is linked to Piazza Erbe by the Arco della Costa, or the Arch of the Rib, named after the whale rib hung beneath it long ago.

The frescoed Renaissance façade of the Loggia del Consiglio on Piazza dei Signori

🔒 Tombs of the Scaligeri
Via Arche Scaligeri.
Beside the entrance to the tiny Romanesque church of **Santa Maria Antica**, once the parish church of the powerful Scaligeri family, lie a profusion of bizarre tombs of the onetime rulers of Verona.

Over the entrance to the church is the impressive tomb of Cangrande I (died 1329), surmounted by an equestrian statue of the ruler, a copy of the original that is now in Castelvecchio (see p137).

The other Scaligeri tombs are next to the church, behind a wrought-iron fence that incorporates the ladder emblem of the family's original name (della Scala, meaning "of the steps"). Towering above the fence are the tombs of Mastino II (died 1351) and Cansignorio (died 1375), splendidly decorated with a profusion of tiny Gothic spires. Other members of the Scaligeri family lie within a series of plainer tombs that stand nearer the church wall.

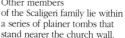

14th-century Scaligeri tomb

🔒 Sant'Anastasia
Piazza Sant'Anastasia. 📞 045 59 28 13. 🔲 daily. 🛈
The huge and lofty church of Sant'Anastasia was begun in 1290. Faded 15th-century frescoes and carved scenes from the life of St. Peter Martyr adorn its Gothic portal.

Inside, there are two notable holy water stoups, supported on figures of beggars, known locally as i gobbi (the hunchbacks). These figures were carved a century apart: the earlier one (on the left) dates from 1495.

The sacristy, off the north aisle, is home to the fine but unfortunately damaged fresco of St. George and the Princess (1433–8) by Pisanello.

ROMEO AND JULIET

The tragic story of Romeo and Juliet, two young lovers from rival families (the Capulets and the Montagues in Shakespeare's play), was written by Luigi da Porto of Vicenza in the 1520s and has inspired countless poems, films, ballets, and dramas.

At the **Casa di Giulietta** (Juliet's house), No. 27 Via Cappello, Romeo is said to have climbed to Juliet's balcony: in reality this is a restored 13th-century inn. Crowds throng to see the simple façade, and stand on the small marble balcony. The run-down house dubbed the **Casa di Romeo** stands a few streets away in Via Arche Scaligeri, east of Piazza dei Signori.

The so-called **Tomba di Giulietta** is displayed in a crypt below the cloister of San Francesco al Corso on Via del Pontiere. The stone sarcophagus lies in an extremely atmospheric setting.

The so-called Casa di Giulietta

↟ Duomo

Piazza Duomo. **[** 045 59 28 13. **◯** Tue–Sun. ◙ &

Verona's cathedral was begun in 1139 and is fronted by a magnificent Romanesque portal carved by Nicolò, one of the two master masons responsible for the façade of San Zeno (see pp140–41). Here he sculpted the sword-bearing figures of Oliver and Roland, two of Charlemagne's knights, whose exploits were much celebrated in medieval poetry. Alongside them stand evangelists and saints with wide eyes and flowing beards. To the south there is a second Romanesque portal carved with Jonah and the Whale and with comically grotesque caryatids.

The highlight of the interior is Titian's lovely *Assumption* (1535–40), and outside there is a Romanesque cloister in which the excavated ruins of earlier churches are visible. The 8th-century baptistry, or San Giovanni in Fonte (St. John of the Spring), was built from Roman masonry; the marble font was carved in 1200.

⋔ Teatro Romano

Rigaste Redentore 2. **[** 045 800 03 60. **◯** Tue–Sun. ◙

This theater was built in the 1st century BC; little now survives of the original stage area, but the semicircular seating area remains largely intact. It offers entrancing views over the city: in the foreground is the only one of three Roman bridges to have survived; it was rebuilt after World War II.

🏛 Museo Archeologico

Rigaste Redentore 2. **[** 045 800 03 60. **◯** 8am–6:30pm Tue–Sun. ◙

An elevator carries visitors from the Teatro Romano up to the monastery above, now an archaeological museum.

The exhibits around the tiny cloister and in the old monks' cells include mosaics, pottery, glass, and tombstones. There is also a fine bronze bust of the ambitious first Roman emperor, Augustus (63 BC–AD 14), who succeeded in overcoming his opponents, including Mark Antony and Cleopatra, to become the sole ruler of the Roman world in 31 BC.

Statuary and formal hedges in the Renaissance Giardino Giusti

♣ Giardino Giusti

Via Giardino Giusti 2. **[** 045 803 40 29. **◯** daily. **●** Dec 25. ◙ &

This is one of Italy's finest Renaissance gardens. It was laid out in 1580 and, as in other gardens of the period, there is a juxtaposition of nature and artifice; the formal lower garden of clipped box-wood hedges, gravel walks, and potted plants contrasts with wilder woods above.

John Evelyn, an English author and diarist who visited Verona in 1661, thought this the finest garden in Europe.

↟ San Giorgio in Braida

Lungadige San Giorgio. **[** 045 834 02 32. **◯** daily.

This lovely domed Renaissance church was begun in about 1530 by Michele Sanmicheli. The altar includes the famous *Martyrdom of St. George* (1566) by Veronese, and above the west door is the *Baptism of Christ*, usually attributed to Tintoretto (1518–94).

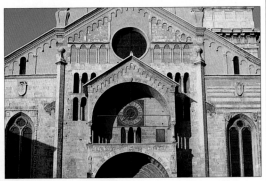

The imposing façade of Verona's duomo, Santa Maria Matricolare

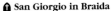

Verona: San Zeno Maggiore

Detail from San Zeno's façade

SAN ZENO, built in 1123–35 to house the shrine of Verona's patron saint, is the most ornate Romanesque church in northern Italy. The façade is adorned with an impressive rose window, marble reliefs, and a graceful porch canopy. The highlight, however, is the fascinating 11th- and 12th-century bronze door panels. A squat tower just north of San Zeno is said to cover the tomb of King Pepin of Italy (777–810).

Nave Ceiling
The nave has a magnificent example of a ship's keel ceiling, so called because it resembles the inside of an upturned boat. This ceiling was constructed in 1386 when the apse was rebuilt.

The bell tower, started in 1045, reached its present height of 72 m (236 ft) in 1178.

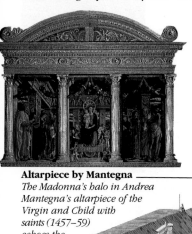

Altarpiece by Mantegna
The Madonna's halo in Andrea Mantegna's altarpiece of the Virgin and Child with saints (1457–59) echoes the shape of the church's rose window.

★ Cloister (1123)
The arches are rounded Romanesque on one side, pointed Gothic on another.

Former washroom

Crypt
The vaulted crypt contains the tomb of San Zeno, appointed first bishop of Verona in AD 362, who died in AD 380.

Nave and Main Altar
The plan of the church is modeled on an ancient Roman basilica, the Hall of Justice. The main altar is situated in the raised sanctuary where the judge's throne would have stood.

VISITORS' CHECKLIST

Piazza San Zeno. **(** 045 59 28 13. **○** Mar–Oct: 9am–6pm Tue–Sat, Sun pm; Nov–Feb: 10am–1pm, 1:30–4pm. **●** Mon, for masses. 🎫 🛉 🔥

BRONZE DOOR PANELS

The 48 bronze panels of the west doors are primitive but forceful in their depiction of biblical stories and scenes from the life of San Zeno. Those on the left date from 1030 and survive from an earlier church on the site; those on the right were made after the earthquake in 1137. The panels are the work of three separate craftsmen, and are linked with masks. Huge staring eyes and Ottoman-style hats, armor and architecture feature prominently. Among the scenes, some of which are unclear, are Adam and Eve, Salome dancing for the head of John the Baptist, and a startling Descent into Limbo.

Descent into Limbo | Christ in Glory | Human head

Striped brickwork is typical of Romanesque buildings in Verona. Courses of local pink brick are alternated with ivory-colored tufa.

The rose window, dating from the early 12th century, symbolizes the Wheel of Fortune: figures on the rim show the rise and fall of human luck.

The Romanesque porch is one of the finest examples of the style in northern Italy. Since 1138 it has shielded biblical bas-reliefs, above the west doors, from the elements.

Marble side panels, which were carved in 1140, depict events from the Life of Christ (to the left of the doors) and scenes from the Book of Genesis (to the right).

★ **West Doors**
Each of the wooden doors has 24 bronze plates nailed on to make the doors look like solid metal. A multi-colored bas-relief above them depicts San Zeno, flanked by the people of Verona, vanquishing the devil.

STAR FEATURES

★ **West Doors**

★ **Cloister**

Lake Garda ❷

GARDA, THE LARGEST AND EASTERNMOST of the Italian lakes, borders three regions: Trentino to the north, Lombardy to the west and south, and the Veneto to the south and east. The low-lying countryside around the southern stretches becomes increasingly dramatic further north, until impressive rocky cliffs, sometimes swathed in pines, hug the shoreline of the northern tip. The numerous sportings facilities, many sights, and splendid scenery of snow-capped mountains help make the lake a favorite summer playground.

VISITORS' CHECKLIST

Brescia, Verona & Trento. ℹ *Via Repubblica 8, Gardone Riviera (0365 203 47).* **FS** *Peschiera del Garda & Desenzano del Garda.* ⛴ *to all towns.* **Villa il Vittoriale**, *Via Vittoriale 12, Gardone.* 🗞 *0365 29 65 01.* ◻ *Tue–Sun.* 🏰 **Rocca Scaligera**, *Sirmione.* 🗞 *030 91 64 68.* ◻ *Tue–Sun.* 🈲 🗞

Eastern tip of Sirmione Peninsula
Beyond the town is a path which follows the rim of the peninsula, passing boiling sulphur springs.

Gardone is noted for its exotically planted park and for the Villa il Vittoriale, the Art Deco home of the poet Gabriele d'Annunzio, which is filled with curiosities.

The Republic of Salò was established here by Mussolini in 1943. The cathedral in this elegant and attractive town of pastel-painted houses contains an altarpiece by Veneziano.

The hydrofoils, *catamarans, and steamers that ply the lake offer glimpses of villas and gardens that cannot be seen from the coastal road.*

Riva's waterfront is dominated by an old fortress of the Scaligeri. Windsurfers favor this resort because of the consistent offshore winds.

The streets of Malcesine cluster below an imposing medieval castle. A cable car climbs to the summit of Monte Baldo (1,745 m/5,725 ft), offering far-reaching views.

0 kilometers 5

0 miles 5

The lake is named after this long-established town.

Bardolino gave its name to the well-known red wine.

Peschiera's attractive enclosed harbor and fortress were built by the Austrians in the 1860s, during the Italian Wars of Independence.

Riva del Garda
Torbole
Limone sul Garda
Tremosine
Campione del Garda
Assenza
Malcesine
Tignale
Brenzone
Gargnano
Castelletto
Bogliaco
Maderno
Gardone Riviera
Salò
Torri del Benaco
Portese
San Felice del Bonaco
Garda
Manerba
Moniga
Bardolino
Padenghe sul Garda
Lazise
Sirmione
Desenzano
Peschiera

KEY

• • Steamer route

• • Car ferry

🏰 Sailing club or center

ℹ Tourist information

🌿 Viewpoint

Sirmione
A fascinating medieval castle, the Rocca Scaligera, dominates the town of Sirmione. At the tip of the peninsula lie Roman ruins.

The 16th-century wooden bridge by Palladio at Bassano del Grappa

Bassano del Grappa ❸

Vicenza. 🏠 39,000. FS 🚌
ℹ Largo Corona d'Italia 35 (0424 52
43 51). 🚪 Thu & Sat am.

THIS PEACEFUL TOWN lies at
the foot of Monte Grappa.
The Brenta River is straddled
by the graceful Ponte degli
Alpini, designed in 1569 by
Palladio. It is built of timber
to allow it to flex when hit by
the waters of the spring thaw.
Bassano is well known for its
majolica products (decorated
and glazed earthenware), some
of which are on display in the
Palazzo Sturm. The town is
also synonymous with the
popular Italian after-dinner
drink, the clear brandy known
as grappa. It is produced from
the lees (graspa) left over from
wine production; information
about the process is given in
the **Museo degli Alpini**.

🏛 Palazzo Sturm
Via Ferracina. **⚑** 0424 52 49 33.
◯ Apr–Oct: Tue–Sun; Nov–Mar:
Fri–Sun. 🖼
🏛 Museo degli Alpini
Via Anagarano 2. **⚑** 0424 50 36 50.
◯ Tue–Sun.

Asolo ❹

Treviso. 🏠 2,000. 🚌 **ℹ** Piazza
d'Annunzio 2 (0423 52 90 46). 🚪 Sat.

ASOLO IS beautifully sited
among the cypress-clad
foothills of the Dolomites. This
tiny walled town was once
ruled by Queen Caterina
Cornaro (1454–1510), the

Venetian wife of the King of
Cyprus, who poisoned her
husband so that Venice would
gain Cyprus. Cardinal Pietro
Bembo, a poet, coined the
verb asolare to describe the
bittersweet life of enforced
idleness she endured in exile
here. Among others who have
fallen in love with the narrow
streets and grand houses was
poet Robert Browning, who
named a volume of poems
Asolanda (1889) after Asolo.

ENVIRONS: At Masèr, 10 km
(6 miles) east of the town,
stands the magnificent **Villa
Barbaro** (see pp76–7). It was
designed by Palladio in about
1555, in conjunction with the
artist Veronese, and perfectly
blends symmetry and light,
airy rooms with sumptuous
trompe l'oeil frescoes.

🏛 Villa Masér
Via Barbano. **⚑** 0423 92 30 04.
◯ Mar–Oct: Tue, Sat, Sun & hols
pm; Nov–Feb: Sat, Sun & hols pm.
● Dec 24–Jan 6, Easter Sun. 🖼

Castelfranco Veneto ❺

Treviso. 🏠 30,000. 🚌
ℹ Via Francesco M Preti 39 (0423
49 50 00). 🚪 Tue am & Fri am.

FORTIFIED IN 1199 by rulers of
Treviso as a defense against
the neighboring Paduans, the
historic core of this town lies
within well-preserved walls. In
the **Casa di Giorgione**, said to
be the birthplace of the painter
Giorgione (1478–1511), about
whom little is known, there is
a museum devoted to his life.
Giorgione innovatively used
landscape to create mood,
adding figures to intensify the
atmosphere – for instance in
his broodingly mysterious but
evocative most famous work,
The Tempest (see p102).
Another of his few directly
attributable works hangs here
in the **duomo**: the Madonna
and Child with Saints Liberal
and Francis (1504).

ENVIRONS: About 8 km (5
miles) northeast of the town,
at the village of Fanzolo, lies
the **Villa Emo** (c.1555).
Designed by Palladio, it is a
typical example of his work: a
cube flanked by two sym-
metrical wings. Inside there
are lavish frescoes by Zelotti.

🏛 Casa di Giorgione
Piazzetta del Duomo. **⚑** 0423 49 12
40. ◯ Tue–Sun. ● public hols. 🖼
🏛 Villa Emo
Fanzolo di Vedelago. **⚑** 0423 47
64 14. ◯ Apr–Oct: Mon–Sat pm,
Sun; Nov–Mar: Sat & Sun pm.
● Dec 23–Jan 15. 🖼

Fresco (c.1561) by Veronese adorning the Villa Barbaro near Asolo

Street-by-Street: Vicenza 6

Face at No. 21 Contrà Porti

VICENZA IS KNOWN as the city of Andrea Palladio (1508–80), who started out as a mere stonemason and became the most influential architect of his time. Walking around the city, it is intriguing to study the evolution of his distinctive style. In the center is the monumental basilica he adapted to serve as the town hall, nearby is the Teatro Olimpico, and all around are the palaces he built for Vicenza's wealthy citizens.

Loggia del Capitaniato
This covered arcade was designed by Palladio in 1571.

Contrà Porti
is bordered by some of the most elegant palazzi in Vicenza.

Palazzo Valmarana Braga
Palladio's impressive building of 1566 is decorated with giant pilasters and sculpted scenes. It was not completed until 1680, 100 years after the architect's death.

San Lorenzo

Piazza Stazione

CORSO ANDREA PALLADIO

CONTRA CAVOUR

VIA BATTISTI

C MUSCHERIA

CONTRÀ LAMPERTICO

CONTRA GARIBALDI

CONTRA PESCHE VE

CONTRA SAN ANTONIO

PIAZZA DEL DUOMO

Duomo
Vicenza's cathedral was rebuilt after bomb damage during World War II left only the façade and choir entirely intact.

Andrea Palladio
This memorial to Vicenza's most famous son is usually surrounded by market stalls.

0 kilometers 2

0 miles 1

KEY

‒ ‒ ‒ Suggested route

STAR SIGHT

★ **Piazza dei Signori**

A large hall is all that remains of the 15th-century Palazzo della Ragione.

Torre di Piazza, built in the 12th century, is an impressive 82 m (269 ft) high.

Santa Corona

Teatro Olimpico Museo Civico

CONTRÀ S BARBARA

The lion of St. Mark gazing down on Piazza dei Signori

★ **Piazza dei Signori**
Palladio's elegant buildings flank the Piazza dei Signori, including the majestic two-tier colonnades of the 16th-century "Basilica," built around the old Palazzo della Ragione.

PIAZZA DELLE BIADE

CONTRÀ CATENA
C GAZZOLE
CONTRÀ PIANCOLI

CONTRÀ SAN PAOLO
CONTRÀ PONTE SAN MICHELE

ERBE

CONTRÀ PESCARIA

RETRONE

The Quartiere delle Barche contains many attractive palaces built in the 14th-century Venetian Gothic style.

Ponte San Michele
This elegant stone bridge, built in 1620, provides lovely views of the surrounding town.

La Rotonda
Monte Berico
Villa Valmarana
ai Nani

Piazza delle Erbe, the city's market square, is overlooked by a 13th-century prison tower.

Casa Pigafetta
This striking 15th-century house was the birthplace of Antonio Pigafetta, who in 1519 set sail round the world with Magellan.

Piazza dei Signori
Basilica 0444 32 36 81.
Tue–Sun.
This square at the heart of Vicenza is dominated by the Palazzo della Ragione, often referred to as the **Basilica**. Its green, copper-clad roof is shaped like an upturned boat with a balustrade bristling with the statues of Greek and Roman gods. The colonnades were designed by Palladio in 1549 as a facing to support the city's 15th-century town hall, which had begun to subside. This was Palladio's first public commission, and a great success. Beside it stands the 12th-century Torre di Piazza.

The **Loggia del Capitaniato**, to the northwest, was built by Palladio in 1571: the Loggia's upper rooms contain the city's council chamber.

Contrà Porti
Contrà (an abbreviation of *contrada*, or district) is the Vicenza dialect word for street. On one side of the Contrà is a series of pretty Gothic buildings with painted windows and ornate balconies, reminiscent of Venice and a reminder that Vicenza was once part of the Venetian empire.

Several elegant Palladian palazzi stand on this street. Palazzo Porto Barbarano (No. 11), Palazzo Thiene (No. 12), and Palazzo Iseppo da Porto (No. 21) illustrate the sheer variety of Palladio's style – all share Classical elements but each is unique. An intriguing detail is that Palazzo Thiene appears to be of stone, though it is in fact built of cheap, light-weight brick, cleverly rendered to look like stone.

Exploring Vicenza

VICENZA, THE GREAT PALLADIAN CITY and one of the wealthiest cities in the Veneto, is celebrated the world over for its splendid and varied architecture; it also offers the visitor elegant shops and cafés to visit.

Carpione's ceiling fresco in the large entrance hall of the Museo Civico

🏛 Museo Civico

Piazza Matteotti. 📞 0444 32 13 48.
🕐 Tue–Sun. 🈂 🚻
The excellent Museo Civico is housed in **Palazzo Chiericati** *(see p76)* by Palladio, built in 1550. Inside is a fresco by Giulio Carpione of a naked charioteer, representing the Sun, who appears to fly over the entrance hall. The upstairs rooms hold many excellent pictures. Among the Gothic altarpieces from churches in Vicenza is Hans Memling's *Crucifixion* (1468–70), the central panel from a triptych whose side panels are now located in New York.

Other rooms contain works by the local artist Bartolomeo Montagna (c.1450–1523).

🔒 Santa Corona

Contrà Santa Corona. 📞 0444 32 36 44. 🕐 daily.
This great Gothic church was built in 1261 to house a thorn donated by Louis IX of France and said to be from Christ's Crown of Thorns. The Cappella Porto houses the tomb of Luigi da Porto (died 1529), author of the novel *Giulietta e Romeo*, on which Shakespeare based his famous play. Notable paintings include Giovanni Bellini's *Baptism of Christ* (c.1500) and the *Adoration of the Magi* (1573) by Paolo Veronese.

🎭 TEATRO OLIMPICO

Piazza Matteotti. 📞 0444 32 37 81.
🕐 Tue–Sun. 🈂 🚻
Europe's oldest surviving indoor theater is a fine and remarkable structure, largely made of wood and plaster, and painted to look like marble. Palladio began work on the design in 1579, but he died the following year. His pupil, Vincenzo Scamozzi, took over the project, completing the theater in time for its opening performance of Sophocles' tragic drama, *Oedipus Rex*, on March 3, 1585.

Odeon Frescoes
The gods of Mount Olympus, after which the theater is named, decorate the Odeon, a room used for music recitals.

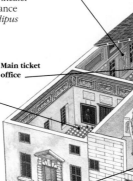

The Anteodeon contains frescoes depicting the theater's opening performance, and oil lamps from the original stage set.

Main ticket office

Stage Set
Scamozzi's scenery represents the Greek city of Thebes. The streets are cleverly painted in perspective and rise at a steep angle to give the illusion of great length.

The Auditorium
was designed by Palladio to resemble the outdoor theaters of ancient Greece and Rome, such as the Arena at Verona *(see p137)*, with a semicircle of "stone" benches and a ceiling painted to portray the sky.

🏛 San Lorenzo

Piazza San Lorenzo. ◯ *daily.*

The portal of this church is a magnificent example of Gothic stone carving, richly decorated with the figures of the Virgin and Child, and St. Francis and St. Clare. Inside there are fine tombs and damaged frescoes. The lovely cloister, north of the church, is an attractive, flower-filled haven of calm.

🏛 Monte Berico

Basilica di Monte Berico. 📞 *0444 32 09 99.* ◯ *daily.*

Monte Berico is the green, cypress-clad hill to the south of Vicenza to which wealthy residents once escaped, in the heat of summer, to enjoy the cooler air and pastoral charms of their country estates. Today, shady *portici*, or colonnades, adorned with shrines, line the wide avenue linking central Vicenza to the basilica on top of the hill. The domed basilica

La Rotonda (1550–52), most famous of all Palladio's works

itself, built in the 15th century and enlarged in the 18th, is dedicated to the Virgin who appeared here during the 1426–8 plague to announce that Vicenza would be spared.

The ornate interior contains a moving *Pietà* fresco (1500) by Bartolomeo Montagna, a fossil collection in the cloister, and Veronese's fine painting, *The Supper of St. Gregory the Great* (1572), in the refectory.

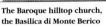

The Baroque hilltop church, the Basilica di Monte Berico

🏛 Villa Valmarana ai Nani

Via dei Nani 12. 📞 *0444 54 39 76.* ◯ *mid-Mar–Nov 5: Tue–Sun.* 🏛

The wall alongside the Villa Valmarana (which was built in 1688 by Antonio Muttoni) is topped by figures of dwarfs that give the building its name *ai Nani* (of the Dwarfs).

Inside, the walls are covered with frescoes by Tiepolo, in which the fleshy and pneumatic gods of Mount Olympus float about on clouds watching scenes from Homer and Virgil.

In the separate Foresteria (guest house), the 18th-century frescoes depicting peasant life and the seasons, painted by Tiepolo's son, Giandomenico, are equally decorative but provide a contrast through their somewhat earthy realism.

The villa can be reached by an enjoyable, ten-minute walk from the basilica on Monte Berico. Head downhill along Via Massimo d'Azeglio to the high-walled convent on the right where the road ends, then take Via San Bastiano.

🏛 La Rotonda

Via Rotonda 25. 📞 *0444 32 17 93.*
Villa ◯ *mid-Mar–Nov 4: Wed.* 🏛
Garden ◯ *Mar–Oct: Tue–Thu.* 🏛

With its perfectly regular, symmetrical forms, this villa, also known as the Villa Capra Valmarana, is the epitome of Palladio's architecture (*see pp76–7*), of which there are several fine examples throughout the Veneto. The design, consisting of a dome rising above a cube, received immediate acclaim for the way it blends so perfectly with its surroundings. A pleasant contrast exists between the terracotta roof tiles, the white walls, and the green lawns.

The villa, built in 1550–52, has inspired many copies in cities as far away as London, St. Petersburg and Delhi. Fans of *Don Giovanni* will enjoy spotting locations used in Joseph Losey's 1979 film.

To reach La Rotonda, follow the path that passes beside the Villa Valmarana ai Nani.

The façade statues of stately toga-clad figures are portraits of sponsors who paid for the theater's construction.

The courtyard giving access to the Teatro is decorated with ancient sculptures. These were donated by members of the Olympic Academy, the learned body that built the theater.

Main entrance

Street-by-Street: Padua **❼**

Pᴀᴅᴜᴀ (PADOVA) is an old university town with an illustrious academic history. Rich in art and architecture, it has two particularly outstanding sights. The magnificent Cappella degli Scrovegni *(see pp150–51)*, north of the city center, is famous for Giotto's lyrical frescoes. Close to the train station, it forms part of the complex incorporating the Eremitani church and museums. The Basilica di Sant'Antonio, which forms the focal point in the southern part of the city, is one of the most popular pilgrimage destinations in Italy.

Palazzo del Capitanio
Built between 1599 and 1605 for the head of the city's militia, the tower incorporates an astronomical clock made in 1344.

Piazza dei Signori is bordered by attractive arcades that house small specialty shops, cafés, and old-fashioned wine bars.

Corte Capitaniato, a 14th-century art school (open for concerts), contains frescoes that include a rare portrait of the poet Petrarch.

Ufficio di Turismo

Loggia della Gran Guardia
This fine Renaissance building dating from 1523 once housed the Council of Nobles. It is now used as a conference center.

PIAZZA CAPITANIATO

VIA SAN CLEMENTE

PIAZZA DEI SIGNORI

VIA MONTE DI PIETÀ

VIA MANIN

PIAZZA DEL DUOMO

V GRITTI

VIA VANDELLI

VIA SON

★ Duomo and Baptistry
The 12th-century baptistry of the duomo contains one of the most complete medieval fresco cycles to survive in Italy, painted by Giusto de' Menabuoi in 1378.

The Palazzo del Monte di Pietà has 16th-century arcades and statues enclosing a medieval building.

KEY	
– – –	Suggested route

0 kilometers   2

0 miles   1

STAR SIGHT
★ Duomo and Baptistry

Caffè Pedrocchi

Built like a Classical temple, the Caffè Pedrocchi has been a famous meeting place for students and intellectuals since it opened in 1831.

VISITORS' CHECKLIST

220,000. **FS** Piazzale della Stazione. **i** Piazza Boschetti (049 875 20 77). daily. Oct–Apr: concert season.

A bronze statue
of a woman (1973) by Emilio Greco stands at the center of this largely pedestrianized square.

Stazione
Chiesa degli Eremitani
Cappella degli Scrovegni
Museo Civico

PIAZZA CAVOUR

VIA GORIZIA

ZZA DELLA FRUTTA

VIA OBERDAN

PTTA GARZERIA

PIAZZA DELLE ERBE

VIA VIII FEBBRAIO

V SAN CANZIANO

Basilica di Sant'Antonio
Orto Botanico

Padua University
Founded in 1222, this is Italy's second oldest university. Elena Piscopia was the first woman graduate, in 1678.

lazzo
ella Ragione,
e medieval court of justice,
ntains magnificent frescoes.

Piazza delle Erbe
There are some excellent views to be had over the market-place from the 15th-century loggia, which runs alongside the 13th-century Palazzo della Ragione.

🏛 Duomo and Baptistry
Piazza Duomo.
Baptistry 049 66 28 14.
daily.

The Duomo was built in 1552 to plans partly by Michelangelo on the site of an earlier 14th-century cathedral. Beside it stands a domed baptistry (c.1200). The interior is entirely decorated with vibrant frescoes painted by Giusto de' Menabuoi, dating from around 1378. The frescoes depict episodes from the Bible, including scenes of the Creation, the Miracles, the Passion, the Crucifixion and the Resurrection of Christ.

🏛 Palazzo della Ragione
Piazza delle Erbe. 049 820 50 06.
Tue–Sun. Jan 1, Dec 25.

The "Palace of Reason," which is also known as the Salone, was built in 1218 to serve as Padua's law court and council chamber. The vast main hall was originally decorated with frescoes by Giotto, but fire destroyed his work in 1420. The Salone is breathtaking in its sheer size. It is the largest undivided medieval hall in Europe, 80 m (262 ft) long, 27 m (89 ft) wide, and 27 m (89 ft) high. Frescoes painted in 1420–25 by Nicola Miretto cover its walls: the fascinating panels – 333 of them – depict the months of the year, with appropriate gods, signs of the zodiac, and seasonal activities. A 1466 copy of the huge Gattamelata statue *(see p152)* by Donatello stands at one end of the hall.

🏛 Caffè Pedrocchi
Via VIII Febbraio 15.
049 878 12 31.
daily.
Caffè Pedrocchi opened in 1831, and became famous throughout Italy as the café that never closed its doors. Today people come as much to talk, play cards, or watch the world go by as to eat or drink. The upstairs rooms, decorated in florid Moorish, Egyptian, medieval, Greek, and other styles, are used for concerts and lectures.

Padua: Cappella degli Scrovegni

ENRICO SCROVEGNI built this chapel in 1303, hoping thereby to spare his dead father, a usurer, from the eternal damnation in hell described by the poet Dante in his *Inferno*. The interior of the chapel is entirely covered with beautiful frescoes of scenes from the life of Christ, painted by Giotto between 1303 and 1305. As works of great narrative force, they exerted a powerful influence on the development of European art.

The Nativity
The naturalism of the Virgin's pose marks a departure from Byzantine stylization, as does the use of natural blue for the sky, in place of celestial gold.

Expulsion of the Merchants
Christ's physical rage, the cowering merchant, and the child hiding his face show an animation that is characteristic of Giotto's style.

The Coretti
Giotto painted the two panels known as the Coretti as an exercise in perspective, creating the illusion of an arch with a room beyond.

View toward altar

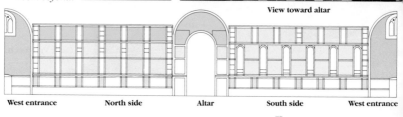

West entrance   North side   Altar   South side   West entrance

GALLERY GUIDE

The scenes, which are depicted in sequence, are fully explained on a small board, printed in several languages with a basic numbered key, which the custodian will offer you on entry to the chapel. Due to the size of the chapel, the number of visitors at any one time is restricted, and as a consequence, long lines can build up at peak times. The duration of visits is also timed when it gets busy, and restricted to 15 minutes per viewing.

KEY

- [ ] Episodes of Joachim and Anna
- [ ] Episodes from the Life of Mary
- [ ] Episodes from the Life and Death of Christ
- [ ] The Virtues and Vices
- [ ] The Last Judgment

The Last Judgment
This scene fills the entire west wall of the chapel. Its formal composition is closer to Byzantine tradition than some of the other frescoes, with parts probably painted by assistants. A model of the chapel is shown (center left, at the bottom) being offered to the Virgin by Scrovegni.

VISITORS' CHECKLIST

Piazza Eremitani. 049 820 45 50. to Piazzale Boschetti. Feb–Oct: 9am–7pm daily; Nov–Jan: 9am–6pm daily. public hols. Adv booking necessary.

View toward entrance

Mary is Presented at the Temple
Giotto sets many scenes against an architectural background, using the laws of perspective to give a sense of three dimensions.

Injustice
The Vices and Virtues are painted in monochrome. Here Injustice is symbolized by scenes of war, murder, and robbery.

Lament over the Dead Christ
Giotto's figures express their grief in different ways: some huddle together, another gestures wildly.

GIOTTO

The great Florentine artist Giotto (1266–1337) is regarded as the father of Western art. His work, with its sense of pictorial space, naturalism, and narrative drama, marks a decisive break with the Byzantine tradition of the preceding 1,000 years. He is the first Italian master whose name has passed into posterity, and although he was regarded in his lifetime as a great artist, few of the works attributed to him are fully documented. Some may have been painted by others, but his authorship of the frescoes in the Scrovegni Chapel need not be doubted.

Exploring Padua

PADUA IS A CITY OF MANY ATTRACTIONS, with a rich history; this is reflected in the major museum complex that occupies a group of 14th-century monastic buildings attached to the church of the Eremitani, a reclusive Augustinian order. The admission ticket includes entry to the Cappella degli Scrovegni *(see pp150–51)*, which stands on the same site. Padua is, in addition, the setting for one of Italy's most important churches – the splendid Basilica di Sant'Antonio – and for one of the earliest universities to be founded in Italy.

🏛 Chiesa degli Eremitani and Museo Civico Eremitani

Piazza Eremitani. 📞 049 820 45 50. ⭘ Mon. 📷

The Eremitani church was built from 1276 to 1306 and contains magnificent roof and wall tombs. Among them is that of Marco Benavides (1489–1582), a professor of law at the city university, whose Renaissance tomb was the work of Ammannati (1511–92), an architect from Florence. Celebrated frescoes (1454–7) by Mantegna, portraying scenes from the lives of St. James and St. Christopher, were destroyed during a bombing raid in 1944. Two scenes from this magnificent series survive in the Cappella Ovetari, south of the sanctuary: *The Martyrdom of St. James* and *The Martyrdom of St. Christopher*.

A 1st-century AD tomb in the archaeological collection

The Museo Civico Eremitani houses a coin collection, an archaeological section, and a wonderful art gallery.

Among the treasures in the Bottacin section there are some very rare Roman medallions and an almost complete set of Venetian coinage.

The rich archaeological collection contains interesting Roman tombs, fine mosaics, and impressive life-size statues. Renaissance bronzes include the comical *Drinking Satyr* by Il Riccio (1470–1532).

The beautiful 14th-century crucifix from the Cappella degli Scrovegni is displayed in the Quadreria Emo Capodilista, along with works by Giotto and 15th- to 18th-century paintings from the Venetian and Flemish schools.

🔒 Basilica di Sant'Antonio

Piazza del Santo.

This exotic church, with its minaret-like spires and Byzantine domes, is also known as Il Santo. It was built from 1232 to house the remains of St. Anthony of Padua, a preacher who modeled himself on St.

15th-century *Angels in Armor* by Guariento, Museo Civico Eremitani

Francis of Assisi. Although he was a simple man who rejected worldly wealth, the citizens of Padua built one of the most lavish churches in Christendom to serve as his shrine.

The influence of Byzantine architecture is clearly visible in the basilica's outline: a cone-shaped central dome rises above seven encircling domes; the façade combines Gothic and Romanesque elements.

Inside, the high altar features Donatello's magnificent reliefs (1444–5) on the miracles of St. Anthony, and his statues of the Crucifixion, the Virgin, and Paduan saints. The tomb of St. Anthony, hung with offerings, lies in the north transept; large marble reliefs depicting the saint's life, carved in 1505–77 by various artists, adorn the walls around it. A lively fresco scene of the Crucifixion by Altichiero da Zevio (1380s) adorns the south transept.

🏇 Statue of Gattamelata

Beside the entrance to the basilica stands one of the great works of the Renaissance: a statue of the mercenary soldier Gattamelata. This gritty portrait was created in 1443–52, in honor of a man who during his life did great service to the Venetian Republic. The artist Donatello won fame for the monument, the first equestrian statue made on such a large scale since Roman times.

The Basilica di Sant'Antonio, and Donatello's statue of Gattamelata

Scuola del Santo and Oratorio di San Giorgio

Piazza del Santo. [049 875 52 35.
Scuola del Santo ○ daily. ● Jan 1, Dec 25. **Oratorio di San Giorgio**
○ daily.

Five excellent frescoes, including the earliest documented paintings by Titian, are to be found in these two buildings. The Scuola del Santo contains two scenes from the life of St. Anthony that were painted by Titian in 1511. The works in the San Giorgio oratory were executed by Altichiero da Zevio and Jacopo Avenzo, who painted them in 1378–84.

Orto Botanico

Via Orto Botanico 15. [049 827 21 19. ○ daily; (Nov–Mar: Mon–Sat am).

Padua's botanical garden, the oldest in Europe, (1545) still retains much of its original appearance. The gardens and hothouses were used to cultivate the first lilac trees (1568), sunflowers (1568), and potatoes (1590) to be grown in Italy.

Palazzo del Bo

Via VIII Febbraio 2. [049 820 97 73. ○ for guided tours only. Tue, Thu, Sat am, Mon, Wed, Fri pm.

The historic main university building originally housed the medical faculty, renowned throughout Europe. Among its famous teachers and students was Gabriele Fallopio (1523–62), after whom the Fallopian tubes are named.

Guided tours include the pulpit Galileo used when he taught physics here from 1592 until 1610 and the wooden anatomy theater, built in 1594 and now the oldest surviving medical lecture theater in the world.

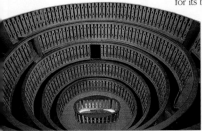

The 16th-century anatomy theater in the old medical school of the university's Palazzo del Bo, Padua

The Euganean Hills, formed by ancient volcanic activity

Euganean Hills ⑧

FS to Terme Euganee, Montegrotto Terme. Viale Stazione 60, Montegrotto Terme (049 79 33 84).

THE CONICAL Euganean Hills, remnants of long-extinct volcanoes, rise abruptly out of the surrounding plain. Hot-water springs bubble up out of the ground at Abano Terme and Montegrotto Terme, where scores of establishments offer thermal treatments, ranging from mud baths to immersion in the hot sulphurated waters. Spa cures originated in Roman times; remains of the original baths and theater are still visible at Montegrotto Terme.

Abbazia di Praglia

Via Abbazia di Praglia, Bresseo di Teolo. [049 990 00 10.
○ Tue–Sun pm. ● Jan.
The Benedictine monastery at Praglia, 6 km (4 miles) west of Abano Terme, is a peaceful haven in the tree-clad hills where the monks grow herbs and restore manuscripts. They also lead guided tours of the dignified Renaissance church (1490–1548), which is noted for its beautiful cloister. There are also richly carved stalls in both the choir and the refectory, and paintings and frescoes by Zelotti, a 16th-century painter from Verona, in the dome of the church and the refectory.

Casa di Petrarca

Via Valleselle 4, Arquà Petrarca. [0429 71 82 94. ○ Tue–Sun.
The picturesque town of Arquà Petrarca, on the southern edge of the Euganean Hills, is named in honor of Francesco Petrarca, the medieval poet known in English as Petrarch (1303–74). Petrarch spent the last few years of his life here, living in a house frescoed with scenes from his lyrical poems, overlooking a landscape of olive groves and vineyards. He lies buried in a simple sarcophagus in front of the church.

The Casa di Petrarca (part 14th century) in Arquà Petrarca

Villa Barbarigo

Valsanzibio. [049 913 00 42.
○ Mar–Nov.
To the north of Arquà is the 18th-century Villa Barbarigo at Valsanzibio, which boasts one of the finest Baroque gardens in the Veneto. These were planned by Antonio Barbarigo in 1669, and are a grandiose mix of statuary, fountains, a maze, formal parterres, lakes, and avenues of cypress trees.

The 16th-century Villa Foscari at Malcontenta, beside the Brenta Canal

Brenta Canal **9**

Padua and Venezia. **FS** *Venezia Mestre, Dolo, Mira.* **🚌** *to Mira, Dolo and Strà.* **ℹ** *Via Don Minzoni, Mira (041 42 49 73).* **Canal trips on *Il Burchiello:** Via Trieste 42, Padua.* **☎** *049 66 09 444.* 🖰

OVER THE CENTURIES, in order to prevent the Venetian lagoon from silting up, the rivers flowing into it were diverted. The Brenta was canalized: the older branch, between Padua and Fusina (just west of Venice), dates back to the 16th century and flows for a total of 36 km (22 miles). Its potential as a transportation route was quickly realized, and fine villas were built along its length.

Today many of these elegant buildings can still be admired – the N11 road runs alongside most of the canal's length – and three of them open their doors to the public. The 18th-century **Villa Nazionale** at Strà has an extravagant frescoed ceiling by Tiepolo. The **Villa Widmann-Foscari** at Mira (itself a pretty village) was built in 1719 but altered in the 19th century, and contains an interior decorated in French Rococo style. In the village of Malcontenta is the well-known **Villa Foscari**, or Villa Malcontenta, one of Palladio's loveliest villas (*see pp76–7*).

It was built in 1560 and the interior was decorated with magnificent frescoes by Zelotti.

These villas may also be visited as part of an indulgent 8½-hour guided tour from Padua, traveling to Venice (or, on alternate days, from Venice to Padua) along the river in a leisurely fashion on board the *Burchiello* motor launch – the cost for the one-way journey, however, is fairly prohibitive.

🏛 Villa Nazionale
Via Pisani, Strà. **☎** *049 50 20 74.* ◯ *daily.* ● *Jan 1, May 1, Dec 25.* 🖰
🏛 Villa Widmann-Foscari
Via Nazionale 420, Mira Porte. **☎** *041 42 41 56.* ◯ *Tue–Sun.* 🖰
🏛 Villa Foscari
Via dei Turisti, Malcontenta. **☎** *041 547 00 12.* ◯ *Tue & Sat am.* ● *Dec–Mar.* 🖰

Treviso **10**

👥 *81,700.* **🚌** **FS** **ℹ** *Piazzetta Monte di Pietà 8 (0422 54 76 32).* **🛒** *Tue & Sat am.*

DESPITE COMPARISONS with Venice, the lovely fortified city of Treviso has its own very distinctive character.

A good place to start a tour of the streets, some lined with attractive balconied houses beside willow-fringed canals, is **Calmaggiore**. The street links the duomo with the Palazzo dei Trecento, the rebuilt 13th-century town hall.

The **duomo** was founded in the 12th century but rebuilt several times. Inside, Titian's *Annunciation* (1570) vies for attention with the striking *Adoration of the Magi* fresco (1520) by Titian's arch rival, Il Pordenone. More paintings by Titian and other artists of the Renaissance may be seen in the **Museo Civico**.

The fish market, which dates from medieval times, is held on an island in the middle of Treviso's Sile River; this allows the remains of the day's trading to be flushed away.

The bulky Dominican church of **San Nicolò**, nestling by the 16th-century city wall, contains interesting tombs and frescoes, including, on a wall of the chapter house, the first-ever depiction of eyeglasses in art. A magnificent tomb (1500) by Antonio Rizzo is framed by a fresco of pageboys (c.1500) by Lorenzo Lotto.

🏛 Museo Civico
Borgo Cavour 24. **☎** *0422 59 13 37.* ◯ *Tue–Sun.* ● *Dec 25.* 🖰

The houses of the medieval town of Treviso overlooking ancient canals

The façade and entrance to the Renaissance Palazzo dei Rettori in Belluno

Conegliano ⓫

Treviso. 🏛 *35,000.* FS 🚌 ℹ️ *Via XX Settembre 61 (0438 212 30).* 🛒 *Fri.*

CONEGLIANO lies among Prosecco-producing vineyards, and winemakers from all over Italy learn their craft at Conegliano's famous wine school. Via XX Settembre, the winding and arcaded main street, is lined with fine 15th- to 18th-century palazzi, many in the Venetian Gothic style or decorated with fading frescoes. The **duomo** contains the town's one great work of art, an altarpiece painted by local artist Cima da Conegliano (1460–1518) depicting the *Virgin and Child with Saints* (1493).

Reproductions of Cima's most famous works are displayed in the **Casa di Cima**, the artist's birthplace. The detailed landscapes in the background of his paintings were based on the hills around the town; the same views can still be seen from the gardens surrounding the Castelvecchio (old castle).

A mythical statue on Conegliano's theater

🏛 Casa di Cima
Via Cima. 📞 *0438 216 60 (call to arrange visit).* 🕐 *Sat & Sun pm.* 📷

Belluno ⓬

🏛 *36,000.* FS 🚌 ℹ️ *Piazza dei Martiri 8 (0437 94 00 83).* 🛒 *Sat.*

PICTURESQUE BELLUNO, capital of Belluno province, serves as a bridge between the two different parts of the Veneto, with the flat plains to the south and the Dolomite peaks to the

north. Both are encapsulated in the views seen from the 12th-century **Porta Ruga** at the southern end of Via Mezzaterra, the main street of the old town. More spectacular still are the views from the bell tower of the 16th-century **duomo** (subsequently rebuilt). The nearby baptistry houses a font cover with the figure of John the Baptist carved by Andrea Brustolon (1662–1732). Brustolon's works also grace the churches of San Pietro (on Via San Pietro) and Santo Stefano (Piazza Santo Stefano). North of Piazza del Duomo stands the city's most elegant building, the **Palazzo dei Rettori** (1491) – once home to the town's Venetian rulers – and the 12th-century **Torre Civica**, all that now survives of a medieval castle.

The **Museo Civico** contains paintings by Bartolomeo Montagna (1450–1523) and Sebastiano Ricci (1659–1734), and a notable archaeological section. North of the museum is Belluno's finest square, the **Piazza del Mercato**, with its arcaded Renaissance palaces and its 1410 fountain.

South of the town are the ski resorts of the Alpe del Nevegal; in the summer a chairlift operates from Faverghera up the flank of the mountain to a height of 1,600 m (5,250 ft) offering extensive views.

🏛 Museo Civico
Piazza Duomo 16. 📞 *0437 94 48 36.* 🕐 *mid-Apr–mid-Oct: Tue–Sun; mid-Oct–mid-Apr: Mon–Sat.* 📷

Cortina d'Ampezzo ⓭

Belluno. 🏛 *6,800.* 🚌 ℹ️ *Piazzetta San Francesco 8 (0436 32 31).* 🛒 *Tue & Fri.*

ITALY'S TOP SKI RESORT, much favored by the smart set from Turin and Milan, is well supplied with restaurants and bars. Cortina is set amid the extremely dramatic scenery of the Dolomites (*see pp78–9*), which explains part of the resort's attraction: all around, crags and spires thrust their distinctive weather-beaten shapes above the trees.

Cortina benefits from better than average sports facilities, thanks to hosting the 1956 Winter Olympics. In addition to downhill and cross-country skiing, there is also a ski jump and a bobsled run for those who want something more adventurous than usual, as well as an Olympic ice stadium, several swimming pools, tennis courts, and riding facilities.

During the summer months, Cortina becomes an excellent base for walkers. Useful information on trails and guided walks is available from the tourist office or, during the summer, from the Guides' office opposite.

Corso Italia in Cortina d'Ampezzo, Italy's most important ski resort

Traditional copper pans on display in the Museo Carnico in Tolmezzo

Tolmezzo ⑭

🏛 *10,000.* 🚌 ℹ️ *Piazza XX Settembre (0433 448 98).*
🔲 *Mon.*

T OLMEZZO IS THE CAPITAL of the Carnia region, named after the Celtic tribe that inhabited the area around the 4th century BC. The town is surrounded by the high peaks of the Carnic Alps, including the pyramidal Monte Amariana (1,906 m/6,253 ft) to the east. The best place to begin a tour of the region is the **Museo delle Arti Popolari**, which has displays of local costumes, crafts, textiles, and agriculture.

Southwest of the town, a scenic road climbs 14 km (8.5 miles) to the ski resort of **Sella Chianzutan**, a good base for walking in the summer. More resorts line the road, west of Tolmezzo, to **Ampezzo**, at which point a minor road heads north through the gorge of the Lumiei River. Following this road to the Ponte di Buso bridge and the **Lago di Sauris** is an excellent introduction to the majestic Carnic Alps.

Above this point the road is often impassable in winter, but in summer there are flower-filled meadows all along the road up to Sella di Razzo, and then back along the **Pesarina Valley**, via Comeglians and Ravascletto. Returning south, **Zuglio** was once the Roman town of Forum Iulii Carnicum, guarding the road over the pass. Today it is worth a detour for the remains of its Ròman basilica, baths, and forum.

🏛 **Museo delle Arti Popolari**
Via della Vittoria 2.
📞 *0433 432 33.* 🕐 *Tue–Sun.* 🔲 *Jan 1, Dec 25.* 🈺

Pordenone ⑮

🏛 *49,000.* 🚉 🚌 ℹ️ *Corso Vittorio Emanuele II 38 (0434 219 12).* 🔲 *Sat am & Wed.*

O LD PORDENONE consists of one long street, the **Corso Vittorio Emanuele**, lined with pretty arcaded houses of pink brick, some with the faded traces of decorative frescoes on their façades. The 13th-century **Palazzo Comunale** forms a striking conclusion to the street with its eccentrically shaped roofline of curves and minaret-like side towers, and its 16th-century clocktower. Opposite is the **Museo Civico**, housed in the 17th-century Palazzo Ricchieri, where works by the local artist Il Pordenone (1484–1539) are on display.

Around the corner stands the **duomo**, which contains the lovely altar painting of the *Madonna della Misericordia* (1515) by Il Pordenone. The bell tower beside the Duomo is a fine example of Roman-esque decorative brickwork.

🏛 **Museo Civico**
Corso Vittorio Emanuele 51. 📞 *0434 39 23 11.* 🕐 *Tue–Fri.* 🔲 *public hols.* 🈺 ♿

Udine ⑯

🏛 *99,000.* 🚉 🚌 ℹ️ *Piazza I Maggio 7 (0432 29 59 72).* 🔲 *Sat.*

U DINE IS A CITY of varied and surprising architecture. In the center lies **Piazza della Libertà**, where the Palazzo del Comune (1448–56), built of pink stone in Venetian Gothic style, stands beside the Art Deco Caffè Contarena (1915). Opposite, the Renaissance symmetry of the Porticato di San Giovanni is interrupted by the Torre dell'Orologio (Clock Tower, 1527) crowned by two bronze Moors who strike the hours. Note also the fountain of 1542, the two 18th-century statues, and the column supporting the Lion of St. Mark.

Rising behind the square is a 26-m (85-ft) hill which offers sweeping views over the city. Beyond the **Arco Bollani**, a gateway designed by Palladio in 1556, steps lead up to the 16th-century castle, now the **Musei Civici e Galleria di Storia e Arte Antica**, which houses the city's fine art and archaeology collections.

South of Piazza Matteotti, where a small market is held, at the end of Via Savorgnana, stands the **Oratorio della Purità**, and the **Duomo** with its octagonal bell tower. Both contain important paintings and frescoes by Giambattista Tiepolo (1696–1770). More of Tiepolo's work can be seen in the **Palazzo Arcivescovile**, which the artist decorated with frescoes.

Lago di Sauris, an artificial lake lying in the Carnic Alps above Tolmezzo

The arcaded Porticato di San Giovanni on Piazza della Libertà, Udine

ENVIRONS: Outside Codroipo, 24 km (15 miles) west, rises the imposing **Villa Manin**. A road passes through the villa's grounds, so its massive size can be seen even when the house – once the retreat of Ludovico Manin, the last doge of Venice (1725–1802) – and its magnificent gardens are closed to the public.

🏛 **Musei Civici e Galleria di Storia e Arte Antica**
Castello di Udine. 🛈 0432 50 28 72. ⏺ Tue–Sat (Sun am). ⬤ Jan 1, Easter, May 1, Dec 25. 📷 ♿
🏛 **Palazzo Arcivescovile**
Piazza Patriarcato 1. 🛈 0432 250 03. ⏺ Wed–Sun. ⬤ Jan 1, Easter, Dec 25. 📷 ♿
🏛 **Villa Manin**
Passariano. 🛈 0432 90 66 57. ⏺ Tue–Sun. ⬤ Jan 1, Dec 25. **Gardens** ⏺ Easter–Oct: Tue–Sun. ♿

Cividale del Friuli ⓱

🏯 11,000. 🚉 🚌 🛈 Corso Paolino Aquileia 10 (0432 73 14 61). ⬤ Sat.

A GATE IN THE medieval walls of Cividale leads down the main street and straight to the dramatic ravine of the Natisone River, which splits the town in two and is spanned by the arch of the medieval **Ponte del Diavolo** (Devil's Bridge).

Above the river's north bank stands the **Tempietto Longobardo** (Lombardic Chapel), a very rare example of an 8th-century church decorated with reliefs of saints, modeled in stucco. The town's history is traced in the excellent **Museo**

Archeologico Nazionale, which contains the excavated remains of buildings from a Roman town, and a collection of Lombardic items including jewelry, ivory, and weapons.

Next door is the **duomo**, rebuilt in 1453 after a fire, with its beautiful silver altarpiece (13th century). The **Museo Cristiano**, off the south aisle, contains sculptures from the original church; of particular interest is the altar donated by Ratchis, the Lombardic Duke of Friuli and later King of Italy (737–44), which is finely carved with scenes from the life of Christ, including a charming Nativity. There is, in addition, the unusual baptismal font of Patriarch Callisto (737–56); this octagonal structure, with a roof supported by pillars, is decorated with symbols of the Evangelists.

The Lion of Venice above the entrance to Gorizia's castle

🏛 **Tempietto Longobardo**
Piazzetta San Biagio. ⏺ daily. 📷

Interior view of the Tempietto Longobardo in Cividale del Friuli

🏛 **Museo Archeologico Nazionale**
Palazzo dei Provveditori Veneti, Piazza del Duomo 13. 🛈 0432 70 07 00. ⏺ Tue–Sun. ⬤ Jan 1, Easter, May 1, Dec 25. 📷 ♿
🏛 **Museo Cristiano**
Piazza del Duomo. 🛈 0432 73 11 44. ⏺ daily. ♿

Gorizia ⓲

🏯 37,000. 🚉 🚌 🛈 Palazzo della Ragione, Via Roma 9 (0481 53 38 70). ⬤ Thu, Fri.

G ORIZIA WAS AT the center of fierce fighting during both world wars and was split in two by the 1947 Treaty of Paris, leaving part in Italy, part in Yugoslavia (now Slovenia).

The town's arcaded streets and pastel-painted houses, have been carefully restored following substantial damage during World War II. A visit to the modern Museo Provinciale della Grande Guerra (Museum of the Great War), housed in the basement of the **Museo Provinciale**, provides a fascinating introduction to the realities of war. The museum uses videos, photographs, and life-size mock-ups of trenches, latrines and gun emplacements to show the waste, squalor, and heroism of war.

Rooms on the upper floor of the museum house temporary exhibitions and items from the town's art collection, which includes works by local artists.

On a mound nearby rises the castle, circled by 16th-century fortifications. From here there are extensive views stretching over the town to the mountains beyond.

ENVIRONS: To the southwest of Gorizia, scenic country roads pass through the foothills of the **Carso**, a limestone plateau stretching down to Trieste. The plateau is dotted with fields enclosed by drystone walls, and gouged with tunnels, caves, and underground rivers.

🏛 **Museo Provinciale**
Borgo Castello 13. 🛈 0481 53 39 26. ⏺ Tue–Sun. ⬤ Jan 1, Dec 25. 📷

The attractive harborside at Grado, along the coast south of Aquileia

Aquileia ⑲

🚶 3,300. 🚌 🛈 *Piazza Capitolo 4 (0431 91 94 91) summer only.* 🚆 *Tue.*

AQUILEIA, now little more than a village but surrounded by the ruins of palatial villas, baths, temples, and market buildings, provides a poignant reminder of the lost splendor of the Roman Empire.

It was here that Emperor Augustus received Herod the Great, King of Judea, in 10 BC, and it was here too, in AD 381, that the early Christian church held a major council attended by the learned saints Ambrose and Jerome to settle doctrinal issues. In the 5th century, however, the town was abandoned following several sackings. Fortunately, substantial parts of the early Christian basilica have survived, that contain the town's particular treasure: ornate floor mosaics.

🎵 Basilica
Piazza Capitolo. 📞 *0431 910 67.* ⭘ *daily.* **Crypt** 🅿️
The basilica was founded in about AD 313 and much of the original structure still survives, including the magnificent floor mosaics of the nave and **Cripta degli Scavi** below. The designs are a mixture of geometric patterns, biblical stories, and scenes from everyday life in ancient Aquileia. There is a lively portrayal of the tale of Jonah, who was swallowed by an extraordinary sea monster: the fishing boats are also surrounded by a rich array of creatures from the deep, including wide-eyed dolphins and squid.

🏛 Museo Archeologico Nazionale
Via Roma 1. 📞 *0431 910 16.* ⭘ *daily.* ● *Jan 1, May 1, Dec 25.* 🅿️ ♿
The mosaics in the basilica continue a tradition of crafts-

manship that flourished in the city from the 2nd century AD. Additional examples of mosaics and stone carvings from the Classical era (1st to 3rd centuries) are on display in this museum, together with glass, amber, and a collection of flies, beautifully worked in gold, that formed the adornment of a Roman matron's veil.

🏛 Museo Paleocristiano
Località Monastero. 📞 *0431 911 31.* ⭘ *daily.* ● *Jan 1, May 1, Dec 25.*
This museum, which stands not far from Aquileia's ancient harbor beside the once-navigable River Natissa, focuses on the development of art during the early Christian era.

ENVIRONS: The resort of **Grado**, like Venice, sits on a group of low islands in the middle of the Adriatic lagoon, attached to the mainland by a long narrow causeway. The town grew into a port for Aquileia in the 2nd century and was used as a haven by Aquileia's citizens during the troubled period of the barbarian invasions. Today, Grado is one of the most popular seaside resorts on the Adriatic, with good seafood restaurants, a long sandy beach, and a yachting harbor.

At the center of the old town stands the **duomo**: the interior contains 6th-century frescoes in the apse, which are similar in style to those covering the vaults of San Marco in Venice (*see pp106–9*). Nearby, in the little church of **Santa Maria delle Grazie**, there are yet more 6th-century mosaics.

SYMBOLISM IN EARLY CHRISTIAN ART

Christians were persecuted until their religion was granted official status by Constantine the Great in AD 313. Prior to this they had developed a language of secret symbols to express their beliefs, many of which can be seen in the mosaics and marble tomb chests of Aquileia. Many of these and other symbols later found their way into popular bestiaries and folk art.

Part of the 4th-century floor mosaic in the basilica at Aquileia

The winged figure of Victory *holding a laurel wreath was a Classical symbol of triumph, and holiness. Later, it came to represent Christ's resurrection, and, more generally, victory over death.*

Trieste ⑳

🏛 *218,000.* ✈ 🚊 🚌 ℹ *Riva III Novembre 9 (040 347 83 12).*
📅 *Tue–Sat.*

T RIESTE IS AN atmospheric city, tucked up next to Slovenia, with a long, bustling harbor lined with handsome buildings and lapped by the waves of the Adriatic Sea.

🏛 Acquario Marino

Molo Pescheria 2. 📞 *040 30 62 01.* 📅 *Tue–Sun (Nov–Mar: am only).* ● *public hols.* 🎫 ♿

The city's aquarium is one of the most popular attractions in Trieste. It contains examples of the fascinating marine life in the Adriatic.

♣ Castello di San Giusto

Piazza Cattedrale 3. 📞 *040 30 93 62.* 📅 *daily.* ● *Jan 1, Dec 25.* 🎫

Up above the harbor stands a hilltop castle – built by the city's Venetian governors from 1368 – set on a terrace from which there are sweeping views over the Gulf of Trieste.

The Castello del Miramare on the bay of Trieste

The interior of the castle now houses a museum containing 19th-century drawings and prints of Trieste, and a collection of weapons and armor.

⛪ Basilica Paleocristiana

Via Madonna del Mare 11. 📞 *040 436 31.* 📅 *Wed am.*

Beside the castle lie the substantial ruins of the Roman basilica or law court built around AD 100. Note the stone magistrates' bench and throne.

⛪ Duomo

Piazza Cattedrale. 📞 *040 30 96 66.* 📅 *daily.* ♿

In the church of **San Giusto**, the city's Duomo, magistrates' bench and throne of the Roman basilica were reinterpreted to become the seat of the bishop and clergy. Because the building was formed in the 14th century by linking two 5th-century churches that stood side by side, there are two thrones and benches here. The two apses are decorated with very fine 13th-century mosaics in the Venetian style.

🏛 Museo di Storia ed Arte ed Orto Lapidario

Via della Cattedrale 15. 📞 *040 31 05 00.* 📅 *Tue–Sun.* ● *public hols.* 🎫

The important archaeological collection held here provides fascinating evidence of Trieste's extensive trade links with the ancient Greek world.

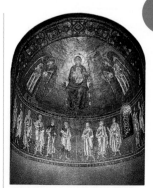

13th-century mosaics in the apse of San Giusto, Trieste's Duomo

ENVIRONS: From **Villa Opicina**, just north of Trieste, there are sweeping views over the city, its bay, and south down the coast of Slovenia. A little beyond, at Borgo Grotta Gigante, lies the **Grotta del Gigante**, a huge cavern filled with stunning "organ pipe" formations and tall columns of stalagmites.

At Grignano, 8 km (5 miles) northwest of the city, stands the **Castello del Miramare**, a white castle set in lush green gardens beside the sparkling blue Adriatic. It was built by the Hapsburg Archduke Maximilian in 1856–60 as his summer retreat, a few years before he was assassinated in Mexico. It is still furnished in contemporary style.

🏞 Grotta del Gigante

Borgo Grotta Gigante.
📞 *040 32 73 12.*
📅 *Tue–Sun (Jul & Aug: daily).* 🎫 🔲
♣ Castello di Miramare

Miramare, Grignano.
📞 *040 22 41 43.* 📅 *daily.* ♿

The Tortoise *hiding in his shell represented darkness and ignorance, while the rooster, who crows at dawn, signified light and enlightenment.*

ICHTHUS, *or fish, was an acronym for* Iesous CHristos THeou Uios Soter – *Jesus Christ, Son of God, Savior, in ancient Greek.*

Colorful birds*, such as peacocks, symbolized immortality and the glorious transformation of the soul when it arrives in Heaven.*

TRENTINO-ALTO ADIGE

THE ITALIAN-SPEAKING *Trentino – named after Trento, the regional capital – and the German-speaking Alto Adige or Südtirol (South Tyrol, the region bordering the upper reaches of the Adige River) differ dramatically in culture. However, they do share one feature in common: the majestic Dolomites that form the backdrop to every town and village, covered in snow for three months of every year and carpeted with exquisite Alpine plants for another three.*

The region's mountains have been cut by glaciers into a series of deep, broad valleys. Many of these face south, so it remains unusually warm and sunny, even in winter. Travelers have passed up and down these valleys for centuries – as confirmed by the extraordinary discovery, in 1991, of a 5,000-year-old man's body found emerging from the surface of a melting glacier in Alto Adige. The frozen corpse wore leather boots, stuffed with hay for warmth, and was armed with a copper ice pick.

The paths that Neolithic man once trod became major road networks under the Romans, when many of the region's cities were founded. By the Middle Ages, Alto Adige had established its very own distinctive culture under the Counts of Tyrol, whose land (later appropriated by the Hapsburgs) straddled both sides of today's Italian/Austrian border. The Tyrolean nobility built the castles that still line the valleys and the mountain passes, in order to protect travelers from brigands.

Another ancient legacy is the tradition of hospitality found in the numerous guesthouses along the valleys. Many of these are built in the distinctive Tyrolean style, with beautiful timber balconies for making the most of the winter sun, and overhanging roof eaves to keep snow at a distance. Cozy in winter, with log fires and warming food, and offering marvelous views, they make the ideal base for enjoying the region's mountain footpaths and ski slopes.

Skiers enjoying the slopes around Monte Spinale, near Madonna di Campiglio, in Trentino

◁ **A typical view of the Dolomites between Bressanone and Ortisei, in Alto Adige**

Exploring Trentino-Alto Adige

TRENTINO-ALTO ADIGE is a region where unspoiled nature is complemented by a wealth of recreational sports. The tributary valleys feeding into the Adige valley contain lakes, rivers and streams, and also woodland, vineyards and Alpine pasture full of butterflies, birds, and flowers. Southeast of the region rise the distinctive limestone peaks of the Dolomites, while farther north the area becomes more mountainous still, enclosed finally by the splendid heights of the Alps.

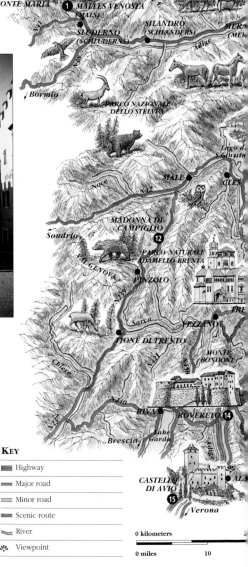

Landeck

Lago di Resia

PARCO NATUR
GRUPPO DI T

ABBAZIA DI
MONTE MARIA ① MALLES VENOSTA
(MALS)

SILANDRO
(SCHLANDERS)

MER
(ME

SLUDERNO
(SCHLUDERNS)

Adige

Bormio

PARCO NAZIONALE
DELLO STELVIO

Lago d
S. Giustin

Noce

MALÈ

CLES

MADONNA DI
CAMPIGLIO

Sondrio

② MALÈ

PARCO NATURALE
ADAMELLO-BRENTA

VAL GENOVA

PINZOLO

TRE

Sarca

ZZANO

TIONE DI TRENTO

MONTE
BONDONE

Chiese

RIVA

ROVERETO ⑭

Lake
Garda

Brescia

CASTELLO
DI AVIO
⑮

AL

Verona

Via Ponte Aquila in Bressanone

SIGHTS AT A GLANCE

KEY

Highway

Major road

Minor road

Scenic route

River

Viewpoint

0 kilometers

0 miles   10

Insbruck

VAL DI RACINES

3 VIPITENO (STERZING)

CAMPO TURES (SAND IN TAUFERS)

RIO DI PUSTERIA (MÜHLBACH)

BRUNICO (BRUNECK) 4

RODENGO (RODENECK)

DOBBIACO (TOBLACH)

Lienz

BRESSANONE (BRIXEN) 5

Rienza

PARCHI NATURALI

VELTURNO (FELDTHURNS)

PARCO NATURALE PUEZ-ODLE

TRE CIME DI LAVAREDO (DREI ZINNEN)

7 MONTE SECEDA

Cortina d'Ampezzo Belluno

ORTISEI (SANKT ULRICH)

6 BOLZANO (BOZEN)

8 CANAZEI

PREDAZZO

PARCO NATURALE

9 TESERO

CAVALESE

ALPE CERMIS

10 SAN MARTINO DI CASTROZZA

DOLOMITI

O VALSUGANA

VAL SUGANA

Brenta

Padova Vicenza

EVICO TERME

Castel Tirolo above the town of Merano

GETTING AROUND

The region's main artery is the Brenner Pass road: it runs from Austria in the north, following the Adige River from Bolzano to Trento, and southward on to Verona. Both the highway and the main road beside it are among the busiest in Europe, and the valley roads can also be congested during the ski season. Winter driving can be hazardous, requiring special tires and snow chains. Trains and buses also serve the main towns, but car transportation is easier.

SEE ALSO

View of the Dolomites from Madonna di Campiglio

Abbazia di Monte Maria, founded in the 12th century, near Malles Venosta

Malles Venosta ●
MALS IM VINSCHGAU

🚌 ℹ️ *Via San Benedetto 1 (0473 83 11 90).* 🚆 *Wed.*

MALLES VENOSTA sits in high border country, close to Switzerland and Austria, and was a customs point during the Middle Ages. The town has several Gothic churches, whose spires and towers give an appealing skyline, mirroring the jagged peaks that rise all around. The oldest is the tiny church of **San Benedetto**, a 9th-century Carolingian building on Via San Benedetto, with frescoes of its patrons.

ENVIRONS: The medieval **Castel Coira** (Churburg) rises at Sluderno (Schluderns), 4 km (2.5 miles) southeast of Malles. It was built to guard the road to Val Venosta, which runs by the Adige River, and it now contains an excellent collection of weapons and armor.

Clinging to the mountainside 5 km (3 miles) north of Malles, just above the town of Burgusio (Burgeis), is the Benedictine **Abbazia di Monte Maria** (Marienberg), founded in the 12th century but enlarged in the 18th and 19th. The church's crypt shelters an outstanding series of 12th-century frescoes.

🔺 **Castel Coira**
Churburg, Sluderno. 📞 *0473 61 52 41.* 🕐 *Mar 20–Nov: Tue–Sun by guided tour only.* 🎟️

🏠 **Abbazia di Monte Maria**
📞 *0473 83 13 06.* 🕐 *Apr–Oct: Mon–Sat; Nov–Mar: groups by appt only.* 🌑 *public hols.* 🎟️ 🎫

Merano ❷
MERAN

🏙️ *35,000.* 🚉 🚌 ℹ️ *Corso della Libertà 45 (0473 23 52 23).* 🚆 *Tue & Fri.*

MERANO IS AN attractive spa town to which Austrians, Germans, and Italians come to drink the waters, take therapeutic baths, and stroll through the riverside gardens – before getting coffee and pastries in one of the Belle Epoque cafés. On Corso Libertà, a street of stylish shops and hotels, stands the **Kurhaus** or Spa Hall built in 1914, now a concert hall. The 15th-century **Castello Principesco** was home to the Hapsburg Archduke Sigismund

The Art Nouveau façade of the Kurhaus in Merano

and is still furnished in period style. Inviting gardens line the Passirio River, which winds its way through the town. The Passeggiata Lungo Passirio d'Inverno (Winter Walk) lines the north bank to the Roman bridge, Ponte Romano; the Passeggiata d'Estate (Summer Walk) on the south bank leads to the medieval Ponte Passirio.

ENVIRONS: The romantic 12th-century **Castel Tirolo**, home of the Counts of Tyrol who gave their name to the Tyrol region, lies 4 km (2.5 miles) to the north. It now houses a museum of Tyrolean history.

🔺 **Castello Principesco**
Via Galilei. 📞 *0473 25 03 29.* 🕐 *Tue–Sun.* 🌑 *Jan, Feb.* 🎟️
🔺 **Castel Tirolo**
Via Castello 24, Tirolo. 📞 *0473 22 02 21.* 🕐 *variable, call to check.* 🎟️ 🎫

Vipiteno ❸
STERZING

🏙️ *5,600.* 🚉 🚌 ℹ️ *Piazza Città 3 (0472 76 53 25).* 🚆 *days vary each month.*

VIPITENO, SURROUNDED by mineral-rich valleys, is very Tyrolean in feel. On Via Città Nuova, lined with fine mansions, rise the Gothic **Palazzo Comunale**, with its Renaissance sculpture and paintings, and the Torre dei Dodici, the symbol of the town. Wood carvings in the

Wrought-iron s Vipiteno

Museo Multscher are by Hans Multscher; the Bavarian sculptor came to Vipiteno in 1456–8 to carve the altar for the parish **church**, which lies just south of the town.

To the west, the charming **Val di Racines** includes waterfalls and a natural rock bridge.

🏛️ **Palazzo Comunale**
Via Città Nuova 21. 📞 *0472 76 51 08.* 🕐 *Mon–Fri.* 🌑 *public hols.*
🏛️ **Museo Multscher**
Via della Commenda. 📞 *0472 76 58 79.* 🕐 *Apr–Oct: Tue–Sat.* 🌑 *public hols.* 🎟️

The medieval castle dominating the town of Brunico

Brunico ❹
BRUNECK

🏠 *13,000.* 🚉 🚌 ⓘ *Via Europa 26 (0474 55 57 22).* 🛒 *Wed.*

THE ATTRACTIVE TOWN of Brunico, overlooked by the imposing form of its medieval **castle** retains 14th-century fortifications and streets so narrow that they must be explored only by walking. The church of **St. Ursula**, northwest of St. Ursula's Gate, contains a series of outstanding mid 15th-century altar reliefs of the Nativity. In the **Museo Etnografico di Teodone** the towns folklore museum, there are displays of traditional agricultural life and local costumes; it also provides visitors with an ideal opportunity to visit a 16th-century farmhouse and barn.

St. Ursula's Gate sundial, Brunico

🏛 **Museo Etnografico di Teodone**
Via Duca Diet 24, Teodone. 📞 *0474 55 20 87.* 🕐 *Easter–Oct: Tue –Sat, Sun pm.* 🌐 🚻 *ground floor.* 🍴

Bressanone ❺
BRIXEN

🏠 *18,000.* 🚉 🚌
ⓘ *Viale Stazione 9 (0472 83 64 01).* 🛒 *Mon.*

THE NARROW MEDIEVAL alleys of Bressanone cluster around the cathedral and the palace of the prince-bishops who ruled the town for much of its history. The **duomo**, on Piazza del Duomo, was rebuilt in the 18th century but retains its 12th-century cloister, decorated with superb 15th-century frescoes. The lavish interiors of Palazzo Vescovile, the bishops' Renaissance palace, house the **Museo Diocesano**. It contains precious items from the Middle Ages, as well as the **Museo dei Presepi**, with its collection of wooden crèche figures that are locally carved .

ENVIRONS: At Velturno (Feldthurns), just 8 km (5 miles) southwest, stands the Renaissance **Castello di Velturno**, the summer retreat of the rulers of Bressanone, noted for its frescoed rooms. A little over 3 km (2 miles) north of Bressanone lies the **Abbazia di Novacella**, a picturesque group of fortified monastic buildings with an outstanding series of cloister frescoes. Farther north up the valley, at **Rio di Pusteria** (Mühlbach), the remains of a 16th-century fortified barrier can be seen to the east of the town. The barrier funneled ancient travelers through the customs post that divided Tyrol from the Görz district.

High above Rio di Pusteria, to the southeast, looms the massive outline of the **Castello di Rodengo** (Rodeneck). The castle contains wonderful 13th-century frescoes showing battle scenes, the Last Judgment, and courtly episodes from the *Iwein* romance by Hartmann von Aue, the medieval poet.

🏛 **Museo Diocesano**
Palazzo Vescovile, Piazza Palazzo Vescovile 2. 📞 *0472 83 05 05.* 🕐 *mid-Mar–Oct: Tue–Sun.* 🌐
🏛 **Museo dei Presepi**
Palazzo Vescovile, Piazza Palazzo Vescovile 2. 📞 *0472 83 05 05.* 🕐 *mid-Mar–Oct: Tue–Sun; Dec–Jan: daily pm.* 🔴 *Dec 24 & 25.* 🌐
⛪ **Castello di Velturno**
Velturno. 📞 *0472 85 55 25.* 🕐 *Mar–Nov: Tue –Sun.* 🌐 🌐
🏠 **Abbazia di Novacella**
Varna. 📞 *0472 83 61 89.* 🕐 *Mon–Sat.* 🔴 *public hols.* 🌐 🌐
⛪ **Castello di Rodengo**
Rodengo. 📞 *0472 45 40 56.* 🕐 *May–mid-Oct: Tue–Sun.* 🌐 🌐

The cloisters of Bressanone Duomo with their 15th-century frescoes

The Baroque interior of the church of St. Ulrich in Ortisei

Bolzano ❻

BOZEN

🏛 98,000. 🚉 🚌 ℹ️ *Piazza Walther 8 (0471 97 06 60).* 🖼 *Sat.*

BOLZANO, THE CAPITAL of the Alto Adige, is the gateway between the Italian-speaking Trentino region and the German-speaking Alto Adige or Südtirol, and has a marked Tyrolean atmosphere. The old center, **Piazza Walther** is dominated by the 15th century Gothic **duomo**, with its multicolored mosaic-patterned roof, and elaborate spire. The "wine door" inside the duomo, is carved with figures at work among vines and reflects the importance of wine to the local economy. In the middle of Piazza Walther stands a statue

The duomo spire, Bolzano

of Walther von der Vogelweide, the 13th-century troubadour – born, according to legend, in the Bolzano area. North of the square, the streets are lined with houses adorned with intricate gables, balconies, and oriel windows; traces of frescoes decorate their pastel-painted façades. The outdoor market, starting at Piazza Grano, forms an inviting array of local produce that continue along the arcaded Via dei Portici. This street continues to the **Museo Civico**, where South Tyrolean history is introduced through domestic interiors, wood carvings, and costumes,

while the new **Museo Archeo-logico** houses the famous 5,000-year-old "Iceman". The **Chiesa dei Domenicani** (Dominican church), on Piazza Domenicani, has 14th-century *Triumph of Death* frescoes and a frescoed cloister.

🏛 **Museo Civico**
Via Cassa di Risparmio 14. 📞 0471 97 46 25. 🕐 Tue – Sat. ⬤ Christmas & Easter. 🖼

🏛 **Museo Archeologico**
Via Museo 43. 📞 0471 98 20 98. 🕐 Tue – Sat. ⬤ Jan 1, May 1, Dec 25. 🖼

Ortisei ❼

SANKT ULRICH

🏛 4,500. 🚌 ℹ️ *Via Rezia 1 (0471 79 63 28).* 🖼 *Fri.*

ORTISEI IS THE prosperous main resort for the pretty Val Gardena and Alpe di Siusi region, and a major center for

woodcarving; good examples of local craftsmanship may be seen in shops in the town, in the **Museo della Val Gardena** (which also focuses on local archaeology), and in the church of **St. Ulrich**.

To the south is the beautiful and popular **Alpe di Siusi** (Seiser Alm) region, noted for its Alpine meadows, balconied farmsteads, and onion-domed churches. The best way to explore the area is by cable-way from Ortisei: to the north-east another cable car runs to 2,518-m (8,260-ft) high Monte Seceda, and walks from here lead into the Odle Dolomites.

🏛 **Museo della Val Gardena**
Via Rezia 83. 📞 0471 79 75 54. 🕐 Feb, Mar: Tue, Fri; Jun, Sep, Oct: Tue–Fri; Jul, Aug: Tue–Sun. 🖼

Canazei ❽

🏛 1,800. 🚌 ℹ️ *Via Roma 34 (0462 60 11 13).* 🖼 *Sat.*

LOCATED AT THE BASE of some of the highest and most awe-inspiring groups of peaks, Canazei is a good base for exploring the Dolomites. In summer, chairlifts climb to viewpoints where the beauty of the encircling mountains can be appreciated to the full. The most popular viewpoints are Pecol and Col dei Rossi, reached by the Belvedere cableway from Via Pareda in Canazei: the cliffs of the Sella group are visible to the north,

Skiers enjoying views of the Dolomites above Canazei

with Sasso Lungo to the west and Marmolada, the highest of the Dolomites at 3,343 m (10,965 ft), to the south.

ENVIRONS: At **Vigo di Fassa**, 13 km (8 miles) southwest, the **Museo Ladino** focuses on the Ladin-speaking people of the Fassa valley. Ladin – a German-influenced Italian dialect – is taught in local schools and the ancient traditions, costumes, and music still thrive.

🏛 **Museo Ladino**
Via della Chiesa 6, San Giovanni, Vigo di Fassa. 🔲 0462 76 42 67. ● until 2001.

Cavalese ⑨

🚶 3,600. 🚌 🚻 Via Fratelli Bronzetti 60 (0462 24 11 11). 🗓 last Tue of month (not Jul).

The frescoed façade of the Palazzo della Magnifica Comunità

CAVALESE IS THE chief town in the Val di Fiemme, a pretty region of flower-filled aromatic pastures, delightful wooded valleys, and Tyrolean architecture. At the center of the town stands the **Palazzo della Magnifica Comunità**. Originally built in the 13th century, this was the seat of the medieval governing council that ruled the area as a semi-autonomous region. Today the paneled interiors contain medieval paintings by local artists, and an archaeology collection. Most visitors come for the excellent summer and winter resort facilities, and to climb, by cable car, to the 2,229 m (7,311 ft) top of **Alpe Cermis**, the mountain that rises to the south of the town.

ENVIRONS: The church in **Tesero**, the next village east, bears a 15th-century fresco by an unknown painter depicting

Vines growing on the terraced slopes of the Cembra valley

Sabbath-breakers. The church itself, dating back to 1450, has a flurry of Gothic vaulting, and a modern representation of the Crucifixion painted against a background of the village.

At **Predazzo**, about 13 km (8 miles) east, the good **Museo Geologico e Mineralogico** explains the local geology.

🏛 **Palazzo della Magnifica Comunità**
Piazza Battisti 2.
🔲 0462 34 03 65. ◯ Jul–Aug: Mon–Sat pm. ● Aug 15. 🅿
🏛 **Museo Geologico e Mineralogico**
Piazza Santi Filippo e Giacomo 1.
🔲 0462 50 23 92.
◯ call to check times.

San Martino di Castrozza ⑩

🚶 470. 🚌 🚻 Via Passo Rolle 165 (0439 76 88 67).

THE RESORT OF San Martino occupies one of the most scenic and accessible valleys in the southern Dolomites, making it very popular with hikers and skiers. Cable cars rise to the peak of **Alpe Tognola** (2,163 m, 7,095 ft), southwest of the town, and up the **Cima della Rosetta** (2,609 m, 8,557 ft) to the east. Both offer magnificent views of the Pale Group of Dolomitic peaks, a stirring sight as the massive rock peaks, split by glaciers,

Piramidi di Segonzano, near Cembra

rise above a sea of green meadows and woodland. San Martino is almost entirely surrounded by forest, which once supplied the Venetian Republic with timber for ships. The forest is now protected, and, as a result, it is possible to see Alpine flowers, mushrooms, birds and other wild-life with relative ease.

Cembra ⑪

🚶 2,500. 🚌 🚻 Piazza Toniolli 2 (0461 68 31 10). 🗓 Wed.

THE WINE-PRODUCING town of Cembra nestles on the terraced slopes of a scenic valley of flower-filled villages. Some 6 km (4 miles) east of Cembra stand the **Piramidi di Segonzano**, a rare series of erosion pillars, some over 30 m (100 ft) high, each topped by a rock. The footpath to the pillars is well marked, with informative noticeboards along the way explaining the formation of the bizarre columns, which are similar in appearance to giant termites' nests. Their setting amid bird-filled woodland makes the steep climb up to the site well worthwhile. A further reward is the fine view, from the top of the hill, along the Cembra valley and westward as far as the Brenta group of Dolomites.

🎿 **Piramidi di Segonzano**
Strada Statale 612 to Cavalese.
🔲 0461 68 31 10. ◯ daily.

The impressive falls of the Cascate di Nardis, Madonna di Campiglio

Madonna di Campiglio 🅬

🏠 *1,300.* 🚌 ℹ️ *Via Pradalago 4 (0465 44 20 00).* 🗓️ *Jun–Sep: Tue & Thu.*

MADONNA DI CAMPIGLIO is the chief resort in the Val Meledrio. Nestling between the Brenta and Adamello groups of Dolomitic peaks, it makes the perfect base for walking or skiing amid the magnificent mountain terrain. Cableways radiate out from the town in every direction, giving easy access to the peaks.

ENVIRONS: The church at **Pinzolo**, 14 km (9 miles) south, has a well-preserved fresco depicting a *Dance of Death* (1539). The inevitable march of the figures, both rich and poor, is underlined by a text written in local dialect.

North of Pinzolo, the road west from Carisolo leads to the verdant and popular, yet unspoiled, **Val Genova**. About 4 km (2 miles) along the valley is the spectacular **Cascate di Nardis**, a waterfall that plunges down 90 m (300 ft). The two masses of rock at the bottom are said to be the forms of petrified demons.

Trento 🅭

🏠 *105,000.* 🚉 🚌 ℹ️ *Via Manci 2 (0461 98 38 80).* 🗓️ *Thu.*

TRENTO, THE CAPITAL of the region to which it gave its name, is also the most attractive town in Trentino: it has a fine Romanesque cathedral and a richly decorated castle, and streets lined with handsome Renaissance mansions. Trento is known for the famous **Council of Trent** (1545–63), set up by the Catholic Church to consider reforms that might encourage breakaway groups, in particular the German Protestants, to return to the fold. The reforms, which ushered in the period of the Counter-Reformation, were only partly successful.

The **duomo**, site of some of the Council meetings, was built in sturdy Romanesque style from the 13th century on. It was three centuries before it was completed, in 1515, but the builders maintained architectural harmony by ignoring Gothic and Renaissance styles entirely. The result is a church of unusual integrity, noble and assured. The duomo stands on **Piazza Duomo**, the city's main square, which was first laid out by the Romans as their central market place or forum. Trento's Roman name, Tridentum, is commemorated in the figure of Neptune who stands holding his trident at the top of the 18th-century fountain, which stands in the middle of the main square.

🏛️ Museo Diocesano Tridentino

Piazza Duomo 18. 📞 *0461 23 44 19.* 🗓️ *Mon–Sat.* 🔴 *Jan 1, Easter, Dec 25.* 🎫 ♿

This museum is housed in the **Palazzo Pretorio**, an imposing medieval building that stands on the eastern side of Piazza Duomo. Its contents include early ivory reliquaries, Flemish tapestries, and paintings depicting the Council of Trent.

♜ Castello del Buonconsiglio

Via Bernardo Clesio 5. 📞 *0461 23 3. 70.* 🗓️ *Tue–Sun.* 🔴 *Jan 1, Nov 1, Dec 25.* 🎫

This large castle, built in the 13th century and later enlarged with additional buildings, is part of the defenses of the town. Trento was an important frontier on the main road linking Italy to northern Europe, and thick walls still encircle the town.

The southern section of the castle consists of the magnificent **Magno Palazzo** (1530), built for the ruling prince-bishops of Trento, who were given extensive powers by the Holy Roman Emperor in order to foster loyalty and discourage defection to the pope. The lavish decoration (which includes frescoes of virile satyrs and nymphs by Gerolamo Romanino, 1531–2) speaks of massive wealth and a luxurious lifestyle. The fine rooms, now the setting for the **Museo Provinciale**, contain paintings, ceramics, and 15th-century wood carvings, and prehistoric, Etruscan and Roman items. The **Torre dell'Aquila** (Eagle Tower) nearby contains frescoes painted around

Inner courtyard of the Magno Palazzo

Palazzo Pretorio and the duomo in Trento's main square

The commanding form of the Ossario del Castel Dante in Rovereto

1400. They depict the Months of the Year in charming detail: the month of January, for instance, has some delightful snowballing scenes.

ENVIRONS: Immediately to the west of Trento a scenic round-trip along a winding road leads up the north flank of **Monte Bondone** and back, via **Vezzano**, down the western slopes. The views along the route are magnificent, in particular from Vaneze and Vason. East of Trento, Pergine marks the start of the **Val Sugana**, a broad valley with attractive and popular lakes. In the hills north of Lake Levico lies the spa town of **Levico Terme**, distinguished by elegant Neo-Classical buildings set amid beautifully wooded parkland.

Rovereto ⑭

🏃 33,000. 🚉 🚌 ℹ️ Via Dante 63 (0464 43 03 63). 🚆 Tue.

ROVERETO WAS at the center of fierce fighting during World War I, after which the Venetian castle (built in 1416) that dominates the town was transformed into the **Museo Storico della Guerra**, a war museum. The displays feature several highlights, among them sections devoted to wartime humor, spying, and propaganda. Contemporary photographs tell the story of this century's two world wars in harrowing detail. Near the entrance to the museum, stairs lead out onto the castle roof for a view of the imposing **Ossario del Castel Dante**.

Some distance away is the **Campana dei Caduti** (Bell of the Fallen). One of the largest bells in Italy, it was cast from melted-down cannons at the end of World War II and mounted in an imposing building above the town; it is rung daily at sunset. From the memorial there are extensive views over the valley. Below the war museum stands the **Museo Civico**, housing collections on archaeology, art, natural history, and folklore.

ENVIRONS: A little over 8 km (5 miles) north of Rovereto is the prominent landmark of **Castel Beseno**, rising on a hill to the east. This enormous castle, by far the largest in the region, was built and rebuilt from the 12th century to the 18th to guard the junction of the three valleys. The ruins are undergoing restoration: 16th-century frescoes may be seen.

To the south of Rovereto, the main road passes through a valley littered with massive house-sized boulders created by landslides; these are known as the **Ruina Dantesca**, because they are mentioned in Dante's *Inferno* (XII, 4–9).

Five kilometers (3 miles) to the south, at Lavini di Marco, fossilized dinosaur footprints have recently been discovered.

🏛 **Museo Storico della Guerra**
Via Castelbarco 7. ☎ 0464 43 81 00. ○ mid-March–Nov: Tue–Sun. 🗓

🏛 **Museo Civico**
Borgo Santa Caterina.
☎ 0464 43 90 55. ○ Tue–Sun. ● public hols. 🗓 ♿

♣ **Castel Beseno**
Besenello. ☎ 0464 83 46 00. ○ Mar–Nov: Tue–Sun. 🗓

Castello di Avio in its lush setting

Castello di Avio ⑮

Via Castello, Sabbionara d'Avio.
☎ 0464 68 44 53. 🚌 🚉 to Vo, then 3 km (2 mile) walk. ○ Feb–Sep: 10am–1pm, 2–6pm Tue–Sun; Oct–Nov: 10am–1pm, 2–5pm Tue–Sun. 🗓

CASTLES LINE THE Adige valley all the way to the Brenner Pass, but few are as accessible as the Castello di Avio, southwest of Ala. It was founded in the 11th century, considerably extended in the 13th, and today offers visitors far-reaching views. Among the numerous frescoes with secular themes is a rare series in the Casa delle Guardie (the Sentry House) depicting 13th-century battle scenes.

The extensive walls enclosing Castel Beseno above Rovereto

NORTHWEST ITALY

Northwest Italy at a Glance

THE NORTHWEST OF ITALY is made up of three very different geological characteristics: the jagged Alps, the flat plain, and the undulating shoreline of the Mediterranean. Within this varied landscape, some of it still wild and unspoiled, lie extremely rich and diverse vestiges of the area's substantial cultural heritage. The major sights, in the regions of Valle d'Aosta and Piedmont, Liguria and Lombardy, are shown on this map.

Valle d'Aosta

Parco Nazionale del Gran Paradiso

Basilica di Sant'Andrea, Vercelli

Mole Antonelliana, Turin

***The Parco Nazionale del Gran Paradiso** is a beautiful wilderness and the habitat of rare Alpine flora and fauna (see pp208–9).*

VALLE D'AOSTA AND PIEDMONT
(See pp202–21)

Piedmont

LIGURIA
(See pp222–35)

***The capital of Piedmont** is Turin, an elegant and bustling city of splendid Baroque architecture. Its skyline is dramatically dominated by the Mole Antonelliana (see p216).*

***San Remo** is a typical Riviera resort, with palm trees and a casino. The onion-domed outline of the Russian church adds an exotic flavor to the town (see p226).*

The casino, San Remo

***The Basilica di Sant'Andrea** in Vercelli is an important Romanesque building, one of the earliest to use Gothic elements (see p220).*

◁ **Typical shuttered Ligurian façades in Santa Margherita Ligure**

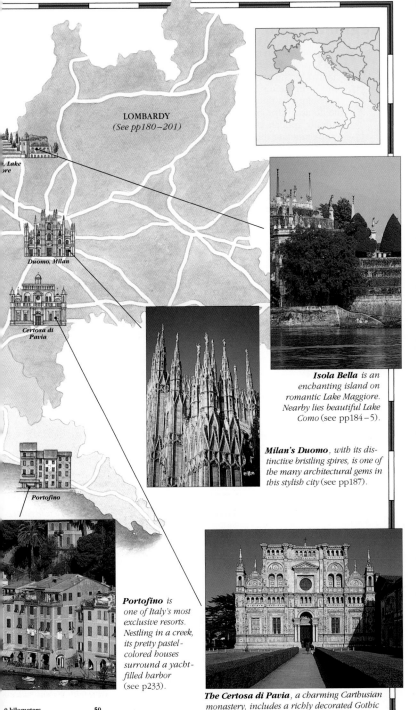

LOMBARDY
(See pp180–201)

, Lake
re

Duomo, Milan

Certosa di Pavia

Portofino

Isola Bella *is an enchanting island on romantic Lake Maggiore. Nearby lies beautiful Lake Como (see pp184–5).*

Milan's Duomo, *with its distinctive bristling spires, is one of the many architectural gems in this stylish city (see p187).*

Portofino *is one of Italy's most exclusive resorts. Nestling in a creek, its pretty pastel-colored houses surround a yacht-filled harbor (see p233).*

The Certosa di Pavia, *a charming Carthusian monastery, includes a richly decorated Gothic church with a magnificent Renaissance façade, and a series of attractive cloisters (see pp196–7).*

0 kilometers   50

0 miles   25

Regional Food: Northwest Italy

RICHNESS AND HEARTINESS characterize the food of northwest Italy, an area dominated by the presence of the Alps. Here, unlike in the rest of Italy, butter is used in cooking as much as oil. The area is the home of rice growing in Italy, and risotto naturally appears prominently on local menus, complementing the ubiquitous pasta dishes. Cheeses are also a specialty, as are truffles – which grow in the clay soil of Piedmont – and nuts of all types. Garlic, saffron, basil, and wine are other favorite ingredients in the aromatic sauces. Grissini, the crisp breadsticks found on every restaurant table, originate in Turin.

Grissini

Onion and Herb Focaccia is *made from dough enriched with olive oil; it may also be baked plain, or with olives or tomato.*

Bresaola, wafer-thin slices of cured raw beef, is served as an antipasto with olive oil and a squeeze of lemon.

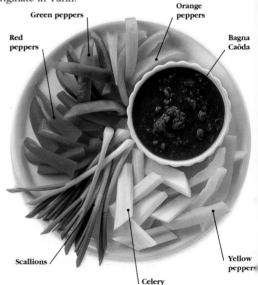

Green peppers

Red peppers

Orange peppers

Bagna Caôda

Scallions

Celery

Yellow peppers

Bagna Caôda is an anchovy-based dip flavored with garlic, olive oil, butter, and sometimes truffles. It is served hot, usually over a warming stove, and eaten with sliced raw vegetables, which are dipped into it. It is a specialty of Piedmont.

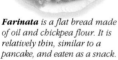

Farinata is a flat bread made of oil and chickpea flour. It is relatively thin, similar to a pancake, and eaten as a snack.

Risotto alla milanese is a rich and delicious Milanese dish of rice, white wine, onion, saffron, and grated Parmesan cheese.

Trenette al pesto, a Genoese specialty, consists of noodles with a sauce of basil, garlic, pine nuts, Parmesan, and oil.

Pansôti with Walnut Sauce is Ligurian, spinach-and-egg-filled pasta, with a sauce of nuts, garlic, herbs, ricotta cheese, and olive oil

Manzo brasato al Barolo *is a Piedmont dish of lean beef marinated in red wine and garlic, then stewed gently until tender.*

Cacciucco, *found on Livorno menus, is a rich stew of mixed fish and seafood cooked with wine, garlic, and herbs.*

Costolette alla milanese *are veal cutlets dipped in egg and breadcrumbs, fried in butter, and served with lemon.*

Ossobuco *is shin of veal with marrowbone in a tomato and wine sauce, with a hint of garlic, anchovy, and lemon.*

Fagiano tartufato – *stuffed pheasant – is filled with white truffles and pork fat; it is then wrapped in bacon and roasted.*

Spezzatino di pollo *is a chicken quarter cooked with tomato sauce containing wine and, sometimes, truffles.*

CHEESE

The lush Alpine meadows in the northwest help to produce some of the finest cheeses in Italy. They include the blue-veined yet mild Gorgonzola; the delicate mascarpone, a cream cheese used in desserts; and Taleggio, a soft, creamy cheese to be eaten young, all from Lombardy. Fontina, a semihard cheese made in the Valle d'Aosta, has a nutty, slightly sweet taste.

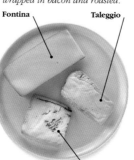

Fontina   Taleggio

Gorgonzola

Spinaci alla Piemontese, *a side order, is a blend of spinach, anchovies, butter, and garlic, with croutons.*

Amaretti *are light and delicious macaroon-type biscuits, usually eaten with coffee, made from almonds and egg whites. They are often wrapped in pretty colored paper.*

Torta di nocciole, *a Piedmontese nut tart, includes hazelnuts, eggs, and butter among its ingredients.*

Zabaione *is a frothy concoction of egg, sugar, and Marsala wine, accompanied by ladyfingers. It is served hot or cold.*

Panettone *from Milan is a light yeast cake that contains candied fruit. It is traditionally eaten at Christmas.*

The Wines of Northwest Italy

Medieval illustration of a grape crusher

Gʀᴀᴘᴇꜱ ᴀʀᴇ ɢʀᴏᴡɴ throughout the northwest – from the cliffs of Liguria to the steep mountainsides of Valle d'Aosta. The best wines, however, come from Piedmont, in particular the Langhe hills southwest of Turin, source of two of Italy's finest reds: the rich, powerful, long-lived Barolo and the Barbaresco. Both of these are now showing the benefits of modern techniques and a renewed interest in high-quality wine making. Lighter, everyday red wines that go well with the local cuisine include Dolcetto and the popular Barbera. Another Piedmont specialty is sparkling *spumante*, Italians' instinctive choice whenever there is something around to celebrate.

Castiglione Falletto in the heart of Piedmo

Barbera d'Alba comes from the adaptable Barbera grape, which can grow on almost any slope. Its ubiquitous nature means that the wines it yields can be light and full of fruit, as well as dense, strong, and full-flavored. Good producers include Aldo Conterno, Voerzio, Pio Cesare, Altare, Gaja, Vaira, and Vietti.

Dolcetto is grown in seven different areas. Dolcetto d'Alba has a delicious perfume and deep purple color. Best drunk within one or two years, it ranges in flavor from fresh and fruity to the rich, concentrated plumminess of some of the top wines, such as those produced by Giuseppe Mascarello.

KEY

☐ Barolo

☐ Barbaresco

☐ Other vineyard areas

0 kilometers	25
0 miles	15

Barolo, prized the world over for its complex array of flavors and firm tannins, is made from the Nebbiolo grape and may take up to 20 years to mature. Vigna Colonnello is a top Barolo from Aldo Conterno, made only in the best years like 1993, 1990, and 1989.

The white truffle of Alba is an autumn specialty from the Langhe hills. Highly prized for its earthy scent, it is excellent with Barolo.

Turin • Chieri

PIEDMONT

MONFERRATO

Canale

Bar

Al

• Bra

Saluzzo

Barolo • Cast Falle

• Dogliani

Cuneo • • Mondovi

LANG

Moscato d'Asti is an excellent aperitivo or light dessert wine made from the aromatic, fruity Moscato grape. It is light in alcohol with a gently sweet finish and may have a slight sparkle. Ideal for refreshing the palate after a hearty Piedmontese meal, Araldica's versatile Moscato is delicious when served well chilled.

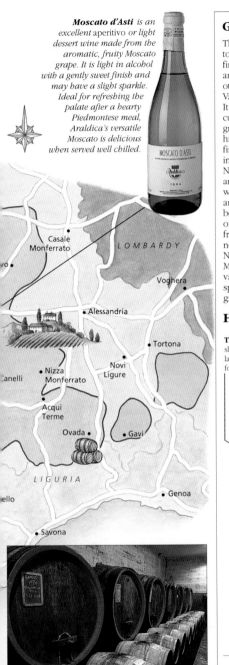

GRAPES OF THE NORTHWEST

The Nebbiolo grape is used to produce two of Italy's finest red wines, Barolo and Barbaresco, as well as other regional wines in the Valtellina and north of Turin. It is a difficult grape to cultivate and requires a long growing season to soften its high acidity. However, the final results are worth it: **Nebbiolo grapes** in the Langhe region the Nebbiolo offers complex perfumes, and a range of flavors, often encased within strong tannins. Easier to handle and lighter, the Dolcetto and Barbera both came from the Monferrato region originally. These reds yield lighter, fruitier wines but, when at their best, no less distinctive than those of the Nebbiolo. Of the white grapes, the Moscato is Piedmont's oldest known variety. Famous for the successful sparkling Asti Spumante, the best grapes are reserved for Moscato d'Asti.

HOW TO READ THE LABEL

The name of the wine is shown in the center of the label: *bricco* is local dialect for a good hilltop vineyard.

The producer's name

Producer's emblem

Year of production

ROCCHE DEI MANZONI
BRICCO MANZONI
1985
IMBOTTIGLIATO DA
PODERE ROCCHE DEI MANZONI
DI VALENTINO
MONFORTE D'ALBA (ITALIA)
VINO DA TAVOLA DELLE LANGHE
13,5% vol.   R 1477/9/CN   75cl.℮

Alcoholic strength

Size of bottle

The official category; in this case a table wine from the Langhe region.

The bottler's name and address

Barolo is aged in wooden casks for at least two years before being put in bottles. This may be done in either the traditional, large botte or the smaller barrique, which imparts a strong, oaky flavor to the wine.

Good Vintages
Barolo and Barbaresco had good years in 1993, 1990, 1989, 1988, 1985.

Understanding Architecture in Northwest Italy

Although the buildings of the northwest tend to be solid and imposing – a result partly of the more severe climate – there is no distinctive architectural stamp as there is around Venice, Florence, or even in Rome. Instead, a variety of buildings in different styles, many borrowed or reinterpreted from elsewhere, are dotted across the area: enchanting medieval castles, outstanding Romanesque and Gothic buildings, unusual Baroque structures. The northwest is also rich in modern architecture – in terms of both design and materials – influenced by the region's industrial developments and its strong flair for innovative design, which also often draws its inspiration from earlier architectural styles.

Castello Sforzesco, 1451–66 (see p186)

CHARACTERISTICS OF NORTHWEST ITALIAN ARCHITECTURE

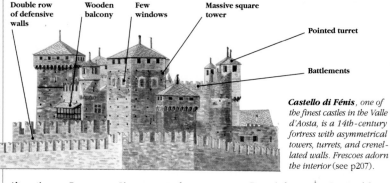

Double row of defensive walls

Wooden balcony

Few windows

Massive square tower

Pointed turret

Battlements

***Castello di Fénis**, one of the finest castles in the Valle d'Aosta, is a 14th-century fortress with asymmetrical towers, turrets, and crenellated walls. Frescoes adorn the interior (see p207).*

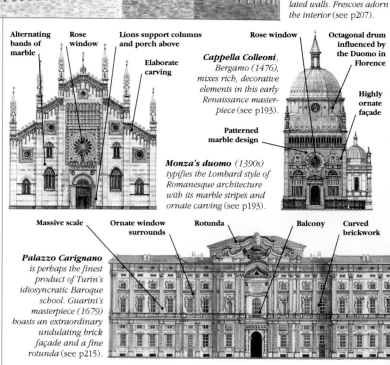

Alternating bands of marble

Rose window

Lions support columns and porch above

Elaborate carving

***Cappella Colleoni**, Bergamo (1476), mixes rich, decorative elements in this early Renaissance masterpiece (see p193).*

Rose window

Octagonal drum influenced by the Duomo in Florence

Highly ornate façade

Patterned marble design

***Monza's duomo** (1390s) typifies the Lombard style of Romanesque architecture with its marble stripes and ornate carving (see p193).*

Massive scale

Ornate window surrounds

Rotunda

Balcony

Curved brickwork

***Palazzo Carignano** is perhaps the finest product of Turin's idiosyncratic Baroque school. Guarini's masterpiece (1679) boasts an extraordinary undulating brick façade and a fine rotunda (see p215).*

WHERE TO SEE THE ARCHITECTURE

The road to Aosta is flanked by numerous medieval castles *(see p206)*, while inspirational Romanesque and Gothic churches are found in Lombardy – at Monza *(p193)*, Pavia *(p195)*, Milan *(pp186–193)*, and Como *(pp184–5)*. The 15th-century Certosa di Pavia *(pp196–7)* is a must, as well as the charming city of Mantova *(p199)*. Turin *(pp212–16)* is famous for its unique Baroque school and Bergamo for its exuberance. Architecture from the last two centuries is best represented in Milan and Turin; in Genoa some exciting redevelopment projects are taking place.

Renzo Piano's mast structure (1992) in Genoa's redeveloped port

19TH–20TH CENTURY ARCHITECTURE

Top reaches 167 m (550 ft)

Aluminium replaces original granite top

Square-sided dome

Galleria Vittorio Emanuele II in Milan, designed by Mengoni in 1865, was the first Italian building to use glass and iron structurally (see p188).

Central dome

Mosaics

Glass balcony

Overhanging upper stories

Struts support the top

The Mole Antonelliana *(1863–97), designed by Antonelli, was the tallest building in the world when it was built (see p216).*

Torre Velasca, Milan *is a 26-floor tower south of the duomo. The design, from the 1950s, was influenced by medieval castles such as the Castello Sforzesco.*

Elliptical shape

Taller windows

Tapering struts

Spiral ramps up to roof

Roof served as test track

Reinforced concrete

The Lingotto building, Turin, *was built in 1915–18 as Fiat's car factory. Made of advanced materials, it was the first large-scale modern building in Italy. The structure of the ramps up to the roof is similar to the interior of Guarini's Baroque dome for San Lorenzo in Turin.*

Milan's Pirelli building, *by Ponti and Nervi, is an elegant and innovative skyscraper built in 1959.*

LOMBARDY

THE REGION OF LOMBARDY *stretches from the Alps, on the border with Switzerland, down through the romantic lakes of Como and Maggiore to the broad, flat plain of the River Po. It is an area of lakeside villas with azalea-filled gardens, of wealthy towns with imposing palazzi and highly decorated churches, and of efficient, modern industry and large-scale agriculture, the financial heart of Italy. At its center stands Milan, the style-conscious capital of Lombardy.*

The region was named after the Lombards or Longobards, a barbarian tribe that invaded Italy in the 6th century AD. During the Middle Ages, Lombardy was part of the Holy Roman Empire, but not always loyal to its German emperors. The Lombards, who had a talent for banking and commerce, resented any outside interference with their prosperity.

The 12th century saw the rise of the Lega Lombarda, or Lombard League, a band of forceful separatists founded to counter the brutal imperialism of Frederick Barbarossa (their most modern incarnation was the Lega Nord political party). Power was seized by the region's great families, most notably the Visconti, and the Sforza of Milan, from the 14th to the early 16th century. These dynasties also became great patrons of the arts, commissioning exquisite palaces, churches, and artwork, many of which can still be seen. Bergamo, Mantova, and Cremona – not to mention Milan itself – contain a remarkably rich array of art treasures. Here are such pinnacles of European civilization as the charterhouse at Pavia, Leonardo da Vinci's *Last Supper,* and the magnificent paintings of the Pinacoteca di Brera in Milan.

Lombardy – famous as the birthplace of Virgil, Monteverdi, Stradivarius, and Donizetti – today offers visitors the contrasting pleasures of lyrical lakeside landscapes (resorts on Lakes Como and Maggiore have attracted poets, aristocrats, and gamblers for centuries) and beautiful, bustling cities.

Strolling through Milan's enormous Galleria Vittorio Emanuele II

◁ **The peaceful shores of the beautiful Lake Como, southwest of Bellagio**

Exploring Lombardy

T HE ENORMOUS PLAIN of the River Po runs through much of
Lombardy, providing a landscape that is flat and perfectly
suited to the consequent expansion of industry in the region.
This is, however, also a region of great contrasts. To the north,
in a still unspoiled setting in the foothills of the mountains,
lie the lakes Como and Maggiore, as well as the dramatic
valleys and peaks of the Parco Nazionale dello Stelvio around
Bormio, Sondrio, and Val Camonica. Farther south, busy
industrialized areas give way
to huge tracts of agriculture
dotted with towns of great
beauty such as Cremona,
Mantova, and Pavia, which
offer a rich and splendid
array of heady pleasures.

SIGHTS AT A GLANCE

SEE ALSO

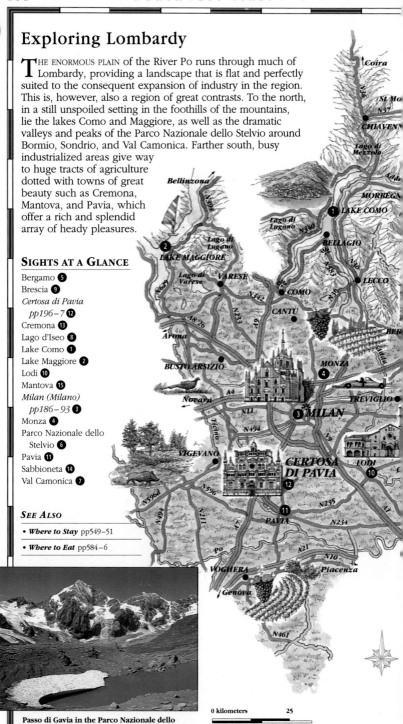

Passo di Gavia in the Parco Nazionale dello
Stelvio on the eastern fringes of Lombardy

0 kilometers   25

0 miles   20

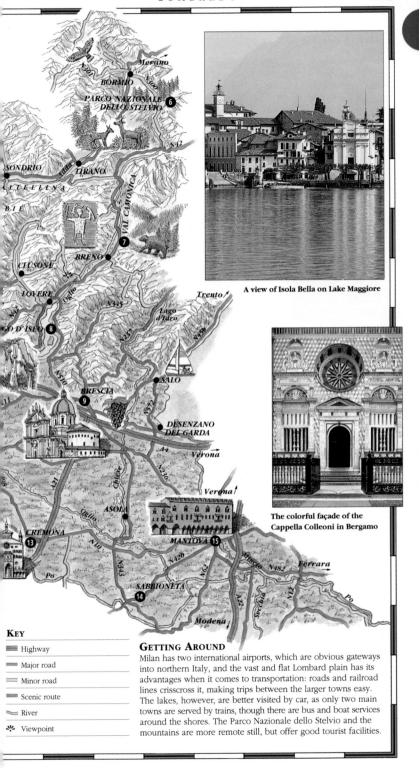

A view of Isola Bella on Lake Maggiore

The colorful façade of the
Cappella Colleoni in Bergamo

KEY

- ▦ Highway
- ▬ Major road
- ▬ Minor road
- ▬ Scenic route
- ≈ River
- ❀ Viewpoint

GETTING AROUND

Milan has two international airports, which are obvious gateways into northern Italy, and the vast and flat Lombard plain has its advantages when it comes to transportation: roads and railroad lines crisscross it, making trips between the larger towns easy. The lakes, however, are better visited by car, as only two main towns are served by trains, though there are bus and boat services around the shores. The Parco Nazionale dello Stelvio and the mountains are more remote still, but offer good tourist facilities.

Lake Como ●

S ET IN AN IDYLLIC LANDSCAPE of mountains and rugged hillsides, and shrouded in an almost eerie calm, Lake Como has for centuries attracted visitors who come here for relaxation, inspiration, walks in the hills, or to go boating. The long and narrow lake, crafted into a wishbone shape by glacial erosion, offers fine views up to the Alps and down to the prosperous towns of Como and Lecco.

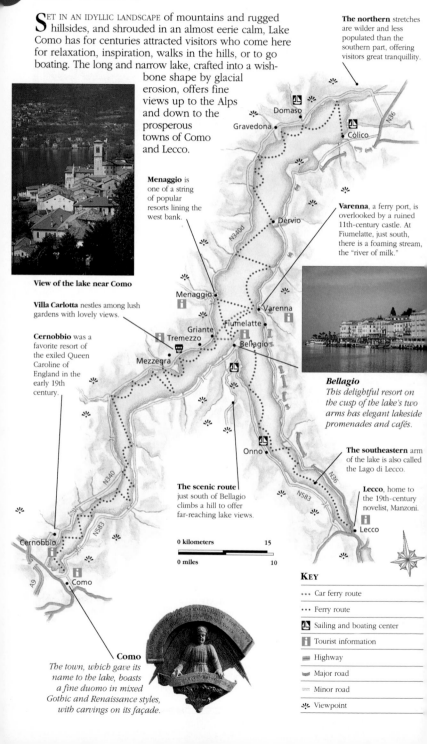

The northern stretches are wilder and less populated than the southern part, offering visitors great tranquillity.

View of the lake near Como

Menaggio is one of a string of popular resorts lining the west bank.

Varenna, a ferry port, is overlooked by a ruined 11th-century castle. At Fiumelatte, just south, there is a foaming stream, the "river of milk."

Villa Carlotta nestles among lush gardens with lovely views.

Cernobbio was a favorite resort of the exiled Queen Caroline of England in the early 19th century.

Bellagio
This delightful resort on the cusp of the lake's two arms has elegant lakeside promenades and cafés.

The southeastern arm of the lake is also called the Lago di Lecco.

Lecco, home to the 19th-century novelist, Manzoni.

The scenic route just south of Bellagio climbs a hill to offer far-reaching lake views.

| 0 kilometers | | 15 |
| 0 miles | | 10 |

Como
The town, which gave its name to the lake, boasts a fine duomo in mixed Gothic and Renaissance styles, with carvings on its façade.

Tadoline's copy (1834) of Canova's
Cupid and Psyche **in Villa Carlotta**

Exploring Lake Como
In the heart of **Como** lies the
elegant Piazza Cavour. Nearby
rises the beautiful 14th-century
duomo, with its 15th- and
16th-century reliefs and paintings, and fine tombs. The
18th-century dome is by
Turin's famous Baroque
architect, Juvarra. Next to the
duomo stand the 13th-century
Broletto (town hall), charmingly striped in white, pink
and grey, and the tall Torre del
Comune. **Villa Carlotta** is an
elegant 18th-century summer-
house, known for its gardens.
In springtime, rhododendrons,
camellias, and azaleas burst
into color in this pretty setting.
Inside, the villa houses a
collection of sculptures.

Lecco, a small industrial
town lying to the south of the
lake's eastern arm, was the
birthplace of the writer
Alessandro Manzoni (1785–
1873). The author's childhood
home, the **Casa Natale di
Manzoni** is devoted to
memorabilia of his life and
works. In Piazza Manzoni, a
monument depicts scenes
from his most famous novel, *I
Promessi Sposi (The Betrothed)*
– set partly in 17th-century
Lecco as well as Milan.

🏛 Villa Carlotta
Tremezzo, Como. **C** 0344 404 05.
⬭ daily. ⬤ Nov–mid-Mar.
🏛 Casa Natale di Manzoni
Via Guanella 1, Lecco. **C** 0341 48
12 47. ⬭ Tue–Sun am. ⬤ Jan 1,
Easter, May 1, Aug 15, Dec 25. 🖼

Lake Maggiore ❷

L AKE MAGGIORE is a long
expanse of water that
nestles right up against the
mountains and stretches away
into Alpine Switzerland; it is
warmer in atmosphere and
more unashamedly romantic
than Lake Como. The gently
sloping shores are dotted with
camellias, azaleas, and ver-
bena vegetation – from
which the ancient
lake derived its Roman
name, Verbanus. In
the center lie the
Borromean islands,
miniparadises named
after the chief patron
of the lake, Cardinal
Carlo Borromeo.

A huge copper statue
of the cardinal stands
in **Arona**, the town
where he was born in
1538. It is possible to
climb up and look out
over the lake through
his eye sockets and
ear holes. Arona also
boasts a ruined castle
and a chapel, Santa
Maria, that was dedi-
cated to the famous
Borromeo family.

Farther up the western coast
of the lake is **Stresa**, the chief
resort and main jumping-off
point for visits to the islands;
the town is full of villas and
verdant gardens, where many
visitors take a stroll. Behind
Stresa, a cable car ride away,
rises Monte Mottarone, a
snow-capped peak offering
spectacular panoramic views

**The statue of Carlo
Borromeo in Arona**

of the surrounding mountains,
including Monte Rosa.

The **Borromean islands**,
lying at the center of the lake
near Stresa, are small jewels
of natural beauty augmented
by artificial grottoes, architectural follies, and landscaped
parks. The **Isola Bella** is
home to the 17th-century
Palazzo Borromeo and its
splendid garden of landscaped
terraces, fountains, peacocks,
statues, and grottoes. Isola
Madre is largely given over to
a botanical garden. San
Giovanni is the
most exclusive and
smallest of the isles,
with a villa which
once belonged to
the conductor
Arturo Toscanini
(1867–1957).

The lake becomes
quieter toward the
Swiss border, but
continues to be
lined with attractive
villas. The **Villa
Taranto**, on the out-
skirts of Verbania,
houses one of the
best exotic botan-
ical collections.

About 3 km (2
miles) west of
Cannobio, a market
town near Switzer-
land, is the dramatic
gorge and tumbling waterfall
of the Orrido di Sant'Anna,
which can be reached by boat.

🏛 Palazzo Borromeo
Isola Bella. 🚢 from Stresa. **C** 0323
305 56. ⬭ Apr–Oct: daily. 🖼
🏛 Villa Taranto
Via Vittorio Veneto 111, Verbania,
Palanza. **C** 0323 55 66 67.
⬭ Apr–Oct: daily. 🖼 🔥

Isola Bella's 17th-century Palazzo Borromeo and garden on Lake Maggiore

Milan ❸

Detail from the Duomo

CENTER OF FASHION, business, and finance Milan has a bustling, businesslike feel about it. It is chic rather than attractive – a city of wealth as opposed to imagination and the heartland of the Italian economy. To the Goths who took it over from the Romans, it was "Mailand," the land of May, a place of warmth and inspiration. It has long been an important trading center at the junction of transalpine routes, and a prize for powerful dynasties. Today, it is the best place to see Italy at its most cosmopolitan and stylish.

Portrait of a Young Woman by Pollaiuolo, Museo Poldi-Pezzoli

♣ Castello Sforzesco

Piazza Castello. ☎ 02 86 46 30 54.
◯ *Tue – Sun.* ◯ *public hols.* ♿
The first castle on this site was built by the Visconti family, but demolished when their reign ended in the mid-15th century. Milan's new ruler, Francesco Sforza, built in its place this Renaissance palace, which combines a forbidding exterior with a delightful interior. The castle is based on a series of courtyards, the most beautiful of which, the Cortile della Rocchetta, is a graceful arcaded square designed by Bramante and Filarete. The palace now contains, together with sections on Applied Arts, Archaeology and Coins, the **Civiche Raccolte d'Arte Antica**. This fine collection of furniture, antiquities, and paintings includes Michelangelo's unfinished sculpture, known as the

Rondanini Pietà. The canvases in the picture collection, dating from the Renaissance to the 18th century, are particularly impressive. The Cappella Ducale contains Gothic frescoes by an unknown artist.

🏛 Museo Poldi-Pezzoli

Via Alessandro Manzoni 12. ☎ 02 79 48 89. ◯ *Tue – Sun.* 🎫
Giacomo Poldi-Pezzoli was a wealthy nobleman who, on his death in 1879, bequeathed his magnificent art collection to the state. Its most famous painting is the 15th-century Renaissance *Portrait of a Young Woman* by Antonio Pollaiuolo, though there are also works by Piero della Francesca, Botticelli, and Mantegna, among others. The applied arts section is richly endowed with fascinating items ranging from rugs and lace to glass, enamels, and porcelain, as well as sculpture, jewelry, and sundials, displayed in fine settings.

Michelangelo's *Rondanini Pietà* (c.1564) in the Castello Sforzesco

SIGHTS AT A GLANCE

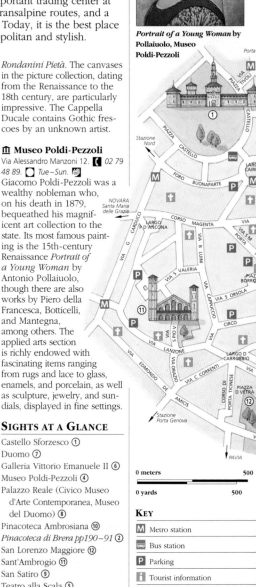

0 meters   500
0 yards   500

🎭 Teatro alla Scala

Piazza della Scala. **C** 02 72 00 37 44.
Museo Teatrale C 02 805 34 18.
⬜ daily. ⬤ Sun in winter, public
hols. 🎫

The Neo-Classical opera
house, known popularly as
La Scala, opened in 1778 and
is one of the most prestigious
opera houses in the world.
It has one of the largest
stages in Europe and hosts
sumptuous productions.

**The façade of the world-famous
Teatro alla Scala**

VISITORS' CHECKLIST

🏠 1,465,000. ✈ Malpensa
55 km (34 miles) NW; Linate 8 km
(5 miles) E. 🚆 Stazione Centrale,
Piazza Duca d'Aosta. 🚌 Piazza
Castello. 🛈 Via Marconi 1 (02 72
52 43 01); Stazione Centrale (02 72
52 43 60). ⬤ daily, major market
on Sat. 🎉 Dec 7: Sant'Ambrogio.

⛪ Duomo

Piazza del Duomo. **C** 02 86 46 34 56.
🎫 for roof. ♿

Situated at the very heart of
Milan is its giant cathedral, one
of the largest Gothic churches
in the world at 157 m (515 ft)
long and, at its widest point,
92 m (301 ft) across. It was
begun in the 14th century
under Prince Gian Galeazzo
Visconti but not completed
until more than 500 years later.

The building's most startling
feature is the extraordinary
roof, with its 135 spires and
innumerable statues and
gargoyles, and from which,
on a clear day, there are far-
reaching views to the Alps.

Below, the façade incor-
porates a dazzling assortment
of styles from Gothic through
to Renaissance and Neo-
Classical. The bronze doors are
faced with bas-reliefs recount-
ing episodes from the life of
the Virgin, the life of Sant'
Ambrogio, and scenes retelling
the history of Milan. Note,
around the apse, the delicate
Gothic tracery of the windows.

Inside, the aisles are divided
by 52 giant pillars and lit from
all sides by remarkable stained
glass. Look for the Visconti
family symbol – a
serpent swallowing
a man – in the fine
tracery of the apse
windows. Among
the many tombs
and statues is a
depiction of San
Bartolomeo Flayed,
carrying his skin.

The treasury,
lying beneath the
main altar, contains
much medieval
gold- and silver-
work. In addition,
excavations have
revealed remains
of the original 4th-
century baptistry.

Tickets
to performances
are usually sold out
months in advance, but you
can visit the adjoining **Museo
Teatrale** to admire sets and
costumes of past productions,
portraits of conductors, and
theatrical items dating back to
Roman times. There is also a
good view of the auditorium,
with its *trompe l'oeil* effects,
gilded box galleries, and its
enormous chandelier.

The Gothic duomo, crowned with spires

Exploring Milan

I N ADDITION TO THE GREAT MONUMENTS in Milan, such as the cathedral and the castle, there is a host of varied and interesting museums, churches, and civic buildings, which provide an enthralling mix of old and new. This chic and busy metropolis offers plenty of opportunities for cultural activities, gastronomic adventures, designer-fashion shopping, or just strolling about, Milan-style.

The glass ceiling and dome covering the Galleria Vittorio Emanuele II

🏛 Galleria Vittorio Emanuele II
Main entrances on Piazza del Duomo and Piazza della Scala.

This ornate shopping arcade, known as *il Salotto di Milano* (Milan's drawing room), was designed by the architect Giuseppe Mengoni in 1865. The galleria had a tragic start, however, as Mengoni fell to his death from the scaffolding not long before its inauguration in 1877 (a year before the arcade was actually finished). The city's glitterati are nevertheless attracted to its stylish shops, cafés, and restaurants, which include Il Salotto, said to serve the finest coffee in all Milan, and the elegant Savini, which is one of the city's most prestigious restaurants.

The galleria itself has a floor plan in the shape of a Latin cross, with an octagonal center adorned with mosaics representing four continents (Europe, America, Africa, and Asia), together with others representing Art, Agriculture, Science, and Industry. Its finest feature is its metal and glass roof, crowned with a magnificent central dome. The roof was the first structure in Italy to use metal and glass in a structural way, rather than just decoratively. The floors are

decorated with mosaics of the signs of the zodiac; locals may be seen stepping on the genitals of Taurus the Bull, in order to bring good luck.

🏛 Museo del Duomo
Palazzo Reale, Piazza del Duomo 14.
📞 *02 86 03 58.* ◻ *Tue–Sun.*
⬤ *public hols.* 🎫

The museum lies south of the duomo in the Palazzo Reale (Royal Palace), for centuries home to the Visconti and other families that ruled Milan. It charts the complicated history of the duomo from its origins

in the 14th century (and the preexisting church on its site) until the 1886 competition held to redesign its façade.

Among the exhibits there are interesting 16th- and 17th-century wooden models of the cathedral, and many of the original medieval sculptures – including figures thought to be Gian Galeazzo Visconti and Galeazzo Maria Sforza. There are in addition stained-glass windows, paintings, tapestries, and a pair of very elaborately carved choir stalls. Another section has displays focusing on some of the 20th-century amendments to the cathedral.

🏛 Civico Museo d'Arte Contemporanea
Palazzo Reale, Piazza del Duomo 12.
📞 *02 62 08 32 19.* ◻ *Tue–Sun.*
⬤ *Easter.* ♿

The Museum of Contemporary Art (or CIMAC), housed on the second floor of the Palazzo Reale, is a refreshingly up-to-date gallery. It opened in 1984 and is still in the process of expanding, but the emphasis is heavily on Italian works: from the 19th century to pieces by members of the Futurist movement (Umberto Boccioni in particular), from abstract art to the more diverse productions of the present day. Look for works by Carlo Carrà (1881–1966), Filippo De Pisis, Giorgio Morandi (1890–1964) and Tancredi, as well as those by more familiar artists such as Modigliani (1884–1920) and De Chirico (1888–1978).

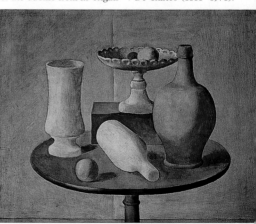

Still Life (1920) by Giorgio Morandi in the Museo d'Arte Contemporanea

Among the non-Italian artists are Post-Impressionists (Van Gogh, Cézanne, Gauguin), Picasso – a bequest of 30 etchings – and Matisse, Klee, Mondrian, and Kandinsky.

🏛 Pinacoteca Ambrosiana

2 Piazza Pio XI. 📞 *02 80 69 21*. ◘ *Tue–Sun.* 🔲

The recently renovated Ambrosiana is home to the magnificent library of Cardinal Federico Borromeo, whose 30,000 manuscripts, including a 5th-century illustrated *Iliad*, early editions of Dante's *Divine Comedy* (1353) and Leonardo's *Atlantic Codex* (15th century), survive to this day.

The building also houses an interesting art gallery, originally bequeathed by Borromeo on his death in 1618. The collection of paintings and sculpture attests to the cardinal's broad-ranging if slightly quirky taste, and now ranges from 14th-century pieces to works of the early 19th century. Among the canvases are the *Portrait of a Musician* by Leonardo da Vinci (1452–1519) and the *Portrait of a Young Woman*, attributed to his pupil, Ambrogio da Predis. Other masterpieces include the *Madonna of the Canopy* by Botticelli (15th century), a cartoon version of Raphael's Vatican fresco, *The*

Fruit Basket (c. 1596) by Caravaggio in the Pinacoteca Ambrosiana

School of Athens (16th century), and Caravaggio's *Fruit Basket* (the first painting in Italy to have a still life as its subject). There is also a strong collection of Venetian art, with paintings by Tiepolo, Titian, Giorgione, and Bassano, and panel paintings by the late 15th-century Lombard painter, Bergognone.

🔒 San Satiro

Via Torino. ◘ *daily*.

This unassuming church, its full title Santa Maria presso San Satiro, is one of the most beautiful Renaissance buildings in Milan. It stands on the site of a 9th-century sanctuary,

little of which remains apart from the Cappella della Pietà (off the left aisle), beside an 11th-century bell tower.

The interior appears to be in the shape of a Greek cross. This, however, is an illusion created by various *trompe-l'oeil* effects in stucco, since space restrictions led Bramante (who was entrusted with its construction in the late 15th century) to choose a T-shaped plan. Above the altar is a 13th-century fresco. An octagonal baptistry containing terra-cottas lies off the right aisle. The church's façade was finished only in the 19th century.

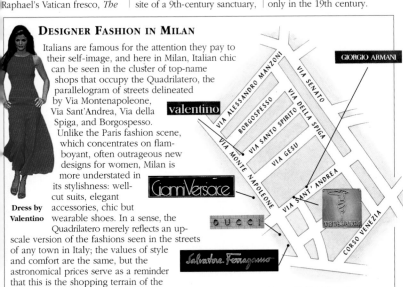

DESIGNER FASHION IN MILAN

Italians are famous for the attention they pay to their self-image, and here in Milan, Italian chic can be seen in the cluster of top-name shops that occupy the Quadrilatero, the parallelogram of streets delineated by Via Montenapoleone, Via Sant'Andrea, Via della Spiga, and Borgospesso.

Unlike the Paris fashion scene, which concentrates on flamboyant, often outrageous new designs for women, Milan is more understated in its stylishness: well-cut suits, elegant accessories, chic but wearable shoes. In a sense, the Quadrilatero merely reflects an up-scale version of the fashions seen in the streets of any town in Italy; the values of style and comfort are the same, but the astronomical prices serve as a reminder that this is the shopping terrain of the glamorous and very well-heeled.

Dress by Valentino

Via Montenapoleone, focus of Milan's best shops

Milan: Pinacoteca di Brera

MILAN'S FINEST art collection is held in an imposing 17th-century building, the Palazzo di Brera. This is where, in the 18th century, the Accademia di Belle Arti was founded; the picture collection developed alongside the academy. Inside the Brera hang some of the finest examples of Italian Renaissance and Baroque painting, including works by Piero della Francesca, Mantegna, Canaletto, Bellini, Raphael, Tintoretto, Veronese, and Caravaggio. The collection also includes 20th-century works by some of Italy's most famous modern artists.

Mother and Son *(1917)*
The metaphysical paintings of Carlo Carrà show a dream world full of strange and obscure symbols.

Portrait of Moisè Kisling
Modigliani's angular portrait of 1915 reflects his interest in African sculpture.

Twin staircases lead up to the first-floor entrance of the Pinacoteca.

The bronze statue (1809) by Canova depicts Napoleon as a demigod with Victory wings in his hand.

★ The Kiss *(1859)*
Francesco Hayez's painting is one of the most reproduced works of Italian 19th-century art. Patriotic and sentimental, it became a symbol of the optimism surrounding the unification of Italy.

KEY TO FLOOR PLAN

- 15th- to 16th-century Italian painting
- 16th- to 17th-century Dutch and Flemish painting
- 17th-century Italian painting
- 18th- to 19th-century Italian painting
- 20th-century Italian painting and sculpture
- Nonexhibition space

Works by Rubens and Van Dyck represent some of the non-Italian artists on show.

★ **Dead Christ by Mantegna**
The subtle lighting and dramatic perspective of this lamentation by Mantegna (1430–1506) make it one of his greatest masterpieces.

VISITORS' CHECKLIST

Via Brera 28. 02 72 26 31.
Lanza, Montenapoleone & Duomo. 60, 61. 9am–6pm Tue–Sat; 9am–8pm Sun & public hols (last adm: 1 hr before closing). Jan 1, May 1, Dec 25.

GALLERY GUIDE

The collection is displayed in 38 rooms, and was built up first by paintings from churches, later from acquisitions. Not all of it is permanently on view – this is due to restoration work and research.

Twinned columns support the arcades in the courtyard.

The stone façade presents a regular and slightly austere appearance.

Madonna della candeletta *(c.1490)*
This painting by Carlo Crivelli was the central part of a polyptych. It is richly detailed with much distinctive ornamentation.

Main entrance from Via Brera

★ **Marriage of the Virgin**
This graceful altarpiece by Raphael was painted in 1504. The circular temple is signed with the artist's name.

STAR PAINTINGS

★ **Dead Christ by Mantegna**

★ **Marriage of the Virgin by Raphael**

Milan: Southwest of the Center

SOME OF MILAN'S FINEST TREASURES are to be found in its religious buildings: the ancient monasteries and churches make up some fine architectural ensembles in themselves, as well as incorporating important ruins and relics dating back to Roman times. It is also in Milan that one of the world's most famous images is found – Leonardo's evocative masterpiece, the *Last Supper*.

San Lorenzo Maggiore viewed from the northeast

The entrance to Sant'Ambrogio, flanked by unequal bell towers

🔒 Sant'Ambrogio
Piazza Sant'Ambrogio 15. [02 86 45 08 95. ◯ daily. ⛾

Sant'Ambrogio, or St. Ambrose, is the patron saint of Milan, a man who was so eloquent that bees were said to fly into his mouth, attracted by his honey tongue. As bishop of Milan in the 4th century, he worked hard to avoid a schism in the church. This is the basilica that he began building in AD 379, though most of it today is 10th-century Romanesque. A medieval gateway leads to the bronze doors of the entrance, flanked by two bell towers. Inside, note the fine rib vaulting and the beautiful pulpit, and the striking 9th-century altar decorated with gold, silver, and precious gems, crowned by a canopy. In a chapel off the south aisle, fine mosaics line a stunning cupola. Down in the crypt lies the tomb of Sant'Ambrogio himself.

Up above the portico, a small museum contains architectural fragments, tapestries, and paintings relating to the church.

🔒 San Lorenzo Maggiore
Corso di Porta Ticinese. [02 89 40 41 29. ◯ daily. ⛾ for the Cappella.

This church contains the most important collection of Roman and early Christian remains in Milan. The octagonal basilica was built in the 4th century, above what was probably a Roman amphitheater, and subsequently rebuilt in the 12th and 16th centuries.

In front of the church stands a row of 16 Roman columns and, in commemoration of his Edict, a statue of the Emperor Constantine. Fine 4th-century mosaics adorn the Cappella di Sant'Aquilino, a Romanesque chapel, which also contains two early Christian sarcophagi. Other Roman architectural elements, which were incorporated into the building of this church, may be seen in a chamber below the chapel.

🔒 Santa Maria delle Grazie
Piazza Santa Maria delle Grazie 2. [02 498 75 88. **Cenacolo** [02 8 42 11 46. ◯ Tue–Sun, booking compulsory. ● public hols. ⛾ 🔒

This beautiful 15th-century Renaissance convent, with its lovely apse and small cloister designed by Bramante, contains one of the key images of western civilization: the *Cenacolo (Last Supper)* by Leonardo da Vinci. The image captures the moment at which Christ tells his disciples that one of them will betray him. Note, however, that the Christ figure is unfinished: Leonardo did not consider himself to be worthy to complete it.

The artist also spurned the standard fresco technique of painting on wet plaster, applying tempera to the dry wall instead. The result is full of subtlety but has deteriorated. The paint is flaking, and restoration has proved difficult. The painting is now protected by an air filtering system.

Leonardo da Vinci's *Last Supper* (1495–7) adorning the refectory wall of Santa Maria delle Grazie

THE EDICT OF MILAN

Milan was colonised by the Romans in 222 BC and quickly grew to be an important city at the junction of different trading routes. As the Roman Empire grew and then split into two, emperors began to neglect Rome for the better-placed Mediolanum (literally, city in the middle of the plain). It was here that Emperor Constantine declared his Edict of AD 313, in which Christianity was officially tolerated, effectively making it a lawful religion.

The emperor is reputed to have been converted as a result of a vision, but by the 4th century adopting Christianity was the only way to unite the now-disparate empire.

Emperor Constantine

Monza ❹

Milano. 🏛 125,000. FS 🚊
ℹ Palazzo Comunale, Piazza Carducci (039 32 32 22). 🚌 Thu & Sat.

THESE DAYS MONZA is merely a satellite of Milan, famous for its international Formula One **Autodromo**, which lies inside a vast and beautiful park on the edge of Monza. The park also includes an elegant Rococo hunting lodge called the Villa Reale, and a large golf course. At one time, however, Monza was one of the most important towns in Lombardy: Theodolinda, the 6th-century Lombard queen, built its first cathedral and bequeathed her treasure to the town.

At the heart of the town center is the present **duomo**, with its notable green and white 14th-century façade and beautiful 15th-century frescoes portraying Theodolinda's life. Behind the high altar is the small Iron Crown, believed to have belonged to Emperor

Constantine. It is prized for the iron strip said to have been one of the nails from the cross of Christ. More local treasures may be found in the duomo's **Museo Serpero**, including a silver hen standing over seven tiny chicks – which symbolize Lombardy and the seven provinces it ruled – and a relic said to be John the Baptist's tooth.

🏁 **Autodromo**
Parco di Monza. 📞 039 248 21.
🔲 daily. ⬤ public hols. ♿ ♿
🏛 **Duomo**
Piazza Duomo. 📞 039 32 34 04. **Museo Serpero** 🔲 Tue–Sun. ▦

Bergamo ❺

🏛 150,000. FS 🚊 ℹ Piazzale Marconi 106 (035 24 22 26).
🚌 Mon.

BERGAMO IS A DELIGHTFUL hilltop town that owes much of its artistic inspiration and architectural splendor to the influence of Venice, which ruled it from the 15th to the late 18th century. The town is divided into two distinct parts: Bergamo Alta crowning the hill, with its cluster of attractive medieval and Renaissance buildings; and the more modern and airy Bergamo Bassa lying below.

The jewel of the upper town is **Piazza Vecchia**, containing one of the most appealing architectural ensembles in the region. Its buildings include the 12th-century Torre del Comune with its fine clock and curfew bell that rings every night at 10pm, the late 16th-century Biblioteca Civica, and the attractive 12th-century Palazzo della Ragione, or law courts, adorned with a statue of the lion of Venice.

The arcades of the Palazzo della Ragione lead to Piazza del Duomo, the square of the Neo-Classical duomo, which is dominated by the façade of the **Cappella Colleoni**

Detail from the Cappella Colleoni

Leonello d'Este (c.1440) by Pisanello, in the Accademia Carrara, Bergamo

(see p178). The chapel was built in 1476 to house the tomb of Bergamo's famous political leader, Bartolomeo Colleoni. The chapel is flanked by two 14th-century buildings: an octagonal baptistry and the porch leading to the Romanesque basilica of Santa Maria Maggiore. The basilica's austere exterior contrasts with its Baroque interior, which contains the tomb of Gaetano Donizetti (1797–1848), the operatic composer who was born in Bergamo.

The **Galleria dell'Accademia Carrara** is the highlight of Bergamo Bassa, a major picture gallery with a fine collection of works by Venetian masters and local artists, as well as masterpieces from the rest of Italy: 15th-century works by Pisanello, Crivelli, Mantegna, Giovanni Bellini, and Botticelli; 16th-century paintings by Titian, Raphael, and Perugino; 18th-century canvases by Tiepolo, Guardi, and Canaletto. Major artists represented from the rest of Europe include Holbein, Dürer, Brueghel, and Velázquez.

🏛 **Galleria dell'Accademia Carrara**
Piazza dell'Accademia. 📞 035 39 96 43. 🔲 Wed–Mon. ⬤ public hols. ▦

A leafy pathway through the Parco Nazionale dello Stelvio

Parco Nazionale dello Stelvio ❻

Trento, Bolzano, Sondrio & Brescia.
🚌 *from Bormio to Santa Caterina & Madonna dei Monti.* 🛈 *Via Roma 56, (0342 90 33 00).*

THE STELVIO, Italy's largest national park, is the gateway from Lombardy to the glacier-strewn Dolomite mountains stretching into Trentino-Alto Adige. The glaciers are dotted with more than 50 lakes, and dominated by craggy peaks such as Gran Zebrù, Cevedale, and Ortles – the tallest mountain here at 3,905 m (12,811 ft). The dramatic, winding roads of the Stelvio are the dread of cyclists in the annual Giro d'Italia, Italy's answer to the Tour de France. For walkers, the area provides virtually unlimited hiking, and access to remote areas populated by ibexes, marmots, chamois, and eagles. The only real population center in the Lombardy part of the parc is at **Bormio**, which boasts plenty of winter and summer sports facilities, and is a good base from which

to explore the area. The town's **Giardino Botanico** displays some of the species of mountain plants found in the region.

🌺 **Giardino Botanico Alpino Retia**
Località Rovinaccia, Bormio.
⭕ *May–Sep: daily.* 📷

Val Camonica ❼

Brescia. 🚆 🚌 *Capo di Ponte.*
🛈 *Via Briscioli, Capo di Ponte (0364 420 80).*

THIS ATTRACTIVE BROAD valley formed by a glacier is the setting for an extraordinary

series of prehistoric carvings on rock. These form an astonishing outdoor mural from the Lago d'Iseo to Capo di Ponte and beyond, and the entire valley has been declared a cultural protection zone by UNESCO. More than 180,000 engravings from the Neolithic era until early Roman times have been discovered, some as recently as the 1970s; the best are in the **Parco Nazionale delle Incisioni Rupestri** around Capo di Ponte. Don't miss the Naquane rock, which is carved with nearly 1,000 figures from the last Ice Age. The **Centro Camuno** focuses on, among other things, the Roman settlement in the valley.

🏛 **Centro Camuno in Studi Preistorici**
Via Mancini 7, Capo di Monte.
📞 *0364 420 91.*
⭕ *Tue–Sun am.* ♿

Lago d'Iseo ❽

Bergamo & Brescia. 🚆 🚌 🚢 *Iseo.*
🛈 *Lungolago Marconi 2, Iseo (030 98 02 09).*

THIS GLACIATED LAKE lying in wine-producing country is not only surrounded by tall mountains and waterfalls, but also boasts a minimountain of its own, in the form of the island of Monte Isola. Along the shores of the lake are a clutch of fishing villages such as Sale Marasino and Iseo itself. From Marone, on the east bank of the lake, a road leads to the village of **Cislano**, about 5 km (3 miles) away. Here, extraordinary spirelike rock formations rise from the

Prehistoric engraving of a mounted hunter and stag in the Val Camonica

The partly Renaissance Ponte Coperto, straddling the Ticino River at Pavia

round, each spire topped by a boulder. These distinctive erosion pillars, one of the strangest and most beautiful natural wonders in Lombardy, are known locally as the Fairies of the Forest."

Brescia ❾

190,000. **FS** **Corso Zanardelli 38 (030 434 18).** Sat.

LOMBARDY'S SECOND city after Milan boasts a rich artistic heritage, ranging from Roman temples to the triumphalist Mussolini-era architecture of its main square, Piazza Vittoriale. The major sights include the Roman ruins around Piazza del Foro, consisting of the **Tempio Capitolino** – a three-part Capitoline temple, now incorporating a museum – and a theater; the **Pinacoteca Civica Tosio Martinengo**, containing works by Raphael, Lorenzo Lotto, and local artists; and the **Duomo** on Piazza Paolo VI, with its 11th-century core and white 17th-century exterior. One of the relics in the duomo is the banner from the *Carroccio*, or sacred ox cart, which served as a symbol for the medieval Lega Lombarda. **Piazza della Loggia**, where the market is held, is named after the Renaissance loggia, built partly by Palladio. The 18th-century church of San Nazaro e San Celso on Via Bronzoni contains a lovely altarpiece by Titian.

Tempio Capitolino
Via Musei 57a. 030 460 31. Tue–Sun. Jan 1, May 1, Nov 1, Dec 25.

Pinacoteca Civica Tosio Martinengo
Via Martinengo da Barco. 030 377 49 99. Tue–Sun. Jan 1, May 1, Nov 1, Dec 25.

Lodi ❿

Milano. 40,000. **FS** *Piazza Broletto 4 (0371 42 13 91).* Wed, Thu, Sat & Sun.

THIS IS A CHARMING medieval town of pastel-colored houses with wrought-iron gateways, pretty courtyards, and gardens. Just off Piazza della Vittoria, the arcaded square on which the 12th-century duomo stands, is the fine Renaissance church of the **Incoronata**. The magnificent octagonal interior is entirely decorated with wall paintings and gilding, and crowned with a dome. One of the chapels has 15th-century works by Bergognone.

Pavia ⓫

81,000. **FS** *Via Fabio Filzi 2 (0382 221 56).* Wed & Sat.

DURING PAVIA'S golden age, the city was the Lombards' capital, and later witnessed coronations of Charlemagne and Frederick Barbarossa. Even after it lost its status to Milan in 1359, Pavia

The Roman Tempio Capitolino in Brescia

remained an important city, and great Romanesque churches, tall towers, and other monuments still reflect this.

As well as the Charterhouse (see pp196–7) just north of Pavia, there is the sandstone **Basilica di San Michele** off Corso Garibaldi. The building was founded in the 7th century but largely rebuilt in the 12th after being struck by lightning. Its façade is decorated with symbols and friezes of fantastic animals, and inside there are intricate carvings on the columns; a chapel to the right of the main altar contains a 7th-century silver crucifix.

In the center of the town, around Piazza della Vittoria, stand several ancient monuments. These include the medieval **Broletto** (town hall) with its 16th-century façade and the recently renovated **Duomo**, originally begun in 1488 and worked on in turn by Amadeo, Leonardo da Vinci, and Bramante. The dome was added in the 1880s. The 11th-century Torre Civica, which stood next to it, collapsed suddenly in 1989. Crossing the river is the **Ponte Coperto**, a Renaissance covered bridge with a consecrated church halfway along it. The bridge was rebuilt after World War II.

Pavia is also the site of one of Europe's oldest (1361) and most respected universities, now residing around a series of Neo-Classical courtyards off Strada Nuova. This road continues northward to the 14th-century castle, now home to Pavia's **Museo Civico**.

Northwest of Piazza Castello is the 12th-century church, **San Pietro in Ciel d'Oro**. It no longer boasts the fine gilded ceiling from which it derives its name, but does still contain a magnificent shrine to St. Augustine, whose bones were allegedly brought to Pavia from Carthage in the 8th century. The body of Boëthius (c.480–524), an important philosopher, is buried down in the crypt.

Museo Civico
Castello Visconteo, Piazza Castello. 0382 338 53. Tue–Fri am & Sat. public hols.

Certosa di Pavia ⑫

THE CHARTERHOUSE 8 km (5 miles) north of Pavia is the pinnacle of Renaissance architecture in Lombardy, a highly decorated Carthusian monastery built over a span of 200 years. It was conceived as a monument to Gian Galeazzo Visconti, the Milanese ruler who founded the complex in 1396 and who had ambitions to become king of all Italy. This splendid shrine was created by the great 15th-century craftsman Giovanni Antonio Amadeo, among others, who used innovative techniques of relief work and multicolored decoration.

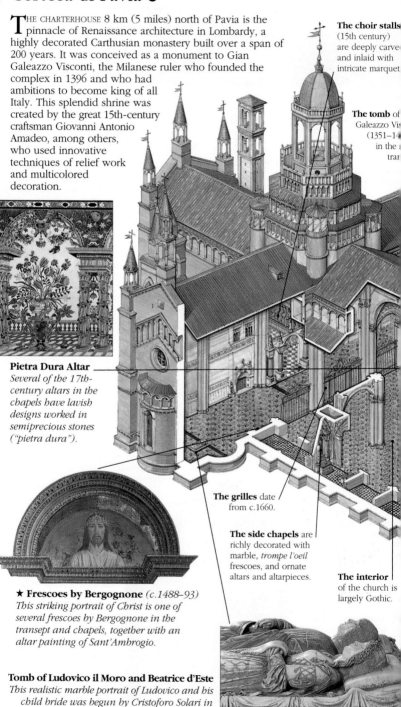

The choir stalls (15th century) are deeply carve⟨d⟩ and inlaid with intricate marquet⟨ry⟩

The tomb of Galeazzo Vis⟨conti⟩ (1351–14⟨ ⟩) in the ⟨ ⟩ tran⟨sept⟩

Pietra Dura Altar
Several of the 17th-century altars in the chapels have lavish designs worked in semiprecious stones ("pietra dura").

The grilles date from c.1660.

The side chapels are richly decorated with marble, *trompe l'oeil* frescoes, and ornate altars and altarpieces.

The interior of the church is largely Gothic.

★ **Frescoes by Bergognone** (c.1488–93)
This striking portrait of Christ is one of several frescoes by Bergognone in the transept and chapels, together with an altar painting of Sant'Ambrogio.

Tomb of Ludovico il Moro and Beatrice d'Este
This realistic marble portrait of Ludovico and his child bride was begun by Cristoforo Solari in 1497, some 11 years before Ludovico's death.

Great Cloister

This huge cloister is reached through the Small Cloister. It is framed on three sides by the two-story monks' cells, each backed by a small garden. A hatch beside the door permits food to be delivered without any communication.

Monk's cell

VISITORS' CHECKLIST

Viale del Monumento, Pavia. ☎ 0382 92 56 13. 🚌 from Pavia. 🚆 Certosa. Both followed by 1 km (half a mile) walk. ⏰ May–Sep: 9–11:30am, 2:30–6pm (Oct–Mar: 4:30pm; Apr: 5:30pm) Tue–Sun & Mon public hols (last adm: 30 mins before closing). **Donation** to guide. 📷 🚻 📷 ♿ ✔

The New Sacristy is painted with colorful ceiling frescoes.

This delightful, arcaded Small Cloister, with fine terra-cotta ornamentation, contains a small garden, planted in formal designs.

★ Renaissance Façade
The 15th-century lower part of the façade is profusely decorated with statues and carvings of Roman emperors, saints (here St. Peter), apostles, and prophets. The upper part dates from 1500.

Main entrance to the Certosa

STAR FEATURES

★ Renaissance Façade

★ Altarpiece by Perugino

★ Frescoes by Bergognone

★ Altarpiece by Perugino
The six-panel altarpiece was painted in 1496 but now only one panel – that depicting God the Father – is original; it is flanked by two paintings by Bergognone.

The duomo on Piazza del Comune, Cremona

Cremona ⑬

🚶 76,000. 🚇 🚌 🅸 *Piazza del Comune 5 (0372 217 22).* 🛒 *Wed & Sat.*

CREMONA, A MAJOR agricultural market, is most famous for music, thanks to native sons such as the composer Claudio Monteverdi (1567–1643) and the violinmaker Stradivari (1644–1737). The town itself is dominated by the beautiful Piazza del Comune, bordered by outstanding buildings.

The main attraction is the exuberant part-Romanesque **duomo**, and its bell tower – said to be the tallest medieval tower in Italy – known as the **Torrazzo**; the two are linked by a Renaissance loggia. The wonderful façade is dominated by the large 13th-century rose window and by a number of intricate touches, including a small portico with statues of the Virgin and saints. Inside, the duomo is sumptuously decorated with magnificent early 16th-century frescoes and Flemish tapestries, as well as paintings in the side chapels. The top of the Torrazzo offers sweeping views. Outside the duomo, note the pulpit where itinerant preachers, including San Bernardino of Siena, used to speak to onlookers.

Next to the duomo stands an octagonal 12th-century baptistry, while on the other side of the piazza rise the arcades of the late 13th-century **Loggia dei Militi** where the town's lords once met, now a war memorial.

The **Palazzo del Comune** is the other major building on the square. It was rebuilt in the 13th century (the windows are more recent) and now contains four rare violins: one each by Guarnieri del Gesù, Andrea and Niccolò Amati, and Stradivari. The **Museo Stradivariano** displays drawings, models, and violins that were made by the master craftsman. The **Museo Civico**, housed in a 16th-century palazzo, contains paintings, wood carvings, the cathedral's treasure, ceramics, and a section on archaeology.

On the eastern outskirts of the town, on the road to Casalmaggiore, lies the Renaissance church of **San Sigismondo**. It was here that Francesco Sforza married Bianca Visconti in 1441, and the church was subsequently rebuilt (from 1463) in honor of the event. The interior is richly decorated with 16th-century paintings, altarpieces, and frescoes by artists of the Cremona school (Camp family, Gatti, and Boccaccino)

🕍 Torrazzo
Piazza del Comune. ⬜ *Easter–Nov daily.* 🈯

🕍 Palazzo del Comune
Piazza del Comune. 📞 *0372 221 38.* ⬜ *Tue–Sun.* ⬛ *public hols.* 🈯 🚻

🏛 Museo Stradivariano
Via Palestro 17. 📞 *0372 46 18 86.* ⬜ *Tue–Sun.* ⬛ *public hols.* 🈯

🏛 Museo Civico
Via Ugolani Dati 4. 📞 *0372 46 18 85.* ⬜ *Tue–Sun.* ⬛ *public hols.* 🈯

Sabbioneta ⑭

Mantova. 🚶 *4,600.* 🚌 *from Mantova.* 🅸 *Piazza d'Armi (0375 22 10 44).* 🛒 *Wed am.* 🈯 *apply to the tourist information center.* 🈯

SABBIONETA is the result of a delightful experiment in the theory of Renaissance architecture. It was built by Vespasiano Gonzaga Colonna (1531–91) as an ideal city, and within its hexagonal walls is a perfect gridwork arrangement of streets and buildings designed on a human scale. The finest buildings include the splendid Teatro All'Antica designed by Scamozzi, the Palazzo Ducale and the frescoed Palazzo del Giardino, which may be visited as part of a tour of the town.

ANTONIO STRADIVARI AND HIS VIOLINS

Cremona is where the violin was developed. The instrument-maker Andrea Amati made the first ones in the 1530s, and they soon became popular with the royal courts throughout Europe because of their superior tone to the medieval fiddle.

It was Antonio Stradivari, known as Stradivarius (1644–1737) – the pupil of Andrea Amati's grandson Niccolò – who raised the level of craftsmanship to genius. He used to go walking in the forests of the Dolomites in search of the perfect wood for his instruments. Stradivarius produced more than 1,100 violins in his workshop, of which more than 400 exist to this day and remain unrivaled by modern techniques or equipment. The main highlights on a Stradivarius tour of Cremona are the Museo Stradivariano, the violin room in the Palazzo del Comune, and the great man's tombstone on Piazza Roma.

19th-century engraving of Antonio Stradivari

The ceiling of the Camera degli Sposi, by Mantegna, in the Palazzo Ducale

Mantova ⑮

🚊 55,000. 🚉 🚌 ℹ *Piazza Andrea Mantegna 6 (0376 32 82 53).* 🚢 *Thu.*

MANTOVA (MANTUA) is a striking if stern-looking place of fine squares and aristocratic architecture, bordered on three sides by lakes formed by the swollen banks of the Mincio River. The climate can be humid as a result, though Mantova more than makes up for it with a fine sense of cultural history: it was the birthplace of the poet Virgil and playground for three centuries of the Gonzaga dukes. It was also the refuge where Shakespeare sent Romeo into exile from Verona, and the setting for Verdi's opera *Rigoletto*. These links are all celebrated in street names, signposts, and monuments around the town. The theatrical connections are enhanced by the 18th-century **Teatro Scientifico Bibiena**, on Via Accademia, which Mozart's father thought was the finest he had ever seen.

Mantova is focused on three attractive main squares: Piazza dell'Erbe, Piazza del Broletto, named after the 13th-century building adorned with a statue of the poet Virgil, and the cobbled Piazza Sordello. On one side of Piazza Sordello is the **duomo**, with an 18th-century façade and fine interior stuccoes by Giulio Romano (c.1492–1546); on another side, the forbidding façade of the Palazzo Bonacolsi, with its tall prison tower. Piazza dell'Erbe is dominated by the **Basilica di Sant'Andrea** (15th century), designed largely by Alberti, the early Renaissance architect and theorist, and now flanked by an arcade of shops. The square is also notable for the appealing 11th-century Rotonda di San Lorenzo, and the part-13th-century Palazzo della Ragione with its 15th-century clock tower.

Detail from the 15th-century clock tower on Piazza dell'Erbe

🏛 Palazzo Ducale

Piazza Sordello. 📞 *0376 32 02 83.* ⏰ *Tue–Sat.* 🔴 *Jan 1, May 1, Dec 25.* 📷 *available upon request from the Tourist Office (0376 32 82 53).* 📷

The highlight of Mantova is the Palazzo Ducale, the vast home of the Gonzaga family that covers the entire northeastern corner of the town and incorporates Castello San Giorgio – a 14th-century fortress – and a basilica, as well as the palace proper. Amid the splendors are many impressive works of art: they include an unfinished series of 15th-century frescoes by Pisanello, retelling episodes from the Arthurian legends; a large portrait by Rubens (17th century) of the ducal family in the Salone degli Arcieri; and – most absorbing of all – the frescoes by Mantegna in the **Camera degli Sposi** (1465–74). These portray Lodovico Gonzaga and members of his family and court in all their magnificence *(pp200–201)*. The entire room is decorated with images of people, animals, and fantastic landscapes, and completed by a light-hearted *trompe l'oeil* ceiling of figures, *putti*, and a blue sky.

🏛 Palazzo Tè

Viale Tè. 📞 *0376 32 32 66.* ⏰ *Mon pm, Tue–Sun.* 🔴 *Jan 1, May 1, Dec 25.* 📷

At the other end of town stands an extraordinary palace, the early 16th-century Palazzo Tè, built by Giulio Romano for the Gonzaga family as a base from which they could go horseback riding. Here the art conspires with the architecture to striking effect: in the **Sala dei Giganti**, for instance, the frescoed Titans appear to be tearing down the pillars of the room itself. Also remarkable is the Sala di Amore e Psiche, decorated with scenes from the *Golden Ass* by Apuleius, and said to celebrate Federico II's love for his mistress. Other rooms are lavishly painted with horses and zodiac signs.

The 13th-century façade of Palazzo Ducale overlooking Piazza Sordello

15th-century fresco, by Mantegna, from the Camera degli Sposi in the Palazzo Ducale ▷

VALLE D'AOSTA AND PIEDMONT

PIEDMONT AND THE NEIGHBORING VALLE D'AOSTA *are – apart from Turin and its cultural splendors – essentially countryside. To the north lie the Alps, with ski resorts such as Courmayeur, and the wild stretches of the Parco Nazionale del Gran Paradiso. To the south lie the vineyard-clad hills around Barolo, and seemingly endless fields of grain and rice, used in the local dish, risotto.*

The northwest is also rich in culture. From the 11th century to the 18th, both the verdant Valle d'Aosta and Piedmont were part of the French-speaking principality of Savoy and enjoyed the influences of both sides of the Alpine divide. Even today, French and dialectal variants are still spoken in the remote valleys of Piedmont and in much of the Valle d'Aosta. It was only under Duke Emanuele Filiberto in the 16th century that the region was brought definitively into the Italian sphere of influence. Later, it was to play the key role in the Risorgimento *(see pp58–9)*, the ambitious movement that united Italy under a king from Piedmont. The vestiges of this history are to be found in the medieval castles of the Valle d'Aosta and the extraordinary clusters of chapels known as *sacri monti* dotted around the foothills of the Alps. Piedmont also spawned a school of painting, which is in evidence in the small parish churches and excellent fine art collections in the region. The most impressive architecture in the northwest, however, is undoubtedly to be found in Turin, a much underrated and surprisingly elegant Baroque city that boasts, among other things, one of the best Egyptian museums in the world. Piedmont is also known for its industry – Fiat in Turin, Olivetti in Ivrea, Ferrero in Alba – but it has not forgotten its agricultural roots, and food and drink play an important role in the life of the region: the hills of southern Piedmont produce many of the great Italian red wines.

Taking vermouth in one of Turin's cafés

◁ **The 13th-century Châtelard castle in the Valle d'Aosta**

Exploring Valle d'Aosta and Piedmont

THE VAST FLAT PLAIN of the Po, covered with the watery expanse of rice fields around Vercelli and Novara, eventually gives way, in the west, to the majestic heights of the Alps. Turin, the largest city in the area and the capital of Piedmont, stands at the edge of the plain, nestling almost in the shadow of the mountains. Further northwest, attractive Alpine valleys headed by dramatic peaks provide the setting for the traditional villages, ancient towns, and castles around Aosta. The Parco Nazionale del Gran Paradiso is an unspoiled tract of breathtaking scenery.

Rice fields around Vercelli

SIGHTS AT A GLANCE

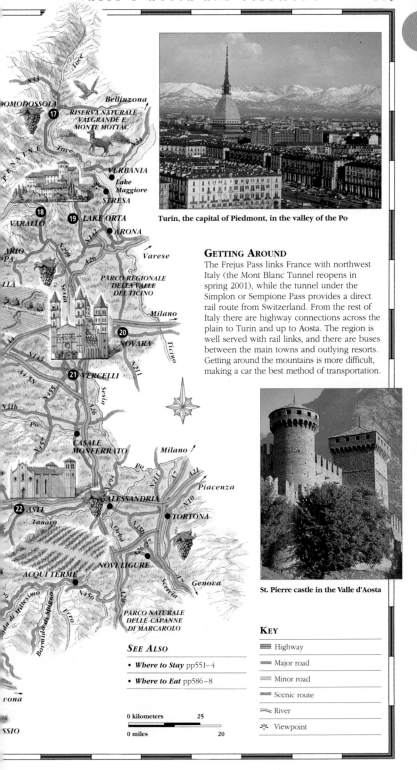

Turin, the capital of Piedmont, in the valley of the Po

GETTING AROUND

The Frejus Pass links France with northwest Italy (the Mont Blanc Tunnel reopens in spring 2001), while the tunnel under the Simplon or Sempione Pass provides a direct rail route from Switzerland. From the rest of Italy there are highway connections across the plain to Turin and up to Aosta. The region is well served with rail links, and there are buses between the main towns and outlying resorts. Getting around the mountains is more difficult, making a car the best method of transportation.

St. Pierre castle in the Valle d'Aosta

SEE ALSO

- *Where to Stay* pp551–4

- *Where to Eat* pp586–8

| 0 kilometers | 25 |
| 0 miles | 20 |

KEY

Highway

Major road

Minor road

Scenic route

River

Viewpoint

Monte Bianco ❶

Aosta. 🚈 *Pré-St-Didier.*
🚌 *Courmayeur.* ℹ️ *Piazzale Monte Bianco 13, Courmayeur (0165 84 20 60).*

MONTE BIANCO – Mont Blanc as it is also known – the tallest mountain in the Alps at 4,810 m (15,780 ft), dominates the western Aosta valley and its attractive all-year resort, **Courmayeur**. A series of cable car rides from Entrèves, 5 km (3 miles) farther north, leads to Chamonix. Passing its highest point (3,842 m, 12,606 ft) at Aiguille du Middi, it offers one of the most spectacular views in the Alps. From Pré-St-Didier, below Courmayeur, the **Little St. Bernard Pass** with its small glaciers, forests, and ravines can be explored.

A St. Bernard dog

Colle del Gran San Bernardo ❷

Aosta. 🚈 🚌 *Aosta.* ℹ️ *Strada Statale Gran San Bernardo 13, Etroubles (0165 785 59).* ⏰ *daily.*

THE GREAT ST. BERNARD pass is synonymous with the hardy mountain rescue dogs that have been trained locally by Catholic monks since the 11th century. The **Monks' Hospice**, founded around 1050 by St. Bernard of Aosta, lies just over the Swiss border (bring your passport), on the shores of a lovely lake; the dogs are still being trained there.

The pretty Great St. Bernard valley itself includes the town of Etroubles, set in a forest of conifers, the hamlet of St-Oyen with its pretty parish church, and the resort of St-Rhémy-en-Bosses.

🏨 **Monks' Hospice**
Colle San Bernardo, Switzerland.
📞 *00 41 277 87 12 36.* ⏰ *daily.*

Monte Cervino ❸

Aosta. 🚈 🚌 *Breuil-Cervinia.* ℹ️ *Via Carrel 29, Breuil-Cervinia (0166 94 91 36).*

THE DISTINCTIVE triangular peak of Monte Cervino (the Matterhorn) rises to 4,478 m (14,691 ft) and is easily recognizable. Below the mountain lies a scattering of attractive villages like Antey-St-André, Valtournenche (which gave its name to the valley), and the resort of **Breuil-Cervinia**. From Breuil a cable car rises to the Plateau Rosa (3,480 m, 11,418 ft) offering dramatic views of the surrounding mountains. This entire area is a paradise for both skiers and hikers.

Monte Rosa ❹

Aosta. 🚈 *Verrès.* 🚌 *St-Jacques.* ℹ️ *Route Varasc, Champoluc (0125 30 71 13).*

MONTE ROSA overlooks the picturesque Gressoney and Ayas valleys. The rolling lower Ayas valley is dominated by the ruins of the 11th-century **Castello di Graines**, perched on a large rock. Higher up, the resort of Champoluc has a cable car connection with the striking **Testa Grigia** (3,315 m, 10,877 ft). The Gressoney valley is home to the Walser people, who speak an obscure German dialect. At the bottom of the valley, near Pont-St-Martin with its Roman bridge, lies **Issime**: the 16th-century church here has a fresco of the Last Judgment on its façade.

⛪ **Castello di Graines**
Graines, Strada Statale 506. ⏰ *daily.*

MEDIEVAL CASTLES AND FORTS IN THE VALLE D'AOSTA

The mountains alone provided insufficient protection to the fragmented kingdoms that covered the Valle d'Aosta in the Middle Ages. The medieval lords, who ruled ruthlessly over their small domains, built castles to enforce their often fragile power. Of the many built, 70 castles survive in some form to this day. You will pass a number of them if you drive into Italy by the Mont Blanc tunnel; they stretch from Aosta to Pont-St-Martin.

Originally Aosta castles were designed to be defensive and threatening, such as the looming tower of **Montmayer**, perched high on a huge rock by the Valgrisenche valley. Nearby, the equally forbidding dark tower of **Ussel** throws a melancholy, brooding watchfulness over the valley.

Fénis and **Verrès** represent an important shift in the function of the feudal castle. Both Fénis, a splendid 14th-century showpiece (*see p178*), and Verrès were not just important military outposts but also examples of palatial opulence and good living. **Issogne**, too, furthered this luxurious trend with its elaborate frescoes, loggias, and fountains.

Decoration was also important to Vittorio Emanuele II, owner of **Sarre**, who turned the halls of his fortress into a plush hunting lodge. The owners of **Châtelard**, set in some of the highest vineyards in Europe, placed fine wine production alongside military aims.

The strategically sited 14th-century castle at Verrès

The 12th-century cloister, with 40 carved columns of darkened marble, in Sant'Orso

Aosta ❺

🚶 37,000. **FS** ➡️ **i** Piazza Chanoux 8 (0165 23 66 27). ➡️ Tue.

LYING ON A PLAIN surrounded by dramatic mountains, the town of Aosta provides a remarkable mixture of ancient culture and spectacular, rich scenery. The Romans captured it from Salassian Gauls in 25 BC, and Aosta is still dotted with fine Roman architecture built in honor of Emperor Augustus – indeed the town was once called *Augusta Praetoria*, and its name only evolved into Aosta over the centuries. The medieval town was later fortified by the Challant family and then by the Dukes of Aosta, who added towers to the old Roman walls.

Modern Aosta is a bustling place with rambling suburbs, a crossroads for local industries and tourists on their way to the mountains. The center, however, still consists of a delightful grid of large squares and surprising architectural treasures, which justify Aosta's nickname of "Rome of the Alps."

🏛 Roman Ruins

Roman Theater, Via Baillage. ⬜ daily. **Amphitheater**, Convento di San Giuseppe, Via dell'Anfiteatro. **(** 0165 26 21 49. ⬜ daily, call convent ahead. 🎟 🚻 **Roman Forum**, Piazza Giovanni XXIII. ⬜ daily.

During Roman times, entry to Aosta was over the **bridge** to the east of the town (beyond the modern bridge) and through the **Arch of Augustus**. This triumphal arch is today marred only by a roof added in the 18th century. Ahead stands the **Porta Pretoria**, its double row of stone arches flanked by a medieval tower; the gateway originally stood about 2.5 m (8 ft) higher than at present. Equally well preserved is the town's **Roman Theater**, with a section of its 20-m (65-ft) high façade. The elliptical **Amphitheater**, a little to the north, is reached through the convent of San Giuseppe. In the old town, next to the cathedral, lies the **Roman Forum**, or market place, with its huge cryptoporticus: the function of this impressive underground gallery, with its massive arches, remains the object of speculation.

Detail of a medieval mosaic on the floor of Aosta's Cattedrale

🏛 Cattedrale

Piazza Giovanni XXIII. ⬜ daily. **Museo del Tesoro** ⬜ Jun–Sep: daily; Oct–May: Sun & public hols pm. 🎟

This relatively modest shrine to St. John the Baptist was first built in the 12th century, but has been altered many times since. The interior is Gothic, with finely carved 15th-century choir stalls, and floor mosaics depicting sacred and pagan scenes. Next door, the **Museo del Tesoro** contains a rich collection of statuettes and reliquaries, and a number of impressive medieval tombs.

🏛 Sant'Orso

Via Sant'Orso. **(** 0165 26 20 26. ⬜ daily. ♿

East of the town walls is the architectural highlight of Aosta: a medieval complex of church buildings. Sant'Orso itself has a simple and unusual Gothic façade characterized by a thin, very tall portal. The interior has 11th-century frescoes, a crypt of the same date holding the tomb of St. Orso, patron saint of Aosta, and a beautiful **cloister** with columns and capitals carved into highly detailed figures and animals.

ENVIRONS: The castle at **Fénis** (*see p206*), 12 km (8 miles) east, is one of the few castles in the Aosta valley with a well-preserved interior, including beautiful frescoes and wooden galleries. **Issogne**, 38 km (23 miles) southeast, is the setting for another highly decorated castle, remodeled about 1490. It is filled with frescoes and decorative motifs, including a wrought-iron fountain in the shape of a pomegranate tree.

♜ Castello di Fénis

Fénis. **(** 0165 76 42 63. ⬜ daily. 🔴 Jan 1, Dec 25. 🎟

♜ Castello di Issogne

Issogne. **(** 0125 92 93 73. ⬜ daily. 🔴 Jan 1, Dec 25. 🎟

Some of the impressive ruins standing in the Roman Forum in Aosta

Parco Nazionale del Gran Paradiso ❻

A BREATHTAKING WILDERNESS of dramatic mountains and lush meadows, the Gran Paradiso is Italy's foremost national park, created in 1922 from part of a former royal hunting estate of the House of Savoy. It is mainly a summer resort for walkers due to its unspoiled scenery, rare wildlife, and unusual Alpine flowers, but there is also cross-country skiing during the winter months. The king of the park is the ibex, a relative of the goat family, all but extinct in the rest of Europe. The park is also prized by naturalists for its chamois, ptarmigan, golden eagles, rare butterflies, and marmots.

Castello di Aymavilles
The 18th-century core of this castle is framed by medieval corner towers.

Goletta Waterfall
is an impressive cascade near the Lago di Goletta.

Male Ibex
The ibex lives mostly above the tree line. Groups are often seen around Col Lauson at dawn and dusk, and also around Pont in June.

Val di Rhêmes-Notre-Dame
This peaceful and broad valley offers magnificent scenery with waterfalls and fast-flowing streams running from the glacier at its head.

ARVIER
VILLENEUVE
Ay
Ponde
Rhêmes-St-George
VAL DI RHÊMES
VALSAVARENCHE
Valsavarenche
Rhêmes-Notre-Dame
Eaux-Rousses
Pont
GRAN PARADISO
4,061 m
(13,320 ft)
Ceresole Reale

Cascata di Lillaz
This tall, dramatic waterfall, situated a little to the east of the rustic village of Lillaz, is best observed after the spring snow melt.

Visitors' Checklist

Piemonte and Valle d'Aosta. *Segreteria Turistica, Via Umberto I 1, Noasca (0124 90 10 70). Other information offices at Ceresole Reale & Cogne.* *Jul, Aug & public hols.* FS *Aosta & Pont Canavese.* *from Aosta or Pont Canavese to the different valleys.* **Paradisia Alpine Garden**, Valnontey, Cogne. *0165 740 40.* *mid-Jun–mid-Sep: daily.*

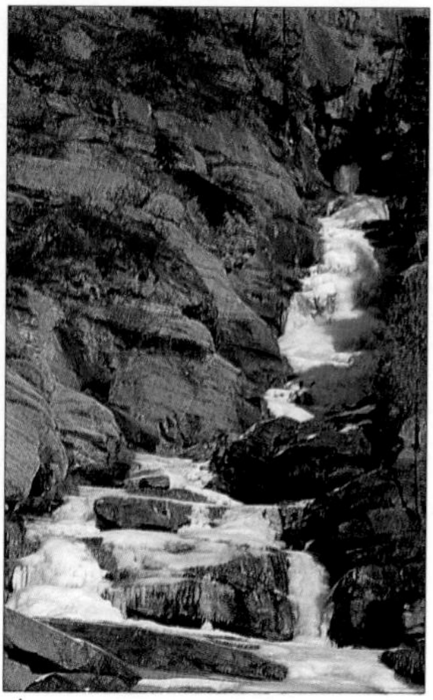

Cogne is the main resort and a good base from which to explore the park. Maps of the park's routes and trails are available here.

Lillaz is sedate and off the beaten track, while Valnontey and Cogne are two of the busiest resorts.

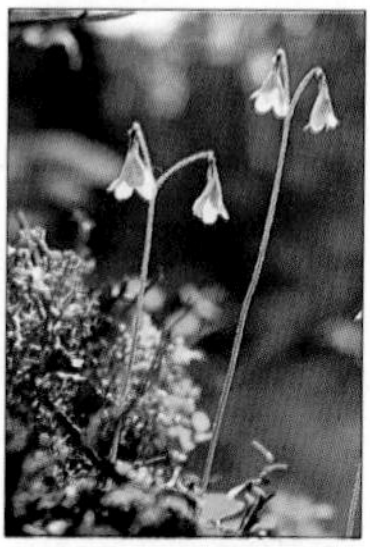

★ Paradisia Alpine Garden
The botanic garden contains a collection of Alpine plants, including the delicate "twinflower."

inel
Cogne
Lillaz
ey
VALLE DI PIANTONETTO
PONT CANAVESE
CUORGNE
PONT CANAVESE
CUORGNE
PONT CANAVESE
CUORGNE
0 kilometers 5
0 miles 5

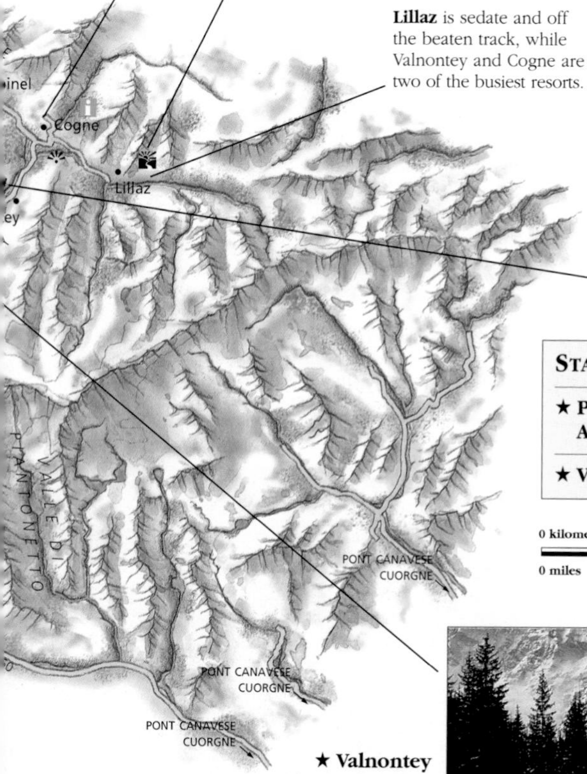

Star Sights

- ★ **Paradisia Alpine Garden**
- ★ **Valnontey**

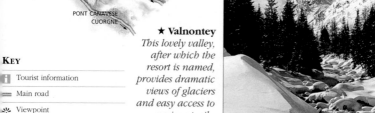

★ Valnontey
This lovely valley, after which the resort is named, provides dramatic views of glaciers and easy access to various trails.

Key

- Tourist information
- Main road
- Viewpoint

The small resort of Ceresole Reale
under winter snow

Lake Ceresole Reale **7**

Torino. 🚌 to Ceresole Reale. 🛈
Corso Vercelli 1, Ivrea (0125 61 81 31);
Comune di Ceresole (0124 95 31 21).

O N THE SOUTHERN, Piedmont side of the extensive Parco Nazionale del Gran Paradiso (*see pp208–9*) lies the small resort of Ceresole Reale, on the shores of a spectacular mountain lake. The route from Cuorgne goes through the rolling countryside of the Canavese and follows the N460 along a narrow gorge with a cascading stream. At **Noasca**, a magnificent waterfall may be seen high above the houses.

Ceresole Reale lies in a basin surrounded by meadows and forests of larch, and framed by mountains – the Gran Paradiso range to the north, Levanna to the southwest – which are reflected in the clear waters of the lake. The lake itself is actually a dammed reservoir, providing energy to supply Turin with electricity. This nevertheless unspoiled corner is a good base for walking, climbing, and hiking, and also offers facilities for skiing during the winter.

Via Lattea **8**

Torino. 🚊 Oulx. 🚌 to Sauze d'Oulx.
🛈 Via Pinerolo 14, Sestriere (0122 75 54 44).

T HE CLOSEST RING of mountain resorts to Turin, and as a result popular for weekend excursions, is known colloquially as the Via Lattea or "milky way." Villages like **Bardonecchia** and **Sauze d'Oulx** preserve traditional old stone and wood buildings that have been features of the region for centuries. The small church in Bardonecchia has, in addition, a fine 15th-century carved choir. In contrast, the supermodern complex at **Sestriere** has been specially built to accommodate skiers in winter and hikers in summer.

From Bardonecchia a chairlift operates some of the way up **Punta Colomion**, which rises immediately to the south of the resort. The summit, at 2,054 m (6,738 ft), offers fine views, and numerous hiking and walking possibilities.

Susa **9**

Torino. 🏠 7,000. 🚊 🚌 🛈 Corso Inghilterra 39 (0122 62 24 70). 🛒 Tue.

T HIS ATTRACTIVE mountain town flourished in Roman times: the **Arch of Augustus**, built in 8 BC and still standing, commemorates the alliance between the local Gallic

The impressive part-Roman
gateway, Porta Savoia, in Susa

chieftain and the Emperor Augustus. Other relics from the Roman period include two arches of an aqueduct, sections of an amphitheater, and traces of the old town walls. **Porta Savoia**, an imposing Roman gateway dating from the 4th century, was remodeled in the Middle Ages.

Most of the historic center of the town is medieval, including the castle of Countess Adelaide and the **duomo**, both originally 11th century. The duomo, much altered since then, houses a polyptych (c.1500) attributed to Bergognone, and a precious 14th-century Flemish triptych portraying the *Virgin and Saints*. South of the town lies the Gothic church of **San Francesco**, surrounded by an area of early medieval houses.

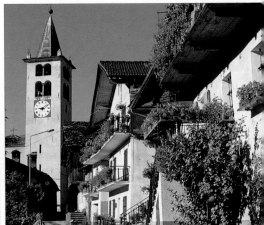

A street in the traditional village of Bardonecchia, on the Via Lattea

Carved capitals on the Porta dello Zodiaco at the Sacra di San Michele

Sacra di San Michele ⑩

Strada Sacra San Michele. 📞 *011 93 91 30.* 🚌 *Jul–Aug from Avigliana & Turin.* ⏰ *9:30am–12:30pm, 3–6pm Tue–Sun, call to arrange group visits.*

THIS SOMEWHAT forbidding abbey complex is perched on a ridge halfway up Monte Pirchiriano, at 962 m (3,156 ft). Its monastic community was founded around the year 1000, possibly on the site of a previous sanctuary, although the exterior looks every bit as much a fortress as the spiritual refuge that it was for 600 years.

During its prime, the abbey attracted pilgrims on their way to Rome, and as a result it grew enormously wealthy and powerful, controlling over 100 other abbeys in Italy, France, and Spain. It was also subsequently attacked and looted several times, despite being fortified, before falling into decline and eventually being suppressed in 1662.

The sanctuary is reached by climbing 154 steep steps hewn out of the rock, which offer wonderful views over the surrounding countryside and up to the Alps. At the very top of this stairway, known as the Scalone dei Morti (Stairway of the Dead), is the Romanesque Porta dello Zodiaco, a doorway profusely carved with creatures and symbols relating to the signs of the zodiac. Beyond the doorway a few more steps lead into the church itself, which dates from the 12th–13th centuries and incorporates traces of an earlier building. The interior houses 15th- and 16th-century paintings and

frescoes, and a 16th-century triptych by the Piedmontese artist Defendente Ferrari. The crypt holds the tombs of the early dukes and princes of the House of Savoy-Carignano.

Avigliana ⑪

Torino. 🚉 *9,500.* 🚆 🚌 ℹ️ *Piazza del Popolo 6 (011 932 86 50).* 🛒 *Thu.*

ON A FINE DAY, this small town perched beside two glacier-fed lakes and encircled by tall mountains looks breathtakingly beautiful. Avigliana is overlooked by a castle, first erected in the mid-10th century but now in ruins, which was once the home of the Counts of Savoy. Until the early 15th century, the town was one of their favorite bases.

The medieval houses here are largely unspoiled, particularly in the two main squares, Piazza Santa Maria and Piazza Conte Rosso. Other buildings of note are the Casa della Porta Ferrata and the 15th-century Casa dei Savoia botj on Via XX Settembre. The church of

San Giovanni (13th–14th century) contains early 16th-century paintings by Defendente Ferrari.

Pinerolo ⑫

Torino. 🚉 *36,000.* 🚆 🚌 ℹ️ *Viale Giolitti 7–9 (0121 79 55 89).* 🛒 *Wed & Sat.*

PINEROLO LIES in an attractive setting beside hills at the confluence of the Lemina and Chisone valleys. The town was the capital of the Acaia family, a branch of the House of Savoy, and in the 14th and 15th centuries it was known for the cultural atmosphere that prevailed here under the family's patronage. However, the town enjoyed none of the stability of Turin; it was occupied by the French five times between the 15th and 18th centuries. During the 17th century the French demolished many of the town's ancient buildings in order to make Pinerolo a defensive stronghold; among the political prisoners allegedly held here was the notorious "Man in the Iron Mask." Today the town is a busy center of commerce.

A number of monumental buildings do remain, however. The **duomo**, at the center of the town, was remodeled in Gothic style in the 15th–16th centuries and has a fine portal and an impressive bell tower. Via Principi d'Acaia climbs up to the 14th-century palace of the Princes of Acaia, and to the 15th-century church of **San Maurizio**, where the Acaia princes are buried; beside it rises a 14th-century bell tower.

The medieval arcades surrounding Piazza Conte Rosso in Avigliana

Turin ⓭

MENTION TURIN (Torino) and most people will think of industry and comfortable north Italian prosperity. It is certainly an economic powerhouse, but it is also a town of enormous grace and charm, with superb Baroque architecture and excellent museums, set against the dramatic scenery of the foothills of the Alps. Turin is also, of course, the home of the famous Turin Shroud, the Fiat car company, and the Juventus soccer team.

Statue of Emperor Augustus in front of the Roman Porta Palatina

Exploring Turin

Although settled by the Romans (**Porta Palatina** is an impressive 1st-century AD relic), and the seat of a university since the Middle Ages, Turin came into its own only after 1563, when Emanuele Filiberto of Savoy moved his capital here. Three centuries of steady prosperity ensued. Turin then became the power base for Italy's unification movement and, from 1861 to 1865, the capital of the newly united country. Subsequently its main

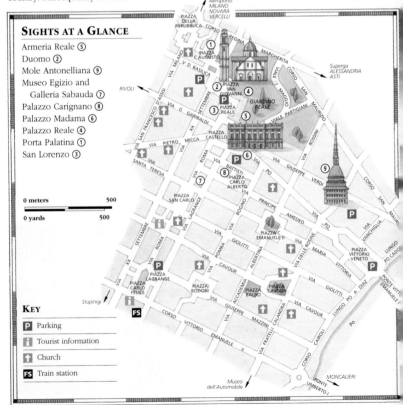

The Fiat car factory logo

power was economic. The car company **Fiat** (Fabbrica Italiana Automobili Torino), was established here in 1899 and grew to be one of the biggest firms in Europe. After World War II, Turin attracted thousands of poor Italians from the south who came to work in its factories. Though there have been social conflicts and labor disputes as a result, managers and workers do unite over soccer: the Juventus team is owned by the much-revered Fiat boss, Gianni Agnelli.

🔒 Duomo

Piazza San Giovanni. ☐ *daily.* ♿
The cathedral, built in 1497–8 and dedicated to St. John the Baptist, is the only example of Renaissance architecture in Turin. The sober square bell

---

SIGHTS AT A GLANCE

Armeria Reale ⑤
Duomo ②
Mole Antonelliana ⑨
Museo Egizio and
  Galleria Sabauda ⑦
Palazzo Carignano ⑧
Palazzo Madama ⑥
Palazzo Reale ④
Porta Palatina ①
San Lorenzo ③

0 meters   500
0 yards   500

KEY

🅿 Parking

ℹ Tourist information

✝ Church

FS Train station

Map labels: Aeroporto MILANO NOVARA VERCELLI, PIAZZA DELLA REPUBBLICA, CORSO REGINA MARGHERITA, PIAZZA C. AUGUSTO, VIA MILANO, V. D. BASILICA, VIA SETTEMBRE, VIA G. GARIBALDI, VIA S. FRANCESCO D'ASSISI, RIVOLI, PIAZZA SAN GIOVANNI, PIAZZA REALE, GIARDINO REALE, VIALE PARTIGIANI, VIA ROSSINI, CORSO SAN MAURIZIO, Superga ALESSANDRIA ASTI, VIA MAGGIO, VIALE, CORSO SAN MAURO, VIA XX SETTEMBRE, VIA PIETRO MICCA, SANTA TERESA, PIAZZA CASTELLO, VIA PO, VIA GIUSEPPE VERDI, VIA BATTISTI, PIAZZA CARLO ALBERTO, Mole Antonelliana, CORSO SAN, PIAZZA SAN CARLO, VIA PRINCIPE AMEDEO, VIA BOGINO, VIA LAGRANGE, PIAZZA C EMANUELE II, VIA ROMA, VIA SETTEMBRE, VIA POMBA, VIA GIOLITTI, VIA CAVOUR, VIA ALBERTINA, VIA DELLE ROSINE, VIA MARIA VITTORIA, PIAZZA VITTORIO VENETO, LUNGO PO DIORA, VIA VANCHIGLIA, PIAZZA CARLO FELICE, PIAZZA LAGRANGE, VIA ACCADEMIA, PIAZZA BODONI, PIAZZA BALBO, PIAZZA CAVOUR, VIA CAVOUR, LUNGO PO V. DIAZ, PONTE V. EMANUELE I, Stupinigi, CORSO VITTORIO EMANUELE II, VIA GIUSEPPE MAZZINI, VIA FRATELLI CALANDRA, CORSO CAIROLI, PONTE UMBERTO I, MONCALIERI, Museo dell'Automobile

---

The 15th-century duomo, with the Cappella della Sacra Sindone beyond

VISITORS' CHECKLIST

1,000,000. ✈ Caselle 15 km (9 miles) N. **FS** Porta Nuova, Piazza Carlo-Felice. Porta Susa, Piazza XVIII Dicembre. 🚌 Corso Inghilterra. **i** Piazza dei Castello 161 (011 53 51 81). Stazione entrance, Porta Nuova (011 53 51 81). 🏛 Sat. 🎭 Jun 24: Festa di San Giovanni.

tower, which predates the rest of the church by 30 years, stands in refreshing contrast to Turin's sumptuous Baroque buildings; its top was designed by Filippo Juvarra in 1720. Inside, the Duomo is heavy with statuary and paintings. Through a black marble arch on the right side of the church is the **Cappella della Sacra Sindone** (Chapel of the Holy Shroud), which is actually incorporated into the Palazzo Reale (see p216). The chapel is a remarkable feat, designed by Guarino Guarini (1624–83) with an extraordinary meshlike cupola; the exterior view is equally eccentric. On top of the altar is the urn containing the famous Shroud.

🏛 Palazzo Madama
Piazza Castello.
⬤ for restoration.

Turin's main square once contained a medieval castle that incorporated elements of the original Roman city walls. The castle was later enlarged and remodeled, and a new façade by Juvarra was added, at the request of a royal widow, in the 18th century. The Palazzo Madama – as it was subsequently renamed – now sits in the center of the square with a stately, balustraded façade.

The interior, with its grand staircase and first floor, both designed by Juvarra, is home to the **Museo Civico d'Arte Antica**. This extensive collection contains treasures that range in date from the Greco-Roman era to the 19th century. The display includes the famous and mysterious Portrait of an Unknown Man by Antonello da Messina (15th century) among the paintings and sculptures, and reproductions of the Duc de Berry's beautiful Book of Hours from c.1420. Other sections contain displays of jewelry, majolica, and glass, complementing the textiles and furniture.

The façade of the Palazzo Madama, designed by Filippo Juvarra in 1718–21

THE TURIN SHROUD

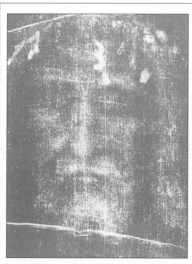

Detail of the mysterious 12th-century Turin Shroud

The most famous – and most dubious – holy relic of them all is kept in Turin's duomo. The shroud, said to be the winding-sheet in which the body of Christ was wrapped after his crucifixion, owes its fame to the fact that the shroud bears the imprint of a crucified man with a wound in his side, and bruises from what might have been a crown of thorns.

The shroud is one of the most famous medieval relics. Its early history is unclear, but the House of Savoy was in possession of it around 1450 and had it displayed in Guarini's chapel from 1694. The "original" shroud – which sits in a silver casket inside an iron box within a marble coffer inside the urn on the chapel altar – is not on view, though a replica is, together with a welter of scientific explanations as to the shroud's possible origins. In 1988, however, the myth of the shroud was exploded: a carbon-dating test showed that it dates back no farther than the 12th century. The shroud nevertheless remains an object of religious veneration.

Exploring Turin

THE CITY OF TURIN IS BLESSED with numerous interesting museums, which are housed in splendid palazzi and civic buildings. The center itself is relatively small, with broad, straight streets, often bordered with historic cafés and shops, which are pleasant places to stroll along. The city is also famous for its innovative cuisine and boasts some of the country's finest restaurants.

Granite statue of Ramses II (13th century BC) in the Museo Egizio

🏛 Museo Egizio
Via Accademia delle Scienze 6.
📞 011 561 77 76. ◯ Tue–Sun.
⬤ Jan 1, May 1, Dec 25. 🈂

Turin owes its magnificent Egyptian Museum – one of the most important in the world – largely to the Piedmont-born Bernardo Drovetti, who was stationed in Egypt as French Consul General at the time of the Napoleonic Wars. It was the booty he brought back that formed the basis of this very fine collection of Egyptian artifacts. On the ground floor, the items on display include monumental sculptures and reconstructed temples; upstairs, there are collections of papyrus and everyday objects. Among the most impressive sculptures are a black granite Ramses II (13th century BC, or 19th dynasty), the slightly earlier Amenophis II, and the basalt figure of Gemenef-Har-Bak, a vizier from the 26th dynasty. The Sala della Nubia contains a breath-taking reconstruction of the 15th-century BC **Rock Temple of Ellessiya**.

Extraordinary wall and tomb paintings are displayed on the upper floor, together with items of daily use such as the tools used for measuring, weaving, fishing, and hunting. The 14th-century BC Tomb of Kha and Merit, complete with the food, tools, and ornaments buried with them for the afterlife, is particularly fascinating. The papyrus collection is beautiful and of enormous interest to scholars: these documents have been vital to modern under-standing of Egyptian language, customs, and history – one document, the *Papiro dei Re* (Royal Papyrus), crucially lists all the pharaohs up to the 17th dynasty, with their dates.

G Ferrari's *St. Peter and a Donor* (16th century), Galleria Sabauda

🏛 Galleria Sabauda
Via Accademia delle Scienze 6.
📞 011 54 74 40. ◯ Tue–Sat am,
Sun. 🈂 ♿

The Palazzo dell'Accademia delle Scienze, the building by Guarini in which the Egyptian Museum is housed, is also home to the House of Savoy's main painting collection. The top two floors are the setting for a stunning array of works by Italian, French, Flemish, and Dutch masters.

The collection was originally begun in the second half of the 15th century and has been expanded over the centuries since. It is grouped in regional schools and contains a section on Piedmontese painting, which is not often represented in other galleries: it includes masterpieces by Gaudenzio Ferrari (c.1480–1546) and two early 16th-century paintings by Defendente Ferrari. Among works of particular interest from other Italian schools are Antonio and Piero Pollaiuolo's 15th-century *Tobias and the*

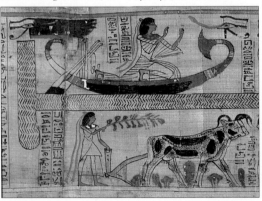

Detail from an 18th-dynasty papyrus Book of the Dead, Museo Egizio

Archangel Raphael,
and the *Ritratto di
Gentiluomo* (portrait
of a nobleman) by
Bronzino. Bellini,
Mantegna, and
Veronese are
among other Italian
artists represented.

The section on
Dutch and Flemish
art includes works
such as Jan Van Eyck's *St.
Francis* (15th century) and
Rembrandt's *Old Man Sleeping* (17th century), as well as
portraits by Van Dyck, which
include a study of Charles I's
children, and his *Principe
Tommaso di Savoia-Carignano*
(1634). Among the French
works on display are 17th-
century landscape paintings
by Claude Lorrain and Poussin.

🏛 Palazzo Carignano

Via Accademia delle Scienze 5.
📞 011 562 11 47. 🕐 Tue–Sun.
🔴 Jan 1, Dec 25. 🏷 &

The main façade of Palazzo Carignano by Guarini

This Baroque palazzo is not
only Guarini's masterpiece, it
is arguably the finest building
in Turin, with its magnificent
brick façade and ornate rotunda. It was built in 1679 for the
Carignano family – an offshoot
of the main House of Savoy
and ancestors of the Italian
kings – but came into its own
in the 19th century, when the
first king of Italy, Vittorio
Emanuele II, was born here in
1829. After Italy was unified
in 1861 by a series of referenda,
the former residence was
used as the first national
parliament building.

The palazzo is now home
to the **Museo Nazionale del
Risorgimento**, which through
paintings and a collection of
artifacts (housed in the rooms
where history was made), tells
the story of unification. It introduces Mazzini, Cavour, and
Garibaldi – key figures in the
Risorgimento (*see pp58–9*).

🚇 Via Roma

Via Roma is Turin's main
street, running through the
heart of the historic center. It
leads from Piazza Castello at
its northern end down through
Piazza San Carlo to the distinctive arched façade of Stazione
Porta Nuova, which forms a
focal point at the southern
end. The station was built in
1868 and looks out over the
green and pleasant gardens
of the 19th-century Piazza
Carlo Felice. The square is
framed by shops and cafés
and provides an excellent
vista up Via Roma
from a calm vantage
point. Via Roma
itself is a magni-
ficent concourse
lined with stylish
shops and shaded
arcades, interrupted
only by cobbled
squares, crisscrossed
by streetcar tracks.
A grid pattern of side streets
branches off either side of Via
Roma, revealing additional
shopping arcades.

🚇 Piazza San Carlo

This square halfway along Via
Roma comprises an ensemble
of Baroque architecture so
sophisticated as to earn it the
nickname of "Turin's drawing
room." At the southern end rise
the twin churches of Santa
Cristina and San Carlo; both
were built in the 1630s, but
Santa Cristina has a Baroque
façade, crowned with statues,
which was designed by Juvarra
in the early 18th century.

At the center of the square
stands a 19th-century statue of
Emanuele Filiberto resheathing
his sword. The work, by Carlo
Marocchetti, has become an
emblem of the city. At the
corners of the square, frescoes
depict the Holy Shroud. The
Galleria San Federico, in the
square's northwestern corner,
is a stylish shopping arcade.

Piazza San Carlo is known
for its society cafés. In one
such establishment, in 1786,
Antonio Benedetto Carpano
invented the drink known as
vermouth, which is still very
popular in Turin today.

🌿 Parco del Valentino

Corso Massimo D'Azeglio. 🕐 *daily.*
Borgo Medioevale 📞 011 669
93 72. 🕐 *daily.* **Orto Botanico**
🕐 *Jun–Sep: Sat & Sun.* 🏷 &
This park beside the river contains the **Borgo Medioevale**,
a complex of buildings
resembling a medieval village
and castle, which was built
for an exhibition in the late
1880s. The buildings show
different types of design and
construction, based on traditional houses and castles,
which can be found scattered
throughout Piedmont and in
the Valle d'Aosta.

The **Orto Botanico**, beside
the medieval complex, is an
impressive botanical garden
in a pleasant setting.

Looking south across the elegant Piazza San Carlo, "Turin's drawing room"

Spacious arcades on Turin's lively Via Roma

Turin: Symbols of the City

Turin's architecture mirrors the city's transition from monarchic power to industrial power. Witness the ostentation of the Baroque apartments of the Savoy royal family and contrast them with the futuristic Mole Antonelliana, a tall structure which heralded the dawn of the modern industrial age. Much of Turin's history in the 20th century has been dominated by the car: Fiat made Turin its home and, despite some industrial unrest, the city's workers replied by rewarding it with success. For the curious, Turin's automobile museum is worth a visit, since it maps out the history of Italian car design.

The 19th-century tower, Mole Antonelliana, dominating Turin

🏛 Mole Antonelliana
Via Montebello 20. 📞 011 817 20 80.
⬤ for restoration. 🖾

This eccentric building is the Turin equivalent of the Eiffel Tower in Paris: a tall, unique landmark that serves no clear purpose except perhaps to act as a signature for the city as a whole. It looks a bit like a glorified lightning conductor; indeed an electric storm struck down the top 47 m (154 ft) in 1954, which was then replaced. The 167-m (548-ft) Mole, by Alessandro Antonelli (1798–1888), was originally planned to be a synagogue, but the city finished it in 1897 and used it to house the Risorgimento museum. The Mole ("massive structure") – for a time the tallest building in the world – became a symbol of Italian unity. Latterly used as an exhibition hall, the building is now the Cinema Museum, designed with the help of British director Peter Greenaway.

Inside the dome of San Lorenzo

🏛 Palazzo Reale
Piazzetta Reale. 📞 011 436 14 55.
🕙 Tue–Sun. ⬤ Jan 1, May 1, Dec 25. 🖾 📷

The Palazzo Reale was the seat of the Savoy royal family from 1660 until the unification of Italy in 1861. Behind the austere façade, designed by Amedeo di Castellamonte, lie richly decorated state apartments – the ceilings were painted by Morello, Miel, and Seyter in the 17th century. The many splendid furnishings, tapestries, and ornaments date from the 17th to the 19th centuries; they include the elaborate Chinese Cabinet, the Alcove Room, the lavishly decorated Throne Room, and the innovative Scala delle Forbici, or Scissor Stairs, created by Juvarra in 1720. Behind the palace are extensive gardens, which extend northward.

To the left of the main entrance to the palace is **San Lorenzo**. This fine Baroque building, begun in 1634 is by architect Guarino Guarini, its ornate interior boasting another of his extraordinary geometric domes.

🏛 Armeria Reale
Piazza Castello 191. 📞 011 54 38 89.
🕙 Tue–Sat am (also Tue & Thu pm).
⬤ Jan 1, May 1, Aug 15, Dec 25. 🖾

One wing of the Palazzo Reale, on the northern side of the main square, provides the splendid setting for one of the most extensive and breathtaking collections of arms and armory in the world.

The armory originally belonged to the House of Savoy, and was opened to the public in 1837. The fine rooms, such as the splendid Galleria Beaumont, designed by Juvarra in 1733, hold treasures ranging in date from Roman and Etruscan times to the 19th century. The collection has some particularly magnificent medieval and Renaissance items from some of the greatest armorers and gunsmiths in the world, including a pistol of Charles V. One section is devoted largely to Oriental arms and armor.

The adjoining but separate Royal Library contains a collection of drawings and manuscripts, including a self-portrait by Leonardo da Vinci.

ENVIRONS: About 3 km (2 miles) out of the city center lies a colossal hall built in the 1960s for the famous **Museo dell'Automobile**. Founded by two automotive pioneers in 1933, it now houses 150 veteran, vintage, and classic cars. The collection includes

A lavishly decorated gallery in the 17th-century Palazzo Reale, a royal home until unification

glorious Bugattis, Maseratis, Lancias, Fiats, and also a number of fine foreign cars. The first gasoline-driven car made in Italy (1896) is kept here, as well as the first Fiat (1899) and the 1929 Isotta Fraschini *coupé de ville* that was used to transport Gloria Swanson in the Hollywood film *Sunset Boulevard*. Note also that a large number of the sports cars from the 1950s have the steering wheel on the right; this brief trend was in deference to the great British car makers such as Aston Martin.

There is also a library and a documentation center which are both open to the public.

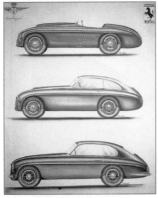

Designs from 1949 for the Ferrari 166 MM

🏛 **Museo dell'Automobile**
Corso Unità d'Italia 40. 📞 *011 67 76 66.* 🔘 *Tue–Sun.* ⬤ *Jan 1, Dec 25.*
♿

Stupinigi ⓮

Piazza Principe Amedeo 7, Stupinigi.
📞 *011 358 12 20.* 🚌 *63 to Piazza Caio Mario & then 41.*
🔘 *Tue–Sun.* ♿

An interior view of the 18th-century Palazzina di Caccia di Stupinigi

I N 1729–30 THE ARCHITECT Filippo Juvarra (1676–1736) designed the magnificent hunting lodge of Stupinigi – known as the Palazzina di Caccia di Stupinigi – at a beautiful location 9 km (5 miles) southwest of Turin. It was created for Vittorio

Amedeo II and is one of the very finest hunting lodges, built on an impressive scale, reminiscent of the palace of Versailles in France.

The dynamic and complex plan incorporates semicircles and an octagon, with the main block consisting of a dome rising above a circular building from which wings jut out, not unlike the arms of a windmill.

The mass of the central section is lightened by balustrading topped with urns and figures, while the dome is crowned with an 18th-century bronze figure of a stag.

The huge interior includes rooms sumptuously decorated with *trompe l'oeil* paintings and frescoes on a hunting theme – the 18th-century *Triumph of Diana*, for instance, in the main *salone*. About 40 of those rooms house the interesting **Museo d'Arte e di Ammobiliamento**, a museum specializing in 17th- and 18th-century furniture and furnishings. Many of the ornate items on display in these rooms were originally kept in other former royal residences.

Outside there are extensive grounds, which feature an elegant combination of spectacular broad avenues, parkland, and colorful formal parterres.

Basilica di Superga ⓯

Strada Basilica di Superga 73, Comune di Torino. 📞 *011 898 00 83.* 🚋
Sassi. 🚋 *79 from Sassi.* 🔘 *May–Sep: 9am–noon, 3–6pm; Oct–Apr: 10am–noon, 3–5pm.* ⬤ *Sep 8.*
Tombs 🔘 *Fri, public hols.* **Donation**.

O N A HILL to the east of Turin, reachable by car or by train, stands the superb Baroque basilica of Superga, built by Juvarra in 1717–31. The commission came from Duke Vittorio Amedeo II, in fulfillment of a vow made to the Virgin Mary in 1706 while the French were besieging the duke and his army in Turin.

The beautiful yellow and white façade is dominated by a large portico designed like a Classical temple, with a 65 m- (213 ft-) high dome immediately beyond. It is flanked by twin bell towers on either side. The interior is magnificent, decorated in light blue and yellow, and contains numerous fine paintings and carvings.

Underneath the basilica lies the great mausoleum that houses the tombs of the kings, princes, and princesses of Savoy from the 18th and 19th centuries. Turin's 1949 aircrash victims, including the city's soccer team, are also remembered on a plaque behind the basilica.

One of the other benefits of visiting the basilica is seeing the views over Turin.

The imposing façade of the 18th-century Baroque Basilica di Superga designed by Filippo Juvarra

The 17th-century Basilica dell'Assunta dominating Sacro Monte, Varallo

Santuario d'Oropa ⑯

Via Santuario d'Oropa 480, Comune di Biella. 📞 015 245 59 20. 🚆 Biella. 🚌 from Biella. 🔘 daily. ♿

ERCHED ABOVE the wool town of Biella stands the tranquil church and hospice complex of Oropa, a series of three squares surrounded by pale buildings with stone-shingled roofs, cut into the forested hillside.

The sanctuary, which dates largely from the 17th and 18th centuries, was originally founded in the 4th century by Sant' Eusebio, Bishop of Vercelli. It was intended as a hospice for the poor and to honor the "Black Madonna," which he had brought back from the Holy Land. The Madonna, said to be the work of St. Luke himself, is the object of some of the biggest and most important pilgrimages in the region.

The statue of the Madonna is kept in the restored **Chiesa Vecchia** (Old Church), whose façade was designed by Filippo Juvarra (1676–1736). Beyond it, at the top of the complex, rises the imposing mass of the Neo-Classical **Chiesa Nuova** (New Church), which was begun in 1885 but completed only in 1960.

Behind this church, a foot-path leads to the cable car up to Monte Mucrone, from where there is good walking countryside and a small, attractive mountain lake. On a hill

southwest of the complex stand 16 chapels, a dozen of which date from between 1620 and 1720. They contain frescoed scenes which depict the life of the Virgin.

Domodossola ⑰

Verbania. 🏘 20,000. 🚆 🚌 ℹ️ Stazione entrance, Piazza Matteotti 24 (0324 24 82 65). 🔘 Sat.

OMODOSSOLA is an attractive mountain town of Roman origin. At its center lies the **Piazza Mercato**, or market square, framed by arcades and houses dating from the 15th and 16th centuries.

The Ossola valley, where the town lies, sits in an Alpine landscape of pasture and forest sliced by rivers and streams, dotted with dams. Pretty villages north of Domodossola include the resort of **Crodo**, with its cold-water mineral spas, and **Baceno**, where the 14th–16th century church – the most important in the region – contains fine frescoes and wood carvings.

Farther north still, the Antigorio and Formazza valleys are planted with fig trees and vineyards. Just before La Frua, spectacular waterfalls from the River Toce drop 145 m (476 ft) when the waters are not being harnessed for power. The idyllic wooded Valle Vigezzo, east of Domodossola, offers breathtaking scenery.

Varallo ⑱

Vercelli. 🏘 7,900. 🚆 🚌 ℹ️ Corso Roma 38 (0163 512 80). 🔘 Tue.

HE SMALL TOWN and tourist resort of Varallo lies half-way up the attractive Sesia valley and boasts a remarkable church, **Santa Maria delle Grazie**. The late 15th-century church is notable for its beautiful frescoed wall depicting the Life of Christ and *trompe l'oeil* architectural elements; the paintings are the work of Gaudenzio Ferrari (1484–1546).

A long stairway behind the church (and also a cableway) climbs up to the even more extraordinary **Sacro Monte**, a religious community built at an altitude of about 610 m (2,000 ft). This "Sacred Mount" was founded as a sanctuary of the New Jerusalem in 1486 and sponsored by the Archbishop of Milan, San Carlo Borromeo.

The Basilica dell'Assunta, with a 19th-century façade, is set in a tranquil courtyard with palm trees and a fountain; the interior is a riot of ornate Baroque architecture. Dotted around it are more than 40 chapels representing the sacred sites of Jerusalem, with statues and painted figures placed in front of frescoed backdrops painted by Gaudenzio Ferrari, Tanzio da Varallo, and others.

Christ Condemned (16th century) in a chapel at Varallo's Sacro Monte

The interior of the church of San Giulio in the middle of Lake Orta

Lake Orta ⑲

Novara. FS 🚌 ⛴ *Orta.*
🛈 *Via Olina 9/11, Orta San Giulio (0322 91 19 37).*

L AKE ORTA IS ONE of Italy's least visited lakes – unjustly, since it is delightfully set among the foothills of the Alps.

The lake's main resort is **Orta San Giulio**, a small town with a historic center containing handsome palazzi and houses decorated with wrought-iron balconies. In the lakeside **Piazza Principale** stands the Palazzo della Comunità, a frescoed building of 1582 resting on arcades. At the top of a mound stands the 15th-century church of **Santa Maria Assunta** (rebuilt in the 17th century), with a Romanesque doorway and an interior that is richly decorated with 17th-century frescoes and paintings.

Above Orta San Giulio is the sanctuary of **Sacro Monte**, built from 1591 to 1770 and dedicated to St. Francis of Assisi. A winding path, offering lovely views of the lake, climbs to the church. The path is lined by 21 chapels, most of them Baroque, in which frescoes and life-size figure groups by various artists depict scenes from the life of St. Francis.

In the middle of the lake rises the picturesque **Isola San Giulio**. The island was said to have been liberated from snakes and monsters by the 4th-century Christian preacher Julius, from whom the island's name derives. A basilica stands on the island to this day; it is notable for its 12th-century black marble pulpit decorated with wild animals and birds, and for the 15th-century frescoes – including one attributed to Gaudenzio Ferrari, of the *Virgin and Child Enthroned.*

Novara ⑳

🏛 *105,000.* FS 🚌 🛈 *Corso Cavour 2 (0321 39 40 59).* 🛒 *Mon, Thu & Sat.*

Fresco detail of a horseman (17th century) by Morazzone in San Gaudenzio, Novara

N OVARA HAS DISTANT origins as the Roman city of Nubliaria – meaning "misty air." Nowadays its delightful arcaded streets and squares, and historic buildings, exude a quiet affluence. Many of the most important buildings stand around Piazza della Repubblica. They include the beautiful Renaissance courtyard of the **Broletto** (town hall), which attracts many art students who come to sketch its graceful 15th-century red-brick arcades and covered stairway. The buildings now house a small **Museo Civico**, comprising an archaeological section, a picture gallery, and a modern art gallery.

Across the piazza rises the **duomo**, rebuilt by the architect Alessandro Antonelli in about 1865 in Neo-Classical style, with a huge central doorway. The interior contains dramatic Renaissance paintings of the Vercelli school and Flemish tapestries, as well as the remains of an earlier sanctuary on this site: these include the frescoed 12th-century chapel of San Siro and the 15th-century cloisters. The octagonal **baptistry** next door dates in part from the 5th century and is painted with medieval frescoed scenes of the Apocalypse.

A few streets away stands the church of **San Gaudenzio**. It is strikingly crowned by an elongated four-tiered dome and spire designed by Antonelli, and reminiscent of his Mole Antonelliana in Turin *(see p216).* At the top of the spire, which is 121 m (397 ft) high, is a statue of San Gaudenzio himself. Inside the late 16th-century church is a fine collection of Renaissance and Baroque paintings by artists from Piedmont: these include a notable 17th-century battle scene by Tanzio da Varallo, a 16th-century altarpiece by Gaudenzio Ferrari, and a fresco painting by Pier Francesco Morazzone (c.1572–1626).

🏛 **Museo Civico**
Via Fratelli Rosselli 20. 📞 *0321 62 70 37.* 🕐 *Tue–Sun.* ⚫ *public hols.* 🖼
🔒 **Baptistry**
Piazza della Repubblica. 📞 *0321 66 16 71.* 🕐 *ask at the Curia Arcivescovile.*

View across Lake Orta to the Isola San Giulio

Vercelli ㉑

🏛 *50,000.* 🚉 🚌 ℹ️ *Viale Garibaldi 90 (0161 25 78 88).* 🗓 *Tue & Fri.*

VERCELLI IS THE RICE capital of Europe, set in a vast plain of paddy fields that produce millions of plates of risotto each year. The paddies provide a sight of shimmering sheets of water stretching far into the distance. Vercelli itself also developed its own school of painting in the 16th century, and has one major architectural treasure, the 13th-century **Basilica di Sant'Andrea**.

The Basilica, standing just across from the train station, is famous as the first example of Italian architecture to be influenced by the Gothic style of northern France – note the beautiful vaulted nave and the flying buttresses, typical Gothic elements. Overall, however, the Basilica remains a stunning achievement in Romanesque architecture, built from 1219 to 1227 as part of an abbey for the papal legate Cardinal Guala Bicheri. The façade, curiously, changes color halfway up, the blue-gray of the lower part turning to red and white in the twin towers; these are linked by a double arcade. A carving attributed to Antelami (12th century) adorns the central lunette.

The three-aisled interior is gently illuminated through rose windows. The muted decoration is largely focused on the vaulting, which is supported by tall, slender shafts. Off the north side is the simple 13th-century cloister, beautifully framed by arcades rising from clustered columns.

Vercelli's other important historic buildings are not far away, including the imposing 16th-century **duomo**, the **Ospedale Maggiore** (13th century), and the church of **San Cristoforo**, with frescoes and a particularly fine Madonna (both c.1529) painted by Gaudenzio Ferrari. The **Museo Civico Borgogna** is the best place to admire the masterpieces of the Vercelli school. The main shopping street, Corso Libertà, has a handful of attractive 15th-century houses and courtyards.

🏛 Museo Civico Borgogna

Via Antonio Borgogna 8. 📞 *0161 25 27 76.* 🕐 *Tue–Fri pm, Sat & Sun am.* ⬤ *Jan 1, Aug 15, Nov 1, Dec 25.* 💶 ✍️

The 13th-century cloisters of the Basilica di Sant'Andrea in Vercelli

Asti ㉒

🏛 *74,000.* 🚉 🚌 ℹ️ *Piazza Alfieri 34 (0141 53 03 57).* 🗓 *Wed & Sat.*

MOST OFTEN ASSOCIATED only with sweet *spumante* (sparkling) wine, Asti is in fact at the center of Italy's most prestigious wine region *(see*

Detail of the carving on the 15th-century porch at the entrance to the duomo in Asti

pp176–7) and also a tranquil and noble city of medieval towers, elegant churches, and warm red roofs.

Just north of the main train station lies the Piazza del Campo del Palio, the largest square in Asti and formerly the site of its annual horse race, now in Piazza Alfieri. The race, held toward the end of September to coincide with the local wine fair, rivals the Palio in Siena *(see p331)* for outrageous horsemanship and medieval pageantry.

Beyond this square lies the triangular-shaped **Piazza Alfieri**. A statue here commemorates the local poet and dramatist Vittorio Alfieri (1749–1803), in whose honor both this square and the main street were renamed.

Corso Alfieri runs the entire length of the old city center. At its eastern end stands the 15th-century church of **San Pietro in Consavia**, with its terra-cotta decoration, 17th-century frescoes, and attractive cloister. Beside it is the circular Romanesque **baptistry** which dates from the 10th–12th centuries; it was once the church of the knights of the Order of St. John of Jerusalem, who had their headquarters here.

West of Piazza Alfieri is the **Collegiata di San Secondo**, (13th–15th century) named after Asti's patron saint, which houses a Renaissance polyptych by Gandolfino d'Asti and 15th-century frescoes. The area around the western section of Corso Alfieri contains a few of the medieval towers for which the town was once famous; they include the Torre dei Comentini, the very elegant Torre Troyana, and at the far

The watery expanses of the rice fields around Vercelli

end, the Torre Ropa. This was built on the ruins of a tower in which San Secondo, a Roman soldier, was held. The nearby 14th-century Gothic **duomo** has a 15th-century porch and, inside, 18th-century frescoes, stoups made from ancient capitals, and two 12th- to 13th-century carvings on the west corner of the transept.

Cuneo ㉓

🏛 *56,000.* 🚉 🚌 ℹ️ *Corso Nizza 17 (0171 69 32 58).* 🛒 *Tue.*

Cuneo derives its name from *cumeo*, meaning wedge-shaped, which describes the sliver of land that the town occupies at the confluence of two rivers, the Gesso and the Stura di Demonte. In early November the town hosts the regional cheese fair, with unusual local cheese varieties.

The market town centers on an enormous main square, **Piazza Galimberti**, with its old arcades, where the traders come to hawk their wares every Tuesday. Much of the town was rebuilt in the 18th and 19th centuries, providing Cuneo with wide, tree-lined boulevards, though the impressive viaduct which takes the railroad line into town dates from the 1930s. The deconsecrated 13th-century church of **San Francesco** has a fine 15th-century portal. The 18th-century church of **Santa Croce** has an unusual concave façade by Francesco Gallo.

Cuneo is a good base for exploring the pretty local valleys, such as the Valle Stura where rare flowers grow.

The Castello di Casotto in the hills above the resort of Garessio

Bossea ㉔

Località Bossea, Comune Frabosa Soprana. 📞 *0174 34 92 40.* 🚉 *Mondovì.* 🚌 *from Mondovì.* 🕐 *daily for guided tours only.* 📷

Some 25 km (16 miles) south of Mondovì, near the end of a scenic route that follows the valley of the Torrente Corsaglia up into the Maritime Alps, are the caves of Bossea, some of the finest in all Italy. The series of caves contain remarkable and beautiful stalactite columns and shapes that have formed over many thousands of years. Guided tours lead through different chambers – some of them surprisingly vast – following the underground rivers and lakes. The skeleton of a prehistoric bear, *Ursus spelaeus*, which was discovered in the caves, may also be seen on display.

Bring a sweater – the temperature rarely rises above 9° C (48° F).

Garessio ㉕

Cuneo. 🏛 *4,000.* 🚉 🚌 ℹ️ *Piazza Carrara 131 (0174 811 22).* 🛒 *Fri.*

One of the prettier resorts of the Maritime Alps, Garessio is no more than a sprinkling of houses spread out over the hills, surrounded by woods of chestnut trees. It is also a popular spa.

According to local legend, the waters here have miraculous powers: in about AD 980 an octogenarian nobleman called Aleramo found instant relief from his painful kidney and circulatory problems by drinking the mineral-rich water. Since then, the waters have been drunk for their remedial properties – linked in particular with the relief of diuretic and digestive problems – and for their refreshing taste.

Environs: About 10 km (4 miles) west of Garessio stands the **Castello di Casotto**, the dramatically sited summer palace used by the House of Savoy. The royal family used to come here to enjoy the local mineral water, the attractive scenery, and the exceptionally pure air of the hills.

The town of **Ormea**, 12 km (7 miles) southwest, is interesting for its ruined 11th-century castle, its church with late 14th-century Gothic frescoes, and its attractive houses.

♠ **Castello di Casotto**
Garessio. 📞 *0174 35 11 31.* 🕐 *daily.* 📷

Market day in the enormous Piazza Galimberti at the center of Cuneo

LIGURIA

LIGURIA IS MADE UP OF A THIN COASTAL STRIP *nestling at the foot of vine-covered mountains. Here pastel-colored houses bask in the Mediterranean sun, while their gardens, enhanced by the mild climate, are a riot of colorful plants. In contrast with resorts like Portofino and even San Remo, the bustling city of Genoa, for centuries a trading port of immense power, is the only major population center.*

Genoa has a long history as a seafaring power, achieving greatness first as a trading post with ancient Greece and Phoenicia, and later as the capital of a small commercial empire that at one stage eclipsed even Venice. The great sea admiral Andrea Doria came from Genoa, as did the 15th-century explorer of the Americas, Christopher Columbus.

Genoa's rise began in the 12th century, when it succeeded in beating back the Saracen pirates that plagued the Ligurian coast. From then on, the maritime republic prospered, profiting from the Crusades to set up trading posts in the Middle East and marshaling its naval might to humble its rivals. The golden age lasted from the 16th to the mid-17th century, and included the glorious reign of Andrea Doria, who enriched the city by financing the wars of Genoa's European allies through the offices of the city's bank. Factionalism among the ruling aristocracy, however, and foreign conquest, by the French in 1668 and the Austrians in 1734, led to the region's decline. It was only in the early 19th century, with unification fervor spreading (thanks to native son Giuseppe Mazzini and the revolutionary Garibaldi), that Liguria ever recaptured a glimpse of its former prominence. Today, sheltered by the steep slopes that rise up from the sea, houses of faded elegance lie all along the coast, particularly in San Remo, where aristocrats came to spend the winter at the end of the 19th century.

Green shutters and rich ocher walls characterize the houses of Portofino

◁ **Rugged cliffs tumble into the sea along Liguria's Riviera Levante**

Exploring Liguria

Liguria divides neatly into two parts. The western coastline, known as the Riviera Ponente, is a thin strip of coastal plain stretching across to the French border, while the eastern coastline, or Riviera Levante, is more rugged and picturesque, descending directly into the sea. Between the two lengths of coast lies the region's capital and biggest port, Genoa (Genova). The faded elegance of the tranquil coastal villages contrasts with this cramped and busy port that snakes along the coast, hemmed in between the sea and the mountains rising steeply behind it.

Stag motif of the city of Cervo, above the cathedral doors

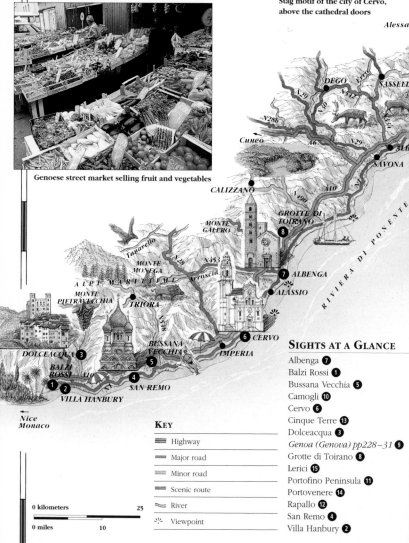

Genoese street market selling fruit and vegetables

Sights at a Glance

Key

Highway

Major road

Minor road

Scenic route

River

Viewpoint

0 kilometers   25

0 miles   10

Nice
Monaco →

The stylish resort of San Remo on the Riviera Ponente, west of Genoa

See Also

- **Where to Stay** pp554–5
- **Where to Eat** pp589

Houses wedged into the cliffs in Riomaggiore, Cinque Terre

GETTING AROUND

If you keep to the coast, travel in Liguria is straightforward. The A10 highway, becoming the A12 at Genoa, and a mainline railroad hug the shore from the French border to Tuscany. The main stations along the route are at Ventimiglia, San Remo, Imperia, Savona, Genoa, and La Spezia. There are good road and rail links between Genoa and Milan and Turin. Access to inland Liguria is harder because of the mountains. Bus services link many of the coastal towns with lovely hill villages. If you have a car you can explore some of the countryside by following the smaller routes, such as the N28 from Imperia toward Garessio in Piedmont, the N334 from Albisola, or the N456 from Voltri toward Milan.

The spectacular gardens of the
Villa Hanbury near Ventimiglia

Balzi Rossi ❶

Imperia. **FS** *Ventimiglia & Mentone.*
*from Ventimiglia to Ponte San
Luigi & then a ten-minute walk.*

Aᴺ ᴜɴᴀssᴜᴍɪɴɢ promontory
is the setting for some of
the most important caves in
northern Italy. Guided tours
lead through the traces of the
cave-dwelling civilization of
pre-Iron Age Liguria. The caves
contain excavated burial sites
where the dead were adorned
with seashells. The **Museo
Nazionale dei Balzi Rossi**
contains tools, weapons, and
stone-etched female figures
dating from 100,000 years
ago. There is also a reproduc-
tion of an etching of a horse
found in one of the caves.

🏛 Museo Nazionale dei Balzi Rossi

Via Balzi Rossi 9, Frazione di Balzi
Rossi. **C** *0184 381 13.* **O** *Tue–Sun.*
● *Jan 1, May 1, Dec 25.*

Villa Hanbury ❷

Corso Monte Carlo 43, Località La
Mortola. **C** *0184 22 95 07.*
FS *Ventimiglia.* *from Ventimiglia.*
O *daily (Oct–Mar: Thu–Tue).*

Iɴ 1867 ᴛʜᴇ ᴇɴɢʟɪsʜ botanist
Sir Thomas Hanbury and
his brother bought this villa on
the Mortola promontory. They
took full advantage of the
exceptionally mild and sunny
Ligurian climate to establish a
garden of exotic plants along
the sloping pathways of the
enchanting seaside villa.

The collection, which
Hanbury had himself gathered
on trips to Africa and Asia, has
since grown to number more
than 3,000 varieties of tropical
flora including rubber trees,
palms, and wild cacti.

The garden is now run by
the state and is one of the
most impressive botanical
gardens in Italy. Even in winter
visitors will find a wealth of
color and vegetation here.

Dolceacqua ❸

Imperia. **▲** *1,800.* **FS** **i** *Via
Patrioti Martiri 22 (0184 20 66 66).*
● *Thu.*

Tʜɪs ᴘʀᴇᴛᴛʏ, wine-producing
village, 8 km (5 miles)
north of Ventimiglia, is built
on either side of the churning
Nervia River, its two halves
joined by an arching 33-m
(108-ft) medieval stone bridge.
The highlight is the ruined
castle (12th–15th century)
inhabited for a while in the
16th century by the powerful
Doria family from Genoa. The

two square towers at the front
dominate the village. The
terraced vineyards in the surrounding hills produce
bunches of grapes for general
consumption as well as for a
robust red wine known as
Rossese or vino di Dolceacqua.

San Remo ❹

Imperia. **▲** *60,000.* **FS**
i *Largo Nuvoloni 1 (0184 57 15 71).*
● *Tue & Sat.*

The Casinò Municipale in San
Remo, completed in 1906

Sᴀɴ ʀᴇᴍᴏ ɪs a pleasant resort
of faded elegance where
late 19th-century aristocrats
first discovered the pleasures
of the Italian Riviera. The
composer Tchaikovsky, Alfred
Nobel (the father of modern
explosives), and the nonsense
poet Edward Lear all stayed in
the stuccoed mansions of the
palm-lined seafront avenue, the
Corso Imperatrice. The focus
of the town, then as now, is
the Casino. A little farther
down the Corso stands the
ornate onion-domed Russian
Orthodox church.

An enchanting flower market
is held on Corso Garibaldi
early in the mornings, while
rising up on the hill called La
Pigna are the winding streets
and pastel-colored shutters of
the old town. A funicular
railway climbs up to Monte
Bignone, which has excellent
views over the Riviera.

Bussana Vecchia ❺

Imperia. Off San Remo–Arma di
Taggià road.

Bᴜssᴀɴᴀ ᴠᴇᴄᴄʜɪᴀ is a marvelously atmospheric ghost
town. In February 1887 an
earthquake shook the village,
reducing its Baroque church

The village of Dolceacqua with its medieval bridge and ruined castle

and surrounding houses to ruins. (One survivor, Giovanni Torre del Merlo, went on to invent the ice-cream cone.)

The town was rebuilt as Bussana Nuova about 2 km (1 mile) closer to the sea. Since then the old village has been taken over by artists, who have restored some interiors, providing a venue for summer concerts and exhibitions.

Cervo ❻

Imperia. 🏘 1,200. FS 🚌
ℹ Piazza Santa Caterina 2 (0183 40 81 97). 🚌 Thu.

CERVO IS THE PRETTIEST of the many old seafront villages just east of Imperia, with a narrow complex of streets and houses rising dramatically up from the shingle beach. At the top of the village stands the concave Baroque façade of **San Giovanni Battista**. In front of the church, in July and August, charming chamber orchestra performances are held. The church is also known as the *"dei corallini,"* after the coral fishing that once brought prosperity for the local people. Now Cervo is an unassuming but characteristic Ligurian holiday resort, with unspoiled hotels near the beach.

San Giovanni Battista at Cervo

Spectacular rock formations in the grottoes of Toirano

Albenga ❼

Savona. 🏘 21,000. FS 🚌
ℹ Vial B Ricci 1 (0182 55 84 44). 🚌 Wed.

UNTIL THE Middle Ages, the Roman port of Albium Ingaunum played an important maritime role. The sea, however, gradually moved farther out, leaving the town, now called Albenga, stranded on the Centa River. Most striking now is its Romanesque brick architecture, in particular the three 13th-century

The 5th-century baptistry at Albenga

towers clustered around the cathedral of **San Michele**. The cathedral's interior was restored to its medieval form in the late 1960s. To the south is an intriguing 5th-century **baptistry** with a ten-sided exterior and octagonal interior. Inside, the original 5th-century blue and white mosaics of doves represent the 12 apostles. To the north of the cathedral is the small Piazza dei Leoni, named after its three stone lions imported from Rome.

In a 14th-century palace on Piazza San Michele is the **Museo Navale Romano,** founded in 1950 following the salvage of a Roman ship that had sunk offshore around 100–90 BC. The museum contains ancient amphorae as well as exhibits salvaged from more recent shipwrecks.

🛈 **Baptistry**
Piazza San Michele. 📞 0182 512 15. 🕐 Tue–Sun. ⬤ Jan 1, Easter, Dec 25. 🆓
🏛 **Museo Navale Romano**
Piazza San Michele 12. 📞 0182 512 15. 🕐 Tue–Sun. ⬤ Jan 1, Easter, Dec 25. 🆓

Grotte di Toirano ❽

Piazzale delle Grotte, Toirano.
📞 0182 980 62. 🚌 from Albenga to Borghetto Santo Spirito. FS to Borghetto Santo Spirito or Loano then bus. 🕐 9am–noon, 2–5pm daily. ⬤ mid-Nov–mid-Dec & Dec 25. 🆓

BENEATH the delightful medieval hill town of Toirano lies a series of extraordinary caves containing relics of Paleolithic life dating from 100,000 BC.

Guided tours through the **Grotta della Basura** (Witch's Cave) reveal remarkable prehistoric human and animal footprints, and a collection of ancient bear bones and teeth in the "bear cemetery."

The **Grotta di Santa Lucia**, which can also be visited by guided tour, reveals the full beauty of the luminous yellow and gray stalactites and stalagmites that have formed there over thousands of years.

The **Museo Preistorico della Val Varatella** at the entrance to the Grotta della Basura has a small display of finds from the caves, as well as a model of a prehistoric bear.

🏛 **Museo Preistorico della Val Varatella**
Piazzale delle Grotte. 📞 0182 980 62. ⬤ for restoration.

Street-by-Street: Genoa ❾

THERE IS SOMETHING refreshingly rough-edged about Genoa (Genova in Italian), Italy's most important commercial port. In contrast to the genteel resorts along the neighboring coast, the narrow streets of the old town are the haunts of sailors and prostitutes.

With its natural harbor and the mountains to protect it, Genoa rose to prominence as a sea-based power. During the 16th century the Andrea Doria cemented Genoa's importance, and also proved astute patrons of the arts.

Palazzo Bianco

Piazza San Matteo
The houses and church of San Matteo were built by the Doria family in 1278. Palazzo Quartara has a bas relief of St. George above the doorway.

PIAZZA CAMPETTO

VIA DI SCURRERIA

PIAZZA SAN MATTEO

SALITA SAN M

VIA ARCHIVESCOVATO

The port and Palazzo Reale

San Lorenzo
The black and white striped Gothic façade of the duomo dates from the early 13th century.

VIA SAN LORENZO

PIAZZA MATTEOTTI

Palazzo Ducale
Once the seat of the doges of Genoa, this elegant building with its two fine 16th-century courtyards and arcades now contains a major arts and cultural center.

SALITA POLLAIUOLI

P ER

San Donato has a splendid 12th-century octagonal bell tower.

Sant'Agostino
The 13th-century church and convent were bombed during World War II, but the bell tower remains. The cloisters now house sculpture like this fragment from the tomb of Margaret of Brabant by Pisano (1312).

VICO TRE RE MAGI

KEY

– – –   Suggested route

| 0 meters | 100 |
| 0 yards | 100 |

Church of Gesù
This Baroque church, built between 1589 and 1606, is also known as the church of Santi Ambrogio e Andrea.

19th-century lion guarding the steps leading to the duomo

Piazza De Ferrari is the site of the Neo-Classical Banco di Roma and the Accademia, as well as the restored Teatro Carlo Felice.

The bronze fountain in Piazza De Ferrari was constructed in 1936.

Porta Soprana
The eastern gateway to the city has curved outer walls and stands close to the site of Christopher Columbus's house.

Sant'Andrea
The 12th-century cloisters standing in a small garden are all that remain of the convent that once stood here.

🏛 San Lorenzo (Duomo)

Piazza San Lorenzo. ☎ 010 247 18 63. ◯ daily. **Museo del Tesoro** ☎ 010 247 18 31. ◯ Mon–Sat. 📷

The duomo, with its black and white striped exterior, blends virtually every architectural style Genoa has ever known, from the 12th-century Romanesque side portal of San Giovanni to the Baroque touches of some of its side chapels. The three portals at the west end are in French Gothic style.

The most sumptuous of the chapels is dedicated to St. John the Baptist, patron saint of Genoa; it includes a 13th-century sarcophagus that once contained the venerated saint's relics.

Steps lead down from the sacristy to the **Museo del Tesoro di San Lorenzo**. It houses such treasures as the Roman green glass dish said to have been used at the Last Supper, and a blue chalcedony plate on which the head of John the Baptist was allegedly served up to Salome.

⚓ The Port

The port is the heart of Genoa and the origin of its wealth and power as a seafaring city state in the 11th and 12th centuries. It is a workaday place, given over to container shipping and ringed by busy roads and 1960s wharves and office buildings.

Among the vestiges of its medieval glory is the **Lanterna** lighthouse (restored in 1543) near the Stazione Marittima. In the old days fires would be lit at the top of the Lanterna to guide ships into port. Today, regeneration of the port is partly due to the modern conference center designed by Renzo Piano (*see p179*). The best way to see the port is from the sea; boats, giving guided tours, depart from Ponte Spinola.

Exploring Genoa

Visitors are well rewarded when they explore Genoa – a city proud of its history and legends. The palaces of the Via Balbi and Via Garibaldi, and the paintings and sculptures dotted around the city in churches and museums, are among the finest in northwestern Italy. The environs, too, provide scenic and relaxing locations for excursions along the coast or in the steep hills behind.

The courtyard of the University on Via Balbi

⚑ Sant'Agostino
Piazza Sarzano 35. **[** 010 251 12 63. ⬤ daily pm. ⬤ public hols.
Museo di Architettura e Scultura Ligure ⬤ Tue–Sat & Sun am. ⬤ public hols. 🎫 ♿

The Gothic church of Sant'Agostino was begun in 1260, but bombed to pieces in World War II. It is now deconsecrated, and all that remains of the original building is the fine Gothic bell tower, decorated with colored tiles. The monastery, of which the church of Sant'Agostino was once a part, was also bombed. What remained were two ruined cloisters – one of which forms the only triangular building in Genoa. The cloisters have recently been reconstructed and converted into the **Museo di Architettura e Scultura Ligure**. It contains the city's collection of architectural pieces and fragments of sculpture, as well as frescoes – all salvaged from Genoa's other destroyed churches. The finest piece is a magnificent fragment from the tomb of Margaret of Brabant. Margaret, who died in 1311, was the wife of Emperor Henry VII, who invaded Italy in 1310. Carved by Giovanni Pisano around 1313, the sculptures from her tomb were restored and repositioned in 1987. The figures, whose garments are arranged in simple folds, seem to be helping Margaret to lie down to rest.

🏛 Palazzo Reale
Via Balbi 10. **[** 010 271 02 72. ⬤ Tue–Sun. ⬤ Mon, Jan 1, Apr 25, May 1, Dec 25. 🎫 ♿

This austere-looking residence, used by the Kings of Savoy from the 17th century onward, has a highly ornate rococo interior – notably the ballroom and the Hall of Mirrors. Among the paintings are works by Parodi and Carlone and a *Crucifixion* by Van Dyck. The lovely garden, which slopes down toward the old port, includes an intriguing cobblestone mosaic around the central fountain, depicting houses and animals.

Opposite the palace is the old **University** (1634) designed by the architect Bartolomeo Bianco, as was much of Via Balbi. The large building brilliantly utilizes Genoa's hilly topography and is constructed on four levels.

🏛 Palazzo Bianco
Via Garibaldi 11. **[** 010 247 63 77. ⬤ Tue–Sun. 🎫 **Palazzo Rosso** **[** 010 247 63 68. ⬤ Tue–Sun. 🎫

The Palazzo Bianco is situated on Genoa's most beautiful street, the **Via Garibaldi**, where there are numerous fine 16th-century mansions and palazzi. The Palazzo Bianco contains the city's prime collection of paintings, including the works of many Genoese artists such as Luca Cambiaso, Bernardo Strozzi, Domenico Piola, and Giovanni Benedetto Castiglione. Better-known artists featured here

A portrait of Columbus, Villa Doria in Pegli

CHRISTOPHER COLUMBUS IN GENOA

The name of Christopher Columbus, the explorer of the New World, is in evidence all over Genoa. His statue greets you as soon as you emerge in Piazza Acquaverde from Porta Principe train station; various public buildings bear his name – even the airport is called Aeroporto Cristoforo Colombo. In the 17th-century Palazzo Belimbau, built on top of the old city walls, is a series of frescoes by the Genoese artist Tavarone celebrating the explorer's life; you can see three of his letters in the Sala del Sindaco in Palazzo Tursi (the city hall) on Via Garibaldi. It is not certain whether Columbus (c.1451– 1506) was born in Genoa, in Savona 15 km (9 miles) to the west, or outside Italy altogether. However, city registers mention his father, a weaver, and different family homes within the city. The small ivy-clad house next to the Porta Soprana may have been Columbus's childhood home, where he first discovered his passion for the sea.

The house where Columbus may have lived

The romantic gardens at Villa Durazzo-Pallavicini in Pegli

include Filippino Lippi (a lovely *Madonna with Saints*), Veronese, Van Dyck, and Rubens. Across the street in the **Palazzo Rosso** are more paintings, including work by Dürer and Caravaggio, as well as ceramics, furniture, and coins. Upstairs in the *piano nobile* the rooms are adorned with 17th-century frescoes by Genoese artists such as de Ferrari and Piola.

⛪ Staglieno Cemetery

Piazzale Resasco, Staglieno. ☎ 010 87 01 84. ◻ *daily*. ● *public hols*. ♿

Fine tomb architecture from the huge Staglieno Cemetery

This grandiose cemetery, just over the hills northeast of Genoa along the Bisagno River, is so big (160 ha, 395 acres) that it has its own internal bus system. Founded in 1844, its tombs and monuments make up an eerie city of miniature cathedrals, Egyptian temples, and Art Nouveau palaces. Its most famous resident is Giuseppe Mazzini, the Genoese revolutionary who died not far from Pisa in 1872.

ENVIRONS: Until World War II, **Pegli**, 6 km (4 miles) west of the city center, was a popular weekend retreat for rich Genoese wanting to get away from it all. Now it forms part of the metropolis, but nevertheless maintains an air of tranquillity, thanks to its parks and two villas, the 19th-century **Villa Durazzo-Pallavicini** and the 16th-century **Villa Doria**. The latter now houses a naval history museum celebrating Genoa's glorious past; you can see globes, compasses, astrolabes, maps, model ships, and a portrait of Columbus ascribed to Ghirlandaio, probably dating from 1525. The Villa Durazzo-Pallavicini houses an archaeological museum, which relates the pre-Roman history of the Ligurian coast. The villa's garden is landscaped with romantic grottoes, pavilions, and fountains.

Nervi, 8 km (5 miles) to the east of the city, is another former resort town, famous for its seafront promenade, the **Passeggiata Anita Garibaldi** (named after Garibaldi's Brazilian wife). The walk crosses the Nervi torrent and follows a route that has been cut into the rock face, giving panoramic views

of the coast. The lush **Parco Municipale** is another feature of Nervi. It once formed the grounds of two aristocratic villas – the Villa Serra and the Villa Gropallo. The gardens contain some rare species of exotic and Mediterranean trees.

The Villa Serra on Via Capolungo now houses the **Galleria d'Arte Moderna** featuring modern Italian painting. The **Villa Luxoro** on Via Aurelia is notable for its collection of clocks, fabrics, furniture, and lace. The area is also famous as Garibaldi's departure point when he set off for Sicily with his *Mille* (the famous "Thousand" men) to bring about the unification of Italy. A large monument at Quarto dei Mille, about 3 km (2 miles) back toward the city, marks the place where the volunteers met in May 1860 to follow the intrepid revolutionary *(see pp58–9)*.

🏛 Villa Doria

Piazza Bonavino 7, Pegli. ☎ 010 696 98 85. ◻ *Tue–Sat & 1st & 3rd Sun of month*. ● *public hols*. 📷 ♿

🏛 Villa Durazzo-Pallavicini

Via Pallavicini 11, Pegli. ☎ 010 698 27 76. ◻ *Tue, Thu–Sat & 2nd & 4th Sun of month*. ● *public hols*. 📷 ♿

🏛 Galleria d'Arte Moderna

Villa Serra, Via Capolungo 3, Nervi. ☎ 010 28 26 41. ◻ *Tue–Sat*.

🏛 Villa Luxoro

Via Mafalda di Savoia 3, Nervi. ☎ 010 32 26 73. ◻ *Tue–Sat*. ● *public hols*. 📷

Pini (c.1920) by Rubaldo Merello in the Galleria d'Arte Moderna at Nervi

Pastel-colored houses near the pebbly beach at Camogli

Camogli ⓾

Genova. 🚶 6,500. 🚉 🚌 ⛴
ℹ️ *Via XX Settembre 33 (0185 77 10
66).* ⛴ *Wed.*

BUILT ON A pinewooded
slope, Camogli is a fishing
village where seashells adorn
the pastel-painted house walls,
and the smell of frying fish
wafts out from the small restaurants into the streets. Near
the pebble beach and fishing
port is the medieval Castello
della Dragonara, a castle now
containing the **Acquario
Tirrenico**, which displays 22
tanks of sea creatures.

Camogli celebrates its
famous festival of the Blessing
of the Fish on the second
Sunday of May when sardines
are fried in a huge pan 4 m
(13 ft) in diameter. The fish is
distributed free to all.

🏛 Acquario Tirrenico
Castello della Dragonara. 📞 *0185
77 33 75.* ⬜ *Tue–Thu am, Fri–Sun &
public hols am & pm.* 📷

Portofino
Peninsula ⓫

Genova. 🚌 ⛴ *Portofino.* ℹ️ *Via
Roma 35 (0185 26 90 24).*

PORTOFINO IS THE most
exclusive harbor and
resort town in Italy, crammed
with the yachts of the wealthy.
You can reach Portofino by

road (cars are not allowed
into the village), or boat, from
the resort of Santa Margherita
Ligure. Above the town is the
church of **San Giorgio**,
containing relics said to be of
the dragonslayer, and a castle.

On the other
side of the
peninsula, which
you have to reach
on foot (a two-
hour walk) or by
boat, is the
**Abbazia di San
Fruttuoso**,
named after a
3rd-century saint
whose followers
were shipwrecked
here and, accord-
ing to local folklore, protected
by three lions. The white
abbey buildings, set among
pines and olive trees, date
mostly from the 11th century,
although the imposing Torre
dei Doria was added 500 years
later. You can take a boat to

try to locate the **Cristo degli
Abissi**, a bronze statue of
Christ that sits on the seabed
near San Fruttuoso, acting as
a protector of sailors. Farther
west along the coast is Punta
Chiappa, a rocky promontory
famous for the changing colors
of the sea.

🏠 Abbazia di San Fruttuoso
San Fruttuoso. 📞 *0185 77 27 03.*
⬜ *Tue–Sun (Dec–Feb: public hols &
the day before only).* ● *Nov.* 📷

Rapallo ⓬

Genova. 🚶 *30,000.* 🚉 🚌 ⛴ ℹ️
Via Diaz 9 (0185 23 03 46). ⛴ *Thu.*

HISTORIANS KNOW Rapallo as
the place where two
treaties – one between Italy
and Yugoslavia, the other between Germany and Russia –
were signed after World War
II. Film buffs might recognize
it as a location for *The Bare-
foot Contessa,* filmed here in
1954. Its villas still have a
patrician feel to
them, as do the
riding stables,
golf course, and
tennis courts.
The palm-lined
esplanade ends
in a small 16th-
century **castle**,
in which art
exhibitions are
now occasionally
held. Above the
village is the
16th-century **Santuario di
Montallegro**, which houses a
Byzantine icon said to possess
miraculous powers.

**The 16th-century castle
jutting into Rapallo harbor**

🏠 Santuario di Montallegro
Montallegro. 📞 *0185 23 90 00.*
⬜ *daily.*

Large yachts moored in Portofino's famous harbor

The dramatic coastline near Corniglia in the Cinque Terre

Cinque Terre ⑬

La Spezia. **FS** to all towns.
Monterosso, Vernazza. **ℹ** Piazza Garibaldi, Monterosso (0187 81 72 04).

THE CINQUE TERRE is a protected stretch of rocky coastline on the Riviera di Levante, which extends from Monterosso al Mare to Riomaggiore at its southeastern tip. The name refers to five dramatically situated villages that apparently cling to the very edge of vertiginous cliffs: Monterosso al Mare, Vernazza, Corniglia, Manarola, and Riomaggiore. The villages were once only accessible by sea, and today there is still no road that links them all. An ancient footpath, known as the Sentiero Azzurro, follows the coast, joining the villages and offering superb views of the distinctive green terraced vineyards that produce the local dry white Cinque Terre wines. The villages remain spectacularly self-contained, hemmed in by steep cliffs, though they are now suffering from some depopulation. Monterosso al Mare, on the northwestern edge of the Cinque Terre, is the largest of the five villages and overlooks a wide bay with its own sandy beach. Vernazza, further down the coast, has streets linked by steep steps *arpaie*. Corniglia, perched on the pinnacle of rocky terraces, seems untouched by the passage of time, as does

Manarola, which is linked by the famous Via dell'Amore, or Lovers' Lane, to **Riomaggiore**, a 15-minute walk away. Riomaggiore, like Monterosso, is one of the more accessible villages by road, allowing it to cater better to visitors.

Portovenere ⑭

La Spezia. **ℹ** 4,600. **▦** **⛴** **ℹ** Piazza Bastreri (0187 79 06 91). **⛴** Mon.

NAMED AFTER VENUS herself, Portovenere is one of the most romantic villages on the Ligurian coast with its cluster of narrow streets lined with pastel-colored houses. In the upper part of the village is the 12th-century church of **San Lorenzo**. A sculpture over the doorway here depicts the martyrdom of the saint who was roasted alive on a grill. On the stone promontory that curls

Above the doorway of San Lorenzo in Portovenere

out into the sea stands the small black and white 13th-century church of **San Pietro**. From here, or from the 16th-century castle on top of the cliffs on the northwestern side of the village, there are glorious views of the Cinque Terre and the small island of Palmaria, which lies about 400 m (1,300 ft) offshore.

Lerici ⑮

La Spezia. **ℹ** 13,000. **▦** **⛴** **ℹ** Via Gerini 40 (0187 96 73 46). **⛴** Sat am.

THIS STRETCH OF COAST, along the Gulf of La Spezia or Poets' gulf, was once popular with such English-language literati as Yeats and DH Lawrence. The village of San Terenzo, across the bay from Lerici, was where the poet Shelley spent the last four years of his life. It was from his home, the Casa Magni, that he set out in 1822 on a fatal voyage to meet Leigh Hunt in Livorno. Tragically, he was shipwrecked near Viareggio and drowned.

Lerici, once a small fishing village and now a popular resort, sits on the edge of a beautiful bay and has a pleasant beach overlooked by pastel-colored houses. It has a forbidding medieval **castle** which was built by the Pisans and later passed to the Genoese. Apparently carved out of the cliff, it dominates the vacation villas below.

⚓ Castello di Lerici
Piazza San Giorgio. **☎** 0187 96 90 42. **◷** Apr–Oct: daily.

The harbor of Vernazza in the Cinque Terre

A stunning view of Manarola on the Sentiero Azzurro, Cinque Terre ▷

CENTRAL ITALY

Central Italy at a Glance

THE CENTRAL REGIONS of Italy are popular with visitors because they offer a range of beautiful landscapes and towns rich in culture and history, including outstanding churches, towers, and palaces. Emilia-Romagna is home to the impressive Po Delta, which provides a haven for wild-life. Tuscany is dominated by Florence, one of Italy's most celebrated centers. Umbria and Le Marche offer gentle pastoral countryside and picturesque hill towns. The major sights of this rewarding area are shown here.

The Leaning Tower *of Pisa and the duomo (see pp314–16), splendid examples of 12th- and 13th-century architecture, are decorated with Arabic-inspired, complex geometric patterns.*

Leaning Tower of Pisa

FLORENCE
(See pp262–303)

TUSC
(See pp-

The Duomo *and the Baptistry, set in the heart of Florence, dominate the city (see pp272–4). The dome dwarfs many surrounding buildings.*

Duomo, Campanile, and Baptistry

Uffizi

Palazzo Pitti

The Uffizi *contains a superb collection of Florentine art from Gothic to High Renaissance and beyond (see pp278–81).*

The Palazzo Pitti, begun in 1457 for the banker Luca Pitti, became the main resi-dence of the Medici. It now houses their trea-sures (see pp294–5).

| 0 kilometers | | 1 |
| 0 miles | 0.5 | |

| 0 kilometers | | |
| 0 miles | | 25 |

◁ **Autumn color in Tuscany, in the hills of the Val d'Orcia, south of Siena**

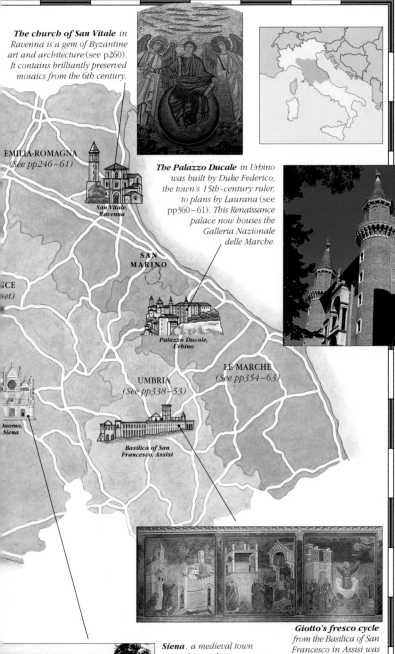

The church of San Vitale in Ravenna is a gem of Byzantine art and architecture (see p260). It contains brilliantly preserved mosaics from the 6th century.

San Vitale, Ravenna

EMILIA-ROMAGNA
(See pp246–61)

NCE
(set)

SAN MARINO

The Palazzo Ducale in Urbino was built by Duke Federico, the town's 15th-century ruler, to plans by Laurana (see pp360–61). This Renaissance palace now houses the Galleria Nazionale delle Marche.

Palazzo Ducale, Urbino

LE MARCHE
(See pp354–63)

UMBRIA
(See pp338–53)

Duomo, Siena

Basilica of San Francesco, Assisi

Siena, a medieval town steeped in tradition, centers around the Campo, the large piazza shaped like a scallop shell (see pp328–33). The lively horse race, the Corsa del Palio, is held here in July and August.

Giotto's fresco cycle from the Basilica of San Francesco in Assisi was executed in the 13th century (see pp344–7). The church is visited by thousands of pilgrims each year.

Regional Food: Central Italy

Artichoke

THE FOOD OF TUSCANY, UMBRIA, and Le Marche is simple but often hearty. Packed with flavor, it is based on peasant cooking that relies heavily on olive oil, tomatoes, beans, hams, and salamis. Meanwhile, the traditional dishes in Emilia-Romagna tend to be more elaborate, using ingredients such as cream, interesting meats – including game, Parma ham, and mortadella – and excellent quality cheeses such as Parmesan. Fresh fish and seafood is available along the coasts, but is often more expensive than meat.

Balsamic vinegar *from Modena in Emilia-Romagna is renowned throughout the world. Aged for up to fourteen years in oak barrels, the dark, smooth vinegar is used to flavor soups, stews, and salad dressings.*

Wild boar salami

Mortadella

Cooked ham (prosciutto cotto)

Parma ham

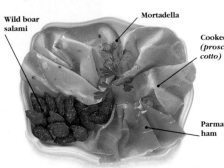

Cured meats and hams *form an important part of the cuisine of central Italy. The most famous is Parma ham from Emilia-Romagna, where the pigs are fattened on the whey left over from making Parmesan cheese.*

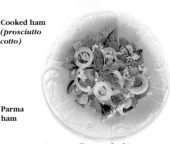

Panzanella, *a refreshing summer salad, is made of juicy tomatoes, onion, garlic, and oil-soaked bread, garnished with fresh basil.*

Liver paste

Tomato paste

Tortelloni, *a larger version of tortellini, may be stuffed with meat or cheese and served with a rich sauce.*

Olive paste

Anchovy paste

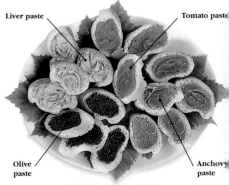

Crostini *are delicious snacks made from rounds of toast topped with anchovy, olive, liver, or tomato paste. Bruschetta is grilled bread rubbed with garlic and drizzled with olive oil.*

Spaghetti al Ragù *is a traditional dish from Bologna. The pasta is topped with a generous portion of beef and tomato sauce.*

Cannelloni *is another form of stuffed pasta. Large pasta tubes may be filled with meat or cheese and spinach, and then coated with tomato or cheese sauce before being baked.*

Baccalà *is a simple, flavorful dish of dried salt cod prepared with garlic and garnished with parsley. In Tuscany, tomatoes are often added.*

Bistecca alla Fiorentina, *grilled over an open fire, is a large, tender steak that can be seasoned with oil and herbs and garnished with fresh lemon.*

Scottiglia di Cinghiale *is prepared with wild boar chops. This dish is particularly popular in the Maremma area of southern Tuscany.*

Pecorino

Parmesan

Torta di Limone *is one of the richer desserts that come from Emilia-Romagna. It is prepared with lemons and fresh cream.*

Torta di Riso *is a traditional Tuscan dessert consisting of rice cake served with a simple fruit sauce and seasonal fruit.*

Cheeses *are used in many recipes, but may also be served with fruit as a main course or at the end of a meal.*

Panforte

Panforte *is a dense, dark cake spiced with cinnamon and cloves. Ricciarelli are made from ground almonds, orange peel, and honey.*

Cantucci *are sweet Tuscan biscuits often served together with vin santo, a traditional dessert wine.*

Ricciarelli

MUSHROOMS AND TRUFFLES

Wild mushrooms are considered a great delicacy in central Italy, and a range of fresh and dried mushrooms are frequently used in cooking. Fresh mushrooms are available in the autumn when restaurants are often packed with locals tasting seasonal mushroom dishes. Prized black truffles *(tartufi neri)* with a rich flavor and firm texture are expensive and used sparingly. Porcini mushrooms may be served grilled as a main course, used on pizza, in stuffed pasta, or served as a vegetable dish, sautéed gently with garlic.

Chanterelle
(Cantarello or Gallinaccio)

Field blewit
(Agarico nudo)

Parasol
(Mazza da Tamburo)

Boletus edulis
(Porcini)

Oyster
(Ostrica)

Black truffle
(Tartufo nero)

The Wines of Central Italy

Roman mosaic of a bird eating grapes

VINEYARDS ARE SEEN EVERYWHERE in Central Italy, from the rolling cypress-fringed hills of Tuscany to the flatter, Lambrusco-producing plains of Emilia-Romagna. The finest red wines are made in the hills of southeastern Tuscany: Chianti Classico, Brunello di Montalcino, and Vino Nobile di Montepulciano. Today's innovative mix of modern and traditional techniques is steadily improving the quality of much of the region's wine.

Chianti Classico is the heart of the Chianti zone. Chianti may be light and fruity or dense and long-lived – price is the usual guide. Rocca delle Macie is very reasonably priced.

Vernaccia di San Gimignano is a Tuscan white wine with a long, distinguished history. Traditionally a golden, often oxidized wine, it is now also produced in a fresher style, for early drinking. Teruzzi e Puthod make consistently good Vernaccia.

Vino Nobile di Montepulciano is made from the same grapes as Chianti. It can be of superior quality, hence its claim to be a "noble wine." The vineyards are set around the delightful hilltop village of Montepulciano.

Brunello di Montalcino is made from Sangiovese, Brunello being its local name. Its firm tannins may need up to ten years to soften before the rich, spicy flavors are revealed. Rosso di Montalcino, on the other hand, can be enjoyed much younger.

0 kilometers 50

0 miles 25

VINO DA TAVOLA

During the 1970s innovative wine makers set out to create new, individual wines, even though under the existing rules they would be labeled as simple table wine. A trend that started with Antinori's Tignanello (a Sangiovese-Cabernet Sauvignon blend), this approach has reinvigorated Tuscan wine, to produce some exciting variations.

Sassicaia, a red wine made from the Cabernet Sauvignon grape

Chianti estate at Badia a Passignano in Tuscany

KEY

☐	Chianti
☐	Chianti Classico
☐	Vernaccia di San Gimignano
☐	Brunello di Montalcino
☐	Vino Nobile di Montepulciano
☐	Orvieto Classico
☐	Orvieto
☐	Verdicchio dei Castelli di Jesi
☐	Lambrusco

Verdicchio is a dry white wine from Le Marche with a crisp, slightly salty taste. In recent years the introduction of the single vineyard Verdicchio, such as Umani Ronchi's CaSal di Serra, has won much acclaim.

Orvieto Classico *is a popular Umbrian white wine. This fresh, dry (Secco) version from the Antinori estate is a good example of a modern-style Orvieto. The wine also comes in a sweeter form, known as* Abboccato.

GRAPES OF CENTRAL ITALY

The versatile Sangiovese grape dominates wine making in Central Italy. It is the main grape in Chianti, in Vino Nobile di Montepulciano, in Brunello di Montalcino, and in many of the new-style *Vino da Tavola* wines. Of the established whites, Trebbiano and Malvasia head the list. Imported varieties such as white Chardonnay and red Cabernet Sauvignon are playing an increasing role, often being used to complement and enhance native varieties.

Sangiovese grapes

HOW TO READ THE LABEL

Producer's name

The DOCG name is a reliable guide to the origin of the wine.

CASTELGIOCONDO
BRUNELLO DI MONTALCINO
denominazione di origine controllata e garantita

1988

Imbottigliato all'origine da Tenuta di Castelgioconda dei Marchesi de' Frescobaldi Montalcino Italia

Year of production

The bottler's name and address are given as a guarantee of the wine's origin.

Alcoholic content

GOOD WINE PRODUCERS

Chianti: Antinori, Badia a Coltibuono, Brolio, Castello di Ama, Castello di Rampolla, Fattoria Selvapiana, Felsina Berardenga, Il Palazzino, Isole e Olena, Monte Vertine, Riecine, Rocca delle Macie, Ruffino, Tenuta Fontodi. **Brunello di Montalcino**: Argiano, Altesino, Caparzo, Castelgiocondo, Costanti, Il Poggione, Villa Banfi. **Vino Nobile di Montepulciano**: Avignonesi, Le Casalte, Poliziano. In **Umbria**: Adanti, Lungarotti.

Good Chianti Vintages
1997, 1995, 1993, 1990, 1988, 1985, 1983, 1975, 1971, 1970, 1967, 1964.

Understanding Architecture in Central Italy

CENTRAL ITALY has countless fine Renaissance buildings, many of them concentrated in and around Florence. Their clear lines, elegant simplicity, and harmonious proportions came out of a reevaluation of the past. Turning their backs on the Gothic style, the architects of the Renaissance returned to Classical Rome for inspiration. Most of the large buildings had been started by the late 15th century, paid for by the Catholic Church or by powerful noble families, such as the Medici of Florence.

The Palazzo Ducale in Urbino (begun 1465)

RELIGIOUS BUILDINGS

Arched bays trisect the façade.

One of 12 roundels by Luca della Robbia

Pope Pius II's coat of arms

Small circular windows

Square plan topped by small dome

Symmetrical floor plan is based on a Greek cross.

Harmonious proportions

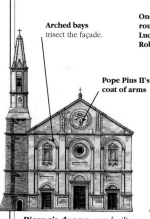

Pienza's duomo was built by Bernardo Rossellino in 1459 for Pope Pius II as part of his vision of the ideal Renaissance city (see p323).

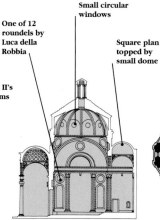

The Pazzi Chapel of Santa Croce in Florence (1433) is one of Brunelleschi's most famous works, decorated with terracotta roundels by Luca della Robbia (see pp276–7).

Santa Maria della Consolazione in Todi, begun in 1508, owes much to the ideas of the architect Bramante (see p349).

TOWN AND COUNTRY HOUSES

The cornice was designed to cast a shadow over the face of the palace around midday.

Wedge-shaped masonry

Strong horizontal line

Square windows are found only on the ground floor.

The Palazzo Strozzi in Florence (1489–1536) is typical of many Tuscan city palaces (see p318). The three stories are given equal importance, and the massive rusticated stonework conveys the impression of strength and power (see p285).

WHERE TO SEE THE ARCHITECTURE

The simple canons of the Renaissance were interpreted differently away from the hotbed of artistic thought and cultural endeavor of Florence, which has the greatest number of churches and palaces. Alberti's Tempio Malatestiano at Rimini (see p258) evokes the sobriety of ancient Roman architecture yet seeks to reinterpret it

Vista in the Boboli Gardens, Florence

in his own unique fashion. Urbino's Palazzo Ducale (pp360–61) perfects the grace and polish of the era and is a truly noble period residence. On a smaller scale are the planned Renaissance centers of elegant towns such as Ferrara (p253), Pienza (p323), and Urbino (p359). All three centres are examples of enlightened patronage, and pay homage to the art of antiquity.

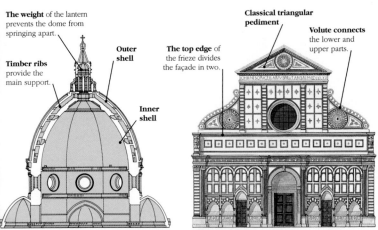

The weight of the lantern prevents the dome from springing apart.

Timber ribs provide the main support.

Outer shell

Inner shell

Classical triangular pediment

The top edge of the frieze divides the façade in two.

Volute connects the lower and upper parts.

The Duomo in Florence is crowned by the revolutionary dome (1436) by Brunelleschi, which had to be built without scaffolding due to its size. The timber structure is covered by an inner and outer shell (see pp272–3).

The façade of Santa Maria Novella in Florence (1458–70) was designed by Leon Battista Alberti. He incorporated some of the existing Gothic features into an overall design typical of the Renaissance (see pp288–9).

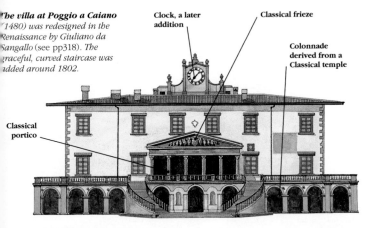

The villa at Poggio a Caiano (1480) was redesigned in the Renaissance by Giuliano da Sangallo (see pp318). The graceful, curved staircase was added around 1802.

Clock, a later addition

Classical frieze

Colonnade derived from a Classical temple

Classical portico

EMILIA-ROMAGNA

EMILIA-ROMAGNA *is the heartland of central Italy, a broad corridor through the hills and plains of the Po Valley that marks the watershed between the cold north of the Alps and the hot Mediterranean south. With its rich agricultural land, historical cities, and thriving industry, it is one of the most prosperous areas in Italy.*

Most of the major towns in Emilia-Romagna lie near the Via Aemilia, a Roman road built in 187 BC linking Rimini on the Adriatic coast with the garrison town of Piacenza. Prior to the Romans, the Etruscans had ruled from their capital, Felsina, located on the site of present-day Bologna. After the fall of Rome, the region's focus moved to Ravenna, which became a principal part of the Byzantine Empire administered from Constantinople.

During the Middle Ages pilgrims heading for Rome continued to use the Via Aemilia. Political power, however, passed to influential noble families – the Malatesta in Rimini, the Bentivoglio in Bologna, the d'Este in Ferrara and Modena, and the Farnese in Parma and Piacenza. Great courts grew up around the families, attracting poets such as Dante and Ariosto, as well as painters, sculptors, and architects. Many of their works still grace the medieval centers of these towns.

Modern Emilia-Romagna, pieced together from separate Papal States in 1860, was given its present borders in 1947. Emilia, covering the western half of the region, is traditionally associated with a more northern outlook and a tendency toward the left in politics. Romagna, with its capital at Ravenna, has always turned to the south for artistic, cultural, and political inspiration.

The entire region has a reputation as a great gastronomic center. Agriculture has long thrived on the Po's alluvial fringes, earning the Pianura Padana (Po Plain) epithets such as the "bread basket" and "fruit bowl" of Italy. Pigs still outnumber humans in many areas, and some of the country's most famous staples – Parma ham and Parmesan cheese – originate here.

The medieval Palazzo del Comune in Ferrara

The Fontana del Nettuno (Neptune's Fountain) in Bologna

Exploring Emilia-Romagna

EMILIA-ROMAGNA is a checkerboard of fields and plains between the Po River to the north and the forest-covered Apennine mountain slopes to the south. The best place to begin a tour of the region is centrally situated Bologna. Modena, its long-time rival, boasts one of the country's loveliest Romanesque cathedrals. Parma has a more provincial feel and Ferrara, too, has an easy-going air. Castell'Arquato offers a taste of the smaller villages that dot the hills south of the Po.

Piazza Cavalli, Piacenza's central square

SEE ALSO

- **Where to Stay** pp555–7
- **Where to Eat** pp590–91

Reed-lined shores along the Po Delta

SIGHTS AT A GLANCE

GETTING AROUND

Excellent road and rail links, aided by predominantly flat terrain, make this region quick and easy to get around. Bologna is connected by the A1 to Florence and by the A13 to Ferrara and Venice. The busy A1 links Bologna with Milan via Piacenza, Fidenza and Parma. The A15 connects Parma with La Spezia, and the A21 joins Piacenza and Cremona. Fast, frequent train services run along almost parallel routes.

The beach at Cesenatico, north of Rimini on the Adriatic coast

KEY

▬▬▬	Highway
▬▬▬	Major road
▬▬▬	Minor road
▬▬▬	Scenic route
≈≈≈	River
☀	Viewpoint

0 kilometers   25

0 miles   20

The 13th-century Palazzo Pretorio in Castell'Arquato

Piacenza ❶

🏛 105,000. 🚊 🚌 ℹ️ *Piazzetta dei Mercanti 7 (0523 32 93 24)*. 🏛 *Wed & Sat*.

Piacenza traces its history back to Roman times. Located near the Po, it served as a fortified camp protecting the Emilian plain from invasion by both Hannibal and the Gauls. The center is still based on the Roman plan.

Little visited by tourists, Piacenza has a pleasantly understated old center that is full of fine medieval and Renaissance buildings. Pride of place goes to two bronze equestrian **statues** in the central Piazza Cavalli, the work of the 17th-century sculptor Francesco Mochi, a pupil of Giambologna. Lauded as masterpieces of Baroque sculpture, the statues represent Alessandro Farnese, a soldier of fortune, and his son, Ranuccio: both were rulers of 16th-century Piacenza.

Behind the statues is the red-brick **Palazzo del Comune**, also known as "Il Gotico," an evocatively battlemented Lombard-Gothic palace begun at the end of the 13th century.

The **duomo**, at the end of Via XX Settembre, has a rather leaden Lombard-Romanesque exterior (begun in 1122), and a 14th-century campanile. The interior features Guercino's painted cupola and medieval frescoes that adorn the apse and transepts. There are also frescoed saints near the main door, painted to resemble members of the congregation.

The **Museo Civico** offers an eclectic mixture of sculpture and paintings – the star among these is the *Madonna and Child with John the Baptist* by Botticelli (1444–1510). There is also an armory and archaeology section. The highlight here is the so-called *Fegato di Piacenza*, an Etruscan bronze representation of the sheep livers once used by priests for divination, inscribed with deities' names.

🏛 **Museo Civico**
Palazzo Farnese, Piazza Cittadella. 【 *0523 32 82 70*. 🕐 *Tue–Sun*. ⬤ *public hols*. 📷

Castell'Arquato ❷

Piacenza. 🏛 *4,500*. 🚌 ℹ️ *Viale Remondini 1 (0523 80 30 91)*. 🏛 *Mon*.

Tucked into the folded hills between Fidenza and Piacenza, Castell'Arquato is among the prettiest of the villages scattered around the countryside south of the Po. Day visitors come at the week-ends to escape Emilia's larger cities, thronging the restaurants and bars around the beautiful **Piazza Matteotti**. The best medieval building on the piazza is the 13th-century **Palazzo Pretorio**, a venerable Romanesque basilica. The impressive **Rocca Viscontea** (14th century), a former Visconti fortress, is situated on Piazza del Municipio. The village's hilltop site offers good views, particularly over the verdant Arda valley to the east.

Fidenza ❸

Parma. 🏛 *23,000*. 🚊 🚌 ℹ️ *Piazza Duomo 2 (0524 840 47)*. 🏛 *Wed & Sat*.

Like many towns hugging the line of the Po, Fidenza owed its early prominence to the Via Aemilia (the old Roman road). The town assumed greater importance as a medieval way station for pilgrims en route to Rome. Today Fidenza is visited for its superb **duomo** on Piazza Duomo (13th century), a composite piece of architecture that embraces Lombard, Gothic and transitional Romanesque elements. The most immediately eye-catching feature is the opulent façade, probably created by the craftsmen who worked with Benedetto Antelami on Parma's duomo. Inside, the walls are dotted with fragments of medieval frescoes, while the crypt contains the relics of San Donnino, the duomo's patron.

Detail from façade of duomo in Fidenza

Interior of Parma Baptistry

Parma ❹

🚶 175,000. 🚆 🚌 ℹ️ *Piazza del Duomo 5 (0521 23 47 35).* 🗓️ *Wed & Sat; Thu (flea market).*

Few Italian towns are as urbane or prosperous as Parma, not only a byword for fine food and good living but also a treasure trove of excellent paintings, superlative sculpture, and fine medieval buildings. It boasts one of Italy's top opera houses and a panoply of elegant shops and first-rate bars and restaurants.

The Lombard-Romanesque **duomo** on Piazza Duomo, among the greatest in northern Italy, is renowned for the painting of the *Assumption* (1534) that fills its main cupola by Emilian artist, Antonio da Correggio. The nave is adorned with the work of pupils of Correggio. The south transept features a carved frieze (1178) by Benedetto Antelami, who was responsible for much of the exquisite **Baptistry** (1196) just south of the cathedral. The reliefs inside and outside the latter – particularly those describing the months of the year – are among the most important of their age in Italy.

East of the duomo is the church of **San Giovanni Evangelista** (rebuilt 1498–1510) whose dome features a fresco (c.1520) of the *Vision of St. John at Patmos* by Correggio. Frescoes by Parmigianino, a pupil of Correggio, can be seen here and in the 16th-century church of **Madonna della Steccata** on Via Dante.

🏛️ Palazzo Pilotta

Piazzale della Pilotta 15. **Galleria** 📞 0521 23 33 09. 🕐 *Tue–Sun.* ⬛ *Jan 1, May 1, Dec 25.* 🎫 ♿ **Museo** 📞 0521 23 37 18. 🕐 *Tue–Sun.* ⬛ *as above.* 🎫

This vast palace was built for the Farnese family during the 16th century, and was rebuilt after bomb damage from World War II. The palace comprises several parts, including the **Teatro Farnese** (1628), a copy of Palladio's ravishing theater in Vicenza, built of wood.

Both Parmigianino and Correggio are represented in the palace's **Galleria Nazionale**. The gallery contains works by Fra Angelico, Bronzino, and El Greco, and two huge paintings by Ludovico Carracci: *Apostles at the Sepulchre* and *Funeral of the Virgin* (both late 16th century).

The **Museo Archeologico Nazionale**, on the lower floor, has exhibits from Velleia, an Etruscan necropolis, and from prehistoric sites in the hills around Parma.

🏛️ Camera di San Paolo

Via Melloni. 📞 *0521 23 33 09.* 🕐 *Tue–Sun.* ⬛ *Jan 1, May 1, Dec 25.* 🎫 ♿

Originally the refectory of the Benedictine convent of San Paolo, this room was frescoed by Correggio in 1518 with mythological scenes.

Campanile and Baptistry in Parma

THE MAKING OF PARMESAN CHEESE AND PARMA HAM

No cheese is as famous or as vital to Italy's cuisine as Parmesan *(Parmigiano)*. There are two types: the superior Parmigiano-Reggiano and the lower-quality Grana. The cheese is made using techniques that have barely altered in centuries. Partially skimmed milk is added to whey, to promote fermentation, and rennet is used to curdle the milk. The cheese is then salted and shaped. Parmesan is not only used in cooking but is delicious eaten on its own, or with pears – an Italian specialty.

Shop selling Parmesan cheese and Parma ham

Parma ham owes its excellence to techniques perfected over many years and to the special conditions in which it is cured. It comes from pigs fattened on whey left over from the making of Parmesan cheese. The meat has a character that requires little more than salt and pepper to produce the famous *prosciutto crudo*. The breezy hills of Langhirino, south of Parma, are ideal for curing the hams, which are aged for up to ten months. Each ham is branded with the five-pointed crown of the old Duchy of Parma.

Flora by Carlo Cignani (1628–1719) in the Galleria Estense in Modena

Modena **❺**

⌂ *175,000.* **FS** **🚌** **ℹ** *Piazza Grande 17 (059 20 66 60).* **🚃** *Mon.*

To MOST ITALIANS Modena means fast cars, for both Ferrari and Maserati have factories in its industrial outskirts. Monuments to an earlier age, however, make this one of Emilia's most enticing historic destinations. A thriving colony since Roman times, the city rose to medieval prominence on the back of its broad agricultural hinterland and the arrival in 1598 of the d'Este nobles from Ferrara. This family continued to rule the city until the 18th century.

🏠 Duomo
Corso Duomo. **☎** *059 21 60 78.* **◯** *daily.*
Modena's superlative **duomo** rises alongside the old Roman Via Aemilia (now Via Emilia). One of the region's greatest Romanesque buildings, it was founded by Countess Matilda of Tuscany, ruler of Modena in the 11th century. It was designed by Lanfranco and dedicated to San Geminiano, the city's patron saint, whose stone coffin lies under the choir. The exterior's most noticeable feature is the **Torre Ghirlandina**, a perilously leaning tower begun at the same time as the duomo and completed two centuries later. It was once home to Modena's famous *Secchia*, a wooden bucket whose theft from Bologna in 1325 supposedly provoked war between the two cities. It also inspired the mock epic poem *La Secchia Rapita* (The Stolen Bucket) by the 17th-century poet Tassoni, and became the symbol of an ongoing rivalry between the cities.

The large reliefs on the duomo's impressive main (west) façade are the work of the mysterious 12th-century sculptor, Wiligelmus.

The highlight of the rather severe interior is a large carved *tribuna* (rood screen) decorated with 12th-century scenes from the Passion.

🏛 Palazzo dei Musei
Largo di Porta Sant'Agostino 337.
Galleria Estense **☎** *059 22 21 45.* **◯** *Tue–Sun (Wed, Thu & Sun am only).* **⬤** *Jan 1, May 1, Dec 25.* **♿**
Biblioteca Estense **☎** *059 22 22 48.* **◯** *Mon–Sat am.* **⬤** *public hols.*
Northwest of the duomo, and reached through an attractive warren of old streets, stands the Palazzo dei Musei. Formerly an arsenal and workhouse, it is now home to the cream of the city's museums and galleries. Its finest section is the **Galleria Estense**, given over to the d'Este's private art collection, which was transferred here when the city of Ferrara, the family's former dominion, became part of the Papal States. Most of the paintings are by Emilian and Ferrarese artists (notably Reni and the Carracci) but there are also works here by Bernini, Velázquez, Tintoretto, and Veronese.

Among the permanent displays in the **Biblioteca Estense**, the d'Este Library, are a 1481 edition of Dante's *Divine Comedy*, and dozens of fascinating maps and diplomatic letters, many dating back centuries. A map dated 1501 was among the first to show the 1492 voyage by Columbus to the New World. The jewel of the collection is the magnificent illuminated Borso d'Este Bible, with gloriously decorated pages containing over 1,200 miniatures by 15th-century artists of the Ferrara school, most notably Taddeo Crivelli and Franco Russi.

The Torre Ghirlandina in Modena

ENVIRONS: The **Ferrari** factory, 20 km (12 miles) to the south, was founded by Enzo Ferrari in 1945. The FIAT-owned manufacturer now produces around 2,500 cars annually. The **Galleria Ferrari** has a small exhibition featuring memorabilia, a reconstruction of the founder's study, classic engines, and many vintage cars.

🏛 Galleria Ferrari
Via Dino Ferrari 43, Maranello.
☎ *0536 94 32 04.* **◯** *Tue–Sun.* **⬤** *Jan 1, Dec 25.* **🌀** **♿**

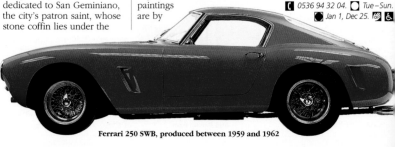

Ferrari 250 SWB, produced between 1959 and 1962

Ferrara ❻

🏛 *140,000.* **FS** 🚌 **ℹ** *Castello
Estense, Largo Castello (0532 20 93
70).* 🍴 *Mon & Fri.*

Façade of the Duomo in Ferrara

THE D'ESTE DYNASTY has left
an indelible mark on
Ferrara, one of the region's
greatest walled towns. The
noble family took control of
the town under Nicolò II in
the late 13th century, holding
power until 1598, when the
family was forced by the
papacy to move to Modena.

♣ Castello Estense

Largo Castello. **▐** *0532 29 92 33.*
🕐 *Tue–Sun.* ⚫ *public hols.* 🔲
The family's dynastic seat,
with its moats, towers, and
battlements (begun 1385),
looms over the town center.
Ferrante and Giulio d'Este were

**The impressive medieval Castello
Estense in Ferrara**

incarcerated in its draughty
dungeons for plotting to over-
throw Alfonso I d'Este. Parisina
d'Este, wife of the ruthless
Nicolò III, was executed here
for having an affair with Ugo,
her illegitimate stepson.

🏛 Palazzo del Comune

Piazza Municipale.
Bronze statues of Nicolò III
and Borso d'Este, one of
Nicolò's reputed 27 children,
adorn this medieval palace
(begun 1243). Both are copies
of the 15th-century originals
by Leon Battista Alberti.

🏛 Museo della Cattedrale

Cattedrale di Ferrara. **▐** *0532 20
74 49.* 🕐 *Tue–Sun.* ⚫ *Mon, public
hols.* **Donation**.
Ferrara's 12th-century **Duomo**
is a Romanesque-Gothic hybrid
designed by Wiligelmus. Fine
reliefs on the façade depict

vivid scenes from the Last
Judgment. The excellent
museum contains a fine
set of marble reliefs of the
Labors of the Months (late
12th century), two painted
organ shutters (1469) of *St.
George* and the *Annunciation*
by Cosmè Tura, and the
Madonna of the Pomegranate
(1408) by Jacopo della Quercia.

🏛 Palazzo Schifanoia

Via Scandiana 23. **▐** *0532 641 78.*
🕐 *daily.* ⚫ *public hols.* 🔲
This d'Este summer retreat,
begun in 1385, is famous for
its Salone dei Mesi (Room of
the Months), whose walls
display murals by Tura and
other Ferrarese painters with
scenes of the different months.
They were commissioned by
Borso d'Este, who appears in
many of the panels.

🏛 Museo Archeologico Nazionale

Palazzo di Ludovico il Moro, Via XX
Settembre 122. **▐** *0532 662 99.*
🕐 *Tue–Sun.* ⚫ *public hols.* 🔲 ♿
The most interesting exhibits
here are artifacts that were
excavated from Spina, a Greco-
Etruscan trading post near
Comacchio on the Po Delta.

🏛 Palazzo dei Diamanti

Palazzo dei Diamanti, Corso Ercole
d'Este 21. **▐** *0532 20 58 44.* 🕐 *Tue–
Sun am.* ⚫ *Jan 1, May 1, Dec 25.* 🔲
Named after the diamond
motifs on its façade, the Palace
of Diamonds houses a modern
art gallery, a museum devoted
to the Risorgimento, and the
Pinacoteca Nazionale, which
contains works from leading
Renaissance exponents of the
Ferrara and Bologna schools.

THE D'ESTE FAMILY DYNASTY

During their medieval heyday, the d'Este family presided
over one of Europe's leading courts, combining the roles
of blood-crazed despots with enlightened Renaissance
patrons. Nicolò III, for example,
had his wife and her lover
brutally murdered. Alfonso I
(1503–34) married Lucrezia
Borgia, descendant of one of
Italy's most notorious families,
while Ercole I (1407–1505)
attempted to poison a nephew
who tried to usurp him (and
eventually had him executed).
At the same time the d'Este court
attracted writers like Petrarch,
Tasso, and Ariosto, and painters
such as Mantegna, Titian, and
Bellini. Ercole I also rebuilt
Ferrara, creating one of Europe's
finest Renaissance cities.

**Portrait of Alfonso I d'Este
by Titian (c.1485–1576)**

Street-by-Street: Bologna ⓿

Detail of façade from San Petronio

THE HISTORIC city center of Bologna is a handsome ensemble of brick buildings and charming porticoed streets. Medieval palaces are clustered around the two central squares, Piazza Maggiore and Piazza del Nettuno, flanked to the south by the churches of San Petronio and San Domenico. Here, too, is the venerable Archiginnasio, part of the university of Bologna, one of the oldest universities in Europe. The skyline is etched by the Asinelli and Garisenda towers, and by the campanile of Santo Stefano.

Fontana di Nettuno
The famous Neptune fountain (1566) was designed by Tommaso Laureti and decorated with magnificent bronze figures by Giambologna.

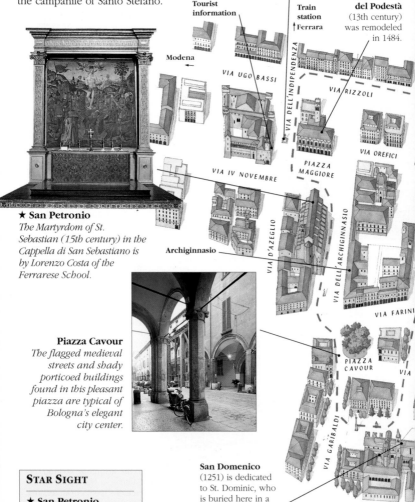

Tourist information

Train station
↑ Ferrara

The Palazzo del Podestà (13th century) was remodeled in 1484.

Modena ←

VIA UGO BASSI

VIA DELL'INDIPENDENZA

VIA RIZZOLI

VIA OREFICI

VIA IV NOVEMBRE

PIAZZA MAGGIORE

★ San Petronio
The Martyrdom of St. Sebastian (15th century) in the Cappella di San Sebastiano is by Lorenzo Costa of the Ferrarese School.

Archiginnasio

VIA D'AZEGLIO

VIA DELL'ARCHIGINNASIO

VIA FARINI

Piazza Cavour
The flagged medieval streets and shady porticoed buildings found in this pleasant piazza are typical of Bologna's elegant city center.

PIAZZA CAVOUR

VIA

VIA GARIBALDI

San Domenico
(1251) is dedicated to St. Dominic, who is buried here in a magnificent tomb.

STAR SIGHT

★ San Petronio

San Giacomo Maggiore
The Triumph of Death fresco by Costa (1483–6) adorns the Cappella Bentivoglio.

⛪ San Giacomo Maggiore

Piazza Rossini. 📞 *051 22 59 70.* ◷ *daily.*

This Romanesque-Gothic church, begun in 1267 but altered substantially since, is visited mainly for the Cappella Bentivoglio, a superb family chapel founded by Annibale Bentivoglio in 1445 and consecrated in 1486. Pride of place naturally goes to a portrait with subtle characterization of the patrons by Lorenzo Costa (1460–1535), who was also responsible for the frescoes of the *Apocalypse*, the *Madonna Enthroned*, and the *Triumph of Death*. The chapel's altarpiece, depicting the *Virgin and Saints with Two Angel Musicians* (1488), is the work of Francesco Francia. The Bentivoglio family is further glorified in the tomb of Anton Galeazzo Bentivoglio (1435) opposite the chapel. It was among the last works of the noted Sienese sculptor, Jacopo della Quercia. The Oratory of Santa Cecilia features frescoes on the lives of Santa Cecilia and San Valeriano by Costa and Francesco Francia (1504–6).

Torri degli Asinelli e Garisenda
The colossal towers are two of the few remaining towers begun by Bologna's important families in the 12th century.

Abbazia di Santo Stefano
The Fontana di Pilato, or Pilate's fountain, in the courtyard features a basin with Lombard inscriptions from the 8th century.

KEY

— — — Suggested route

```
0 meters        150
0 yards         150
```

The Bentivoglio tomb (1435) by Jacopo della Quercia

Exploring Bologna

Mᴏɴᴜᴍᴇɴᴛꜱ ᴛᴏ ʙᴏʟᴏɢɴᴀ'ꜱ rich cultural heritage are scattered across the city, from the leaning towers and the church of San Petronio in the old center to the Pinacoteca Nazionale in the university district.

🏛 Torri degli Asinelli e Garisenda

Piazza di Porta Ravegnana. ◯ *daily*. 🖼

The famous Torri Pendenti, or leaning towers – Torre degli Asinelli and Torre Garisenda – are among the few survivors of the original 200 that once formed the skyline of Bologna. Both were begun in the 12th century, though there were probably earlier towers on the site – Dante mentioned a pair of towers here in his *Inferno*. Torre Garisenda was shortened as a safety measure within only a few years of its construction, and still leans some 3 m (10 ft) from the vertical. At 97 m (318 ft) tall, Torre Asinelli is the fourth highest tower in Italy after those in Cremona, Siena, and Venice. Its 500-step ascent offers fine views over Bologna's pantiled rooftops to the hills beyond.

🔒 Abbazia di Santo Stefano

Via Santo Stefano 24.
📞 *051 22 32 56*. ◯ *daily*.

Santo Stefano is a curious collection of four medieval churches (originally seven) jumbled together under one roof. The 11th-century church of the Crocifisso provides little

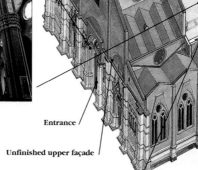

Exterior of the Abbazia di Santo Stefano

🔒 SAN PETRONIO

Piazza Maggiore. 📞 *051 22 21 12*. ◯ *daily*. ♿

Dedicated to the city's 5th-century bishop, this church ranks among the greatest of Italy's brick-built medieval buildings. Founded in 1390, it was originally intended to be larger than St. Peter's in Rome, but its size was scaled down when the church authorities diverted funds to the nearby Palazzo Archiginnasio. The resulting financial shortfall left the church decidedly lopsided, with a row of columns on its eastern flank that were intended to support an additional internal aisle. The project's financial profligacy, nonetheless, was said to have been instrumental in turning Martin Luther against Catholicism.

The altarpiece of the *Martyrdom of St. Sebastian* is from the late Ferrarese School.

The pink and white interior adds to the overall light and airy effect.

The canopied main portal features beautiful biblical reliefs (1425–38) by Jacopo della Quercia.

Gothic Interior
The interior is airy, with graceful pillars supporting the roof. Twenty-two chapels, shielded by screens, open off the nave. In 1547 the Council of Trent (see p168) was temporarily moved here due to the plague.

Entrance

Unfinished upper façade

The meridian line, along the 60th meridian between the north and south poles, was traced in 1655 by the astronomer Gian Domenico Cassini.

The stained glass windows (1464–6) in this chapel are by Jacob of Ulm.

more than a corridor to polygonal San Sepolcro, the most appealing of the quartet. Also dating from the 11th century, its centerpiece is the tomb of St. Petronius, a marvelously overstated affair modeled on the Holy Sepulchre of Jerusalem. The courtyard contains the so-called Fontana di Pilato, an 8th-century basin.

Santi Vitale e Agricola dates originally from the 5th century, making it the oldest church in the city. It was rebuilt in the 8th and 11th centuries. Inside are the sarcophagi of Saints Vitalis and Agricola, martyred in the 4th century. Santa Trinità features a small museum of minor paintings and religious artifacts, including wooden statues of the *Adoration of the Magi* painted by Simone dei Crocifissi (c.1370).

Bell tower

Choir Stalls
The exquisite inlaid choir stalls of the Chapel of the Holy Sacrament were made by Raffaello da Brescia in 1521.

🏛 Pinacoteca Nazionale

Via delle Belle Arti 56.
📞 051 24 32 49.
🕐 Tue–Sun.
⬤ Jan 1, May 1, Aug 15, Dec 25. 🎟 ♿

Bologna's principal art gallery, and one of northern Italy's most important collections, stands on the edge of the city's university district, a bustling area of bars, bookshops, and cheap restaurants. The gallery is mainly dedicated to work by Bolognese painters, notably Vitale da Bologna, Guido Reni, Guercino, and the Carracci family. Members of the Ferrarese School are also represented, in particular Francesco del Cossa and Ercole de' Roberti. The two highlights are Perugino's *Madonna in Glory* (c.1491) and Raphael's famous *Ecstasy of St. Cecilia*, painted around 1515, both artists having worked in Bologna.

The *Ecstasy of St. Cecilia* (c.1515) by Raphael in Bologna's Pinacoteca Nazionale

🏛 Museo di Anatomia Umana Normale

Palazzo Poggi, Via Zamboni 33. 📞 051 209 93 69. 🕐 Mon–Fri. ⬤ Dec 25, Jan 1, Easter, 1 May, public hols.

Although well off the standard tourist itineraries, the Museum of Human Anatomy is one of the more memorable of Bologna's smaller museums. The collection includes occasionally gruesome visceral waxworks and numerous models of organs, limbs, and flayed bodies. Sculpted rather than made from casts, they have an artistic as well as scientific appeal. The models were used as medical teaching aids until the 19th century. The contents of the museum recently moved to Palazzo Poggi, which also contains the Museo Cartageographica.

🏠 San Domenico

Piazza di San Domenico 13.
📞 051 640 04 11. 🕐 daily. ♿

Bologna's San Domenico can lay claim to being the most important of Italy's many Dominican churches. Begun in 1221, after St. Dominic's death, it was built to house the body of the saint, who died here and lies buried in a tomb known as the Arca di San Domenico. A magnificent composite work, the tomb's statues were executed by Nicola Pisano; the reliefs of scenes from the *Life of St. Dominic* were the work of Nicola Pisano and his assistants; the canopy (1473) is attributed to Nicola di Bari; while the figures of the angels and Saints Proculus and Petronius are early works by Michelangelo. The reliquary (1383) behind the sarcophagus contains St. Dominic's head.

Arca di San Domenico in the Basilica di San Domenico

Fresco of Malatesta and St. Sigismund (1451) by Piero della Francesca in the Tempio Malatestiano, Rimini

Faenza ❽

Ravenna. 👥 *54,000*. 🚉 🚌
ℹ️ *Piazza del Popolo 1 (0546 252 31).*
🗓️ *Tue, Thu & Sat.*

FAENZA IS SYNONYMOUS with the **faïence** ceramic ware to which it gave its name. Renowned across Europe for over 500 years, the pottery, with its distinctive blue and ocher coloring, is still made in countless small factories around the town.

The highlight of Faenza is the **Museo Internazionale delle Ceramiche**, one of the largest ceramic collections in Italy. Its exhibits feature not only examples of local ware, but also pottery from other countries and other periods, including Roman ceramics and medieval majolica. There is also a section devoted to the modern ceramic art of Picasso, Matisse, and Chagall.

🏛️ Museo Internazionale delle Ceramiche
Viale Baccarini 19. 📞 *0546 212 40.*
🗓️ *Tue–Sun.* ⬤ *Jan 1, May 1, Aug 15, Dec 25.* ♿ 📷

Rimini ❾

👥 *130,000*. 🚉 🚌 ℹ️ *Piazza Fellini 3 (0541 569 02).* 🗓️ *Wed & Sat.*

RIMINI WAS ONCE a quaint seaside resort, whose innocent charms were celebrated in the early films of Federico Fellini, the director

born and raised here. Today it is the largest beach resort in Europe. The seafront, which continues unbroken for almost 15 km (9 miles), is lined with clubs, restaurants, and bars. The crowded beaches are clean and well groomed, though entrance fees are charged at the private beaches.

Rimini's old quarter, by contrast, is pleasantly quiet. Its charming cobbled streets gather around **Piazza Cavour**, dominated by the 14th-century **Palazzo del Podestà**. The town's finest building is the **Tempio Malatestiano**, built as a Franciscan church but converted in 1450 by Leon Battista Alberti, the great Florentine architect, into one of Italy's great Renaissance monuments. The work was commissioned by Sigismondo Malatesta (1417–68), a descendant of Rimini's ruling medieval family, and reputedly one of the most debauched and evil men of his

time. Ostensibly designed as a chapel, the Tempio eventually became little more than a monument to Malatesta. Inside there are sculptures by Agostino di Duccio and a fresco (1451) by Piero della Francesca of Malatesta kneeling before St. Sigismund (1451).

The entwined initials of Malatesta and his fourth wife, Isotta degli Atti, provide a recurring decorative motif, and there are reliefs depicting scenes of bacchanalian excess and oddities such as strangely posed elephants (a Malatesta family emblem). All this led Pope Pius II to condemn the building as "a temple of devil-worshippers", and to burn Malatesta's effigy for what the papal charge against him described as acts of "murder, violation, adultery, incest, sacrilege and perjury."

ENVIRONS: Further along the coast, away from Rimini, the resorts become relatively quieter. **Cesenatico**, 18 km (11 miles) north, offers all the usual facilities but the beaches are less crowded.

🏛️ Tempio Malatestiano
Via IV Novembre. ⬤ *daily.* ♿

Ravenna ❿

👥 *90,000*. 🚉 🚌 ℹ️ *Via Salara 8–12 (0544 354 04).* 🗓️ *Wed & Sat.*

MOST PEOPLE VISIT Ravenna for its superb mosaics from the Byzantine period *(see pp260–61)*, but the town itself is a surprisingly pleasant medley of old streets, fine shops, and peaceful piazzas.

Façade of the Renaissance Tempio Malatestiano in Rimini

Piazza del Popolo, Ravenna's central square

The **Museo Nazionale** features a wide range of icons, paintings, and archaeological displays. The best place to relax and take a break from sightseeing is Piazza del Popolo, a lovely ensemble of medieval buildings.

🏛 **Museo Nazionale**
Via Fiandrini. 📞 0544 344 24.
🕐 Tue–Sun. 📷 ⛔

Po Delta ⓫

Ferrara. 🚆 Ferrara Ostellata.
🚌 to Goro or Gorino. ⛴ from Porto Garibaldi, Goro & Gorino.
ℹ Via Buonafede 12, Comacchio (0533 31 01 47).

THE PO IS ITALY'S longest river. Its vast basin covers some 15 percent of the country and supports around a third of the nation's population. Although ravaged in many places by industrial pollution, at its finest it offers beautifully subtle landscapes – rows of poplar trees across misty fields and long views over soft brown earth.

There are wide vistas over the shifting sands of its vast delta, an estuary of marshes, dunes, and islands.

The Po Delta is known to Italian naturalists as the "Italian Camargue." There are plans to turn the entire region – some 30,000 ha (74,000 acres) – into a national park that would stretch from the edge of the Venetian lagoon to the coastal pine woods that lie around Ravenna.

Wetland areas such as the **Valli di Comacchio** north of Ravenna are already nature preserves, a winter home to thousands of breeding and migrating birds. Ornithologists gather here to see gulls, coots, bean geese, and black terns, and far rarer species such as the white egret, hen harrier, and pygmy cormorant. **Comacchio**, the nearest settlement, is one of several fishing villages dotted around the area. Its most famous catch is eels, often caught using methods like water gates that date back as far as Roman times.

Other nature reserves include the **Bosco della Mesola**, a tract of ancient woodland planted by the Etruscans and cared for by generations of monks. You can walk or bike through it, with excellent opportunities for spotting deer.

For a good look at the entire region, follow the N309 – part of the old Via Romea pilgrimage trail to Rome – that runs north to south through some 100 km (62 miles) of the proposed park. Numerous smaller lanes branch off into the wilderness. There are also boat trips to some of the delta's more remote corners: key departure points include the villages of Ca' Tiepolo, Ca' Vernier and Taglio di Po.

Hen harrier, found in the Po Delta

The peaceful landscape along the banks of the river in the Po Delta

A Tour of Ravenna

RAVENNA ROSE to power in the 1st century BC under the Emperor Augustus, who built a port and naval base at nearby Classis. As Rome's power declined, Ravenna was made the capital of the Western Empire (AD 402), a prominence it retained during the Ostrogoth and Byzantine rule in the 5th and 6th centuries. Ravenna is renowned for its early Christian mosaics – the town had converted to Christianity in the 2nd century AD and was made a bishopric in the 4th century AD. The mosaics span the years of Roman and Byzantine rule, offering comparisons between Classically inspired designs and later Byzantine motifs.

Mosaic detail from San Vitale

The Good Shepherd ②
This mosaic adorns the tiny Mausoleo di Galla Placidia. Begun in 430, this exquisite building probably never received the remains of Placidia, wife of a Barbarian emperor.

San Vitale ①
San Vitale's apse mosaics (526–547) show Christ, San Vitale (being handed a martyr's crown), two angels, and Bishop Ecclesius, who founded the church (see pp46–7).

Baptism of Jesus ③
The 5th-century Battistero Neoniano (Neonian Baptistry) is named after the bishop who may have commissioned its decoration, including this beautiful mosaic. It was built near the remains of a Roman bathhouse and is Ravenna's oldest monument.

Battistero degli Ariani ⑤
The cupola of this late 5th-century baptistry has a mosaic showing the Apostles ringed around a centerpiece depicting the Baptism of Christ.

VISITORS' CHECKLIST

San Vitale & Mausoleo di Galla Placidia, Via Fiandrini. ☎ 0544 21 99 38. ☐ Apr–Sep: 9am–7pm daily; Oct–Mar: 9:30am–4:30pm (last adm: 15 mins before closing). ● Jan 1, Dec 25. 📷 ♿
Battistero Neoniano, Via Battistero. ☎ 0544 21 85 59. ☐ as above. ● Jan 1, Dec 25. 📷
Tomba di Dante, Via Dante Aleghieri. ☐ Apr–Sep: 9am–7pm daily; Oct–Mar: 9am–noon, 2–5pm daily (last adm: 15 mins before closing). ● Jan 1, Dec 25. ♿
Battistero degli Ariani, Via degli Ariani. ☎ 0544 344 24.
☐ Apr– Sep: 9am–7pm daily; Oct–Mar: 9:30am–4:30pm daily (last adm: 15 mins before closing). ● Jan 1, May 1. ♿
Sant'Apollinare Nuovo, Via di Roma. ☎ 0544 390 81.
☐ Apr–Sep: 9am–7pm daily; Oct–Mar: 9:30am–4:30pm (last adm: 15 mins before closing). ● Jan 1, Dec 25. 📷 ♿
Combined ticket also available.

Sant'Apollinare Nuovo ⑥
This glorious 6th-century church, named after Ravenna's first bishop, is dominated by two rows of mosaics. Both show processions of martyrs and virgins bearing gifts for Christ and the Virgin.

Tomba di Dante ④
Dante's wanderings around Italy after his exile from Florence eventually brought him to Ravenna, where he died in 1321. A lamp in his sepulchre (1780) is fed by oil given by the city of Florence.

KEY

– – – Suggested route

🅿 Parking

ℹ Tourist information

0 meters   200

0 yards   200

FLORENCE

F LORENCE IS A VAST AND BEAUTIFUL *monument to the Renaissance, the artistic and cultural reawakening of the 15th century. Writers such as Dante, Petrarch, and Machiavelli contributed to its proud literary heritage, but it was the paintings and sculptures of artists such as Botticelli, Michelangelo, and Donatello that turned the city into one of the world's greatest artistic capitals.*

While the Etruscans had long settled the hills around Fiesole, Florence first sprang to life as a Roman colony in 59 BC. Captured by the Lombards in the 6th century, the city later emerged from the Dark Ages as an independent city state. By the 13th century a burgeoning trade in wool and textiles, backed by a powerful banking sector, had turned the city into one of Italy's leading powers. Political control was wielded first by the guilds, and later by the Florentine Republic. In time, power passed to leading noble families, of which the most influential were the Medici, a hugely wealthy banking dynasty. Florence, and later Tuscany, remained under the family's almost unbroken sway for three centuries. During this time the city was at the cultural and intellectual heart of Europe, its cosmopolitan atmosphere and wealthy patrons providing the impetus for a period of unparalleled artistic growth. Artists, sculptors, and architects flocked to the city, filling its streets, churches, and palaces with some of the world's greatest Renaissance works. By 1737 the Medici had died out, leaving the city under Austrian (and briefly Napoleonic) control until Italian Unification in 1860. Between 1865 and 1871 Florence was the capital of the new Kingdom of Italy. In recent history its streets and artistic heritage were ravaged by the Arno floods of November 1966.

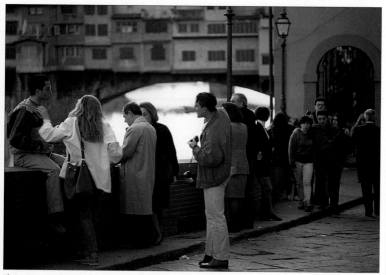

Florentines strolling in front of Ponte Vecchio (1345), the old bridge lined with shops spanning the Arno

◁ The dome of Florence's Duomo, completed in 1436, designed by Brunelleschi

Exploring Florence

H ISTORIC FLORENCE is a surprisingly compact area, and the majority
of the sights described on the following pages can easily be
reached on foot. Most visitors head for the Duomo, the city's
geographical and historical focus, ideally placed to explore
the Campanile, Baptistry, and Museo dell'Opera del Duomo.
To the south is Piazza della Signoria, long the city's political
heart, flanked by the Palazzo Vecchio, Florence's town
hall, and the Uffizi, one of Italy's leading art galleries.
To the east lies the church of Santa Croce, home
to frescoes by Giotto and the tombs of some of
Florence's greatest men. To the west stands
Santa Maria Novella, the city's other great
church, also adorned with fresco-filled
chapels. Across the Ponte Vecchio, and
the Arno – the river that bisects the city –
is the district of Oltrarno, dominated
by Santo Spirito and the vast Pitti
Palace, containing galleries

Bell tower, with works by great Renais-
Palazzo sance artists including
Vecchio Raphael and Titian.

GETTING AROUND

Florence has excellent bus service,
including electric buses, making
public transportation both
convenient and fast. The compact
city center, closed to traffic, is easily
negotiated on foot.

KEY

■	Street-by-Street: Around San Marco pp266–7
■	Street-by-Street: Around the Duomo pp270–71
■	Street-by-Street: Around Piazza della Repubblica pp284–5
■	Street-by-Street: Around Oltrarno pp292–3
FS	Train station
P	Parking
i	Tourist information
—	City walls

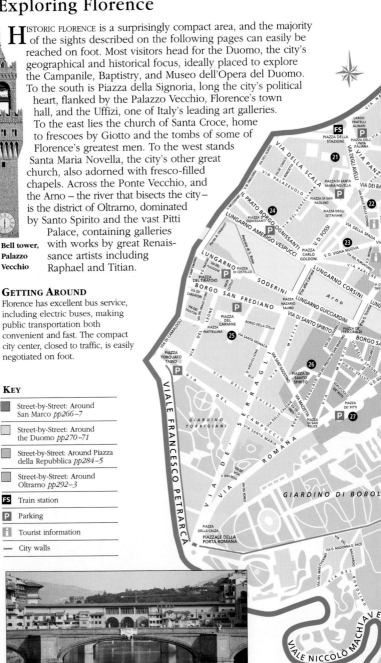

Ponte Vecchio with Ponte Santa Trìnita in the foreground

LOCATOR MAP

SIGHTS AT A GLANCE

Churches

Cappella Brancacci pp290–91 25

Cappelle Medicee 19

Convento di San Marco 2

Duomo and Baptistry pp272–4 7

Ognissanti 24

Orsanmichele 8

Santissima Annunziata 3

Santa Croce 10

Santa Felicita 28

San Lorenzo 18

Santa Maria Novella 21

San Miniato al Monte 30

Santo Spirito 26

Buildings, Monuments and Squares

Mercato Centrale 20

Palazzo Antinori 22

Palazzo Davanzati 16

Palazzo Rucellai 23

Palazzo Strozzi 17

Palazzo Vecchio 15

Piazza della Signoria 14

Piazzale Michelangelo 29

Ponte Vecchio 12

Spedale degli Innocenti 5

Museums and Galleries

Bargello 9

Galleria dell'Accademia 1

Museo Archeologico 4

Museo dell'Opera del Duomo 6

Museo di Storia della Scienza 11

Palazzo Pitti pp294–5 27

Uffizi pp278–81 13

SEE ALSO

0 meters   500

0 yards   500

Street-by-Street: Around San Marco

T HE BUILDINGS in this part of Florence once stood on the fringes of the city, serving as stables and barracks. The Medici menagerie of lions, elephants, and giraffes was housed here. Today it is a student quarter and the streets are often busy with young people attending the university or the Accademia di Belle Arti, the world's oldest art school, founded in 1563.

Santissima Annunziata
This fine Renaissance church has an opulent Baroque interior ❸

Palazzo Pandolfini
was designed by Raphael in 1516.

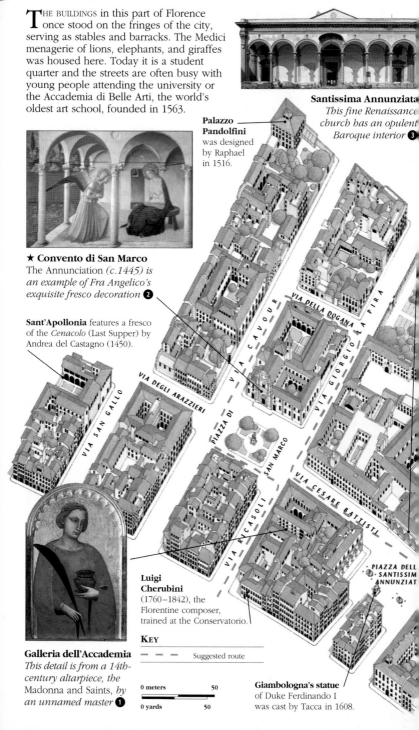

★ **Convento di San Marco**
The Annunciation (c.1445) is an example of Fra Angelico's exquisite fresco decoration ❷

Sant'Apollonia features a fresco of the *Cenacolo* (Last Supper) by Andrea del Castagno (1450).

Luigi Cherubini (1760–1842), the Florentine composer, trained at the Conservatorio.

KEY

– – – Suggested route

0 meters   50

0 yards   50

Galleria dell'Accademia
This detail is from a 14th-century altarpiece, the Madonna and Saints, *by an unnamed master* ❶

Giambologna's statue of Duke Ferdinando I was cast by Tacca in 1608.

LOCATOR MAP
*See Florence Street Finder
map 2*

Spedale degli Innocenti
Opened in 1444, the city orphanage by Brunelleschi was decorated with cameos by Andrea della Robbia **5**

The Giardino dei Semplici
was opened in 1543.

Museo Archeologico
Many of the Etruscan objects in the museum were originally in the Medici collections **4**

STAR SIGHTS

★ **Convento di San Marco**

★ **Galleria dell'Accademia**

Part of the 15th-century *Cassone Adimari* by Lo Scheggia in the Accademia

Galleria dell'Accademia ❶

Via Ricasoli 60. **Map** 2 D4. 📞 055 238 86 09. ⏰ *Jun–Sep: 8:30am–6:50pm Tue–Fri, 8:30am–10pm Sat, 8:30am–7pm Sun; Oct–May: 8:30am–6:50pm Tue–Sat, 8:30am–7pm Sun.* ⏰ *Mon, public hols.* 🎫 📷 ♿

T HE ACADEMY OF FINE ARTS, founded in 1563, was the first school established in Europe specifically to teach the techniques of drawing, painting, and sculpture. The art collection displayed here was formed in 1784 to provide material for students to study and copy.

The most famous work is Michelangelo's *David* (1504), a colossal nude of the biblical hero who killed the giant Goliath. The sculpture was commissioned by the city for Piazza della Signoria, but it was moved to the Accademia for safekeeping in 1873. One copy now stands in its original position *(see pp282–3)* and a second is on Piazzale Michelangelo. The *David* statue established Michelangelo, at the age of 29, as the foremost sculptor of his time.

Michelangelo's other masterpieces in the Accademia include the *Quattro Prigioni* (the Four Prisoners), sculpted between 1521 and 1523 and intended to adorn the tomb of Pope Julius II. The statues

Michelangelo's *David*

were presented to the Medici family in 1564 by the artist's nephew, Leonardo. The muscular figures struggling to free themselves from the stone are among the most dramatic of Michelangelo's works. The statues were then moved to the Grotta Grande in the Boboli Gardens, where casts of the originals can now be seen.

The Accademia also contains an important collection of paintings by 15th- and 16th-century Florentine artists, among them Filippino Lippi, Fra Bartolomeo, Bronzino, and Ridolfo del Ghirlandaio. The major works include the *Madonna del Mare* (Madonna of the Sea), attributed to Botticelli (1445–1510), and *Venus and Cupid* by Jacopo Pontormo (1494–1556), based on a preparatory drawing by Michelangelo. Also here is an elaborately painted wooden chest, the *Cassone Adimari* (1440–45) by Lo Scheggia. Originally part of a wealthy bride's trousseau, it is decorated with details of Florentine life, clothing, and architecture. A scene of the bridal party appears on the chest in front of the Baptistry.

The Salone della Toscana (Tuscany Room) features more modest paintings and sculptures by 19th-century members of the Accademia and plaster models by the sculptor, Lorenzo Bartolini.

The light and airy former library, designed by Michelozzo

Convento di San Marco ❷

Piazza di San Marco. **Map** 2 D4.
📞 055 287 628. ⏰ 7am–noon,
4–8pm. 🎫 📷 **Museo di San Marco**
📞 055 238 86 08. ⏰ 8:30am–1:50pm
daily (later Sat, Sun). 🚫 Jan 1, May 1,
Dec 25, 2nd & 4th Mon and 1st, 2nd
& 5th Sun of each month. 🅿 📷

T HE CONVENT OF SAN MARCO
was founded in the 13th
century and enlarged in 1437
when Dominican monks from
nearby Fiesole
moved there
at the
invitation of Cosimo il Vecchio.
He paid a considerable sum to
have the convent rebuilt by his
favorite architect, Michelozzo,
whose simple cloisters and
cells provide the setting for a
remarkable series of devotional
frescoes (c.1438–45) by Florentine painter and Dominican
friar, Fra Angelico. The convent
and art collections form the
Museo di San Marco.

Beyond the ticket office lies
the magnificent **Chiostro di
Sant'Antonino** by Michelozzo,
a cloister named after the
convent's first prior,
Antonino Pierozzi
(1389–1459), who
later became the
Archbishop of
Florence. Most
of the faded
frescoes here
describe scenes
from the saint's
life by
Bernardino
Poccetti. The
panels in the
corner are by Fra Angelico.
A door in the right side of the
cloister leads to the **Ospizio
dei Pellegrini** (Pilgrims'
Hospice).Today it houses the
museum's free-standing paintings, including
two famous
master-

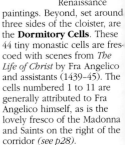

A detail from Fra Angelico's poignant Deposition (c. 1440)

pieces: Fra Angelico's moving
Deposition (c.1435–40), an
altarpiece painted for the
church of Santa Trinità, and
the *Madonna dei Linaiuoli*,
commissioned by the Linaiuoli
(flaxworkers' guild) in 1433.

In the courtyard, right of
the convent's former bell, is
the vaulted **Sala Capitolare**
(Chapter House), decorated
with a noted but over-restored
Crucifixion and Saints (1440)
painted by Fra Angelico.

Covering one wall of the
small **Refettorio** (refectory)
is a fresco of the *Last Supper*
(c.1480) by Domenico
Ghirlandaio. Stairs
from the courtyard
lead to the first
floor, where you
suddenly see
Fra Angelico's
Annunciation
(c.1445), thought
by many to be
among the city's
most beautiful
Renaissance
paintings. Beyond, set around
three sides of the cloister, are
the **Dormitory Cells**. These
44 tiny monastic cells are frescoed with scenes from *The
Life of Christ* by Fra Angelico
and assistants (1439–45). The
cells numbered 1 to 11 are
generally attributed to Fra
Angelico himself, as is the
lovely fresco of the Madonna
and Saints on the right of the
corridor *(see p28)*.

Cells 12–14 were once
occupied by Savonarola, the
zealous Dominican monk who
became Prior of San Marco in
1491. Among other deeds,
Savonarola incited Florentines
to rebel against the Medici
and was responsible for
burning many works of art.
Denounced as a heretic, he
was burned at the stake in
Piazza della Signoria in 1498.

Along the third corridor
lies an airy colonnaded hall,
formerly a public **library**
designed by Michelozzo in
1441 for Cosimo il Vecchio.
Beyond it lie two cells (38
and 39) that were used by
Cosimo when he went on
retreat here. Each is decorated
with two frescoes (the other
cells have only one) and they
are both larger than any of
the neighboring rooms.

**Fra Angelico's allegorical fresco, the *Mocking of Christ* (c. 1442), shows
Jesus blindfolded and being struck by a Roman guard**

The Birth of the Virgin (1514) by del Sarto in Santissima Annunziata

Santissima Annunziata ❸

Piazza della Santissima Annunziata.
Map 2 E4. 055 239 80 34.
7:30am–12:30pm, 4–6:30pm
daily.

FOUNDED BY the Servite order in 1250, the church of the Holy Annunciation was later rebuilt by Michelozzo between 1444 and 1481. Its atrium contains frescoes by the Mannerist artists Rosso Fiorentino, Andrea del Sarto, and Jacopo Pontormo. Perhaps the finest of its panels are *The Journey of the Magi* (1511) and *The Birth of the Virgin* (1514) by Andrea del Sarto.

The heavily decorated, dark interior has a frescoed ceiling completed by Pietro Giambelli in 1669. Here is one of the city's most revered shrines, a painting of the Virgin Mary begun by a monk in 1252 but miraculously completed by an angel, according to devout Florentines. Newlywed couples traditionally visit the shrine (on the left as you enter the church) to present a bouquet of flowers to the Virgin and to pray for a long, fruitful marriage.

A door from the north transept leads to the **Chiostrino dei Morti** (Cloister of the Dead), so called because it was originally used as a burial ground. Today it is best known for del Sarto's beautiful fresco, *The Madonna del Sacco* (1525).

The church is situated on the northern flank of **Piazza della Santissima Annunziata**, one of the finest Renaissance squares in Florence. Designed by Brunelleschi, the delicate nine-bay arcade fronts the Spedale degli Innocenti to its right, while at the center of the square stands a bronze equestrian statue of Duke Ferdinando I. Started by Giambologna, it was finished in 1608 by his assistant Pietro Tacca (who designed the squares bronze fountains).

Museo Archeologico ❹

Via della Colonna 36. **Map** 2 E4.
055 235 75. 2–7pm Mon,
9am–7pm Tue–Fri, Sun, 9am–2pm Sat.
2nd & 4th Mon and 1st, 3rd &
5th Sun of each month.

THE ARCHAEOLOGICAL MUSEUM in Florence is in a palazzo built by Giulio Parigi for the Princess Maria Maddalena de' Medici in 1620. It now exhibits an outstanding collection of Etruscan, Greek, Roman, and Egyptian artifacts, although parts of the collection are being restored following the flood of 1966. The first floor contains a splendid series of Etruscan bronzes as well as the famous *Chimera* (4th century BC), a mythical lion with a goat's head imposed on its body and a serpent for a tail. Equally impressive is the 1st-century *Arringatore* bronze

Etruscan warrior, Museo Archeologico

found near Lake Trasimeno in Umbria. It is inscribed with the name of Aulus Metellus. A large section on the second floor is dedicated to Greek vases, notably the famed François Vase, found in an Etruscan tomb near Chiusi.

Spedale degli Innocenti ❺

Piazza della Santissima Annunziata 12.
Map 2 E4. 055 249 17 08.
8:30am–2pm Mon, Tue, Thu–Sat.
public hols.

Part of Brunelleschi's arcaded loggia, Spedale degli Innocenti

NAMED AFTER Herod's biblical Massacre of the Innocents, the "Hospital" opened in 1444 as Europe's first orphanage. Part of the building is still used for this purpose. Brunelleschi's arcaded loggia is decorated with glazed terra-cotta roundels, added by Andrea della Robbia around 1498, showing babies wrapped in swaddling bands. To the left of the portico is the *rota*, a rotating stone cylinder on which mothers could anonymously place their unwanted children and ring the bell for them to be admitted to the orphanage.

Within the building lie two elegant cloisters: the **Chiostro degli Uomini** (Men's Cloister), built between 1422 and 1445 and decorated with *sgraffito* roosters and cherubs, and the smaller Women's Cloister (1438). A small upstairs gallery contains a handful of fine works, including terra-cottas by della Robbia and pictures by Botticelli, Piero di Cosimo, and Domenico Ghirlandaio.

Street-by-Street: Around the Duomo

WHILE MUCH OF FLORENCE was rebuilt during the Renaissance, the eastern part of the city retains a distinctly medieval feel. With its maze of tiny alleys, it is an area that would still be familiar to Dante (1265–1321), whose birthplace probably lay somewhere among its hidden lanes. The poet would recognize the Badia Fiorentina where he first glimpsed Beatrice, as well as the gaunt outlines of the Bargello opposite. He would also be familiar with the Baptistry, one of the city's oldest buildings, though he would not know the Campanile or the Duomo, whose foundations were laid in the poet's old age.

Stained-glass window from the Duomo

★ Duomo and Baptistry
The exteriors of the Duomo and Baptistry are richly decorated with marbles and reliefs, such as this detail from the Duomo's façade **⑦**

The Loggia del Bigallo (1358) is where abandoned children were once left. They were then sent to foster homes if they remained unclaimed.

Orsanmichele
The church's niche carvings depict patron saints of trade guilds, such as this copy of Donatello's St. George **⑧**

PIAZZA DI SAN GIOVANNI

PIAZZA DEL DUOMO

VIA DELL OCHE

VIA S. ELISABETTA

VIA

VIA DE' MEDICI

VIA ROMA

VIA D. SPEZIALI

VIA DE' CALZAIUOLI

VIA DE' CERC

V.D.TAVOLINI

V.D.CIMATOR

V. DE' LAMBERTI

CALIMALA

VIA PORTA ROSSA

VIA D

KEY

– – – Suggested route

| 0 meters | 100 |
| 0 yards | 100 |

Via dei Calzaiuoli, lined with chic shops, is the city's liveliest street.

Piazza della Signoria ↓

Museo dell'Opera del Duomo

Works from the Duomo, Campanile, and Baptistry are displayed in this museum **6**

Pegna sells a range of fine wines, oil, and honey.

LOCATOR MAP
See Florence Street Finder map 6

Badia Fiorentina, the abbey church founded in 978, is home to *The Virgin Appearing to St. Bernard* (1485) by Filippino Lippi.

Casa di Dante, a restored medieval house, is reputedly Dante's birthplace.

★ **Bargello**
The city's old prison is home to a rich collection of applied arts and sculpture, including this figure of Mercury *by Giambologna (1564)* **9**

STAR SIGHTS

★ **Duomo and Baptistry**

★ **Bargello**

Carving from Luca della Robbia's choir loft in the Museo dell'Opera

Museo dell'Opera del Duomo **6**

Piazza del Duomo 9. **Map** 2 D5 (6 E2).
(055 230 28 85. **◯** 9:30am–6:30pm Mon–Sat; 8am–2pm Sun, hols (last adm: 40 mins before closing). **◯** Jan 1, Easter, Dec 25.

THE CATHEDRAL Works Museum, second only to the Bargello in its collection of sculpture, houses items removed over the years from the exteriors of the Duomo, Campanile, and Baptistry.

Its first two rooms are devoted to Brunelleschi and to the Duomo's construction, displaying tools used by 15th-century masons and a model created during the building of the cathedral dome.

The main ground floor room has a facsimile of Arnolfo di Cambio's original façade for the cathedral, together with statues such as Donatello's *St. John* (1408–15) and Arnolfo di Cambio's striking *Madonna of the Glass Eyes* (1296), both originally created for its niches. Michelangelo's *Pietà* (before 1555) has pride of place on the staircase, a fitting prelude to the magnificent white marble lofts by Donatello and Luca della Robbia on the upper floor. The former dwarfs Donatello's remarkable *La Maddalena* statue (1455), a counterpoint to his figure of the prophet Abakuk (1423–5), in the same room. Close by stand four of Ghiberti's cleaned and restored Baptistry door panels *(see p274)*, surrounded by a beautiful medley of paintings and silverware.

Duomo and Baptistry ●7

Sir John Hawkwood by Paolo Uccello, in the Duomo

RISING ABOVE THE heart of the city, the richly-decorated Duomo – Santa Maria del Fiore – and its orange-tiled dome have become Florence's most famous symbols. Typical of the Florentine determination to lead in all things, the cathedral is Europe's fourth largest church, and to this day it still remains the city's tallest building. The Baptistry, with its celebrated bronze doors, may date back to the 4th century, making it one of Florence's oldest buildings. The Campanile, designed by Giotto in 1334, was completed in 1359, 22 years after his death.

Campanile
At 85 m (276 ft), the Campanile is 6 m (20 ft) shorter than the dome. It is clad in white, green and pink Tuscan marble.

Gothic windows

The Neo-Gothic marble façade echoes the style of Giotto's Campanile, but was only added in 1871–87.

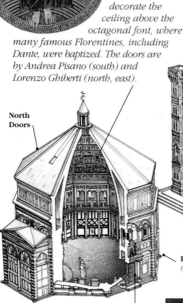

★ Baptistry
Colorful 13th-century mosaics illustrating the Last Judgment *decorate the ceiling above the octagonal font, where many famous Florentines, including Dante, were baptized. The doors are by Andrea Pisano (south) and Lorenzo Ghiberti (north, east).*

North Doors

East Doors
(See p274)

Main entrance

South Doors

Campanile Reliefs
Copies of reliefs by Andrea Pisano on the Campanile's first level depict the Creation of Man, and the Arts and the Industries. The originals are kept in the Museo dell'Opera del Duomo (see p271).

The top of the dome offers spectacular views over the city.

★ Dome by Brunelleschi
Brunelleschi's dome, finished in 1463, was the largest of its time to be built without scaffolding. The outer shell is supported by a thicker inner shell that acts as a platform for it.

The *Last Judgment* frescoes (1572–4) by Vasari were completed by Zuccari.

Bricks were set between marble ribs in a self-supporting herringbone pattern – a technique Brunelleschi copied from the Pantheon in Rome.

Chapels at the East End
The three apses, crowned by smaller copies of the dome, have five chapels each. The 15th-century stained glass is by Ghiberti.

Entrance leading to the dome

The marble sanctuary around the High Altar was created by Baccio Bandinelli in 1555.

Marble Pavement
The colorful, intricately inlaid pavement (16th century) was designed in part by Baccio d'Agnolo and Francesco da Sangallo.

Dante Explaining the Divine Comedy *(1465)*
This painting by Michelino shows the poet outside Florence against a backdrop of Purgatory, Hell, and Paradise.

STAR FEATURES

★ **Dome by Brunelleschi**

★ **Baptistry**

The East Doors of the Baptistry

Lorenzo Ghiberti's famous bronze Baptistry doors were commissioned in 1401 to mark the city's deliverance from the plague. Ghiberti was chosen to make a set of new doors after a competition that involved seven leading artists, including Donatello, Jacopo

Ghiberti's winning panel

della Quercia, and Brunelleschi. The trial panels by Ghiberti and Brunelleschi are so different from Florentine Gothic art of the time, notably in the use of perspective and individuality of figures, that they are often regarded as the first works of the Renaissance.

"GATE OF PARADISE"

Having spent 21 years working on the North Doors, Ghiberti was commissioned to make the East Doors (1424–1452). Michelangelo enthusiastically dubbed them, the "Gate of Paradise." The original ten relief panels showing scriptural subjects are now exhibited in the Museo dell'Opera del Duomo *(see p271)*; those on the Baptistry are copies.

Abraham and the Sacrifice of Isaac
The jagged modeled rocks symbolizing Abraham's pain are carefully arranged to emphasize the sacrificial act.

Joseph Sold into Slavery
Ghiberti, a master of perspective, formed the architectural elements in shallower relief behind the figures to create the illusion of depth in the scene.

KEY TO THE EAST DOORS

1	2
3	4
5	6
7	8
9	10

1 Adam and Eve are Expelled from Eden
2 Cain Murders his Brother, Abel
3 The Drunkenness of Noah and his Sacrifice
4 Abraham and the Sacrifice of Isaac
5 Esau and Jacob
6 Joseph Sold into Slavery
7 Moses Receives the Ten Commandments
8 The Fall of Jericho
9 The Battle with the Philistines
10 Solomon and the Queen of Sheba

Detail of carvings by Donatello on the wall of Orsanmichele

Orsanmichele ⑧

Via dell'Arte della Lana. **Map** 3 C1
(6 D3). ◻ 9am–noon, 4–6pm daily.
● 1st and last Mon of each month,
Jan 1, May 1, Dec 25.

BUILT IN 1337 as a grain
market, Orsanmichele was
later converted into a church
that took its name from *Orto
di San Michele*, a monastic
garden long since vanished.
The arcades of the market
became windows, which are
today bricked in, but the
original Gothic tracery can still
be seen. The decoration was
entrusted to Florence's major
Arti (guilds). Over 60 years
they commissioned sculptures
of their patron saints to adorn
the 14 exterior niches, though
today many of the
figures are copies.
Among the sculp-
tors were Lorenzo
Ghiberti, Donatello,
and Verrocchio.

The beautifully
tranquil interior
contains an opulent
14th-century altar
by Andrea Orcagna,
a *Virgin and Child*
by Bernardo Daddi
(1348), and a statue
of the *Madonna
and Child with St. Anne* by
Francesco da Sangallo (1522).

Bargello ⑨

Via del Proconsolo 4. **Map** 4 D1
(6 E3). 📞 055 238 86 06. 🚌 19.
◻ 8:30am–1:50pm daily. ● 1st &
3rd Sun and 2nd & 4th Mon of each
month, Jan 1, May 1, Dec 25.
💶 📷 ♿

FLORENCE'S second-ranking
museum after the Uffizi, the
Bargello contains a wonderful
medley of applied arts and
Italy's finest collection of

Renaissance sculpture.
Begun in 1255, the
fortresslike building
was initially the town
hall, (making it the
oldest seat of gov-
ernment in the
city) but later
became a prison
and home to the
chief of police
(the *Bargello*). It
also became known
for its executions
that took place in the
main courtyard until
1786, when the death
sentence was abolished
by Grand Duke Pietro
Leopoldo. Following
extensive renovation,
the building opened as
one of Italy's first
national museums in
1865.

The key exhibits
range over three
floors, beginning
with the Michelangelo Room,
superbly redesigned after
extensive damage during the
1966 flood. Three contrasting
works by Michelangelo lie
dotted around the room, the
most famous a tipsy-looking
Bacchus (1497), the
sculptor's first
large free standing
work. Close by is
a powerful bust of
Brutus (1539–40),
the only known
portrait bust by
Michelangelo,
and a beautifully
delicate circular
relief depicting
the *Madonna and
Child* (1503–5).
Countless works
by other sculptors occupy the
same room. Among them is
an exquisite *Mercury* (1564)
by the Mannerist genius,
Giambologna, as well as
several virtuoso bronzes by
the sculptor and goldsmith,
Benvenuto Cellini (1500–71).

Across the courtyard, full
of fragments and the coats of
arms of the Bargello's various
incumbents, two more rooms
contain exterior sculptures
removed from sites around
the city. The courtyard's
external staircase leads to
the first floor, which opens
with a wonderfully eccentric

**Donatello's *David*
(c.1430) in the Bargello**

**Brunelleschi's
Sacrifice of Isaac
(1402) in the Bargello**

bronze menagerie by
Giambologna. To the
right is the Salone del
Consiglio Generale,
a cavernous for-
mer courtroom
that contains
the cream of
the museum's Early
Renaissance sculpture.
Foremost among its
highlights is Donatello's
heroic *St. George* (1416) –
the epitome of "youth,
courage and valor of
arms" in the words of
Vasari. Commissioned
by the Armorers'
Guild, the statue was
brought here from
Orsanmichele in
1892. At the center
of the room, in
direct contrast,
is Donatello's
androgynous
David (c.1430),
famous as the
first free standing nude by a
Western artist since antiquity.
Among the room's more easily
missed works, tucked away
on the right wall, are two
reliefs depicting *The Sacrifice
of Isaac* (1402). Created by
Brunelleschi and Lorenzo
Ghiberti respectively, both
were entries in the competition
to design the Baptistry doors.

Beyond the Salone, the
Bargello's emphasis shifts to
the applied arts, with room
after room devoted to rugs,
ceramics, silverware
and a host of other
beautiful
objets d'art.
The most
celebrated of
these rooms is
the Salone del
Camino on the
second floor,
which features the
finest collection
of small bronzes
in Italy. Some
are reproduc-
tions of antique
models, others are
small copies of
Renaissance statues.
Giambologna,
Cellini, and
Antonio del
Pollaiuolo are
among those
represented.

**Bacchus (1497)
by Michelangelo**

Santa Croce ⑩

The GOTHIC CHURCH of Santa Croce contains the tombs and monuments of many famous Florentines, among them Michelangelo, Galileo, and Machiavelli, as well as radiant early 14th-century frescoes by Giotto and his gifted pupil Taddeo Gaddi. In the cloister alongside the church stands the Cappella de' Pazzi (Pazzi Chapel), a Renaissance masterpiece designed by Filippo Brunelleschi.

Tomb of Leonardo Bruni (1447)
Rossellino's effigy of this great humanist was unusual in its sensitive realism and lack of monumental pomp.

Annunciation by Donatello (15th century)

Tomb of Michelangelo *(1570)*
Vasari's tomb figures represent Painting, Sculpture, and Architecture.

Tomb of Machiavelli

The Neo-Gothic façade by Niccolò Matas was added in 1863.

Tomb of Galileo

Entrance to church

Exit

Entrance to Cloister and Cappella de' Pazzi

Entrance to Museo

Cimabue's Crucifixion
Badly damaged in the flood of 1966, this 13th-century masterpiece is among the highlights of the museum (museo), *as is Taddeo Gaddi's magnificent* Last Supper *(c.1355–60).*

★ Cappella de' Pazzi
Brunelleschi's domed chapel with Classical proportions was begun in 1443. The roundels (c.1442–52) are by Luca della Robbia.

**The Neo-Gothic
campanile** was
added in 1842.

The Cappella Baroncelli,
frescoed by Taddeo Gaddi
between 1332 and 1338,
contains the first true night
scene in Western art.

Sacristy

★ Cappella Bardi Frescoes
*Giotto frescoed the Bardi
and Peruzzi chapels to the
right of the high altar
between 1315 and 1330.
This touching scene from
the left hand wall of the
chapel shows* The Death
of St. Francis *(1317).*

STAR FEATURES

★ **Cappella Bardi
Frescoes**

★ **Cappella de' Pazzi**

Museo di Storia della Scienza ⓫

Piazza de' Giudici 1. **Map** 4 D1 (6 E4).
☎ 055 239 88 76. 🕐 9:30am–
1pm, 2–5pm Mon–Sat. 🕐 public
hols. 🈲

THIS LIVELY and superbly
presented museum devotes
numerous rooms on two floors
to different scientific themes,
illustrating each with many
fine displays and a panoply
of old and beautifully made
scientific instruments. It is
also something of a shrine to
the Pisa-born scientist, Galileo
Galilei (1564–1642),
and features two of
his telescopes, as
well as large-
scale reconstruc-
tions of his
experiments
into motion,
weight, velocity,
and acceleration.
These are some-
times demonstrated
by the attendants. Other
exhibits come from
the Accademia del
Cimento (Academy
for Experimentation),
which was founded in 1657
by Grand Duke Ferdinand II
in memory of Galileo.

**Astrolabe,
Museo di Storia
della Scienza**

The first few rooms are
devoted to astronomical,
mathematical, and navigational
instruments, with galleries
concentrating on Galileo,
telescopes, and optical games.
Some of the loveliest exhibits
are in Room 7, which is
crammed with early maps,
globes, and astrolabes, and
among the antique micro-
scopes, thermometers and
barometers in the rooms
beyond. The second floor is
slightly less arresting, but
there are some fine old clocks,
mathematical instruments,
calculators, a horrifying
collection of 19th-century
surgical instruments, weights
and measures, and some
graphic anatomical models.

Ponte Vecchio ⓬

Map 4 D1 (6 E4).

PONTE VECCHIO, the oldest
surviving bridge in the city,
was built in 1345, the last in a
succession of bridges and fords
on the site that dated back to
Roman times. Designed by
Giotto's pupil Taddeo
Gaddi, its pictur-
esque shops were
originally the
domain of
blacksmiths,
butchers, and tan-
ners (who used
the river as a con-
venient place for
disposing of waste).
They were reviled for
their noise and stench
and were eventually
evicted in 1593 by
Duke Ferdinando I –
replaced by jewelers and
goldsmiths who were able to
pay higher rents. The
elevated Corridoio Vasariano
runs along the eastern side of
the bridge, above the shops.
Giorgio Vasari designed the
corridor in 1565 to allow the
Medici family to move about
their residences without
having to mix with the public.
This was the city's only bridge
to escape destruction during
World War II, and visitors
today come as much to admire
the views as to browse among
the antique shops and
specialized jewelry shops.

Ponte Vecchio viewed from the Ponte Santa Trìnita

Uffizi ⑬

THE UFFIZI, Italy's greatest art gallery, was built in 1560–80 to house offices (uffici) for Duke Cosimo I. The architect Vasari used iron as reinforcement, which enabled his successor Buontalenti to create an almost continuous wall of glass on the upper story. This was used as a gallery for Francesco I to display the Medici art treasures. The collection was divided up in the 19th century: ancient objects went to the archaeological museum and sculpture to the Bargello, leaving the Uffizi with a matchless collection of paintings.

Main staircase

Entrance hall

Entrance

Bacchus (c.1589)
Caravaggio's early work depicts the god of wine as a pallid, debauched youth. The mood of dissipation is echoed in the decaying fruit, one of Western art's earliest still-life paintings.

Corridor ceilings are frescoed with 1580s "grotesques" inspired by Roman grottoes.

Annunciation (1333)
The Sienese painter Simone Martini was strongly influenced by French Gothic art, and this is one of his masterpieces. The two saints are by Martini's pupil and brother-in-law, Lippo Memmi.

Buontalenti staircase

GALLERY GUIDE

The Uffizi art collection is on the top floor of the building. Greek and Roman sculptures are displayed in the broad corridors (East, Arno, West) running around the inner side of the building. The paintings are hung in rooms off the corridors in chronological order to reveal the development of Florentine art from Byzantine to High Renaissance and beyond. Gothic art is in rooms 2–6; Early Renaissance in 7–14; High Renaissance and Mannerism in 15–29; and later paintings in 30–45.

Ognissanti Madonna (c.1310)
Giotto's grasp of spatial depth and substance in this altarpiece was a milestone in the mastery of perspective.

KEY TO FLOORPLAN

☐	East Corridor
☐	West Corridor
☐	Arno Corridor
☐	Gallery rooms 1–45
☐	Nonexhibition space

VISITORS' CHECKLIST

Loggiata degli Uffizi 6. **Map** 4
D1 (6 D4). [phone] 055 238 86 51.
[bus] B, 23. [clock] 8:30am–9pm
Tue–Sat (7pm Oct–May), 8:30am–
8pm Sun, hols (last adm: 60 mins
before closing). [closed] Jan 1, Dec
25. [icons] Rooms 38,
41, 43, 44, 45 [icon] for restoration.

The Duke and Duchess of Urbino (c.1465–70)
*Piero della Francesca's portraits of Federico da Montefeltro
and his wife Battista Sforza were painted after Battista died
at 26. Her portrait was probably based on her death mask.*

The Tribune,
decorated in
red and gold,
contains the
works most
valued by
the Medici.

The Birth of Venus (c.1485)
*Botticelli shows the goddess of love flanked by
Zephyrus, god of the west wind, who blows
the risen Venus to shore on a half shell. The
myth may symbolize the birth of beauty
through the divine fertilization of matter.*

The Holy Family (1507)
*Michelangelo's paint-
ing, the first to break
with the convention
of showing Christ
on the Virgin's lap,
inspired Mannerist
artists through its
expressive handling
of color and posture.*

Vasari's Classical Arno
façade (begun 1560)

The Vasari Corridor
is a passageway
across the Arno to
the Pitti Palace.

**The Venus of
Urbino** (1538)
*Titian's sensuous nude,
inspired by Giorgione's
Sleeping Venus, may in
fact be a portrait of a
courtesan deemed
sufficiently beautiful
to be a goddess.*

Exploring the Uffizi

THE UFFIZI offers not only the chance to see the world's greatest collection of Italian Renaissance paintings but also the opportunity to enjoy masterpieces from as far afield as Holland, Spain, and Germany. Accumulated over the centuries by the Medici, the collection was first housed in the Uffizi in 1581, and eventually bequeathed to the Florentine people by Anna Maria Lodovica, the last of the Medici.

GOTHIC ART

PAST THE STATUES and antiquities of Room 1, the Uffizi proper opens in style with three altarpieces of the *Maestà*, or Madonna Enthroned, by Giotto, Duccio, and Cimabue, some of Italy's greatest 13th-century painters. Each work marks a stage in the development of Italian painting away from the stilted conventions of Byzantium to the livelier traditions of Gothic and Renaissance art. The shift is best expressed in Giotto's version of the subject (known as the *Ognissanti Madonna*), where new feeling for depth and naturalistic detail is shown in the range of emotion displayed by the saints and angels, and by the carefully evoked three-dimensionality of the Virgin's throne.

Giotto's naturalistic influence can also be seen among the paintings of Room 4, which is devoted to the 14th-century Florentine School, an interesting counterpoint to the Sienese paintings of Duccio and his followers in Room 3. Among the many fine paintings here are works by Ambrogio and Pietro Lorenzetti, and Simone Martini's *Annunciation*.

Room 6 is devoted to International Gothic, a highly decorative style that represented the height of Gothic expression. It is exemplified by Gentile da Fabriano's exquisite, glittering *Adoration of the Magi* painted in 1423.

EARLY RENAISSANCE

A NEW UNDERSTANDING of geometry and perspective during the 15th century increasingly allowed artists to explore the complexities of space and depth. None became more obsessed with these new compositional possibilities than Paolo

Madonna and Child with Angels (1455–66) by Fra Filippo Lippi

Uccello (1397–1475), whose picture of *The Battle of San Romano* (1456) in Room 7 is one of the gallery's most fevered creations.

Room 7 also contains two panels from 1460 by Piero della Francesca, another artist preoccupied with the art of perspective. The panels, which are among the earliest Renaissance portraits, depict the Duke and Duchess of Urbino on one side and representations of their virtues on the other.

While such works can seem coldly experimental, Fra Filippo Lippi's *Madonna and Child with Angels* (1455–66), in Room 8, is a masterpiece of warmth and humanity.

Sandro Botticelli's allegorical painting, *Primavera* (1480)

Like many Renaissance artists, Lippi uses a religious subject to celebrate earthly delights such as landscape and feminine beauty. A similar approach is apparent in the works of Botticelli, whose famous paintings in Rooms 10–14 may be the highlight of the gallery. In *The Birth of Venus*, for example, Venus takes the place of the Virgin, expressing a fascination with Classical mythology common to many Renaissance artists. The same is true of the *Primavera* (1480), which breaks with Christian religious painting by illustrating a pagan rite of spring.

Detail from *The Annunciation* (1472–5) by Leonardo da Vinci

HIGH RENAISSANCE AND MANNERISM

ROOM 15 FEATURES works attributed to the young Leonardo da Vinci, notably a sublime *Annunciation* (1472–5), which reveals hints of his still emerging style, and the *Adoration of the Magi* (1481), which remained unfinished when he left Florence for Milan to paint *The Last Supper* (1495–8).

Room 18, better known as the Tribune, was designed in 1584 by Buontalenti in order to accommodate the best-loved pieces of the Medici collection. Its most famous work is the so-called Medici Venus (1st century BC), a Roman copy of a Greek statue deemed to be the most erotic in the ancient world. The copy proved equally salacious and was removed from Rome's Villa Medici by Cosimo III to keep it from corrupting the city's art students. Other highlights in

Room 18 include Agnolo Bronzino's portraits of *Cosimo I* and *Eleonora di Toledo*, both painted around 1545, Pontormo's *Charity* (1530) and the portrait of *Cosimo il Vecchio* (1517).

Rooms 19 to 23 depart from the gallery's Florentine bias, demonstrating how rapidly Renaissance ideas and techniques spread beyond Tuscany. Painters from the German and Flemish schools, including Albrecht Dürer, are well represented together with painters from Umbria like Perugino, but perhaps the most captivating works are the paintings by Venetian and northern Italian artists such as Mantegna, Carpaccio, Correggio, and Bellini.

Room 25, which returns to the Tuscan mainstream, is dominated by Michelangelo's *Holy Family* or Doni Tondo (1456), notable for its vibrant colors and the Virgin's unusual twisted pose. The gallery's only work by Michelangelo, it was to prove immensely influential with the next generation of painters, especially Bronzino (1503–72), Pontormo (1494–1556), and Parmigianino (1503–40). The last of these was responsible for the *Madonna of the Long Neck* (c.1534) in Room 29. With its contorted anatomy, unnatural colors, and strange composition, this painting is a masterpiece of the style that came to be called Mannerism. Earlier, but no less remarkable masterpieces in Rooms 26 and 28 include Raphael's sublime

Madonna of the Goldfinch (1506) by Raphael

Madonna of the Long Neck (c.1534) by Parmigianino

Madonna of the Goldfinch (1506) and Titian's notorious *Venus of Urbino* (1538), censured by Mark Twain as the "foulest, the vilest, the obscenest picture the world possesses." Others hold it to be one of the most beautiful nudes ever painted.

LATER PAINTINGS

VISITORS, already sated by a surfeit of outstanding paintings, are often tempted to skim through the Uffizi's final rooms. The paintings in Rooms 30 to 35 – which are mainly from the Veneto and Emilia-Romagna – are mostly unexceptional, but the gallery's last rooms (41–45) contain paintings that compare favorably with those in previous rooms. Room 43 has three works by Caravaggio: *Medusa* (1596–8), painted for a Roman cardinal; *Bacchus* (c.1589), one of the artist's earliest works; and the *Sacrifice of Isaac* (c.1590), whose violent subject is belied by the painting's gentle background landscape. Room 44, dedicated to Rembrandt and northern European painting, features Rembrandt's *Portrait of an Old Man* (1665) and two self-portraits of the artist as a young and old man (painted in 1634 and 1664, respectively). Canaletto, Goya, Tiepolo, and other 18th-century artists bring the gallery to its conclusion.

Piazza della Signoria ⓮

Savonarola (1452–98)

Pɪᴀᴢᴢᴀ ᴅᴇʟʟᴀ sɪɢɴᴏʀɪᴀ and Palazzo Vecchio have been at the heart of Florence's political and social life for centuries. The great bell once used to summon citizens to *parlamento* (a public meeting) here, and the square has long been a popular promenade for both visitors and Florentines. The piazza's statues (some are copies) commemorate the city's major historical events, but its most famous episode is celebrated by a simple pavement plaque near the loggia: the execution of the religious leader Girolamo Savonarola, who was burned at the stake.

David
This copy of the famous Michelangelo statue symbolizes triumph over tyranny. The original (see p267) stood in the piazza until 1873.

Heraldic Frieze
The crossed keys on this shield represent Medici papal rule.

Sala dei Gigli

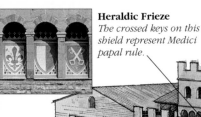

Salone dei Cinquecento *(1495)*
This vast chamber contains a statue of Victory by Michelangelo and frescoes by Vasari describing Florentine triumphs over Pisa and Siena.

Fontana di Nettuno, Ammannati's fountain (1575) of the Roman sea god surrounded by water nymphs, commemorates Tuscan naval victories.

The Marzocco is a copy of the heraldic lion of Florence carved by Donatello in 1420. The original is in the Bargello.

★ Palazzo Vecchio *(completed 1332)*
This Republican frieze over the palace entrance is inscribed with the words, "Christ is King," implying that no mortal ruler has absolute power.

★ The Rape of the Sabine Women by Giambologna
(1583) The writhing figures in Giambologna's famous statue were carved from a single block of flawed marble.

The Uffizi

The Loggia dei Lanzi
(1382), designed by Orcagna, is named after the Lancers, the bodyguards of Cosimo I who were billeted here.

Roman statues, possibly of emperors, line the Loggia.

★ Perseus by Cellini
This bronze statue (1554) of Perseus beheading Medusa was intended to warn Cosimo I's enemies of their probable fate.

STAR FEATURES

★ **Palazzo Vecchio**

★ **Perseus by Cellini**

★ **The Rape of the Sabine Women by Giambologna**

Palazzo Vecchio ⑮

Piazza della Signoria (entrance on via della Ninna). **Map** 4 D1 (6 D3). ☎ 055 276 83 25. 🚌 A, B. ◯ 9am–7pm Mon–Wed, Fri & Sat, 9am–2pm Thu & Sun (last adm: 45 mins before closing). ⬤ Jan 1, Easter, May 1, Aug 15, Dec 25. 🏛 ♿

T HE "OLD PALACE" still fulfills its original role as Florence's town hall. It was completed in 1322 when a huge bell, used to call citizens to meetings or warn of fire, flood, or enemy attack, was hauled to the top of the imposing bell tower. While retaining much of its medieval appearance, the interior was remodeled for Duke Cosimo I when he moved into the palace in 1540. Leonardo and Michelangelo were asked to redecorate the interior, but it was Vasari who finally undertook the work, incorporating bombastic frescoes (1563–5) of Florentine achievements. Michelangelo's *Victory* statue (1525) graces the Salone dei Cinquecento, which also has a tiny Studiolo (study) decorated in 1569–1573 by 30 of Florence's leading Mannerist painters. Other highlights include the Cappella di Eleonora, painted by Bronzino (1540–45); the loggia, with its views over the city; and the Sala dei Gigli (Room of Lilies) containing Donatello's *Judith and Holofernes* (c.1455) and frescoes of Roman heroes (1485) by Ghirlandaio.

A copy of Verrocchio's Putto fountain in Vasari's courtyard

Street-by-Street: Around Piazza della Repubblica

UNDERLYING THE STREET PLAN of modern Florence is the far older pattern of the ancient Roman city. Nowhere is this more evident than in the grid of narrow streets around Piazza della Repubblica, site of the old Roman forum. This pivotal square housed the city's main food market until the 1860s, when redevelopment tidied up the area, and added the triumphal arch that now stands in today's café-filled square.

Santa Trinita has frescoes by Ghirlandaio on the Life of St. Francis (1486), depicting events that took place in this area. Here, a child is revived after falling from the Palazzo Spini-Ferroni.

Palazzo Spini-Ferroni

Ponte Santa Trìnita was built in wood in 1290 and then rebuilt by Ammannati in 1567 to celebrate the defeat of Siena.

Palazzo Strozzi
This monumental palazzo dominates the square ⑰

Santi Apostoli
was reputedly founded by Charlemagne.

Palazzo Davanzati
Frescoes with exotic birds decorate the Sala dei Pappagalli, which was once the dining room of this 14th-century palazzo ⑯

KEY

– – – Suggested route

0 meters	200
0 yards	200

LOCATOR MAP
See Florence Street Finder maps 5, 6

Piazza della Repubblica, which dates from the 19th century, is lined by some of Florence's oldest and best-known cafés.

Mercato Nuovo, the "New Market" (1547), now deals mainly in souvenirs.

Palazzo di Parte Guelfa was the headquarters of the Guelphs, the dominant political party of medieval Florence.

Ponte Vecchio
(See p277)

Detail of a frieze illustrating a medieval romance in Palazzo Davanzati

Palazzo Davanzati ⑯

Via Porta Rossa 13. **Map** 3 C1 (5 C3).
📞 *055 238 86 10.* 🔵 *for renovation.*

THIS WONDERFUL MUSEUM, also known as the Museo dell'Antica Casa Fiorentina, uses original fittings and furniture to recreate the ambience of a typical well-to-do 14th-century town house. The peaceful inner courtyard, linked by stairs to the upper floors, contains a well and a pulley system, something of a luxury in medieval Florence, when most households drew their water from public fountains. All the rooms have something of interest, but the most beautiful are the Sala dei Pappagalli, named after its frescoed parrot (*pappagallo*) motifs; the gloriously decorated Sala Pavoni, or Camera Nuziale (Wedding Room); and the upper floor kitchen, a room decorated in rustic style and which has wonderful views.

Palazzo Strozzi ⑰

Piazza degli Strozzi. **Map** 3 C1 (5 C3).
Piccolo Museo di Palazzo Strozzi 🔵 *for restoration.*

SHEER SIZE accounts for the impact of the Palazzo Strozzi, and although it is only three stories high, each floor exceeds the height of a normal palazzo. It was commissioned by the wealthy banker Filippo Strozzi, who had 15 buildings demolished to make way for the palazzo; he hoped it would rival the Medici palaces elsewhere in the city. Strozzi died in 1491, just two years after the first stone was laid.

Work on the building continued until 1536, with three major architects contributing to its design – Giuliano da Sangallo, Benedetto da Maiano, and Simone del Pollaiuolo (also known as Cronaca). The exterior, built of huge rusticated masonry blocks, remains unspoiled. Look for the original Renaissance torch-holders, lamps, and the rings for tethering horses that still adorn the corners and façades. A small museum off the courtyard records the building's history, but the palace is now primarily used as an exhibition hall (a large antique fair is held here biennially in late September).

Exterior of Palazzo Strozzi, with masonry block rustication

San Lorenzo ⑱

SAN LORENZO was the parish church of the Medici family, and in 1419 Brunelleschi was commissioned to rebuild it in the Classical style of the Renaissance. Almost a century later Michelangelo submitted some plans for the façade, and began work on the Medici tombs in the Sagrestia Nuova. He also designed a library, the Biblioteca Mediceo-Laurenziana, to house the family's collection of manuscripts. The lavish family mausoleum, the Cappella dei Principi, was started in 1604.

Cappella dei Principi
The Medici mausoleum, behind the high altar, was begun in 1604 by Matteo Nigetti, and forms part of the Cappelle Medicee.

The huge dome by Buontalenti echoes that of the Duomo *(see pp272–3).*

The Old Sacristy was designed by Brunelleschi and decorated by Donatello.

Campani

Biblioteca Staircase
Michelangelo's Mannerist staircase, one of the artist's most innovative designs, was built by Ammannati in 1559.

Michelangelo designed the desks and ceiling of the Biblioteca, where exhibitions of Medici manuscripts are often held.

The cloister garden is planted with boxwood hedges, pomegranate, and orange trees.

The Martyrdom of St. Lawrence
Bronzino's vast Mannerist fresco of 1659 is a bravura, choreographed study of the human form, rather than a reverential response to the agony of the saint.

Entrance to church

A simple stone slab
marks the modest grave
of Cosimo il Vecchio
(1389–1464), founder
of the Medici dynasty.

The Cappelle Medicee
complex comprises the
Cappella dei Principi and its
crypt, the Sagrestia Nuova
(see p287).

Pulpits by Donatello
The bronze pulpits in the
nave were Donatello's last
works. Completed by his
pupils in 1460, the reliefs
capture the flinching pain of
Christ's Passion and the
glory of the Resurrection.

**St. Joseph and Christ
in the Workshop**, a
striking work showing
the young Christ with
his father, is by Pietro
Annigoni (1910–88),
one of the few modern
artists whose work is
seen in Florence.

Michelangelo submitted
several designs for the
façade of San Lorenzo, but
it remains unfinished.

***The Tomb of the Duke of Nemours
(1520–34) by Michelangelo in the
Cappelle Medicee's New Sacristy***

Cappelle
Medicee ⑲

Piazza di Madonna degli Aldobrandini.
Map 1 C5 (6 D1). 🔔 055 238 86 02.
🚌 many routes. ⏰ 8:30am–5pm
daily (1:50pm public hols) (last adm:
30 mins before closing). ⏰ 1st, 3rd
& 5th Mon of each month, Jan 1,
May 1, Dec 25. 🎫 📷 ♿

THE MEDICI CHAPELS divide
into three distinct areas.
Beyond the entrance hall lies
a low-vaulted crypt, a suitably
subdued space for the brass-
railed tombs of many lesser
members of the Medici
family. From here steps lead
to the octagonal **Cappella dei
Principi** (Chapel of Princes),
a vast family mausoleum
begun by Cosimo I in 1604.
It is opulently decorated: the
ceiling is garishly frescoed and
the walls are smothered in
huge swathes of semiprecious
pietre dure (inlaid stone).
Spaced around the walls are

the tombs of six Medici Grand
Dukes. A corridor leads to
Michelangelo's **New Sacristy**,
designed as a counterpoint
to Brunelleschi's Old Sacristy
in San Lorenzo. Three groups
of statues, all carved by
Michelangelo between 1520
and 1534, stand around the
walls: that on the near left
hand wall is *The Tomb of the
Duke of Urbino* (grandson
of Lorenzo the Magnificent).
Opposite is *The Tomb of the
Duke of Nemours* (Lorenzo's
third son). Close to the
unfinished *Madonna and
Child* (1521) is a simple tomb
containing Lorenzo the
Magnificent and his murdered
brother, Giuliano (died 1478).

Mercato Centrale ⑳

Piazza del Mercato Centrale. **Map** 1 C4
(5 C1). ⏰ 7am–2pm Mon–Sat.

AT THE HEART of the San
Lorenzo street market is
the bustling Mercato Centrale,
Florence's busiest food
market. It is housed in a vast
two-story building of cast-iron
and glass, built in 1874 by
Giuseppe Mengoni.
The ground floor stalls sell
meat, poultry, fish, salamis,
hams, cheeses, and excellent
olive oils. There are also
Tuscan takeout foods such as
porchetta (roast suckling pig),
lampredotto (pig's intestines),
and trippa (tripe). Fresh fruit,
vegetables, and flowers are
sold on the top floor: look for
wild mushrooms and truffles
in the autumn, and broad
beans, peas and baby
artichokes in early spring.

Yellow zucchini flowers and other vegetables in the Mercato Centrale

Santa Maria Novella ㉑

THE CHURCH of Santa Maria Novella was built by the Dominicans between 1279 and 1357. The lower Romanesque part of its façade was incorporated into one based on Classical proportions by the pioneering Renaissance architect Leon Battista Alberti in 1456–70. The Gothic interior contains superb frescoes, including Masaccio's powerful *Trinity*. The famous Green Cloister, frescoed with perspective scenes by Paolo Uccello, and the dramatically decorated Spanish Chapel now form a museum.

The arcade arches are emphasized by gray and white banding.

Monastic buildings

The Nave
The piers of the nave are spaced closer together at the altar end. This trick of perspective creates the illusion of an exceptionally long church.

Cappellone degli Spagnuoli, the chapel used by the Spanish courtiers of Eleonora of Toledo, has frescoes of salvation and damnation.

Chiostro Verde takes its name from the green base used in Uccello's frescoes, which were badly damaged by the 1966 floods.

Entrance

Entrance to museum

Trinity by Masaccio
This pioneering fresco (c.1428) is renowned as a masterpiece of perspective and portraiture. The kneeling figures flanking the arch are the painting's sponsors, judge Lorenzo Lenzi and his wife.

Cappella Strozzi
The 14th-century frescoes by Nardo di Cione and his brother Andrea Orcagna were inspired by Dante's epic poem, The Divine Comedy.

*Ghirlandaio's **Madonna della Misericordia** (1472) in Ognissanti*

The Strozzi Tomb is
by Benedetto
da Maiano
(1493).

**Cappella di
Filippo Strozzi**
features Filippino
Lippi's frescoes of St. John
raising Drusiana from the dead
and St. Philip slaying a dragon.

Cappella Tornabuoni
*Ghirlandaio's famous fresco
cycle*, The Life of John the
Baptist *(1485), peoples the
biblical episodes with
Florentine aristocrats in
contemporary dress.*

Palazzo Antinori ㉒

Via de' Tornabuoni. **Map** 1 C5 (5 C2).
⛔ to the public. **Cantinetta
Antinori** 📞 055 29 22 34. ⏰
12:30–2:30pm, 7–10:30pm Mon–Fri.

Palazzo Antinori was built
in 1461–6 and is one of
the finest small Renaissance
palazzi in Florence. It was
acquired by the Antinori in
1506 and has remained with
the family ever since. The
dynasty owns many estates
all over Tuscany and Umbria,
producing a range of wines,
oils, and liqueurs that can be
sampled – along with fine
Tuscan dishes – in the wine
bar off the main courtyard,
called the Cantinetta Antinori.

Palazzo Rucellai ㉓

Via della Vigna Nuova 16. **Map** 1 C5
(5 B2). ⛔ to the public.
Archivio Alinari Largo Fratelli Alinari
15. 📞 055 239 51. ⏰ 9am–6pm
Mon–Fri. ⛔ public hols. 🚫

Built in 1446–57, this is
one of the most ornate
Renaissance palaces in the
city. It was commissioned
by Giovanni Rucellai,
whose enormous wealth
derived from the import of
a rare and costly red dye
made from lichen found
only on Majorca. The dye
was called *oricello*, from which
the name Rucellai is derived.

Giovanni commissioned
several buildings from the
architect Leon Battista Alberti,
who designed this palace as a
virtual textbook illustration of
the major Classical orders.

The palazzo used to house
the Museo Alinari, but the
collection has recently moved
to Largo Alinari 15 and is now
known as the Archivio Alinari.
The Alinari brothers began
taking pictures of Florence in
the 1840s. They supplied high-
quality prints, postcards, and
art books to foreigners on the
Grand Tour who flocked to
Florence in the 19th century.
The museum offers a vivid
insight into the social history
of Florence at that time.

Ognissanti ㉔

Borgo Ognissanti 42. **Map** 1 B5 (5 A2).
📞 055 239 87 00. ⏰ 8am–noon,
4–7pm Mon–Sat, 4–6pm Sun. ⛔
first and last Mon of each month. ♿

Ognissanti, or All Saints,
was the parish church of
the Vespucci, one of whose
members, the 15th-century
navigator Amerigo, gave his
name to the New World. The
young Amerigo is depicted in
Ghirlandaio's fresco of the
Madonna della Misericordia
(1472) in the second chapel
on the right between the Virgin
and the man in the red cloak.
Amerigo realized that the land
discovered by Columbus was
a new continentand made
two voyages there. The letters
he sent back enabled carto-
graphers to draw the first maps
of the new land.

Ognissanti is also the burial
place of Botticelli. His fresco
of *St. Augustine* (1480) is on
the south wall. Alongside the
church is a cloister and refectory with Ghirlandaio's fresco
of *The Last Supper* (1480).

Cappella Brancacci ㉕

T HE CHURCH of Santa Maria del Carmine is famous for
the Brancacci Chapel, which contains frescoes on
The Life of St. Peter commissioned by the Florentine
merchant Felice Brancacci around 1424. Although the
paintings were begun by Masolino in 1425, many of the
scenes are by his pupil Masaccio (who died before
completing the cycle) and by Filippino Lippi, who
completed the work in 1480. Masaccio's revolutionary
use of perspective, his narrative drama, and the tragic
realism of his figures placed him in the vanguard of
Renaissance painting. Many great artists, including
Leonardo and Michelangelo,
later visited the chapel to
study his pioneering work.

In every scene, St. Peter
is distinguished from the
crowds as the figure in
the orange cloak.

St. Peter Healing the Sick
*Masaccio's realistic portrayal
of cripples and beggars was
revolutionary in his time.*

The grouping of stylized
figures in Masaccio's frescoes
reflects his interest in the
sculpture of Donatello.

Masaccio's simple style
allows us to focus on the
figures central to the frescoes
without distracting detail.

Expulsion of Adam and Eve
*Masaccio's ability to express
emotion is well illustrated by
his harrowing portrait of
Adam and Eve being driven
out of the Garden of Eden,
their faces wracked by
misery, shame, and the
burden of self-knowledge.*

KEY TO THE FRESCOES: ARTISTS AND SUBJECTS

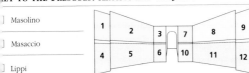

☐ Masolino

☐ Masaccio

☐ Lippi

Expulsion of Adam and Eve
The Tribute Money
St. Peter Preaching
St. Peter Visited by St. Paul
Raising the Emperor's Son;
St. Peter Enthroned
St. Peter Healing the Sick

7 St. Peter Baptizing the Converts
8 St. Peter Healing the Cripple;
  Raising Tabitha
9 Temptation of Adam and Eve
10 St. Peter and St. John Giving Alms
11 Crucifixion; Before the Proconsul
12 The Release of St. Peter

VISITORS' CHECKLIST

Piazza del Carmine. **Map** 3 A1
(5 A4). ☎ 055 238 21 95.
🚌 D. ◐ 10am–5pm Mon,
Wed–Sat, 1–5pm Sun (arrive
early). ● public hols. 📷

**Masolino's *Temptation
of Adam and Eve* is**
gentle and decorous, in
contrast with the
emotional force of
Masaccio's painting on
the opposite wall.

St. Peter is depicted
against a background
of Florentine buildings.

Woman in a Turban
*The freshness of Masaccio's
original colors is seen in
this rediscovered roundel,
hidden behind the altar
for 500 years.*

Two Figures
*Masolino's work tends to be more
formal, less naturalistic and
animated than that of Masaccio.*

Before the Proconsul
*Filippino Lippi was called in to complete the cycle of
frescoes in 1480. He added this emotional scene
showing the Proconsul sentencing St. Peter to death.*

Street-by-Street: Oltrarno

Medici coat of arms

FOR THE MOST PART, the Oltrarno is a homey area of small houses, quiet squares, and shops selling antiques, bric-a-brac, and foodstuffs. The Via Maggio, a busy thoroughfare, breaks this pattern, but step into the side streets and you escape the bustle to discover a corner of old world Florence. The restaurants serve authentic, reasonably priced food, and the area is full of studios and workshops restoring antique furniture. Among the things to see are Santo Spirito and Palazzo Pitti, one of the city's largest palaces, whose medley of museums contains an art collection second only to that of the Uffizi.

Santo Spirito
Brunelleschi's simple church was completed after the architect's death ㉖

Ponte Santa Trinita

Cenacolo di Santo Spirito, the old refectory of a monastery that once stood here, contains a dramatic fresco attributed to Orcagna (c.1360).

Palazzo Guadagni (1500) was the first in the city to be built with a rooftop loggia, setting a trend among the aristocracy.

Palazzo di Bianca Cappello (1579) is covered in ornate *sgraffito* work and was the home of the mistress of Grand Duke Francesco I.

Masks and murals are handmade at this shop, Frieze of Papier Mâché.

LOCATOR MAP
See Florence Street Finder
maps 3, 5

The 16th-century fountain
and gargoyle in Piazza de' Frescobaldi were
designed by Buontalenti, as was the façade
(1593–4) of the nearby church of Santa Trìnita.

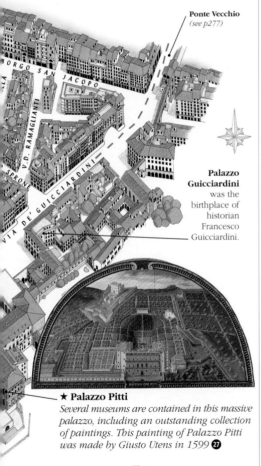

Ponte Vecchio
(see p277)

**Palazzo
Guicciardini**
was the
birthplace of
historian
Francesco
Guicciardini.

★ **Palazzo Pitti**
*Several museums are contained in this massive
palazzo, including an outstanding collection
of paintings. This painting of Palazzo Pitti
was made by Giusto Utens in 1599* ㉗

KEY

– – – Suggested route

STAR SIGHTS

★ **Palazzo Pitti**

0 meters   100

0 yards   100

Santo Spirito ㉖

Piazza di Santo Spirito. **Map** 3 B2
(5 B4). 🚌 D. 📞 055 21 00 30. ⏰
8am–noon, 4–6:30pm Thu–Tue,
8:30am–noon Wed.

THE AUGUSTINIAN foundation
of this church dates from
1250. The present building,
dominating the northern end
of the pretty Piazza di Santo
Spirito, was designed by the
architect Brunelleschi in 1435,
but not completed until the
late 15th century. The unfinished modest façade was
added in the 18th century.

Inside, the harmony of the
proportions has been somewhat spoiled by the elaborate
Baroque baldacchino and the
High Altar, which was finished
in 1607 by Giovanni Caccini.
The church has 38 side
altars, decorated with 15th-
and 16th-century Renaissance
paintings and sculpture,
among them works by
Cosimo Rosselli, Domenico
Ghirlandaio, and Filippino
Lippi. The latter painted a
magnificent *Madonna and
Child* (1466) for the Nerli
Chapel in the south transept.

In the north aisle, a door
beneath the organ leads to
a vestibule with an ornate
coffered ceiling. It was
designed by Simone del
Pollaiuolo, more commonly
known as Cronaca, in 1491.
The sacristy adjoining the
vestibule, in which 12 huge
columns are crammed into a
tiny space, was designed by
Giuliano da Sangallo in 1489.

**Interior of Santo Spirito with
colonnaded aisle**

Palazzo Pitti 🅮

THE PALAZZO PITTI was originally built for the banker
Luca Pitti. The huge scale of the building, begun in
1457 and attributed to Brunelleschi, illustrated Pitti's
determination to outrival the Medici family through its
display of wealth and power. Ironically, the Medici
later purchased the palazzo when building costs
bankrupted Pitti's heirs. In 1550 it became the main
residence of the Medici, and subsequently all the rulers
of the city lived here. Today the richly decorated rooms
exhibit countless treasures from the Medici collections.

Judith (1620–30) by Artemisia
Gentileschi

**The Three Ages of Man (c.1510),
attributed to Giorgione**

GALLERIA PALATINA

THE PALATINE GALLERY, which
forms the heart of the Pitti
museum complex, contains
many masterpieces by artists
such as Botticelli, Titian,
Perugino, Andrea del Sarto,
Tintoretto, Veronese, Giorgione,
and Gentileschi. The works of
art, accumulated by the
Medici Grand Dukes, are still
hung much as the Medici
wished, regardless of subject
or chronology. The gallery
consists of 11 main salons, the
first five of which are painted
with allegorical ceiling frescoes
glorifying the Medici. Begun
by Pietro da Cortona in 1641,
they were completed in 1665
by his pupil, Ciro Ferri. Room 1

(Sala di Venere) contains
Antonio Canova's statue of
the *Venus Italica* (1810),
commissioned by Napoleon
to replace the *Venus de'
Medici* (which was to be
taken to Paris). Room 2
(Sala di Apollo) features
Titian's *Portrait of a
Gentleman* (1540), perhaps
the finest of several
paintings by the
artist in the
gallery. Still finer
pictures adorn
rooms 4 and 5,
including some
canvases by
Perugino, Andrea
del Sarto, and a host
of paintings by
Raphael. The most
beautiful of the last
group are Raphael's

High Renaissance *Madonna
della Seggiola* or Madonna
of the Chair (c.1514–15), and
the *Donna Velata* or Veiled
Woman (c.1516), whose
model was reputedly
the artist's mistress.
Other excellent
paintings in the
remaining gallery
rooms include
Fra Filippo
Lippi's lovely
*Madonna and
Child*, painted in the
mid-15th century, and
The Sleeping Cupid
(1608) by Caravaggio.

**Madonna of the
Chair (c.1515) by
Raphael**

Galleria Palatina

**The Museo degli
Argenti,** or the
silverware museum,
also displays
precious objets
d'art.

**The
Boboli
Gardens**

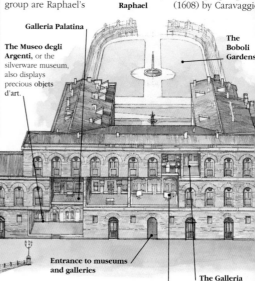

**Entrance to museums
and galleries**

Brunelleschi designed the
palace façade, which was
eventually extended to three
times its original length.

**Appartamenti
Monumentali**

**The Galleria
d'Arte Moderna**
is a 30-room
gallery featuring
paintings from the
years 1784 to 1924.

e Palmieri Rotonda by Giovanni Fattori (1825–1908)

APPARTAMENTI MONUMENTALI

THE STATE APARTMENTS on the first floor of the south wing the palazzo were built in e 17th century. They are corated with frescoes by rious Florentine artists, a ries of portraits of the Medici the Flemish painter Justus stermans, who worked at e court between 1619 and 81, and a group of 18th-ntury Gobelins tapestries. In e late 18th and early 19th centuries, the apartments were completely revamped in Neo-Classical style by the Dukes of Lorraine when they succeeded the Medici dynasty as the rulers of Florence.

The apartments are lavishly appointed with ornate gold and white stuccoed ceilings and rich decoration, notably on the walls of the Parrot Room, which are covered with an opulent crimson fabric detailed with a bird design. The apartments have been extensively restored in accordance with the original plans and designs.

e Throne Room of the ppartamenti Monumentali

Galleria del Costume

OTHER COLLECTIONS

THE MUSEO degli Argenti (Silverware Museum) is housed in rooms formerly used by the Medici as summer apartments. The family's lavish and occasionally dubious taste is reflected in the vast array of precious objects on display. These embrace beautiful examples of Roman glassware, ivory, carpets, crystal, amber, and fine works by Florentine and German goldsmiths. Pride of place goes to 16 *pietre dure* vases (decorated with hard or semiprecious inlaid stone), once owned by Lorenzo the Magnificent.

The Galleria del Costume, which opened in 1983, re-flects the changing taste in the courtly fashion of the late 18th century up to the 1920s, but is currently closed for extensive restoration.

The highlights of the Galleria d'Arte Moderna (Modern Art Gallery) are the paintings of the *Macchiaioli* (spot-makers), a group of Tuscan artists with a style similar to the French Impressionists.

Piazza della Signoria
depicted in precious stones

THE BOBOLI GARDENS

A copy of Giambologna's
Oceanus Fountain (1576)

The Boboli Gardens, a lovely place to escape the rigors of sightseeing, were laid out for the Medici after they bought the Palazzo Pitti in 1549. An excellent example of stylized Renaissance gardening, they were opened to the public in 1766. The formal parts of the garden, nearest the palazzo, consist of box-wood hedges clipped into symmetrical geometric patterns. These lead to wilder groves of oak and cypress trees, planted to create a contrast between artifice and nature. Countless statues adorn the gardens, particularly along the Viottolone, an avenue of cypress trees planted in 1637. High above the gardens stands the Forte di Belvedere, designed by Buontalenti in 1590 for the Medici Grand Dukes.

The Virgin from *The Annunciation* **(1528) by Pontormo**

Santa Felicita ㉘

Piazza di Santa Felicita. **Map** 3 C2 (5 C5). D. 055 21 30 18. 9am–noon, 3:30–6pm Mon–Sat; 4:30–6pm Sun.

THERE HAS BEEN a church on this site since the 4th century. The present structure, begun in the 11th century, was remodeled in 1736–9 by Ferdinando Ruggieri, who retained Vasari's earlier porch (added in 1564) as well as many of the church's original Gothic features.

The Capponi family chapel to the right of the entrance contains two works by Jacopo da Pontormo: *The Deposition* and *The Annunciation* (1525–28). The frescoes' strange composition and remarkable coloring make them two of Mannerism's greatest masterpieces.

Piazzale Michelangelo ㉙

Piazzale Michelangelo. **Map** 4 E3. 12, 13.

OF ALL THE GREAT Florentine viewpoints – such as the Duomo and Campanile – none offer such a magnificent panorama of the city as Piazzale Michelangelo. Laid out in the 1860s by Giuseppe Poggi and dotted with copies of Michelangelo's statues, its lofty balconies attract endless tour buses, countless visitors, and the inevitable massed ranks of souvenir sellers. Nonetheless, this bustling square remains an evocative spot, particularly at dusk, when the sun sets over the Arno and distant Tuscan hills.

San Miniato al Monte ㉚

Via del Monte alle Croci. **Map** 4 E3. 055 234 27 31. 12, 13. 8am–7:30pm daily (Oct–Mar: 8am–5:30pm). public hols.

SAN MINIATO is one of the most beautiful Romanesque churches in Italy. Begun in 1018, it was built over the shrine of San Miniato (St. Minias), a rich Armenian merchant beheaded for his beliefs by Emperor Decius in the 3rd century. The façade, begun around 1090, has the geometric marble patterning typical of Pisan-Romanesque architecture. The statue on the gable shows an eagle carrying a bale of cloth, the symbol of the powerful Arte di Calimala (guild of wool importers), who financed the church in the Middle Ages.

The façade of the church of San Miniato al Monte

The 13th-century mosaic shows Christ, the Virgin, and St. Minias. The same protagonists appear in the apse mosaic inside the church, which sits above a crypt supported by columns salvaged from ancient Roman buildings. The floor of the nave is covered with seven mosaic panels of animals and signs of the zodiac (1207).

Other highlights in the church include Michelozzo's freestanding Cappella del Crocifisso (1448) and the Renaissance Cappella del Cardinale del Portogallo (1461) with terra-cotta roundels (1466) on the ceiling by Luca della Robbia. There is a fresco cycle of *Scenes from the Life of St. Benedict* (1387) by Spinello Aretino in the sacristy.

Ponte Vecchio and the Arno from the heights of Piazzale Michelangelo

FLORENCE STREET FINDER

MAP REFERENCES given for sights in the Florence section refer to the maps on the following pages. Where two references are provided, the one in brackets relates to the large-scale maps, 5 and 6. References are also given for Florence hotels *(see pp557–9)* and restaurants *(see pp591–3)*, and for useful addresses in the *Travelers' Needs* and *Survival Guide* sections at the back of the book. The map below shows the area of Florence covered by the *Street Finder*. The symbols used for sights and other features on the *Florence Street Finder* maps are listed below. Streets in Florence have double sets of numbers: red numbers are for businesses, and black or blue for domestic residences.

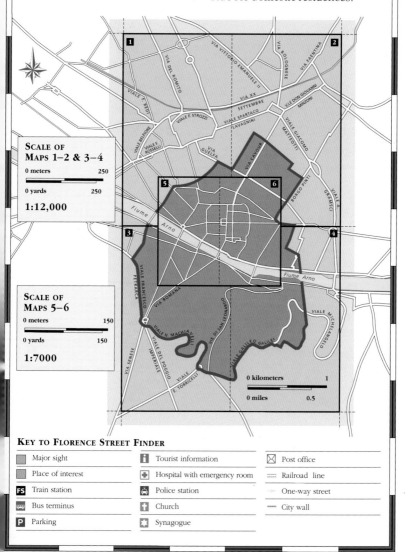

SCALE OF
MAPS 1–2 & 3–4

| 0 meters | 250 |
| 0 yards | 250 |

1:12,000

SCALE OF
MAPS 5–6

| 0 meters | 150 |
| 0 yards | 150 |

1:7000

| 0 kilometers | 1 |
| 0 miles | 0.5 |

KEY TO FLORENCE STREET FINDER

▩	Major sight	ⓘ	Tourist information	⊠	Post office
▩	Place of interest	✚	Hospital with emergency room	══	Railroad line
FS	Train station	▣	Police station	—	One-way street
▦	Bus terminus	✝	Church	—	City wall
P	Parking	✡	Synagogue		

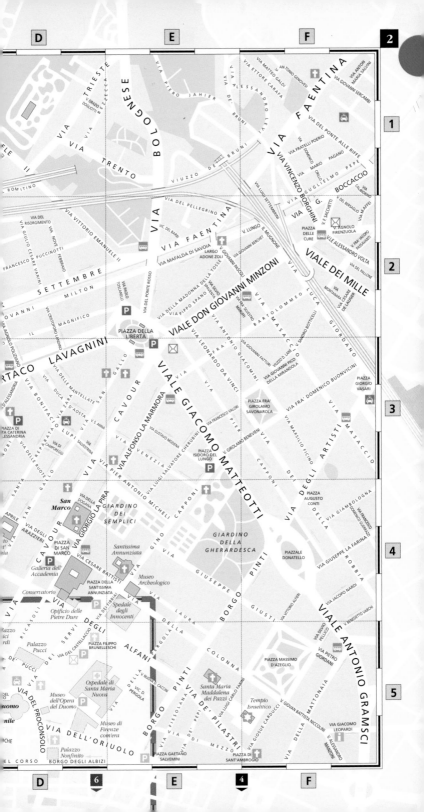

3

A **1** **B** **5** **C**

SEE PAGES 5, 6 FOR ENLARGEMENT OF THIS AREA

1

PIAZZA DI VERZAIA

BORGO SAN FREDIANO

VIA LUDOVICO ARIOSTO

VIA SAN GIOVANNI

PIAZZA DE' NERLI

VIA DELL'ORTO

VIA LORENZO BARTOLINI

VIA SANTONINO

VIA DEI CARDATORI

VIA DEL LEONE

PIAZZA DEL TIRATOIO

LUNGARNO SODERINI

San Frediano in Cestello

PIAZZA DI CESTELLO

Pescaia di S. Rosa

PIAZZA CARLO GOLDONI

V. D. VIGNA NUOVA

Palazzo Corsini

VIA DEL PURGATORIO

VIA PARIONE

LUNGARNO CORSINI

Santa Trinita

P. DI S. TRINITA

PIAZZA DEGLI STROZZI

Palazzo Strozzi

V. D. ANSELMI

V. P.TA ROSSA

PIAZZA DE' DAVANZATI

Palazzo Davanzati

PIAZZA TORQUATO TASSO

VIA DEL TESSITORI

Cappella Brancacci (Santa Maria del Carmine)

PIAZZA DEL CARMINE

PIAZZA PIATTELLINA

VIA SANTA MONACA

BORGO DELLA STELLA

PIAZZA NAZARIO SAURO

VIA DI SANTO SPIRITO

LUNGARNO GUICCIARDINI

PIAZZA DI FRESCOBALDI

Palazzo di Parte Guelfa

Palazzo Spini-Ferroni

Santi Apostoli

LUNGARNO D. ACCIAIUOLI

2

VIA VILLANI

VIA DI SAN FRANCESCO DI PAOLA

VIA MINIMA

VIA GIANO DELLA BELLA

VIALE FRANCESCO PETRARCA

VIA DEL CAMPUCCIO

VIA D'ARDIGLIONE

VIA SANT'AGOSTINO

VIA SANTA MARIA

VIA DELLA CHIESA

VIA DEL CASONE

GIARDINO TORRIGIANI

VIA DELLE CALDAIE

Cenacolo di Santo Spirito

Santo Spirito

PIAZZA DI SANTO SPIRITO

VIA MAZZETTA

VIA DE' COVERELLI

VIA MAGGIO

VIA DEL PRESTO DI SAN MARTINO

VIA DE' VELLUTI

VIA DELLO SPRONE

BORGO SAN JACOPO

PIAZZA DE' FRESCOBALDI

SDRUCCIOLO DE' PITTI

Palazzo Pitti

PIAZZA DE' PITTI

PIAZZA DI SAN FELICE

PIAZZA DE' VELLUTI

VIA GUICCIARDINI

PIAZZA DI SANTA FELICITA

Santa Felicita

VIA ROMANA

Museo La Specola

3

VIA IPPOLITO PINDEMONTE

VIA VINCENZO MONTI

VIA UGO FOSCOLO

VIA PIETRO METASTASIO

VIA GIOVANNI PRATI

VIA DELLE CAMPORA

PIAZZA DELLA CALZA

PIAZZALE DELLA PORTA ROMANA

VIA DEL RONCO

V. SERUMIDO

VIA DEL MORO

GIARDINO DI BOBOLI

Forte di Belvedere

VIA DEL MADONNA D. PACE

VIA DEL MASCHERINO

VIA DEL BOBOLINO

4

V. DI SANTILARIO A COLOMBAIA

VIALE NICCOLÒ MACHIAVELLI

VIA DANTE DA CASTIGLIONE

VIA FARINATA DEGLI UBERTI

VIA MICHELE DI LANDO

VIALE NICCOLÒ MACHIAVELLI

VIA SENESE

VIA CANTAGALLI

VIA BENEDETTO DA FOIANO

VIALE DEL POGGIO

PIAZZALE GALILEO

VIA DI SAN LEONARDO

5

R. PAOLO MA SCAGNI

VIA LORENZO BELLINI

VIA BENEDETTO CASTELLI

VIALE LORENZO MAGALOTTI

VIA GIOVANNI ALFONSO BORELLI

VIA DEL GELSOMINO

VIALE LEONARDO XIMENES

VIALE EVANGELISTA TORRICELLI

V.LE EVANGELISTA TORRICELLI

IMPERIALE

VIA DI SAN LEONARDO

VIA V. VIVIANI

VIA GUGLIELMO RIGHINI

VIA SENESE

A **B** **C**

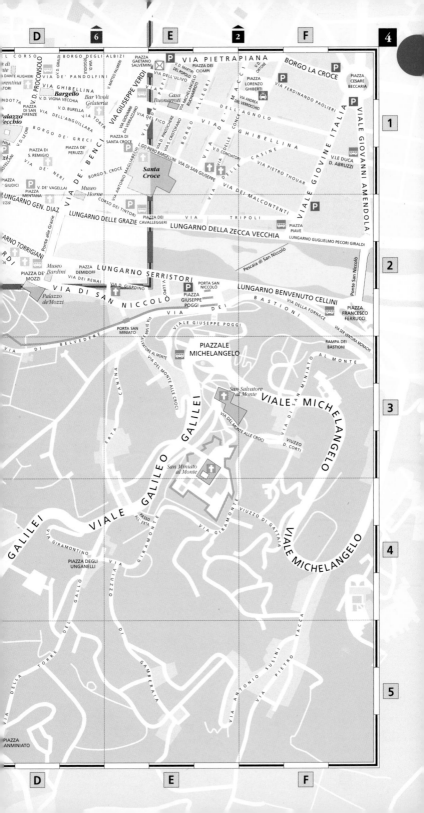

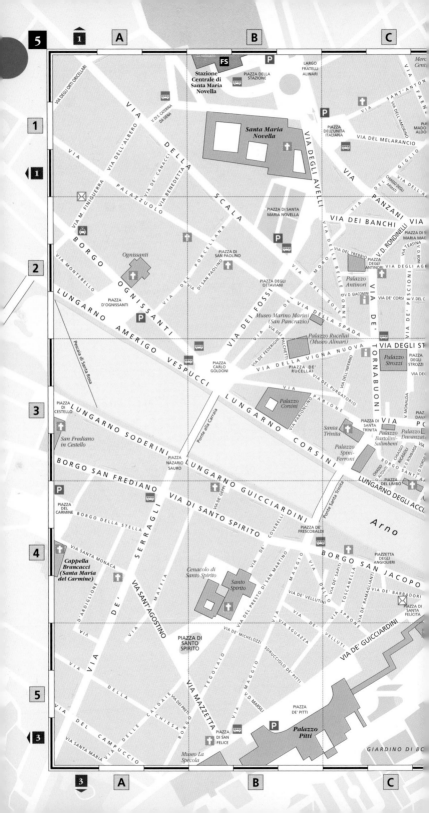

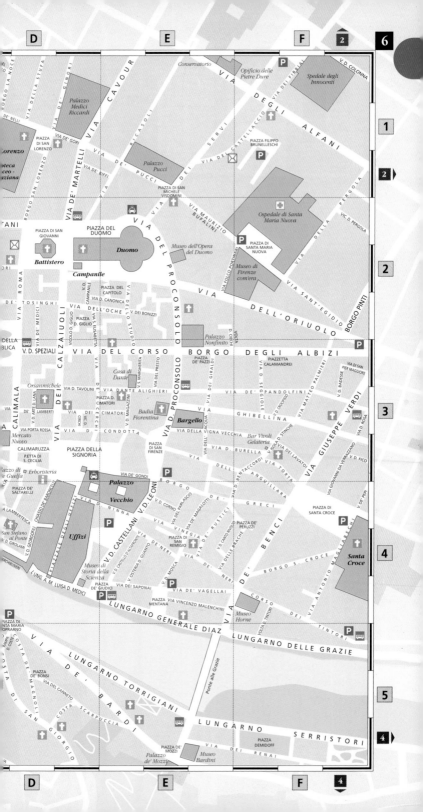

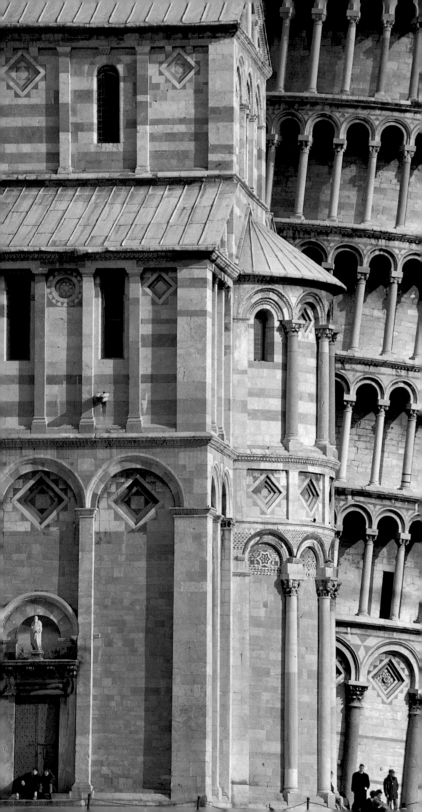

TUSCANY

....

R ENOWNED FOR ITS ART, *history, and evocative landscape, Tuscany is a region where the past and present merge in pleasant harmony. Hill towns gaze across the countryside from on high, many* encircled by Etruscan walls and slender cypress trees. Handsome palaces testify to the region's wealth, and medieval town halls indicate a long-standing tradition of democracy and self-government.

In the countryside, among the vineyards and olive groves, there are hamlets and farmhouses, as well as fortified villas and castles that symbolize the violence and intercommunal strife that tore Tuscany apart during the Middle Ages. Several imposing castles and villas were built for the Medici family, the great patrons of the Renaissance who supported eminent scientists such as Galileo.

Northern Tuscany, and the heavily populated plain between Florence and Lucca, is dominated by industry, with intensively cultivated land between the cities and the wild mountainous areas.

The area centered around Livorno and Pisa is now the region's economic hub. Pisa, at the height of its powers, dominated the western Mediterranean from the 11th to the 13th centuries. Its navy opened up extensive trading routes with North Africa and brought to Italy the benefits of Arabic scientific and artistic achievement. During the 16th century the Arno estuary began to silt up, ending Pisan power.

At the heart of central Tuscany lies Siena, which was involved in a long feud with Florence. Its finest hour came with its victory in the Battle of Montaperti in 1260, but it was devastated by the Black Death in the 14th century and finally suffered a crushing defeat by Florence in the siege of 1554–5.

Northeastern Tuscany, with its mountain peaks and woodland, provided refuge for hermits and saints, while the east was home to Piero della Francesca, the early Renaissance painter whose timeless and serene works are imbued with an almost religious perfection.

A timeless view and way of life in Casole d'Elsa, near San Gimignano in central Tuscany

◁ **The complex architecture of Pisa's duomo (begun in 1063) and the Leaning Tower (begun in 1173)**

Exploring Tuscany

TUSCAN CITIES such as Florence, Siena, and Pisa, together with smaller towns like Lucca, Cortona, and Arezzo, contain some of Italy's most famous artistic treasures. Medieval villages such as San Gimignano, with its famous towers, or Pienza, a tiny Renaissance jewel, sit at the heart of the glorious pastoral countryside for which the region is equally renowned. Elsewhere landscapes range from the spectacular mountains of the Alpi Apuane to the gentle hills of Chianti.

SIGHTS AT A GLANCE

View of Cortona in eastern Tuscany

0 kilometers   25

0 miles   20

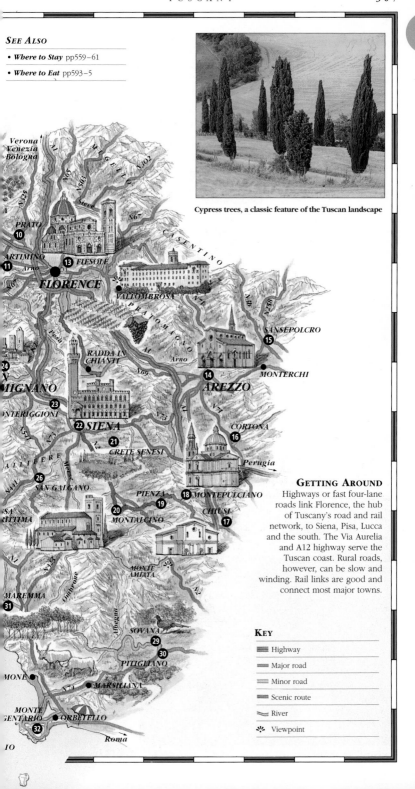

SEE ALSO

- **Where to Stay** pp559–61
- **Where to Eat** pp593–5

Cypress trees, a classic feature of the Tuscan landscape

Verona
Venezia
Bologna

MUGELLO

PRATO
10

ARTIMINO
11

FIESOLE
13

Arno

FLORENCE

CASENTINO

VALLOMBROSA

PRATOMAGNO

RADDA IN
CHIANTI

24

MIGNANO

SANSEPOLCRO
15

MONTERCHI

AREZZO
14

23

MONTERIGGIONI

SIENA
22

21

CRETE SENESI

CORTONA

16

Perugia

SAN GALGANO
26

PIENZA
19

MONTEPULCIANO
18

CHIUSI
17

MONTALCINO
20

MASSA
MARITTIMA

MONTE
AMIATA

GETTING AROUND

Highways or fast four-lane
roads link Florence, the hub
of Tuscany's road and rail
network, to Siena, Pisa, Lucca
and the south. The Via Aurelia
and A12 highway serve the
Tuscan coast. Rural roads,
however, can be slow and
winding. Rail links are good and
connect most major towns.

MAREMMA
31

SOVANA
29

PITIGLIANO
30

MONE

MARSILIANA

MONTE
ARGENTARIO

ORBETELLO

32

Roma

KEY

▰▰▰	Highway
▰▰▰	Major road
▰▰▰	Minor road
▰▰▰	Scenic route
〰	River
⁂	Viewpoint

Carrara ❶

Massa Carrara. 🏘 *70,000.* FS 🚌
ℹ *Viale XX Settembre (localitá
Stadio) (0585 84 44 03).* 🗓 *Mon.*

INTERNATIONALLY renowned for
its marble quarries, Carrara's
almost flawless white stone
has been prized for centuries
by famous sculptors from
Michelangelo to Henry Moore
(the stone for Michelangelo's
David came from Carrara). The
region's 300 or more quarries
date back to Roman times,
making this one of the oldest
industrial sites in continuous
use in the world. Many of the
town's marble-sawing mills
and workshops welcome
visitors, offering them the
chance to see the ways in
which marble and quartz are
worked. These techniques –
along with marble artifacts old
and new – can be seen at the
Museo Civico del Marmo.

Local marble is put to good
use in the town's **duomo** in
Piazza del Duomo, particularly
in the fine Pisan-Romanesque
façade with its delicate rose
window. The cathedral square
also contains Michelangelo's
house, used by the sculptor

A quarry in the marble-bearing hills around Carrara

during his visits to select blocks
of marble. The town has some
lovely corners to explore, in
particular the elegant Piazza
Alberica. Most visitors head
for the stone quarries that are
open to the public at nearby
Colonnata and at **Fantiscritti**
(take one of the regular town
buses or follow the signs to
the "Cave di Marmo"). The
latter features a small museum
with displays of various marble
quarrying techniques.

🏛 **Museo Civico del Marmo**
Viale XX Settembre. 📞 *0585 84 57
46.* 🕐 *Mon–Sat (Nov–Apr: am only).*

The Parco Naturale delle Alpi Apuane on the edge of the Garfagnana

Garfagnana ❷

Lucca. FS 🚌 *Castelnuovo di
Garfagnana.* ℹ *Castelnuovo di
Garfagnana (0583 64 43 54).*

A LOVELY VERDANT, silent
valley wedged between
the Orecchiella mountains
and the Alpi Apuane, the
Garfagnana region can be
explored from **Seravezza**,
Barga or **Castelnuovo di
Garfagnana**. While the town
of Barga makes the prettiest
base, thanks to its tawny
stone cathedral and charming
streets, Castelnuovo is more
convenient for drives and
walks in the surrounding
mountains. **San Pellegrino in
Alpe** in the Orecchiella has a
fascinating folklore museum,
the **Museo Etnografico**. It is
easily seen in conjunction with
the **Orto Botanico Pania di
Corfino** at the headquarters
of the **Parco dell'Orecchiella**
at Pania di Corfino, with its
collection of local Alpine trees.

To the west is the Parco
Naturale delle Alpi Apuane, an
area whose spectacular jagged
peaks and wooded valleys are
crisscrossed by hiking trails
and scenic mountain roads.

🏛 **Museo Etnografico**
Via del Voltone 15, San Pellegrino in
Alpe. 📞 *0583 64 90 72.*
🕐 *Tue–Sun.* ⬤ *public hols.* 🖼
♣ **Parco dell'Orecchiella**
Centro Visitatori, Orecchiella.
📞 *0583 61 90 98.* 🕐 *Jul–Aug:
daily; Jun & Sep: Sat–Sun; Apr–May &
Oct–Nov: Sun.* ♿
♣ **Orto Botanico Pania
di Corfino**
Parco dell'Orecchiella. 📞 *0583 61 90
98.* 🕐 *May–Sep: Sun (Jul–Aug: daily).*

One of many seaside cafés lining the waterfront in the popular beach resort of Viareggio

Bagni di Lucca ❸

Lucca. 🅰 7,400. 🚌 🅸 *Via del Casino 4 (0583 46 99 64).* 🅰 *Wed & Sat.*

A LL OVER TUSCANY there are hot springs of volcanic origin, like Bagni di Lucca. The Romans first exploited the springs and built bath complexes where army veterans, who settled in towns including Florence and Siena, could relax. More spas came into prominence in the Middle Ages and the Renaissance and have continued to be recommended for relieving a variety of ailments, such as arthritis.

Tuscan spas really came into their own in the early 19th century, when Bagni di Lucca reached its heyday as one of Europe's most fashionable spas, frequented by emperors, kings, and aristocrats. Visitors came not only for thermal cures, but also for the **Casino** (1837), one of Europe's first licensed gambling houses. These days the town is rather sleepy, and its main sights are the 19th-century monuments, including the Neo-Gothic **English Church** (1839) on Via Crawford and the **Cimitero Anglicano** (Protestant Cemetery) on Via Letizia.

ENVIRONS: Southeast of Bagni di Lucca lies another popular spa town, **Montecatini Terme**. Developed in the 18th century, this town is one of the most interesting with a wide range of spa architecture, from Neo-Classical to Art Nouveau spa establishments.

Viareggio ❹

Lucca. 🅰 55,000. 🚆 🚌 🅸 *Viale Carducci 10 (0584 96 22 33).* 🅰 *Thu.*

K NOWN FOR ITS CARNIVAL, held in January and early February, this is also the most popular of the resorts on the Versilia coast. Its famous "Liberty" (Art Nouveau) style of architecture can be seen in the grand hotels, villas, and cafés built in the 1920s after the resort's original boardwalk and timber chalets went up in flames in 1917. The finest example of the architecture is the **Gran Caffè Margherita** at the end of Passeggiata Margherita, designed by the prolific father of Italian Art Nouveau, Galileo Chini.

Torre del Lago Puccini ❺

Lucca. 🅰 11,500. 🚆 🚌 🅸 *Via Marconi 225 (0584 35 98 93).* 🅰 *Fri (Jul & Aug: also Sun).*

A GLORIOUS AVENUE of lime trees, the Via dei Tigli, connects Viareggio with Torre del Lago Puccini, once the home of the opera composer Giacomo Puccini (1858–1924). He and his wife are buried in their former home, now the **Museo Villa Puccini**, a small museum that features the piano on which the maestro composed many of his best-known works. Equal prominence is given to the villa's original fittings, including the gun room that housed Puccini's hunting rifle. **Lago Massaciuccoli**, an important nature preserve for rare and migrant birds, provides a pretty backdrop for open-air performances of Puccini's works.

🏛 **Museo Villa Puccini**
Piazzale Belvedere Puccini 64.
🅲 *0584 34 14 45.* ⬜ *daily.* 🌍 ♿

Near Puccini's lakeside home at Torre del Lago Puccini

Street-by-Street: Lucca ❻

L UCCA'S REGULAR GRID OF STREETS still follows the pattern of the former Roman colony founded in 180 BC. Great, solid ramparts, built in the 16th to 17th century, help to shut out traffic, making the city a pleasant place to explore on foot. San Michele in Foro – one of the town's many fine Pisan-Romanesque churches – stands on the site of the Roman forum (foro), the city's main square laid out in ancient times. It is still Lucca's main square today.

Casa di Puccini
Giacomo Puccini (1858–1924), composer of some of the world's most popular operas, including La Bohème, *was born in this house.*

Tourist information

San Frediano / Palazzo Pfanner

Piazza Napoleone
This sprawling square is named after Napoleon, whose sister, Elisa Baciocchi, ruled Lucca from 1805 to 1815.

Train station

★ San Michele in Foro
The extraordinary Pisan-Romanesque façade (11th to 14th century) has three tiers of twisted or carved columns, each one different from the rest.

San Giovanni

The Museo dell'Opera del Duomo,
a new museum, features treasures removed from San Martino.

STAR SIGHTS
★ **San Martino**
★ **San Michele in Foro**

KEY

– – – Suggested route

0 meters   300
0 yards   300

In Via Fillungo,
Lucca's main
shopping street,
several shop fronts
are decorated
with Art Nouveau
details.

anfiteatro
Romano

**Torre dei
Guinigi**

**Villa
Bottoni**

**Pinacoteca
Nazionale**

Giardino Botanico

Martino

*'s beautiful 11th-century
o is one of the outstand-
amples of the exuberant
-Romanesque style.*

Apostles from the mosaic on the façade of San Frediano in Lucca

🔒 San Frediano

Piazza San Frediano. ⏰ *daily.*
San Frediano's striking façade
features a colorful 13th-
century mosaic, *The Ascension*,
a fine prelude to the church's
wonderfully atmospheric interior. Pride of place goes to a
splendid Romanesque font on
the right, its sides carved with
scenes from the life of Christ
and the story of Moses. Note
the scene of Moses and his
followers (dressed as medieval
knights) as they pass through
the divided Red Sea. In the
second chapel in the north
aisle, Aspertini's frescoes
(1508–9) tell the story of
Lucca's precious relic, the
Volto Santo – a carving said
to date from the time of the
Crucifixion. The fine altarpiece
(1422) in the fourth chapel of
San Frediano's north aisle is
by Jacopo della Quercia.

🔒 San Michele in Foro

Piazza San Michele. ⏰ *daily.*
Built on the site of the old
Roman forum (*foro*), San
Michele's wonderfully rich
mixture of twisted marble
columns and Cosmati work
(inlaid marble) adorns one of
the most exuberant Pisan-
Romanesque façades in
Tuscany. Built between the
11th and 14th centuries, its
decoration is overwhelmingly
pagan. Only the huge winged
figure of St. Michael on the
pediment marks this out as a
church. The interior has little

of interest except for the
beautiful painting of *Saints
Helena, Jerome, Sebastian,
and Roch* by Filippino Lippi
(1457–1504).

🏛 Casa di Puccini

Via di Poggio. 📞 *0583 58 40 28.*
⏰ *Tue–Sun.* 🔴 *Jan 1, Dec 25.* 🎫
The fine 15th-century house
in which Giacomo Puccini
(1858–1924) was born is now
a shrine to the great opera
composer. It contains portraits
of Puccini, costume designs
for his operas, and the piano
he used when composing his
last opera, *Turandot*.

🏛 Via Fillungo

Lucca's principal shopping
street winds its way through
the heart of the city toward
the Anfiteatro Romano. A good
place to stroll, its northern
end has several shops with
Art Nouveau ironwork, and
halfway down lies the de-
consecrated church of San
Cristoforo, built in the 13th
century, with a lovely interior.

**One of the many bars and shops
along Via Fillungo**

Exploring Lucca

L UCCA'S PEACEFUL NARROW LANES wind among the medieval buildings, opening suddenly to reveal churches, tiny piazzas, and many other reminders of the city's long history, including a Roman amphitheater.

Medieval buildings mark the outline of Lucca's old Roman amphitheater

piazza until 1830, when it was cleared on the orders of Marie Louise, the city's Bourbon ruler of that time. It was then that the amphitheater's original shape was revealed, a graphic and evocative reminder of Lucca's rich Roman heritage. Low archways at the piazza's cardinal points mark the gates through which beasts and gladiators would once have entered the arena.

🏛 Museo dell'Opera del Duomo

Via Arcivescovado. 📞 0583 49 05 30. ⭕ daily. 🈺 🅱

The museum, housed in the former Archbishop's Palace (14th century), displays the treasures of the duomo of San Martino. These include the 11th-century carved stone head

🏛 Anfiteatro Romano

Piazza del Anfiteatro.
Roman *Luca* was founded in 180 BC, and stones from the ancient Roman amphitheater have been ransacked over the centuries to build churches and palaces, leaving only a handful of original fragments studded into today's arena-shaped Piazza del Mercato. Slum housing clogged the

🏛 SAN MARTINO

Piazza San Martino. 📞 0583 95 70 68. ⭕ daily.
Lucca's extraordinary cathedral, dedicated to St. Martin, was built subsequent to the campanile, hence the façade's cramped and asymmetric appearance. The main portals contain outstanding 13th-century carvings by Nicola Pisano and Guidetto da Como. The Tempietto inside houses the Volto Santo, a revered 13th-century effigy believed by medieval pilgrims to have been carved at the time of the Crucifixion.

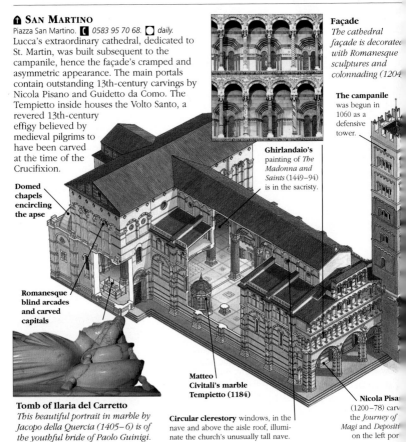

Façade
The cathedral façade is decorated with Romanesque sculptures and colonnading (1204

The campanile was begun in 1060 as a defensive tower.

Ghirlandaio's painting of *The Madonna and Saints* (1449–94) is in the sacristy.

Domed chapels encircling the apse

Romanesque blind arcades and carved capitals

Tomb of Ilaria del Carretto
This beautiful portrait in marble by Jacopo della Quercia (1405–6) is of the youthful bride of Paolo Guinigi.

Matteo Civitali's marble Tempietto (1184)

Circular clerestory windows, in the nave and above the aisle roof, illuminate the church's unusually tall nave.

Nicola Pisa (1200–78) carv the *Journey of Magi* and *Depositi* on the left por

Baroque gods and goddesses in the garden of the Palazzo Pfanner

of a king, removed from the cathedral façade, and a 12th-century Limoges casket, possibly created for a relic of St. Thomas à Becket. The Croce dei Pisani, made by Vincenzo di Michele in 1411, is a masterpiece of the goldsmith's art. It shows Christ on the Tree of Redemption, surrounded by angels, the Virgin, St. John, and the other evangelists.

🏛 Palazzo Pfanner
🔵 for restoration.
The elegant Palazzo Pfanner, an imposing house built in 1667, has a beautiful outside staircase. It also boasts one of Tuscany's most delightful formal gardens. Laid out in the 18th century, the central avenue of the garden is lined with Baroque statues of the gods and goddesses of ancient Roman mythology. The garden can also be viewed while walking along the ramparts.

The house itself contains a collection of court costume of the 18th and 19th centuries. Many garments are made of silk, whose production accounted for much of Lucca's medieval wealth.

🏛 Ramparts
One of the pleasures of visiting Lucca is strolling along the ramparts – the magnificent city walls, whose tree-lined promenade offers some entrancing views of the city.

Work on the ramparts began around 1500, when advances in military technology made the old medieval defenses ineffective. On their completion in 1645, the walls were some of the most advanced of their time. One of their most curious features was the open space that lay beyond them, and which survives to this day, cleared to prevent the enemy taking cover in trees and undergrowth. Ironically, the walls never actually had to be defended, and they were eventually converted into a public park in the early 19th century.

Romanesque lion in the Museo Nazionale Guinigi

Part of the imposing 17th-century ramparts that encircle Lucca

🏛 Santa Maria Forisportam
Piazza di Santa Maria Forisportam.
🔵 daily.
This church was built at the end of the 12th century, beyond the Roman walls of Lucca. Its name, Forisportam, means "outside the gate." The unfinished marble façade, in Pisan-Romanesque style, has blind arcading. Above the central portal is a relief of the *Coronation of the Virgin* (17th century). The interior was redesigned in the early 16th century, resulting in the nave and transepts being raised. The fourth altar of the south aisle contains a painting of *St. Lucy,* and the north transept has an *Assumption,* both by Guercino (1591–1666).

🏛 Museo Nazionale di Villa Guinigi
Via della Quarquonia. 📞 0583 49 60 33. 🔵 Tue–Sun. 🔵 Dec 25. 📷
This massive Renaissance villa was built in 1418 for Paolo Guinigi, leading light of the powerful noble family who ruled Lucca in the early 15th century. A familiar landmark of the city is the battlemented tower, the Torre dei Guinigi, with oak trees growing at the top. It offers good views over the city and the Apuan Alps. The garden features traces of a Roman mosaic, together with a pride of Romanesque lions removed from the city's walls.

Inside, the museum's first floor is devoted to sculptures and archaeological displays. The highlights are works by Matteo Civitali, Jacopo della Quercia, and fine Romanesque reliefs removed from several of Lucca's churches. Most of the paintings in the gallery on the floor above are by minor local artists, with the exception of two works by Fra Bartolomeo (c.1472–1517): *God the Father with Saints Catherine and Mary Magdalene* and the *Madonna della Misericordia.* The floor also has furnishings, church vestments, and choir stalls from Lucca's cathedral, inlaid with marquetry views of the city carved in 1529.

Pisa ⑦

Inlaid marble, duomo façade

FOR MUCH OF THE MIDDLE AGES, Pisa's powerful navy ensured its dominance of the western Mediterranean. Trading links with Spain and North Africa in the 12th century brought vast mercantile wealth and formed the basis of a scientific and cultural revolution that is still reflected in Pisa's splendid buildings – especially the duomo, baptistry and campanile (Leaning Tower). Pisa's decline began in 1284, with its defeat by Genoa, and was hastened by the silting up of the harbor. The city fell to the Florentines in 1406, but suffered its worst crisis in 1944 when it fell victim to Allied bombing.

A detail from the duomo pulpit

The circular baptistry, a graceful counterpoint to the duomo, was begun in 1152 along Romanesque lines, and finished a century later – after a delay caused by a shortage of money – in a more ornate Gothic style by Nicola and Giovanni Pisano. The former was responsible for the magnificent marble pulpit (1260) in the interior, carved with reliefs of the *Nativity*, the *Adoration of the Magi*, the *Presentation*, the *Crucifixion,* and the *Last Judgment*. The pillars that support the pulpit feature statues of the Virtues. The inlaid marble font (1246) is by Guido da Como.

The baptistry, duomo and Leaning Tower in Pisa's Campo dei Miracoli

🏛 Leaning Tower
See p316.

🏛 Duomo and Baptistry
Piazza Duomo. ☎ 050 56 09 21.
🕐 *daily.*

Pisa's famous Leaning Tower is now the best-known building in the Campo dei Miracoli (Field of Miracles). Originally, however, it was intended as a campanile to complement the duomo, which was begun by Buscheto almost a century earlier in 1064. Today the duomo stands as one of the finest Pisan-Romanesque buildings in Tuscany, its wonderful four-tiered façade a

medley of creamy colonnades and intricate blind arcades. Buscheto's tomb is in the left arch of the façade. Other important features of the exterior include the Portale di San Ranieri (leading to the south transept) and the bronze doors (1180), decorated with reliefs cast by Bonanno Pisano, the first architect of the Leaning Tower. Inside, the highlights are the carved pulpit (1302–11) by Giovanni Pisano, the *Tomb of Emperor Henry VII* (1315) by Tino da Camaino, and a mosaic of *Christ in Majesty* in the apse, completed by Cimabue in 1302.

🏛 Camposanto
Piazza dei Miracoli. ☎ 050 56 05 47.
🕐 *daily.* ● *Jan 1, Dec 25.*

The Camposanto – the "Holy Field," or cemetery – is the fourth element in the Campo dei Miracoli's lovely medieval ensemble. Begun in 1278 by Giovanni di Simone, the vast marble arcades of this long, rectangular building are said to enclose soil brought back from the Holy Land. Bombs in World War II all but destroyed its once famous frescoes, leaving only traces of scenes depicting *The Triumph of Death* (1360–80).

A fresco from the *Triumph of Death* cycle in the Camposanto

Santa Maria della Spina alongside the River Arno in Pisa

🅐 Museo dell'Opera el Duomo

azza del Duomo 6. [050 56 05 7.] daily. 🎞 &

oused in the cathedral's 13th-entury former Chapter House, is excellent modern museum isplays exhibits removed over e years from the duomo, aptistry, and Camposanto. mong the highlights is n imposing 10th-century ippogriff (half horse, alf griffin). Cast in ronze by Moorish raftsmen, this statue as looted by Pisan dventurers during e wars against the aracens. There are so works by both icola and Giovanni isano, notably

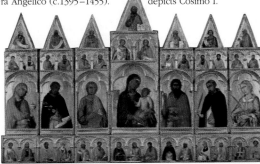

10th-century bronze hippogriff

iovanni's ivory *Virgin and hild* (1300), carved for the uomo's high altar. Other xhibits include paintings, oman and Etruscan remains, nd ecclesiastical treasures.

🅐 Museo Nazionale di an Matteo

ungarno Mediceo, Piazza San Matteo . [050 54 18 65.] Tue–Sun. 🎞

his museum is located on e banks of the Arno in San latteo, an elegantly fronted edieval convent that also erved as a prison in the 19th entury. Much of the building as been closed for years, ith the result that several of e rooms have no numbers nd some of the exhibits are oorly labeled. Nevertheless, e museum presents a unique pportunity to examine the omplete sweep of Pisan and orentine art from the 12th to e 17th centuries.

The first rooms are devoted to sculpture and early Tuscan paintings. The best exhibits include a 14th-century polyptych by Francesco Traini of *Scenes from the Life of St. Dominic*, Simone Martini's fine polyptych of *The Madonna and Saints* (1321), and a 14th-century statue of the *Madonna del Latte*, attributed to Andrea Pisano, another member of Pisa's talented school of medieval sculptors. The half-length statue, in gilded marble, shows Christ feeding at his mother's breast. In Room 6 are some of the highlights of the museum, including Masaccio's *St. Paul* (1426), Gentile da Fabriano's radiant 15th-century *Madonna of Humility*, and Donatello's reliquary bust of *San Rossore* (1424–7). Additional rooms contain paintings by Guido Reni, Benozzo Gozzoli, Rosso Fiorentino, and an important picture of *Christ* attributed to Fra Angelico (c.1395–1455).

🅐 Santa Maria della Spina

Lungarno Gambacorti. [050 53 24 74.] by permission only.

The roofline of this tiny church, located just beyond the Ponte Solferino, bristles with spiky Gothic pinnacles, miniature spires, and niches sheltering statues of apostles and saints. The decoration reflects the history of the church, which was built between 1230 and 1323 to house a thorn *(spina)* from Christ's Crown of Thorns, the gift of a Pisan merchant. The church was once even closer to the Arno, but was rebuilt on the present site in 1871 to protect it from flooding.

🏛 Piazza dei Cavalieri

The huge building on the north side of this square is the Palazzo dei Cavalieri, home to one of Pisa University's most prestigious colleges: the Scuola Normale Superiore. Designed by Vasari in 1562, the building, which is covered in exuberant black and white *sgraffito* decoration (designs scratched into wet plaster), served as the headquarters of the Cavalieri di Santo Stefano, an order of knights created by Cosimo I in 1561. The imposing statue outside depicts Cosimo I.

The Virgin and Child (1321) by Simone Martini in the Museo Nazionale

The Leaning Tower of Pisa

Begun in 1173 on sandy silt subsoil, the Leaning Tower (Torre Pendente) started to tilt even before the third level was finished in 1274. Despite the shallow foundations, construction continued and the structure was completed in 1350. The tower's apparent flouting of the laws of gravity has attracted many visitors over the centuries, including the Pisan scientist Galileo, who climbed to the top to conduct his famous experiments on the velocity of falling objects. Recently its tilt has increased alarmingly: the tower now leans in excess of 5 m (16.5 ft), and remains closed for restoration and underpinning.

Galileo Galilei (1564–1642)

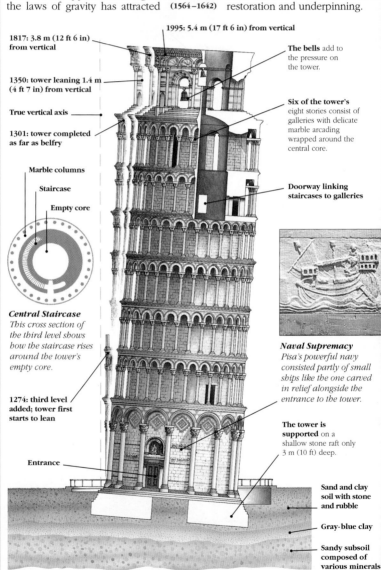

1995: 5.4 m (17 ft 6 in) from vertical

1817: 3.8 m (12 ft 6 in) from vertical

1350: tower leaning 1.4 m (4 ft 7 in) from vertical

True vertical axis

1301: tower completed as far as belfry

Marble columns

Staircase

Empty core

Central Staircase
This cross section of the third level shows how the staircase rises around the tower's empty core.

1274: third level added; tower first starts to lean

Entrance

The bells add to the pressure on the tower.

Six of the tower's eight stories consist of galleries with delicate marble arcading wrapped around the central core.

Doorway linking staircases to galleries

Naval Supremacy
Pisa's powerful navy consisted partly of small ships like the one carved in relief alongside the entrance to the tower.

The tower is supported on a shallow stone raft only 3 m (10 ft) deep.

Sand and clay soil with stone and rubble

Gray-blue clay

Sandy subsoil composed of various minerals

Vinci

Florence. 🏛 1,500. 🚌 🅿 Wed.

FAMOUS AS THE BIRTHPLACE OF
Leonardo da Vinci (1452–
1519), this hilltop town
celebrates the genius in the
Museo Leonardiano, housed
in the 13th-century castle.
Among the displays are
wooden models of Leonardo's
machines and inventions, most
of them based on drawings
from his notebooks, shown
alongside. These include a
bicycle, his conception of a
car, an armored tank, and
even a machine gun.

🏛 Museo Leonardiano
Castello dei Conti Guidi.
(0571 560 55. ◯ daily. 🔳

**Model bicycle based on designs
by Leonardo, Museo Leonardiano**

Pistoia 🟡

🏛 93,000. 🚊 🚌 ℹ Palazzo dei
Vescovi, Piazza del Duomo (0573 216
22). 🅿 Wed & Sat.

PISTOIA'S CITIZENS WERE
once known for violence
and intrigue, a reputation
grounded in the medieval
disputes between the city's
rival factions, the Bianchi
and Neri (Whites and Blacks).
Their favored weapon was a
tiny, locally made dagger
known as a *pistola*. Long a
center of metalwork, everything from buses to mattress
springs are now made here.
In the center, several fine historic buildings are preserved.

🏛 Duomo
Piazza del Duomo. ◯ daily.
Piazza del Duomo, Pistoia's
main square, is dominated by
the duomo (San Zeno) and
its bulky 12th-century campanile, originally built as a
watchtower in the city walls.
The interior of the duomo is

Detail of frieze (1514–25) by Giovanni della Robbia, Ospedale del Ceppo

rich in funerary monuments.
The finest of these, in the
south aisle, is the tomb of
Cino da Pistoia. He was a
friend of Dante and fellow
poet, and is depicted in a
relief (1337) lecturing to a
class of young boys.
   Nearby is the chapel of St.
James and its extraordinary
silver altar decorated with
more than 600 statues and
reliefs. Although the earliest
of these dates from 1287, the
altar was not completed
until 1456. One of the
craftsmen involved was
Brunelleschi, who began
his career as a silver-
smith before turning to
architecture. Also in
the Piazza del Duomo
is the octagonal baptistry,
completed in 1359.

🏛 Ospedale del Ceppo
Piazza Giovanni XXIII.
This hospital and orphanage,
founded in 1277, was named
after the *ceppo* (hollowed-out
tree trunk) that was used to
collect donations for its work.
The main façade features
colored terra-cotta panels
(1514–25) by Giovanni della
Robbia illustrating the *Seven
Works of Mercy*. The portico
is by Michelozzo.

**The Pisan-Romanesque façade of
Pistoia's Duomo (San Zeno)**

🏛 Cappella del Tau
Corso Silvano Fedi 70.
◯ Mon–Sat am.
The Cappella del Tau (1360)
is so called because the
monks who built it wore on
their cloaks the letter T (tau
in Greek), symbolizing a
crutch and their work with
the sick and disabled. Inside
there are frescoes by Niccolò
di Tommaso on *The Creation*
and the *Life of St. Anthony
Abbot* (1370). Two doors down
the **Palazzo Tau** has work by
Marino Marini, Pistoia's best-
known 20th-century artist.

**The Fall (1372) by Niccolò di
Tommaso in the Cappella del Tau**

🏛 San Giovanni Fuorcivitas
Via Cavour. ◯ daily.
Built in the 12th to 14th
centuries, the striking church
of San Giovanni Fuorcivitas
(literally "St. John Outside the
City") once stood beyond the
city walls. Its north flank is
clad in banded marble and
there is a Romanesque relief
of the Last Supper over the
portal. Inside, the holy water
stoup, carved in marble with
figures of the Virtues, is by
Giovanni Pisano (1245–1320).
A masterly pulpit, carved
in 1270 with scenes from
the New Testament, is by
Guglielmo da Pisa. Both are
among the finest works of
this period, when artists were
reviving the art of carving.

Prato ⑩

Florence. 🏛 170,000. 🚌 ℹ Via Cairoli 48 (0574 241 12). 🗓 Mon.

WHILE TEXTILE factories gird Prato's outskirts, the city's historic center retains several important churches and museums. The **duomo** (begun 1211) is flanked by the Pulpit of the Holy Girdle (1434–8), designed by Donatello and Michelozzo, used once a year to display a girdle, reputedly given to Thomas the Apostle before the Assumption of the Virgin. Inside the Duomo is a masterpiece by Fra Filippo Lippi, *The Life of John the Baptist* (1452–66), and a fresco cycle (1392–5) by Agnolo Gaddi describing how the Virgin's girdle reached Prato. The *Madonna del Ceppo* (15th century), also painted by Lippi, is kept in the **Museo Civico**.

Other sights include **Santa Maria delle Carceri** in Piazza delle Carceri, a Renaissance church designed by Giuliano da Sangallo; the **Castello dell' Imperatore**, a fortress built by Emperor Frederick II in 1237; and the **Museo del Tessuto**, which traces the history of Prato's textile industry.

🏛 **Museo Civico**
Palazzo Pretorio, Piazza del Comune.
📞 0574 45 23 02 24.
⬤ for restoration.
⛪ **Castello dell'Imperatore**
Piazza delle Carceri. ⬤ Wed–Mon.
🏛 **Museo del Tessuto**
Piazzo del Comune.
📞 0574 531 71. ⬤ Mon, Wed–Sat.

Madonna del Ceppo by Fra Filippo Lippi in Prato's Museo Civico

Buontalenti's Villa di Artimino, or "Villa of a Hundred Chimneys"

Artimino ⑪

Prato. 🏛 400. 🚌

A SMALL FORTIFIED hamlet, Artimino is remarkable for the unspoiled Romanesque church of **San Leonardo**. Outside the walls lies the **Villa di Artimino**, designed by Buontalenti in 1594 for Grand Duke Ferdinando I. Also known as the "Villa of a Hundred Chimneys" – after the chimney pots crowding the roofline – it houses the **Museo Archeologico Etrusco**, a collection of archaeological exhibits.

ENVIRONS: For lovers of Pontormo's paintings, the church of **San Michele** in Carmignano, 5 km (3 miles) north of Artimino, contains *The Visitation* (1530). East of here lies the villa of **Poggio a Caiano**. Built in 1480 by Giuliano da Sangallo for Lorenzo de' Medici *(see p245)*, it was the first Italian villa to be designed in the Renaissance style.

🏛 **Villa di Artimino**
Viale Papa Giovanni 23. **Villa** 📞 .055 879 20 30. ⬤ by appt. **Museum** 📞 055 871 80 81. ⬤ 9am–4pm (12:30pm Sun) Thu–Tue. 🚫
🏛 **Poggio a Caiano**
Piazza Medici. 📞 055 87 70 12. ⬤ Tue–Sun. 🚫 🚫 🚫

San Miniato ⑫

Pisa. 🏛 3,900. 🚌 ℹ Piazza del Popolo 3 (0571 427 45). 🗓 Tue.

THIS HILLTOP TOWN manages to remain aloof from the vast industrial sprawl of the Arno valley. Its key building is the semiderelict Rocca (castle), built for Frederick II, German Holy Roman Emperor, in the 13th century. Close by stands the **Museo Diocesano** which is home to a *Crucifixion* (c.1430) attributed to Filippo Lippi, a terra-cotta bust of Christ attributed to Verrocchio (1435–88), and the *Virgin of the Holy Girdle* by Andrea del Castagno (c.1417–57). Next door, the redbrick Romanesque façade of the **duomo** dates from the 12th century. Its strange inset majolica plates evidence of trade with Spain or North Africa, probably represent the North Star and the constellations of Ursa Major and Minor (all three were key points of reference for early navigators).

🏛 **Museo Diocesano**
Piazza Duomo. 📞 0571 41 82 71.
⬤ Easter–Jan 5: Sat & Sun; Jan 6–Easter: Tue–Sat. 🚫

Façade of the duomo in San Miniato

Fiesole ⑬

Florence. 🏛 15,000. 🚌 ℹ Via Portigiani 3/5 (055 59 87 20). 🗓 Sat.

FIESOLE STANDS IN rolling hilly countryside 8 km (5 miles) north of Florence. Idyllically situated among olive groves, it is a popular retreat from the city – thanks to its hilltop position, which attracts cool breezes. Founded in the 7th century BC, the original Etruscan colony was a powerful force in central Italy, only

A view over the hills and rooftops of Fiesole from Via di San Francesco

surrendering its supremacy after the foundation of Florence (1st century BC).

The **duomo** of San Romolo in Piazza Mino da Fiesole was begun in 1028. It has a massive bell tower and a bare Romanesque interior with columns topped with re-used Roman capitals. Behind the duomo, an archaeological area contains the remains of a 1st-century BC **Roman Theater**, traces of **Etruscan walls** from the 4th century BC, and the **Museo Faesulanum**, with a collection of bronzes, ceramics, and jewelry dating from the Bronze Age.

Via di San Francesco, a steep lane offering lovely views, leads to the Franciscan friary of **San Francesco** (14th century) and the interesting 9th-century church of **Sant'Alessandro**, with Neo-Classical façade.

Via Vecchia Fiesolana leads to the little hamlet of **San Domenico**. Here the 15th-century church of the same name contains a painting of the *Madonna with Angels and Saints* (c.1430) by Fra Angelico, and the Chapter House contains a fresco of *The Crucifixion* (c.1430), also by him. Close by, on the Via della Badia dei Roccettini, stands the pretty Romanesque church of the **Badia Fiesolana** with its striped marble façade and interior of local gray sandstone, *pietra serena*.

ⅲ Museo Faesulanum
Via Portigiani 1. 055 594 77.
daily (Oct–Mar: Wed–Mon).

Arezzo ⑭

92,000. 🚌 ℹ *Piazza della Repubblica (0575 37 76 78).* 🛒 *Sat.*

AREZZO IS ONE of Tuscany's wealthiest cities, its prosperity based on a thriving jewelry industry. Although much of its medieval center was destroyed during World War II, resulting in extensive rebuilding and many medieval alleys being replaced by broad avenues, the city preserves some outstanding sights: foremost are Piero della Francesca's famous frescoes in the church of **San Francesco** *(see pp320–21)*. Close to the church on Corso Italia, the main street, stands the **Pieve di Santa Maria**, which boasts one of the most ornate Romanesque façades in the region. To its rear stretches the steeply sloping **Piazza Grande**, flanked by an arcade (1573) designed by Vasari, and by

the **Palazzo della Fraternità dei Laici** (1377–1552). The latter features a *Madonna* relief by Bernardo Rossellino. The huge **duomo** to the north is best known for its 16th-century stained glass and a small fresco of *Mary Magdalene* by Piero della Francesca (1416–92). The **Museo del Duomo** features three wooden crucifixes, dating from the 12th and 13th centuries, a bas relief of *The Annunciation* (1434) by Rossellino, and paintings by Vasari. More works by Vasari can be seen in the **Casa di Vasari**, a house built by the artist in 1540. Still more frescoes by him are displayed in the **Museo d'Arte Medioevale e Moderna**, a museum that is famed for its excellent collection of majolica pottery.

The **Fortezza Medicea**, a ruined Medici castle built by Antonio da Sangallo during the 16th century, has fine views.

ⅲ Museo del Duomo
Piazzetta del Duomo 13. 0575 239 91. Thu–Sat am by appt.
⛪ Casa di Vasari
Via XX Settembre 55. 0575 30 03 01. Wed–Mon.
ⅲ Museo d'Arte Medioevale e Moderna
Via di San Lorentino 8. 0575 30 03 01. Tue–Sun.
♜ Fortezza Medicea
Parco il Prato. 0575 37 76 66.
daily.

The monthly antique market held in Arezzo's Piazza Grande

Arezzo: San Francesco

THE 13TH-CENTURY CHURCH of San Francesco houses one of Italy's greatest fresco cycles, the *Legend of the True Cross* (1452–66), the masterpiece of Piero della Francesca. The famous scenes on the walls of the choir describe the history of the cross used to crucify Christ from sprig to Tree of Knowledge, to its use as a bridge during the reigns of Solomon and the Queen of Sheba, and ultimately its discovery by Helena, mother of Constantine, the first Christian emperor.

A Group of Onlookers
These figures kneel in wonder while Heraclius returns the True Cross to Jerusalem.

Excavation of the Cross
The town, meant to be Jerusalem, gives a fair representation of 15th-century Arezzo.

The Cross returns to Jerusalem.

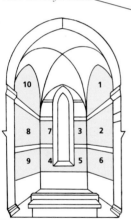

KEY TO FRESCOES

1 The Death of Adam; a sprig from the Tree of Knowledge is planted over his grave; 2 The Queen of Sheba visits Solomon and foresees that a bridge made from the Tree will be used to crucify the greatest king in the world; 3 Solomon, assuming he is the greatest king in the world, orders the bridge to be buried; 4 The Annunciation: Christ's death is foreshadowed in the panel's cruciform structure; 5 Constantine has a vision of the Cross and hears a voice saying "In this sign you shall conquer"; 6 Constantine defeats his rival Maxentius; 7 The Levite Judas is tortured and reveals the location of the True Cross; 8 Three crosses are dug up; Constantine's mother Helena recognizes the True Cross; 9 The Persian king Chosroes is defeated after stealing the Cross; 10 The True Cross is returned to Jerusalem.

The Defeat of Chosroes depicts the defeat of a Persian king who had stolen the Cross.

Judas reveals where the Cross is hidden.

Painted Crucifix
The 13th-century Crucifix forms the focal point of the fresco cycle. The figure at the foot of the Cross represents St. Francis, to whom the church is dedicated.

The Death of Adam
*Piero's vivid portrayal of Adam
and Eve in old age shows an
adept treatment of anatomy. He
was one of the first Renaissance
artists to paint nude figures.*

VISITORS' CHECKLIST

Piazza San Francesco, Arezzo.
[0575 206 30. **□** 8:30am–
noon, 2:30–6:30pm daily.
✝ daily. **&**

The prophets appear to play
no part in the narrative cycle;
their presence may be for
purely decorative reasons.

The buildings
in the fresco reflect
the newly fashionable
styles of Renaissance
architecture.

The wood of the
Cross is buried
in a pit.

Constantine dreams
of the Cross on the eve
of battle against rival
emperor Maxentius.

Constantine leads his
cavalry into battle.

The Queen of Sheba
recognizes the wood
of the Cross.

Solomon's Handshake
*The handshake between
the Queen of Sheba and
Solomon, King of Israel,
portrays 15th-century
hopes for a union
between the Orthodox
and Western churches.*

Piero's *The Resurrection* (1463) in Sansepolcro

Sansepolcro ⓯

Arezzo. 🏠 *16,000.* 🚌 ℹ️ *Piazza Garibaldi 2 (0575 74 05 36).* 🚪 *Tue, Sat.*

SANSEPOLCRO IS the birthplace of Piero della Francesca (1410–92). The town's **Museo Civico** contains two of his masterpieces: *The Resurrection* (1463) and the *Madonna della Misericordia* (1462). It also has a 15th-century *Crucifixion* by Luca Signorelli. In the church of **San Lorenzo** on Via Santa Croce there is a *Deposition* in the Mannerist style by Rosso Fiorentino (1494–1541).

Another famous painting by Piero della Francesca, the *Madonna del Parto* (1460), can be seen at Via Reglia 1 in Monterchi, 13 km (8 miles) southwest of Sansepolcro.

🏛 **Museo Civico**
Via Aggiunti 65. 📞 *0575 73 22 18.* 🕐 *daily.* ⬤ *public hols.* 🎫

Cortona ⓰

Arezzo. 🏠 *23,000.* 🚆 🚌 ℹ️ *Via Nazionale 42 (0575 63 03 52).* 🚪 *Sat.*

CORTONA WAS FOUNDED by the Etruscans and apart from being one of the oldest hill towns in Tuscany, it is also one of the most scenic. A major power in the Middle Ages, it was able to hold its own against Siena and Arezzo. Today it is a charming maze of old streets and medieval

buildings, like the **Palazzo Comunale** on Piazza Signorelli. The town's early history is traced in the **Museo dell'Accademia Etrusca**, which contains Etruscan artifacts and a wide variety of Egyptian and Roman remains. The small **Museo Diocesano** features several fine paintings, in particular a *Crucifixion* by the Renaissance artist Pietro Lorenzetti, a *Deposition* (1502) by Luca Signorelli, and a sublime *Annunciation* (c.1434) by Fra Angelico. Signorelli, born in Cortona, is buried in the church of **San Francesco** (built in 1245), which contains an *Annunciation* painted in Baroque style by Pietro da Cortona, another native artist. The other well-known church in Cortona is the **Madonna del Calcinaio** (1485), a gem of Renaissance architecture located on the southern outskirts of town.

The 13th-century Palazzo Comunale in Cortona

🏛 **Museo dell'Accademia Etrusca**
Palazzo Casali, Piazza Signorelli 9. 📞 *0575 63 04 15.* 🕐 *Tue – Sun.* 🎫
🏛 **Museo Diocesano**
Piazza del Duomo 1. 📞 *0575 628 30.* 🕐 *Tue – Sun.* 🎫

Chiusi ⓱

Siena. 🏠 *10,000.* 🚆 🚌 ℹ️ *Via Porsenna 73 (0578 22 76 67).* 🚪 *Tue.*

CHIUSI IS NOW a mostly modern town, but in the past it was one of the most powerful cities in the Etruscan league, reaching the height of its influence in the 7th and 6th centuries BC *(see p41).* Numerous Etruscan tombs lie dotted about the surrounding countryside, the source of the exhibits in the town's **Museo Nazionale Etrusco**. Founded in 1871, the museum is packed with cremation urns, vases decorated with black figures, and Bucchero ware, burnished to resemble bronze.

The Romanesque **duomo** in Piazza del Duomo incorporates recycled Roman pillars and capitals. The wall decorations in the nave, resembling frescoes, were painted by Arturo Viligiardi in 1887. There is a Roman mosaic underneath the high altar. Visits can be made to several Etruscan tombs under the town from the **Museo della Cattedrale**, a museum in the cloister of the duomo that also features displays of Roman, Lombardic, and medieval sculpture from the region.

🏛 **Museo Nazionale Etrusco**
Via Porsenna 17. 📞 *0578 201 77.* 🕐 *daily.* 🎫
🏛 **Museo della Cattedrale**
Piazza del Duomo. 📞 *0578 22 64 90.* 🕐 *daily.* 🎫

Etruscan frieze in the Museo Nazionale Etrusco in Chiusi

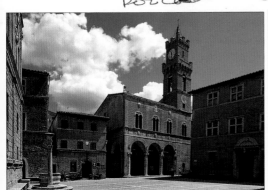

Pienza's Piazza Pio II, designed by Bernardo Rossellino (1459)

Montepulciano ⓘ

Siena. 🏛 *14,000.* 🚌 🛈 *Via Ricci 9 (0578 75 73 41).* 🛒 *Thu.*

THIS IS ONE of Tuscany's highest hill towns, its walls and fortifications offering broad views over Umbria and southern Tuscany, and the vineyards providing the Vino Nobile wine that has made its name famous. The streets are brimming with Renaissance palazzi. The steep main street, the Corso, climbs to the **duomo** (1592–1630), the setting for one of the masterpieces of the Sienese School, the *Assumption* (1401) by Taddeo di Bartolo. The High Renaissance church, **Tempio di San Biagio** (1518–34), lies off the road to Pienza.

Pienza ⓘ

Siena. 🏛 *2,300.* 🚌 🛈 *Corso il Rossellino 59 (0578 74 90 71).* 🛒 *Fri.*

PIENZA IS A delightful village whose intimate little center was almost completely re-designed in the 15th century by Pope Pius II. Born as Aeneas Sylvius Piccolomini in 1405, when the village was known as Corsignano, he became a leading Humanist scholar and philosopher. Elected pope in 1458, Pius II decided to rebuild his birthplace a year later, renaming it Pienza in his own honor. The Florentine architect and sculptor, Bernardo Rossellino, was commissioned to build a cathedral, papal palace, and

town hall (all completed in the three years from 1459 to 1462), but the grander scheme for a planned model Renaissance town was never realized. Some idea of what might have been, however, can still be gained from the **Palazzo Piccolomini**, the former papal palace, which continued to be inhabited by Pius's descendants until 1968. The rooms open to the public include Pius's bedroom and library, but the highlight of a visit is the superb panorama from the loggia and arcaded courtyard at the palace's rear.

Pleasant walks and more great views can be had from the village walls. The airy **duomo** *(see p244)* next door contains six altarpieces of the *Madonna and Child*, each commissioned from the leading Sienese painters of the day. Rossellino was forced to build the duomo on a cramped site with poor foundations, and cracks appeared

in the building before it was even completed. Today the church's eastern end suffers from severe settling.

🏛 Palazzo Piccolomini
Piazza Pio II. 🕻 *0578 74 85 03.* 🔲 *Tue–Sun.* 🗐

Montalcino ⓘ

Siena. 🏛 *5,100.* 🚌 🛈 *Costa del Municipio 8 (0577 84 93 31).* 🛒 *Fri.*

HILLTOP MONTALCINO sits at the heart of vineyards that produce Brunello, one of Italy's finest red wines. It can be sampled in the Enoteca (wine shop) situated in the 14th-century **Fortezza** with its impressive ramparts. The town's timeless streets are a pleasure to wander, and there are some buildings of interest. On the way from the fortress into town is the monastery of Sant' Agostino and its 14th-century church with an attractive rose window and, just beyond, the Palazzo Vescovile. On Piazza del Popolo the slim tower of the Palazzo Communale, constructed in the 13th and 14th centuries, stands tall above the town.

♣ Fortezza
Piazzale della Fortezza. 🕻 *0577 84 92 11.* 🗐 *for ramparts.*
  Enoteca 🔲 *Apr–Oct: 9am–8pm daily; Nov–Mar: 9am–6pm Tue–Sun.*

The Tempio di San Biagio on the outskirts of Montepulciano

The landscape of the Crete Senesi

Crete Senesi ㉑

Asciano. **FS** 🚌 **ℹ** *Corso Matteotti (0577 71 95 10).*

TO THE SOUTH of Siena and central Tuscany is the area known as the Crete Senesi, characterized by round clay hillocks eroded by heavy rains over the centuries. Dubbed the "Tuscan desert," it is almost completely barren. Cypress and pine trees, planted to provide windbreaks along roads and around isolated farm houses, are an important feature in this empty, primeval landscape. Shepherds tend flocks of sheep here; the milk is used to produce the strongly flavored *pecorino* cheese that is popular throughout Tuscany.

Siena ㉒

See pp328–33.

Monteriggioni ㉓

Siena. 🏠 *7,000.* 🚌

MONTERIGGIONI is a gem of a medieval hilltop town. It was built in 1203 and ten years later became a garrison town. It is completely encircled by high walls with 14 heavily fortified towers, built to guard the northern borders of Siena's territory against invasion by Florentine armies.

Dante was sufficiently impressed to use Monteriggioni as a simile for the deepest abyss at the heart of his *Inferno*, which compares the town's "ring-shaped citadel...crowned with towers" with giants standing in a moat. The perfectly preserved walls are best viewed from the Colle di Val d'Elsa road. Within the walls, the sleepy town consists of a large piazza, a pretty Romanesque church (on the piazza), a few houses, a couple of craft shops, restaurants, and shops selling many of the locally produced Castello di Monteriggioni wines.

ENVIRONS: West of Monteriggioni by 3 km (2 miles) lies the former Cistercian Abbey of **Abbadia dell' Isola** (12th century). This Romanesque church was largely rebuilt in the 18th century, after the cupola fell apart. It contains frescoes by Taddeo di Bartolo and Vincenzo Tamagni and a Renaissance altarpiece.

San Gimignano ㉔

See pp334–5.

Volterra ㉕

Pisa. 🏠 *13,000.* 🚌 **ℹ** *Via Giusto Turazza 2 (0588 861 50).* 🍴 *Sat.*

LIKE MANY Etruscan cities, Volterra is situated on a high plateau, offering fine views over the surrounding hills. In many places the ancient Etruscan walls still survive. The famous **Museo Guarnacci** contains one of the best collections of Etruscan artifacts in Italy. Of special interest is the group of over 600 Etruscan cinerary urns, made from alabaster or terracotta, many of which were gathered from local tombs.

The **Palazzo dei Priori**, the medieval seat of government on Piazza dei Priori, is the oldest of its kind in Tuscany. It was begun in 1208 and there are 14th-century frescoes inside. The Pisan-Romanesque **duomo**, located on Piazza San Giovanni, has a fine 13th-century pulpit with sculptured panels.

Detail from the pulpit in Volterra's Duomo

Volterra's excellent art gallery and museum, the **Pinacoteca e Museo Civico**, features works by Florentine artists. Ghirlandaio's *Christ in Majesty* (1492) shows Christ hovering above an idealized Tuscan landscape. Luca Signorelli's *Madonna and Child with Saints* (1491) states his debt to Roman art through the reliefs on the base of the Virgin's throne. Painted in the same year, his *Annunciation* is a beautifully balanced composition. Another highlight is Rosso Fiorentino's Mannerist painting, *The Deposition* (1521).

The city is famous for its craftsmen who carve elaborate white statues and *objets d'art* from locally mined alabaster.

The beautifully preserved walls of Monteriggioni in central Tuscany

The ruined abbey at San Galgano, surrounded by dense woodland

Museo Guarnacci
Via Don Minzoni 15. 0588 863 47.
daily. Jan 1, Dec 25.
Pinacoteca e Museo Civico
Via dei Sarti 1. 0588 875 80.
daily. Jan 1, Dec 25.

San Galgano ㉖

Siena. from Siena. 0577 75
6 11. **Abbey & oratory** daily.

THE REMOTE Cistercian abbey at San Galgano lies in a superb setting. San Galgano 1148–81) was a brave but dissolute young knight who turned to God, renouncing the material world. When he tried to break his sword against a rock as a symbol of his rejection of war, it was swallowed by the stone. This he interpreted as a sign of God's approval. He built a hut on a hill above the abbey (the site of today's beehive-shaped chapel at **Montesiepi**, built c.1185). Here he later died a hermit. Pope Urban III declared him a saint and an example to Christian knights.

The abbey, begun in 1218, is Gothic in style, reflecting the French origins of the Cistercian monks who designed it. They avoided contact with the outside world and divided their lives between prayer and labor. Despite an emphasis on poverty, the monks became wealthy from the sale of wood, and by the middle of the 14th century the abbey was corruptly administered and gradually fell into decline.

In the late 14th century, the English mercenary Sir John Hawkwood sacked the abbey, and by 1397 the abbot was its sole occupant. It was eventually dissolved in 1652.

St. Galgano's sword stands embedded in a stone just inside the door of the circular **oratory**. The 14th-century stone walls of the side chapel are covered with worn frescoes showing scenes from Galgano's life by Ambrogio Lorenzetti (1344).

Massa Marittima ㉗

Grosseto. 9,500. Amatur, Via Norma Paventi 22 (0566 90 27 56). Wed.

SET IN THE Colline Metallifere (metal-bearing hills) where lead, copper, and silver ores were mined as early as Etruscan times, Massa Marittima is far from being a grimy industrial town. Excellent examples of Romanesque architecture survive from the period when the town became an independent republic (1225–1335). The Romanesque-Gothic **duomo** in Piazza Garibaldi is dedicated to St. Cerbone, a 6th-century saint whose story is sculpted in stone above the main portal. Inside the building, the *Maestà* is attributed to Duccio (c.1316).

The interesting **Museo della Miniera** (museum of mining) is located partially inside a former mine shaft and has exhibits explaining mining techniques, tools, and locally found minerals.

The **Museo Archeologico**, housed in a 13th-century building, has material from Paleolithic to Roman times. There is also a picture gallery.

Museo della Miniera
Via Corridoni. 0566 90 22 89.
Tue–Sun (Jul & Aug: daily).
Museo Archeologico
Palazzo del Podestà, Piazza Garibaldi.
0566 90 22 89. Tue–Sun.

View across the rooftops of Massa Marittima

Denuded hillocks of clay in the Crete Senesi area southeast of Siena ▷

Street-by-Street: Siena ㉒

Unicorn Contrada

S IENA'S PRINCIPAL SIGHTS cluster in the maze of narrow streets and alleys around the fan-shaped Piazza del Campo. One of Europe's greatest medieval squares, the piazza sits at the heart of the city's 17 *contrade*, a series of parishes whose ancient rivalries are still acted out in the twice-yearly Palio *(see p331)*. Loyalty to the *contrada* of one's birth is fierce, and as you wander the streets you will see the parishes' animal symbols repeated on flags, plaques, and carvings. Siena's hilly position also means that city walks offer delightful hidden corners and countless sudden views.

The duomo dominating Siena's skyline

Via della Galluzza leads to the house of St. Catherine.

The baptistry has fine frescoes and a font with reliefs by Donatello, Jacopo della Quercia, and Ghiberti.

★ Duomo
Striped black and white marble pillars, surmounted by a carved frieze of the popes, support the duomo's vaulted ceiling, painted blue with gold stars to resemble the night sky.

Each tier of the duomo's bell tower has one more window than the floor below.

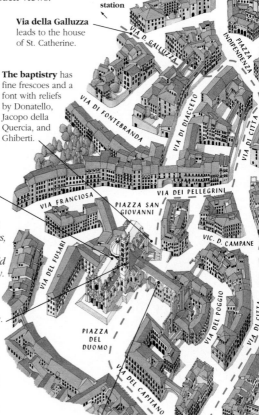

Bus station ↑

Train station ↘

VIA D. GALLUZZA

PIAZZA INDIPENDENZA

VIA DI FONTEBRANDA

VIA DI DIACCETO

VIA DI CITTÀ

VIA FRANCIOSA

VIA DEI PELLEGRINI

PIAZZA SAN GIOVANNI

VIC. D. CAMPANE

VIA DEL FUSARI

VIA DEL POGGIO

VIA DI CITTÀ

PIAZZA DEL DUOMO

VIA DEL CAPITANO

Museo dell'Opera del Duomo
Duccio's Maestà, *one of the greatest Sienese paintings, was paraded around Siena's streets on its completion in 1311, and influenced the city's painters for decades to come.*

KEY

– – – Suggested route

| 0 meters | 300 |
| 0 yards | 300 |

Loggia della Mercanzia
Built in 1417, the arcade is where Siena's medieval merchants and money dealers carried out their business.

VISITORS' CHECKLIST

60,000. FS *Piazzale Rosselli.*
Piazza San Domenico.
ℹ *Piazza del Campo 56 (0577 28 05 51).* 🕐 *Wed.* 🐎 *Palio: Jul 2, Aug 16; Settimana Musicale Chigiana (Classical music concerts): Jul.*

🏛 **Piazza del Campo**
Italy's loveliest piazza occupies the site of the old Roman forum, and for much of Siena's early history was the city's principal marketplace. It began to assume its present shape in 1293, when the Council of Nine, Siena's ruling body at the time, began to acquire land with a view to creating a grand civic piazza. The redbrick paving was begun in 1327 and completed in 1349, its distinctive nine segments designed to reflect the authority of the Council of Nine and to symbolize the protective folds of the Madonna's cloak. The piazza has been the focus of city life ever since, a setting for executions, bullfights, and the twice-yearly drama of the Palio *(see p331),* a festival centered around a bareback horse race. Cafés, restaurants, and fine medieval palazzi now line the Campo's fringes, dominated by the **Palazzo Pubblico** (1297–1342) and **Torre del Mangia,** built in 1348 *(see p330).* This imposing ensemble tends to overshadow the little **Fonte Gaia** on the piazza's northern edge. The fountain is a 19th-century copy of an original carved by Jacopo della Quercia in 1409–19. Its reliefs depict the *Virtues, Adam and Eve,* and the *Madonna and Child* (the originals are on the rear loggia of the Palazzo Pubblico). The fountain's water is still supplied by a 500-year-old aqueduct.

The Logge del Papa, or Pope's colonnade, was built in honor of Pius II in 1462.

Drummer in Siena's Palio

Tourist information

VIA BANCHI DI SOTTO
VIA DI PANTANETO
VIA RINALDINA
ZZA EL CAMPO
VIA DEL PORRIONE
VIA DI SALICOTTO
PIAZZA DEL MERCATO
VIA DUPRE

Fonte Gaia
These reliefs are 19th-century copies of originals by Jacopo della Quercia.

★ **Palazzo Pubblico**
The graceful Gothic town hall was completed in 1342. At 102 m (335 ft), the bell tower, Torre del Mangia, is the second highest medieval tower ever built in Italy.

STAR SIGHTS

★ **Duomo**

★ **Palazzo Pubblico**

The Piazza del Campo and Fonte Gaia from the Torre del Mangia

Exploring Siena

ONCE A CAPITAL to rival Florence, Siena is still unspoiled and endowed with the grandeur of the age when it was at its peak (1260–1348). The best place to begin an exploration of its historic center is Piazza del Campo and the surrounding maze of medieval streets.

Lorenzetti's *Allegory of Good Government* (1338), Palazzo Pubblico

🏛 Palazzo Pubblico

Piazza del Campo 1. 📞 *0577 29 22 63.* **Museo Civico & Torre del Mangia** ⬜ *daily.* 📷

Although it continues in its ancient role as Siena's town hall, the Palazzo Pubblico's medieval rooms, some decorated with paintings of the Sienese School, are open to the public. The **Museo Civico** is housed here. The main council chamber, or Sala del Mappamondo, is named after a map of the world painted by Ambrogio Lorenzetti in the early 14th century. One wall is covered by Simone Martini's recently restored fresco of the *Maestà* (1315), which depicts the Virgin in Majesty as the Queen of Heaven, attended by the Apostles, saints, and angels. Opposite is a fresco (attributed to Simone Martini, but possibly later) of the mercenary *Guidoriccio da Fogliano* (1330). The walls of the chapel alongside have frescoes of the *Life of the Virgin* (1407) by Taddeo di Bartolo; the choir stalls (1428)

are decorated with wooden panels inlaid with biblical scenes. The Sala della Pace contains the famous *Allegory of Good and Bad Government*, two frescoes by Ambrogio Lorenzetti, finished in 1338. They form one of the most important series of secular paintings from the Middle Ages. In the *Good Government* fresco civic life flourishes, while the *Bad Government* reveals rubbish-strewn streets and ruins.

The Sala del Risorgimento is covered with late 19th-century frescoes illustrating the events leading up to the unification of Italy under King Vittorio Emanuele II.

In the palace courtyard is the entrance to the magnificent **Torre del Mangia**, the palace's huge bell tower. Rising 102 m (335 ft), it is a prominent feature of Siena's skyline. Built by

the brothers Muccio and Francesco di Rinaldo between 1138 and 1148, it was named after the first bell-ringer, whose idleness led to the nickname *Mangiaguadagni* (literally "eat the profits"). There are 505 steps to the top of the tower, which has wonderful views of the Tuscan countryside.

🏛 Casa di Santa Caterina

Costa di Sant'Antonio. 📞 *0577 441 77.* ⬜ *daily.*

Siena's patron saint, Catherine Benincasa (1347–80), was the daughter of a tradesman. At the age of eight she devoted herself to God and had many visions, as well as later receiving the stigmata (wounds of Christ). Like her namesake, St. Catherine of Alexandria, she was believed to have been betrothed to the Christ child in a vision – a scene that inspired many artists. Her eloquence persuaded Pope Gregory XI to return the seat of the papacy to Rome in 1376, after 67 years of exile in Avignon. St. Catherine died in Rome and was canonized in 1461.

Today Catherine's house is surrounded by chapels and cloisters. Among them is the Church of the Crucifixion, which was built in 1623 in her orchard to house the late 12th-century Crucifixion, in front of which she received the stigmata in 1375. The house is decorated with paintings of events from her life by artists including her contemporaries Francesco Vanni and Pietro Sorri.

Cloister of Casa di Santa Caterina, birthplace of Siena's patron saint

🏛 Palazzo Piccolomini

Via Banchi di Sotto 52. 📞 *0577 24 71 45.* 🕐 *Mon–Sat am.*

Siena's most imposing private palazzo was built for the wealthy Piccolomini family in the 1460s by the Florentine architect and sculptor Bernardo Rossellino. It now contains the Sienese state archives, account books, and financial records dating back to the 13th century. Some of the leading artists of their day were employed to paint the wooden bindings used to enclose the financial records. The paintings, now on display in the Sala di Congresso, often show scenes of Siena itself, bristling with towers, or episodes from the city's past.

Other records include a will attributed to Boccaccio and the council's contract with Jacopo della Quercia for the Fonte Gaia *(see p329).*

A detail from Martini's *Blessed Agostino Novello* (c.1330)

🏛 Pinacoteca Nazionale

Via San Pietro 29. 📞 *0577 28 11 61.* 🕐 *daily.* 🈲 🚫

This fine gallery, that is housed in the 14th-century Palazzo Buonsignori, contains an unsurpassed collection of paintings by artists of the Sienese School. Arranged in chronological order, from the 13th century through to the Mannerist period (1520–1600), highlights include Duccio's *Madonna dei Francescani* (1285) and Simone Martini's masterpiece *The Blessed Agostino Novello and Four of His Miracles* (c.1330). Pietro Lorenzetti's *Two Views*, from the 14th century, are early examples of landscape painting, and Pietro da Domenico's *Adoration of the Shepherds* (1510) shows how the art of

Siena remained visibly influenced by its Byzantine roots long after the naturalism of the Renaissance had reached the rest of Europe.

🏛 San Domenico

Piazza San Domenico. 🕐 *daily.*

The preserved head of the city's patroness, St. Catherine of Siena (1347–80), can be seen in a gilded tabernacle on the altar of a chapel ded-

The austere exterior of the church of San Domenico (begun 1226)

icated to her in the huge, barnlike Gothic church of San Domenico (begun 1226). The chapel itself was built in 1460 for this purpose and is dominated by Sodoma's frescoes (1526), to the right and left of the altar, showing Catherine in states of religious fervor. The church has the only portrait of St. Catherine considered authentic, painted by her friend Andrea Vanni.

THE SIENESE PALIO

The Palio is Tuscany's most celebrated festival and it occurs in the Campo each year on July 2 and August 16. It is a bareback horse race first recorded in 1283, but it may have had its origins in Roman military training. The jockeys represent Siena's 17 *contrade* (districts); the horses are chosen by lottery and are blessed at the local *contrada* churches. Preceded by days of colorful

A *contrada* symbol

pageantry, costume processions, and heavy betting, the races themselves last only 90 seconds each. Thousands of spectators crowd into the piazza to watch the race, and rivalry between competitors is intense. The winner is rewarded with a silk *palio* (banner). Festivities for the winners, and recriminations among the losers, can last for weeks.

The Sienese displaying their flag-throwing skills before the Palio

Siena: Duomo

SIENA'S DUOMO (1136–1382) is one of Italy's greatest cathedrals, a spectacular mixture of sculpture, paintings, and Pisan-influenced Romanesque-Gothic architecture. Had 14th-century plans to create a new nave come to fruition, the building would have become the largest church in Christendom. However, the plan came to nothing, abandoned when the plague of 1348 virtually halved the city's population. Among the duomo's treasures are sculptural masterpieces by Nicola Pisano, Donatello, and Michelangelo, a fine inlaid floor and a magnificent fresco cycle by Pinturicchio.

A symbol of the Risen Christ on the façade

Baptismal Font
This Renaissance font by della Quercia and Donatello stands in the baptistry.

Pulpit Panels
Carved in 1265–8 by Nicola Pisano, with help from Arnolfo di Cambio and his son Giovanni, the panels on the octagonal pulpit depict scenes from the Life of Christ.

In the nave, black-and-white marble pillars support the vault.

Chapel of St. John the Baptist

The north aisle contains sculptures by Michelangelo of Saints Peter, Pius, Gregory, and Paul (1501–4).

Inlaid Marble Floor
The Massacre of the Innocents *is one of a series of scenes in the inlaid marble floor. The marble is usually uncovered during September each year.*

Piccolomini Library
Pinturicchio's frescoes (1509) portray the life of the Piccolomini pope, Pius II. Here he presides at the betrothal of Frederick III to Eleonora of Portugal.

The Museo dell'Opera del Duomo occupies the side aisle of the unfinished nave, which was roofed over to house the museum.

The Campanile was added in 1313.

Archway leading to the baptistry

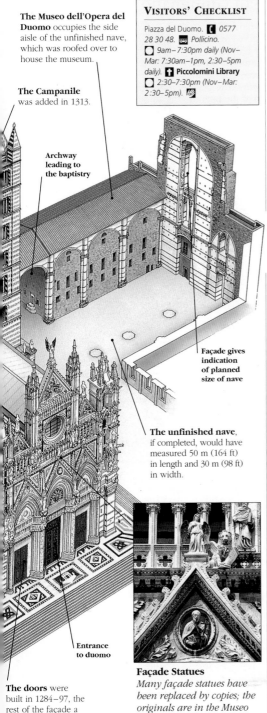

Façade gives indication of planned size of nave

The unfinished nave, if completed, would have measured 50 m (164 ft) in length and 30 m (98 ft) in width.

Entrance to duomo

The doors were built in 1284–97, the rest of the façade a century later.

Façade Statues
Many façade statues have been replaced by copies; the originals are in the Museo dell'Opera del Duomo.

🏛 Museo dell'Opera del Duomo

Piazza del Duomo 8. ☎ *0577 28 30 48.* ◷ *daily.* ● *public hols.* 🖼

Part of this museum is devoted to sculpture removed from the exterior of the duomo, including a Renaissance medallion of a *Madonna and Child*, probably by Donatello, as well as several badly eroded Gothic statues by Giovanni Pisano and Jacopo della Quercia. The highlight is Duccio's huge *Maestà* (1308–11), one of the Sienese School's finest works. It depicts the Madonna and Child on one side, and scenes from the Life of Christ on the other. It was originally placed on the duomo's high altar, where it replaced the striking *Madonna of the Large Eyes* (1220–30), by an anonymous Sienese painter, also in the museum.

Statues from the duomo now on show in the Museo dell'Opera

🏰 Fortezza Medicea

Viale Maccari.
Fortezza ◷ *daily.* **Enoteca** ◷ *3pm–midnight Mon–Sat.* 🖼

This huge redbrick fortress was built for Cosimo I by Baldassarre Lanci in 1560, following Siena's defeat by the Florentines in the 1554–5 war. After an 18-month siege, during which more than 8,000 Sienese died, the town's banking and wool industries were suppressed by the Florentine masters and all major building work ended.

The fortress now houses the Enoteca Italica, a wine shop offering visitors the chance both to taste and to buy from a comprehensive list of quality wines from all over Italy.

Street-by-Street: San Gimignano ②

THE THIRTEEN TOWERS that dominate San Gimignano's majestic skyline were built by rival noble families during the 12th and 13th centuries, when the town's position – on the main pilgrim route from northern Europe to Rome – brought it great prosperity. The plague of 1348, and later the diversion of the pilgrim route, led to its economic decline as well as its preservation. Street by street it remains mostly medieval. For a small town, San Gimignano is rich in works of art, good shops, and restaurants.

San Gimignano's famous skyline, almost unchanged since the Middle Ages

Collegiata
This 11th-century church's interior is full of frescoes, including The Creation *(1367) by Bartolo di Fredi.*

Palazzo del Popolo
The council chamber of the town hall (1288–1323) features a large Maestà *(1317) by Lippo Memmi.*

The Annunciation by Ghirlandaio
This painting, completed in 1482, is located in a courtyard loggia alongside the Collegiata.

↘ Sant'Agostino

Tourist information

VIA SAN MATTEO

VIA CAPASSI

VIA DIACCETO

PIAZZA NOMI

PIAZZA DEL DUOMO

PIAZZA DELLA CISTERN

VIA DELLA COSTERELLA

VIA DI QUERCECCHIO

VIA BERIGNANO

VIA SAN GIOVANNI

Bus station ↓

Via San Giovanni
is lined with shops selling local goods.

VISITORS' CHECKLIST

Siena. ▓ 7,000. ▦ Porta San
Giovanni. ▐ Piazza del Duomo 1
(0577 94 00 08). ◢ Thu.
◪ Patron saints' festivals: San
Gimignano Jan 31 & Santa Fina
Mar 12; Carnival: varying dates in
Feb; Fiera di Santa Fina: 1st Mon
in Aug; Fiera di Sant'Agostino:
Aug 12; Festa della Madonna di
Panacole: Sep 8; Fiera della
Bertesca: Sep 15.

Among the Piazza del
Duomo's historic buildings
is the Palazzo Vecchio
del Podestà (1239),
whose tower is
probably the
town's oldest.

Piazza della Cisterna

*This square is
named after
the well at its
center and
is the heart
of the old
town.*

CASTELLO

OCENTI

NDORNELLA

**The Museo
Civico** provides
access to the tallest of the
town's 13 remaining towers.

KEY

- - - Suggested route

meters   250

yards   250

▥ Museo Civico

Palazzo del Popolo, Piazza del
Duomo. ▐ 0577 94 00 08.
Museum & tower ◯ daily. ◪
Frescoes in the courtyard of
this museum feature the coats
of arms of city mayors and
magistrates, as well as a 14th-
century *Virgin and Child* by
Taddeo di Bartolo.

The first public room is the
Sala di Dante, where an
inscription recalls a visit by
the poet in 1300. The walls
are covered with hunting
scenes and a huge *Maestà*
fresco (1317) by Lippo
Memmi. The floor above has
an art collection, which
includes excellent works by
Pinturicchio, Bartolo di
Fredi, Benozzo Gozzoli,
and Filippino Lippi. The
famous *Wedding Scene*
frescoes by Memmo di
Filippucci (early 14th
century) show a couple
sharing a bath and going
to bed – an unusual
record of life in 14th-
century Tuscany.

⛪ Collegiata

Piazza del
Duomo. ◯ daily.
This 12th-century
Romanesque church
contains a feast of
frescoes. In the
north aisle the
frescoes comprise
26 episodes from
the Old Testament
(1367) by Bartolo di Fredi.
The opposite wall features
scenes from the *Life of Christ*
(1333–41) by Lippo Memmi,
while at the back of the church

**Bartolo di Fredi's
Christ, Sant'Agostino**

**The ceiling of the Collegiata,
painted with gold stars**

there are scenes from the *Last
Judgment* painted by Taddeo
di Bartolo. Frescoes (1475) by
Ghirlandaio adorn both the
tiny Chapel of Santa Fina and
the nearby loggia.

⛪ Sant'Agostino

Piazza Sant'Agostino. ◯ daily.
Consecrated in 1298, this
church has a simple façade,
contrasting markedly with the
heavily decorated Rococo
interior (c.1740) by Vanvitelli.
Above the main altar is
the *Coronation of the
Virgin* by Piero del
Pollaiuolo, dated
1483. The choir is
entirely covered in
a cycle of frescoes
of *The Life of St.
Augustine* (1465)
executed by the
Florentine artist
Benozzo Gozzoli.

In the Cappella di San
Bartolo, on the right of the
main entrance, is an elaborate
marble altar completed by
Benedetto da Maiano in 1495.

**Fresco from the early 14th-century *Wedding Scene* cycle by
Memmo di Filippucci in the Museo Civico**

Elba 🄮

Livorno. 🚶 30,000. ⛴ Portoferraio
🚌 ℹ Calata Italia 26 (0565 91 46
71). 🛒 Portoferraio: Fri.

Eᴸʙᴀ's ᴍᴏsᴛ ғᴀᴍᴏᴜs resident
was Napoleon, who spent
nine months here after the
fall of Paris in 1814. Today
the island is mainly populated
by vacationers, who come by
ferry from Piombino, 10 km
(6 miles) away on the
mainland. The main town is
Portoferraio, with an old port
and a modern seafront of
hotels and fish restaurants.

The landscape of the island
is varied. On the west coast,
which tends to be a little
quieter, there are sandy
beaches suitable for all water
sports. The east coast,
centered on the town of
Porto Azzurro, the island's
second port, is more rugged,
with high cliffs and stony
beaches. Inland, olive groves
and vineyards line hillsides,
and vegetation covers the
mountains. One of the best
ways to see the interior is to
take the road from Marciana
Marina to the old medieval
village of Marciana Alta. Close
by, a minor road leads to a
cable car that runs to Monte
Capanne (1,018 m/3,340 ft), a
magnificent viewpoint.

Marciana Marina on Elba

Sovana 🄯

Grosseto. 🚶 100.

Sᴏᴠᴀɴᴀ ɪs ᴏɴᴇ of southern
Tuscany's prettiest villages.
Its single little street ends in
Piazza del Pretorio, home to
the ancient church of Santa

View over Pitigliano and the town's dramatic cliffs and caves

Maria, whose lovely interior
contains frescoes and a 9th-
century altar canopy. A lane
beyond leads through olive
groves to the Romanesque
duomo, filled with reliefs and
carvings from an earlier church
on the site. Tuscany's finest
Etruscan tombs lie in the surrounding countryside, many
of them clearly marked and
easily visited from the village.

Pitigliano 🄰

Grosseto. 🚶 4,400. 🚌 ℹ Via
Roma 6 (0564 61 70 19). 🛒 Wed.

Pɪᴛɪɢʟɪᴀɴᴏ ɪs spectacularly
situated high above the
cave-riddled cliffs of the Lente
valley. Its maze of tiny
medieval streets includes a
small Jewish ghetto, formed
in the 17th century by Jews

Maremma 🄱

Grosseto. ℹ Maremma Centro Visite,
Alberese (0564 40 70 98). **Marginal
Areas** 🚌 to entrances from Alberese.
⭕ daily. 🎟 🚫 **Inner Park Areas**
🚌 from Alberese to tour departure
point. ⭕ 9am–1 hr before sunset
Wed, Sat, Sun, public hols. 🎟 only
Jun–Sep: walking tours at 7am (4
hrs) & 4pm (3 hrs). 🚫

Tʜᴇ ᴇᴛʀᴜsᴄᴀɴs,
followed by the
Romans, were the first
to cultivate the marshes
and low hills of the
Maremma. Following the
collapse of the Roman Empire,
however, the area fell prey to
flooding and malaria, twin
scourges that left it virtually
uninhabited until the 18th
century. The land has since
been reclaimed, the irrigation
canals unblocked, and farming
developed on the fertile soil.
The stunning Parco Naturale
della Maremma was set up in
1975 to preserve the area's
native flora and fauna, and to
prevent development on one
of Italy's few pristine stretches
of coastline. Entrance to much
of the park is restricted to
access on foot or by a park
bus from Alberese. Other more
marginal areas, however, such
as the excellent beach at
Marina di Alberese, and the
countryside around Talamone
in the south, are easier to see.

The Ombrone estuary is a mixture
of pines, marsh, and dunes and is
home to birds such as the flamingo,
sea eagle, roller, and bee-eater.

Kᴇʏ

═══	Roads
▭	Paths
▭	Canals and rivers
- -	Itineraries

0 kilometers   2

0 miles   1

Monte Argentario

Grosseto. 🏘 *13,000.* 🚌 🛈 *Corso Umberto 55, Porto Santo Stefano (0564 81 42 08).* 🛒 *Tue.*

Meeing from Catholic persecution. The **Palazzo Orsini** has its water supply brought in by an impressive aqueduct, built in 1545. It houses the **Museo Zuccarelli** with its small exhibition of work by artist Francesco Zuccarelli (1702–88), who lived locally. He also painted two of the altarpieces in the medieval **duomo** in Piazza San Gregorio. The **Museo Etrusco** contains finds from ancient local settlements.

🏛 **Museo Zuccarelli**
Palazzo Orsini, Piazza della Fortezza Orsini 4. 📞 *0564 61 55 68.* 🕐 *Mar–Jul: Tue–Sun; Aug: daily; Sep–Dec: Sat & Sun.* 🎟
🏛 **Museo Etrusco**
Piazza della Fortezza Orsini. 📞 *0564 61 70 19.* 🕐 *Tue–Sun.*

MONTE ARGENTARIO was an island until the early 18th century, when the shallow waters separating it from the mainland began to silt up, creating two sandy spits of land, known as *tomboli*, which enclose the Orbetello lagoon. **Orbetello** itself, a lively and relatively unspoiled little town, was linked to the island in 1842, when a dike was constructed from the mainland. The two harbor towns of **Porto Ercole** and **Porto Santo Stefano** are both upscale resorts, busy with visitors in

Porto Ercole, Monte Argentario

summer. Interior roads, however – notably the Strada Panoramica – offer more peaceful drives past rocky coves, cliffs, and bays.

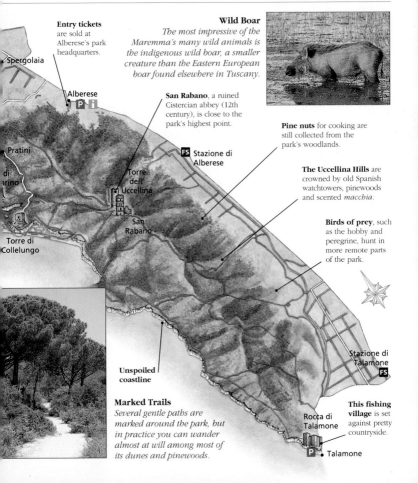

Entry tickets are sold at Alberese's park headquarters.

Spergolaia

Alberese 🅿 🛈

Pratini

di arino

Torre di Collelungo

Wild Boar
The most impressive of the Maremma's many wild animals is the indigenous wild boar, a smaller creature than the Eastern European boar found elsewhere in Tuscany.

San Rabano, a ruined Cistercian abbey (12th century), is close to the park's highest point.

🚆 **Stazione di Alberese**

Torre dell' Uccellina

San Rabano

Pine nuts for cooking are still collected from the park's woodlands.

The Uccellina Hills are crowned by old Spanish watchtowers, pinewoods and scented *macchia*.

Birds of prey, such as the hobby and peregrine, hunt in more remote parts of the park.

Stazione di Talamone 🚆

Unspoiled coastline

Marked Trails
Several gentle paths are marked around the park, but in practice you can wander almost at will among most of its dunes and pinewoods.

Rocca di Talamone 🅿 • Talamone

This fishing village is set against pretty countryside.

UMBRIA

....

LONG DISMISSED AS *Tuscany's "gentler sister," Umbria has recently emerged from the shadow of its more famous western neighbor. Forming an expanse of gentle pastoral countryside and high mountain wilderness, the picturesque region has been dubbed the "Green Heart of Italy." Umbria is also well known for the beauty and profusion of its medieval hill towns.*

The region was inhabited in the 8th century BC by the Umbrians, a peaceable farming tribe, and later colonized by the Etruscans and Romans. In the Middle Ages, the Lombards established a dukedom centered around Spoleto. By the 13th century much of the region was scattered with independent city-states, most of them eventually absorbed by the Papal States, where they remained until Italian unification in 1860.

Today the old towns are Umbria's chief glory. In Perugia, the region's capital, and the smaller centers of Gubbio, Montefalco, and Todi, there are numerous Romanesque churches, civic palaces, vivid fresco cycles, and endless medieval nooks and crannies. Spoleto, famous for its summer arts festival, blends grandiose medieval monuments with Roman remains and some of Italy's oldest churches. The surrounding Vale of Spoleto is a checkerboard of agricultural countryside and fascinating traditional villages.

Assisi, the birthplace of St. Francis, contains the Basilica di San Francesco, frescoed in part by Giotto. At Orvieto, magnificently situated on its volcanic crag, there are Etruscan remains and one of Italy's finest Romanesque-Gothic cathedrals.

Umbria's oak woods, ice-clear streams, and rich soils yield many delicacies. Chief among these are trout and truffles, olive oils to rival those of Tuscany, prized lentils from Castelluccio, cured meats from Norcia, and tangy mountain cheeses. A variety of well-regarded wines are produced from the vineyards of Torgiano and Montefalco.

A shop in Norcia selling a selection of Italy's finest hams, sausages, and salamis

A street scene in the ancient town of Todi

Exploring Umbria

Assisi and Spoleto, Umbria's loveliest towns, are the most convenient and charming bases for exploring the region. Both these medieval gems are must-sees, as is the old center of Perugia, the region's capital, and the alluring hill towns of Gubbio, Spello, Montefalco, and Todi. Umbria's landscapes are as compelling as its towns, from the eerie wastes of the Piano Grande and the mountain splendor of the Monti Sibillini national park (best reached from Norcia) to the gentler countryside of the Valnerina and the beach-fringed shores of Lake Trasimeno.

SIGHTS AT A GLANCE

Assisi pp344–5 **2**
Gubbio **1**
Lake Trasimeno **4**
Montefalco **8**
Monti Sibillini **10**
Norcia **11**
Orvieto **5**
Perugia **3**
Spello **9**
Spoleto **7**
Todi **6**
Valnerina **12**

SEE ALSO

- *Where to Stay* pp561–3

- *Where to Eat* pp595–7

Olive harvest in the Umbrian countryside near Orvieto

GETTING AROUND

Excellent road, rail, and bus links exist in the region. The A1 from Florence passes Orvieto, which is linked to Todi by the N448. The N75 connects Perugia, Assisi, and Spello, then the N3 continues to Trevi, Spoleto, and Terni. Rome–Florence trains serve Orvieto, and Rome–Ancona trains serve Spoleto, with branch lines connecting Perugia, Spello, and Assisi.

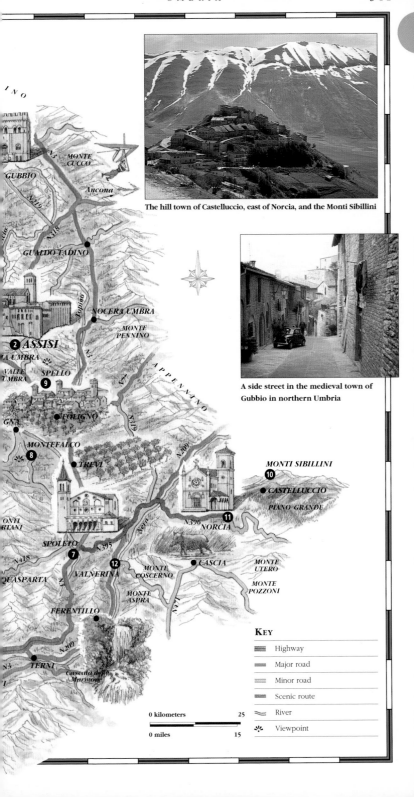

The hill town of Castelluccio, east of Norcia, and the Monti Sibillini

A side street in the medieval town of Gubbio in northern Umbria

GUBBIO

MONTE CUCCO

N3

Ancona

GUALDO TADINO

Topino

NOCERA UMBRA

MONTE PENNINO

2 ASSISI

A UMBRA

VALLE UMBRA

9 SPELLO

FOLIGNO

GNA

MONTEFALCO

8 TREVI

APPENNINO

N319

N209

MONTI SIBILLINI

10 CASTELLUCCIO

PIANO GRANDE

ONTI RTANI

Nera

11 N396 NORCIA

SPOLETO

7 N395

12 VALNERINA

MONTE COSCERNO

CASCIA

MONTE UTERO

MONTE POZZONI

QUASPARTA

N418

MONTE ASPRA

N471

FERENTILLO

N209

N3 TERNI

Cascata delle Marmore

KEY

▤	Highway
▤	Major road
▤	Minor road
▤	Scenic route
≈	River
✲	Viewpoint

0 kilometers 25

0 miles 15

Gubbio ❶

Perugia. 🏛 *33,000.* 🚉 *Fossato di Vico-Gubbio.* 🚌 ℹ *Piazza Oderesi 6 (075 922 06 93).* 🏛 *Tue.*

G UBBIO VIES with Assisi for the title of Umbria's most medieval town. The beauty of its twisting streets and terra-cotta-tiled houses is enhanced by the forest-swathed Apennines. Founded by the Umbrians in the 3rd century BC as Tota Ikuvina, it assumed greater prominence in the 1st century AD as the Roman town, Eugubium. It emerged as an independent commune in the 11th century having spread up the slopes of Monte Ingino. From 1387 to 1508 Gubbio was ruled from Urbino by the Dukes of Montefeltro.

The 13th-century **Duomo** is distinguished by a wagon-vaulted ceiling whose curved arches symbolize hands in prayer. Medieval Via dei Consoli leads to the 13th-century **Palazzo del Bargello** – a stone-faced building formerly the headquarters of the chief of police. Also here is the **Fontana dei Matti** (Fountain of the Mad), named after the tradition that anyone who walks around it three times will go insane.

Macabre legends surround the walled-up **Porte della Morte** (Doors of Death) that can be seen in Via dei Consoli and elsewhere in the town. Reputedly used for the passage of coffins from houses, the doors, once tainted, were sealed and never used again.

It is now thought their purpose was probably defensive. In the lower town, the church of **San Francesco** (1259–82)

Façade of the Palazzo dei Consoli in Gubbio

is known for 17 faded frescoes showing scenes from the *Life of the Virgin*, painted between 1408 and 1413 by Ottaviano Nelli. Opposite is the **Tiratoio** (Weavers' Loggia). Wool was stretched out to dry in its shady arcade. West of here are the ruins of a 1st-century AD Roman amphitheater.

🏛 Palazzo dei Consoli

Piazza Grande. ☎ *075 927 42 98.* ○ *daily.* ● *May 15, Dec 25.* 🌀 Dominating the skyline of Gubbio is this mighty civic palace, begun in 1332 by Gattapone. Its Salone dell'Arengo houses the Museo Civico, best known for the Eugubine Tablets (250–150 BC). Discovered in 1444, the seven bronze slabs are inscribed with Etruscan and Roman characters, probably a phonetic translation of prayers and rituals from the ancient Umbrian and Etruscan languages. Upstairs a small art gallery contains works by local painters.

One of the Eugubine Tablets in Gubbio

🏛 Palazzo Ducale

Via Federico da Montefeltro. ☎ *075 927 58 72.* ○ *daily.* ● *Jan 1, May 1, Dec 25 & 1st Mon of each month.* 🌀 🚹 Attributed to Francesco di Giorgio Martini, this palace was built in 1470 for the Montefeltro as a copy of the family home in Urbino *(see pp360–61)*. It also has a Renaissance courtyard.

The interior of Perugia's San Pietro, rebuilt in the 15th century

Assisi ❷

See pp344–5.

Perugia ❸

🏛 *160,000.* 🚉 🚌 ℹ *Piazza IV Novembre 3 (075 572 33 27).* 🏛 *da*

P ERUGIA'S OLD CENTER hinge around Corso Vannucci, named after the local painter Pietro Vannucci (Perugino). A its northern end lie Piazza IV Novembre dominated by the **Fontana Maggiore** a 13th-century fountain by Nicola and Giovanni Pisano

To the rear rises Perugia's 15th-centur **duomo**, its entrance flanked by a statue c Pope Julius II (1555 and a pulpit built fo Siena's San Bernardino (1425) The Cappella del Santo Anell inside contains the Virgin's "wedding ring," a weighty piece of agate said to change color according to the character of the person wearing it A pillar in the nave, festooned in votive offerings, holds a Renaissance painting of the *Madonna delle Grazie* by Gian Nicola di Paolo. The figure is credited with miracu lous powers, and mothers bring newly baptized childre to kneel before it. Buried in the transepts are Popes Urba IV and Martin IV.

Away from the Corso is the **Oratorio di San Bernardine** (1457–61) on Piazza San Francesco, with a colorful façade by Agostino di Duccio

eyond the old city walls on
orgo XX Giugno stands **San
ietro**, Perugia's most extrav-
gantly decorated church.
ounded in the 10th century
d rebuilt in 1463, the best
ature of the fine interior is
e wooden choir (1526).
Piazza Giordano Bruno is
ome to **San Domenico**
305–1632), Umbria's largest
urch, which is known for
e Gothic tomb of Benedict
(c.1304) and decoration
y Agostino di Duccio.

**Museo Archeologico
azionale dell'Umbria**

n Domenico, Piazza Giordano Bruno.
075 572 71 41. ◯ daily (Sun am).
Jan 1, May 1, Dec 25. 🗓 🔥

oused in the cloisters of San
omenico, this museum ex-
bits prehistoric, Etruscan,
nd Roman artifacts.

Palazzo dei Priori

orso Vannucci 19.
075 574 12 47.
daily. ● Jan 1, May
Dec 25 & 1st Mon
ch month. 🗓 🔥

he monumental
alls and bristling
renellations of this
alace mark it as
mbria's finest
ublic building *(see
p50–51)*. Among
s finely decorated
ooms is the Sala
ei Notari (c.1295), the former
awyers' hall, which is vividly
rescoed with scenes from the
ld Testament – the work of
follower of Pietro Cavallini.
he raised doorway is guarded
y a pair of large bronzes
ade in 1274: a Guelph lion
nd a griffin, the medieval

Medieval street in Perugia

emblem of Perugia. The Sala
di Udienza del Collegio della
Mercanzia, built around 1390,
was formerly used by the
Merchants' Guild. This room
is late Gothic in style, with
exquisite paneling and 15th-
century inlaid wood.
   Also in the palace
is the Collegio del
Cambio, Perugia's
former money ex-
change, which
began in 1452. This
room was used by
the Bankers' Guild.
Its walls are covered
with superlative
frescoes (1498–1500)
by Perugino, works
that are devoted to
a mixture of Classical and
religious scenes. A glum self-
portrait scowls down from the
center of the left wall, while
the hand of Perugino's pupil
Raphael may be evident in
some panels on the right wall.

**Entrance of Palazzo
dei Priori, Perugia**

🏛 **Galleria Nazionale
dell'Umbria**

Palazzo dei Priori, Corso Vannucci 19.
075 574 12 47. ◯ daily.
● Jan 1, Dec 25. 🗓 🔥

Umbria's greatest collection of
paintings is displayed here on
the third floor of the palace.
Most of the works are 13th-
to 18th-century paintings by
local artists, but the highlights
are altarpieces by Piero della
Francesca and Fra Angelico.

Lake Trasimeno ➍

Perugia. 🚋 🚌 Castiglione del Lago.
ℹ Piazza Mazzini 10, Castiglione del
Lago (075 965 24 84).

Edged with low hills and
gentle farming country,
this is Italy's fourth-largest
lake. Its miles of placid water
and reed-lined shores have a
tranquil, melancholy beauty.
   Drainage of the lake began
under the Romans, but today
the lake is gently drying up of
its own accord. The town of
Castiglione del Lago, jutting
out on a fortified promontory,
has an easy-going atmosphere
and small sandy beaches. The
16th-century **castle** is used for
summer concerts. The church
of **Santa Maria Maddalena**,
begun in 1836, has a fine
Madonna and Child (c.1500)
by Eusebio di San Giorgio.
   Passignano sul Trasimeno
has a bustling promenade and,
like Castiglione, offers boat
trips to **Isola Maggiore**. The
island's charming village is
known for lacemaking.

**19th-century engraving
of General Hannibal**

THE BATTLE OF
LAKE TRASIMENO

In 217 BC the Romans
suffered one of their worst-
ever military defeats on the
shores of Lake Trasimeno.
The Carthaginian general,
Hannibal, lured the Romans
(who were led by the consul
Flaminius) into a masterful
ambush close to present-day
Ossaia (Place of Bones) and
Sanguineto (Place of Blood).
Some 16,000 legionaries perished, hacked down on the lake's
marshy fringes. Hannibal, by contrast, lost only 1,500 men.
Today you can explore the battlefield, which includes over
100 mass graves found near Tuoro sul Trasimeno.

**Colorful façade of Perugia's
Oratorio di San Bernardino**

Assisi: Basilica di San Francesco

THE BURIAL PLACE of St. Francis, this basilica was begun in 1228, two years after the saint's death. Over the next century its Upper and Lower Churches were decorated by the foremost artists of their day, among them Cimabue, Simone Martini, Pietro Lorenzetti, and Giotto, whose frescoes on the *Life of St. Francis* are some of the most renowned in Italy. The basilica, which dominates Assisi, is one of the great Christian shrines and receives vast numbers of pilgrims throughout the year.

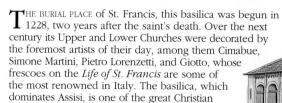

The campanile
was built in 1239.

Faded paintings
by Roman artists
line the walls
above Giotto's
Life of St. Francis.

The choir (1501)
features a 13th-
century stone
papal throne.

St. Francis
*Cimabue's simple
painting (c.1280)
captures the humility
of the revered saint,
who stood for
poverty, chastity,
and obedience.*

**★ Frescoes by
Lorenzetti**
*The bold composition
of Pietro Lorenzetti's
fresco, titled* The
Deposition *(1323),
is based around the
truncated Cross,
focusing attention
on the twisted figure
of Christ.*

**Steps to the
Treasury**

The crypt contains
the tomb of St. Francis.

Lower Church
*Side chapels were created here in
the 13th century to accommodate
the growing number of pilgrims.*

STAR FEATURES

★ Frescoes by Giotto

★ Frescoes by
Lorenzetti

★ Cappella di San
Martino

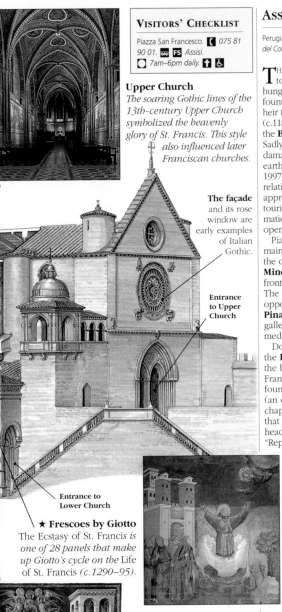

Upper Church
The soaring Gothic lines of the 13th-century Upper Church symbolized the heavenly glory of St. Francis. This style also influenced later Franciscan churches.

The façade and its rose window are early examples of Italian Gothic.

Entrance to Upper Church

Entrance to Lower Church

★ Frescoes by Giotto
The Ecstasy of St. Francis is one of 28 panels that make up Giotto's cycle on the Life of St. Francis (c.1290–95).

★ Cappella di San Martino
The frescoes in this chapel on the Life of St. Martin (1315) are by the Sienese painter Simone Martini. This panel shows the Death of the Saint. Martini was also responsible for the fine stained glass in the chapel.

VISITORS' CHECKLIST

Piazza San Francesco. 075 81 90 01. Assisi.
7am–6pm daily.

Assisi ②

Perugia. 25,000. Piazza del Comune (075 81 25 34). Sat.

THIS BEAUTIFUL medieval town, with its geranium-hung streets, lovely views, and fountain-splashed piazzas, is heir to the legacy of St. Francis (c.1181–1226), who is buried in the **Basilica di San Francesco**. Sadly the town suffered serious damage when it was hit by an earthquake on September 26, 1997, but restoration was relatively swift– completed in approximately two years. The tourist office can give information on which sights are open to visitors.

Piazza del Comune, Assisi's main square, is dominated by the columns of the **Tempio di Minerva**, a Roman temple-front from the Augustan age. The Palazzo Comunale, opposite, is home to the **Pinacoteca Comunale**, an art gallery with works by local medieval artists.

Down Corso Mazzini lies the **Basilica di Santa Chiara**, the burial place of St. Clare – Francis's companion and the founder of the Poor Clares (an order of nuns). One of its chapels contains the crucifix that is said to have bowed its head and ordered Francis to "Repair God's church." It came from **San Damiano**, a sublime church set amid olive groves south of the Porta Nuova.

The **duomo (San Rufino)**, built during the 12th and 13th centuries, has a superb Roman-esque façade. Inside is a small museum of paintings, and there are archaeological items in the crypt. From the duomo, Via Maria delle Rose leads to the **Rocca Maggiore** (rebuilt in 1367), an evocative but much-restored castle.

Thirteenth-century **San Pietro**, on Piazza San Pietro, is a simple and carefully restored Romanesque church. The nearby **Oratorio dei Pellegrini**, a 15th-century pilgrims' hospice, contains well-preserved frescoes by Matteo da Gualdo.

Giotto's fresco, *St. Francis Appearing to the Friars at Arles* (c.1295), in the Basilica di San Francesco, Assisi ▷

Orvieto **⑤**

Terni. 🚶 *22,000.* FS 🚌 🛈 *Piazza Duomo 24 (0763 34 17 72).* 🛒 *Thu & Sat.*

ORVIETO IS MAGNIFICENT from any angle. Perched on a 300-m (984-ft) plateau, it looks down from its cliff-edged balcony over a vineyard-dotted plain. Visitors flood into the town to admire the **duomo**, among the greatest of all Italy's Romanesque-Gothic cathedrals.

The tiny 13th-century church of **San Lorenzo in Arari** is at the end of Via Scalza. Its walls feature frescoes describing the martyrdom of St. Lawrence, who was grilled to death. The altar is made from an Etruscan sacrificial slab. Via Malabranca leads to **San Giovenale** at Orvieto's western tip, a church that is beautifully and almost completely covered in detailed frescoes from the 15th and 16th centuries. It offers broad views over the surrounding countryside. **Sant'Andrea**, in Piazza della Repubblica, is distinguished by a curious 12-sided campanile, part of the original 12th-century building.

🏛 **Museo dell' Opera del Duomo**
Piazza Duomo. 📞 *0763 34 24 77.* ⏰ *call to check times.*
This interesting little museum contains an eclectic collection of treasures given to the duomo. Among the highlights are paintings by Lorenzo Maitani (died 1330) and sculptures by Andrea Pisano (c.1270–1348).

🏛 **Museo Archeologico Faina and Museo Civico**
Piazza Duomo 29. 📞 *0763 34 15 11.* ⏰ *daily; Oct–Mar Tue–Sun.* ⚫ *Jan 1, Dec 25.* 📷 🅿 ♿
The first of these two museums has a well-known, low-key collection of Etruscan remains including many Greek vases

View into the Pozzo di San Patrizio in Orvieto

that were found in Etruscan tombs in the area. The Museo Civico contains ancient Greek artifacts, as well as Etruscan copies of Greek art.

🏛 **Museo d'Arte Moderna "Emilio Greco"**
Palazzo Soliano, Piazza Duomo. 📞 *0763 34 46 05.* ⏰ *Tue–Sun.* ⚫ *Jan 1, Dec 25.* ♿
This museum is devoted to the modern Sicilian sculptor, Emilio Greco, who made the bronze doors (1964–70) of the duomo in Orvieto.

🔒 **DUOMO OF ORVIETO**
Piazza Duomo. 📞 *0763 34 11 67.* ⏰ *daily.* ♿ 📷
Some 300 years in the building, Orvieto's duomo (begun 1290), with its breathtaking façade, is one of Italy's greatest cathedrals. It was inspired by the Miracle of Bolsena in which real blood from a consecrated host supposedly fell on the altar cloth of a church in nearby Bolsena.

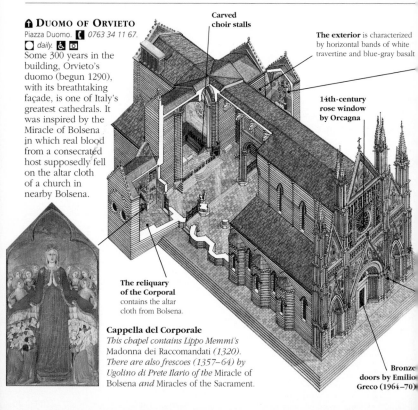

Carved choir stalls

The exterior is characterized by horizontal bands of white travertine and blue-gray basalt

14th-century rose window by Orcagna

The reliquary of the Corporal contains the altar cloth from Bolsena.

Cappella del Corporale
This chapel contains Lippo Memmi's Madonna dei Raccomandati *(1320). There are also frescoes (1357–64) by Ugolino di Prete Ilario of the* Miracle of Bolsena *and* Miracles of the Sacrament.

Bronze doors by Emilio Greco (1964–70)

🏛 Pozzo di San Patrizio

Viale San Gallo. 📞 *0763 34 37 68.*
🕐 *daily.* ⬤ *Jan 1, Dec 25.* 🏷

Orvieto's vast well was commissioned in 1527 by Pope Clement VII and designed by the Florentine architect Antonio da Sangallo to provide the town with a water supply in case of attack. Two 248-step staircases drop into its dank interior, cleverly arranged as a double helix (spiral) so as not to intersect. The 62-m (203-ft) shaft, built out of tufa blocks and bricks, took ten years to complete.

🏛 Necropoli del Crocifisso del Tufo

Strada Statale 71, km 1,600.
📞 *0763 34 36 11.* 🕐 *daily.* 🏷 ♿

This Etruscan necropolis from the 6th century BC has burial chambers built of blocks of tufa. Etruscan words, which are thought to be the names of the deceased, are inscribed on the tombs.

Cappella Nuova
Luca Signorelli's great fresco cycle of the Last Judgment (1499–1504) features prominently in this chapel. Fra Angelico and Benozzo Gozzoli worked here before Signorelli.

The Façade
There are detailed carvings (c.1320–30) at the base of its four main pilasters. By Lorenzo Maitani, they depict scenes from the Old and New Testaments, including hell and damnation.

View of the hill town of Todi in southern Umbria

Todi ❻

Perugia. 🏘 *17,000.* FS ⬛ ℹ
Piazza Umberto I 6 (075 894 33 95).
🚌 *Sat.*

LOOKING DOWN over the Tiber valley from its hilltop eyrie, Todi is one of the most strikingly situated of Umbria's famous hill towns. An ancient Etruscan, and then Roman settlement, it still preserves an uncorrupted medieval air, with several tiny churches, three austere public palaces and many sleepy corners.

Most people are drawn by the **Piazza del Popolo**, the main square, flanked by the lovely plain-faced **duomo**. Built in the 13th century on the site of a Roman temple to Apollo, it has a dusky interior and one of Umbria's finest choirs (1521–30). Note Ferraù da Faenza's huge painting (1596) on the rear wall, mediocre copy of Michelangelo's *Last Judgment*, and the altarpiece at the end of the right aisle by Giannicola di Paolo (a follower of Perugino).

Also flanking the piazza are the **Palazzo dei Priori** (1293–1337) and the linked **Palazzo del Capitano** (1290) and **Palazzo del Popolo** (1213). In the Palazzo del Capitano, distinguished by its formidable medieval interior, lies the **Museo Etrusco-Romano**.

The museum contains a collection of local Etruscan and Roman artifacts. There are altarpieces and sacred objects in the **Pinacoteca Comunale**, also housed in the palace.

A few steps from the piazza rises **San Fortunato** (1292–1462), named after Todi's first bishop, with a florid Gothic doorway (1415–58). The high vaulted plan is based on German Gothic "hall" churches and the "barn" churches of Tuscany, characterized by a low-pitched vault, polygonal apse, and naves and aisles of equal height. The choir (1590) is superb, but the church's most famous work is a *Madonna and Child* (1432) by Masolino da Panicale (fourth chapel on the right). The crypt contains the tomb of Jacopone da Todi (c.1228–1306), a noted medieval poet and mystic.

To the right of the church are some shady gardens, from which a path (past the tiny castle) drops through the trees to emerge in front of **Santa Maria della Consolazione** (1508–1607), near the N79. One of central Italy's finest Renaissance churches, and based on a Greek cross, it may have been built to a plan by Bramante. The stark, chill interior is overshadowed by the harmonious exterior.

🏛 Museo Etrusco-Romano and Pinacoteca Comunale

Palazzi Comunali. 📞 *075 895 61.*
🕐 *Tue–Sun (Apr: daily).* 🏷 ♿

Santa Maria della Consolazione in Todi

Spoleto ❼

Perugia. 🏃 *38,000.* 🚉 🚌
ℹ️ *Piazza della Libertà 7 (0743 22
03 11).* 🛒 *Tue & Fri.*

FOUNDED BY THE UMBRIANS,
Spoleto became one of
central Italy's most important
Roman colonies, a prominence
maintained by the Lombards,
who in the 7th century made
it the capital of one of their
three Italian dukedoms. After
a period as an independent
city state, the town fell to the
papacy in 1354.

Spoleto, within its wooded
setting, is the loveliest of the
Umbrian hill towns. Its urbane
atmosphere is enhanced by its
superb monuments and by the
Festival dei Due Mondi, one of
Europe's leading arts festivals
held annually in June and July.

At the southern end of
Piazza del Mercato is the

Arco di Druso, a 1st-century
AD Roman arch. It is flanked
by the church of **Sant'Ansano**,
whose crypt is covered in
frescoes that may date from
the 6th century. Via Aurelio
Saffi, at the piazza's northern
end, leads to **Sant'Eufemia**.
This utterly simple 10th-
century Romanesque church
is known for its matroneum
(women's gallery), once used
to segregate the congregation.

A short way beyond, the
fan-shaped Piazza del Duomo
opens out to reveal Spoleto's
12th-century **Duomo**, graced
with one of the most elegant
façades in Italy. Filling the
apse of the Baroque interior
is a great, newly restored
fresco cycle. The final work of
Fra Lippo Lippi, from 1467–9,
it describes episodes from
the *Life of the Virgin*. The
Cappella Erioli is adorned
with Pinturicchio's unfinished
*Madonna and
Child* (1497).

The best of
the exceptional
churches in the
lower town is
4th-century
San Salvatore,
located in the
main cemetery,
a spot suited
to the church's
eerie sense of
antiquity. Near-
by stands **San
Ponziano**,
fronted by a
captivating
three-tiered

Ponte delle Torri, Spoleto

Façade of San Pietro in Spoleto

Romanesque façade typical of
Umbria. It has a 10th-century
crypt, supported by odd little
columns and decorated with
Byzantine frescoes.

Romanesque **San Gregorio**
in Piazza Garibaldi dates from
1069, but its cramped façade
and stolid campanile incorporate fragments of Roman
buildings. Inside is a raised
presbytery and a lovely
multicolumned crypt. Well-
preserved patches of fresco dot
the walls, interspersed with
austere stone confessionals.
Some 10,000 Christian martyrs
are supposedly buried near the
church. They were reputedly
slaughtered in the town's
Roman **amphitheater**, traces
of which can be seen in the
barracks on Via del Anfiteatro.

🏛 **Ponte delle Torri**
This magnificent 14th-century
aqueduct, the "bridge of
towers," is 80 m (262 ft)
high. Designed by
Gattapone (from

ROMANESQUE CHURCHES IN UMBRIA

Umbria's church-building tradition had its roots in ancient
Roman basilicas and in the chapels built over the shrines of its
many saints and martyrs. The region's Romanesque façades are
usually divided into three tiers, often with three rose windows
arranged above a trio of arched portals.
The three doors usually correspond to
the interior's nave and two aisles, which
derive from the simple barnlike plan
of Roman basilicas. Inside, the
presbytery is often raised in
order to allow for the building
of a crypt, which usually contained the relics of a saint or
martyr. Many of the churches
took centuries to build, or
were repeatedly modified
over time, often acquiring
elements of Gothic, Baroque,
or Renaissance styles.

San Lorenzo di Arari *in
Orvieto takes its name from an
Etruscan altar* (arari). *This
14th-century church has a
very simple façade (see p348).*

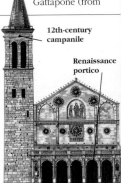
**12th-century
campanile**

**Renaissance
portico**

Spoleto's duomo *(1198) has
eight rose windows, a mosaic
(1207), and a Renaissance
portico (1491). The tower was
built from old Roman remains.*

Gubbio), it is the town's single most famous monument. From the bridge, there are views of the bastions of the **Rocca Albornoz**, a huge papal fortress built in 1359–64, also by Gattapone. Unfortunately, the fortress is closed to the public. Across the bridge a path leads to the Strada di Monteluco and the church of **San Pietro**, which is renowned for the fascinating 12th-century carvings on its façade.

🏛 Pinacoteca Comunale
Palazzo Comunale, Piazza del Municipio.
📞 0743 21 81. **◯** Tue–Sun.
● Jan 1, Dec 25.
Spoleto's art gallery has four beautifully appointed rooms with works by Perugino and his Spoletan protégé, Lo Spagna (c.1450–1528), including a painting of the Madonna and Child with Saints.

Montefalco ❽

Perugia. 👥 4,900. 🚌 🚍 Mon.

MONTEFALCO, whose name (Falcon's Mount) draws inspiration from its lofty position and sweeping views, is the best of the fascinating villages in the Vale of Spoleto. Crisscrossed by streets almost too narrow for cars, it takes less than five minutes to walk through the village. Yet you might happily spend a morning here, most of it in the polished new **Museo Civico**, housed in the former church

A panel from Gozzoli's fresco cycle (1452) in Montefalco's Museo Civico

of San Francesco. Its highlight is Benozzo Gozzoli's *Life of St. Francis* (1452), a radiant fresco cycle that borrows heavily from Giotto's cycle in Assisi *(see pp344–7)*. Other painters represented here are Perugino, Tiberio d'Assisi, and Nicolò Alunno, all leading medieval Umbrian artists.

The simple Gothic church of **Sant'Agostino** (begun 1279) on Corso Mameli is dotted with frescoes from the 14th–16th centuries. The church also contains three mummies.

In the main square local wines on sale include the rich, red Sagrantino di Montefalco. Just outside the town walls, the church of **Sant'Illuminata** is covered with charming frescoes, the work of the local 16th-century artist Francesco

Melanzio. About 2 km (1 mile) beyond, the prettily situated church of **San Fortunato** is decorated with frescoes by Gozzoli and Tiberio d'Assisi.

ENVIRONS: The village in the Vale of Spoleto with the most spectacular setting is **Trevi**. The churches of **San Martino** (16th century), on Passeggiata di San Martino, and **Madonna delle Lacrime** (1487–1522), south of Trevi on the road into the village, contain paintings by Perugino and Tiberio d'Assisi, among others.

🏛 Museo Civico di San Francesco
Via Ringhiera Umbra 9. **📞** 0742 37 95 98. **◯** Mar–Oct: daily; Nov–Feb: Tue–Sun. **●** Jan 1, Dec 25.

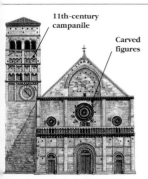

The duomo (1253) in Assisi is a fine example of the three-tiered façades found across central Italy (see p345). It has a pointed arch and a row of arcading.

11th-century campanile

Carved figures

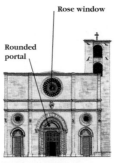

Todi's duomo was begun in the 12th century, but work on its windows and portals continued until the 17th century (see p349).

Rose window

Rounded portal

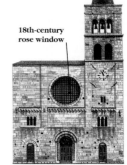

San Michele (c.1195) in Bevagna has a beautiful portal that combines both Romanesque and old Roman fragments (see p352).

18th-century rose window

Spello ❾

Perugia. 🏘 8,000. 🚉 📟
ℹ️ Piazza Matteotti 3 (0742 30 10 09). 🔺 Wed.

Spello is one of the better-known villages in the Vale of Spoleto. It is renowned for a fresco cycle by Pinturicchio in the Cappella Baglioni of the church of **Santa Maria Maggiore** (12th–13th century) on Via Consolare. Executed around 1500, the frescoes depict scenes from the New Testament. Toward the center of the village is the Gothic church of **Sant'Andrea** (13th century) on Via Cavour. This road becomes Via Garibaldi, which leads to **San Lorenzo**, a Baroque gem of a church dating from the 12th century.

Spello also boasts Roman ruins from the age of Augustus: the **Porta Consolare** at the end of Via Consolare, and the twin-towered **Porta Venere** by Via Torri di Properzio.

The road to Assisi over **Monte Subasio** offers stunning views from the top of the mountain above Spello.

ENVIRONS: The least-known village in the Vale of Spoleto is **Bevagna.** Like Spello, it sprang to life as a way station on the Via Flaminia (the Roman road that ran through this part of Umbria). The medieval Piazza Silvestri is the setting for two Romanesque churches.

The lofty peaks of the Monti Sibillini in eastern Umbria

San Silvestro (1195) is the more atmospheric of the pair, thanks to its shadowy interior and ancient crypt, but **San Michele** (late 12th century) has an elegant portal, famed for the little gargoyles on either side. Both churches are the work of Maestro Binello.

Monti Sibillini ❿

Macerata. 🚉 Spoleto. 📟 Visso.
ℹ️ Largo Giovanni Battista Antinori 1, Visso (0737 955 26).

Recently awarded national park status, the Monti Sibillini in eastern Umbria provide the region's wildest and most spectacular scenery. A range 40 km (25 miles) long, the mountains form part of the Apennines, a chain that runs the length of the Italian peninsula. **Monte Vettore** is the loftiest point, and the peninsula's third highest; it stands at 2,476 m (8,123 ft), a great whale-backed peak close to the cave of the mythical sibyl that gave the region its name.

Good maps and trails make this a superb walking area, while drivers can follow hairpin roads to some of Italy's most magical landscapes. Chief of these is the **Piano Grande**, a huge upland plain surrounded by a vast amphitheater of mountains. Bare but for flocks of sheep and bedraggled haystacks, the plain blazes with wild flowers in spring and with lentils later in the year. The only habitation is **Castelluccio**, a beautiful, neglected mountain village now being restored. It can be reached by road from Norcia and Arquata del Tronto.

Storefront in Norcia displaying the town's varied meats

Norcia ⓫

Perugia. 🏘 4,700. 📟 ℹ️ Piazza San Benedetto (0743 82 81 73). 🔺 Thu.

The birthplace of St. Benedict, Norcia is a robust mountain town and an excellent base for exploring Valnerina and Monti Sibillini. One of Italy's culinary capitals, it is renowned for truffles and some of the country's best hams, sausages, and salamis.

Norcia's main sights are in **Piazza San Benedetto**. Occupying the eastern flank, the church of **San Benedetto** has a 14th-century portal adorned with statues of Benedict and his sister (Santa Scolastica). Legend claims that the church marks the site of Benedict's birth – indeed there are the remains of a 5th-century building in the crypt. However, the

Pinturicchio's Annunciation **(c.1500) in Spello's Santa Maria Maggiore**

The 8th-century monastery of San Pietro in Valle, set in the beautiful Valnerina

church is more likely to have been built over the site of an old Roman temple, since the forum of the Roman colony of Nursia once occupied this spot.

Left of the church stands the newly-renovated **Palazzo Comunale**, a monument to the town's period as a free commune during the 13th and 14th centuries. On the opposite side of the square, still dominating the town, rises the **Castellina** (1554), a blunt papal fortress designed by Vignola to help impose order on an unruly mountain district. The **duomo** (1560), to the left of the Castellina, has been ravaged by earthquakes over the centuries. Indeed, Norcia has been the victim of successive earthquakes, and its houses are low and heavily buttressed with thick walls to protect them from further damage.

Piazza San Benedetto has enticing food shops, fronted by boars' heads, hams, and strings of sausages. Nearby **Sant'Agostino** on Via Anicia features a range of good 16th-century frescoes. A little way beyond, the **Oratorio di Sant'Agostinaccio** in Piazza Palatina contains a superb 17th-century ceiling. Via Umberto shelters the **Edicola** (1354), a strange tabernacle believed to have been carved for a Holy Week procession.

Valnerina ⑫

Perugia. **FS** *Spoleto, then bus.* **ℹ** *Piazza Garibaldi, Cascia (0743 711 47).*

THE VALNERINA (Little Valley of the Nera River) curves through a broad swathe of eastern Umbria, draining the mountains around Norcia and the Sibillini before emptying into the Tiber beyond Terni. It is edged with craggy, tree-covered slopes and dotted with countless upland villages and fortified hamlets.

The high spot is **San Pietro in Valle**, an idyllically situated monastery in the hills above the village of Colleponte. Founded in the 8th century, it is one of the few surviving memorials to the Lombards, whose central Italian duchy had its capital in Spoleto. The main body of the monastery church dates from this period, as does the high altar, an outstanding piece of Lombard work. The nave walls are covered in a wealth of 12th-century frescoes.

More popular than the monastery are the **Cascate delle Marmore** near Terni, among Europe's highest waterfalls at 165 m (541 ft). Created by the Romans during drainage work, their waters are now diverted to produce hydroelectric power on all but a few special days. You can view the falls from Marmore village or the N209.

🏠 San Pietro in Valle
Località Ferentillo, Terni. **📞** *0744 78 03 16.* **◯** *daily.*

🏞 Cascate delle Marmore
7 km (4 miles) along N209 Valnerina, Terni. **◯** *sporadically. Ask at tourist information.*

Piazza San Benedetto and the church of San Benedetto in Norcia

LE MARCHE

Tucked away *in a remote corner between the Adriatic Sea and the Apennine mountains, Le Marche (the Marches) is an enchanting rural patchwork of old towns, hill country, and long, sandy beaches. In pre-Christian times the area was settled by the Piceni, a tribe eventually assimilated by the Romans.*

In the 4th century BC, exiles from Magna Graecia colonized much of the region. The most notable town was Ancona, also the northernmost point of Greek influence on the Italian peninsula. During the early Middle Ages the region marked the edge of the Holy Roman Empire, giving rise to its present name (*march* meant border area).

The region's historical peak was reached in the 15th century under Federico da Montefeltro, whose court at Urbino became one of Europe's leading cultural centers. Much of Urbino's former grandeur survives, particularly in Federico's magnificent Renaissance Palazzo Ducale, now home to a regional art collection. Ascoli Piceno is almost as enchanting as Urbino, its central Piazza del Popolo among the most evocative old squares in Italy. Smaller towns like San Leo and Urbania and the republic of San Marino also boast fine medieval monuments.

Today probably as many people come to Le Marche for its beaches and towns as for its hilly, unspoiled interior. Especially beautiful are the snowcapped peaks of the Monti Sibillini, situated in magnificent walking and skiing country.

Regional cuisine encompasses the truffles and robust cheeses of the mountains, tender hams and salamis, *olive ascolane* (olives stuffed with meat and herbs), and *brodetto*, fish soup made in several versions up and down the coast. Dry, white Verdicchio is the best known wine, although more unusual names, such as Bianchello del Metauro, are gaining in popularity.

A field of poppies and olive trees in the heart of Le Marche's countryside

◁ **Medieval gates and ramparts surrounding the hilltop republic of San Marino**

Exploring Le Marche

THE MEDIEVAL TOWNS of Urbino and Ascoli Piceno are the highlights of the region, but the rolling hills of the interior contain an abundance of smaller towns and all but undiscovered villages. San Leo, with its dramatic fortress, is one of the best. Most of the countryside is a pretty mixture of woods and remote hills, rising in the west to the majestic Monti Sibillini. Ancona and the attractive town of Pèsaro are the pivotal points of the vast coastline.

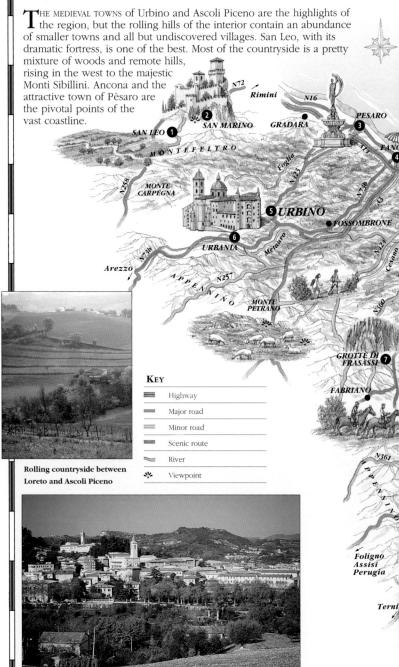

N72
Rimini
N16
SAN MARINO
PESARO
GRADARA
SAN LEO
FANO
MONTEFELTRO
A258
Foglia
N73b
MONTE CARPEGNA
N23
A5
URBINO
FOSSOMBRONE
Arezzo
URBANIA
Metauro
N73b
N257
APPENNINO
Cesano
N360
Mauro
MONTE PETRANO
GROTTE DI FRASASSI
FABRIANO
N361
APPENNINO
Foligno
Assisi
Perugia
Terni

KEY

▬▬▬	Highway
▬▬▬	Major road
▬▬▬	Minor road
▬▬▬	Scenic route
～	River
✹	Viewpoint

Rolling countryside between Loreto and Ascoli Piceno

View of Ascoli Piceno, one of the prettiest towns in Le Marche

Sights at a Glance

Ancona 9
Ascoli Piceno 12
Conero Peninsula 10
Fano 4
Grotte di Frasassi 7
Jesi 8
Loreto 11
Pèsaro 3
San Marino 2
San Leo 1
Urbania 6
Urbino pp360–61 5

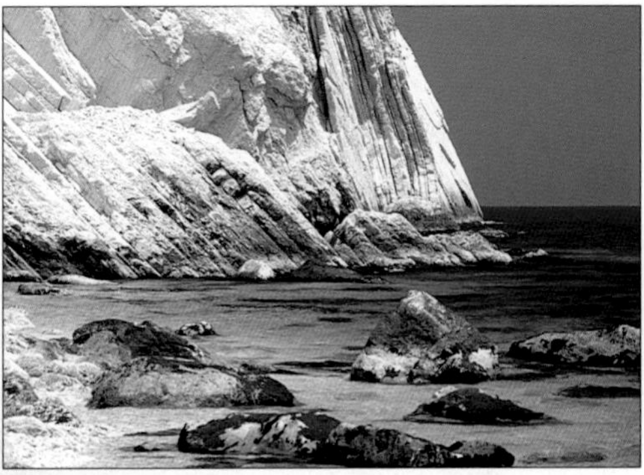

The rocky reef near Portonovo on the Conero Peninsula

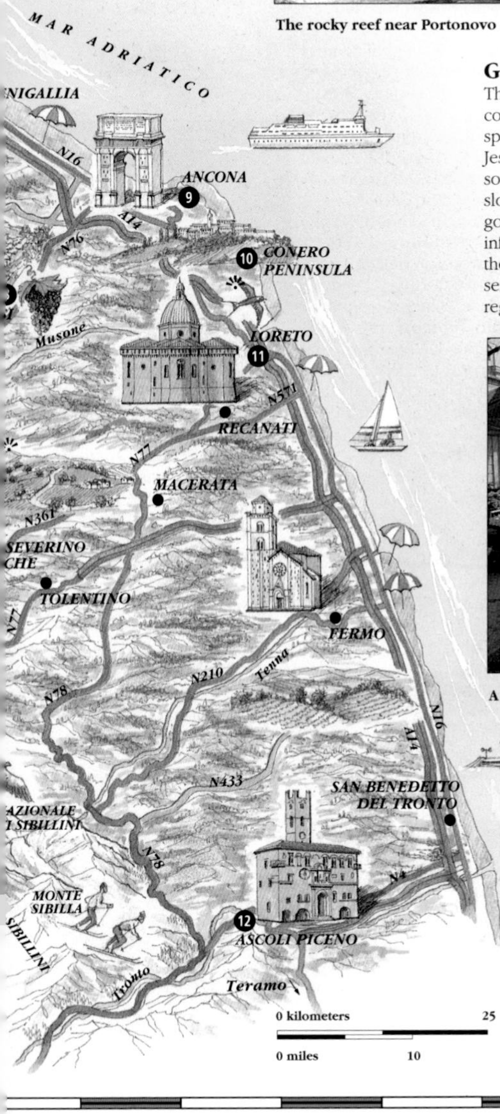
MAR ADRIATICO
NIGALLIA
N16
ANCONA
9
A14
N76
10
CONERO PENINSULA
Musone
LORETO
11
N571
RECANATI
N77
MACERATA
N361
SEVERINO
CHE
TOLENTINO
N77
FERMO
Tenna
N210
N78
N16
A14
N433
SAN BENEDETTO DEL TRONTO
AZIONALE
I SIBILLINI
N78
N4
MONTE SIBILLA
SIBILLINI
12
ASCOLI PICENO
Tronto
Teramo
0 kilometers 25
0 miles 10

Getting Around

The A14 provides easy access to the coastal resorts. Two-lane highway spurs from the A14 lead to Urbino, Jesi, and Ascoli Piceno, but north-south roads in the interior can be slow. Bus services are generally good, but in the interior can be infrequent. The train service along the coast is excellent, with good service through the heart of the region, although it can be slow.

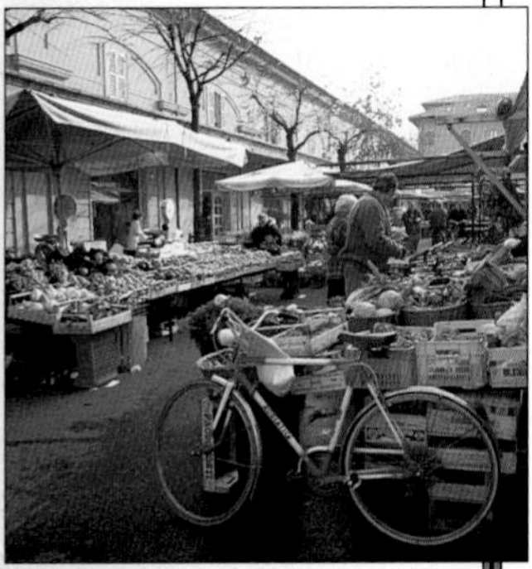

A market scene in Fano

See Also

- ***Where to Stay*** pp564–5
- ***Where to Eat*** pp597–8

The bell tower of the duomo rising above the village of San Leo

San Leo ❶

Pèsaro. 🛈 *Piazza Dante 10 (0541 91 62 31).* 🚌 *from Rimini, change at Villanova.*

F EW CASTLES are as impressive as the great **fortress** that towers over the village of San Leo. Dante used this crag-top site as a model for the landscapes of *Purgatorio,* while Machiavelli considered the citadel to be the finest piece of military architecture in Italy. Its rocky ramparts once contained the Mons Feretrius, a Roman temple dedicated to Jupiter.

An earlier Roman fortress on the site became a papal prison in the 18th century. Its most famous inmate was the larger-than-life Conte di Cagliostro. A swindler, womanizer, necromancer, quack, and alchemist, Cagliostro was imprisoned for heresy in the 1790s. His cell was specially built so that its window faced the village's two churches. It is still visible, together with a small picture gallery, state rooms, and the majestic Renaissance ramparts, built by Francesco di Giorgio Martini for the dukes of Montefeltro in the 15th century.

Duty-free shop in San Marino

The captivating village has a quaint cobbled square with a superb 9th-century **Pieve** (parish church). Built partly with stone from the ruined Mons Feretrius, the church was raised over the site of a 6th-century chapel.

Just behind lies the 12th-century **duomo**, a fine Romanesque building with Corinthian capitals and Roman columns from the Mons Feretrius. The lid of St. Leo's sarcophagus is in the crypt. Ancient pagan carvings can be seen on the wall behind the altar.

♣ Fortress
Via Leopardi. 📞 *0541 91 62 31.* 🕐 *daily.*

San Marino ❷

🏘 *26,000.* 🚌 *San Marino Città (fr Rimini).* 🛈 *Contrada Omagnano 20, San Marino (0549 88 24 00).*

E UROPE'S OLDEST republic, tiny San Marino was reputedly founded by St. Marinus, a 4th-century monk and stonemason forced to flee the religious persecution of the Emperor Diocletian. With him was St. Leo, the founder of the nearby town of San Leo. Dramatically situated on the slopes of Monte Titano, the country has its own mint, stamps, soccer team – even its own 1,000-strong army.

There are no customs formalities in this small country, whose borders are just 12 km (7 miles)

apart at the widest point. Sadly, the capital, also known as **San Marino**, is thronged with visitors for much of the year and its streets are clogged with souvenir stands. Garibaldi, who sought shelter here after fleeing Venice in 1849, is honored by a monument in Piazza Garibaldi. **Borgomaggiore**, the largest town, lies at the foot of Monte Titano, with a cable car to the capital above.

Pèsaro ❸

🏘 *85,000.* 🚉 🚌 🛈 *Via Trieste 164 (0721 693 41).* 🗓 *Tue & 1st Thu of month.*

Detail of the *Coronation of the Virgin* by Bellini (c.1470) in the Musei Civici

O NE OF THE ADRIATIC'S larger seaside resorts, Pèsaro has managed to retain a stylish air. Behind the promenade and the wall of white stucco hotels is a lively, attractive medieval area.

The art gallery of the **Musei Civici** contains Giovanni Bellini's sumptuous polyptych, the *Coronation of the Virgin* (c.1470). The museum also features Renaissance ceramics.

The **Museo Archeologico Oliveriano** presents historical displays from Roman remains to Iron Age artifacts from the necropolis of nearby Novilara.

The best of the town's churches is **Sant'Agostino** on Corso XI Settembre, remarkable for its choir stalls, each a patchwork of inlaid landscapes and narrative scenes.

Pèsaro is also a point of musical pilgrimage. In 1792 the composer Gioachino Rossini was born here. His home, **Casa Rossini**, contains memorabilia, while his piano and some original manuscripts lie in the **Conservatorio Rossini**. His operas are performed in the **Teatro Rossini** in Piazza Lazzarini during the annual August music festival.

🏛 **Musei Civici**
Piazza Mosca 29. 📞 0721 312 13.
⏰ Tue, Wed am; Thu–Sun. 📷
🏛 **Museo Archeologico Oliveriano**
Via Mazza 97. 📞 0721 333 44.
⏰ Mon–Sat am by appt. ♿
🏠 **Casa Rossini**
Via Rossini 34. 📞 0721 38 73 57.
⏰ Tue–Sun. 📷
🏠 **Conservatorio Rossini**
Piazza Olivieri 5. 📞 0721 336 70.
⏰ Mon–Sat am, but call first to arrange. ● public hols.

Fano ❹

Pèsaro. 🚶 54,000. 🚉 🚌 ⛴
🛈 Via Cesare Battisti 10 (0721 80 35 34). 🛒 Wed & Sat.

Aᴺᴄɪᴇɴᴛ ꜰᴀɴᴏ stands out from the string of beach resorts south of Pèsaro, thanks to its fine old center and historic monuments. Named after Fanum Fortunae, a pagan temple to the goddess Fortuna, it became the terminus of the Via Flaminia (an important consular road from Rome) and the largest Roman colony on the Adriatic coast. The **Arco d'Augusto** (AD 2), on Via Arco d'Augusto, is Fano's most significant ancient monument, having narrowly escaped destruction at the hands of Federico da Montefeltro in 1463. He destroyed its upper section while besieging the town as a papal *condottiere*.

The 16th-century **Fontana della Fortuna**, in Piazza XX Settembre, is dedicated to the goddess Fortuna. The large **Palazzo Malatesta** that rises up to its rear was built around 1420 and enlarged in 1544 for Fano's rulers, the Rimini-based Malatesta family. Inside is the small **Museo Civico** and the **Pinacoteca Malatestiana**, with works by Guercino, Guido Reni, and the Venetian artist, Michele Giambono.

🏛 **Museo Civico and Pinacoteca Malatestiana**
Piazza XX Settembre.
📞 0721 82 83 62. ⏰ Tue–Sun (Oct–Mar: Tue–Sun am). ● Jan 1, Dec 25, 26. 📷

Entrance to the Palazzo Ducale in Urbania

Urbino ❺

See pp360–61.

Urbania ❻

Pèsaro. 🚶 7,200. 🚌 🛈 Corso Vittorio Emanuele 24 (0722 31 31 40). 🛒 Thu.

Uʀʙᴀɴɪᴀ, ᴡɪᴛʜ ɪᴛꜱ elegant arcaded center, takes its name from Pope Urban VIII (1623–44), who entertained the notion of converting the old medieval village known as Castel Durante into a model Renaissance town.

Its chief attraction is a monument from an earlier age, the huge **Palazzo Ducale**, built by the dukes of Montefeltro as one of several residential alternatives to the Palazzo Ducale in nearby Urbino. It was begun in the 13th century, and then rebuilt in the 15th and 16th centuries. Beautifully situated alongside the Metauro river, it houses a small art gallery, a modest museum, old maps and globes, and the remnants of Duke Federico's famous library.

🏛 **Palazzo Ducale**
Palazzo Ducale. 📞 0722 31 99 85.
⏰ Tue–Sun (Oct–Mar: ask at library). ● public hols. 📷

Fontana della Fortuna in Fano

Urbino: Palazzo Ducale

ITALY'S MOST BEAUTIFUL Renaissance palace was
built for Duke Federico da Montefeltro, the
ruler of Urbino between 1444 and 1482, known
for his prowess as a mercenary soldier. Federico
was a man of the arts as well as a soldier, and
his palace, with its library, paintings, and refined
architecture, is a monument to the high artistic
and intellectual ideals of the Renaissance.

**★ The Flagellation by
Piero della Francesca**
*Dramatic perspective creates an
unsettling effect in this 15th-century
painting of the scourging of Christ.*

Towers attributed to Laurana

**The palace rising
above Urbino**

**The simple
east side** of
the palace was
designed by Maso di
Bartolomeo before 1460.

Cortile d'Onore
*This early Renaissance
courtyard was designed by
the Dalmatian-born artist
Luciano Laurana (1420–79).*

entr

The Lib
was one
Europe's
in its da

Ideal City
*Attributed to Luciano
Laurana, this 15th-century
painting of an imaginary
Renaissance city is notable
for its measured perspective
and lack of people.*

★ Studiolo
*The former study of Federico
da Montefeltro is decorated with
intarsia (inlaid wood), some
of it designed by Botticelli.*

**Duke Federico by
Pedro Berruguete**
*The duke, shown
here with his son in
this 15th-century
painting, was always
portrayed in left
profile after an
injury to his face.*

**Hanging
garden**

The rooms in
this wing are
known as the
Appartamento
della Duchessa.

★ La Muta by Raphael
The Mute Woman *may be a
portrait of Maddalena Doni,
a Florentine noblewoman.*

STAR EXHIBITS

**★ The Flagellation by
Piero della Francesca**

★ La Muta by Raphael

★ Studiolo

VISITORS' CHECKLIST

Piazza Duca Federico 13.
📞 0722 27 60. 🚌 *Piazza del
Mercatale.* ⭕ *Jun–Oct: 9am–
2pm Mon, 9am–7pm Tue–Sat,
9am–1pm Sun; Nov–May: call
for winter schedule. Last adm:
30 mins before closing.* ⭕ *Jan 1,
Dec 25.* 🎫 📷 ♿

Urbino ❺

Pèsaro. 👥 *16,000.* 🚌 ℹ️ *Via
Rinascimento 1 (0722 26 13).* 🗓 *Sat.*

AMID URBINO'S TANGLE of
medieval and Renaissance
streets stands the Neo-Classical
duomo, on Piazza Federico,
built in 1789. Of special interest
is the painting of the *Last
Supper* by Federico Barocci
(c.1535–1612). The
Museo Diocesano
contains a collection
of ceramics, glass, and
religious artifacts.

Urbino's famous son,
the painter Raphael
(1483–1520), lived in
the **Casa Natale di
Raffaello**. It has a
highly evocative
interior, especially the
kitchen and courtyard.

In Via Barocci stands
the medieval **Oratorio
di San Giuseppe**,
known for its *presepio*
(Christmas scene), and
the 14th-century
**Oratorio di San
Giovanni Battista**,
whose interior is
smothered in 15th-
century frescoes of the
Crucifixion and the *Life of John
the Baptist* by Giacomo and
Lorenzo Salimbeni.

The 15th-century **Fortezza
dell'Albornoz** on Viale Bruno
Buozzi is the defensive focus of
Urbino's surviving 16th-century
walls and bastions.

🏛 **Museo Diocesano**
Piazza Pascoli 2. 📞 *0722 28 50.*
⭕ *Mon–Sat (Oct–Mar: ask Duomo
custodian).* 🎫 ♿
🏛 **Casa Natale di Raffaello**
Via di Raffaello 57. 📞 *0722 32 01 05.*
⭕ *daily (Sun am only).* ⭕ *Jan 1,
Dec 25.* 🎫

**A street scene in the medieval
town of Urbino**

Fresh seafood and fishing boats in the harbor at Ancona

Grotte di Frasassi **7**

Ancona. **C** 0732 972 11. **FS** Genga San Vittore Terme. **O** for guided tours only (1 hr 15 mins). **O** Jan 1, Dec 4 & 25.

SOME OF EUROPE'S largest publicly accessible caverns lie in the cave network gouged out by the Sentino River southwest of Jesi. Of the vast network of 18 km (11 miles), an area of about 1,000 m (3,281 ft) is open to the public. The colossal **Grotta del Vento** is large enough to contain Milan cathedral – its ceiling extends to a height of 240 m (787 ft). This cavern has been used for a range of experiments, from sensory deprivation to an exploration of the social consequences of leaving a group of people alone in its depths for long periods.

Jesi **8**

Ancona. **M** 41,000. **FS** **P** Piazza della Repubblica 11 (0731 597 88). **O** Wed & Sat.

PERCHED ON A LONG, rocky ridge, Jesi lies in the heart of the verdant hill country where Verdicchio is produced. A crisp, white wine renowned for centuries, Verdicchio is bottled in unique containers – glass models of the terra-cotta amphorae once used to export the wine to ancient Greece. No wine is made in Jesi itself, but there are many vineyards in the surrounding countryside.

Housed in the town's 18th-century Palazzo Pianetti is the **Pinacoteca e Musei Civici**,

which contains fine late-period paintings by Lorenzo Lotto. Almost as alluring as the gallery's paintings, however, is the great central salon – an orgy of Rococo decoration that once formed the centerpiece of the Palazzo Pianetti. The nearby **Palazzo della Signoria** features an interesting little collection of archaeological finds, while beyond the old town's Renaissance walls stands the 14th-century church of **San Marco**, known for its collection of well-preserved Giottesque frescoes.

m Pinacoteca e Musei Civici
Via XV Settembre. **C** 0731 53 83 43. **O** Tue–Sun.
H Palazzo della Signoria
Piazza Colocci. **C** 0731 53 83 45. **O** call to check times.

Ancona **9**

M 98,000. **FS** **H** Via Thaon de Revel 4 (071 35 89 91). **O** Tue & Fri.

THE CAPITAL OF LE MARCHE and its largest port, Ancona, dates back to at least the 5th century BC, when it was settled by Greek exiles from Siracusa. Its name derives from *ankon* (Greek for elbow), a reference to the rocky spur that juts into the sea to form the town's fine natural harbor.

Heavy bombing during World War II, however, destroyed much of the medieval town. The 15th-century **Loggia dei Mercanti** (merchants' exchange) on Via della Loggia survives as a monument to the town's medieval heyday.

Just north of the loggia is the Romanesque church of **Santa Maria della Piazza**, with a lovely façade. The nearby **Pinacoteca Comunale F Podesti e Galleria d'Arte Moderna** includes canvases by Titian, Lorenzo Lotto, and Carlo Crivelli, among others. In the **Museo Archeologico Nazionale delle Marche**, the town's best museum, there are displays of Greek, Gallic, and Roman art and artifacts. The **Arco di Traiano**, by the harbor, was erected in AD 115 and is one of Italy's better preserved Roman arches.

An impressive cavern in the cave system of the Grotte di Frasassi

The beach at the village of Sirolo on the Conero Peninsula

⌂ Pinacoteca Comunale ⌂ Podesti e Galleria d'Arte Moderna

Via Pizzecolli 17. ☎ 071 222 50 41. ☐ Tue–Sat daily (Sun pm & Mon am). ● public hols. ♿

⌂ Museo Archeologico Nazionale delle Marche

Palazzo Ferretti, Via Ferretti 1. ☎ 071 20 75 90. ☐ daily (Oct–May: daily am). ● Jan 1, Dec 25. 🎫 ♿

Conero Peninsula ⑩

Ancona. 🚉 🚢 Ancona. 🚌 from Ancona to Sirolo or Numana. 🛈 Via Thaon de Revel 4, Ancona (071 35 89 91).

THE BEAUTIFUL cliff-edged Conero Peninsula is the only natural feature to disturb the almost unbroken line of beaches along the coast of Le Marche. Easily accessible from Ancona to the north, it is a semiwild area known for its scenery, its wines (notably Rosso del Conero), and for a collection of coves, beaches, and picturesque little resorts.

The best of these resorts is **Portonovo**, above whose beach stands **Santa Maria di Portonovo**, a pretty 11th-century Romanesque church mentioned by Dante in Canto XXI of *Paradiso*. The villages of **Sirolo** and **Numana** are busier and more commercialized, but you can escape the summer crowds by hiking the lower-swathed slopes of Monte Conero, which stands at 572 m (1,877 ft), or by taking a boat trip to the smaller beaches beyond the resorts.

Loreto ⑪

Ancona. 🚶 11,000. 🚉 🚌 🛈 Via Solari 3 (071 97 02 76). 🚢 Fri.

LEGEND SAYS that in 1294 the house of the Virgin Mary (**Santa Casa**) miraculously uprooted itself from the Holy Land and was brought by angels to a laurel grove *(loreto)* south of Ancona. Each year three million pilgrims visit the

Santa Casa in Loreto

Santa Casa in Loreto and its **Basilica**. Begun in 1468, the basilica was designed and built in part by Renaissance architects Bramante, Sansovino, and Giuliano da Sangallo. Its paintings include works by Luca Signorelli. The **Museo-Pinacoteca** has 16th-century paintings by Lorenzo Lotto.

⌂ Basilica and Santa Casa

Piazza Santuario. ☎ 071 97 01 04. ☐ daily. ♿

⌂ Museo-Pinacoteca

Palazzo Apostolico. ☎ 071 97 77 59. ☐ Tue–Sun daily. 🎫

Ascoli Piceno ⑫

🚶 54,000. 🚉 🛈 Piazza del Popolo (0736 25 30 45). 🚢 Wed & Sat.

THIS ALLURING TOWN takes its name from the Piceni, a tribe eventually conquered by the Romans in 89 BC. The gridiron plan of Roman Asculum Picenum is visible in the streets today, but it is the town's medieval heritage that attracts most visitors.

The enchanting **Piazza del Popolo** is dominated by the 13th-century **Palazzo dei Capitani del Popolo**, whose façade was designed by Cola dell'Amatrice, and the church of **San Francesco**, a large and faintly austere Gothic ensemble built between 1262 and 1549.

Via del Trivio leads north to a medieval district overlooking the River Tronto. Along Via Cairoli lies the 13th-century Dominican church of **San Pietro Martire**. Opposite is the church of **Santi Vincenzo e Anastasio** (11th century), with an ancient crypt built over a spring said to cure leprosy.

Around Piazza dell'Arringo is the 12th-century **duomo**, spoiled by a Baroque overlay. Its Cappella del Sacramento contains a polyptych by the 15th-century painter, Carlo Crivelli. The **Pinacoteca Civica** has more works by Crivelli and by Guido Reni, Titian, and Alemanno. The **Museo Archeologico** contains Roman, Piceni and Lombard artifacts.

⌂ Pinacoteca Civica

Palazzo Comunale, Piazza Arringo. ☎ 0736 29 82 13. ☐ daily. ● Jan 1, Dec 25. 🎫 ♿

⌂ Museo Archeologico

Palazzo Panighi, Piazza Arringo. ☎ 0736 25 35 62. ☐ daily. ● Jan 1, May 1, Dec 25. 🎫 ♿

A view of the medieval town of Ascoli Piceno

ROME AND LAZIO

Rome and Lazio at a Glance

T HE FIRST SETTLEMENTS IN THE REGION can be traced back
to the early Etruscan civilization in northern Lazio.
Rome grew to rule a vast empire and, as the empire
began to divide, the region became the center of the
Christian world. Artists and architects flocked to
work for the popes and their families, notably in
the Renaissance and Baroque periods when some
magnificent architectural works were created. The
legacy of this uninterrupted history can be seen all
over the city and the surrounding area.

St. Peter's, *with its majestic dome
by Michelangelo, is a magnificent
and sumptuous 16th-century
basilica (see pp408–9).*

Piazza Navona, *flanked by
cafés, contains three Baroque
fountains, including the
colossal Fontana dei
Quattro Fiumi, one
of Bernini's finest
works (see p389).*

St. Peter's

PIAZZA
NAVONA
(See pp386–

Fontana dei Quattro Fiumi

**Santa Maria in
Trastevere**, *probably
the first Christian
church in Rome, holds
some remarkable mo-
saics such as this detail
from Cavallini's* Life of
the Virgin *which dates
from 1291 (see p418).*

THE VATICAN
AND TRASTEVERE
(See pp404–19)

*Santa Maria in
Trastevere*

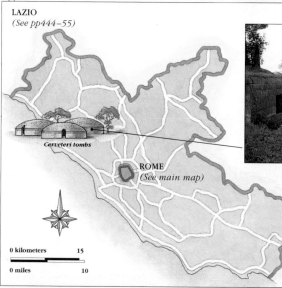

LAZIO
(See pp444–55)

Cerveteri tombs

ROME
(See main map)

0 kilometers   15

0 miles   10

Cerveteri *is one of
the many necropolises
left by the Etruscan
civilization in northern
Lazio. The larger
tumulus tombs often
contained frescoes and
utensils useful for the
afterlife (see p450).*

◁ Bernini's allegorical Fountain of the Four Rivers at the center of Piazza Navona

The Pantheon, built between AD 118–125, is a marvel of Roman engineering with its huge dome hidden behind the Classical portico (see p394).

SEE ALSO

- **Where to Stay** pp565–9
- **Where to Eat** pp599–602

NORTHEAST ROME
(See pp396–403)

Santa Maria Maggiore

Santa Maria Maggiore's richly decorated interior blends different architectural styles, such as this baldacchino from the 18th century (see p403).

heon

THE ANCIENT CENTER
(See pp372–85)

Capitoline Museums

Colosseum

San Giovanni in Laterano

AVENTINE AND LATERAN
(See pp420–27)

San Giovanni in Laterano, the Cathedral of Rome, incorporates the elaborate Corsini Chapel built in the 1730s (see p426).

The Capitoline Museums have held treasures of the Classical world since the Renaissance, including this colossal 4th-century head of Constantine (see pp376–7).

| 0 meters | 750 |
| 0 yards | 750 |

The Colosseum was constructed in AD 80 by Emperor Vespasian. His aim was to gain popularity by staging deadly gladiatorial combats and wild animal fights for public viewing (see p383).

Regional Food: Rome and Lazio

THE TRADITIONAL *cucina romanesca* has always relied on fresh seasonal produce from the nearby countryside bought in the local markets. Mushrooms, in autumn, and artichokes, in spring, are served in dozens of different ways, and the *mesticanza*, a fresh mix of salad leaves including the peppery *rughetta* (arugula) and *puntarelle* (curly endive shoots), is also delicious when it is in season in the summer months. Many of the genuinely Roman dishes are highly seasoned with onions, garlic, rosemary, sage, and bay leaves. The typical Roman meat dish, based on the so-called *quinto quarto* (fifth quarter) – head, tail, feet, and so on – is flavored with olive oil, herbs, *pancetta* (bacon), and *guanciale* (pigs' cheek) and is a culinary delight. *Pecorino*, a tangy sheep's milk cheese, is often sprinkled on dishes as seasoning, and the blander *ricotta* is a filling for pizzas as well as the Roman dessert *torta di ricotta*.

Sage leaves

Suppli di Riso *are fried rice croquettes stuffed with mozzarella. They are typically Roman and make an excellent snack.*

Batter-fried artichoke hearts

Batter-fried zucchini flowers

An antipasto *starts the meal and is usually a selection of appetizers based on the vegetables that are in season. The vegetables may be fresh, grilled, or preserved in aromatic oils or vinegar. Artichoke hearts and zucchini flowers are excellent in spring, and are used in a variety of dishes, including the fritto misto, a selection of local ingredients fried in batter.*

Filetti di Baccalà, *deep-fried cod fillets, were originally a Jewish specialty, and now a feature of Roman cuisine.*

Gnocchi alla Romana, *small semolina dumplings, can be eaten with tomato sauce or just with butter.*

Risotto alla Romana *is a rice dish made with a sauce of liver, sweetbreads, and Marsala, a fortified wine from Sicily.*

Bucatini all'Amatriciana *is hollow spaghetti-like pasta with bacon, tomatoes, and onion sprinkled with cheese.*

Spaghetti alla Carbonara, *devised in Rome, is made with pancetta, eggs, Parmesan cheese, and black pepper.*

Coda alla Vaccinara is a traditional Roman dish made from braised oxtail served with herbs and a tomato sauce.

Torta di Ricotta, a popular dessert from Rome, is a delicious cheesecake filled with ricotta, Marsala, and lemon.

Saltimbocca alla Romana is a tasty dish of veal with ham and sage. It can also be served rolled and skewered.

Fave al Guanciale are young spring fava beans, simmered in olive oil with pigs' cheeks (guanciale) and onion.

WHAT TO DRINK IN ROME AND LAZIO

Vines thrive in the warm climate and fertile land of Lazio, keeping up the wine-producing tradition that was started around the hills of Rome over 2,000 years ago by the ancient Romans. Today, wine is usually drunk with meals as a matter of course, and the region offers abundant supplies of inexpensive dry white wine for the city's restaurants and cafés. Of local bottled white wines, Frascati is the best known, but Castelli Romani, Marino, Colli Albani, and Velletri are very similar in style. All are made from one grape variety, the Trebbiano, though better quality versions contain a dash of Malvasia for perfume and flavor. Local red wine is rarer and most reds come from other parts of Italy. As well as the usual range of digestives and apéritifs, such as Campari, beer is also widely available; the popular Italian lager is Nastro Azzurro. Fruit juices are also good, and bars squeeze fresh orange juice *(spremuta)*. Rome's drinking water, another debt to the ancient Romans, is particularly good, fresh and sweet, and in abundant supply.

Frascati, the best known local white

Torre Ercolana, one of the few red wines produced in Lazio, is made in small quantities and generally regarded as one of the region's best wines. It is made from both the local Cesanese grapes and the more robust Cabernet, and should be aged for at least five years.

Drinking water in Rome, unlike many other Mediterranean cities, is excellent. The city benefits from a constant supply of fresh drinking water, piped down from the hills through a system of pipes and aqueducts that has changed very little since ancient Roman times. At regular intervals throughout the city, ornate fountains pump delicious fresh water for general use as well as for drinking. Only if there is a sign saying acqua non potabile *is the water not safe to drink.*

One of Rome's many fresh water drinking fountains

Coffee is almost more important to Roman life than wine. Drink espresso *for a shot of strong black coffee at any time of the day, sit with a* milky *cappuccino for breakfast or mid afternoon, or sip a caffe latte in a glass for extra milk.*

Espresso

Cappuccino

Caffe latte

Understanding Architecture in Rome and Lazio

THE ARCHITECTURE of Imperial Rome, a combination of Etruscan and Classical Greek styles, gradually developed new and uniquely Roman forms based on the arch, the vault, and the dome. During the early Christian period, simple rectangular basilicas were built, forms that by the 12th century had been incorporated into the stark Romanesque style. The Renaissance, inspired by the example of Florence, saw a return to Classical ideals of simplicity and harmonious proportions, but it was to be in the flamboyance of the 17th-century Baroque that Rome once again found great architectural expression.

The extravagant Baroque style of the Fontana di Trevi, Rome

FROM ETRUSCAN TO CLASSICAL ROME

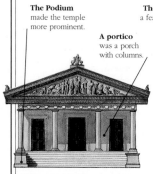

The Podium made the temple more prominent.

A portico was a porch with columns.

The arch became a feature of Roman architecture.

Reliefs were scavenged from earlier monuments.

Three naves divided the interior of the basilica.

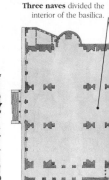

Etruscan temples, based on Greek models, inspired early Roman architecture. A front portico was the only entrance.

The Arch of Constantine (AD 315) is typical of triumphant Imperial Roman architecture (see p379). It stands at a colossal 25 m (82 ft).

Early Christian basilicas (4th century) were based on a rectangular floor plan.

FROM RENAISSANCE TO BAROQUE

Doric columns recall Classical architecture.

Bramante adopted the circular form of ancient temples.

Rustication, massive blocks divided by deep joints, was used for palazzi.

Ionic pilasters lend an air of elegance to the imposing upper stories.

The elliptical staircase was a typical feature of Mannerist houses.

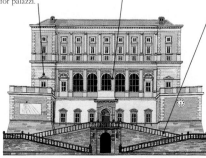

The Tempietto at San Pietro in Montorio, Rome (1502) is a model of Renaissance architecture: simple and perfectly proportioned (see p419).

Palazzo Farnese at Caprarola, a pentagonal building completed in 1575 (see p449), combines some Mannerist tricks of architecture with the strict geometric proportions characteristic of the Renaissance.

WHERE TO SEE THE ARCHITECTURE

A walk through the back streets of the center of Rome will reveal masterpieces of virtually every architectural age. The most ancient treasures are seven obelisks stolen from Egypt. One stands on the back of Bernini's elephant *(see p394)*. Highlights from Ancient Rome include triumphal arches and temples such as the Pantheon *(see p394)*. Romanesque elements survive in the church of San Clemente *(see p425)*, while the Renaissance finds expression in the dome of St. Peter's *(see pp408–9)*. Magnificent Baroque treasures dot the entire city, in particular flamboyant fountains that adorn the squares. Outside the city the outstanding sights are the late Renaissance villas such as Caprarola *(see p449)*.

Part of Bernini's elephant supporting an ancient Egyptian obelisk

---

Coffering reduces the weight of the dome.

The oculus, a hole at the top of the dome, provides the only light.

The portico dates from an earlier temple.

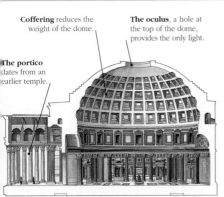

The Pantheon *(see p394) is one of the cardinal buildings of late Roman architecture. Completed in AD 125, it reveals how the form of the Greek temple was elaborated upon to create a masterpiece of perfect proportions.*

Corinthian capitals were decorated with acanthus leaves.

Doric columns had straight capitals.

Ionic columns had scrolled capitals.

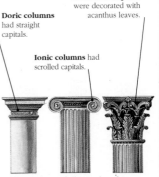

The orders *of Classical architecture were building styles based on ancient Greek models, identified by the column capitals.*

Columns around the altar draw attention away from the prominent lateral axis.

A concave portico reflects the oval body of the church.

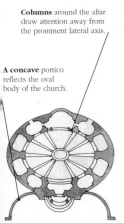

The oval floor plan *of the Baroque Sant'Andrea al Quirinale (see p401) makes ingenious use of restricted space.*

Engaged pillars replace the flat pilasters of the Renaissance.

Deep recesses create complex effects of light and shade.

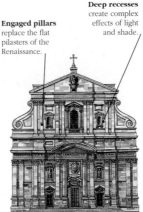

The Gesù *façade (1584) epitomizes Counter-Reformation architecture and has been imitated throughout the Catholic world (see p393).*

Two superimposed equilateral triangles form the complex hexagonal floor plan.

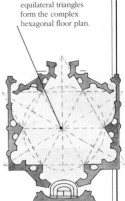

Sant'Ivo alla Sapienza's *floor plan (1642) favored grandiose design over Classical form (see p390).*

THE ANCIENT CENTER

THE CAPITOL, the southern summit of the Capitoline Hill, was the symbolic center of the Roman world and home to the city's three most important temples. These were dedicated to the god Jupiter Optimus Maximus, protector of Rome; Minerva, goddess of wisdom and war; and Juno Moneta, a guardian goddess. Below the Capitol lies

Capitoline Wolf with Romulus and Remus

the Forum, once the focus of political, social, legal, and commercial life; the Imperial Fora, built when Rome's population grew; and the Colosseum, the center of entertainment. Overlooking the Forum is the Palatine Hill, where Romulus is said to have founded Rome in the 8th century BC and emperors lived for over 400 years.

SIGHTS AT A GLANCE

GETTING THERE

The Capitoline is in walking distance of Piazza Venezia, the hub of the city bus routes, while the Forum, Colosseum, and Palatine are close to Metro Colosseo. Buses 81, 87, and 186 link Piazza Venezia and the Colosseum with Corso Rinascimento, in the heart of the *centro storico*.

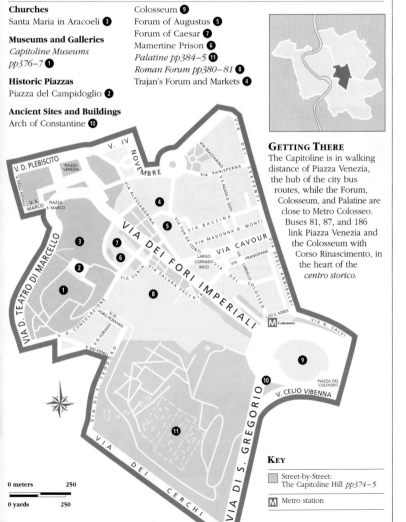

0 meters 250
0 yards 250

KEY

Street-by-Street: The Capitoline Hill *pp374–5*

M Metro station

◁ **View of the Colosseum rising behind the Forum**

Street-by-Street: The Capitoline Hill

THE CAPITOL, citadel of ancient Rome, was designed by Michelangelo in the 16th century. He was responsible for the trapezoid Piazza del Campidoglio as well as the Cordonata, the broad flight of steps leading up to it. The piazza is flanked by Palazzo Nuovo and Palazzo dei Conservatori, housing the Capitoline Museums, with their fine collections of sculpture and paintings. It is also well worth walking behind the museums to the Tarpeian Rock, for a fine view of the Forum lying below.

The Victor Emmanuel Monument was begun in 1885 and inaugurated in 1911 in honor of Victor Emmanuel II, the first king of unified Italy.

PIAZZA VENEZIA

San Marco, dedicated to the patron saint of Venice, has splendid 9th-century mosaics in the apse.

VIA DEL TEATRO DI MARCELLO

The Aracoeli Staircase was completed in 1348 to commemorate the end of the plague.

Palazzo Venezia, once the home of Mussolini, now holds a museum of fine and decorative arts. Exhibits include this medieval gilt and enamel angel.

The Cordonata is presided over by the colossal statues of Castor and Pollux.

★ **Capitoline Museums**
The collections of art and ancient sculpture include this statue of the Emperor Marcus Aurelius, a replica of which stands in the center of the piazza ❶

STAR SIGHT

★ **Capitoline Museums**

KEY

— — — Suggested route

0 meters   75

0 yards   75

Santa Maria in Aracoeli

The brick façade hides treasures such as this 15th-century fresco of the Funeral of San Bernardino *by Pinturicchio* ❸

LOCATOR MAP
See Rome Street Finder map 3

Palazzo Nuovo was made into a public museum in 1734.

Palazzo Senatorio, the splendid Renaissance seat of the city government, is built on the ruins of the ancient Tabularium.

Piazza del Campidoglio
Michelangelo designed the geometric paving and the façades of the buildings ❷

PIETRO IN CARCERE

Palazzo dei Conservatori

The Temple of Jupiter, represented on this coin, was dedicated to Jupiter Optimus Maximus, the most important of the Roman gods. He was believed to have the power to protect or destroy the city.

VIA DEL TEMPIO DI GIOVE

The Tarpeian Rock is a cliff from which traitors were believed to have been thrown to their death in ancient Rome.

Steps to the Capitoline

Capitoline Museums ❶

See pp376–7.

Piazza del Campidoglio ❷

Map 3 B5. 🚌 *40, 64, 65, 70, 75.*

WHEN EMPEROR CHARLES V announced he was to visit Rome in 1536, Pope Paul III Farnese asked Michelangelo to give the Capitoline a face-lift. He redesigned the piazza, renovated the façades of its palaces, and built a new staircase, the Cordonata. This gently rising ramp is now crowned with the massive statues of Castor and Pollux.

Santa Maria in Aracoeli ❸

Piazza d'Aracoeli. **Map** 3 B5.
📞 *06 679 81 55.* 🚌 *64, 65, 70, 75.*
🕐 *7am–6pm daily.*

THIS CHURCH STANDS on the site of the Temple of Juno, on the northern summit of the Capitoline Hill, and dates back at least to the 6th century. The church is famous today for its ornate gilded ceiling and a very fine series of frescoes by Pinturicchio, dating from the 1480s. They depict scenes from the life of San Bernardino of Siena. The miracle-working *Santo Bambino* fiure was stolen in 1994 but has been replaced by a replica.

The marble staircase and austere façade of Santa Maria in Aracoeli

Capitoline Museums: ❶
Palazzo Nuovo

A COLLECTION of Classical sculptures has been kept on the Capitoline Hill since Pope Sixtus IV donated a group of bronze sculptures to the city in 1471. Paintings as well as sculpture are now housed in two palaces designed by Michelangelo. The Palazzo Nuovo, first opened to the public in 1734 by Pope Clement XII, contains a fine selection of Greek and Roman sculptures.

LOCATOR MAP

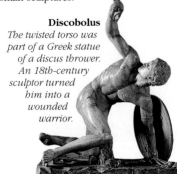

Discobolus
The twisted torso was part of a Greek statue of a discus thrower. An 18th-century sculptor turned him into a wounded warrior.

Alexander Severus as Hunter
In this marble of the 3rd century AD, the emperor's pose is a pastiche of the mythical hero, Perseus, holding up the head of Medusa the Gorgon after he had killed her.

Mosaic of the Doves
This 1st-century AD naturalistic mosaic once decorated the floor of Hadrian's Villa at Tivoli (see p452).

Stairs to ground floor

Stairs to first floor

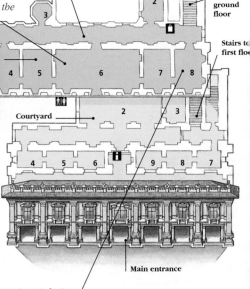

Courtyard

Main entrance

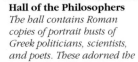

Hall of the Philosophers
The ball contains Roman copies of portrait busts of Greek politicians, scientists, and poets. These adorned the homes of wealthy Romans.

Dying Galatian
Great compassion is conveyed in this Roman copy of a Greek work of the 3rd century BC.

KEY TO FLOORPLAN

☐ Ground floor
☐ First floor
☐ Second floor
☐ Nonexhibition space

Palazzo dei Conservatori

THE PALAZZO DEI CONSERVATORI was the seat of the city's magistrates during the late Middle Ages. Its frescoed halls are still used occasionally for political meetings, and the ground floor houses the municipal registry office. While much of the palazzo is given over to sculpture, including fragments of a huge sculpture of Constantine, the art galleries on the second floor hold works by Veronese, Tintoretto, Caravaggio, Van Dyck, and Titian.

VISITORS' CHECKLIST

Musei Capitolini, Piazza del Campidoglio. **Map** 3 B5.
📞 06 67 10 20 71. 🚌 40, 63, 64, 70, 73, 81, 87 & many other routes through Piazza Venezia.
🕐 9am–7pm Tue–Sun, 9am–1:45pm public holidays.
⬤ Jan 1, May 1, Dec 25.
🎟 free last Sun of every month; entrance ticket is valid for both museums. 📷

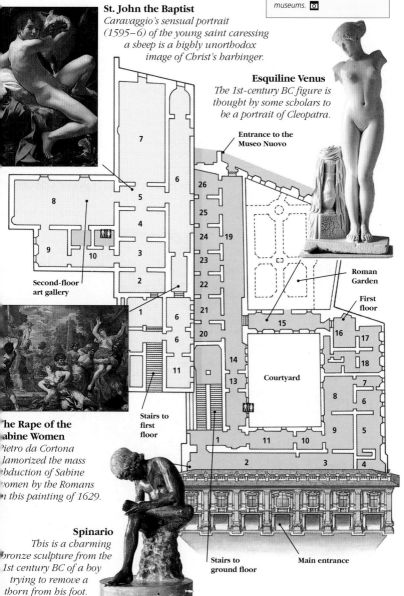

St. John the Baptist
Caravaggio's sensual portrait (1595–6) of the young saint caressing a sheep is a highly unorthodox image of Christ's harbinger.

Esquiline Venus
The 1st-century BC figure is thought by some scholars to be a portrait of Cleopatra.

Entrance to the Museo Nuovo

Second-floor art gallery

Roman Garden

First floor

Courtyard

Stairs to first floor

The Rape of the Sabine Women
Pietro da Cortona glamorized the mass abduction of Sabine women by the Romans in this painting of 1629.

Spinario
This is a charming bronze sculpture from the 1st century BC of a boy trying to remove a thorn from his foot.

Stairs to ground floor

Main entrance

Trajan's Forum and Markets ❹

Map 3 B4. **Trajan's Forum**, Via dei Fori Imperiali. ● *to the public.*
Trajan's Markets, Via IV Novembre.
📞 *06 679 00 48.* ⏱ *9am–6:30pm Tue–Sat, 9am–2pm Sun.* ● *Mon, public hols.* 📷 ♿

TRAJAN BEGAN to build his forum in AD 107 to commemorate his final conquest of Dacia (present day Romania) after successful campaigns in AD 101–2 and 105–6. His new forum was the most ambitious yet, with a vast colonnaded open space centering on an equestrian statue of the emperor, a huge basilica, and two big libraries. Dominating the ruins today is **Trajan's Column**, which originally stood between the two libraries.

Trajan's Column

Spiraling up its 30-m-high (98 ft) stem are minutely detailed scenes from the Dacian campaigns, beginning with the Romans preparing for war and ending with the Dacians being ousted from their homeland. The subtly modeled reliefs were designed to be seen from viewing platforms on the libraries, and are consequently difficult to interpret from ground level. If you want to examine the scenes in detail there are casts in the Museo della Civiltà Romana *(see p432).* The **market** complex, which is situated directly behind the forum, was begun slightly earlier. Like the forum it was probably designed by Apollodorus of Damascus, and was the

Via Biberatica, the main street through Trajan's Markets

ancient Roman equivalent of the modern shopping center. There were about 150 shops selling everything from orient silks and spices to fruit, fresh fish, and flowers. It was also here that the *annone*, or grai dole, was distributed. This wa a free ration of grain given to Roman men, a practice that was introduced in the Republ by politicians who wanted to buy votes and prevent unres during periods of famine.

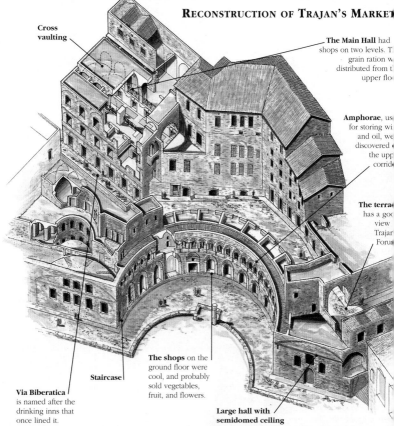

RECONSTRUCTION OF TRAJAN'S MARKE

Cross vaulting

The Main Hall had shops on two levels. T grain ration w distributed from t upper flo

Amphorae, us for storing wi and oil, we discovered the upp corrid

The terra has a goo view Trajar Foru

Via Biberatica is named after the drinking inns that once lined it.

Staircase

The shops on the ground floor were cool, and probably sold vegetables, fruit, and flowers.

Large hall with semidomed ceiling

Forum of Augustus ❺

Piazza del Grillo 1. **Map** 3 B5.
🚌 87, 186. ⭕ by appt. 🎫 includes entry to Trajan's Markets.

T HE FORUM of Augustus, which once stretched from a high wall at the foot of sleazy Suburra to the edge of Caesar's Forum, was built to celebrate Augustus's victory in 41 BC over Brutus and Cassius, the assassins of Julius Caesar. As a consequence the temple in its center was dedicated to Mars the Avenger. The temple, with its cracked steps and four Corinthian columns, is easily identified. Originally it had a statue of Mars that looked very like Augustus, but in case anyone failed to notice the resemblance, a colossal statue of the emperor himself was placed against the wall of the Suburra quarter.

19th-century engraving of the Mamertine Prison

Mamertine Prison ❻

Clivo Argentario 1. **Map** 3 B5.
📞 06 69 94 10 20. 🚌 84, 85, 87, 175, 186. ⭕ 9am–noon, 2–5pm daily. **Donation**. 📷

B ELOW THE 16th-century church of San Giuseppe dei Falegnami is a dank dungeon in which, according to Christian legend, St. Peter and St. Paul were imprisoned. They are said to have caused a spring to bubble up into the

Podium of the Temple of Mars the Avenger, Forum of Augustus

cell, and to have used the water to baptize two prison guards. The prison was in an old cistern with access to the city's main sewer (the Cloaca Maxima). The lower cell was used for executions, and corpses were thrown into the sewer. However, the inmates, who received no food, often died of starvation.

Forum of Caesar ❼

Via del Carcere Tulliano. **Map** 3 B5.
📞 06 678 29 28. 🚌 84, 85, 87, 175,186, 810, 850. ⭕ by appt only: permit needed (see p614).

T HE FIRST of Rome's Imperial fora was built by Julius Caesar to relieve congestion in the Roman Forum when Rome's population boomed. He spent a fortune – most of it booty from his recent conquest of Gaul – buying up and demolishing houses on the site. Pride of place went to a temple dedicated in 46 BC to Venus Genetrix (Venus the Ancestor) since Caesar claimed to be descended from the goddess. The temple contained statues of Caesar and Cleopatra as well as of Venus, but all that remains today is a platform and three Corinthian columns. The forum was once enclosed by a double colonnade, under which was sheltered a row of shops. However, this burned down in AD 80 and was rebuilt by Domitian and Trajan. The latter also added the

Basilica Argentaria – which became an important financial exchange – as well as shops and a heated public lavatory.

Roman Forum ❽

See pp380–81.

Colosseum ❾

See p383.

Arch of Constantine ❿

Between Via di San Gregorio and Piazza del Colosseo. **Map** 7 A1.
🚌 75, 85, 87, 110, 175, 673, 810.
🚋 13. Ⓜ Colosseo.

T HIS TRIUMPHAL ARCH is one of Imperial Rome's last monuments, built in AD 315, a few years before Constantine moved the capital of the Empire to Byzantium. It was built to celebrate Constantine's victory in AD 312 over his co-emperor Maxentius at the Battle of the Milvian Bridge. Constantine attributed the victory to a dream in which he was told to mark his men's shields with *chi-rho*, the first two Greek letters of Christ's name. Christian tradition prefers a version in which the emperor has a vision of the Cross, mid-battle. There is nothing Christian about the arch; most of the reliefs were from earlier pagan monuments.

Palatine ⓫

See pp384–5.

The north side of the Arch of Constantine

Roman Forum ❽

IN THE EARLY REPUBLIC, the Forum was a chaotic place, with food stalls and brothels as well as temples and the Senate House. By the 2nd century BC it was decided that Rome required a more salubrious center, and the food stores were replaced by business centers and law courts. The Forum remained the ceremonial center of the city under the Empire, with emperors renovating old buildings and erecting new temples and monuments.

Arch of Septimius Severus
This triumphal arch was erected in AD 203, the 10th anniversary of Emperor Septimius Severus' accession.

The Temple of Antonin **and Faustina** is no incorporated into the church of Sa Lorenzo Miranda

Temple of Saturn

The Rostra was the orator's tribune from which speeches were made.

The Curia, or ancient Roman Senate House, has been reconstructed.

Basilica Julia
Named after Julius Caesar, who began its construction in 54 BC, this was the seat of the civil magistrates court.

Basilica Aemilia was a meeting hall for business and money exchange.

Temple of Vesta

Temple of Castor and Pollux
Although there has been a temple here since the 5th century BC, the columns and elaborate cornice date from AD 6 when the temple was rebuilt.

0 meters   75

0 yards   75

★ **House of the Vestal Virgins**
The priestesses who tended the sacred flame in the Temple of Vesta lived here. The house was a large rectangular building around a central garden.

★ Basilica of Constantine and Maxeritius
The basilica's three vast barrel vaults are all that remain of the Forum's largest building. Like other basilicas, it was used for the administration of justice and conducting business.

VISITORS' CHECKLIST

Entrances: Largo Romolo e Remo and near the Arch of Titus on Via Sacra. **Map** 3 B5.
📞 06 699 01 10. 🚌 75, 81, 85, 87, 117, 175, 186, 810, 850. Ⓜ Colosseo. 🚋 13. 🕐 9am–1 hr before sunset daily. ⬤ Jan 1, May 1, Dec 25.
📷 🚻 ♿ 🛒

The Temple of Romulus, now part of the church of Santi Cosma e Damiano that stands behind it, retains its original 4th-century bronze doors.

Arch of Titus
This arch was erected by Emperor Domitian in AD 81 to commemorate the sack of Jerusalem by his father, Vespasian, and brother Titus, 13 years earlier.

VIA DEI FORI IMPERIALI

VIA SACRA

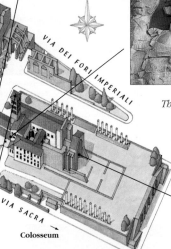

Antiquarium Forense
This small museum contains finds from the Forum. Exhibits range from Iron Age burial urns to this frieze of Aeneas from the Basilica Aemilia.

The Temple of Venus and Rome was built in AD 135, and was largely designed by Hadrian.

VIA SACRA
Colosseum ←

Palatine

Santa Francesca Romana
The Romanesque bell tower of Santa Francesca Romana towers over one of a number of churches built among the ruins of the Forum.

THE VESTAL VIRGINS

The cult of Vesta, the goddess of fire, dates back to at least the 8th century BC. Romulus and Remus were allegedly born of the Vestal priestess Rhea and the god Mars. Six virgins kept the sacred flame of Vesta burning in her circular temple. The girls, who came from noble families, were selected when they were between six and ten years old, and served for 30 years. They had high status and financial security, but were buried alive if they lost their virginity and whipped by the high priest if the sacred flame died out. Although they were permitted to marry after finishing their service, few did so.

Honorary statue of a Vestal Virgin

Exploring the Roman Forum

To appreciate the layout of the Roman Forum before wandering through its confusing patchwork of ruined temples, triumphal arches, and basilicas, it is best to view the whole area from the Capitoline Hill above. From there you can make out the more substantial ruins, and the course of the Via Sacra (Sacred Way), the route followed through the Forum by religious and triumphal processions making their way up to the Capitol to give thanks at the Temple of Jupiter (see p375).

Corinthian columns of the Temple of Castor and Pollux

The Main Sights

The first building you come to on entering the Forum is the **Basilica Aemilia**. A rectangular hall built in 179 BC, it was a meeting place for moneylenders, businessmen, and tax collectors. Although little more remains of it than a pastel marble pavement fringed with column stumps, you can still find splashes of verdigrised bronze, reputedly the remains of coins that melted when the Visigoths invaded Rome and burned down the basilica in the 5th century.

Inside the Curia – the stark brick building next to the basilica – are the **Plutei of Trajan**, relief panels commissioned by either Trajan or Hadrian to decorate the Rostra, the public oratory platform. On one panel are piles of books holding tax records, which Trajan had destroyed in order to free citizens from debts. The **Arch of Septimius Severus** is the best preserved of the Forum's monuments. The marble relief panels depict the military triumphs of the emperor in Parthia (modern-day Iran and Iraq) and Arabia.

The **Temple of Saturn** was the focus of the annual Saturnalia celebrations, when, for up to a week in December, schools closed, slaves dined with their masters, presents were exchanged, and a fair and market were held.

Soaring above the remains of the **Basilica Julia** are three delicately fluted columns and a finely carved slab of entablature taken from the **Temple of Castor and Pollux**. This striking relic is dedicated to the twin brothers of Helen of Troy, who were supposed to have appeared at the battle of Lake Regillus in 499 BC, aiding the Romans in their defeat of the Etruscans.

The elegant circular **Temple of Vesta** was one of ancient Rome's most sacred shrines and was dedicated to the goddess of the hearth. The flame, kept alive by the Vestal Virgins, symbolized the perpetuity of the state, and its extinction prophesied doom for the city. The building was

Restored section of Temple of Vesta

partly reconstructed in 1930, but the circular form goes back to the Latin mud huts that originally occupied the site. Just behind is the **House of the Vestal Virgins**, the living quarters of the priestess and the Vestals. This enormous complex of 50 rooms was once annexed to the Temple. Best preserved are the rooms overlooking a pretty courtyard, ornamented with statues of Vestals, ponds of waterlilies, and rose trees.

On the other side of the Forum lie the impressive remains of the **Basilica of Constantine**. It was begun in AD 308 by Maxentius and is therefore also known as the Basilica of Maxentius.

Constantine completed it after he defeated his rival at the battle of the Milvian Bridge in AD 312. The remains of the huge arches and ceilings give an indication of the original scale and grandeur of the forum's public buildings. Three enormous coffered vaults remain, which originally measured up to 35 m (115 ft) and were faced with marble. The interior walls, which held niches for statues, were also covered with marble below and stucco above. Remains of a spiral staircase that once led to the roof can be found scattered on the ground.

The basilica's apse and hexagonal arches were often used as models by Renaissance architects striving to re-create a Classical symmetry and nobility in their work. They include Michelangelo, who allegedly studied the basilica's architecture when working on the dome of St. Peter's.

Central courtyard of the House of the Vestal Virgins

Colosseum 9

Gladiator's shield

ROME'S GREATEST amphitheater was commissioned by Emperor Vespasian in AD 72. Deadly gladiatorial combats and wild animal fights were staged by emperors and wealthy citizens, largely to gain popularity. Slaughter was on a huge scale; at the inaugural games in AD 80, over 9,000 wild animals were killed. The Colosseum could hold up to 55,000 people, who were seated according to rank.

The Velarium, a huge sailcloth awning that sheltered spectators from the sun, was supported by poles on the upper story.

VISITORS' CHECKLIST

Piazza del Colosseo. **Map** 7 B1.
📞 06 39 74 99 07. 🚌 75, 81,
85, 87, 117, 175, 673, 810. Ⓜ
Colosseo. 🚊 13, 30b to Piazza
del Colosseo. ◻ 9am–7pm (4pm
in winter) Thu–Tue, 9am–1pm Wed
& public hols. ◼ Jan 1, May 1,
Dec 25. 🎫 for upper level. 📷 🎧.

Internal Corridors
These allowed the large and often unruly crowd to move freely and be seated quickly.

The Colossus of Nero
This gilt bronze statue from Nero's palace, over which the Colosseum was built, may have given the amphitheater its name.

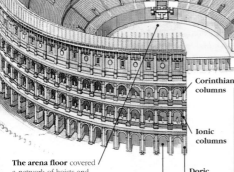

Entry routes
and stairs led to seats at the various levels. The emperor and consul had their own, separate entrances.

Corinthian columns

Ionic columns

The arena floor covered a network of hoists and cages for wild animals.

Doric columns

Doric, Ionic, and Corinthian Tiers
The tiers inspired many Renaissance architects, who plundered the building, using its travertine marble to build palaces and part of St. Peter's.

Entrances

Roman Gladiators
These were originally soldiers in training. Their combat became a sport, and slaves, prisoners of war, or criminals were forced to fight men or wild animals to the death.

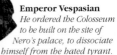

Emperor Vespasian
He ordered the Colosseum to be built on the site of Nero's palace, to dissociate himself from the hated tyrant.

Palatine ⓫

Statue of the Goddess Cybele

The PALATINE, once the residence of emperors and aristocrats, is the most pleasant of Rome's ancient sites. The ruins range from the simple house in which Augustus is thought to have lived, to the Domus Flavia and Domus Augustana, the public and private wings of a luxurious palace built by Domitian.

The House of Augustus is thought to have been the public part of the emperor's modest home.

The Huts of Romulus, indicated by holes left by the supporting posts, were reputedly founded by Romulus in the 9th century BC.

Temple of Cybele, Goddess of fertility

★ House of Livia
Many of the wall paintings have survived in the private quarters of the house where Augustus is believed to have lived with his wife, Livia.

★ Domus Flavia
The courtyard of the Domus Flavia was lavishly paved with colored marble. The Roman poets praised this villa as the most splendid.

Domus Augustana was the private home of the emperors.

STAR SIGHTS

★ Domus Flavia

★ House of Livia

0 meters   75
0 yards   75

Emperor Septimius Severus
During his reign (AD 193–211), he extended the Domus Augustana and built an impressive bath complex.

Cryptoporticus
This underground gallery, elaborately decorated with stuccoed walls, was built by Emperor Nero.

A HISTORY OF THE PALATINE HILL

Romans of the Decadence by Thomas Couture (1815–79)

The courtyard of the Domus Flavia was lined by Domitian with mirrorlike marble, so he could spot would-be assassins.

The exedra of the stadium may have housed a balcony.

↗ **Forum entrance**

Stadium
Part of the Imperial palace, this enclosure may have been used by the emperors as a private garden.

The Palace of Septimius Severus
This extension of the Domus Augustana projected beyond the hillside, supported on giant arches.

The Founding of Rome
According to legend the twins Romulus and Remus were brought up on the Palatine by a wolf. Here Romulus, having killed his brother, is said to have founded the village that was destined to become Rome. Traces of mud huts dating back to the 8th century BC have been found on the hill, lending archaeological support to the legend.

The Republic
By the 1st century BC the Palatine was the most desirable address in Rome and home to the leading citizens of the Republic. Its residents, including the erotic poet Catullus and the orator Cicero, were notoriously indulgent, and their villas were magnificent dwellings with doors of ivory, floors of bronze, and frescoed walls.

The Empire
Augustus was born on the Palatine in 63 BC, and lived there in a modest house after becoming emperor. The hill was therefore an obvious choice of abode for future emperors. Domitian's ambitious house, the Domus Flavia (1st century AD), and its private quarters, the Domus Augustana, remained the official residence of future emperors (who were re-ferred to as *Augustus*) for more than 300 years.

Around Piazza Navona

Detail of an 18th-century street shrine

HE AREA around Piazza Navona, known as the *centro storico*, has been inhabited for at least 2,000 years. Piazza Navona stands above an ancient stadium; the Pantheon has been a temple since AD 27; and the Theater of Marcellus in the Ghetto has been converted into fine apartments. The area's heyday began in the 15th century, when the papacy returned to Rome. Throughout the Renaissance and Baroque eras princes, popes, and cardinals settled here, as did the artists and artisans they commissioned to build and adorn lavish palaces, churches, and fountains.

SIGHTS AT A GLANCE

Churches and Temples
Chiesa Nuova ❻
Gesù ⓭
La Maddalena ⓴
Sant'Ignazio di Loyola ⓱
Sant'Ivo alla Sapienza ❷
San Luigi dei Francesi ❸
Santa Maria sopra Minerva ⓯
Santa Maria della Pace ❺

Museums and Galleries
Palazzo Doria Pamphilj ⓮
Palazzo Spada ❿

Ancient Sites and Buildings
Area Sacra di Largo Argentina ⓬
Pantheon ⓰

Historic Buildings
Palazzo Altemps ❹
Palazzo della Cancelleria ❼
Palazzo Farnese ❾

Historic Piazzas and Areas
Campo de' Fiori ❽
Ghetto and Tiber Island ⓫
Piazza Colonna ⓲
Piazza di Montecitorio ⓳
Piazza Navona ❶

GETTING THERE

Corso Vittorio Emanuele II, Largo Argentina, and Corso Rinascimento are main bus arteries, but only minibus 116 runs along the narrow streets of the *centro storico*.

KEY

Street-by-Street: Around Piazza Navona *pp388–9*

Street-by-Street: Around the Pantheon *pp392–3*

P Parking

0 meters 250
0 yards 250

◁ **Piazza Navona, with the Fontana del Moro (1653) and the 17th-century church of Sant'Agnese in Agone**

Street-by-Street: Around Piazza Navona

No OTHER PIAZZA in Rome can rival the theatricality of Piazza Navona. The luxurious cafés are the social center of the city, and day and night there is always something going on in the pedestrian area around the three flamboyant Baroque fountains. The Baroque is also represented in many of the area's churches. To discover an older Rome, walk along Via del Governo Vecchio to admire the façades of Renaissance buildings, browse in the fascinating antique shops, and lunch in one of the many trattorias.

The Torre dell'Orologio by Borromini (1648) formed part of the Oratorio dei Filippini.

Chiesa Nuova
This church was rebuilt in 1575 for the order founded by San Filippo Neri ❻

The Vatican

VIA DEL CORALLO

VIA DEL GOVERNO VECCHIO

VIA DI PARIONE

At the Oratorio dei Filippini (1637) biblical stories were sung and the congregation responded with a chorus: thus, the origin of the oratorio.

Via del Governo Vecchio preserves a large number of fine Renaissance houses.

CORSO VITTORIO EMANUELE II

PIAZZA DI PASQUINO

Santa Maria della Pace
This Renaissance church has frescoes of the Four Sibyls by Raphael and a refined courtyard by Bramante. The Baroque portico is by Pietro da Cortona ❺

STAR SIGHTS

★ **Piazza Navona**

Pasquino is a 3rd-century BC Hellenistic statue of Menelaus. Romans have been hanging satirical verses at its feet since the 16th century.

Palazzo Braschi, a late 18th-century building designed by Cosimo Morelli, has a splendid balcony overlooking the piazza.

Palazzo Pamphilj

Fontana del Moro

Campo de' Fiori

KEY

--- — Suggested route

| 0 meters | 75 |
| 0 yards | 75 |

Sant'Andrea della Valle, begun in 1591, has a flamboyant Baroque façade flanked by angels with outstretched wings by Ercole Ferrata. The church is the setting of the first act of Puccini's *Tosca*.

Sant'Agnese in Agone
by Borromini (1657)
is allegedly built
on the site where,
in AD 304, the
young St. Agnes
was exposed
naked to force
her to renounce
her faith.

LOCATOR MAP
*See Rome Street Finder
map 2*

**Fontana dei
Quattro Fiumi**

San Luigi dei Francesi
*This church, which was
completed in 1589, is best
known for three paintings
by Caravaggio* ❸

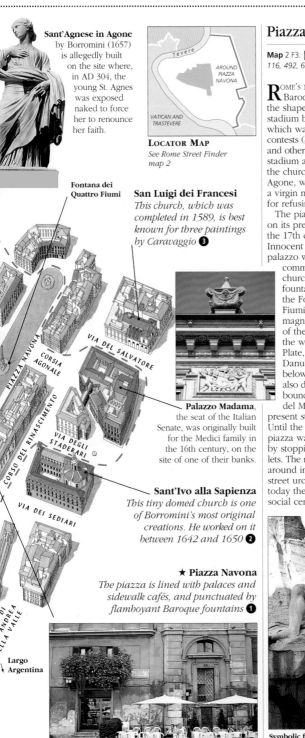

Palazzo Madama,
the seat of the Italian
Senate, was originally built
for the Medici family in
the 16th century, on the
site of one of their banks.

Sant'Ivo alla Sapienza
*This tiny domed church is one
of Borromini's most original
creations. He worked on it
between 1642 and 1650* ❷

★ Piazza Navona
*The piazza is lined with palaces and
sidewalk cafés, and punctuated by
flamboyant Baroque fountains* ❶

Largo
Argentina

Piazza Navona ❶

Map 2 F3. 🚌 *40, 46, 62, 64, 81, 87,
116, 492, 628, 810.*

ROME'S MOST BEAUTIFUL
Baroque piazza follows
the shape of a 1st-century AD
stadium built by Domitian,
which was used for athletic
contests (*agones*), chariot races,
and other sports. Traces of the
stadium are still visible below
the church of Sant'Agnese in
Agone, which is dedicated to
a virgin martyred on the site
for refusing to marry a pagan.

The piazza began to take
on its present appearance in
the 17th century, when Pope
Innocent X, whose family
palazzo was on the piazza,
commissioned a new
church, palace, and
fountain. The fountain,
the Fontana dei Quattro
Fiumi, is Bernini's most
magnificent, with statues
of the four great rivers of
the world (the Nile, the
Plate, the Ganges, and the
Danube) sitting on rocks
below an obelisk. Bernini
also designed the muscle-
bound Moor in the Fontana
del Moro, though the
present statue is a copy.
Until the 19th century, the
piazza was flooded in August
by stopping the fountain outlets. The rich would splash
around in carriages, while
street urchins paddled. Even
today the piazza remains the
social center of the city.

Symbolic figure of the Nile River on
Bernini's Fontana dei Quattro Fiumi

Sant'Ivo alla Sapienza ❷

Corso del Rinascimento 40. **Map** 2 F4.
📞 06 686 49 87. 🚌 40, 46, 64, 70,
81, 87, 116, 186, 492, 628. ⬜ 9am–
noon, 6–8pm Sat (Sun am for mass).
🔲 Jul–Aug. 📷 🛗

H IDDEN IN the courtyard of
Palazzo della Sapienza,
seat of the old University of
Rome, Sant'Ivo's spiral belfry
is nevertheless a distinctive
landmark on Rome's skyline.
Built by Borromini in 1642–60,
the church is astonishingly
complex, an ingenious combination of concave and convex
surfaces. The work spanned
the reigns of three popes, and
incorporated in the design are
their emblems: Urban VIII's
bee, Innocent X's dove and
olive branch, and the star and
hills of Alexander VII.

San Luigi dei Francesi ❸

Via Santa Giovanna d'Arco. **Map** 4 F4
& 12 D2. 📞 06 688 27 1. 🚌 70,
81, 87, 116, 180, 186, 492, 628.
⬜ 8:30am–12:30pm, 3:30–7pm
daily. 🔲 Thu pm. 📷

T HE FRENCH NATIONAL church
in Rome, San Luigi is a
16th-century building, best
known for three magnificent
canvases by Caravaggio in the
Cerasi chapel. Painted between
1597 and 1602, these were
Caravaggio's first significant
religious works: *The Calling
of St. Matthew, Martyrdom of
St. Matthew,* and *St. Matthew
and the Angel.* The first version
of this last was initially rejected
because it depicted the saint
as an old man with dirty feet.

**Detail from Caravaggio's *The Calling of St.
Matthew* (1597–1602) in San Luigi dei Francesi**

**Side relief of the Ludovisi Throne,
on display in the Palazzo Altemps**

Palazzo Altemps ❹

Via di Sant'Apollinare 46. **Map** 2 F3.
📞 06 39 74 99 07. 🚌 70, 81, 87,
115, 280, 628. ⬜ 9am–6:45pm
Tue–Sat, 9am–7:45pm Sun. 🎫

A N EXTRAORDINARY collection
of Classical sculpture is
housed in this branch of the
Museo Nazionale Romano
(see p402). Restored as a
museum during the 1990s, the
palazzo was originally built
for Girolamo Riario, nephew
of Pope Sixtus IV in 1480. In
the popular uprising that
followed the pope's death in
1484, the building was
sacked and Girolamo
fled the city. In 1568
the palazzo
was bought
by Cardinal
Marco
Sittico
Altemps.
and renovated
in the 1570s by
Martino Longhi
the Elder, who
added the obe-
lisk-crowned
belvedere
and marble
unicorn.
The Altemps
family were keen
collectors; the
courtyard and its
staircase are lined with ancient
sculptures, which complement
the Ludovisi sculp-
tures. One of the
highlights is the
statue of *Galatea's
Suicide,* a marble
copy of the bronze
original, in the Sal-
one del Camino.
Also on the first
floor is the Greek,
5th-century BC
Ludovisi Throne.
One of the carved
reliefs shows a
woman represent-
ing Aphrodite.

***Galatea's Suicide* in
the Palazzo Altemps**

Santa Maria della Pace ❺

Vicolo dell'Arco della Pace 5. **Map** 2
E3. 📞 06 686 11 56. 🚌 46, 62, 6
70, 81, 87, 116, 492, 628, 810. ⬜
newly open; call to check. 📷 🛗

D ESIGNED IN 1656 by Pietro
da Cortona, the façade
of Santa Maria della Pace
embraces an intimate piazza.
The church itself, named by
Pope Sixtus IV to celebrate
the peace he hoped to bring
to Italy, dates from the 1480s
The refined cloister,
Bramante's first work in
Rome, was added in 1504.

Chiesa Nuova ❻

Piazza della Chiesa Nuova. **Map**
2 E4. 📞 06 687 52 89. 🚌 46,
64. ⬜ 8am–noon, 4:30–
6:30pm daily. 📷 🛗

S AN FILIPPO NERI
commissioned
this church in 1575
to replace the dilap
idated medieval
church his Order
had been given by
Pope Gregory XIII.
Neri required his
followers to humble
themselves, and set
aristocratic young
men to work as la-
borers on the church.
Against Neri's wishes,
the nave, dome,
and apse were
flamboyantly
frescoed after
his death by
Pietro da Cortona.
There are also
three paintings by
Rubens around the altar. The
first versions were rejected, so
Rubens repainted them on
slate, placing the originals
above his mother's tomb.

Palazzo della Cancelleria ❼

Piazza della Cancelleria. **Map** 2 E4.
📞 06 69 89 34 91. 🚌 46, 62, 64, 70
81, 87, 116, 492. ⬜ 4–8pm Mon–
Sat with permit from Vatican only.

A SUPREME EXAMPLE of the
confident delicacy of
early Renaissance architecture,

his palazzo was begun in 485, allegedly financed by he proceeds of a single night's ambling by Raffaele Riario, a ephew of Pope Sixtus I. In 478 Riario was involved in he Pazzi conspiracy against he Medici, and when Giovanni de'Medici became Pope Leo XIII in 1513, he took elated revenge, seizing the Riario palace and turning it nto the papal chancellery.

Tiber Island, with Ponte Cestio, built in 46 BC, linking it to Trastevere

Campo de' Fiori ⑧

Map 2 F4. 🚌 116 & routes to Largo i Torre Argentina.

CAMPO DE' FIORI (field of flowers), was one of the veliest and roughest areas of nedieval and Renaissance Rome. Cardinals and nobles ningled with fishmongers nd foreigners in the piazza's narket; Caravaggio killed his pponent after losing a game f tennis on the square; and he goldsmith Cellini murdered business rival nearby. Today, he area continues to be a hub f secular activity. The colorful narket, trattorias and down-o-earth bars retain the original nimated atmosphere.

In the Renaissance the iazza was surrounded by nns, many of which were wned by the 15th-century ourtesan Vannozza Catanei, nistress of Pope Alexander VI.

The square was also a place f execution. The hooded tatue in its center is the

philosopher Giordano Bruno, burnt at the stake for heresy on this spot in 1600 for suggesting the earth moved around the sun.

Palazzo Farnese ⑨

Piazza Farnese. **Map** 2 E5. 🚌 23, 116, 280 & routes to Largo di Torre Argentina. ⬛ to the public.

ORIGINALLY CONSTRUCTED for Cardinal Alessandro Farnese, who became Pope Paul III in 1534, this palazzo was started by Antonio da Sangallo the Younger, and continued after his death by Michelangelo, who created the cornice on the façade and the courtyard's third story.

The palace, now the French Embassy, is closed to the public, but when the chandeliers are lit at night you may be able to glimpse the ceiling of the Galleria, an illusionistic masterpiece by Annibale Carracci (1597–1603) based on Ovid's *Metamorphoses*.

Palazzo Spada ⑩

Piazza Capo di Ferro 13. **Map** 2 F5. 📞 06 686 11 58. 🚌 23, 116, 280 & routes to Largo di Torre Argentina. ⬛ 9am–7pm Tue–Sat, 9am–1pm Sun. ⬛ Jan 1, May 1, Dec 25. 🖼 📷 ⬛

A STUCCO extravaganza studded with reliefs of illustrious Romans and swags of flowers, Palazzo Spada was built in 1550, but bought in 1637 by Cardinal Bernardino Spada. A keen patron of the arts, he commissioned Borromini to create an illusionistic tunnel from the courtyard that appears four times longer than it is. The cardinal's superb art collection, which is now shown in the Galleria Spada, includes works by Guercino, Dürer, and Artemisia Gentileschi.

Ghetto and Tiber Island ⑪

Map 3 A5. 🚌 23, 63, 280, 780 and routes to Largo di Torre Argentina.

THE FIRST JEWS came to Rome as traders in the 2nd century BC and were greatly appreciated for their financial and medical skills during the Roman Empire. Persecution began in the 16th century, when Pope Paul IV forced all Jews to live within a walled enclosure, an area later to form the hub of the present-day Ghetto. Today Via del Portico d'Ottavia, the district's main street, leads to Rome's central synagogue, passing restaurants and shops selling Roman Jewish food. Ponte Fabricio links the Ghetto with Tiber Island, a centre of healing since 293 BC when a Temple to Aesculapius was founded. The island is now home to a hospital.

ruit stands at Campo de' Fiori's lively morning market

Street-by-Street: Around the Pantheon

THE MAZE OF NARROW STREETS around the Pantheon is a mixture of lively restaurants and cafés, and some of Rome's finest sights. This is also the city's financial and political district, home to Parliament, government offices, and the stock exchange. The Pantheon itself, with its awe-inspiring domed interior, has long been a symbol of the city.

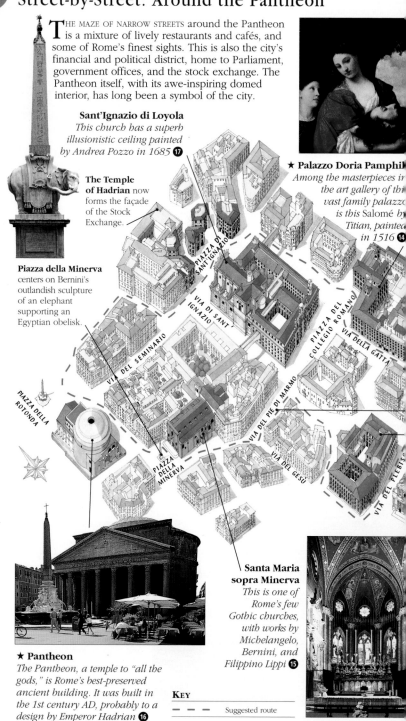

Sant'Ignazio di Loyola
This church has a superb illusionistic ceiling painted by Andrea Pozzo in 1685 ⓲

The Temple of Hadrian now forms the façade of the Stock Exchange.

★ Palazzo Doria Pamphilj
Among the masterpieces in the art gallery of this vast family palazzo is this Salomé *by Titian, painted in 1516* ⓮

Piazza della Minerva
centers on Bernini's outlandish sculpture of an elephant supporting an Egyptian obelisk.

PIAZZA DI SANT'IGNAZIO

VIA DI SANT'IGNAZIO

VIA DEL SEMINARIO

PIAZZA DEL COLLEGIO ROMANO

VIA DELLA GATTA

PIAZZA DELLA ROTONDA

VIA DEL PIÈ DI MARMO

PIAZZA DELLA MINERVA

VIA DEL GESÙ

VIA DEL PLEBISCITO

Santa Maria sopra Minerva
This is one of Rome's few Gothic churches, with works by Michelangelo, Bernini, and Filippino Lippi ⓯

★ Pantheon
The Pantheon, a temple to "all the gods," is Rome's best-preserved ancient building. It was built in the 1st century AD, probably to a design by Emperor Hadrian ⓰

KEY

– – – – Suggested route

LOCATOR MAP
*See Rome Street Finder
map 3*

Via della Gatta is overlooked by this marble statue of a cat *(gatta)* that gives the narrow street its name.

The Pie' di Marmo, an ancient marble foot, is probably part of a giant statue from the temple to the Egyptian goddess Isis.

Palazzo Altieri incorporates the hovel of an old woman who refused to allow her house to be demolished when this palace was built in the 17th century.

Gesù
Built in the late 16th century, this Jesuit church served as a model for the Order's churches throughout the world ⑬

STAR SIGHTS

★ **Pantheon**

★ **Palazzo Doria Pamphilj**

0 meters   75
0 yards   75

Area Sacra di Largo Argentina ⑫

Largo di Torre Argentina. **Map** 2 F5. 🚌 *40, 46, 62, 64, 70, 81, 87, 186, 492.* ⬭ *with permit only (see p614).*

THE REMAINS of four temples were discovered in the 1920s at the center of Largo Argentina, now a busy bus terminus and traffic junction. They date from the era of the Republic, and are among the oldest found in Rome. For the purpose of identification, they are known as A, B, C, and D. The oldest (temple C) dates from the early 3rd century BC. It was placed on a high platform preceded by an altar and is typical of Italic temple plans as opposed to the Greek model. Temple A is from the 3rd century BC, but in medieval times the small church of San Nicola di Cesarini was built over its podium and the remains of its two apses are still visible. The column stumps to the north belonged to a great portico, known as the Hecatostylum (portico of 100 columns). In Imperial times two marble latrines were built here – the remains of one are visible behind temple A.

Behind temples B and C, near Via di Torre Argentina, are the remains of a great platform of tufa blocks. These have been identified as part of the Curia of Pompey, a rectangular building where the Senate met, and where Julius Caesar was assassinated by Brutus, Cassius, and their followers on March 15, 44 BC.

Area Sacra, with the ruins of circular temple B

Baroque *Triumph of Faith over Idolatry* by Pierre Legros, Gesù

Gesù ⑬

Piazza del Gesù. **Map** 3 A4. ☎ *06 69 70 01.* 🚌 *H, 44, 46, 62, 64, 70, 81, 87, 186, 492, 628 & other routes.* ⬭ *6am–12:30pm, 4–7:15pm daily.* 📷

BUILT BETWEEN 1568 and 1584, the Gesù was Rome's first Jesuit church. The Jesuit order was founded in Rome in 1537 by a Basque soldier, Ignatius Loyola, who became a Christian after he was wounded in battle. The order was austere, intellectual, and heavily engaged in missionary activity and religious wars.

The much-imitated design of the Gesù typifies Counter-Reformation architecture, with a large nave with side pulpits for preaching to crowds, and a main altar as the centerpiece for the Mass. The illusionistic decoration on the nave ceiling and dome was added by Il Baciccia in the 17th century.

The nave depicts the *Triumph of the Name of Jesus* and its message is clear: faithful, Catholic worshipers will be joyfully uplifted to heaven while Protestants and heretics are flung into the fires of hell. The message is reiterated in the Cappella di Sant'Ignazio, a rich display of lapis lazuli, serpentine, silver, and gold. The Baroque marble by Legros, *Triumph of Faith over Idolatry*, shows a female "Religion" trampling on the head of the serpent Idolatry, while in Théudon's *Barbarians Adoring the Faith*, an angel aims a kick toward a decrepit old barbarian couple entangled with a snake.

Palazzo Doria Pamphilj

Piazza del Collegio Romano 1/a.
Map 5 A4. **C** 06 679 73 23. ☎ 64, 70, 81, 85, 117, 119, 492. ○ 10am–5pm Fri–Wed. ● Jan 1, May 1, Dec 25. 🖼 ♿ 🎫 by appt for private apartments.

PALAZZO DORIA PAMPHILJ is a vast edifice whose oldest parts date from 1435. When the Pamphilj family took over in 1647 they built a new wing, a splendid chapel, and a theater.

The family art collection has over 400 paintings dating from the 15th–18th century, including a portrait of Pope Innocent X by Velázquez and works by Titian, Guercino, Caravaggio, and Claude Lorrain. The opulent rooms of the private apartments retain many of their original furnishings, including Brussels and Gobelins tapestries, Murano chandeliers, and a gilded crib.

Velázquez's *Pope Innocent X* (1650)

Santa Maria sopra Minerva ⑮

Piazza della Minerva 42. **Map** 4 F4.
C 06 679 39 26. ☎ 116 & many other routes. ○ 7am–noon daily.

ONE OF ROME'S rare Gothic buildings, this church was built in the 13th century over what were thought to be the ruins of a Temple of Minerva. It was a stronghold of the Dominicans, who produced some of the Church's most infamous inquisitors, and who tried the scientist Galileo in the adjoining monastery.

Inside, the church has a superb collection of art and sculpture, ranging from 13th-century Cosmatesque tombs to

a bust by Bernini. Highlights include Antoniazzo Romano's *Annunciation* featuring Cardinal Juan de Torquemada, uncle of the vicious Spanish Inquisitor, and the Carafa Chapel whose frescoes by Filippino Lippi have recently been restored.

In the Aldobrandini Chapel are the tombs of the 16th-century Medici popes, Leo X and his cousin Clement VII, and near the steps of the choir is a stocky *Risen Christ*, begun by Michelangelo.

The church also contains the tombs of many famous Italians, such as St. Catherine of Siena who died in 1380 and Fra Angelico, the Dominican friar and painter, who died in 1455. Outside, Bernini's spectacular sculpture of an elephant holds an obelisk on its back.

Simple vaulted nave of Santa Maria sopra Minerva

Pantheon ⑯

Piazza della Rotonda. **Map** 3 F4. **C** 06 68 30 02 30. ☎ 116 & many routes. ○ 9am–6:30pm daily (7pm Sun). ● Jan 1, May 1, Dec 25. 📷 ♿

THE PANTHEON, the Roman "temple of all the gods," is the most extraordinary and best preserved ancient building in Rome. The first temple on the site was a conventional rectangular affair erected by Agrippa between 27 and 25 BC; the present structure was built and possibly designed by Emperor Hadrian in AD 118.

The temple is fronted by a massive pedimented portico screening what appears to be a cylinder fused to a shallow dome. Only from the inside can the true scale and beauty of this building be appreciated: a vast hemispherical dome equal in radius to the height of the cylinder giving perfectly harmonious proportions to the building. A circular opening, the *oculus*, lets in the only light.

In the 7th century Christians claimed to be plagued by demons as they passed by, and permission was given to make the Pantheon a church. Today it is lined with tombs, ranging from a restrained monument to Raphael to huge marble and porphyry sarcophagi holding the bodies of Italian monarchs.

Interior of the Pantheon, burial place for Italian monarchs

Sant'Ignazio di Loyola ⑰

Piazza di Sant'Ignazio. **Map** 3 A4.
📞 06 679 44 06. 🚌 116, 117, 492.
🕐 7:30am–12:30pm, 4– 7:15pm
daily. 📷 ♿

THIS CHURCH was built by Pope Gregory XV in 1626 in honor of St. Ignatius of Loyola, founder of the Society of Jesus (Jesuits) and the man who most embodied the zeal of the Counter-Reformation.

Together with the Gesù (see p393), Sant'Ignazio forms the nucleus of the Jesuit area of Rome. It is one of the most extravagant Baroque churches and its vast interior is plated with precious stones, marble, stucco, and gilt, creating a thrilling sense of theater. The church has a Latin-cross plan, with an apse and many side chapels. A cupola was planned but never built, since the nuns from a nearby convent objected that it would obscure the view from their roof garden. Instead the space was filled by a perspective painting of a dome on a flat disk.

Even more striking is the illusionistic ceiling created by the Jesuit artist Andrea Pozzo in 1685, a propagandist extravaganza extolling the success of Jesuit missionaries throughout the world. Above four women, representing Asia, Europe, America, and Africa, lithe angels and beautiful youths are drawn into a heaven of fluffy clouds.

Detail from the AD 180 Column of Marcus Aurelius, Piazza Colonna

Piazza Colonna ⑱

Map 3 A3. 🚌 116.

HOME TO Palazzo Chigi, official residence of the prime minister, Piazza Colonna is dominated by and named after the majestic Column of Marcus Aurelius. This was erected after the death of Marcus Aurelius in AD 180 to commemorate his victories over the barbarian tribes of the Danube. It is clearly an imitation of Trajan's Column (see p378) with scenes from the emperor's wars spiraling in reliefs up the column. The 80-year lapse between the two works produced a great artistic change: the wars of Marcus Aurelius are rendered with simplified pictures in stronger relief, sacrificing Classical proportions for the sake of clarity and immediacy.

Piazza di Montecitorio ⑲

Map 3 A3. 📞 06 676 01. 🚌 116.
🕐 10am–5:30pm 1st Sun of month.

THE OBELISK in the center of Piazza Montecitorio formed the spine of a giant sundial brought back from Heliopolis in Egypt by Augustus. It vanished some time in the 9th century, and was rediscovered under medieval houses during the reign of Julius II (1503–13).

The piazza is dominated by the rugged façade of Palazzo di Montecitorio, designed by Bernini and completed in 1697, after his death, by Carlo Fontana. It has been the seat of Italy's Chamber of Deputies since the late 19th century.

La Maddalena's stuccoed façade

La Maddalena ⑳

Piazza della Maddalena. **Map** 3 A3.
📞 06 679 77 96. 🚌 116 & many
other routes. 🕐 7:30am–noon,
5–7:45pm daily. 📷

SITUATED IN a small piazza near the Pantheon, the Maddalena's Rococo façade, built in 1735, epitomizes the love of light and movement of the late Baroque. The façade has been restored, despite the protests of Neo-Classicists who dismissed its painted stucco as cake frosting.

The diminutive dimensions of the church did not deter 17th- and 18th-century decorators from filling the interior with paintings and ornaments from the floor to the top of the elegant cupola.

Baroque illusionistic ceiling by Andrea Pozzo in Sant'Ignazio di Loyola

NORTHEAST ROME

THIS AREA stretches from the exclusive shopping streets around Piazza di Spagna to the Esquiline Hill, once bourgeois, but now a poor, often seedy area full of early Christian churches. The Piazza di Spagna and Piazza del Popolo district grew up in the 16th century, when the increase in the influx of pilgrims

Lion fountain in Piazza del Popolo

was such that a road was built to channel them as quickly as possible to the Vatican. About the same time, the Quirinal Hill became the site of a papal palace. When Rome became capital of Italy in 1870, Via Veneto became a lavish residential area, and the Esquiline was covered with apartments for the new civil servants.

SIGHTS AT A GLANCE

Churches
Sant'Andrea al Quirinale 7
San Carlo alle Quattro Fontane 8
Santa Maria della Concezione 10
Santa Maria Maggiore 15
Santa Maria del Popolo 3
Santa Maria della Vittoria 11
San Pietro in Vincoli 14
Santa Prassede 13

Museums and Galleries
Museo Nazionale Romano 12
Palazzo Barberini 9

Ancient Sites and Buildings
Ara Pacis 4
Mausoleum of Augustus 5

Historic Buildings
Villa Medici 2

Piazzas and Fountains
Piazza di Spagna and the Spanish Steps 1
Trevi Fountain 6

GETTING THERE
Metro stations Repubblica, Barberini, and Spagna (line A) cover the area between Termini and Piazza del Popolo. Bus 16 runs from Termini to Santa Maria Maggiore and down Via Merulana.

KEY

	Street-by-Street: Piazza di Spagna pp398–9
FS	Train station
M	Metro station
P	Parking
i	Tourist information
---	City walls

0 meters 250
0 yards 250

◁ **The Spanish Steps with their spring display of azaleas**

Street-by-Street: Piazza di Spagna

THE NETWORK OF NARROW STREETS around Piazza di Spagna forms one of the most exclusive areas in Rome, drawing droves of tourists and Romans to the elegant shops around Via Condotti. The square and its nearby coffee houses have long attracted those who want to see and be seen. In the 18th century the area was full of hotels for frivolous aristocrats doing the Grand Tour, as well as artists, writers, and composers, who took the city's history and culture more seriously.

Caffè Greco is an 18th-century café once frequented by writers and musicians such as Keats, Goethe, Byron, Liszt, and Wagner.

Spagna

VIALE TRINITÀ DEI MONTI

PIAZZA DI SPAGNA

VIA CONDOTTI

PIAZZA MIGNANELLI

VIA DI PROPAGANDA

Trinità dei Monti is a 16th-century church at the top of the Spanish Steps. There are fine views of Rome from the stairway.

Babington's Tea Rooms, founded by two English spinsters in 1896, still serves English teas.

★ **Piazza di Spagna and the Spanish Steps**
These have been at the heart of tourist's Rome since the 18th century ❶

The Keats-Shelley Memorial House, where the poet Keats died in 1821, is now a museum honoring English Romantic poets.

The Colonna dell' Immacolata, erected in 1857, commemorates Pope Pius IX's doctrine of the Immaculate Conception.

The Collegio di Propaganda Fide, built for the Jesuits in 1662, has a superb façade designed by Francesco Borromini

KEY

– – – Suggested route

| 0 meters | 75 |
| 0 yards | 75 |

LOCATOR MAP
See Rome Street Finder map 3

AROUND PIAZZA NAVONA

NORTHEAST ROME

THE ANCIENT CENTER

Sant'Andrea delle Fratte
contains two angels by
Bernini (1669) made for
Ponte Sant'Angelo, which Pope
Clement X thought
too lovely to expose
to the weather.

The Fontana della Barcaccia at the
foot of the Spanish Steps

Piazza di Spagna and the Spanish Steps ❶

Map 3 A2. 🚌 *116, 117.* Ⓜ *Spagna.*

SHAPED LIKE a crooked bow
tie, and surrounded by
muted, shuttered façades,
Piazza di Spagna is crowded
all day and (in summer) most
of the night. The most famous
square in Rome, it takes its
name from the Palazzo di
Spagna, built in the 17th
century to house the Spanish
Embassy to the Holy See.

The piazza has long been
the haunt of foreign visitors
and expatriates. In the 18th
and 19th centuries the square
stood at the heart of the city's
main hotel district. Some of the
travelers came in search of
knowledge and inspiration,
although most were more
interested in collecting statues
to adorn their family homes.
When the Victorian novelist
Charles Dickens visited, he
reported that the Spanish Steps

were crowded with models
dressed as Madonnas, saints
and emperors, hoping to attract
the attention of foreign artists.

The steps were built in the
1720s to link the square with
the French church of Trinità
dei Monti above. The French
wanted to place a statue of
Louis XIV at the top, but the
pope objected, and it was not
until the 1720s that the Italian
architect Francesco de Sanctis
produced the voluptuous
Rococo design that satisfied
both camps. The Fontana
Barcaccia, sunk into the
paving at the foot of the steps
due to low water pressure,
was designed by Bernini's
less famous father, Pietro.

Villa Medici ❷

Accademia di Francia a Roma, Viale
Trinità dei Monti 1. **Map** 3 B1.
📞 *06 679 83 81.* 🚌 *117.*
Ⓜ *Spagna.* **Accademia and
gardens** ◻ *10:30am, 11:30am Sat,
Sun spring & autumn.* 🎫 ✔ *only.*

SUPERBLY POSITIONED on the
Pincio Hill, this 16th-century
villa has retained the name
that it assumed when Cardinal
Ferdinando de' Medici bought
it in 1576. It is now home to
the French Academy, which
was founded in 1666 to give
artists the chance to study in
Rome. Since 1803 musicians
have been allowed to study
there too; both Berlioz and
Debussy were students.

The villa is only open for
exhibitions, but the formal
gardens, with a beautifully
frescoed pavilion and copies
of ancient statues, can be
visited in certain months.

19th-century engraving of the inner façade of the Villa Medici

---

STAR SIGHT

★ Piazza di Spagna and
the Spanish Steps

Pinturicchio's fresco of the *Delphic Sibyl* (1509) in Santa Maria del Popolo

Santa Maria del Popolo ❸

Piazza del Popolo 12. **Map** 2 F1. 📞 *06 361 08 36.* 🚌 *95, 117, 119, 490, 495, 628, 926.* Ⓜ *Flaminio.* ⚪ *7am–7pm Mon–Sat, 8am–1:30pm, 4:30–7:30pm Sun.* 📷

SANTA MARIA DEL POPOLO was one of the first Renaissance churches in Rome, commissioned by Pope Sixtus IV della Rovere in 1472. Lavish endowments by Sixtus's descendants and other powerful families has made it one of Rome's greatest artistic treasures.

Shortly after Sixtus died in 1484, Pinturicchio and his pupils frescoed two chapels (first and third right) for the della Rovere family. On the altar of the first chapel there is a lovely *Nativity* from 1490 that depicts a stable at the foot of a Classical column.

In 1503 Sixtus IV's nephew Giuliano became Pope Julius II and had Bramante build a new apse. Pinturicchio was called in again to paint its vaults with Sibyls and Apostles framed in an intricate tracery of freakish beasts.

In 1513 Raphael created the Chigi chapel (second left) for the wealthy banker Agostino Chigi. The design is an audacious Renaissance fusion of the sacred and profane; there are pyramid-like tombs and a ceiling mosaic of God holding the signs of the zodiac describing Chigi's horoscope. Raphael died before the chapel was finished, and it was completed by Bernini who added the dynamic statues of Daniel and Habakkuk. In the

Cerasi chapel, left of the altar, there are two realistic works painted by Caravaggio in 1601: the *Conversion of St. Paul* and the *Crucifixion of St. Peter.* The artist uses daringly exaggerated lighting effects and foreshortening techniques to intensify the dramatic effect.

Detail of the Ara Pacis frieze

Ara Pacis ❹

Via di Ripetta. **Map** 2 F2. 📞 *06 68 80 68 48.* 🚌 *70, 81, 117, 119, 186.* ⚫ *for restoration.*

PAINSTAKINGLY reconstructed over many years from scattered fragments, the exquisitely carved Ara Pacis (Altar of Peace) celebrates the peace created throughout the Mediterranean by Emperor Augustus. Commissioned by the Senate in 13 BC and completed four years later, the altar stands in a square enclosure of Carrara marble, carved with realistic reliefs of such high quality that experts think the craftsmen may have been Greek.

The reliefs on the north and south walls depict a procession that took place on July 4, 13 BC, in which the members of the emperor's

family can be identified, including Augustus's grandson, Lucius, who is the toddler clutching at the skirts of his mother, Antonia.

Mausoleum of Augustus ❺

Piazza Augusto Imperatore. **Map** 2 F2. 📞 *06 67 10 20 70.* 🚌 *81, 117, 492, 628, 913, 926.* ⚪ *by appt only, permit needed (see p614).* 📷 ⚫ ♿

NOW JUST A WEEDY mound ringed with cypresses and strewn with litter, this was once the most prestigious burial place in Rome. Augustus had the mausoleum built in 28 BC, the year before he became sole ruler, as a tomb for himself and his descendants. The circular building was 87 m (285 ft) in diameter with two obelisks (now in Piazza del Quirinale and Piazza dell' Esquilino) at the entrance. Inside were four concentric passageways linked by corridors where urns holding the ashes of the Imperial family were placed, including those of Augustus who died in AD 14.

Trevi Fountain ❻

Piazza di Trevi. **Map** 3 B3. 🚌 *116 & many other routes.*

NICOLA SALVI's theatrical design for Rome's largest and most famous fountain was completed in 1762. The central figures are Neptune, flanked by two Tritons, one trying to

Rome's largest and most famous fountain, the Trevi

master an unruly seahorse, the other leading a quieter beast, symbolizing the two contrasting moods of the sea.

The site originally marked the terminal of the Aqua Virgo aqueduct, built by Augustus' right-hand man and son-in-law, Agrippa, in 19 BC to channel water to Rome's new bath complexes. One of the reliefs on the first level shows a young girl, Trivia, after whom the fountain may have been named. She is said to have first shown the spring, 22 km (14 miles) from the city, to thirsty Roman soldiers.

The dome of San Carlo alle Quattro Fontane, by Borromini

Interior, Sant'Andrea al Quirinale

Sant'Andrea al Quirinale ❼

Via del Quirinale 29. **Map** 3 C3.
🕿 06 48 90 31 87. 🚌 116, 116T, 117. 🕒 9am–noon, 4–7pm Wed–Mon. ⬤ Aug pm. ⌀

Sant'Andrea was designed for the Jesuits by Bernini and executed by his assistants between 1658 and 1670. The site was wide but shallow, so Bernini took the radical step of pointing the long axis of his oval plan toward the sides, and leading the eye around to the altar by means of a strong horizontal cornice. At the altar he combined sculpture and painting to create a theatrical crucifixion of Sant'Andrea (St. Andrew); the diagonally crucified saint on the altarpiece looks up at a stucco effigy of himself ascending to the lantern, where the Holy Spirit and cherubs await him in heaven.

San Carlo alle Quattro Fontane ❽

Via del Quirinale 23. **Map** 3 C3.
🕿 06 488 32 61. 🚌 116T & routes to Piazza Barberini.
⬤ for restoration.

In 1638, Borromini was commissioned by the Trinitarians to design a church and convent on a tiny cramped site at the Quattro Fontane crossroads. The church, so small that it is said it would fit inside one of the piers of St. Peter's, is designed with bold fluid curves on both the façade and interior to give light and life to the diminutive building. One of the most cunning features is the dome, whose concealed windows, illusionistic coffering, and tiny lantern are designed to make it look higher than it really is.

Palazzo Barberini ❾

Via delle Quattro Fontane 13. **Map** 3 C2. 🕿 06 482 41 84. 🚌 52, 53, 61, 62, 63, 80, 95, 116, 175, 492, 590. Ⓜ Barberini. 🕒 9am–7pm Tue–Sun. ⬤ Mon & public hols. ⌀ 📷 🔇 ♿ ⬆ (elevator).

When Maffei Barberini became Pope Urban VIII in 1623, he decided to build a grand family palazzo. Designed by Carlo Maderno as a typical country villa on the fringes of

the city, it now overlooks Piazza Barberini, where traffic hurtles around Bernini's Triton fountain. Maderno died shortly after the foundations had been laid, and Bernini and Borromini took over.

The most dazzling room is the Gran Salone, with an illusionistic ceiling frescoed by Pietro da Cortona in 1633–9. The palazzo also houses part of the Galleria Nazionale d'Arte Antica with works by Filippo Lippi, Titian, Artemisia Gentileschi, and Caravaggio. The most famous is a portrait of a courtesan, reputedly Raphael's lover, *La Fornarina*, said to be the daughter of a baker, although not painted by the artist himself.

Ceiling fresco detail in Palazzo Barberini (1633)

Santa Maria della Concezione ❿

Via Veneto 27. **Map** 3 C2. 🕿 06 487 11 85. 🚌 52, 53, 61, 62, 63, 80, 95, 116, 175. Ⓜ Barberini. **Crypt** 🕒 9am–noon, 3–6pm Fri–Wed. ⌀

Below this unassuming church on Via Veneto is a crypt decked with the dismembered skeletons of 4,000 Capuchin monks. They form a macabre reminder of the transience of life, with vertebrae wired together to make sacred hearts and crowns of thorns, and, in one chapel, the poignant skeleton of a tiny Barberini princess.

Santa Maria della Vittoria ⑪

Via XX Settembre 17. **Map** 4 D2. 🕾
06 482 61 90. 🚌 61, 62, 84, 175,
495, 910. Ⓜ Repubblica. ☐ 7am–
noon, 4:30–7pm daily. ⬤ August.

Santa Maria della Vittoria is
an intimate Baroque church
with a lavish, candlelit interior.
Inside the Cornaro chapel is
one of Bernini's most ambitious sculptures, the *Ecstasy of
St. Teresa* (1646). The physical
nature of St. Teresa's ecstasy is
apparent as she appears collapsed on a cloud with her
mouth half open and eyes
closed, struck by the arrow of
a smiling angel. Ecclesiastical
members, past and present,
of the Venetian Cornaro family,
who commissioned the chapel,
sit in boxes as if watching and
discussing the scene being
played out in front of them.

**Bernini's *Ecstasy of St. Teresa* in
Santa Maria della Vittoria**

Museo Nazionale Romano ⑫

Palazzo Massimo, Largo di Villa Peretti
1 (1 of 5 sites). **Map** 4 E3. 🕾 06 39
74 99 07. 🚌 all routes to Termini.
Ⓜ Repubblica. ☐ 9am–6:45pm
Tue–Sat; 9am–7:45pm Sun. 🎫
ticket valid for all sites. 🔊 ♿ 🎦

Founded in 1899, the Museo
Nazionale Romano – one of
the world's leading museums
of Classical art – houses most
of the antiquities found in
Rome since 1870, as well as
important older collections.

During the
1990s it
underwent
a major
reorganization
and now has
five branches:
the Palazzo
Altemps *(see
p390)*; the
Baths of
Diocletian; the
Aula Ottagona;
the Crypta
Balbi, and the
Palazzo
Massimo. In
the latter
exhibits dating
from the 2nd
century BC to
the late 4th
century AD
are displayed in a series of
rooms over three floors. Highlights of the collection include
the exquisite *Quattro Aurighe*
mosaics from a villa in northern Rome, a Greek statue, the
Generale di Tivoli, depicting a
Roman soldier from the Asian
wars, and the famous statue
of Emperor Augustus.

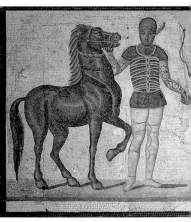

**One of the finely detailed Quattro Aurighe mosaics on
display at the Museo Nazionale Romano**

Santa Prassede ⑬

Via Santa Prassede 9a. **Map** 4 D5.
🕾 06 488 24 56. 🚌 16, 70, 71, 75,
714. Ⓜ Vittorio Emanuele. ☐
7am–noon, 4–6:30pm daily. 📷 ♿

The church was founded by
Pope Paschal II in the 9th
century and decorated by
Byzantium artists with the most
important, glittering mosaics in
Rome. In the apse Christ stands
between Santa Prassede and
her sister, dressed as Byzantine
empresses, among white-robed
elders, lambs, feather-mop
palms, and bright red poppies.
The Cappella di San Zeno is
even lovelier, a jewel box of

9th-century mosaic, Santa Prassede

a mausoleum, built by Pope
Paschal II for his mother,
Theodora. Her square halo
shows that she was still alive
when the mosaic was created.

San Pietro in Vincoli ⑭

Piazza di San Pietro in Vincoli. **Map** 4
D5. 🕾 06 488 28 65. 🚌 75, 84,
117. Ⓜ Colosseo. ☐ 7am–
12:30pm, 3:30–7pm (Oct–Mar: 6pm)
Mon–Sat, 8:45am–11:45am Sun. ♿

The church's name means
St. Peter in Chains; so called
because it houses what are said
to be the chains with which
St. Peter was shackled in the
Mamertine Prison *(see p379)*.
According to tradition, one set
of chains was sent to Constantinople by Empress Eudoxia;
when it was returned to Rome
some years later it miraculously fused with its partner.

San Pietro is now best known
for the Tomb of Julius II, commissioned from Michelangelo
by the pope in 1505. Much to
the artist's chagrin, Julius soon
became more interested in the
building of a new St. Peter's and
the tomb project was laid to
one side. After the pope died
in 1513, Michelangelo resumed
work on the tomb, but had
only completed the statues of
the *Dying Slaves* (now in found
in Paris and Florence) and
Moses when he was called
away to paint the *Last Judgment* in the Sistine Chapel.

Santa Maria Maggiore ⑮

A CONFIDENT BLEND of architectural styles, ranging from Early Christian to late Baroque, Santa Maria is also famous for its superb mosaics. Founded in about AD 420, it retains the original colonnaded triple nave, lined with panels of rare 5th-century mosaics. The Cosmatesque marble floor and bell tower are medieval, as are the spectacular mosaics on the triumphal arch and in the loggia. The lavish coffered ceiling is Renaissance; the façades, domes, and chapels Baroque.

VISITORS' CHECKLIST

Piazza di Santa Maria Maggiore.
Map 4 E4. 📞 06 48 31 95.
🚌 16, 70, 71, 714. 🚋 14.
Ⓜ Cavour. 🕐 7am–7pm daily.
✝ 📷

Coronation of the Virgin
This is one of the wonderful 13th-century mosaics in the apse by Jacopo Torriti.

Bell tower

5th-century mosaics

Tomb of Cardinal Rodriguez
This Gothic tomb, which dates from 1299, contains magnificent marblework by the Cosmati.

18th-century façade by Ferdinando Fuga

13th-century mosaics

Cappella Paolina
Flaminio Ponzio, architect of the Villa Borghese, designed this sumptuous chapel in 1611 for Pope Paul V who is buried here.

Column in Piazza Santa Maria Maggiore
In 1611 a bronze of the Virgin and Child was added to this ancient marble column that came from the Basilica of Constantine.

Cappella Sistina
This chapel was built for Pope Sixtus V (1584–7) by Domenico Fontana and was opulently plated with ancient marble. It houses the pope's tomb.

THE VATICAN AND TRASTEVERE

ATICAN CITY, the world capital of Catholicism, is the world's smallest state. It occupies 43 ha (106 acres) within high walls watched over by the Vatican guard. It was the site where St. Peter was martyred (c.AD 64) and buried, and it became the residence of the popes who succeeded him. The papal palaces, next to the great basilica of St. Peter's, are home to the

Pope Urban VIII's coat of arms in St. Peter's

Sistine Chapel and the eclectic collections of the Vatican Museums, as well as being the residence of the pope. Neighboring Trastevere is quite different, a picturesque old quarter, whose inhabitants consider themselves to be the only true Romans. Sadly, the proletarian identity of the place is in danger of being destroyed by the proliferation of trendy restaurants, clubs, and shops.

SIGHTS AT A GLANCE

GETTING THERE

The quickest way to the Vatican is by Metro Line A to Ottaviano, just north of Piazza San Pietro. The 40 and 64 buses link it with Termini and the 81 links it with the Colosseum. The J buses are also a useful link. Trastevere is a short walk from Campo de' Fiori across Ponte Sisto.

Churches

San Francesco a Ripa ⑨
San Pietro in Montorio and the Tempietto ⑩
Santa Cecilia in Trastevere ⑧
Santa Maria in Trastevere ⑦
St. Peter's pp408–9 ②

Museums and Galleries

Palazzo Corsini and the Galleria Nazionale d'Arte Antica ⑤
Vatican Museums pp410–17 ③

Historic Buildings

Castel Sant'Angelo ①
Villa Farnesina ④

Parks and Gardens

Botanical Gardens ⑥

KEY

A Tour of the Vatican
pp406–7

P Parking

Tourist information

— City walls

0 meters 250
0 yards 250

View of St. Peter's with the Ponte Sant'Angelo in the foreground

A Tour of the Vatican

Crucifix in the Vatican

THE VATICAN, a sovereign state since February 1929, is ruled by the pope, Europe's only absolute monarch. About 500 people live here and, as well as accommodations for staff and ecclesiasts, the city has its own post office, banks, currency, judicial system, radio station, shops, and a daily newspaper, *l'Osservatore Romano*.

Vatican Radio broadcasts in 20 languages throughout the world from this tower, part of the 9th-century Leonine Wall.

★ St. Peter's
Most of the great architects of the Renaissance and Baroque had a hand in the design of the Basilica of St. Peter's, one of the most famous churches in Christendom (see pp408–9).

★ Sistine Chapel
Michelangelo frescoed the ceiling with scenes from Genesis (1508–12), and the altar wall with the Last Judgment (1534–41). The chapel is used by cardinals when electing a new pope (see p414).

The Papal Audience Chamber

Information office

PIAZZA DEL SANT'UFFIZIO

★ Raphael Rooms
Raphael frescoed this suite in the early 16th century. Works like The School of Athens *established his reputation, to equal that of his contemporary Michelangelo (see p417).*

Piazza San Pietro
was laid out by Bernini between 1656 and 1667.

To Via della Conciliazione

This staircase up to the museums, designed in 1932 by Giuseppe Momo, is in the form of a double helix, consisting of two spirals: one to walk up and one to walk down.

LOCATOR MAP
See Rome Street Finder map 1

Entrance to Vatican Museums

★ **Vatican Museums**
This marble group of the Laocoön (AD 1) is one of many prestigious works of art in the Vatican (see p410).

The Cortile della Pigna is named after a bronze pine cone from an ancient fountain.

VIA DI PORTA ANGELICA

The Vatican Gardens, open for guided tours, make up a third of the Vatican's territory.

meters   75
yards   75

Castel Sant'Angelo ❶

Lungotevere Castello. **Map** 2 D3.
📞 06 39 08 07 30. 🚌 23, 34, 64, 280. Ⓜ Lepanto. 🕐 9am–8pm Tue–Sun (last entry 7pm). 🔴 public hols, 2nd & 4th Tue of month. 🖼 🎧

THE MASSIVE FORTRESS of Castel Sant'Angelo takes its name from the vision of the Archangel Michael by Pope Gregory the Great in the 6th century as he led a procession across the bridge, praying for the end of the plague.

The castle began life in AD 139 as the Emperor Hadrian's mausoleum. Since then it has been a bridgehead in the Emperor Aurelian's city wall, a medieval citadel and prison, and a place of safety for popes during times of political unrest. A corridor links it with the Vatican Palace, providing an escape route for the pope. From dank cells to fine apartments of Renaissance popes, the museums cover all aspects of the castle's history, including the Sala Paolina, with illusionistic frescoes (1546–8) by Pellegrino Tibaldi and Perin del Vaga and the Courtyard of Honor.

St. Peter's ❷

See pp408–9.

Vatican Museums ❸

See pp410–17.

View of Castel Sant'Angelo from the Ponte Sant'Angelo

STAR SIGHTS

★ **St. Peter's**

★ **Vatican Museums**

★ **Sistine Chapel**

★ **Raphael Rooms**

St. Peter's ②

CATHOLICISM'S most sacred shrine, the sumptuous, marble-clad Basilica of St. Peter, draws pilgrims and tourists from all over the world. It holds hundreds of precious works of art, some salvaged from the original 4th-century basilica built by Constantine, others commissioned from Renaissance and Baroque artists. The dominant tone is set by Bernini, who created the baldacchino twisting up below Michelangelo's huge dome. He also created the Cathedra in the apse, with four saints supporting a throne that contains fragments once thought to be relics of the chair from which St. Peter delivered his first sermon.

Dome of St. Peter's
The 136.5 m (448 ft) high dome, designed by Michelangelo, was not completed in his lifetime.

A staircase of 537 steps leads to the summit of the dome.

Baldacchino
Commissioned by Pope Urban VIII in 1624, Bernini's extravagant Baroque canopy stands above St. Peter's tomb.

The church is 186 m (610 ft) long.

Entrance to Treasury and Sacristy

Stairs to the dome

The Papal Altar stands over the crypt where St. Peter is reputedly buried

HISTORICAL PLAN OF THE BASILICA OF ST. PETER

St. Peter was buried in AD 64 in a necropolis near the site of his crucifixion in the Circus of Nero. In AD 324 Constantine constructed a basilica over the tomb. The old church was rebuilt in the 15th century, and throughout the 16th and 17th centuries various architects developed the existing structure. The new church was inaugurated in 1626.

KEY
- ☐ Circus of Nero
- ☐ Constantinian
- ☐ Renaissance
- ☐ Baroque

Monument to Pope Alexander VII
Bernini's last work in St. Peter's was finished in 1678 and shows the Chigi pope among the allegorical figures of Truth, Justice, Charity, and Prudence.

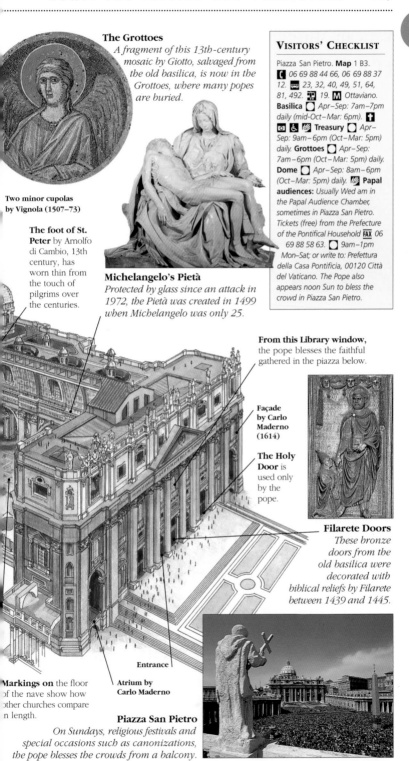

The Grottoes
A fragment of this 13th-century mosaic by Giotto, salvaged from the old basilica, is now in the Grottoes, where many popes are buried.

Two minor cupolas by Vignola (1507–73)

The foot of St. Peter by Arnolfo di Cambio, 13th century, has worn thin from the touch of pilgrims over the centuries.

Michelangelo's Pietà
Protected by glass since an attack in 1972, the Pietà was created in 1499 when Michelangelo was only 25.

VISITORS' CHECKLIST

Piazza San Pietro. **Map** 1 B3.
06 69 88 44 66, 06 69 88 37 12. 23, 32, 40, 49, 51, 64, 81, 492. 19. Ottaviano.
Basilica Apr–Sep: 7am–7pm daily (mid-Oct–Mar: 6pm).
Treasury Apr–Sep: 9am–6pm (Oct–Mar: 5pm) daily. **Grottoes** Apr–Sep: 7am–6pm (Oct–Mar: 5pm) daily.
Dome Apr–Sep: 8am–6pm (Oct–Mar: 5pm) daily. **Papal audiences:** Usually Wed am in the Papal Audience Chamber, sometimes in Piazza San Pietro. Tickets (free) from the Prefecture of the Pontifical Household FAX 06 69 88 58 63. 9am–1pm Mon–Sat; or write to: Prefettura della Casa Pontificia, 00120 Città del Vaticano. The Pope also appears noon Sun to bless the crowd in Piazza San Pietro.

From this Library window, the pope blesses the faithful gathered in the piazza below.

Façade by Carlo Maderno (1614)

The Holy Door is used only by the pope.

Filarete Doors
These bronze doors from the old basilica were decorated with biblical reliefs by Filarete between 1439 and 1445.

Markings on the floor of the nave show how other churches compare in length.

Entrance

Atrium by Carlo Maderno

Piazza San Pietro
On Sundays, religious festivals and special occasions such as canonizations, the pope blesses the crowds from a balcony.

Vatican Museums ❸

Ｈ OME TO the Sistine Chapel and Raphael Rooms
as well as to one of the world's most important
art collections, the Vatican Museums are housed in
palaces originally built for Renaissance popes such
as Julius II, Innocent VIII, and Sixtus IV. Most of
the later additions were made in the 18th century,
when priceless works of art accumulated by
earlier popes were first displayed.

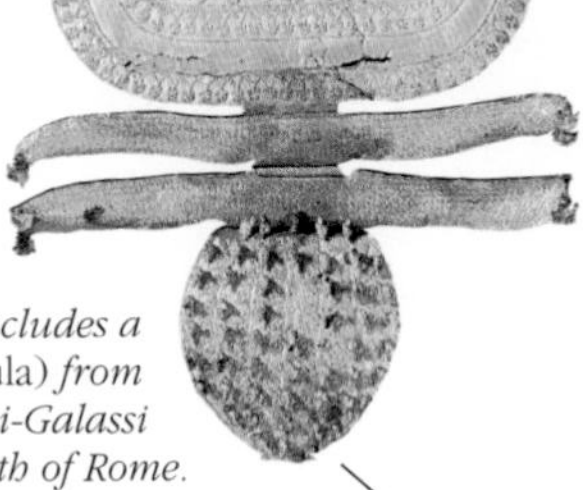

Etruscan Museum
*The Etruscan collection includes a
woman's gold clasp (fibula) from
the 7th-century BC Regolini-Galassi
tomb at Cerveteri, north of Rome.*

Gallery of Maps
*The Siege of Malta is one of 40
maps of the Church's territories,
frescoed by the 16th-century cartographer
Ignazio Danti on the gallery's walls.*

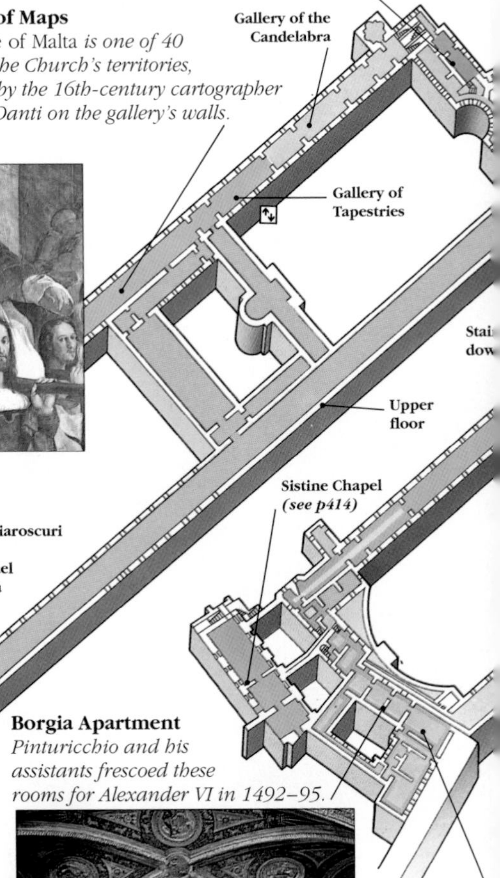

**Gallery of the
Candelabra**

Raphael Rooms
*This is a detail of
the Expulsion of
Heliodorus from
the Temple, one
of many frescoes
painted by
Raphael and his
pupils for Julius
II's private
apartments
(see p417).*

**Gallery of
Tapestries**

**Stai
dow**

**Upper
floor**

Sala dei Chiaroscuri

**Raphael
Loggia**

**Sistine Chapel
(see p414)**

Borgia Apartment
*Pinturicchio and his
assistants frescoed these
rooms for Alexander VI in 1492–95.*

GALLERY
GUIDE
*The museum
complex is vast; the Sistine Chapel
is 20–30 minutes' walk from the
entrance, so allow plenty of time.
There is a strict one-way system,
and it is best to be selective or
choose one of four color-coded
itineraries, which vary from 90
minutes to a five-hour marathon.*

**Modern
religious art**
on view here
was sent to the
popes by artists
worldwide, such
as Bacon, Ernst,
and Carrà.

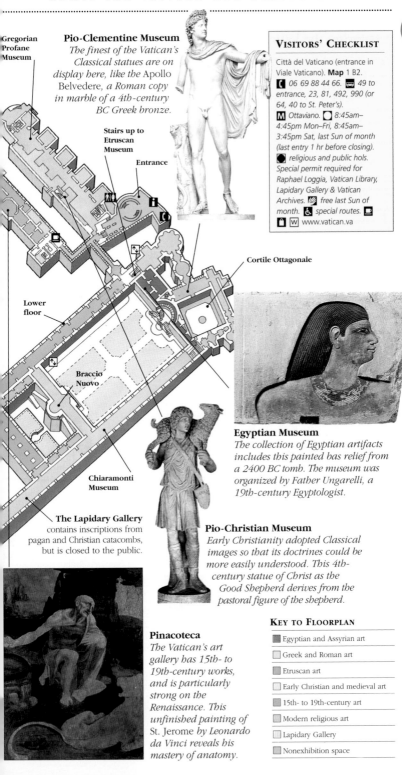

Gregorian Profane Museum

Pio-Clementine Museum
The finest of the Vatican's Classical statues are on display here, like the Apollo Belvedere, *a Roman copy in marble of a 4th-century BC Greek bronze.*

Stairs up to Etruscan Museum

Entrance

VISITORS' CHECKLIST

Città del Vaticano (entrance in Viale Vaticano). **Map** 1 B2.
📞 06 69 88 44 66. 🚌 49 to entrance, 23, 81, 492, 990 (or 64, 40 to St. Peter's).
Ⓜ Ottaviano. 🕐 8:45am–4:45pm Mon–Fri, 8:45am–3:45pm Sat, last Sun of month (last entry 1 hr before closing).
⬤ religious and public hols. Special permit required for Raphael Loggia, Vatican Library, Lapidary Gallery & Vatican Archives. 🎫 free last Sun of month. ♿ special routes. 📷
📱 🖥 www.vatican.va

Cortile Ottagonale

Lower floor

Braccio Nuovo

Chiaramonti Museum

The Lapidary Gallery contains inscriptions from pagan and Christian catacombs, but is closed to the public.

Egyptian Museum
The collection of Egyptian artifacts includes this painted bas relief from a 2400 BC tomb. The museum was organized by Father Ungarelli, a 19th-century Egyptologist.

Pio-Christian Museum
Early Christianity adopted Classical images so that its doctrines could be more easily understood. This 4th-century statue of Christ as the Good Shepherd derives from the pastoral figure of the shepherd.

Pinacoteca
The Vatican's art gallery has 15th- to 19th-century works, and is particularly strong on the Renaissance. This unfinished painting of St. Jerome *by Leonardo da Vinci reveals his mastery of anatomy.*

KEY TO FLOORPLAN

▨	Egyptian and Assyrian art
☐	Greek and Roman art
▨	Etruscan art
☐	Early Christian and medieval art
▨	15th- to 19th-century art
☐	Modern religious art
☐	Lapidary Gallery
☐	Nonexhibition space

Exploring the Vatican's Collections

THE VATICAN'S GREATEST TREASURES are its superlative Greek and Roman antiquities, together with the magnificent artifacts excavated from Egyptian and Etruscan tombs during the 19th century. Some of Italy's greatest artists, such as Raphael, Michelangelo, and Leonardo da Vinci, are represented in the Pinacoteca (art gallery) and parts of the former palaces, where they were employed by popes to decorate sumptuous apartments and galleries.

Head of an athlete in mosaic from the Baths of Caracalla, AD 217

EGYPTIAN AND ASSYRIAN ART

THE EGYPTIAN COLLECTION contains finds from 19th- and 20th-century excavations in Egypt, as well as statues that were brought to Rome in Imperial times. There are also Roman imitations of Egyptian art from Hadrian's Villa *(see p452)* and from temples in Rome devoted to Egyptian gods and goddesses, such as Isis and Serapis.

The genuine Egyptian works, displayed on the lower floor next to the Pio-Clementine Museum, include statues, mummies, mummy cases, and a Book of the Dead. One of the main treasures is a colossal granite 13th-century statue of Queen Mutuy, the mother of Rameses II, which was found on the site of the Horti Sallustiani gardens near Via Veneto. Also noteworthy are the head of a statue of Mentuhotep IV (21st century BC), the beautiful mummy case of Queen Hetep-heret-es, and the tomb of Iri, who was the guardian of the Pyramid of Cheops. This dates back to the 22nd century BC.

Roman copy of the Greek *Doryphoros*

GREEK, ETRUSCAN, AND ROMAN ART

THE GREATER PART of the Vatican Museums is dedicated to Greek and Roman art. However, the Etruscan Museum houses a superb collection of Etruscan *(see p40)* and pre-Roman artifacts from Etruria and the Greek colonies of southern Italy. Here, the most famous exhibits are the gold jewelry and bronze throne, bed, and funeral cart, found in the 650 BC Regolini-Galassi tomb in Cerveteri *(see p450)*.

Prize Greek and Roman pieces form the nucleus of the Pio-Clementine Museum. These include high-quality Roman copies of 4th-century BC Greek statues, such as the *Apoxyomenos* (an athlete wiping his body after a race) and the *Apollo del Belvedere*. The splendid *Laocoön* (1st century AD), originally from Rhodes, was found in 1506 in the ruins of Nero's Golden House. Works such as these inspired Michelangelo and other Renaissance artists.

The much smaller Chiaramonti Museum is lined with ancient busts, and its extension, the Braccio Nuovo, has a 1st-century BC statue of Augustus from the villa of his wife, Livia. It is based on the *Doryphoros* (spear-carrier) by the 5th-century BC Greek sculptor Polyclitus. There is also a Roman copy of this on display opposite it. The Gregorian Profane Museum, housed in a new wing, follows the evolution of Roman art from reliance on Greek models to a recognizably Roman style.

In this museum, original Greek works include large marble fragments from the Parthenon in Athens. Among the Roman pieces are two reliefs, the *Rilievi della Cancelleria*, commissioned by Domitian in AD 81 to glorify the military parades of his father, Emperor Vespasian. There are also fine Roman floor mosaics, two from the Baths of Caracalla *(see p427)*, and one, in the Round Room, dated 3rd century AD, from the Baths of Otricoli in Umbria.

In the Vatican Library is the 1st-century AD *Aldobrandini Wedding*, a beautiful Roman fresco depicting a bride being prepared for her marriage.

Roman mosaic from the Baths of Otricoli, Umbria, in the Round Room

EARLY CHRISTIAN AND MEDIEVAL ART

THE MAIN COLLECTION of early Christian antiquities is in the Pio-Christian Museum, which contains inscriptions and sculpture from catacombs and early Christian basilicas. The sculpture consists chiefly of reliefs from sarcophagi, though the most striking work is a freestanding 4th-century statue of the *Good Shepherd*. The sculpture's chief interest lies in the way it blends Biblical episodes with pagan mythology. The idealized pastoral figure of the shepherd became Christ himself, while bearded philosophers turned into the Apostles.

The first two rooms of the Pinacoteca are dedicated to late medieval art, mostly wooden altarpieces painted in tempera. The outstanding work is Giotto's *Stefaneschi Triptych* of about 1300, which decorated the main altar of the old St. Peter's.

The Vatican Library has a number of medieval treasures including reliquaries, textiles, enamels, and icons.

Detail of Giotto's *Stefaneschi Triptych* (1330) in the Pinacoteca

15TH- TO 19TH-CENTURY ART

MANY RENAISSANCE popes were connoisseurs of the arts who considered it their duty to sponsor the leading painters, sculptors, and

Pietà (c.1471–4) by the Venetian artist Giovanni Bellini in the Pinacoteca

goldsmiths of the age. Between the 16th and the 19th centuries, the galleries around the Cortile del Belvedere were decorated by great artists.

The Gallery of Tapestries is hung with tapestries woven in Brussels to designs by students of Raphael. The Apartment of Pope Pius V has beautiful 15th-century Flemish tapestries, and the Gallery of Maps is frescoed with 16th-century maps of ancient and contemporary Italy.

Alongside the Raphael Rooms *(see p417)* are the Room of the Chiaroscuri and Pope Nicholas V's private chapel. This was frescoed between 1447 and 1451 by Fra Angelico. Also worth seeing is the Borgia Apartment, decorated in the 1490s by Pinturicchio and his pupils for the Borgia pope, Alexander VI. Another set of fascinating frescoes can

Pinturicchio's *Adoration of the Magi* (1490), Borgia Apartment

be found in the Loggia of Raphael, but a visit here requires special permission.

The Pinacoteca has many important Renaissance works. Highlights from the 15th century are a fine *Pietà* by Giovanni Bellini, part of his *Coronation of the Virgin* altarpiece in Pèsaro *(see p358)* and Leonardo da Vinci's unfinished *St. Jerome*, discovered, after being long lost, in two halves. One was being used as a coffer lid in an antique shop, the other as the seat of a stool in a shoemaker's. Exceptional pieces from the 16th century include eight tapestry cartoons, the *Transfiguration* and *Madonna of Foligno* by Raphael, in a room devoted to the artist; a *Deposition* by Caravaggio; an altarpiece by Titian; and *St. Helen* by Veronese, which shows the saint as a sumptuously dressed aristocrat.

Sistine Chapel: The Ceiling

MICHELANGELO FRESCOED the ceiling for Pope Julius II between 1508 and 1512, working on specially designed scaffolding. The main panels, which chart the Creation of the World and Fall of Man, are surrounded by subjects from the Old and New Testaments – except for the Classical Sibyls who are said to have foreseen the birth of Christ. In the 1980s the ceiling was restored revealing colors of an unsuspected vibrancy.

Libyan Sibyl
The pagan prophet reaches for the Book of Knowledge. Like most female figures Michelangelo painted, the beautiful Libyan Sibyl was probably modeled on a man.

Illusionistic architecture

30	19	10	26	12	21	14	28	16	23	32
18	1	2	3	4	5	6	7	8	9	24
31	25	11	20	13	27	15	22	17	29	33

Creation of the Sun and Moon
Michelangelo depicts God as a dynamic but terrifying figure commanding the Sun to shed light on the Earth.

KEY TO CEILING PANELS

GENESIS: 1 God Dividing Light from Darkness; **2** Creation of the Sun and Moon; **3** Separating Waters from Land; **4** Creation of Adam; **5** Creation of Eve; **6** Original Sin; **7** Sacrifice of Noah; **8** The Deluge; **9** Drunkenness of Noah.

ANCESTORS OF CHRIST: 10 Solomon with his Mother; **11** Parents of Jesse; **12** Rehoboam with Mother; **13** Asa with Parents; **14** Uzziah with Parents; **15** Hezekiah with Parents; **16** Zerubbabel with Parents; **17** Josiah with Parents.

PROPHETS: 18 Jonah; **19** Jeremiah; **20** Daniel; **21** Ezekiel; **22** Isaiah; **23** Joel; **24** Zechariah.

SIBYLS: 25 Libyan Sibyl; **26** Persian Sibyl; **27** Cumaean Sibyl; **28** Erythrean Sibyl; **29** Delphic Sibyl.

OLD TESTAMENT SCENES OF SALVATION: 30 Punishment of Haman; **31** Moses and the Brazen Serpent; **32** David and Goliath; **33** Judith and Holofernes.

Original Sin

This shows Adam and Eve tasting the forbidden fruit from the Tree of Knowledge, and their expulsion from Paradise. Michelangelo represents Satan as a snake with the body of a woman.

The *ignudi* are athletic male nudes whose significance is uncertain.

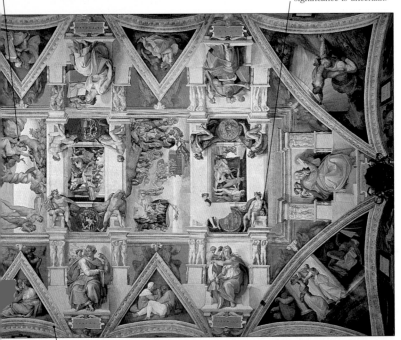

The lunettes are devoted to frescoes of the ancestors of Christ, like Hezekiah.

RESTORATION OF THE SISTINE CEILING

The recent restorers of the Sistine Chapel used computers, photography, and spectrum technology to analyse the fresco before cleaning began. They separated Michelangelo's work from that of later restorers and discovered that the restorers had attempted to clean the ceiling with materials ranging from bread to retsina wine. The new restoration revealed the familiarly

A restorer cleaning the Libyan Sibyl

dusky, eggshell-cracked figures to have creamy skins, lustrous hair and to be dressed in brightly colored, luscious robes. "A Benetton Michelangelo" mocked one critic, claiming that a layer of varnish, which the artist had added to darken the colors, had been removed. However, after examining the work, most experts agreed that the new colors probably matched those painted by Michelangelo.

Sistine Chapel: The Walls

THE MASSIVE WALLS of the Sistine Chapel, the main chapel in the Vatican Palace, were frescoed by some of the finest artists of the 15th and 16th centuries. The 12 paintings on the side walls, by artists including Perugino, Ghirlandaio, Botticelli, and Signorelli, show parallel episodes from the life of Moses and of Christ. The decoration of the chapel walls was completed between 1534 and 1541 by Michelangelo, who added the great altar wall fresco, *The Last Judgment*.

KEY TO THE FRESCOES: ARTISTS AND SUBJECTS

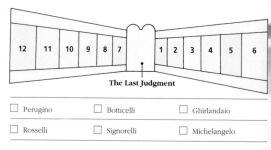

| 12 | 11 | 10 | 9 | 8 | 7 | | 1 | 2 | 3 | 4 | 5 | 6 |

The Last Judgment

☐ Perugino   ☐ Botticelli   ☐ Ghirlandaio

☐ Rosselli   ☐ Signorelli   ☐ Michelangelo

1 Baptism of Christ in the Jordan
2 Temptations of Christ
3 Calling of St. Peter and St. Andrew
4 Sermon on the Mount
5 Handing over the Keys to St. Peter
6 Last Supper

7 Moses's Journey into Egypt
8 Moses Receiving the Call
9 Crossing of the Red Sea
10 Adoration of the Golden Calf
11 Punishment of the Rebels
12 Last Days of Moses

THE LAST JUDGMENT BY MICHELANGELO

REVEALED IN 1993 after a year's restoration, *The Last Judgment* is considered to be the masterpiece of Michelangelo's mature years. It was commissioned by Pope Paul III Farnese, and required the removal of some earlier frescoes and two windows over the altar. A new wall was erected that slanted inward to stop dust from settling on it. Michelangelo worked alone on the fresco for seven years, until its completion in 1541.

The painting depicts the souls of the dead rising up to face the wrath of God, a subject that is rarely used for an altar decoration. The pope chose it as a warning to Catholics to adhere to their faith in the turmoil of the Reformation. In fact the work conveys the artist's own tormented attitude to his faith. It offers neither the certainties of Christian orthodoxy, nor the ordered view of Classicism.

In a dynamic, emotional composition, the figures are caught in a vortex of motion. The dead are torn from their graves and hauled up to face Christ the Judge, whose athletic, muscular figure is the focus of all the painting's movement. Christ shows little sympathy for the agitated saints around him, clutching the instruments of their martyrdom. Neither is any pity shown for the damned, hurled down to the demons in hell. Here Charon, pushing people off his boat into the depths of Hades, and the infernal judge Minos, are taken from Dante's *Inferno*. Minos has ass's ears, and is a portrait of courtier Biagio da Cesena, who had objected to the nude figures in the fresco. Michelangelo's self-portrait is on the skin held by the martyr St. Bartholomew.

Souls meeting the wrath of Christ in Michelangelo's *The Last Judgment*

Raphael Rooms

POPE JULIUS II'S PRIVATE APARTMENTS were built above those of his hated predecessor, Alexander VI, who died in 1503. Julius was impressed with Raphael's work and chose him to redecorate the four rooms *(stanze)*. Raphael and his pupils began in 1508, replacing works by better-known artists, including Raphael's teacher, Perugino. The new frescoes quickly established the young artist's reputation in Rome, but the project took 16 years to complete and he died before it was finished.

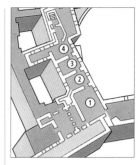

Detail from Raphael's *The Mass of Bolsena* (1512)

HALL OF CONSTANTINE

THE FRESCOES IN THIS room were started in 1517 and completed in 1525, five years after Raphael's death, and are largely the work of the artist's pupils. The theme of the decoration is the triumph of Christianity over paganism, and the four major frescoes show scenes from the life of Constantine, the first Christian emperor. These include the *Vision of the Cross* and the emperor's victory over his rival, Maxentius, at *The Battle of the Milvian Bridge*, for which Raphael had provided a preparatory sketch.

ROOM OF HELIODORUS

RAPHAEL DECORATED this private antechamber between 1512 and 1514. The main frescoes all contain thinly veiled references to the protective powers of the papacy. The room's name refers to the fresco on the right, *The Expulsion of Heliodorus from the Temple*, showing Heliodorus felled by a horseman as he tries to rob the Temple in Jerusalem. It alludes to Pope Julius II's victory over foreign armies in Italy. *The Mass of Bolsena* on the left wall refers to a miracle that occurred in 1263, in which a priest who doubted the doctrine of the Holy Host was said to have seen blood issue from it at the moment of sacrifice.

ROOM OF THE SEGNATURA

COMPLETED BETWEEN 1508 and 1511, the frescoes here are the most harmonious in the series. The scheme followed by Raphael, dictated by Pope Julius II, reflected the Humanist belief that there could be perfect harmony between Classical culture and Christianity in the search for truth. The most famous work, *The School of Athens*, centers on the debate about truth between the Greek philosophers Plato and Aristotle. Raphael depicted some of his contemporaries as philosophers, including Leonardo da Vinci, Bramante, and Michelangelo.

KEY TO FLOORPLAN

① Hall of Constantine

② Room of Heliodorus

③ Room of the Segnatura

④ Room of the Fire in the Borgo

ROOM OF THE FIRE IN THE BORGO

THIS WAS ORIGINALLY the dining room, but when the decoration was completed under Pope Leo X, it became a music room. All the frescoes exalt the reigning pope by depicting events in the lives of his 9th-century namesakes, Leo III and IV. The main frescoes were designed by Raphael, but finished by his assistants between 1514 and 1517. The most famous, *The Fire in the Borgo*, shows a miracle of 847, when Pope Leo IV put out a fire by making the sign of the cross. Raphael draws a parallel between this and the legendary flight of Aeneas from Troy, recounted by Virgil. Aeneas appears in the foreground, carrying his father Anchises on his back.

The School of Athens (1511) showing philosophers and scholars

Villa Farnesina **4**

Via della Lungara 230. **Map** 2 E5.
[06 68 80 17 67. **[** 23, 280.
[9am–1pm Mon–Sat.

THE FABULOUSLY WEALTHY
Sienese banker Agostino
Chigi commissioned this villa
in 1508 from his fellow
Sienese Baldassare Peruzzi.
Chigi's main home was across
the Tiber, and the villa was
designed purely for lavish
banquets. Artists, poets,
cardinals, princes, and the
pope himself were entertained
here in magnificent style.
Chigi also used the villa for
sojourns with the courtesan
Imperia, who allegedly inspired one of the *Three Graces*
painted by Raphael in the
Loggia of Cupid and Psyche.
  The simple harmonious
design of the Farnesina, with
a central block and projecting
wings, made it one of the first
true villas of the Renaissance.
Peruzzi decorated some of
the interiors himself, such as
the Sala della Prospettiva
upstairs, in which the illusionistic frescoes create the
impression of looking out
over 16th-century Rome
through a marble colonnade.
  Other frescoes, by Sebastiano
del Piombo and Raphael and
his pupils, illustrate Classical
myths, while the vault of the
main hall, the Sala di Galatea,
is adorned with astrological
scenes showing the position
of the stars at the time of
Chigi's birth. After his death
the business collapsed, and in
1577 the villa was sold off to
the Farnese family.

**Raphael's *Three Graces* in the
Villa Farnesina**

**Queen Christina of Sweden's
bedroom in the Palazzo Corsini**

Palazzo Corsini
and the Galleria
Corsini **5**

Via della Lungara 10. **Map** 2 D5.
[06 328 10. **[** 23, 280.
[9am–7pm Tue–Fri, 9am–2pm Sat,
9am–1pm Sun & public hols (last
adm: 30 mins before closing).
[Jan 1, May 1, Aug 15, Dec 25.

BUILT FOR Cardinal Domenico
Riario in 1510–12, the
Palazzo Corsini has numbered
Bramante, the young Michelangelo, Erasmus, and the
mother of Napoleon among
its guests. Queen Christina
of Sweden died here in 1689.
The palazzo was rebuilt by
Ferdinando Fuga, who
planned the façade to be
viewed from an angle, as Via
della Lungara is too narrow
for a full frontal view.
  When the palazzo was
bought by the state in 1893,
the Corsini family donated
their paintings, which formed
the core of the national art
collection, and was soon
augmented. The collection is
now split between Palazzo
Barberini and Palazzo Corsini.
Although the best works are
in the Barberini, there are fine
paintings by Van Dyck, Rubens,
Murillo, Reni, and Caravaggio,
notably an androgynous *St.
John the Baptist* (c.1604) by
Caravaggio, and a *Salome*
(1638) by Reni. The strangest
work is a portrait of the rotund
Queen Christina as the goddess
Diana by J Van Egmont.

Botanical
Gardens **6**

Largo Cristina di Svezia 24. **Map** 2 D5.
[06 49 91 71 06. **[** 23, 280. **[**
9:30am–6:30pm (Oct–Mar: 5:30pm)
Tue–Sat. **[** public hols.

SEQUOIAS, PALM TREES, orchids,
and bromeliads are among
the 7,000 plants from all over
the world represented in the
Botanical Gardens *(Orto
Botanico)*. Indigenous and
exotic species are grouped to
illustrate their botanical families and their adaptation to
different climates and eco-
systems. There are also some
curious plants like the ginkgo
that have survived almost
unchanged from earlier eras.

**Palm trees in the Botanical
Gardens, Trastevere**

Santa Maria in
Trastevere **7**

Piazza Santa Maria in Trastevere.
Map 5 C1. **[** 06 581 48 02. **[** H,
23, 44, 75, 280, 780. **[** 7:30am–
1pm, 4–7pm daily.

SANTA MARIA IN TRASTEVERE
was probably the first
Christian place of worship in
Rome, founded by Pope
Callixtus I in the 3rd century,
when emperors were still
pagan and Christianity a
minority cult. According to
legend, it was built on the
site where a fountain of oil
had miraculously sprung up
on the day that Christ was
born. The basilica became
the focus of devotion to the
Madonna, and although
today's church and its
remarkable mosaics date
largely from the 12th and
13th centuries, images of the

Apse mosaic of the *Coronation of the Virgin*, Santa Maria in Trastevere

Virgin continue to dominate. The façade mosaics probably date from the 12th century, and show Mary, Christ, and ten lamp-bearing women. Inside in the apse is a stylized 12th-century *Coronation of the Virgin*, and below, a series of realistic scenes from the life of the Virgin by the 13th-century artist Pietro Cavallini. The oldest image of the Virgin is a 7th-century icon, the *Madonna di Clemenza*, which depicts her as a Byzantine empress flanked by a guard of angels. It sits above the altar in the Cappella Altemps.

Santa Cecilia in Trastevere **8**

Piazza di Santa Cecilia. **Map** 6 D2.
☎ 06 589 92 89. **🚌** H, 23, 44, 280.
◻ 9am–1pm, 2–7pm daily.
Cavallini fresco ◻ 10–11:30am
Tue & Thu, 11:30am–noon Sun.

ST. CECILIA, aristocrat and patron saint of music, was martyred here in AD 230. After an unsuccessful attempt to suffocate her by locking her in the hot steam-bath of her house for three days, she was beheaded. A church was built, possibly in the 4th century, on the site of the saint's house (still to be seen beneath the church, along with the remains of a Roman tannery). For a long time her body was lost, but it turned up again in the Catacombs of San Callisto (*see p432*). In the 9th century it was reburied here by Pope Paschal I, who rebuilt the church.

A fine apse mosaic survives from this period. The altar canopy by Arnolfo di Cambio and the fresco of *The Last Judgment* by Pietro Cavallini can be reached through the adjoining convent; they date from the 13th century, one of the few periods when Rome had a distinctive artistic style.

In front of the altar is a delicate statue of St. Cecilia by Stefano Maderno, which is based on sketches made of her perfectly preserved relics when they were briefly disinterred in 1599.

San Francesco a Ripa **9**

Piazza San Francesco d'Assisi 88.
Map 6 D2. **☎** 06 581 90 20.
🚌 H, 23, 44, 75, 280. ◻
7:30am–noon, 4–7pm daily. ♿

ST. FRANCIS OF ASSISI lived here in a hospice when he visited Rome in 1219 and his stone pillow and crucifix are preserved in his cell. The church was built by a follower, a local nobleman called Rodolfo Anguillara, who is

portrayed on his tombstone wearing the Franciscan habit.

Entirely rebuilt in the 1680s by Cardinal Pallavicini, the church is rich in 17th- and 18th-century sculptures. Not to be missed in the Altieri chapel (fourth left, along the nave) is Bernini's exquisite late work, the *Ecstasy of Beata Ludovica Albertoni* (1674).

San Pietro in Montorio and the Tempietto **10**

Piazza San Pietro in Montorio 2. **Map** 5 B1. **☎** 06 581 39 40. **🚌** 44, 75, 100. ◻ 7:30am–noon, 4–6pm daily (**Tempietto ●** for restoration).
📷

Bramante's circular Tempietto at San Pietro in Montorio

THE TEMPIETTO, a diminutive masterpiece of Renaissance architecture completed by Bramante in 1502, stands in the courtyard of San Pietro in Montorio. The name means "little temple" and its circular shape echoes early Christian *martyria*, chapels built on the site of a saint's martyrdom. This was erroneously thought to be the spot in Nero's Circus where St. Peter was crucified. Bramante ringed the chapel with Doric columns, a Classical frieze, and fine balustrade.

Bernini's *Ecstasy of Beata Ludovica Albertoni*, San Francesco a Ripa

AVENTINE AND LATERAN

THIS IS ONE of the greenest parts of the city, taking in the Celian and Aventine Hills, as well as the very congested area around San Giovanni in Laterano. The Celian, now scattered with churches, was a fashionable place to live in Imperial Rome. Some of the era's splendor is still apparent in the ruins of the Baths of Caracalla.

Mosaic fragment, Baths of Caracalla

Behind the Baths rises the Aventine Hill, a peaceful, leafy area, with the superb basilica of Santa Sabina, and lovely views across the river to Trastevere and St. Peter's. In the valley below, cars and Vespas skim around the Circus Maximus, following the ancient charioteering track, while to the south lies Testaccio, a lively working-class district.

SIGHTS AT A GLANCE

Churches
San Clemente ❻
San Giovanni in Laterano ❼
Santa Maria in Cosmedin ❷
Santa Maria in Domnica ❸
Santi Quattro Coronati ❺
Santa Sabina ⓫
Santo Stefano Rotondo ❹

Ancient Sites and Buildings
Baths of Caracalla ❽
Temples of the Forum Boarium ❶

Monuments and Tombs
Protestant Cemetery ❿
Pyramid of Caius Cestius ❾

KEY

	Street by Street: Piazza della Bocca della Verità pp422–3
FS	Train station
M	Metro station
P	Parking
	City walls

GETTING THERE
Bus 95 runs from Piramide to Piazza della Bocca della Verità. The Celian is near Metro Colosseo and Circo Massimo; tram 3 and buses 81, 160, and 715 are all good routes to the Aventine area.

0 meters 250
0 yards 250

◁ **Pines and orange trees in the Aventine's Parco Savelli, with the dome of St. Peter's in the distance**

Street-by-Street: Piazza della Bocca della Verità

THE SITE OF ROME'S FIRST PORT and its busy cattle market, this is an odd little corner of the city, stretching from the heavily trafficked road running along the Tiber to the southern spur of the Capitoline Hill, a place of execution from ancient times until the Middle Ages. Although best known for the Bocca della Verità (Mouth of Truth) in Santa Maria in Cosmedin, which is supposed to snap shut on the hands of liars, there are many other sites in the area, notably two temples from the Republican era. In the 6th century the area became home to a Greek community that founded the churches of San Giorgio in Velabro and Santa Maria in Cosmedin.

The Casa dei Crescenzi, studded with ancient fragments, incorporates the ruins of a 10th-century tower built by the powerful Crescenzi family to guard the Tiber River.

Sant'Omobono stands on an archaeological site where finds date back to the 6th century.

★ **Temples of the Forum Boarium**
These two buildings are the best preserved of Rome's Republican temples ❶

Ponte Rotto, as this forlorn ruined arch in the Tiber is called, simply means "broken bridge." Built in the 2nd century BC, its original name was the Pons Aemilius.

The Fontana dei Tritoni, built by Carlo Bizzaccheri in 1715, shows the strong influence of Bernini.

★ **Santa Maria in Cosmedin**
The Bocca della Verità, *a medieval drain cover, is set into the portico* ❷

San Giovanni Decollato belonged to a confraternity that encouraged condemned prisoners to repent.

KEY

― ― ― Suggested route

0 meters 75

0 yards 75

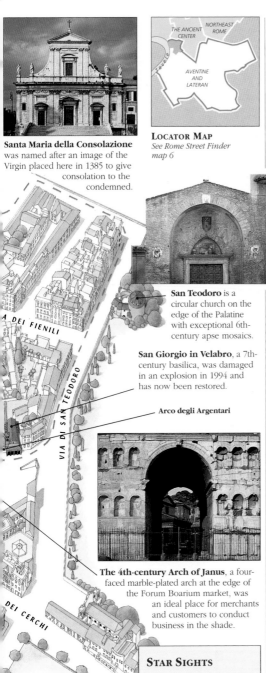

Santa Maria della Consolazione was named after an image of the Virgin placed here in 1385 to give consolation to the condemned.

LOCATOR MAP
See Rome Street Finder map 6

THE ANCIENT CENTER

NORTHEAST ROME

AVENTINE AND LATERAN

San Teodoro is a circular church on the edge of the Palatine with exceptional 6th-century apse mosaics.

San Giorgio in Velabro, a 7th-century basilica, was damaged in an explosion in 1994 and has now been restored.

Arco degli Argentari

A DEI FIENILI

VIA DI SAN TEODORO

The 4th-century Arch of Janus, a four-faced marble-plated arch at the edge of the Forum Boarium market, was an ideal place for merchants and customers to conduct business in the shade.

DEI CERCHI

STAR SIGHTS

★ Santa Maria in Cosmedin

★ Temples of the Forum Boarium

Temples of the Forum Boarium ❶

Piazza della Bocca della Verità.
Map 6 E1. 🚌 *23, 44, 63, 81, 95, 160, 170, 280, 628, 715, 716, 780.*

THESE WONDERFULLY well-preserved Republican temples are at their best at moonlight, standing in their grassy enclave beside the Tiber sheltered by umbrella pines. During the day, they look less romantic, stranded in a sea of traffic. They date from the 2nd century BC, and were saved from ruin by being consecrated as Christian churches in the Middle Ages by the Greek community then living in the area. The rectangular temple, formerly known as the Temple of Fortuna Virilis, was probably dedicated to Portunus, the god of rivers and ports. Set on a podium it has four Ionic travertine columns fluted at the front and 12 half-columns embedded in the tufa wall of the *cella* – the room that housed the image of the god. In the 9th century the Temple was converted into the church of Santa Maria Egiziaca, after a 5th-century prostitute who re-formed and became a hermit.

The smaller circular Temple, which is made of solid marble and surrounded by 20 fluted columns, was dedicated to Hercules, though it was long believed to be a Temple of Vesta because of its similarity to the one in the Forum.

The Ionic façade of the Republican era Temple of Portunus

Apse mosaic from the 9th century of the Virgin and Child in Santa Maria in Domnica

Santa Maria in Cosmedin ②

Piazza della Bocca della Verità. **Map** 6 E1. 06 678 14 19. 23, 44, 63, 81, 95, 160, 170, 280, 628, 715, 716, 780. 9am–6pm daily (10am–noon, 3–5pm winter).

THIS BEAUTIFUL church was built in the 6th century on the site of the ancient city's food market. The Romanesque bell tower and portico were added during the 12th century. In the 19th century a Baroque façade was removed and the church restored to its original simplicity. It contains fine examples of Cosmati work, in particular the mosaic flooring, the raised choir, the bishop's throne, and the canopy over the main altar.

Set into the wall of the portico is the Bocca della Verità (Mouth of Truth), a grotesque marble face, thought to have

The nave of Santa Maria in Cosmedin with its Cosmati floor

been an ancient drain cover. Medieval tradition had it that the jaws would snap shut on liars – a useful way of testing the faithfulness of spouses.

Santa Maria in Domnica ③

Piazza della Navicella 12. **Map** 7 B2. 06 700 15 19. 81, 117, 673. Colosseo. 9am–noon daily (pm sometimes).

SANTA MARIA IN DOMNICA was probably founded in the 7th century, and renovated in the 9th century. By this time the Romans had lost the art of making mosaics, so Pope Paschal I imported mosaicists. They created an exquisite apse mosaic showing the Virgin, Child, and angels in a delicate garden of paradise. Paschal I appears kneeling at the Virgin's feet wearing a square halo, indicating that he was alive when it was made.

In 1513 Andrea Sansovino added a portico decorated with lions' heads, a punning homage to Pope Leo X.

Santo Stefano Rotondo ④

Via di Santo Stefano Rotondo 7. **Map** 9 B2. 06 70 49 37 17. 81, 117, 673. for restoration, call Ministro del Collegio Germanico (06 42 11 99) for details.

SANTO STEFANO ROTONDO was built between 468 and 483 on a circular plan with four chapels in a cruciform. It has

a circular inner area enclosed by two concentric corridors. A third, outer corridor was demolished on the orders of Leon Battista Alberti in 1453. In the 16th century Niccolò Pomarancio, Antonio Tempesta, and others covered the walls with 34 frescoes, gruesomely detailing the martyrdoms of saints by Roman emperors.

Cloister of Santi Quattro Coronati

Santi Quattro Coronati ⑤

Via dei Santi Quattro Coronati 20. **Map** 7 C1. 06 70 47 54 27. 85, 117, 850. 30b. 9:30am–noon, 3:30–6pm daily.

THIS FORTIFIED convent was built in the 4th century to house the relics of four Persian stonemasons, martyred after they refused to make a statue honoring the pagan god Aesculapius. It was rebuilt after invading Normans set fire to it in 1084.

Highlights are a delightful garden cloister and the Chapel of St. Sylvester, where 12th-century frescoes recount the legend of Constantine's conversion to Christianity.

San Clemente ❻

I N 1857 FATHER MULLOOLY, the Irish Dominican prior of
San Clemente, began excavations beneath the
existing 12th-century basilica. Directly underneath he
and his successors discovered a 4th-century church,
and below that a number of ancient Roman buildings.
Both basilicas are dedicated to St. Clement, the fourth
pope. On the lowest level is a temple devoted to the
cult of Mithras, a mystical all-male religion imported
from Persia that rivaled Christianity for popularity.

VISITORS' CHECKLIST

Via di San Giovanni in Laterano.
Map 7 B1. **☏** 06 70 45 10 18.
🚌 85, 87, 117, 186, 810, 850.
Ⓜ Colosseo. 🚋 30.
⏰ 9am–12:30pm, 3–6pm daily
(Sun 10am opening).
🎫 to excavations. ✝ 📷

Cappella di Santa Caterina
*Recently restored frescoes
by the 15th-century artist
Masolino da Panicale show
scenes from the life of St.
Catherine of Alexandria.*

Entrance

Apse Mosaic
The 12th-century Triumph
of the Cross *includes
finely detailed animals
and acanthus leaves.*

**Paschal
Candlestick**
*This splendid 12th-
century spiraling
candlestick, striped
with glittering multi-
colored
mosaic, is
the work of
the Cosmati.*

**12th-century
basilica**

**18th-century
façade**

Piscina

**Schola
Cantorum**

**4th-century
basilica**

**Temple
of Mithras**

Life of San Clemente
*Faded frescoed episodes
from the life of the fourth
pope decorate the lower
church. This one tells the
story of a boy found alive
in his tomb under the sea.*

Triclinium
*An altar to the god
Mithras, showing him
slaying a bull, stands in
the dank triclinium,
a room used for ritual
banquets by cult members.*

San Giovanni in Laterano ⑦

Sᴀɴ ɢɪovᴀɴɴɪ, the cathedral of Rome, was founded by Emperor Constantine in the early 4th century. It has been rebuilt several times, notably in 1646 when Borromini restyled the interior, but retains its original basilica form. Before the papacy moved to Avignon in 1309, the adjoining Lateran Palace was the official papal residence. The present structure dates from 1589, but older parts survive, like the Scala Santa (Holy Staircase) that Christ is said to have climbed at his trial.

VISITORS' CHECKLIST

Piazza di San Giovanni in Laterano.
Map 8 D2. **[** 06 69 88 64 52.
[16, 81, 85, 87, 650. **[** 3.
M San Giovanni. **Cathedral**
[7am–6:45pm daily (Oct–Mar:
6pm). **Cloisters [** 7am–
7:30pm daily. **Museum [**
9am–1pm Sat & 1st Sun of
month. **[** **[** **[** **[**
Baptistry [for restoration.

Baptistry
Though much restored, the octagonal baptistry contains some beautiful 5th-century mosaics.

North façade

East Façade
The main entrance, on the east façade (1735), is adorned with statues of Christ and the Apostles.

Apse

Museum entrance

Lateran Palace

Papal Altar
The Gothic baldacchino, which rises over the papal altar, is decorated with 14th-century frescoes.

On Maundy Thursday the Pope, as Bishop of Rome, gives a blessing from the loggia of the city's main cathedral.

Main entrance

The Corsini Chapel
was built in the 1730s for Pope Clement XII Corsini, who lies buried in a porphyry tomb from the Pantheon.

Cloisters
Built by the Vassalletto family in about 1220, the cloisters are remarkable for their twisted columns and inlaid marble mosaics.

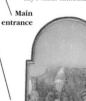

Boniface VIII Fresco
Possibly by Giotto, this fragment shows the pope announcing the Holy Year of 1300, which attracted about two million pilgrims.

Part of one of the gymnasia in the Baths of Caracalla

Baths of Caracalla ⑧

Viale delle Terme di Caracalla 52.
Map 7 A3. 06 39 74 99 07.
160, 628. 3. ☐ 9am–1 hr before
sunset Tue–Sun, 9am–2pm Mon.
Jan 1, May 1, Dec 25.

R EARING UP at the foot of the
Aventine Hill are the
monolithic redbrick ruins of
the Baths of Caracalla. Begun
by Emperor Septimius Severus
in AD 206, and completed by
his son Caracalla in AD 217,
they remained in use until the
6th century, when the Goths
sabotaged the city's aqueducts.

Going for a bath was one of
the social events of the day in
ancient Rome. Large com-
plexes such as Caracalla, with
a capacity for 1,600 bathers,
were not simply places to get
washed, but also offered an
impressive array of facilities:
art galleries, gymnasia, gardens, libraries, conference
rooms, lecture rooms, and
shops selling food and drink.

A Roman bath was a long
and complicated business,
beginning with a form of
Turkish bath, followed by a
spell in the *calidarium*, a large
hot room with pools of water
to moisten the atmosphere.
Then came the lukewarm
tepidarium, followed by a
visit to the large central
meeting place known as the
frigidarium, and finally a
plunge into the *natatio*, an
open-air swimming pool. For
the rich, this was followed by
a rubdown with scented
woolen cloth.

Most of the rich marble
decorations of the baths were
scavenged by the Farnese
family in the 16th century to

adorn the rooms of Palazzo
Farnese *(see p391)*. There are,
however, statues and mosaics
from the Baths in the Museo
Nazionale Archeologico in
Naples *(see pp474–5)* and in
the Vatican's Gregorian
Profane Museum *(see p412)*.

So dramatic and so
theatrically vivid is the setting
that for many years it was the
regular place for the open-air
opera season in August.

Pyramid of Caius Cestius ⑨

Piazzale Ostiense. **Map** 6 E4.
23, 95, 280. 3. Ⓜ *Piramide.*

C AIUS CESTIUS was a wealthy
but unimportant 1st-
century BC *praetor*, or senior
magistrate. At the time,
inspired by the Cleopatra
scandals, there was a craze
for all things Egyptian, and
in 12 BC, Caius decided to
commission himself a
pyramid as a tomb. Set into
the Aurelian Wall near Porta
San Paolo, it is built of brick
and faced with white marble;
according to an inscription, it
took just 330 days to build.

**The Pyramid of Caius Cestius on
Piazzale Ostiense**

Protestant Cemetery ⑩

Cimitero Acattolico, Via di Caio Cestio.
Map 6 E4. 06 574 19 00. 23,
280. 3. ☐ Apr–Sep: 9am–5:30pm
(Oct–Mar: 4:30pm) Tue–Sun (last adm:
30 mins before closing). **Donation.**

N ONCATHOLICS have been
buried in this peaceful
cemetery behind the Aurelian
Wall since 1738. In the oldest
part (on the left as you enter)
is the grave of the poet John
Keats, who died in 1821 in a
house on Piazza di Spagna
(see p398). He wrote his own
epitaph: "Here lies one whose
name was writ in water." Not
far away from here rest the
ashes of Percy Bysshe Shelley,
who drowned in 1822.

The interior of Santa Sabina

Santa Sabina ⑪

Piazza Pietro d'Illiria 1. **Map** 6 E4.
06 574 35 73. 23, 44, 95,
170, 781. ☐ 6:30am–12:45pm,
3:30–7pm daily.

H IGH ON THE AVENTINE stands
an early Christian basilica,
founded by Peter of Illyria in
AD 425 and later given to the
Dominican order. It was restored to its original simplicity in
the early 20th century. Light fil-
ters through 9th-century windows on to a nave framed by
pale Corinthian columns.
Above the main door is a blue
and gold 5th-century mosaic
inscription to Peter. In the side
portico outside is a 5th-century
paneled door carved with biblical scenes, notably one of the
oldest images of the Crucifixion (top left-hand corner).

Farther Afield

IT IS WELL WORTH making the effort to see some of Rome's outlying sights. Highlights are the Villa Giulia, home to a magnificent Etruscan museum, and the Museo Borghese on the splendid Villa Borghese estate, with its extraordinary collection of virtuoso statues by Bernini. Other sights range from ancient churches and catacombs, to the more modern suburb of EUR, a strange architectural medley begun by Mussolini in the 1930s.

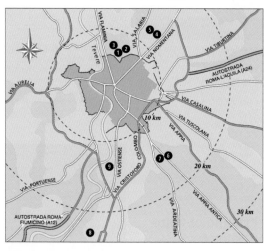

KEY

▥	Central Rome
▢	Suburbs
▰	Highway
▬	Major road
▭	Minor road
⎯	City walls

10 km = 6 miles

Villa Borghese ❶

Map 3 B1. ☎ 06 321 65 64. ⛐ 52, 53, 88, 95, 116, 490. ⛟ 3, 19. ◯ Mar–Oct: 9:30am–6pm; Nov–Feb: 9:30am–5pm daily. ⬤ Jan 1, Dec 25.

THE VILLA AND ITS PARK were designed in 1605 for Cardinal Scipione Borghese, the sybaritic nephew of Pope Paul V. An extravagant patron of the arts, he amassed one of Europe's finest collections of paintings, statues, and antiquities, many of which are still displayed in the villa that he built especially to house his antique sculptures.

The **park** was one of the first of its kind in Rome, its formal gardens divided by avenues and graced with statues. It contained 400 newly planted trees, garden sculpture by Bernini's father, Pietro, along with many ingenious fountains, "secret" flower gardens, enclosures of exotic animals and birds, and even a grotto with artificial rain. There was also a speaking robot and a trick

chair, which trapped anyone who sat in it. At first the grounds were open to the public, but after a visitor was shocked by the collection of erotic paintings, Paul V decided to keep the park private.

In 1773 work began on redesigning the park in the wilder, Romantic style made fashionable by landscape artists like Claude Lorrain and Poussin. Over the next few

Temple of Aesculapius, an 18th-century folly, at the Villa Borghese

years mock-Classical temples, fountains and *casine* (summerhouses) were added. In 1901, the park and villa were acquired by the state, and in 1911 the area was chosen as the site for the International Exhibition. Pavilions were built by many of the world's nations, the most impressive of which is the **British School at Rome** by Edwin Lutyens. In the northeastern corner of the park lie the Museo Zoologico and a small redeveloped zoo, known as the Bioparco, where the emphasis is on conservation. Today the estates of the Villa Borghese, Villa Giulia and the Pincio gardens form one vast park, with the **Giardino del Lago**, at its center, named after an artificial boating lake. Its main entrance is marked by an 18th-century copy of the Arch of Septimius Severus, while on the lake's island is a fake Ionic temple to the Greek god of health, Aesculapius, designed by the 18th-century architect Antonis Aspurucci.

A circular Temple of Diana folly lies between the Porta Pinciana, at the top of Via Veneto, and Piazza di Siena, a grassy amphitheater which hosts Rome's international horse show in May. Its umbrella pines inspired the composer Ottorino Respighi to write *The Pines of Rome* (1924). The open-air opera season is also held in the park.

To the northwest of the park is the Galleria Nazionale d'Arte Moderna, which houses a large but somewhat uninspiring collection of 19th- and 20th-century paintings.

Sacred and Profane Love by Titian (1514), in the Galleria Borghese

Museo e Galleria Borghese ❷

Villa Borghese, Piazzale Scipione Borghese 5. 📞 06 328 10. 🚌 52, 53, 116, 910. 🚋 3, 19. 🕐 9am–7pm Tue–Sat, 9am–8pm Sun (reservations needed for Sat & Sun). ⚫ public hols. 🈳 🅿️

Scipione Borghese's villa was designed in 1605 as a typical Roman country house, with its wings projecting into the surrounding gardens. It was built by Flaminio Ponzio, Pope Paul V's architect, and was used by Scipione for entertaining guests and for displaying his impressive collection of paintings and sculpture. Between 1801 and 1809 Prince Camillo Borghese, husband to Napoleon's sister Pauline, unfortunately sold many of the family paintings

to his brother-in-law, and swapped 200 of Scipione's Classical statues for an estate in Piedmont. These statues are still in the Louvre and, as a consequence, the remaining antique Classical collection is less interesting than it might once have been. However, the hedonistic cardinal was an enthusiastic patron of the arts and the sculptures he commissioned from artists such as the young Bernini now rank among their most famous works.

The eight rooms of the ground floor of the Villa Borghese are set around a central hall, the Salone. The most famous statue is one of Bernini's finest works, *Apollo and Daphne* (1624) in room 3, which shows the nymph Daphne with bay leaves sprouting from her out-stretched fingers, roots growing from her toes, and rough bark enfolding her smooth body, as she begins to metamorphose into a laurel tree to escape being abducted by the god Apollo. Abduction is also the theme of *Rape of Proserpina*, again by Bernini, in room 4. Depicting Pluto, the god of the underworld, carrying Proserpina, daughter of Ceres, off to be his bride, the sculpture is a virtuoso piece in which Bernini contrasts the taut musculature of Pluto with the soft yielding flesh of Proserpina, whose thigh dimples in his iron grip.

The third famous Bernini piece, which dates from 1623, is *David* in room 2. The artist captures the tensed, grimacing youth the moment before he releases the stone that slew Goliath. It is said that Pope Urban VIII held a mirror up to Bernini so that the sculptor could model David's face on

Detail of *Rape of Proserpina* by Bernini (1622), Museo Borghese

his own. In the next alcove is the Villa Borghese's most infamous work – a sculpture, executed in 1805 by Canova, of Pauline Borghese as *Venus Victrix* (Venus the Conqueror). The seminaked Pauline reclining on a chaise longue shocked those who saw it and Pauline's husband kept the statue locked away, even denying Canova access to it.

The next room holds a selection of antiquities, notably a Roman copy of a plump *Bacchus* by the 4th-century BC Greek sculptor Praxiteles, and frag-ments of a 3rd-century AD mosaic found on one of the Borghese estates in Torrenova, showing gladiators battling with wild animals.

The Galleria Borghese, on the upper floor, houses some superb Baroque and Renaissance paintings, which could fomerly be seen at the Complesso San Michele in Trastevere while the gallery was closed for renovation. Works includes Raphael's masterpiece, the *Deposition*, various works by Caravaggio, the graceful *Danäe* by the 16th-century artist Correggio, as well as works by Pinturicchio, Barocci, Rubens, and Titian.

Bernini's *Apollo and Daphne* (1624)

Villa Giulia ❸

T HIS VILLA WAS BUILT in 1551 as a country retreat for
Pope Julius III. Designed by Vignola and Ammannati,
with contributions by Michelangelo and Vasari, it was
intended for entertaining guests of the Vatican, such as
Queen Christina of Sweden, rather than as a permanent
home. The gardens were planted with 36,000 trees and
peppered with pavilions and fountains. The villa once
housed an outstanding collection of statues: 160 boats
filled with statues
and ornaments
were sent to the
Vatican after the
pope died in 1555.

Since 1889 the villa
has been home to
the Museo Nazionale
Etrusco, an impressive
collection of pre-Roman
antiquities from
central Italy.

VISITORS' CHECKLIST

Piazzale di Villa Giulia 9.
📞 06 482 41 84 (info).
📞 06 328 10 (reservations)
🚌 52, 95. 🚊 3, 19.
🕐 9am–7pm Tue–Sat, 9am–
8pm Sun. ⬤ Jan 1, May 1,
Dec 25. ♿ 📷 with seven days'
notice. 🎵 **Concerts** at the
Ninfeo (Nypheum) on Saturdays
in Jul & Aug.
🎵

Rooms 24–29 contain finds from the Ager
Faliscus, an area between the Tiber and
Lake Bracciano, in particular temples from
Falerii Vetere, the principal Faliscan town.

Spiraled Faliscan Crater
*Painted in the free style of the 4th century
BC, this spiral handled vase was used to
hold wines or oil. The Falisci were an
Italic tribe influenced by the Etruscans.*

Room 19 exhibits finds from
the Castellani collection,
including early 6th-century
ceramics and bronzes.

Rooms 11–18,
the Antiquarium
collection, display
domestic and votive
objects and ceramics,
including the Chigi
vase from 6th-
century BC
Corinth.

Ficoroni Cist
*Engraved and
beautifully
illustrated, this
4th-century BC
bronze
marriage coffer
held mirrors
and other body-
care implements*

**Ninfeo
(Nympheum)**

**Husband and Wife
Sarcophagus**
*This 6th-century BC
tomb from Cerveteri
shows a deceased
couple banqueting
in the afterlife. Their
tender expression bears
witness to the skill
of Etruscan artists.*

Rooms 30–34 exhibit finds
from various sites including the
Temple of Diana at Nemi.

Rooms 1–10
are arranged by
site, with
Vulci (most import-
antly articles from the
Warrior's Tomb) and including
Bisenzio, Veii, and Cerveteri.

Entrance

KEY TO FLOOR PLAN

☐	Ground floor
☐	First floor
☐	Nonexhibition space

Apse mosaic in Sant'Agnese, showing the saint flanked by two popes

Sant'Agnese fuori le Mura ❹

Via Nomentana 349. ☎ 06 861 08 40. 🚌 36, 60, 84, 90. ⏰ 9am–noon, 4–6pm Tue–Sat, 4–6pm Sun, 9am–noon Mon. 🎫 to catacombs. 📷 ♿ ✍

SANT'AGNESE FUORI LE MURA was built in the 4th century above the crypt of the 13-year-old martyr St. Agnes, and although much altered, it retains the form of the original basilica. According to legend it was founded by Constantine's daughter Constantia, who was cured of leprosy after sleeping beside Agnes's tomb.

In the 7th-century apse mosaic, St. Agnes appears as a bejeweled Byzantine empress in a stole of gold and a violet robe. Tradition has it that she appeared like this eight days after her death holding a white lamb. On January 21 two lambs are blessed in the church and a vestment called a *pallium* is woven from their wool, to be given to a new archbishop.

Santa Costanza ❺

Via Nomentana 349. ☎ 06 861 08 40. 🚌 36, 60, 84, 90. ⏰ 9am–noon, 4–6pm Tue–Sat, 4–6pm Sun, 9am–noon Mon. 📷 ♿ ✍

THIS CIRCULAR church was built in the early 4th century as a mausoleum for Emperor Constantine's daughters, Constantia and Helena. The dome and its drum are supported by an arcade that rests on 12 magnificent pairs of granite columns, while the encircling ambulatory has a barrel-vaulted ceiling decorated with the world's earliest surviving Christian mosaics. Dating from the 4th century, they are thought to have been copied from a secular Roman floor and include flowers, animals, and birds. There is even a charming scene of a Roman grape-harvest, though the wine is said by Christians to represent Christ's blood.

In a niche on the far side of the church is a replica of Constantia's ornate porphyry sarcophagus, carved with cherubs crushing grapes. The original was moved to the Vatican Museums in 1790.

Circular interior of the 4th-century church of Santa Costanza

The sanctity of Constantia is somewhat debatable. Described by the historian Marcellinus as a fury incarnate, constantly goading her equally unpleasant husband, Hannibalianus, to violence, her canonization was probably the result of some confusion with a saintly nun of the same name.

Via Appia Antica ❻

🚌 218, 760.

Cypresses lining the Via Appia

THE FIRST PART of the Via Appia was built in 312 BC by Appius Claudius Caecus. In 190 BC, when it was extended to the ports of Taranto and Brindisi, the road became Rome's link with its empire in the East. It was the route taken by the funeral processions of the dictator Sulla (78 BC) and Emperor Augustus (AD 14), and it was along this road that St. Paul was led as a prisoner to Rome in AD 56. The church of Domine Quo Vadis? marks the spot where St. Peter is said to have met Christ when fleeing Rome.

The road is lined with ruined family tombs, decaying monuments, and collective burial places (*columbaria*). Beneath the fields on either side lies a maze of catacombs, including those of San Callisto and San Sebastiano.

Catacombs ❼

Via Appia Antica 110. 🚌 *218, 660, 760.* **San Callisto** 📞 *06 513 01 51.* 🕐 *9am–noon, 2:30–5:30pm Fri–Wed.* ⬤ *Jan 1, Feb & Nov, Easter Sun, Dec 25.* 🎫 ⛪ 🚫 🏛

I N BURYING THEIR DEAD in underground cemeteries outside the city walls, the early Christians were simply obeying the laws of the time. They were not forced to use them because of persecution, as later popular myth has suggested. Many saints were buried there, and the catacombs later became shrines and places of pilgrimage.

Today several catacombs are open to the public. The vast Catacombs of San Callisto, hewn from volcanic tufa, contain niches, or *loculi*, which held two or three bodies, as well as the burial places of several early popes. Close by, walls in the Catacombs of San Sebastiano are covered in graffiti invoking St. Peter and St. Paul, whose remains may once have been moved here.

Engraving of Christian ceremony in Catacombs of San Callisto (AD 50)

EUR ❽

🚌 *170, 671, 714.* Ⓜ *EUR Fermi, EUR Palasport.* **Museo della Civiltà Romana** 📞 *06 592 60 41.* 🕐 *9am–6pm Tue–Sat, 9am–1pm Sun & public hols.* ⬤ *Jan 1, May 1, Dec 25.* 🎫

T HE ESPOSIZIONE UNIVERSALE di Roma (EUR), a suburb to the south of the city, was originally built for an international exhibition, a kind of "Work Olympics," which was

EUR's Palazzo della Civiltà del Lavoro, the "Square Colosseum"

planned for 1942, but never took place because of the outbreak of war. The architecture was intended to glorify Fascism, as a result the bombastic style of the buildings can look overblown and rhetorical to modern eyes. Of all the buildings the best known is probably the Palazzo della Civiltà del Lavoro (the Palace of the Civilization of Work), an unmistakable landmark for people arriving from Fiumicino airport.

The project was eventually completed in the 1950s. Despite the area's dubious architecture, EUR has been a planning success, and people are still eager to live here. As well as residential housing, the vast marble halls along the wide boulevards are also home to a number of government offices and museums. Best among the latter is the Museo della Civiltà Romana, famous for its casts of the reliefs from the Column of Trajan, and for a large scale

model depicting 4th-century Rome with all the buildings which then stood within the Aurelian walls. The south of the suburb features a lake and shady park, and the huge domed Palazzo dello Sport, built for the 1960 Olympics.

San Paolo fuori le Mura ❾

Via Ostiense 186. 🚌 *23, 128, 170, 670, 702, 707, 761, 766.* Ⓜ *San Paolo.* 📞 *06 541 03 41.* 🕐 *7am–7pm daily (6:30pm winter).* ⛪ 📷 ♿ 🏛

T ODAY'S CHURCH is a faithful if soulless reconstruction of the great 4th-century basilica destroyed by fire in 1823. Only a few fragments of the earlier church survived, most notably the cloister (1241), with its pairs of colorful inlaid columns, considered one of the most beautiful in Rome.

Elsewhere, the church's triumphal arch is decorated on one side with heavily restored 5th-century mosaics, and on the other with mosaics by Pietro Cavallini, originally on the façade. The equally fine mosaics (1220) in the apse represent the figures of Christ with St. Peter, St. Andrew, St. Paul and St. Luke.

The single most outstanding work of art is the fine marble canopy over the high altar, the work of Arnolfo di Cambio (1285), with the possible assistance of Pietro Cavallini. Below the altar is the *confessio* where it is alleged St. Paul was once buried. To its right is an impressive Paschal candlestick dating from the 12th century by Nicolò di Angelo and Pietro Vassalletto.

19th-century mosaic on façade of San Paolo fuori le Mura

ROME STREET FINDER

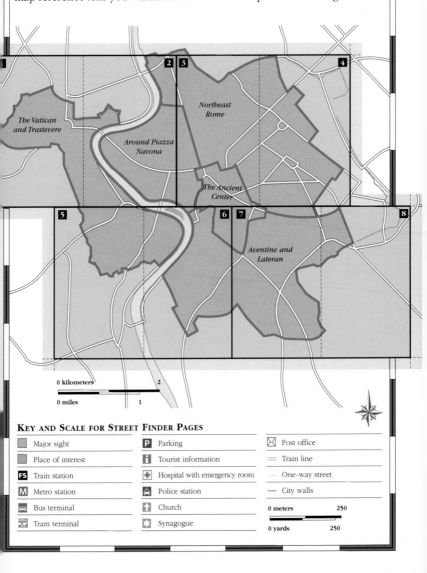

M AP REFERENCES given with sights described in the Rome chapters relate to the maps on the following pages. Map references are also given for hotels *(see pp542–75)* and restaurant listings *(see pp578–609)* and for useful addresses in the *Travelers' Needs* and *Survival Guide* sections at the back of the book. The first figure in the map reference tells you which Street

Finder map to turn to, and the letter and number that follow refer to the grid reference on that map. The small map below shows the area of Rome covered by each of the six maps, and the corresponding map, number is given in black. All the major sights are sketched out on the maps, and symbols, listed in the key below, are used to indicate the location of other important buildings.

The Vatican and Trastevere

Around Piazza Navona

Northeast Rome

The Ancient Center

Aventine and Lateran

0 kilometers   2

0 miles   1

KEY AND SCALE FOR STREET FINDER PAGES

■	Major sight	P	Parking	⊠	Post office
■	Place of interest	ℹ	Tourist information	=	Train line
FS	Train station	✚	Hospital with emergency room	→	One-way street
M	Metro station	Ⓟ	Police station	—	City walls
▬	Bus terminal	✝	Church		
▦	Tram terminal	✡	Synagogue		

0 meters   250

0 yards   250

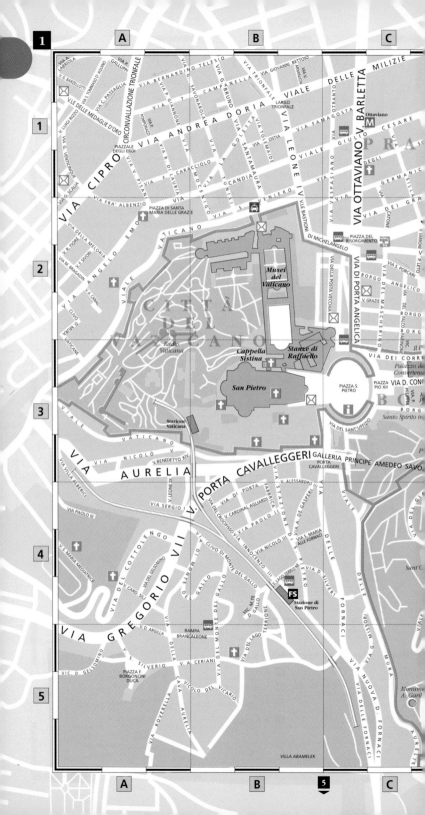

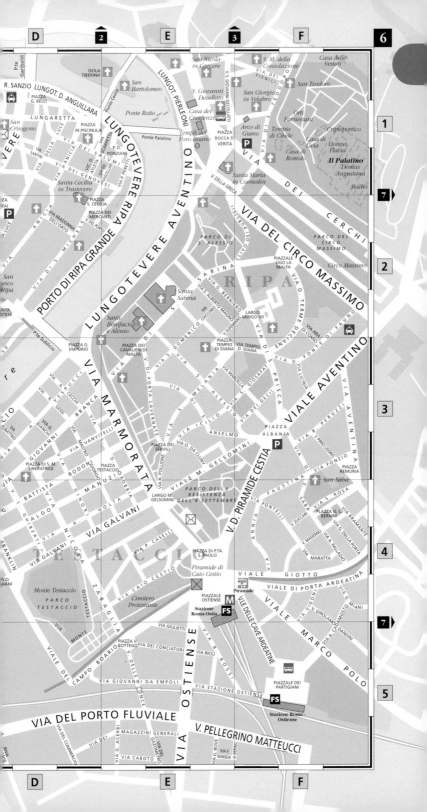

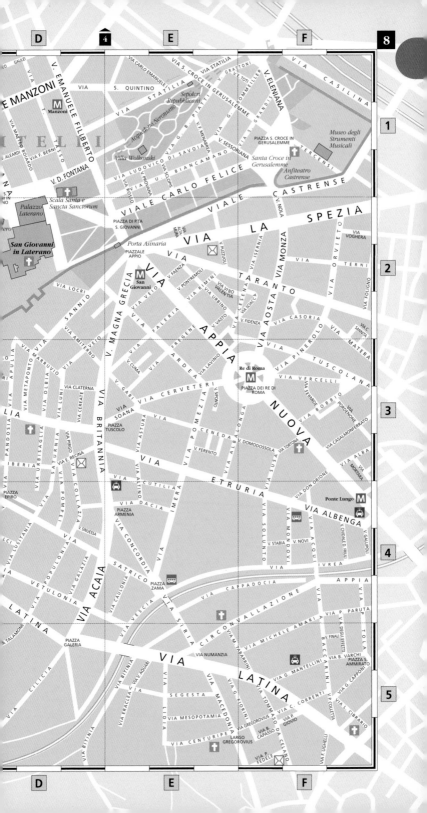

442

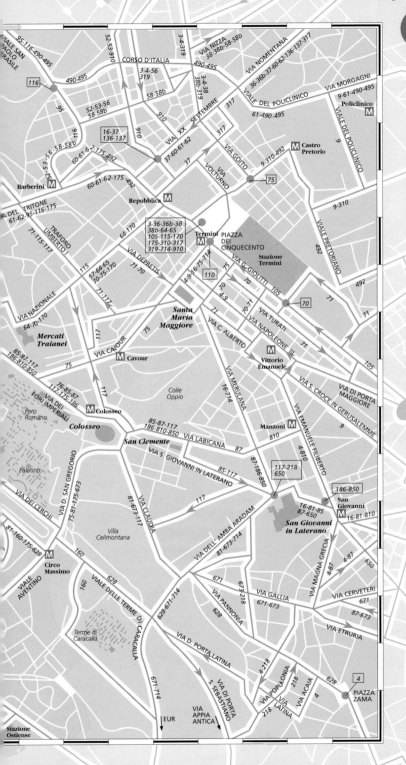

LAZIO

LYING BETWEEN *the Apennines and the Tyrrhenian Sea, Lazio is a varied region of volcanic lakes, mountains, ravines, vineyards, and olive groves. Before the rise of Rome, it was populated by the Etruscans and various Italic tribes, including the Latins, after whom the region is named. Besides rich archaeological sites, Lazio also offers skiing, and swimming and watersports in the lakes and sea.*

Lazio was inhabited at least 60,000 years ago, although the first signs of a substantial civilization date back to the 10th century BC. By the 7th century BC a flourishing Etruscan and Sabine civilization based on trade and agriculture existed in the north, while the region's south-ern margins were colonized by the Latins, Volsci, and Ernici. History mingles with myth in Virgil's writings, whose stories tell how Aeneas landed on Lazio's coast where he married the daughter of the King of the Latins. From this alliance, Romulus and Remus (legend-ary founders of Rome) were descended.

With the rise of Rome as a power, the Etruscan and Latin peoples were, in time, overwhelmed and the focus of the region turned to the city of Rome. Great roads and aqueducts extended out of the city like spokes of a wheel, and the wealthy built lavish villas in the countryside.

The early Middle Ages saw the rise of the Church's temporal power and, with the foun-dation of monasteries at Subiaco and Montecassino, Lazio became the cradle of western monasticism, and even-tually part of the Papal States. In the 16th and 17th centuries, wealthy papal families competed with one another to build luxurious villas and gardens, hiring some of the best archi-tects of the Renaissance and Baroque.

Throughout its history, however, Lazio has been eclipsed and neglected by Rome. The Pontine marshes were a malaria-ridden swamp until the 1920s, when Mussolini had them drained and brought new roads and agricultural improvements to the area.

Looking out over Caprarola during the early evening *passeggiata*

◁ **Vignola's graceful Renaissance parterre gardens and fountains in Villa Lante, Viterbo**

Exploring Lazio

MUCH OF LAZIO'S LANDSCAPE WAS FORMED by the eruption of four volcanoes that showered the area with lava. Lakes formed in the craters, and the soil, rendered fertile by the lava, nourished vines, olives, fruit, and nut trees. The volcanic activity also left Lazio with hot springs, notably around Tivoli, Viterbo, and Fiuggi. Rome dominates the area, dividing the wooded hills of the north from the reclaimed Pontine marshes in the south. Swimming and sailing are possible in lakes Bracciano, Bolsena, and Albano, and Lazio's best beaches lie between Gaeta and Sabaudia in the Parco Nazionale del Circeo.

SIGHTS AT A GLANCE

Anagni **15**
Bomarzo **4**
Caprarola **5**
Cerveteri **7**
Frascati and
   the Castelli Romani **10**
Gaeta **19**
Lake Bracciano **8**
Montecassino **14**
Montefiascone **3**
Ostia Antica **9**
Palestrina **12**
ROME pp372–443
Sermoneta and Ninfa **16**
Sperlonga **18**
Subiaco **13**
Tarquinia **6**
Terracina **17**
Tivoli **11**
Tuscania **1**
Viterbo **2**

SEE ALSO

• **Where to Stay** pp568–9

• **Where to Eat** pp601–2

The Tolfa hills southwest of Lake Bracciano

KEY

▨	Highway
▬	Major road
▭	Minor road
▬	Scenic route
～	River
✲	Viewpoint

The old quarter overlooking the beach at Sperlonga

GETTING AROUND

Rome's two international airports at Fiumicino and Ciampino serve the region. The main highways are the *Autostrada del Sole* (A1) from Firenze–Roma and Roma–Napoli, and the Roma–L'Aquila (A24). The ring road *(raccordo anulare)* around Rome connects the highways and main roads.

The Lazio bus service, COTRAL, serves all the main towns with changeover points for the smaller locations in Rome and at Latina, Frosinone, Viterbo, and Rieti. Train routes into the region from other Italian cities are efficient, although within the region the services are slower and less frequent.

Palestrina's terraces climbing up the hill

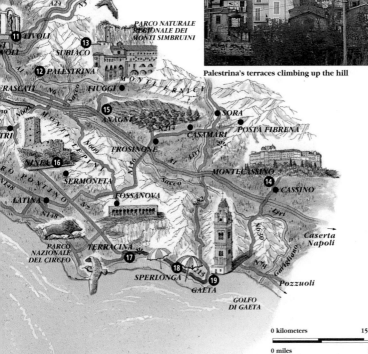

Carved loggia of the Palazzo Papale, Viterbo

Tuscania ❶

Viterbo. 🏠 7,500. 🚌 ℹ️ Largo del Teatro (0761 43 63 71). 🏛 Fri am.

TUSCANIA'S TRIM WALLS and towers are visible from afar on the empty low-lying plains between Viterbo and Tarquinia. Although shaken by an earthquake in 1971, its medieval and Renaissance buildings have since been carefully re-constructed. Just outside the city walls, on the rocky Colle San Pietro, two remarkable churches dating from the Lombard-Romanesque period occupy the site of Tuscana, a major Etruscan center con-quered by Rome in 300 BC.

Santa Maria Maggiore, at the foot of the hill, has a typically Lombard-Romanesque asymmetric façade with blind arcades and a bold rose

Façade of San Pietro, Tuscania

window. Over the central door lies a simple marble Madonna and Child, framed by abstract motifs and biblical scenes. Inside, a rare 12th-century full-immersion bap-tismal font stands in the aisle. The Lombard-Romanesque church of **San Pietro**, on top of the hill, is a striking building of ocher-hued tufa and white marble details. It stands on a grassy piazza, along with two medieval towers and a bishop's palace. The façade features an intri-cately inlaid rose window flanked by strange reliefs, including three-headed bearded demons. The interior is true to its 8th-century form, with squat columns, toothed arches, capitals carved with stylized plants, and a Cosmati floor. Below the church lies a strange mosquelike crypt.

Viterbo ❷

🏠 60,000. 🚉 🚌 ℹ️ Piazza San Carluccio 5 (0761 30 47 95). 🏛 Sat.

VITERBO WAS AN important Etruscan center before falling to the Romans in the 4th century BC. Its heyday, however, came in the 13th century when it briefly became the papal seat (1257–81). During World War II it was devastated, but the austere gray stone medieval core, still encircled by walls, and many of the town's churches, have been carefully restored.

In **San Pellegrino**, Viterbo's oldest and best preserved quarter, medieval houses with towers, arches, and external staircases line narrow streets running between little piazzas decorated with fountains.

On Piazza San Lorenzo the 12th-century **duomo** boasts an elegant black- and white-striped bell tower, a solemn 16th-century façade, and a stark Romanesque interior. The adjacent 13th-century **Palazzo Papale**, with a finely carved loggia, was built for popes on their visits to the city.

The town's civic buildings border the main square, Piazza del Plebiscito. The most inter-esting is the 15th-century **Palazzo dei Priori**, frescoed inside by Baldassare Croce with scenes from the town's history and mythological past.

Outside the city walls, on Viale Capocci, the Romanesque **Santa Maria della Verità** has wonderful 15th-century fres-coes by Lorenzo da Viterbo.

Villa Lante's small but splendid Renaissance gardens, considered Vignola's masterpiece

ENVIRONS: The **Villa Lante**, northeast of Viterbo, was begun in 1562 by Vignola for Cardinal Gambara. The main attractions are the outstanding Renaissance gardens and fountains. Be careful not to be a victim of a 16th-century practical joke: many of the fountains will sprinkle people without warning.

Palazzo dei Priori
Piazza Plebiscito. [0761 30 46 43.] daily. ● public hols. &

Villa Lante
Bagnaia. [0761 28 80 08.] Tue–Sun. ● Jan 1, May 1, Dec 25. & to gardens.

Montefiascone ❸

Viterbo. 🏠 13,000. FS 📧 i Largo Plebiscito (0761 83 20 60). ● Wed.

Carved 11th-century capital in San Flaviano, Montefiascone

THIS PRETTY TOWN is perched on the edge of a defunct volcanic crater between the shores of Lake Bolsena, over which there are splendid views, and the Via Cassia. It is dominated by the octagonal bulk of its cathedral, **Santa Margherita**, whose dome, created in the 1670s by Carlo Fontana, is second in size only to St. Peter's.

On the town's outskirts, along the Via Cassia toward Orvieto, lies **San Flaviano**, a lovely double-decker building with a 12th-century church oriented east over an 11th-century church pointing west. Inside are some fine 14th-century frescoes and freely carved capitals, thought to have been inspired by the traditions of Etruscan art.

The main façade of the pentagonal Palazzo Farnese at Caprarola

ENVIRONS: The popular lakeside beach resort of **Bolsena**, 15 km (9 miles) north on Lake Bolsena, has a medieval castle, as well as boats to the islands of Bisentina and Martana.

Bomarzo ❹

Parco dei Mostri, Bomarzo. [0761 92 40 29. FS to Viterbo. 📧 from Viterbo.] 8am–sunset. &

THE SACRO BOSCO beneath the town of Bomarzo was created between 1522 and 1580 by Duke Vicino Orsini as a bizarre memorial to his late wife. Far from designing a meticulous Renaissance garden, Orsini embraced the artificiality and distortion of the Mannerist period by creating lopsided buildings and sculpting huge boulders of stone into fantastic creatures and vast allegorical monsters.

One of the bizarre stone monsters in Bomarzo's Sacro Bosco

Caprarola ❺

Viterbo. 🏠 4,900. 📧 i Via Filippo Nicolai 2 (0761 64 61 57). ● Tue.

PERHAPS THE GRANDEST of the country villas created during the 17th century by the wealthy families of Rome, **Palazzo Farnese** (see p370) is the focal point of the medieval village of Caprarola. Designed by Vignola, it was built between 1559 and 1575 and takes its star shape from the foundations of a large pentagonal fortress, designed by Antonio da Sangallo the Younger half a century earlier. On the main floor, reached by an elaborately stuccoed spiral staircase, the rooms were frescoed, largely by the Zuccari brothers in 1560, with scenes depicting heroic episodes from the life of Hercules and the Farnese family.

ENVIRONS: Created, according to legend, by the god Hercules ramming his club into the ground, **Lago di Vico**, 4 km (3 miles) west of Caprarola, in fact occupies the remnants of a volcanic crater. An idyllic enclave, the lake is encircled by the wooded slopes of the Cimini Hills (much of which is a nature preserve). A scenic road runs around the lake, and the best place for swimming is on the southeast shore.

Palazzo Farnese
Caprarola. [0761 64 60 52.] Tue–Sun. ● Jan 1, May 1, Dec 25.

Etruscan tumulus tombs from the necropolis at Cerveteri

Tarquinia ❻

Viterbo. 🏠 *14,000.* **FS** 🚌 **i** *Piazza Cavour (0766 85 63 84).* 🍴 *Wed.*

ANCIENT TARQUINIA (Tarxuna) was one of Etruria's most important centers. It occupied a strategic position to the northeast of the present town, on a ridge dominating the coastal plain, until the 4th century BC when it fell to Rome.

Tarquinia itself is worth seeing for its crumbling medieval churches and spacious main square, although the main reason to visit is the **Museo Archeologico e Necropoli**, which has one of Italy's better collections of Etruscan finds. Relaxed, reclining statues of the deceased adorn the sarcophagi on the ground floor, but the star attraction, on the mezzanine, is a group of terra-cotta winged horses dating from the 4th century BC.

On a hilltop 2 km (1 mile) southeast of town are the frescoed tombs of the **necropolis** dug into the soft volcanic tufa. There are almost 6,000

tombs but only about 15 can be visited at a time. The frescoes that decorate them, designed to remind the dead of life, range from frenetic dancing figures in the Tomba delle Leonesse to the diners reclining in the Tomba dei Leopardi.

🏛 Museo Archeologico e Necropoli

Piazza Cavour. **C** *0766 85 60 36.* 🕐 *Tue–Sun.* ● *Jan 1, May 1, Dec 25.* 🎫 *valid also for necropolis.* ♿

Cerveteri ❼

Roma. 🏠 *30,000.* **FS** 🚌 **i** *Piazza Risorgimento (06 995 18 58).* 🍴 *Fri.*

IN THE 6TH century BC Cerveteri (ancient Kysry) was one of the most populated and culturally rich towns of the Mediterranean, trading with Greece and controlling a large area along the coast. The **necropolis**, a city of the dead 2 km (1 mile) outside town, is a network of streets lined with tombs dating from the 7th to the 1st century BC. Some of the larger tumulus tombs, like the Tomba degli Scudi e delle Sedie, are arranged like houses with rooms, doors, and corridors. The Tomba dei Rilievi is decorated with plaster reliefs of tools, pets, and mythological figures.

Although the best finds from the necropolis are in museums such as the Vatican Museums, Villa Giulia and the British Museum in London, some are in the small **Museo Nazionale Cerite** in the center of town.

ENVIRONS: There are more traces of the Etruscans to be seen at **Norchia**, where the tombs are carved out of a rock face, and **Sutri**, whose amphitheater is one of the few relics of the living Etruscans.

⋔ Necropolis
Via delle Necropoli. **C** *06 994 00 01.* 🕐 *Tue–Sun.* ● *public hols.* 🎫
🏛 Museo Nazionale Cerite
Piazza Santa Maria. **C** *06 994 13 54.* 🕐 *Tue–Sun.* ● *Public hols.* 🎫

Lake Bracciano ❽

Roma. **FS** 🚌 *Bracciano.* **i** *Via Claudia 72, Bracciano (06 99 84 00 69).*

Medieval Anguillara on Lake Bracciano

BRACCIANO is a large lake famous for its fish, and popular for water sports and lakeside lunches.

Medieval **Anguillara**, to the south, is the prettiest of the lakeside towns with romantic views over the water. The main town, **Bracciano**, on the east shore, is dominated by the Orsini-Odescalchi fortress, a pentagonal 15th-century structure with frescoes by Antoniazzo Romano and other Tuscan and Umbrian artists.

♠ Castello Orsini-Odescalchi
Via del Castello. **C** *06 99 80 43 48.* 🕐 *Tue–Sun.* ● *Jan 1, Dec 25.* 🎫 🎫

Dancers from the 4th-century BC frescoed Tomba del Triclinio in the Museo Archeologico, Tarquinia

Ostia Antica **9**

Viale dei Romagnoli 717, Ostia.
[06 328 10. **M** Magliana on line
B then **FS** to Ostia Antica.
Excavations & Museum
○ 9am–7pm Tue–Sun (6pm
winter). **●** Jan 1, May 1,
Dec 25. **[**

F OR OVER 600 years
Ostia was Rome's
main port and a busy
trading centre, until the
5th century AD when a
disastrous combination
of malaria and com-
mercial competition
brought the town into
decline. Silt preserved
its buildings, and it
now lies 5 km
(3 miles) inland.

The ruins of Ostia give a
vivid idea of life in Classical
times. The main thoroughfare,
the **Decumanus Maximus**,
runs through the Forum,
which houses Ostia's largest
temple, the **Capitol**, and past
the restored **theater**, still used
for open-air concerts in
summer. The road is lined
with baths, shops, and multi-
story buildings. There is even
a **Thermopolium**, or bar, with
a marble counter and paintings
advertising food and drink.

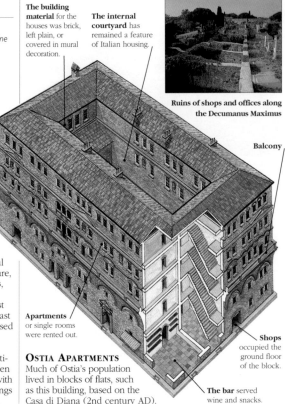

**The building
material** for the
houses was brick,
left plain, or
covered in mural
decoration.

**The internal
courtyard** has
remained a feature
of Italian housing.

Ruins of shops and offices along
the Decumanus Maximus

Balcony

Apartments
or single rooms
were rented out.

Shops
occupied the
ground floor
of the block.

The bar served
wine and snacks.

OSTIA APARTMENTS
Much of Ostia's population
lived in blocks of flats, such
as this building, based on the
Casa di Diana (2nd century AD).

Frascati and the
Castelli Romani **10**

Roma. **FS** 🚌 Frascati. **ℹ** Piazza
Marconi 1, Frascati (06 942 03 31).
Villa Aldobrandini ○ Mon–Fri with
permission from tourist office only.

T HE ALBAN HILLS have long
been a country retreat for
Romans. In Classical times they
were scattered with villas; in
the Middle Ages with fortified
castles (hence the name); and
in the 16th and 17th centuries
with luxurious country residences and their spectacular
parks and gardens. During
World War II German defenses
were based in the Alban hills
and many Castelli towns were
damaged by Allied bombs.
Although partly protected by
a nature preserve, the hilltop
towns are popular day-trip
destinations, as well as being
famous for their white wine.

Frascati's central piazza is a
belvedere overlooked by the
Villa Aldobrandini, a majestic
17th-century building set in
a splendid park of secret
grottoes, fountains, and statues.

The fortified Abbazia di San
Nilo in **Grottaferrata**, 3 km
(2 miles) south, was founded
in 1004 and contains some
lovely 17th-century frescoes by
Domenichino in the chapel.

Overlooking Lake Albano,
6 km (4 miles) south, **Castel
Gandolfo** is the site of the
pope's summer palace. When
in residence the pope addresses
the crowd from the balcony.

Gathered around a sturdy
9th-century castle, and famed
for its strawberries, **Nemi**, 10
km (6 miles) southeast, looks
down onto the glassy dark
blue waters of Lake Nemi.

The forested shores around the small, volcanic Lake Nemi

Tivoli, a favorite place to escape the heat of the Roman summer

Tivoli ⑪

Roma. 🏛 *57,000.* 🚋 🚌 ℹ️ *Largo
Garibaldi (0774 33 45 22).* 🛒 *Wed.*

Hill town Tivoli, now
probably the most
popular excursion from
Rome, was once a favored
resort of the ancient Romans,
attracted by its fresh water and
sulfur springs, and beautiful
countryside. The temples that
once covered Tivoli's hilltop
are still visible in places. Some
are half buried in medieval
buildings, others, such as the
Temples of Sibyl and Vesta,
inside the gardens of the
Sibilla restaurant (on Via
Sibilla), are relatively intact.

**Splendors from around the world
reproduced in Hadrian's Villa**

The town's most famous sight
is the **Villa d'Este**, a sumptuous country residence created
in the 16th century by Pirro
Ligorio for Cardinal Ippolito
d'Este from the shell of a
Benedictine monastery. It is
known primarily for its gardens,
steeply raked on terraces, and
studded with spectacular, if
somewhat faded and moss-
hung, fountains. Although
suffering from reduced water-
pressure and polluted water
due to centuries of neglect,
the gardens give a vivid
impression of the frivolous
luxury enjoyed by the papal
families. Highlights include
the Viale delle Cento Fontane
and the Fontana dell'Organo
Idraulico, which, thanks to a
hydraulic system, once played
music. At the other end of
town, the **Villa Gregoriana**,
now a hotel, is set in a lush
wooded valley where paths
wind down into a deep ravine.

Environs: About 5 km (3
miles) west of Tivoli are the
ruins of **Hadrian's Villa**.
Easily seen in conjunction
with a visit to the town, this
is one of the largest and most
spectacular villas ever built
in the Roman Empire (it once
covered an area greater than
the center of Imperial Rome).
Hadrian's aim in creating
the villa was to reproduce
some of the wonders he, an
inveterate traveler, had seen
around the world. The Stoa
Poikile, for example, a walkway around a rectangular
pool and garden, recalls the
painted colonnade of the
Stoic philosophers in Athens,
while the Canopus evokes the
grand sanctuary of Serapis in

Alexandria. There are also
ruins of two bath complexes,
a Latin and a Greek library, a
Greek theater, and a private
study on a little island known
as the Teatro Marittimo.

Today the rambling ruins,
full of shady nooks and hidden
corners, make a lovely place
to relax, picnic or explore.

🏛 **Villa d'Este**
Piazza Trento. 📞 *0774 31 20 70.*
⏱ *Tue–Sun.* ⬤ *Jan 1, May 1, Dec 25.*

🏛 **Villa Gregoriana**
Piazza Massimo. ⏱ *daily.* 📷

⛩ **Hadrian's Villa**
Villa Adriana. 📞 *0774 53 02 03.*
⏱ *daily.* ⬤ *Jan 1, May 1, Dec 25.* 📷

Palestrina ⑫

Roma. 🏛 *16,000.* 🚌 ℹ️ *Piazza
Santa Maria degli Angeli (06 957 31
76).* ⬤ *Sat & 15th of the month.*

**Mosaic fragment of Nile in flood,
Archaeological Museum, Palestrina**

Medieval Palestrina grew
up over the terraces of a
huge temple dedicated to the
goddess Fortuna Primigenia,
the mother of all gods. The
temple, founded in the 8th
century BC and rebuilt in the
2nd century BC by Sulla,
housed one of the most important oracles of ancient times.
The terraces of the sanctuary,
littered with fragments of
columns and porticoes, lead
up to the curved **Palazzo
Barberini**. Built over the site
of a circular temple, it now
houses the **Museo Nazionale
Archeologico**, best known
for a 1st-century BC mosaic,
portraying the Nile in flood.

🏛 **Museo Nazionale
Archeologico**
Via Barberini. 📞 *06 953 81 00.*
⏱ *daily.* ⬤ *Jan 1, May 1, Dec 25.*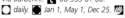

Subiaco ⓲

Roma. 🏛 *9,000.* 🚌 ℹ️ *Via Cadorna 59 (0774 82 20 13).* 🚍 *Sat.*

I N THE 6th century, weary of the decadence of Rome, St. Benedict left the city to become a hermit in a cave above Subiaco. Others joined him, and eventually there were 12 monasteries in the area.

Only two now survive: **Santa Scolastica**, dedicated to Benedict's sister, is organized around three cloisters, one Renaissance, one early Gothic, and the third Cosmatesque. Higher up, the 12th-century **San Benedetto** is a more rewarding destination. Overhanging a deep gorge, it comprises two churches built on top of each other. The upper is decorated with 14th-century Sienese frescoes; the lower, built over several levels, incorporates the original cave where Benedict spent three years after fleeing Rome.

🏛 **Santa Scolastica**
3 km (2 miles) E of Subiaco.
📞 *0774 855 25.* 🕐 *daily.* 🚫 ♿

🏛 **San Benedetto**
3 km (2 miles) E of Subiaco.
📞 *0774 850 39.* 🕐 *daily.* 🚫 ♿

Montecassino ⓳

Cassino. 📞 *0776 31 15 29.* 🚆 *Cassino then bus.* 🕐 *8:30am–noon, 3:30–6pm daily (Nov–Feb 5pm).*

T HE ABBEY of Montecassino, mother church of the Benedictine order and a center of medieval art, was founded in 529 by St. Benedict over the ruins of an ancient acropolis. By the 8th century it was an important center of learning, and by the 11th century had become one of the richest monasteries in Europe.

In 1944 it was a German stronghold and a target for Allied bombs. Most of the complex was devastated, including the lavish Baroque church, but the walls remained intact and the abbey resisted for three months before falling to the Allies. The adjoining war cemeteries commemorate the 30,000 soldiers killed.

THE MONASTERIES OF LAZIO

Rose window, Fossanova

St. Benedict founded the Abbey of Montecassino around 529 and there wrote his famous Rule. Based on the principles of prayer, study, and manual labor, this became the fundamental monastic code of western Europe. The Cistercian Order, an offshoot of the Benedictines, came to Italy from Burgundy in the 12th century. The Cistercians were followers of St. Bernard, whose creed was based on austerity and self-sufficiency, qualities that were reflected in the simple, early Gothic architecture of their monasteries. Their first abbey was at Fossanova. Other Cistercian abbeys in Lazio include Valvisciolo (northeast of Sermoneta) and San Martino in Cimino (near Lago di Vico).

The Abbey of Montecassino, *destroyed during World War II, was rebuilt as a replica of its 17th-century predecessor.*

The Abbey of San Benedetto, *Subiaco, was founded in the 11th century over St. Benedict's cave. A staircase carved in the rock leads to the grotto where he preached to shepherds.*

The Abbey of Casamari, *14 km (8 miles) east of Frosinone, was founded by Benedictine monks in 1035 and handed over to the Cistercians who rebuilt it in 1203.*

The abandoned medieval village of Ninfa, now a beautiful garden

Anagni ⓯

Frosinone. 🏛 19,000. FS 🚌
ℹ Piazza Innocenzo III (0775 72 78 52). 🛒 Wed.

ACCORDING TO LEGEND Saturn founded five towns in southeast Lazio, including Anagni, Alatri, and Arpino. This area is now known as La Ciociaria, from *ciocie*, the bark clogs worn in the area until about 20 years ago.

Before the Romans conquered this part of Lazio it was inhabited by several different tribes: the Volsci, the Sanniti, and the Hernici. Little is known of them, apart from the extraordinary walls with which they protected their settlements. In later years these were believed to have been built by the Cyclops, a mythical giant, which gave them their present name of Cyclopean walls.

Anagni was the most sacred Hernician center until its destruction by the Romans in 306 BC. In the Middle Ages it was the birthplace and family seat of several popes, an era from which many buildings survive, most notably Boniface VIII's 13th-century mullion-windowed palace.

The beautiful Romanesque **duomo**, Santa Maria, built over the ancient Hernician acropolis, boasts a fine Cosmati mosaic floor from the 13th

century as well as 14th-century Sienese frescoes. The crypt of San Magno is frescoed with one of the most complete surviving cycles of the 12th and 13th centuries.

ENVIRONS: Alatri, perched on an olive-covered slope 28 km (17 miles) east of Anagni, was an important Hernician town. It preserves an impressive double set of Cyclopean walls, 2 km (1 mile) long and 3 m (10 ft) high, from its 7th-century BC acropolis. In the medieval town below the walls is the Romanesque church of Santa Maria Maggiore, greatly restored in the 13th century.

Arpino, 40 km (25 miles) east of Alatri, is a bustling town with a medieval core, and was the birthplace of the

An unusual pointed arch in the Cyclopean walls at Arpino

Roman orator, Cicero. About 3 km (2 miles) above Arpino, at the site of the ancient town of Civitavecchia, is a tremendous stretch of Cyclopean walls, which includes a rare gateway with a pointed arch.

Sermoneta and Ninfa ⓰

Latina. FS Latina Scalo. 🚌 from Latina. ℹ Via Duca del Mare 19, Latina (0773 69 54 04 17).
Ninfa ⭕ Apr–Oct: 1st Sat & Sun of the month. 🌿

SERMONETA IS A LOVELY hilltop town overlooking the Pontine Plains, with narrow cobbled streets winding around medieval houses, palaces, and churches. The **duomo** has a fine 15th-century panel by Benozzo Gozzoli showing the Virgin cradling Sermoneta in her hands. At the top of the town rises the moated fairy-tale Castello Caetani, frescoed with mythological scenes by a pupil of Pinturicchio.

In the valley below lies the romantic abandoned medieval village of **Ninfa**, restored and converted into lush botanical gardens by the Caetani family in 1921. Streams and waterfalls punctuate the picturesque garden laid out among the crumbling buildings.

Terracina **17**

Latina. 🏘 *40,000.* 🚆 🚌 ℹ️ *Via Leopardi (0773 72 77 59).* 🛒 *Thu.*

ROMAN TERRACINA was an important commercial center on the Via Appia (the Appian Way). Today it is a popular seaside resort, with a fascinating collage of medieval buildings and Roman ruins in its historic center, perched on the slopes of the Ausonian Hills. The more modern part of town by the sea is full of restaurants, bars, and hotels.

Bombing during World War II uncovered many of the town's ancient structures, notably a stretch of the Appian Way and the original paving of the Roman Forum in Piazza del Municipio. The 11th-century **duomo** was built in the shell of a Roman temple and is still entered by the temple's steps. The medieval portico is adorned with a lovely 12th-century mosaic, and the interior preserves the 13th-century mosaic pavement. Next door, the modern town hall houses the **Museo Archeologico**, devoted to local Greek and Roman finds.

Duomo at Terracina with original Roman steps

Three kilometers (2 miles) above the town are the podium and foundations that once supported the Temple of Jove Anxur, dating back to the 1st century BC. This huge arcaded platform is illuminated at night and offers vertiginous views of Terracina and its bay.

🏛 Museo Archeologico
Piazza Municipio. 📞 *0773 70 22 20.* ⬜ *daily.* ⬤ *public hols.*

Sperlonga **18**

Latina. 🏘 *4,000.* 🚌 ℹ️ *Piazza della Rimembranza (0771 55 70 00).* 🛒 *Sat.*

SPERLONGA IS a popular seaside resort surrounded by sandy beaches. The old town sits on a rocky promontory, a picturesque labyrinth of whitewashed buildings, narrow alleyways, piazzettas, and balconies offering an occasional glimpse of the sea below. It is now full of bars, restaurants, and boutiques. The modern part of town lies down on the seafront.

The area around Sperlonga was a favorite retreat for the ancient Romans during the hot summer months. They built villas along the coast and converted the natural caves in the nearby cliffs into places to dine and relax. In 1957 archaeologists excavating the huge complex of Tiberius's luxury villa, 1 km (half a mile) on the southern outskirts of town, found some marvelous 2nd-century BC Hellenistic sculptures in a large cave open to the sea. These sculptures, representing

12th-century bell tower at Gaeta

incidents from Homer's *Odyssey*, are thought to be by the same artists from Rhodes (where the Emperor Tiberius once lived) who were responsible for the Laocoön *(see p407).* They are displayed, along with other local finds, in the **Museo Archeologico Nazionale,** which is part of the archaeological zone.

🏛 Zona Archeologica
Via Flacca. 📞 *0771 540 28.* ⬜ *daily.* ⬤ *Jan 1, May 1, Dec 25.* 🏷

Gaeta **19**

Latina. 🏘 *22,000.* 🚌 ℹ️ *Piazza Traniello 19 (0771 46 27 67).* 🛒 *Wed.*

ACCORDING TO VIRGIL, Gaeta was named after Aeneas's wet nurse Caieta, who was allegedly buried here. The town sits on the southern headland of the gulf of Gaeta, wedged under Monte Orlando. The historic center is dominated by a mighty Aragonese castle and the pinnacles of mock-Gothic San Francesco. To the north, the modern quarter links Gaeta to the bay of Serapo, a popular and picturesque beach resort.

Gaeta's most beautiful feature is the **duomo**'s elegant late Romanesque bell tower, its lofty summit topped by a roof of colored ceramic tiles. On the seafront lies the tiny 10th-century church of **San Giovanni a Mare,** with faded frescoes, a hemispherical dome, and a sloping floor to let the sea flow out after flooding.

Stretches of sandy beach along the coast between Gaeta and Terracina

SOUTHERN ITALY

Southern Italy at a Glance

VㅁISITORS TO SOUTHERN ITALY find a rich array of archaeological remains. Although those of the Romans at Pompeii are high on everyone's list, Greek ruins litter Sicily and the southern coast, and there are mysterious ancient structures, called *nuraghi*, in Sardinia. Campania, Puglia, and Sicily are admired for their architecture, and across the south there are magnificent landscapes, abundant wildlife, and endless opportunities for outdoor activities. The cuisine alone, with its eclectic heritage and diversity of tastes, provides the excuse to dawdle on the coast or in the mountain villages.

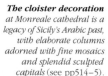

The Parco Nazionale d'Abruzzo, a vast wilderness, is home to wolves, bears, and many species of birds (see pp490–91).

Su Nuraxi at Barumini, built about 1500 BC, is the most celebrated of Sardinia's mysterious stone nuraghe sites (see p533).

Su Nuraxi

SARDINIA
(See pp528–35)

The cloister decoration at Monreale cathedral is a legacy of Sicily's Arabic past, with elaborate columns adorned with fine mosaics and splendid sculpted capitals (see pp514–5).

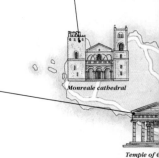

Monreale cathedral

Temple of C...

Sicily's Valley of the Temples at Agrigento contains some of the best ruins outside Greece. Mostly Doric in construction and style, they date from the 5th and 6th centuries BC (see p520).

0 kilometers   100

0 miles   50

◁ **Grapes and citrus trees growing along Campania's scenic Costiera Amalfitana (Amalfi Coast)**

The Museo Archeologico Nazionale in Naples is one of Italy's most important museums. It houses the treasures of Pompeii, including sculptures, vases, and everyday artifacts that provide a detailed glimpse of Roman life (see pp474–5).

ABRUZZO, MOLISE, AND PUGLIA
(See pp484–497)

NAPLES
CAMPANIA
pp466–483

Archeologico Nazionale

Puglia

Basilicata

Pompeii

Santa Croce

BASILICATA
AND CALABRIA
(See pp498–505)

Calabria

Pompeii's Roman ruins include streets, houses, and an amphitheater (see pp478–9).

The church of Santa Croce in Lecce is an excellent example of the exuberant Lecce Baroque style, from its elaborate rose window to the intricately carved capitals (see pp496–7).

Mount Etna

SICILY
(See pp506–527)

Mount Etna, one of the world's largest volcanoes, is still active, with lava erupting from fissures that dot its flanks. The nearby town of Catania has suffered repeatedly from volcanic damage (see p523).

Regional Food: Southern Italy

SOUTHERN ITALIAN FOOD is as varied as the landscape, each region having its own specialties. While pasta, for example, is eaten throughout Italy, nothing matches the handmade *orecchiette* of Puglia. Think of Naples, and wafer-thin pizza springs to mind. Sicilian food is both rustic and voluptuous. Across the south, the dishes are enlivened with seafood, fruity green olive oil, and dry white wine and, together with fresh green vegetables and huge, bursting tomatoes, they supply one of the most enviably healthy diets in Europe.

Dried chillies

Some of Italy's best olives *come from Puglia. Green and black olives may be served in piquant oil and garlic.*

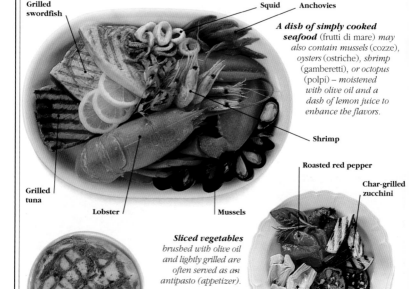

Grilled swordfish

Squid   **Anchovies**

A dish of simply cooked seafood *(frutti di mare) may also contain mussels (cozze), oysters (ostriche), shrimp (gamberetti), or octopus (polpi) – moistened with olive oil and a dash of lemon juice to enhance the flavors.*

Shrimp

Grilled tuna

Lobster   **Mussels**

Roasted red pepper

Char-grilled zucchini

Sliced vegetables *brushed with olive oil and lightly grilled are often served as an antipasto (appetizer).*

Pizza Napoletana *is a simple thin pizza topped with tomato, garlic, basil, and anchovies.*

Marinated artichoke hearts

Chargrilled eggplant

Maccheroncini con le sarde, *a Sicilian classic, contains sardines, fennel, raisins, pine nuts, breadcrumbs, and saffron.*

Pesce spada *(swordfish steak), grilled or panfried with lemon and oregano, is a favorite in Campania, Puglia and Sicily.*

Agnello arrosto *(juicy roast lamb) is a Sardinian specialty, roasted on a spit or in casseroles with rosemary and thyme.*

Sicilian cassata is ice cream made with ricotta cheese, candied fruit, pistachios, sugar, and chocolate in a sponge cake.

Nougat is a sweet Sardinian specialty that can be made simply with nuts, or flavored with chocolate.

Cannoli

Sicilian almond biscuits

Many biscuits and cakes are made in honor of a religious festival or saint's day. They might be deep-fried in oil, soaked in honey, crusted with almonds, or stuffed with ricotta, like the tube shaped cannoli *biscuits much favored in Sicily.*

TYPICAL SOUTHERN SEASONINGS

The food of the south is simple but often served with aromatic herbs like oregano, rosemary, basil, mint, sage, and thyme, as well as garlic, capers, sundried tomatoes, anchovies, and sardines.

Rosemary

Oregano   **Capers**

Sardines   **Sundried tomatoes**

SOUTHERN CHEESES

Cheese exists in almost infinite varieties. Delicate mozzarella di bufala, made with buffalo milk, is delicious eaten on its own. Scamorza, a similar spun cheese, is exceptional – especially from Basilicata. It is also served smoked. Hard-textured Provolone can be mild or piquant; ricotta, from sheep's milk, is creamy.

Provolone

Scamorza

Ricotta

Mozzarella

Smoked Scamorza

WINE

The south's sunny hillsides have produced wine since the Bronze Age. Puglia produces more wine than any other region in Italy, and Sicily boasts some of the south's finest wines. Good producers include Regaleali, Rapitalà, Corvo, and Donnafugata. Marsala, a classic desert wine also from Sicily (*see p518*), was devised in the 18th century and made famous by Admiral Nelson. Pellegrino is an excellent producer.

OLIVE OIL

Some of the finest olive oils (*olio di oliva*) in Italy come from the south. The words *extra vergine* (extra virgin) refer to the pure, unblended oil from the first pressings of the olives. A variation is chili oil (*olio santo*), soaked with red chili peppers, resulting in a rich, spicy oil with a red hue.

Sicilian white wine

Sweet Marsala

Chili oil (Olio santo)

Olive oil (Olio di oliva)

Understanding the Architecture of Southern Italy

THE ROMANESQUE STYLE of southern Italy owes much to the Normans, who brought from France, in the 11th century, both form and style in architecture and sculpture. In the southeast, the style has hefty Byzantine overtones; in Sicily it is characterized by strong traditional Islamic motifs and a love of rich color, pattern and ornamentation. These elements surface later in Sicily's Baroque style and are allied to a dynamism that originates in the Baroque of Rome – though in Sicily it is more vivacious. Neapolitan Baroque is more sophisticated and displays a greater interest in the creative use of space.

Baroque carving on Bagheria's Villa Palagonia

BYZANTINE AND ROMANESQUE FEATURES

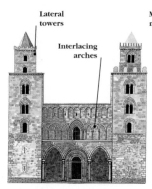

Lateral towers

Interlacing arches

Multicolored marble

Glass and plaster mosaics on gold

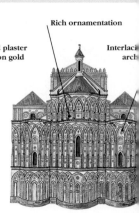

Rich ornamentation

Interlacing arches

Cefalù, begun in 1131 by Roger II, is one of Sicily's great Norman cathedrals (see p519). Its west front exhibits many northern Romanesque features, such as the massive towers.

Christ Pantocrator, a Byzantine apse mosaic (c.1132), adorns the Cappella Palatina (see p510).

The east end of the Norman cathedral of Monreale, founded in 1172 by William II, is built of multicolored materials with interlacing arches (see pp514–15).

BAROQUE FEATURES

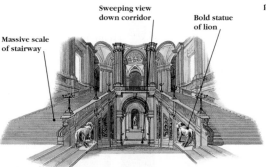

Massive scale of stairway

Sweeping view down corridor

Bold statue of lion

Lifelike putti

Brilliant realism of drapery

Caserta's Palazzo Reale, a sumptuous royal palace begun by Charles III in 1752, is characterized by its monumental scale (see p480). The richly decorated interior is prefaced by several huge entrances and impressive staircases offering views. The enormous building was designed by Luigi Vanvitelli.

Giacomo Serpotta's stucco reliefs (c.1690) in Palermo's Oratorio di Santa Zita illustrate Sicilians' love of exuberant decoration (see p513).

WHERE TO SEE THE ARCHITECTURE

The best places to see Romanesque architecture are Puglia and the cathedral cities of northwestern Sicily. Puglia's best churches are those at Trani *(see p493)* and nearby Canosa, Molfetta, and Bitonto; Ruvo di Puglia *(p494)*, San Leonardo di Siponto on the Gargano Peninsula, and Martina Franca, near Alberobello. The Baroque style of the south is epitomized by the villas, palaces,

The duomo portal in Ruvo di Puglia

and churches of Naples and Sicily, and by the deeply encrusted ornamentation found on church façades in Lecce *(pp496–7)*, in Puglia. In Sicily, the Baroque of Palermo *(pp510–13)*, Bagheria *(p516)*, Noto, Modica and Ragusa *(p527)*, and Siracusa *(pp526–7)* is well known. Less so are churches at Piazza Armerina *(p521)*, Trapani *(p516)*, Palazzolo Acreide, close to Siracusa, and Acireale, near Catania.

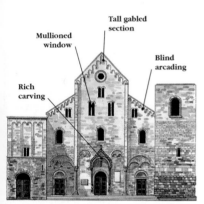

Mullioned window

Tall gabled section

Rich carving

Blind arcading

Bari's Basilica di San Nicola *(founded 1087) was the model for subsequent churches in Puglia* (see p494). *Based on Norman architecture, its façade is flanked by towers and divided vertically into three, reflecting the tripartite nature of its plan.*

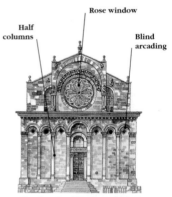

Rose window

Half columns

Blind arcading

The façade of Troia cathedral *(1093–1125) owes its design to Pisan architecture and its rich ornamentation to Byzantine and Arab models* (see pp492–3).

Carved scroll

Protruding columns

The façade *of Siracusa's duomo, begun in 1728 by Andrea Palma, is animated by broken or curved elements* (see pp526–7).

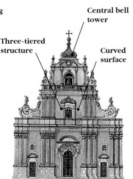

Central bell tower

Three-tiered structure

Curved surface

San Giorgio in Ragusa *(1744) has a façade by Gagliardi with layers of ornamentation culminating in the tower* (see p527).

Stone-carved decoration

Lecce's Chiesa del Rosario *(begun 1691) was built by Lo Zingarello of soft local sandstone in the Lecce Baroque style of profuse carving* (see pp496–7).

The Ancient Greeks in Southern Italy

SOME OF THE BEST ruins of the ancient Greek world are in Southern Italy. Syracuse, Selinunte, Segesta and Gela are among the better known Sicilian sites, while those on the mainland include Croton, Locri and Paestum. Magna Graecia is the collective name given to these scattered colonies of ancient Greece, the earliest of which were founded in the Naples area in the 11th century BC. Many great figures of the age – including Pythagoras, Archimedes, and Aeschylus – lived in these far-flung settlements, and it was here that the ancient winemaker's art flourished. Artifacts from this age are exhibited in the excellent archaeological museums of Naples, Syracuse, and Taranto.

KYME
Cuma

NEAPOLIS
Napoli

HERA
Ercola

Herculaneum was named after its patron deity, the mighty Hercules. It was buried by the eruption of Mount Vesuvius in AD 79 (see p479).

POSEIDON
Paestu

Poseidonia (today's Paestum), was the city of Poseidon, God of the Sea. Its ruins, dating from the 6th century BC, include the hulks of two well preserved Doric temples (see pp482–3).

Mount Etna was believed to have been the forge of Hephaistos (Vulcan) – God of Fire – or the Cyclops, the one-eyed giant (see p523).

Tyndaris was one of the last Greek cities founded on Sicily.

LIPA
Lip

TYND
Tir

PANORMOS
Palermo

SOLUS
Soluto

Eryx, founder of the town, was the son of Aphrodite and Poseidon.

ERYX
Erice

EGESTA
Segesta

HIMERA
Himera

SELINUS
Selinunte

Valley
of the
Temples

HENNA
Enna

K

MEGARA HY
M

The legendary founder of Agrigento was Daedalus, who created wings for himself and his son, Icarus, so they could fly.

AKRAGAS
Agrigento

GELA
Gela

Archeo
Reg
Paol

Gela prospered under the ruler Hippocrates in the 5th century BC.

Egesta (built 426–416 BC) was colonized by the Elymians who may have originated at Troy. Among the ruins of this town are a half-completed temple and a theater (see p518). *Ancient Greeks used theaters for plays; the Romans preferred combat in arenas.*

0 kilometers   100

0 miles   50

Aeschylus, the dramatist, died in Gela in 456. Considered the father of Greek tragedy, his plays include Seven Against Thebes, Women of Aetna, *and* Prometheus Bound.

Metapontion (Metapontum) was home to Pythagoras after his expulsion from Croton. Its ruins include Doric temples, the Tavole Palatine and a theater *(see p503)*.

Taras was home to the philosopher and scientist, Archytas, and Aristoxenes, author of the earliest treatise on music.

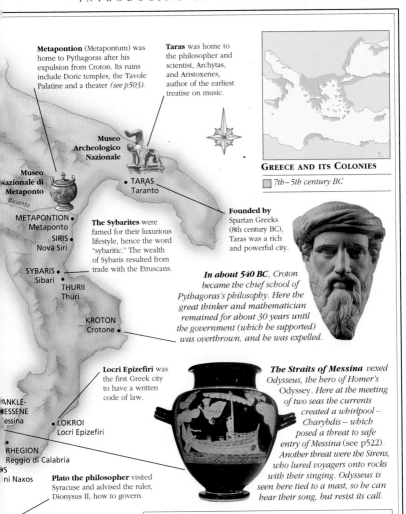

GREECE AND ITS COLONIES

☐ 7th–5th century BC

Museo Archeologico Nazionale

Museo Nazionale di Metaponto

Basento

METAPONTION •
Metaponto

SIRIS •
Nova Siri

SYBARIS •
Sibari

THURII
Thuri

KROTON
Crotone •

TARAS
Taranto

The Sybarites were famed for their luxurious lifestyle, hence the word "sybaritic." The wealth of Sybaris resulted from trade with the Etruscans.

Founded by Spartan Greeks (8th century BC), Taras was a rich and powerful city.

In about 540 BC, Croton became the chief school of Pythagoras's philosophy. Here the great thinker and mathematician remained for about 30 years until the government (which he supported) was overthrown, and he was expelled.

Locri Epizefiri was the first Greek city to have a written code of law.

ANKLE-
MESSENE
Messina

LOKROI
Locri Epizefiri

RHEGION
Reggio di Calabria
ni Naxos

The Straits of Messina vexed Odysseus, the hero of Homer's Odyssey. Here at the meeting of two seas the currents created a whirlpool – Charybdis – which posed a threat to safe entry of Messina *(see p522)*. Another threat were the Sirens, who lured voyagers onto rocks with their singing. Odysseus is seen here tied to a mast, so he can hear their song, but resist its call.

Plato the philosopher visited Syracuse and advised the ruler, Dionysius II, how to govern.

KOUSAI
sa

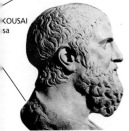

The mathematician and inventor, Archimedes, was born in Syracuse c.287 BC. His inventions included the famous Archimedean screw and various weapons to stave off the Romans *(see pp526–7)*.

DEMETER AND PERSEPHONE

The complex web of Greek mythology was part of the daily life of the ancients. Enna was once the seat of the cult of Demeter, the earth goddess, and in 480 BC a temple was erected there in her honor. According to the legend, Persephone, the daughter of Demeter and Zeus, was abducted in the nearby fields by Hades who carried her off into the Underworld. Demeter then left Olympus and wandered the world searching in vain for her daughter. Discovering that Zeus had allowed the abduction to happen, Demeter put a blight on Sicily: it would remain barren until Persephone returned. Finally Hades allowed her return from the Underworld, but only for a few months of each year – from spring to autumn. Demeter, satisfied with the result, ensured that Sicily became the most fertile place on earth.

Sculpture of Persephone

NAPLES AND CAMPANIA

THE CAPITAL OF CAMPANIA, *Naples is one of the few European cities of the ancient world that has never been completely extinguished. Founded by Greeks, it was embellished and enlarged* by the Romans and in subsequent centuries was the much-prized booty of foreign invaders and Imperialists – most prominently the Normans, Hohenstaufen, French, and Spanish.

Naples today is a chaotic yet spectacular, often crime-ridden metropolis that sprawls noisily and dirtily around the edge of the beautiful Bay of Naples. To one side is Mount Vesuvius; facing from the sea are the pretty islands of Capri, Ischia and Procida. Pompeii and Herculaneum, lying in the shadow of the volcano that destroyed them, contain the most revealing Roman ruins in Italy.

For centuries Naples has dominated the Italian south – the *Mezzogiorno*, or land of the midday sun. The problems of poverty, crime, and unemployment are magnified here, but there is also an attractive, rude ebullience.

The ancient history of Campania is associated with the Etruscans and the Greeks, whose gigantic ruins can be seen at Paestum. Next came a time of great prosperity under Roman leadership; archaeological evidence of this still exists at Benevento and Santa Maria Capua Vetere. The hinterland, with its rich, well-cultivated plains, is eclipsed by the Amalfi coastline with its breathtaking views and the dramatic seaboard of the Cilento. The mountainous interior, remote and unvisited, contains small towns that were settled by the Greeks, developed by the Romans, and often abandoned in the wake of malaria and Saracen attacks.

A glimpse into the narrow streets of Naples' Quartieri Spagnoli (Spanish Quarter)

◁ **The old fishing quarter on the island of Procida in the Bay of Naples**

Exploring Naples and Campania

THE MAIN CENTER FROM WHICH to explore Campania is the anarchic metropolis of Naples (Napoli). To the north, verdant plains sweep down to Santa Maria Capua Vetere. To the east is the lonely, mountainous province of Benevento. Tragic, earthquake-ravaged Avellino and its province lurk on a plain beyond Vesuvius. The northern coastline is not as enticing as the Roman ruins lining it at such places as Cuma. The Costiera Amalfitana, south of Naples, is stunning. Beyond the tip of the Sorrentine Peninsula and along the Cilento coast there is good swimming, as on Capri, Ischia, and Procida in the Gulf of Naples.

SIGHTS AT A GLANCE

Benevento **5**
Capri **9**
Caserta **4**
Costiera Amalfitana **6**
Ischia and Procida **10**
Naples (Napoli) pp470–77 **1**
Paestum **8**
Pompeii pp478–9 **2**
Salerno **7**
Santa Maria Capua Vetere **3**

Typical Naples street viewed from Santa Maria Maggiore

KEY

▨	Highway
▨	Major road
▨	Minor road
▨	Scenic route
∿	River
☼	Viewpoint

0 kilometers   25

0 miles   20

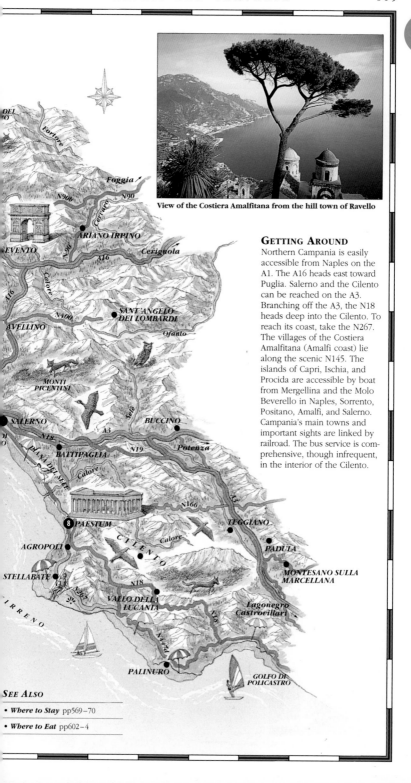

View of the Costiera Amalfitana from the hill town of Ravello

GETTING AROUND

Northern Campania is easily accessible from Naples on the A1. The A16 heads east toward Puglia. Salerno and the Cilento can be reached on the A3. Branching off the A3, the N18 heads deep into the Cilento. To reach its coast, take the N267. The villages of the Costiera Amalfitana (Amalfi coast) lie along the scenic N145. The islands of Capri, Ischia, and Procida are accessible by boat from Mergellina and the Molo Beverello in Naples, Sorrento, Positano, Amalfi, and Salerno. Campania's main towns and important sights are linked by railroad. The bus service is comprehensive, though infrequent, in the interior of the Cilento.

Naples ❶

T HE COMPACT CENTER of Naples, filled with palaces, churches, convents, and monasteries, revolves around just a few streets. From the Piazza del Plebiscito, Via Toledo (also called Via Roma) proceeds north toward Piazza Dante. To the east, narrow Via del Tribunale and Via San Biagio dei Librai penetrate the historic and noisy heart of the city, the *Spaccanapoli* (split Naples). South of Palazzo Reale is the Santa Lucia district. To the west is the port of Mergellina and overlooking the city is the Vomero district.

San Gennaro, protector of Naples

View of the Bay of Naples and Mount Vesuvius

Exploring Northeast Naples

Many of the city's gems of art and architecture can be found here, including the Museo Archeologico Nazionale and its Roman treasures from Herculaneum and Pompeii. The buildings provide a wide range of architectural styles from the French-Gothic of the duomo to the Florentine-Renaissance style of the Porta Capuana.

Tomb of Ladislas, San Giovanni a Carbonara

including Marco and Andrea da Firenze's masterpiece, the Tomb of Ladislas, behind the church's high altar. Built to house the body of King Ladislas of Naples (1386–1414), who enlarged the church, the tomb is a three-story confection of statues and arches topped by an equestrian figure.

🔒 San Giovanni a Carbonara
Via Carbonara 5. **(** 081 29 58 73.
◻ Mon–Sat.
A great and rare success story in the annals of Neapolitan building restoration, San Giovanni a Carbonara (built 1343) is open again after suffering damage in 1943, long closure, and neglect. Within are glorious medieval and Renaissance monuments,

🚇 Porta Capuana and Castel Capuano
Piazza Enrico de Nicola.
(081 223 71 11.
Between the Aragonese towers of the Capua Gate and facing a huge market is a rare sculpture in the Florentine-Renaissance manner. Created by Giuliano da Maiano (finished in 1490 by Luca Fancelli) as a defensive gate, the Porta Capuana is perhaps Italy's finest Renaissance gateway. The nearby Castel Capuano, begun by Norman King William I and completed by Frederick II, was used as a royal palace until 1540 when it became the Court of Justice. It has been renovated, and functions as a courthouse today.

The beautiful Renaissance gate of Porta Capuana

| 0 meters | 250 |
| 0 yards | 250 |

MUSEO DI CAPODIMONTE

CATACOMBE DI SAN GENNARO

PIAZZA CAVOUR

PIAZZA MUSEO NAZIONALE

VIA ENRICO PESSINA

VICO SANTO GAUDIOSO

VIA LUIGI DE CRECCHIO

VIA SANTA MARIA DI COSTANTINOPOLI

VIA CONTE DI RUVO

VIA SAPIENZA

VIA DEL SOLE

PIAZZA DANTE

PIAZZA LUIGI MIRAGLIA

PIAZZA SAN DOMENICO MAGGIORE

VIA TOLEDO ROMA

VIA DOMENICO CAPITELLI

VIA BENEDETTO CROCE

PIAZZA DEL GESU NUOVO

VIA SANTA CHIARA

CALATA TRINITA MAGGIORE

PIAZZA MONTEOLIVETO

PIAZZA CARITA

VIA MONTEOLIVETO

VIA DONNALBINA

VIA CESARE BATTISTI

PIAZZA MATTEOTTI

PIAZZA BANCO NUOVO

VIA SEDILE

MUSEO NAZIONALE DI SAN MARTINO

VILLA FLORIDIANA

VIA ARMANDO DIAZ

VIA TOLEDO (ROMA)

VIA ROBERTO BRACCO

VIA G. SANFELICE

RUA CATALANA

VIA M CERVANTES

VIA MEDINA

VIA AGOSTINO DEPRETIS

VIA SAN GIACOMO

VIA PAOLO EMILIO IMBRIANI

PIAZZA MUNICIPIO

VICO D'AFFLITTO

VIA SANTA BRIGIDA

VIA SANTA MATTIA

VIA SERGENTE MAGGIORE

PIAZZA TRENTO E TRIESTE

VIA SAN CARLO

VIA CHIAIA

VIA AMMIRAGLIO ACTON

MUSEO PRINCIPE DI ARAGONA PIGNATELLI CORTES

PIAZZA DEL PLEBISCITO

VIA CESARIO CONSOLE

CASTEL DELL'OVO MERGELLINA

POZZUOLI

POZZUOLI

Sights at a Glance

Interior of the duomo

🛐 Duomo
Via Duomo 147. 📞 081 44 90 97.
◷ *daily.* ⬤ *Sep 19.*

Built between 1294 and
1323, the duomo of San
Gennaro lies behind a
mostly 19th-century façade.
The nave is lined with
ancient columns, and there
is an interesting array of
monuments to past rulers,
together with paintings by
Lanfranco and Domenichino.

The duomo houses the
relics of San Gennaro, the
protector of Naples, who was
martyred in AD 305. The
ornate Cappella San Gennaro
contains his head, within a
silver-gilt bust, and phials of
his congealed blood, which
miraculously liquefies three
times annually. According to
tradition, if the blood should
fail to liquefy, the city will
have bad luck. The Cappella
Carafa, a Renaissance masterpiece built from 1497 to 1506,
contains the saint's tomb.

Accessible from the duomo's
north aisle is the Basilica di
Santa Restituta, founded in the
4th century on the site of a
former Temple of Apollo and
rebuilt in the 14th century. It
has ceiling paintings by Luca
Giordano (1632–1705). At the
end of the right aisle is the 5th-
century baptistry.

Visitors' Checklist

🏙 *1,300,000.* ✈ *4 km (2.5
miles) NW Capodichino.* 🚉
Napoli Centrale, Piazza Garibaldi.
🚌 *Piazza Garibaldi.* ⛴ *Stazione
Marittima, Molo Beverello &
Mergellina.* ℹ *Piazza del Gesù
Nuovo (081 551 27 01).* ⬤ *daily.*
🎉 *San Gennaro: Sep 19.*

🛐 Monte della Misericordia
Via Tribunali 253. 📞 081 44 69 73.
◷ *Mon–Sat am.*

The 17th-century octagonal
church belonging to this
charitable foundation houses
Caravaggio's huge *Seven Acts
of Mercy* (1607). Also here, in
the art gallery, is an important
collection of paintings, including works by Luca Giordano
and Mattia Preti.

🛐 Cappella Sansevero
Via Francesco de Sanctis 19. 📞 081
551 14 15. ◷ *daily.* ⬤

This small 16th-century
chapel is the burial sepulchre
of the Princes of Sangro di
Sansevero. It possesses both
Christian and Masonic symbolism, giving the chapel
an unusual character.

Remarkable 18th-century
sculpture fills the chapel.
Antonio Corradini's ironic
Modesty is a voluptuous
female, carefully veiled. *The
Resurrection of the Prince*,
by an unknown artist, is
mirrored by that of Christ,
above the altar. Giuseppe
Sammartino's *The Dead
Christ* is an alabaster figure
beneath a marble veil, and
is a work of breathtaking
technical virtuosity.

Eccentric Prince Raimondo,
an 18th-century alchemist, is
associated with the chapel.
He performed gruesome
experiments on human
bodies, for which he was
excommunicated. The results
of some of his experiments
can be seen in the crypt.

Key

Ⓜ Metro

🚡 Funicular

ℹ Tourist information

🛐 Church

Sammartino's *The Dead Christ* (1753) in the Cappella Sansevero

Exploring Central Naples

THE PART OF SANTA LUCIA bordered by Via Duomo to the east, Via del Tribunale to the north, Via Toledo (Roma) to the west, and the water to the south, is the old heart of Naples. Especially rich in 14th- and 15th-century churches, the area offers visitors an abundance of sights.

Interior of San Gregorio Armeno

🏛 San Lorenzo Maggiore
Via Tribunali 316. 📞 081 45 49 48.
Church ⬜ daily. 🈁 ♿
Excavations ⬜ Mon–Sat.
This mainly 14th-century Franciscan church (with an 18th-century façade) was built during the reign of Robert the Wise of Anjou. The storyteller Giovanni Boccaccio (1313–75) reputedly based the character Fiammetta on King Robert's daughter Maria, whom he saw here on Easter Eve, 1334. For

Naples, San Lorenzo Maggiore is a rare Gothic edifice. Its nave and the apse ambulatory have a magnificent period simplicity. The church houses some interesting medieval tombs, most notably the Gothic tomb of Catherine of Austria, who died in 1323, by a pupil of Giovanni Pisano. Excavations in the monastic cloister, where the lyric poet and scholar Petrarch (1304–74) once stayed, have revealed the remains of a Roman basilica. Important Greek and medieval excavations are also under way.

🏛 San Gregorio Armeno
Via San G Armeno 1. 📞 081 552 01 86. ⬜ am daily.
Benedictine nuns still preside over this church. The convent attached to it earned a reputation for luxury since the nuns, traditionally from noble families, were accustomed to lavish living, which continued here.
The sumptuous Baroque interior of the church holds frescoes by the prolific Luca Giordano. The cloister is a quiet haven in a

neighborhood noisy with vendors of Neapolitan crèche figures (presepi), whose workshops line the Via San Gregorio Armeno.

🏛 Museo Filangieri
Palazzo Cuomo, Via Duomo 288.
📞 081 20 31 75. ⬜ Tue–Sun.
⬛ Mon, Jan 1. 🈁
The 15th-century Renaissance Palazzo Cuomo houses the Museo Filangieri. Founded in 1881, the original museum collections put together by Prince Gaetano Filangieri were destroyed during World War II. The new collection contains interesting and varied objects, including porcelain, embroidery, manuscripts, Italian and Spanish arms, objects from local archaeological excavations, and paintings by such artists as Luca Giordano, Ribera, and Mattia Preti.

🏛 Sant'Angelo a Nilo
Piazzetta Nilo. 📞 081 551 62 27.
⬜ daily.

Renaissance tomb of Cardinal Brancaccio, Sant'Angelo a Nilo

This 14th-century church contains a fine work of Renaissance sculpture: the Tomb of Cardinal Rinaldo Brancaccio. Designed by Michelozzo, it was sculpted in Pisa, and then shipped to Naples upon completion in 1428. Donatello reputedly carved the right-hand angel drawing back the curtain, the shallow relief *Assumption*, and the cardinal's head.

The simple Gothic interior of San Lorenzo Maggiore, looking down the nave to the apse

San Domenico Maggiore

Piazza San Domenico Maggiore.
081 55 73 11. daily.

This Gothic church (1289–1324) contains some of the finest Renaissance monuments and sculpture in Naples. The tomb slab of John of Durazzo (died 1335), by Tino da Camaino, is in the south transept. In the sacristy are the 18th-century *Apotheosis of Faith* ceiling frescoes by Solimena. The choir features a paschal candlestick (1585) supported by figures by da Camaino. The Cappellone del Crocifisso contains a medieval painting of the *Crucifixion,* which supposedly spoke to St. Thomas Aquinas. The grand Brancaccio tomb by Jacopo della Pila (1492) is in the Chiesa Antica. Also of interest is the Cappella Saluzzo.

Detail of the embossed façade of Gesù Nuovo

Santa Chiara

Via Benedetto Croce. 081 552 62 80. daily.

This 14th-century church was badly bombed in World War II, but a reconstruction uncovered the original austere Provençal-Gothic structure. The most interesting monuments are the tombs of the Angevin monarchs. The tomb of Robert the Wise (died 1343) is by Giovanni and Pacio Bertini; that of Robert's son, Charles of Calabria (died 1328), is by Tino da Camaino, and the tomb of Charles' wife, Mary of Valois (died 1331) is by da Camaino and his followers. Adjacent is a convent with a peaceful Angevin cloister designed by Vaccaro (1742) and adorned with splendid majolica tiles.

Gesù Nuovo

Piazza del Gesù Nuovo 2. 081 551 86 13. daily. Jan 31, Nov 16.

The 16th-century Jesuit church was constructed by Valeriano (and later Fanzago and Fuga) out of the Severini palace (15th century), of which only the curious embossed stone façade survives. The ebullient decoration of the interior (17th century) is fully in accordance with the needs of the Jesuits, who attracted the faithful through drama and direct appeal to the emotions. It is resplendent with colored marble and paintings, including some by Ribera and Solimena. In 1688 an earthquake destroyed Lanfranco's dome – the present one is 18th century.

Monteoliveto

Piazza Monteoliveto. 081 551 33 33. daily.

Built in 1411 and restored after bomb damage from World War II, this church is a rich repository of Renaissance art.

Guido Mazzoni's *Pietà* (1492) in the church of Monteoliveto

Entering, past the tomb (1627) of Domenico Fontana (the architect who completed the dome of St. Peter's in Rome after Michelangelo's death), the richness of the interior soon becomes clear.

The Cappella Mastrogiudice contains an *Annunciation* panel by Florentine sculptor Benedetto da Maiano (1489) and the Cappella Piccolomini contains Antonio Rossellino's monument (c.1475) to Maria d'Aragona (completed by da Maiano). The Cappella del Santo Sepolcro houses a vividly realistic *Pietà* by Guido Mazzoni (1492). Its eight terra-cotta figures are considered life-size portraits of the artist's contemporaries. The old Sacristy, frescoed by Vasari (1544), has inlaid stalls by Giovanni da Verona (1510).

Majolica tiles decorated with scenes of rural life in the cloisters of Santa Chiara

Naples: Museo Archeologico Nazionale

T HIS MUSEUM IS ONE of the world's most important. The building that houses it, a former military barracks, then university seat, was remodeled in 1790 to receive the treasures of Pompeii and Herculaneum *(see pp478–9)*. It also acquired the fabulous Farnese collections, containing Classical sculpture, which Charles of Bourbon inherited from his mother Elizabeth. The 1980 earthquake caused heavy damage to the collections while dust and chaos engulfed the rest. Restoration work has now revitalized the museum.

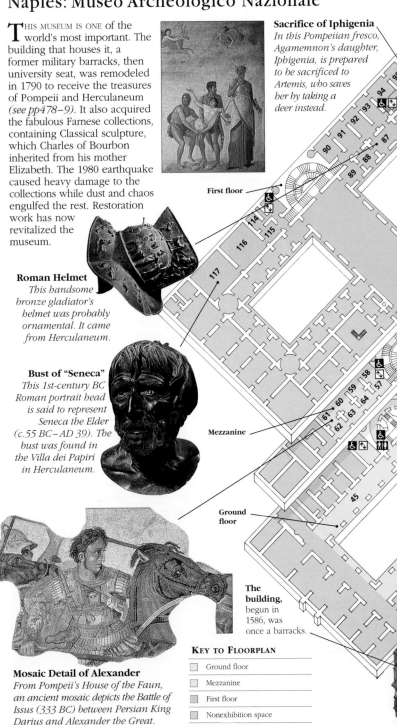

Sacrifice of Iphigenia
In this Pompeiian fresco, Agamemnon's daughter, Iphigenia, is prepared to be sacrificed to Artemis, who saves her by taking a deer instead.

First floor

Roman Helmet
This handsome bronze gladiator's helmet was probably ornamental. It came from Herculaneum.

Bust of "Seneca"
This 1st-century BC Roman portrait head is said to represent Seneca the Elder (c.55 BC – AD 39). The bust was found in the Villa dei Papiri in Herculaneum.

Mezzanine

Ground floor

The building, begun in 1586, was once a barracks.

Mosaic Detail of Alexander
From Pompeii's House of the Faun, an ancient mosaic depicts the Battle of Issus (333 BC) between Persian King Darius and Alexander the Great.

KEY TO FLOORPLAN

☐	Ground floor
☐	Mezzanine
☐	First floor
☐	Nonexhibition space

Blue Vase
Found in a tomb at Pompeii, this glass vase is a fine example of the cameomaker's art. Grape-gathering cupids are cut on to a superimposed white glass paste over the vase, creating a striking, complex design.

VISITORS' CHECKLIST

Piazza Museo Nazionale 19.
081 44 01 66.
185, 42. Piazza Cavour.
9am–7pm Wed–Mon
(last adm: 1 hr before closing).
Tue, Jan 1, Dec 25.

Spring Fresco
From Stabiae comes the ancient fresco of "Spring," a delicate, dreamlike image of a robed girl gathering flowers. The colors remain soft and fresh.

Stairs down to
Egyptian Collection

Farnese Bull
Excavated in the Baths of Caracalla (see p427) in Rome, this is the largest sculptural group (c.200 BC) to have survived from antiquity. It represents Amphion and Zethus tying Dirce to the horns of a bull.

GALLERY GUIDE
The ground floor contains the Farnese collections and sculpture from Herculaneum, Pompeii, and the Campanian cities. On the mezzanine level there are Pompeiian mosaics. The first floor has domestic items, weapons, bronzes, and murals from Pompeii and Herculaneum. A lower ground-floor level houses the Egyptian Collection. Be prepared for areas of the museum to be closed occasionally and without warning. Some will be opened on request, including coins and erotic art from Pompeii.

Entrance

Farnese Hercules
An ancient Roman copy of a Greek original by Lysippus, this huge statue is the finest in the Farnese collections. Napoleon is said to have regretted leaving it when he removed his booty from Italy in 1797.

Exploring Southeast Naples

THE AREA SOUTH of Via A Diaz is home to Naples' castles and royal palace as well as the densely packed Spanish Quarter. On the outskirts of the old town are a number of museums in historic buildings.

♠ Castel Nuovo
Piazza Municipio. **C** 081 551 96 62. ◯ Mon–Sat. ● some public hols. ♿
Museo Civico ◯ Mon–Sat. ▨
Also known as the Maschio Angioino, this Angevin fortress was built for Charles of Anjou in 1279–82. However, apart from the squat towers and the Cappella Palatina (with Francesco Laurana's *Madonna* of 1474 above the portal), most of the structure is Aragonese.

The castle was once the main royal residence. In the Sala dei Baroni, Ferdinand I of Aragon brutally suppressed the ringleaders of the Baron's Revolt of 1486. The Aragonese were capable of acts of terror, but they were also inspired patrons of the arts.

The triumphal arch of the castle's entrance (begun 1454) is theirs. Commemorating Alfonso of Aragon's entry to Naples in 1443, this ingenious application of the ancient triumphal arch design was worked on, at least in part, by Laurana. The original bronze doors by Guillaume le Moine (1468) are kept in the Palazzo Reale. Part of the building houses the **Museo Civico**.

The colorful and compact Quartieri Spagnoli

▦ Quartieri Spagnoli
Via Toledo (Roma) to Via Chiaia.
The Spanish Quarter – the neighborhood west of Via Toledo, sloping up to San Martino and Vomero – is one of the city's most densely populated areas. It was named after the Spanish troops who laid out its grid of narrow streets in the 17th century. This is where the archetypal Neapolitan scene comes to life, in which laundry hung above the streets crowds out the sun. This area is lively by day, slightly sinister by night.

⛫ Museo Nazionale di San Martino
Largo di San Martino 5. **C** 081 578 17 69. ◯ Tue–Sun am. ▨ ♿
High above Santa Lucia, the Baroque Certosa di San Martino, founded in the 14th century as a Carthusian monastery, has magnificent views of the Bay of Naples. It houses an excellent museum that features a variety of *presepi*, Christmas crèches of Neapolitan tradition. The cloister was completed in 1623–9 by Cosimo Fanzago (the creator of Neapolitan Baroque) to the 16th-century designs of Dosio. The church and choir are other remarkable examples of his virtuosity.

Next to the Certosa is Castel Sant'Elmo, which was built from 1329–43 and rebuilt in the 16th century, and offers stunning views over the bay.

⛫ Museo Principe di Aragona Pignatelli Cortes
Riviera di Chiaia 200. **C** 081 761 23 56. ◯ Tue–Sun. ● 1 Jan. ▨
Lower down, in the Chiaia neighborhood, the Neo-Classical Villa Pignatelli houses this museum and its interesting collection of porcelain, period furniture, paintings, and sculpture.

The bold Castel Nuovo, with the triumphal arch entrance

🏛 Galleria Umberto I

Via Toledo. 📞 081 797 23 03.
🕐 daily am. 🔴 Jan 1, Easter, Aug
7–21, Dec 25. 🔲

Once a focus for fashionable
Neapolitans, the arcades of the
Galleria Umberto I were built
in 1887 and rebuilt after World
War II. Still handsome, though
shabby, they face Italy's largest
opera house: the **Teatro San
Carlo**. Built for Charles of
Bourbon in 1737, and later
rebuilt, the magnificent interior
has a luxurious auditorium
that once aroused great envy
in the courts of Europe.

**Magnificent glass-roofed interior
of the Galleria Umberto I**

🏛 Palazzo Reale

Piazza Plebiscito. **Museo** 📞 081 41
38 88. 🕐 Thu–Tue. 🔴 Jan 1, May 1,
Dec 25. 🔲 **Biblioteca** 📞 081 42
71 77. 🕐 Mon–Fri. 🔴 public hols.

Begun by Domenico Fontana
for the Spanish Viceroys in
1600, and expanded and
embellished by subsequent
residents, Naples' royal palace
is a handsome edifice with
great halls filled with furniture,
tapestries, paintings, and porcelain. The small private Teatro
di Corte (1768) was built by
Ferdinando Fuga. A large part
of the building contains the

Painting of *Lavinia Vecellio* (c.1540) by Titian in the Museo di Capodimonte

Biblioteca Nazionale. The
exterior of the palace has
been partly restored – note
the 19th-century statues representing the dynasties of
Naples. The huge Piazza del
Plebiscito facing it has been
cleaned up and cleared of
traffic. The great colonnades
sweep toward 19th-century
San Francesco di Paola,
modeled on Rome's Pantheon.

🏛 Villa Floridiana

Via Cimarosa 77. 📞 081 578 84 18.
🕐 Tue–Sun am. **Park** 🕐 daily.
🔴 Jan 1, May 1, Dec 25. 🔲 🔲

Set in handsome gardens,
this Neo-Classical villa houses
the **Museo Nazionale della
Ceramica Duca di Martina**,
which is famous for its collection of ceramics, including
porcelain and majolica.

🏛 Museo di Capodimonte

Parco di Capodimonte. 📞 081 744
13 07. 🕐 Tue–Sun. 🔲

Begun in 1738 by the Bourbon
king Charles III as a hunting
lodge, the **Palazzo Reale di
Capodimonte** houses this
museum with magnificent
collections of Italian paintings.
Included are works by Titian,

Botticelli, Perugino, Raphael,
and Sebastiano del Piombo,
much of it originating in the
Farnese family collections.
There is also a gallery of 19th-
century art, largely from
southern Italy.

⛪ Catacombs of San Gennaro

Via di Capodimonte 16. 📞 081 741
10 71. 🕐 daily. 🔲 🔲

These catacombs – the original
burial place of San Gennaro –
are located near the church of
San Gennaro in Moenia. The
small church was founded in
the 8th century, and is adjoined
by a 17th-century workhouse.
Two tiers of catacombs dating
from the 2nd century penetrate
the tufa, and there are mosaics
and early Christian frescoes.
Farther along the street, the
Catacombs of San Gaudioso
commemorate the 5th-century
saint who founded a monastery on the spot. Above is the
17th-century church of Santa
Maria della Sanità.

♟ Castel dell'Ovo

Borgo Marinari. 🕐 for exhibitions.

Away from the center, Castel
dell'Ovo occupies a small
island facing, and joining, the
Santa Lucia district – once
the site of Naples' shellfish
market. The castle was begun
in 1154. Under the Normans
and Hohenstaufen it was a
royal residence, but today it
belongs to the military.

Beneath its ramparts, tiny
Porta Santa Lucia is filled with
seafood restaurants, and the
Via Partenope running past it
is a lovely promenade that
leads west to Mergellina.

The façade of the Palazzo Reale, Naples' royal palace

Pompeii ❷

ANCIENT POMPEII SPRAWLS in a decrepit heap at the foot of Mount Vesuvius, which erupted in AD 79, destroying the town. Stones and ash buried it, and it lay undiscovered until the 17th century. In 1748 excavation began, revealing a city frozen in time. All around, buildings have survived, often replete with paintings and sculpture. Graffiti is still on walls, streets are paved; the ghosts of that distant past are almost tangible on the site.

House of the Mysteries

★ House of the Vettii

This partly reconstructed patrician villa of the wealthy merchants, Aulus Vettius Conviva and Aulus Vettius Restitutus, contains frescoes (see pp44–5).

Forum Baths

★ House of the Faun

This famous villa of the wealthy patrician Casii is named after its bronze statuette. The mosaic Battle of Alexander, in the Museo Archeologico Nazionale in Naples, originated here.

0 meters 100
0 yards 100

Forum

Sacrarium of the Lares

Facing the Forum, and by the Temple of Vespasian, this building housed the statues of Pompeii's guardian deities, the Lares Publici.

In the bakery of Modesto, carbonized loaves of bread were found.

Macellum
Pompeii's market place was an important focus for the commercial activity of the town.

STAR SIGHTS

★ House of the Vettii

★ House of the Faun

Last Days of Pompeii
Used as a backdrop for an opera of the same name, this dramatic 19th-century painting by Sanquirico shows the people of Pompeii fleeing as Mount Vesuvius erupts violently.

WESTERN POMPEII

This detailed western area contains impressive Roman ruins, some remarkably intact. Parts of eastern Pompeii still await excavation.

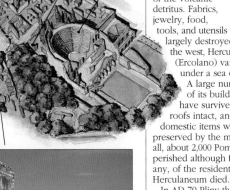

Palestra

Teatro Grande

Via dell'Abbondanza
This was one of the original and most important roads through ancient Pompeii. Many inns lined the route.

EXTENT OF ARCHAEOLOGICAL SITE

WESTERN POMPEII

LOCATOR MAP

VESUVIUS AND THE CAMPANIAN TOWNS

Nearly 2,000 years after the eruption of Mount Vesuvius, the Roman towns in its shadow are still being released from the petrification that engulfed them. Both Pompeii and Stabiae (Castellammare di Stabia), to the southeast of Naples and the volcano, were suffocated by hot ash and volcanic pumice-stone. The roofs of the buildings collapsed under the weight of the volcanic detritus. Fabrics, jewelry, food, tools, and utensils were largely destroyed. To the west, Herculaneum (Ercolano) vanished under a sea of mud. A large number of its buildings have survived, their roofs intact, and many domestic items were preserved by the mud. In all, about 2,000 Pompeians perished although few, if any, of the residents of Herculaneum died.

In AD 79 Pliny the Elder, the Roman soldier, writer, and naturalist, was the commander of a fleet stationed off Misenum (present-day Miseno, west of Naples) and observed the impending eruption from afar. He related the information to his nephew, Pliny the Younger. Eager to see this natural catastrophe closer to hand, Pliny the Elder proceeded to Stabiae, but was overcome by

Pompeiian vase in Museo Nazionale Archeologico

fumes and died. Pliny the Elder's detailed account of the first hours of that eruption, described in letters from his nephew to Tacitus, has been referred to ever since by scientists.

Much of our knowledge of the daily lives of the ancient Romans derives from the excavations of both Pompeii and Herculaneum. Most of the artifacts from them as well as Stabiae have been moved to the Museo Archeologico Nazionale in Naples (see pp474–5), contributing to one of the world's most outstanding and fascinating archaeological collections.

Mount Vesuvius has not erupted since 1944, and today interested visitors are quite safe to visit it by train or car. There is so much to see at Pompeii that you will probably need a day to explore it.

Casts of a dying mother and child in the museum in Naples

Santa Maria Capua Vetere ❸

Caserta. 👥 *34,000.* 🚉 🚌
ℹ️ *Via Albana (0823 79 95 89).*
🛒 *Thu & Sun.*

T HE BEST REASON to visit this town is the ruined Roman **amphitheater** (1st century AD), once Italy's largest after the Colosseum. Better preserved is the series of tunnels beneath it. The town occupies the site of ancient Capua, an Etruscan city and then a flourishing center during the Roman Empire. It was the scene of the revolt of the gladiators, led by Spartacus in 73 BC. Nearby is a **Mithraeum** (2nd–3rd century) with well-preserved frescoes. Finds from the sites can be seen in the **Museo Archeologico dell' Antica Capua** in Capua.

⋔ Amphitheater
Piazza Adriano. 📞 *0823 79 88 64.*
⏰ *Tue–Sun.* 🎟️ *valid also for*
Mithraeum ⏰ *Tue–Sun.*
🏛 Museo Archeologico dell' Antica Capua
Via Roma, Capua. 📞 *0823 84 42 06.*
⏰ *Tue–Sun.* ● *Jan 1, Dec 25.* 🖼️

Tunnels under the amphitheater in Santa Maria Capua Vetere

Caserta ❹

👥 *66,000.* 🚉 🚌 ℹ️ *Palazzo Reale (0823 32 60 00).* 🛒 *Wed & Sat.*

M AGNIFICENTLY OPULENT, the colossal **Palazzo Reale**, likened in scale to Versailles, dominates Caserta. Built for the extravagant Bourbon King Charles III, it boasts over 1,000 rooms, grand staircases,

A fountain in the gardens of the Palazzo Reale at Caserta

and several richly adorned royal apartments. The massive construction was designed by the architect Luigi Vanvitelli, and construction started in 1752. The vast surrounding park is a showpiece in itself, with fountains, ornamental waterworks, and statuary. The scale is overwhelming.

ENVIRONS: The little medieval town of **Caserta Vecchia** lies 10 km (6 miles) to the northeast. Its 12th-century cathedral is a fine example of southern Norman architecture. **San Leucio**, 3 km (2 miles) northwest of Caserta, is a model town built by Ferdinand IV. It remains the seat of a silk industry, which was also founded by the king.

🏯 Palazzo Reale
Viale Douhet. 📞 *0823 32 14 00.*
⏰ *Tue–Sun.* ● *Jan 1, Dec 25.* 🖼️ ♿

Benevento ❺

👥 *62,000.* 🚉 🚌 ℹ️ *Piazza Roma 11 (0824 31 99 38).* 🛒 *Fri & Sat.*

B ENEVENTO, set in a lonely, mountainous province, is home to one of southern Italy's most interesting ancient Roman monuments: the **Arch of Trajan** on Via Traiano. The Roman city, Beneventum, was an important

center. It stood at the end of the first extension of the Via Appia from Capua, and the Arch was erected across the old road in honor of Trajan. Built from AD 114–166 of Parian marble, it is extremely well preserved. The relief sculpture adorning it – scenes from the life of Trajan and mythological subjects – is in excellent condition.

Elsewhere, evidence of the Romans is to be found in the ruined **Roman theater**, built during Hadrian's reign, and in the **Museo del Sannio**, which contains artifacts from the region, from ancient Greek finds to modern art.

During World War II, the city stood directly in the way of the Allied advance from the south. It was heavily bombed, hence its largely modern appearance today. The duomo, a 13th-century building reconstructed after the war, has a sculpted façade that, though badly damaged, has since been restored. The remains of its Byzantine bronze doors are within.

The ornate 2nd-century Roman arch in Benevento, built to honor Trajan

The town has centuries-old associations with pagan worship, and a liqueur called Strega (witch) is made here.

♪ Roman Theater
Piazza Gaio Ponzio Telesino. ⬛ *Tue–Sun.* ⬤ *public hols.* 🎦 &

🏛 Museo del Sannio
Piazza Santa Sofia. 🕿 *0824 218 18.*
⬛ *Tue–Sun.* ⬤ *public hols.* 🎦 &

Costiera Amalfitana ❻

Salerno. 🚌 ⛴ *Amalfi.* 🚹 *Corso delle Republiche 27, Amalfi (089 87 11 07).*

The small town of Atrani on the Costiera Amalfitana

THE MOST enchanting and most visited route in Campania is that skirting the southern flank of Sorrento's peninsula: the Costiera Amalfitana (Amalfi Coast). Among the popular pleasures here are dining on locally caught grilled fish and sipping icy Lacrima Christi from the vineyards on the slopes of Vesuvius, interspersed with beach-hopping and trips to coastal summits to admire the breathtaking views.

From **Sorrento**, a well-developed vacation resort, the road winds down to **Positano**, a village clambering down a vertiginous slope to the sea. Expensive, it is nonetheless a good place to swim, or to catch the hydrofoil or ferry to Capri. Farther on, **Praiano** is just as fashionable.

Amalfi is the coast's largest town. Its chief glory is a lovely 10th-century duomo fronted by a rich, colored façade (13th century). Amalfi was a maritime power before it was subdued in 1131 by King Roger of Naples. Its most illustrious citizens were buried in the 13th-century Chiostro del Paradiso, flanking the duomo, a magnificent 9th-century structure facing the town from the top of a long flight of steps. The style is Lombard-Norman, though the cloisters have a Saracenic-inspired appearance. Amalfi is a tremendously popular resort.

Ravello has the best views on this coast. Poised on a shelf above Amalfi, the best vantage points are the gardens of Villa Cimbrone and Villa Rufolo. Views from the latter provided inspiration for Wagner's *Parsifal*. The 11th-century duomo has entrance doors by Barisano da Trani (1179) and an ornate 13th-century ambo (pulpit) held aloft by six spiral columns. The chapel of San Pantaleone contains the blood of its 4th-century namesake, which liquefies annually in May and August.

Farther on, beyond **Atrani**, the ruins of a Roman villa at **Minori** serve as a reminder that this coastline has always been a popular holiday spot.

A breathtaking view of the steep village of Positano on the Costiera Amalfitana

Salerno ❼

Salerno. FS 🚌 ⛴ Salerno. ℹ Piazza Ferrovia (089 23 14 32).

SALERNO IS A BIG, busy port. Here the Allies landed in 1943, leaving in their wake a much bombed, ruined city. Once famous for its School of Medicine (12th century), it is visited today for its **duomo**, an 11th-century structure built on a 10th-century foundation. Its best feature is the Atrium, whose columns came from nearby Paestum. In the crypt is the Tomb of St. Matthew, which was brought here in 954.

The **Museo Diocesano** is home to most of the cathedral treasures, including an 11th-century ivory altar-front called the Paliotto. Before wandering off down the bustling Corso Vittorio Emanuele, visit the **Museo Provinciale** for local archaeological finds.

ENVIRONS: The **Cilento** is a mountainous region south of Salerno with a remote interior and a lovely, quiet coastline that is only slightly more populous. Among the towns along the coast, **Agropoli** is a busy little seaside resort 42 km (25 miles) south of Salerno. Outside Castellammare di Velia, a further 28 km (17 miles) to the southeast, are the ruins of the Greek town of **Elea** (founded 6th century BC), once famous for its school of philosophy. It was much visited by the Romans – Cicero was here and Horace came on his doctor's orders to undergo a treatment of sea bathing.

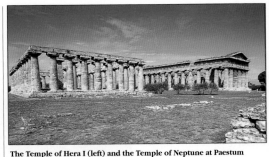

The Temple of Hera I (left) and the Temple of Neptune at Paestum

Excavations have revealed a magnificent 4th-century Roman gateway: the Porta Rosa, Roman baths, the foundations of a temple, and the remains of the ancient acropolis.

🏛 **Museo Diocesano**
Via Duomo. 📞 089 23 91 26.
⬜ daily.
🏛 **Museo Provinciale**
Via San Benedetto. 📞 089 23 11 35.
⬜ daily. ⬤ 1st & 3rd Mon of month.

Paestum ❽

Zona Archeologica. 📞 0828 81 10 16. 🚌 from Salerno. FS Paestum. ⬜ 9am–1 hr before sunset daily. **Museum** ⬤ 1st & 3rd Mon of month & some public hols. 🎫 ♿

THIS IS THE MOST important ancient Greek site south of Naples in Campania. The Greeks, who founded this city on the edge of the Piana del Sele in the 6th century BC,

Capri ❾

Napoli. ⛴ Capri. ℹ Piazza Umberto I, Capri (081 837 06 86). **Grotta Azzurra** ⛴ from Marina Grande. ⬜ in calm sea. **Certosa** Via Certosa, Capri. 📞 081 837 62 18. ⬜ Tue–Sun am. ♿ **Villa Jovis** Via Tiberio. ⬜ daily. 🎫

CAPRI'S ENDURING reputation as a sybaritic paradise is nearly eclipsed by its notoriety as a tourist trap. However, the great views are unmarred by the throng. The home of emperors, seat of monasteries, place of

exile, former haunt of goats and fishermen, its fortunes changed during the 19th century when English and German expatriates discovered its charms. Today it barely has an "off season"; farmers run little hotels, and fishermen rent pleasure boats. Capri has constant sunshine and enjoys a well-deserved reputation as a Garden of Eden.

The Grotta Azzurra, or the Blue Grotto, is a cave bathed in iridescent blue light, which can be reached by tour boat from Marina Grande.

Anacapri is Capri's second town.

0 kilometers   1

0 miles   0.5

The busy port of Salerno

knew it as Poseidonia, the City of Poseidon. The Romans took and renamed it in 273 BC. It fell into decline and was abandoned in the 9th century AD due to malaria and a Saracen assault. It was re-discovered in the 18th century.

Today Paestum is visited for three massive surviving Doric temples in an excellent state of repair: the **Basilica** or **Temple of Hera I** (mid-6th century BC); the **Temple of Neptune** (5th century BC), the largest and most complete at Paestum; and the **Temple of Ceres**, thought to date between its two neighbors.

Excavations have revealed the remains of the ancient city, its public and religious buildings, roads, and protective walls. A **museum** contains the extensive finds from the site, including tomb paintings, tomb treasures, some terra-cotta votive offerings, architectural fragments, and sculpture.

A view from the highest point of Procida, called Terra Murata

Ischia and Procida ⑩

Napoli. 🚢 Ischia Porto & Procida Porto.
ℹ Via Iasolino, Ischia (081 99 11 46).
Via Roma, Procida (081 810 19 68).

I SCHIA IS THE BIGGEST island in the Bay of Naples and, with its beach resorts, thermal springs, therapeutic sands, and cheap hotels, it is nearly as

popular as its more glamorous neighbor, Capri. Ferries dock at **Ischia Porto**, the harbor and modern part of the main town, **Ischia**. **Ischia Ponte**, the older part, is a short walk away. The northern and the western shores are developed; the southern flank of the island is the quietest. Here, the village of **Sant'Angelo** is dominated by the hulk of a long-extinct volcano, **Monte Epomeo**, whose summit of 788 m (2,585 ft) offers terrific views back across the bay to Naples.

Procida is the odd one next to Ischia and Capri, and it is small – only 3.5 km (2 miles) long – and less visited by holiday crowds. Nevertheless, the swimming is good at **Chiaiolella** and, as at Ischia, there are inexpensive places to stay. The ramshackle main town, also called **Procida**, is home to the main ferry port – the **Marina Grande**.

There are views toward Vesuvius and the Bay of Naples from the north of the island.

Capri is the main town on the island.

Marina Grande
This is Capri's main port of call for ferries from Naples and other ports on the Tyrrhenian coast. An array of colorful houses overlooks the harbor.

I Faraglioni

Marina Piccola
is reached by dramatic Via Krupp.

Villa Jovis
Covering an enormous area, this was the Imperial villa from which Tiberius ruled the Roman Empire during his final years.

Certosa di San Giacomo
Founded in 1371 on the site of one of Tiberius's villas, this Carthusian monastery was suppressed in 1808 and is now in part a school. The distant rocks are I Faraglioni.

ABRUZZO, MOLISE, AND PUGLIA

P UGLIA IS THE "HEEL" *of the Italian boot, the Gargano Peninsula is its "spur" and Abruzzo and Molise together form the "ankle." Hugging the southeastern seaboard of Italy and looking toward the Balkans, the mountainous regions of Abruzzo and Molise, united until 1963, differ considerably from Puglia, the richest of the three.*

Abruzzo and Molise are sparsely populated, quiet places where the wild landscape exerts a strong influence. Settled by various Apennine tribes in the Middle Bronze Age, the areas were later subdued by the Romans, united under the Normans in the 12th century and, thereafter, ruled by a succession of dynasties based in Naples. Abruzzo, dominated by the Apennines, is a brooding, introspective land of shepherds. Vertiginous drops preface the ascent to ramshackle hill towns clinging to the sides of high mountains, semi-abandoned and poor. Molise is less dramatic, but life in both regions is primitive. Legends of witches persist, as do strange fertility rites and rituals celebrating the changing seasons.

Puglia's advantage over its poverty-stricken neighbors is that it is nearly all flat and highly fertile. It produces the largest amounts of olive oil and wine in Italy, and its big cities – Lecce, Bari, and Taranto – are lively commercial centers.

The region experienced a long-lasting Greek influence, though the golden age of Puglia's past was under the rule of the Normans, followed by Frederick II who, between his return from Germany as emperor in 1220 and his death 30 years later, only spent four years away from here.

Puglia has glorious architecture, particularly in the churches and castles of the north. The curious *trulli* houses in central Puglia, the florid Baroque of Lecce, and the Levantine atmosphere of its merchant cities complete the picture of an ancient land subject to more influences from outside the Italian peninsula than from within it.

Traditional dress worn in the town of Scanno in Abruzzo

◁ **The curious *trulli* buildings found in central Puglia, particularly around Alberobello and Locorotondo**

Exploring Abruzzo, Molise, and Puglia

DOMINATED BY THE PROLIFIC Apennine mountain range, the hinterland of Abruzzo and Molise forms one of Italy's last wildernesses. At 2,912 m (9,554 ft), the highest peak is the Gran Sasso. Parts of Abruzzo are covered in endless tracts of forest. Molise is characterized by high plains, soft valleys, and lonely peaks. The spectacular Gargano Peninsula in Puglia (Apulia) has a lovely seaboard. Reaching south is the fertile Tavoliere plain, and farther south a series of upland plateaus (the Murge) descend towards the dry Salentine Peninsula and the Adriatic.

The exotic *trulli* houses in Alberobello in central Puglia

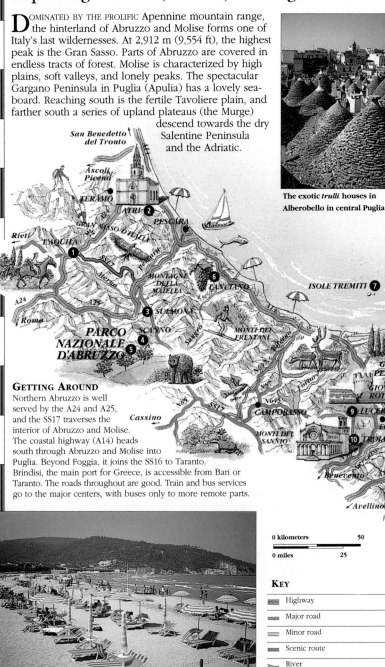

GETTING AROUND

Northern Abruzzo is well served by the A24 and A25, and the SS17 traverses the interior of Abruzzo and Molise. The coastal highway (A14) heads south through Abruzzo and Molise into Puglia. Beyond Foggia, it joins the SS16 to Taranto. Brindisi, the main port for Greece, is accessible from Bari or Taranto. The roads throughout are good. Train and bus services go to the major centers, with buses only to more remote parts.

San Benedetto del Tronto
Ascoli Piceno
TERAMO
ATRI
PESCARA
GRAN SASSO D'ITALIA
Rieti
L'AQUILA
Roma
A24
A25
MONTAGNE DELLA MAIELLA
LANCIANO
SULMONA
SCANNO
PARCO NAZIONALE D'ABRUZZO
MONTI DEL FRENTANI
ISOLE TREMITI
Cassino
CAMPOBASSO
MONTI DEL SANNIO
LUCERA
TROIA
Benevento
Avellino

The coast at Vieste on the beautiful Gargano Peninsula in Puglia

0 kilometers 50

0 miles 25

KEY

	Highway
	Major road
	Minor road
	Scenic route
	River
	Viewpoint

The high peaks of the Gran Sasso, north of L'Aquila in Abruzzo

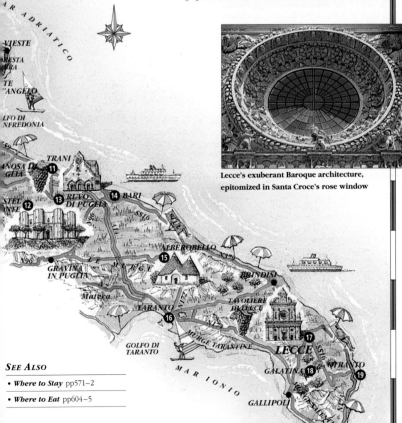

Lecce's exuberant Baroque architecture, epitomized in Santa Croce's rose window

The pink and white stone façade of Santa Maria di Collemaggio in L'Aquila

L'Aquila ❶

64,000. FS *Via XX Settembre (0862 223 06). daily.*

ABRUZZO'S CAPITAL lies at the foot of the **Gran Sasso**, the highest point of the Italian mainland south of the Alps (and good for skiing). Its ancient streets are peppered with churches and mansions. The beautifully domed **Santa Giusta** (1257), off Via Santa Giusta, has a rose window and a *Martyrdom of St. Stephen* (1615) by Cavalier d'Arpino. **Santa Maria di Paganica,** off Via Paganica has a 14th-century façade and a carved portal. The **duomo** (1257) in Piazza del Duomo was rebuilt and enlargedin the 18th century.

The church of **Santa Maria di Collemaggio**, on Piazza di Collemaggio, is a massive structure with a façade of pink and white stone. It was built in the 13th century by Pietro dal Morrone, who later became Pope Celestine V. In the chapel to the right of the apse is the tomb of the founder who, in 1313, was canonized as St. Peter Celestine.

San Bernardino, on Via di San Bernardino, houses the tomb (1505) of San Bernardino of Siena by Silvestro dell'Aquila. The church, built from 1454 to 1472, has a façade (1527) by Cola dell'Amatrice and an 18th-century carved ceiling by Ferdinando Mosca. The second chapel in the south aisle has an altarpiece by Andrea della Robbia, the Renaissance artist.

Detail of Fontanelle delle Novantanove Cannelle in L'Aquila

The medieval **Fontanelle delle Novantanove Cannelle** at the end of Via San Iacopo is a fountain commemorating the 99 villages that Frederick II supposedly united when he founded L'Aquila in 1240.

The **Museo Nazionale d'Abruzzo**, in the 16th-century castle, contains the remains of a prehistoric elephant, Roman artifacts, and religious works.

ENVIRONS: North of L'Aquila are the ruins of a **theater** and **amphitheater** of ancient **Amiternum**, a Sabine, then Roman town, and the birthplace of Sallust (86–c.35 BC), the Roman historian and politician who helped to develop the monograph.

Museo Nazionale d'Abruzzo

Castello Cinquecentesco. *0862 63 31.* *Tue–Sun.* *Jan 1, Easter, Dec 25.*

Atri ❷

Teramo. *11,000.* *Mon.*

THE PRETTIEST in a series of small hill towns in Abruzzo, Atri is a warren of stepped streets, alleys, and passages bound by mostly brick and stone churches and houses. The 13th-century **duomo** occupies the site of a Roman bath; the crypt was once a swimming pool, and fragments of the original mosaic floor are visible in the apse. Also in the apse is Andrea Delitio's great 15th-century fresco cycle, in which he combined landscape and architecture in a variety of religious scenes from the Old and New Testaments. The cloister has views of the 15th-century brick campanile.

ENVIRONS: South of Atri is the hill town of **Penne**. Street by street it is remarkably homogeneous with its buildings of reddish brick, which give the town a warm glow. East of Atri, **Loreto Aprutino** is known for the *Last Judgment* fresco (14th century) in Santa Maria in Piano.

Detail from 15th-century fresco by Andrea Delitio in Atri's Duomo

Sulmona ❸

L'Aquila. *24,000.* FS *Corso Ovidio 208 (0864 532 76).* *Wed & Sat.*

THIS TOWN is famous as the home of both Ovid and *confetti* (sugared almonds). After a wedding ceremony in Abruzzo, the happy couple is pelted with *confetti* in an effort to see them on the road to good fortune. Sulmona is filled with ancient buildings, especially along medieval **Via dell'Ospedale**, imparting a beguiling atmosphere. The greatest treasure is the palace of the **Annunziata** on Corso Ovidio. Founded in 1320, the building combines Gothic and Renaissance styles. It houses the **Museo Civico**, which contains local antiquities, paintings, and the work of goldsmiths. The adjacent church of the **Annunziata**, with a robust Baroque façade, was rebuilt in the 18th century.

At the end of Viale Matteotti is the cathedral of **San Panfilo**, built over a Roman temple. **San Francesco della Scarpa**, in Piazza del Carmine, has a 13th-century portal. Winding past it to the **Fontana del Vecchio** (1474) is an aqueduct that once fueled local industry.

ENVIRONS: East of Sulmona is the Maiella, a massif of 61 peaks and deep, forested valleys offering walking, bird-watching, climbing, and skiing. To the west, Cocullo is the scene of the May Processione dei Serpari (Festival of Snakes) in which a statue of the patron saint, Domenico Abate, is draped with snakes and carried through the town. In the 11th century he is said to have freed the area from venomous snakes.

🏛 Museo Civico
Palazzo dell'Annunziata, Corso Ovidio.
📞 0864 21 02 16. **🕐** Tue–Sun.

OVID, THE LATIN POET

Born in 43 BC, Ovid (Publius Ovidius Naso) was Sulmona's most illustrious son. Not much survives there to remind you of his presence, however, apart from a **Corso Ovidio**, a 20th-century statue of him in Piazza XX Settembre and, just outside the town, a ruin traditionally known as **Ovid's Villa**. Known as one of the greatest poets of Classical Rome, his subjects included love (*Ars Amatoria*) and mythology (*Metamorphoses*). In AD 8 he was banished into exile at the Black Sea, the far edge of the Roman Empire, after being implicated in a scandal of adultery with Julia, the granddaughter of Emperor Augustus (*see pp44–5*). Ovid continued to write of his hardships, and died in exile in AD 17.

Scanno ❹

L'Aquila. 🏘 *2,400.* 🚌 **ℹ** *Piazza Santa Maria della Valle 12 (0864 743 17).* 🛒 *Tue.*

CHARMINGLY well-preserved, this medieval hill town set in beautiful, wild countryside is one of Abruzzo's most popular attractions. There are alleys and narrow flights of steps, oddly shaped courtyards into which small churches have been pressed, and ancient mansions in whose windows the women can be seen making lace or embroidering.

Traditional costume still worn in Scanno

In the shadow of Apennine peaks and beside lovely **Lago di Scanno**, the town is also a favored stop on the way to the Parco Nazionale d'Abruzzo (*see pp490–91*). The summer months are the busiest, with a variety of amusements from riding, boating, and camping by the lake, to the August classical music festival. During the January Festa di Sant'Antonio Abate, a large lasagna is cooked outside **Santa Maria della Valle**, built on the remains of a pagan temple. The food is doled out to whoever comes along first.

High Apennine peaks looming above the medieval hill town of Scanno in Abruzzo

Parco Nazionale d'Abruzzo ❺

Iris

THIS VAST PARK was inaugurated in 1992 and has a rich landscape of high peaks, rivers, lakes, and forests, is one of Europe's most important nature preserves. Until 1877 it formed part of a royal hunting preserve, but today it is a refuge for over 40 species of mammal, 30 types of reptile, and 300 species of bird, including the golden eagle and white-backed wood-pecker. Walkers can choose from an extensive network of paths; there are opportunities for riding, skiing, and canoeing, making the park popular with visitors.

Golden eagles may be seen near the Sangro river.

Young Chamois
Dense forests of beech and maple hide the Apennine chamois. There are also red and roe deer in the park.

Forests of beech and black pine provide beautiful scenery.

Pescasseroli
At the heart of the park, this town is a major center for information on the region. It has good tourist facilities, including a number of hotels, and ski facilities are nearby.

Apennine Wolves
The park guarantees protection for the Apennine wolf, and about 30 wolves survive here. The chances of seeing one, however, are fairly remote.

Marsican Brown Bear
Once hunted almost to extinction, the park now boasts between 80 and 100 brown bears.

Horseback Riding
Pony trekking is an excellent way to explore more remote areas of the park.

The Camosciara is a spectacular area, home to many wild animals.

Lake Barrea
Created by the artificial damming of the River Sangro, this lake is surrounded by valleys and forests offering walking and pony trekking.

ANNO
MONA

N479

Villetta Barrea

Barrea

LAGO DI BARREA

Civitella Alfedena

N83

ALFEDENA
ISERNIA

MONTI DELLA META

MONTE PETROSO
▲
2,247 m
(7,372 ft)

LA META
▲
2,241 m
(7,352 ft)

Dense Forests
Beech and maple forests, dotted with black hornbeam, ash, hawthorn, cherry, wild apple, and pear, protect the once persecuted bears and wolves.

KEY

▬▬▬	Major road
▬▬▬	Minor road
▬ ▬	Walking path
☆	Viewpoint
🛈	Tourist information

0 kilometers 5

0 miles 5

Lanciano 🌀

Chieti. 🏛 *50,000.* 🚍 🚌
🛈 *Piazza Plebiscito (0872 71 49 59).*
📅 *Wed & Sat.*

GREAT CHUNKS of Lanciano's ancient nucleus are left in the Middle Ages. In the crumbling Civitanova quarter is the 13th-century church of **Santa Maria Maggiore**, with a magnificent 14th-century portal and a silver processional cross (1422) by Nicola da Guardiagrele. Also in this area are **Sant'Agostino** (14th century) and the now vacant **San Biagio** (begun c.1059), near the 11th-century **Porta San Biagio** – a rare surviving town gate. The **duomo**, with its 17th-century bell tower, is situated on top of the remains of a Roman bridge that dates from the period of Diocletian.

The Ripa Sacca (Jewish ghetto) was a busy commercial center in the Middle Ages – the period of Lanciano's greatest prosperity. The hefty walls of the **Torri Montanara** were built then by the Aragonese as a bulwark against attack.

Isole Tremiti 🌀

Foggia. 🚢 *San Nicola.* 🛈 *Via Perrone 17, Foggia (0881 72 36 50).*

OF ALL ITALY'S coastal islands, these are the least visited by foreigners. **San Domino** is the largest of the group, with a sandy beach and coves. Here in AD 8, Julia, granddaughter of Augustus, was exiled for adultery and died in AD 28. The poet Ovid was supposedly involved *(see p489)*.

San Nicola, the administrative center of the group of islands, has an important 11th-century monument: **Santa Maria a Mare**. An abbey-fortress founded in the 8th century, it was turned into a prison late in the 18th century and ultimately became a place of detention for political prisoners, a role it kept until 1945.

Both islands are popular with Italians. The swimming is good, though the coastline of San Nicola is rocky.

The coast near Peschici on the Gargano Peninsula

Gargano Peninsula ❽

Foggia. **FS** 🚌 **i** *Piazza del Popolo 11, Manfredonia (0884 58 19 98).*

A HIGH, ROCKY SPUR jutting into the Adriatic Sea, the Gargano is a dramatic wilderness dotted with coves and cliffs. Its coastal towns of **Rodi Garganico**, **Peschici**, **Vieste**, and **Manfredonia** are popular with vacationers. To the east lies the **Foresta Umbra**, a vast woodland of beech, oak, yew, and pine, and to the north the salt lakes of **Lesina** and **Varano**, havens for waterfowl.

Typical street scene in the town of Vieste on the Gargano Peninsula

Plunging through the Gargano is an old pilgrim route (N272) from **San Severo** in the west to the shrine at **Monte Sant' Angelo** in the east. The first stop is **San Marco in Lamis**, which is dominated by a huge 16th-century convent. Farther along, **San Giovanni Rotondo** is a focus for pilgrims in search of a cure from Padre Pio (1887–1968), a miracle-worker who is buried here. The last stop is **Monte Sant'Angelo** with its grotto where in 493, according to tradition, the Archangel Michael appeared to the Bishop of Sipontum.

To the south of Manfredonia, beside the ruins of the ancient town of Siponto, is the oriental-inspired 12th-century church of **Santa Maria di Siponto**.

Lucera ❾

Foggia. 🏠 *43,000.* 🚌 🚆 *Wed.*

T HIS WAS ONCE a prosperous Roman colony and, on the northeast edge of town, the ruins of a Roman **amphitheater** survive. Lucera was rebuilt in the 13th century by Frederick II, who peopled it with 20,000 Muslims from Sicily. It became one of the strongest fortresses in southern Italy, and its **castle** is one of Puglia's most magnificent. Built by Frederick II in 1233, and enlarged by Charles I after 1269, its fortified wall of 900 m

(2,953 ft) is interspersed with 24 towers. Of Frederick's original palace within, only the base and some vaulting remains.

In 1300 Charles II, who massacred most of Lucera's Muslim population, began the **duomo** on the site of their main mosque, blending Gothic and Romanesque styles. The high, soaring nave is filled with 15th- and 16th-century frescoes and carvings.

The **Museo Civico Fiorelli** has displays of episodes from throughout Lucera's history.

🏛 **Museo Civico Fiorelli**
Via de Nicastri 44. 📞 *0881 54 70 41.* ⭘ *daily.* 🚫

The remains of Lucera castle

Troia ❿

Foggia. 🏠 *33,000.* 🚌 🚆 *1st & 3rd Sat of month.*

F OUNDED IN 1017 as a Byzantine fortress against the Lombards, Troia fell to the Normans in 1066. Until Frederick II destroyed it in 1229, the town had been ruled by a succession of powerful bishops who were responsible for producing some of Puglia's most remarkable buildings, including Troia's **duomo** *(see pp462–3).*

Begun in 1093 and constructed over the following 30 years, it exhibits an extraordinary diversity of styles. It successfully blends elements of Lombard, Saracenic, and Byzantine style with that of the Pisan-Romanesque.

Elegant blind arcading distinguishes the duomo's lower story. The upper sections are characterized by powerfully carved sculpture – projecting lions and bulls. The upper façade displays a rose window with Saracenic-style detailing.

The main entrance, with bronze doors by Oderisio da Beneventano (1119), is dominated by carved capitals and an architrave, both Byzantine in style. Within the duomo is a Romanesque pulpit (1169).

Trani ⓫

Lecce. 🚶 45,000. **FS** 🚤
🛈 *Piazza Palmieri, Piazza Trieste 10 (0883 58 88 30).* 🛍 *Tue.*

The façade of Trani's duomo

D URING THE MIDDLE AGES this small, lively whitewashed port bustled with mercantile activity and was filled with merchants and traders from Genoa, Amalfi, Pisa, and Ravello. It reached its peak of prosperity under Frederick II.

Today it is visited for its Norman **duomo** in Piazza Duomo, built mainly from 1159 to 1186 over an earlier church whose predecessor, the Ipogei di San Leucio, dates from the 7th century. It is dedicated to St. Nicholas the Pilgrim, a little-remembered miracle-worker (d. 1094) who was canonized as an act of rivalry against the town of Bari, which possessed the bones of another, more memorable St. Nicholas. The duomo's most notable external characteristics are its sculptures, particularly surrounding the rose window and the arched window below it, and the richly adorned entrance portal with bronze doors (1175–9) by Barisano da Trani. The vigor of the interior has recently been revealed following restoration.

Next to the duomo is the **castle** (1233–49) that was founded by Frederick II. Rebuilt in the 14th and 15th centuries, it is a well-preserved edifice with one wall dropping sheer into the sea.

Elsewhere in Trani the 15th-century Gothic-Renaissance town house, the **Palazzo Caccetta** in Piazza Trieste, is a rare survival. Nearby, on Via Ognissanti, the 12th-century Romanesque church of the **Ognissanti**, the chapel of the Knights Templar erected in the courtyard of their hospital, is notable for its original portico.

Castel del Monte ⓬

Località Andria, Bari. 🛈 *Commune (0883 56 98 48).* ⏰ *Apr–Sep: 9am–5pm Tue–Sat; Oct–Mar: 9am–1pm Tue–Sat.* ⬤ *Dec 25.* 📷 🅾

Frederick II

R EMOTE IN THE endless plains near Ruvo di Puglia, Castel del Monte, begun in 1240, outclasses every other castle associated with Frederick II. It is also one of the most sophisticated secular buildings of the Middle Ages. The emperor had broad intellectual interests, and he used his castles as hunting lodges where he could retire from court life with his falcons, books, and correspondence. Inside there are two floors, each with eight rib-vaulted rooms, some still lined with marble. This, and the marble moldings on the entrance and the upper floor, as well as sophisticated lavatory arrangements, mark the castle as a palace.

Octagonal satellite tower

Graceful arched windows

Thick and impenetrable walls

Octagonal courtyard

The main entrance portal is in the style of a Roman triumphal arch.

FLOOR PLAN OF THE CASTLE

The building is a harmonious geometrical study with two stories of eight rooms each. The reasons for such precise planning of this giant octagon remain a mystery to this day.

The castle standing alone on the summit of a low hill

Ruvo di Puglia ⑬

Bari. 👥 24,000. 🚉 🚌 ⛴ Sat.

ONCE CELEBRATED for its vases, Ruvo di Puglia's ceramics industry, producing "Apulian" ware, flourished until the 2nd century BC. Using Archaic Corinthian and Attic models, the style was based on the striking red and black colors of the originals. An excellent exhibit can be seen in the **Museo Archeologico Nazionale Jatta**.

The 13th-century **duomo** is a bold example of the Apulian-Romanesque style with a portal that blends Byzantine, Saracenic, and Classical motifs.

🏛 Museo Archeologico Nazionale Jatta

Piazza Bovio 35. 📞 081 81 28 48.
🕐 daily. ⬤ Jan 1, May 1, Dec 25. ♿

Bari ⑭

👥 400,000. ✈ 🚉 🚌
⛴ ℹ Piazza Aldo Moro 33a (080 524 22 44).
⛴ daily.

ROMAN BARIUM was simply a commercial center, but the city became the regional capital under the Saracens in 847, and was subsequently the seat of the *catapan*, the Byzantine governor of southern Italy. Under the Normans, to whom it fell in 1071, Bari became a center of maritime significance rivaling Venice. Today it is Puglia's lively capital.

The **Basilica di San Nicola**, one of Puglia's first great Norman churches (begun 1087), was a model for others. Its plain exterior has a tall gabled section flanked by towers. The entrance portal is Apulian-Romanesque, with carving on the door jambs and arch in Arabic, Byzantine, and Classical styles. Beyond the choir screen is a fine 12th-century altar canopy and an episcopal throne (c.11th century). The relics of St. Nicholas – patron saint of Russia, children, and sailors – are buried in the crypt.

The late 12th-century Apulian-Romanesque **duomo** is based on San Nicola, with a dome and one surviving tower (the other tower collapsed during an earthquake in 1613). The Baroque portals on the entrance façade incorporate 12th-century doorways. The

Portal detail of Ruvo di Puglia's duomo

Sculpture at Bari castle

interior has been restored to its medieval simplicity. The canopy over the high altar, the pulpit, and the episcopal throne are reconstructions from fragments of the originals. The sacristy, which was built as a baptistry, is known as the *Trulla*. The crypt houses the remains of San Sabino, Bari's original patron saint.

The city's **castle**, founded by Roger II, was adapted by Frederick II in 1233–9. In the vaulted hall is a collection of plaster casts of sculpture and architectural fragments from various Romanesque monuments in the region.

Bari castle, situated in the old district known as the Città Vecchia, where most of the town's sites are clustered

Alberobello **15**

Bari. **FS** *to Alberobello & Ostuni.*
i *Piazza del Popolo (080 432 54 91).*

IN THE DRY, almost arid landscape called the **Murge dei Trulli**, there is a profusion of olive groves, orchards, vineyards, and *trulli*. Strange circular buildings with conical roofs and domed within, *trulli* are built from local limestone stacked without using mortar. The walls and openings are generally whitewashed, while the stone roof tiles are either bare or have religious or folk symbols painted on them. Some have been converted into modern houses; others are farm buildings or storage barns. Their origins are obscure, though the name is traditionally applied to ancient round tombs found in the Roman countryside.

Alberobello is the *trulli* capital and, inevitably, a tourist haunt. Here the strange white buildings crowd the narrow streets, and there are *trulli* restaurants, shops, and even a *trulli* cathedral.

ENVIRONS: The whitewashed hill town of **Locorotondo** is one of the region's prettiest places, although labyrinthine **Martina Franca** may be the most elegant, with streets enlivened by Rococo balconies. In late July or early August there is a music festival here, the Festivale della Valle d'Itria.

Aphrodite in museum in Taranto

![Whitewashed and sunbaked *trulli* in Alberobello]
Whitewashed and sunbaked *trulli* in Alberobello

Taranto **16**

▨ *245,000.* **FS ▤ i** *Corso Umberto 113 (099 453 23 92).*
▤ *Mon & Fri.*

LITTLE REMAINS OF the ancient city of Taras, founded by Spartans in 708 BC. It enjoyed its greatest prosperity under the philosopher and scientist Archytas in the mid-4th century BC. The **Museo Archeologico Nazionale** has artifacts that shed light on much of the region's early history. Taranto suffered greatly due to heavy bombing in World War II and is garlanded by heavy industry, especially in the Borgo area. The picturesque **Città Vecchia**, an island dividing the Mare Grande from the Mare Piccolo, was the site of the Roman citadel of Tarentum. There is an ebullient fish market that still offers the shellfish for which the city was once famous. Here, too, is the **duomo**. Founded in 1071, it has been the subject of subsequent rebuilding. The most interesting features include the catacomb-like crypt, with its sarcophagi and fragmented frescoes, and the antique marble columns of the nave. Behind it is the 11th-century **San Domenico Maggiore**, which later gained a high double-approach Baroque staircase. The huge **castle** built by Frederick of Aragon (15th century) covers the eastern corner of the Città Vecchia, with a pivot bridge connecting it to the mainland.

🏛 Museo Archeologico Nazionale
Corso Umberto 141. **(** *099 471 11 99.* **●** *for restoration.*
🌐 ♿

THE TARANTELLA

Italy's lively and graceful folk dance, the Tarantella, grew out of tarantism – the hysteria that appeared in 15th- to 17th-century Italy, and was prevalent in Taranto. Alleged victims of the tarantula spider's bite could supposedly cure themselves through frenzied dancing, which sweated out the poison. The dance is characterized by light, quick steps and a "teasing" flirt. The strange ritual can be experienced annually on 28–29 June at the celebrations for the Feast of Saints Peter and Paul in Galatina. This remains the only place on the Salentine Peninsula where the phenomenon of tarantism has survived.

Street-by-Street: Lecce ⑰

Façade detail, Santa Croce

THIS TOWN, tucked away on the Salentine Peninsula, was the site of the Greek Messapi settlement. It became an important center of the Roman Empire, and during the Middle Ages a strong tradition of scholarship was established. Much of the architecture is in the Lecce Baroque style, which flourished in the 17th century. Characterized by rich sculptural decoration, this style was possible due to the building material, *pietra di Lecce* – an easily carved stone. Giuseppe Zimbalo (lo Zingarello) was the greatest master of the style.

★ Palazzo Vescovile and Duomo
The bishop's palace (rebuilt in 1632), the adjoining duomo by lo Zingarello (after 1659), and a seminary enclose the Piazza Duomo.

Chiesa del Rosario
Said to be the finest work by lo Zingarello (begun 1691), the exterior is ornate and idiosyncratic in its detail.

Porta Rudiae
This 18th-century city gate leads to the suburbs and to the ruins of Roman Rudiae.

The Seminary once supplied the Vatican with *castrato* singers – eunuchs noted for their high voices.

Chiesa del Carmine

STAR SIGHTS
★ Santa Croce
★ Palazzo Vescovile and Duomo

KEY

– – – Suggested route

0 meters   100

0 yards   100

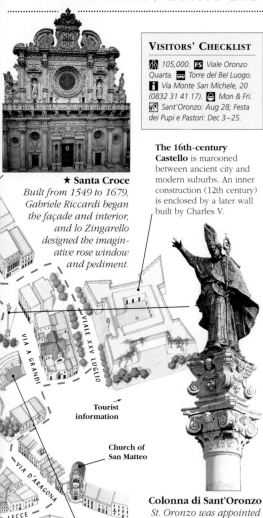

★ **Santa Croce**
*Built from 1549 to 1679,
Gabriele Riccardi began
the façade and interior,
and lo Zingarello
designed the imagin-
ative rose window
and pediment.*

**The 16th-century
Castello** is marooned
between ancient city and
modern suburbs. An inner
construction (12th century)
is enclosed by a later wall
built by Charles V.

**Tourist
information**

**Church of
San Matteo**

VIALE XXV LUGLIO

VIA A GRANDI

VIA D'ARAGONA

LECCE

Colonna di Sant'Oronzo
*St. Oronzo was appointed
Bishop of Lecce by St. Paul in
AD 57, and later martyred by
the Roman emperor Nero. This
bronze statue dates from 1739.*

**A Roman
theater** was
excavated nearly
intact with its
orchestra and
seats.

way
on

Roman Amphitheater
*Excavated in 1938, only part of this
1st-century BC amphitheater is visible.
The lower tier of seats has survived.*

Detail of a 15th-century fresco in
Santa Caterina d'Alessandria

Galatina ⑱

Lecce. 🏛 28,000. 🚆 🚌 🛒 Thu.

An important Greek colony
in the Middle Ages, this
town retains a distinctive
Greek flavor. It is the center
of one of Puglia's chief wine-
producing regions, although
it is more famous for its lively
tarantella dance, performed
on June 28–29 (see p495).

The Gothic church of **Santa
Caterina d'Alessandria** on
Piazza Orsini was built by
Raimondello del Balzo Orsini
(begun 1384). This lovely
church contains early 15th-
century frescoes with scenes
from the Old and New
Testaments that glorify the
Orsini, who were feudal lords.
Orsini's tomb is in the chancel.

Otranto ⑲

Lecce. 🏛 4,800. 🚆 🚌 ⛴
ℹ️ *Piazza Castello (0836 80 14 36).*
🛒 Wed.

Today otranto is a mere
shadow of its former self. It
was one of Republican Rome's
main ports for trade with Asia
Minor and Greece, and under
the Byzantines was an important toehold of the Eastern
Empire in Italy. In 1070 it fell
to the Normans. Turks
attacked in 1480 and
slaughtered its inhabi-
tants. The 800 survivors
were promised their
lives if they renounced
Christianity: all refused.

The Norman **duomo**
(founded 1080) on Via
Duomo houses the
bones of the martyrs.
There is a 12th-century
mosaic floor and a fine
crypt. A **castle** (1485–98)
built by the Aragonese at the
center of town, overlooking the
port, adds to Otranto's charm.

BASILICATA AND CALABRIA

R EMOTE AND WILD, *Basilicata is one of the poorest regions in Italy. It is underdeveloped and undervisited, and so remains unspoiled. Neighboring Calabria has been immortalized in the drawings of Edward Lear who, traveling through on a donkey in 1847, was transfixed by the "horror and magnificence" of its savage landscape.*

Today these regions are mutually distinct, but they share a common history and, along with Sicily and Puglia, were part of Magna Graecia. Ancient Metaponto in Basilicata was an important center, as were Crotone and Locri Epizefiri in Calabria. Their ruins evoke a confident past.

After the Greeks came the Romans, followed by the Byzantines. The Cattolica at Stilo is a beautiful reminder of Byzantine rule. Then came eastern Christian Basilian monks, whose religious establishments make up a core of interesting monuments. Matera, for example, where the monks took refuge in caves, is a strange and fascinating place, decaying yet ebullient.

Many of the historic remains are Norman, but sporadic evidence of Svevi, Angevin, Aragonese, and Spanish occupation also exists.

Centuries of rule by Naples led to the marginalization of Basilicata and Calabria. Today Calabria has a terrifying reputation due to the *'ndrangheta*, the ferocious first cousin to the Mafia, whose activities are a constant menace. Banditry does still exist, but the sensible traveler should have little to fear.

Due to emigration, Basilicata and Calabria are sparsely populated and have as much to offer in unspoiled countryside as in historic centers. The vast coastline boasts sandy beaches, while the interior features the rugged Aspromonte and Sila mountain ranges.

The remote landscape has kept change at bay. Isolated Pentedattilo, for example, preserves customs of Byzantine origin while around San Giorgio Albanese there live close-knit communities of Albanians, descended from 15th-century refugees.

Sparsely populated, rugged countryside surrounding Stilo in southern Calabria

◁ **The silent Sassi district in Matera, where dwellings are scooped out of the rock**

Exploring Basilicata and Calabria

Mostly upland country, Basilicata is scattered with Greek ruins (like those at Metaponto), medieval abbeys, Norman castles (such as Melfi's), and isolated hill towns. Matera, its most interesting city, stands amid an arid lunar landscape of denuded valleys. Calabria is often described as the mountains between the seas. The lovely beaches and virgin landscape around Tropea and Maratea are popular with visitors. The Ionian coast's chief attractions are its Greek ruins, including Sybaris and Locri Epizefiri, and the hill towns, like Gerace and Stilo, that eventually replaced them.

SIGHTS AT A GLANCE

Gerace ⑩
Lagopesole ③
Maratea ⑥
Matera ④
Melfi ①
Metaponto ⑤
Reggio di Calabria ⑪
Rossano ⑦
Stilo ⑨
Tropea ⑧
Venosa ②

Repairing nets in the town of Pizzo, northeast of Tropea

The picturesque hill town of Rivello, north of Maratea in Basilicata

KEY

▬▬	Highway
▬▬	Major road
▬▬	Minor road
▬▬	Scenic route
〜	River
❉	Viewpoint

0 kilometers   50

0 miles   25

The port of Maratea on the Tyrrhenian coast of Basilicata

GETTING AROUND

Calabria's Tyrrhenian coast is well served by the A3, a spur of which extends to Potenza in Basilicata. To reach the Ionian coast, it is best is to skirt the Aspromonte via the N106 from Reggio to Basilicata. Although the mountains can be crossed, namely on the N280 to Catanzaro, the roads are narrow and pass through isolated countryside. Much of Basilicata is even less accessible, and Matera is more easily reached from Puglia. There are airports at Reggio di Calabria, Lamezia (west of Catanzaro), and Brindisi (Puglia). Trains connect the bigger centers and country buses serve the small towns.

SEE ALSO

• *Where to Stay* p572

• *Where to Eat* p606

The countryside near Miglionico, south of Matera

The impressive castle at Melfi, showing evidence of both Angevin and later construction

Melfi ❶

Potenza. 🏛 *15,000.* **FS** 🚌
🍴 *Wed & Sat.*

A BROODING and now almost deserted medieval town, Melfi is crowned by the formidable **castle** where Pope Nicholas II conducted the investiture of Robert Guiscard in 1059, thus legitimizing the Normans in the south. Melfi subsequently became the Norman capital. Here, too, Frederick II proclaimed his *Constitutiones Augustales* (1231) which unified his kingdom as a state. The castle houses the **Museo Nazionale del Melfese**, with its collection of Byzantine jewelry.

The **duomo**, off Via Vittorio Emanuele, was begun in 1155 by William the Bad but rebuilt in the 18th century. Only the campanile survives.

🏛 Museo Nazionale del Melfese
Castello di Melfi, Via Normanna.
☎ *0972 23 87 26.* ◯ *daily.*
⬤ *May 1, Dec 25.* 🎦 ♿

Venosa ❷

Potenza. 🏛 *12,000.* **FS** 🚌 **ℹ** *Via Garibaldi 42 (open occasionally).*
🍴 *1st Sat & 3rd Thu of month.*

V ENOSA WAS ONE of the most important Roman colonies around 290 BC, and remains of **baths** and an **amphitheater** survive in the archaeological

zone along Via Vittorio Emanuele. It was also the birthplace of the Latin poet, Horace (65–8 BC), and the site where the Roman general Marcellus died at the hands of Hannibal in 208 BC. Marcellus' reputed **tomb** is in Via Melfi.

The **duomo**, also on Via Vittorio Emanuele, and the huge **castle** in Piazza Umberto I date from the 16th century.

Occupying the site of a Roman temple is **La Trinità**, a partially ruined abbey complex formed by an older church, possibly early Christian (5th–6th century). It is backed by an unfinished 11th-century construction, in which Robert Guiscard (d. 1085) was buried with his half-brothers and Alberada, his first wife. Only her tomb has survived.

Lagopesole ❸

Potenza. ☎ *0971 860 83.* **FS** *to Lagopesole Scalo then bus to town.*
◯ *9:30am–1pm, 4–7pm daily.*
♿

R ISING DRAMATICALLY on a hill with a village huddled at its feet, Lagopesole's **castle** is the most striking in Basilicata. Dating from 1242–50, it was the last castle Frederick II built and was used as a hunting lodge. There is interesting decoration, particularly the carved heads above the portal of the keep. One is said to be Frederick Barbarossa (the grandfather of Frederick II),

and the other is reputedly Barbarossa's wife, Beatrice. Inside, the royal apartments and chapel can be visited.

Matera ❹

🏛 *56,000.* **FS** 🚌 **ℹ** *Via de Viti de Marco 9 (0835 33 19 83).* 🍴 *Sat.*

The Sassi district of Matera

P ERCHED ON THE EDGE of a deep ravine, this town consists of the bustling upper district and the silent lower **Sassi** (cave) district, divided into the Sasso Barisano and the more picturesque Sasso Caveoso. The people of Matera once lived here in dwellings scooped out of the rock. The two parts are odd neighbors, making Matera one of the most fascinating cities in southern Italy.

For the best overview, walk along the **Strada Panoramica dei Sassi** and look down into the caves. From the 8th to the

13th centuries, such caves probably provided refuge for monks from Basilicata. Many chapels, which were gouged out of the rock, were taken over in the 15th century by peasants. Subsequently, a cave-dwelling Matera evolved and by the 18th century some buildings fronting the caves had become fairly grand mansions and convents. By the 1950s and 1960s the Sassi were overtaken by squalor and poverty, and the inhabitants were forcibly rehoused. Carlo Levi (1912–75) drew attention to their miserable living conditions in his book *Christ Stopped at Eboli*, comparing Sassi districts with Dante's *Inferno*. Today the warren of streets and steps amid the mostly empty Sassi are silent.

Of the 120 *chiese rupestri* (rock-cut churches) in the Sassi and the Agri district outside the town, **Santa Maria di Idris** in the Monte Errone area and **Santa Lucia alle Malve** in the Albanian quarter both contain 13th-century frescoes.

The **Museo Nazionale Ridola** provides a background to Matera and the Sassi. Many Neolithic trench villages, necropoli, and other ancient sites have been discovered, and artifacts from them are displayed here.

The Apulian-Romanesque **duomo** (13th century) in Piazza Duomo has interesting sculpture and an anonymous 12th-century painting of the *Madonna della Bruna*, the patroness of Matera, who is celebrated on July 2. Via Duomo leads toward **San Francesco d'Assisi** (13th century with Baroque overlay), which commemorates St. Francis's visit to Matera in 1218. Other churches to visit are **San Domenico** and **San Giovanni Battista** on Via San Biagio (both 13th century), and the **Purgatorio** (1770) on Via Ridola.

🏛 **Museo Nazionale Ridola**
Via Ridola 24. 📞 0835 31 00 58.
🌑 *for restoration.* 📷

The Tavole Palatine in Metaponto

Metaponto ❺

Zona Archeologica, Matera. 📞 0835 74 53 27. 🚌 🚆 *to Metaponto.*
🕓 *9am–1 hr before sunset daily.*
🌑 *Jan 1, Easter, Dec 25.* 📷 ♿

FOUNDED IN THE 7th century BC, ancient Metapontum was once the center of a wealthy city-state with a philosophical tradition expounded by Pythagoras, who settled here after his expulsion from Croton. Its ruins include the **Tavole Palatine** (6th century BC) at the Bradano River bridge, and a Doric temple, probably dedicated to Hera, with 15 columns standing. The **Museo Nazionale di Metaponto** displays artifacts from the site. The ruins of a theater and the Doric **Temple of Apollo Lycius** (6th century

Church of San Francesco in Matera

BC) are in the **Archaeological Zone**. Farther south, modern **Policoro** occupies the site of ancient Heracleia (founded 7th –5th century BC). Its **Museo Nazionale della Siritide** has finds from this and other sites.

🏛 **Museo Nazionale di Metaponto**
Metaponto Borgo. 📞 0835 74 53 27.
🌑 *daily.* 🌑 *public hols.* 📷 *also valid for archaeological zone.* ♿

🏛 **Museo Nazionale della Siritide**
Via Colombo 8, Policoro. 📞 0835 97 21 54. 🌑 *daily.* 🌑 *Jan 1, May 1, Dec 25.* 📷 ♿

Maratea ❻

Potenza. 🏘 5,000. 🚆 🚌
ℹ *Piazza del Gesù 40 (0973 87 69 08).* 🚌 *1st & 3rd Sat of month.*

A TINY STRETCH of Basilicata meets the Tyrrhenian Sea in the Gulf of Policastro. This unblemished coast is home to Maratea. Its small port (Maratea Inferiore) is beneath the old center (Maratea Superiore), which straddles the flank of a hill. From here the road climbs Monte Biagio to a summit with breathtaking views, where a huge statue of the **Redeemer** stands.

ENVIRONS: Dramatically sited **Rivello**, 23 km (14 miles) to the north, once had a largely Greek population. Byzantine influences can be seen in the churches of **San Nicola dei Greci** and **Santa Barbara**.

The small port of Maratea Inferiore with fishing boats

*A page from the precious Codex
Purpureus Rossanensis*

Rossano ⁊

Cosenza. 32,000. FS
2nd & 4th Fri of month.

THIS HANDSOME hill town was
one of the main centers of
Byzantine civilization in
Calabria. It assumed power
when Reggio di Calabria fell
to the Saracens in the 9th,
10th, and 11th centuries. The
Museo Diocesano houses the
Codex Purpureus Rossanensis,
a rare 6th-century Greek
Gospel with silver lettering and
splendidly detailed miniatures.

The Baroque **cathedral**
contains the *Madonna
Acheropita* fresco, a much
venerated Byzantine relic of
the 8th or 9th century.

ENVIRONS: On a hilltop to the
southeast of Rossano is the
five-domed Greek church of
San Marco (10th century). The
12th-century **Panaglia**, another
Greek church, lies off Via
Archivescovado. Both contain
fragments of early frescoes.
Santa Maria del Patirion
is magnificently adorned with
colored brickwork, tile, and
stone. It is situated on a
hilltop 18 km (11 miles) to
the west. It offers wonderful
views over the Piana di Sibari
(Plain of Sibari), the presumed
location of the fabled city of
Sybaris that was destroyed in
510 BC. The church has
remained virtually unaltered
since it was built around 1095.

🏛 **Museo Diocesano**
Palazzo Arcivescovile. 0983 52 02
82. Tue–Sun.

Tropea ⑧

Vibo Valenzia. 7,000. FS
Piazza Ercole. Sat.

ONE OF THE MOST picturesque
towns on Calabria's largely
built-up Tyrrhenian coast is
Tropea, which offers superb
views of the sea and beaches.
The old town hangs on to a
cliffside facing a large rock
that was formerly an island.
The rock is topped by **Santa
Maria dell'Isola**, a former
medieval Benedictine sanctuary. The **cathedral** at the end
of Via Roma is of Norman
origin, although it has been
rebuilt several times. Inside is
a 14th-century painting, the
Madonna di Romania, by
an unknown artist.

Casa Trampo (14th century)
and **Palazzo Cesareo** (early
20th century) in Vicolo Manco
are the most interesting of the
small palaces in Tropea. The
latter has a splendid balcony
adorned with carvings.

Below the town are pretty
beaches and a good choice of
places to eat. Other seaside
towns to visit are **Palmi** to the
south, and **Pizzo** to the north.

Stilo ⑨

Reggio di Calabria. 3,000. FS
Tue.

A SHORT DISTANCE from the
coast, Stilo is a ramshackle
and earthquake-damaged
town clamped to the side of

Monte Consolino. Standing on
a ledge looking out over the
olive trees is the **Cattolica**,
which has made Stilo a focus
of dedicated pilgrimage for
lovers of Byzantine architecture. Built in the 10th
century by Basilian monks,
the brick building with its
terra cotta-tiled roof is based
on a Greek cross-in-a-square
plan. Four antique, mis-
matched marble columns
divide the interior into nine
quadrants. The capitals are
placed at the base of the
columns instead of on top
to indicate the triumph of
Christianity over paganism.
The frescoes within, discovered and restored in 1927,
date from the 11th century.

The Cattolica dominates the
town, but on Via Tommaso
Campanella there is a medieval **duomo** as well as the
17th-century ruins of the
Convent of San Domenico,
where the philosopher and
Dominican friar Tommaso
Campanella (1568–1639)
lived. The church of **San
Francesco**, built about 1400,
has an ornate carved wooden
altar and a lovely 16th-century
painting of the *Madonna del
Borgo* (unknown origin). The
church of **San Giovanni**
(11th century) in Bivongi,
northwest of Stilo, although
generally closed, is open
during Easter week.

🏠 **Cattolica**
2 km (1 mile) above Stilo on Via
Cattolica. daily.

The beautiful and unspoiled coastline at Tropea

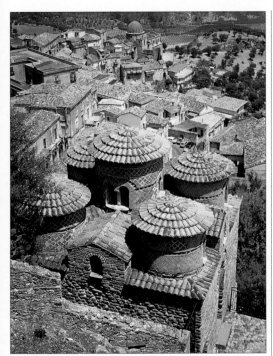

The distinctive five-domed Cattolica in Stilo

Gerace ⑩

Reggio di Calabria. 🏛 *3,000.* 🚌

Occupying an impregnable crag on the northeastern flank of the Aspromonte, this ancient place was founded by refugees from **Locri Epizephiri** who fled in the 9th century to escape Saracen attack. Its defensive character is reinforced by the medieval town walls and the remains of the once impregnable castle.

Apart from the slow pace of life here – where you are as likely to meet a flock of sheep in an alley as a Fiat 500 – the main attraction is Calabria's grandest **Duomo**. This massive structure indicates the importance of Gerace at least up to the time of the Normans. Constructed not later than the early 12th century, rebuilt in the 13th century, and restored in the 18th century, the crypt is its chief treasure. Both crypt and church are simple, adorned by a series of antique colored marble and granite columns probably stolen from the site of ancient Locri Epizephyrii. At the end of Via Cavour is 12th-century **San Giovanello**, part Byzantine and part Norman. Nearby is the Gothic church of **San Francesco d'Assisi**, which contains a Baroque marble altar (1615) and the Pisan-style tomb of Niccolò Ruffo (d. 1372), a member of a prominent Calabrian family.

ENVIRONS: The vast site of **Locri Epizephiri**, the first Greek city to have a written code of law (660 BC), was a well-known center of the cult of Persephone. There are remains of **temples**, a **theater**, and Greek and Roman **tombs**. The **Museo** displays a ground plan of the site and a collection of votive statues, coins, inscriptions, and sculptural fragments – evidence of Greek and Roman occupation of the site.

⋔ Locri Epizephiri
Southwest of Locri on the N106, Contrada Marasà. 【 *0964 39 00 23.* ☐ *Tue–Sun.* **Museo** ☐ *daily.* ● *Jan 1 & 6, May 1, Nov 25, Dec 25.*

Reggio di Calabria ⑪

🏛 *175,000.* ✈ 🚇 FS 🚌 🚢 🛈 *Corso Garibaldi 329 (0965 89 20 12).* 🛒 *Fri.*

This is a run-down city, but one reason to make a visit is to see the outstanding **Museo Nazionale della Magna Grecia**. The museum houses a fine collection of artifacts from ancient Rhegion – an important Greek city on the site of the present town – and from other Greek sites.

Chief among its treasures are the Greek bronzes, larger-than-life statues of warriors dredged from the sea off Riace Marina in 1972. Statue A (460 BC) is thought to be by Phidias, the Athenian sculptor and chief exponent of the idealizing, Classical style. If true, it is a rare survivor because his works, praised in the highest terms by ancient writers, were hitherto only known to us from Roman copies. Statue B (430 BC) has been attributed to the sculptor Polyclitus. It is possible that the statues originated from the Temple of Delphi, the Athenians' monument to the victory of Marathon.

🏛 Museo Nazionale della Magna Grecia
Piazza de Nava 26. 【 *0965 81 22 55.* ☐ *daily (Sun and public hols am only).* 🈲

Riace Bronzes (6th and 5th century BC) in Reggio's Museo Nazionale

SICILY

················

O N A CROSSROADS *in the Mediterranean, part of Europe and Africa yet belonging to neither, Sicily was tramped across by half the ancient civilized world. As conquerors came and went, they left behind a rich and varied cultural deposit. This has resulted in a quirky mixture in almost every aspect of the local culture from language, customs, and cooking to art and the interesting and diverse architecture of the island.*

During the 6th and 5th centuries BC, there cannot have been much difference between Athens and the Greek cities of Sicily. Their ruins are among the most spectacular of the ancient Greek world. The Romans took over in the 3rd century BC, followed by the Vandals, Ostrogoths, and Byzantines. Not much that is tangible has survived from the days of the Arabs, who ruled from the 9th to 11th centuries, though Palermo's Vucciria is more souk than market. The Norman era, beginning in 1060, spawned brilliant artistic achievements, such as the cathedrals of Monreale and Cefalù, while the eclecticism of that period's architecture is best seen at Santi Pietro e Paolo outside Taormina.

The Sicilian Baroque of the 17th and 18th centuries is just as individual. The palaces and churches of Palermo, reflecting the elaborate ritual of the Spanish Viceregal court, tend toward extravagant display. At Noto, Ragusa, Modica, Siracusa, and Catania the buildings are a useful vehicle for the Sicilians' love of ornamentation, itself a remnant from the island's early fling with the Arab world. The style is an expression of the nature of Sicilians, whose sense of pomp and pageantry is both magnificent and extreme.

Sicily is a curiosity, and the legacy of the past is redolent everywhere. The fact that it is an island has intensified the cultural impact of each successive occupier. They say that today there's less Italian blood in Sicilian veins than there is Phoenician, Greek, Arabic, Norman, Spanish, or French. The resulting mixture – exotic, spicy, and highly flammable – has created a separate nation at the foot of Italy.

Detail of a 12th-century mosaic from the Palazzo dei Normanni in Palermo

◁ **The beautifully preserved doric Temple of Concord (c.430 BC) in the Valley of the Temples at Agrigento**

Exploring Sicily

THE VAST COASTLINE of Sicily (Sicilia) provides many magnificent beaches, particularly at Taormina and the Golfo di Castellammare by Capo San Vito – part of a huge nature preserve. Sicily's varied interior is characterized by remote hill towns and plains punctuated by mountain ranges known for spring flowers and wildlife. Among the most spectacular sights is Mount Etna, an active volcano whose lava flows over the centuries have left the land immensely fertile, supporting an abundance of walnut trees, citrus groves, and vineyards.

Fishermen at work in their boats at Siracusa

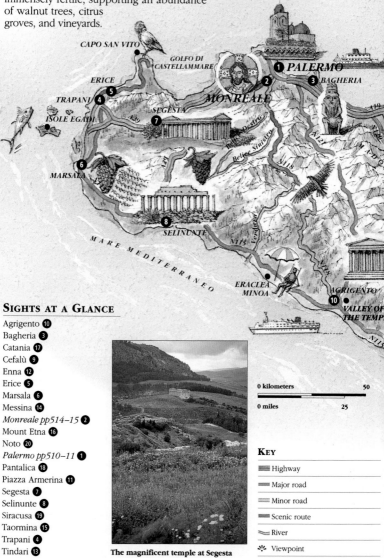

CAPO SAN VITO

GOLFO DI CASTELLAMMARE

ERICE

TRAPANI ④

ISOLE EGADI

MONREALE

① PALERMO

② ③ BAGHERIA

⑤

SEGESTA ⑦

MARSALA ⑥

SELINUNTE ⑧

ERACLEA MINOA

AGRIGENTO

⑩ VALLEY OF THE TEMPL

MARE MEDITERRANEO

SIGHTS AT A GLANCE

The magnificent temple at Segesta

| 0 kilometers | 50 |
| 0 miles | 25 |

KEY

▬▬	Highway
▬▬	Major road
▬▬	Minor road
▬▬	Scenic route
≈	River
⚜	Viewpoint

SEE ALSO

• *Where to Stay* pp573–5

• *Where to Eat* pp607–8

ISOLE EOLIE
(LIPARI)

The Norman duomo in Palermo

TRENO

A20

MESSINA ⑭

TINDARI ⑬

STRETTA DI
MESSINA

TROINA

NICOSIA

⑮ TAORMINA

N120

⑯

MOUNT ETNA

MARIONIO

⑫ ENNA

⑰ CATANIA

GOLFO DI
CATANIA

PIAZZA ARMERINA

⑪

CALTAGIRONE

PANTALICA

GOLFO DI
AUGUSTA

⑱

SIRACUSA

⑲

GELA

PALAZZOLO
ACREIDE

FO DI GELA

VITTORIA

COMISO

RAGUSA

⑳ NOTO

GOLFO DI
NOTO

GETTING AROUND

The A19 connects
Palermo and Catania, the A18
links Catania and Messina, and the
A20 (Palermo to Messina) is under construction. The west is accessible from Palermo,
on the A29. Ferry routes run from Messina
to Reggio di Calabria, and from Palermo
to Genoa or Naples. Between the larger
towns, train services are efficient, but for
smaller towns the buses are better. Catania
and Palermo have international airports.

The scenic town of Cefalù, dominated by a huge rock

Palermo ❶

Mosaic detail from Cappella Palatina

Nestling on the protective flank of Monte Pellegrino with Monte Alfano to the east, Palermo lies in a natural amphitheater called the Conca d'Oro (Golden Shell). Against La Cala harbor, the setting is beautiful and the city, a mix of Asian and European, is without equal despite reduced circumstances. The architecture, ranging in style from Arabic to Norman, Baroque, and Art Nouveau, is without comparison in Sicily, making this exotic city an exciting place to explore.

✚ Gesù

Piazza Casa Professa. ⬜ daily.

In the poor, bomb-devastated Albergheria quarter, near the colorful market of Piazza Ballarò, lies this important Baroque church (1564–1633). Also known as the church of the Casa Professa, the interior is an excellent example of the virtuosity of Sicilian craftsmen in the treatment of marble carving and inlay. The oldest Jesuit church in Sicily, it was heavily restored after suffering extensive bomb damage in World War II.

Ruined cloister with the red domes of San Giovanni degli Eremiti behind

✚ San Giovanni degli Eremiti

Via dei Benedettini. 📞 091 651 50 19. ⬜ daily. 🈳

Reflecting Islamic architectural tradition with bulbous domes, corner arches, and filigreed windows, this deconsecrated Norman church (1132–48) was built in the grounds of a mosque. Beyond church and mosque, a ruined cloister from a 13th-century monastery encloses a pretty garden.

✚ Palazzo Reale

Piazza Indipendenza. 📞 091 705 43 17. **Palazzo Reale** ⬜ daily am. 📞 091 656 17 32. **Cappella Palatina** ⬜ daily. ⬛ Easter, Apr 25, May 1, Dec 25. 🈳

Also called the Palazzo dei Normanni, this site has been the focus of power since the days of Byzantine rule and is now home to Sicily's regional government. The nucleus of the present building was constructed by the Arabs, but after the Norman conquest of the city (1072), it was enlarged and embellished for the Norman court. See the luxurious royal apartments, especially the Sala di Ruggero and the splendid Cappella Palatina. Built by Roger II (1132–40), this dazzling chapel blends Byzantine, Islamic, and Norman styles of craftsmanship. It is lavishly adorned with mosaics, as well as marble inlaid with gold, stone, and glass. Next to the palace is the eccentrically decorated Porta Nuova (1535).

Sumptuous interior of the Cappella Palatina, Palazzo Reale

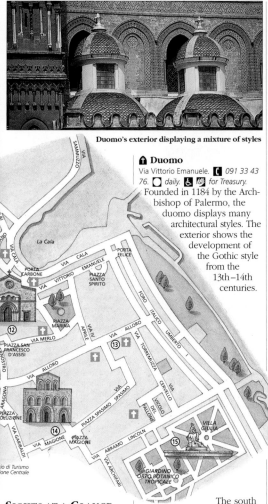

Duomo's exterior displaying a mixture of styles

VISITORS' CHECKLIST

730,000. ✈ *Punta Raisi 32 km (20 miles) W.* FS *Stazione Centrale, Piazza Giulio Cesare.* 🚌 *Via Balsamo.* ⚓ *Stazione Marittima, Molo Vittorio Veneto.* ℹ️ *Piazza Castelnuovo 35 (091 58 58 47).* 🚻 *Mon–Sat.* 🎭 *U Festinu for the city's patron saint, S. Rosalia: Jul 10–15; Pilgrimage to grotto of Santa Rosalia: Sep 4; Greek Orthodox celebrations in Martorana church: Easter.*

🔒 Duomo

Via Vittorio Emanuele. 🔲 091 33 43 76. ⭕ daily. ♿ 🏛 for Treasury.

Founded in 1184 by the Archbishop of Palermo, the duomo displays many architectural styles. The exterior shows the development of the Gothic style from the 13th–14th centuries.

porch are the remains of Emperor Frederick II; his wife, Constance of Aragon; his mother, Constance, daughter of Roger II (also entombed here); and his father, Henry VI. The Treasury houses the 12th-century Imperial Diadem of Constance of Aragon, which was removed from her tomb in the 18th century.

Fontana Pretorio with Santa Caterina in the background

The south porch (1453) is a masterpiece of the Catalan style, and at the apse end, sturdy Norman work can be seen through a decorative Islamic-inspired overlay. The dome is 18th century.

Within the much-altered interior are the tombs of Sicily's kings. Squeezed into an enclosure by the south

🔒 Santa Caterina

Piazza Bellini. ⚫ for restoration.

Although begun in 1566, most of the internal decoration of this unique church dates from the 17th and 18th centuries. A powerful example of the Palermitan Baroque, it overwhelms with colors, textures, sculpture, and marble inlay. There are illusionistic ceiling frescoes (18th century) by Filippo Randazzo in the nave and Vito d'Anna in the dome.

The church is flanked by Piazza Pretorio, which is dominated by the monumental Mannerist Fontana Pretorio, erected here in 1544.

SIGHTS AT A GLANCE

KEY

🅿️ Parking

✝️ Church

0 meters   250

0 yards   250

Exploring Palermo

EAST OF THE Quattro Canti, where Via Maqueda and
Corso Vittorio Emanuele meet, the city is sprinkled
with ornate palaces and more churches. Squeezed
behind them are labyrinthine medieval quarters where
ancient buildings with crumbling walls still survive.

🔒 La Martorana
Piazza Bellini. 📞 *091 616 16 92.*
⬜ *daily.*
Also called Santa Maria dell'
Ammiraglio, this church was
built around 1140 by George
of Antioch, Roger II's admiral
and also an orthodox Greek
Christian. The design derives
from Norman and Islamic traditions with mosaics possibly
by Greek artisans. In the right
aisle, King Roger receives the
Imperial Diadem from Christ;
in the left aisle, George of
Antioch is portrayed.

A nearby convent, founded
by Eloisa Martorana in 1193,
was the site where the Sicilian
Parliament met in 1295 and
decided, in the wake of the
Sicilian Vespers, to hand the
crown of Sicily to Frederick of
Aragon. The church was presented to the convent in 1433.

**Mosaic of Christ with Four Angels
in the dome of La Martorana**

📿 Vucciria
Via Roma. ⬜ *Mon–Sat.*
Nowhere is Palermo's Arabic
past more apparent than in
this medieval casbah-style
market that burrows through
the ruinous Loggia district
below Via Roma. Merchants,
hawkers, shoppers, and pickpockets crowd an area once
the haunt of artisans. The
alleys all around are named
after their professions, such
as silversmiths, dyers, and
keymakers. This busy market,
the largest in Palermo, offers
the usual market ware from
daily objects to junk, as well
as a wide selection of fresh
fruit, vegetables, and fish.

**Stuccoed interior of the Oratorio
del Rosario di San Domenico**

🔒 Oratorio del Rosario di
San Domenico
Via Bambinai 2. 📞 *091 32 05 59.*
⬜ *Mon–Sat.*
The interior of this tiny 16th-
century chapel displays elegant
Baroque decoration by the
master of stucco, Giacomo
Serpotta. Created around
1720–30, this was his latest
and possibly his finest work.
Serpotta's technical virtuosity,
not to mention the sensory
indulgence and whimsical
fantasy in evidence here, are
remarkable. The altarpiece is
the famous *Madonna of the*

Rosary (1624–8) by Anthony
Van Dyck, and there are wall
paintings by Luca Giordano
and Pietro Novelli.

🔒 San Domenico
Piazza San Domenico. 📞 *091 32
95 88.* ⬜ *Mon–Fri am.* **Museo del
Risorgimento** 📞 *091 58 27 74.* ⬜
Mon, Wed, Fri–Sun am. ⬛ *Jul & Aug.*
Although the present building
was begun in 1640, there has
been a Dominican church on
the site since the 14th century.
The architect responsible for
the exuberant church façade
(1726) and square in front
(1724) was Tommaso Maria
Napoli, one of the masters
of Sicilian Baroque.

Within, the most interesting
feature is Antonello Gagini's
bas-relief of *Santa Caterina*
(1528) in the third chapel on
the left. Next to the church is
the 14th-century cloister, part
of the original monastery that
gives access to the Museo del
Risorgimento.

🏛 Museo Archeologico
Regionale
Piazza San Domenico 1. 📞 *091 58
27 74.* ⬜ *Mon, Wed, Fri.* 🈂
Housed in a former monastery
of the Filippini, Sicily's most
important museum contains
sculpture, architectural fragments, and artifacts, including
ceramics, glassware, bronzes,
jewelry, terra-cottas, and
weapons. The collection is
taken from the island's great
Phoenician, Greek, and Roman
sites of antiquity – Tindari,
Termini Imerese, Agrigento,
Siracusa, Selinunte, and Mozia.
The highlights are sculptures
from the friezes of the ancient
Greek temples at Selinunte.

Palermo's noisy, bustling Vucciria market east of Via Roma

🏛 Oratorio del Rosario di Santa Zita

Via Valverde 3. 📞 *091 33 27 79.*
⭘ *Mon–Sat.*

This small chapel is dedicated to the Virgin of the Rosary after her miraculous intervention at the Battle of Lepanto (*see pp54–5*). The stucco relief decoration, again, is the work of Giacomo Serpotta (after 1688); the panel on the rear wall depicts the battle, and other reliefs show scenes from the New Testament, all portrayed with extravagant realism. The neighboring 16th-century church of Santa Zita, from which the oratory takes its name, is filled with sculptures by Antonello Gagini (1517–27).

Ornate interior of the Oratorio di Santa Cita

🏛 Oratorio di San Lorenzo

Via Immacolatella 5. ⭘ *daily am.*

Lining the walls of this tiny oratory are incredible stucco scenes from the lives of St. Francis and St. Lawrence, and allegorical figures and putti by Giacomo Serpotta (1699–1706). These remarkable, expressive works exhibit the virtuosity of their creator in the handling of his medium. Caravaggio's *Nativity with St. Francis and St. Lawrence* (1609) graced the space above the altar until it was stolen in 1969. The oratory lies hidden next to the medieval church of San Francesco d'Assisi (13th century), which is brimming with excellent sculpture. The undoubted highlight of the church is the triumphal arch (1468) by Pietro da Bonitate and Francesco Laurana in the Cappella Mastrantonio.

The Palazzina Cinese (c.1799) set in the Parco della Favorita

🏛 Palazzo Abatellis and Galleria Regionale di Sicilia

Via Alloro 4. 📞 *091 623 00 11.*
⭘ *daily am.* 🈲

Matteo Carnelivari built this palace combining elements of Spanish late-Gothic and Italian Renaissance styles in the 15th century. It is home to the Galleria Regionale di Sicilia, which houses Antonello da Messina's *Vergine Annunziate* (1476), Francesco Laurana's marble head of Eleanor of Aragon (15th century), and sculptures by the Gagini. Nearby, the 15th-century church of Santa Maria degli Angeli (or La Gancia) contains works by Antonello Gagini and Giacomo Serpotta.

Annunciation (1476) by da Messina in the Galleria Regionale di Sicilia

🏛 La Magione

Via Magione 44. 📞 *091 617 05 96.*
⭘ *daily.*

Badly damaged in World War II, later restorations have revealed the ancient structure of this church. It was founded in 1150 by Matteo d'Aiello, Roger II's chancellor. With its simple, tall nave flanked by fine Gothic columns, La Magione is a major feature of any tour of Norman Sicily.

♣ Villa Giulia

Via Abramo Lincoln. ⭘ *daily.* 🚻
Orto Botanico 📞 *091 740 40 28.*
⭘ *daily.* ⬤ *public hols.* 🚻

The formal gardens of the villa were established in the 18th century. Once, with their statues and fountains, they were an exotic evocation of the antique world; the writer Goethe thought they were "wonderful." Nowadays, both the tropical flora and sense of faded grandeur make them a delightful setting for walks. In the adjacent Orto Botanico (botanical gardens) there are magnificent tropical plants. In Léon Dufourny's Neo-Classical Gymnasium (1789), plant specimens can be examined.

♣ Parco della Favorita

Entrance on Piazza Leoni & Piazza Generale Cascino. ⭘ *daily.* 🚻 **Museo Etnografico Siciliano Pitré**, Via Duca degli Abruzzi 1. 📞 *091 740 48 93.*
⭘ *Sat–Thu.* ⬤ *Fri, public hols.*

This park, laid out as a hunting ground in 1799 by the Bourbon Ferdinand IV, was surrounded by summer villas of the aristocracy. One of these, the Palazzina Cinese (c.1799), was built in a Chinese style for Ferdinand III and Maria Carolina, the sister of Marie Antoinette.

The Museo Etnografico Siciliano Pitré, in the stables of the Palazzina Cinese, has an outstanding collection of objects from Sicilian life.

Monreale ❷

MAGNIFICENTLY ADORNED, and with a splendid view of the Conca d'Oro, the Duomo at Monreale is one of the great sights of Norman Sicily. Founded in 1172 by the Norman King William II, it flanks a monastery of the Benedictine Order. The interior of the cathedral glitters with mosaics designed by Sicilian and Byzantine artists – the inspiration of a king who wanted to rival the power of the Archbishop of Palermo. Like Cefalù, and later Palermo, it was to serve as a royal sepulchre.

Capital from cloister column

★ Christ Pantocrator
The cathedral's Latin-cross plan focuses on the imposing mosaic of the all-powerful Christ (12th–13th century).

Nave and aisles separated by Roman columns

Magnificent gilded wood ceiling

Apse Exterior
With their rich multi-colored ornamentation in tufa and marble, the three apses represent the apogee of Norman decoration.

Entrance to Cappella del Crocifisso and Treasury

Original Cosmati floor in choir

The royal tomb of William II, in white marble, flanks the porphyry tomb of William I in the corner of the transept.

Barisano da Trani's bronze door (1179) on the north side is shielded by a portico designed by Gian Domenico and Fazio Gagini (1547–69).

★ Mosaic Cycle
Completed in 1182, the rich mosaics show scenes from the Old Testament (nave), Teachings of Christ (aisles, choir, and transepts), and the Gospels (side apses). The story of Noah's Ark is depicted here.

★ Cloisters
A masterpiece of Norman artistic expression from the time of William II, the columns – plain, carved, or inlaid with richly lustered tiles – support elaborate capitals from which spring Saracenic-style arches.

VISITORS' CHECKLIST

Piazza Vittorio Emanuele. 🚌 809, 8/9 & many others going W.
Church ☎ 091 640 24 24.
⏰ 8am–7pm daily. ♦ 🔲 ⚿
Cloister ☎ 091 640 44 03. ⏰
Apr–Sep: 9am–7pm Mon–Fri, 9am–12:30pm Sat & Sun; Oct–Mar: 9am–1pm Mon–Fri (also: 3–5pm Mon & Thu), 9am–12:30pm Sat & Sun. 🔲 ⚿ for Treasury,

The south wall and cloisters survive as elements from the Benedictine monastery.

Small Oriental-inspired fountain

Column Detail
Craftsmen from Campania, Puglia, Lombardy, and Sicily worked on the cloister columns. The detail here shows Adam and Eve.

The 18th-century porch is surrounded by two squat towers.

Bronze Door Panel
Bonanno da Pisa's fine bronze door (1185), signed by him, depicts 42 scenes from the Bible set within elaborate borders. The lion and griffin are symbols of the Norman kingdom.

STAR FEATURES

★ Cloisters

★ Mosaic Cycle

★ Christ Pantocrator

Bagheria ❸

Palermo. 🚶 40,000. 🚉 🚌
ℹ️ Comune di Bagheria, Via
Mattarella (091 90 54 38). 🛒 Wed.

Fishing and pleasure boats moored in the harbor of Trapani

ODAY BAGHERIA is almost a suburb of Palermo, though open countryside with olive and orange groves once separated them. In the 17th century Giuseppe Branciforte, Prince of Butera, built a summer retreat there, starting a fashion that was quickly followed by other Palermitan aristocrats. The town's core is sprinkled with their Baroque and Neo-Classical villas.

The **Villa Palagonia** was designed in 1705 by the architect Tommaso Maria Napoli for Ferdinando Gravina, the Prince of Palagonia. It has remarkable architectural qualities: a complex open-air staircase leads to the first floor, and the principal rooms, all with unusual shapes, are arranged around a curved axis. A later prince adorned the perimeter wall with the grotesque stone monsters that amused the 18th-century traveler Patrick

Stone figure on Villa Palagonia

Brydone, and horrified Goethe, who also traveled here and called this the "Palagonian madhouse." Across the piazza are **Villa Valguarnera** (begun in 1713 by Napoli), set in its own park, and **Villa Trabia** (mid-18th century), but neither is open to the public. **Villa Cattolica** (18th century) houses a modern art gallery.

🏛 **Villa Palagonia**
Piazza Garibaldi. 📞 091 93 20 88.
⏰ daily. 📷
🏛 **Villa Cattolica**
Via Consolare. 📞 091 90 54 38.
⏰ Tue–Sun. 📷

Trapani ❹

🚶 73,000. 🚉 🚌 ⛴ ℹ️ Piazza
Saturno (0923 290 00).
🛒 daily.

OLD TRAPANI occupies a narrow peninsula. The best buildings in this lively quarter are the churches, especially the **Cathedral of San Lorenzo** (1635) and **Chiesa del Collegio dei Gesuiti** (c.1614–40). The façades of both, and that of the **Palazzo d'Ali** (17th century) on Via Garibaldi, display magnificently the curious ebullience of west Sicilian Baroque architecture.

The 17th-century **Purgatorio** on Via San Francesco d'Assisi contains 18th-century *Misteri* – realistic, life-sized wooden statues used annually in the Good Friday procession. **Santa Maria del Gesù** on Via Sant' Agostino should be visited for the *Madonna degli Angeli* by Andrea della Robbia (1435–1525) and Antonello Gagini's canopy (1521). In the Jewish quarter, west of Via XXX Gennaio, the **Palazzo della Giudecca** (16th century) has a strangely textured façade.

The **Museo Pepoli** has a comprehensive collection of local antiquities. Of greatest interest are the coral objects and the Christmas crib figures *(presepi)*, modern versions of which are made here. Next to the museum, the **Santuario di Maria Santissima Annunziata** contains the *Madonna di Trapani*, a statue revered by fishermen and sailors for its legendary miraculous powers.

🏛 **Museo Nazionale Pepoli**
Via Conte Agostino Pepoli. 📞 0923
55 32 69. ⏰ daily. 📷

Open-air staircase of the eccentric Villa Palagonia in Bagheria

Erice ⑤

Trapani. 🏛 29,000. 🚌 ℹ️ Viale Conte Pepoli 11 (0923 86 93 88). 🗓 Mon.

POISED ON A CRAG overlooking Trapani, Erice was once the seat of the cult of the fertility goddess Venus Erycina. Her temple stood on the present site of the Norman **castle**, beyond the **Villa Balio** public gardens. The ancient town of Eryx was renamed Gebel-Hamed by the Arabs and then it became Monte San Giuliano under the Normans. It was not until 1934 that Mussolini adopted the present name.

Erice is medieval throughout. The **Duomo** (14th century) has a 15th-century porch and an earlier battlemented campanile used as a watchtower by the Aragonese. Inside is a lovely *Madonna and Child* (c.1469), attributed to either Francesco Laurana or Domenico Gagini. Deconsecrated 13th-century **San Giovanni Battista** on Viale Nunzio Nasi is home to Antonello Gagini's *St. John the Evangelist* (1531) and Antonino Gagini's *St. John the Baptist* (1539). **San Cataldo**, a plain 14th-century building on Via San Cataldo, contains a holy water stoup from the workshop of Domenico Gagini (c.1474). The **Museo Cordici** houses Antonello Gagini's *Annunciation* (1525) and an interesting variety of Classical remains.

🏛 Museo Cordici
Piazza Umberto I. ☎ 0923 86 00 48. 🕐 daily. ⬤ public hols.

A typical medieval street in the small hilltown of Erice

SICILIAN ISLANDS

Surrounding Sicily are several island groups. The Isole Eolie or Lipari (Aeolian Islands), to which Panaria, Lipari, Vulcano, and Stromboli belong, are a mass of extinct or nearly extinct volcanoes poking out of the sea off the coast of Milazzo. The Isole Egadi (Egadi Islands), off the coast of Trapani, have a distinctly Arabic flavor. They include Favignana, Levanzo (which has Paleolithic and Neolithic paintings and drawings), and Marettimo – the smallest and most unspoiled. Ustica, renowned for its marine life and popular among divers, lies north of Palermo. To the south are the remarkably tourist-free Isole Pelagie (Pelagic Islands) – Lampedusa and Linosa, which are North African in character. Remote Pantelleria is nearer Tunisia than Sicily.

The biggest and most popular of the Isole Eolie is Lipari, which has a pretty port and a good range of bars, restaurants and hotels. Nearby sulfur-scented Vulcano offers hot mudbaths and black beaches.

Favignana, the largest and most populous of the Isole Egadi, is the scene of the traditional tuna harvest – la mattanza. This takes place, as it has for centuries, in May. These fishermen are bringing in the nets following the harvest.

Part of the Isole Pelagie, Lampedusa was once owned by the family of Giuseppe Tomasi di Lampedusa, author of The Leopard, *Sicily's most famous novel. The island is nearer to Malta than Sicily and has clean water and great beaches.*

USTICA

ISOLE EOLIE (LIPARI)

Palermo

ISOLE EGADI

SICILY

PANTELLERIA

0 kilometers   100

0 miles   50

ISOLE PELAGIE

Marsala

Trapani. 🏛 *85,000.* 🚊 🚌 ⛴ ℹ️
Via XI Maggio 100 (0923 71 40 97).
🚌 *Tue.*

THE PORT OF MARSALA is the home of a thick, strong, sweet wine that has been in production here since the 18th century. In 1798 Admiral Nelson ordered vast quantities of it following the Battle of the Nile. Its early production was presided over by three British families living in Sicily. One of the old warehouses where the wine was produced is now the **Museo Archeologico di Baglio Anselmi**, housing important Phoenician artifacts.

Among other important attractions are the ruins of **Lilybaeum**, an outpost of the Phoenician Empire, founded in 397 BC. It was peopled by the survivors of the massacre by Dionysius I of Siracusa at Mozia (ancient Motya) – the island used by the Phoenicians as a commercial center. Best of all are the unique reconstructed remains of a Punic ship thought to have been active in the First Punic War (263–241 BC). The **Museo di Mozia** in the Whitaker villa contains a remarkable early 5th-century BC statue of a Greek youth.

The excavations here are important; what we know of the Phoenicians today comes

Statue of a Greek youth in Museo di Mozia

mostly from the Bible, and from Mozia. The **Duomo**, begun in the 17th century, was built on the site of an earlier church; both were dedicated to Marsala's patron saint, Thomas Becket of Canterbury. Its interior is full of sculptural works by members of the Gagini family. The small **Museo degli Arazzi**, behind the Duomo, contains several magnificent 16th-century Brussels tapestries.

🏛 **Museo Archeologico di Baglio Anselmi**
Via Lungomare. 📞 *0923 95 25 35.* 🕐 *daily.* &

🏛 **Museo degli Arazzi**
Via Garappa. 📞 *0923 71, 29 03.* 🕐 *Tue–Sun.* 📷

🏛 **Museo di Mozia**
Isola di Mozia. 📞 *0923 71 25 98.* 🕐 *daily am.* 📷 &

Segesta

Trapani. 🚌 *from Trapani & Palermo.*
🕐 *9am–1 hr before sunset.*

ACCORDING TO LEGEND, the ancient town of Segesta – still largely unexcavated – was founded by Trojan followers of Aeneas. It presents one of the most spectacular sights on the island: a massive unfinished **temple** stranded on a remote hillside. Its construction was started between 426 and 416 BC, and it was left incomplete following the devastation of Selinunte by the Carthaginians in 409 BC. Archaeologists

regard the temple as a good example of "work in progress." Nearby, close to the summit of Monte Barbaro, the ruins of an ancient theater (3rd century BC) can be visited. Summer concerts are now held here.

Selinunte

Trapani. 📞 *0924 462 77.*
🚊 *Castelvetrano then bus.*
🕐 *9am–1 hr before sunset. Ticket office closes at 7pm.* 📷

FOUNDED IN 651 BC, Selinunte became one of the great cities of Magna Graecia – the part of southern Italy that was colonized by ancient Greece – and its toppled ruins are among Sicily's most important historic sites. Its ancient name, Selinus, derives from the wild celery that still grows here. The city was an important port, and its wall defenses can still be seen around the Acropolis. The Carthaginians, under Hannibal, completely destroyed the city in 409 BC in a battle famous for its epic and spectacularly savage proportions.

While the city itself has virtually disappeared, eight of its temples are distinguishable, particularly the so-called **Eastern Temples** (E, F and G). Of these, the columns of huge Doric **Temple E** (490–480 BC) have been partially re-erected. **Temple F** (c.560–540 BC) is in ruins. **Temple G** (late 6th century BC), which had 17 massive side columns, was one of the greatest Greek temples ever built.

Higher on the Acropolis lie the remains of **Temples A, B, C, D,** and **O**. Metope sculpture from **Temple C** (early 6th century), originally located on the frieze between the triglyphs, can be seen in the Museo Archeologico Regionale in Palermo *(see p512)*, along with ceramics, jewelry, and other artifacts found here. A small **museum** on the site houses less important finds, as does one in Castelvetrano, 14 km (8.5 miles) north of Selinunte. The ancient city is still being excavated; its **North Gate** entrance is well preserved and further north there is also a **necropolis**.

The spectacularly situated, unfinished Doric temple at Segesta

Cefalù **9**

Palermo. 14,000. 🚆 🚌 ℹ️ Corso Ruggero 77 (0921 42 10 50). 🚢 Sat.

THIS PRETTY, unspoiled seaside town with good beaches and many hotels and restaurants is dominated by a huge rock – once the site of a Temple of Diana – and by one of the finest Norman cathedrals in Sicily. Begun in 1131 by Roger II, the **duomo** was intended as the principal religious seat in Sicily. Though it failed to fulfil this function, the building's magnificence has never been eclipsed. Its splendid mosaics (1148), which feature a huge image of Christ Pantocrator in the apse, are remarkable and often celebrated as purely Byzantine works of art on Sicilian soil.

The **Museo Mandralisca** houses a fine *Portrait of a Man* (c.1465) by Antonello da Messina and an interesting collection of artifacts that includes coins, ceramics, vases, minerals, and shells.

🏛 **Museo Mandralisca**
Via Mandralisca. 📞 0921 42 15 47.
🔵 daily; Sun & public hols am only. 🖼

The twin-towered façade of the Norman duomo in Cefalù

The lavish apse of Cefalù's Duomo

Agrigento **10**

57,000. 🚆 🚌 ℹ️ Via Empedocle 73 (0922 203 91). 🚢 Fri.

MODERN AGRIGENTO occupies the site of Akragas, an important city of the ancient Greek world. Founded by Daedalus, according to legend, it was famed for the luxurious lifestyle of its inhabitants, and was a great power and rival to Siracusa. In 406 BC it fell to the Carthaginians, who sacked and burned it following the flight of its citizens and soldiers.

The historic core of the city, with its narrow medieval streets, focuses on the Via Atenea. **Santo Spirito** (13th century) houses stuccoes by Giacomo Serpotta (1695). **Santa Maria dei Greci** was built on the remains of a 5th-century BC temple – see the flattened columns in the nave. The **duomo**, founded in the 14th century and altered in the 16th and 17th centuries, exhibits a unique mixture of Arab, Norman, and Catalan detailing.

ENVIRONS: The chief reason to visit Agrigento nowadays is to see the archaeological zone known as the Valley of the Temples (*see p520*). The **Museo Regionale Archeologico** houses an interesting display of artifacts from the temples and the city, including an outstanding collection of vases, coins, and Greek and Roman sculpture.

🏛 **Museo Regionale Archeologico**
Contrada San Nicola, Viale Panoramica.
📞 0922 40 15 65. 🔵 daily am. 🖼

THE MAFIA

An international organization founded in Sicily, the Mafia (meaning hostility to law) developed against a background of a cruel State, exploitative nobility, and severe poverty. By the late 19th century it had become a criminal organization thriving on property speculation and drug trafficking. Since the "singing" of Tommaso Buscetta and the capture of Toto Riina, the Mafia has been on the defensive against a State that has doubled its efforts against it. Although violence is common, it is not aimed at tourists. Indeed, Sicilians on the whole are known for their hospitality.

Mafia assassination depicted in this scene from the film *The Godfather Part III* (1990)

Valley of the Temples

STRADDLING A LOW RIDGE to the south of Agrigento, the Valley of the Temples (Valle dei Templi) ranks among the most impressive complexes of ancient Greek buildings outside Greece. Its Doric temples, dating from the 5th century BC, were destroyed in part by Carthaginians (406 BC).

In the 6th century pious Christians, believing the temples to be pagan, wreaked further havoc on them, as did subsequent earthquakes. The extraordinary ruins in this archaeological zone can be covered in a day, though crowd-free early morning and evening visits are recommended.

Telamone from the Temple of Olympian Zeus

Temple of Hephaistos ①
Apart from a couple of incomplete columns still standing, very little remains of this temple, built c.430 BC. It is also called the Temple of Vulcan.

Sanctuary of the Chthonic Divinities ②
At this group of shrines, the forces of nature were worshipped.

(see p519)
Museo Regionale Archeologico •
San Nicola •

Via dei Templi

• Hellenistic and Roman Quarter

San Biagio

Rock Sanctuary of Demeter

Strada Panoramica

Temple of Herakles ⑥
This is the oldest temple in the valley (late 6th century BC).

• Catacombs

Ⓟ Parking

Via Sacra

Temple of Asklepios

N115

Temple of Olympian Zeus ④
Begun c.480 BC, this was the biggest Doric temple ever built. Unfinished at the time of the Carthaginian attack, it is now a toppled ruin. Giant figures known as telamones were used in its construction.

Temple of Juno ⑧
Built around 450 BC, this temple still has many intact columns.

Tomb of Theron ⑤
Here are the ruins of a Roman tomb (1st century AD).

Temple of Castor and Pollux ③
This is an incorrect assemblage of pieces from other buildings, erected in the 19th century. Modern Agrigento (see p519) is in the background.

KEY

– – Suggested route

Ⓟ Parking

—— Ancient walls

0 meters 500
0 yards 500

Temple of Concord ⑦
This beautifully preserved temple (c.430 BC) was converted into a Christian church in the 4th century AD, thus saved from destruction.

Piazza Armerina ⑪

Enna. 🚶 22,000. 🚌 ℹ️ Via Cavour 15 (0935 68 02 01). 🛒 Thu.

THIS ACTIVE, ebullient provincial town is half medieval and half Baroque. The 17th-century **duomo**, at its highest point, is the most interesting of the Baroque buildings.

In August, the lively *Palio dei Normanni* festival attracts many visitors, but the main reason to visit Piazza Armerina is to see the early 4th-century mosaics in the **Villa Romana del Casale**, 5 km (3 miles) southwest of the town.

It is thought that this huge, once sumptuous villa with its public halls, private quarters, baths, and courtyards, belonged to Maximianus Herculeus, Diocletian's co-emperor, from AD 286 to 305. His son and successor, Maxentius, probably continued its decoration, with Constantine taking over on Maxentius's death in 312.

Although little remains of the building fabric, the floors are decorated with some of the finest surviving mosaics from Roman antiquity. The hunting, mythological, and domestic scenes, and exotic landscapes, all exhibit astonishingly realistic attention to detail.

🏛️ Villa Romana del Casale

Contrada Paratorre. 📞 0935 68 00 36. 🕐 daily. 🎟️

Roman *Girls in Bikinis* from the Villa Romana del Casale

Enna ⑫

🚶 28,000. 🚊 🚌 ℹ️ Piazza Colaianni 6 (0935 50 08 75). 🛒 Tue.

IMPREGNABLE on a crag above a fertile landscape where Persephone, mythological daughter of Demeter, once played, Sicily's highest town has been coveted by successive invaders since its earliest days. The venerated seat of the Cult of Demeter (Patroness of Fertility) was at Enna. Her temple stood on the **Rocca Cerere**, not far from the huge **Castello di Lombardia** (13th century) built by Frederick II.

Most of Enna's sights are clustered at the core of the old town among the warren of ancient streets that open out of the Via Roma. The church of **San Francesco** has a 16th-century tower. **Piazza Crispi**, with its fine views to nearby Calascibetta, is dominated by a copy of Bernini's *Rape of Persephone*. The 14th-century **duomo**, altered and adorned in later centuries, contains parts of Demeter's temple.

The **Museo Alessi** houses the Cathedral Treasury and an interesting coin collection. The **Museo Varisano** has exhibits on the area's history, from Neolithic to Roman. Away from the center, the octagonal **Torre di Federico II** (13th century) is a former watchtower.

ENVIRONS: The ancient hill town of **Nicosia**, northeast of Enna, was damaged in the 1967 earthquake, but still contains a smattering of churches. San Nicola, built in the 14th century and subsequently haphazardly readorned, has a magnificent, carved entrance portal. Inside there is a much-venerated wooden crucifix (17th century) by Fra Umile di Petralia. Santa Maria Maggiore houses a 16th-century marble polyptych by Antonello Gagini and a throne reputedly used by Charles V in 1535. Farther east is **Troina**. It was captured in 1062 by the Normans, whose work survives in the Chiesa Matrice. Southeast of Enna, **Vizzini** commands fine views of the countryside.

🏛️ Museo Alessi

Via Roma. 📞 0935 50 31 65. 🕐 daily.

🏛️ Museo Varisano

Piazza Mazzini. 📞 0935 50 03 31. 🕐 daily. 🎟️

A view from the hills overlooking Vizzini, southeast of Enna

Taormina's magnificently situated Greek theater, with Mount Etna in the distance

Tindari ⓭

Messina. **C** *0941 36 90 23.*
FS *Patti or Oliveri then bus.*
⊙ *9am–1 hr before sunset daily.* &

POISED ON THE EDGE of a cliff
overlooking the Golfo di
Patti are the ruins of **Tyndaris**,
almost the last Greek city to
have been founded in Sicily
(395 BC) and strategically
important to this coast. Apart
from the city walls, the ruins
are mostly Roman, including
the huge **basilica**, **theater**,
and houses. An **antiquarium**
holds artifacts from the site.
   Tindari is better known for
its shrine to a Byzantine icon,
the **Black Madonna** on
Piazzale Belvedere.

Messina ⓮

M *275,000.* **FS** **⛴** **H** *Piazza
Cairoli 45 (090 293 52 92).* ⊖ *daily.*

NO SICILIAN CITY has suffered
more than Messina, the
victim of earthquakes and the
bombs of World War II. The
Museo Regionale houses
treasures from many of the
buildings no longer standing.
**Santissima Annunziata dei
Catalani** in Piazza Catalani
displays the typical eclecticism
of 12th-century Norman

architecture, with rich decoration. It surpasses the **duomo**
(begun 1160) that, despite
faithful rebuilding after the war,
is a ghost of its former self.
   Outside, GA Montorsoli's
Fontana d'Orione (1547) is
the finest fountain of its kind
from 16th-century Sicily. His
Fontana di Nettuno (1557)
celebrates Messina's foundation
and position in the world as a
principal commercial port.

🏛 **Museo Regionale**
Via della Libertà 465. **C** *090 36 12 92.*
⊙ *Mon–Sat.* 📷

**Antonello da Messina's *Madonna
and Child* (1473), Museo Regionale**

Taormina ⓯

Messina. **M** *10,000.* **FS** **⛟**
H *Palazzo Corvaja, Piazza Santa
Caterina (0942 232 43).* ⊖ *Wed.*

SPLENDIDLY SITUATED, Taormina
is Sicily's window on the
modern world. It is a delight to
visit, filled with a wide range of
restaurants and hotels, with
sandy beaches far below.
   The most illustrious relic of
the past is the **theater**. Begun
in the 3rd century BC by the
Greeks, it was subsequently
rebuilt by the Romans. Among
other Classical remains are
the ruins of the **odeon** (for
musical performances) and
the **naumachia** (an artificial
lake for mock-battles). On
Piazza Vittorio Emanuele (site
of the Roman Forum), **Palazzo
Corvaia** (14th century) was
built using stone from a temple
that once stood here. The 13th-
century **duomo** (renovated in
1636) is a fortresslike building.

ENVIRONS: Taormina's main
beach, **Mazzarò**, has a beautiful, clear sea and can be
easily reached from the town.
South of Taormina at **Capo
Schisò** are the ruins of ancient
Naxos. To the west is **Gole
dell'Alcantara**, a 20-m (66-ft)
deep gorge of basalt rock, with
an ice-cold river and waterfalls.

Mount Etna 🔟

Catania. **FS** to Linguaglossa or
Randazzo; Circumetnea railroad from
Catania to Riposto. 🚌 to Nicolosi.
ℹ️ Piazza Vittorio Emanuele 32,
Nicolosi (095 91 44 88).

ONE OF THE WORLD'S largest
active volcanoes, Mount
Etna was thought by the
Romans to have been the forge
of Vulcan (god of fire). The
authorities are always on the
watch for violent eruptions–
like those that devastated
Catania in the past. To view it
in comfort, the Circumetnea
railroad runs around the base
from Catania to Riposto.

Catania 🔟

🏛️ 365,000. ✈️ **FS** 🚌 ℹ️ Via Cimarosa 12 (095 730 62 11). 🛒 Mon–Sat
(general); Sun (antique & bric-a-brac).

HAVING BEEN DECIMATED by
the earthquake of 1693,
Catania was comprehensively
rebuilt, and today contains
some of the most imaginative

The façade of Catania's duomo

lava-built Baroque buildings
in Sicily. From **Piazza del
Duomo**, featuring a lava
elephant (Catania's symbol)
carrying an Egyptian obelisk,
there is a dramatic vista to
Mount Etna. In 1736 the
Norman **duomo** was given a
new façade by Vaccarini, who
also worked on the **Municipio**
(finished 1741). A vigorous
plasticity of form is his hall-
mark – see the façade of
Sant'Agata (1748), and the
designs of **Collegio Cutelli**,

probably built by a pupil
around 1779, and **Palazzo
Valle** (c.1740–50).
Carrying on the Vaccarini
tradition is Stefano Ittar's **San
Placido** (around 1768). The
frenzied stone carving on the
Palazzo Biscari (early 18th
century) is exceeded by
Antonino Amato's unres-
trained decoration of the vast
Benedictine **convent** (1704)
and the adjacent huge church
of **San Niccolò** (1730).
On Via Vittorio Emanuele is
the **Museo Belliniano**, birthplace of composer Vincenzo
Bellini (1801–35). The lava
ruins of the **Teatro Romano**
(21 BC) are at Piazza Stesicono.
Verga's House, home of the
great Sicilian novelist Giovanni
Verga (1840–1922), is on Via
Sant' Anna. Via Crociferi is
home to 18th-century churches
San Francesco Borgia, **San
Benedetto**, and **San Giuliano**,
whose interior is Vaccarini's
masterpiece (1760). Farther
along Via Crociferi, the church
of **Santo Carcere** contains the
prison of St. Agatha, who was
martyred in AD 253.

INFLUENCES ON TRADITIONAL SICILIAN CUISINE

Sicily has one of Italy's
most varied cuisines. The
island's unique location –
marooned between North
Africa, Europe, and the
eastern Mediterranean –
and the invaders it attracted,
are responsible for this.
The earliest Western cook-
book, the now lost *Art of
Cooking* (5th century BC),
was written by Mithaecus,
a Siracusan Greek. Sicily's
fertility attracted Greek
colonists, who exported
oil, wheat, honey, cheese,
fruit, and vegetables to their
homeland. To the Romans,
Sicily was merely a bread-
basket. The Arabs, however,
introduced oranges, lemons,
eggplants, and sugar cane.
Their love of sweets

An impressive selection of olives displayed in a Palermo market stall

provided the inspiration for
granita, a form of flavored
ice. The Sicilians love to
claim an Arabic origin for
their ice cream, but the
Greeks and Romans had
created an earlier
version by chilling
their wine with snow
from Mount Etna.
Traditionally, the
peasants existed on a
subsistence diet while

the aristocracy enjoyed
extravagant fare, and one of
the peculiarities of Sicilian
food today is that it can be
both frugal and handsomely
ornate. All of the usual
Italian dishes are available,
but more interesting are
the variations using local
ingredients like swordfish,
sardines, ricotta cheese, red
chilies, eggplants, capers,
olives, and almond paste.

Marzipan fruits made from almond paste

Overlooking the beach at Mazzarò near Taormina ▷

Shorefront in Siracusa, one of the most beautiful cities of the ancient Greek world

Pantalica ⓲

Siracusa. 📞 0931 46 24 52. 🚌 from
Siracusa to Sortino then 5 km (3 miles)
walk to entrance or bus from Siracusa
to Ferla then 10 km (6 miles) walk to
entrance. **Necropolis** ◯ 7am–sunset
(Oct–Mar: 6pm). ♿

R EMOTE IN THE desolate
Monti Iblei and over-
looking the Anapo River is
the prehistoric **necropolis** of
Pantalica – today a pleasant
place to walk and picnic. The
dead of a large, unexcavated
village (which was occupied
from 13th–8th century BC)
were buried here in deep,
cavelike tombs cut into the
rock. More than 5,000 of
these tombs were arranged in
tiers with a single flat stone
sealing each opening.
  The inhabitants of Pantalica
are thought to have come
from coastal **Thapsos**, which
was abandoned after raids by
warlike tribes from mainland
Italy. The site was reinhabited
in the Byzantine period when
some tombs were made into

**Rock-cut tombs in the prehistoric
necropolis of Pantalica**

cave dwellings and chapels.
Artifacts from the necropolis
are displayed in Siracusa's
Museo Archeologico Regionale.

Siracusa ⓳

🏛 125,000. 🚉 🚌 🚢 Via San
Sebastiano 43 (0931 677 10). 🛒 Wed.

Interior of duomo in Siracusa

S IRACUSA (SYRACUSE) was the
most important and power-
ful Greek city from the 5th to
3rd centuries BC, and, according to the Roman consul
Cicero, the most beautiful. The
peninsula **Ortigia** is the self-
contained hub of the old city.
On the mainland, **Achradina,
Tyche,** and **Neapolis** have
been occupied almost without
a break since the expansion
of the city in 480 BC. These
were the years of Gelon,
tyrant of Gela, when Siracusa
was enriched with new
temples, theaters, and
dockyards. The city was a
powerful force until 211 BC,

when it fell to the Romans in
a battle that also killed the
mathematician Archimedes,
its most famous inhabitant.
  The highlight of Ortigia is
the extraordinary **duomo**,
begun in 1728 by architect
Andrea Palma. Its Baroque
façade masks the **Temple of
Athena** (5th century BC),
which has been absorbed
into the duomo. Facing the
Ponte Nuovo are the ruins of
Sicily's earliest Doric temple,
the **Temple of Apollo**, which
had monolithic columns.
  Across from the duomo is
the **Palazzo Beneventano
del Bosco** (1778–88), a bold
example of Siracusan Baroque,
as is **Santa Lucia alla Badia**
(1695–1703). In the Municipio
a small museum records the
history of Ionic temples and
the coin collection of the
Galleria Numismatica records
Siracusa's past wealth. The
delightful **Fonte Aretusa** is
often referred to by Classical
writers as the point where
Aretusa emerged from the
ground, having been changed
into a spring by Artemis to
help her escape from her
lover Alpheus.
  At Ortigia's farthest point
is the **Castello Maniace**, built
by Frederick II about 1239.
Here too is the **Gallerie Regionale di Palazzo Bellomo**,
with sculpture and paintings,
including the *Burial of St.
Lucy* (1608) by Caravaggio.
  The painting comes from
the church of **Santa Lucia** in
the Achradina quarter. This
area was flattened during

World War II, but the church survived. It is mostly 17th century with a Norman campanile, and occupies the site where St. Lucy, patron saint of Siracusa, was martyred in AD 304. Achradina is now the center of modern Siracusa.

To the north, in Tyche, is the **Museo Archeologico Regionale Paolo Orsi**, with its important collection of artifacts from the Paleolithic to the Byzantine era, taken from southeastern sites in Sicily. Included are vases, coins, bronzes, votive objects, busts, sculpture, and fragments from Siracusan temples.

The Neapolis quarter and its **Parco Archeologico** feature the Teatro Romano, the Altar of Hieron II, and the spectacular Teatro Greco, carved from the hillside. Beyond the Nymphaeum is the 2nd-century AD Roman amphitheater and the stone quarries – the Latomia del Paradiso featuring the **Ear of Dyonisius**. It is thought that 7,000 Athenians were incarcerated here and left to die after their calamitous defeat in 413 BC, in a battle described by Thucydides as "the greatest action in Hellenic history."

ENVIRONS: At **Epipolae**, 8 km (5 miles) north of Neapolis is the **Castle of Euryalus** – the most important ancient Greek fortification to have survived.

🏛 **Gallerie Regionale di Palazzo Bellomo**
Palazzo Bellomo, Via Capodieci 16.
📞 *0931 695 11.* ⏰ *Tue–Sat am.*
🏛 **Museo Archeologico Regionale Paolo Orsi**
Viale Teocrito 66. 📞 *0931 46 40 22.*
⏰ *Tue–Sat am.*

Noto ⑳

Siracusa. 🏠 *24,000.* 🚈 🚌 ℹ️
Piazza XVI Maggio (0931 83 67 44).
📅 *Mon & 1st & 3rd Tue of the month.*

NOTO WAS BUILT from scratch in the early 18th century to replace Noto Antica, which was devastated by an earthquake in 1693. The town was comprehensively designed in Baroque style, using the local white tufa, a limestone that has turned a honey-brown

The façade of the duomo in Noto rises above a huge staircase

color from the sun.
It is now one of the most enchanting towns in Sicily.

The twin-towered **Duomo** (completed 1770s), that dominates Noto, suffered damage in 1996 when the dome of the main chapel collapsed. The Duomo is attributed to the architect Rosario Gagliardi, who also designed the eccentric tower façade of the seminary of **San Salvatore** (18th century) in Piazza Municipio, the convex façade of **San Domenico** (1730s) in Piazza XVI Maggio,

and the oval interior of **Santa Chiara** (1730) on Corso Vittorio Emanuele. The magnificent **Palazzo Trigona** (1781) stands on Via Cavour behind the Duomo. The **Palazzo Villadorata** (1730s) on Via Nicolaci is set off by a splendid façade adorned with elaborate stone carvings. At the north end of Via Nicolaci, the **Monastery of Montevergine** has a striking curved façade. Gagliardi's church of the **Crocifisso** (1728) stands on the town's summit, containing sculpture of the Madonna by Francesco Laurana (1471). The **Municipio** (1740s), facing the duomo, has a fine "billowing" ground floor design.

ENVIRONS: The earthquake of 1693 also devastated the towns of **Modica**, about 30 km (19 miles) to the west, and **Ragusa**, a short distance farther. Like Noto, they were rebuilt in the region's rich, Baroque style. Gagliardi worked on Modica's **San Giorgio** (early 18th century), on Ragusa's **San Giorgio** (begun around 1746, and one of his masterpieces), and **San Giuseppe** (mid-18th century).

Boisterous carving on the façade of the Palazzo Villadorata in Noto

SARDINIA

I<small>N HIS TRAVELOGUE,</small> Sea and Sardinia, *DH Lawrence wrote that Sardinia was "left outside of time and history." Indeed, the march of time has been slow here, and traditions from ancient Europe have survived – the legacy of invasion by Phoenicians, Carthaginians, Romans, Arabs, Byzantines, Spanish, Savoyards, and Italians.*

These traditions are displayed in Sardinia's many festivals – some soberly Christian, others with pagan roots. Several different dialects and languages are spoken in Sardinia. Catalan can be heard in Alghero, and on the island of San Pietro, there is a Ligurian dialect. Even remnants of Phoenician and Etruscan survive. In the south, the traditional influences are Arab and Spanish, while pure native strains of people and language survive in the Gennargentu mountains. Peopled by shepherds in isolated communities, this region is so impenetrable that invaders have never bothered it.

Of particular interest are the prehistoric *nuraghe* castles, villages, temples, and tombs that litter the countryside – most notably around Barumini, north of Cagliari, and in the Valle dei Nuraghe, south of Sassari. The *nuraghe* were built by a people whose origins constitute one of the Mediterranean's great mysteries. In Cagliari, the capital of Sardinia, there is a museum with an excellent archaeological collection that offers insight into this enigmatic people.

Sassari, Oristano, Alghero, and Olbia are all centers of areas marked by their individuality. Some remarkable Pisan-Romanesque churches are located around Sassari and here too dialects reveal close links with the languages of Tuscany. Olbia is a boom town made rich by tourism and the proximity of the jet-setting Costa Smeralda. Sober Nuoro with its province in the shadow of the Gennargentu mountains, by contrast, has little in common with the Sardinia of tourist brochures.

Relaxing during the day in the tiny resort of Carloforte on the Isola di San Pietro, next to Sant'Antioco

◁ **The Bay of Simius east of Cagliari in the southeast corner of Sardinia**

Exploring Sardinia

THIS ISLAND, called Sardegna in Italian, is characterized by an interior of dramatic, rolling uplands covered in *macchia* – grassland mingled with myrtle, wild thyme, prickly pears, and dwarf oaks – and a coastline of beguiling, translucent sea, isolated coves, long sandy beaches, and caves. The Gennargentu mountains, with the highest peak at 1,834 m (6,017 ft), shield a nearly impenetrable area of rural villages. In the northeast, mountains fall away dramatically to the Costa Smeralda, Sardinia's most exclusive coastal area. Farther south, the shoreline around the Golfo di Orosei is unspoiled. Around Oristano in the west the land is flat, leading to the plain of Campidano where the island's grain, fruits and vegetables grow.

SIGHTS AT A GLANCE

Alghero ❸
Bosa ❹
Cagliari ❾
Cala Gonone ❻
Costa Smeralda ❶
Nuoro ❺
Oristano ❼
Sant'Antioco ❽
Sassari ❷

**Prehistoric nuraghic remains
at Su Nuraxi near Barumini**

A typical scene of clothes hanging out to dry in Alghero

SEE ALSO

• *Where to Stay* p575
• *Where to Eat* p609

0 kilometers   50

0 miles   25

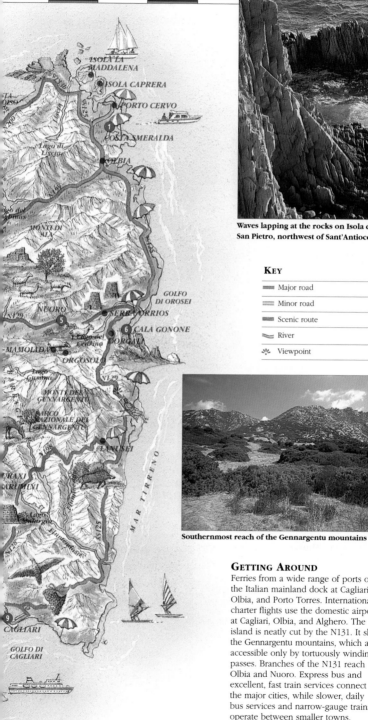

Waves lapping at the rocks on Isola di San Pietro, northwest of Sant'Antioco

KEY

- Major road
- Minor road
- Scenic route
- River
- Viewpoint

Southernmost reach of the Gennargentu mountains

GETTING AROUND

Ferries from a wide range of ports on the Italian mainland dock at Cagliari, Olbia, and Porto Torres. International charter flights use the domestic airports at Cagliari, Olbia, and Alghero. The island is neatly cut by the N131. It skirts the Gennargentu mountains, which are accessible only by tortuously winding passes. Branches of the N131 reach Olbia and Nuoro. Express bus and excellent, fast train services connect the major cities, while slower, daily bus services and narrow-gauge trains operate between smaller towns.

The extravagantly beautiful, *macchia*-scented Costa Smeralda

Costa Smeralda ●

Sassari. 🚆 ⛴ Olbia. 🚌 Porto
Cervo. ℹ Via Catello Piro 1, Olbia
(0789 214 53).

THE FORMERLY WILD, lonely
Costa Smeralda, stretching
from the Golfo di Cugnana to
the Golfo di Arzachena, was
developed at the end of the
1950s by a consortium of
magnates, including the Aga
Khan, into one of the world's
most lucrative vacation resorts.
Its pristine appearance is now
strictly controlled.

In **Porto Cervo**, the main
town, boutiques jostle with
nightclubs, fine restaurants,
and luxury hotels. It caters to
the seriously rich – billionaires,
crowned heads, and pop stars.

ENVIRONS: If this leaves you
cold, head north to rural **Baia
Sardinia** and **Cannigione**.
From **Palau** ferries leave for
La Maddalena and **Isola
Caprera**, the home of
Garibaldi and the **Museo
Nazionale Garibaldino**.

🏛 **Museo Nazionale
Garibaldino**
Frazione Caprera, Maddalena.
📞 0789 72 71 62. 🕐 daily am.
⬤ Jan 1, May 1, Dec 25. 💶 ♿

Sassari ●

🏠 130,000. 🚇 🚆 🚌 ℹ Viale
Caprera 36 (079 29 95 44). 🛒 Mon.

FOUNDED BY GENOESE and
Pisan merchants early in
the 13th century, Sassari is
known for its spectacular

Cavalcata Sarda festival on
Ascension Day. There is a
raucous, throbbing, tight,
church-filled medieval quarter
around the **duomo** (11th
century with later,
mostly Baroque,
additions), and to the
north is the
handsome **Fonte
Rosello**, a huge late-
Renaissance fountain.
The **Museo Archeo-
logico Nazionale
"GA Sanna"** is a
good starting point
from which to
begin a fascinating
investigation
into the region's
nuraghic history.

ENVIRONS: To the
southeast along the
N131 is the Pisan-Romanesque
church of **Santissima Trinità
di Saccargia** (1116), which
contains the only extant cycle
of 13th-century frescoes in
Sardinia. Farther on is the
church of **San
Michele di
Salvenero**
(12th century),
and at **Ardara**
the basalt-built
Romanesque
**Santa Maria
del Regno**,
or "Black
Cathedral."

🏛 **Museo
Archeologico
Nazionale
"GA Sanna"**
Via Roma 64.
📞 079 27 22 03.
🕐 daily am. 💶

**Façade of Santissima
Trinità di Saccargia**

Alghero ●

Sassari. 🏠 41,000. 🚇 🚆 🚌 ⛴
ℹ Piazza Porta Terra 9 (079 97 90 54).
🛒 Wed.

FOUNDED ON A PENINSULA
facing the Bay of Alghero
early in the 12th century, and
taken from the Genoese
Dorias by the Aragonese in
1353, Alghero was peopled
by settlers from Barcelona
and Valencia. Its original
occupants – Ligurians and
Sardinians – were expelled
with such thoroughness that
today the Catalan language
and culture is enjoying a
revival and the look of old
Alghero is consistently Spanish.

Filled with labyrinthine alleys
and cobbled streets, the lively
port of old Alghero is flanked
by battlemented walls and
defensive towers on all but
the landward section. Facing
the Giardino Pubblico is the
massive 16th-century **Torre di
Porta Terra**, also known as
the Jewish Tower after
its builders. Around
the periphery of the
old town are more
towers, including
**Torre dell'Espero
Reial** and **Torre
San Giacomo**
on Lungomare
Colombo, and
**Torre della
Maddalena** on
Piazza Porta Terra.
The 16th-century **Duomo** at
the bottom of Via Umberto is
predominantly Catalan-Gothic
with an Aragonese portal.
Off Via Carlo Alberto, **San
Francesco** (14th century)

A typical house in Alghero

The waterfront at Bosa

has a delightful cloister and octagonal campanile which towers over Alghero, and Baroque **San Michele** has a bright, handsome tiled dome. In Via Principe Umberto is the **Casa Doria**, the house where the pre-Hispanic rulers of Alghero lived. It has a beautiful Renaissance portal and Gothic-arched window.

ENVIRONS: Boat or car trips can be made to the spectacular **Grotta di Nettuno** around the point of Capo Caccia, a deep natural cave, or the nearby **Grotta Verde**.

Bosa ❹

Nuoro. 🏠 8,500. ⬛ ⬛ 🚹 Corso
Vittorio Emanuele 59 (0785 37 61 07).
🔼 Tue.

BOSA IS A SMALL, picturesque seaside town at the mouth of Sardinia's only navigable river, the Temo. The historic **Sa Costa** district struggles up the side of a low hill capped by the **Castello di Serravalle**, built in 1122 by the Malaspina family. The narrow passages and alleys here have changed little since the Middle Ages. By the Temo are **Sas Conzas** – the former dyers' houses and workshops.

Languishing on the riverside, the **Sa Piatta** district is more cosmopolitan than the rest of Bosa. It houses the Aragonese-Gothic **duomo** (15th century) and Romanesque **San Pietro** (11th century), with a Gothic façade added by Cistercian monks in the 13th century.

NURAGHE IN SARDINIA

The dominant feature of Sardinia is the 7,000 or so *nuraghe* dotted around the island. Dating from 1500 to 400 BC, these strange, truncated cone structures were built without any bonding from huge basalt blocks taken from extinct volcanoes. Almost nothing is known about the identity of the nuraghic people. They must have been well organized and possessed remarkable engineering skills, judging by their buildings, but appear to have left no written word. The mystery of these enigmatic people has plagued Sardinians for centuries.

The individual nuraghe are fairly small. A few were fortresses, equipped with wells and other defensive features.

Su Nuraxi at Barumini (above), Serra Orrios, near Dorgali, and Santu Antine at Torralba are among the most important nuraghe complexes. Houses, temples, tombs, and even a theater have been identified.

This bronze figure of a hero with four eyes and four arms is among the many objects and statues discovered on nuraghic sites and associated with the nuraghic people.

KEY

• Nuraghic sites

0 kilometers 100

0 miles 50

Nobel Prize-winning novelist Grazia Deledda from Nuoro

Nuoro ❺

🏃 38,000. **FS** 🚌 ℹ️ *Piazza d'Italia 19 (0784 300 83).* 🔼 *Fri & Sat.*

T HIS TOWN, in a spectacular setting beneath the gaze of Monte Ortobene and the dramatic Sopramonte, has been the home of some of Sardinia's most important men and women of letters. Among these literary figures is Grazia Deledda, who won the Nobel Prize for Literature in 1926 in recognition of her understanding portrayal of the power and passions in the primitive communities around her. A comprehensive collection of ethnic items, such as traditional Sardinian costumes and jewelry, can be seen in the excellent **Museo della Vita e delle Tradizioni Popolari Sarde**. Attending the *Sagra del Redentore* festival is the best way to witness the region's dancing and dialects.

ENVIRONS: Nuoro is on the edge of the Barbagia region, which has isolated villages of shepherds who have never experienced the hand of any overlord, so impenetrable are the **Gennargentu** mountains. This region was known to the Romans as Barbaria, an area they were never able to subdue. Traces of the traditional lawlessness of the Barbagia can be seen in **Orgosolo**, with its wall murals calling for Sardinia's independence. Rival clans were locked in bloody vendetta for almost 50 years, and the deeds of native bandits form part of local folklore.

In **Mamoiada**'s *Feast of the Mamuthones*, men in sinister masks and traditional costume perform a ritual dance ending with a symbolic "killing" of a scapegoat. The passion and fervor of the event is indicative of the survival of a fierce folkloric tradition and deep resistance to change.

🏛 **Museo della Vita e delle Tradizioni Popolari Sarde**
Via Mereu 56. 🅲 *0784 314 26.*
🕐 *9am–1pm, 3–7pm daily.*
♿

Cala Gonone ❻

Nuoro. 🏃 800. 🚌 ℹ️ *Viale Buemarino (0784 93 61 96).* 🔼 *daily.* 🚢 *to grottoes (Apr–mid-Oct).* 🅲 *0784 933 05.*

E AST OF NUORO, squeezed between the sea and the base of high mountains, is the hamlet of Cala Gonone – a bustling seaside resort and fishing port, with magnificent beaches. Along the unspoiled coast are the isolated coves of **Cala di Luna** and **Cala Sisine** as well as deep natural caves, including the famous **Grotta del Bue Marino,** which is adorned with weird rock formations. The area around Cala Gonone is good for walking and hiking, especially down to Cala Sinisi, and the road from Dorgali to Baunei and Tortoli is spectacular.

Oristano ❼

Cagliari. 🏃 32,000. **FS** 🚌
ℹ️ *Via Cagliari 278 (0783 741 91).*
🔼 *Tue & Fri.*

Ruins of Tharros near Oristano

T HE PROVINCE of Oristano corresponds roughly with historical Arborea, over which Eleonora ruled *(see opposite).* She is commemorated by an 18th-century statue in **Piazza Eleonora**. On Corso Vittorio Emanuele is the 16th-century **Casa di Eleonora**, and nearby the **Antiquarium Arborense**, which has Neolithic, nuraghic, Punic, and Roman artifacts. The **Torre di San Cristoforo** (1291) in Piazza Roma once formed part of Oristano's fortifications. The **duomo** (13th century) was later rebuilt in the Baroque style. More interesting are the churches of **Santa Chiara** (1343) on Via Garibaldi and 14th-century **San Martino** on Via Cagliari.

ENVIRONS: The 12th-century Pisan-Romanesque **Cathedral** at Santa Giusta has interior columns probably taken from

Entrance to the Grotta del Bue Marino, south of Cala Gonone

The tiny resort of Carloforte, the capital of Isola di San Pietro

Tharros, an 8th-century BC Punic settlement whose extensive ruins lie 20 km (12 miles) west of Oristano on the Sinis peninsula.

🏛 Antiquarium Arborense
Via Parpaglia 37. **☎** 0783 79 12 62.
◯ daily. **📷 ♿**

Sant'Antioco ⑧

Cagliari. **FS** **🚌** **ℹ** Piazza Repubblica (0781 820 31).

THE MAIN TOWN on this unspoiled island is **Sant' Antioco**. It was a Phoenician port known as Sulcis and an important Roman base. Proof of almost continual occupation is clear at the **catacombs**, a Phoenician burial place later used by Christians, under the 12th-century basilica of **Sant' Antioco Martire**. The **Anti-quarium** contains Phoenician artifacts. The Punic **Tophet** (sanctuary of the goddess Tanit) and the **necropolis** are nearby. The small **Isola di San Pietro** can be reached by ferry from Calasetta.

� Catacombs
Piazza Parrocchia.
☎ 0781 830 44.
◯ daily. **📷** only.
● Easter, Aug 15,
Dec 25. **📷**

🏛 Antiquarium
Via Regina Margherita
113. **☎** 0781 835 90.
◯ daily. **●** Jan 1, Easter,
Dec 8, 25 & 26. **📷**

Cagliari ⑨

👥 250,000. **✈ FS 🚌 ⚓**
ℹ Piazza Matteotti 9 (070 66 92 55).
📅 daily; also Sun (flea) and second Sun of month (antiques).

THE CAPITAL of Sardinia, this site was occupied by the Phoenicians, Carthaginians, and Romans, and extensive ruins of the Phoenician city of Nora lie to the southwest of Cagliari. A 2nd-century **amphitheater** survives from the Roman era, cut from rock. The best indication of the town's earlier history is to be found in the **Cittadella dei Musei**. Fashioned from the former royal arsenal, it houses several museums including the **Museo Nazionale Archeologico**. The nuraghic items are the most interesting in the collection, especially the bronze votive statuettes. Also in the Cittadella dei Musei is the **Pinacoteca**, an art gallery.

The 6th-century church of San Saturnino in Cagliari, built on a Greek-cross plan

The compact old core of Cagliari has an appealing North African character. In the high **Castello** district, the Romans and, much later, Pisans built defenses. The gracious **Bastione San Remy** on Piazza Costituzione offers magnificent views over the city and surrounding countryside. The **duomo** is a 20th-century rehash of a Romanesque building. Flanking the entrance are two 12th-century pulpits originally destined for the cathedral in Pisa.

Nearby is the Pisan tower **Torre San Pancrazio** (14th century). From the partially ruined **Torre dell'Elefante** on Via dell'Università to the port lies the **Marina** quarter, that expanded from the old town in the 16th to 17th centuries. In Piazza San Cosimo, the 6th-century church of **San Saturnino** is a rare monument to Byzantine occupation.

♫ Amphitheater
Viale Sant'Ignazio. **◯** Tue–Sun.
🏛 Cittadella dei Musei
Piazza Arsenale. **Museo Nazionale Archeologico ☎** 070 65 59 11.
◯ Tue–Sun. **📷 Pinacoteca ☎** 070 67 01 57. **◯** daily. **●** Jan 1, May 1, Dec 25. **📷 ♿**

ELEONORA OF ARBOREA

A champion against rule from abroad, Eleonora was governing *giudicessa* (judge) of Arborea, one of four administrative divisions of Sardinia, from 1383 to 1404. Her marriage to Brancaleone Doria consolidated Genoese interests in Sardinia. She rallied the island to bar Spanish invaders who tried to claim land that had been given to the Aragonese King James II. Her greatest legacy was the completion of the codifying of laws begun by her father. Written in Sardinian, they called for community property in marriage and the right of women to seek redress from rape.

TRAVELERS' NEEDS

WHERE TO STAY

PEOPLE COME FROM all over the world to visit Italy, and the majority of Italians choose to spend their vacations there as well, particularly in the mountains or by the sea. This means that there is a dazzling range of accommodation options offered, from splendid hotels in old palazzi and historic residences, to simple family-run *pensioni* and hostels. Those who want efficiency apartments are also well

Sign for a
3-star hotel

served with everything from stately, isolated villas in Tuscany to special apartments in or near busy seaside resorts. Italian hotels are notorious for being expensive and short of services, but you can nevertheless find excellent value in all price ranges. The hotels listed on pages 542–75 have been selected from every price category as among the best value in each area for style, comfort, or location.

The Gritti Palace, one of Venice's historic palazzi *(see p544)*

GRADINGS

HOTELS IN ITALY are graded with one to five stars. Grading depends on facilities offered rather than atmosphere and each region awards stars according to slightly different criteria. Sometimes a hotel has a lower rating than it deserves. This may be because the local tourist office hasn't upgraded it yet or the hotel itself has opted to stay in a lower category to avoid higher taxes.

ALBERGHI

ALBERGO IS ITALIAN for hotel but the term tends to refer to the upper categories. Room sizes vary considerably: in city centers even expensive hotels can have far smaller rooms than their counterparts in other countries, whereas outside the city your room may be more like a small suite. In general, *alberghi* will have private showers in all rooms and the more luxurious have baths.

In city centers you may come across the sign *albergo diurno*. This is a day hotel without accommodation but with bathroom, showers, hairdressing, drying, and other cleaning facilities you may need when traveling. Day hotels are usually situated at or near the main train station.

PENSIONI

ALTHOUGH THE TERM *pensione* is no longer in official use it still describes one- and two-star hotels, most of which are small and family-run. On the whole you'll meet immaculate standards of cleanliness and

Street sign showing the direction and location of hotels

friendly, helpful service with basic, although perfectly functional, rooms. However, as *pensioni* are often in old buildings, historic charm may be paid for with noisy, erratic plumbing and dark rooms. Many do not have public rooms other than a sparsely furnished breakfast room. Most will offer at least some rooms with a private shower, but rarely a bath. If you intend to be out late, check that you'll be able to get back into the *pensione*. Not all of them have night porters after midnight or 1am, but most will at least be able to provide a key to the main door.

If you are planning to stay in a *pensione* in winter, check that it has central heating. Not all of them do, and, even in the south, temperatures are low from November to February.

A *locanda* was traditionally an inn, offering cheap food and a place to sleep for the traveler. The word is still in use, particularly in central and northern Italy, but is now synonymous with *pensione* and may be more of an affectation for the benefit of the tourist.

CHAIN HOTELS

THERE ARE VARIOUS Italian chain hotels at the upper end of the market, as well as the usual big internationals. **Ciga** hotels, now part of the Sheraton Corporation, have a turn-of-the-century opulence. **Jolly** are more akin to the international luxury chains, while **Notturno Italiano** cater for the more modest budget.

◁ Popular café in Piazza Navona, Rome

Romantic Hotel Villa Pagoda in Nervi, Genova *(see p555)*

can expect a good range of facilities, a pleasant or central location, and often a lot of local or historic charm. Hotels in the major cities and resorts are likely to be more expensive.

By law hotels have to display their rates in every bedroom. Variation between high and off season can be 100 percent or more in resorts.

Also, beware of extras: the mini-bar can be extortionate as can charges for parking, laundry, or phoning directly from your hotel bedroom.

Relais et Châteaux run charming hotels in historic castles, villas, and monasteries with facilities to match.

MEALS AND FACILITIES

ITALIAN HOTELS TEND TO guarantee fewer special facilities than those in many other countries. In spite of the warm summers, for example, air-conditioning is rare in all but five-star hotels, as is 24-hour room service.

Some hotels may insist on full board *(pensione completa)* or half board *(mezza pensione)* in peak season. However, avoid this if you can: unless it's very isolated, there will almost certainly be a good range of places to eat nearby. Most hotel rates include breakfast, which in four- and five-star hotels will consist of a large buffet; the *pensioni* breakfast will probably consist of coffee and biscuits or brioches with butter and jam. Once again, try to avoid this as breakfast at a local bar is an enjoyable Italian institution.

For a double room, stipulate whether you want twin beds *(letti singoli)* or a double bed *(matrimoniale)*. Bathrooms in all but the most expensive hotels will tend to have showers rather than baths so state your preference.

CHILDREN

ITALIANS ACCEPT CHILDREN as an ordinary part of life and, although there may not be many special facilities, they are always welcome. Some of the cheaper hotels may not be able to provide cribs. However,

virtually all hotels, from the simplest to the most grand, will put a small bed or two into a double room for families traveling together. The price of this is usually an extra 30–40 percent of the double room rate per bed. Most of the large hotels will also offer a regular babysitting service.

PRICES

HOTELS IIN ITALY are not cheap, although prices vary between places and seasons. Prices, which include tax and service and are quoted per room, start at around L90,000 for a double room without a bath-room, and can rise to at least L130,000 with a bath, even for a very basic hotel. A single room will cost about two-thirds of a double. Around L200,000 will get you something comfortable and often picturesque, although not particularly luxurious. For L400,000 and upward you

Hotel Sant'Anselmo's garden, Rome *(see p565)*

BOOKING

BOOK AS SOON AS possible, particularly if you have special requests such as a room with a view, off the street, or with a bath. Two months should be ample, but during the high season popular hotels can be fully booked six months in advance. August is very busy at beach resorts and February at mountain resorts. The same goes for cities and towns depending on their particular cultural calendars *(see pp62–5)*.

You will be asked for a deposit when you book; this can usually be paid for by credit card (even in places that do not accept credit cards for final payment); otherwise by cash or international money order. Under Italian law the hotel must issue you with a receipt *(ricevuta fiscale)* for final payment, which you must keep until you leave Italy.

Mirrored entrance hall of the hotel Campo de' Fiori in Rome *(see p565)*

Vaulted central entrance of Hotel Porta Rossa in Florence *(see p557)*

CHECKING IN AND OUT

O N ARRIVAL the management will take your passport to register you with the police. This is a mere formality and it should be returned within an hour or two. You will also have to authorize the hotel to transfer calls to your room.

Check-out time is usually before noon, and may be earlier in small hotels. The room must be vacated, but most places will allow you to leave luggage in the reception to be picked up later on in the day.

Albergo al Sole, Venice *(see p544)*

APARTMENTS AND AGRITURISMO

I F YOU INTEND to be based in one area, efficiency accommodations often enjoy marvelous locations and are generally of a high standard.

Across rural Italy there are more than 2,000 farms, villas, and mountain chalets offering reasonably priced apartments or hotel-style accommodations as part of the **Agriturismo** plan. Facilities range from those of a first-class hotel in beautifully kept villas or ancient castles to basic rooms with the family on a working farm. Some have excellent restaurants that serve farm and local produce, others can arrange riding, fishing, or other activity vacations *(see p624)*. There may be a minimum-stay requirement, especially in peak season. The booklets *Guida dell'Ospitalità Rurale* can be found in the central office in Rome or the regional offices. Other self-catering options can be arranged through specialized agencies such as **Vacanze in Italia**, **Italian Rentals**, **Cuendet USA**, and others before you leave for Italy, but again, make sure you call in advance; they can be booked up for months.

There are also so-called *residence*, found in the **ENIT** accommodation lists. These are halfway between a hotel and efficiency apartments and may offer cooking facilities or restaurant service.

For stays of several months or more, accommodation agencies for apartments in the city center as well as the nearby countryside can be found under *Immobiliari* in the *Pagine Gialle* (Yellow Pages).

BUDGET ACCOMMODATION

A S WELL AS THE International Youth Hostel Association (**AIG** in Italy), tourist offices in the major cities have lists of privately run hostels. Prices, at around L15,000 per person per night, are considerably less than even the cheapest *pensioni* but accommodations are in single-sex dormitories and washing facilities may be over-stretched. A room in a private house is another cheap option, offering often small but clean rooms. Bed-and-breakfast accomodation is increasing rapidly but is of variable quality, so only rely on trust-worthy recommendations.

The **Centro Turistico Studentesco** can help students find rooms in university dormitories across Italy. This is not limited to students taking courses, particularly in the summer when resident students are on vacation.

A peaceful alternative is to stay in a convent or monastery with guest facilities. The rooms are clean, if a little spartan, and they are usually in a secluded area or behind cloister walls. However, strict rules may be a price to pay: most have early curfews and many will not admit members of the opposite sex even when with their spouses. Contact the "Arcivescovado" in the city you want to visit or write to the tourist office in New York for a partial list.

A suitcase boat carrying visitors' luggage to a hotel in Venice

MOUNTAIN REFUGES AND CAMPSITES

BASIC ACCOMMODATION in huts and shelters is available in mountainous areas where there is hill-walking and hiking. Most of these huts are owned and run by the **Club Alpino Italiano,** whose offices are in Rome.

Campsites abound in the mountains and around the coastal regions. Many of them offer basic accommodations in family-sized cabins *(bungalow)* as well as spaces for tents,

Villa San Michele, a former monastery in Fiesole, Tuscany *(see p559)*

The highest shelter in the Valsesia alps, Rifugio Francesco Pastore

campers, and trailers, with basic facilities such as water, electricity, and toilets. There is usually a restaurant and, especially in campsites by the sea, there may also be sports facilities such as swimming pools, boat and water sports equipment rental, and tennis courts. The **Touring Club Italiano** publishes a full list in *Campeggi e Villaggi Turistici in Italia* (L32,000), as does **Federcampeggio**.

DISABLED TRAVELERS

FEW HOTELS IN ITALY have special facilities for disabled travelers. Those that do are indicated with the appropriate symbol in the hotels listings on pages 542–75. In many cases, however, hotels without special facilities will do all they can to accommodate people in wheelchairs by giving them downstairs rooms (when available) and help with elevators or stairs.

FURTHER INFORMATION

THE ITALIAN STATE TOURIST office (**ENIT**) has accommodation lists for every region. They are reprinted annually but may not be updated and prices may have changed. Rooms can also be booked at the local **APT** (Azienda Provinciale per il Turismo).

DIRECTORY

GENERAL

ENIT (Ente Nazionale Italiano per il Turismo)
Via Marghera 2–6,
00185 Rome.
(06 497 11.
FAX 06 446 99 07.
W www.enit.it

Italian Government Office
630 Fifth Avenue,
New York, NY 10111.
(212 245 4822.
FAX 212 586 9249.

CHAIN HOTELS

Ciga Hotels
Piazza della Repubblica 20,
20124 Milano.
(02 6230 2018.
FAX 02 659 58 38.
W www.sheraton.com

Jolly Hotels
Via Bellini 6, Valdagno
36078, Vicenza.
(0445 41 00 00.

Notturno Italiano
(0578 75 60 70.
FAX 0578 75 60 06.
W www.notturno.it

Relais et Châteaux
11 East 44th Street, Suite
104, New York, NY 10017.
(212 856 0115.
FAX 212 856 0193.

APARTMENTS

Agriturismo
Corso Vittorio Emanuele II
89, 00186 Rome.
(06 685 23 42.
FAX 06 685 24 24.
W www.agriturist.it

Grand Lux International
165 Chestnut Street,
Allendale, NJ 07401.
(201 327 2333.
FAX 201 825 2664.

Hometours International
P.O.Box 11503
Knoxville,
TN 37939.
(800 367 4668.

Vacanze in Italia
22 Railroad Street,
Great Barrington,
MA 01230.
(413 528 6610.
FAX 413 528 6222.

MOUNTAIN HUTS AND CAMPSITES

Club Alpino Italiano
Corso Vittorio Emanuelle
305, Rome.
(06 68 61 01 11.
FAX 06 68 80 34 24.

Federcampeggio
Via Vittorio Emanuele 11,
50041 Calenzano, Firenze.
(055 88 23 91.
FAX 055 882 59 18.

Touring Club Italiano
Corso Italia 10,
20122 Milano.
(02 852 61.
FAX 02 852 63 62.
W www.touringclub.it

BUDGET ACCOMMODATION

AIG (Associazione Italiana Alberghi per la Gioventù)
Via Cavour 44,
00184 Rome.
(06 487 11 52.
FAX 06 488 04 92.
W www.hostel-aig.org

Centro Turistico Studentesco
Via Genova 16,
00184 Rome.
(06 44 11 11.
FAX 06 462 04326.
W www.cts.it

Choosing a Hotel

THE HOTELS in this guide have been selected from a wide price range for their good value or exceptional location, comfort, and style. The chart highlights some of the factors that may influence your choice and gives a brief description of each hotel. Entries are listed by price category within the towns, with color-coded thumb tabs to indicate the regions covered on each page.

	NUMBER OF ROOMS	RESTAURANT	SWIMMING POOL	GARDEN OR TERRACE

VENICE

CANNAREGIO: *Abbazia* ⓁⓁ
Calle Priuli, 66–68. **Map** 1 C4. **☎** 041 71 73 33. **FAX** 041 71 79 49. **@** abbazia@iol.it
Quietly situated just off the lively Lista di Spagna area. The rooms are comfortable, and drinks are served in the delightful garden. 🛏 📺 📇 🌿
39 — — — ■

CANNAREGIO: *Giorgione* ⓁⓁⓁ
Santi Apostoli, 4587. **Map** 3 B5. **☎** 041 522 58 10. **FAX** 041 523 90 92. **@** giorgione@hotelgiorgione.com
Well-situated for the Rialto area. This is a recently refurbished hotel in a delightful color-washed building with a spacious lobby. 🛏 📺 🌿
68 — — — ■

CANNAREGIO: *Continental* ⓁⓁⓁⓁ
Lista di Spagna, 166. **Map** 2 D4. **☎** 041 71 51 22. **FAX** 041 524 24 32. **@** continental@ve.nettuno.it
A large, well-equipped, modern hotel. Some rooms overlook the Grand Canal, while others are quieter with views of a tree-shaded square. 🛏 📺 📇 🌿
93 ■ — — ■

CASTELLO: *Paganelli* ⓁⓁ
Riva degli Schiavoni, 4686. **Map** 8 D2. **☎** 041 522 43 24. **FAX** 041 523 92 67. **@** hotelpag@tin.it
Excellent views of St. Mark's Basin from cozy old-fashioned rooms; those situated in the *dipendenza* (annex) are less attractive but quieter. 🛏 📺 🌿
22 — — — ■

CASTELLO: *Pensione Wildner* ⓁⓁⓁ
Riva degli Schiavoni, 4161. **Map** 8 D2. **☎** 041 522 74 63. **FAX** 041 526 56 15.
A family-run hotel with simple yet immaculate rooms offering stunning views across to San Giorgio Maggiore. There is also a small bar. 🛏 📺 📇 🌿
16 ■ — — ■

CASTELLO: *Londra Palace* ⓁⓁⓁⓁ
Riva degli Schiavoni, 4171. **Map** 8 D2. **☎** 041 520 05 33. **FAX** 041 522 50 32. **@** info@hotellondra.it
A lovely stone-faced hotel, the comfortable bedrooms are very traditional and are decorated with antique furniture. The best ones are on the lagoon. Tchaikovsky composed his Fourth Symphony here in 1877. 🛏 📺 📇 🌿
53 ■ — — ■

CASTELLO: *Danieli* ⓁⓁⓁⓁⓁ
Riva degli Schiavoni, 4196. **Map** 7 C2. **☎** 041 522 64 80. **FAX** 041 520 02 08.
This luxurious hotel was the palace of the Dandolo family and has strong literary and musical connections. Service is impeccable. 🛏 📺 📇 🌿
235 ■ — — ■

DORSODURO: *Agli Alboretti* ⓁⓁ
Rio Terrà Antonio Foscarini, 884. **Map** 6 E4. **☎** 041 523 00 58. **FAX** 041 521 01 58. **@** alborett@gpnet.it
A great favorite with English and American visitors, this modern hotel has a cozy wood paneled lobby and a warm atmosphere. The pergola is enchanting, and the best rooms look onto the interior gardens. 🛏 📇 📺 🌿
24 ■ — — ■

DORSODURO: *Montin* ⓁⓁ
Fondamenta Eremite, 1147. **Map** 6 D3. **☎** 041 522 71 51. **FAX** 041 520 02 55.
These few rooms above one of Venice's best restaurants (*see p578*) are full of charm and character. Book well ahead of your visit. 🌿
10 ■ — — ■

DORSODURO: *American* ⓁⓁⓁ
Fondamenta Bragadin, San Vio 628. **Map** 6 E4. **☎** 041 520 47 33. **FAX** 041 520 40 48.
A comfortable hotel tucked away beside a small canal near the Accademia. The rooms are well appointed, and the management is friendly. 🛏 📺 📇 🌿
28 — — — ■

DORSODURO: *Pausania* ⓁⓁⓁ
Rio di San Barnaba, 2824. **Map** 6 D3. **☎** 041 522 20 83. **FAX** 041 522 29 89.
Offering respite from city life, the reasonable prices and friendly staff, make the Pausania a pleasant place to stay during the busy summer months. 🛏 📺 📇 🌿
26 — — — ■

LIDO DI VENEZIA: *Villa Mabapa* ⓁⓁⓁ
Riviera San Nicolo 16. **☎** 041 526 05 90. **FAX** 041 526 94 41. **@** info@villamabapa.com
Originally built as a private residence in the 1930s, this lovely villa on the promenade by the lagoon retains its original style and atmosphere. 🛏 📺 📇 🌿
70 ■ — — ■

	NUMBER OF ROOMS	RESTAURANT	SWIMMING POOL	GARDEN OR TERRACE
Price categories for a standard double room for one night, including tax and service charges but not including breakfast: ⓛ under L100,000 ⓛⓛ L100–200,000 ⓛⓛⓛ L200–300,000 ⓛⓛⓛⓛ L300–400,000 ⓛⓛⓛⓛⓛ over L400,000. **RESTAURANT** A restaurant within the hotel sometimes reserved for residents. **SWIMMING POOL** Hotel swimming pools are usually quite small and are outdoors unless otherwise stated. **GARDEN OR TERRACE** A garden, courtyard, or terrace belonging to the hotel, often providing tables for eating outside. **CREDIT CARDS** The major credit cards VISA, MasterCard (Access), and American Express are accepted in hotels with the credit card symbol.				
LIDO DI VENEZIA: *Excelsior Palace* ⓛⓛⓛⓛ Lungomare Marconi 41. (041 526 02 01. FAX 041 526 72 76. @ res077_excelsior@sheraton.com With a flamboyantly Moorish exterior (even the beach huts are styled like Arabian tents), the service and comfort of this hotel are equally splendid.	196	■	●	■
LIDO DI VENEZIA: *Hotel des Bains* ⓛⓛⓛⓛ Lungomare Marconi 17. (041 526 59 21. FAX 041 526 01 13. @ res078_desbains@sheraton.com This was the setting for Luchino Visconti's film *Death in Venice*, and it was here that Thomas Mann wrote the original novel. Reception rooms are in Art Deco style, bedrooms are spacious and service superb.	191	■	●	■
RIALTO: *Rialto* ⓛⓛⓛ San Marco 5149. **Map** 7 A1. (041 520 91 66. FAX 041 523 89 58. @ info@rialtohotel.com From its spectacular position by the Rialto bridge, the hotel looks out onto the bustle of the city center and graceful gondolas.	79	■		■
SAN MARCO: *Ai Do Mori* ⓛⓛ Calle Larga San Marco, 658. **Map** 7 B2. (041 528 92 93. FAX 041 520 53 28. This friendly little pensione is clean and quaint and offers good value. Some rooms have superb views.	11			
SAN MARCO: *Al Gambero* ⓛⓛ Calle dei Fabbri, 4687. **Map** 7 B2. (041 522 43 84. FAX 041 520 04 31. @ hotgamb@tin.it Situated on one of Venice's main shopping streets, close to the piazza, the Gambero has simple rooms, several with views over the canal.	27	■		
SAN MARCO: *La Fenice et des Artistes* ⓛⓛⓛ Campiello Fenice, 1936. **Map** 7 A2. (041 523 23 33. FAX 041 520 37 21. @ fenice@fenicehotels.it This pretty hotel is made up of two houses joined together by a small patio. Rooms are comfortable and furnished with antiques.	68			■
SAN MARCO: *Flora* ⓛⓛⓛ Calle Larga XXII Marzo, 2283a. **Map** 7 A3. (041 520 58 44. FAX 041 522 82 17. @ info@hotelflora.it A charming and quiet hotel on a secluded alley near Piazza San Marco. During the summer breakfast is served in the flower-filled garden.	44			■
SAN MARCO: *Panada* ⓛⓛⓛ San Marco, 646. **Map** 7 A2. (041 520 90 88. FAX 041 520 96 19. @ info@panada.com Set in a quiet location, this recently renovated 17th-century mansion has an intimate bar lined with antique mirrors.	48			
SAN MARCO: *Santo Stefano* ⓛⓛⓛ Campo Santo Stefano, 2957. **Map** 6 F3. (041 520 01 66. FAX 041 522 44 60. This tall narrow hotel has good views over the Santo Stefano quarter. Traditional furnishings, but some rooms are cramped.	11			
SAN MARCO: *Concordia* ⓛⓛⓛⓛ San Marco 367. **Map** 7 B2. (041 520 68 66. FAX 041 520 67 75. @ venezia@hotelconcordia.it The main feature of this hotel is its view over St Mark's Square. While this can be enjoyed at breakfast, rooms with the same view must be booked well in advance.	57	■		
SAN MARCO: *Europa & Regina* ⓛⓛⓛⓛ San Marco 2159. **Map** 7 A3. (041 520 04 77. FAX 041 523 15 33. @ marconilocco@sheraton.com Once the residence of the 18th-century Italian painter Tiepolo, this splendid property has been completely restyled. The terrace overlooking the Grand Canal houses a flamboyant bar and restaurant.	185	■		■
SAN MARCO: *Metropole* ⓛⓛⓛⓛ Riva Schiavoni 4149. **Map** 8 D2. (041 520 50 44. FAX 041 522 36 79. @ hotelmetropole@venere.it This characterful hotel has is furnished throughout with myriad antique pieces. The restaurant is famous for only offering buffet service, but with a very wide choice of delicious specialities.	72	■		■

For key to symbols see back flap

				NUMBER OF ROOMS	RESTAURANT	SWIMMING POOL	GARDEN OR TERRACE

Price categories for a standard double room for one night, including tax and service charges but not including breakfast:
Ⓛ under L100,000
ⓁⓁ L100–200,000
ⓁⓁⓁ L200–300,000
ⓁⓁⓁⓁ L300–400,000
ⓁⓁⓁⓁⓁ over L400,000.

RESTAURANT
A restaurant within the hotel sometimes reserved for residents.
SWIMMING POOL
Hotel swimming pools are usually quite small and are outdoors unless otherwise stated.
GARDEN OR TERRACE
A garden, courtyard, or terrace belonging to the hotel, often providing tables for eating outside.
CREDIT CARDS
The major credit cards VISA, MasterCard (Access), and American Express are accepted in hotels with the credit card symbol.

SAN MARCO: *Bauer*   ⓁⓁⓁⓁⓁ | 196 | ■ | | ■
Campo San Moisè, 1459. **Map** 7 A3. 📞 *041 520 70 22.* 📠 *041 520 75 57.* @ booking@bauervenezia.it
A luxury hotel in the heart of Venice, it has been recently refurbished and can offer unique accommodations overlooking the Grand Canal. 🛏 📺 🍽 🌿

SAN MARCO: *Gritti Palace*   ⓁⓁⓁⓁⓁ | 93 | ■ | | ■
Santa Maria del Giglio, 2467. **Map** 6 F3. 📞 *041 79 46 11.* 📠 *041 520 09 42.*
An elegant, sumptuous hotel housed in the 15th-century palazzo that once belonged to the Gritti family. Rooms are superb and the hotel is charmingly old-fashioned. Ernest Hemingway stayed here while in Venice. 🛏 📺 🍽 🌿

SAN MARCO: *Monaco and Grand Canal*   ⓁⓁⓁⓁ | 71 | ■ | | ■
Calle Vallaresso, 1325. **Map** 7 B3. 📞 *041 520 02 11.* 📠 *041 520 05 01.* @ mailbox@hotelmonaco.it
An elegant hotel in an 18th-century palazzo overlooking the Grand Canal. Public rooms are intimate, and bedrooms are beautifully decorated. 🛏 📺 🍽 🌿

SAN MARCO: *Saturnia & International*   ⓁⓁⓁⓁⓁ | 95 | ■ | | ■
Via XXII Marzo 2399. **Map** 7 A3. 📞 *041 520 83 77.* 📠 *041 520 58 58.* @ saturnia@italyhotel.com
Set in an ancient palace this luxury hotel is decorated throughout with antique furniture. There is a charming courtyard with restaurant. 🛏 📺 🍽 🌿

SAN POLO: *Alex*   Ⓛ | 11 | | | ■
Rio Terrà Frari, 2606. **Map** 6 E1. 📞 *041 523 13 41.* 📠 *041 523 13 41.*
A family-run hotel that makes up for its limited facilities with a friendly welcome and excellent value for money, Ideally located near the Frari.

SAN POLO: *Hotel Marconi*   ⓁⓁⓁ | 26 | | |
San Polo, 729. **Map** 7 A1. 📞 *041 522 20 68.* 📠 *041 522 97 00.* @ info@hotelmarconi.it
A refurbished 16th-century palazzo with opulently Venetian reception rooms. Bedrooms are plainer, but some have views of the Grand Canal. 🛏 📺 🍽 🌿

SANTA CROCE: *Falier*   ⓁⓁ | 19 | | | ■
Salizzada San Pantalon, 130. **Map** 5 C1. 📞 *041 71 08 82.* 📠 *041 520 65 54.* @ falier@tin.it
On the edge of the student district, the reasonably priced Falier is away from the main hotel area of Venice. It has recently been restored. 🛏 📺 🍽 🌿

SANTA CROCE: *Al Sole*   ⓁⓁⓁ | 80 | | | ■
Fondamenta Minotta, 136. **Map** 5 C1. 📞 *041 71 08 44.* 📠 *041 71 43 98.* @ info@corihotels.it
This 14th-century building is conveniently situated in a quiet corner near the station. It has pleasant rooms and a marble-floored lobby. 🛏 🍽 🌿

TORCELLO: *Locanda Cipriani*   ⓁⓁ | 6 | ■ | | ■
Piazza Santa Fosca 29. 📞 *041 73 01 50.* 📠 *041 73 54 33.* @ info@locandacipriani.com
A perfect place to stay away from the crowds. Be sure to sample the cuisine, especially the fish; meals are served in the garden or gallery. The impeccable service and comfort make it essential that you book in advance. 🛏 🍽 🌿

THE VENETO AND FRIULI

BARDOLINO: *Kriss International*   Ⓛ | 40 | ■ | | ■
Lungolago Cipriani 3, 37011. 📞 *045 621 24 33.* 📠 *045 721 02 42.* @ kriss@kriss.it
A modern hotel, attractively placed on a promontory jutting into the lake with balconies in every room. Train travelers are met at the station. 🛏 📺 🍽 🌿 P

BASSANO DEL GRAPPA: *Victoria*   Ⓛ | 23 | | |
Viale Diaz 33, 36061. 📞 *0424 50 36 20.* 📠 *0424 50 31 30.* @ victoriahotel@pn.itnet.it
Just outside the city walls, this pleasant hotel has comfortable rooms. It is a busy hotel that can be noisy, but is well placed for sightseeing. 🛏 📺 🍽 🌿 P

BASSANO DEL GRAPPA: *Belvedere*   ⓁⓁ | 87 | ■ | |
Piazzale G Giardino 14, 36061. 📞 *0424 52 98 45.* 📠 *0424 52 98 49.* @ belvederehotel@bonotto.it
Set on one of Bassano's main squares, this busy hotel is the best equipped in the area. Rooms are comfortable (if noisy) and service is good. 🛏 📺 🍽 🌿 P

BELLUNO: *Astor*   Ⓛ   32
Piazza dei Martiri 26e, 32100. 【 *0437 94 20 94.* FAX *0437 94 24 93.*
Centrally situated, this hotel is popular with skiers in winter. The rooms are
well designed and comfortable, offering good value for money. 🛏 TV 🍴

CHIOGGIA: *Grande Italia*   ⓁⓁⓁ   57
Piazza Vigo 1, 30015. 【 *041 40 05 15.* FAX *041 40 01 85.* @ hg@hotelgrandeitalia.com
This unpretentious old-fashioned hotel, at the head of the main street, has
comfortable rooms and is well situated for boats running to Venice. 🛏 TV 🍽 🍴 P

CIVIDALE DEL FRIULI: *Locanda al Castello*   ⓁⓁ   17
Via del Castello 20, 33043. 【 *0432 73 32 42.* FAX *0432 70 09 01.* @ castello@ud.nettuno.it
An attractive historic building, this was once a castle and a
Jesuit monastery before its most recent incarnation as a welcoming,
friendly hotel with wonderful views. 🛏 TV 🍴 P

CONEGLIANO: *Canon d'Oro*   Ⓛ   38
Via XX Settembre 129, 31015. 【 *0438 342 46.* FAX *0438 342 46.* @ canondoro@sevenonline.it
On the main street of the town, this hotel offers solid comfort and a warm
welcome. Relax in the lovely garden with a glass of Prosecco. 🛏 TV 🍽 🍴 P

CORTINA D'AMPEZZO: *Cavallino*   ⓁⓁ   7
Corso Italia 142, 32043. 【 *0436 26 14.* FAX *0436 87 99 09.*
This centrally located hotel has spotless rooms and
breathtaking mountain views from the front rooms.
🛏 🍴 P

CORTINA D'AMPEZZO: *Menardi*   ⓁⓁⓁ   53
Via Majon 110, 32043. 【 *0436 24 00.* FAX *0436 86 21 83.* @ hmenardi@sunrise.it
The Menardi family have run this well-managed hotel since 1900.
Originally a farmhouse, it is tastefully furnished with antiques and
has a welcoming atmosphere. 🛏 TV 🍴 P

GARDA: *Bisesti*   Ⓛ   90
Corso Italia 34, 37016. 【 *045 725 57 66.* FAX *045 725 59 27.* @ bisesti@infogarda.com
Well placed near the town center and the lake. Many rooms in this modern
vacation hotel have their own balcony and there is a private beach. 🛏 TV 🍽 P

GARDA: *Locanda San Vigilio*   ⓁⓁⓁⓁⓁ   7
San Vigilio, 37016. 【 *045 725 66 88.* FAX *045 725 65 51.* @ sanvigilio@gardanews.it
One of the loveliest, most exclusive hotels on Lake Garda. Comfort and
service live up to all expectations and there is a private beach. 🛏 TV 🍽 🍴 P

MALCESINE: *Sailing Center Hotel*   ⓁⓁ   32
Località Molini Campagnola 3, 37018. 【 *045 740 00 55.* FAX *045 740 03 92.*
A modern hotel just outside town, away from the crowds. Rooms are cool
and pleasant; there is a tennis court and private beach. 🛏 TV 🍴 P

PADUA: *Leon Bianco*   Ⓛ   22
Piazzetta Pedrocchi 12, 35122. 【 *049 875 08 14.* FAX *049 875 61 84.* @ leonbianco@toscanelli.com
A centrally situated hotel overlooking the Caffé Pedrocchi. Rooms are small
but staff are friendly and welcoming. Book well in advance. 🛏 TV 🍽 🍴 P

PADUA: *Augustus Terme*   ⓁⓁ   130
Viale Stazione 150, Montegrotto Terme 35036. 【 *049 79 32 00.* FAX *049 79 35 18.*
One of the best hotels at Montegrotto Terme, this is a big,
functional, and comfortable hotel. In addition to the usual facilities it
has tennis courts and hot thermal springs. 🛏 TV 🍴 P

PADUA: *Donatello*   ⓁⓁ   49
Via del Santo 102, 35123. 【 *049 875 06 34.* FAX *049 875 08 29.*
A modern hotel in an old building with big comfortable bedrooms, named after
the sculptor of the equestrian statue of Gattamelata in the square. 🛏 TV 🍽 🍴 P

PADUA: *Plaza*   ⓁⓁ   142
Corso Milano 40, 35139. 【 *049 65 68 22.* FAX *049 66 11 17.* @ plazapd@gpnet.it
An established and efficiently run hotel with a deserved good reputation.
It provides a full range of services and a warm welcome. 🛏 TV 🍽 🍴 P

PESCHIERA DEL GARDA: *Peschiera*   Ⓛ   30
Via Parini 4, 37010. 【 *045 755 05 26.* FAX *045 755 04 44.*
This modern hotel, built in the local architectural style, is set in its own
grounds, with lofty, cool bedrooms. It is five minutes from the A4 highway,
or the friendly staff will pick up train travelers from the station. 🛏 🍴 P

Price categories for a standard double room for one night, including tax and service charges but not including breakfast:
- Ⓛ under L100,000
- ⓛⓛ L100–200,000
- ⓛⓛⓛ L200–300,000
- ⓛⓛⓛⓛ L300–400,000
- ⓛⓛⓛⓛⓛ over L400,000

RESTAURANT
A restaurant within the hotel sometimes reserved for residents.

SWIMMING POOL
Hotel swimming pools are usually quite small and are outdoors unless otherwise stated.

GARDEN OR TERRACE
A garden, courtyard, or terrace belonging to the hotel, often providing tables for eating outside.

CREDIT CARDS
The major credit cards VISA, MasterCard (Access), and American Express are accepted in hotels with the credit card symbol.

	NUMBER OF ROOMS	RESTAURANT	SWIMMING POOL	GARDEN OR TERRACE
PORDENONE: *Palace Hotel Moderno* ⓛⓛ Viale Martelli 1, 33170. ☎ 0434 282 15. FAX 0434 52 03 15. A comfortable, recently refurbished traditional hotel with a good range of facilities in all bedrooms. It is centrally located close to the station. The restaurant specializes in traditional cuisine, particularly fish dishes.	100	■		
SAN FLORIANO DEL COLLIO: *Romantik Golf Hotel* ⓛⓛ Via Oslavia 2, 34070. ☎ 0481 88 40 51. FAX 0481 88 40 52. A lovely 18th-century building furnished with antiques and set in its own well-kept grounds with a nine-hole golf course and tennis courts.	14	■	●	■
TORRI DEL BENACO: *Hotel Gardesana* ⓛⓛ Piazza Calderini 20, 37010. ☎ 045 722 54 11. FAX 045 722 57 71. @ gardesana@easynet.it The 15th-century harbormaster's house overlooking Lake Garda has been converted into a friendly, comfortable hotel. Ask for a room on the third floor; they are quieter and have wonderful views of the lake.	34	■		■
TREVISO: *Ca' del Galletto* ⓛⓛ Via Santa Bona Vecchia 30, 31100. ☎ 0422 43 25 50. FAX 0422 43 25 10. Set on its own grounds and only ten minutes' walk from the city walls, this efficiently run hotel has good-sized modern, bedrooms.	58	■		■
TREVISO: *Villa Cipriani* ⓛⓛⓛⓛ Via Canova 298, Asolo. ☎ 0423 52 34 11. FAX 0423 95 20 95. @ gianpaolo_burattin@sheraton.com This superbly comfortable hotel is set in a 16th-century villa where Robert Browning once lived. A popular feature is its beautiful garden which has a lovely view. A good base for exploring a wider area.	31	■		■
TRIESTE: *Jolly* ⓛⓛ Corso Cavour 7, 34132. ☎ 040 760 00 55. FAX 040 36 26 99. A modern hotel aiming at business as well as vacation clientele. The well-equipped rooms are spacious if slightly impersonally decorated.	174	■		
TRIESTE: *Grand Hotel Duchi d'Aosta* ⓛⓛⓛ Piazza Unità d'Italia 2, 34121. ☎ 040 760 00 11. FAX 040 36 60 92. A palace from a bygone era, this hotel has enormous rooms fitted with modern conveniences. It is set in the old part of town, near the fort.	55	■		
UDINE: *Quo Vadis* ⓛ Piazzale Cella 28, 33100. ☎ 0432 210 91. FAX 0432 210 92. A comfortable hotel on a tranquil tree-lined street. The decor is mixed (some rooms have rather fussy wallpaper), and there are plenty of plants.	26			■
VERONA: *Il Torcolo* ⓛ Vicolo Listone 3, 37121. ☎ 045 800 75 12. FAX 045 800 40 58. This friendly hotel is close to the Arena and is popular during the opera season. It has a breakfast terrace, and some pretty and traditional rooms.	19			■
VERONA: *Accademia* ⓛⓛ Via Scala 12, 37121. ☎ 045 596 222. FAX 045 800 84 40. @ accademia@accademiavr.it Blending modern and ancient architecture, this ornate 17th-century building has a central location. The well-known restaurant offers regional cuisine.	98	■		
VERONA: *Giulietta e Romeo* ⓛⓛ Vicolo Tre Marchetti 3, 37121. ☎ 045 800 35 54. FAX 045 801 08 62. @ giuliettaeromeo@easynet.it Situated in a quiet street just behind the Arena, the bedrooms are spacious and comfortable with modern furnishings. Breakfast is served in the bar.	31			
VERONA: *Due Torri Hotel Baglioni* ⓛⓛⓛⓛ Piazza Sant'Anastasia 4, 37121. ☎ 045 59 50 44. FAX 045 800 41 30. Right in the heart of medieval Verona, this is one of Italy's most eccentric hotels. The huge bedrooms are each decorated and furnished in the style of a different era. Many of the walls and ceilings are frescoed.	91	■		

VICENZA: *Casa San Raffaele* Ⓛ | 29
Viale X Giugno 10, 36100. [0444 54 57 67. FAX 0444 54 22 59.
A tranquil hotel with excellent views, set on the slopes of Monte Berico. The comfortable rooms make this one of the best budget choices in the area. 🛏 🍽 🖼 🄿

VICENZA: *Campo Marzo* ⓁⓁ | 35
Via Roma 27, 36100. [0444 54 57 00. FAX 0444 32 04 95. @ hcm@tradenet.it
A stylish hotel with good facilities near the city center. Bedrooms are large, light, and well furnished, and the location is peaceful. 🛏 📺 🍽 🖼 🄿

VICENZA: *Castello* ⓁⓁ | 20
Contrà Piazza del Castello 24, 36100. [0444 32 35 85. FAX 0444 32 35 83.
Very near the cathedral, this is also an excellent choice for train travelers. Rooms are pleasant and the location is fairly quiet. 🛏 📺 🍽 🖼 🄿

TRENTINO - ALTO ADIGE

BOLZANO (BOZEN): *Engel* ⓁⓁ | 30
Via San Valentino, Nova Levante 39056. [0471 61 31 31. FAX 0471 61 34 04.
In a small town near Bolzano, the Engel is a good choice for families and the sporty, with hiking and skiing nearby. 🛏 🖼 🄿

BOLZANO (BOZEN): *Luna-Mondschein* ⓁⓁ | 60
Via Piave 15, 39100. [0471 97 56 42. FAX 0471 97 55 77. @ info@hotel-luna.it
One of the oldest hotels in Bolzano, the Luna-Mondschein dates from 1798, although the buildings have been much added to since then. It is set near the town center with a pleasant garden for summer dining. 🛏 📺 🖼 🄿

BOLZANO (BOZEN): *Asterix* ⓁⓁⓁ | 24
Piazza Mazzini 35, 39100. [0471 27 33 01. FAX 0471 26 00 21.
Set in the newer part of central Bolzano, the Asterix is a simple but comfortable town hotel which is excellent value for money. 🛏 📺 🄿

BRESSANONE (BRIXEN): *Elefante* ⓁⓁ | 44
Via Rio Bianco 4, 39042. [0472 83 27 50. FAX 0472 83 65 79. @ elephant.brixen@acs.it
A smart, traditional hotel that dates from the 16th century and, while offering all modern comforts, has retained a strong historical atmosphere. 🛏 📺 🖼 🄿

BRESSANONE (BRIXEN): *Dominik* ⓁⓁⓁ | 28
Via Terzo di Sotto 13, 39042. [0472 83 01 44. FAX 0472 83 65 54.
One of the luxurious Relais et Châteaux group, the Dominik is attractively furnished with antiques, although the buildings themselves date from the 1970s. It is peacefully set near the Rienza River and the Rapp gardens. 🛏 📺 🖼 🄿

BRUNICO (BRUNECK): *Andreas Hofer* ⓁⓁ | 54
Via Campo Tures 1, 39031. [0474 55 14 69. FAX 0474 55 12 83. @ peter.s@pass.dnet.it
A welcoming family-run chalet hotel that has been fitted out with wood paneling and wooden Alpine-style furniture. The Andreas Hofer is quietly set in its own garden; some of the rooms have balconies. 🛏 📺 🖼 🄿

CALDARO (KALTERN): *Leuchtenburg* Ⓛ | 19
Campi al Lago 100, 39052. [0471 96 00 93. FAX 0471 96 01 55. @ pensionleuchtenburg@iol.it
Set in a beautiful 16th-century farmhouse surrounded by vineyards. Some of the simple bedrooms are furnished with traditional painted furniture. 🛏 📺 🖼 🄿

CANAZEI: *Park Hotel Faloria* Ⓛ | 36
Via Pareda 103, 38032. [0462 60 11 18. FAX 0462 60 27 15.
Surrounded by its own well-kept gardens, this friendly hotel is managed by its owners. Some bedrooms have balconies overlooking the grounds. 🛏 📺 🖼 🄿

CASTELROTTO (KASTELRUTH): *Cavallino d'Oro* ⓁⓁ | 21
Piazza Kraus 1, 39040. [0471 70 63 37. FAX 0471 70 71 72. @ cavallino@cavallino.it
This charming hotel is set in a pretty village 26 km (16 miles) from Bolzano, where traditional costume is still worn. The rooms are well kept. 🛏 📺 🖼 🄿

CAVALESE: *Fiemme.* Ⓛ | 15
Via Cavazzal 27, 38033. [0462 34 17 20. FAX 0462 23 11 51.
A modern hotel in a peaceful setting with good views, conveniently close to the town center and the bus station; the hotel offers a sauna. 🛏 📺 🖼 🄿

COLFOSCO: *Cappella* ⓁⓁ | 63
Strada Pecei 17, 39030. [0471 83 61 83. FAX 0471 83 65 61. @ cappella@altabadia.it
A chalet in the Dolomites, opened by the present owner's grandfather. The pioneer spirit lives on, and the hotel has now opened an art gallery. 🛏 📺 🖼 🄿

Price categories for a standard double room for one night, including tax and service charges but not including breakfast: Ⓛ under L100,000 ⓁⓁ L100–200,000 ⓁⓁⓁ L200–300,000 ⓁⓁⓁⓁ L300–400,000 ⓁⓁⓁⓁⓁ over L400,000.	**RESTAURANT** A restaurant within the hotel sometimes reserved for residents. **SWIMMING POOL** Hotel swimming pools are usually quite small and are outdoors unless otherwise stated. **GARDEN OR TERRACE** A garden, courtyard, or terrace belonging to the hotel, often providing tables for eating outside. **CREDIT CARDS** The major credit cards VISA, MasterCard (Access), and American Express are accepted in hotels with the credit card symbol.		

	NUMBER OF ROOMS	RESTAURANT	SWIMMING POOL	GARDEN OR TERRACE
FIE ALLO SCILIAR: *Turm* ⓁⓁ Piazza della Chiesa 9, 39050. ☎ 0471 72 50 14. ☒ 0471 72 54 74. @ turmwirt@cenida.it The owner's art collection, displayed on the hotel walls, is one of the main attractions at this friendly Alpine hotel with cozy bars and two pools. 📺 P	26	■	●	
MADONNA DI CAMPIGLIO: *Grifone* ⓁⓁ Via Vallesinella 7, 38084. ☎ 0465 44 20 02. ☒ 0465 44 05 40. A modern wooden chalet set near the lake in the Madonna di Campiglio ski resort. Although rather simply decorated and furnished, it offers an excellent range of facilities ideal for winter sports vacations. Full board only. 📺 P	42	■		■
MALLES VENOSTA (MALS IM VINSCHGAU): *Garberhof* Ⓛ Via Nazionale 25, 39024. ☎ 0473 83 13 99. ☒ 0473 83 19 50. @ info@garberhof.com A modern chalet-style hotel with extensive panoramic terraces. It is surrounded by meadows and has a good range of sports and leisure facilities. 📺 ≣ P	29	■	●	■
MERANO (MERAN): *Castel Rundegg* ⓁⓁⓁⓁ Via Scena 2, 39012. ☎ 0473 23 41 00. ☒ 0473 23 72 00. @ rundegg@tophotels.net A fairy-tale whitewashed castle, parts of which date from the 12th century, set in pretty gardens. Inside, the romantic atmosphere continues with traditional wood furniture, beamed ceilings, and parquet floors. 📺 P	30	■	●	■
MERANO (MERAN): *Castel Schloss Labers* ⓁⓁ Via Labers 25, 39012. ☎ 0473 23 44 84. ☒ 0473 23 41 46. A romantic castle is the setting for this high-class country hotel. There are wonderful views over the surrounding vineyards and woods. 📺 P	35	■	●	■
MERANO (MERAN): *Der Punthof* ⓁⓁ Via Steinach 25, 39022. ☎ 0473 44 85 53. ☒ 0473 44 99 19. Set in peaceful and attractive gardens, this farmhouse dates back to the Middle Ages. Inside, wooden floors and ceilings match the Alpine furniture. 📺 P	12	■	●	■
ORTISEI (SANKT ULRICH): *Hell* ⓁⓁ Via Promenade 3, 39046. ☎ 0471 79 67 85. ☒ 0471 79 81 96. @ hotelhell@val-gardena.com A pleasant hotel that is open for the skiing season and during the summer. It has a sauna and a gym, and is set in a peaceful part of town. 📺 P	25	■		■
PERGINE VALSUGANA: *Castel Pergine* Ⓛ Via al Castello 10, 38057. ☎ 0461 53 11 58. ☒ 0461 53 13 29. @ castelpergine@valsugana.com Set in a 13th-century castle with exquisite views over the countryside. The interior is simply decorated and has traditional wooden furnishings. P	21	■		■
RASUN ANTERSELVA (RASEN ANTHOLZ): *Ansitz Heufler* ⓁⓁ Rasun di Sopra 37, 39030. ☎ 0474 49 85 82. ☒ 0474 49 80 46. @ ansitz.heufler@dnet.it In the historic center of town close to the main monuments, this beautifully decorated 16th-century castle has large rooms and a pleasant garden. P	8	■		■
RIVA DEL GARDA: *Europa* ⓁⓁ Piazza Catena 9, 38066. ☎ 0464 55 54 33. ☒ 0464 52 17 77. @ europa@rivadelgarda.com A turn-of-the-century color-washed building right next to the lake and near the bustling town center. Many of the simply furnished bedrooms have views over the lake. 📺 ≣ P	63	■		■
RIVA DEL GARDA: *Lido Palace* ⓁⓁ Viale Carducci 10, 38066. ☎ 0464 55 26 64. ☒ 0464 55 19 57. @ lidopalace@anthesi.com Centrally located, this is an immaculately run hotel set in magnificent gardens. Diners are treated to stunning views out onto the garden and Lake.Garda. There are tennis courts nearby. 📺 P	63	■	●	■
SAN PAOLO (ST PAULS): *Schloss Korb* ⓁⓁ Via Castel d'Appiano 5, Missiano 39050. ☎ 0471 63 60 00. ☒ 0471 63 60 33. Partly set in a 13th-century castle, this simply decorated and prettily furnished hotel also has a more modern annex, and tennis courts for residents. 📺 P	50	■	●	■

TIRES (TIERS): *Stefaner* ⓁⓁ 16
San Cipriano 88d, 39050. 📞 *0471 64 21 75.* 📠 *0471 64 23 02.* @ stefaner@rolmail.it
A friendly chalet hotel on the edge of the western Dolomites. Bedrooms are light, spacious, and simple. Balconies are decked with flowers. 🍴 📺 🅿

TRENTO: *Accademia* ⓁⓁ 43
Vicolo Colico 4–6, 38100. 📞 *0461 23 36 00.* 📠 *0461 23 01 74.* @ info@accademiahotel.it
Set in a well-restored medieval building right in the historic center of Trento. The interior of this relaxing hotel, although essentially modern, retains many original features. The restaurant is also very good. 🍴 📺 🍽 🖃 🅿

VIPITENO (STERZING): *Hotel Schwarzer Alder* ⓁⓁ 35 ●
Piazza Città 1, 39049. 📞 *0472 76 40 64.* 📠 *0472 76 65 22.*
A comfortable hotel for winter sports or summer hiking vacations with many leisure facilities, including a sauna, gym, and a famous restaurant. 🍴 📺 🖃 🅿

LOMBARDY

BELLAGIO: *La Pergola* Ⓛ 11
Piazza del Porto 4, 22021. 📞 *031 95 02 63.* 📠 *031 95 02 53.*
An attractive hotel tucked away to the south of Lake Como, charmingly furnished in an old-fashioned style with a rustic and friendly atmosphere. 🍴 📺 🖃

BELLAGIO: *Florence* ⓁⓁ 32
Piazza Mazzini 46, 22021. 📞 *031 95 03 42.* 📠 *031 95 17 22.*
This friendly hotel has a bar, and its rooms overlook the lively port of Lake Como. The hotel has plenty of charm and tastefully furnished rooms. 🍴 📺 🖃

BRATTO DELLA PRESOLANA (BERGAMO): *Hotel Milano* ⓁⓁ 63
Via Silvio Pellico 3, 24020. 📞 *034 631 211.* 📠 *034 636 236.* @ hotelmilano@tin.it
In the foothills of the alps, this hotel offers a large array of sports to its guests. The less energetic are pampered with eight styles of pillow and a cigar menu. 🍴 📺 🅿

BRESCIA: *Park Hotel Ca' Noa* ⓁⓁ 80 ●
Via Triumplina 66, 25127. 📞 *030 39 87 62.* 📠 *030 39 87 64.* @ hotelca'noa@tin.it
A beautiful modern hotel set in its own grounds with tasteful and bright decor, large, spacious public rooms, and excellent service. 🍴 📺 🖃 🅿

BORMIO: *Palace* ⓁⓁ 80 ●
Via Milano 54, 23032. 📞 *0342 90 31 31.* 📠 *0342 90 33 66.* @ palace@valtline.it
A recently built hotel with a wide range of business and leisure facilities that include a gym, sunbeds, a discotheque, and a piano bar. 🍴 📺 🖃 🅿

CERVESINA: *Castello di San Gaudenzio* ⓁⓁ 45
Via Mulino 1, Frazione San Gaudenzio 27050. 📞 *0383 33 31.* 📠 *0383 33 34 09.*
A wonderful, almost kitsch hotel in a building with parts dating from the 15th century. Furnishings are from a variety of periods; some are French 18th century, others are heavier and more 16th-century baronial. 🍴 📺 🍽 🖃 ♿ 🅿

COLOGNE FRANCIACORTA: *Cappuccini* ⓁⓁ 6
Via Cappuccini 54, 25033. 📞 *030 715 72 54.* 📠 *030 715 72 57.*
A converted convent (built in 1569), which has been restored. Long hallways and white rooms create a pleasant, monastic atmosphere. 🍴 📺 🍽 🖃 🅿

COMO: *Metropole & Suisse au Lac* ⓁⓁ 9
Piazza Cavour 19, 22100. 📞 *031 26 94 44.* 📠 *031 30 08 08.*
Hotel established in 1892 by the lake and recently renovated. Excellent location for strolling or shopping. Facilities include a restaurant with outside terrace. 🍴 📺 🍽 🖃 🅿

CREMONA: *Duomo* Ⓛ 23
Via Gonfalonieri 13, 26100. 📞 *0372 352 42.* 📠 *0372 45 83 92.*
Unsurprisingly, given its name, this hotel is right next to the cathedral in Cremona's historic center. Some of the rooms have good views. 🍴 📺 🍽 🖃 🅿

CREMONA: *Continental* ⓁⓁ 57
Piazza della Libertà 26, 26100. 📞 *0372 43 41 41.* 📠 *0372 45 48 73.*
This luxurious hotel has been owned and run by the Ghiraldi family since 1920 and is excellently situated for Cremona's main places of interest. Rooms are comfortable, and the restaurant is one of the best in the city. 🍴 📺 🍽 🖃 🅿

DESENZANO DEL GARDA: *Piroscafo* Ⓛ 32
Via Porto Vecchio 11, 25015. 📞 *030 914 11 28.* 📠 *030 991 25 86.*
An attractive old hotel, well placed for all the town's amenities. Bedrooms at the front have balconies overlooking the busy old port. 🍴 📺 🖃

Price categories for a standard double room for one night, including tax and service charges but not including breakfast: Ⓛ under L100,000 ⓁⓁ L100–200,000 ⓁⓁⓁ L200–300,000 ⓁⓁⓁⓁ L300–400,000 ⓁⓁⓁⓁⓁ over L400,000.	**RESTAURANT** A restaurant within the hotel sometimes reserved for residents. **SWIMMING POOL** Hotel swimming pools are usually quite small and are outdoors unless otherwise stated. **GARDEN OR TERRACE** A garden, courtyard, or terrace belonging to the hotel, often providing tables for eating outside. **CREDIT CARDS** The major credit cards VISA, MasterCard (Access), and American Express are accepted in hotels with the credit card symbol.		

	NUMBER OF ROOMS	RESTAURANT	SWIMMING POOL	GARDEN OR TERRACE
GARDONE RIVIERA: *Villa Fiordaliso* ⓁⓁⓁ Corso Zanardelli 132, 25083. ☎ 0365 201 58. FAX 0365 29 00 11. This beautiful, eclectic villa overlooking Lake Garda has comfortable rooms. It was once the private residence of Clara Petacci, Mussolini's lover. 📺 TV 📋 💳 P	7	■		■
GARDONE RIVIERA: *Villa Del Sogno* ⓁⓁⓁⓁ Via Zanardelli 107, 25083. ☎ 0365 29 01 81. FAX 0365 29 02 30. A turn-of-the-century villa set in beautiful gardens and furnished with antiques of various periods. All rooms are spacious and light and it's a good choice for those seeking luxurious tranquillity. 📺 TV 📋 💳 P	32	■	●	■
LIMONE SUL GARDA: *Capo Reamol* ⓁⓁ Via IV Novembre 92, 25010. ☎ 0365 95 40 40. FAX 0365 95 42 62. A stunning location on the edge of the lake below the main road. Rooms are spacious and all have their own terrace. Sports and leisure facilities are excellent for families and include private beach, gym, and jacuzzi. 📺 TV 💳 P	60	■	●	■
LIVIGNO: *Camana Veglia* ⓁⓁ Via Ostaria 107, 23030. ☎ 0342 99 63 10. FAX 0342 99 69 04. @ camanaveglia@livnet.it Set in a typical chalet that dates from the beginning of the century. The interior is wood-paneled and furnished in Alpine style. 📺 TV 💳 P	12	■		■
MANTOVA: *Broletto* ⓁⓁ Via Accademia 1, 46100. ☎ 0376 32 67 84. FAX 0376 22 12 97. A small, immaculate hotel in a renovated 16th-century town house. Rooms are bright with attractive modern furnishings and polished marble floors. 📺 TV 📋 💳	16			
MANTOVA: *Rechigi* ⓁⓁ Piazza Concordia 14, 46100. ☎ 0376 32 07 81. FAX 0376 22 02 91. Although located in the historical city center, the hotel is innovatively modern. Decorated with contemporary art, it regularly houses exhibitions. 📺 TV 📋 💳 💷 P	60	■		■
MANTOVA: *Villa dei Tigli* ⓁⓁⓁ Via Cantarana 20, 46040. ☎ 0376 65 06 91. FAX 0376 65 06 49. @ hotel.villadeitigli@interbusiness.it A charming villa set in a quiet park in the country. The hotel has a gym with swimming pools and sauna, and runs a shuttle service to the city. 📺 TV 📋 💳 P	27	■	●	■
MILAN: *Antica Locanda Solferino* ⓁⓁ Via Castelfidardo 2, 20121. ☎ 02 657 01 29. FAX 02 657 13 61. Excellent value at this surprisingly rustic old inn. Bedrooms are small but nicely decorated with old furniture, paintings, and flowery wallpaper. There is also an informal bistro next door to the hotel. Book in advance. 📺 TV 💳	11			
MILAN: *Zurigo* ⓁⓁⓁ Corso Italia 11a, 20122. ☎ 02 72 02 22 60. FAX 02 72 00 00 13. @ brerahotels@citylightsnews.com A modern, innovative hotel whose central location appeals to both business and vacation travelers. Guests can borrow bicycles for sightseeing. 📺 TV 📋 💳 P	41	■		■
MILAN: *Capitol Millennium* ⓁⓁⓁ Via Cimarosa 6. ☎ 02 48 00 30 50. FAX 02 469 47 24. @ capitol@tin.it After major restructuring this hotel now boasts excellent facilities. The rooms are wood-panelled and the marble bathrooms have a jacuzzi shower or tub. The public spaces are tastefully decorated and there is a gym, restaurant, and bar. TV 📋 💳 ♿	66	■		
MILAN: *Cavour* ⓁⓁⓁ Via Fatebenefratelli 21, 20121. ☎ 02 657 20 51. FAX 02 659 22 63. Very well placed for Milan's main sights, this modern city hotel has good-sized, comfortable rooms. The management is friendly. 📺 TV 📋 💳 P	113	■		
MILAN: *Pierre Milano* ⓁⓁⓁ Via de Amicis 32, 20123. ☎ 02 72 00 05 81. FAX 02 805 21 57. A very luxurious hotel that blends traditional and modern styles in its interior design and furnishings. The restaurant is one of the best in Milan. 📺 TV 📋 💳 ♿	49	■		

PAVIA: *Moderno*   ⓛⓛ   54
Viale Vittorio Emanuele 41, 27100. 📞 *0382 30 34 01.* 📠 *0382 252 25.*
Set in a restored palazzo, the Moderno is a calm, well-run establishment
with a welcoming atmosphere and comfortable rooms. 🛌 📺 ▤ 🗐 🕭 🅿

RANCO: *Sole*   ⓛⓛⓛ   15
Piazza Venezia 5, 21020. 📞 *0331 97 65 07.* 📠 *0331 97 66 20.* @ ivanet@tin.it
The restaurant is the highlight of the Sole, which has been in the same family
for five generations. The few rooms are in newly built suites, and some have
lovely views over Lake Maggiore (these do cost slightly more). 🛌 📺 ▤ 🗐 🅿

RIVA DEL GARDA: *Luise*   ⓛⓛ   69
Viale Rovereto 9. 📞 *0464 55 27 96.* 📠 *0464 55 42 50.*
A few minutes away from the lake this hotel has a well-tended garden and tennis
courts.The hotel also offers facilities for mountain-biking enthusiasts. 🛌 📺 🗐 🅿

RIVA DI SOLTO: *Miranda da Oreste*   ⓛ   25
Via Cornello 8, 24060. 📞 *035 98 60 21.* 📠 *035 98 00 55.* @ miranda@intercom.it
A family-run pensione offering simple, modern accommodations. The restaurant
serves good local cuisine on a terrace with views of Lake Iseo. 🛌 📺 ▤ 🕭 🅿

SABBIONETA: *Al Duca*   ⓛ   10
Via della Stamperia 18, 46018. 📞 *0375 524 74.* 📠 *0375 22 00 21.*
A plain but comfortable family-run pensione in a much-converted Renaissance
palazzo, located in the historic center. Prices are very reasonable. 🛌 📺 ▤ 🗐

SALÒ: *Romantik Hotel Laurin*   ⓛⓛⓛⓛ   38
Viale Landi 9, 25087. 📞 *0365 220 22.* 📠 *0365 223 82.*
A family hotel in a pretty lakeside villa on a sheltered bay. Spacious bedrooms
and a happy atmosphere, as well as a beach and tennis courts. 🛌 📺 🗐 🅿

SIRMIONE SUL GARDA: *Villa Cortine Palace Hotel*   ⓛⓛⓛⓛ   54
Via Grotte 6, 25019. 📞 *030 990 58 90.* 📠 *030 91 63 90.*
Huge, frescoed rooms furnished with antiques in this luxurious and tranquil
hotel set in a Classical villa. Excellent service and comfort. 🛌 📺 ▤ 🗐 🅿

TREMEZZO: *San Giorgio*   ⓛⓛ   26
Via Regina 81, Località Lenno 22016. 📞 *0344 404 15.* 📠 *0344 415 91.*
Set in its own large garden on the shores of Lake Como, the San Giorgio is
a traditional lakeside hotel with elegant terraces and public rooms. Ask for
a room with a balcony for wonderful views of the lake. 🛌 🗐 🅿

VALSOLDA: *Stella d'Italia*   ⓛⓛ   35
Piazza Roma 1, San Mamete 22010. 📞 *0344 681 39.* 📠 *0344 687 29.*
An exquisite setting with a shady terrace right on the edge of Lake Lugano.
Rooms have lake views and are prettily decorated with floral prints and bright
bedspreads. Guests can use the swimming area and the hotel library. 🛌 📺 🗐 🅿

VARENNA: *Hotel du Lac*   ⓛⓛ   18
Via del Prestino 4, 22050. 📞 *0341 83 02 38.* 📠 *0341 83 10 81.*
There are wonderful views from this delightfully peaceful hotel overlooking
Lake Como. Furnishings are simple but comfortable and modern. 🛌 📺 ▤ 🗐 🅿

VALLE D'AOSTA AND PIEDMONT

ALESSANDRIA: *Domus*   ⓛⓛ   27
Via Castellani 12, 15100. 📞 *0131 433 05.* 📠 *0131 23 20 19.* @ efuganti@tin.it
Very centrally located and close to the station, the Domus is, however, quiet
and peaceful inside. All the rooms have double beds. 🛌 📺 ▤ 🗐 🅿

AOSTA: *Europe*   ⓛⓛ   71
Piazza Narbonne 1, 11100. 📞 *0165 23 63 63.* 📠 *0165 40 566.* @ hoteleurope@tiscalinet.it
In the historical city center, this modern hotel offers excellent hospitality, a
renowned restaurant, and a fitness centre. 🛌 📺 ▤ 🗐 🅿

AOSTA: *Milleluci*   ⓛⓛ   33
Località Porossan Roppoz 15, 11100. 📞 *0165 23 52 78.* 📠 *0165 23 52 84.*
An old farmhouse, carefully and attractively restored, is the setting for this
pleasant hotel. The lounge has a wonderful open fireplace. 🛌 📺 🗐 🕭 🅿

ARONA: *Giardino*   ⓛ   56
Corso Repubblica 1, 28041. 📞 *0322 459 94.* 📠 *0322 24 94 01.*
A friendly, comfortable lakeside hotel. A large terrace offers spectacular views
over Lake Maggiore, and bedrooms are tastefully furnished. 🛌 📺 ▤ 🗐

Price categories for a standard double room for one night, including tax and service charges but not including breakfast:
Ⓛ under L100,000
ⓁⓁ L100–200,000
ⓁⓁⓁ L200–300,000
ⓁⓁⓁⓁ L300–400,000
ⓁⓁⓁⓁⓁ over L400,000.

RESTAURANT
A restaurant within the hotel sometimes reserved for residents.
SWIMMING POOL
Hotel swimming pools are usually quite small and are outdoors unless otherwise stated.
GARDEN OR TERRACE
A garden, courtyard, or terrace belonging to the hotel, often providing tables for eating outside.
CREDIT CARDS
The major credit cards VISA, MasterCard (Access), and American Express are accepted in hotels with the credit card symbol.

	NUMBER OF ROOMS	RESTAURANT	SWIMMING POOL	GARDEN OR TERRACE
ASTI: *Aleramo* ⓁⓁ Via Emanuele Filiberto 13, 14100. ☎ 0141 59 56 61. ⒻⒶⓍ 0141 300 39. A slick, modern hotel in the center of town and close to the station. Rooms have a good range of facilities, including hair driers and safes. 🛏 TV ▤ ✉ ♿ 🅿	42			
ASTI: *Lis* ⓁⓁ Viale Fratelli Roselli 10, 14100. ☎ 0141 59 50 51. ⒻⒶⓍ 0141 35 38 45. Centrally but peacefully located opposite the town's public gardens and close to the historic center. Rooms are modern and well-equipped. 🛏 TV ▤ ✉ 🅿	29			
ASTI: *Salera* ⓁⓁ Via Monsignor Marello 19, 14100. ☎ 0141 41 01 69. ⒻⒶⓍ 0141 41 03 72. A modern, comfortable hotel well placed for the highway. Rooms are simply but attractively furnished, and all are equipped with minibar. 🛏 TV ▤ ✉ 🅿	50	■		
BREUIL-CERVINIA: *Les Neiges d'Antan* ⓁⓁ Frazione Cret-Perrères, 11021. ☎ 0166 94 87 75. ⒻⒶⓍ 0166 94 88 52. A delightful mountain chalet hotel attached to one of the best restaurants in the area. Both are run by the friendly and enthusiastic Bich family. Inside it's all clean white walls and original wooden beams. 🛏 TV ✉ 🅿	28	■		■
BREUIL-CERVINIA: *Hermitage* ⓁⓁⓁ Via Piolet, 11021. ☎ 0166 94 89 98. ⒻⒶⓍ 0166 94 90 32. Those looking for luxury and charm will find it here. This well-equipped modern hotel has bright and flower-filled rooms. 🛏 TV ✉ 🅿	36	■	●	■
CANNERO RIVIERA: *Cannero* ⓁⓁ Lungo Lago 2, Verbania 28821. ☎ 0323 78 80 46 (Nov–Mar: 78 81 13). ⒻⒶⓍ 0323 78 80 48. The hotel, set in a former monastery, has been in the same family for four generations and, although modernized, it has retained the atmosphere of other times. It also has tennis courts and a good restaurant. 🛏 TV ✉ ♿ 🅿	40	■	●	■
CANNOBIO: *Pironi* ⓁⓁ Via Marconi 35, 22822. ☎ 0323 706 24. ⒻⒶⓍ 0323 721 84. Housed in a 15th-century palazzo in a pedestrian zone in the historic center, the hotel retains many original features such as the inner courtyard. Bedrooms are comfortable, with views over the lake or old town. 🛏 ✉ 🅿	12			
CHAMPOLUC: *Villa Anna Maria* Ⓛ Via Croues 5, 11020. ☎ 0125 30 71 28. ⒻⒶⓍ 0125 30 79 84. A simple country hotel in a 1920s chalet-style house with lots of wood paneling. The restaurant offers simple but excellent food. TV ✉ 🅿	21	■		■
COGNE: *Bellevue* ⓁⓁ Rue Grand Paradis, 11012. ☎ 0165 748 25. ⒻⒶⓍ 0165 74 91 92. This is a beautifully situated hotel surrounded by meadows and with excellent views of the Gran Paradiso. Modified American Plan (MAP). 🛏 TV ✉ ♿ 🅿	33	■	●	■
COURMAYEUR: *La Grange* ⓁⓁ Strada la Brenva 1, Entreves 11013. ☎ 0165 86 97 33. ⒻⒶⓍ 0165 86 97 44. A restructured barn, which has been in the same family since the 14th century, is the setting for this clean, bright Alpine hotel. Furnishings are new but based on traditional designs, and the atmosphere is cozy and homey. 🛏 TV ✉ 🅿	23			■
COURMAYEUR: *Palace Bron* ⓁⓁⓁ Via Plan Gorret 41, 11013. ☎ 0165 84 67 42. ⒻⒶⓍ 0165 84 40 15. @ hotelpb@tin.it An elegant family-run hotel that is furnished in the style of a smart home. Most of the rooms have balconies with wonderful views. 🛏 TV ✉ 🅿	27	■		■
COURMAYEUR: *Gallia Gran Baita* ⓁⓁⓁ Strada Larzey Courmayeur, 11013. ☎ 0165 84 40 40. ⒻⒶⓍ 0165 84 48 05. A modern luxury hotel catering to the upmarket skier; it has saunas, a fitness center, beauty parlor, and free rides to the slopes. 🛏 TV ✉ ♿ 🅿	53	■	●	■

CUNEO: *Smeraldo* Ⓛ 21
Corso Nizza 27, 12100. **(** 0171 69 63 67. **FAX** 0171 69 80 76.
A reasonably priced hotel located on one of the main roads of central Cuneo; the historic center is easily reached by bus or on foot. 🛌 TV 🛒 P

DOMODOSSOLA: *Corona* Ⓛ 32
Via Marconi 8, 28037. **(** 0324 24 21 14. **FAX** 0324 24 28 42.
Set in the center of town, the Corona combines tradition with modern convenience. The restaurant offers a range of local cuisine. 🛌 TV ▤ 🛒 ♿ P

IVREA: *Castello San Giuseppe* ⓁⓁ 16
Località Castello San Giuseppe, Chiaverano 10010. **(** 0125 42 43 70. **FAX** 0125 64 12 78.
Originally a convent, this pretty, peaceful hotel has a lovely garden. The simple rooms are attractively furnished in traditional style. 🛌 TV 🛒 P

LAKE MAGGIORE: *Verbano* ⓁⓁ 12
Via Ugo Ara 1, Isola dei Pescatori 28049. **(** 0323 304 08. **FAX** 0323 331 29.
A rambling villa is the setting for this friendly hotel with views over the lake. All of the prettily decorated bedrooms have their own balcony. 🛌 🛒

NOVARA: *Bussola* ⓁⓁ 93
Via Boggiani 54, 28100. **(** 0321 45 08 10. **FAX** 0321 45 27 86. **@** bussola@msoft.it
The modern Bussola hotel is pleasantly and comfortably decorated. The popular restaurant holds dinner dances on Saturday nights. 🛌 TV 🛒 P

NOVARA: *Italia* ⓁⓁ 63
Via Paolo Solaroli 8, 28100. **(** 0321 39 93 16. **FAX** 0321 39 93 10.
Located in the center of Novara next to the cathedral, the Italia is comfortable and well run. The hotel's restaurant is also very good. 🛌 TV ▤ 🛒 P

ORTA SAN GIULIO: *Bussola* ⓁⓁ 16
Orta San Giulio, 28016. **(** 0322 91 19 13. **FAX** 0322 91 19 34.
The hotel is a traditional villa set in a pretty flower-filled garden with views over the lake. Guests are expected to take MAP in summer. 🛌 TV 🛒 P

ORTA SAN GIULIO: *Leon d'Oro* Ⓛ 36
Piazza Motta 42, 28016. **(** 0322 91 19 91. **FAX** 0322 903 03. **@** leond'oro@alycosmail.com
Beautifully located on the shores of Lake Orta, the bedrooms have functional, if rather bland, decor, and some have balconies with views. 🛌 TV 🛒

ORTA SAN GIULIO: *Orta* ⓁⓁ 35
Piazza Motta 1, 28016. **(** 0322 902 53. **FAX** 0322 90 56 46.
Set on the main piazza of Orta San Giulio, the hotel terrace overlooks the lake. It has a pleasant old-fashioned atmosphere and spacious rooms. 🛌 🛒

PONT-SAINT-MARTIN: *Ponte Romano* Ⓛ 13
Piazza IV Novembre 14, 11026. **(** 0125 80 43 29. **FAX** 0125 80 71 08.
Attractively located next to an ancient Roman bridge, this small, comfortable, family-run hotel is conveniently close to the center of town. 🛌 TV 🛒 P

SAN GIORGIO MONFERRATO: *Castello San Giorgio* ⓁⓁ 11
Via Cavalli d'Olivola 3, 15020. **(** 0142 80 62 03. **FAX** 0142 80 65 05.
An elegant, refined hotel with an excellent restaurant in a pretty castle set in its own grounds 6 km (4 miles) from Casale Monferrato. 🛌 TV ▤ 🛒 P

SAUZE D'OULX: *Il Capricorno* ⓁⓁ 7
Case Sparse 21, Le Clotes 10050. **(** 0122 85 02 73. **FAX** 0122 85 00 55.
Set on the wooded hills above the village, this is a delightfully traditional chalet hotel with traditional wooden beams and furniture. 🛌 TV 🛒 P

SESTRIERE: *Principe di Piemonte* ⓁⓁⓁ 100
Via Sauze di Cesana, 10058. **(** 0122 79 41. **FAX** 0122 75 54 11.
This was once the grand hotel of Sestriere, and it is still plush and extremely comfortable. It has everything you will need from sauna to shops. 🛌 TV 🛒 P

SUSA: *Napoleon* Ⓛ 62
Via Mazzini 44, 10059. **(** 0122 62 28 55. **FAX** 0122 319 00.
The Napoleon is a modern, clean hotel that has always been run by the same family. It is well placed in the town center. 🛌 TV 🛒 ♿ P

TURIN: *Conte Biancamano* ⓁⓁ 25
Corso Vittorio Emanuele II 73, 10128. **(** 011 562 32 81. **FAX** 011 562 37 89. **@** cbhtl.to@iol.it
A centrally placed family-run hotel, whose public rooms are decorated with paintings and chandeliers. Bedrooms are light and spacious. 🛌 TV 🛒 P

For key to symbols see back flap

<table>
<tr><td>

Price categories for a standard double room for one night, including tax and service charges but not including breakfast:
Ⓛ under L100,000
ⓁⓁ L100 – 200,000
ⓁⓁⓁ L200 – 300,000
ⓁⓁⓁⓁ L300 – 400,000
ⓁⓁⓁⓁⓁ over L400,000

</td><td>

RESTAURANT
A restaurant within the hotel sometimes reserved for residents.
SWIMMING POOL
Hotel swimming pools are usually quite small and are outdoors unless otherwise stated.
GARDEN OR TERRACE
A garden, courtyard, or terrace belonging to the hotel, often providing tables for eating outside.
CREDIT CARDS
The major credit cards VISA, MasterCard (Access), and American Express are accepted in hotels with the credit card symbol.

</td></tr>
</table>

		NUMBER OF ROOMS	RESTAURANT	SWIMMING POOL	GARDEN OR TERRACE
TURIN: *Genova e Stazione* Via Sacchi 14b, 10128. 【 011 562 94 00. FAX 011 562 98 96. Well placed in the city center, close to the station. Bedrooms are decorated in a mixture of styles including Art Deco and 18th century. 🔲 TV 🔳 🔳 🔳 P	ⓁⓁ	58			▪
TURIN: *Victoria* Via Nino Costa 4, 10123. 【 011 561 19 09. FAX 011 561 18 06. The comfortable, pretty rooms in this modern hotel combine function with innovative decor; choose the Egyptian or New Orleans rooms. 🔲 TV 🔳 🔳	ⓁⓁ	96			
TURIN: *Grand Hotel Sitea* Via Carlo Alberto 35. 【 011 51 70 171. FAX 011 54 80 90. This elegant, traditional hotel located in the heart of the city offers excellent standards of service and a renowned restaurant. 🔲 TV 🔳 🔳 🔳 P	ⓁⓁⓁ	118	▪		▪
TURIN: *Turin Palace* Via Sacchi 8, 10128. 【 011 562 55 11. FAX 011 561 21 87. Dating from 1872, Turin's smartest hotel has an impressive array of modern facilities. The sumptuous rooms are furnished with antiques. 🔲 TV 🔳 🔳 🔳 P	ⓁⓁⓁ	121	▪		
TURIN: *Villa Sassi-El Toulà* Strada al Traforo del Pino 47, 10132. 【 011 898 05 56. FAX 011 898 00 95. Set in a beautiful 17th-century villa, this luxurious hotel just outside Turin still has many original features such as candelabra and marble floors. 🔲 TV 🔳 🔳 P	ⓁⓁⓁ	17	▪		▪
VARALLO SESIA: *Vecchio Albergo Sacro Monte* Regione Sacro Monte 14, 13019. 【 0163 542 54. FAX 0163 511 89. A peaceful hotel in a restored 16th-century building at the entrance to the Sacro Monte. Many of the original features have been retained. 🔲 TV 🔳 P	Ⓛ	24	▪		▪
LIGURIA					
CAMOGLI: *Casmona* Saleto Pineto 13. 【 0185 770015. FAX 0185 775030. This simple and friendly hotel enjoys a good location overlooking the sea. Spacious rooms and a restaurant specialising in fish dishes add to its charm. 🔲 TV 🔳 P	ⓁⓁ	26	▪		▪
CAMOGLI: *Cenobio dei Dogi* Via Cuneo 34, 16032. 【 0185 72 41 00. FAX 0185 77 27 96. A vast luxurious hotel that offers everything you would expect for the price. It has tennis courts, panoramic terrace, and its own beach. 🔲 TV 🔳 🔳 P	ⓁⓁⓁ	107	▪	●	▪
FINALE LIGURE: *Punta Est* Via Aurelia 1, 17024. 【 019 60 06 11. FAX 019 60 06 11. An 18th-century villa overlooking the sea is the setting for this elegant hotel. The interior is spacious and furnished with antiques, while the terraces and gardens offer some wonderful views. MAP is normally offered. 🔲 TV 🔳 P	ⓁⓁ	40	▪	●	▪
GARLENDA: *La Meridiana* Via ai Castelli, 17033. 【 0182 58 02 71. FAX 0182 58 01 50. This elegant country villa hotel with comfortable rooms is set in peaceful gardens. Guests come here to play golf at the course next door, and the hotel offers tennis, bikes, and a sauna. Mini-apartments are also available. 🔲 TV 🔳	ⓁⓁⓁ	30	▪	●	▪
GENOA: *Nuovo Astoria* Piazza Brignole 4, 16122. 【 010 87 33 16. FAX 010 831 73 26. A simple, no frills, modern hotel in the center of Genoa, very close to the station and a short walk from the city's main sights. 🔲 TV 🔳 P	ⓁⓁ	69			
GENOA: *Best Western Hotel Metropoli* Piazza Fontane Marose, 16123. 【 010 246 88 88. FAX 010 246 86 86. Conveniently placed for both business and sightseeing, the hotel offers tastefully decorated rooms equipped with minibars and hair driers. 🔲 TV 🔳 🔳 P	ⓁⓁ	48			

GENOA: *Britannia* ⓛⓛ 97
Via Balbi 38. 【 010 26991. FAX 010 246 29 42.
Centrally situated this hotel has an excellent range of facilities including valet service, a sauna and solarium, and a gym fitted with the latest equipment. 🛏 TV 🗐 P

MONTEROSSO AL MARE: *Porto Roca* ⓛⓛⓛ 43
Via Corone 1, 19016. 【 0187 81 75 02. FAX 0187 81 76 92.
Set on a cliff overlooking the sea in a charming village in the Cinque Terre, the decor in this hotel is a congenial combination of different styles. 🛏 TV 🗐 🗐

NERVI: *Villa Pagoda* ⓛⓛ 17
Via Capolungo 15, 16167. 【 010 372 61 61. FAX 010 32 12 18.
A splendidly romantic early 19th-century villa set in spectacular gardens. Rooms are large, and the decor is bright and clean. 🛏 TV 🗐 P

RAPALLO: *Stella* ⓛ 30
Via Aurelia Ponente 10, 16035. 【 0185 503 67. FAX 0185 27 28 37. @ hotelstella@tigullio.net
A tall, thin, pink villa with good panoramic views of the sea from the roof terrace. The decor is a little stark, but the owners are particularly friendly and welcoming. 🛏 TV 🗐 P

PORTOFINO: *Eden* ⓛⓛ 9
Via Dritto 18, 16034. 【 0185 26 90 91. FAX 0185 26 90 47. @ eden@ifree.it
Conveniently located just behind the piazza of the pretty harbor, the Eden is, as its name suggests, set in an attractive garden. Bedrooms are simple but well equipped. 🛏 TV 🗐 🗐

PORTOVENERE: *Genio* ⓛ 7
Piazza Bastreri 8, 19025. 【 0187 79 06 11. FAX 0187 79 06 11.
A delightful hotel built into the walls of the medieval castle in 1924. Rooms are simple, but it is one of the best value hotels in the area. 🛏 TV

SAN REMO: *Nyala Suite* ⓛⓛ 81
Via Strada Solero 134, 18038. 【 0184 667 668. FAX 0184 666 059.
Located in a quiet residential area and surrounded by a tropical garden, the hotel offers a swimming pool and very spacious rooms. The restaurant has a special vegetarian menu. 🛏 TV 🗐 🗐 P

SAN REMO: *Royal* ⓛⓛⓛ 142
Corso Imperatrice 80, 18038. 【 0184 53 91. FAX 0184 66 14 45. @ royal@royalhotelsanremo
A traditional deluxe seaside hotel that has been owned by the same family since 1872. The comfortable bedrooms are decorated with delicate floral patterns, and there is a range of sports and leisure facilities. 🛏 TV 🗐 🗐 P

SESTRI LEVANTE: *Grand Hotel dei Castelli* ⓛⓛⓛ 30
Penisola 26, 16039. 【 0185 48 72 20. FAX 0185 447 67. @ htl.castelli@rainbownet.it
Set in spectacular gardens rising from the sea, this converted castle is decorated with mosaics and Moorish columns. The service is very cordial. 🛏 TV 🗐 🗐 P

EMILIA-ROMAGNA

BOLOGNA: *Orologio* ⓛⓛ 32
Via IV Novembre 10, 40123. 【 051 23 12 53. FAX 051 26 05 52. @ hotoro@tin.it
Set in the medieval historic center, nearly all of the rooms in this quiet town hotel have exceptional views over Piazza Maggiore. 🛏 TV 🗐 🗐 P

BOLOGNA: *Commercianti* ⓛⓛⓛ 34
Via de Pignattari 11, 40124. 【 051 23 30 52. FAX 051 22 47 33.
This was Bologna's first town hall in the 12th century and sympathetic refurbishment has retained some of its medieval features; some bedrooms are in the tower. 🛏 TV 🗐 🗐 P

BOLOGNA: *Corona d'Oro 1890* ⓛⓛⓛ 35
Via Oberdan 12, 40126. 【 051 23 64 56. FAX 051 26 26 79. @ hotcoro@tin.it
Parts of the building date back to the 14th century, and there has been a hotel here for more than 100 years. Today it has a turn-of-the-century elegance, with Art Nouveau friezes combined with all conveniences. 🛏 TV 🗐 🗐 P

BUSSETO: *I Due Foscari* ⓛⓛ 20
Piazza Carlo Rossi 15, 43011. 【 0524 93 00 39. FAX 0524 916 25.
Decorated and furnished in Hollywood medieval style with mock Gothic windows and wood beams, this hotel is popular with film stars who come here especially for the annual opera season in June and July. 🛏 TV 🗐 🗐 P

		Price categories			

<table>
<tr><td colspan="2">Price categories for a standard double room for one night, including tax and service charges but not including breakfast:
Ⓛ under L100,000
ⓁⓁ L100–200,000
ⓁⓁⓁ L200–300,000
ⓁⓁⓁⓁ L300–400,000
ⓁⓁⓁⓁⓁ over L400,000.</td><td colspan="4">RESTAURANT
A restaurant within the hotel sometimes reserved for residents.
SWIMMING POOL
Hotel swimming pools are usually quite small and are outdoors unless otherwise stated.
GARDEN OR TERRACE
A garden, courtyard, or terrace belonging to the hotel, often providing tables for eating outside.
CREDIT CARDS
The major credit cards VISA, MasterCard (Access), and American Express are accepted in hotels with the credit card symbol.</td></tr>
</table>

	NUMBER OF ROOMS	RESTAURANT	SWIMMING POOL	GARDEN OR TERRACE
CASTELFRANCO: *Villa Gaidello Club* ⓁⓁ Via Gaidello 18, 41013. 【 *059 92 68 06.* FAX *059 92 66 20.* The "club" consists of just three pleasantly furnished suites in a lovely 18th-century farmhouse set amid peaceful grounds with a lake. 📶 TV 🗂 P	6	■		■
CESENATICO: *Miramare* ⓁⓁ Viale Carducci 2, 47042. 【 *0547 800 06.* FAX *0547 847 85.* @ miramare@emiliaromagna.it Excellently placed for both beach fans and those who want to explore the surrounding countryside, the Miramare has a good range of sports and leisure facilities and hosts an important local tennis training ground. 📶 TV ▤ 🗂 P	30	■	●	■
FAENZA: *Vittoria* ⓁⓁ Corso Garibaldi 23, 48018. 【 *0546 215 08.* FAX *0546 291 36.* @ hvittoria@connectivy.it The hotel, in the historic center and close to the station, is Art Nouveau in style and has frescoes in the hall and some of the bedrooms. 📶 TV ▤ 🗂 P	49	■		■
FERRARA: *Carlton* ⓁⓁ Via Garibaldi, 93. 【 *0532 211 130.* FAX *0532 205 766.* @ hotelcarlton@sestantenet.it Close to the monuments of the city, this modern and efficient hotel is well-run and well-equipped. Service is always attentive and courteous. 📶 TV ▤ 🗂 P	66			
FERRARA: *Ripagrande* ⓁⓁ Via Ripagrande 21, 44100. 【 *0532 76 52 50.* FAX *0532 76 43 77.* A very attractively restored Renaissance palace is the setting for this smart, well-run hotel. Rooms are light, and many are furnished with antiques; those with balconies have lovely views over Ferrara. 📶 TV ▤ 🗂 P	40	■		
FERRARA: *Duchessa Isabella* ⓁⓁⓁⓁ Via Palestro 70, 44100. 【 *0532 20 21 21.* FAX *0532 20 26 38.* @ isabellad@tin.it A splendid hotel set in a 15th-century palazzo in the center of Ferrara, named after Isabella d'Este, who was famous for her parties. Impeccable service and luxurious bedrooms that look out onto a garden full of birds. 📶 TV ▤ 🗂 P	27	■		■
MARINA DI RAVENNA: *Bermuda* ⓁⓁ Viale della Pace 363, 48023. 【 *0544 53 05 60.* FAX *0544 53 16 43.* @ hotelbermuda@libero.it Set in the pine woods near the beach 10 km (6 miles) from Ravenna, this modern family-run hotel is basic but clean and welcoming. 📶 TV ▤ 🗂	23	■		■
MODENA: *Canalgrande* ⓁⓁ Corso Canalgrande N 6, 41100. 【 *059 217 160.* FAX *059 221 674.* @ info@canalgrandehotel.it Located in the city centre, this former monastery is an outstanding piece of Neo-Classical architecture, richly decorated and featuring original paintings. TV 🗂 P	70	■		
PARMA: *Torino* ⓁⓁ Via Angelo Mazza 7, 43100. 【 *0521 28 10 46.* FAX *0521 23 07 25.* A restuctured former convent, the Torino has been in the same family for three generations and offers peaceful accommodations in the heart of Parma. Bed-rooms and public rooms are furnished with Art Nouveau artifacts. 📶 TV ▤ 🗂 P	33			■
PARMA: *Grand Hotel Baglioni* ⓁⓁⓁ Viale Piacenza 12c, 43100. 【 *0521 29 29 29.* FAX *0521 29 28 28.* @ ghb.parma@baglionihotel.com A modern hotel in the center of Parma, this example of industrial architecture dating from 1921 has a full range of facilities on offer. 📶 TV ▤ 🗂 P	169	■		
PIACENZA: *Florida* Ⓛ Via Cristoforo Colombo 29, 29100. 【 *0523 59 26 00.* FAX *0523 59 26 72.* A reasonably priced pensione located just outside the historic center and within easy reach of the train station. 📶 TV 🗂 P	65			
PORTICO DI ROMAGNA: *Al Vecchio Convento* Ⓛ Via Roma 7, 47010. 【 *0543 96 70 53.* FAX *0543 96 71 57.* @ vecchioconvento@mail.asianet.it An exquisite hotel, tastefully furnished with simple antiques and white linen, all combining to create an impression of space and tranquillity. 📶 TV 🗂 P	15	■		■

RAVENNA: *Argentario* Ⓛ 28
Via di Roma 45, 48100. ☎ *0544 355 55.* FAX *0544 351 47.*
Well situated in the heart of Ravenna, close to its main monuments and the
public gardens, this is a well-equipped hotel with attractive rooms. 🛏 📺 🗐 🥗

RAVENNA: *Bisanzio* ⓁⓁ 38
Via Salara 30, 48100. ☎ *0544 21 71 11.* FAX *0544 325 39.*
A faded façade hides a welcoming, modern interior overlooking a pretty
garden, conveniently located in the center of Ravenna. 🛏 📺 🗐 🥗

REGGIO NELL'EMILIA: *Hotel Posta* ⓁⓁ 43
Piazza del Monte 2, 42100. ☎ *0522 43 29 44.* FAX *0522 45 26 02.* @ info@hotelposta.re.it
Located in the historic center, this comfortable hotel has very original decor. An
austere medieval façade hides an embellished Rococo interior. 🛏 📺 🗐 🥗 🅿

RICCIONE: *Hotel des Nations* ⓁⓁⓁ 32
Lungomare Costituzione 2, 47838. ☎ *0541 647 878.* FAX *0541 645 154.*
New Age hotel on the oceanfront, decorated in soft colours to harmonize body and
spirit. Various therapies available on request such as reflexology, aromatherapy,
massage, and meditation. Private yacht available for excursions. 🛏 📺 🗐 🥗 🅿

RIMINI: *Rosabianca* Ⓛ 50
Viale Tripoli 195, 47037. ☎ *0541 39 06 66.* FAX *0541 39 06 66.*
A modern, recently renovated hotel close to both the beach and the historic
center of Rimini. Guests can make use of the private beach huts. 🛏 📺 🗐 🥗

RIMINI: *Ambasciatori* ⓁⓁⓁ 66
Viale Vespucci 22, 47037. ☎ *0541 555 61.* FAX *0541 237 90.*
This elegant and modern hotel is well situated and most rooms have a sea
view. The roof-garden offers a panoramic vista of the coast. 🛏 📺 🗐 🥗 🅿

RIMINI: *Grand Hotel* ⓁⓁⓁⓁ 117
Via Ramuscio 1, 47900. ☎ *0541 560 00.* FAX *0541 568 66.* @ info@grandhotelrimini.com
Conveniently situated near the seafront, the port, and the station, this large, well-
equipped, smart hotel has tennis courts and its own beach. 🛏 📺 🗐 🥗 🅿

SANTARCANGELO DI ROMAGNA: *Hotel della Porta* Ⓛ 22
Via Andrea Costa 85, 47822. ☎ *0541 62 21 52.* FAX *0541 62 21 68.*
Set a few miles out of Rimini in a region steeped in references to Dante's
Divine Comedy (see pp30–31), this hotel is divided into two houses. Ornate
frescoes and antique furniture decorate some of the rooms. 🛏 📺 🗐 🥗 ♿ 🅿

FLORENCE

FLORENCE: *Pensione Maxim* Ⓛ 22
Via del Calzaivoli 111B, 50123. **Map** 6 D2. ☎ *055 21 74 74.* FAX *055 28 37 29.* @ homaxim@tin.it
Stairs lead up from a side street to the reception. Some of the bedrooms in
this third-floor hotel look on to the pedestrianized Via dei Calzaiuoli. 🛏 🥗 🅿

FLORENCE: *Ariele* ⓁⓁ 39
2 km (1 mile) W, Via Magenta 11, 50123. **Map** 1 A4. ☎ *055 21 15 09.* FAX *055 26 85 21.*
Located on a residential side street, the lounge in this homey hotel is
furnished with antiques. Bedrooms are spacious but austere. 🛏 📺 🗐 🥗 🅿

FLORENCE: *Hotel Porta Rossa* ⓁⓁ 80
Via Porta Rossa 19, 50123. **Map** 3 C1 (5 C3). ☎ *055 28 75 51.* FAX *055 28 21 79.*
Italy's second-oldest hotel, it dates from 1386 and has a warm and welcoming
atmosphere. The huge bedrooms are airy and pleasantly decorated, and the
vaulted entrance hall is furnished with fine leather furniture. 🛏 📺 🗐 🥗

FLORENCE: *Hotel Silla* ⓁⓁ 36
Via dei Renai 5, 50125. **Map** 4 D2 (6 E5). ☎ *055 234 28 88.* FAX *055 234 14 37.* @ hotelsilla@tin.it
This 16th-century hotel is approached through an elegant courtyard with
a grand staircase. There is a pretty terrace giving views of the Arno. 🛏 📺 🗐 🥗 🅿

FLORENCE: *Hotel Villa Liberty* ⓁⓁ 17
Viale Michelangelo 40, 50125. **Map** 4 F3. ☎ *055 68 10 81.* FAX *055 681 25 95.*
This turn-of-the-century villa lies on a tree-lined street in the southeast of
town. Curving steps lead into a homey, old-fashioned interior. 🛏 📺 🗐 🥗 🅿

FLORENCE: *Splendor* ⓁⓁ 31
Via San Gallo 30, 50129. **Map** 2 D4. ☎ *055 48 34 27.* FAX *055 46 12 76.* @ info@hotelsplendor.it
A family hotel with dark red decor and frescoed, stuccoed ceilings that give
it the impression of a grand mansion. It shows some signs of wear. 🛏 📺 🗐 🥗

Price categories			

Price categories for a standard double room for one night, including tax and service charges but not including breakfast:
Ⓛ under L100,000
ⓁⓁ L100 – 200,000
ⓁⓁⓁ L200 – 300,000
ⓁⓁⓁⓁ L300 – 400,000
ⓁⓁⓁⓁⓁ over L400,000.

RESTAURANT
A restaurant within the hotel sometimes reserved for residents.
SWIMMING POOL
Hotel swimming pools are usually quite small and are outdoors unless otherwise stated.
GARDEN OR TERRACE
A garden, courtyard, or terrace belonging to the hotel, often providing tables for eating outside.
CREDIT CARDS
The major credit cards VISA, MasterCard (Access), and American Express are accepted in hotels with the credit card symbol.

	NUMBER OF ROOMS	RESTAURANT	SWIMMING POOL	GARDEN OR TERRACE
FLORENCE: *Hotel Hermitage* ⒶⒷⒷ Vicolo Marzio 1, 50122. Map 6 D4. ☎ 055 28 72 16. FAX 055 21 22 08. Spectacular views from the more expensive top-floor rooms of this medieval building a few yards from the Ponte Vecchio. This small hotel has comfortable rooms, each one decorated in a different style.	28			▪
FLORENCE: *Hotel Loggiato dei Serviti* ⓁⓁⓁ Piazza della SS Annunziata 3, 50122. Map 2 D4. ☎ 055 28 95 92. FAX 055 28 95 95. Built in 1527, the reception areas in this hotel near the Spedale degli Innocenti have vaulted ceilings and a bar area flanked by stone columns.	29			▪
FLORENCE: *Hotel Tornabuoni Beacci* ⓁⓁⓁ Via de' Tornabuoni 3, 50123. Map 1 C5 (5 C2). ☎ 055 21 26 45. FAX 055 28 35 94. @ info@bthotel.it This former palazzo is situated on a busy central street. Wide carpeted hallways lead to lounge areas furnished with antiques and tapestries. Bedrooms are luxurious with beds piled high with pillows.	28	▪		▪
FLORENCE: *Hotel Villa Belvedere* ⓁⓁⓁ Via Benedetto Castelli 3, 50124. Map 3 A5. ☎ 055 22 25 01. FAX 055 22 31 63. A spacious 1930s villa set in landscaped grounds near the Boboli Gardens. The first-floor terraces have good views of the garden.	26		●	▪
FLORENCE: *Londra* ⓁⓁⓁ Via Jacopo da Diacceto, 16–18, 50123. Map 1 B4. ☎ 055 238 27 91. FAX 055 21 06 82. Conveniently located near the train station, this hotel is equipped for the business or leisure traveler: some rooms are provided with PC, fax and modem: there is a gym and sauna: bikes can be hired: special services for children.	158	▪		▪
FLORENCE: *Morandi alla Crocetta* ⓁⓁⓁ Via Laura 50, 50121. Map 2 E4. ☎ 055 234 47 47. FAX 055 248 09 54. @ hmorandi@dada.it A lovely former convent run by an Englishwoman who has lived here since the 1920s. The interior is decorated with plants and antique rugs.	10			
FLORENCE: *Pensione Annalena* ⓁⓁⓁ Via Romana 34, 50125. Map 3 A3. ☎ 055 22 24 02. FAX 055 22 24 03. @ info@hotelannalena.it A 15th-century hotel with spacious, simply but attractively decorated bedrooms. The public areas are all contained in one great hall.	20			
FLORENCE: *Rivoli* ⓁⓁⓁ Via della Scala 33, 50123. Map 1 A4 (5 A1). ☎ 055 28 28 53. FAX 055 29 40 41. The weathered façade gives a clue to the age of this 15th-century hotel. It is generally spacious, cool, and decorated to a high standard, combining both modern and Classical styles with unfussy elegance.	60		●	▪
FLORENCE: *Hotel Brunelleschi* ⓁⓁⓁⓁ Piazza Santa Elisabetta 3, 50122. Map 6 D2. ☎ 055 273 70. FAX 055 21 96 53. This unique hotel was built inside a Byzantine tower. It is therefore wonderfully atmospheric with stunning views over Florence from the roof terrace.	96	▪		
FLORENCE: *Hotel Continental* ⓁⓁⓁⓁ Lungarno degli Acciaiuoli 2, 50123. Map 3 C1 (5 C4). ☎ 055 272 62. FAX 055 28 31 39. In a prime location near the Ponte Vecchio, the hotel's bar and top-floor suites overlook the river. The walls are decorated with a marble effect.	48			▪
FLORENCE: *Hotel Helvetia e Bristol* ⓁⓁⓁⓁ Via de' Pescioni 2, 50123. Map 1 C5 (5 C2). ☎ 055 28 78 14. FAX 055 28 83 53. A luxurious 18th-century hotel a few steps from the Duomo, with antiques, a domed, stained-glass ceiling, and a splendid wood and marble bar.	49	▪		
FLORENCE: *Hotel Monna Lisa* ⓁⓁⓁⓁ Borgo Pinti 27, 50121. Map 2 E5. ☎ 055 247 97 51. FAX 055 247 97 55. @ monnalis@ats.it An impressive stone courtyard leads into this Renaissance palazzo. Some of the bedrooms are huge, with old furniture and high ceilings.	30			▪

FLORENCE: *Hotel Montebello Splendid* ⓁⓁⓁ 49
Via Montebello 60. **Map** 1 A5 (5 A2). **[** 055 23 98 05. **FAX** 055 21 18 67.
A 19th-century villa elegantly transformed into an intimate hotel near the city center.
Lovely garden and restaurant with outdoor seating. 🔒 TV 🗐 🖉 P

FLORENCE: *Torre di Bellosguardo* ⓁⓁⓁⓁ 16
Via de' Michelozzi 2, 50124. **Map** 5 B5. **[** 055 229 81 45. **FAX** 055 22 90 08.
A long, sweeping road leads to this 14th-century tower and adjoining 16th-
century villa. Inside, colossal wooden doors lead to huge rooms filled with
antiques and Persian rugs. There are spectacular views over Florence. 🔒 🖉 P

FLORENCE: *Villa Carlotta* ⓁⓁⓁ 32
Via Michele di Lando 3, 50125. **Map** 3 B4. **[** 055 233 61 34. **FAX** 055 233 61 47.
This gracious 19th-century building, hidden in a remote, secluded area,
is an attractive, homey villa decorated in Neo-Classical style. 🔒 TV 🗐 🖉 P

FLORENCE: *Grand Hotel Villa Cora* ⓁⓁⓁⓁ 48
Viale Machiavelli 18, 50125. **Map** 3 A3. **[** 055 229 84 51. **FAX** 055 22 90 86. **@** info@villacora.com
A stunning Renaissance building with balustraded terraces segregated by
Classical pillars and tall windows. Inside, the reception rooms are decorated
with frescoed ceilings and varnished wooden floors. 🔒 TV 🗐 🖉 P

FLORENCE: *Hotel Excelsior* ⓁⓁⓁⓁ 168
Piazza d'Ognissanti 3, 50123. **Map** 1 B5 (5 A2). **[** 055 26 42 01. **FAX** 055 21 02 78.
Occupying two houses rebuilt in 1815, the hotel is decorated with gracious
marble floors and stained-glass with lovely views over the Arno. 🔒 TV 🗐 🖉 P

FLORENCE: *Hotel J and J* ⓁⓁⓁⓁ 20
Via di Mezzo 20, 50121. **Map** 2 E5. **[** 055 234 50 05. **FAX** 055 24 02 82. **@** jandj@dada.it
This pretty, peaceful hotel is set in a former 16th-century monastery and
has windows set between old stone arches and frescoed ceilings. 🔒 🗐 TV 🖉

FLORENCE: *Hotel Regency* ⓁⓁⓁⓁ 33
Piazza Massimo d'Azeglio 3, 50121. **Map** 2 F5. **[** 055 24 52 47. **FAX** 055 234 67 35.
Behind the modest exterior of a Florentine town house lies a grand, Classical-
style reception area and bar with wood-paneling decor. 🔒 TV 🗐 🖉 P

FLORENCE: *Villa La Massa* ⓁⓁⓁⓁ 34
Via la Massa 24, Candeli 50012. **[** 055 626 11. **FAX** 055 63 31 02. **@** villamassa@galacteca.it
On a riverside setting 6 km (4 miles) northeast of Florence, this luxurious 17th-
century hotel has elegant rooms with antique furniture. 🔒 TV 🗐 🖉 P

TUSCANY

AREZZO: *Castello di Gargonza* Ⓛ 7
Gargonza, Monte San Savino, 52048. **[** 0575 84 70 21. **FAX** 0575 84 70 54.
A sweeping tree-lined driveway curves around the walls of this castle guest-
house, which also has 18 efficiency apartments. The views are magnificent,
and weekly services are held in the pretty frescoed chapel. 🔒 🖉 P

CORTONA: *Hotel San Luca* Ⓛ 60
Piazzale Garibaldi 2, 52044. **[** 0575 63 04 60. **FAX** 0575 63 01 05.
This hillside hotel has simple bedrooms, but the comfortable reception
rooms offer good panoramas over the surrounding valleys. 🔒 TV 🖉 P

CORTONA: *Hotel San Michele* ⓁⓁ 40
Via Guelfa 15, 52044. **[** 0575 60 43 48. **FAX** 0575 63 01 47.
A beautifully restored Renaissance palazzo on a narrow street. A maze of
corridors leads to comfortable bedrooms and a superb attic suite. 🔒 TV 🗐 🖉 P

CASTELLINA IN CHIANTI: *Tenuta di Ricavo* ⓁⓁⓁ 23
Località Ricavo, 53011. **[** 0577 74 02 21. **FAX** 0577 74 10 14.
A charming hotel occupying the entire hamlet and furnished with a mixture of
antiques and rustic furniture. Many rooms are in old country houses. 🔒 🖉 P

ELBA: *Airone del Parco e delle Terme* ⓁⓁ 85
Località San Giovanni, 57037. **[** 0565 92 91 11. **FAX** 0565 91 74 84. **@** airone@elbalink.it
This hotel provides a complete range of facilities: park, a beach, two swimming
pools, spa, beauty center, and a private boat for excursions. 🔒 TV 🗐 🖉 P

ELBA: *Capo Sud* ⓁⓁ 40
Località Lacona, 57037. **[** 0565 96 40 21. **FAX** 0565 96 42 63. **@** caposud@elbalink.it
A villagelike resort with excellent bay views. The rooms are housed in a
complex of villas, and the restaurant serves produce from its orchard. 🔒 TV P

For key to symbols see back flap

Price categories for a standard double room for one night, including tax and service charges but not including breakfast: Ⓛ under L100,000 ⓁⓁ L100–200,000 ⓁⓁⓁ L200–300,000 ⓁⓁⓁⓁ L300–400,000 ⓁⓁⓁⓁⓁ over L400,000.	**RESTAURANT** A restaurant within the hotel sometimes reserved for residents. **SWIMMING POOL** Hotel swimming pools are usually quite small and are outdoors unless otherwise stated. **GARDEN OR TERRACE** A garden, courtyard, or terrace belonging to the hotel, often providing tables for eating outside. **CREDIT CARDS** The major credit cards VISA, MasterCard (Access), and American Express are accepted in hotels with the credit card symbol.	**NUMBER OF ROOMS**	**RESTAURANT**	**SWIMMING POOL**	**GARDEN OR TERRACE**

	NUMBER OF ROOMS	RESTAURANT	SWIMMING POOL	GARDEN OR TERRACE
FIESOLE: *Hotel Villa Bonelli* ⓁⓁ Via F Poeti 1, 50014. **☎** 055 595 13. **FAX** 055 59 89 42. **@** info@hotelvillabonelli.com This simple, friendly hotel is pleasantly furnished and has excellent views of Florence. Guests may take dinner if they want. 🔲 TV 🔲 🔲 P	20	▪		
FIESOLE: *Villa San Michele* ⓁⓁⓁⓁ Via Doccia 4, 50014. **☎** 055 567 82 00. **FAX** 055 59 87 34. **@** villasanmichele@firenze.net Allegedly designed by Michelangelo, the beautiful monastery has extensive grounds and beautiful panoramas over the city from the loggia. 🔲 TV 🔲 🔲 P	41	▪	●	▪
GAIOLE IN CHIANTI: *Castello di Spaltenna* ⓁⓁⓁ Via Spaltenna 13, 53013. **☎** 0577 74 94 83. **FAX** 0577 74 92 69. A beautiful, fortified former monastery with spacious rooms overlooking a courtyard; some rooms have jacuzzis. The restaurant is excellent. 🔲 TV 🔲 🔲 P	37	▪	●	▪
GIGLIO PORTO: *Castello Monticello* ⓁⓁ Via Provinciale, 58013. **☎** 0564 80 92 52. **FAX** 0564 80 94 73. A castle hotel, it was originally built on this pretty island as a private house. It sits on a hill, and there are superb views from the bedrooms. 🔲 TV 🔲 🔲 P	29	▪		▪
LUCCA: *Piccolo Hotel Puccini* Ⓛ Via di Poggio 9, 55100. **☎** 0583 554 21. **FAX** 0583 534 87. **@** info@hotelpuccini.com Housed in a lovely old stone building, this stylish small hotel has an attractive bar that overlooks the pretty, narrow street outside. 🔲 TV 🔲	14			
LUCCA: *Hotel Universo* ⓁⓁ Piazza del Giglio 1, 55100. **☎** 0583 49 36 78. **FAX** 0583 95 48 54. This big, but slightly worn hotel was built in the 19th century. It has large and comfortable bedrooms, some with pleasant views over the quiet square. The big luxurious bathrooms are an added attraction. 🔲 TV 🔲 🔲 P	60	▪		▪
LUCCA: *Locanda L'Elisa* ⓁⓁⓁⓁ Via Nuova per Pisa 1952, 55050. **☎** 0583 37 97 37. **FAX** 0583 37 90 19. **@** locanda.elisa@lunet.it There is a peaceful and luxurious atmosphere in this stately home that imitates 18th-century Parisian style. Bedrooms are beautifully decorated with antiques, and there are two elegant drawing rooms. 🔲 TV 🔲	10	▪	●	▪
MONTERIGGIONI: *Albergo Casalta* Ⓛ Località Strove, 53035. **☎** 0577 30 10 02. **FAX** 0577 30 10 02. Housed in a 1,000-year-old building, a central hearth in the reception adds to the warm and welcoming atmosphere. The restaurant is also very elegant. 🔲 🔲	10	▪	●	
PISA: *Royal Victoria Hotel* ⓁⓁ Lungarno Pacinotti 12, 56126. **☎** 050 94 01 11. **FAX** 050 94 01 80. **@** rvh@csinfo.it A dignified hotel originally built in the 19th century. It retains several original features, including exquisite trompe l'oeil drapery and wood paneled doors. 🔲 TV 🔲 P	48	▪		▪
PISA: *Duomo* ⓁⓁⓁ Via S Maria 94. **☎** 050 56 18 94. **FAX** 050 56 04 18. **@** hotelduomo@csinfo.it This very comfortable hotel has a spectacular view of the Tower and the other monuments of the city from its roof garden. 🔲 TV 🔲 P	93	▪		▪
PISTOIA: *Albergo Patria* Ⓛ Via Crispi 8, 51100. **☎** 0573 251 87. **FAX** 0573 36 81 68. An ancient hotel with a dark, modern interior and 1970s bedrooms. It is on a pretty street in the center of Pistoia, well placed for sightseeing. Upper bedrooms have excellent views of the Romanesque duomo. 🔲 TV 🔲	23	▪		
PISTOIA: *Hotel Piccolo Ritz* Ⓛ Via Vannucci 67, 51100. **☎** 0573 267 75 16. **FAX** 0573 277 98. Near the station in the historic center of Pistoia, this small hotel lives up to its name and has a pleasant, frescoed café-style bar. 🔲 TV 🔲	21			

PORTO ERCOLE: *Il Pellicano*   ⓁⓁⓁⓁ   41
Località Sbarcatello, 58018. 📞 0564 83 38 01. FAX 0564 83 34 18.
Luxurious and exclusive with its own rocky beach, this old-style Tuscan villa
is covered with vines and has wonderful views from the terraces descending
to the sea. Rooms are elegantly furnished with antiques. 🛏 TV 🍽 🇪 🅿

RADDA IN CHIANTI: *Villa Miranda*   ⓁⓁ   49
Siena 53017. 📞 0577 73 80 21. FAX 0577 73 86 68.
Run by the same family since the original building (the Post House) was
built in 1842. Bedrooms have beamed ceilings and brass bedsteads. 🛏 🍽 🇪 🅿

SAN GIMIGNANO: *Hotel Leon Bianco*   ⓁⓁ   25
Piazza della Cisterna 13, 53037. 📞 0577 94 12 94. FAX 0577 94 21 23.
Airy rooms with pleasant views and terra-cotta floors typify this former
palazzo. Parts of the original stone wall can still be seen. 🛏 TV 🍽 🇪 🅿

SAN GIMIGNANO: *Hotel Villa Belvedere*   ⓁⓁ   12
Via Dante 14, 53037. 📞 0577 94 05 39. FAX 0577 94 03 27.
A pretty terra-cotta villa set in a cypress-filled garden with hammocks.
Light, modern bedrooms are painted in soothing pastel shades. 🇪 🅿

SAN GIMIGNANO: *Villa San Paolo*   ⓁⓁ   18
Strada per Certaldo, 53037. 📞 0577 95 51 00. FAX 0577 95 51 13.
An attractive hillside villa set in terraced gardens with tennis courts.
Inside there are pretty bedrooms and intimate lounges. 🛏 TV 🍽 🇪 🅿

SIENA: *Hotel Chiusarelli*   ⓁⓁ   49
Viale Curtatone 15, 53100. 📞 0577 28 05 62. FAX 0577 27 11 77. @ chiusare@tin.it
A pretty villa that still looks slightly the worse for wear in spite of its recent
restoration. The pleasant garden is filled with palm trees. 🛏 TV 🍽 🇪 🅿

SIENA: *Santa Caterina*   ⓁⓁ   19
Via Enea Silvio Piccolomini 7, 53100. 📞 0577 22 11 05. FAX 0577 27 10 87. @ hsc@sienanet.it
The comfortable rooms overlook the marvelous flower garden, which has
charming views of the red roofs of Siena. The Santa Caterina, situated near
the Porta Romana, was once a privately owned villa. 🛏 TV 🍽 🇪 🅿

SIENA: *Villa Patrizia*   ⓁⓁⓁ   33
Via Fiorentina 58, 53100. 📞 0577 504 31. FAX 0577 504 42. @ info@villapatrizia.it
A rambling old villa on the city's northern outskirts. The bedrooms,
all of which look out onto the gardens, are simply furnished but
comfortable. 🛏 TV 🍽 🇪 🅿

SIENA: *Villa Scacciapensieri*   ⓁⓁⓁ   31
Via di Scacciapensieri 10, 53100. 📞 0577 414 41. FAX 0577 27 08 54. @ villasca@tin.it
Set in attractive grounds, this villa features an old-fashioned lounge with a huge
stone fireplace. The spacious bedrooms have views of Siena. 🛏 TV 🍽 🇪 🅿

SIENA: *Hotel Certosa di Maggiano*   ⓁⓁⓁⓁⓁ   17
Strada di Certosa 82, 53100. 📞 0577 28 81 80. FAX 0577 28 81 89. @ certosa@relaischateaux.fr
A former Carthusian monastery built in 1314 and turned into an exclusive,
peaceful retreat. The rooms are adorned with antique paintings. 🛏 TV 🍽 🇪 🅿

SINALUNGA: *Locanda L'Amorosa*   ⓁⓁⓁ   20
L'Amorosa, 53048. 📞 0577 67 94 97. FAX 0577 63 20 01. @ locanda@amorosa.it
An enchanting stone and pink terra-cotta building is the setting for this beautiful
inn. The luxurious bedrooms are quiet and comfortable. 🛏 TV 🍽 🇪 🅿

VIAREGGIO: *Hotel President*   ⓁⓁ   37
Viale Carducci 5, 55049. 📞 0584 96 27 12. FAX 0584 96 36 58.
A chic seaside hotel with attractively refurbished and comfortable bedrooms.
There are excellent sea views from the rooftop restaurant. 🛏 TV 🍽 🇪

VOLTERRA: *Albergo Villa Nencini*   Ⓛ   32
Borgo Santo Stefano 55, 56048. 📞 0588 863 86. FAX 0588 806 01.
A stone country hotel set in a park a few minutes from the town. Cool, light
bedrooms, a chic breakfast room, basement trattoria, and terrace. 🛏 TV 🇪 🅿

UMBRIA

ASSISI: *Umbra*   Ⓛ   25
Via degli Archi 6, 06081. 📞 075 81 22 40. FAX 075 81 36 53. @ humbra@mail.caribusiness.it
A friendly hotel in an atmospheric back street in the historic center. Furnishings
are comfortable and there is a charming terrace for outside dining. 🛏 TV 🇪

<table>
<tr><td>

Price categories for a standard double room for one night, including tax and service charges but not including breakfast:
Ⓛ under L100,000
ⒺⓁ L100–200,000
ⓁⓁⓁ L200–300,000
ⓁⓁⓁⓁ L300–400,000
ⓁⓁⓁⓁⓁ over L400,000.

</td><td>

RESTAURANT
A restaurant within the hotel sometimes reserved for residents.
SWIMMING POOL
Hotel swimming pools are usually quite small and are outdoors unless otherwise stated.
GARDEN OR TERRACE
A garden, courtyard, or terrace belonging to the hotel, often providing tables for eating outside.
CREDIT CARDS
The major credit cards VISA, MasterCard (Access), and American Express are accepted in hotels with the credit card symbol.

</td></tr>
</table>

	NUMBER OF ROOMS	RESTAURANT	SWIMMING POOL	GARDEN OR TERRACE
ASSISI: *Country House* ⓁⓁ Via San Pietro Campagna 178, Località Valecchie, 06081. ☏ 075 81 63 63. FAX 075 81 61 55. A convenient 700 m (half a mile) from the center of Assisi, this 1920s villa is set amid peaceful countryside. Rooms are furnished with antiques. �'TV 🔲 🗐 P	15			■
ASSISI: *Dei Priori* ⓁⓁ Corso Mazzini 15, 06081. ☏ 075 81 22 37. FAX 075 81 68 04. Set in a 17th-century building in the historic center, the bedrooms are pretty and fresh, and there is a lovely vaulted dining room. 🚗 TV 🔲 🗐 P	34	■		■
ASSISI: *Romantik Hotel Le Silve* ⓁⓁ Località Armenzano di Assisi, 06081. ☏ 075 801 90 00. FAX 075 801 90 05. @ hotellesilve@tin.it Located about 12 km (7 miles) from Assisi, the Romantik has wonderful views of the Umbrian hills as well as an excellent range of sports and leisure facilities. 🚗 TV 🗐 P	15	■	●	■
CAMPELLO SUL CLITUNNO: *Il Vecchio Molino* ⓁⓁ Via del Tempio 34, Località Pissignano 06042. ☏ 0743 52 11 22. FAX 0743 27 50 97. Set in a converted mill on an island in the river, the bedrooms are spacious and comfortable. A Roman temple can be seen from the garden. 🚗 🔲 🗐 P	13			■
CASTIGLIONE DEL LAGO: *Miralago* Ⓛ Piazza Mazzini 6, 06061. ☏ 075 95 11 57. FAX 075 95 19 24. @ miralago@ftbcc.it Set in the center of this town on the shores of Lake Trasimeno, the Miralago is a small hotel run by a family from Kenya who extend a friendly welcome to all guests. Fresh fish from the lake is served in the restaurant. 🚗 TV 🔲 🗐	19	■		■
FONTIGNANO: *Villa di Monte Solare* ⓁⓁ Via Montali 7, Colle San Paolo 06007. ☏ 075 83 23 76. FAX 075 835 54 62. A beautiful 18th-century villa set in its own grounds with many original features such as terra-cotta floors, period furniture, and frescoes. Colle San Paolo is 25 km (15 miles) from Perugia through beautiful Umbrian landscape. 🚗 TV 🗐 P	20	■	●	■
GUBBIO: *Oderisi-Balestrieri* Ⓛ Via Mazzatinti 2/12, 06024. ☏ 075 922 06 62. FAX 075 922 06 63. A hotel in the medieval town center; the rooms are pleasantly furnished with modern wooden beams, bedsteads, and tables. 🚗 TV 🗐 P	35			
GUBBIO: *Bosone Palace* ⓁⓁ Via XX Settembre 22, 06024. ☏ 075 922 06 88. FAX 075 922 01 59. Set in the Palazzo Raffaelli, one of the oldest palazzi in the historic center, the Bosone has a mixture of bedrooms from the spectacular to the ordinary. All of them, however, have a wonderfully historic atmosphere. 🚗 TV 🗐	30	■		
GUBBIO: *Villa Montegranelli* ⓁⓁ Località Monteluiano, 06024. ☏ 075 922 01 85. FAX 075 927 33 72. An elegant country villa about 4 km (2 miles) from Gubbio with attractive bedrooms and a highly recommended restaurant (see p596). 🚗 TV 🗐 P	21	■		■
LAKE TRASIMENO: *Hotel da Sauro* Ⓛ Isola Maggiore, 06060. ☏ 075 82 61 68. FAX 075 82 51 30. @ hotelsauro@libero.it A basic hotel with friendly staff in an exceptional location. Isola Maggiore remains fairly isolated, making this a quiet and simple retreat. 🚗 🗐	12	■		■
MONTEFALCO: *Ringhiera Umbra* Ⓛ Via G Mameli 20, 06036. ☏ 0742 37 91 66. FAX 0742 37 91 66. A simple yet immaculately kept hotel in a historic building in the center of Montefalco. The reasonably priced restaurant is in a vaulted room. 🚗 TV 🗐	20	■		
MONTEFALCO: *Villa Pambuffetti* ⓁⓁⓁ Via della Vittoria 20, 06036. ☏ 0742 37 94 17. FAX 0742 37 92 45. @ villabianca@interbusiness.it The spacious and comfortable bedrooms in this hotel are all different. The tower room has wonderful views of the surrounding country. 🚗 TV 🔲 🗐 P	15	■	●	■

NORCIA: *Garden* Ⓛ 45
Viale XX Settembre 2b, 06046. **(** *0743 81 66 87.* **FAX** *0743 81 66 87.*
A simple hotel close to the center of Norcia, with basic but comfortable
rooms. The Garden is a good base from which to explore the city. 🛏 TV 🌐 P

ORVIETO: *Villa Ciconia* ⓁⓁ 10
Via dei Tigli 69, 05019. **(** *0763 30 55 82.* **FAX** *0763 30 20 77.*
Set in lovely grounds a short distance out of Orvieto, this 16th-century country
house makes a peaceful base from which to explore Umbria. 🛏 TV ▤ 🌐 P

ORVIETO: *Virgilio* ⓁⓁ 15
Piazza Duomo 5–6, 05018. **(** *0763 34 18 82.* **FAX** *0763 34 37 97.* **@** virgilio@orvienet.it
Located in central Orvieto, this simple hotel was converted by the owner from
what was once his home. Some rooms have views of the cathedral. 🛏 TV 🌐

ORVIETO: *La Badia* ⓁⓁ 26
Località la Badia 8, 05019. **(** *0763 30 19 59.* **FAX** *0763 30 53 96.*
Housed in a spectacular former monastery, parts of which date back to the
12th century, modern comfort is combined with medieval splendor. 🛏 TV ▤ 🌐 P

PERUGIA: *Lo Spedalicchio* Ⓛ 25
Piazza Bruno Buozzi 3, Ospedalicchio 06080. **(** *075 801 03 23.* **FAX** *075 801 03 23.*
Built within the walls of a 14th-century fortress, the rooms are simply but
comfortably decorated in keeping with the style of the building. 🛏 TV 🌐 P

PERUGIA: *Locanda della Posta* ⓁⓁ 40
Corso Vannucci 97, 06100. **(** *075 572 89 25.* **FAX** *075 573 25 62.* **@** novelber@tin.it
This elegant 200-year-old hotel is housed in a charming old palazzo on
the pedestrianized main street of the historic center. 🛏 TV ▤ 🌐

PERUGIA: *Locanda della Rocca* ⓁⓁ 7
Viale Roma 4, 06060. **(** *075 83 02 36.* **FAX** *075 83 02 36.*
An old Umbrian mansion with a mill has been transformed into this small, charming,
family-run hotel. The attentive service lends a warm atmosphere. 🛏 TV ▤ 🌐

PERUGIA: *Tiferno* ⓁⓁ 38
Piazza Rafaello Sanzio 13, 06012 Citta di Castello. **(** *0758 55 03 31.* **FAX** *0758 52 11 96.*
A 17th-century palace that was turned into a monastery; it has been a hotel since
1895.The restructuring has respected the original architecture. 🛏 TV ▤ 🌐 P

PERUGIA: *Brufani* ⓁⓁⓁⓁ 82
Piazza Italia 12, 06100. **(** *075 573 25 41.* **FAX** *075 572 02 10.* **@** brufani@tin.it
Opened in 1884, the public rooms of this exclusive hotel were painted by Lillis,
the German interior designer. The views are spectacular. 🛏 TV ▤ 🌐 P

SPELLO: *La Bastiglia* Ⓛ 33
Piazza Vallegloria 7, 06038. **(** *0742 65 12 77.* **FAX** *0742 30 11 59.* **@** fancelli@labastiglia.com
An adapted old mill is the setting for this airy, homey hotel whose extensive
terraces give excellent views over the surrounding countryside. 🛏 TV ▤ 🌐 P

SPELLO: *Palazzo Bocci* ⓁⓁ 23
Via Cavour 17, 06038. **(** *0742 30 10 21.* **FAX** *0742 30 14 64.* **@** bocci@bcsnet.it
Set in a much restored 14th-century palazzo in the center of Spello, this
hotel combines modern convenience with traditional charm. 🛏 TV ▤ 🌐 P

SPOLETO: *Aurora* Ⓛ 15
Via Apollinare 3, 06049. **(** *0743 22 03 15.* **FAX** *0743 22 18 85.* **@** hotelaurora@virgilio.it
A good value hotel in the historic center. It is connected to the Apollinare
restaurant and (unusually for this price) all rooms have minibars. 🛏 TV 🌐 P

SPOLETO: *Charleston* Ⓛ 21
Piazza Collicola 10, 06049. **(** *0743 22 00 52.* **FAX** *0743 22 20 10.* **@** hotelcharleston@edisons.it
A 17th-century building in the center of Spoleto. The modern and traditional
furnishings in this hotel create an uncluttered yet homey feel. 🛏 TV ▤ 🌐 P

SPOLETO: *Gattapone* ⓁⓁ 15
Via del Ponte 6, 06049. **(** *0743 22 34 47.* **FAX** *0743 22 34 48.* **@** gattapone@mail.caribusiness.it
A smart hotel, built on the highest point of the town, five minutes' walk
from the center with excellent views of the Ponte delle Torri. 🛏 TV 🌐 P

TODI: *Bramante* ⓁⓁ 43
Via Orvietana 48, 06059. **(** *075 894 83 81.* **FAX** *075 894 80 74.* **@** bramante@hotelbramante.it
Although rebuilt, parts of the 13th-century convent remain, and the simple
furnishings of this quiet hotel add to the peaceful atmosphere. 🛏 TV ▤ 🌐 P

		NUMBER OF ROOMS	RESTAURANT	SWIMMING POOL	GARDEN OR TERRACE
TODI: *Hotel Fonte Cesia* ⓛ ⓛ Via Lorenzo Leonj 3, 06059. 📞 075 894 37 37. FAX 075 894 46 77. @ f.cesia@full_service.it A beautiful 17th-century palazzo is the setting for this elegant and intimate hotel that combines traditional charm with all modern comforts. 📺 🅿		36			■
TORGIANO: *Le Tre Vaselle* ⓛ ⓛ Via G Garibaldi 48, 06089. 📞 075 988 04 47. FAX 075 988 02 14. @ 3vaselle@3vaselle.it Set in a 17th-century country house, the hotel has retained its terra-cotta floor tiles and beamed ceilings and is furnished with rustic antiques. 📺 🅿		61	■	●	■

LE MARCHE

		NUMBER OF ROOMS	RESTAURANT	SWIMMING POOL	GARDEN OR TERRACE
ANCONA: *Emilia* ⓛ ⓛ Poggio di Portonovo, 60020. 📞 071 80 11 45. FAX 071 80 13 30. @ info@hotelemilia.com A refined hotel with bright and pretty interior decorations. As well as hosting concerts for the Ancona Jazz festival in its elegant garden, the Emilia organizes an annual art prize and has a collection of contemporary art. 📺 🅿		29	■	●	■
ANCONA: *Grand Hotel Palace* ⓛ ⓛ Lungomare Vanvitelli 24. 📞 071 20 18 13. FAX 071 207 48 32. @ palace.ancona@tiscalinet.it Once the private palace of a noble family, this stylish hotel is located near the harbor. There is a beautiful panorama from the roof terrace. 📺		40			■
AQUAVIVA PICENA: *Hotel O'Viv* ⓛ Via Marziale 43, 63030. 📞 0735 76 46 49. FAX 0735 76 50 54. Set in an attractive palazzo in the medieval town center, the bedrooms in this traditional hotel are spacious with wonderful views from the terrace. 📺		12	■		■
FOLIGNANO: *Villa Pigna* ⓛ ⓛ Viale Assisi 33, 63040. 📞 0736 49 18 68. FAX 0736 49 21 79. A modern, efficiently run hotel in the center of town. The public rooms are attractive and the bedrooms, if unexceptional, are satisfactory. 📺 🅿		54	■		
JESI: *Federico II* ⓛ ⓛ Via Ancona 100, 60035. 📞 0731 21 10 79. FAX 0731 572 21. @ htl.federico@pieralisi.it A slick postmodern hotel offering a massive range of facilities: indoor pool, gym, and a conference center. A little impersonal, but comfortable. 📺 🅿		124	■	●	■
MONTECASSIANO: *Villa Quiete* ⓛ ⓛ Località Vallecascia, 62010. 📞 0733 59 95 59. FAX 0733 59 95 59. A country villa hotel set in its own beautiful gardens. Some of the pretty rooms have antique furnishings. There are also two suites. 📺 🅿		38	■		
PESARO: *Villa Serena* ⓛ ⓛ Via San Nicola 6–3, 61100. 📞 0721 552 11. FAX 0721 559 27. This 17th-century mansion, set in its own well-kept grounds, is a very comfortable, friendly hotel where no two rooms are alike. 🅿		9	■		■
PESARO: *Vittoria* ⓛ ⓛ ⓛ Via A Vespucci 2, Piazzale Libertà 2, 61100. 📞 0721 343 43. FAX 0721 652 04. @ info@viphotels.it The Vittoria is a perfect combination of old-fashioned charm and modern convenience. It has a good range of facilities and is close to the sea. 📺 🅿		27	■	●	■
PORTONOVO: *Fortino Napoleonico* ⓛ ⓛ ⓛ Via Poggio 166, 60020. 📞 071 80 14 50. FAX 071 80 14 54. @ fortino@fastnet.it Built to protect the coast from marauding English during the Napoleonic wars, the fortress has been comfortably restored with tasteful decor and antiques, and has its own beach. Now even the English are welcome. 📺 🅿		30	■		
SAN BENEDETTO DEL TRONTO: *Sabbia D'Oro* ⓛ Viale Marconi 46, 63039. 📞 0735 819 11. FAX 0735 849 17. A modern beach hotel in this busy, fashionable resort. Rooms are well-designed and comfortable, and each has a minibar and safe. 📺 🅿		63	■	●	■

SAN LEO: *Castello* ⓛ 14
Piazza Dante Alighieri 12, 61018. 【 *0541 91 62 14.* ⟦FAX⟧ *0541 92 69 26.*
Housed in a restored 16th-century town building in the town center, the white
tiles and light colors in the interior create an airy atmosphere. 🛏 TV 🖎

SAN MARINO: *Panoramic* ⓛ 27
Via Voltone 89, 47890. 【 *0549 99 23 59.* ⟦FAX⟧ *0549 99 03 56.*
A family-run hotel in a tranquil part of this independent republic in the middle
of Italy. The Panoramic is particularly proud of its restaurant. 🛏 TV 🖎 P

SIROLO: *Monte Conero* ⓛⓛ 60
Via Monteconero 26, 60020. 【 *071 933 05 92.* ⟦FAX⟧ *071 933 03 65.* @ monteconero.hotel@fastnet.it
Splendid sea views from this hotel in an 11th-century monastery with a
Romanesque church. Rooms are bright and have their own balconies. Guests
must use American or MAP during July and August. 🛏 TV 🖎 P

URBINO: *Locanda la Brombolona* ⓛ 12
Località Sant'Andrea in Primicilio 22, 61029. 【 *0722 535 01.* ⟦FAX⟧ *0722 535 01.*
Pleasantly located in the rolling hills above Urbino, this charming little hotel
makes a peaceful rural base from which to explore the surroundings. Inside
it is simply furnished, and rooms have views over the countryside. 🛏 ▤ 🖎 P

URBINO: *Bonconte* ⓛⓛ 23
Via delle Mura 28, 61029. 【 *0722 24 63.* ⟦FAX⟧ *0722 24 63.*
A recently refurbished old villa; furnishings include some antiques among
the more modern suites. The bright rooms are well equipped. 🛏 TV ▤ 🖎

ROME

AVENTINE: *Sant'Anselmo* ⓛⓛⓛ 46
Piazza Sant'Anselmo 2, 00153. Map 6 E3. 【 *06 574 35 47.* ⟦FAX⟧ *06 578 36 04.*
A pretty villa on the peaceful Aventine within walking distance of the
Colosseum. It has a secluded garden and hand-painted furniture. 🛏 TV 🖎 P

AVENTINE: *Domus Aventino* ⓛⓛⓛ 26
Via di Santa Prisca 11b, 00153. Map 6 E3. 【 *06 57 461 35.* ⟦FAX⟧ *06 57 30 00 44.*
Situated in a 14th-century convent at the foot of the Aventine Hill, the hotel
offers large, simply decorated rooms, most of them with balconies. 🛏 ▤ TV 🖎

CAMPO DE' FIORI: *Piccolo* ⓛⓛ 15
Via dei Chiavari 32, 00186. Map 2 F4. 【 *06 68 80 25 60.*
A cool, serene family-run hotel with clean, simple rooms and a TV in
the breakfast room. It is one of the cheapest hotels in the area. 🖎

CAMPO DE' FIORI: *Teatro di Pompeo* ⓛⓛⓛ 13
Largo del Pallaro 8, 00186. Map 2 F4. 【 *06 68 30 01 70, 687 25 66.* ⟦FAX⟧ *06 68 80 55 31.*
A small courteously run hotel whose basement breakfast room is in the ruins
of Pompey's Theater. Bedrooms have beamed ceilings. 🛏 TV 🖎 P

FORUM: *Forum* ⓛⓛⓛⓛ 76
Via Tor de' Conti 25, 00184. Map 3 C5. 【 *06 679 24 46.* ⟦FAX⟧ *06 678 64 79.*
An old-fashioned hotel with wood-paneled public rooms and a sunny
roof-terrace restaurant with views over the archaeological zone. 🛏 TV ▤ 🖎 P

GIULIA: *Ponte Sisto* ⓛⓛⓛ 106
Via dei Pettinari 64. Map 2 F5. 【 *06 681 946 05.* ⟦FAX⟧ *06 686 55 98.*
Newly opened luxurious hotel set within a historic building. There is a gourmet
indoor restaurant and another in the charming private garden. 🛏 TV 🖎 P

NAZIONALE: *Artemide* ⓛⓛ 23
Via Nazionale 22, 00184. Map 3 C4. 【 *06 48 99 11.* ⟦FAX⟧ *06 489 917 00.*
Stylish hotel harmonizing turn-of-the-century architecture and Art Nouveau motifs.
Impeccable, sound-proof rooms offer every modern facility. The adjoining
"Caffetteria Nazionale" is a popular two-level coffee shop/restaurant. 🛏 TV ▤ 🖎

PANTHEON: *Abruzzi* ⓛ 25
Piazza della Rotonda 69, 00186. Map 2 F4. 【 *06 679 20 21.*
Terra-cotta–tiled floors in an ocher-colored palazzo overlooking the Pantheon.
The Abruzzi provides clean, simple but pleasant rooms. No breakfast.

PANTHEON: *Santa Chiara* ⓛⓛⓛ 97
Via di Santa Chiara 21, 00186. Map 2 F4. 【 *06 687 29 79.* ⟦FAX⟧ *06 687 31 44.*
A conveniently located hotel with cool, marble reception area and
well-furnished bedrooms. Rooms facing the street can be noisy. 🛏 TV ▤ 🖎

Price categories for a standard double room for one night, including tax and service charges but not including breakfast:
Ⓛ under L100,000
ⓁⓁ L100 – 200,000
ⓁⓁⓁ L200 – 300,000
ⓁⓁⓁⓁ L300 – 400,000
ⓁⓁⓁⓁⓁ over L400,000.

RESTAURANT
A restaurant within the hotel sometimes reserved for residents.
SWIMMING POOL
Hotel swimming pools are usually quite small and are outdoors unless otherwise stated.
GARDEN OR TERRACE
A garden, courtyard, or terrace belonging to the hotel, often providing tables for eating outside.
CREDIT CARDS
The major credit cards VISA, MasterCard (Access), and American Express are accepted in hotels with the credit card symbol.

	NUMBER OF ROOMS	RESTAURANT	SWIMMING POOL	GARDEN OR TERRACE
PANTHEON: *Nazionale* ⓁⓁⓁⓁ Piazza di Montecitorio 131, 00186. Map 3 A3. 📞 06 69 50 01. FAX 06 678 66 77. Opposite the Chamber of Deputies, the Nazionale's comfortable and sometimes huge rooms are furnished with British and Italian antiques. The hotel is popular with business travelers and well-heeled tourists. 🛏 TV 🗐	87	▪		
PANTHEON: *Sole al Pantheon* ⓁⓁⓁⓁ Piazza della Rotonda 63, 00186. Map 2 F4. 📞 06 678 04 41. FAX 06 69 94 06 89. A historic hotel dating from 1467. Some of its beautiful modernized rooms have painted paneled ceilings and magical views of the Pantheon. 🛏 TV 🗐 🗐	25			
PANTHEON: *Holiday Inn Crowne Plaza Minerva* ⓁⓁⓁⓁⓁ Piazza della Minerva 69, 00186. Map 3 A4. 📞 06 69 52 01. FAX 06 679 41 65. The interior, with its semitranslucent Venetian glass and marble, was designed by postmodern architect Paolo Portoghesi, and the bedrooms are spacious and bright. The roof terrace commands magnificent views. 🛏 TV 🗐 🗐 🗐	134	▪		▪
PIAZZA NAVONA: *Navona* ⓁⓁ Via dei Sediari 8, 00186. Map 2 F4. 📞 06 686 42 03. FAX 06 68 80 38 02. Book well in advance for this superbly located, good value hotel run by the owner's friendly Australian son-in-law. Rooms are basic but satisfactory. 🛏 🗐 🗐	31			
PIAZZA NAVONA: *Due Torri* ⓁⓁⓁ Vicolo del Leonetto 23–25, 00186. Map 2 F3. 📞 06 687 69 83. FAX 06 686 54 42. An amiable hotel tucked into an alleyway in the artisans' district. Rooms vary in size and style. Public rooms have a country house feel. 🛏 TV 🗐 🗐	26			▪
PIAZZA NAVONA: *Raphael* ⓁⓁⓁⓁ Largo Febo 2, 00186. Map 2 F3. 📞 06 68 28 31. FAX 06 687 89 93. @ info@raphaelhotel.com An ivy-clad luxury hotel whose lobby is full of antique statues and modern sculpture. It has a restaurant and elegantly furnished bedrooms. 🛏 TV 🗐 🗐	71	▪		
PIAZZA DI SPAGNA: *Jonella* Ⓛ Via della Croce 41, 00187. Map 3 A2. 📞 06 679 79 66. FAX 06 446 23 68. @ jonella@lodgingitaly.com The low prices and location on one of the main shopping streets of the Piazza di Spagna area make this simple pensione well worth considering.	5			
PIAZZA DI SPAGNA: *Margutta* ⓁⓁ Via Laurina 34, 00187. Map 3 A1. 📞 06 322 36 74. FAX 06 320 03 95. Pretty rooms on a quiet street. Book in advance if you want one of the three attic rooms that share a roof terrace. Public rooms are airy and bright. 🛏 🗐	24			
PIAZZA DI SPAGNA: *Condotti* ⓁⓁⓁ Via Mario de' Fiori 37, 00187. Map 3 A2. 📞 06 679 46 61. FAX 06 679 04 57. A comfortable, welcoming hotel in the heart of the designer shopping district. Rooms are medium to large and well decorated. One room has its own small terrace and three others share one. 🛏 TV 🗐 🗐	16			▪
PIAZZA DI SPAGNA: *Homs* ⓁⓁⓁ Via della Vite 71–72, 00187. Map 3 A2. 📞 06 679 29 76. FAX 06 678 04 82. Clean, pleasant rooms on one of the area's quieter, less pretentious shopping streets. The breakfast room opens onto a pleasant terrace. 🛏 TV 🗐 🗐 P	50			▪
PIAZZA DI SPAGNA: *Gregoriana* ⓁⓁⓁⓁ Via Gregoriana 18, 00187. Map 3 B2. 📞 06 679 50 57. FAX 06 678 42 58. This stylish hotel, popular with writers and artists in the 19th century, has an interesting variety of decoration, including some unusual leopard-spotted wallpaper. Bedrooms, however, are flowery and fresh. 🛏 TV 🗐	19			
PIAZZA DI SPAGNA: *Hassler* ⓁⓁⓁⓁⓁ Piazza Trinità dei Monti 6, 00187. Map 3 B2. 📞 06 69 93 40. FAX 06 678 99 91. Venetian glass chandeliers and wood-paneled bathrooms retain the air of a more extravagant era. Magnificent views from the roof terrace. 🛏 TV 🗐 🗐 P	100	▪		▪

PIAZZA DI SPAGNA: *Scalinata di Spagna* ⓛⓛⓛⓛ 16
Piazza Trinità dei Monti 17, 00187. **Map** 3 B2. ☎ 06 679 30 06. ꜰᴀx 06 69 94 05 98.
A convivial hotel in a small 18th-century villa at the top of the Spanish Steps.
The rooms that open onto the terrace have exquisite views. 🛏 📺 🗒 🄴

TERMINI: *Katty* ⓛ 12
Via Palestro 35, 00185. **Map** 4 E1. ☎ 06 444 12 16. ꜰᴀx 06 444 12 16.
The Katty has clean, basic rooms with an occasional piece of antique furniture.
It is extremely popular with British and American students, so book early.

TERMINI: *Restivo* ⓛ 6
Via Palestro 55, 00185. **Map** 4 F2. ☎ 06 446 21 72.
Alongside the Mari, this small hotel (only six rooms) is beautifully
maintained. Guests return again and again.

TERMINI: *Mari 2* ⓛⓛ 27
Via Calata Fini 38, 00185. **Map** 4 E1. ☎ 06 474 03 71. ꜰᴀx 06 482 83 13.
A friendly hotel run by three women. It has clean pleasant rooms with no frills.
Guests can be accommodated at a nearby pensione when this one is full. 🄴

TERMINI: *Canada* ⓛⓛ 70
Via Vicenza 58, 00185. **Map** 4 F2. ☎ 06 445 77 70. ꜰᴀx 06 445 07 49. ⓐ canada@italyhotel.com
A good, midrange hotel behind Termini station, which has a pleasant lounge-bar
with attractive cane seats and squashy sofas. Courteous service. 🛏 📺 🗒 🄴 🅿

TERMINI: *Kennedy* ⓛⓛ 51
Via Filippo Turati 64, 00185. **Map** 4 F2. ☎ 06 446 53 73. ꜰᴀx 06 446 54 17.
Close to Termini station, this recently renovated hotel has friendly young staff.
Ample breakfasts are served and some rooms have great views. 🛏 📺 🗒 🄴

TERMINI: *Diana* ⓛⓛ 188
Via Principe Amedeo 4. **Map** 4 E3. ☎ 06 482 75 41. ꜰᴀx 06 48 69 98.
This pleasant hotel offers tastefully furnished rooms. The restaurant offers traditional
Italian cuisine, served on the roof terrace in summer. 🛏 📺 🗒 🄴

VATICAN: *Alimandi* ⓛⓛ 35
Via Tunisi 8, 00192. **Map** 3 D1. ☎ 06 39 72 63 00. ꜰᴀx 06 39 72 39 43. ⓐ alimandi@tin.it
A simple pensione near the entrance to the Vatican museums. It has a large
terrace where you can have barbecues if you ask in advance. 🛏 📺 🗒 🄴 🅿

VATICAN: *Colombus* ⓛⓛⓛ 100
Via della Conciliazione 33, 00193. **Map** 1 C3. ☎ 06 686 48 74. ꜰᴀx 06 686 54 34.
Occupying a former monastery near St. Peter's Square, the hotel's banquet
room is in the old refectory and has retained its original frescoes. 🛏 📺 🗒 🄴 🅿

VATICAN: *Hotel dei Mellini* ⓛⓛⓛⓛ 80
Via Muzio Clementi 81. **Map** 2 F2. ☎ 06 32 47 71. ꜰᴀx 06 32 47 78 01. ⓐ info@hotelmellini.com
The cool style of this smart hotel attracts international travelers. Contemporary
works of art adorn the interior public spaces. 🛏 📺 🗒 🄴 🅿

VATICAN: *Visconti Palace* ⓛⓛⓛ 247
Via Federico Cesi 37, 00193. **Map** 2 E2. ☎ 06 36 84. ꜰᴀx 06 32 00 551.
This modern and efficient hotel is in an ideal location and provides large common
spaces and well-decorated rooms. There is a piano bar nightly. 🛏 📺 🗒 🄴 🅿

VIA VENETO: *Merano* ⓛⓛ 30
Via Veneto 155, 00187. **Map** 3 C1. ☎ 06 482 17 808. ꜰᴀx 06 482 18 10.
A bonus feature of this very friendly hotel in a 19th-century palazzo
is its sunny, parquet-floored breakfast room. 🛏 🄴

VIA VENETO: *Alexandra* ⓛⓛⓛ 58
Via Veneto 18, 00187. **Map** 3 C1. ☎ 06 488 19 43. ꜰᴀx 06 487 18 04. ⓐ alexandra@venere.it
A good value hotel on this expensive street, the Alexandra has a pleasant
breakfast room, and each bedroom has been decorated differently. 🛏 📺 🗒 🄴

VIA VENETO: *Residenza* ⓛⓛⓛ 29
Via Emilia 22–24, 00187. **Map** 3 C1. ☎ 06 488 07 89. ꜰᴀx 06 48 57 21.
An elegant, courteously run hotel in a quiet villa, with stylish public rooms,
comfortable bedrooms, and a delightful canopied terrace. 🛏 📺 🗒 🄴 🅿

VIA VENETO: *Ambasciatori Palace* ⓛⓛⓛⓛ 150
Via Vittorio Veneto 62, 00187. **Map** 3 C1. ☎ 06 474 93. ꜰᴀx 06 474 36 01.
This hotel offers hospitality in the grand tradition. Set within a historical
building, the plush furnishings add to the air of luxury. 🛏 📺 🗒 🄴

	NUMBER OF ROOMS	RESTAURANT	SWIMMING POOL	GARDEN OR TERRACE

Price categories for a standard double room for one night, including tax and service charges but not including breakfast:
Ⓛ under L100,000
ⓁⓁ L100–200,000
ⓁⓁⓁ L200–300,000
ⓁⓁⓁⓁ L300–400,000
ⓁⓁⓁⓁⓁ over L400,000.

RESTAURANT
A restaurant within the hotel sometimes reserved for residents.
SWIMMING POOL
Hotel swimming pools are usually quite small and are outdoors unless otherwise stated.
GARDEN OR TERRACE
A garden, courtyard, or terrace belonging to the hotel, often providing tables for eating outside.
CREDIT CARDS
The major credit cards VISA, MasterCard (Access), and American Express are accepted in hotels with the credit card symbol.

		NUMBER OF ROOMS	RESTAURANT	SWIMMING POOL	GARDEN OR TERRACE
VIA VENETO: *Excelsior* ⓁⓁⓁⓁ Via Veneto 125, 00187. **Map** 3 C1. **(** 06 47 081. **FAX** 06 482 62 05. This extravagant hotel has sumptuous public rooms with marble floors and brocade furnishings. Bedrooms are elegant and spacious. 📷 TV 🍴 💳 P		321	■		
VILLA BORGHESE: *Villa Borghese* ⓁⓁⓁ Via Pinciana 31, 00198. **(** 06 854 96 48. **FAX** 06 841 41 00. **@** hotel.villaborghese@quipo.it This pleasant hotel has the atmosphere of a private home rather than a hotel. Rooms are small but comfortable and are tastefully decorated. 📷 TV 🍴 💳 P		31			■
VILLA BORGHESE: *Lord Byron* ⓁⓁⓁⓁ Via Notaris 5, 00197. **(** 06 322 04 04. **FAX** 06 322 04 05. **@** info@lordbyronhotel.com A small, refined hotel housed in a former stately house in the Parioli district, the Lord Byron has lavishly decorated public rooms. 📷 TV 🍴 💳		37	■		■

LAZIO

	NUMBER OF ROOMS	RESTAURANT	SWIMMING POOL	GARDEN OR TERRACE
ANAGNI: *Villa La Floridiana* ⓁⓁⓁ Via Casilina, km 63,700, 03012. **(** 0775 76 99 60. **FAX** 0775 77 45 27. **@** floridiana@applicazioni.it A beautiful medieval village is the setting for this charming villa with a traditional faded pink façade, green shutters, and large, comfortable rooms. 📷 TV 🍴 💳 P	9	■		■
BAGNI DI TIVOLI: *Grand Hotel Duca d'Este* ⓁⓁⓁ Via Tiburtina Valeria 330, 00011. **(** 0774 3883. **FAX** 0774 38 81 01. **@** ducadeste@ducadeste.com A modern well-equipped hotel near Tivoli and Villa Adriana and within easy reach of Rome by road or rail. Suites have satellite TV and jacuzzis. 📷 TV 🍴 💳 P	184	■	●	■
FORMIA: *Castello Miramare* ⓁⓁ Via Balze di Pagnano, 04023. **(** 0771 70 01 38. **FAX** 0771 70 01 39. **@** info@hotelcastellomiramare.it The castle was built in 1910 on a hill in the center of Formia with fine views over the sea. Spacious bedrooms are decorated in Spanish style. 📷 TV 🍴 💳 P	10	■		■
GROTTAFERRATA: *Villa Fiorio* ⓁⓁⓁ Viale Dusmet 25, 00046. **(** 06 94 54 80 07. **FAX** 06 94 54 80 09. **@** villafiorio@tin.it Built as a summer residence at the turn of the century, this pretty villa, which retains some original frescoes, has large, cool, quiet rooms. 📷 TV 🍴 💳 P	24	■	●	■
ISOLA DI PONZA: *Cernia* ⓁⓁⓁ Via Panoramica, Chiaia di Luna 04027. **(** 0771 804 12. **FAX** 0771 80 99 54. **@** pagreca@tin.it A beautiful setting for this modern but stylish hotel with a dense garden. Wicker furniture and rocking chairs create a friendly atmosphere. 📷 TV 🍴 💳 P	50	■	●	■
LADISPOLI: *La Posta Vecchia* ⓁⓁⓁⓁⓁ Località Palo Laziale, 00055. **(** 06 994 95 01. **FAX** 06 994 95 07. **@** postavecchia@caerenet.it A magnificent 17th-century villa on the sea, it was restored by John Paul Getty as his Italian residence and is now one of Italy's most luxurious hotels. All rooms are exquisitely and individually decorated with antiques. 📷 TV 🍴 💳 P	17	■	●	■
PALESTRINA: *Stella* Ⓛ Piazzale della Liberazione 3, 00036. **(** 06 953 81 72. **FAX** 06 957 33 60. **@** info@hotelstella.it A friendly, peaceful hotel in the historic center of Palestrina close to the town's sights and with an excellent restaurant. 📷 TV 🍴 💳 P	28	■		
SABAUDIA: *Oasi di Kufra* ⓁⓁ Via Lungomare, 04016. **(** 0773 515 775. **FAX** 0773 51 55 98. **@** oasikufra@tin.it Luminous hotel lying amid sandy dunes. With its own private beach it offers a host of sports and balconies in most rooms overlooking the sea. 📷 TV 🍴 💳 P	105	■		■
SAN FELICE CIRCEO: *Punta Rossa* ⓁⓁⓁ Via delle Batterie 37, 04017. **(** 0773 54 80 85. **FAX** 0773 54 80 75. **@** punta_rossa@iol.it A charming hotel set in a garden that leads down to the sea. Rooms are in various buildings, all have terraces and sea views, and there is a covered salt-water swimming pool as well as a second pool by the sea. 📷 TV 🍴 💳 P	33	■	●	■

SUBIACO: *Livata*   Ⓛ   84
Località Monte Livata, 00028. 0774 82 60 31. FAX 0774 82 60 33.
A good choice if you're visiting the monastery of San Benedetto, the Livata is a friendly country hotel with tennis courts and attractive gardens.

TARQUINIA LIDO: *La Torraccia*   ⓁⓁ   18
Viale Mediterraneo 45, 01010. 0766 86 43 75. FAX 0766 86 42 96. @ torraccia@tin.it
A modern, comfortable hotel set in pinewoods 200 m (656 ft) from the sea. All rooms have a terrace and there is a private beach.

VITERBO: *Balletti Park*   ⓁⓁ   136
Via Umbria 2, San Martino al Cimino 01030. 0761 37 71. FAX 0761 37 94 96. @ info@balletti.it
A modern hotel set in its own extensive gardens. There are sports facilities and a health center as well as some independent apartments.

VITERBO: *Balletti Palace*   ⓁⓁ   105
Via Molini 8, 01100. 0761 34 47 77. FAX 0761 34 50 60.
A modern hotel set in Viterbo's historic center with elegant bedrooms and suites. There is no restaurant, but the Grenier Café serves light meals.

NAPLES AND CAMPANIA

AMALFI: *Marina Riviera*   ⓁⓁ   22
Via P Comite 33, 84011. 089 87 11 04. FAX 089 87 10 24.
This mediterranean-style seaside hotel offers simple, tasteful rooms, and an attractive patio overlooking the beach for leisurely breakfasts.

AMALFI: *Luna Convento*   ⓁⓁⓁ   40
Via Comite 33, 84011. 089 87 10 02. FAX 089 87 13 33.
This tastefully furnished 13th-century monastery overlooking the sea makes a luxurious, peaceful base from which to explore the countryside.

AMALFI: *Santa Caterina*   ⓁⓁⓁⓁ   66
Via SS Amalfitana 9, 84011. 089 87 10 12. FAX 089 87 13 51. @ info@hotelsantacaterina.it
This is a luxurious property set amid lemon groves. Two elevators can whisk you from the spectacular suites to the private beach in seconds. Enjoy the ocean view from the hotels terraces or the high tech gym.

BAIA DOMIZIA: *Hotel della Baia*   ⓁⓁ   56
Via dell'Erica, 81030. 0823 72 13 44. FAX 0823 72 15 56.
A charming, friendly hotel run by three sisters with its own private beach. The pretty bedrooms are comfortable and all have sea views.

BENEVENTO: *Grand Hotel Italiano*   ⓁⓁ   71
Viale Principe di Napoli 137, 82100. 0824 241 11. FAX 0824 217 58.
The Italiano family are justly proud of the hotel's reputation for courtesy and good service. Public areas are spacious and elegant.

CAPRI: *Villa Sarah*   ⓁⓁ   20
Via Tiberio 3a, 80073. 081 837 78 17. FAX 081 837 72 15. @ info@villasarah.it
A peaceful family-run villa hotel set among the island's vineyards. Rooms are clean and pretty, and home produce is served for breakfast.

CAPRI: *Punta Tragara*   ⓁⓁⓁⓁ   45
Via Tragara 57, 80073. 081 837 08 44. FAX 081 837 77 90. @ hotel.tragara@capri.it
A sumptuous hotel built into a cliff over the sea, designed by Le Corbusier, with all the comforts of a luxury residence. No children under 12.

CASERTA: *Europa*   ⓁⓁ   60
Via Roma 29, 81100. 0823 32 54 00. FAX 0823 32 54 11. @ hotel.europa@tin.it
A smart modern hotel conveniently placed in central Caserta. The Europa also has several miniapartments with cooking facilities for longer stays.

ISCHIA: *Pensione Il Monastero*   Ⓛ   20
Castello Aragonese 3, Ischia Ponte 80070. 081 99 24 35.
A charming, simple pensione set in a converted monastery overlooking the town of Ischia. The walls are hung with paintings, and furniture is plain but attractive. Guests are expected to use MAP in summer.

ISCHIA: *La Villarosa*   ⓁⓁ   37
Via Giacinto Gigante 5, Porto d'Ischia 80070. 081 99 13 16. FAX 081 99 24 25.
An enchanting, elegant hotel set in a beautiful tropical garden. Many of the discreetly charming rooms have balconies filled with luxuriant bougainvilleas.

<table>
<tr><td colspan="2">

Price categories for a standard double room for one night, including tax and service charges but not including breakfast:
Ⓛ under L100,000
ⓁⓁ L100–200,000
ⓁⓁⓁ L200–300,000
ⓁⓁⓁⓁ L300–400,000
ⓁⓁⓁⓁⓁ over L400,000.

RESTAURANT
A restaurant within the hotel sometimes reserved for residents.
SWIMMING POOL
Hotel swimming pools are usually quite small and are outdoors unless otherwise stated.
GARDEN OR TERRACE
A garden, courtyard, or terrace belonging to the hotel, often providing tables for eating outside.
CREDIT CARDS
The major credit cards VISA, MasterCard (Access), and American Express are accepted in hotels with the credit card symbol.

</td></tr>
</table>

	NUMBER OF ROOMS	RESTAURANT	SWIMMING POOL	GARDEN OR TERRACE
NAPLES: *Britannique* ⓁⓁ Corso Vittorio Emanuele 133, 80121. 📞 *081 761 41 45.* FAX *081 66 04 57.* A smart, modern hotel in the center of Naples. Bedrooms are attractively decorated, and there are spectacular views from the roof terrace. Some suites with cooking facilities are available for longer stays. 🛏 TV ▤ 🗭 **P**	86	▦		▦
NAPLES: *Rex* ⓁⓁ Via Palepoli 12, 80132. 📞 *081 764 93 89.* FAX *081 764 92 27.* A friendly, family hotel on the seafront of Naples, well placed for theaters and beaches. Public rooms are elegantly furnished with wicker chairs. 🛏 TV ▤ 🗭	35			
NAPLES: *Grand Hotel Parker's* ⓁⓁⓁ Corso Vittorio Emanuele 135, 80121. 📞 *081 761 24 74.* FAX *081 66 35 27.* @ ghparker@tin.it This elegant and intimate hotel is beautifully furnished in different styles, from Louis XVI to Empire. From the excellent rooftop restaurant, clients enjoy a sweeping view of the bay. 🛏 TV ▤ 🗭 **P**	80	▦	●	▦
NAPLES: *Grande Albergo Vesuvio* ⓁⓁⓁⓁ Via Partenope 45, 80121. 📞 *081 764 00 44.* FAX *081 764 44 83.* @ info@vesuvio.it Founded in 1882, the Grande Hotel overlooks the marina in central Naples. It is well decorated and furnished with marble bathrooms and antiques, and includes a "baby" room with a rocking horse, mobiles, and toys. 🛏 TV ▤ 🗭 **P**	163	▦		▦
PAESTUM: *Le Palme* Ⓛ Via Sterpinia 33, 84063. 📞 *0828 85 10 25.* FAX *0828 85 15 07.* This pleasant, peaceful seaside hotel is set in attractive grounds with tennis courts and its own beach. Rooms are comfortable. 🛏 TV ▤ 🗭 **P**	72	▦	●	▦
POSITANO: *L'Ancora* ⓁⓁ Via Colombo 36, 84017. 📞 *089 87 53 18.* FAX *089 81 17 84.* Excellent value in expensive Positano from this modern, central hotel with sea views. The good-sized bedrooms are comfortable. 🛏 TV ▤ 🗭 **P**	16			▦
POSITANO: *Palazzo Murat* ⓁⓁⓁⓁ Via dei Mulini 23, 84017. 📞 *089 87 51 77.* FAX *089 81 14 19.* @ hpm@starnet.it A pretty 18th-century palazzo in central Positano, near the cathedral. Rooms have traditional wooden furniture, and some have balconies. 🛏 TV ▤ 🗭	30	▦		▦
RAVELLO: *Graal* ⓁⓁ Via della Repubblica 8, 84010. 📞 *089 85 72 22.* FAX *089 85 75 51.* @ info@hotelgraal.it The hotel has a wonderful swimming pool with attractive views over Ravello. The restaurant serves good local specialties. 🛏 ▤ TV 🗭 **P**	36	▦	●	▦
RAVELLO: *Palumbo* ⓁⓁⓁⓁⓁ Via San Giovanni del Toro 16, 84010. 📞 *089 85 72 44.* FAX *089 85 81 33.* @ palumbo@amalfinet.it This 12th-century palazzo has been run as a hotel by the same family for more than 100 years. Furnishings are elegant, and there are antiques in some bedrooms. Rooms in the modern annex are cheaper. 🛏 TV ▤ 🗭 **P**	18	▦		▦
SALERNO: *Fiorenza* ⓁⓁ Via Trento 145, 84131. 📞 *089 33 88 00.* FAX *089 33 88 00.* @ fiorealb@tin.it A 1960s hotel overlooking the sea on the outskirts of Salerno. All the rooms are modern and have private safes, minibars, and satellite TV. 🛏 TV ▤ 🗭 **P**	30			
SAPRI: *Tirreno* Ⓛ Corso Italia 73, 84073. 📞 *0973 39 10 06.* FAX *0973 39 11 57.* A good value pensione facing the sea. Inside it is airy and light, and bedrooms have their own balconies. The restaurant serves local specialties. 🛏 TV 🗭 **P**	44	▦		▦
SAPRI: *Mediterraneo* ⓁⓁ Via Verdi, 84073. 📞 *0973 39 17 74.* FAX *0973 39 11 57.* @ htlmediterraneo@tiscalinet.it Excellent value at this comfortable, no frills hotel built right next to the rocky beach with garden and terrace overlooking the sea. 🛏 TV 🗭 **P**	20	▦		▦

SORRENTO: *Bellevue Syrene*　　　　　　　　　　Ⓛ Ⓛ | 73
Piazza della Vittoria 5, 80067. 【 *081 878 10 24.* FAX *081 878 39 63.* @ bellevue@sorrentopalace.it
A typical grand beach hotel, now slightly faded. It is perched on the cliffs with an
elevator to take guests to the private beach. Sumptuous bedrooms. 🛏 TV 🍽 🛥 P

SORRENTO: *Grand Hotel Cocumella*　　　　　Ⓛ Ⓛ Ⓛ Ⓛ | 50
Via Cocumella 7, 80065. 【 *081 878 29 33.* FAX *081 878 37 12.* @ hcocum@tin.it
Opulent elegance from another era characterizes this peaceful hotel on the
Amalfi coast set in fragrant and peaceful gardens. The sea is nearby, and the
hotel sailing boat will take guests to Capri for the day. 🛏 TV 🍽 🛥 P

ABRUZZO, MOLISE AND PUGLIA

ALBEROBELLO: *Colle del Sole*　　　　　　　　　　　Ⓛ | 37
Via Indipendenza 63, 70011. 【 *080 432 18 14.* FAX *080 432 13 70.* @ colledelsol@libero.it
A comfortable, modern hotel with a balcony for every bedroom. Art and
photo exhibitions are sometimes arranged in the restaurant. 🛏 TV 🛥 P

ALBEROBELLO: *Dei Trulli*　　　　　　　　　　Ⓛ Ⓛ Ⓛ | 19
Via Cadore 32, 70011. 【 *080 432 35 55.* FAX *080 432 35 60.* @ htrulli@inmedia.it
The hotel is set in a minivillage of *Trulli (see p495).* Furnishings are simple,
even stark, but the grounds are pleasant. MAP in summer. 🛏 TV 🍽 🛥 P

BARI: *Boston*　　　　　　　　　　　　　　　　Ⓛ Ⓛ | 70
Via Piccinni 155, 70122. 【 *080 521 66 33.* FAX *080 524 68 02.* @ boston@inmedia.it
A modern hotel near the historic center of Bari. Furnishings are stylish and
functional, and there is much dark wood paneling. MAP. 🛏 TV 🍽 🛥 P

BARI: *Palace Hotel*　　　　　　　　　　　　Ⓛ Ⓛ Ⓛ | 197
Via Lombardi 13, 70122. 【 *080 521 65 51.* FAX *080 521 14 99.* @ palaceh@tin.it
With rooms that cater to most specialized needs, this hotel provides excellent service.
The delicious buffet breakfast also has something for everyone. 🛏 TV 🍽 🛥 P

GARGANO PENINSULA: *Seggio*　　　　　　　　　　Ⓛ | 30
Via Vesta 7, Vieste 71019. 【 *0884 70 81 23.* FAX *0884 70 87 27.* @ hotel.seggio@tiscalinet.it
Perched on a small cliff over its own private bay, this restored 17th-century
building was the original town hall. Bedrooms are simple. 🛏 TV 🍽 🛥 P

ISOLE TREMITI: *Kyrie*　　　　　　　　　　　Ⓛ Ⓛ Ⓛ | 27
San Domino, 71040. 【 *0882 46 32 41.* FAX *0882 46 34 15.*
The largest and best-equipped of the Tremiti hotels. It is in the pinewoods
next to the sea. Open from June to September only. 🛏 TV 🍽 🛥

L'AQUILA: *Amiternum*　　　　　　　　　　　　　　Ⓛ | 60
Bivio Sant'Antonio 67100. 【 *0862 31 57 57.* FAX *0862 31 59 87.* @ hotel.amiternum@worldtel.it
Comfortable hotel in a pretty location near the heart of the city.
🛏 TV 🛥 P

L'AQUILA: *Grand Hotel e del Parco*　　　　　　　Ⓛ Ⓛ | 42
Corso Federico II 74, 67100. 【 *0862 41 32 48.* FAX *0862 659 38.*
A comfortable, modern hotel in the center of L'Aquila, within easy reach
of the ski slopes and hiking trails of the Gran Sasso. The hotel also has a
health center, complete with saunas and Turkish baths. 🛏 TV 🛥 P

LECCE: *Grand Hotel*　　　　　　　　　　　　　　Ⓛ | 70
Viale Oronzo Quarta 28, 73100. 【 *0832 30 94 05.* FAX *0832 30 98 91.*
This Art Nouveau villa was converted into an elegant hotel in the 1930s.
Although some of the rooms are rather shabby, it is still charming. 🛏 TV 🛥 P

LECCE: *Hotel President*　　　　　　　　　　　Ⓛ Ⓛ | 150
Via Salandra No 6. 【 *0832 31 18 81.* FAX *0832 37 22 83.*
Large and modern hotel with a good reputation and good service.
The excellent restaurant has a well-stocked wine cellar. 🛏 TV 🍽 🛥 P

MARINA DI LESINA: *Maddalena Hotel*　　　　　　　Ⓛ | 80
Via Saturno 82, 71010. 【 *0882 99 50 76.* FAX *0882 999 54 34.*
A modern beach hotel with a range of sports and leisure facilities, including
a private beach. The restaurant serves a variety of local fish dishes. 🛏 TV 🛥 P

MONOPOLI: *Il Melograno*　　　　　　　　　　Ⓛ Ⓛ Ⓛ | 37
Contrada Torricella 345, 70043. 【 *080 690 90 30.* FAX *080 74 79 08.* @ melograno@melograno.com
A luxurious oasis of tranquillity in a peaceful, verdant corner of Puglia.
The sumptuous interior of this restored 16th-century residence is furnished
with antiques; there are tennis courts and a private beach. 🛏 TV 🍽 🛥 P

Price categories for a standard double room for one night, including tax and service charges but not including breakfast: (L) under L100,000 (L)(L) L100–200,000 (L)(L)(L) L200–300,000 (L)(L)(L)(L) L300–400,000 (L)(L)(L)(L)(L) over L400,000.	**RESTAURANT** A restaurant within the hotel sometimes reserved for residents. **SWIMMING POOL** Hotel swimming pools are usually quite small and are outdoors unless otherwise stated. **GARDEN OR TERRACE** A garden, courtyard, or terrace belonging to the hotel, often providing tables for eating outside. **CREDIT CARDS** The major credit cards VISA, MasterCard (Access), and American Express are accepted in hotels with the credit card symbol.	**NUMBER OF ROOMS**	**RESTAURANT**	**SWIMMING POOL**	**GARDEN OR TERRACE**

RUVO DI PUGLIA: *Talos* Via Rodolfo Morandi 12, 70037. [080 361 16 45. FAX 080 361 16 45. A simple, modern hotel that is good value for travelers on a budget. It is well placed for exploring the surrounding countryside. 🔧 📺 ▤ 🅲 🅿	(L)	25	▦		▦
SCANNO: *Mille Pini* Via Pescara 2, 67038. [0864 74 72 64. FAX 0864 74 98 18. A friendly, budget chalet hotel at the foot of Monte Rotondo chairlift. Facilities are simple and rustic but comfortable, and there is a restaurant. 🔧 🅿	(L)	22	▦		▦
SULMONA: *Italia* Piazza Salvatore Tommasi 3, 67039. [0864 523 08. FAX 0864 523 08. A charming ivy-covered town house in a quiet square. Furnishings vary from modern utility to antique, giving a lived-in feeling to this friendly hotel. 🔧 📺	(L)	27			
TARANTO: *Plaza* Via d'Aquino 46, 74100. [099 459 07 75. FAX 099 459 06 75. A big, city hotel that is very well placed in the newer part of Taranto near the major sights. Both business and vacation guests are welcome. 🔧 📺 ▤ 🅲 🅿	(L)(L)	112	▦		

BASILICATA AND CALABRIA

COSENZA: *Royal* Via Molinella 24e, 87100. [0984 41 21 65. FAX 0984 41 17 77. @ royalhot@tin.it One of the best modern hotels in Cosenza, conveniently located in the center of town, not far from the station. 🔧 📺 ▤ 🅲 🅿	(L)	44	▦		▦
MARATEA: *Romantik Hotel, Villa Cheta Elite* Strada Statale 18, 85046. [0973 87 81 34. FAX 0973 87 81 35. An elegant, Liberty-style villa with stunning views over a picturesque bay. The comfortable rooms are attractively furnished in traditional southern Italian style; staff and service are friendly and polite. 🔧 📺 ▤ 🅲 🅿	(L)(L)	17	▦		▦
MATERA: *De Nicola* Via Nazionale 158, 75100. [0835 38 51 11. FAX 0835 38 51 13. @ hotelden@tin.it A large modern hotel in central Matera close to the station and easily accessible from the highway. Bedrooms are functional. 🔧 📺 ▤ 🅲 🅿	(L)(L)	104	▦		▦
METAPONTO LIDO: *Turismo* Viale delle Ninfe 5, 75010. [0835 74 19 18. FAX 0835 74 19 17. A functional, if unexceptional, seaside hotel with its own beach and bar. The restaurant has outside tables for summer dining. 🔧 ▤ 🅲 🅿	(L)	60	▦		▦
PARGHELIA: *Baia Paraelios* Località Fornaci, 88035 (nr Tropea). [0963 60 03 00. FAX 0963 60 00 74. A little village of 72 bungalows, each with terrace and sitting room, with superb views over the beach and sea. The restaurant is on a beach terrace. 🔧 🅲 🅿	(L)(L)(L)	87	▦	●	▦
REGGIO DI CALABRIA: *Grand Hotel Excelsior* Via Vittorio Veneto 66, 89100. [0965 81 22 11. FAX 0965 89 30 84. This hotel has some of the best facilities in southern Italy. Situated in the center of town, it appeals to business as well as vacation guests. 🔧 📺 ▤ 🅲 🅿	(L)(L)	84	▦		▦
ROSSANO SCALO: *Murano* Viale Mediterraneo 2, 87068. [0983 51 17 88. FAX 0983 53 00 88. Set in its own grounds over the sea, the Murano has a private beach and rooms with sea views. There is a piano bar and an outside pizzeria as well as a traditional restaurant serving Calabrian specialties. 🔧 📺 🅲 🅿	(L)	37	▦		▦
STILO: *San Giorgio* Via R Citarelli 1, 89049. [0964 77 50 47. FAX 0964 77 50 47. Set in the heart of Stilo, this comfortable hotel is located in a restored 17th-century palazzo and furnished with some 18th-century antiques. 🔧 📺 🅲 🅿	(L)	15	▦	●	▦

TROPEA: *La Pineta*　　　　　　　　　　　　　　　　　　　ⓁⓁ | 43
Via Marina 150, 89861. **☎** *0963 617 77.* **FAX** *0963 622 65.*
This typical resort hotel is open only from June to September. The decor
is fairly ordinary but La Pineta does have tennis courts. 🛏 ▤ 🛋 **P**

VENOSA: *Il Guiscardo*　　　　　　　　　　　　　　　　　　　　Ⓛ | 35
Via Accademia dei Rinascenti 106, 85029. **☎** *0972 32 362.* **FAX** *0972 32 916.*
There are wonderful views from the terrace over the red roofs of Venosa's
historic center. Bedrooms are elegant and public rooms spacious. 🛏 📺 ▤ 🛋 **P**

SICILY

ACIREALE: *Excelsior Palace*　　　　　　　　　　　　　　　　ⓁⓁ | 230
Via delle Terme 103, 95024. **☎** *095 604 444.* **FAX** *095 605 441.*
Well placed for visiting the sights of east Sicily and close to the Santa Venera Spa,
this hotel set in a 19th-century building offers all modern comforts. 🛏 📺 ▤ 🛋 **P**

AGRIGENTO: *Colleverde Park Hotel*　　　　　　　　　　　ⓁⓁ | 48
Via dei Templi, 92100. **☎** *0922 295 55.* **FAX** *0922 290 12.* **@** hotcolle@iol.it
A peaceful modern hotel in the Valley of the Temples, with stunning views.
The facilities include safes in the bedrooms and a gym. 🛏 📺 ▤ 🛋 **P**

AGRIGENTO: *Grand Hotel dei Templi*　　　　　　　　　　ⓁⓁ | 146
Viale L Sciascia, Villaggio Mose 92100. **☎** *0922 61 01 75.* **FAX** *0922 60 66 85.*
One of the modern, efficient Jolly chain, this large, well-equipped hotel lies
just outside Agrigento. Rooms are comfortably furnished. 🛏 📺 ▤ 🛋 **P**

AGRIGENTO: *Villa Athena*　　　　　　　　　　　　　　　Ⓛ Ⓛ Ⓛ | 40
Via Panoramica dei Templi 33, 92100. **☎** *0922 59 62 88.* **FAX** *0922 40 21 80.*
Set in an 18th-century villa just outside Agrigento. The decor is modern but
the gardens are exquisite, with views of the Temple of Concord. 🛏 📺 ▤ 🛋 **P**

CATANIA: *Nettuno*　　　　　　　　　　　　　　　　　　　ⓁⓁ | 80
Viale Ruggero di Lauria 121, 95127. **☎** *095 712 52 52.* **FAX** *095 49 80 66.*
A well-equipped, modern hotel in a quiet location. The Nettuno overlooks
the sea and has a breakfast terrace above the outdoor swimming pool.
The comfortable rooms also have balconies. 🛏 📺 ▤ 🛋 **P**

CEFALÙ: *Riva del Sole*　　　　　　　　　　　　　　　　　ⓁⓁ | 28
Viale Lungomare Cefalù 25, 90015. **☎** *0921 421 12 30.* **FAX** *0921 42 19 84.*
A hotel on the seafront with good panoramic views. Bedrooms are on the
basic side but there is a terrace for sunbathing and a shadier internal courtyard
with tables. 🛏 📺 ▤ 🛋 **P**

ISOLE EGADI: *Egadi Favignana*　　　　　　　　　　　　　　　Ⓛ | 12
Via Colombo 17, Favignana 91023. **☎** *0923 92 12 32.* **FAX** *0923 92 12 32.*
A small, friendly pensione attached to one of the best restaurants on the island.
Favignana is famous for its tuna, which comes from the local fisheries. 🛏 📺 ▤ 🛋

ISOLE EOLIE: *Pensione Villa Diana*　　　　　　　　　　　　　Ⓛ | 12
Via Diana Tufo, Lipari 98055. **☎** *090 981 14 03.* **FAX** *090 981 14 03.*
A comfortable family hotel with antiques in some rooms, and spacious
gardens and terraces. The hotel is open from April to October. 🛏 🛋 **P**

ISOLE EOLIE: *La Sciara Residence*　　　　　　　　　　　　ⓁⓁ | 62
Via Soldato Cincotta, Isola Stromboli 98050. **☎** *090 98 60 05.* **FAX** *090 98 62 84.*
A splendid garden full of bougainvilleas is the setting for this spacious
and comfortable hotel. Mini efficiencies are also available. 🛏 📺 🛋

ISOLE EOLIE: *Raya*　　　　　　　　　　　　　Ⓛ Ⓛ Ⓛ Ⓛ | 36
Via San Pietro, Isola Panarea 98050. **☎** *090 98 30 13.* **FAX** *090 98 31 03.* **@** htlraya@netnet.it
This modern, fashionable hotel consists of pink and white houses on terraces
descending to the sea. The restaurant and bar overlook the port. 🛏 🛋

ERICE: *Moderno*　　　　　　　　　　　　　　　　　　　ⓁⓁ | 41
Via Vittorio Emanuele 63, 91016. **☎** *0923 86 93 00.* **FAX** *0923 86 91 39.*
A family-run hotel that has some attractively old-fashioned bedrooms as well
as some more modern ones. Excellent views from the terrace. 🛏 📺 🛋

ERICE: *Elimo*　　　　　　　　　　　　　　　　　　Ⓛ Ⓛ Ⓛ | 21
Via Vittorio Emanuele 75, 91016. **☎** *0923 86 93 77.* **FAX** *0923 86 92 52.* **@** elimoh@comeg.it
This 18th-century villa retains several original features including traditional
Sicilian wall, ceiling, and floor tiles. The hotel is located in the center of
Erice and has spectacular views as far as the Egadi Islands. 🛏 📺 ▤ 🛋 **P**

For key to symbols see back flap

<table>
<tr><td colspan="2">

Price categories for a standard double room for one night, including tax and service charges but not including breakfast:
Ⓛ under L100,000
ⓁⓁ L100 – 200,000
ⓁⓁⓁ L200 – 300,000
ⓁⓁⓁⓁ L300 – 400,000
ⓁⓁⓁⓁⓁ over L400,000.

RESTAURANT
A restaurant within the hotel sometimes reserved for residents.
SWIMMING POOL
Hotel swimming pools are usually quite small and are outdoors unless otherwise stated.
GARDEN OR TERRACE
A garden, courtyard, or terrace belonging to the hotel, often providing tables for eating outside.
CREDIT CARDS
The major credit cards VISA, MasterCard (Access), and American Express are accepted in hotels with the credit card symbol.

</td></tr>
</table>

	NUMBER OF ROOMS	RESTAURANT	SWIMMING POOL	GARDEN OR TERRACE
GIARDINI-NAXOS: *Arathena Rocks* ⓁⓁ Via Calcide Eubea 55, 98035. 0942 513 49. FAX 0942 516 90. A friendly hotel near the beach and slightly out of this busy resort. Rooms are bright and airy with sea or garden views. Half board required.	49	■	●	■
MARSALA: *President* ⓁⓁ Via Nino Bixio 1, 91025. 0923 99 93 33. FAX 0923 99 91 15. About 1 km (half a mile) from the center of town this modern, comfortable hotel serves Sicilian and international cuisine in the restaurant.	128	■	●	■
MESSINA: *Paradis* ⓁⓁ Via Consolare Pompea 441, 98168. 090 31 06 82. FAX 090 31 20 43. About 3 km (2 miles) out of central Messina, the Paradis has good views and an excellent restaurant. Rooms are basic but satisfactory.	88	■		
PALERMO: *San Paolo Palace* ⓁⓁ Via Messina Marine 91. 091 621 11 12. FAX 091 621 53 00. @ hotel@sanpaolopalace.it This large, modern building overlooking the bay offers a complete range of services: roof terrace with swimming pool, panoramic restaurant, piano bar, spacious gym, and sauna.	284	■	●	■
PALERMO: *Splendid Hotel La Torre* ⓁⓁ Via Piano Gallo 11, Mondello 90151. 091 45 02 22. FAX 09145 00 33. @ latorre@latorre.com A big, traditional seaside hotel, set on a promontory with its own private beach. Some bedrooms have their own balcony with sea views.	179	■	●	■
PALERMO: *Grand Hotel Villa Igiea* ⓁⓁⓁ Salita Belmonte 43, 90142. 091 54 37 44. FAX 091 54 76 54. @ villa-igea@thi.it An exquisite hotel dating from the beginning of the century with Art Nouveau stained glass and wall paintings. It's set by the sea in gardens with their own ancient ruins. An elegant cocktail bar opens onto the terrace.	114	■	●	■
SCIACCA: *Grand Hotel delle Terme* ⓁⓁ Viale Nuove Terme 1, 92019. 0925 231 33. FAX 0925 87002. @ ghterme@sc.trinakria.it A spa hotel with access (for an extra charge) to the local mineral springs that were used by the Phoenicians more than 2,000 years ago. Many of the clientele come for various treatments and cures.	77	■	●	■
SIRACUSA: *Gran Bretagna* Ⓛ Via Savoia 21, 96100. 0931 687 65. FAX 0931 687 65. A small, friendly, family-run hotel with comfortable rooms. The restaurant has special family menus and serves Sicilian and Italian specialties.	12			
SIRACUSA: *Grand Hotel Villa Politi* ⓁⓁ Via Maria Politi Laudien 2, 96100. 0931 41 21 21. FAX 0931 360 61. A slightly shabby old-fashioned hotel whose vast reception rooms belong to another era. The hotel dates from the turn of the century.	100	■	●	■
SIRACUSA: *Villa Lucia* ⓁⓁ Trav. Mondello 1, 1 Contrada Isola, 96100. 0931 72 10 07. FAX 0931 72 15 87. This beautiful villa, situated in the middle of a mediterranean park close to the sea, offers a relaxing stay in pretty surroundings.	14		●	■
TAORMINA: *Villa Belvedere* ⓁⓁ Via Bagnoli Croci 79, 98039. 0942 237 91. FAX 0942 62 58 30. @ info@villabelvedere.it A very comfortable, family hotel in the center of Taormina. Some rooms have sea views and balconies. Light meals are served by the pool.	47	■	●	■
TAORMINA: *Romantik Villa Ducale* ⓁⓁⓁ Via Leonardo da Vinci 60, 98039. 0942 281 53. FAX 0942 287 10 This elegant villa is now a comfortable hotel. The rooms are all different, furnished with antiques and with excellent views of Etna and the sea. The library has books on the region for guests to browse through.	15			■

TAORMINA: *Timeo*   ⓁⓁⓁ   56
Via Teatro Greco 59, 98039. 【 094 22 38 01. FAX 094 262 85 01. @ framon@framon-hotels.com
Since 1884 this exclusive villa has attracted such guests as Marconi, Gide and de
Maupassant. All guests can enjoy a complimentary afternoon tea. 🔲 TV 🗒 ✉ P

TAORMINA: *San Domenico Palace*   ⓁⓁⓁⓁ   111
Piazza San Domenico 5, 98039. 【 0942 237 01. FAX 0942 62 55 06.
A peaceful, 15th-century monastery restored and furnished with genuine
antiques. This is one of the most luxurious hotels in Sicily, and it has a
beautiful formal garden as well as an elegant swimming pool. 🔲 TV 🗒 ✉ P

TRAPANI: *Vittoria*   Ⓛ   65
Via Francesco Crispi 4, 91100. 【 0923 87 30 44. FAX 0923 298 70.
Very conveniently placed in the center of Trapani, this modern functional
hotel has very simple, well-designed furnishings. 🔲 TV 🗒 ✉

TRAPANI: *Astoria Park*   ⓁⓁ   91
Lungomare Dante Alighieri, 91100. 【 0923 56 24 00. FAX 0923 56 74 22.
A modern hotel on the seafront with all you need for a beach vacation (tennis,
discotheque). A good base from which to explore the region. 🔲 TV 🗒 ✉ P

SARDINIA

ALGHERO: *Villa las Tronas*   ⓁⓁ   29
Lungomare Valencia 1, 07041. 【 079 98 18 18. FAX 079 98 10 44.
A mustard-colored villa on a promontory is the setting for this comfortable,
elegantly decorated hotel. Public rooms are full of gilt and 18th-century
French-style furniture; bedrooms are simpler but pretty. 🔲 TV 🗒 ✉ P

CAGLIARI: *Italia*   Ⓛ   113
Via Sardegna 31, 09124. 【 070 66 05 10. FAX 070 65 02 40.
Housed in two much-restored palazzi in central Cagliari, this slightly shabby
hotel is a convenient base from which to explore the countryside. 🔲 TV 🗒 ✉

CAGLIARI: *Sardegna*   ⓁⓁ   90
Via Lunigiana 50, 09122. 【 070 28 62 45. FAX 070 29 04 69.
A modern hotel close to the town center and 2 km (1 mile) from the
airport. The rooms are comfortably but simply decorated. 🔲 TV 🗒 ✉ P

ISOLA DI SAN PIETRO: *Hotel Paola e Primo Maggio*   Ⓛ   20
Tacca Rossa, Carloforte 09014. 【 0781 85 00 98. FAX 0781 85 01 04.
A modern pensione overlooking the sea with lovely views and charging
very reasonable prices. There is a shady terrace for outside dining. 🔲 ✉ P

NUORO: *Grazia Deledda*   Ⓛ   72
Via Lamarmora 175, 08100. 【 0784 312 57. FAX 0784 312 58.
A well-equipped modern hotel in a central location with an American-style
bar. The restaurant serves Sardinian and Italian specialties. 🔲 TV 🗒 ✉ P

OLIENA: *Su Gologone*   ⓁⓁⓁ   68
Località Su Gologone, 08025. 【 0784 28 75 12. FAX 0784 28 75 52.
A rambling villa in the mountainous Barbagia region is the setting for this
delightfully peaceful hotel, which offers a good range of sports. 🔲 TV 🗒 ✉ P

PORTO CERVO: *Balocco*   ⓁⓁⓁ   35
Località Liscia di Vacca, 07020. 【 0789 915 55. FAX 0789 915 10.
An attractive, airy hotel surrounded by palm-filled grounds and terraces for
every room. It offers comparatively good value for the fashionable Costa
Smeralda, but beware: prices double for the summer season. 🔲 TV 🗒 ✉ P

PORTO CERVO: *Capriccioli*   ⓁⓁⓁ   40
Località Capriccioli, 07020. 【 0789 960 04. FAX 0789 964 22.
One of the best value hotels on the expensive Costa Smeralda. This family-run
hotel is close to the beach and has an excellent restaurant. 🔲 TV 🗒 ✉ P

PORTO ROTONDO: *Sporting*   ⓁⓁⓁ   27
Porto Rotondo, 07026. 【 0789 340 05. FAX 0789 343 83.
An oasis of comfort in the Costa Smeralda region. It has its own beach and
tranquil grounds and bedrooms have flower-filled terraces. 🔲 TV 🗒 ✉ P

SASSARI: *Leonardo da Vinci*   ⓁⓁ   117
Via Roma 79, 07100. 【 079 28 07 44. FAX 079 285 72 33
A large, comfortable hotel a few minutes' walk from the city center. Furnishings
are functional but there is a sense of space and tranquillity. 🔲 TV 🗒 ✉ P

WHERE TO EAT

OOD IS A serious subject in Italy. The Italians are justly proud of their fine cuisine and wines and many sociable hours are spent around the table. One of the great pleasures of traveling in Italy is exploring regional variations in pasta, breads, and cheeses. Whether it is spinach-filled *tortelloni* from the north or stuffed sweet red peppers from the south, restaurants will rarely serve anything other than

Waiter at Alberto Ciarla *(see p601)*

Italian specialties. You don't have to head to the most expensive places for good food; a simple trattoria, which has to answer to the local clientele, will often serve much better fare than the nearby international restaurant. However, whether it's a crowded osteria or a terrace with sea views, this introduction gives a few practical tips on types of restaurants, ordering, and service to help you enjoy eating out in Italy.

TYPES OF RESTAURANTS AND SNACK BARS

TRADITIONALLY a trattoria and an osteria were cheaper and more popular alternatives to the smarter ristorante. These days, however, the terms are interchangeable and high cost is not always indicative of memorably delicious food.

A pizzeria is usually an inexpensive place to eat (as little as L15,000 with beer), and many serve pasta, meat, and fish dishes as well as pizzas. Pizzerie are often open in the evening only, especially those with wood-fired ovens *(forni a legna)*. A birreria is another option, serving pasta and snacks such as sausages and hamburgers. An enoteca, or vineria, is in fact a place to taste wine. Since Italians will rarely drink without eating, there will normally be a range of light dishes offered as well as a fine selection of wines. Prices vary and tend not to be cheap for the quantities served.

El Gato restaurant, Chioggia, famous for its fish *(see p580)*

At lunch time and in the early evening rosticcerie sell roast chicken, slices of pizza *(pizza al taglio)*, and other snacks to take out. Pizza al taglio, with various different toppings, can also be bought straight from the baker. Bars have filled rolls *(panini)* and sandwiches *(tramezzini)*, and some have a *tavola calda* counter with hot dishes for under L10,000.

Stop at a *gelateria* for ice cream, with a sometimes mesmerizing choice of different flavors, or a *pasticceria* for one of a dazzling variety of sweet and savory pastries, cakes and cookies.

EATING HOURS

LUNCH IS generally served between 1pm and 2:30pm and, particularly in the south, all other activity stops between these hours. Dinner is at about 8pm and goes on until 11pm or later (in the south eating hours tend to be later). It is not unusual to see tables still full from lunch at 4pm or diners sipping *digestivi* well after midnight.

RESERVATIONS

GOOD RESTAURANTS in Italy are likely to be popular, so reserve a table if you can. Otherwise, get there early to avoid having to line up. Many restaurants close for a few weeks either in winter or the summer holiday season so phone first if in doubt.

THE MENU

ITALIAN MEALS consist of at least three or four courses, and restaurants generally expect you to eat at least two. The *antipasto* (starter), is followed by the *primo*, of pasta, rice, or soup. The *secondo* is the main meat or fish course with vegetables or salad (as *contorni*). Fruit, cheese, or dessert follow, with coffee and a *digestivo* such as *grappa* or a bitter *amaro* to finish the meal.

Menus usually change with the season to make use of the best and freshest local produce, and the day's specials may be recited to you by the waiter rather than written down.

Villa Crespi in Piedmont, inspired by the Arabian Nights *(see p587)*

Persevere, if you don't immediately understand, using the
menu decoders explained at
the beginning of each section.

VEGETARIANS

WHILE FEW PLACES advertise
specifically vegetarian
meals, you're unlikely to have
much trouble choosing from an
Italian menu. Many pasta and
antipasto dishes use no meat
at all, and for a main course
you can ask for a selection of
vegetables from the *contorni*.
Vegetarians eat particularly
well in spring when the first
new vegetables come into the
markets, and in autumn when
wild mushrooms abound.

WINE AND DRINKS

MANY REGIONS have their
own *aperitivo* for before
the meal and a *digestivo* for
afterward. Universal alternatives are *prosecco* (dry fizzy
white wine) or an *analcolico*
(nonalcoholic) aperitif and
grappa as a digestive. House
wine (red or white) will be a
simple local wine served by
the liter or fraction thereof
and will generally be perfectly
palatable. In addition, all but
the cheapest places have a
range of other local and
regional wines specially
selected to accompany the
food on the menu. For this
reason, it is unusual to come
across many non-Italian wines.
   Tap water *(acqua del
rubinetto)* is always drinkable
and often very good, but Italy
has a massive range of mineral
waters. Fizzy ones *(frizzante)*
may contain carbon dioxide

The 11th-century Badia a Coltibuono in Gaiole in Chianti *(see p594)*

while *naturale* can mean still
or naturally sparkling. The
popular *Ferrarelle* lies somewhere between the two. If
you particularly want a still
water ask for *non gassata*.

PAYING

TAX AND SERVICE are included
in the menu prices but it
is normal to leave a small tip
(from L2,000 to L10,000).
Take note of the cover charge
(coperto): an unavoidable
extra that basically covers
bread (whether you eat it or
not) and is charged per person.
   Credit cards are not always
accepted in Italy, particularly
in smaller towns, and it is
wise to check before you eat.

DRESS

ITALIANS GENERALLY tend to
look stylish but don't neces-
sarily expect visitors to do the
same. In most places you
won't be expected to dress
up; however, very scruffy or
dirty clothes are unlikely to
get you good or particularly
friendly service.

CHILDREN

CHILDREN ARE welcome in all
but the most upscale
spots and throughout Italy
restaurants are likely to be
filled with extensive Italian
families for Sunday lunch.
Facilities such as high chairs
or special menus are rare, but
most places will provide
cushions and small portions.

**Roman trattoria, Sora Lella, on
Tiber Island** *(see p599)*

SMOKING

SMOKING IS POPULAR in Italy,
and it is common for
people to light up between
courses or while others are
still eating. Be warned: non-
smoking sections are rare, and
if somebody else's cigarette is
bothering you, you are the
one who will have to move.

WHEELCHAIR ACCESS

FEW RESTAURANTS have special
facilities for people in
wheelchairs, but let them know
you are coming in advance so
they can reserve a suitable
table and be ready to help if
necessary when you arrive.

La Marinella restaurant overlooking the Amalfi coast *(see p603)*

Choosing a Restaurant

THE RESTAURANTS in this guide have been selected across a wide range of price categories for their good value, exceptional food, and interesting location. This chart lists the restaurants by region, starting with Venice. The thumb tabs on the side of the page use the same color-coding as the corresponding regional chapter in the main section of the guide.

	FIXED-PRICE MENU	GOOD WINE LIST	FORMAL DRESS	OUTDOOR TABLES

VENICE

BURANO: *Ai Pescatori*   ⑰⑰⑰⑰

	●	▪		

Piazza Galuppi 371, 30012. **(** 041 73 06 50.
A welcoming restaurant whose menu includes lobster and *tagliolini* (flat pasta) with cuttlefish. In winter the menu includes excellent game. The extensive wine list offers foreign as well as Italian wines. ● *Wed; Jan.* 🗲 ▤

BURANO: *Da Romano*   ⑰⑰⑰⑰

	●			▪

Via Galuppi 221, 30012. **(** 041 73 00 30.
A pretty restaurant founded in the 1800s, now run by a descendant of the original owner. The cooking is traditional and the fish is excellent. ● *Tue; mid-Dec–Feb.* 🗲 ▤

CANNAREGIO: *Osteria al Bacco*   ⑰⑰⑰

				▪

Fondamenta delle Cappuccine 3054, 30121. **Map** 2 D2. **(** 041 71 74 93.
A rustic restaurant with a pretty shaded courtyard. The menu serves mainly fish, and includes *spaghetti* with black cuttlefish-ink sauce. ● *Mon; 2weeks Jan, 2 weeks Aug.* 🗲

CANNAREGIO: *Fiaschetteria Toscana*   ⑰⑰⑰⑰

		▪		▪

Salizzada San Giovanni Crisostomo 5719, 30131. **Map** 3 B5. **(** 041 528 52 81.
The Busatto family offer many Venetian dishes such as warm salad of lagoon fish, and turbot with black butter and capers. ● *Mon lunch, Tue; mid-Jul–mid-Aug.* 🗲 ▤

CANNAREGIO: *Vini Da Gigio*   ⑰⑰⑰

		▪		

Fondamenta San Felice 3628a, 30131. **Map** 3 A4. **(** 041 528 51 40.
A cozy restaurant serving traditional Venetian cuisine with a difference. The *risotto* of shrimp and grilled cuttlefish is particularly good. ● *Mon; mid-Jan–Feb, late Aug.* 🗲 ▤

CASTELLO: *Da Remigio*   ⑰⑰⑰

Salizzada dei Greci 3416, 30122. **Map** 8 D2. **(** 041 523 00 89.
A lively local fish restaurant with a robust and straightforward menu.
Booking is advisable. ● *Mon eve, Tue; Dec 20–Jan 24, last wk Jul.* 🗲 ▤

CASTELLO: *La Corte Sconta*   ⑰⑰⑰⑰

		▪		▪

Calle del Pestrin 3886, 30122. **Map** 8 E2. **(** 041 522 70 24.
This simple eating house has become one of the city's top restaurants. The fish and the homemade pasta are both superb. ● *Sun, Mon; Jan 7–Feb 7, Jul 21–Aug 16.* 🗲 ▤

CASTELLO: *Arcimboldo*   ⑰⑰⑰⑰

		▪		▪

Calle dei Furlani 3219, 30122. **Map** 8 D1. **(** 041 528 65 69.
Named after the 16th-century painter who used vegetables and fruit to create portraits of people. The food is similarly innovative today; try sea bass with tomatoes or marinated salmon with citrus fruit. ● *Tue (in winter); 3 wks Aug.* 🗲 ▤

DORSODURO: *Da Silvio*   ⑰⑰

				▪

Calle San Pantalon 3748, 30123. **Map** 6 D2. **(** 041 520 58 33.
A genuine local restaurant with a lovely garden for summer eating. The menu has no surprises, but the food is fresh and homemade. ● *Sun, Sat lunch.* 🗲

DORSODURO: *Taverna San Trovaso*   ⑰⑰

	●			

Fondamenta Priuli 1016, 30123. **Map** 6 E3. **(** 041 520 37 03.
A cheerful, bustling restaurant between the Accademia and the Zattere.
The cooking is straightforward and includes pizzas. ● *Mon.* 🗲 ▤

DORSODURO: *Locanda Montin*   ⑰⑰⑰⑰

		▪		▪

Fondamenta Eremite 1147, 30123. **Map** 6 D3. **(** 041 522 71 51.
A famous restaurant with artistic and literary connections. Food and service can vary in quality but there is a lively atmosphere. ● *Tue eve, Wed.* 🗲

DORSODURO: *Ai Gondolieri*   ⑰⑰⑰

		▪		

San Vio 366, 30123. **Map** 6 F4. **(** 041 528 63 96.
Housed in a sympathetically restored old inn, friendly hosts offer good regional specialties including *sformati* (soufflés) with wild herbs and mushroom soups. ● *Tue.* 🗲 ▤

<table>
<tr><td>

Average prices for a three-course meal for one, including a half bottle of house wine, tax and service:
Ⓛ up to L35,000
ⓁⓁ L35–55,000
ⓁⓁⓁ L55–75,000
ⓁⓁⓁⓁ L75–100,000
ⓁⓁⓁⓁⓁ over L100,000.

</td><td>

FIXED-PRICE MENU
A fixed-price menu offered, usually with three courses.
GOOD WINE LIST
Denotes a wide range of good quality wines.
FORMAL DRESS
Some restaurants require men to wear a jacket and tie.
OUTDOOR TABLES
Tables for eating outdoors, often with a good view.
CREDIT CARDS
The symbol shows that major credit cards are accepted.

</td></tr>
</table>

		FIXED-PRICE MENU	GOOD WINE LIST	FORMAL DRESS	OUTDOOR TABLES

GIUDECCA: *Cipriani* — ⓁⓁⓁⓁⓁ | ● | ■ | ● | ■
Guidecca 10, 30122. ☎ 041 520 77 44.
One of the most exclusive restaurants in Venice, *Cipriani* offers impeccable food and service in elegant surroundings. Panoramic terrace. ● *Nov–Mar.* 💳 ▤

GIUDECCA: *Harry's Dolci* — ⓁⓁⓁⓁ | | ■ | | ■
Fondamenta San Biagio 773, 30133. **Map** 6 D5. ☎ 041 522 48 44.
Originally a bar and tearoom, this is now a restaurant serving similar food to Harry's Bar in San Marco. Try *carpaccio* (marinated, sliced raw beef), the pasta and beans, and the house chocolate cake. ● *Tue; Nov–Mar.* 💳

MAZZORBO: *Antica Trattoria alla Maddalena* — ⓁⓁ | | | | ■
Fondamente Santa Caterina 7c, 30131. ☎ 041 73 01 51.
This modest restaurant, popular with the locals, acts as a local bar as well as an eating house. It has a tranquil atmosphere, however, and the wild duck served with *polenta* is famous throughout the area. ● *Thu.* 💳

SAN MARCO: *Al Conte Pescaor* — ⓁⓁⓁ | ● | ■ | · | ■
Piscina San Zulian 544a, 30124. **Map** 7 B1. ☎ 041 522 14 83.
A little restaurant with a superb fish menu. The clientele are mainly local people, which guarantees the high quality of the food. ● *Sun; Jan 7–Feb 7.* 💳

SAN MARCO: *Da Raffaele* — ⓁⓁⓁⓁ | | ■ | | ■
Ponte delle Ostreghe 2347, 30124. **Map** 7 A3. ☎ 041 523 23 17.
A romantic setting in which to eat regional dishes. Try the *granseola* (spider crab), *risotto* with scampi, and *rombo alla Raffaele* (turbot). ● *Thu; Dec–early Feb.* 💳 ▤

SAN MARCO: *Antico Martini* — ⓁⓁⓁⓁ | | ■ | | ■
Campo San Fantin 1983, 30124. **Map** 7 A2. ☎ 041 522 41 21.
Overlooking the Fenice theater, this smart restaurant serves until 1am. The cooking is creative: try the lamb with caper sauce. ● *Tue (winter only).* 💳 ▤

SAN MARCO: *Da Arturo* — ⓁⓁⓁⓁⓁ | | ■ | |
Calle degli Assassini 3656, 30124. **Map** 7 A2. ☎ 041 528 69 74.
This restaurant must be the only place in Venice that does not serve fish, but the menu does include a variety of meat dishes and vegetarian salads. ● *Sun; Aug.* ▤

SAN MARCO: *La Caravella* — ⓁⓁⓁⓁ | ● | ■ | | ■
Calle Larga XXII Marzo 2398, 30124. **Map** 7 A3. ☎ 041 520 89 01.
Now the only restaurant in the Hotel Saturnia, *La Caravella* has a beautiful setting with a waterside terrace by the Grand Canal. The food is outstanding with specialty dishes including lobster soup. 💳 ▤

SAN MARCO: *Harry's Bar* — ⓁⓁⓁⓁ | | ■ | |
Calle Vallaresso 1323, 30124. **Map** 7 B3. ☎ 041 528 57 77.
People come here because it's so famous. The wine list and cocktails are good, but the food is not particularly exciting for the price. 💳 ▤

SAN POLO: *Antica Trattoria Poste Vecie* — ⓁⓁⓁⓁ | ● | | | ■
Rialto Pescheria 1608, 30123. **Map** 3 A5. ☎ 041 72 18 22.
This stylish restaurant near the fish market claims to be the oldest in Venice. Dishes include homemade pasta as well as lovely desserts. ● *Tue.* 💳 ▤

SAN POLO: *Da Fiore* — ⓁⓁⓁⓁ | | ■ | |
Calle del Scaleter 2202a. **Map** 2 E5. ☎ 041 72 13 08.
Fish specialties include a wonderful seafood antipasto, grilled fish, and *fritto misto* (mixed fried fish). Try the house white wine. ● *Sun, Mon; 2 wks Aug, 2 wks Dec.* 💳 ▤

TORCELLO: *Locanda Cipriani* — ⓁⓁⓁⓁ | | ■ | | ■
Piazza Santa Fosca 29, 30121. ☎ 041 73 01 50.
Transformed from a fishermen's inn in the 1930s, dishes include *fritto misto* and a *risotto* with vegetables from the kitchen garden. At weekends, a boat launch collects diners from Piazza San Marco. ● *Tue; Jan.* 💳 ▤

Average prices for a three-course meal for one, including a half bottle of house wine, tax and service:
Ⓛ up to L35,000
ⓁⓁ L35–55,000
ⓁⓁⓁ L55–75,000
ⓁⓁⓁⓁ L75–100,000
ⓁⓁⓁⓁⓁ over L100,000.

FIXED-PRICE MENU
A fixed-price menu offered, usually with three courses.
GOOD WINE LIST
Denotes a wide range of good quality wines.
FORMAL DRESS
Some restaurants require men to wear a jacket and tie.
OUTDOOR TABLES
Tables for eating outdoors, often with a good view.
CREDIT CARDS
The symbol shows that major credit cards are accepted.

	FIXED-PRICE MENU	GOOD WINE LIST	FORMAL DRESS	OUTDOOR TABLES

THE VENETO AND FRIULI

ASOLO: *Villa Cipriani*   ⓁⓁⓁⓁ
Via Canova 298, 31011. ☎ *0423 95 21 66.* 🖷 *0423 95 20 35.*
Set in one of the grand hotels of the Veneto. Local ingredients are used in the creative cuisine with dishes such as gnocci of ricotta with rosemary. 🍴▤
— Good Wine List ■ · Formal Dress ● · Outdoor Tables ■

BELLUNO: *Terracotta*   ⓁⓁ
Via Garibaldi 61. ☎ *0437 94 26 44.*
Regional specialties include *pappardelle* (wide ribbon pasta) with smoked ricotta, radicchio and speck, or chick pea and prawn soup. ● *Wed.* 🍴
— Good Wine List ■ · Outdoor Tables ■

BREGANZE: *Al Toresan*   ⓁⓁ
Via Zabarella 1, 36042. ☎ *0445 87 32 60.*
In the autumn the locals flock here for the wild mushroom dishes. The cooking is hearty and is complemented by local wines. ● *Thu; end Jul–Aug 25.* 🍴
— Outdoor Tables ■

CAORLE: *Duilio*   ⓁⓁⓁ
Via Strada Nuova 19, 30021. ☎ *0421 810 87.*
A spacious restaurant where the fish-based regional cuisine is given a creative slant. Try the dried cod with *polenta*. ● *Mon (winter); Jan 10–15.* 🍴
— Good Wine List ■ · Formal Dress ● · Outdoor Tables ■

CASTELFRANCO: *Barbesin*   ⓁⓁ
Via Montebelluna 41, 31033. ☎ *0423 49 04 46.*
A restaurant serving regional specialties, including *risotto* with fish, or vegetables, or *porcini* mushrooms. ● *Wed eve, Thu; 2 weeks Jan, 2 weeks Aug.* 🍴
— Good Wine List ■

CHIOGGIA: *El Gato*   ⓁⓁⓁ
Campo Sant'Andrea 653, 30015. ☎ *041 40 18 06.*
Classic cooking based on seafood in an elegant, slightly restrained setting. The delicious deserts are highly recommended. ● *Mon, Tue lunch; Jan–mid-Feb.* 🍴
— Good Wine List ■ · Outdoor Tables ■

CIVIDALE DEL FRIULI: *Zorutti*   ⓁⓁⓁ
Borgo Ponte 9, 33043. ☎ *0432 73 11 00.*
A family-run restaurant with a well-deserved reputation for good, regional cuisine served in generous portions. The house specialty is buzara, a local specialty of *spaghetti* with seafood, giant shrimp, or lobster. ● *Mon.* ▤🍴
— Good Wine List ■

CONEGLIANO: *Al Salisà*   ⓁⓁⓁ
Via XX Settembre 2, 31015. ☎ *0438 242 88.*
An elegant restaurant set in a medieval house with a pretty veranda for eating outdoors. The traditional menu includes homemade pastas served with a range of vegetarian sauces. ● *Tue pm, Wed.* 🍴
— Good Wine List ■ · Outdoor Tables ■

CORTINA D'AMPEZZO: *Baita Fraina*   ⓁⓁⓁ
Località Fraina 1, 32043. ☎ *0436 36 34.*
An elegant alpine restaurant, with wood fittings and a panoramic terrace. The food is robust and extremely good value. ● *Mon (Jan–mid-Mar); May, Jun, Oct, Nov.* 🍴
— Good Wine List ■ · Outdoor Tables ■

DOLO: *Alla Posta*   ⓁⓁⓁ
Via Ca' Tron 33, 30031. ☎ *041 41 07 40.*
This superb restaurant in an old Venetian posthouse prepares regional specialties with fresh ingredients and well-blended flavors. ● *Mon; 2 wks Jan, 2 wks Jun–Jul.* 🍴▤
— Fixed-Price Menu ● · Good Wine List ■ · Outdoor Tables ■

GORIZIA: *Nanut*   Ⓛ
Via Trieste 118, 34170. ☎ *0481 205 95.*
A long-established trattoria in the industrial zone. It serves good local food; *gnocchi*, market vegetables, meats, and fish on Friday. ● *Sat, Sun; Aug.* 🍴▤
— Outdoor Tables ■

GRADO: *Trattoria de Toni*   ⓁⓁ
Piazza Duca d'Aosta 37, 34073. ☎ *0431 801 04.*
A traditional trattoria in the historic center, the house specialty is *boreto alla Gradese*, a fish stew cooked in oil and vinegar. ● *Nov–Mar: Wed; Jan, Dec.* 🍴♿
— Good Wine List ■ · Outdoor Tables ■

GRANCONA: *Isetta* Ⓛ Ⓛ
Via Pederiva 96, 36040. ⟨ *0444 88 99 92.*
Regional food, with the emphasis on grilled meats and good puddings,
in Galdino Gianesin's restaurant in the Berici hills. ● *Tue eve, Wed; Jul.*

LAKE GARDA: *Antica Locanda Mincio* Ⓛ Ⓛ Ⓛ
Via Michelangelo 12, Località Borghetto, Valeggio sul Mincio 37067. ⟨ *045 795 00 59.*
Once a wayside inn, this is now a delightful restaurant with frescoed walls and
open fireplaces. Serves good regional food. ● *Wed, Thu; 2 wks Feb, 2 wks Nov.*

LAKE GARDA: *Locanda San Vigilio* Ⓛ Ⓛ Ⓛ Ⓛ
Località San Vigilio, Garda 37016. ⟨ *045 725 66 88.*
This excellent restaurant overlooking Lake Garda has an antipasto buffet and
an astounding range of freshwater fish and seafood dishes. ● *Nov–Mar.*

MONTECCHIA DI CROSARA: *Baba-jaga* Ⓛ Ⓛ Ⓛ
Via Cabalao 11, 37030. ⟨ *045 745 02 22.*
Black-truffle *risotto* and shrimp with zucchinis, tomatoes and leeks are a good
choice in the Soave wine-producing area. ● *Sun eve, Mon; Jan, 2 wks Aug.*

NOVENTA PADOVANA: *Boccadoro* Ⓛ Ⓛ
Via della Resistenza 49, 35100. ⟨ *049 62 50 29.*
Good Paduan food is served in this family-run restaurant. The goose
is well-worth sampling. ● *Tue eve, Wed; 2 weeks Jan, 2 weeks Aug.*

ODERZO: *Dussin* Ⓛ Ⓛ
Via Maggiore 60, Località Piavon, 31046. ⟨ *0422 75 21 30.*
Good value, traditional cuisine is served in this lively restaurant. Fish is a specialty,
with such dishes as seafood *risotto* and grilled tuna. ● *Mon eve, Tue; Jan, Aug.*

PADUA: *La Braseria* Ⓛ Ⓛ
Via Tommaseo 48, 35100. ⟨ *049 876 09 07.*
A friendly restaurant with straightforward cooking. *Penne* with *porcini* mushrooms
and smoked bacon are recommended. ● *Sat lunch, Sun; eves Aug.*

PADUA: *Osteria L'Anfora* Ⓛ Ⓛ
Via dei Soncin 13, 35122. ⟨ *049 65 66 29.*
Traditional Veneto cuisine, with elements originally brought by Renaissance
merchants from far afield, is served in a lively atmosphere. ● *Sun; Jan 1–6, 2 wks Aug.*

PADUA: *San Pietro* Ⓛ Ⓛ
Via San Pietro 95, 35149. ⟨ *049 876 03 30.*
The perfect place to try the regional specialties, cooked with fresh, local ingredients.
The service is friendly and attentive, and the atmosphere informal. ● *Sun; Jul.*

PADUA: *Antico Brolo* Ⓛ Ⓛ Ⓛ
Corso Milano 22. ⟨ *049 66 45 55.*
This quietly elegant restaurant delivers appropriately elegant food, such as
ravioli stuffed with courgette flowers. ● *Mon; Aug.*

PORDENONE: *Vecia Osteria del Moro* Ⓛ Ⓛ
Via Castello 2, 33170. ⟨ *0434 286 58.*
A refined restaurant set in a beautifully restored 13th-century convent. Daily
specials include rabbit with *polenta*. ● *Sun; 2 weeks Jan, 2 weeks Aug.*

ROVIGO: *Cauccio* Ⓛ
Viale Oroboni 50, 45100. ⟨ *0425 316 39.*
An old-fashioned trattoria, serving unpretentious, traditional Italian cuisine, such as
lasagne, *cannelloni* and *vitello tonnató* (veal with tuna and caper sauce). ● *Mon.*

TREVISO: *Osteria Snack Bassanello* Ⓛ Ⓛ
Viale Cairoli 133, 31100. ⟨ *0422 26 06 23.*
Excellent local cuisine is served in this popular osteria. In season, *radicchio* (endive)
is used in numerous ways including the digestive, grappa. ● *Mon; 2 wks Aug.*

TREVISO: *Toni del Spin* Ⓛ Ⓛ
Via Inferiore 7, 31100. ⟨ *0422 54 38 29.*
A homey restaurant serving regional fare. House specialties include pasta and
fagioli (beans), baked tripe, and *tiramisù*. ● *Sun, Mon lunch; 3 wks Aug.*

TREVISO: *Ristorante Beccherie* Ⓛ Ⓛ Ⓛ
Piazza Ancillotto 10, 31100. ⟨ *0422 54 08 71.*
Housed in a lovely building reminiscent of Venetian splendor. The guinea
fowl in pepper sauce is a particular delicacy. ● *Sun eve, Mon; Jul 15–30.*

For key to symbols see back flap

	FIXED-PRICE MENU	**GOOD WINE LIST**	**FORMAL DRESS**	**OUTDOOR TABLES**

Average prices for a three-course meal for one, including a half bottle of house wine, tax and service:
Ⓛ up to L35,000
ⓁⓁ L35–55,000
ⓁⓁⓁ L55–75,000
ⓁⓁⓁⓁ L75–100,000
ⓁⓁⓁⓁⓁ over L100,000.

FIXED-PRICE MENU
A fixed-price menu offered, usually with three courses.
GOOD WINE LIST
Denotes a wide range of good quality wines.
FORMAL DRESS
Some restaurants require men to wear a jacket and tie.
OUTDOOR TABLES
Tables for eating outdoors, often with a good view.
CREDIT CARDS
The symbol shows that major credit cards are accepted.

Restaurant	Price	FIXED-PRICE MENU	GOOD WINE LIST	FORMAL DRESS	OUTDOOR TABLES
TRIESTE: *Al Bragozzo* Riva Sauro 22, 34124. 📞 *040 30 30 01.* The menu changes from week to week, depending on the local produce available. This lively restaurant is popular with locals. ● *Sun. Mon; 2 weeks Jan, 2 weeks Jul.* 🗎 ▤	ⓁⓁ		▨		▨
TRIESTE: *Harry's Grill* Piazza Unità d'Italia 2, 34121. 📞 *040 36 56 46.* This restaurant is distinguished by its central position and high-class cuisine. Try *bigoli* pasta with duck or beef fillet with *bordolese* sauce. ● *Sun eve.* 🗎 ▤	ⓁⓁⓁⓁ		▨		▨
UDINE: *Agli Amici* Via Liguria 250, Località Godia, 33100. 📞 *0432 56 54 11.* Friulian dishes, such as *polenta* with smoked ricotta and walnuts, or *cjarsons* (ravioli) with wild herbs, are cooked with flair here. ● *Sun eve, Mon; Jan, Jul.* 🗎 ▤	ⓁⓁⓁ	●	▨		
VERONA: *Al Bersagliere* Via dietro Pallone 1, 37121. 📞 *045 800 48 24.* Traditional Veronese food in an old wood-lined dining room. Dishes include mixed boiled meats and *polenta* with wild mushrooms. ● *Sun.* 🗎	ⓁⓁ		▨		
VERONA: *Arche* Via Arche Scaligere 6, 37100. 📞 *045 800 74 15.* A long-established fish restaurant serving *spaghetti* with clams in *cartoccio* and rock lobster in *serenissima saor* marinade. ● *Sun, Mon lunch.* 🗎 ▤	ⓁⓁⓁⓁ	●	▨		
VERONA: *Il Desco* Via dietro San Sebastiano 5–7, 37121. 📞 *045 59 53 58.* One of Italy's best restaurants, set in a 16th-century palazzo. Imaginative dishes include veal with ginger and lobster *risotto*. ● *Sun, Mon; 2 wks Jan, 2 wks Jun.* 🗎 ▤	ⓁⓁⓁⓁ	●	▨		
VICENZA: *Antica Trattoria Tre Visi* Corso Palladio 25, 36100. 📞 *0444 32 48 68.* The building, in the historic center, dates from 1483. Diners can see into the kitchen where the excellent local dishes are prepared. ● *Sun eve, Mon; Jul.* 🗎	ⓁⓁ	●	▨		▨
VICENZA: *Cinzia e Valerio* Piazzetta Porta Padova 65–67, 36100. 📞 *0444 50 52 13.* A stylish restaurant within the city walls, serving nothing but fish. Dishes include a mixed plate of scampi and squid. ● *Sun eve, Mon; Dec 26–Jan 5, 3 weeks Aug.* 🗎	ⓁⓁⓁ	●	▨		
VICENZA: *Taverna Aeolia* Piazza Conte da Schio 1, Costozza di Longare 36023. 📞 *0444 55 50 36.* This restaurant is housed in an elegant villa with a beautiful frescoed ceiling. The menu spacializes in creative meat dishes. ● *Tue; Nov 1–15.* 🗎	ⓁⓁⓁ	●	▨		

TRENTINO-ALTO ADIGE

Restaurant	Price	FIXED-PRICE MENU	GOOD WINE LIST	FORMAL DRESS	OUTDOOR TABLES
ARCO: *Alla Lega* Via Vergolano 4, 38062. 📞 *0464 51 62 05.* A lively, family-run restaurant housed in a rustically elegant 18th century building with a beautiful courtyard. The food is traditional, including such dishes as *risottos*, cured meats and trout with *polenta*. ● *Wed; Feb, Mar.* 🗎 ▤	ⓁⓁ		▨		▨
BOLZANO (BOZEN): *Domino* Piazza Walther 1, 39100. 📞 *0471 98 16 10.* This town center wine bar is a good stop for a delicious lunch time snack or a glass of wine in the evening. ● *Sun; 1week Jul.* 🗎	ⓁⓁ		▨		▨
BOLZANO (BOZEN): *Da Abramo* Piazza Gries 16, 39050. 📞 *0471 28 01 41.* This elegant restaurant offers splendid river views across the Talvera. The cuisine features richly seasoned fish and meat dishes. ● *Sun; 2 weeks Jan, 2 weeks Aug.* 🗎 ▤	ⓁⓁ	●	▨		

BOLZANO (BOZEN): *Rastbichler*
Via Cadorna 1, 39100. (0471 26 11 31.
This restaurant is known for its excellent fish and generously served grilled
meats. Typical South Tyrol decor. ● Sat lunch, Sun.
ⓁⓁⓁ

BRESSANONE (BRIXEN): *Oste Scuro-Finsterwirt*
Vicolo Duomo 3, 39042. (0472 83 53 43.
One of the oldest buildings in the historic center, it specializes in regional
cuisine using local produce in imaginative ways. ● Sun eve, Mon. 🌣 ⓖ
ⓁⓁ

BRESSANONE (BRIXEN): *Fink*
Via Portici Minori 4, 39042. (0472 83 48 83.
Popular with locals who come to sample the immaculately prepared dishes
such as black *polenta* or *knödel* (a kind of dumpling). ● Tue eve, Wed. 🌣 ⚡ ⓖ
ⓁⓁ

BRUNICO (BRUNECK): *Oberraut*
Via Ameto 1, Località Amaten, 39031. (0474 55 99 77.
Set in woods, this Tyrolean-style restaurant specializes in local game and
seasonal dishes. There is a tantalizing dessert list. ● Thu (winter); Jan. 🌣 ⓖ
ⓁⓁ

CARZANO: *Le Rose*
Via XVIII Settembre 35, 38050. (0461 76 61 77.
This popular Valsugana restaurant concentrates on fish and seasonal
produce. Try the *tortelli* of fish with *porcini* mushrooms. ● Mon. 🌣
ⓁⓁⓁ

CAVALESE: *Costa Salica*
Via Costa dei Salici 10, 38033. (0462 34 01 40.
A popular restaurant with specialties such as homemade pasta with finferli,
mushrooms, marinated venison, and pear strudel. ● Mon lunch, Tue. 🌣 ⓖ
ⓁⓁⓁ

CIVEZZANO: *Maso Cantanghel*
Via della Madonnina 33, Località Forte 38045. (0461 85 87 14.
An excellent restaurant just outside Trento. Food is simple yet delicious; garden
vegetables, roasted meats and homemade pasta. ● Sat, Sun; 1 week Aug. 🌣
ⓁⓁ

LEVICO TERME: *Boivin*
Via Garibaldi 9, 38056. (0461 70 16 70.
This excellent trattoria is one of the best places to taste authentic local cuisine;
booking is essential. Only open evenings and for Sunday lunch. ● Mon. 🌣
ⓁⓁ

MADONNA DI CAMPIGLIO: *Hermitage*
Via Castelletto Inferiore 63, 38084. (0465 44 15 58.
Set in a private park at the foot of the Dolomites, the Hermitage serves imagin-
atively regional cuisine, with fresh-flavored, tasty dishes. ● May–Jun, Oct–May. 🌣 ⚡
ⓁⓁⓁ

MALLES VENOSTA (MALS IM VINSCHGAU): *Greif*
Via Generale Verdross 40a, 39024. (0473 83 14 29.
Here the chef creates Tyrolean dishes using organic produce. The restaurant also
serves a vegetarian menu. ● Mon; 2 weeks Jun, 2 weeks Dec. 🌣 ⚡ ⓖ
ⓁⓁⓁ

MALLES VENOSTA (MALS IM VINSCHGAU): *Weisses Kreuz*
Località Burgusio 82, 39024. (0473 83 13 07.
This excellent value restaurant serves traditional fare such as *knödel*
(dumplings), roasted meats and fruit strudels. ● Thu, Fri lunch. 🌣 ⓖ
ⓁⓁⓁ

MERANO (MERAN): *Artemis*
Via Giuseppe Verdi 72, 39012. (0473 44 62 82.
Good Italian and international food is served here. Live classical music
accompanies Sunday brunch. ● Jan–Mar. 🌣
ⓁⓁⓁⓁ

MERANO (MERAN): *Sissi*
Via Galilei 44, 39012. (0473 23 10 62.
A 19th-century building close to the town center, the Sissi offers a refined,
seasonal menu combining traditional and modern dishes. ● Mon. 🌣 ▤
ⓁⓁⓁ

MOENA: *Malga Panna*
Via Costalunga 29, 38035. (0462 57 34 89.
Mushrooms and game are served at this romantic restaurant in a rustic setting
about 1 km (half a mile) from the center of Moena. ● Dec–Apr: Mon; May; Nov. 🌣 ⓖ
ⓁⓁⓁⓁ

ROVERETO: *Novecento*
Corso Rosmini 82d, 38068. (0464 43 54 54.
A refined restaurant, part of a hotel in the middle of Rovereto, serving
some carefully prepared local dishes. ● Sun; 3 weeks Aug. 🌣 ▤ ⚡
ⓁⓁⓁ

For key to symbols see back flap

Average prices for a three-course meal for one, including a half bottle of house wine, tax and service:
Ⓛ up to L35,000
ⓁⓁ L35–55,000
ⓁⓁⓁ L55–75,000
ⓁⓁⓁⓁ L75–100,000
ⓁⓁⓁⓁⓁ over L100,000.

FIXED-PRICE MENU
A fixed-price menu offered, usually with three courses.

GOOD WINE LIST
Denotes a wide range of good quality wines.

FORMAL DRESS
Some restaurants require men to wear a jacket and tie.

OUTDOOR TABLES
Tables for eating outdoors, often with a good view.

CREDIT CARDS
The symbol shows that major credit cards are accepted.

	FIXED-PRICE MENU	GOOD WINE LIST	FORMAL DRESS	OUTDOOR TABLES
ROVERETO: *Al Borgo* ⓁⓁⓁⓁ Via Garibaldi 13, 38068. ▌ *0464 43 63 00.* Centrally situated, Al Borgo is one of the best restaurants in the Trentino region, offering creative dishes using local produce. ● *Sun eve, Mon; Jan 20–30, 3 wks Jul.* 🗐 ▤	●	▪		
TRENTO: *Al Tino* Ⓛ Via Santissima Trinità 10, 38100. ▌ *0461 98 41 09.* Situated in an historic building in the centre of Trento, this traditional trattoria is lively and popular so booking is adivisable. The food and wine are good value. ● *Sun.* 🗐 ▤	●	▪		
TRENTO: *Al Castello* ⓁⓁ Via Val Gola 2–4, Località Ravina 38040. ▌ *0461 92 33 33.* This family-run restaurant concentrates on good basics, including homemade pasta, and *strangolapreti* of potato, ricotta, and spinach. ● *Sun eve, Mon.* 🗐		▪		▪
TRENTO: *Osteria A le Due Spade* ⓁⓁⓁⓁ Via Don Rizzi 11, 38100. ▌ *0461 23 43 43.* A welcoming cellar restaurant near the duomo, serving traditional Trentino cuisine, including game and freshwater fish dishes. ● *Sun, Mon lunch.* 🗐 ▤	●	▪		▪
VAL DI VIZZE (PFITCH): *Pretzhof* ⓁⓁⓁ Località Tulve 259, 39040. ▌ *0472 76 44 55.* Karl and Ulli Mair run this peaceful country inn, using fresh produce from their own farm to concoct Tyrolean specialties. ● *Mon, Tue; end Jan–mid-Feb, end Jun–1st wk Jul.* 🗐				▪
VIPITENO (BOLZANO): *Kleine Flamme* ⓁⓁⓁ Città Nuova 31, 39049. ▌ *0472 76 60 65.* A high standard of creative cuisine is matched by attentive service and attention to detail at this small, chic restaurant in a 16th century building. ● *Sun eve, Mon.* 🗐 ▤	●	▪		▪

LOMBARDY

	FIXED-PRICE MENU	GOOD WINE LIST	FORMAL DRESS	OUTDOOR TABLES
BELLAGIO: *Silvio* ⓁⓁ Via Carcano 12, 22021. ▌ *031 95 03 22.* Silvio and his son Cristian catch much of the lake fish that is used for patés, pasta sauces, *ravioli*, and *risottos*. There is a relaxed atmosphere in this lovely restaurant and hotel with beautiful lakeside views. ● *Jan, Feb.* 🗐	●			▪
BERGAMO: *Vineria Cozzi* ⓁⓁ Via Colleoni 22, 24129. ▌ *035 23 88 36.* An attractive, old wine shop decorated in 19th-century style, the Cozzi has a spectacular list of wines and a range of light dishes and cheeses to accompany them. Try *polenta* with truffled cheese. ● *Wed; 2 wks Jan, 2 wks Aug.* 🗐		▪		▪
BERGAMO: *Taverna del Colleoni dell'Angelo* ⓁⓁⓁⓁ Piazza Vecchia 7, 24129. ▌ *035 23 25 96.* An elegant taverna. Specialties include pasta with squid, shrimp with light *polenta*, and delicious desserts. ● *Mon; 2 wks Aug.* 🗐 ▤ 🔀	●	▪	●	▪
BORMIO: *Taulà* ⓁⓁⓁ Via Dante 6, 23032. ▌ *0342 90 47 71.* A restaurant in a 17th-century barn. It serves local cuisine with specialties based on game, mushrooms and cured meats. ● *Tue; Wed lunch; May–Jun. Oct–Nov.* 🗐				
BRESCIA: *Trattoria Mezzeria* ⓁⓁⓁ Via Trieste 66, 25121. ▌ *030 403 06.* A busy trattoria serving homemade pasta or squash *gnocchi*, with main dishes such as boiled rabbit *alle Bresciana*. ● *Sun; Jul–Aug.* 🗐 ♿		▪		
CASTELVECCANA: *Sant'Antonio* ⓁⓁ Località Sant'Antonio, 21010. ▌ *0332 54 84 42.* This restaurant is set in a delightful 10th-century village with views of Lake Maggiore. The menu includes an excellent *polenta* with boiled meats. ● *Sep–May: Mon–Fri.*	●			▪

COMO: *Sant'Anna 1907*   Ⓛ Ⓛ Ⓛ
Via Turati 3, 22100. 【 031 50 52 66.
This restaurant has been run by the Fontana family for three generations.
The traditional dishes include fish *risotto* and veal in an olive crust.
⬤ *Sat lunch; Aug; 1 week Dec.* 🎫 ▤ ♿

CREMONA: *Mellini*   Ⓛ Ⓛ
Via Bissolati 105, 26100. 【 0372 305 35.
A cosy, family-run restaurant with a good choice of dishes prepared with great flair,
using exclusively fresh and local ingredients and seafish of the highest quality. Try the
pumpkin *tortelli, risotto* with mushrooms or bass with potatoes. ⬤ *Sun eve, Mon; Aug.*

CREMONA: *Osteria Porta Mosa*   Ⓛ Ⓛ Ⓛ
Via Santa Maria in Betlem 11, 26100. 【 0372 41 18 03.
A refined trattoria with excellent wines and simple dishes, such as *ravioli*, smoked
sword fish, and *polenta* with seasonal sauces. Wine shop. ⬤ *Sun; Aug.* 🎫 ▤

GARGNANO DEL GARDA: *La Tortuga*   Ⓛ Ⓛ Ⓛ Ⓛ
Via XXIV Maggio 5, Porticciolo di Gargnano, 25084. 【 0365 712 51.
A charming lakeside location for light imaginative cuisine. Try the *coregone*
with tomatoes and capers. ⬤ *lunch; Mon eve (Oct–May), Tue; Jan, Feb.* 🎫 ▤

LAKE COMO: *Locanda dell'Isola Comacina*   Ⓛ Ⓛ Ⓛ
Isola Comacina, 22010. 【 0344 550 83.
Set by the water's edge on an otherwise uninhabited island. A wonderful
five-course set menu of fish dishes is served. ⬤ *Tue (Sep 16–Jun 14); Nov–Mar.*

LECCO: *Casa di Lucia*   Ⓛ Ⓛ
Via Lucia 27, Località Acquate 22053. 【 0341 49 45 94.
In a 17th century house, traditional fare such as salami, *bresaola* (cured beef),
rabbit, and *pasta e fagioli* is served with good national wines. ⬤ *Sat lunch; Sun; Aug.*

MANERBA DEL GARDA: *Capriccio*   Ⓛ Ⓛ Ⓛ Ⓛ
Piazza San Bernardo 6, Località Montinelle, 25080. 【 0365 55 11 24.
Excellent lake views is an extra bonus at this restaurant that uses the local
fish and olive oil in its cuisine. Desserts include a muscat-grape gelatin with
peach sauce. ⬤ *lunch; Tue (mid-Sep–mid-Jun); Jan–Feb.* 🎫 ▤

MANTOVA: *L'Ochina Bianca*   Ⓛ Ⓛ
Via Finzi 2, 46100. 【 0376 32 37 00.
A simple restaurant serving some of the less well-known local specialties
such as meat parcels with sausage and cheese. ⬤ *Mon, Tue lunch; 1st wk Jan.* 🎫

MANTOVA: *Ai Ranari*   Ⓛ Ⓛ
Via Trieste 11, 46100. 【 0376 32 84 31.
A simple trattoria. Dishes are Mantuan and include pumpkin *tortelli* with
butter sauce and meat *polenta*. ⬤ *Mon; 2 weeks Jul, 1 week Aug.* 🎫

MANTOVA: *Il Cigno Trattoria dei Martini*   Ⓛ Ⓛ Ⓛ
Piazza Carlo d'Arco 1, 46100. 【 0376 32 71 01.
Fine Mantuan cuisine is accompanied by excellent wines. Try *bottargo*
(tuna roe) and *tortelli di zucce* (pumpkin). ⬤ *Mon, Tue; Aug, 1st wk Jan.* 🎫 ▤

MILAN: *Geppo*   Ⓛ
Viale Morgagni 37, 20124. 【 02 29 51 48 62.
A fun atmosphere and wide range of pizzas are on offer in this restaurant. Try the
valdostane (spinach, tomato, mozzarella and taleggio cheese). ⬤ *Sun lunch.*

MILAN: *Premiata Pizzeria*   Ⓛ
Alzaia Nauiglio Grande 2, 20144. 【 02 89 40 04 68.
This lively, informal restaurant is always busy but the service is efficient and friendly.
The dining room is spacious and fitted with antiques; in the summer the tables are
laid outside in the beautiful courtyard. ⬤ *Tue.* 🎫 ▤

MILAN: *Ba Ba Reeba*   Ⓛ Ⓛ
Via Orti 7, 20122. 【 02 55 01 12 67
This is different, in that its cuisine is exclusively Spanish. Specialties include
baccalà (dried salt cod) and fillet in red wine sauce. ⬤ *Sun, Mon lunch; 3 weeks Aug.* ▤

MILAN: *La Capanna*   Ⓛ Ⓛ
Via Donatello 9, 20131. 【 02 29 40 08 84.
Don't be put off by the plain appearance; the food, based on Tuscan
cuisine, is exceptional; fresh pasta and homemade puddings.
⬤ *Sat; Aug.* 🎫 ▤

For key to symbols see back flap

<table>
<tr><td>

Average prices for a three-course meal for one, including a half bottle of house wine, tax and service:
Ⓛ up to L35,000
ⓁⓁ L35–55,000
ⓁⓁⓁ L55–75,000
ⓁⓁⓁⓁ L75–100,000
ⓁⓁⓁⓁⓁ over L100,000.

</td><td>

FIXED-PRICE MENU
A fixed-price menu offered, usually with three courses.
GOOD WINE LIST
Denotes a wide range of good quality wines.
FORMAL DRESS
Some restaurants require men to wear a jacket and tie.
OUTDOOR TABLES
Tables for eating outdoors, often with a good view.
CREDIT CARDS
The symbol shows that major credit cards are accepted.

</td></tr>
</table>

	FIXED-PRICE MENU	GOOD WINE LIST	FORMAL DRESS	OUTDOOR TABLES
MILAN: *Lucca* ⓁⓁⓁ Via Castaldi 33, 20100. ☎ 02 29 52 66 68. Great for business lunches and popular for dinner, the cuisine is Tuscan and Mediterranean in style. 🗷 ▤		■		
MILAN: *Aimo e Nadia* ⓁⓁⓁⓁ Via Montecuccoli 6, 20147. ☎ 02 41 68 86. A small, chic restaurant which is famed for its delicious, imaginative dishes, prepared with select, seasonal ingredients. ● *Sat lunch, Sun; Aug; 1 wk Dec.* 🗷 ▤	●	■	●	
MONTE ISOLA: *La Foresta* ⓁⓁ Località Peschiera Maraglio 174, 25050. ☎ 030 988 62 10. Lake fish form the basis of the menu, making this popular with lovers of all sorts of local freshwater fish. ● *Wed; Oct–Nov.* 🗷 ▤	●	■		■
PAVIA: *Locanda Vecchia Pavia al Mulino* ⓁⓁⓁⓁ Via al Monumento 5, Località Certosa, 27012. ☎ 0382 92 58 94. Frothy desserts follow creative dishes that bring a light touch to local specialties. The service is cordial and attentive. ● *Mon, Wed lunch; 3 wks Jan, 2 wks Aug.* 🗷 ▤	●	■		
SALÒ: *Alla Campagnola* ⓁⓁ Via Brunati 11, 25087. ☎ 0365 221 53. A mother and sons team offer interesting traditional recipes including pasta stuffed with pumpkin or eggplant. ● *Mon, Tue lunch; Jan.* 🗷	●	■		■

VALLE D'AOSTA AND PIEDMONT

	FIXED-PRICE MENU	GOOD WINE LIST	FORMAL DRESS	OUTDOOR TABLES
ACQUI TERME: *La Schiavia* ⓁⓁⓁ Vicolo della Schiavia, 15011. ☎ 0144 559 39. An elegant family run restaurant on the ground floor of a 17th-century palazzo. Cuisine is regional including a delicious mix of vegetables and fish. ● *Sun; Aug.* 🗷		■		
ALBA: *Porta San Martino* ⓁⓁⓁ Via Einaudi 5, 12051. ☎ 0173 36 23 35. Excellent value at this refined restaurant with good service and a menu of Piedmontese and Albese specialties: *vitello tonnato* (veal with a sauce of tuna and capers) and *brasato* (meat) in Barbaresco wine sauce. ● *Mon; 2 wks Jul, 2 wks Aug.* 🗷		■		
ALESSANDRIA: *Il Grappolo* ⓁⓁⓁ Via Casale 28, 15100. ☎ 0131 25 32 17. Piedmontese cuisine with a few borrowed touches. Try the *agnolotti* (stuffed pasta) *all'Alessandrina.* ● *Mon eve, Tue; 1 wk Jan, 2 wks Aug.* 🗷 🗷	●	■		■
AOSTA: *Grotta Azzurra* ⓁⓁ Via Croix de Ville 97, 11100. ☎ 0165 26 24 74. This good pizzeria also serves excellent fish, pasta, and *risotto.* Try the seafood salad, *risotto,* or fish soup as a first course. ● *Wed; Jul.* 🗷 ▤		■		■
AOSTA: *Le Foyer* ⓁⓁⓁ Corso Ivrea 146, 11100. ☎ 0165 321 36. Popular with locals, this trattoria serves excellent fish including salmon *carpaccio,* *risotto* of shrimp, and arugula and zucchini flan. ● *Mon eve, Tue; Jan, 2 wks Jul.* 🗷	●			
AOSTA: *Vecchia Aosta* ⓁⓁ Piazza Porta Pretoria 4c, 11100. ☎ 0165 36 11 86. Set into the old Roman wall, the Vecchia Aosta offers typical regional dishes such as vegetable terrines and *ravioli.* ● *Wed.* 🗷	●	■		■
ASTI: *Gener Neuv* ⓁⓁⓁⓁ Lungotanaro 4, 14100. ☎ 0141 55 72 70. A peacefully rustic restaurant about 1 km (half a mile) from the town center. The Gener Neuv serves carefully prepared local dishes, and the family who run it give attentive service. ● *Sun eve, Mon; 2 wks Aug, 2 wks over Christmas.* 🗷	●	■	●	

BRA: *Osteria Boccondivino*   ⓁⓁ
Via Mendicità Istruita 14, 12042. ☎ *0172 42 56 74.*
An informal restaurant with Piedmontese cuisine. Try stuffed veal, rabbit in white
wine sauce and *panna cotta* (crème brûlée). ● *Sun, Mon lunch; Feb, 2 weeks Aug.* 🗎

BREUIL-CERVINIA: *Les Neiges d'Antan*   ⓁⓁⓁⓁ
Frazione Cret de Perrères 10, 11021. ☎ *0166 94 87 75.*
Elegantly rustic, this restaurant has beautiful mountain views and serves
carefully prepared rich mountain fare. 🗎 🗲

CANNOBIO: *Del Lago*   ⓁⓁⓁⓁⓁ
Via Nazionale 2, Località Carmine Inferiore 28052. ☎ *0323 705 95.*
A lovely lakeside restaurant where the imaginative cuisine combines
sometimes surprising flavors to great effect. ● *Tue, Wed lunch; Nov–Feb.* 🗎

CASALE MONFERRATO: *La Torre*   ⓁⓁⓁⓁ
Via Garoglio 3, 15033. ☎ *0142 702 95.*
An elegant restaurant with panoramic views near the town center. The creative cuisine
uses seasonal ingredients. ● *Wed; 3 weeks Aug, 1 week Dec, 1 week Jan.* 🗎 ⑤ 📃

COGNE: *Lou Ressignon*   ⓁⓁ
Rue Mines de Cogne 22, 11012. ☎ *0165 740 34.*
A 17th-century inn where an open fireplace creates an old-world feeling. Rustic cuisine
with salamis, *polenta*, and grilled meats. ● *Mon, Tue; 2 wks Jun, 2 wks Sep, Nov.* 🗎 ⑤

COSTIGLIOLE D'ASTI: *Collavini*   ⓁⓁ
Via Asti-Nizza 84, 14055. ☎ *0141 96 64 40.*
A comfortable atmosphere, good service and carefully prepared simple food combine
to make the Collavini a popular spot. ● *Tue lunch, Wed; 3 wks Jan, 3 wks Aug.* 🗎

COURMAYEUR: *Pierre Alexis 1877*   ⓁⓁⓁ
Via Marconi 54, 11013. ☎ *0165 84 35 17.*
A converted barn in the historic center with dishes based on local traditions;
beef in four sauces and *ravioli di cacciagione* (game). ● *Mon; Oct–Nov.* 🗎

CUNEO: *Osteria della Chiocciola*   ⓁⓁ
Via Fossano 1, 12100. ☎ *0171 662 77.*
An excellent restaurant where seasonal fare is combined with the appropriate
wines. Winter has full-bodied reds. ● *Sun; 1 wk Jan, 1 wk Aug.* 🗎

DOMODOSSOLA: *Piemonte da Sciolla*   ⓁⓁ
Piazza della Convenzione 4, 28037. ☎ *0324 24 26 33.*
Immaculately prepared regional specialties such as *gnocchi* with rye and
chestnuts, set in a historic building. ● *Wed; 2 weeks Jan, 1 week Aug, 1 week Sep.* 🗎 🗲

FEISOGLIO: *Piemonte da Renato*   ⓁⓁ
Via Firenze 19, 12050. ☎ *0173 83 11 16.*
A family atmosphere at this trattoria serving seasonal specialties, especially
dishes with white and black truffles. Booking is advisable. ● *Dec – Easter.* ⑤

IVREA: *La Trattoria*   ⓁⓁ
Via Aosta 47, 10015. ☎ *0125 489 98.*
A bright restaurant where the food is simple and based on regional cuisine.
Try the smoked fish in vegetable sauce. ● *Sun eve, Mon; 2 weeks Aug.* 🗎 📃

NOVARA: *La Famiglia*   ⓁⓁⓁ
Via Solaroli 9, 28100. ☎ *0321 39 95 29.*
A small, peaceful restaurant, its walls painted with frescoes of Lake Maggiore.
The cuisine specializes in fresh fish and *risottos*. 🗎

NOVARA: *Osteria del Laghetto*   ⓁⓁⓁⓁ
Case Sparse 11, Località Veveri, 28100. ☎ *0321 62 15 79.*
Set in a park, the flower-filled Laghetto specializes in dishes using fresh
fish, mushrooms, and truffles. Booking is advisable. ● *Sat lunch, Sun.* 🗎 ⑤

ORTA SAN GIULIO: *Villa Crespi*   ⓁⓁⓁⓁⓁ
Via Generale Fava 8 – 10, 28016. ☎ *0322 91 19 02.*
The decor is based on the Arabian Nights. The imaginative cuisine uses seasonal
truffles and *foie gras* (liver pâté). ● *Tue (Oct–Mar); 3 wks Jan, 1 wk Feb.* 🗎 ⑤ 📃

SAINT VINCENT: *Nuovo Batezar*   ⓁⓁⓁⓁⓁ
Via Marconi 1, 11027. ☎ *0166 51 31 64.*
An excellent restaurant serving classic cuisine with special touches (*ravioli* with
lobster sauce, pheasant in *polenta* crust). ● *Wed, Mon – Fri lunch; 3 wks Jun, 2 wks Nov.* 🗎

Average prices for a three-course meal for one, including a half bottle of house wine, tax and service:
Ⓛ up to L35,000
ⓁⓁ L35–55,000
ⓁⓁⓁ L55–75,000
ⓁⓁⓁⓁ L75–100,000
ⓁⓁⓁⓁⓁ over L100,000.

FIXED-PRICE MENU
A fixed-price menu offered, usually with three courses.
GOOD WINE LIST
Denotes a wide range of good quality wines.
FORMAL DRESS
Some restaurants require men to wear a jacket and tie.
OUTDOOR TABLES
Tables for eating outdoors, often with a good view.
CREDIT CARDS
The symbol shows that major credit cards are accepted.

	FIXED-PRICE MENU	GOOD WINE LIST	FORMAL DRESS	OUTDOOR TABLES
SAN SECONDO DI PINEROLO: *La Ciau* ⓁⓁⓁ Via Castello di Miradolo 2, 10060. 📞 *0121 50 06 11.* Care and innovation go into the preparation of regional dishes. Try the *agnolotti* (pasta) stuffed with meat and the home-baked bread. ● *Wed; Jan.* 🎫 ▤	●	▦		▦
SESTRIERE: *Braciere del Possetto* ⓁⓁⓁ Via Agnelli 11–12, 01058. 📞 *0122 761 29.* This is one of the best places to taste Piedmontese dishes, exquisitely prepared, as well as a range of Italian and French cheeses. ● *Wed; May, Oct, Nov.* 🎫		▦		
SORISO: *Al Sorriso* ⓁⓁⓁⓁ Via Roma 18, 28016. 📞 *0322 98 32 28.* One of the most acclaimed restaurants in Italy. The cuisine makes use of what's in season locally and draws on a wide range of traditions from Italy and abroad. ● *Mon, Tue lunch; 2 weeks Jan, 3 weeks Aug.* 🎫 ⚡	●	▦	●	
STRESA: *La Piemontese* ⓁⓁⓁⓁ Via Mazzini 25, 28049. 📞 *0323 302 35.* A refined but unstuffy restaurant with impeccable service. The cuisine is creative, and the prices are very fair. ● *Mon, Sun eve (Oct–May); 2 wks Jan, 2 wks Dec.*		▦		▦
TURIN: *Birilli* ⓁⓁ Strada Val San Martino 6, 10131. 📞 *011 819 05 67.* A friendly, cheerful restaurant opened in 1991 as part of a family-run chain whose first branch opened in Los Angeles in 1929. Simple dishes include meats and the house pasta *Birilli* (with tomato and bacon). ● *Sun (winter).* 🎫 ♿				▦
TURIN: *Porto di Savona* ⓁⓁ Piazza Vittorio Veneto 2, 10100. 📞 *011 817 35 00.* A friendly restaurant set in an 18th-century building in central Turin. The regional cuisine includes such dishes as *gnocchi* with gorgonzola, and meats braised in Barolo wine. ● *Mon, Tue lunch; 2 weeks Aug.* ▤	●	▦		▦
TURIN: *Saletta* ⓁⓁ Via Belfiore 37, 10125. 📞 *011 668 78 67.* A warm, friendly atmosphere in central Turin. House specialties include meat braised in Barolo wine, and a fluffy *zabaglione.* ● *Sun; Aug.* 🎫 ▤	●	▦		
TURIN: *Spada Reale* ⓁⓁⓁ Via Principe Amedeo 53, 10123. 📞 *011 817 13 63.* This restaurant provides a traditional, rustic setting in which to try the Piedmontese dishes. Run by a family, it is lively and informal, serving good value food. ● *Sun, Sat lunch; Aug.*		▦		
TURIN: *Neuv Caval 'd Brôns* ⓁⓁⓁⓁ Piazza San Carlo 151, 10123. 📞 *011 562 74 83.* An elegant, spacious restaurant offering excellent food from a range of cuisine including vegetarian dishes. Specialties include the famous mint and chocolate pudding *Santa Vittoria.* ● *Sat lunch, Sun.* 🎫 ⚡	●	▦	●	
VERBANIA PALLANZA: *Milano* ⓁⓁⓁⓁ Corso Zanitello 2, 28048. 📞 *0323 55 68 16.* Close to the town center, the Milano has lake views and a romantic interior. Dishes include *tagliolini* and lake fish. ● *Tue; Jan, 1 week Jun.* 🎫		▦		▦
VERCELLI: *Il Paiolo* ⓁⓁ Viale Garibaldi 72, 13100. 📞 *0161 25 05 77.* A country trattoria in the historic center, it specializes in local cuisine. The Vercellese *risotto* is particularly recommended. ● *Thu; mid-Jul–mid-Aug.* 🎫		▦		
VERCELLI: *Il Giardinetto* ⓁⓁⓁⓁ Via Sereno 3, 13100. 📞 *0161 25 72 30.* The restaurant of an elegant villa hotel, it specializes in cuisine with truffles and mushrooms. Try the *foie gras* with apple and wine sauce. ● *Mon; 3 weeks Aug.* 🎫 ▤		▦		▦

VILLARFOCCHIARDO: *La Giaconera*　　　　　Ⓛ Ⓛ Ⓛ
Via Antica di Francia 1, 10050. 📞 *011 964 50 00.*
This elegantly restored coach house makes good use of seasonal ingredients such
as truffles, game and choice vegetables. ● *Mon, Tue; 2 weeks Jan, 2 weeks Aug.* 📧 ♿

LIGURIA

CAMOGLI: *La Cucina di Nonna Nina*　　　　　Ⓛ Ⓛ Ⓛ
Via Molfino 126, San Rocco di Camogli 16032. 📞 *0185 77 38 35.*
"If you're in a hurry" says the menu, "relax; our food is prepared according
to traditional methods." The atmosphere is friendly and there are wonderful
views of the Golfo Paradiso. ● *Wed; 1 week Jan, 1 week Oct.* 📧

CAMOGLI: *Rosa*　　　　　Ⓛ Ⓛ Ⓛ Ⓛ
Largo Casabona 11, 16032. 📞 *0185 77 34 11.*
Set in a pretty villa on the Golfo Paradiso, the menu offers exquisitely prepared fish
such as pasta with fresh anchovies. ● *Tue; mid-Jan–mid-Feb, 2 wks Nov.* 📧

CERVO: *San Giorgio*　　　　　Ⓛ Ⓛ Ⓛ Ⓛ
Via Volta 19, 18010. 📞 *0183 40 01 75.*
Booking is absolutely essential at this popular spot for regional cuisine with a
different twist. The dishes are mainly fresh fish and seafood; the *branzino* (sea bass)
with rosemary and beans is exceptional. ● *Mon eve (winter), Tue; 3 wks Jan, Nov.*

DOLCEACQUA: *Gastone*　　　　　Ⓛ Ⓛ Ⓛ
Piazza Garibaldi 2, 18035. 📞 *0184 20 65 77.*
Home-made pasta and regional meat dishes are two of the attractions
at this elegant restaurant in the historic center. ● *Mon eve, Tue; 3 weeks Jan.* 📧

GENOA: *Da Genio*　　　　　Ⓛ Ⓛ
Salita San Leonardo 61r, 16128. 📞 *010 58 84 63.*
Popular with locals, this restaurant has a animated atmosphere. The food is delicious,
and includes grilled swordfish and anchovies stuffed with capers. ● *Sun; Aug.* 📧

GENOA: *Do' Colla*　　　　　Ⓛ Ⓛ
Via alla Chiesa di Murta 10, Località Bolzaneto. 📞 *010 740 85 79.*
It's worth heading the few miles out of Genoa to taste the exquisite home-style
Ligurian cooking of this simple trattoria. ● *Sun eve, Mon; 2 weeks Jan, Aug.*

LEVANTO: *Tumelin*　　　　　Ⓛ Ⓛ Ⓛ
Via Grillo 32, 19015. 📞 *0187 80 83 79.*
The restaurant is 100m (300ft) from the sea and the menu includes a selection
of wonderful seafood appetisers. Friendly service. ● *Thu; Jan.* 📧

MANAROLA: *Marina Piccola*　　　　　Ⓛ Ⓛ Ⓛ
Via Lo Scalo 16, 19010. 📞 *0187 92 01 03.*
There are wonderful sea views from this restaurant, whose menu of regional
specialties includes seafood antipasti, pesto, and grilled fish. ● *Tue; Nov.* 📧 ♿

NERVI: *Astor*　　　　　Ⓛ Ⓛ Ⓛ
Viale delle Palme 16–18, 16167. 📞 *010 32 90 11.*
This hotel restaurant offers a good selection of dishes including pesto, fish,
and the local pasta dish *(pansotti)* with wild herbs and nut sauce. 📧 🍽 ♿

PORTOFINO: *Puny*　　　　　Ⓛ Ⓛ Ⓛ Ⓛ
Piazza Martiri Olivetta 5, 16034. 📞 *0185 26 90 37.*
A spectacular view of the bay of Portofino accompanies the well-prepared regional
dishes accompanied by crisp Ligurian wines. ● *Thu; Jan, Feb, 2 weeks Dec.*

PORTOVENERE: *Taverna del Corsaro*　　　　　Ⓛ Ⓛ Ⓛ Ⓛ
Calata Doria 102, 19025. 📞 *0187 79 06 22.*
Reinterpreted regional recipes form the basis of the exclusively fish menu. Set on the
tip of the Portovenere Peninsula with views over the sea. ● *Mon; Nov–Dec.* 📧

RAPALLO: *Roccabruna*　　　　　Ⓛ Ⓛ Ⓛ
Via Sotto la Croce 6, Località Savagna 16035. 📞 *0185 26 14 00.*
Set on a pretty terrace away from the crowds on the seafront, this restaurant
simply serves the menu of the day, from the antipasti to the wines. ● *Sun eve, Mon.* 📧

SAN REMO: *Paolo e Barbara*　　　　　Ⓛ Ⓛ Ⓛ Ⓛ
Via Roma 47, 18038. 📞 *0184 53 16 53.*
One of the most renowned restaurants in Liguria, the cuisine here is
based on local and Mediterranean specialties, especially fish and seafood.
● *Wed, Thu lunch.* 📧 🍽

		FIXED-PRICE MENU	GOOD WINE LIST	FORMAL DRESS	OUTDOOR TABLES

Average prices for a three-course meal for one, including a half bottle of house wine, tax and service:
Ⓛ up to L35,000
ⓁⓁ L35–55,000
ⓁⓁⓁ L55–75,000
ⓁⓁⓁⓁ L75–100,000
ⓁⓁⓁⓁⓁ over L100,000.

FIXED-PRICE MENU
A fixed-price menu offered, usually with three courses.
GOOD WINE LIST
Denotes a wide range of good quality wines.
FORMAL DRESS
Some restaurants require men to wear a jacket and tie.
OUTDOOR TABLES
Tables for eating outdoors, often with a good view.
CREDIT CARDS
The symbol shows that major credit cards are accepted.

	FIXED-PRICE MENU	GOOD WINE LIST	FORMAL DRESS	OUTDOOR TABLES
VERNAZZA: *Gambero Rosso* ⓁⓁⓁ Piazza Marconi 7, 1901 8. 【 0187 81 22 65. Rice with lemon and shrimp, roast anchovies, *gamberoni in pigiama* (deep-fried shrimp), and *pansotti (see p174)* with cocoa and thyme are only some of the imaginatively interpreted Ligurian dishes here. ● Mon; Dec–Feb. 🗐 🕭	●			▨

EMILIA-ROMAGNA

	FIXED-PRICE MENU	GOOD WINE LIST	FORMAL DRESS	OUTDOOR TABLES
BOLOGNA: *Antica Trattoria Spiga* Ⓛ Via Broccaindosso 21a, 40125. 【 051 23 00 63. A homely, authentic trattoria, with immaculately prepared traditional cuisine. Specialties include *lasagne*, *tortellini* and *gnocchi*. ● Mon eve, Sun; Aug. 🗐	●			
BOLOGNA: *Antica Trattoria del Cacciatore* ⓁⓁⓁⓁ Via Caduti di Casteldebole 25, 40132. 【 051 56 42 03. A country inn near the airport. The menu is a mix of local and international dishes with homemade bread. ● Sun eve, Mon; 1 week Jan, 2 weeks Aug. 🗐 ▤		▨		
BOLOGNA: *Pappagallo* ⓁⓁⓁⓁ Piazza Mercanzia 3c, 40125. 【 051 23 28 07. Housed in a 14th-century palazzo in the historic center, this elegant resturant serves Bolognese dishes: *tortellini* and *lasagna*. ● Sun; Aug. 🗐		▨		
CASTELL'ARQUATO: *Da Faccini* ⓁⓁ Località Sant' Antonio 10, 29014. 【 0523 89 63 40. Pasta and game are the highlights. Try *gnocchi* with carrots, duck and truffle *ravioli* and rabbit with mustard. ● Wed; 1 week Jul, 1 week Jan. 🗐 🕭		▨		
CASTELL'ARQUATO: *Maps* ⓁⓁⓁ Piazza Europa 3, 29014. 【 0523 80 44 11. In a restructured medieval mill in the historic center, fish is the mainstay of the menu that changes according to the market. ● Mon pm, Tue; Jul; 1 week Jan, 1 week Dec. 🗐 ▤		▨		▨
FAENZA: *Le Volte* ⓁⓁ Corso Mazzini 54, 48018. 【 0546 66 16 00. Housed in an atmospheric building in the historic center. The food is delicious with a strong Pugliese influence. Try green gnocchi with tomato and basil, and chicken with olives. ● Sun; 2 weeks Jul, 2 weeks Aug. 🗐 ▤	●	▨		▨
FERRARA: *La Sgarbata* ⓁⓁ Via Sgarbata 84, 44100. 【 0532 71 21 10. An country trattoria on the outskirts of Ferrara which serves specialty fish dishes as well as rich and tasty pizzas. ● Mon, Tue; Aug. 🗐	●	▨		▨
FERRARA: *Quel Fantastico Giovedì* ⓁⓁ Via Castelnuovo 9, 44100. 【 0532 76 05 70. A bright restaurant whose varied and creative menu, which changes every week, includes Japanese-style sushi of salmon. ● Wed; Aug, 2 weeks Jan. 🗐 ▤ 🗲	●	▨		
FIDENZA: *Del Duomo* ⓁⓁ Via Micheli 27, 43036. 【 0524 52 42 68. Near the cathedral, the menu includes homemade *spaghetti* with mushrooms, and tripe alla parmigiana. ● Mon; 1 week Jul, 3 weeks Aug. 🗐		▨		
GORO: *Ferrari* ⓁⓁⓁ Via Antonio Brugnoli 240–4, 44020. 【 0533 99 64 48. Next to the fish market, the menu changes every day to make use of the best of the day's catch; the menu is almost entirely fish. ● Wed. ▤	●	▨		▨
MODENA: *Al Boschetto* Ⓛ Via Due Canali Nord 198, 41100. 【 059 25 17 59. A rustic restaurant set in a vast park. Specialties include *tortellini* in chicken broth, *ragù* sauce, and spit-roasted meats. ● Sun eve, Wed; 2 weeks Aug. 🗐 🗲	●	▨		▨

MODENA: *Fini* $\textcircled{L}\textcircled{L}\textcircled{L}\textcircled{L}$
Piazzetta San Francesco, 41100. **[** 059 22 33 14.
A mainstay of local cuisine with exquisite dishes: *tortellini, lasagna di maccheroni* and delicious desserts. ● Mon, Tue; late Jul–late Aug. 🗺 ≣

PARMA: *Aldo* $\textcircled{L}\textcircled{L}$
Piazzale Inzani 15, 43100. **[** 0521 20 60 01.
A trattoria serving classics with interesting touches: smoked roast beef, and guinea fowl with orange sauce. ● Sun eve, Mon; mid-Jul–mid-Aug. 🗺

PARMA: *Le Viole* $\textcircled{L}\textcircled{L}\textcircled{L}$
Strada Nuova 60a, Località Castelnuovo Golese 43031. **[** 0521 60 10 00.
A delightful place to eat offering a successful mix of modern ideas and tradition. Try the *fagottini* (parcels) of turkey with vegetables, and the homemade desserts. ● Wed, Thu lunch; 2 weeks Jan, 1 week Feb, 1 week Aug. 🗺

PIACENZA: *Don Carlos* $\textcircled{L}\textcircled{L}\textcircled{L}$
Strada Aguzzafame 85, 29100. **[** 0523 499 80 00.
The excellent cuisine in this elegant restaurant uses fresh seasonal ingredients and includes a seafood and bean salad, and pickled salmon. ● Mon; 2 weeks Aug. 🗺

PIACENZA: *Antica Osteria del Teatro* $\textcircled{L}\textcircled{L}\textcircled{L}\textcircled{L}$
Via Verdi 16, 29100. **[** 0523 32 37 77.
An excellent wine list accompanies a menu of imaginative dishes prepared with immense flair from the best of local produce. The setting, in a 15th-century palazzo in the historic center, is also pleasant. ● Sun, Mon. 🗺 ≣

RAVENNA: *Trattoria Capannetti* $\textcircled{L}\textcircled{L}\textcircled{L}$
Vicolo Capannetti 21, 48100. **[** 0544 666 81.
Creative, regional homemade cuisine that changes with the season. It's a peaceful restaurant in the historic center. ● Sun eve, Mon. 🗺

RAVENNA: *Tre Spade* $\textcircled{L}\textcircled{L}\textcircled{L}$
Via Faentina 136, 48100. **[** 0544 50 05 22.
Set in a 19th-century villa in a park. The chef's specialties include *tortelli* with duck sauce and lamb with seafood salad. ● Sun eve, Mon. 🗺 🗾 ⛊ ≣

RIMINI: *Il Melograno* $\textcircled{L}\textcircled{L}\textcircled{L}$
Viale Vespucci 16, 47037. **[** 0541 522 55.
The restaurant of the Holiday Inn hotel serves mainly fish (turbot in a potato crust, red mullet with rosemary) as well as grilled meats. 🗺 🗾 ≣

RIMINI: *Europa* $\textcircled{L}\textcircled{L}\textcircled{L}\textcircled{L}$
Via Roma 51, 47037. **[** 0541 287 61.
Fish forms the basis of the menu here, with dishes including salad of warm fish with *radicchio*, seafood *spaghetti*. ● Sun; 1 week Aug. 🗺 ⛊ ≣

FLORENCE

FLORENCE: *La Maremmana* $\textcircled{L}$
Via de' Macci 77r, 50100. **Map** 4 E1. **[** 055 24 12 26.
A basic trattoria with traditional fare, off the main tourist circuit and close to Santa Croce. The fixed-price menu is particularly recommended. ● Sun. 🗺

FLORENCE: *Palle D'Oro* $\textcircled{L}$
Via Sant'Antonino 43r, 50123. **Map** 1 C5 (5 C1). **[** 055 28 83 83.
Sparse, simple, spotlessly clean trattoria. The food is basic but cooked well and there is a very good carry-out sandwich bar at the front. ● Sun; Aug. 🗺 ≣

FLORENCE: *Trattoria Mario* $\textcircled{L}$
Via Rosina 2r, 50123. **Map** 1 C4. **[** 055 21 85 50.
A popular lunch-time trattoria. Specials change daily; on Thursday there is *gnocchi* and on Friday, fish. ● eves, Sun. ≣

FLORENCE: *Acquacotta* $\textcircled{L}\textcircled{L}$
Via de' Pilastri 51r, 50124. **Map** 2 E5. **[** 055 24 29 07.
An inexpensive, three-roomed restaurant named after a Florentine vegetable soup. Grilled meats and other Tuscan dishes are also featured. ● Sun. 🗺

FLORENCE: *Buca dell'Orafo* $\textcircled{L}\textcircled{L}$
Volta de' Girolami 28r, 50122. **Map** 6 D4. **[** 055 21 36 19.
This friendly hole-in-the-wall is a long-time favorite with Florentines. The homey cooking is based on homemade pasta, and daily specials include the typically Tuscan *ribollita* (vegetable soup), pasta and *fagioli* (beans). ● Sun, Mon; Aug. ≣

	FIXED-PRICE MENU	GOOD WINE LIST	FORMAL DRESS	OUTDOOR TABLES
Average prices for a three-course meal for one, including a half bottle of house wine, tax and service: Ⓛ up to L35,000 ⓁⓁ L35–55,000 ⓁⓁⓁ L55–75,000 ⓁⓁⓁⓁ L75–100,000 ⓁⓁⓁⓁⓁ over L100,000.	**FIXED-PRICE MENU** A fixed-price menu offered, usually with three courses. **GOOD WINE LIST** Denotes a wide range of good quality wines. **FORMAL DRESS** Some restaurants require men to wear a jacket and tie. **OUTDOOR TABLES** Tables for eating outdoors, often with a good view. **CREDIT CARDS** The symbol shows that major credit cards are accepted.			

FLORENCE: *Da Pennello* ⓁⓁ Via Dante Alighieri 4r, 50100. **Map** 4 D1. 〔 055 29 48 48. Book well ahead or risk a long wait for a table. This popular restaurant is famous for its extensive antipasti, a meal in themselves. ● *Sun eve, Mon; Aug, 1 week on Dec.*	●	▨		▨
FLORENCE: *Dino* ⓁⓁ Via Ghibellina 51r, 50122. **Map** 4 D1 (6 E3). 〔 055 24 14 52. A well-regarded restaurant in a beautiful 14th-century palazzo. It has one of the best wine lists in Florence and a menu of regional dishes such as onion soup and *pici* (pasta) *alle Senese.* ● *Sun eve, Mon.* 🍴 ▤		▨		
FLORENCE: *Enoteca Fuori Porta* ⓁⓁ Via Monte alle Croci 10r, 50122. **Map** 4 3E. 〔 055 234 24 83. This wine bar is very popular with locals and visitors alike for its excellent *crostini* with assorted toppings and, of course, the wide-ranging wine list. ● *Sun.*				
FLORENCE: *Le Mossacce* ⓁⓁ Via del Pronconsolo 55r, 50122. **Map** 2 D5 (6 E2). 〔 055 29 43 61. Don't be put off by the multilingual menus, the paper tablecloths, and the chaos; the 100-year-old Mossacce serves robust Tuscan food. ● *Sat, Sun.* 🍴	●			
FLORENCE: *San Zanobi* ⓁⓁ Via San Zanobi 33r, 50100. **Map** 1 C4. 〔 055 47 52 86. Delicate, inventive food served in a sedate, refined dining room. The dishes, based on a Florentine theme, are light and well presented. ● *Sun.* 🍴		▨		
FLORENCE: *Trattoria Angiolino* ⓁⓁ Via di Santo Spirito 36r, 50125. **Map** 3 B1. 〔 055 239 89 76. An attractive restaurant with a typically Florentine, bustling atmosphere. The food is traditional Tuscan style, from vegetable soups to grilled meats. In winter an iron stove in the middle of the restaurant is lit. ● *Nov–Mar: Mon.* 🍴		▨		
FLORENCE: *Trattoria Zà Zà* ⓁⓁ Piazza del Mercato Centrale 26r, 50123. **Map** 1 C4. 〔 055 21 54 11. A canteenlike restaurant that is always packed. The food is Tuscan. Excellent soups include *ribollita* (vegetables), and *passata di fagioli* (bean purée). ● *Sun.* 🍴	●			▨
FLORENCE: *Buca Mario* ⓁⓁ Piazza degli Ottaviani 16r, 50100. **Map** 1 B5. 〔 055 21 41 79. A crowded restaurant where it is normal to book or line up for a table. Enjoy the homemade pasta and grilled meats at good prices. ● *Wed, Thu lunch; Aug.* 🍴		▨		
FLORENCE: *Cafaggi* ⓁⓁ Via Guelfa 35r, 50123. **Map** 1 C4. 〔 055 29 49 89. This classic Tuscan trattoria serves oil and wines from the family farm. *Crostini* (toasts), *zuppa di certosina* and *involtini* (roulade) are particularly good dishes on a varied menu. ● *Sun; 2 weeks Jul, 2 weeks Aug.* 🍴	●	▨		
FLORENCE: *Da Ganino* ⓁⓁⓁ Piazza dei Cimatori 4r, 50100. **Map** 6 D3. 〔 055 21 41 25. A small, friendly restaurant popular with locals, da Ganino offers all the basics of local fare, including *ravioli* with butter and sage. ● *Sun.* 🍴		▨		▨
FLORENCE: *Francescano* ⓁⓁ Via San Guiseppe 26r, 50120. **Map** 4 E1. 〔 055 24 16 05. A smartly fitted restaurant of wood, marble, and objets d'art. The menu is based on seasonal ingredients and changes weekly. ● *Oct–Apr: Tue.* 🍴 ▤		▨		
FLORENCE: *I Quattro Amici* ⓁⓁⓁ Via degli Orti Oricellari 29, 50100. **Map** 1 A5. 〔 055 21 54 13. Four friends with many years in the business created this fish restaurant. The interior is cool and spartan but the fish, which comes from Porto Santo Stefano, is always excellent. 🍴 ▤	●	▨		

FLORENCE: *La Taverna del Bronzino* Ⓛ Ⓛ Ⓛ
Via delle Ruote 27r, 50129. **Map** 2 D3. 055 49 52 20.
Named after the Florentine painter who had connections with the 15th-century
palazzo that houses this restaurant. Finest quality cooking. ● *Sun; Aug.*

FLORENCE: *Paoli* Ⓛ Ⓛ Ⓛ
Via dei Tavolini 12r, 50100. **Map** 6 D3 (4 D1). 055 21 62 15.
A spectacular setting: the dining room is a vaulted hall smothered in medieval
frescoes. The restaurant specializes in typically Tuscan dishes. ● *Tue; Aug.*

FLORENCE: *Alle Murate* Ⓛ Ⓛ Ⓛ Ⓛ
Via Ghibellina 52r, 50122. **Map** 4 E1. 055 24 06 18.
Popular with locals, this refined restaurant offers a great range of creative,
Tuscan dishes. The food combines Italian staples with more far-flung Mediterranean
cuisines and there are light and interesting desserts. ● *lunch, Mon; 1 week Dec.*

FLORENCE: *Cibreo* Ⓛ Ⓛ Ⓛ Ⓛ
Via Andrea del Verrocchio 8r, 50122. **Map** 4 E1. 055 234 11 00.
Superbly prepared Tuscan food in an informal atmosphere. There is no pasta,
but specialties include tripe and kidneys. For the squeamish there are many
delicious alternatives such as duck stuffed with raisins. ● *Sun, Mon; Aug.*

FLORENCE: *Enoteca Pinchiorri* Ⓛ Ⓛ Ⓛ Ⓛ Ⓛ
Via Ghibellina 87, 50122. **Map** 1 A4 (5 A1). 055 24 27 77.
Often described as Italy's best restaurant with the finest wine cellar in Europe, the
Pinchiorri is on the ground floor of a 15th-century palazzo. The Tuscan- and French-
inspired dishes includes a wonderful mix of dishes. ● *Sun, Mon, Wed lunch; Aug.*

FLORENCE: *Sabatini* Ⓛ Ⓛ Ⓛ Ⓛ
Via Panzani 9a, 50123. **Map** 1 C5 (5 C1). 055 21 15 59.
Once Florence's best restaurant, the cuisine (Italian and international) is
sometimes excellent, and the ambience and service are good. ● *Mon.*

TUSCANY

AREZZO: *Buca di San Francesco* Ⓛ Ⓛ
Via San Francesco 1, 52100. 0575 232 71.
The medieval atmosphere and position alongside the church of Piero della
Francesca's fresco cycle make this an obvious choice. ● *Mon eve, Tue.*

ARTIMINO: *Da Delfina* Ⓛ Ⓛ Ⓛ
Via della Chiesa 1, 50041. 055 871 80 74.
A lovely restaurant outside a walled medieval village. Game is a specialty,
as is pork with fennel and black Tuscan cabbage. ● *Sun eve, Mon.*

BAGNI DI LUCCA: *Dandini* Ⓛ Ⓛ
Via Dorati, Localita Granaiola. 0583 88 10 81.
This small, simple restaurant clings to a hillside and serves up excellent roasted
meats and delicious desserts. Local game and mushrooms in season. ● *Mon; Nov.*

CAPALBIO: *Da Maria* Ⓛ Ⓛ Ⓛ
Via Comunale 3, 58011. 0564 89 60 14.
Vacationing politicians from Rome sit down with locals to enjoy soundly cooked
Maremma specialties like wild boar and pasta with truffles. ● *Oct–Apr: Tue.*

CASTELNUOVO BERARDENGA: *La Bottega del Trenta* Ⓛ Ⓛ Ⓛ Ⓛ
Via Santa Caterina 2, Villa a Sesta 53019. 0577 35 92 26.
A tasteful restaurant serving adventurous cooking including duck breast with
wild fennel and delicious desserts. ● *Tue, Wed, Mon–Sat lunch; 2 weeks Jan, 2 weeks Feb.*

COLLE DI VAL D'ELSA: *L'Antica Trattoria* Ⓛ Ⓛ Ⓛ Ⓛ
Piazza Arnolfo 23, 53034. 0577 92 37 47.
A homey, family-run restaurant dedicated to traditional regional cuisine. The setting
is medieval and the service lively and attentive. ● *Tue; 1 week Jan, 1 week Dec.*

CORTONA: *La Loggetta* Ⓛ Ⓛ
Piazza Pescheria 3, 52044. 0575 63 05 75.
Set in a quaint medieval loggia, the atmosphere is cool and sedate and the
homemade *ravioli* stuffed with fondue, delicious. ● *Oct–May: Mon; Nov, Dec.*

ELBA: *Publius* Ⓛ Ⓛ Ⓛ
Piazza XX Settembre, Poggio di Marciana 57030. 0565 992 08.
A pleasant trattoria with one of the best wine cellar on Elba. In addition to fish,
you can eat wild mushrooms, game, and wild boar. ● *Nov–Mar.*

Average prices for a three-course meal for one, including a half bottle of house wine, tax and service:
(L) up to L35,000
(L)(L) L35–55,000
(L)(L)(L) L55–75,000
(L)(L)(L)(L) L75–100,000
(L)(L)(L)(L)(L) over L100,000.

FIXED-PRICE MENU
A fixed-price menu offered, usually with three courses.

GOOD WINE LIST
Denotes a wide range of good quality wines.

FORMAL DRESS
Some restaurants require men to wear a jacket and tie.

OUTDOOR TABLES
Tables for eating outdoors, often with a good view.

CREDIT CARDS
The symbol shows that major credit cards are accepted.

	FIXED-PRICE MENU	GOOD WINE LIST	FORMAL DRESS	OUTDOOR TABLES
GAIOLE IN CHIANTI: *Badia a Coltibuono* (L)(L)		■		■
LIVORNO: *La Chiave* (L)(L)(L)		■		
LUCCA: *Buca di Sant'Antonio* (L)(L)				
MASSA MARITTIMA: *Bracali* (L)(L)(L)(L)				
MONTALCINO: *Taverna dei Barbi* (L)(L)		■		■
MONTECATINI TERME: *Gourmet* (L)(L)(L)(L)	●	■	●	
MONTEPULCIANO: *Il Marzocco* (L)(L)	●	■		■
MONTERIGGIONI: *Il Pozzo* (L)(L)(L)		■		■
ORBETELLO: *Osteria del Lupacante* (L)(L)	●	■		
PESCIA: *Cecco* (L)(L)		■		■
PIENZA: *Da Falco* (L)(L)	●	■		■
PISA: *Al Ristoro dei Vecchi Macelli* (L)(L)(L)		■		

GAIOLE IN CHIANTI: *Badia a Coltibuono*   (L)(L)
Badia a Coltibuono, 53013. (0577 74 94 24.
Set in front of an 11th-century abbey, in the heart of a vineyard whose oils and wines are used in the restaurant. The menu includes spit-roasted meats and delicious desserts. Tours of the estate are offered for wine-tasters. ● *Mon; Nov–Feb.*

LIVORNO: *La Chiave*   (L)(L)(L)
Scali delle Cantine 52, 57100. (0586 88 86 09.
Refined and elegant dining from a menu that includes traditional Tuscan meat and fish cuisine and is changed every two weeks. ● *lunch; Wed; Aug.*

LUCCA: *Buca di Sant'Antonio*   (L)(L)
Via della Cervia 3, 55100. (0583 558 81.
This is Lucca's most famous restaurant of traditional rustic cooking. It serves a range of local dishes, such as *fettucine sul piccione* (pasta and pigeon). ● *Sun eve, Mon; Jul.*

MASSA MARITTIMA: *Bracali*   (L)(L)(L)(L)
Frazione Ghirlanda 2, 58024. (0566 90 23 18.
Mouth-watering Maremma cooking in a family restaurant; thinly sliced wild boar, pigeon with honey, and guinea fowl with white grapes. ● *Tue; Jan, Nov.*

MONTALCINO: *Taverna dei Barbi*   (L)(L)
Località Podernovi, 53024. (0577 84 92 82.
Superb country cooking, served with Brunello wines, in a renowned restaurant that also has wonderful views over the surrounding hills. ● *Tue eve, Wed; Jan.*

MONTECATINI TERME: *Gourmet*   (L)(L)(L)(L)
Via Amendola 6, 51016. (0572 77 10 12.
This is an elegant restaurant in a wonderful 19th century building. The atmosphere is relaxing, the fiah dishes are sublime. ● *2 weeks Jan, 3 weeks Aug.*

MONTEPULCIANO: *Il Marzocco*   (L)(L)
Piazza Savonarola 18, 53045. (0578 75 72 62
Part of a 19th-century hotel, this is a pleasant family-run restaurant that offers well-presented local dishes in unpretentious surroundings. ● *Wed; Nov–Easter.*

MONTERIGGIONI: *Il Pozzo*   (L)(L)(L)
Piazza Roma 2, 53035. (0577 30 41 27.
A stone-walled restaurant in the charming medieval village of Monteriggioni. The Tuscan food is simple and enthusiastically prepared, and the homemade desserts are well-known in the surrounding region. ● *Sun eve, Mon; 3 weeks Jan, 1 week Feb.*

ORBETELLO: *Osteria del Lupacante*   (L)(L)
Corso Italia 103, 58015. (0564 86 76 18.
The cooking concentrates on fish and seafood specialties with some touches of adventure; look out for mussels in Marsala sauce, grilled shrimp and zucchini flowers with squid. ● *Oct–May: Tue.*

PESCIA: *Cecco*   (L)(L)
Via Francesca Forti 94–96, 51017. (0572 47 79 55.
A friendly local restaurant where the food is often outstanding. Try the local Pescia asparagus, and *cioncia* (the house main course). ● *Mon; Jan, Jul.*

PIENZA: *Da Falco*   (L)(L)
Piazza Dante Alighieri 3, 53026. (0578 74 85 51.
A friendly local restaurant with excellent antipasti and a magnificent choice of primi and secondi from a menu of local specialties. ● *Fri.*

PISA: *Al Ristoro dei Vecchi Macelli*   (L)(L)(L)
Via Volturno 49, 56126. (050 204 24.
Innovative dishes in a pleasant, intimate restaurant that serves light Tuscan food with an adventurous twist. Fish, seafood, and game specialties are delicately prepared and the desserts are a delight. ● *Wed; 2 weeks Aug.*

POPPI: *Il Cedro* ⓁⓁ
Via di Camaldoli 20, Località Moggiona, 52010. [0575 55 60 80.
Venison, wild boar, and guinea fowl in wine are among some of the excellently
cooked specialties of Il Cedro. This good-value restaurant stands in a
wonderful setting that overlooks forests and mountains. ● *Mon.*

PORTO ERCOLE: *Bacco in Toscana* ⓁⓁⓁ
Via San Paolo 6, 58018. [0564 83 30 78.
An intimate restaurant that serves an array of excellent seafood dishes; scampi
with lemon and *spaghetti alle vongole* (clams). ● *lunch; Wed; Nov–Mar.* 🗗

PORTO SANTO STEFANO: *La Bussola* ⓁⓁⓁ
Viale Marconi, 58019. [0564 81 42 25.
The menu includes some excellent seafood pastas as well as simpler grilled
fish. From the terrace there are fine views of the sea. ● *Wed; Nov.* 🗗 ▤

PRATO: *Il Piraña* ⓁⓁⓁⓁ
Via Valentini 110, 50047. [0574 257 46.
Rated as one of the best fish and seafood restaurants in Tuscany; don't be
put off by its setting or too-precious modern interior. ● *Sat lunch, Sun; Aug.* 🗗

SAN GIMIGNANO: *Le Terrazze* ⓁⓁⓁ
Albergo la Cisterna, Piazza della Cisterna 24, 53037. [0577 94 03 28.
Set within the medievil walls, with views over the rolling hills of southern Tuscany,
one of the dining rooms forms part of a 13th-century palazzo. Good for regional
specialties with some novelties. ● *Tue, Wed lunch.* 🗗 ▤

SANSEPOLCRO: *Paola e Marco Mercati* ⓁⓁⓁ
Via Palmiro Togliatti 68, 52037. [0575 73 48 75.
A new restaurant whose dishes include Tuscan black cabbage cooked with white truf-
fles, vegetable *ravioli*, roast pigeon, and *gnocchi*. ● *Lunch; Sun; 2 weeks Jun, 2 weeks Jul.* 🗗

SATURNIA: *I Due Cippi da Michele* ⓁⓁ
Piazza Vittorio Veneto 26a, 58050. [0564 60 10 74.
One of the region's most popular restaurants, it is a touchstone for Maremma
cuisine and its traditional offerings are a good value. ● *Oct–Jun: Tue; 1 week Dec.* 🗗

SIENA: *Al Marsili* ⓁⓁⓁ
Via del Castoro 3, 53100. [0577 471 54.
Set in an 11th century building, Al Marsili, long regarded as one of the best
restaurants in Siena, offers good regional specialties. ● *Mon.* 🗗 ▤

SIENA: *Osteria le Logge* ⓁⓁⓁ
Via del Porrione 33, 53100. [0577 480 13.
Siena's prettiest restaurant, with dark wood and marble interior. Home-
produced oils and Montalcino wines accompany dishes that include
guinea fowl, duck and fennel, and rabbit with capers. ● *Sun; Nov.* 🗗

SOVANA: *Taverna Etrusca* ⓁⓁ
Piazza del Pretorio 16, 58010. [0564 61 61 83.
A small restaurant with medieval dining area. The carefully produced cuisine
is Tuscan with sophisticated touches. ● *Mon; 3 weeks Jan, 1 week Feb.* 🗗 ▤

VIAREGGIO: *Romano* ⓁⓁⓁⓁ
Via Mazzini 120, 55049. [0584 313 82.
This is one of Tuscany's best fish and seafood restaurants. The service is
courteous and friendly and the wines are well priced. ● *Mon; Jan.* 🗗

UMBRIA

AMELIA: *Anita* Ⓛ
Via Roma 31, 05022. [0744 98 21 46.
This simple restaurant offers no-frills local food, such as *crostini* (toasted bread with
toppings), roasted meats, pasta with *porcini* mushrooms, and wild boar. ● *Mon.* 🗗

ASSISI: *Medioevo* ⓁⓁⓁ
Via Arco dei Priori 4b, 06081. [075 81 30 68.
An elegant restaurant in old Assisi. Pastas are homemade (try them with black
truffles in season). Meats are cooked to traditional recipes. ● *Wed, Sun eve; Jul.* 🗗 ▤

ASSISI: *San Francesco* ⓁⓁⓁ
Via San Francesco 52, 06081. [075 81 23 29.
A carefully chosen menu includes *carpaccio* of *porcini* mushrooms (raw,
thinly sliced), homemade pâté, and beef fillet with truffles. ● *Wed; 2 weeks Jul.* 🗗 ▤

For key to symbols see back flap

Average prices for a three-course meal for one, including a half bottle of house wine, tax and service: Ⓛ up to L35,000 ⓁⓁ L35–55,000 ⓁⓁⓁ L55–75,000 ⓁⓁⓁⓁ L75–100,000 ⓁⓁⓁⓁⓁ over L100,000.	**FIXED-PRICE MENU** A fixed-price menu offered, usually with three courses. **GOOD WINE LIST** Denotes a wide range of good quality wines. **FORMAL DRESS** Some restaurants require men to wear a jacket and tie. **OUTDOOR TABLES** Tables for eating outdoors, often with a good view. **CREDIT CARDS** The symbol shows that major credit cards are accepted.	**FIXED-PRICE MENU**	**GOOD WINE LIST**	**FORMAL DRESS**	**OUTDOOR TABLES**

BASCHI: *Vissani* ⓁⓁⓁⓁ Strada Statale 448, Todi-Baschi, 05023. [0744 95 02 06. Gianfranco Vissani is famous throughout Italy for his wonderful haute cuisine. The surroundings are elegant – you can choose your own music. ● *Thu lunch, Sun eve.* 🔲▤	●	▦	●	
CITTÀ DI CASTELLO: *Amici Miei* Ⓛ Via del Monte 2, 06012. [075 855 99 04. Set in the storerooms of a 16th-century palazzo in the historic center, the menu is based on regional cuisine. Try the *tagliatelle* with rabbit. ● *Wed.*	●	▦		
CITTÀ DI CASTELLO: *Il Bersaglio* ⓁⓁ Via Vittorio Emanuele Orlando 14, 06012. [075 855 55 34. A traditional Umbrian restaurant with specialties including *gnocchetti* (little *gnocchi*) with truffles. ● *Wed; Jan, 2 weeks Jul.* 🔲	●	▦		▦
CAMPELLO SUL CLITUNNO: *Trattoria Pettino* ⓁⓁ Frazione Pettino 31, 06042. [0743 27 60 21. Set in the middle of the mountains in an old restored house. The *bruschetta* and, in season, the plethora of dishes with truffles are delicious. ● *Tue.*				▦
FOLIGNO: *Villa Roncalli* ⓁⓁⓁ Via Roma 25, 06034. [0742 39 10 91. A charming country inn set in its own garden 1 km (half a mile) from Foligno. Regional specialties are well prepared using fresh ingredients. ● *Mon; Jan, Aug.* 🔲▤	●	▦	●	▦
GUBBIO: *Alcatraz* ⓁⓁ Località Santa Cristina 53, 06020. [075 922 99 38. An Agriturist center about 25 km (15 miles) southwest of Gubbio, the simple food is produced on the farm, including the olive oil, pastas, and wines. 🔲				▦
GUBBIO: *Villa Montegranelli* ⓁⓁⓁ Località Monteluiano, 06024. [075 922 01 85. Set in an 18th-century villa with an elegantly rural atmosphere. Exquisitely made specialties include *crostini* (toasts) with *porcini* mushroom terrine and chestnut flour pancakes with melted cheese and ricotta. 🔲⚡	●	▦		▦
MAGIONE: *Associazione Agrituristica Montemelino* Ⓛ Via dei Montemelini 22, Località Montemelino, 06063. [075 84 36 06. Another of the simple, reliable Agriturist restaurants. This one serves sea fish, grilled meats and, in season, *ravioli* of *porcini* mushrooms. ● *Mon.* 🔲	●	▦		▦
NARNI: *Monte del Grano 1696* ⓁⓁⓁ Strada Guadamello 128, Località San Vito 05030. [0744 74 91 43. Much care goes into creating a pleasant atmosphere in which to sample the excellent regional dishes,. In season, try the truffles and *porcini* mushrooms. ● *Mon; Tue–Fri lunch; Nov.* 🔲	●	▦		
NORCIA: *Dal Francese* ⓁⓁ Via Riguardati 16, 06046. [0743 81 62 90. A country-style trattoria in the center of Norcia. It offers regional specialties such as a truffle-based menu-degustazione in season. ● *Nov–Jul: Fri.* 🔲▤ ⛟				
ORVIETO: *La Volpe e L'Uva* Ⓛ Via Ripa Corsica 1, 05018. [0763 34 16 12. A popular trattoria in the center of Orvieto offering a large variety of regional dishes that change with the season at reasonable prices. ● *Mon; Jan.* 🔲▤	●	▦		
ORVIETO: *I Sette Consoli* ⓁⓁⓁ Piazza Sant'Angelo 1a, 05018. [0763 34 39 11. A comfortable, friendly restaurant with a garden for summer dining. Try *baccalà* (salt cod) marinated in cider vinegar with potato salad, stuffed rabbit, bean soup with fennel, and fish *ravioli*. ● *Wed.* 🔲▤	●	▦		▦

PASSIGNANO SUL TRASIMENO: *Cacciatori da Luciano* ⓁⒺⓁ
Lungolago Pompili 11, 06065. [075 82 72 10.
The menu is based on sea fish, including scampi salad, fish *carpaccio*
(raw, thinly sliced fish), *risotto* of different types of shrimp, and grilled
sole. Some of the desserts are made with wild fruits. ● *Wed.* 🗐 ▤

PERUGIA: *Aladino* ⓁⒺ
Via delle Prome 11, 06122. [075 572 09 38.
In the historic center, the Aladino offers wonderful cuisine with emphasis on
Sardinian specialties. Try the roasted wild boar. ● *lunch daily; Mon; 2 weeks Aug.* 🗐 ▤

PERUGIA: *Giò Arte e Vini* ⓁⒺ
Via Ruggero d'Andreotto 19, 06124. [075 573 11 00.
Famous for its spectacular selection of wines and well-chosen regional
dishes with special touches. The pumpkin *ravioli* and the *trecciola
di agnello* (lamb) are particularly good. ● *Sun eve, Mon lunch.* 🗐 ▤

PERUGIA: *Osteria del Bartolo* ⓁⒺⓁⒺⓁ
Via Bartolo 30, 06122. [075 573 15 61.
An elegant restaurant that is one of the mainstays of the Perugian eating
tradition. Many items are homemade. ● *Wed lunch, Sun.* 🗐 ▤

SPOLETO: *Le Casaline* ⓁⒺ
Località Poreta di Spoleto, Frazione Casaline, 06042. [0743 52 11 13.
An oasis of calm in a restored 18th-century mill. Try the *gnocchi* stuffed with
mushrooms, wild boar *alla cacciatora* (in wine and tomato sauce). ● *Mon.* 🗐

SPOLETO: *Il Tartufo* ⓁⒺⓁ
Piazza Garibaldi 24, 06049. [0743 402 36.
The floor of one of the dining rooms is ancient Roman. Well-tried regional
specialties, including, not surprisingly, truffles, as well as other delights such as
barley soup and duck in Sagrantino wine sauce. ● *Sun eve, Mon; 2 weeks Jul.* 🗐 ▤

TERNI: *Da Carlino* ⓁⒺ
Via Piemonte 1, 05100. [0744 42 01 63.
Robust rustic food, such as *crostini* with local salami, *tagliatelle* with truffles
or duck sauce, lamb, and some fish dishes. ● *Mon; 2 weeks Aug.*

TODI: *La Mulinella* Ⓛ
Località Pontenaia 29, Località Vasciano, 06059. [075 894 47 79.
In the countryside about 2 km (1 mile) from Todi serving simple, reliable
dishes. The homemade pastas and roasted meats are recommended. ● *Wed.* 🗐 ▤

TODI: *Lucaroni* ⓁⒺ
Via Cortesi 7, 06059. [075 88 73 70.
Regional fish, meat, and game (including hare, duck and lamb with truffles).
Desserts, such as *crema* with warm chocolate, are also good. ● *eves; Tue.* 🗐

TREVI: *La Taverna del Pescatore* ⓁⒺⓁ
Via della Chiesa Tonda 50, Località Pigge, 06039. [0742 78 09 20.
The freshest of local produce is combined and cooked in simple yet exquisite
recipes, and the atmosphere is relaxed with attentive service. ● *Wed; Jan.* 🗐

MARCHE

ANCONA: *La Moretta* ⓁⒺⓁ
Piazza Plebiscito 52, 60124. [071 20 23 17.
A lovely traditional restaurant serving excellent local dishes; *polenta* with
calamari and truffles, and lamb with artichokes. ● *Sun; 1week Jan.* 🗐 ▤ ▤

ANCONA: *Passetto* ⓁⒺⓁ
Piazza IV Novembre 1, 60124. [071 332 14.
Outside eating with splendid views of the sea in the summer. The meat
dishes are good – the fish excels. ● *Sun eve, Mon; 2 weeks Aug.* 🗐

ASCOLI PICENO: *C'era Una Volta* Ⓛ
Via Piagge 336, Località Piagge, 63100. [0736 26 17 80.
This restaurant offers simple but tasty dishes in a homely and pleasant atmosphere.
There are beautiful views of the town from the farmhouse garden. 🗐

FABRIANO: *Villa Marchese del Grillo* ⓁⒺ
Via Rocchetta 73, Frazione Rocchetta. [0732 62 56 90.
Set in a restored 18th-century villa, this restaurant combines attentive service with
relaxed informality. The food is superbly prepared. ● *Sun eve, Mon; Jan.* 🗐

Average prices for a three-course meal for one, including a half bottle of house wine, tax and service:
Ⓛ up to L35,000
ⓁⓁ L35–55,000
ⓁⓁⓁ L55–75,000
ⓁⓁⓁⓁ L75–100,000
ⓁⓁⓁⓁⓁ over L100,000.

FIXED-PRICE MENU
A fixed-price menu offered, usually with three courses.

GOOD WINE LIST
Denotes a wide range of good quality wines.

FORMAL DRESS
Some restaurants require men to wear a jacket and tie.

OUTDOOR TABLES
Tables for eating outdoors, often with a good view.

CREDIT CARDS
The symbol shows that major credit cards are accepted.

	FIXED-PRICE MENU	GOOD WINE LIST	FORMAL DRESS	OUTDOOR TABLES
FANO: *Darpetti Quinta* ⓁⓁ Viale Adriatico 42, 61032. 📞 0721 80 80 43. An excellent, basic trattoria where the daily menu consists of simple but delicious cuisine, including many dishes of fresh fish. ● Sun. 🔲				▣
FANO: *Ristorantino da Giulio* ⓁⓁⓁ Viale Adriatico 100, 61032. 📞 0721 80 56 80. A quiet restaurant situated just opposite the beach. The cuisine is basically regional, with the chef's personal touches. Fish antipasti are especially good. ● Tue; Nov. 🔲 ♿				▣
JESI: *Tana Liberatutti* ⓁⓁⓁ Piazza Pontelli 1, 60035. 📞 0731 592 37. A dignified restaurant where Mediterranean dishes are prepared with care. Try the fish *risotto*, or the baked fish. ● Sun; 1 wk Jan, 1 wk Aug. 🔲 ▤				▣
LORETO: *Andreina* ⓁⓁⓁ Via Buffolareccia 14, 60025. 📞 071 97 01 24. A mother-and-daughter-team prepare traditional cuisine with homemade pasta, chicken, rabbit, and game, followed by tempting desserts. ● Tue. 🔲 ▤		▣		▣
MACERATA: *Da Secondo* ⓁⓁ Via Pescheria Vecchia 26–28, 62100. 📞 0733 26 09 12. The regional cuisine, such as *vincisgrassi alla Macerata* (local *lasagna*) and *frittura mista* (batter-fried fish and vegetables) is recommended at this restaurant. ● Mon. 🔲 ▤ 🍴	●			▣
NUMANA: *La Costarella* ⓁⓁⓁ Via IV Novembre 35, 60026. 📞 071 736 02 97. Booking is advisable in this specialty fish restaurant; pasta with black cuttlefish ink and fried fish with zucchini flowers. ● Oct–Easter. 🍴	●	▣		
PESARO: *Rifugio del Gabbiano* ⓁⓁⓁⓁ Strada Panoramica San Bartolo, Località Santa Marina Alta 61100. 📞 0721 27 98 45. Pèsaro traditional dishes are presented with flair. Fish is the mainstay of the menu; try pasta in squid ink, fish *ravioli*, and baked fish. ● Tue. 🔲 ▤	●	▣		▣
PESARO: *Da Teresa* ⓁⓁⓁ Viale Trieste 180, 61100. 📞 0721 302 22. A gracious restaurant offering imaginatively prepared dishes strongly based on local cuisine. As well as exquisite fish and seafood there are a few meat dishes, and delightful desserts follow. ● lunch, Sun eve, Mon; Dec–Jan. 🔲 ▤ ♿	●	▣		
PESARO: *Da Alceo* ⓁⓁⓁⓁ Via Panoramica Ardizio 101, 61100. 📞 0721 513 60. A famous fish restaurant with a spectacular panoramic terrace serving *gnocchi* with shellfish, and *risotto*. Desserts are homemade and tasty. ● Sun eve; Mon. 🔲	●	▣		▣
SENIGALLIA: *Uliassi* ⓁⓁⓁ Via Banchina di Levante 6, 60020. 📞 071 654 63. Run by a brother and sister, this is a friendly restaurant offering a high standard of cuisine. Try the specialty pasta with shrimp and asparagus. ● Mon; Jan–Feb. 🔲	●	▣		
SIROLO: *Rocco* ⓁⓁⓁ Via Torrione 1, 60020. 📞 071 933 05 58. Open during the spring and summer evenings only, Rocco serves delicious (mainly fish) dishes such as *gnocchi* with clams, fried mixed fish and vegetables, and sea bass with a sauce of lettuce and balsamic vinegar. ● lunch; Nov–Mar. 🔲	●			▣
URBANIA: *Big Ben* ⓁⓁ Corso Vittorio Emanuele 61, 61049. 📞 0722 31 97 95. In the historic center of town, Big Ben's specialties include *tagliolini* (pasta) with truffles, grilled lamb and homemade desserts. ● lunch; Wed. 🔲 🍴		▣		▣

URBINO: *Vecchia Urbino* $Ⓛ$$Ⓛ$$Ⓛ$
Via del Vasari 3–5, 61029. $\blacksquare$ *0722 44 47.*
A restaurant with views over the historic center, serving simply prepared
traditional rustic dishes from the region, including *vincisgrassi* (the local *lasagne*),
rabbit, and *polenta* with herbs. $\bullet$ *Tue.* $\blacksquare$ $\blacksquare$

ROME

AVENTINE: *Perilli a Testaccio* $Ⓛ$$Ⓛ$$Ⓛ$
Via Marmorata 39, 00153. **Map** 6 E3. $\blacksquare$ *06 574 63 18.*
An archetypal noisy Roman trattoria serving a regular clientele with robust Roman
fare that includes artichokes and *rigatoni alla pajata.* $\bullet$ *Wed; Aug.* $\blacksquare$ $\blacksquare$ $\blacksquare$

AVENTINE: *Checchino dal 1887* $Ⓛ$$Ⓛ$$Ⓛ$$Ⓛ$
Via di Monte Testaccio 30, 00153. **Map** 6 D4. $\blacksquare$ *06 574 63 18.*
Roman cuisine served at old tables under vaulted ceilings with an open fire in
winter. $\bullet$ *Oct–May: Mon, Sun eve; Jun–Sep: Mon eve, Sun; Aug, 1 week Dec.* $\blacksquare$ $\blacksquare$

CAMPO DE' FIORI: *Al Pompiere* $Ⓛ$$Ⓛ$
Via Santa Maria dei Calderari 38, 00186. **Map** 2 F5. $\blacksquare$ *06 686 83 77.*
In the heart of the Jewish ghetto, on the first floor of the Palazzo Cenci
Bolognetti with frescoed, beamed ceilings. The food is classically Roman,
including fried zucchini flowers and *rigatoni alla pajata.* $\bullet$ *Sun; Aug.* $\blacksquare$ $\blacksquare$

CAMPO DE' FIORI: *Le Maschere* $Ⓛ$$Ⓛ$
Via Monte della Farina 29, 00186. **Map** 2 F5. $\blacksquare$ *06 687 94 44.*
A tiled hall opens onto a rustic indoor terrace with a pleasant country
feel. The house wine and the fiery food are Calabrian. $\bullet$ *lunch; Mon; Aug.* $\blacksquare$ $\blacksquare$ $\blacksquare$

CAMPO DE' FIORI: *Il Drappo* $Ⓛ$$Ⓛ$$Ⓛ$$Ⓛ$
Vicolo del Malpasso 9, 00186. **Map** 2 E4. $\blacksquare$ *06 687 73 65.*
An intimate restaurant, serving Sardinian cuisine; *seadas* (sweet cheese-filled
ravioli) and *mirto* liqueur. $\bullet$ *lunch, Sun; 2 weeks Aug, 2 weeks Sep.* $\blacksquare$ $\blacksquare$ $\blacksquare$

CAMPO DE' FIORI: *Sora Lella* $Ⓛ$$Ⓛ$$Ⓛ$$Ⓛ$
Via di Ponte Quattro Capi 16, 00186. **Map** 6 D1. $\blacksquare$ *06 686 16 01.*
Situated on the picturesque Tiber Island, this restaurant is popular with the locals.
Traditional Roman dishes are served in elegant surroundings. $\bullet$ *Sun; Aug.* $\blacksquare$ $\blacksquare$

CAMPO DE' FIORI: *Camponeschi* $Ⓛ$$Ⓛ$$Ⓛ$$Ⓛ$$Ⓛ$
Piazza Farnese 50, 00186. **Map** 2 E5. $\blacksquare$ *06 687 49 27.*
Modern and regional Italian cooking, and French specialties, served in a lush interior
on one of the most beautiful piazzas in Rome. $\bullet$ *lunch, Sun; 3 weeks Aug.* $\blacksquare$ $\blacksquare$ $\blacksquare$

ESQUILINE: *Trattoria Monti* $Ⓛ$$Ⓛ$
Via di San Vito 13a, 00185. **Map** 4 E4. $\blacksquare$ *06 446 65 73.*
Delicate dishes from the Marches are prepared by Franca Camerucci. Specialties are
fried olives stuffed with meat, and *ravioli di ricotta.* $\bullet$ *Tue; Aug, Dec–Jan.* $\blacksquare$ $\blacksquare$ $\blacksquare$

ESQUILINE: *Agata e Romeo* $Ⓛ$$Ⓛ$$Ⓛ$$Ⓛ$
Via Carlo Alberto 45, 00185. **Map** 4 E4. $\blacksquare$ *06 446 61 15.*
Agata cooks predominantly Roman and southern Italian fare while Romeo
serves. Tables are well spaced and the atmosphere is tranquil. $\bullet$ *Sat, Sun.* $\blacksquare$ $\blacksquare$ $\blacksquare$

JANICULUM: *Antico Arco* $Ⓛ$$Ⓛ$$Ⓛ$
Via San Pancrazio 1, 00152. **Map** 5 A1. $\blacksquare$ *06 581 52 74.*
A highly recommended restaurant, set in elegant surroundings. The traditional food has
creative touches, such as guinea fowl with apples and *foie gras.* $\bullet$ *Sun; Aug.* $\blacksquare$ $\blacksquare$ $\blacksquare$

LATERAN: *Alfredo a Via Gabi* $Ⓛ$$Ⓛ$
Via Gabi 36–38, 00183. **Map** 8 E3. $\blacksquare$ *06 77 20 67 92.*
A spacious trattoria with cheerful service and ample portions. Try *spaghetti* with sword-
fish sauce, *straccetti all'ortica* (meat in nettle sauce), and *panna cotta.* $\bullet$ *Tue; Aug.* $\blacksquare$

PANTHEON: *Da Gino* $Ⓛ$$Ⓛ$
Vicolo Rosini 4, 00186. **Map** 3 A3. $\blacksquare$ *06 687 34 34.*
An ancient, traditional Roman trattoria full of journalists, politicians,
and the initiated. Daily dishes include *gnocchi* and *ossobuco* and
baccalà, as well as some classic sturdy soups. $\bullet$ *Sun; Aug.*

PANTHEON: *Sangallo* $Ⓛ$$Ⓛ$$Ⓛ$$Ⓛ$
Vicolo della Vaccarella 11a, 00186. **Map** 2 F3. $\blacksquare$ *06 686 55 49.*
Small bistro specializing in regional fish dishes and a huge array of antipasti,
including many types of vegetables and seafood. $\bullet$ *lunch; Sun; Aug.* $\blacksquare$ $\blacksquare$

For key to symbols see back flap

Average prices for a three-course meal for one, including a half bottle of house wine, tax and service:
Ⓛ up to L35,000
ⓁⓁ L35–55,000
ⓁⓁⓁ L55–75,000
ⓁⓁⓁⓁ L75–100,000
ⓁⓁⓁⓁⓁ over L100,000.

FIXED-PRICE MENU
A fixed-price menu offered, usually with three courses.
GOOD WINE LIST
Denotes a wide range of good quality wines.
FORMAL DRESS
Some restaurants require men to wear a jacket and tie.
OUTDOOR TABLES
Tables for eating outdoors, often with a good view.
CREDIT CARDS
The symbol shows that major credit cards are accepted.

	FIXED-PRICE MENU	GOOD WINE LIST	FORMAL DRESS	OUTDOOR TABLES
PANTHEON: *El Toulà* — ⓁⓁⓁⓁ Via della Lupa 29b, 00186. **Map** 2 F3. 06 687 34 98. One of the most exclusive and traditional restaurants in Rome. The cuisine is mainly Venetian, the service and wines are superb. ● *Sat lunch; Mon lunch; Sun; Aug.*	●	■	●	
PIAZZA NAVONA: *La Taverna da Giovanni* — ⓁⓁ Via del Banco di Santo Spirito 58, 00186. **Map** 2 D3. 06 686 41 16. A crowded Roman trattoria with a family atmosphere. The *rigatoni all'amatriciana* (pasta with spicy bacon and tomato) is a specialty, as are the traditional *gnocchi, baccalà* (salt cod), and tripe on Thursday, Friday, and Saturday respectively. ● *Mon.*	●	■		■
PIAZZA NAVONA: *Papà Giovanni* — ⓁⓁⓁⓁ Via dei Sediari 4–5, 00186. **Map** 2 F4. 06 686 53 08. Giovanni's son now runs this restaurant with an excellent cellar. New, lighter Roman cuisine is served with traditional dishes. ● *Sun.*		■		
PIAZZA DI SPAGNA: *Birreria Viennese* — ⓁⓁ Via della Croce 21, 00187. **Map** 3 A2. 06 679 55 69. Traditional beers and Austrian specialties have been served in this long and crowded room for more than 60 years. In the atmospheric setting, try the sausages, goulash, sauerkraut, or the Wienerschnitzel.	●			■
PIAZZA DI SPAGNA: *Al 34* — ⓁⓁⓁ Via Mario de' Fiori 34, 00187. **Map** 3 A2. 06 679 50 91. The perfect setting for a comfortable chat or a romantic tête-à-tête. The extensive menu offers mostly southern Italian cuisine. ● *Mon; Aug.*	●			■
PIAZZA DI SPAGNA: *Mario alla Vite* — ⓁⓁⓁ Via della Vite 55, 00187. **Map** 3 A2. 06 678 38 18. Simple, honest Tuscan fare. The service can be haphazard but the *ribollita, fagioli al fiasco* (beans), steaks, and desserts make up for it. ● *Sun; Aug.*		■		■
PIAZZA DI SPAGNA: *Porto di Ripetta* — ⓁⓁⓁⓁ Via di Ripetta 250, 00187. **Map** 2 F2. 06 361 23 76. A friendly restaurant serving wonderful dishes with fish and seafood brought in daily. Try the swordfish or the fish soup. ● *Sun; Aug.*	●	■	●	
QUIRINAL: *Colline Emiliane* — ⓁⓁ Via degli Avignonesi 22, 00187. **Map** 3 C3. 06 481 75 38. A small, family trattoria serving specialties from Emilia-Romagna; homemade pasta, salami, boiled meat, and *salsa verde* (parsley, onion, and anchovy sauce), and Emilian wines. ● *Fri; Aug.*		■		
QUIRINAL: *Il Posto Accanto* — ⓁⓁⓁ Via del Boschetto 36a, 00184. **Map** 3 C4. 06 474 30 02. This elegant family-run restaurant owes its success to a carefully chosen menu based on homemade pasta, fish, and meat. ● *Sat lunch; Sun; Aug.*		■		
QUIRINAL: *Al Moro* — ⓁⓁⓁⓁ Vicolo delle Bollette 13, 00185. **Map** 3 B3. 06 678 34 95. A reliable choice for traditional Roman cooking in this typical and crowded trattoria. Fresh local ingredients are used to make dishes such as *bucatini all'amatriciana* and *spaghetti alla Moro* (a version of carbonara). ● *Sun; Aug.*			●	■
TERMINI: *Gemma alla Lupa* — Ⓛ Via Marghera 39, 00185. **Map** 4 F3. 06 49 12 30. A typical, modest Roman trattoria serving real Roman cuisine in a bustling atmosphere. Excellent value with speedy service. ● *Sun, Aug.*	●			■
TRASTEVERE: *Da Lucia* — Ⓛ Vicolo del Mattonato 2b, 00153. **Map** 5 C1. 06 580 36 01. A popular, crowded trattoria serving basic Roman cuisine. Try the *pasta e ceci* and the *spaghetti alla gricia* (pecorino, pancetta, and pepper). ● *Mon; 2 weeks Aug.*				■

TRASTEVERE: *Ascinotto* ⓛⓛⓛ
Via dei Vascellari 48. **Map** 8 D1. 06 589 89 85.
This casually elegant restaurant offers imaginative cooking with dishes such as aubergine, arugula, and nettle *ravioli* and sea bass with truffle. ● *3 weeks Jan.* ▨ ▤

TRASTEVERE: *Da Paris* ⓛⓛⓛⓛ
Piazza San Calisto 7a, 00153. **Map** 5 C1. 06 581 53 78.
A Roman-Jewish restaurant popular with locals. Homemade pasta and traditional dishes include *minestra di arzilla* (skate), tripe, and exquisite *fritto misto* (batter-fried fish) with vegetables. ● *Sun eve, Mon; 2 weeks Aug.* ▨ ▤

TRASTEVERE: *La Cornucopia* ⓛⓛⓛ
Piazza in Piscinula 18. **Map** 6 D1. 06 580 03 80.
Come here for excellent antipasti and simply cooked fish dishes such as *spigola al vapore* (steamed sea bass). Candlelight adds to the ambience. ● *Tue.* ▨ ▤

TRASTEVERE: *Romolo nel Giardino della Fornarina* ⓛⓛⓛ
Via Porta Settimiana 8, 00153. **Map** 2 E5. 06 581 82 84.
La Fornarina was Raphael's mistress and this is said to have been her home. In summer the Roman food is served in the courtyard. ● *Mon, Aug.* ▨

TRASTEVERE: *Alberto Ciarla* ⓛⓛⓛⓛ
Piazza San Cosimato 40, 00153. **Map** 5 C1. 06 581 86 68.
This is the place to enjoy fish and seafood. From oysters to scampi, the menu is based on the day's fish from the market. The decor is elegant and dramatic. ▨ ▰ ▤

VATICAN: *Macondo* ⓛⓛ
Via Marianna Dionigi 37, 00193. **Map** 2 E2. 06 321 26 01.
This is one of the best restaurants in Rome for exotic cuisine. The specialty is Caribbean dishes, such as turkey with orange and pineapple or *pabellon criollo* (rice, beef, beans and bananas). Choose from a selection of rum and beers. ● *Sun.* ▤

VATICAN: *Les Etoiles* ⓛⓛⓛⓛ
Via dei Bastioni 1, 00193. **Map** 2 D2. 06 687 32 33.
This rooftop restaurant sits atop the Atlante Star hotel. Specialty dishes include *tagliolini* (pasta) with clams, and in season, game and truffles. ▨ ♿ ▤

VIA VENETO: *Cantina Cantarini* ⓛⓛ
Piazza Sallustio 12, 00187. **Map** 4 D1. 06 48 55 28.
A popular local trattoria with friendly service. Meat is served from Monday to Thursday lunch time, fish for the rest of the week. ● *Sun; 2 weeks Aug; 1 week Dec.* ▨

VIA VENETO: *Tullio* ⓛⓛⓛ
Via San Nicola da Tolentino 26, 00187. **Map** 3 C2. 06 474 55 60.
A genuine Tuscan restaurant frequented by an enthusiastic crowd. Typical dishes include *porcini* mushrooms in numerous ways. ● *Sun, Aug.* ▨ ♿ ▤

VIA VENETO: *Giovanni* ⓛⓛⓛ
Via Marche 64, 00187. **Map** 3 C1. 06 482 18 34.
A crowded restaurant popular with locals. Traditional food from Lazio and the Marches, including fresh fish, pasta, and *ossobuco*. ● *Fri eve, Sat; Aug.* ▨ ▤

VIA VENETO: *George's* ⓛⓛⓛⓛ
Via Marche 7, 00187. **Map** 3 C1. 06 42 08 45 75.
A survivor from the Dolce Vita era with a nostalgic air of luxurious elegance. Service is impeccable and there is a tempting selection of international dishes. ● *Sun; Aug.* ▨ ▤

VILLA BORGHESE: *Al Ceppo* ⓛⓛⓛ
Via Panama 2, 00198. 06 841 96 96.
Run by two sisters who serve a strictly seasonal menu of traditional dishes with flashes of inspiration in a hospitable atmosphere. ● *Mon; Aug.* ▨ ♿ ▤

VILLA BORGHESE: *Relais le Jardin dell'Hotel Lord Byron* ⓛⓛⓛⓛ
Via de Notaris 5, 00198. 06 322 45 41.
High prices are matched by impeccable service and haute cuisine at its best. Inspired cooking draws on tradition with delicious mixtures of fruit, herbs, and vegetables combined with top-quality meats and fish. ● *Aug.* ▨ ▤ ▰

LAZIO

ALATRI: *La Rosetta* ⓛ
Via del Duomo 35, 03011. 0775 43 45 68.
A quiet restaurant near the 6th-century BC acropolis. Try the *maccheroni alla ciociaria* (wine, herb, bacon and meat sauce). ● *Oct–May: Tue; 2 weeks Feb, 2 weeks Nov.* ▨ ▤ ▰ ♿

	FIXED-PRICE MENU	GOOD WINE LIST	FORMAL DRESS	OUTDOOR TABLES

Average prices for a three-course meal for one, including a half bottle of house wine, tax and service:
Ⓛ up to L35,000
ⓁⓁ L35–55,000
ⓁⓁⓁ L55–75,000
ⓁⓁⓁⓁ L75–100,000
ⓁⓁⓁⓁⓁ over L100,000.

FIXED-PRICE MENU
A fixed-price menu offered, usually with three courses.
GOOD WINE LIST
Denotes a wide range of good quality wines.
FORMAL DRESS
Some restaurants require men to wear a jacket and tie.
OUTDOOR TABLES
Tables for eating outdoors, often with a good view.
CREDIT CARDS
The symbol shows that major credit cards are accepted.

CERVETERI: *Da Fiore* Ⓛ Località Procoio di Ceri 6, 00052. 📞 *06 99 20 42 50.* A simple country trattoria: specialties include home-cooked pastas with *ragù*, rabbit, and grilled meats. The *bruschette* and pizzas are also good. ● *Tue; Sep.*				▨
FRASCATI: *Enoteca Frascati* ⓁⓁ Via Diaz 42, 00044. 📞 *06 941 74 49.* A good range of light dishes accompany the more than 400 wines in this enoteca: smoked fish, soups, and *carpaccio* (thin slices) of duck. ● *Sun; Aug.* 🗗 ⚡		▨		
GAETA: *La Cianciola* Ⓛ Vico 2 Buonomo 16, 04024. 📞 *0771 46 61 90.* A charming trattoria hidden up a little alley into which tables are tightly packed. Try the pasta with eggplants and shellfish. ● *Oct–May: Mon; Nov.* 🗗 ▤	●			▨
NETTUNO: *Cacciatori Dal 1896* ⓁⓁⓁ Via Matteotti 27–29, 00048. 📞 *06 988 03 30.* A large, rustically furnished restaurant with a veranda overlooking the sea. Fish is caught daily, and the dishes are inspired by regional recipes. ● *Wed; Aug.* 🗗 ♿ ▤		▨		▨
OSTIA ANTICA: *Il Monumento* ⓁⓁⓁ Piazza Umberto I 8, 00119. 📞 *06 565 00 21.* A fish-based menu; the house specialty, *spaghetti monumento*, is served with seafood sauce. ● *Mon; 2 weeks Aug.* 🗗				
SPERLONGA: *La Bisaccia* ⓁⓁⓁ Via Romita 25, 04029. 📞 *0771 545 76.* Linguine with wild asparagus and shrimp is a highlight of this restaurant that also makes use of local fish for soups and grills. ● *Tue; Nov.* 🗗 ♿ ▤				▨
TERRACINA: *L'Incontro Da Baffone* ⓁⓁⓁ Via Appia, km 104,500, 04029. 📞 *0773 72 60 07.* This popular restaurant along the beautiful beach of Terracina is a peaceful place to sample some good local fish dishes. ● *Oct–Apr: Wed.*		▨		▨
TIVOLI: *Villa Esedra* ⓁⓁⓁ Via di Villa Adriana 51, Località Villa Adriana 00011. 📞 *0774 53 47 16.* Typical menu with imaginative antipasti such as fish salad and *carpaccio* of smoked meat. In the evening there are also pizzas. ● *Mon (in winter).* 🗗 ▤ ⚡	●			▨
TREVIGNANO: *Ristorante Il Palazzetto* ⓁⓁⓁ Piazza Vittorio Emanuele III 20, 00069. 📞 *06 999 92 54.* A little restaurant with views over Lake Bracciano. The excellent menu makes good use of sea and lake fish, including *ravioli al persico* (perch), and delicious scampi soups. Desserts are homemade. ● *Wed.* 🗗		▨		▨
TUSCANIA: *Al Gallo* ⓁⓁⓁ Via del Gallo 22, 01017. 📞 *0761 44 33 88.* An unusual interpretation of regional dishes has created an exceptionally good menu. Warm atmosphere and charming service. ● *Mon; 2 weeks Jan.* 🗗 ▤ ♿	●	▨		
VITERBO: *Porta Romana* ⓁⓁ Via della Bontà 12, 01100. 📞 *0761 30 71 18.* A simple trattoria where a wide range of classic dishes are immaculately prepared. In the winter, try *pignataccia*, a Viterbo specialty of mixed veal, beef, and pork cooked on a slow fire with celery, carrots, and potatoes. ● *Sun; Aug.* ▤				

NAPLES AND CAMPANIA

AGROPOLI: *Il Ceppo* ⓁⓁⓁ Via Madonna Del Carmine 31, 84043. 📞 *0974 84 30 36.* A wonderful range of local fish and homemade pastas and pizzas: try the *spaghetti* with seafood, shrimp in lemon sauce, or the fish soups. ● *Mon; Feb, Nov.* 🗗 ▤		▨		▨

AMALFI: *La Marinella* Ⓛ Ⓛ
Via Lungomare dei Cavalieri di San Giovanni di Gerusalemme 1, 84011. 〖 *089 87 10 43*.
A lively, friendly restaurant overlooking the the Amalfi coast. Much fish is
served as well as the traditional local specialties. ● *Fri; Jan–Feb, lunch in summer.* 🍴 &

AMALFI: *Eolo* Ⓛ Ⓛ Ⓛ
Via Comite 3, 84011. 〖 *089 87 12 41*.
Situated in the historic centre of Amalfi, this restaurant's menu changes every fortnight to
make use of seasonal ingredients. The food is of a high standard. ● *Tue; Nov–May.* 🍴 ▤

BENEVENTO: *Pina e Gino* Ⓛ
Via dell'Università, 82100. 〖 *0824 249 47*.
In the heart of the historic center; try *cardone* (a type of thistle), *sfoglia al forno*
(meat baked in a parcel), pasta with broccoli. ● *Sun.* 🍴 & ▤

CAPRI: *La Savardina da Eduardo* Ⓛ Ⓛ
Via Lo Capo 8, 80073. 〖 *081 837 63 00*.
This is one of the most traditional restaurants in Capri, with orange trees, sea views,
and regional specialties, such as homemade *ravioli*. ● *lunch; Wed; Nov–Feb.* 🍴

CAPRI: *Quisi del Grand Hotel Quisisana* Ⓛ Ⓛ Ⓛ Ⓛ Ⓛ
Via Camerelle 2, 80073. 〖 *081 837 07 88*.
The atmosphere is elegant and the food is delightful. Try the succulent roast
duck with peaches and hot apple pie with Calvados. ● *lunch; Nov–Mar.* 🍴 ▤

CASERTA: *La Brace* Ⓛ Ⓛ
Piazza Madonna delle Grazie 9, Località Vaccheria 81020. 〖 *0823 36 17 44*.
An old-fashioned country inn in a village outside Caserta. Try *pasta e fagioli*
(with beans) and grilled fish. ● *Tue; Aug.* 🍴 ▤ 🏊 &

ISCHIA: *Da Peppina* Ⓛ Ⓛ Ⓛ
Via Montecorvo 42, Località Forio 80075. 〖 *081 99 83 12*.
Basic fare served in this simple trattoria; *pasta e fagioli*, soups, grilled meats
and pizzas cooked in a wood oven. ● *Thu; Nov–Mar.* 🍴 &

ISCHIA: *La Tavernetta* Ⓛ Ⓛ Ⓛ
Via Sant'Angelo 77, Località Serrara Fontana 80070. 〖 *081 99 92 51*.
You can relax in this peaceful corner, where you find a good choice of pasta
with Mediterranean sauces, salads, or fried fish. ● *Nov–Feb.* 🍴

FAICCHIO: *La Campagnola* Ⓛ
Via San Nicola 36, Località Massa 82030. 〖 *0824 81 40 81*.
Set in a village 38 km (23 miles) northwest of Benevento, serving simple, tasty cuisine.
Try *torciglioni alle melanzane* (pasta with eggplant). ● *Wed; 2 weeks Sep.* 🍴 &

NAPLES: *Gorizia* Ⓛ
Via Bernini 29, 80129. 〖 *081 578 22 48*.
This is one of the oldest and most renowned pizzerias in Naples. The food is
excellent, from the home-made pizzas to the fish antipasti. ● *Wed; Aug.* 🍴 & ▤

NAPLES: *California* Ⓛ Ⓛ
Via Santa Lucia 101, 80132. 〖 *081 764 97 52*.
Well-presented stalwarts are offered such as *spaghetti alla carbonara* and *bucatini
amatriciana* as well as American-style sandwiches. ● *Sun; 10 days Aug.* 🍴 ▤

NAPLES: *La Chiacchierata* Ⓛ Ⓛ
Piazzetta Matilde Serao 37, 80100. 〖 *081 41 14 65*.
A traditional trattoria popular with the locals. Among Neapolitan specialties
are *orecchiette* (ear-shaped pasta) with chickpeas, and octopus. ● *lunch; Sun; Aug.* 🍴

NAPLES: *La Sacrestia* Ⓛ Ⓛ Ⓛ Ⓛ
Via Orazio 116, 80122. 〖 *081 66 41 86*.
An attractive setting with views of the Gulf of Naples. The food is excellent,
and the atmosphere elegant but informal. ● *Mon; 2 weeks Aug.* 🍴 & ▤

NAPLES: *La Cantinella* Ⓛ Ⓛ Ⓛ Ⓛ Ⓛ
Via Cuma 42, 80132. 〖 *081 764 86 84*.
One of Naples' most famous restaurants, with an astounding reputation for its
carefully and successfully prepared regional cuisine. ● *Sun; 3 weeks Aug.* 🍴 ▤ 🏊

NERANO: *Taverna del Capitano* Ⓛ Ⓛ Ⓛ Ⓛ
Piazza delle Sirene 10, 80068. 〖 *081 808 10 28*.
A refined restaurant on the beach, serving regional specialties with some creative
touches; try the fish in breadcrumbs and herbs. ● *Mon; Jan, Feb.* 🍴 ▤ 🏊

Average prices for a three-course meal for one, including a half bottle of house wine, tax and service:
- L up to L35,000
- L L35–55,000
- L L L55–75,000
- L L L L75–100,000
- L L L L L over L100,000.

FIXED-PRICE MENU
A fixed-price menu offered, usually with three courses.
GOOD WINE LIST
Denotes a wide range of good quality wines.
FORMAL DRESS
Some restaurants require men to wear a jacket and tie.
OUTDOOR TABLES
Tables for eating outdoors, often with a good view.
CREDIT CARDS
The symbol shows that major credit cards are accepted.

	FIXED-PRICE MENU	GOOD WINE LIST	FORMAL DRESS	OUTDOOR TABLES
PAESTUM: *La Pergola* LL Via Nazionale, Capaccio Scalo 84040. 0828 72 33 77. Innovative regional cuisine that makes use of seasonal specialties in a rustic restaurant 3 km (2 miles) from the ruins of Paestum. ● *Mon (except Aug); 3 wks Oct.*		■		■
POMPEII: *Il Principe* LLLLL Piazza B Longo 8, 80045. 081 850 55 66. An airy, refined restaurant close to the excavations. Its cuisine is based on fish and includes fish-filled *ravioli* and turbot with vegetables. ● *Mon (eve only Mar–Oct), Sun.*		■		■
POSITANO: *Da Adolfo* LL Località Laurito 40, 84017. 089 87 50 22. A boat leaves Positano harbor every half hour for this charming trattoria serving *spaghetti* with clams or zucchini with grilled mozzarella. ● *Sat in Jul, Aug, Sep–May.*	●			■
POSITANO: *La Sponda* LLLLL Via Colombo 30, 84017. 089 87 50 66. A sumptuous restaurant where guests are treated like family friends and offered a tempting range of modern and traditional dishes based on fresh fish. ● *Dec–Mar.*	●	■		■
SALERNO: *Pizzeria Vicolo della Neve* L Vicolo della Neve 24, 84100. 089 22 57 05. A pizzeria in the historic center also serving a range of dishes such as pasta and *fagioli, baccalà* casserole, and sausages with broccoli. ● *lunch; Wed.*				
SALERNO: *Al Cenacolo* LLL Piazza Alfano I 4, 84100. 089 23 88 18. Dedicated cuisine with a menu that changes daily to make good use of local ingredients. Pasta and bread are homemade. ● *Sun eve, Mon; Aug.*		■		
SANT'AGATA SUI DUE GOLFI: *Don Alfonso 1890* LLLLL Piazza Sant'Agata 11, 80064. 081 878 00 26. Set in elegant gardens, dishes include seafood and fish specialties and delicious traditional desserts. ● *Mon, Tue; Jan, Feb.*	●	■		
SICIGNANO DEGLI ALBURNI: *La Taverna* LL Via Nazionale 139, Frazione Scorzo 84029. 0828 97 80 50. An 18th-century country inn, near Salerno. The regional cuisine includes salamis, bean and chickpea soups, and grilled meats. ● *Wed; Jul.*		■		
SORRENTO: *Antico Frantoio* LL Via Casarlano 5, Località Casarlano 80067. 081 878 58 45. A great variety of dishes for all courses, made from local ingredients. Try the pizzas, the corn bread and the beer brewed at the next-door *birreria.*				■

ABRUZZO, MOLISE, AND PUGLIA

	FIXED-PRICE MENU	GOOD WINE LIST	FORMAL DRESS	OUTDOOR TABLES
ALBEROBELLO: *Il Poeta Contadino* LLLL Via Indipendenza 21, 70011. 080 432 19 17. An elegant restaurant where the excellent service matches the high standard of both food and wine. The cuisine makes imaginative use of fresh local ingredients, offering both fish and meat dishes. ● *Mon; 2 weeks Jan.*	●	■		
BARI: *Borgo Antico* LL Piazza del Ferrarese 10–11, 70123. 080 523 58 52. This elegant restaurant is in the center of the old town, just by the old harbor. The cuisine is mainly Pugliese and Mediterranean. ● *Mon; Nov.*		■		■
BARI: *Villa Rosa* LL Lungomare Starita 64, 70123. 080 534 76 10. A homey trattoria and pizzeria on the seafront. Specialties include *orecchiette* (ear-shaped pasta) with arugula, fish and meat kebabs. ● *Wed; Dec 15–Jan 15.*				■

GALLIPOLI: *Capriccio* ⓁⓁⓁ
Viale Bovio 14/16. 📞 *0833 26 15 45.*
This restaurant serves up classical regional cuuisine including plenty of fresh fish.
⬤ *Mon (winter); Nov.* 🅮

ISOLE TREMITI: *Al Gabbiano* ⓁⓁⓁ
San Domino, 71040. 📞 *0882 46 34 10.*
The food here is based on the best fish from the sea. Try fresh fish
roasted in a case of salt and the traditional fish soup. 🅮 ▤

L'AQUILA: *Ernesto* ⓁⓁ
Piazza Palazzo 22, 67100. 📞 *0862 210 94.*
A peaceful, sophisticated place to eat. The menu is a tasty, creative mix of
different inspirations and there is a wine bar attached. ⬤ *Sun, Mon.* 🅮

LECCE: *Barbablú* ⓁⓁⓁ
Via Umberto 7, 73100. 📞 *0832 24 11 83.*
An old palazzo in the historic center is the perfect setting for imaginative
and delicious dishes that use only fresh local ingredients. ⬤ *Mon.* 🅮 ▤

LOCOROTONDO: *Centro Storico* ⓁⓁ
Via Eroi di Dogali 6, 70010. 📞 *080 431 54 73.*
Hidden among the winding streets of the historic center, this little trattoria
offers some excellent Pugliese cuisine often with creative touches. ⬤ *Wed.* 🅮

OTRANTO: *Vecchia Otranto* ⓁⓁⓁ
Corso Garibaldi 96, 73028. 📞 *0836 80 15 75.*
Good marine and other regional specialties in this traditional trattoria include
pasta with sea urchin and pepper sauce. ⬤ *Thu; Nov, 1 week Jan.* 🅮 ♿ ▤

OVINDOLI: *Il Pozzo* ⓁⓁ
Via dell'Alpino, 67046. 📞 *0863 71 01 91.*
Wonderful mountain setting for this atmospheric restaurant in the historic center
of town. The food is traditional and robust. ⬤ *Wed; Sep–Oct.* 🅮

PORTO CESAREO: *L'Angolo di Beppe* ⓁⓁ
Via Zanella 24, Località Torre Lapillo, 73050. 📞 *0833 56 53 05.*
A cozy atmosphere and elegant decor with a large open fire in winter. The cuisine
is based on fish, and mixes local and international traditions. ⬤ *Mon.* 🅮 ▤

ROCCA DI MEZZO: *La Fiorita* Ⓛ
Piazza Principe di Piemonte 3, 67048. 📞 *0862 91 74 67.*
Efficient, friendly service in this family-run trattoria where the food is based
on local products from the Abruzzi mountains. ⬤ *Tue; 2 wks Sep.* 🅮 ♿

SULMONA: *Rigoletto* ⓁⓁ
Via Stazione Introacqua 46, 67039. 📞 *0864 555 29.*
A short walk from the center of town, reliable homemade pastas are served
with beans, *scamorza*, rabbit, and truffles. ⬤ *Mon; Jun, Jul.* 🅮 ♿ ▤

TARANTO: *Le Vecchie Cantine* ⓁⓁ
Via Girasoli 23, Frazione Lama 74020. 📞 *099 777 25 89.*
Set in restored storerooms just outside Taranto. A tasty fish and seafood menu, such
as *carpaccio* of swordfish and fusilli with sardines. ⬤ *lunch; Wed (in winter); Jan.* 🅮

TARANTO: *Al Faro* ⓁⓁⓁ
Via Galeso 126, 74100. 📞 *099 471 44 44.*
The menu is exclusively marine, using locally caught fish and seafood for
antipasti, soups, *risotti*, and grills. ⬤ *Sun; 2 weeks Jan, 2 weeks Dec.* 🅮 ♿ ▤

TERMOLI: *Z'Bass* ⓁⓁ
Via Oberdan 8, 86039. 📞 *0875 70 67 03.*
This friendly, welcoming trattoria offers a high level of cuisine using fresh, seasonal
ingredients. There is also an extensive wine list available. ⬤ *Mon (in winter).* 🅮 ▤ ♿

TRANI: *Torrente Antico* ⓁⓁⓁⓁ
Via Fusco 3, 70059. 📞 *0883 48 79 11.*
Exquisite, lightly prepared dishes based on traditional regional cuisine with modern
touches. The wine list is also extensive. ⬤ *Sun eve, Mon; 1 wk Jan, 2 wks Jul.* 🅮 ▤

VIESTE: *Il Trabucco dell'Hotel Pizzomunno* ⓁⓁⓁⓁ
Lungomare di Pizzomunno km 1, 71019. 📞 *0884 70 87 41.*
Surrounded by gardens and very close to the sea. The cuisine has some
creative touches and the dishes are light and tasty. ⬤ *Nov–Mar.* 🅮 🈂 ▤

Average prices for a three-course meal for one, including a half bottle of house wine, tax and service:
Ⓛ up to L35,000
ⓁⓁ L35–55,000
ⓁⓁⓁ L55–75,000
ⓁⓁⓁⓁ L75–100,000
ⓁⓁⓁⓁⓁ over L100,000.

FIXED-PRICE MENU
A fixed-price menu offered, usually with three courses.

GOOD WINE LIST
Denotes a wide range of good quality wines.

FORMAL DRESS
Some restaurants require men to wear a jacket and tie.

OUTDOOR TABLES
Tables for eating outdoors, often with a good view.

CREDIT CARDS
The symbol shows that major credit cards are accepted.

	FIXED-PRICE MENU	GOOD WINE LIST	FORMAL DRESS	OUTDOOR TABLES

VILLETTA BARREA: *Trattoria del Pescatore* — Ⓛ
Via B Virgilio 175, 67030. 0864 892 74.
A simple, family-run trattoria in the Abruzzo National Park. Regional dishes include trout and homemade *chitarrini* (pasta cut like guitar strings). ● Thu (in winter).

BASILICATA AND CALABRIA

BIVONGI: *Vecchia Miniera* — Ⓛ
Contrada Perrocalli, 89040. 0964 73 18 69.
Regional cuisine such as pasta with *sugo di capra* (goat sauce), a favorite ancient Roman dish, in this village just outside Stilo. ● Mon.
(Outdoor Tables)

MARATEA: *Taverna Rovita* — ⓁⓁⓁ
Via Rovita 13, 85046. 0973 87 65 88.
An elegant country restaurant with white walls and tiled floors serving regional cuisine. Try the *risotto* of asparagus and venison. ● Oct–Apr: Tue; Jan.
(Good Wine List)

MATERA: *Al Casino del Diavolo* — ⓁⓁ
Via La Martella, 75100. 0835 26 19 86.
Excellent Matera fare at this elegant, traditional restaurant just outside the town. Try *orecchiette* (ear-shaped pasta) with broccoli. ● Mon.
(Outdoor Tables)

MATERA: *Il Terrazzino* — ⓁⓁ
Vicolo San Giuseppe 7, 75100. 0835 33 25 03.
In the Sassi district *(see p502)*, the restaurant has a panoramic terrace. Try soups of grains and chickpeas, or grilled lamb *involtini* (lamb parcels). ● Tue; 1 week Jun.
(Fixed-Price Menu, Outdoor Tables)

MATERA: *Venusio* — ⓁⓁⓁ
Via Lussemburgo 2, Borgo Venusio 75100. 0835 25 90 81.
An elegant restaurant 6 km (4 miles) south of Matera. Specialties include fish baked in a bread case, fish *tortelli*, mushrooms and various antipasti.
● Mon; Aug.
(Fixed-Price Menu, Good Wine List, Outdoor Tables)

MELFI: *Vaddone* — ⓁⓁ
Contrada Sant'Abruzzese, 85025. 0972 243 23.
A well-known trattoria serving delicious soups of legumes and grilled meats. The menu also includes fish dishes. ● Mon eve.
(Fixed-Price Menu, Outdoor Tables)

POTENZA: *Z' Mingo* — Ⓛ
Contrada Botte 2, 85100. 0971 44 59 29.
This simple trattoria is the perfect place to join the locals in eating regional fare. The menu includes fresh pasta, roasted meats and local cheeses and salamis. ● Mon; 2 weeks Aug.

REGGIO DI CALABRIA: *Villegianti* — Ⓛ
Via Eremo-Condera 31, Località Mariannazzo, 89125. 0965 250 21.
A Reggio Calabrian institution where good simple fare is well prepared and served informally. Try *spaghetti* with broccoli or rich, spicy sausages. ● Mon (in winter).
(Fixed-Price Menu, Outdoor Tables)

ROSSANO: *Antiche Mura* — Ⓛ
Via Prigioni 40, 87067. 0983 52 00 42.
A friendly trattoria, housed in the stable of an 18th-century palazzo. The dining room has a vaulted ceiling. The menu includes stuffed eggplant and roasted goat. ● lunch; Wed.
(Outdoor Tables)

SCILLA: *La Grotta Azzurra* — ⓁⓁ
Via Cristoforo Colombo, 89058. 0965 75 48 89.
A wonderful setting on the beach where, according to legend, Ulysses came ashore. This basic trattoria serves mainly fish. ● Mon lunch; 2 weeks Dec.
(Good Wine List, Outdoor Tables)

TROPEA: *Pimm's* — ⓁⓁ
Corso Vittorio Emanuele, 88038. 0963 66 61 05.
A beautiful setting in the historic center. Simple, local fare, well prepared and pleasantly served. Start with seafood *crostini* or smoked swordfish, then try pasta with sea urchins and stuffed, grilled squid. ● Oct–Apr: Mon; Jan.
(Good Wine List)

VENOSA: *Taverna Ducale* Ⓛ Ⓛ
Piazza Municipio 2, 85029. 【 0972 369 44.
The 15th-century building sets the scene for a cuisine based on rediscovered ancient dishes such as *preferito di Orazio* (the favorite of the Latin poet Horace) and *triticum* (a mixture of legumes and vegetables). ● *Mon.* 🥗 ⤢ ♿

SICILY

AGRIGENTO: *Le Caprice* Ⓛ Ⓛ
Via Panoramica dei Templi 51, 92100. 【 0922 264 69.
A good restaurant in an exquisite setting in the Valley of the Temples. Regional cuisine is carefully prepared; the antipasto buffet is a specialty. ● *Fri; 2 weeks Jul.* 🥗 ♿ ▤

AGRIGENTO: *Trattoria del Pescatore* Ⓛ Ⓛ
Lungomare Falcone e Borsellino 20, Località Lido di San Leone 92100. 【 0922 41 43 43.
The chef chooses the fish daily and uses it, sometimes raw, in simple but delicious dishes with oil and lemon juice. The pasta specialty is *spaghetti* with swordfish, eggplant, and basil. ● *Wed; Oct.* 🥗 ▤

AGRIGENTO: *Kalos* Ⓛ Ⓛ Ⓛ
Piazza San Calogero 1, 92100. 【 0922 263 89.
A bright restaurant with original and well-prepared cuisine. Try pasta with pistachio and gorgonzola, grilled fish, and *cassata* of ricotta. ● *Sun.* 🥗 ▤

BAGHERIA: *Don Ciccio* Ⓛ
Via del Cavaliere 87, 90011. 【 091 93 24 42.
This town-center trattoria concentrates on regional specialties. Watch for pasta with sardines, broccoli, tuna, and other sauces. ● *Sun, Wed; Aug.* 🥗 ▤ ♿

CATANIA: *I Vicere* Ⓛ Ⓛ
Via Grotte Bianche 97, 95129. 【 095 32 01 88.
Outside dining on a terrace with spectacular views. Good food, particularly the succulent pork fillet in mandarin sauce. ⤢ ▤ ♿

CEFALÙ: *L'Antica Corte* Ⓛ
Corso Ruggero 155, 90015. 【 0921 42 32 28.
A trattoria-pizzeria in an old courtyard in the historic center, the cuisine is local with influences from almost-forgotten old Sicilian recipes. ● *Thu; Jan, Nov.* 🥗 ▤

ENNA: *Ariston* Ⓛ Ⓛ
Via Roma 353, 94100. 【 0935 260 38.
In the heart of Enna, with a selection of fish dishes as well as meat specialties, such as stuffed lamb, or bean and pea soup and *frittata* (omelette). ● *Sun; Aug.* 🥗 ▤

ERICE: *Osteria di Venere* Ⓛ Ⓛ
Via Roma 6, 91016. 【 0923 86 93 62.
A delightful restaurant in an attractive 17th-century building. The menu is basically Sicilian and Mediterranean. ● *Jan–Feb: Wed.* ▤

ERICE: *Monte San Giuliano* Ⓛ Ⓛ
Via San Rocco 7, 91016. 【 0923 86 95 95.
Located in the center of town, the menu is based on Sicilian traditions and includes fresh pasta with sardines, and couscous with fish. ● *Mon; Jan, Nov.* 🥗

ISOLE EOLIE: *Filippino* Ⓛ Ⓛ
Piazza del Municipio, Lipari 98055. 【 090 981 10 02.
An essentially Sicilian, sea-based menu includes swordfish, homemade *maccheroni*, and some excellent *cassata Siciliana*. ● *Oct–Apr: Mon; 2 weeks Nov, 2 weeks Dec.* 🥗 ▤ ⤢

MARSALA: *Delfino* Ⓛ Ⓛ
Via Lungomare Mediterraneo 672, 91025. 【 0923 96 95 65.
Three lovely rooms all with views over either the sea or the garden. Try the sunflower *spaghetti* or swordfish *alla Messinese*. ● *Tue.* 🥗 ▤ ⤢ ♿

MARSALA: *Mothia* Ⓛ Ⓛ
Contrada Ettore Infersa 13, 91016. 【 0923 74 52 55.
Simple, delicious cooking with homemade bread, pasta, rich desserts, and cakes. The *tagliatelle* with lobster sauce are particularly recommended. ● *Wed; Jan–Feb.* 🥗 ▤ ♿

PALERMO: *Simpaty* Ⓛ Ⓛ
Via Piano Gallo 18, Località Mondello 90151. 【 091 45 44 70.
The dining room has good views over the popular bay of Mondello, and the menu is almost exclusively fish. Try *ricci* (little sea urchins) – served as antipasto or as a pasta sauce, octopus, and squid. ● *Fri.* 🥗 ▤

	FIXED-PRICE MENU	GOOD WINE LIST	FORMAL DRESS	OUTDOOR TABLES

Average prices for a three-course meal for one, including a half bottle of house wine, tax and service:
Ⓛ up to L35,000
ⓁⓁ L35–55,000
ⓁⓁⓁ L55–75,000
ⓁⓁⓁⓁ L75–100,000
ⓁⓁⓁⓁⓁ over L100,000.

FIXED-PRICE MENU
A fixed-price menu offered, usually with three courses.
GOOD WINE LIST
Denotes a wide range of good quality wines.
FORMAL DRESS
Some restaurants require men to wear a jacket and tie.
OUTDOOR TABLES
Tables for eating outdoors, often with a good view.
CREDIT CARDS
The symbol shows that major credit cards are accepted.

Restaurant	FIXED-PRICE MENU	GOOD WINE LIST	FORMAL DRESS	OUTDOOR TABLES
PALERMO: *La Scuderia* ⓁⓁⓁ Viale del Fante 9, 90146. 〖 091 52 03 23. Set in the Parco della Favorita, this elegant restaurant sticks to traditional Sicilian cuisine that is carefully and deliciously prepared. ● Sun; 2 weeks Aug. 🗎🗎🗎		■		
PALERMO: *Temptation* ⓁⓁⓁ Via Torretta 94, Località Sferracavallo 90148. 〖 091 691 11 04. This trattoria offers an all-inclusive menu of seafood antipasti, and the pasta with eggplant and fried fish is particularly recommended. ● Thu. 🗎🗎	●			
RAGUSA: *La Ciotola* ⓁⓁ Via Archimede 23, 9710. 〖 0932 22 89 44. An elegant, modern restaurant in the city center serving well-prepared specialties such as *maccheroncini* with eggplant, and lots of fish. ● Mon; Aug. 🗎🗎🗎		■		
SCIACCA: *Hostaria del Vicolo* ⓁⓁⓁ Vico Sammaritano 10, 92019. 〖 0925 230 71. The menu is Sicilian, with dishes such as *tagliatelle* with shrimp, eggplant and *bottarga* (tuna eggs), and tasty desserts. ● Sun eve, Mon eve; Oct. 🗎🗎🗎		■		
SELINUNTE: *Lido Azzurro* ⓁⓁ Via Marco Polo 51, Località Marinella 91022. 〖 0924 462 11. A bustling trattoria with views of the top of the acropolis from the terrace. There's a wide range of buffet-style antipasti. ● Nov–Feb. 🗎				■
SIRACUSA: *La Foglia* ⓁⓁ Via Capodieci 29, 96100. 〖 0931 662 33. Vegetables and legumes are the mainstay of the menu at this restaurant in the historic center. Try fresh pasta with vegetables or fish and the soups. ● Tue. 🗎🗎				
SIRACUSA: *Minerva* ⓁⓁ Piazza Duomo 20, 96100. 〖 0931 694 04. A pizzeria right in the historic center, with a wide and imaginative range of pizzas on offer. Tables are outside in the cathedral square. ● Mon. 🗎🗎				■
SIRACUSA: *Jonico 'a Rutta 'e Ciauli* ⓁⓁⓁ Riviera Dionisio il Grande 194, 96100. 〖 0931 655 40. The attractive, bright dining room has walls that are covered with Sicilian ceramics and some old, agricultural artifacts The cuisine is regional and traditional. ● Tue. 🗎🗎		■		■
TAORMINA: *Pizzeria Vecchia Taormina* Ⓛ Vico Ebrei 3, 98039. 〖 0942 62 55 89. A traditional pizzeria in the old Jewish quarter of Taormina. There's a massive range of Sicilian-style pizzas and delicious antipasti. ● Wed; Nov–Dec. 🗎🗎🗲				■
TAORMINA: *Al Duomo* ⓁⓁⓁ Vico Ebrei 11, 98039. 〖 0942 62 56 56. A typical Sicilian trattoria, dishes include tuna and swordfish. ● Wed (in winter); Feb. 🗎🗎		■		■
TAORMINA: *La Giara* ⓁⓁⓁⓁ Vicolo La Floresta 1, 98039. 〖 0942 233 60. A pretty restaurant with beautiful views over the bay of Taormina. Try *ravioli* with eggplant and wild fennel *involtini* (parcels). ● Mon; Nov–Mar: Mon–Fri; Jan, Feb. 🗎		■	●	■
TRAPANI: *Da Peppe* ⓁⓁⓁ Via Spalti 50, 91100. 〖 0923 282 46. Trapani specialties served as well as house dishes established over the years. The mainstay is fish, including locally caught tuna. ● Sun eve; Jan, Dec. 🗎🗎		■		■
TRAPANI: *P&G* ⓁⓁ Via Spalti 1, 91100. 〖 0923 54 77 01. This restaurant has become an institution in Trapani. During the annual tuna *mattanza*, fresh tuna is served in a huge variety of ways. ● Sun; Aug. 🗎🗎🗎				

SARDINIA

ALGHERO: *Al Tuguri* ⓁⓁⓁ
Via Maiorca 113, 07041. █ 079 97 67 72.
A pretty restaurant in a 15th-century building in the historic center, with an interesting menu of delicious Mediterranean specialties. ● *Sun; Dec–Jan.* ✎ ⚡ ▤

ALGHERO: *La Lepanto* ⓁⓁⓁ
Via Carlo Alberto 135, 07041. █ 079 97 91 16.
Regional dishes, such as *bottarga* (tuna roe) and lobster and other creative dishes: warm octopus, and scampi with pecorino. ● *Mon.* ✎ ▤ ♿

BOSA: *Mannu Da Giancarlo e Rita* ⓁⓁ
Viale Alghero, 08013. █ 0785 37 53 06.
A smart, modern restaurant offering extremely good local fish specialties; Bosa is famous for fresh lobster, which is served here in a celery sauce. ✎ ▤

CAGLIARI: *Nuovo Saint Pierre* ⓁⓁ
Via Coghinas 13, 09122. █ 070 27 15 78.
Traditional dishes include wild boar with lentils, wild asparagus *risotto*, roasted lamb, and stuffed beef. Fish is served in summer. ● *Sun; Aug.* ✎ ▤

CAGLIARI: *Dal Corsaro* ⓁⓁⓁ
Viale Regina Margherita 28, 09124. █ 070 66 43 18.
Good service and a pleasant atmosphere in which to enjoy carefully prepared regional dishes (fish *ravioli*), original creations (*tagliatelle* with zucchini and clams), and some rediscovered Cagliari classics. ● *Sun; Aug; 2 weeks Dec.* ✎ ♿ ▤

CALASETTE: *Da Pasqualino* ⓁⓁ
Via Roma 99, 09011. █ 0781 884 73.
Delicious local fish-based specialties are served in this simple and relaxed trattoria, including fish soups, *bottarga* (tuna roe) and lobster. ● *Tue (in winter); Nov.* ✎ ▤ ♿

NUORO: *Canne al Vento* ⓁⓁ
Viale Repubblica 66, 08100. █ 0784 20 17 62.
Dishes available at this regional restaurant include roast meats, excellent cheeses, octopus salad, and a hot *seadas* (honey dessert). ● *Sun; 2 wks Aug, 2 wks Dec.* ✎ ▤ ♿

OLBIA: *Bacchus* ⓁⓁⓁ
Centro Commerciale Martini, Via Gabriele d'Annunzio 2nd floor, 07026. █ 0789 216 12.
An elegant restaurant with sea views. Creative cooking with regional undertones includes fish, lamb with artichokes, and crab. ● *Mon; 3 wks Nov.* ✎ ▤ ⚡ ♿

OLIENA: *CK* ⓁⓁ
Corso ML King 2/4, 08025. █ 0784 28 80 24.
Typical local specialties in this family-run restaurant include game and herbs, fresh cheese *ravioli* and honey desserts. ✎ ▤ ♿

ORISTANO: *Faro* ⓁⓁⓁⓁ
Via Bellini 25, 09170. █ 0783 700 02.
One of Sardinia's best restaurants, serving regional dishes based on what is fresh in the market that day, particularly fish and seafood. ● *Sun; 2 weeks Jul, Dec 22–Jan 15.* ✎ ▤ ♿

PORTO CERVO: *Gianni Pedrinelli* ⓁⓁⓁⓁ
Località Piccolo Pevero, 07020. █ 0789 924 36.
The menu is regional serving much fish. Try the house specialty, a typically Sardinian dish, *porcettu allo spiedo* (pork on the spit). ● *Oct–Feb.* ✎

PORTO ROTONDO: *Da Giovannino* ⓁⓁⓁⓁ
Piazza Quadra, 07026. █ 0789 352 80.
Popular with Italian politicos and media types, who dine on expensive but delicious (and attentively served) Mediterranean specialties, which are accompanied by superb wines. ● *Mon, Sun eve (in winter); 2 wks Nov, 2 wks Dec.* ✎ ⚡ ▤ ♿

PORTOSCUSO: *La Ghinghetta* ⓁⓁⓁⓁ
Via Cavour 26, Località Sa Caletta, 09010. █ 0781 50 81 43.
Set in a charming fishing village, the almost exclusively fish-based menu adds a different twist to local specialties. ● *Sun; Nov–Apr.* ✎ ⚡

SASSARI: *Florian* ⓁⓁⓁ
Via Bellieni 27, 07100. █ 079 23 62 51.
The menu here offers the very best of sea and land regional specialties according to the season: there are mushrooms in autumn, seafood in summer, and appropriate vegetables year-round. ● *Aug.* ✎ ▤ ♿

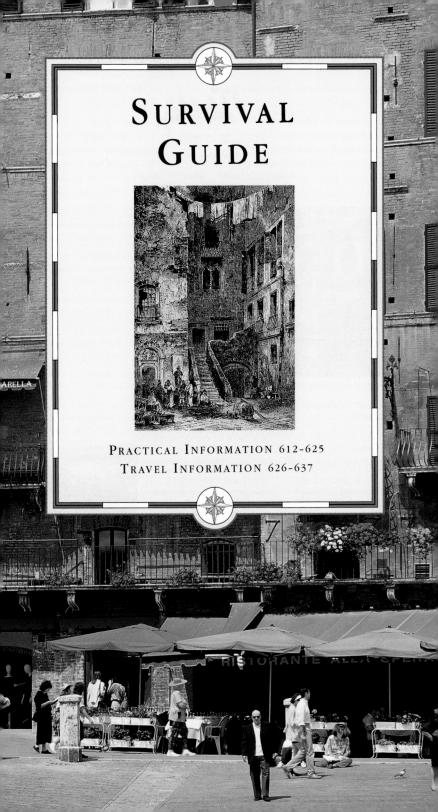

SURVIVAL
GUIDE

PRACTICAL INFORMATION

SK ANY ITALIAN and they will almost certainly tell you that Italy is the most beautiful country in the world. They may not be far wrong. However, the charm and allure of Italy may help to veil some of her numerous practical problems. Getting information is rarely straightforward; public

ENTE NAZIONALE ITALIANO PER IL TURISMO

Tourist board logo

offices and banks are nearly always crippled by long lines and bureaucracy, and the postal service is famous for its inefficiency. This section, together with some forward planning and a little patience, should help you cope with some of Italy's idiosyncrasies.

Tourists crossing the Ponte della Paglia in Venice *(see p105)*

VISAS AND PERMESSO DI SOGGIORNO

EUROPEAN UNION nationals and citizens of the US, Canada, Australia, and New Zealand do not need visas for stays of up to three months. Most European Union (EU) visitors need only a valid identity document, but visitors from UK, Ireland, Denmark, and Sweden do need a passport. All other visitors are required to present a full passport on entry and, officially, declare themselves to the Italian police within eight days of arrival. If you are staying in a hotel or campsite, this will be done for you; otherwise contact the local *Questura* (police station).

Anyone wishing to stay in Italy for more than three months (eight days for non-EU citizens) will have to obtain a *permesso di soggiorno* (permit to stay). You can apply for a permit at any main police station, *Questura di Provincia*. You must apply for the correct permit, either a permit to work *(lavoro)* or a permit to study *(studio)*. For each permit you will need to submit a written application *(domanda)*, pass-

port-style photographs, and photocopies of your passport. If you are looking for work, these items need to be accompanied by proof of your future employment in Italy or other means of financial support.

If you are applying for a study permit, it is necessary to obtain a letter from the relevant school or university giving details of your course. This then has to be sent to the Italian consulate in your country of origin to obtain an official covering letter, or declaration. You will also need some form of guarantee that your medical bills will be paid should you become ill or have an accident. A comprehensive insurance policy *(see p616)* would be sufficient.

WHEN TO VISIT

ITALY'S TOWNS and historic sites are extremely popular attractions, and it is worth considering this when planning your trip. Rome, Florence, and Venice are all crowded from spring to October, and it is advisable to book a hotel well in advance. In August the cities are generally slightly

less busy, abandoned by their inhabitants in the summer heat. At Easter, Rome is overrun by pilgrims and tourists, and in February, Venice triples its population during Carnevale *(see p65)*. Seaside resorts fill up over the months of July and August, whereas June and September can be equally hot but far less crowded. The seas and beaches are notably cleaner at the beginning of summer. December to March is the time of year for skiing, although the first snow often falls as early as November. Most sights are open all year, except on some public holidays *(see p65)* and often two Mondays each month *(see p614)*.

Rome's renowned Tazza d'Oro café, an ideal rest stop after sightseeing

SEASONAL DIFFERENCES

THE NORTHERN PART of Italy is generally more temperate than the south, which has a Mediterranean climate. June to September is hot and in high summer, also humid. Summer storms can be quite dramatic, but often last only a few hours. Spring and autumn are ideal for visiting cities; temperatures are mild. Winter can be bitterly cold, especially in the north. *The Climate of Italy* on pages 68–9 takes a detailed look at the country's regional weather.

◁ **The beautiful Piazza del Campo in Siena, meeting place for visitors and locals**

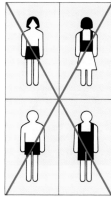

**Unacceptable dress in church:
both sexes are required to
cover torsos and upper arms**

ETIQUETTE AND TIPPING

PEOPLE IN ITALY ARE, on the whole, friendly toward foreign visitors. On entering a shop or bar it is customary to greet people with a general *buon giorno* (good morning) or *buona sera* (good evening), and the same applies when leaving. They will also try to be helpful when asked directions in the street. If your Italian is slight, *scusi* followed by the name of the place you wish to go to will often suffice. *Grazie* (thank you) is always replied to with *prego* (not at all).

Tipping in restaurants is expected when the 15 percent service is not included. However, as much as 10 percent would be considered generous and a tip is often not expected at all in family-run restaurants. Taxi drivers and hotel porters expect a couple of thousand lire if they have been helpful. You could simply round the bill up to the nearest L5,000.

Italians are very dress conscious, and unusual or risqué clothes do get noticed. Strict dress codes are enforced in many places of worship, where your torso and upper arms must be covered; shorts and skirts must reach below the knee.

CUSTOMS

ON JUNE 30, 1999, the intra-EU Duty and Tax Free Allowances, better known as Duty-Free and mainly affecting such luxury items as alcohol, perfumes, and tobacco, were abolished. However, for EU residents the amount of these goods that can be imported for personal used has increased

Consulates can generally provide up-to-date information on particular customs regulations. To find out what you can take back from Italy to non-EU countries, contact the particular country's customs department, who will be able to advise you.

TAX EXEMPTION

VALUE ADDED TAX (IVA in Italy) ranges from 12–35 percent, depending on the item. Non-European Union citizens can obtain an IVA refund for each purchase over L300,000, but be prepared for a long process. It is easier to get a refund if you shop where you see the "Euro Free Tax" sign, rather than from a market stall, for example. After showing your passport to the shop assistant and completing a form, the IVA will be deducted from your bill. The alternative is to present a customs officer with your purchases and their receipts on your departure. He or she will stamp the receipts, which you then send back to the vendor. A refund will eventually be mailed to you.

The clock of San Giacomo di Rialto in Venice (see p93)

ITALIAN TIME

ITALY IS SIX hours ahead of Eastern Standard Time (EST). The clocks are put forward one hour in March and back in September (like Daylight Savings Time). From Italy: New York: -6 hours; London: -1 hour; Ottawa: -6 hours; Sydney: +10 hours.

ELECTRICAL ADAPTORS

THE VOLTAGE IN ITALY is 220 volts, with two-pin round-pronged plugs. US electrical equipment will need an adaptor; for European appliances, the plug can simply be changed over. Italian plugs come in many different sizes, for no apparent reason, and you can buy adaptors or even just swap plugs. It is worth buying travel plugs before you leave since they are difficult to find in Italy. Most hotels with three or more stars have hair driers and outlets for shavers in all bedrooms, but check the voltage first, to be safe.

Standard Italian plug

BOOKING TICKETS

THEATERS IN ITALY do not generally take bookings over the telephone – you have to visit the box office in person. However, there are agencies, such as **Box Office** and **Virtours**, that will book tickets for you (for a fee). Opera tickets are sold months in advance, with just a few held back until two days before the performance. Tickets for rock and jazz concerts are also sold at some record shops whose names appear on the publicity posters.

DIRECTORY

TICKET AGENCIES

Box Office
Viale Giulio Cesare 88, Rome.
Map 3 C1. *Tickets for classical music, rock, pop & jazz concerts & some sporting events*
📞 06 372 02 16.

Virtours
Galleria Pellicciae, Verona.
📞 045 800 51 12.
FAX 045 59 54 54.

TOURIST INFORMATION

THE NATIONAL tourist board, **ENIT**, has branches in capital cities worldwide and offers general information on Italy. For more specific requests, contact the local tourist offices. The addresses and telephone numbers are listed under each town or city, directly under the title, and they are plotted on the town and city maps. An EPT *(Ente Provinciale di Turismo)* has information on its town and surrounding province, whereas an APT *(Azienda di Promozione Turistica)* deals exclusively with individual towns. Both offices help with practical information such as hotel bookings and tours. They also provide free maps and guidebooks in various languages. The EPT and APT can refer you to local tour guides and advise on trips and excursions. Small towns will have a *Pro Loco*, a tourist office run by the local administration, which is sometimes open only during the tourist season. It is usually located in the town hall *(comune)*, or occasionally in someone's private residence.

Sign for tourist information

TOURS

MANY TOUR COMPANIES organize coach trips with English-speaking guides, which include all the main tourist attractions in Italy. American Express offices in

A student relaxing in the sun in Gaiole in Chianti

Rome, Florence, Venice, and Milan organize local trips and **CIT** offers coach tours that go all over the country. If you are looking for something a little more personal and off the beaten track, check the local pages of national newspapers for tour groups or organizations. Local tourist boards will also be able to advise you. Always employ official guides and be sure to establish the fee in advance. For information on various special vacations, turn to pages 624–5.

SIGHTSEEING PERMITS

TO VISIT CERTAIN SITES in Rome, such as the Vatican library, you need a written permit, which can be obtained from:

Comune di Roma Soprintendenze Comunale
Piazza Campitelli 7, Rome. **Map** 3 A5.
📞 *06 67 10 32 38.*
📠 *06 679 22 58.*

SIGHTSEEING OPENING HOURS

ITALIAN MUSEUMS are gradually conforming to new regulations, particularly in the north, opening from 9am–7pm daily, except for two Mondays each month. In winter, however, many revert to 9am–1pm Tuesday to Saturday, and 9am–12:30pm on Sunday, but it is best to check. Privately run and smaller museums have their own times, so always phone in advance. Archaeological sites are generally open from 9am until one hour before

A guided group tour through the streets of Florence

sunset, Tuesday to Sunday. Churches are usually open from around 7am–12:30pm and 4–7pm. However, they often prefer not to let tourists in during services, so Sunday is not the best day to visit.

Daytime sightseeing on a tranquil canal in Venice

ADMISSION CHARGES

SIGHTSEEING FEES generally range from about L4,000 to L14,000 (but churches are usually free). Reductions for students are not always offered, but many state-run museums and archaeological sites allow free entry for people under 24 and over 60 years of age. Large groups are often entitled to a discount as well. If reductions are available, you will need to show a valid piece of identification, such as a student card or passport.

STUDENT INFORMATION

THE NATIONAL STUDENT travel organization, **CTS** (Centro Turistico Studentesco), has branches throughout Italy and the rest of Europe. They issue the International Student Identity Card (ISIC); the Council on International Educational Exchange also offers international ID cards. Both can be used, in conjunction with a passport, for discounts at museums and other attractions. The ISIC card also

ISIC card

gives access to a 24-hour telephone helpline providing general information. As well as issuing ID cards, CTS and CIEE offer discount car rentals, rail passes, and cultural tours. For details

about youth hostels, contact the **Associazione Italiana Alberghi per la Gioventù** (the Italian YHA), as long as you are a current member.

TRAVELING WITH CHILDREN

O N THE WHOLE, Italians love children, to an extent that sometimes seems over-indulgent. Most trattorias and pizzerias welcome them, and there are no rules excluding children from bars. Hotels also welcome children, but smaller establishments usually have limited facilities. Some of the more upscale hotels may offer a babysitting service. It is a common sight to see children playing outside fairly late at night, especially in summer. Most towns have playgrounds, and many have summer fun-fairs. For young swimmers, the calm Mediterranean is ideal.

Fascinated child feeding pigeons at Piazza Navona, Rome

DISABLED TRAVELERS

P UBLIC AWARENESS of the needs of the disabled is low, but improving. Some towns now have buses for the disabled, and ramps and lifts are slowly being added to museums and some churches. **CO.IN** (Consorzio Cooperative Intergrale) provides information on hotels, services, and general assistance.

A mechanically operated wheelchair ramp across a bridge

RELIGIOUS SERVICES

A LMOST 85 PERCENT of the population is Catholic. Sunday mass is celebrated throughout the country, and in the principal churches services are also held during the week. In major cities some churches, such as the church of San Silvestro (Piazza San Silvestro) in Rome, offer services and confession in English. For some visitors, a trip to Rome will include an audience with the pope (p409).

Although Italy is predominantly Catholic, all the main religious beliefs are represented. For details contact the main centers in Rome.

CONVERSION CHART

US Standard to Metric
1 inch = 2.54 centimeters
1 foot = 30 centimeters
1 mile = 1.6 kilometers
1 ounce = 28 grams
1 pound = 454 grams
1 US quart = 0.947 liter
1 US gallon = 3.6 liters

Metric to US Standard
1 centimeter = 0.4 inch
1 meter = 3 feet 3 inches
1 kilometer = 0.6 mile
1 gram = 0.04 ounce
1 kilogram = 2.2 pounds
1 liter = 1.1 US quarts

Personal Security and Health

Although Italy is generally a safe place for visitors, it is wise to keep a watchful eye on your personal belongings, especially in the larger towns and cities. There is a conspicuous police presence throughout the country, and in the event of an emergency or crime, any of the police officers described in this section will be able to assist you and tell you where to go to report an incident. If you fall ill, pharmacies are a good first stop where medically trained staff can give advice or tell you where to find further help. In an emergency, the emergency room (*Pronto Soccorso*) of any hospital will treat you.

Commissariato di Polizia – a police station

Police car

Green Cross ambulance in Venice

Roman fire engine

PERSONAL PROPERTY

Petty theft such as pickpocketing, purse snatching, and car theft is rife. In the event of a theft you must report it within 24 hours to the nearest *questura* or *commissariato* (police station).

Avoid leaving anything visible in an unattended car, including a car radio. If you have to leave luggage in a car, find a hotel that has private parking. When making a purchase, always check your change and do not keep wallets in back pockets, especially on buses or in other crowded places. "Fanny packs" and money belts are a favorite target for pickpockets, so try to keep them hidden. When walking, hold bags and cameras to the inside of the sidewalk so as not to tempt motorized snatchers; do not show expensive cameras and video equipment in areas off tourist routes. The safest way to carry large sums of money is to use travelers' checks. Try to keep your receipts and credit card separate, together with a photocopy of vital documents, in case of loss or theft. It is also advisable to get comprehensive travel insurance that covers theft of personal possessions in addition to covering cancellation/delay of flights, loss/damage of luggage, money, and other valuables, as well as personal liability and accidents. If you do need to make an insurance claim for stolen or lost property, you must get a copy of the report (*denuncia*) from the police station when you report the incident. In case of lost passports, go to your embassy or consulate; for lost travelers' checks contact the issuing company's nearest office.

LEGAL ASSISTANCE

A comprehensive insurance package should include coverage for legal assistance and advice. If you do not have insurance coverage, contact your embassy as soon as possible after an incident occurs. The embassy can offer advice and should provide you with a list of English- and Italian-speaking lawyers who are knowledgeable about both the Italian and English legal systems.

PERSONAL SECURITY

Although petty crime in the cities is frequent, violent crime in Italy is rare. However, it is common for people to raise their voices aggressively during an argument. Usually, remaining calm and being polite will help to defuse the situation. Always be wary of unofficial tour guides, taxi drivers, or strangers who wish to assist you or advise you on accommodations, restaurants, or shops since they may expect money in return.

WOMEN TRAVELERS

Women traveling on their own in Italy are likely to meet with a lot of attention. Although this is often more of an irritation than a danger, it is best to keep away from lonely, unlit streets and areas

A team of *carabinieri* in traffic police uniform

near train stations at night. Walking quickly and purposefully is a good way to avoid any unwanted attention. The staff at hotels and restaurants generally treat their single female guests and customers with extra care and attention.

THE POLICE

THERE ARE SEVERAL different police forces in Italy and each one fulfills a particular role. The state police, *la polizia*, wear blue uniforms and drive blue cars. They deal with most crimes. The *carabinieri* are militarily trained and wear dark blue and black uniforms with red striped trousers. These officers deal with a variety of offences from organized crime to speeding and can also conduct random security checks. The *guardia di finanza* are the financial police force (the fraud squad), and wear gray uniforms with yellow striped trousers. The *vigili urbani*, or the municipal traffic police, wear blue and white uniforms in winter and white during the summer. Even though they are not official police officers, the *vigili urbani* can issue heavy fines for traffic and parking offences. They can usually be spotted patrolling the streets, enforcing laws, or directing traffic. Officers from any of the forces will be able to help.

Municipal policeman

INTERPRETERS

INDEPENDENT INTERPRETERS and translators often advertise their services in newspapers and foreign-language bookshops. You will find agencies listed in the Yellow Pages (*Pagine Gialle*), and the AITI (*Associazione Italiana di Traduttori e Interpreti*) has a list of qualified translators and interpreters. In an emergency, your embassy will be able to provide an interpreter.

Outside a Florentine pharmacy with a red cross sign

MEDICAL TREATMENT

IF YOU ARE in need of urgent medical attention, go to the *Pronto Soccorso* (emergency room) of the nearest hospital. Standards of health care are generally better in the north than those in the south of Italy, although not as high as in the US or Britain. Visitors from the US should check with their insurance companies before leaving home to be sure they are covered if medical care is needed. Many medical facilities will require you to pay for your treatment in full at the time of service. Be sure to get an itemized bill to submit to your insurance company. In some cases, insruance companies require you to provide an official translation before they will reimburse you. Travelers may wish to take out additional, private travel insurance against the cost of any emergency hospital care, doctors' fees, and repatriation.

No inoculations are needed for Italy, but mosquito repellent is advisable in summer.

EMERGENCY SUPPLIES

VARIOUS MEDICAL products, including homeopathic medicines, are available in any pharmacy (*farmacia*), but a prescription is often required. Thanks to a 24-hour service, (*servizio notturno*), there is always a pharmacy open in all cities and most

DIRECTORY

EMBASSIES AND CONSULATES

US
Via Vittorio Veneto 119A, Rome.
C 06 467 41. Lungarno Amerigo Vespucci 46, Florence.
C 055 239 82 76. Piazza della Repubblica, Naples. **C** 081 583 81 11. **W** www.usis.it

Canada
Via G B De Rossi, Rome.
C 06 44 59 81.
W www.canada.it

EMERGENCY NUMBERS

General Emergency
C 113.
Police (Carabinieri)
C 112.
Fire Service
C 115.
Medical Emergencies
C 118.

towns. Those that are open at night are listed in the local pages of daily newspapers and on all pharmacy doors. *Tabacchi* (tobacco) shops are a source of many useful supplies and are easily recognized by their "T" signs (see below). Apart from tobacco, cigarettes, and matches, you can buy razors, batteries, bus and metro tickets, phone cards, and parking cards. At some, you can also purchase postage stamps and get packages weighed and priced.

A Tabacchi shop, with its characteristic white "T" sign

Banking and Local Currency

Eurocheque logo

VIRTUALLY ALL ITALIAN HOTELS, many shops, large restaurants, and gas stations now accept major credit cards and travelers' checks. Eurocheques, available only to travelers with European bank accounts, can be used in cash machines with the Eurocheque logo. When you pay with credit cards, you may be asked to show identification. Currency can be changed in the often crowded banks, but service is not always fast. All banks will cash travelers' checks and ATM's *(bancomat)* will accept cash cards. Some machines may also accept MasterCard (Access), VISA, and American Express cards. Cash cards for US bank accounts may be used in cash machines displaying the appropriate system logo.

Electronic exchange machine

Cash dispenser that also accepts VISA and MasterCard (Access)

CHANGING MONEY

BANKING HOURS are somewhat restrictive and can also be slightly erratic so it is safest to acquire some local currency before you arrive in Italy. Exchange rates will vary from place to place.

Once you arrive, the most convenient way to change money is to use the electronic exchange machines, which are located at all major airports, train stations, and banks. The machines have multilingual instructions and the exchange rate is clearly displayed on the screen. You simply feed in up to ten bills of the same foreign currency and you will receive lire in return.

Bureaux de change can be found in all main towns. Although they are easier to use, they tend to have higher exchange rates and charge more commission than banks.

TRAVELER'S CHECKS

TRAVELER'S CHECKS are probably the safest way to carry large sums of money. Choose a name that is well known such as Thomas Cook, American Express, or checks issued through a major bank. There is usually a minimum commission charge, which may make changing small sums of money uneconomical. Some establishments will charge you for each check.

Check the exchange rates before you travel and decide whether dollar or lire traveler's checks are more appropriate for your trip.

REGIONAL DIFFERENCES IN COST OF LIVING

THE NORTH is generally more expensive than the south, but there are many exceptions. Look for local producers, including those with special items to sell. Their goods are often of better quality.

Metal-detecting security doors found at most banks

BANKING HOURS

BANKS ARE USUALLY open between 8:30am and 1:30pm, Monday to Friday. Most also open for an hour in the afternoon, from about 2:15pm to 3pm or 2:30pm until 3:30pm, depending on the bank. All banks close on weekends and for public holidays, and they also close early the day before a major holiday. Bureaux de change are often open all day, and in some places, also late at night.

USING BANKS

FOR SECURITY PURPOSES, most banks have electronic double doors with metal detectors, allowing one person in at a time. Metal objects and bags should first be deposited in lockers situated in the foyer. Press the button to open the outer door, then wait for it to close behind you. The inner door then opens automatically. Do not be alarmed by the heavily armed guards that patrol most banks in Italy.

Changing money at a bank can at times be a frustrating process, as it can involve endless forms and standing in line. First you have to go to the window that displays the *cambio* sign and then you will have to go to the *cassa* to obtain your Italian money. If in doubt, ask someone in order to avoid waiting in the wrong line.

If you need to have money sent to you in Italy, banks at home can telex money to an Italian bank, but it takes about a week. American Express, Thomas Cook, and Western Union all provide faster money transfer services, with a charge to the sender.

CURRENCY

ITALY'S CURRENCY is the *lira* (plural *lire*) and is usually written as L or £. *Lira* means pound, so the English pound is referred to as the *lira sterlina*.

The thousands of units of currency may seem confusing at first but the distinctive colors of the bills makes it easy to distinguish between them. You will find that the last three zeros are often ignored in spoken Italian: *cinquanta* will usually mean L50,000 and not, as you may think, L50. Shop and bar owners are reluctant to accept high-value bills for small purchases, so get some small denomination bills when changing money.

On January 1, 1999, the Euro became legal currency in 11 European Union countries, including Italy. From January 1, 2002, national currencies will be replaced gradually by the Euro. Each state will adorn coins with its own national designs, and the currency can be used in each of the 11 member states.

Bank Notes

All bills are issued by the Banca d'Italia. Each denomination is a different color and carries a portrait of a historic person, like Caravaggio, on the L100,000 bill. As a further aid to identification, the denominations above L2,000 increase in size according to their value. The lira itself is never subdivided.

1,000 lire

2,000 lire

5,000 lire

10,000 lire

50,000 lire

100,000 lire

50 lire (old)   100 lire (old)   50 lire (new)   100 lire (new)   200 lire

Coins

Coins, shown here at actual size, are in denominations of L1,000, L500, L200, L100, and L50. Three versions of the L100 and L50 coins are still in circulation, the two types shown here and an older design. All three are likely to remain legal tender until the introduction of the Euro as the single European currency.

500 lire

1,000 lire

Communications

Telephone company logo

ALTHOUGH THE ITALIAN POSTAL service is known for being particularly slow, Italy's other forms of communication, at least in the cities, are more efficient. Fax machines, courier services, and telephones are widespread and Internet points are available throughout Italy. Foreign-language newspapers and magazines are available in all cities and most large towns. Both state-run and privately owned television stations exist, but only satellite television and radio stations broadcast foreign-language programs.

PUBLIC TELEPHONES

THE ITALIAN NATIONAL telephone company is Telecom Italia. Coin-operated telephones are being replaced by new card-operated machines. Although many of the new telephones will take both cards and coins, some only accept a Telecom credit card. You can buy phone cards *(carta* or *scheda telefonica)* from bars, newspaper kiosks, post offices, and *tabacchi.* International telephone cards are also on sale at *tabacchi* and newsstands and offer

Telephone sign

considerable savings. The latest public telephones have instructions in four languages (Italian, English, French, and German). To select a language, push the top right-hand button.

Coin telephones, usually located in bars and restaurants, accept L100, L200, and L500. A local call costs L200. When making long-distance or international calls have at least L2,000 in change at hand. If you don't put enough coins in to start with, you will be disconnected and lose your money. An alternative is to look for a *telefono a scatti,* or metered phone. Ask the bar or restaurant owner if

you can phone and the call will be metered. You then pay when you have finished.

Many main towns have telephone offices *(Telefoni)* where you are assigned a booth and pay after your calls. Although no premium is charged, it is wise to check the rate before making a call.

Using one of Italy's public telephones or *interurbani*

USING A COIN AND CARD TELEPHONE

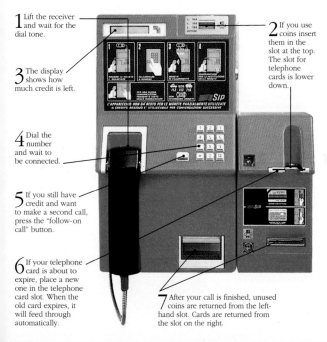

1 Lift the receiver and wait for the dial tone.

3 The display shows how much credit is left.

4 Dial the number and wait to be connected.

5 If you still have credit and want to make a second call, press the "follow-on call" button.

6 If your telephone card is about to expire, place a new one in the telephone card slot. When the old card expires, it will feed through automatically.

2 If you use coins insert them in the slot at the top. The slot for telephone cards is lower down.

7 After your call is finished, unused coins are returned from the left-hand slot. Cards are returned from the slot on the right.

Telephone cards have values of L5,000 or L10,000.

To use a card, break off the marked corner and insert, arrow first.

L500

L200

L100

DIRECTORY

For operator-assisted calls from a public phone, insert L200, which will be returned after the call:

To calculate the cost of a call from a private phone, dial * 40 # before and after the call and the number of units will be read to you.

From 1998, the full area code must always be included, even when phoning within a city.

USEFUL NUMBERS

Directory Assistance
📞 12.

International Directory Assistance
📞 176.

Italcable
📞 170 (for reverse charge and calling card calls).

American Operators
📞 172 10 11 (AT&T).
📞 172 10 22 (MCI Worldphone).
📞 172 18 77 (Sprint).

British Operator
📞 172 00 44.

Australian Operators
📞 172 10 61 (Telstra).
📞 172 11 61 (Optus).

COUNTRY CODES

To call Italy from the US:
📞 011-39 then the full area code (incl. 0) and the number.

To call the US from Italy:
📞 001 then area code and number.

TV AND RADIO

Television channels in Italy include the state-owned RAI (Uno, Due, and Tre) and Fininvest (Retequattro, Canale Cinque, and Italia Uno). There are also many local channels. Most foreign programs are dubbed into Italian, although satellite channels, such as Sky, CNN, and RTL, show news and sports programs in a variety of languages. There are three national radio stations and hundreds of local stations. The BBC World Service is on 15.070MHz (short wave) in the mornings and 648KHz (medium wave) at night.

NEWSPAPERS

The main national daily newspapers are *La Stampa*, *Il Corriere della Sera*, and *La Repubblica*. Papers with the most detailed news of Italy's major cities include *Il Mattino* for Naples, *Il Messaggero* for Rome, and *Il Giornale* for Milan. All newspapers have local pages and listings for movies, theaters and main concerts. In Rome and Milan, *La Repubblica* publishes "what's on and where to go" supplements called *TrovaRoma* and *Vivi-Milano*. Florence's *Firenze Spettacolo* and Rome's *RomaC'è* and *Time out in Rome* are weekly entertainment listings magazines. Foreign papers, such as the *International Guardian*, *International Herald Tribune*, and *USA Today*, arrive in the main cities at or shortly after midday.

Newspaper stand selling national and international publications

POST OFFICE

Post offices and also some tobacconists weigh and price letters and sell stamps. Local post offices open from 8:25am–1:50pm weekdays, and from 8:25am–12 noon on Saturday. Main post offices are open from 8:25am–7pm

City letters   **Other destinations**

Italian mail box

Post Office sign

nonstop. The Vatican City and the state of San Marino have their own postal system and stamps. Letters and postcards destined for Europe cost the same as mail within Italy. The red mail boxes (blue in the Vatican) usually have two slots labeled *per la città* (for the city only) and *tutte le altre destinazioni* (for all other destinations). Italian mail is famous for its unreliability and letters can take from four days to two weeks to arrive.

For a faster service, send letters express (*espresso*). More reliable are registered delivery (*raccomandata*) and registered delivery with an arrival receipt (*raccomandata con ricevuta di ritorno*). However, anything of value should be sent by insured mail (*assicurata*).

For urgent communications, try state couriers *Posta celere* and *Cai post*, which are based at all main post offices. They guarantee delivery within 24–72 hours and are far cheaper than private couriers. Main post offices also provide telegram, telex, and fax services. The fax service, however, is not available for certain countries. Post offices also provide a *fermo posta* service (poste restante) for a small collection fee. Send letters to the central post office, c/o Fermo Posta. You will need to show some identification when picking up the letters.

REGIONS OF ITALY

Italy consists of 20 regions that are divided into provinces. Each province has a *capoluogo* (an administrative capital) and a *sigla*, the initials of the capital. For example, FI stands for the *capoluogo* of Florence (*Firenze*). The *sigla* appears on car licence plates registered before 1994 and denotes the origins of the vehicle owner. The code can also be used to address letters, appearing after the town name.

Shopping

ITALY IS KNOWN FOR ITS QUALITY designer goods, ranging from chic clothing and sleek cars to stylish household items. There is a strong tradition of craftsmanship, often from family-run businesses, and there are numerous markets selling regional specialties. Apart from the town markets, it is not a country for bargains, but the joys of window shopping will offer plenty of compensation.

Fresh vegetables on display at a Florentine market stall

OPENING HOURS

OPENING TIMES for shops are usually 9:30am–1pm and around 3:30–8pm, Tuesday to Saturday and Monday afternoons. However, shopkeepers are increasingly keeping more flexible hours. There are not that many large department stores, but most large towns will have a Standa, Upim, and perhaps a Coin or Rinascente. These stores are often open nonstop (*orario continuato*) from 9am–8pm, Monday to Saturday. Boutiques generally open later; music and bookshops sometimes stay open after 8pm and on Sundays.

FOOD STORES

EVEN THOUGH there are supermarkets throughout Italy, the specialty shops, although more expensive, are still the most interesting way to shop. A *forno* has the best bread and a *macellaio* has the finest meat (go to a *norceria* for pork products). Vegetables are freshest from market stalls or the *fruttivendolo*. You can buy cakes at the *pasticceria*, milk at the *latteria*, and pasta, ham, cheese, and general foods at the often impressively stocked *alimentari*. Here you can also buy wine, but for a wider choice, head for the *enoteca*, *vineria*, or *vinaio*, where you can sometimes taste the wine before purchasing.

MARKETS

ALL TOWNS HAVE regional markets that take place each week. Large towns will have several small daily markets followed by a weekly flea market, usually held on a Sunday. In this guide the main market days are listed under each town. Traders set up at 5am and start to clear away at about 1:30pm. Food is sold by the *etto* (100 grams) and the *chilo* (kilo) (*see p615*), or in numbers (two onions, etc). Food stalls selling seasonal products generally have fresher and less expensive produce than the stores. Bargaining is not usually done when buying food, but it is worth asking for a discount (*sconto*) for clothes and other items.

SEASONAL PRODUCE

TO MAKE THE MOST of Italian food, try to buy and eat what is in season. Grapes and mushrooms are best in autumn, whereas spring is the season for asparagus, strawberries, and Roman artichokes. In winter, vegetables such as cauliflower and broccoli are at their best, as are lemons from Amalfi and Sicilian blood oranges. Summer is the time for plums, pears, and cherries, as well as zucchini, eggplant, tomatoes, and melon.

CLOTHES AND DESIGNER SHOPS

ITALY IS FAMOUS worldwide for its fashion industry. Milan is the fashion capital and Via Monte Napoleone, in the city center, is lined with the most famous of the designer boutiques. All large towns will have a selection of designer shops, usually situated near each other. Less expensive clothes are available in markets and many department stores where the styles tend to be

Protective bag with designer label

Souvenir shop in Ostuni, near Brindisi, Puglia

more conventional and classical. Sales, called *saldi*, are held during summer and winter. Second-hand shops are often quite expensive, but the quality and condition of the clothes can be very good. Larger markets have stands piled high with used clothes priced between L1,000 and L10,000. Rummage through and you will often find bargains. Many markets sell fake Rayban sunglasses, Lacoste T-shirts and Levi's jeans. Some shops have signs that read *ingresso libero*, meaning "browsers welcome," but do not be surprised if a sales assistant assails you as soon as you walk in.

An elegant designer clothes boutique in Treviso

Colorful shop display of leather handbags in Florence

JEWELRY AND ANTIQUE SHOPS

Glitzy gold jewelry is very popular in Italy and every *gioielleria* (jewelry shop) will have a wide selection. For more unusual items, try the *bigiotteria* or artisan shops (*oreficeria*). Antique stores like *Antichità* and *Antiquariato* sell furniture and ornaments of varying quality and prices. You will rarely find bargains in Italy, except perhaps at the *Fiere dell'Antiquariato* (antique fairs), held throughout the year all over the country.

INTERIOR DESIGN AND HOUSEHOLD WARES

Interior design is another Italian sector where top names demand extravagant prices, with many shops concentrating on modern, high-tech styles.

There are household shops in cities and towns throughout the country. Italian kitchenware is particularly striking, with its stainless steel and copper pots, pans, and utensils. For the lowest prices, avoid the tourist shops and, if possible, buy directly from the manufacturer. Less expensive items include the characteristic brown espresso and cappuccino cups sold in all markets.

REGIONAL SPECIALITIES

Many of Italy's regional specialties are world famous: Parma ham, Chianti wine, olive oil, and grappa. Regional sweets, including the Sienese *panforte* and Sicilian marzipan, are also well-known, as are cheeses such as Gorgonzola from Lombardy, and Parmesan from Emilia-Romagna. Traditional crafts are still practiced in Italy and range from delicate lacework and glassware in the Veneto to leatherwork, jewelry and marbled paper in Florence. Italian ceramics include elaborate Tuscan pottery, hand-painted dishes around Amalfi, and De Simone's stylized designer plates from Sicily.

Display of decorative glazed pottery from Tuscany

SIZE CHART
For Australian sizes follow the British and American conversions.

Women's dresses, coats and skirts

Italian	40	42	44	46	48	50	52
British	8	10	12	14	16	18	20
American	6	8	10	12	14	16	18

Women's shoes

Italian	36	37	38	39	40	41
British	3	4	5	6	7	8
American	5	6	7	8	9	10

Men's suits

Italian	44	46	48	50	52	54	56	58 (size)
British	34	36	38	40	42	44	46	48 (inches)
American	34	36	38	40	42	44	46	48 (inches)

Men's shirts (collar size)

Italian	36	38	39	41	42	43	44	45 (cm)
British	14	15	15½	16	16½	17	17½	18 (inches)
American	14	15	15½	16	16½	17	17½	18 (inches)

Men's shoes

Italian	39	40	41	42	43	44	45	46
British	6	7	7½	8	9	10	11	12
American	7	7½	8	8½	9½	10½	11	11½

Special Vacations and Outdoor Activities

Exploring the country-side on horseback

ITALY OFFERS AN AMAZING variety of cultural, sports and leisure activities. However, many schools and groups require annual membership and short-term activities are often expensive and difficult to find. Information on current leisure and sports events in a specific region is available from the tourist office listed for each town in this guide. For details on annual festivals, see *Italy Through the Year* on pages 62–5. The following suggestions include some of the most popular as well as the more unusual pursuits.

Cycling on the tree-lined flatlands of the Po Delta

WALKING, BICYCLING, AND HORSEBACK RIDING

SOME ITALIAN BRANCHES of the World Wide Fund for Nature (WWF) organize walks and treks. **Club Alpino Italiano (CAI)** runs trekking and climbing excursions and the **Italian Birds Protection League (LIPU)** arranges nature walks and bird-watching trips. The military *IGM* maps are the most detailed but unfortunately are only available from specialty map shops.

Biking is a national sport despite the country's mountainous landscape. The Po Delta, however, has miles of flat and stunningly beautiful cycling areas. Travel bookshops stock publications with suggested bike routes.

Many riding schools organize trips and outings, even on a daily basis, which are also advertised in the local press. For general information, contact the **Federazione Italiana di Sport Equestre**.

MOUNTAIN SPORTS

THE MOST WELL-EQUIPPED and famous ski resorts are in the Dolomites. Smaller and less expensive resorts, however, are in the Apennines and in Sicily.

Ski lift near the desolate Falzarego Pass, in the heart of the Dolomites

Package ski holidays, arranged from outside Italy, offer the best deals. The **Federazione Arrampicata Sportiva Italiana** has a list of mountain-climbing schools that organize climbs for people at all levels.

ARCHAEOLOGICAL DIGS

THE BRITISH MONTHLY magazine *Archaeology Abroad*, available in the UK, gives a comprehensive list of archaeology groups and digs worldwide. In Italy, the **Gruppo Archeologico Romano** runs two-week digs in various regions. There are summer and winter digs, for both adults and children. The group has contacts with local archaeological organizations as well.

ITALIAN LANGUAGE AND CULTURE

FOR A WIDE SELECTION of material on courses and schools in Italy, contact the Italian consulate in your home country. The **Società Dante Alighieri** provides courses in the Italian language, history of art, literature, and culture. There are both full- and part-time courses available, for every level. Language schools abound in Italy's main cities and are advertised in the Yellow Pages *(Pagine Gialle)* or foreign language bookshops and newspapers. For young students, **Intercultura** will organize weekly, monthly, and year-long exchanges including language courses, accommodations with Italian families, and enrollment in Italian schools.

Group hiking tour in the Dolomites of Trentino-Alto Adige *(see p78)*

A lesson in Italian cookery in Sicily

In recent years, cooking holidays run by English-speaking experts in Italian cooking have become very popular. **Tasting Places**, for example, does wine tours and week-long courses in Italian cuisine, and provides beautiful private accommodations. The course locations include the Veneto, Sicily, Tuscany, and Piedmont. Wine-tasting tours are organized by local tourist boards. The Università per Stranieri in Perugia runs courses on Italian culture, history, and cooking.

WATER SPORTS

Most LAKES AND many seaside resorts rent sailing boats, canoes, and windsurfing equipment. Lessons and courses are organized by clubs, which usually require membership. For a list of authorized associations, contact the **Federazione Italiana di Canoa e Kayak** and the **Federazione Italiana di Vela**. Weekend and weekly sailing vacations and courses are featured in the magazine *Avventure nel Mondo* and most travel agents have a selection of sailing vacations.

Swimming pools are expensive in Italy and many do not accept people on a daily basis. You often have to pay a membership fee and a monthly tariff. Some of the luxurious hotels open their pools to the public in summer, but at pricey rates. Water parks are popular and provide pools, slides, wave machines, and games.

Before diving into any lakes or rivers (and even the sea near main towns) it is best to check that the water is not polluted. The **Federazione Italiana di Attività Subacquee**

runs underwater diving courses, and can provide helpful information on all local centers.

AIR SPORTS

There are schools nationwide that offer hang gliding and flying courses, but the minimum duration of each course is one month. For information and a list of schools contact the **Aeroclub d'Italia**. You must be licensed before you can fly, and all craft must be registered with the Aeroclub.

OTHER SPORTS

Golf IS A POPULAR sport in Italy and there are plenty of courses to choose from. Home membership and handicap are often required for daily access to a club.

Italian tennis clubs usually operate on a membership basis, unless you are invited as a member's guest. The national **Federazione Italiana di Tennis** has a list of all the clubs in Italy.

Soccer is an Italian obsession and you will see friendly, noisy games in every park, beach or open space. It is possible to rent courts at most sports centers, but for a more relaxed game you can get a group of friends together or join in a game with other people.

Sailing in Italy, a popular leisure activity and competitive sport

DIRECTORY

Aeroclub d'Italia
Via Roberto Ferruzzi 38, 00143 Rome. 06 51 95 97 01.
www.aeci.it

Club Alpino Italiano
Corso Vittorio Emanuele II 305, 00186 Rome. 06 68 61 01 11.

Federazione Arrampicata Sportiva Italiana
Via San Secondo 92, Turin.
011 568 31 54.

Federazione Italiana Attività Subacquee
Via Vittoria Colonna 27, 00193 Rome. 06 36 85 82 20.

Federazione Italiana di Canoa e Kayak
Viale Tiziano 70, 00196 Rome.
06 36 85 83 16.

Federazione Italiana di Sport Equestre
Viale Tiziano 74, 00196 Rome.
06 94 43 64 49.

Federazione Italiana di Tennis
Viale Tiziano 74, 00196 Rome.
06 36 85 85 73.

Federazione Italiana di Vela
Viale Prigata Pisanio 2–17, 1610029 Genova.
010 58 94 31.

Gruppo Archeologico Romano
Via degli Scipioni 30a, 00192 Rome. 06 39 73 36 37.

Intercultura
Ufficio di Segretaria Generale, Corso Vittorio Emanuele 187, 00186 Rome. 06 687 72 41.
www.intercultura.it

Italian Birds Protection League (LIPU)
Via Trento 49, 40300 Parma.
0521 23 34 14.

Società Dante Alighieri
Piazza Firenze 27, Rome.
06 687 36 94.
www.soc-dante-alighieri.it

Tasting Places Cooking and Wine Tours
Bus Space, Unit 40, Colan Street, London W10 5AP, UK.
020 7460 0077.

World Wide Fund for Nature
Via Garigliano 57, 00198 Rome.
06 84 49 71. www.wwf.it

TRAVEL INFORMATION

ITALY HAS TRANSPORTATION systems of varying efficiency, from the modern road, bus, and rail networks of the north to the slower and more antiquated systems of the south. Many airlines operate flights to several of the country's major airports, while within Italy itself the national carrier Alitalia, and several smaller companies, provide an extensive network of internal flights.

Alitalia aircraft

Connections by road to the rest of Europe are good, but Alpine roads can be adversely affected by the weather. Highways and other roads within the country are generally good, but can be busy on weekends and peak periods. Italy also has an efficient system of ferries connecting Sicily, Sardinia, and many of the smaller offshore islands. Many of these are car ferries and are busy in summer.

Arriving by Air

ROME'S LEONARDO DA VINCI (Fiumicino) and Milan's Malpensa are the key airports for long-haul flights into Italy. Milan's Linate airport handles some European flights, and most European airlines also fly to Venice, Turin, Naples, and Pisa (for Florence). Many airlines are now flying regularly to smaller cities such as Florence, Genoa, Bologna, Verona, and Bergamo, while charter flights serve summer destinations in peak season such as Catania, Olbia, and Rimini.

Part of the extension to Fiumicino airport, Rome

one of the major airports is usually necessary. As internal flights are expensive, and busy at peak periods, it is worth trying the train as an alternative to domestic flights. Note that flights to airports in the north, particularly Milan and Turin, can be disrupted by fog in autumn and winter.

TICKETS AND FARES

APEX, PEX OR SUPERPEX fares generally offer the best deals on scheduled flights to Italy, but they must be purchased well in advance; some require minimum stays, and all, however, are subject to penalty clauses, so it is advisable to take out insurance against unforeseen cancellation.

It is well worth scouring the small ads in the Travel Section of newspapers for discount charters and heavily discounted scheduled flights. Many discount flights may

LONG-HAUL FLIGHTS

IF YOU ARE FLYING from the United States, TWA, Delta, and Continental operate regular direct scheduled flights to Rome, with services from New York, Washington, Los Angeles, Boston, and Chicago. Canadian Airlines flies from Montréal and Toronto, and Qantas flies from Sydney and Melbourne.

The Italian state airline, Alitalia, has regular service between Rome and New York, San Francisco, Philadelphia, Boston, Chicago, Detroit, Washington, Montréal, Toronto, and Sydney. It may, however, be more convenient and cheaper for

Alitalia flight tickets

long-haul passengers to take a budget flight to London, Frankfurt, Paris, or Amsterdam and then continue with their journey to Italy (by airplane or train) from there.

NATIONAL FLIGHTS

ALITALIA RUNS regular services between many Italian cities. Long-haul passengers can easily transfer to domestic flights in Rome and Milan. Passengers from European destinations should find scheduled flights to most big cities, with the notable exceptions of Sicily's two major cities, Palermo and Catania, where a change of flight at

AIRPORT
Rome (Fiumicino)
Rome (Ciampino)
Milan (Linate)
Milan (Malpensa)
Pisa (Galileo Galilei)
Venice (Marco Polo)
Venice (Treviso)

The entrance hall at Pisa airport

depart and land at a city's second (and often less convenient) airport. Fares tend to vary greatly during the year, but the most expensive periods are during the summer months and over the Christmas and Easter holidays. Where possible ask for available student or senior citizen discounts.

PACKAGE HOLIDAYS

P ACKAGE HOLIDAYS to Italy are usually cheaper than traveling independently, unless you are traveling on a tight budget and are prepared to make use of youth hostels and campsites. Rome, Florence, and Venice are often offered as separate or linked package deals, and many operators have packages to the Tuscan and Umbrian countryside, Sicily, the Italian Lakes, the Italian Riviera, Naples, and the Amalfi coast. In winter, ski packages are available to many Alpine resorts. Specialty packages, such as cooking, walking, and art tours, are becoming increasingly common. In cities, different tour operators may use different hotels, so it is worth shopping around for the most pleasant (and centrally located) hotels. Many operators transport you free of charge from the airport to your hotel. Some will include a tour guide.

Shuttle bus to car hire lots at Fiumicino

FLY-DRIVE DEALS

M ANY TRAVEL AGENTS and car rental firms will organize special fly-drive packages that enable you to book a flight and have a rental car waiting for you at your destination. This is usually cheaper and involves fewer formalities than renting a car on arrival. Most major car rental firms such as Hertz, Avis, and Budget have offices located at all of the major Italian airports.

DIRECTORY

AIRLINES

Alitalia
(800 223 5730.
(800 625 4825.

American
(800 433 7300.

British Airways
(800 247 9297.

Canadian Airlines
(800 426 7000.

Continental
(800 231 0856.

Delta
(800 241 4141.

Northwest (KLM)
(800 447 4747.

Qantas
(800 227 4500.

TWA
(800 892 4141.

Airport Information
(Florence 055 37 34 98.
(Rome 06 659 51.
(Venice 041 260 61 11.

The quayside at Venice's Marco Polo airport

INFORMATION	DISTANCE TO CITY CENTER	TAXI FARE TO CITY CENTER	PUBLIC TRANSPORT TO CITY CENTER
06 65 95 44 55	35 km (22 miles)	L85,000	FS 30 mins
06 79 49 41	15 km (9 miles)	L60,000	M 50 mins
02 28 10 63 06	10 km (6 miles)	L25–30,000	20 mins
02 26 80 06 13	40 km (25 miles)	L100–120,000	1 hr
050 50 07 07	2 km (1 mile)	L15,000 to Pisa	FS to Pisa: 5 mins FS to Florence: 1 hr
041 260 92 60	13 km (8 miles)	L130,000 by Water Taxi	90 mins 20 mins
0422 31 51 11	30 km (18 miles)	L80,000 to Venice	to Treviso: 20 mins to Venice: 30 mins

Arriving by Sea, Rail, and Coach

VENICE SIMPLON ORIENT-EXPRESS

Orient Express logo

ITALY IS SERVED BY AN EXTENSIVE network of roads, railroads, and international ferry lines. Road and rail links cross into the country from France, Switzerland, Austria, and Slovenia, and there are through train services from as far afield as Moscow, London, and Barcelona. Road connections into the country are generally of highway standard, though delays can occur at some of the many Alpine passes and tunnels during bad weather or peak summer holiday periods.

Computerized kiosks with train information on screens

Ticket windows at Florence's Santa Maria Novella station

ARRIVING BY CAR

MOST ROADS into Italy from the rest of Europe involve Alpine crossings by tunnel or mountain passes. The notable exceptions are the approach from Slovenia in the northeast (on the A4 highway) and the route along the French Riviera that enters Italy as the A10 highway at Ventimiglia.

The most popular route from Geneva and southeast France is via the Mont Blanc tunnel and A5 highway, entering Italy close to Aosta and Turin. Another busy approach (from Switzerland) uses the St. Bernard Pass and tunnel, also entering Italy close to Aosta.

Farther east, the main route from Austria and southern Germany crosses the Brenner Pass and goes down to Verona on the A22 highway via Trento and the Adige valley. Weather conditions rarely close the passes, but snow and fog can make progress slow on the winding roads through the mountains. Most highways are tollroads; you pay as you exit the highway.

ARRIVING BY TRAIN

AFTER AIR TRAVEL, arriving by train is the least painful way to reach Italy. Countless through services (including many sleepers) link Italian towns and cities with places as far afield as Brussels, Moscow, and Barcelona. Connections from Paris and London run to Milan, Venice or along Italy's west coast to Rome and Naples. Services also operate from German, Swiss, and other northern European cities to Milan, Turin, Venice, and Verona.

BINARIO 17

Platform sign

← **uscita**

Exit sign

The sleeping car on an international Eurocity train

There are also direct services from Vienna, Spain, and the south of France. Car-rail connections exist from several northern European centers and the Channel ports.

Despite its convenience, international train travel is usually not much cheaper than air travel, particularly for longer trips such as those from the UK or France. Special discount fares, however, are often available for senior travelers and for people under 26. Trains can be extremely busy during peak periods, particularly on Friday and Sunday evenings, and during the Christmas and Easter holiday periods. July and August can also be frantically busy, especially on routes from Germany and ports connecting with Greek ferries in the south. Reservations on most services are inexpensive and advisable.

ARRIVING BY BOAT

MOST PEOPLE arriving in Italy by boat do so from Greece, which is linked by services from Corfu and Patras to Brindisi and other ports in southeast Italy. Services are particularly crowded in the summer months, as are the connecting train services from Brindisi to the rest of Italy.

Other international ferry connections include boats from Malta, Tunisia, and other North African ports to Palermo, Naples and various southern Italian ports. Boats also run from towns in the south of France to Genoa, Livorno, and ports on the Italian Riviera.

ARRIVING BY COACH

COACH TRAVEL to Italy is relatively cheap (though often not much cheaper than trains), but long travel times make it one of the least comfortable ways to travel. Some coach companies have now introduced plane-coach deals, whereby you can travel by coach on one leg of your trip and by air on the other. At the moment there are thrice-weekly services in summer from the UK to Turin, Milan,

Bologna, and Rome. The journey time from London to Milan is about 27 hours, and about 36 hours to Rome. A night on the road is thus unavoidable. **National Express Eurolines** run weekly coaches from London's Victoria Coach Station to all of Italy's major cities as far as Rome. Buses travel via Dover, Calais, Paris, and Lyon, and it

SITA coach arriving at the station in Florence

is useful to take some French francs with you for the probable stops en route.

Traveling Around by Ferry

ITALY'S LARGE NUMBER of off-shore islands mean that it has a large and well-developed network of ferries, as well as services to the rest of Europe, and North Africa.

One of the Moby Lines car ferries that sail the Mediterranean

FERRIES

CAR FERRIES are a convenient link with the beautiful islands scattered off the Italian mainland. Boats for Sardinia leave from Civitavecchia (north of Rome), Livorno, and Genoa, and depart for Sicily from Naples and Reggio di Calabria. Ferries run from the major Sicilian ports to the Egadi and the Aeolian archipelagoes, as well as to countless other small

islands around Sicily (although ferries to the smaller islands do not always carry cars).

Boats also sail between Elba and Piombino, as well as the smaller islands of the Tuscan archipelago such as Capraia. Ferries run from ports close to Rome to Ponza and its surrounding islands, and from Naples to Capri and Ischia. On the east coast the Tremiti islands are linked to ports on the Gargano Peninsula.

Hydrofoils are increasingly complementing conventional ferries on many routes, particularly on the busy services to Capri and Ischia.

Ferries to many destinations are usually crowded in the summer, and you should book well ahead if you wish to travel to Sardinia in July or August, especially if taking a car. Reservations can often be made through travel agents, as well as a ferry line's agents in your own country.

ROUTE	FERRY COMPANY	TELEPHONE INFORMATION
Piombino – Elba	Moby Lines	(0586 826 823 (Livorno)
Livorno – Elba	Moby Lines	(0565 93 61 (Portoferraio)
Genoa – Sardinia	Tirrenia	(070 66 60 65 (Cagliari) (0789 20 71 06 (Olbia) (010 269 81 (Genoa)
Livorno – Sardinia	Sardinia Ferries Moby Lines	(0789 252 00 (Olbia) (010 59 33 01 (Genoa) (0789 279 27 (Olbia)
Genoa/Livorno – Palermo	Grandi Traghetti	(091 58 78 32 (Palermo)
Naples – Palermo	Tirrenia	(091 602 12 14 (Palermo)
Naples – Cagliari	Tirrenia	(070 66 60 65 (Cagliari)

Traveling Around by Train

FS Logo

TRAIN TRAVEL is one of the best ways to explore Italy. Tickets are cheap, services frequent, and rolling stock some of the most modern in Europe. Services can be busy, but the days of rampant overcrowding are mostly over. Lines often run through lovely countryside, from mountain lakes to rolling plateau, and they provide more convenient links between cities than roads or air travel. Only in the south, or deeply rural areas, are services slow and infrequent.

A Eurostar– Italy's fastest train

The atrium of Stazione Termini, at Piazza dei Cinquecento, Rome

THE NETWORK

THE BULK OF ITALY'S rail network is an integrated state-run system operated by the Ferrovie dello Stato (FS). A few privately run lines fill crucial gaps left by the FS, but through tickets are generally available where travel involves both networks. FS and private lines often (but not always) share the same main station *(stazione)*, and also charge similar fares.

TRAINS

THE FS IS IN THE PROCESS of changing the categories of trains, but in practice the same broad divisions will continue to apply. The fast Eurostar and a handful of other special high-speed trains almost always require prebooking of seats. Intercity (IC) trains and Eurocity (EC) trains stop only at major stations and require the payment of a first- or second-class supplement *(un supplemento)* on top of the standard ticket (supplements can be bought on the train, but are more expensive). *Espresso* (Espr) and *Diretto* (Dir) trains make more stops and require no supplement (you may also find

these trains called *Regionali* and *Interregionali). Locali* stop at all stations.

Rolling stock has improved in recent years, especially on Intercity trains, which are now usually modern and air-conditioned. Branch line carriages can still be ancient. Facilities for the disabled exist on many Intercity trains.

FS train in Verona station

TICKETS AND FARES

TICKETS (BIGLIETTI) are available as single *(andata)* or round-trip *(andata e ritorno)* in first *(prima)* or second class *(seconda classe)*. They can be bought at some travel agents or at any station ticket office *(la biglietteria)*. Automatic ticket machines are being introduced, and

increasingly you can buy tickets for journeys of up to 250 km (155 miles) from newsstands or station tobacconists (such a ticket is known as *un biglietto a fascia chilometrica)*. Be sure to validate all tickets on both outbound and return trips, or you will be fined. A ticket's validity usually starts on the day of purchase, so be sure to specify the day of travel when buying tickets in advance. The fares are calculated on kilometric basis and are among the cheapest in western Europe. Round-trip fares offer a 15 percent discount on trips of up to 250 km (155 miles).

Although in theory tickets can be refunded, it is a very complicated process and refunds are very difficult to obtain. It is important, therefore, to buy the correct ticket before traveling.

PASSES

THE FS PROVIDES three basic passes: the Biglietto Chilometrico, valid for two months, allowing 3,000 km (1,865 miles) of travel for up to five people for a maximum of 20 trips; the Flexipass, permitting unlimited travel for four days within a nine-day period, eight days within a 21-day period, or 12 days within any month; and the Biglietto Turistico Libera Circolazione (BTLC), a travel-at-will pass for 8, 15, 21, or 30 days.

TIMETABLES

IT IS WORTH picking up a time-table *(un orario)* if you plan to use trains often. The official FS timetable is comprehensive but heavy and sells out very fast. A far better buy is the small *Pozzorario*, issued twice yearly. It is available from station kiosks and newsstands.

DIRECTORY

RAILROAD INFORMATION

Italian State Railroad Information Office
Toll-free number within Italy; information for traveling all over Italy. ☎ *1478 880 88.*
🌐 www.fs-on-line.it

ENIT US
☎ *212 245 4822 (New York).*

VALIDITY AND RESERVATIONS

Single or round-trip tickets are valid for up to two months from the date of purchase. If a seat reservation is made with the ticket, however, the date you wish to travel will be stamped automatically on the ticket. Undated tickets for up to 250 km (155 miles) can also be purchased at newsstands, and must be validated on the day of travel. Reservations are a good idea on and around public holidays and can be made at most main stations for the high-speed trains. Larger stations generally have separate windows for making reservations *(prenotazioni)*.

DISCOUNTS

Discounts of 20 percent are available with a *Carta Verde*, for travelers aged between 12 and 26; and with a *Carta d'Argento*, for travelers over 60. Passes are not valid during Christmas and at certain periods in high summer. They can be bought from main line stations and are valid for a year.

BAGGAGE ROOMS

Main city stations usually have baggage rooms. Most are manned (but the smaller stations have self-service lockers), and you may need to present a passport or other form of identification when depositing or picking up bags. Fees are calculated per bag.

Baggage Room logo

MACHINES FOR FS RAIL TICKETS

These self-service machines are simple and easy to use. Most have instructions in four languages on a printed panel.

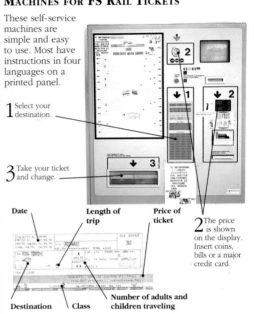

1 Select your destination.

2 The price is shown on the display. Insert coins, bills or a major credit card.

3 Take your ticket and change.

Date

Length of trip

Price of ticket

Destination

Class

Number of adults and children traveling

ITALY'S PRINCIPAL FS NETWORK

The Italian state rail network operates various different types of service. Check what is available before buying your ticket.

KEY

● Main stations

○ Other stations

— Principal rail route

-- Route over water

Traveling Around by Car

The classic Fiat 500

A MOTORING TOUR OF ITALY is the most practical way of exploring the country, but you should take into account high gas prices, the difficulty of parking in many medieval towns, and the Italians' occasionally erratic approach to driving. A car is invaluable in the countryside and for extensive touring, but less useful if you are only visiting a few major towns and cities, since the traffic congestion makes driving slow.

Blue signs showing main roads and green signs showing highways

Busy routes include the A1 from Bologna to Florence and between Bologna, Parma, and Milan. Tolls are payable on all but a handful of highways, again leading to congestion at tollbooths *(Alt Stazione)* on weekends and busy holiday periods. Payment is made at the end of the journey in cash or prepaid magnetic cards called VIAcards, available from tobacconists and the ACI.

Secondary roads are known as Nazionali (N) or as Strade Statali (SS), and vary enormously in quality, the worst being in the south. Mountain roads are usually good, but distances can be deceptive on winding roads, and in winter snow chains are obligatory on many higher routes. Some back roads (known as *strade bianche*, or "white roads") have only a gravel surface, but are still marked on motoring maps. These are slow, but usually passable to cars, if you drive carefully.

Automatic tollbooths on the highway outside Florence

WHAT TO TAKE

DRIVERS FROM OUTSIDE Italy bringing their own foreign-registered cars into the country must be at least 18 years old and carry a Green Card (for insurance purposes), all the vehicle's registration documents, and a full, valid driver's licence *(patente* in Italian). (Any UK or other EU nationals who do not have the standard EU "pink" licence and are planning to stay for more than six months need an Italian translation of their licence, obtainable from most auto clubs or from the Italian government tourist office in your home country.) A red warning triangle must also be carried at all times, for use in the event of a breakdown.

GASOLINE

GAS *(benzina)* in Italy is some of the most expensive in Europe (diesel, or *gasolio*, is a little cheaper). Although many gas stations are now self-service, it is still common to be served by an attendant. Most gas stations follow normal shop hours so make sure you have a full tank before lunchtime or

public holidays. On highways gas stations tend to be open 24 hours a day. Credit cards are rarely accepted.

ROADS

ITALY HAS A GOOD network of highways, although many have a total of only four lanes, often leading to congestion.

Rules and Regulations
Italy uses standard European road signs. Drive on the right and yield to traffic from the right. Seat belts are compulsory in the front and the back, and children should be properly restrained. The speed limit in urban areas is 50 km/h (30 mph); outside urban areas it is 110 km/h (70 mph) on divided roads and 90 km/h on all other secondary roads. On highways (autostrade) *the limit is 130 km/h (80 mph) for vehicles over 1100cc and 110 km/h (70 mph) for all vehicles under 1100cc. All documentation must be carried with you.*

One-way street

No stopping

End of speed restriction

Pedestrianized street – no traffic

Yield to oncoming traffic

No parking

Danger (often with description)

Car rental offices at Fiumicino airport, Rome

CAR RENTAL

CAR RENTAL (autonoleggio) is expensive in Italy and should be organized beforehand through fly-drive deals (see p627) or prebooked with firms who have branches in Italy. For on the spot rental Italian firms may be cheaper than big international names. Agencies are listed in Yellow Pages (Pagine Gialle) under Autonoleggio. Most airports have rental offices on site.

To rent a car in Italy you must be over 21 and have held a valid driver's license for at least a year. Visitors from outside the EU require an international license, though in practice not all rental firms insist on this. Check the small print of the agreement for insurance coverage.

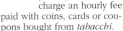

Parking disk

CAR RENTAL NUMBERS

Avis (Rome)
06 419 99.

Europcar (Rome)
06 65 01 08 79.

Hertz
02 48 23 36 63.

Maggiore Budget (Rome)
06 22 93 51.

Sixt (Rome)
06 65 96 51.

ACCIDENTS AND BREAKDOWNS

IF YOU HAVE AN ACCIDENT or a breakdown, switch on your hazard warning lights and place a warning triangle 50 m (164 ft) behind your car. Then (for breakdowns) call the ACI emergency number (116) or the emergency services (112 or 113). The ACI will tow any foreign-registered car free to

the nearest ACI-affiliated garage. They also do free repairs for members of affiliated associations, such as the AAA in the US.

If you have an accident, keep calm and do not admit liability or make any statements that might incriminate you later. Simply swap car and insurance details, names, and addresses.

PARKING

PARKING IN MOST Italian cities and large towns is a problem. Many historic centers have restricted daytime access and baffling one-way systems. Other areas may be reserved for residents' parking (marked riservato ai residenti). Most towns have metered parking areas that charge an hourly fee paid with coins, cards or coupons bought from tabacchi.

Cars can be towed away or booted – especially in areas marked zona rimozione (particularly on street-cleaning days). Call the Municipal Police (Vigili) to retrieve your car.

SAFETY

CAR THEFT IS RIFE in Italy. Never leave anything in your car, and (if possible) always remove radio-cassette players. Leave your car in a guarded parking lot whenever you can. Be especially careful driving at night, when Italian driving is more cavalier than usual, and when many traffic lights switch to flashing amber. Hitchhiking (autostop) is not a good idea (and is not common), certainly never for women on their own.

Official parking area patrolled by attendant

DISTANCE CHART

10 Distance in kilometers
10 Distance in miles

ROME											
286 178	ANCONA										
748 465	**617** 383	AOSTA									
383 238	**219** 136	**401** 249	BOLOGNA								
645 401	**494** 307	**449** 279	**280** 174	BOLZANO							
278 173	**262** 163	**470** 292	**106** 66	**228** 367	FLORENCE						
510 317	**506** 315	**245** 152	**291** 181	**422** 262	**225** 140	GENOA					
601 373	**614** 382	**1220** 758	**822** 511	**1097** 682	**871** 541	**1103** 685	LECCE				
575 357	**426** 265	**181** 113	**210** 130	**295** 183	**299** 186	**145** 90	**1029** 639	MILAN			
219 136	**409** 254	**959** 596	**594** 369	**856** 532	**489** 304	**714** 444	**393** 244	**786** 488	NAPLES		
673 418	**547** 340	**110** 68	**382** 206	**410** 255	**395** 245	**170** 106	**1150** 715	**138** 86	**884** 549	TURIN	
530 329	**364** 226	**442** 275	**154** 96	**214** 133	**255** 158	**397** 247	**967** 601	**273** 170	**741** 460	**402** 250	VENICE

Traveling within Cities

THE BEST WAYS of getting around Italian cities differ from place to place. In Rome buses are most useful, in Milan the metro is more efficient, and in Venice you will need to take a boat to get around. **Pedestrian zone sign** Trams still run in some cities, such as Milan and Rome. Cars are a liability almost everywhere; walking is, in most cases, the easiest way to negotiate the tight historic cores of Italian towns and cities. Florence has a large limited-traffic zone, and most towns now have a pedestrian area in the center.

Bus stop displaying the route

A Roman tram in the orange livery of ATAC

One of the distinctive orange city buses, central Verona

BUSES AND TRAMS

VIRTUALLY EVERY ITALIAN city and large town has a bus system. Most are cheap, comprehensive, and as efficient as traffic and narrow streets will allow, and vary only slightly from city to city. Bus stops are known as *fermate*, and increasingly (notably in Rome) list full details of the routes they serve. Buses *(autobus)* usually run from about 6am to midnight, and there are night buses *(servizio notturno)* in larger cities. Note that if you arrive in a town by train, stations are invariably linked to the center by shuttle buses from the station forecourt (tickets are usually available from the station bar or tabacconist).

TICKETS

TICKETS *(biglietti)* must usually be bought before boarding the bus, and are available from kiosks belonging to the bus company (ATAC in Rome, ATAF in Florence), bars, newsstands or tobacconists *(tabacchi)* displaying the bus company's sticker. A few places, like Florence, also have on-street vending machines around the city's main transport hubs. It is worth buying more than one ticket at a time, especially as outlets often close in the afternoon or early evening. Discounted tickets *(un blocchetto)*, or day- or week-long visitors' tickets and passes *(una tessera* or *tesserino)* are also available. In some cities, notably Rome and Florence, tickets are valid for any number of trips within a given time.

USING BUSES AND TRAMS

YOU BOARD BUSES via the front and rear doors, and exit via the central doors. Buses usually only have a driver and no conductor (though night buses may have a conductor from whom tickets can be bought). Tickets must therefore be validated by punching them in machines at the front or rear of the bus. There are large on-the-spot fines if you are caught without a properly validated ticket. Most larger cities have transportation information offices at the main train station or larger piazzas providing free maps, timetables, and tickets.

The majority of city buses are painted bright orange and display the final destination *(capolinea)* on the front.

METROPOLITANA

SUBWAY systems, known as *metropolitana (la metro* for short), are found in Rome and Milan. Rome's network amounts to just two lines, A and B, which converge at Stazione Termini, the city's central train station. Several stations are useful for key sights, although the system is designed primarily to ferry commuters. At peak times, however, the lines provide the best way of crossing the city quickly. Stations are fairly dingy – though rarely dangerous – and train carriages can be stiflingly hot in summer. In Milan the network is more extensive, with three principal lines – MM1 (the red line), MM2 (green) and MM3 (yellow) – that meet at the hub stations of Stazione Centrale, Duomo, Cadorna, and Lima. These three lines

Metro sign

Termini Metro station, Rome

Waiting for a fare at an official stand in Florence

give easy access to the majority of the city's main sights.

Metro tickets in both cities are available from the same sources as bus and tram tickets, and from machines and ticket offices in subway stations. Tickets in Rome are valid for one trip only, though the special *BIG* ticket offers a day's travel on bus, tram, and metro. In Milan, by contrast, ordinary metro tickets are valid for 75 minutes for any number of journeys and can also be used on the buses and trams.

Never buy tickets from people outside stations, since they are invariably already used or otherwise invalid.

WALKING

WALKING can be a wonderful way to explore Italy's historic towns and cities, most of whose historic centers are smaller than you might expect. Traffic can be a curse, however, especially in narrow streets (Rome is worst in this respect), but many cities are introducing pedestrianized areas or cutting down on car access around key tourist sights. On certain Sundays (*Domenica a Piedi*), entire town centers may be designated traffic-free zones.

Italian towns have plenty of shady squares and cafés to escape the heat of the summer sun, and churches and cathedrals also provide cool retreats from the rigors of sightseeing. Most sights are well marked (churches,

Stay on the pavement at all costs

Marginally less dangerous to cross

museums, and other places of interest are often indicated by yellow signs). Don't try to do too much, however, especially in the heat of summer, and always carry your valuables well out of sight. The best times to walk are in the cool of the morning or in the early evening, when you can join in the predinner stroll known as the *passeggiata*.

TAXIS

ONLY ACCEPT RIDES in official taxis. These may be of different colours in the different cities, but all will have a "Taxi" sign on the roof. Contrary to rumor, most drivers are honest (if not terribly friendly), but there is a wide range of supplements that are legitimate. These vary, but generally an extra charge is made for each piece of luggage placed in the trunk, for rides between 10pm and 7am, on Sundays and public holidays, and for trips to and from airports. It is worth fixing a price before you set off to or from airports, especially in Rome or Naples.

In the event of any dispute, note the cab's number and ask the nearest policeman to arbitrate. It is hard to hail a cab in the street, but they can be found at the station, main piazza, or close to key tourist sights. If you call a cab, the meter will run from your call.

CYCLE RENTAL

MANY TOWNS and cities, especially those popular with visitors, have stands and shops offering bikes and scooters for rent. You can usually rent hourly or by the day, and you may have to leave your passport with the shop as a deposit. Be very careful, however, if riding a bike in the busy traffic of the larger towns and cities.

INTER-CITY TRANSPORTATION: COACHES

Long-haul coaches (*pullman* or *corriere*) between towns operate in a similar way to local buses, though you can usually buy tickets on board, and services are often run by different companies in different-colored buses (blue is the most common color for *pullman*, orange for city buses). Coaches in some

Rome – Gubbio bus

areas may be run by several companies (notably around Florence and in Tuscany), and not all operate from the same terminals. Services often depart from outside train stations, or from a town's main piazza. If in doubt, ask at local tourist offices. A reduced service may operate on weekends, when offices are shut.

Rome	**Tuscany**	**National**
Cotral	Lazzi	Lazzi
800 43 17 84.	055 21 51 55.	055 21 51 55.
Lazzi	Sita	Sita
06 884 08 40.	055 21 47 21.	055 29 49 55.
Appian	Tra-In	
06 48 78 61.	0577 20 42 45.	

Traveling Around Venice

For visitors to Venice, the *vaporetti* or water buses *(see pp130–31)* provide a pleasant form of public transportation, although most journeys within the city can usually be covered more quickly on foot. The main route through the city for the *vaporetti* is the Grand Canal. Water buses also supply a useful service connecting outlying points on the periphery of Venice, and linking the city to the islands in the lagoon. The most important service from a visitor's point of view is the No. 1. This operates from one end of the Grand Canal to the other, traveling slowly enough for you to admire the parade of palaces at the waterside *(see pp84–9)*.

Vaporetto stop at the Giardini Pubblici, Venice

A *vaporetto* pulling into San Marco

The smaller, sleeker and quicker *motoscafo*

The Boats

The original *vaporetti* were steam-powered (*vaporetto* means little steamer); today they are diesel-run motor boats. Although all the boats tend to be called *vaporetti*, the word only really applies to the large wide boats used on slow routes, such as No. 1. These boats provide the best views. *Motoscafi* are the slimmer, smaller, and faster boats that look old but go at a fair pace. *Motonavi* are two-tier boats that run to the islands.

Types of Ticket

The price of a ticket depends not on the length of your trip but on the particular line you are taking.

Tickets purchased on board, rather than at the kiosk found at each stop, are more expensive. If you buy a book of 10 or 20 tickets, the cost is no cheaper than single tickets, but it avoids lining up at a ticket office for each trip.

You can save money, however, by buying a 24-hour or 72-hour ticket, which entitles the holder to unlimited travel on most lines. If you are staying more than just a few days, you can also save money by buying a weekly or monthly season ticket (*abbonamento*), which is available from ticket offices. Holders of Rolling Venice cards (offering information packs and discounts to 14- to 30-year-olds) can buy a *Tre Giorni Giovane*, or three-day youth pass.

The new "Isles Ticket" enables you to travel on the No. 12 for a one-way run and stay for the day on the islands of Murano, Mazzorbo, Burano, and Torcello (but you must buy a ticket for the return trip).

You may have to buy a ticket for each piece of large luggage, and you must remember to date-stamp your tickets.

Hours of Service

The main routes run every 10 to 20 minutes until the early evening. Services are reduced at night, particularly after 1am. From June to September the services are more frequent and certain routes are extended. Details of main lines are also given in the booklet *Un Ospite di Venezia*. From May to September the main routes and island boats are very crowded.

Vaporetto Information

ACTV (Information Office)
Piazzale Roma, Venice.
Map 5 B1.
C 041 528 78 86.

Traghetti

Traghetti are gondola ferries that cross the Grand Canal at seven different points, providing a useful service for pedestrians. Few tourists make use of this cheap (L600 per trip), constant service. Points where *traghetti* cross the Grand Canal are marked on the Street Finder maps *(see pp120–29)*. A gondola on yellow street signs points to *traghetti* stops.

A two-tier *motonave* on its way to Torcello

GONDOLAS

GONDOLAS are a luxury form of transportation used only by visitors and Venetians at weddings. Before boarding, check the official tariffs and agree on a price with the gondolier. Official costs are around L100,000 for 45 minutes, rising to L150,000 after 8pm. During the off season, you may also be able to negotiate a lower fee, and a ride shorter than the usual 50 minutes.

WATER TAXIS

FOR THOSE with little time and sufficient funds, the fastest and most practical means of getting from A to B is by water taxi. The boats are sleek, white or polished wood motorboats, all equipped with a cabin. They zip to and from the airport in only 20 minutes. There are 16 water taxi ranks, including one at the airport and the Lido. Be aware of extra charges for luggage, waiting,

A water taxi

night service, and for calling for a taxi. When the *vaporetti* go on strike, taxis are scarce.

WATER TAXI STANDS

Radio Taxi (all of Venice)
📞 *041 522 23 03.*

Ferrovia (Santa Lucia)
Map 1 C5. 📞 *041 71 62 86.*

Piazzale Roma
Map 5 B1. 📞 *041 71 69 22.*

San Marco
Map 7 B3. 📞 *041 522 97 50.*

Crossing the Grand Canal by *traghetto*

THE MAIN ROUTES

① Confusingly called the *Accelerato*, this is the slow boat down the Grand Canal, stopping at every landing stage. The route starts at Piazzale Roma, travels the length of the Grand Canal, then from San Marco it heads east to the Lido.

⑧② The No. 82 is the faster route down the Grand Canal, making only six stops. The route is circular, starting at San Zaccaria, continuing westward along the Giudecca Canal to Tronchetto and Pizzale Roma, then down the Grand Canal back to San Zaccaria, from there out to the Lido.

⑤① ⑤② The 51 and 52 skirt the periphery of Venice and have been extended to the Lido. The cirular *Giracittà* route provides a scenic tour of Venice, though to do the whole circuit you have to change boats at Fondamente Nuove.

⑫ This line departs from the Fondamente Nuove and runs to the main islands in the northern lagoon: Murano, Mazzorbo, Burano, and Torcello ending at Punta Sabbioni.

USING THE VAPORETTI

1 Tickets are available at most landing stages, some bars, shops, and tobacconists displaying the ACTV sign. The price of a ticket remains the same whether you are going one stop or travelling the whole line, but some routes are more expensive than others, and some prices go up in summer.

2 Signs on the landing stage tell you at which end you should board the boat.

3 Tickets should be punched at the automatic machines on the landing stages before each journey. Inspectors rarely board the boats and this makes it surprisingly easy for tourists (and Venetians) to hop on and off the boats without a validated ticket. However, there are steep fines for any passengers caught without tickets.

4 An indicator board at the front of each boat gives the line number and main stops. (Ignore the black numbers on the boat's side.)

5 Each landing stage has its name clearly marked on a yellow board. Most stops have two landing stages and it is quite easy, particularly if it is crowded and you can't see which way the boat is facing, to board a boat traveling in the wrong direction. It is helpful to watch which direction the boat is approaching from; if in doubt, check with the boatman.

General Index

Collegio di Propaganda Fide (Rome)
  Street-by-Street map 398

Acknowledgments

DORLING KINDERSLEY would like to thank the following people whose contributions and assistance have made the preparation of this book possible.

CONTRIBUTORS

Paul Duncan is an expert on art and architectural history and has published a guide to Sicily as well as one on Italy's hilltowns.
Tim Jepson, formerly Rome correspondent for the *Sunday Telegraph*, has written guides to Tuscany, Umbria, Rome, and Venice, a complete guide to Italy, *Italy by Train* and *Wild Italy*, a guide to Italy's nature preserves.
Andrew Gumbel, former Reuters correspondent in Rome, has written a number of guide books and is the correspondent for the *Independent* in Rome.
Christopher Catling has written guides to Florence and Tuscany, the Veneto and the Italian Lakes and is particularly interested in archaeology.
Sam Cole works for Reuters in Rome, where he has lived for some years, and contributes regularly to guidebooks on Rome and the Lazio region.

ADDITIONAL CONTRIBUTORS

Dominic Robertson, Mick Hamer, Richard Langham Smith.

ADDITIONAL PHOTOGRAPHY

Peter Chadwick, Andy Crawford, Philip Dowell, Mike Dunning, Philip Enticknap, Steve Gorton, Dave King, Neil Mersh, Roger Moss, Poppy, Kim Sayer, James Stevenson, Clive Streeter, David Ward, Matthew Ward.

ADDITIONAL ILLUSTRATIONS

Andrea Corbella, Richard Draper, Kevin Jones Associates, Chris Orr and Associates, Robbie Polley, Martin Woodward.

CARTOGRAPHIC RESEARCH

Jane Hugill, Samantha James, Jennifer Skelley.

DESIGN AND EDITORIAL ASSISTANCE

Gillian Allan, Gaye Allen, Douglas Amrine, Emily Anderson, Hilary Bird, Samantha Borland, Isabel Boucher, Caroline Brooke, Margaret Chang, Elspeth Collier, Cooling Brown, Gary Cross, Felicity Crowe, Mandy Dredge, Michael Ellis, Danny Farnham, Angela-Marie Graham, Caroline Greene, Vanessa Hamilton, Sally-Ann Hibbard, Tim Hollis, Gail Jones, Steve Knowlden, Siri Lowe, Sarah Martin, Georgina Matthews, Ferdie McDonald, Rebecca Milner, Adam Moore, Jennifer Mussett, Alice Peebles, Tamsin Pender, David Pugh, Jake Reimann, David Roberts, Evelyn Robertson, Carolyn Ryden, Simon Ryder, Giuseppina Russo, Alison Stace, Hugh Thompson, Elaine Verweymeren, Ingrid Vienings, Veronica Wood.

DORLING KINDERSLEY would also like to thank the following for their assistance: Azienda Autonoma di Soggiorno Cura e Turismo, Napoli; Azienda Promozione Turistica del Trentino, Trento; Osservatorio Geofisico dell'Università di Modena; Bell'Italia; Enotria Winecellars.

PHOTOGRAPHY PERMISSION

DORLING KINDERSLEY would like to thank the following for their assistance and kind permission to photograph at their establishments: Assessorato Beni Culturali Comune di Padova. Le Soprintendenze Archeologiche di Agrigento, di Enna, di Etruria Meridionale, per il Lazio, di Napoli, di Pompei, di Reggio Calabria e di Roma. Le Soprintendenze per i Beni Ambientali e Architettonici di Bolzano, di Napoli, di Potenza, della Provincia di Firenze e Pistoia, di Ravenna, di Roma, di Siena e di Urbino. Le Soprintendenze per i Beni Ambientali, Architettonici, Artistici e Storici di Caserta, di Cosenza, di Palermo, di Pisa, di Salerno e di Venezia. Le Soprintendenze per i Beni Artistici e Storici della Provincia di Firenze e Pistoia, di Milano e di Roma. Also all the other churches, museums, hotels, restaurants, shops, galleries, and sights too numerous to thank individually.

PICTURE CREDITS

t = top; tl = top left; tc = top center; tr = top right; cla = center left above; ca = center above; cra = center right above; cl = center left; c = center; cr = center right; clb = center left below; cb = center below; crb = center right below; bl = bottom left; b = bottom; bc = bottom center; br = bottom right.

Works of art have been reproduced with the permission of the following copyright holders:
© ADAGP, Paris and DACS, London 1996 *Bird in Space* by Constantin Brancusi 101cl; © DACS, 1996 *Mother and Son* by Carlo Carrà 190t.

DORLING KINDERSLEY would like to thank the following for their assistance: Eric Crighton: 79cra, FIAT: 212c, Gucci Ltd: 35cr, Prada, Milan: 35c, National Archaeological Museum, Naples: 479b, National Maritime Museum 36c, Royal Botanic Gardens, Kew: 79ca, Science Museum: 36cla, Telecom Italia: 620tc.

The publisher would like to thank the following individuals, companies, and picture libraries for permission to reproduce their photographs:

ACCADEMIA ITALIANA: Sue Bond 479c; AFE, Rome: 34clb, 34cb, 35tl; Giuseppe Carfagna 188b, 194b, 210tl, 210b, 214tl, 216b, 217t, 227t; Claudio Cerquetti 64t, 65bl, 65t; Enrico Martino 54cl, 62tr; Roberto Merlo 228b, 231t, 231b; Piero Servo 259t,

261b; Gustavo Tomsich 219b; Archivio APT Monregalese 221t; Action Plus: Mike Hewitt 66ca; Glyn Kirk 67tr; Alitalia: 626t, 626b; Allsport: Mark Thompson: 67cl; Simon Bruty: 67tl; Ancient Art and Architecture: 39t, 465br; Archiv für Kunst und Geschichte, London: 24bl, 30b, *Rossini* (1820), Camuccini, Museo Teatrale alla Scala, Milan 32br, 33bl, 37br, *Pope Sixtus IV Naming Platina Prefect of the Library*, Melozzo da Forlì (1477), Pinacoteca Vaticana, Rome 38, 40tl, *Statue of Augustus from Prima Porta* (1st century AD) 45tl, *The Gift of Constantine* (1246), Oratorio di San Silvestro, Rome 46cl, *Frederick I Barbarossa as a Crusader* (1188), Biblioteca Apostolica Vaticana, Rome 49bl, 52tl, *Giving the Keys to St. Peter*, Perugino (1482), Sistine Chapel, Vatican, Rome 52cla, 52bl, *Machiavelli*, Santi di Tito, Palazzo Vecchio, Florence 53br, *Andrea Palladio*, Meyer 54cb, *Goethe in the Campagna*, Tischbein (1787), Stadelsches Kunstinstitut, Frankfurt 56cl, *Venetian Carnival in the Eighteenth Century*, Anon (19th century) 56clb, *Bonaparte Crossing the Alps*, David, Schloss Charlottenburg, Berlin 57cr, 57bl, 102t, 102b, 191b, 346–7, 450b, *Archimedes*, Museo Capitolino, Rome 465bl, 489t, 493c; Stefan Diller *St. Francis Appearing to the Brothers at Arles* (1295–1300), San Francesco, Assisi 49tl; Erich Lessing *Margrave Gualtieri of Saluzzo Chooses the Poor Farmer's Daughter, Griseldis, for his Wife*, di Stefano, Galleria dell'Accademia Carrara, Bergamo 30crb, *The Vision of St. Augustine* (1502), Carpaccio, Chiesa di San Giorgio degli Schiavoni, Venice 53cr, 214b, 260b, 475b; Archivio IGDA, Milan: 196t, 196c, 197b, 505bl, 505br; Emporio Armani: 20cl, 35tc; Artemide, GB Ltd: 35clb.

Mario Bettella 519c, 526c; Frank Blackburn: 259c; Osvaldo Böhm, Venice: 85t, 90c, 107t; Bridgeman Art Library, London: Ambrosiana, Milan 189t; Bargello, Florence 271b, 275c; Bibliothèque Nationale, Paris: *Marco Polo with Elephants and Camels Arriving at Hormuz, Gulf of Persia, from India*, Livre des Merveilles Fr 2810 f.14v 37t; British Museum, London *Etruscan Vase Showing Boxers Fighting* 41tl, *Flask Decorated with Christian Symbols* 46tl, *Greek Attic Red-Figure Vase depicting Odysseus with the Sirens*, Stamnos 465cb; Galleria dell'Accademia Carrara, Bergamo 193t; Galleria degli Uffizi, Florence 22tl, 25tl, 25br, *Self Portrait*, Raphael Sanzio of Urbino 53bl, 279b, 281b: K & B News Photo, Florence 268tl; Santa Maria Novella, Florence 289b; Museo Civico, Prato 318b; Louvre, Paris *Statuette of Herakles Brandishing his Club*, Classical Greek, Argive period 464t; Mausoleo di Galla Placidia, Ravenna 260tr; Museo di San Marco, Florence 289b; Musée d'Orsay, Paris - Giraudon *Les Romains de la Decadence*, Thomas

Couture 385t; Museo delle Sinopie, Camposanto, Pisa 23clb; Palazzo dei Normanni, Palermo *Scene with Centaurs from the Room of King Ruggero* 507b; Pinacoteca di Brera, Milan 190c, 190b, 191t, Private Collection *Theodoric I* (455–526 AD) *Ostrogothic King of Italy* 46b; San Francesco, Arezzo 23tr; San Francesco, Assisi 345c; San Sebastiano, Venice 25crb; San Zaccaria, Venice 29c, 29tr, 95c; Santa Croce, Florence 276bl, 277cb; Santa Maria Gloriosa dei Frari, Venice 24tr; Santa Maria Novella, Florence 23cla; Scrovegni (Arena) Chapel, Padua 22tr; Scuola di San Giorgio degli Schiavoni, Venice 116b; Staatliche Museen, Berlin *Septimius Severus and Family* 45b; Vatican Museums and Galleries, Rome 411b; Walker Art Gallery, Liverpool *Aeschylus and Hygieia* 464b; British Museum, London: 42cl.

Cephas Picture Library Mick Rock: 2–3, 19t, 20t, 176tr, 177b, 177tr, 234–5, 243tl, 243tr, 456–7, 610–1; JL Charmet, Paris: 343br, 479t; Ciga Hotels: 87cb; Foto Elio e Stefano Ciol: 73cra, 158bl, 158br, 159bl, 159bc, 159br; Comune di Asti: 64cl; Stephani Colasanti: 72bl; Joe Cornish: 18t, 78tr, 132, 154t, 236–7, 304, 354, 445b, 521b; Giancarlo Costa: 9c, 30t, 31cr, 31tr, 31tl, 71c, 171c, 176tl, 457c, 537c, 611c.

Il Dagherrotipo: Archivio Arte 199t; Archivio Storico 31b, 198b, 253b; Salvatore Barba 490t; Alberto Berni 217bl; Riccardo Catani 485b; Marco Cerruti 172t, 205b, 207b, 208b; Antonio Cittadini 182b, 186b, 194t ; Gianni Dolfini 534b; Riccardo d'Errico 66tr, 239t, 260c; Maurizio Fraschetti 480; Diane Haines 167br, 625br; Maurizio Leoni 63c; Marco Melodia 490cb, 491b, 531t, 624tl, 624cl; Stefano Occhibelli 65c, 246; Giorgio Oddi 239cr, 244t, 497tr; Bruno Pantaloni 67bl; Donato Fierro Perez 517cb; Marco Ravasini 164t, 533c; Giovanni Rinaldi 62bl, 63tl, 173bl, 223b, 357t, 363t, 450c, 466, 483t, 490bl, 490br, 491c, 517cr, 535t, 535c; Lorenzo Scaramella 452c; Stefania Servili 166t; James Darell: 338; CM Dixon: 411cb; Chris Donaghue The Oxford Photo Library: 113t.

Electa: 150c, 151c, 151t; Empics: John Marsh 66b; ET Archive: 32bc, 41c, 42tl, 45cr, 48cr–49cl, 53tl, 55tl, 59b, 465t, 515b; Mary Evans Picture Library: 30clb, 31cl, 37ca, 58b, 58crb, 59cr, 60cb, 76tr, 237c, 310t, 316t, 381ca, 383bl, 399b, 432c, 495cr, 534t.

Archivio Storico Fiat, Turin: 60tr; Ferrari: 34b; APT Folignate e Nocera Umbra: 351t; Werner Forman Archive: 41br, 47tr, 425br; Consorzio Frasassi: 362b.

Studio Gavirati, Gubbio: 342c; APT Genova: Roberto Merlo 230bl; Giraudon, Paris: *Aphrodite*

Persuading Helen to Follow Paris to Troy, Museo Nazionale di Villa Giulia, Rome 41clb, *Pharmacy,* Museo della Civiltà Romana 44cb, *Grandes Chroniques de France; Coronation of Charlemagne in St. Peter's by Leon III,* Musée Goya, Castres 47tl, *Taking of Constantinople,* Basilica of St. John the Evangelist, Ravenna 49cr, *Dante's Hell with Commentary of Guiniforte delli Bargigi* (Ms2017 fol 245), Bibliothèque Nationale, Paris 50cb, *Portrait of St. Ignatius of Loyola,* Rubens, Musée Brukenthal, Sibiu 55ca, *Charles III's Fleet at Naples 6th October 1759,* Joli de Dipi, Museo del Prado, Madrid 56tr, *Inauguration of the Naples-Portici Railway,* Fergola (1839), Museo Nazionale di San Martino, Naples 58clb, *Piedmontese and French at the Battle of San Martino in 1859* Anon, Museo Centrale del Risorgimento, Rome 59tl, 102c, 103t, 191c, 260tl; ALINARI-GIRAUDON: *St. Mark Appearing to the Venetians Looking for His Body,* Tintoretto (1568), Brera Art Gallery, Milan 25tr, *Shrine,* House of the Vettii, Pompeii 45cb, *St. Gregory in his Study* (Inv 285), Pinacoteca Nazionale, Bologna 47bl, *Portrait of Victor Emmanuel II,* Dugoni (1866), Galleria d'Arte Moderna, Palazzo Pitti, Florence 58tl, 103b, 190t, *Louis II of Gonzaga and his Court,* Andrea Mantegna (1466–74), Museo di Palazzo Ducale, Mantova 200–201, 279tl-tr, *History of Pope Alexander III: Building of the City of Alexandria,* Aretino Spinello (1407), Palazzo Pubblico, Siena 51cr; ALINARI-SEAT-GIRAUDON: 219c; FLAMMARION-GIRAUDON: *Poem by Donizo in Honour of Queen Matilda,* Biblioteca Apostolica, Vatican 48ca; LAUROS-GIRAUDON: *Portrait of Francis Petrarch* 50b, *Liber notabilium Philippi Septimi, francorum regis a libris Galieni extractus* (Ms 334 569 fig17), Guy of Pavia (1345), Musée Condé, Chantilly 51b, *Gallery of Views of Ancient Rome,* Pannini (1758), Musée du Louvre, Paris 56cr, 57cl, *Portrait of the Artist,* Bernini, Private Collection 54tl, *Four Angels and Symbols of the Evangelists,* 28tr–29tcr; ORSI-BATTAGLINI-GIRAUDON: *Madonna of the Shadow,* Museum of San Marco, Florence 28c, *Supplice de Savonarola* Anon 52cl; THE RONALD GRANT ARCHIVE: 61b; Paramount *The Godfather Part III* (1990) 519b; Riama *La Dolce Vita* (1960) 61tl; TCF *Boccaccio '70* (1962) 19cl, *The Name of the Rose* (1986) 30cla; PALAZZO VENIER DEI LEONI, PEGGY GUGGENHEIM COLLECTION, VENICE: 87cla.

PHOTO HALUPKA: 116t; ROBERT HARDING PICTURE LIBRARY: 1c, 66tl, 185b, 262, 380cl, 404, 409b, 615b, 624b; Richard Ashworth 21t; Dumrath 261c; HP Merton 160, 624tr; Roy Rainford 483cr; JOHN HESELTINE: 451t; MICHAEL HOLFORD: 43ca, 374b; HOTEL PORTA ROSSA: 540t; HOTEL VILLA PAGODA: 539t; THE HULTON DEUTSCH COLLECTION: 60br, 85cla, 86cla, 86br, 151br, 365c; Keystone 60ca, Reuter/Luciano Mellace 35tr.

THE IMAGE BANK, London: 324b; Marcella Pedone 181b; Andrea Pistolesi 247b; Guido Rossi 10b, 43cb; IMPACT: 305b; INDEX, Florence: 274c, 317t, 317cr; ISTITUTO E MUSEO DI STORIA DELLA SCIENZA DI FIRENZE: Franca Principe 36b, 277c.

TIM JEPSON: 341t.

FRANK LANE PICTURE AGENCY: 208t, 209t, 209c, 209b; M Melodia/Panda 490ca.

MAGNUM, London: Abbas 61clb; THE MANSELL COLLECTION: 48cl, 383tl; MARCONI LTD 36t; MASTERSTUDIO, Pescara: 488c; su concessione del MINISTERO PER I BENI CULTURALI E AMBIENTALI: *The Last Supper,* da Vinci, Leonardo 192b; MIRROR SYNDICATION INTERNATIONAL: 36clb; MOBY LINES: 629b; FOTO MODENA: 258t, 361c; TONY MOTT: 449b, 454t; MUSEO DIOCESANO DI ROSSANO 504t.

NHPA: Laurie Campbell 79crb; Gerard Lacz 79br; Silvestris Fotoservice 79cr; BY COURTESY OF THE NATIONAL PORTRAIT GALLERY, London: (detail) *Percy Bysshe Shelley,* Amelia Curran (1819) 56tl; GRAZIA NERI: 48tl; Marco Bruzzo 64br; Cameraphoto 104bl; Marcello Mencarini 84br; NIPPON TELEVISION NETWORK: 414c–415c, 414t, 414b–415bl, 415t, 415br, 416b; PETER NOBLE: 308t, 326–7, 331b, 616b.

L'OCCHIO DI CRISTALLO/STUDIO FOTOGRAFICO DI GIORGIO OLIVERO: 221b; APT ORVIETO: Massimo Roncella 348t; OXFORD SCIENTIFIC FILMS: Stan Osolinski 337c.

PADOVA - MUSEI CIVICI - CAPPELLA SCROVEGNI: 73cr, 150t, 150cla, 150clb, 151cra, 151crb, 151bl; PADOVA - MUSEI CIVICI AGLI EREMITANI: 152t, 152c; LUCIANO PEDICINI - ARCHIVIO DELL'ARTE: 352b, 394t, 459t, 470tl, 474t, 474ca, 474cb, 474b, 475t, 475ca, 475cr, 477t, 514b; APT PESARO - LE MARCHE: 358c; PICTURES COLOUR LIBRARY: 530b, 532l; ANDREA PISTOLESI: 16; POPPERFOTO: 60tl, 61ca, 61cb.

SARAH QUILL, Venice: 86t, 90b, 96tl.

RETROGRAPH ARCHIVE: 33c; REX FEATURES: 33t.

SCALA, Florence: 22b, 23b, 24br, 25ca, 25bl, 32tl, *Portrait of Claudio Monteverdi,* Domenico Feti, Accademia, Venice 32bl, *Portolan of Italy* (16th century), Museo Correr, Venice 39b, *Etruscan Bronze Liver,* Museo Civico, Piacenza 40cl, *Earrings,* Museo Etrusco Guarnacci, Volterra 40br, 40cr–41cl, *Crater from Pescia Romana,* Museo Archeologico, Grosseto 41bc, *Terracotta Vase in the Shape of an Elephant,* Museo Nazionale, Naples 42cr, *Cicero denounces Catiline,* Palazzo Madama, Rome 43tl, 43bl, *Circus Scene Mosaic -*

Gladiator Fight, Galleria Borghese, Rome 44t, 44br, *Theodolinda Melts the Gold for the New Church* (15th century), Famiglia Zavattari, Duomo, Monza 46clb, 46cr–47cl, 47b, *Tomb Relief depicting a School,* Matteo Gandoni, Museo Civico, Bologna 48b, *Detail from an Ambo of Frederick II* (13th century), Cattedrale, Bitonto 49cb, *Guidoriccio da Fogliano at the Siege of Note Massi,* Simone Martini, Palazzo Pubblico, Siena 50cl, 51tl, *Return of Gregory XI from Avignon* Giorgio Vasari, Sala Regia, Vatican 51cb, 52br, 52cr–53cl, 53crb, *Clement VII in Conversation with Charles V,* Giorgio Vasari, Palazzo Vecchio, Florence 54cla, *Portrait of Pierluigi da Palestrina,* Istituto dei Padri dell'Oratorio, Rome 54br, *Revolt at Masaniello,* Domenico Gargiulo, Museo di San Martino, Naples 55crb, 56br, 57tl, 57crb, 58cla, 58cr–59cl, 59crb, 91c, 96c, 114br, 140c, 214tr, 218b, 252t, 255t, 257t, 261t, 266c, 266b, 267t, 268c, 268b, 269t, 269b, 272, 274tr, 275tr, 275b, 278t, 278c, 278b, 279ca, 279cb, 280t, 280b, 281t, 282c, 283bl, 284t, 284b, 285t, 285b, 286t, 286c, 287t, 288bl, 290t, 290cl, 290cra, 290crb, 290b, 291t, 291cla, 291clb, 291cr, 291bl, 291br, 293bl, 294tr, 294tl, 294c, 295t, 295cl, 295b, 315c, 315b, 320t, 320cla, 320c, 320ca, 320cr-321cl, 320cb, 320b, 321cr, 321cb, 321cra, 321t, 321b, 322t, 322b, 328b, 330t, 331cl, 334cla, 335b, 344t, 344c, 345b, 348b, 349c, 360t, 360b, 361t, 361bl, 367br, 374c, 390bl, 392t, 394c, 401c, 406tl, 406c, 406b, 407t, 408b, 409t, 410t, 410cb, 411c, 413t, 413c, 413b, 417t, 417b, 495c, 497tl, 513b, 514tr, 520t, 521t, 522b, 533b; SCIENCE PHOTO LIBRARY: 11t; Argonne National Laboratory 37cr; JOHN FERRO SIMS: 20b, 21b, 80, 170–171, 355b, 364–365, 444, 526b; AGENZIA SINTESI, ROME: 616tl; MARIO SOSTER DI ALAGNA: 541c; FRANK SPOONER PICTURES: Diffidenti 532b; Gamma 61cr, 61tc; Daniel Simon 189b; SPORTING PICTURES: 66clb, 66crb, 67cb, 67cra; TONY STONE IMAGES: 79cla; Stephen Studd 27tr, 179cr; AGENZIA FOTOGRAFICA STRADELLA, Milan: Bersanetti

185c; Lamberto Caenazzo 530t; Francesco Gavazzini 208c; F Giaccone 510c; Mozzati 360clb; Massimo Pacifico 491t; Ettore Re 483crb; Ghigo Roli 483b; Giulio Vegi 517t; Amedeo Vergani 202, 206b, 226t, 249t; SYGMA: 63tr.

TASTING ITALY: Martin Brigdale 625t; TATE GALLERY PUBLICATIONS: 60bl; APT DELL'ALTA VALLE DEL TEVERE: Museo del Duomo 50tl; TOURING CLUB OF ITALY: 196b, Cresci 518t; ARCHIVIO CITTÀ DI TORINO Settore Turismo: 213t, 213b; Davide Bogliacino 205t; FOTOTECA APT del TRENTINO: Foto di Banal 168t; Foto di Faganello 167t, 169c.

VENICE-SIMPLON ORIENT EXPRESS: 628tl; VILLA CRESPI: 576b.

CHARLIE WAITE: 17b; GRAHAM WATSON: 66cr; EDIZIONE WHITE STAR: Marcello Bertinetti 81b; Giulio Veggi 8–9, 70–71, 133b; FIONA WILD: 524–5; PETER WILSON: 5t, 88–89; WORLD PICTURES: 536–7.

Front Endpaper:
JOE CORNISH: Lcrb, Rc, Rtcr; IL DAGHERROTIPO: Marco Melodia Lbl; Stefano Occhibelli Rtl; Giovanni Rinaldi Rbl; JAMES DARELL: Rcl; ROBERT HARDING PICTURE LIBRARY: Lc, H.P. Merton Rtcl; JOHN FERRO SIMS: Ltr, Rbc; AGENZIA FOTOGRAFICA STRADELLA, Milan: Amedeo Vergani Ltl.

Back Endpaper:
ROBERT HARDING PICTURE LIBRARY: Rolf Richardson Lt.

COVER:
FERRARI: bl; GIRAUDON: Nicolò Orsi Battaglini crb; HULTON DEUTSCH COLLECTION: Reuter cra.

BACK COVER:
PETER WILSON: bl.

Phrase Book

IN EMERGENCY

Help!	**Aiuto!**	eye-**yoo**-toh
Stop!	**Fermate!**	fair-**mah**-teh
Call a doctor.	**Chiama un medico.**	kee-**ah**-mah oon **meh**-dee-koh
Call an ambulance.	**Chiama un' ambulanza.**	kee-**ah**-mah oon am-boo-**lan**-tsa
Call the police.	**Chiama la polizia.**	kee-**ah**-mah lah pol-ee-**tsee**-ah
Call the fire department.	**Chiama i pompieri.**	kee-**ah**-mah ee pom-pee-**air**-ee
Where is the telephone?	**Dov'è il telefono?**	dov-**eh** eel teh-**leh**-foh-noh?
The nearest hospital?	**L'ospedale più vicino?**	loss-peh-**dah**-leh pee-oo **vee**-**chee**-noh?

COMMUNICATION ESSENTIALS

Yes/No	**Sì/No**	see/ noh
Please	**Per favore**	pair fah-**vor**-eh
Thank you	**Grazie**	**grah**-tsee-eh
Excuse me	**Mi scusi**	mee **skoo**-zee
Hello	**Buon giorno**	bwon **jor**-noh
Goodbye	**Arrivederci**	ah-ree-veh-**dair**-chee
Good evening	**Buona sera**	**bwon**-ah **sair**-ah
morning	**la mattina**	lah mah-**tee**-nah
afternoon	**il pomeriggio**	eel poh-meh-**ree**-joh
evening	**la sera**	lah **sair**-ah
yesterday	**ieri**	ee-**air**-ee
today	**oggi**	**oh**-jee
tomorrow	**domani**	doh-**mah**-nee
here	**qui**	**kwee**
there	**la**	**lah**
What?	**Quale?**	**kwah**-leh?
When?	**Quando?**	**kwan**-doh?
Why?	**Perché?**	pair-**keh**?
Where?	**Dove?**	**doh**-veh?

USEFUL PHRASES

How are you?	**Come sta?**	**koh**-meh stah?
Very well, thank you.	**Molto bene, grazie.**	**moll**-toh **beh**-neh **grah**-tsee-eh
Pleased to meet you.	**Piacere di conoscerla.**	pee-ah-**chair**-eh dee coh-**noh**-shair-lah
See you later.	**A più tardi.**	ah pee-oo **tar**-dee
That's fine.	**Va bene.**	va **beh**-neh
Where is/are ...?	**Dov'è/Dove sono ...?**	dov-**eh**/doveh **soh**-noh?
How long does it take to get to ...?	**Quanto tempo ci vuole per andare a ...?**	**kwan**-toh **tem**-poh chee voo-**oh**-leh pair an-**dar**-eh ah ...?
How do I get to ...?	**Come faccio per arrivare a ...?**	koh-meh **fah**-choh pair arri-**var**-eh ah...?
Do you speak English?	**Parla inglese?**	**par**-lah een-**gleh**-zeh?
I don't understand.	**Non capisco.**	non ka-**pee**-skoh
Could you speak more slowly, please?	**Può parlare più lentamente, per favore?**	pwoh par-**lah**-reh pee-oo len-ta-**men**-teh pair fah-**vor**-eh?
I'm sorry.	**Mi dispiace.**	mee dee-spee-**ah**-cheh

USEFUL WORDS

big	**grande**	**gran**-deh
small	**piccolo**	**pee**-koh-loh
hot	**caldo**	**kal**-doh
cold	**freddo**	**fred**-doh
good	**buono**	**bwoh**-noh
bad	**cattivo**	kat-**tee**-voh
enough	**basta**	**bas**-tah
well	**bene**	**beh**-neh
open	**aperto**	ah-**pair**-toh
closed	**chiuso**	kee-**oo**-zoh
left	**a sinistra**	ah see-**nee**-strah
right	**a destra**	ah **dess**-trah
ahead	**sempre dritto**	**sem**-preh **dree**-toh
near	**vicino**	vee-**chee**-noh
far	**lontano**	lon-**tah**-noh
up	**su**	**soo**
down	**giù**	**joo**
early	**presto**	**press**-toh
late	**tardi**	**tar**-dee
entrance	**entrata**	en-**trah**-tah
exit	**uscita**	oo-**shee**-ta
toilet	**il gabinetto**	eel gah-bee-**net**-toh
free, unoccupied	**libero**	**lee**-bair-oh
free, no charge	**gratuito**	grah-**too**-ee-toh

MAKING A TELEPHONE CALL

I'd like to place a long-distance call.	**Vorrei fare una interurbana.**	vor-**ray far**-eh oona in-tair-oor-**bah**-nah
I'd like to make a collect call.	**Vorrei fare una telefonata a carico del destinatario.**	vor-**ray far**-eh oona teh-leh-fon-**ah**-tah ah **kar**-ee-koh dell dess-tee-nah-**tar**-ree-oh
I'll try again later.	**Ritelefono più tardi.**	ree-teh-**leh**-foh-noh pee-oo **tar**-dee
Can I leave a message?	**Posso lasciare un messaggio?**	**poss**-oh lash-**ah**-reh oon mess-**sah**-joh?
Hold on.	**Un attimo, per favore**	oon **ah**-tee-moh, pair fah-**vor**-eh
Could you speak up a little please?	**Può parlare più forte, per favore?**	pwoh par-**lah**-reh pee-**oo for**-teh, pair fah-**vor**-eh?
local call	**telefonata locale**	te-leh-fon-**ah**-tah loh-cah-leh

SHOPPING

How much does this cost?	**Quant'è, per favore?**	kwan-**teh**, pair fah-**vor**-eh?
I would like ...	**Vorrei ...**	vor-**ray**...
Do you have ...?	**Avete ...?**	ah-**veh**-teh.. ?
I'm just looking.	**Sto soltanto guardando.**	stoh sol-**tan**-toh gwar-**dan**-doh
Do you take credit cards?	**Accettate carte di credito?**	ah-chet-**tah**-teh **kar**-teh dee **creh**-dee-toh?
What time do you open/close?	**A che ora apre/ chiude?**	ah keh **or**-ah **ah**-preh/kee-**oo**-deh?
this one	**questo**	**kweh**-stoh
that one	**quello**	**kwell**-oh
expensive	**caro**	**kar**-oh
cheap	**a buon prezzo**	ah bwon **pret**-soh
size, clothes	**la taglia**	lah **tah**-lee-ah
size, shoes	**il numero**	eel **noo**-mair-oh
white	**bianco**	bee-**ang**-koh
black	**nero**	**neh**-roh
red	**rosso**	**ross**-oh
yellow	**giallo**	**jal**-loh
green	**verde**	**vair**-deh
blue	**blu**	bloo

TYPES OF SHOPS

antique dealer	**l'antiquario**	lan-tee-**kwah**-ree-oh
bakery	**il forno /il panificio**	eel **forn**-oh /eel pan-ee-**fee**-choh
bank	**la banca**	lah **bang**-kah
bookstore	**la libreria**	lah lee-breh-**ree**-ah
butcher	**la macelleria**	lah mah-chell-eh-**ree**-ah
delicatessen	**la salumeria**	lah sah-loo-meh-**ree**-ah
department store	**il grande magazzino**	eel **gran**-deh mag-gad-**zee**-noh
drugstore	**la farmacia**	lah far-mah-**chee**-ah
fish market	**il pescivendolo**	eel pesh-ee-**ven**-doh-loh
florist	**il fioraio**	eel fee-or-**eye**-oh
greengrocer	**il fruttivendolo**	eel froo-tee-**ven**-doh-loh
grocery	**alimentari**	ah-lee-men-**tah**-ree
hairdresser	**il parrucchiere**	eel par-oo-kee-**air**-eh
ice cream parlor	**la gelateria**	lah jel-lah-tair-**ree**-ah
market	**il mercato**	eel mair-**kah**-toh
newsstand	**l'edicola**	leh-**dee**-koh-lah
pastry shop	**la pasticceria**	lah pas-tee-chair-**ee**-ah
post office	**l'ufficio postale**	loo-**fee**-choh pos-**tah**-leh
shoe store	**il negozio di scarpe**	eel neh-**goh**-tsioh dee **skar**-peh
supermarket	**il supermercato**	eel su-pair-mair-**kah**-toh
tobacco shop	**il tabaccaio**	eel tah-bak-**eye**-oh
travel agency	**l'agenzia di viaggi**	lah-jen-**tsee**-ah dee vee-**ad**-jee

SIGHTSEEING

art gallery	**la pinacoteca**	lah peena-koh-**teh**-kah
bus stop	**la fermata dell'autobus**	lah fair-**mah**-tah dell **ow**-toh-booss
church	**la chiesa**	lah kee-**eh**-zah
	la basilica	lah bah-**seel**-i-kah
closed for the public holiday	**chiuso per le ferie**	kee-**oo**-zoh pair leh **fair**-ee-eh
garden	**il giardino**	eel jar-**dee**-no
library	**la biblioteca**	lah beeb-lee-oh-**teh**-kah
museum	**il museo**	eel moo-**zeh**-oh
railroad station	**la stazione**	lah stah-tsee-**oh**-neh
tourist information	**l'ufficio di turismo**	loo-**fee**-choh dee too-**ree**-smoh

STAYING IN A HOTEL

Do you have any vacant rooms?	**Avete camere libere?**	ah-**veh**-teh **kah**-mair-eh **lee**-bair-eh?
double room	**una camera doppia**	oona **kah**-mair-ah **doh**-pee-ah
with double bed	**con letto matrimoniale**	kon **let**-toh mah-tree-moh-nee-**ah**-leh
twin room	**una camera con due letti**	oona **kah**-mair-ah kon **doo**-eh **let**-tee
single room	**una camera singola**	oona **kah**-mair-ah **sing**-goh-lah
room with a bath, shower	**una camera con bagno, con doccia**	oona **kah**-mair-ah kon **ban**-yoh, kon **dot**-chah
porter	**il facchino**	eel fah-**kee**-noh
key	**la chiave**	lah kee-**ah**-veh
I have a reservation.	**Ho fatto una prenotazione.**	oh **fat**-toh oona preh-noh-tah-tsee-**oh**-neh

EATING OUT

Have you got a table for ...?	**Avete una tavola per ... ?**	ah-**veh**-teh oona **tah**-voh-lah pair ...?
I'd like to reserve a table.	**Vorrei riservare una tavola.**	vor-**ray** ree-sair-**vah**-reh oona **tah**-voh-lah
breakfast	**colazione**	koh-lah-tsee-**oh**-neh
lunch	**pranzo**	**pran**-tsoh
dinner	**cena**	**cheh**-nah
The check, please.	**Il conto, per favore.**	eel **kon**-toh pair fah-**vor**-eh
I am a vegetarian.	**Sono vegetariano/a.**	**soh**-noh veh-jeh-tar-ee-**ah**-noh/nah
waitress	**cameriera**	kah-mair-ee-**air**-ah
waiter	**cameriere**	kah-mair-ee-**air**-eh
fixed price menu	**il menù a prezzo fisso**	eel meh-**noo** ah **pret**-soh **fee**-soh
dish of the day	**piatto del giorno**	pee-**ah**-toh dell **jor**-no
appetizer	**antipasto**	an-tee-**pass**-toh
first course	**il primo**	eel **pree**-moh
main course	**il secondo**	eel seh-**kon**-doh
vegetables	**il contorno**	eel kon-**tor**-noh
dessert	**il dolce**	eel **doll**-cheh
cover charge	**il coperto**	eel koh-**pair**-toh
wine list	**la lista dei vini**	lah **lee**-stah day **vee**-nee
rare	**al sangue**	al **sang**-gweh
medium	**al puntino**	al poon-**tee**-noh
well done	**ben cotto**	ben **kot**-toh
glass	**il bicchiere**	eel bee-kee-**air**-eh
bottle	**la bottiglia**	lah bot-**teel**-yah
knife	**il coltello**	eel kol-**tell**-oh
fork	**la forchetta**	lah for-**ket**-tah
spoon	**il cucchiaio**	eel koo-kee-**eye**-oh

MENU DECODER

l'acqua minerale gassata/naturale	lah-kwah mee-nair-**ah**-leh gah-**zah**-tah/ nah-too-rah-leh	mineral water fizzy/still
agnello	ah-**niell**-oh	lamb
aceto	ah-**cheh**-toh	vinegar
aglio	**al**-ee-oh	garlic
al forno	al **for**-noh	baked
alla griglia	ah-lah **greel**-yah	grilled
l'aragosta	lah-rah-**goss**-tah	lobster
arrosto	ar-**ross**-toh	roast
la birra	lah **beer**-rah	beer
la bistecca	lah bee-**stek**-kah	steak
il brodo	eel **broh**-doh	broth
il burro	eel **boor**-oh	butter
il caffè	eel kah-**feh**	coffee
i calamari	ee kah-lah-**mah**-ree	squid
i carciofi	ee kar-**choff**-ee	artichokes
la carne	la **kar**-neh	meat
carne di maiale	**kar**-neh dee mah-**yah**-leh	pork
la cipolla	la chip-**oh**-lah	onion
i contorni	ee kon-**tor**-nee	vegetables
i fagioli	ee fah-**joh**-lee	beans
il fegato	eel **fay**-gah-toh	liver
il finocchio	eel fee-**nok**-ee-oh	fennel
il formaggio	eel for-**mad**-joh	cheese
le fragole	leh **frah**-goh-leh	strawberries
il fritto misto	eel free-toh **mees**-toh	mixed fried dish
la frutta	la **froot**-tah	fruit
frutti di mare	**froo**-tee dee mah-reh	seafood
i funghi	ee **foon**-ghee	mushrooms
i gamberi	ee **gam**-bair-ee	shrimp
il gelato	eel jel-**lah**-toh	ice cream
l'insalata	leen-sah-lah-tah	salad

il latte	eel **laht**-teh	milk
lesso	**less**-oh	boiled
il manzo	eel **man**-tsoh	beef
la melanzana	lah meh-lan-**tsah**-nah	eggplant
la minestra	lah mee-**ness**-trah	soup
l'olio	loh-lee-oh	oil
il pane	eel **pah**-neh	bread
le patate	leh pah-**tah**-teh	potatoes
le patatine fritte	leh pah-tah-**teen**-eh **free**-teh	french fries
il pepe	eel **peh**-peh	pepper
la pesca	lah **pess**-kah	peach
il pesce	eel **pesh**-eh	fish
il pollo	eel **poll**-oh	chicken
il pomodoro	eel poh-moh-**dor**-oh	tomato
il prosciutto cotto/crudo	eel pro-**shoo**-toh **kot**-toh/**kroo**-doh	ham cooked/cured
il riso	eel **ree**-zoh	rice
il sale	eel **sah**-leh	salt
la salsiccia	lah sal-**see**-chah	sausage
le seppie	leh **sep**-pee-eh	cuttlefish
secco	**sek**-koh	dry
la sogliola	lah **soll**-yoh-lah	sole
i spinaci	ee spee-**nah**-chee	spinach
succo d'arancia/ di limone	**soo**-koh dah-**ran**-chah/ dee leh-**moh**-neh	orange /lemon juice
il tè	eel **teh**	tea
la tisana	lah tee-**zah**-nah	herbal tea
il tonno	eel **ton**-noh	tuna
la torta	lah **tor**-tah	cake/tart
l'uovo	loo-**oh**-voh	egg
vino bianco	**vee**-noh bee-**ang**-koh	white wine
vino rosso	**vee**-noh **ross**-oh	red wine
il vitello	eel vee-**tell**-oh	veal
le vongole	leh **von**-goh-leh	clams
lo zucchero	loh **zoo**-kair-oh	sugar
gli zucchini	lyee dzu-**kee**-nee	zucchini
la zuppa	lah **tsoo**-pah	soup

NUMBERS

1	**uno**	**oo**-noh
2	**due**	**doo**-eh
3	**tre**	treh
4	**quattro**	**kwat**-roh
5	**cinque**	**ching**-kweh
6	**sei**	**say**-ee
7	**sette**	**set**-teh
8	**otto**	**ot**-toh
9	**nove**	**noh**-veh
10	**dieci**	dee-**eh**-chee
11	**undici**	**oon**-dee-chee
12	**dodici**	**doh**-dee-chee
13	**tredici**	**tray**-dee-chee
14	**quattordici**	kwat-**tor**-dee-chee
15	**quindici**	**kwin**-dee-chee
16	**sedici**	**say**-dee-chee
17	**diciassette**	dee-chah-**set**-teh
18	**diciotto**	dee-**chot**-toh
19	**diciannove**	dee-chah-**noh**-veh
20	**venti**	**ven**-tee
30	**trenta**	**tren**-tah
40	**quaranta**	kwah-**ran**-tah
50	**cinquanta**	ching-**kwan**-tah
60	**sessanta**	sess-**an**-tah
70	**settanta**	set-**tan**-tah
80	**ottanta**	ot-**tan**-tah
90	**novanta**	noh-**van**-tah
100	**cento**	**chen**-toh
1,000	**mille**	**mee**-leh
2,000	**duemila**	**doo**-eh mee-lah
5,000	**cinquemila**	**ching**-kweh mee-lah
1,000,000	**un milione**	oon meel-**yoh**-neh

TIME

one minute	**un minuto**	oon mee-**noo**-toh
one hour	**un'ora**	oon or-ah
half an hour	**mezz'ora**	medz-**or**-ah
a day	**un giorno**	oon **jor**-noh
a week	**una settimana**	oona set-tee-**mah**-nah
Monday	**lunedì**	loo-neh-**dee**
Tuesday	**martedì**	mar-teh-**dee**
Wednesday	**mercoledì**	mair-koh-leh-**dee**
Thursday	**giovedì**	joh-veh-**dee**
Friday	**venerdì**	ven-air-**dee**
Saturday	**sabato**	**sah**-bah-toh
Sunday	**domenica**	doh-**meh**-nee-kah

COUNTRY GUIDES

AUSTRALIA • CANADA • CRUISE GUIDE TO EUROPE AND THE
MEDITERRANEAN • FRANCE • GERMANY • GREAT BRITAIN
GREECE: ATHENS & THE MAINLAND • THE GREEK ISLANDS
IRELAND • ITALY • JAPAN • MEXICO • POLAND
PORTUGAL • SCOTLAND • SINGAPORE
SOUTH AFRICA • SPAIN • THAILAND
GREAT PLACES TO STAY IN EUROPE
A TASTE OF SCOTLAND

REGIONAL GUIDES

BALI & LOMBOK • BARCELONA & CATALONIA • CALIFORNIA
FLORENCE & TUSCANY • FLORIDA • HAWAII
JERUSALEM & THE HOLY LAND • LOIRE VALLEY
MILAN & THE LAKES • NAPLES WITH POMPEII & THE AMALFI
COAST • NEW ENGLAND • NEW ZEALAND
PROVENCE & THE COTE D'AZUR • SARDINIA
SEVILLE & ANDALUSIA • SICILY • VENICE & THE VENETO

CITY GUIDES

AMSTERDAM • BERLIN • BOSTON • BRUSSELS • BUDAPEST
CHICAGO • CRACOW • DELHI, AGRA & JAIPUR • DUBLIN
ISTANBUL • LISBON • LONDON • MADRID
MOSCOW • NEW YORK • PARIS • PRAGUE • ROME
SAN FRANCISCO • STOCKHOLM • ST PETERSBURG
SYDNEY • VIENNA • WARSAW • WASHINGTON, DC

NEW FOR AUTUMN 2001

EGYPT • EUROPE • A TASTE OF TUSCANY
NEW ORLEANS • SOUTHWEST USA & LAS VEGAS

FOR UPDATES TO OUR GUIDES, AND INFORMATION ON
TRAVEL PLANNERS, CITY MAPS, &
DK EYEWITNESS TRAVEL GUIDES
PHRASEBOOKS

VISIT US AT
eyewitnesstravel.dk.com

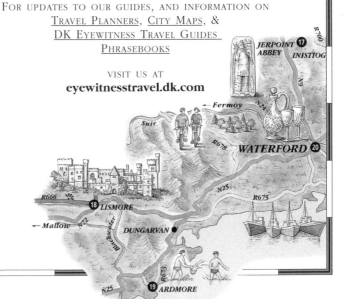

Central Rome

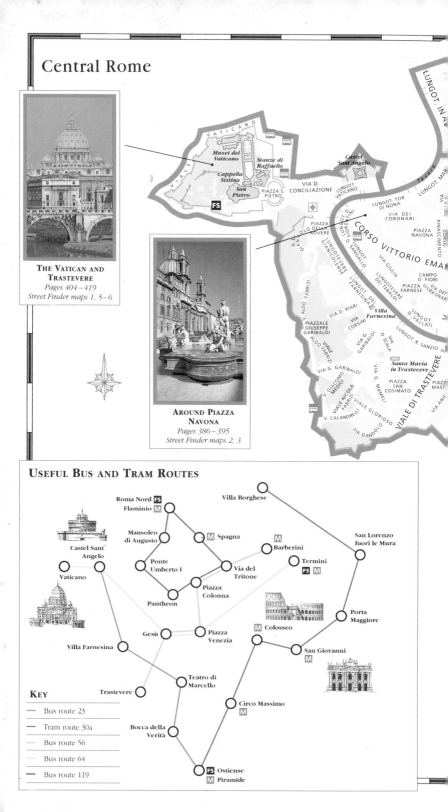

THE VATICAN AND TRASTEVERE
Pages 404–419
Street Finder maps 1, 5–6

AROUND PIAZZA NAVONA
Pages 386–395
Street Finder maps 2, 3

USEFUL BUS AND TRAM ROUTES

Villa Borghese

Roma Nord **FS**
Flaminio **M**

Mausoleo di Augusto

Castel Sant' Angelo

Vaticano

Ponte Umberto I

Spagna **M**

Barberini **M**

San Lorenzo fuori le Mura

Termini **FS M**

Via del Tritone

Piazza Colonna

Pantheon

Gesù

Villa Farnesina

Piazza Venezia

Porta Maggiore

Colosseo **M**

San Giovanni **M**

Trastevere

Teatro di Marcello

Circo Massimo **M**

Bocca della Verità

FS Ostiense
M Piramide

KEY

— Bus route 23

— Tram route 30a

— Bus route 56

— Bus route 64

— Bus route 119